John Milton

An Annotated Bibliography, 1968-1988

compiled by Calvin Huckabay

edited by Paul J. Klemp

DUQUESNE UNIVERSITY PRESS
Pittsburgh, Pennsylvania

Published in the United States of America by

DUQUESNE UNIVERSITY PRESS
600 Forbes Avenue
Pittsburgh, Pennsylvania 15282-0101

Library of Congress Cataloging in Publication Data

Huckabay, Calvin.
    John Milton: an annotated bibliography, 1968–1988 / compiled by
Calvin Huckabay and edited by P. J. Klemp.
       p.   cm.
    Includes index.
    ISBN 0-8207-0272-2 (alk. paper)
    1. Milton, John, 1608–1674—Bibliography.   I. Klemp, P. J.
II. Title.
Z8578.H82   1996
[PR3581]
016.821'4—dc20   95-49712
                                        CIP

CONTENTS

PREFACE

This bibliography is an updating of my earlier work, *John Milton: An Annotated Bibliography, 1929–1968* (No. 46). This publication was a supplement to David H. Stevens's *A Reference Guide to Milton from 1800 to the Present Day* (Huckabay No. 60) and Harris Fletcher's *Contributions to a Milton Bibliography, 1800–1930* (No. 34). The references to "Stevens" and "Huckabay" are to our previous works and consist mostly of reprints, which indicate continuing interest in earlier scholarship; references that state simply "No." refer to the present volume.

As in the earlier bibliography, my purpose has been to list editions and translations of Milton's works and to cite the books, essays, notes, and dissertations and other studies that have been published about the writer and his works. The terminal date for the present undertaking is 1988. Some items published during 1968 are listed here, especially those items that appeared too late for review, and some early 1989 publications are included. Some references from after 1988 are also included to identify abstracts, reviews, reprints, or subsequent editions of studies that fall within my chronological restrictions. However, the intent was to cover a twenty-year period, which is one of the most productive eras in the history of Milton criticism in terms of output. An updating to cover the years after 1988 is already underway.

Whenever we could, either I or one of my assistants examined and annotated each item, except for the reprints, which are listed in the OCLC bibliographic network. Although I have attempted to be comprehensive, not selective, some publications were not available, especially those printed in non-English speaking countries. However, copies of those publications are easier to obtain today than they were in the past, even from the former Soviet bloc countries. Although there are obvious exceptions, the annotations are intended to describe content and not to be evaluations. If a published essay had no title, I provided one in brackets.

We have checked all of the annual lists of Milton studies from 1968 to 1988 and other publications listed in the bibliography section of this work. Much of the research has taken place at the Fondren Library of Rice University and at the Bodleian Library in Oxford. Jon Suter, the Director of Libraries at Houston Baptist University, has taken a special interest in the project and has located and obtained many volumes through interlibrary loan. Also, his uncanny skill at locating holdings of journals through electronic search produced photocopies of essays about Milton and his writing.

vii

Unfortunately, comprehensive lists of reviews have been difficult to locate. I have relied mainly on those contained in the Modern Humanities Research Association annual bibliography (No. 82), the *Book Review Index*, and *General Periodicals on Disc*, a CD/ROM service from University Microfilms. In many instances, every issue of individual journals has been checked. The reviews in *Milton Quarterly* and *Seventeenth-Century News* have been especially helpful. Whenever their names were available, the authors of reviews are indexed in this bibliography. With the exception of journals which we have personally checked, book reviews have not been verified.

Modern criticism of Milton probably dates from Walter Raleigh's *Milton* (Stevens No. 2226). What scholars now need is a comprehensive critical study comparable to Harry Redman's recent *Major French Milton Critics of the Nineteenth Century* (Pittsburgh, PA: Duquesne Univ. Press, 1994), which would be international in focus, chronological, and topical. During the twenty years covered in this bibliography, there was a proliferation of Milton studies. The Yale *Complete Prose Works* (No. 366) was finished, as was the most useful nine-volume *Milton Encyclopedia* (No. 49), with the ninth volume containing a substantial amount of recent bibliographical information. *Milton Quarterly* (No. 78) and *Milton Studies* (No. 80) provided convenient outlets for scholarly publication. Milton criticism went in many directions. In recent years, political interpretations of the major poems became commonplace, and feminist critics thoroughly explored Milton's views on women and his attitude toward marriage, with little agreement and obviously more studies to come. Controversy concerning the God of *Paradise Lost*, which began with Samuel Johnson (Huckabay No. 3226), continued, with attacks focused mainly on the point of view expressed by William Empson (No. 2175). Scholarship on William Blake and Milton flourished, as did studies of *Comus* and *Lycidas*. William B. Hunter, Jr., recently questioned Milton's authorship of the *Christian Doctrine* (*SEL*, 32, 1992, 129–42) and his point of view is already causing some debate. An obvious trend is the psychological approach to Milton as a person and to his works, with some critics finding oedipal and other problems in his personality. Several discussions of the current state of Milton criticism are listed in the general criticism section of this bibliography. See especially the essays by Jacques Blondel (No. 484), Roy Flannagan (Nos. 598–99), Ian Fletcher (No. 607), Michael Lieb (Nos. 789, 792–93), and Joseph A. Wittreich, Jr. (Nos. 1141, 1144, 1148–49).

Many individuals have assisted me in the present updating, which has taken several years. My greatest debt is to Paul J. Klemp, an associate editor of *Milton Quarterly* and the compiler of the *Essential Milton* (No. 55). During the process of compilation and annotation, the need for an associate editor became apparent. He has checked most of the entries in this volume, has made many good suggestions, and has prepared the final copy. Rosemary Fojtik, my secretary, has served tirelessly at the word processor and printer. Randall Wuensche checked for reviews, and Scott Shaw handled interlibrary loan requests. Fumio Ochi sent copies of *MCJ News* (No. 65) annually from Kyoto and made me keenly aware of the developing interest in Milton in Japan. In addition to Jon Suter, mentioned above, David Vaisey, Bodley's Librarian, has been of great assistance. Archie Burnett of Oxford Brookes University and former reviewer of the Milton section for the *Year's Work in English Studies* (Huckabay No. 15) read the manuscript and offered suggestions, as did William B. Hunter, Jr., and John Shawcross, who supplied a list of items that I had overlooked. John Gillespie, a former student and a specialist in Japanese literature, annotated many of the articles written in Japanese, and Makiko Menow Pinkney annotated some of the others. Several friends and colleagues in the Houston academic community have assisted in the annotation of foreign language items, especially those from eastern Europe. Wallace Hooker proofread the copy. This bibliography represents a group effort.

Finally, I owe a word of thanks for institutional support. The administrative officials of Houston Baptist University have understood the value of the present undertaking and the difficulties encountered by a dean on a small liberal arts campus in obtaining books and articles that only large research libraries have. They have provided plenty of secretarial and student help, computer services, and ample funding for me to obtain any needed materials. To them, I am grateful.

I trust that this work will be useful to beginning students of Milton as well as to seasoned Milton scholars.

Calvin Huckabay
Houston, Texas
June, 1994

EDITOR'S ACKNOWLEDGMENTS

I want to thank Calvin Huckabay not only for giving me the opportunity to work on this bibliography but also for welcoming my efforts with such a generous spirit. And I am grateful to the many scholars and librarians who answered questions and provided information about various books and articles. My thanks go to the University of Wisconsin—Oshkosh, for funding a faculty and student collaborative research grant. But I am especially grateful to Jeanne Kuhaupt and Stephen Beers, who were the other recipients of the grant and the research assistants who contributed so much work to this bibliography.

P. J. Klemp
Oshkosh, Wisconsin
June 1995

LIST OF ABBREVIATIONS

ABU	Aberdeen University Review
AHR	American Historical Review
AI	American Imago: A Psychoanalytic Journal for Culture, Science, and the Arts
AJES	Aligarh Journal of English Studies
AL	American Literature: A Journal of Literary History, Criticism, and Bibliography
ALIL	Anuar de Lingvistica si Istorie Literara
Anglia	Anglia: Zeitschrift für Englische Philologie
ANQ	ANQ: A Quarterly Journal of Short Articles, Notes, and Reviews (supersedes American Notes and Queries)
AN&Q	American Notes & Queries
AnRS	Annual Reports of Studies (Kyoto, Japan)
AnUBLG	Analele Universitatii Bucuresti Limbi Germanice
Apollo	Apollo: The International Magazine of Art and Antiques
ARBA	American Reference Books Annual
Archiv	Archiv für das Studium der Neueren Sprachen und Literaturen
ArielE	Ariel: A Review of International English Literature
ArlQ	Arlington Quarterly
ArQ	Arizona Quarterly: A Journal of American Literature, Culture, and Theory
ART	Art International
ArtSci	Arts and Sciences
AULLA	Australasian Universities Language and Literature Association
AUMLA	AUMLA: Journal of the Australasian Universities Language and Literature Association
BA	Books Abroad
BB	Bulletin of Bibliography
BBaud	Bulletin Baudelairien
BBN	British Book News
BC	Book Collector
BG	Bungaku (Tokyo)
BHR	Bibliothèque d'Humanisme et Renaissance
Blake	Blake: An Illustrated Quarterly
BlakeN	Blake Newsletter

BlakeS   Blake Studies
BLR   Bodleian Library Record
BNYPL   Bulletin of the New York Public Library
BP   Banasthali Patrika
BRH   Bulletin of Research in the Humanities
BSEAA   Bulletin de la Société d'Études Anglo-Américaines des XVIIᵉ et
                XVIIIᵉ Siècles
BSNotes   Browning Society Notes
BSUF   Ball State University Forum
BuR   Bucknell Review: A Scholarly Journal of Letters, Arts and
                Sciences
BWVACET   Bulletin of the West Virginia Association of College English
                Teachers
BYUS   Brigham Young University Studies
CA   Cuadernos Americanos
CahiersE   Cahiers Elisabéthains: Études sur la Pré-Renaissance et la Ren-
                aissance Anglaises
CAIEF   Cahiers de l'Association Internationale des Études Françaises
CanL   Canadian Literature
CarnM   Carnegie Magazine
CaudaP   Cauda Pavonis: Studies in Hermeticism
CCrit   Comparative Criticism: A Yearbook
CCTEP   Conference of College Teachers of English Proceedings
CdS   Corriere della Sera
CE   College English
CEA   CEA Critic: An Official Journal of the College English Association
CEMF   Collected Essays by the Members of the Faculty (Kyoritsu Wom-
                en's Junior College)
CentR   Centennial Review
CF   Classical Folia: Studies in the Christian Perpetration of the
                Classics
CH   Church History
CHA   Cuadernos Hispanoamericanos: Revista Mensual de Cultura
                Hispanica (Madrid)
ChildL   Children's Literature: An International Journal
CHum   Computers and the Humanities
CIFM   Contributi dell'Istituto di Filologia Moderna
Cithara   Cithara: Essays in the Judaeo-Christian Tradition
CJ   Classical Journal
CL   Comparative Literature
C&L   Christianity and Literature
CLAJ   College Language Association Journal
CLAQ   Children's Literature Association Quarterly

CLIO	CLIO: A Journal of Literature, History, and the Philosophy of History
CLJ	Cornell Library Journal
CLQ	Colby Library Quarterly
CLS	Comparative Literature Studies
CML	Classical and Modern Literature: A Quarterly
CollL	College Literature
Colóquio	Colóquio/Letras (Portugal)
Compass	Compass: A Provincial Review
CompD	Comparative Drama
Comunità	Comunità: Revista di Informazione Culturale
Conradiana	Conradiana: A Journal of Joseph Conrad
Cowrie	Cowrie: A Chinese Journal of Comparative Literature
CP	Concerning Poetry
CPe	Castrum Peregrini (Amsterdam)
CQ	Cambridge Quarterly
CQR	Church Quarterly Review
CR	Critical Review
CRCL	Canadian Review of Comparative Literature
CREL	Cahiers Roumains d'Études Littéraires: Revue Trimestrielle de Critique, d'Esthétique et d'Histoire Littéraires
CritI	Critical Inquiry
CritQ	Critical Quarterly
CritS	Critical Survey
CSLBull	CSL: The Bulletin of the New York C. S. Lewis Society
CSR	Christian Scholar's Review
CV	Città di Vita: Bimestrale di Relgione Arte e Scienza
DA	Dissertation Abstracts
DAI	Dissertation Abstracts International
DDJ	Deutsches Dante-Jahrbuch
Diacritics	Diacritics: A Review of Contemporary Criticism
DLN	Doris Lessing Newsletter
DQR	Dutch Quarterly Review of Anglo-American Letters
DQu	Dickens Quarterly
DR	Dalhousie Review
DSN	Dickens Studies Newsletter
DUJ	Durham University Journal
EA	Études Anglaises: Grande-Bretagne, Etats-Unis
EAA	Estudos Anglo-Americanos (Brazil)
EAL	Early American Literature
ECLife	Eighteenth-Century Life
ECS	Eighteenth-Century Studies
Edda	Edda: Nordisk Tidsskrift for Litteraturforskning (Oslo)

EDH	Essays by Divers Hands
EHR	English Historical Review
EIC	Essays in Criticism: A Quarterly Journal of Literary Criticism
EigoS	Eigo Seinen (Tokyo)
EIRC	Explorations in Renaissance Culture
ELH	ELH: A Journal of English Literary History
ELN	English Language Notes
ELR	English Literary Renaissance
ELWIU	Essays in Literature (Western Illinois Univ.)
EM	English Miscellany: A Symposium of History, Literature and the Arts
EngR	English Record
EngRev	English Review of Salem College
EnlE	Enlightenment Essays
ES	English Studies: A Journal of English Language and Literature
E&S	Essays and Studies
ESA	English Studies in Africa: A Journal of the Humanities (Johannesburg)
ESC	English Studies in Canada
ESELL	Essays and Studies in English Language and Literature
Expl	Explicator
Extracta	Extracta: Resumeer af Specialeopgaver fra det Filosofiske Fakultet ved Københavns Universitet
FLS	Foreign Literature Studies (China)
ForumH	Forum (Houston, TX)
GaR	Georgia Review
GGA	Göttingische Gelehrte Anzeigen
GHJ	George Herbert Journal
Glyph	Glyph Textual Studies
Greyfriar	Greyfriar: Siena Studies in Literature
GyS	Gypsy Scholar
HAB	Humanities Association Bulletin
HAR	Humanities Association Review
HLQ	Huntington Library Quarterly: A Journal for the History and Interpretation of English and American Civilization
HSE	Hungarian Studies in English
HSELL	Hiroshima Studies in English Language and Literature
HSL	University of Hartford Studies in Literature: A Journal of Interdisciplinary Criticism
HT	History Today
HTR	Harvard Theological Review
HudR	Hudson Review
HumLov	Humanistica Lovaniensia: Journal of Neo-Latin Studies

HUS	Harvard Ukrainian Studies
HUSL	Hebrew University Studies in Literature and the Arts
IHT	International Herald Tribune
IJIAC	Interpretations: A Journal of Ideas, Analysis, and Criticism
IJPP	Interpretation: A Journal of Political Philosophy
IK	Irodalomtörténeti Közlemények (Budapest)
ILQ	Illinois Quarterly
IndL	Indian Literature
INH	Inmun Nonchong
IT	Index to Theses Accepted for Higher Degrees by the Universities of Great Britain and Ireland
JA	Journal of Aesthetics and Art Criticism
JAF	Journal of American Folklore
JAS	Journal of American Studies
JC	Journal of Communication
JCSS	Journal of Cultural and Social Science
JDECU	Journal of the Department of English (Calcutta Univ.)
JDJ	John Donne Journal: Studies in the Age of Donne
JDSG	Jahrbuch der Deutschen Schillergesellschaft
JEGP	JEGP: Journal of English and Germanic Philology
JELL	Journal of English Language and Literature (Seoul)
JELLC	Journal of the English Language and Literature, Chungchong (Daejeon, Korea)
JEngL	Journal of English Linguistics
JEP	Journal of Evolutionary Psychology
JES	Journal of European Studies
JETS	Journal of the Evangelical Theological Society
JGE	Journal of General Education
JGH	Journal of Garden History
JHI	Journal of the History of Ideas
JHS	Journal of Historical Studies
JIWE	Journal of Indian Writing in English
JJQ	James Joyce Quarterly
JMH	Journal of Modern History
JMJ	James Madison Journal
JMRS	Journal of Medieval and Renaissance Studies
JNT	Journal of Narrative Technique
JQ	Journalism Quarterly
JR	Journal of Religion
JRMMRA	Journal of the Rocky Mountain Medieval and Renaissance Association
JTS	Journal of Theological Studies
JWCI	Journal of the Warburg and Courtauld Institutes

Káñina	Káñina: Revista de Artes y Letras de la Universidad de Costa Rica
KN	Kwartalnik Neofilologiczny
KR	Kenyon Review
KSJ	Keats-Shelley Journal: Keats, Shelley, Byron, Hunt, and Their Circles
KSMB	Keats-Shelley Memorial Bulletin
KSR	Keats-Shelley Review
KyR	Kentucky Review
Lang&C	Language and Culture (Hokkaido Univ.)
LangQ	Language Quarterly
Lang&S	Language and Style: An International Journal
LauR	Laurel Review
L&B	Literature and Belief
LCrit	Literary Criterion (Univ. of Mysore, India)
LCUT	Library Chronicle of the University of Texas
LeS	Lingua e Stile: Trimestrale di Linguìstica e Critica Letteraria (Bologna)
LeuB	Leuvense Bijdragen: Contributions in Linguistics and Philology (Louvain)
LFQ	Literature/Film Quarterly
L&H	Literature and History: A New Journal for the Humanities
LHR	Lock Haven Review
LHY	Literary Half-Yearly
L&I	Literature and Ideology
Library	Library: The Transactions of the Bibliographical Society
Linguistics	Linguistics: An Interdisciplinary Journal of the Language Sciences
LitR	Literary Review: International Journal of Contemporary Writing
LJ	Library Journal
LOS	Literary Onomastics Studies
L&P	Literature and Psychology
LRB	London Review of Books
LRN	Literary Research Newsletter
L&S	Language and Speech
L&T	Literature and Theology: An Interdisciplinary Journal of Theory and Criticism
LURev	Lakehead University Review
MA	Master Abstracts
Matatu	Matatu: Journal for African Culture and Society
MCJ	Milton Center of Japan
MFS	Modern Fiction Studies
MGW	Manchester Guardian Weekly

MHLS	Mid-Hudson Language Studies
MHRA	Modern Humanities Research Association
MiltonN	Milton Newsletter
MiltonQ	Milton Quarterly (formerly Milton Newsletter)
MiltonS	Milton Studies
MLA	Modern Language Association
MLN	MLN: Modern Language Notes
MLQ	Modern Language Quarterly
MLR	Modern Language Review
MLS	Modern Language Studies
ModA	Modern Age: A Quarterly Review
Moreana	Moreana: Bulletin Thomas More
Mosaic	Mosaic: A Journal for the Interdisciplinary Study of Literature
MP	Modern Philology: A Journal Devoted to Research in Medieval and Modern Literature
MQR	Michigan Quarterly Review
MR	Medieval and Renaissance Drama in England: An Annual Gathering of Research, Criticism and Reviews
M&R	Milton and the Romantics
MS	Mediaeval Studies
MSE	Massachusetts Studies in English
MSEx	Melville Society Extracts
MTJ	Mark Twain Journal
NCF	Nineteenth-Century Fiction
NConL	Notes on Contemporary Literature
NDEJ	Notre Dame English Journal: A Journal of Religion
NDQ	North Dakota Quarterly
NEMLA	New England Modern Language Association
NemlaIS	Nemla Italian Studies
Neohelicon	Neohelicon: Acta Comparationis Litterarum Universarum
NEQ	New England Quarterly: A Historical Review of New England Life and Letters
NHJ	Nathaniel Hawthorne Journal
NLH	New Literary History: A Journal of Theory and Interpretation
NM	Neuphilologische Mitteilungen: Bulletin de la Société Néophilologique
NMAL	Notes on Modern American Literature
N&Q	Notes and Queries
NR	New Republic: A Journal of Politics and the Arts
NRam	New Rambler: Journal of the Johnson Society of London
NYRB	New York Review of Books
NYTB	New York Times Book Review

Oberon	Oberon: Magazine for the Study of English and American Literature (Tokyo)
Odyssey	Odyssey: A Journal of the Humanities
OL	Orbis Litterarum: International Review of Literary Studies
OLR	Oxford Literary Review
Orev	Occasional Review: A Journal of Contemporary Thought in the Humanities, Arts and Social Sciences
OT	Oral Tradition
PAPS	Proceedings of the American Philosophical Society Held at Philadelphia for Promoting Useful Knowledge
PBSA	Papers of the Bibliographical Society of America
PCP	Pacific Coast Philology
PFSCL	Papers on French Seventeenth Century Literature
PLL	Papers on Language and Literature: A Journal for Scholars and Critics of Language and Literature
PMASAL	Papers of the Michigan Academy of Science, Arts, and Letters
PMLA	PMLA: Publications of the Modern Language Association of America
PMPA	Publications of the Missouri Philological Association
PN	Poe Newsletter
POMPA	Publications of the Mississippi Philological Association
PPMRC	Proceedings of the PMR Conference: Annual Publication of the International Patristic, Mediaeval and Renaissance Conference
PQ	Philological Quarterly
Proverbium	Proverbium: Yearbook of International Proverb Scholarship
PrS	Prairie Schooner
PSt	Prose Studies: History, Theory, Criticism
PULC	Princeton University Library Chronicle
QFSK	Quellen und Forschungen zur Sprach- und Kulturgeschichte der Germanischen Völker
QJS	Quarterly Journal of Speech
QLL	Quaderni di Lingue e Letterature
QQ	Queen's Quarterly
RaJAH	Rackham Journal of the Arts and Humanities
RAR	Raritan: A Quarterly Review
RBPH	Revue Belge de Philologie et d'Histoire
RCam	Revista Camoniana
RCEI	Revista Canaria de Estudios Ingleses
Renascence	Renascence: Essays on Value in Literature
RenB	Renaissance Bulletin
RenD	Renaissance Drama
Rendezvous	Rendezvous: Journal of Arts and Letters

RenP	Renaissance Papers
RenQ	Renaissance Quarterly
Ren&R	Renaissance and Reformation
RenSt	Renaissance Studies: Journal of the Society for Renaissance Studies
RES	Review of English Studies: A Quarterly Journal of English Literature and the English Language
Rev	Review (Blacksburg, VA)
R&L	Religion and Literature
RLC	Revue de Littérature Comparée
RLV	Revue des Langues Vivantes (Brussels)
RMM	Revue de Métaphysique et de Morale
RMR	Rocky Mountain Review of Language and Literature
RMS	Renaissance and Modern Studies
RN	Revue Nouvelle (Brussels)
RoLit	Romînia Literara: Saptaminal de Literatura si Arta Editat de Uniunea Scriitorilor din Republica Socialista Romînia (Bucharest)
RPP	Romanticism Past and Present
RRCNU	Research Review of Chungbuk National University (Chongju, Korea)
RS	Research Studies
RSR	Religious Studies Review
RUO	Revue de l'Université d'Ottawa
RUS	Rice University Studies
SAB	South Atlantic Bulletin
SAP	Studia Anglica Posnaniensia: An International Review of English Studies (Poznan)
SAQ	South Atlantic Quarterly
SatR	Saturday Review
SB	Studies in Bibliography: Papers of the Bibliographical Society of the University of Virginia
SBrown	Studies in Browning and His Circle: A Journal of Criticism, History, and Bibliography
SCB	South Central Bulletin
SCJ	Sixteenth Century Journal
ScLJ	Scottish Literary Journal
SCMLA	South Central Modern Language Association
SCN	Seventeenth-Century News
SCR	South Carolina Review
SCRev	South Central Review: The Journal of the South Central Modern Language Association

SCUL	Soundings: Collections of the University Library, University of California, Santa Barbara
SECC	Studies in Eighteenth-Century Culture
SEL	SEL: Studies in English Literature, 1500–1900
SELit	Studies in English Literature (Tokyo)
Seminar	Seminar: A Journal of Germanic Studies
SES	Sophia English Studies
ShakS	Shakespeare Studies
ShN	Shakespeare Newsletter
SHR	Southern Humanities Review
SIcon	Studies in Iconography
SIR	Studies in Romanticism
SLitI	Studies in the Literary Imagination
SLRev	Stanford Literature Review
SMLit	Studies in Mystical Literature (Taiwan)
SMy	Studia Mystica
SN	Studia Neophilologica: A Journal of Germanic and Romance Languages and Literature
SNL	Satire Newsletter
SoAR	South Atlantic Review
SocSJ	Social Science Journal
SoQ	Southern Quarterly: A Journal of the Arts in the South
SoR	Southern Review
SoRA	Southern Review: Literary and Interdisciplinary Essays (Adelaide, Australia)
SP	Studies in Philology
SpenN	Spenser Newsletter
SPWVSRA	Selected Papers from the West Virginia Shakespeare and Renaissance Association
SQ	Shakespeare Quarterly
SR	Sewanee Review
SSCJ	Southern Speech Communication Journal
SSF	Studies in Short Fiction
SSL	Studies in Scottish Literature
StHum	Studies in the Humanities
StIR	Stanford Italian Review
SXX	Secolul 20 (Bucharest)
TCBS	Transactions of the Cambridge Bibliographical Society
TES	Times Educational Supplement
TEXT	Text: Transactions of the Society for Textual Scholarship
TFSB	Tennessee Folklore Society Bulletin
THA	Thomas Hardy Annual

THES   Times Higher Education Supplement (London)
Thought   Thought: A Review of Culture and Idea
TJQ   Thoreau Journal Quarterly
TLS   Times Literary Supplement
TPB   Tennessee Philological Bulletin: Proceedings of the Annual Meeting of the Tennessee Philological Association
TQ   Texas Quarterly
TRB   Tennyson Research Bulletin
TriQ   TriQuarterly
Triveni   Triveni: Journal of Indian Renaissance
TSE   Tulane Studies in English
TSL   Tennessee Studies in Literature
TSLL   Texas Studies in Literature and Language
TWA   Transactions of the Wisconsin Academy of Sciences, Arts, and Letters
UCTSE   University of Cape Town Studies in English
UDR   University of Dayton Review
UES   Unisa English Studies: Journal of the Department of English
UMSE   University of Mississippi Studies in English
UR   University Review (Kansas City)
USSE   University of Saga Studies in English
UTQ   University of Toronto Quarterly: A Canadian Journal of the Humanities
UWR   University of Windsor Review
Ventures   Ventures: Magazine of the Yale Graduate School
VIA 8   Via 8: Architecture and Literature
VMU   Vestnik Moskovskogo Universiteta
VP   Victorian Poetry: A Critical Journal of Victorian Literature
VQR   Virginia Quarterly Review: A National Journal of Literature and Discussion
VR   Vox Romanica: Annales Helvetici Explorandis Linguis Romanicis Destinati
Vsesvit   Literaturno-Mystets'kyi ta Hromads' ko-Politychnyi Zhumal (USSR)
WascanaR   Wascana Review
WC   Wordsworth Circle
WHR   Western Humanities Review
WLWE   World Literature Written in English
WTJ   Westminster Theological Journal
WVUPP   West Virginia University Philological Papers
XUS   Xavier University Studies
YCC   Yearbook of Comparative Criticism

YES   Yearbook of English Studies
YFS   Yale French Studies
YR   Yale Review
YWES   Year's Work in English Studies
ZAA   Zeitschrift für Anglistik und Amerikanistik
ZRL   Zagadnienia Rodzajów Literackich: Woprosy Literaturnych
           Zanrov (Poland)

BIBLIOGRAPHY AND REFERENCE WORKS

1 **Abstracts of English Studies.** Oxford and New York: Basil Blackwell.
Published four times a year for the Editorial Board, English Department, Univ. of Calgary. Latest vol. 34, 1991.

2 **[Allen, Don Cameron.]** "Bibliography of Books and Articles by Don Cameron Allen." *ELH*, 36, 1969, 291–95.
Lists sixteen studies on Milton.

3 **Amory, Hugh.** "Things Unattempted Yet: A Bibliography of the First Edition of *Paradise Lost*." *BC*, 32, 1983, 41–66.
Analyzes the order of printing of the first six issues of the first edition of *Paradise Lost*, examining their structural differences, title pages, and binding orders and creating a timeframe for printings and revisions.

4 **Arai, Akira.** "A Select Bibliography of Milton." *Studies in Milton* (Tokyo: Kinseido, 1974), pp. 1–24.
In Japanese, except for English titles.

5 **[Barker, Arthur Edward.]** "Selected List of Publications and Lectures of Arthur Edward Barker." *Familiar Colloquy: Essays Presented to Arthur Edward Barker.* Ed. by Patricia Brückmann (Toronto: Oberon Press, 1978), pp. 227–30.
Compiled by Jane Couchman. Includes lists of theses and dissertations supervised.

6 **Bentley, Christopher.** "The Earliest Milton Word-Index." *MiltonQ*, 9, 1975, 47–48.
On the *Verbal Index to "Paradise Lost"* (1741), attributed to Alexander Cruden. "In spite of some shortcomings, it is in general a worthy predecessor of the modern literary concordance, and an interesting sidelight on Milton scholarship in the earlier eighteenth century."

7 **Bergeron, David M.** *Twentieth-Century Criticism of English Masques, Pageants, and Entertainments: 1558–1642.* San Antonio, TX: Trinity Univ. Press, 1972. xvi, 67pp.
Contains 143 items of twentieth-century criticism of *Comus*, pp. 17–26.

8 **"Bibliography of Doctoral Dissertations in British and American Literature."** *GyS*, 5, No. 3, 1978.
A special issue that lists several recent dissertations.

9 **Boswell, Jackson Campbell.** *Milton's Library: A Catalogue of the Remains of John Milton's Library and an Annotated Reconstruction of Milton's Library and Ancillary Readings.* New York and London: Garland Publishing, 1975. xv, 263pp.
A list by author and title of 1,520 books which survive from Milton's library or which he mentions in the *Commonplace Book* or cites in his works. Includes some doubtful entries and is admittedly a preliminary work. See also Nos. 190 and 789. Reviews: *MiltonQ*, 9, 1975, 84–85; Michael Lieb, *Cithara*, 17, No. 1, 1977, 65–67.

10 **Bradshaw, John.** *A Concordance to the Poetical Works of John Milton.* Boston, MA: Longwood, 1977; Ann Arbor, MI: Univ. Microfilms International, 1980 Books on Demand Reprints.
Reprints of Stevens No. 24, originally published in 1894.

11 **British Columbia. University Library.** *Critical Studies of John Milton and His Works, 1958–1963.* Vancouver: Univ. of British Columbia, 1964. 15pp.

Supplements the 1960 edition of Huckabay's Milton bibliography (Huckabay No. 28). An unannotated, alphabetical list. Additional supplement, 1968. 15pp.

12 ["British Museum Exhibition."] *SCN*, 33, 1975, 103–04.

Lists items displayed for the tercentenary exhibition of the publication of *Paradise Lost*.

13 Bush, Douglas. "Milton, 1608–1674." *English Poetry: Select Bibliographical Guides*. Ed. by A. E. Dyson (London and New York: Oxford Univ. Press, 1971), pp. 76–95.

Includes comments on editions and criticism, as well as a list of standard references.

14 Camé, Jean-François. "Milton: *Paradise Lost*, Books IV and IX: Bibliographie Sélective et Commentée." *BSEAA*, 13, 1981, 9–42.

A highly selective classified list.

15 Cameron, William J. *A Perfectible Milton Bibliography: An Experiment in Collocation of the Machine-Readable Bibliographic Records of the HPB Project*. London, Ontario: School of Library and Information Science, Univ. of Western Ontario, 1972. viii, 88pp.

Explains the methodology being used to compile a perfectible Milton bibliography. "It is our aim in this publication to describe our attempts to provide an even more sophisticated series of Milton catalogs . . . that will be equal to or better than the British Museum Catalogue as a tool for providing access for the Milton scholar to existing collections of Milton and Miltoniana up to and including 1800." The final product will be a computerized checklist and union catalog of pre-1801 editions of Milton and Miltoniana. Contains two illustrative inserts. Review: James L. Harner, *SCN*, 31, 1973, 76–77.

16 [Cameron, William J., ed.] *A Short Title Catalog of Milton and Miltoniana*

Transferred from Special Collections of the School of Library and Information Science to the G. William Stuart Collection of the D. B. Weldon Library, the University of Western Ontario. Western Hemisphere Short Title Catalog No. 1. December, 1981. iii, 20pp.

Revised, January, 1982.

17 [Cameron, William J., ed.] *A Short-Title Catalogue of Seventeenth and Eighteenth Century Editions of the Writings of John Milton in Special Collections, Douglas Library, Queen's University, Kingston, Ontario*. Western Hemisphere Short Title Catalog No. 2. January, 1982. iii, 17pp.

Revised, March, 1982.

18 [Cameron, William J., ed.] *A Short-Title Catalog of Seventeenth and Eighteenth Century Editions of the Writings of John Milton in Special Collections, Mills Memorial Library, McMaster University, Hamilton, Ontario*. Western Hemisphere Short Title Catalog No. 3. April, 1982. iii, 38pp.

19 Cleveland, Charles Dexter. *A Complete Concordance to the Poetical Works of John Milton*. Folcroft, PA: Folcroft Library Editions, 1970, 1976, 1978; Norwood, PA: Norwood Editions, 1977.

Reprints of Stevens No. 11, originally published in 1867.

20 Cohen, Michael M., and **Robert E. Bourdette, Jr.** "Richard Bentley's Edition of *Paradise Lost* (1732): A Bibliography." *MiltonQ*, 14, 1980, 49–54.

Arranges items according to texts, biography and correspondence, critical methods, contemporary critical reactions to Bentley's edition, and modern criticism.

21 Coleridge, K. A. *A Descriptive Catalogue of the Milton Collection in the Alexander Turnbull Library, Wellington, New Zealand*. Wellington: Oxford Univ. Press, 1980. xxv, 536pp.

Provides extensive bibliographical descriptions of 224 editions and translations of Milton's works printed before 1801, as well as less detailed descriptions of 223 other works, the more important Miltoniana in the Alexander Turnbull Library. Includes 60 facsimiles of title pages. Review: Leo Miller, *MiltonQ*, 15, 1981, 126–28.

22 Comprehensive Dissertation Index, 1861–1972. Ann Arbor, MI: Univ. Microfilms International.

Lists title, author, date, university, and *DAI* citation. Comprised mainly of dissertations written in North America. Vol. 30, 1972, pp. 72–75. Ten-year Cumulation: Vol. 30, 1973–1982, 1984, pp. 70–72.

23 Dahiyat, Eid Abdallah. "Bibliography of Writings in Arabic Pertaining to Milton." *John Milton and the Arab-Islamic Culture* (Amman: Shukayr and Akasheh, 1987), pp. 120–21.

Lists fifteen items of criticism and six brief translations.

24 Diekhoff, John S. "Appendix: The Text of *Comus*, 1634 to 1645." *"A Maske at Ludlow": Essays on Milton's "Comus."* Ed. by Diekhoff (Ann Arbor, MI: Univ. Microfilms International, 1980 Books on Demand Reprints), pp. 251–75.

Reprint of Huckabay No. 2446, originally published in 1968.

25 [Diekhoff, John S.] "Bibliography." *MiltonQ*, 4, 1970, 19.

Compiled by James G. Taaffe. Includes only items about Milton.

26 [Diekhoff, John S.] "John S. Diekhoff: A Bibliography." *Calm of Mind: Tercentenary Essays on "Paradise Regained" and "Samson Agonistes" in Honor of John S. Diekhoff.* Ed. by Joseph Anthony Wittreich, Jr. (Cleveland, OH, and London: Press of Case Western Reserve Univ., 1971), pp. xix–xxiv.

Compiled by Jane Cerny. Lists Diekhoff's publications on Milton.

27 Dillon, John B. "Milton's Latin and Greek Verse: An Annotated Bibliography." *MiltonS*, 19, 1984, 227–307.

An extensive list, with ample annotations. Part 1: Reference and Bibliography; Part 2: Editions, Translations, Illustrations, and Comment (General and Multiple); Part 3: Individual Poems (and Groups Thereof); Part 4: Reputation and Influence; Index Nominum.

28 Dissertation Abstracts International. Ann Arbor, MI: Univ. Microfilms International.

Published annually since 1938. The "A" volume includes abstracts of dissertations in English literature. Restricted mainly to universities in the United States and Canada.

29 Elliott, V. G., comp. *John Milton: An Exhibition of Seventeenth-Century Editions.* Wellington: Alexander Turnbull Library, 1974. 28pp.

A catalog of an exhibition mounted as a tercentenary tribute to Milton and as a tribute to Alexander Turnbull, who started the Milton collection in Wellington. Contains seventy-six items.

30 Enozawa, Kazuyoshi, and **Miyo Takone.** *Bibliography of English Renaissance Studies in Japan: I, 1961–1970.* Tokyo: Renaissance Institute, Sophia Univ., 1979. v, 218pp.

Lists items chronologically according to author. Discusses Milton scholarship in Japan, pp. 29–46.

31 An Exhibit of Seventeenth-Century Editions of Writings by John Milton. Preface by William Riley Parker. Note by David A. Randall. Bloomington, IN: The Lilly Library, 1969. N. pag.

A checklist of seventeenth-century editions of Milton's work. All items exhibited are from the Lilly Library.

32 Fallon, Robert Thomas. "Miltonic Documents in the Public Record Office, London." *SB*, 32, 1979, 82–100.

Provides an annotated list of Milton documents found in the Public Record Office. Finds that Milton spent most of his time as a public servant corresponding with foreign powers.

33 [Flannagan, Roy C.] *"Milton Quarterly."* *MiltonQ*, 4, 1970, 1.

A talk given by the editor before the Milton Society of America on December 27, 1969. On the transition of *Milton Newsletter* to *Milton Quarterly* and on the publication's purposes.

34 Fletcher, Harris Francis. *Contributions to a Milton Bibliography 1800–1930, Being a List of Addenda to Stevens's "Reference Guide to Milton."* Univ. of Illinois Studies in Language and Literature, 16. Urbana: Univ. of Illinois Press, 1966; New York: Russell and Russell, 1967; New York: Johnson Reprint Corp., 1968; Folcroft, PA: Folcroft Library Editions, 1969, 1973.

Reprints of Huckabay No. 19, originally published in 1931.

35 Gabel, Gernot U., and **Gisela R. Gabel,** comps. *Dissertations in English and American Literature: Theses Accepted by Austrian, French, and Swiss Universities, 1875–1970.* Hamburg: Gernot Gabel Verlag, 1977. 198pp.

36 Gabler, Hans Walter. *English Renaissance Studies in German, 1945–1967.* Heidelberg: Quelle and Meyer, 1971. 77pp.

A checklist of German, Austrian, and Swiss academic theses, monographs, and book publications on English language and literature, c. 1500–1650. Supplies translations of titles into English and contains an index in English. See No. 39.

37 [Gardner, Dame Helen.] "A Select List of the Published Writings of Dame Helen Gardner, DBE, MA, DLitt, FBA, FRSL." *English Renaissance Studies Presented to Dame Helen Gardner in Honour of Her Seventieth Birthday.* [Ed. by John Carey] (Oxford: Clarendon Press, 1980), pp. 291–98.

Compiled by Helen Peters. Lists selected publications from 1933 to 1979, including Gardner's Milton studies and reviews.

38 Gilbert, Allan H. *A Geographical Dictionary of Milton.* New York: Russell and Russell, 1968; Folcroft, PA: Folcroft

Library Editions, 1969; Norwood, PA: Norwood Editions, 1977; Philadelphia, PA: R. West, 1978.

Reprints of Stevens No. 64, originally published in 1919.

39 Habicht, Werner, ed. *English and American Studies in German.* Summaries of Theses and Monographs. A Supplement to *Anglia.* Tübingen: Max Niemeyer Verlag, 1969.

Takes up where No. 36 leaves off. Published annually.

40 Hanford, James Holly, and **William A. McQueen,** comps. *Milton.* Goldentree Bibliographies in Language and Literature. Second edition. Arlington Heights, IL: Harlan Davidson, 1979. x, 111pp.

An updating of Huckabay No. 26. Contains 1,650 unannotated items.

41 Hanford, James Holly, and **James G. Taaffe.** *A Milton Handbook.* Fifth edition. Revised. New York: Appleton-Century-Crofts, 1970. xiii, 374pp.

A revision of Huckabay No. 25, whose first edition appeared in 1926. Bibliography, pp. 343–64. Reviews: *MiltonQ,* 4, 1970, 42–43; James H. Sims, *SCN,* 29, 1971, 62–64.

42 Himy, Armand. "J. Milton: Bibliographie Sélective et Critique." *BSEAA,* 3, 1976, 7–20.

Provides brief annotations for 140 items, with a focus on *Samson Agonistes.*

43 Howard, Patsy C. *Theses in English Literature, 1894–1970.* Ann Arbor, MI: Pierian Press, 1973.

Unpublished baccalaureate and masters' theses. John Milton, pp. 187–99.

44 Howard-Hill, T. H. *Bibliography of British Literary Bibliographies.* Vol. 1 of *Index to British Literary Bibliography.* Oxford: Clarendon Press, 1969. xxv, 570pp. Revised and enlarged edition. Oxford: Clarendon Press, 1987.

Lists thirty items, pp. 410–12.

45 Howard-Hill, T. H. *British Bibliography and Textual Criticism: A Bibliography.*

Vols. 4–5. Oxford: Clarendon Press, 1979. Vol. 6, An Index, 1980.

For Milton, see vol. 5, pp. 304–14, and vol. 6, pp. 295–96.

46 Huckabay, Calvin, comp. *John Milton: An Annotated Bibliography, 1929–1968.* Revised edition. Duquesne Studies, Philological Series, vol. 1. Pittsburgh, PA: Duquesne Univ. Press; Louvain: Editions E. Nauwelaerts, 1969. xvii, 392pp.

John T. Shawcross (*MiltonQ*, 5, 1971, 64–65) lists nineteen omitted items. Reviews: Purvis E. Boyette, *SCB*, 30, 1970, 148–49; J. Max Patrick, *SCN*, 28, 1970, 25–26; C. A. Patrides, *SN*, 42, 1970, 471–73.

47 Hudson, Gladys W. *"Paradise Lost": A Concordance.* Detroit, MI: Gale Research Co., 1970. viii, 361pp.

Compiled with a Honeywell 1200 computer. Reviews: *MiltonQ*, 5, 1971, 80; J. Max Patrick, *SCN*, 29, 1971, 64, 66; R. E. C. Houghton, *N&Q*, 19, 1972, 185–87; Jason P. Rosenblatt, *CHum*, 7, 1973, 421–24; Edward R. Weismiller, *RenQ*, 27, 1974, 255–57.

48 Hunter, William B. "A Bibliographical Excursus into Milton's Trinity Manuscript." *MiltonQ*, 19, 1985, 61–71. Reprinted in *The Descent of Urania: Studies in Milton, 1946–1988* (Lewisburg, PA: Bucknell Univ. Press; London and Toronto: Associated Univ. Presses, 1989), pp. 246–60.

Discusses the textual and bibliographical questions raised by the Trinity Manuscript of Milton's poetry. Concentrates on Comus.

49 Hunter, William B., Jr., gen. ed. *A Milton Encyclopedia.* 9 vols. Lewisburg, PA: Bucknell Univ. Press; London: Associated Univ. Presses, 1978–83.

"This compilation attempts to bring together all of the important information and opinion concerning the life and works of John Milton." Vol. 1, Ab-By, 1978, 208pp.; vol. 2, C-Ec, 1978, 206pp.; vol. 3, Ed-Hi, 1978, 199pp.; vol. 4, Ho-La, 1978, 218pp.; vol. 5, Le-N, 1979, 206pp.; vol. 6, O-Po, 1979, 216pp.; vol. 7, Pr-Sl, 1979, 208pp.; vol. 8, Sm-Z, 1980, 205pp.; vol. 9, Bibliography and Indexes and a few additional entries, 1983, 170pp. See No. 54. Reviews of vol. 1: *MiltonQ*, 12, 1978, 110–11; John Mulryan, *Cithara*, 17, No. 2, 1978, 68–69; David S. Berkeley, *SCB*, 38, 1979, 128. Review of vols. 1–4: C. A. Patrides, *RES*, 30, 1979, 215–17. Review of vols. 2–4: *MiltonQ*, 12, 1978, 148–50. Review of vol. 5: Albert C. Labriola, *MiltonQ*, 14, 1980, 25–27. Review of vol. 8: Edward Le Comte, *MiltonQ*, 15, 1981, 62–64 (a summary view with emphasis on vol. 8). Review of vols. 1–9: John Mulryan, *Cithara*, 24, No. 1, 1984, 75–76.

50 Hunter, William B., ed. *Milton's English Poetry: Being Entries from "A Milton Encyclopedia."* Lewisburg, PA: Bucknell Univ. Press; London: Associated Univ. Presses, 1986. 248pp.

Contains twenty-three entries from No. 49, some of which have been revised, about Milton's biography and poetry. The bibliography (pp. 226–43), by John T. Shawcross, is selective. Review: Charles Martindale, *TLS*, Feb. 5–11, 1988, p. 142.

51 Ingram, William, and **Kathleen Swaim,** eds. *A Concordance to Milton's English Poetry.* Oxford: Clarendon Press; New York: Oxford Univ. Press, 1972. xvii, 683pp.

Compiled with an IBM 360/67. Reviews: R. E. C. Houghton, *N&Q*, 19, 1972, 185–87; *MiltonQ*, 6, No. 2, 1972, 42–43: J. Max Patrick, *SCN*, 31, 1973, 76; Jason P. Rosenblatt, *CHum*, 7, 1973, 421–24.

52 James, Brian, ed. *A Catalogue of The Tract Collection of Saint David's University College, Lampeter.* Introduction by Julian Roberts. London: Mansell, 1975. xix, 316pp.

Deals with works printed between 1520 and 1843, many from the collection amassed by the Bowdler family. Contains twelve Milton items.

53 Johnson, William C. *Milton Criticism: A Subject Index.* Folkestone: Dawson, 1978. xviii, 450pp.

"This work presents a detailed and relatively complete index to subjects referred to, or covered in, a carefully selected group of 150 books of criticism pertaining to the life and writings of John Milton." Reviews: Edward Jones, *MiltonQ*, 13, 1979, 55–56; Archie Burnett, *N&Q*, 26, 1979, 249-51; Albert C. Labriola, *SCN*, 37, 1979, 10–11; Roger Lejosne, *EA*, 34, 1981, 221–22.

54 Kelley, Maurice. "A Review of Four Entries on the Milton Mss. in *A Milton Encyclopedia.*" *MiltonQ*, 20, 1986, 32.

Questions entries in No. 49 under autographs, amanuenses, Milton's library, and Milton's marginalia.

55 Klemp, P. J. *The Essential Milton: An Annotated Bibliography of Major Modern Studies.* Boston, MA: G. K. Hall, 1989. xiv, 474pp.

Contains 1,021 annotated citations to "the most significant Milton scholarship published between 1900 and 1987." Excludes theses, dissertations and studies written in foreign languages. Reviews: John T. Shawcross, *Analytical and Enumerative Bibliography*, 3, 1989, 180–84; Roy Flannagan, *Literary Research*, 14, 1989, 34–37; Robert E. Brown, *LJ*, 114, 1989, 52; Albert W. Fields, *BB*, 47, 1990, 247–49; Janet R. Ivey, *ARBA*, 21, 1990, 501; William B. Hunter, Jr., *MiltonQ*, 25, 1991, 30–31; Robert C. Evans, *SCJ*, 22, 1991, 154.

56 Klemp, P. J. "Numerology and English Renaissance Literature: Twentieth-Century Studies." *BB*, 40, 1983, 231–41. Contains twelve Milton items.

57 Kuroda, Kenjiro. "A Note on Milton Bibliography in Japan—A Review of Dr. Miyanishi's *Milton Studies in Japan.*" *Kobe Miscellany*, 6, 1972, 33–43.

58 Kuroda, Kenjiro, comp. *Nihon no Milton Bunken: Shiryo to Kaidai.* Tokyo: Kazama Shobo, 1978. 917pp.

Materials on Milton published in Japan in the Meiji period. See also Irene Samuel in *MiltonQ*, 13, 1979, 66–67, and Nos. 77 and 81.

59 Le Comte, Edward. "The *Index* to the Columbia Milton: Its Virtues and Defects." *Greyfriar*, 28, 1987, 3–17. Reprinted in *Milton Re-Viewed: Ten Essays* (New York and London: Garland Publishing, 1991), pp. 103–18.

Discusses several indices and concordances and concludes that the Columbia Index (see No. 295) "may and does have rivals, but it has no substitutes."

60 Lockwood, Laura E. *Lexicon to the English Poetical Works of John Milton.* New York: Burt Franklin, 1968; Folcroft, PA: Folcroft Library Editions, 1970; Norwood, PA: Norwood Editions, 1975.

Reprints of Stevens No. 40 and Huckabay No. 40, originally published in 1907. Review: Michael Lieb, *Cithara*, 14, No. 1, 1974, 132–33.

61 Luey, Beth E., ed. *"Milton Studies" Index: Volumes I–XII.* Pittsburgh, PA: Univ. of Pittsburgh Press, 1980. viii, 105pp.

Contains three sections: Explanatory Notes; Articles by Subject; and the Index itself. "There is more repetition in this index than in most, but this seemed preferable to making it difficult or impossible to find a topic that could be indexed in several different ways."

62 MacLaren, I. S. "Milton's Nativity Ode: The Function of Poetry and Structures of Response in 1629 (with a Bibliography of Twentieth-Century Criticism)." *MiltonS*, 15, 1981, 181–200.

"A chronological ordering has been chosen to indicate more readily the kind of critical attention which the Nativity ode has attracted at different periods in this century." Lists approximately eighty-eight items. See also No. 1557.

63 [Marilla, Esmond Linworth.] "Publications of Esmond Linworth Marilla." *Essays in Honor of Esmond Linworth Marilla.* Ed. by Thomas Austin Kirby and William John Olive. Louisiana State Univ. Studies, Humanities Series, no. 19 (Baton Rouge: Louisiana State Univ. Press, 1970), pp. ix–xi.

Includes Marilla's Milton studies.

64 Masters Abstracts. *Abstracts of Selected Masters Theses on Microfilm.* Ann Arbor, MI: Univ. Microfilms International, 1962.

65 MCJ News. Published by the Milton Center of Japan, English Department, Doshisha Women's College of Liberal Arts, Kyoto.

Ed. by Fumio Ochi. Vol. 1, 1976, 10–24, contains "Milton Bibliography in Japan (1972–1975)" and addenda and corrigenda to No. 81. Each volume includes an annual bibliography of Milton studies in Japan; latest bibliography (for 1991), vol. 14, 1993, 21–23.

66 McKenzie, D. F. "Milton's Printers: Matthew, Mary and Samuel Simmons." *MiltonQ*, 14, 1980, 87–91.

Offers evidence that Matthew, Mary, and Samuel Simmons were father, mother, and son.

67 McNamee, Lawrence F. *Dissertations in English and American Literature, Supplement One: Theses Accepted by American, British, and German Universities, 1964–1968.* New York and London: R. R. Bowker Co., 1969.

Chapter 8 lists eighty-six dissertations on Milton. Review: J. Max Patrick, *SCN*, 28, 1970, 12.

68 McNamee, Lawrence F. *Dissertations in English and American Literature, Supplement Two: Theses Accepted by American, British, British Commonwealth, and German Universities. 1969–1973.* New York and London: R. R. Bowker Co., 1974. ix, 690pp.

Chapter 8 lists ninety-nine dissertations on Milton.

69 McNamee, Lawrence F. *Ninety-Nine Years of English Dissertations.* Commerce: East Texas State Univ., 1969. 123pp.

Contains information on Milton dissertations, pp. 38–39.

70 Mikolajczak, Michael Allen. "Reading Milton: A Summary of Illuminating Efforts." *The Cambridge Companion to Milton.* Ed. by Dennis Danielson (Cambridge and New York: Cambridge Univ. Press, 1989), pp. 277–89.

Surveys useful tools for the study of Milton.

71 Mikolajczak, Michael Allen, ed. *A Selected Catalog of Books in the Seventeenth-Century Research Collection of the University of Wisconsin, Milwaukee, with "A Bibliographer's 'Apologia Pro Vita Sua'" by Harrison T. Meserole.* Milwaukee: The Golda Meir Library, Univ. of Wisconsin, 1982. xii, 72pp.

Introductory comments by Joseph Anthony Wittreich, Jr., William F. Halloran, and Donald C. Emerson. Preface by William C. Roselle, and Foreword by Mikolajczak. Consists mostly of tributes to J. Max Patrick, whose gift of some six-hundred rare books formed the nucleus of the collection.

72 Miller, Leo. "Miltoniana: Some Hitherto Unrecognized Items." *PBSA*, 70, 1976, 107–10.

"The recent transfer of the G. William Stuart, Jr. collection of Miltoniana . . . to the Alexander Turnbull Library, New Zealand, has brought to light three items which have hitherto not been recorded in Milton studies": a 1653 Flemish/Dutch translation of *Regii Sanguinis Clamor*; an edition of *Pro Populo Anglicano Defensio*, a presentation copy given to Henry Darley, M.P., member of the Council of State in 1651; and a volume (1727) partly composed and edited by Jenkin Thomas Philipps and containing a "modernized" version of *Of Education*.

73 Miller, Leo. "National Union Catalogue." *MiltonQ*, 10, 1976, 94.

Describes what can and cannot be

found on Milton in the catalog, vol. 385, pp. 243–392.

74 Milton and the Romantics. Georgia Southern College, Statesboro, Georgia. Ed. by Luther L. Scales. Beginning in 1975, an annual journal on notes and relationships between Milton and the Romantics. Now published as *Romanticism Past and Present* at Northeastern University.

75 "Milton Encyclopedia." *MiltonQ*, 4, 1970, 11.

The Board of Directors met at the 1969 MLA Convention in Denver and discussed the project with interested individuals.

76 "Milton in France." *MiltonQ*, 13, 1979, 64–65.

Describes the accomplishments of French Miltonists and lists recent publications about Milton in *Études Anglaises* and *Cahiers Elisabéthains*.

77 "Milton in Japan." *MiltonQ*, 13, 1979, 66–67.

Reports on the activities of the Milton Center of Japan and on individual studies and translations.

78 Milton Quarterly. Ohio Univ., Athens, Ohio.

Ed. by Roy C. Flannagan. Published quarterly. Started in 1967 as *Milton Newsletter*. Changed title in 1970 and published since 1986 by Medieval and Renaissance Texts and Studies at the State Univ. of New York, Binghamton.

79 "Milton Society of America." Annual Dinner and Meeting.

An annual booklet containing business reports, the society's constitution, biographical material on a given year's honored scholar, work-in-progress, and membership list. Albert C. Labriola is the current editor.

80 Milton Studies. Pittsburgh, PA: Univ. of Pittsburgh Press. Ann Arbor, MI: Univ. Microfilms International.

Started in 1969. Ed. by James D. Simmonds; Albert C. Labriola became editor in 1992. An annual collection of essays, with an occasional special volume. See No. 485.

81 Miyanishi, Mitsuo. *Milton in Japan, 1871–1971.* Tokyo: Kinseido, 1975. 312pp.

In Japanese. Contents: Milton in the Meiji Era (1868–1912); Milton in the Taisho and Showa Eras; Conclusion: Milton and Japan; Milton Bibliography in Japan (1841–1971). A concise and revised edition of *Milton Studies in Japan for a Hundred Years Since the Meiji Restoration* (1971). Provides "brief but pertinent criticism on the principal research works in respect to their historical significance and literary merits." See Nos. 57 and 65. Reviews: Frank L. Huntley, *MiltonQ*, 9, 1975, 83–84; Fumio Ochi, *EigoS*, 121, 1975, 313–14.

82 Modern Humanities Research Association. *Annual Bibliography of English Language and Literature.*

Since 1921. Contains a section on Milton. Latest vol. 67, 1992, 412–19.

83 Modern Language Association. *MLA International Bibliography of Books and Articles on the Modern Languages and Literatures.*

Since 1922. Contains a section on Milton. Latest is for 1993 (vol. 1, pp. 50–52).

84 Mulryan, John. "John Milton, 1608–1674." *Research Guide to Biography and Criticism.* Ed. by Walton Beacham. 6 vols. (Washington, DC: Research Publishing, 1985–91), vol. 2, pp. 830–34.

Lists standard editions of Milton's works, selected biographies, selected volumes of criticism, and dictionaries and encyclopedias.

85 "Our Index and Illustrations." *MiltonQ*, 11, 1977, 123.

Announces that starting with the current issue, *Milton Quarterly* will be indexed in the *Arts and Humanities Citation Index*. Notes the source of this issue's illustrations.

86 Parker, William Riley. "Milton's Commonplace Book: An Index and Notes." *MiltonN*, 3, 1969, 41–54.

An edition by John T. Shawcross of Parker's alphabetical index to the *Commonplace Book*, with an analysis of its entries. The index was not complete when Parker died.

87 Patrides, C. A. *An Annotated Critical Bibliography of John Milton.* Brighton: Harvester; New York: St. Martin's Press, 1987. xii, 200pp.

Highly selective. Contains 1,145 items, most published within the past four decades. No annotations for many items. Reviews: *BBN*, Apr. 1987, p. 223; *ARBA*, 19, 1988, 489; *Library Review*, 37, 1988, 64; Michael Fixler, *RES*, 39, 1988, 604; Thomas F. Healy, *MLR*, 84, 1989, 717–18.

88 Patrides, C. A. "John Milton." *The New Cambridge Bibliography of English Literature.* Ed. by George Watson (Cambridge: Cambridge Univ. Press, 1974), vol. 1, pp. 1237–96.

89 Patrides, C. A. "A Reading List on the Language of Theology." *Bright Essence: Studies in Milton's Theology.* By W. B. Hunter, Patrides, and J. H. Adamson (Salt Lake City: Univ. of Utah Press, 1971), pp. 179–81.

A bibliography of modern studies pertinent to Milton's theology.

90 Pinto, V. De Sola. *The English Renaissance, 1510–1688.* With a Chapter on Literature and Music by Bruce Pattison. Third revised edition. London: Cresset Press, 1966. 403pp.

Includes bibliographical section on Milton, pp. 354–72.

91 Pironon, Jean. *Bibliographies; Encyclopedies Miltoniennes; Editions de la Poésie de Milton de 1968 à 1978 Inclus. La Critique de la Poésie Miltonienne: 1942–1978.* Doctoral diss., Université Paul Valéry, Montpellier, 1979. 2 vols. 760pp.

An extensive bibliography which includes Milton encyclopedias, editions of his poetry published from 1968 to 1978, works of literary history concerning him, new criticism, and works on the theory of criticism.

92 Rosenblatt, Jason P. "Three New Milton Concordances." *CHum*, 7, 1973, 421–24.

Review article. Discusses the merits of the *Context Concordance to John Milton's "Paradise Lost,"* by Linda D. Misek (No. 2740); *A Concordance to Milton's English Poetry,* by William Ingram and Kathleen Swaim (No. 51); and *"Paradise Lost": A Concordance,* by Gladys W. Hudson (No. 47). Concludes that Misek's work (with a UNIVAC 1108) gives little human judgment on the text; Ingram and Swaim's is generated by an IBM 360/67, and is definitive; and Hudson's is comprehensive but outdated.

93 Schlösser, Leonard B. "John Milton: The Poet Illustrated." *Gazette of the Grolier Club*, 20–21, 1974, 14–45.

Catalog of the Milton memorial exhibition, December 19, 1973 through February 14, 1974, with commentary. A catalog was printed separately for distribution at the exhibit itself, which was held in commemoration of the three-hundredth anniversary of Milton's death and of the second edition of *Paradise Lost.*

94 Shafer, Ronald G., ed. *The Newsletter of the Friends of Milton's Cottage, 1977.* Printed at the Armstrong Campus, Indiana Univ. of Pennsylvania.

Issued intermittently. Contains information about the restoration and refurbishing of the cottage at Chalfont St. Giles.

95 Shawcross, John T., comp. *The Collection of the Works of John Milton and Miltoniana in the Margaret I. King Library, the University of Kentucky.* Foreword by Thomas B. Stroup. [Univ. of Kentucky Libraries, Occasional Papers, No. 8.] Lexington: The Press of the Library, Univ. of Kentucky, 1985. 113pp.

"Compiled here in three sections are

works by Milton or those of a secondary nature which discuss him, allude to him, or imitate his writing, from the seventeenth and eighteenth centuries, arranged chronologically (I: Milton and Miltoniana, 1641–1799); selected important works by or about him from the nineteenth and twentieth centuries, arranged by classification (II: Selected Later Editions, Biographies, Reference Works, and Criticism); and some few seventeenth-century items significant for a fuller study, arranged chronologically (III: Some Important Contemporary Volumes for a Study of Milton)."

96 Shawcross, John T. "Early Milton Bibliography, Its Nature and Implications." *TEXT*, 2, 1985, 173–80.

Discusses seventeenth-century Milton bibliography.

97 Shawcross, John T., comp. *Milton: A Bibliography for the Years 1624–1700.* Medieval and Renaissance Texts and Studies, vol. 30. Binghamton, NY: Medieval and Renaissance Texts and Studies, 1984. xiv, 452pp.

"The present bibliography tries to bring together all manuscripts and editions of the works and all studies and critical statements concerning Milton's life and works, all allusions and quotations, and all significant imitations during the years 1624–1700." Contents: Primary Bibliography; Secondary Bibliography; Indices: Milton: His Works and Related Subjects; State Papers; Non-Miltonic Titles; Authors of Non-Miltonic Works, Editors, Translators, Booksellers (Cataloguers); Designers and Engravers; Printers, Publishers, and Booksellers; Owners of Printed Copies Cited; Manuscript Holdings of Cited Items. See Nos. 98 and 99. Reviews: Roy Flannagan, *MiltonQ*, 19, 1985, 20–21; Gillian Avery, *TLS*, Mar. 22, 1985, p. 316; *AN&Q*, 23, 1985, 93–94; *ARBA*, 17, 1986, 461.

98 Shawcross, John. *"Milton: A Bibliography for the Years 1624–1700*: Corrigenda and Addenda." *MiltonQ*, 19, 1985, 21–22.

See No. 97. These corrigenda and addenda are included in No. 99.

99 Shawcross, John T., comp. *"Milton: A Bibliography for the Years 1624–1700" : Corrigenda and Addenda.* Medieval and Renaissance Texts and Studies, vol. 30A. Binghamton, NY: Medieval and Renaissance Texts and Studies, 1990. i, 34pp.

See No. 97. Includes material in No. 98.

100 Shawcross, John T. "Research and the State of Milton Studies." *LRN*, 7, 1982, 143–53.

Surveys and evaluates the basic research tools for Milton studies. Emphasizes the need for an updated bibliography.

101 Shawcross, John T. "Select Bibliography." *Milton's English Poetry: Being Entries from "A Milton Encyclopedia"* (Lewisburg, PA: Bucknell Univ. Press; London and Toronto: Associated Univ. Presses, 1986), pp. 226–43.

Suggests that readers see also the bibliographies for individual poems within the essays themselves.

102 Shawcross, John T. "Some Inferences about Literary History from the John Milton Collection in the Margaret I. King Library." *KyR*, 2, No. 3, 1981, 85–99.

Examines and comments on the Milton collection in the library of the University of Kentucky and concludes, "It should be clear from the preceding that literary history is always subject to change, and most significant is revision which derives from the kind of factual evidence we have glanced at here. For Milton a painstaking bibliography of primary and secondary materials for the years leading up to 1800 is manifestly needed."

103 Shawcross, John T. "There's Always Something To Be Learned through Bibliographic Study: The Case of Milton." *MiltonQ*, 11, 1977, 94.

Abstract of a paper presented at the 1977 NEMLA Convention. "A seventeenth-century primary and secondary bibliography of works by and about John Milton can lead to a variety of data."

104 Sterne, Laurence, and **Harold H. Kollmeier,** gen. eds. *A Concordance to the English Prose of John Milton.* Medieval and Renaissance Texts and Studies, vol. 35. Binghamton, NY: Medieval and Renaissance Texts and Studies, 1985. xxii, 1491pp.

This concordance takes the place of an index originally planned for the Yale *Complete Prose Works* (No. 366). Does not include English translations. Reviews: Roy Flannagan, *MiltonQ,* 20, 1986, 103–05; Michael Fixler, *RES,* 38, 1987, 594.

105 The Renaissance Bulletin. Sophia Univ., Tokyo, 1975.

Contains a bibliography of studies in Japan from 1961–63.

106 Thompson, Claud A. " 'Coded' Signatures: A Printer's Clue to the Bibliographical Tangle of *The Doctrine and Discipline of Divorce* (1644)." *PBSA,* 68, 1974, 297–305.

Collates various copies of the work's second edition (1644) and summarizes the various states of correction in the five gatherings.

107 Thompson, Claud A. *"The Doctrine and Discipline of Divorce,* 1643–1645: A Bibliographical Study." *TCBS,* 7, 1977, 74–93.

Reviews the pamphlet's publication history and presents a bibliographical analysis and description of its four editions.

108 Thompson, Claud Adelbert. "Milton's *The Doctrine and Discipline of Divorce*: A Bibliographical Study." Doctoral diss., Univ. of Wisconsin, 1971. 146pp. Abs., *DAI,* 32, 1971, 1487A.

Studies four early editions of Milton's pamphlet to affirm "William Riley Parker's general conclusions" concerning its publication and to "identify the corrected states of . . . variant sheets" in the second edition.

109 Thompson, Elbert Nevius Sebring. *John Milton: A Topical Bibliography.* Folcroft, PA: Folcroft Library Editions, 1969; Norwood, PA: Norwood Editions, 1978.

Reprints of Stevens No. 63 and Huckabay No. 64, originally published in 1916.

110 Van Dorsten, J. A. "A Critical Bibliography of English Literature: Sixteenth and Seventeenth Centuries, Part I." *DQR,* 5, 1975, 54–60; "[Part II]," *DQR,* 7, 1977, 214–26.

Contains brief remarks on recent studies.

111 Watson, George, ed. *The Shorter New Cambridge Bibliography of English Literature.* Cambridge: Cambridge Univ. Press, 1981. xivpp., 1612 cols.; index, pp. 1615–22.

A condensed version of the five-volume *New Cambridge Bibliography* (1969–77; see No. 88), with some additions and corrections. Milton section, cols. 145–52, 352.

112 "Western Ontario Acquisition." *MiltonN,* 3, 1969, 21.

Notes the University of Western Ontario's acquisition of "a collection of seventeenth and eighteenth century works by and about Milton that ranks as the sixth most outstanding collection of Miltoniana in the world." The collection consists of 451 rare books and is reported to be "the world's last great private Milton collection." Lists several of the most valuable items.

113 The Year's Work in English Studies. Atlantic Highlands, NJ: Humanities Press; Oxford: Basil Blackwell.

From Oxford Univ. Press, starting in 1919; published annually. Latest vol. 72, 1991, 221–30 (Milton section by Thomas N. Corns).

BIOGRAPHY

114 Andrew Marvell: Poet and Politician, 1621–78: An Exhibition To Commemorate the Tercentenary of His Death. British Library Reference Division, July 14–October 1, 1978. Catalog compiled by Hilton Kelliher. London: British Museum Publications Limited for the British Library, 1978. 128pp.

Several items illustrate Marvell's relationship to Milton.

115 Arai, Akira. "Milton: A Short Biography." *Miscellaneous Essays on Milton* (Tokyo: Chukyo Shuppan, 1979), pp. 9–20.

In Japanese. A chronological survey of Milton's life and writings.

116 Arai, Akira. "Milton and the Restoration." *Miscellaneous Essays on Milton* (Tokyo: Chukyo Shuppan, 1979), pp. 45–71.

In Japanese. Discusses Milton's views of the Restoration, a "free commonwealth," and a "commonality."

117 Arai, Akira. "Milton and Thomas Young." *The Bulletin of the Tokyo University of Education, Literature Department*, 83, 1971, 1–14.

In Japanese; English summary, pp. 15–16. Believes that Young influenced Milton's decision to become a serious poet. Abs., *MiltonQ*, 5, 1971, 61.

118 Asahi, Satoru. "Milton's Britain and Italy." *MCJ News*, 3, 1979, 27–28.

Abstract of a paper presented at the Fourth Colloquium of MCJ in December, 1977. "I tried to elucidate some aspects of Milton's life and works" with photographs of such places as Ludlow Castle and Fiesole.

119 Barker, Arthur Edward. *Milton's Schoolmasters*. Folcroft, PA: Folcroft Library Editions, 1972, 1973.

Reprints of Huckabay No. 3102, originally published in 1937.

120 Belloc, Hilaire. *Milton*. London: Cassell, 1970.

Reprint of Huckabay No. 3104, originally published in 1935.

121 Bentley, G. E., Jr. "A Portrait of Milton Engraved by William Blake 'When Three Years of Age'? A Speculation by Samuel Palmer." *UTQ*, 51, 1981, 28–35.

On Samuel Palmer's statement that Blake reengraved the head of Giovanni Cipriani's portrait of Milton. Abs., *MiltonQ*, 16, 1982, 53.

122 Berry, William Grinton. *John Milton*. Folcroft, PA: Folcroft Library Editions, 1970, 1973; Norwood, PA: Norwood Editions, 1975; Philadelphia, PA: R. West, 1977.

Reprints of Stevens No. 2332, originally published in 1909.

123 Boswell, Jackson Campbell. "A Lost Book." *MiltonQ*, 7, 1973, 38–39.

Suggests Milton's possible ownership of *Navigation du Roy d'Écosse Jacques V* (1583), a geography book published in Paris by Nicolas de Nicolay.

124 Brennecke, Ernest, Jr. *John Milton the Elder and His Music*. New York: Octagon Books, 1973.

Reprint of Huckabay No. 3107, originally published in 1938.

125 Broadbent, John. "Inside Milton." *John Milton: Introductions*. Ed. by Broadbent (Cambridge: Cambridge Univ. Press, 1973), pp. 108–19.

Concerned with Milton's family, erotic feelings, friends, views of love, marriage and subsequent divorce pamphlets, handling of middle age, and fears at the time of the Restoration.

126 Brooke, Stopford A. *Milton*. Folcroft, PA: Folcroft Library Editions, 1971; New York: AMS Press, 1973; Norwood, PA: Norwood Editions, 1975, 1977; Philadelphia, PA: R. West, 1977.

Reprints of Stevens No. 2103, originally published in 1879.

127 Brown, Eleanor Gertrude. *Milton's Blindness*. New York: Columbia Univ. Press, 1967; New York: Octagon Books, 1968; Folcroft, PA: Folcroft Library Editions, 1973; Norwood, PA: Norwood Editions, 1975; Philadelphia, PA: R. West, 1977; Darby, PA: Arden Library, 1978.

Reprints of Huckabay No. 3111, originally published in 1934.

128 Brydges, Sir Samuel Egerton. *The Life of John Milton*. Ann Arbor, MI: Univ. Microfilms International, 1980 Books on Demand Reprints.

Reprint of Stevens No. 1667, originally published in 1835.

129 Bush, Douglas. "Plainly Built To Last." *VQR*, 43, 1967, 162–65.

Review essay on William Riley Parker's *Milton: A Biography* (No. 230).

130 Campbell, Gordon. "Milton and the Lives of the Ancients." *JWCI*, 47, 1984, 234–38.

Notes that Milton was familiar with the lives of many ancient writers and sees many parallels between Milton's own life and that of his master, Virgil.

131 Campbell, Gordon. "Nathaniel Tovey: Milton's Second Tutor." *MiltonQ*, 21, No. 3, 1987, 81–90.

Traces the biography of Nathaniel Tovey. Concludes that, based on Tovey's anti-Puritan leanings and positive relationship with Milton as his tutor, "Milton was not the radical which he was later to become."

132 Carey, John, ed. *Andrew Marvell: A Critical Anthology*. Harmondsworth: Penguin, 1969. 351pp.

Reprints Milton's letter recommending Marvell to John Bradshaw, dated February, 1653. Other references to Milton appear throughout.

133 Carpenter, William. *The Life and Times of John Milton*. Folcroft, PA: Folcroft Library Editions, 1971, 1976; Norwood, PA: Norwood Editions, 1977; Philadelphia, PA: R. West, 1978; Ann Arbor, MI: Univ. Microfilms International, 1980 Books on Demand Reprints.

Reprints of Stevens No. 1953, originally published in 1836.

134 Chaney, Edward. *The Grand Tour and the Great Rebellion: Richard Lassels and "The Voyage of Italy" in the Seventeenth Century*. Geneva: Slatkine, 1985. 479pp.

Appendix: "Further Notes on Milton's Travels in Italy, 1638–39." Questions the validity of several of Milton's statements concerning his Italian journey. Review: Roy Flannagan, *MiltonQ*, 23, 1989, 73–77; response by Chaney, pp. 77–81.

135 Channing, William Ellery. *Remarks on the Character and Writings of John Milton*. Folcroft, PA: Folcroft Library Editions, 1969, 1976; Norwood, PA: Norwood Editions, 1977; Philadelphia, PA: R. West, 1978.

Reprints of Stevens No. 1282, originally published in 1826.

136 Chelline, Warren H. "John Milton's American Friend." *PMPA*, 6, 1981, 39–42.

"At least we know that they [Roger Williams and Milton] knew each other intimately, and the possibilities, even strong probabilities, of their close fellowship and full communication are rife, for all their lives." Wonders about their mutual influence.

137 Chelline, Warren Herman. "On the Relationship of Roger Williams and John Milton: A Review of Selected Historical and Critical Comment, with an Investigation of Various Reciprocities and Mutualities." Doctoral diss., Univ. of

Kansas, 1982. 294pp. Abs., *DAI*, 43, 1983, 3593A.

Uses documents, mutual friends, and supporting anecdotes to assert the reality of a friendship between Milton and Williams, but notes the reciprocal influence of each writer's ideology.

138 Cooke, John. *John Milton, 1608–1674.* Folcroft, PA: Folcroft Library Editions, 1974.

Reprint of Stevens No. 2298, originally published in 1908.

139 Copley, J. "Cowper on Johnson's *Life of Milton.*" *N&Q*, 24, 1977, 311–17.

Most likely made when Cowper was attempting to produce "a new edition of Milton in the early 1790s," these comments are largely Cowper's objections to what he felt were Johnson's biases against Milton. This article reproduces Cowper's remarks side by side with Johnson's text.

140 Corns, Thomas N. "Milton's Quest for Respectability." *MLR*, 77, 1982, 769–79.

Examines how Milton defined his relationships to the sectaries of the 1640s.

141 Daiches, David. *Milton.* London: Hutchinson Univ. Library, 1968, 1970.

Reprints of Huckabay No. 3135, originally published in 1957.

142 "The Diaries of Hermann Mylius." *MiltonQ*, 14, 1980, 72–73.

Reports that Leo Miller obtained the photocopies of Mylius's complete diaries from the Oldenburg archives, which will make possible a definitive and complete account of this episode in Milton's secretaryship. See Nos. 210 and 212.

143 Doyle, Charles Clay. "Milton's Monolingual Woman and Her Forebears." *Proverbium*, 5, 1988, 15–21.

Discusses Dr. John Ward's report that Deborah Milton told him that her father often said "one tongue was enough for a woman." Questions the report's authenticity, but discusses contemporary and near-contemporary variations of the saying.

144 Duncan-Jones, E. E. "Milton's Admirer, Du Moulin of Nîmes." *English Renaissance Studies Presented to Dame Helen Gardner in Honour of Her Seventieth Birthday.* [Ed. by John Carey] (Oxford: Clarendon Press, 1980), pp. 245–53.

Identifies the Du Moulin of Nîmes, whom Milton mentions in a letter to Jean Labadie, as James Molins, M.A., of Aberdeen.

145 Edmonds, Cyrus R. *John Milton: A Biography.* Folcroft, PA: Folcroft Library Editions, 1969; Norwood, PA: Norwood Editions, 1976; Philadelphia, PA: R. West, 1976.

Reprints of Stevens No. 1678, originally published in 1851.

146 Ellis, Anthony. "Eyeless in Chalfont St. Giles." *The Observer Magazine* (London), July 5, 1981, p. 10.

Announces the reenactment of the Milton family's arrival at Chalfont St. Giles, to take place on July 11.

147 Emerson, Everett H. "John Milton (1608–1674)." *English Puritanism from John Hooper to John Milton* (Durham, NC: Duke Univ. Press, 1968), pp. 279–93.

Focuses on Milton's career and works as they relate to Puritanism as a "dominant force in his life." Reviews (of book): Roger L. Emerson, *CH*, 38, 1969, 379; Charles F. Mullett, *AHR*, 74, 1969, 1578–79; Darrett B. Rutman, *NEQ*, 42, 1969, 294–96; David Underdown, *RenQ*, 22, 1969, 419–20; Joan Webber, *ELN*, 7, 1969, 141–43; Richard W. Etulain, *Gordon Review*, 11, 1970, 302–03; Harold P. Levitt, *HSL*, 2, 1970, 92–93; John M. Wallace, *ShakS*, 5, 1970, 316–17; Hilton Landry, *SCN*, 31, 1973, 3–4.

148 Emerson, Everett H. "A Note on Milton's Early Puritanism." *Essays in Honor of Esmond Linworth Marilla.* Ed. by Thomas Austin Kirby and William John Olive. Louisiana State Univ.

Studies, Humanities Series, no. 19 (Baton Rouge: Louisiana State Univ. Press, 1970), pp. 127–34.

Concentrates on Milton's views in the early 1640s. Concludes that "on the verge of that Revolution Milton was a Puritan Activist alert to the needs of reformation in church and state, a revolutionary and a utopian."

149 **Fackler, Mark,** and **Clifford G. Christians.** "John Milton's Place in Journalism History: Champion or Turncoat?" *JQ*, 57, 1980, 563–70.

Suggests that reformers "can 'stand against' or 'work from within.' Milton chose the latter; his choice should not be interpreted as contradiction or even compromise." Examines the nature of his responsibility for *Mercurius Politicus*.

150 **Fallon, Robert Thomas.** "Filling the Gaps: New Perspectives on Mr. Secretary Milton." *MiltonS*, 12, 1978, 165–95.

Investigates the gaps in the documentation of Milton's career as Secretary for Foreign Tongues. Proposes that questionable documents should not be dismissed out of hand; nor should gaps in Milton's public record cause scholars to leap to conclusions concerning his political allegiance or philosophy. Abs., *MiltonQ*, 11, 1977, 94.

151 **Fallon, Robert T.** "John Milton and the Honorable Artillery Company." *MiltonQ*, 9, 1975, 49–51.

Concludes that the John Milton listed in the *Great Vellum Book* of the Honorable Artillery Company of London and in other records is not the poet, who was never a member of the company.

152 **Fenton, Elijah.** *The Life of John Milton.* Introduction by Edward Le Comte. Norwood, PA: Norwood Editions, 1977.

Reprint of the 1725 edition. See *MiltonQ*, 12, 1978, 154.

153 **Fix, Stephen.** "Distant Genius: Johnson and the Art of Milton's Life." *MP*, 81, 1984, 244–64.

Rejects both the idea that Samuel Johnson in his *Life of Milton* "crudely reached for biographical interpretations of specific poems" and the idea that "Johnson's personal antipathy toward Milton made him unable to appreciate his art." Argues, conversely, "that Johnson found in Milton's life and character the best evidence to explain his unusual combination of artistic talents and deficiencies."

154 **Flannagan, Roy.** "Bate's *Samuel Johnson* and Johnson's *Life of Milton*: Puckish or Perverse? A Review Article." *MiltonQ*, 12, 1978, 147–48.

Review essay on Walter Jackson Bate's *Samuel Johnson* (1977). "What I am anxious to discover . . . is the reason why Johnson felt the need to blacken almost all of Milton's works and perpetually slur the character of the man."

155 **Flannagan, Roy.** "Milton's Gout." *MiltonQ*, 15, 1981, 123–24.

Describes the disease's symptoms and questions John Aubrey's statement that Milton remained cheerful and sang "even in his goutefitts."

156 **Fletcher, Harris Francis.** *The Intellectual Development of John Milton.* Ann Arbor, MI: Univ. Microfilms International, 1980 Books on Demand Reprints.

Reprint of Huckabay No. 3156, originally published in 1956.

157 **Frank, Joseph.** *Cromwell's Press Agent: A Critical Biography of Marchamont Nedham, 1620–1678.* Lanham, MD: Univ. Press of America, 1980. viii, 205pp.

An appendix considers Milton's relationship to the editor of *Mercurius Politicus*, but finds no evidence that either man influenced the other, despite their long acquaintanceship.

158 **Freeman, James.** "Milton and His Military Shadow." *MiltonQ*, 14, 1980, 71.

Abstract of a paper presented at the Florida State Comparative Literature Conference in Tallahassee on January 25, 1980. Contends that in *Paradise Lost*, Milton denigrated the arts of war to justify his own vocation and to exorcise "the presence of a second John Milton, who was a soldier from 1635 until at least 1648."

159 Freeman, James A. "Milton's Roman Connection: Giovanni Salzilli." *MiltonS*, 19, 1984, 87–104.

Proposes that the content and style of several Italian academic societies influenced Milton. Focuses on Milton's relation to Giovanni Salzilli in *Ad Salsillum*.

160 French, J. Milton, ed. *The Life Records of John Milton*. 5 vols. Ann Arbor, MI: Univ. Microfilms International, 1980 Books on Demand Reprints.

Reprint of Huckabay No. 3168, originally published in 1949–58. See Nos. 218, 221, and 4404–05.

161 Frye, Roland Mushat. "Milton's Florentine Friend, Bishop Frescobaldi: A Biographical Note and Portrait." *MiltonQ*, 7, 1973, 74–76.

Offers information from the Frescobaldi family archives and gives the location of the family palace and three other palaces known to have belonged to Milton's Florentine friends. See Nos. 218, 221, and 4404.

162 Fuller, Edmund. *John Milton*. London: Victor Gollancz, 1969.

Reprint of Huckabay No. 3186, originally published in 1944. Review: *TLS*, July 10, 1969, p. 749.

163 Garcia Amescua, Magdalena. "Breve Semblanza de John Milton." *Ensayos sobre John Milton: Epopeya y Drama.* Ed. by María Enriqueta González Padilla. Facultad de Filosofía y Letras, Centro de Investigaciones de Letras Modernas y Arte Dramático (Mexico, D.F.: Universidad Nacional Autónoma de México, 1976), pp. 7–12.

Discusses Milton's life and major works.

164 Graham, James John George, ed. *Autobiography of John Milton; or, Milton's Life in His Own Words*. Folcroft, PA: Folcroft Library Editions, 1972; Norwood, PA: Norwood Editions, 1977.

Reprints of Stevens No. 1228, originally published in 1872.

165 Grose, Christopher. "'Unweapon'd Creature in the Word': A Revision in Milton's *Letter to a Friend*." *ELN*, 21, No. 1, 1983, 29–34.

Behind both versions of the letter lies the notion of a special calling that indicates Milton's concern about his mission in life. Feels that there are reasons for retaining the phrase "unweapon'd creature in the word," which pertains to the young poet's hopes and fears in his long preparation for pastoral work.

166 Gum, Coburn. "Lawes Folio." *MiltonN*, 3, 1969, 4–5.

Describes a folio volume at the British Library which contains five songs from *Comus* in Henry Lawes's handwriting.

167 Hamilton, John Arthur. *The Life of John Milton, Englishman*. Folcroft, PA: Folcroft Library Editions, 1970.

Reprint of Stevens No. 2303, originally published in 1908.

168 Hamilton, W. Douglas, ed. *Original Papers Illustrative of the Life and Writings of John Milton*. New York: AMS Press, 1968; Folcroft, PA: Folcroft Library Editions, 1976; Norwood, PA: Norwood Editions, 1977; Philadelphia, PA: R. West, 1978.

Reprints of Stevens No. 1221A, originally published in 1859.

169 Harned, Jon William. "John Milton, 1632–1642: A Psychobiographical Study." Doctoral diss., Univ. of Virginia, 1977. 212pp. Abs., *DAI*, 38, 1978, 4181A.

Uses Erik Erikson's ego psychology to interpret Milton's quest for an adult identity, vocational indecision, conflict with his father's wishes, desire for knowledge and fame, and pursuit of intimacy.

170 Harris, William Melville. *John Milton, Puritan, Patriot, Poet*. Folcroft, PA: Folcroft Library Editions, 1971, 1977; Norwood, PA: Norwood Editions, 1978.

Reprints of Stevens No. 2340, originally published in 1909.

171 Hayley, William. *The Life of Milton.* Introduction by Joseph Anthony Wittreich, Jr. Gainesville, FL: Scholars' Facsimiles and Reprints, 1970; Folcroft, PA: Folcroft Press, 1970, 1976; New York: Garland Publishing, 1971; Norwood, PA: Norwood Editions, 1977. xxxvii, 328pp.

A facsimile of the second edition (1796). Wittreich stresses the importance of Hayley's biography because he was one of the first to deal objectively with Milton's emphasis on liberty. "This biography managed to create a new 'impression' and its Milton became the Milton of Blake, Wordsworth, Coleridge, and Shelley."

172 Henry, Nathaniel H. "John Milton, Anglican." *RenP*, 1969, pp. 57–66.

Points out Milton's Anglican connections and contends that "the environmental and intellectual influences of the Church of England were pervasive in the life and work of John Milton."

173 Hill, Christopher. "Conclusion: Milton and the Experience of Defeat." *The Experience of Defeat: Milton and Some Contemporaries* (New York: Viking; London: Faber and Faber, 1984), pp. 297–328.

Discusses Milton's reaction to the defeat of the revolution. In *Samson Agonistes*, the Philistines represent the gentry and aristocracy who were to control England for the next two hundred years. Reviews (of book): Eric Christiansen, *Spectator*, 253, 1984, 21; Henry Horwitz, *NYTB*, Nov. 18, 1984, p. 46; Alan Howkins, *New Statesman*, 108, 1984, 22; J. G. A. Pocock, *TLS*, Dec. 28, 1984, p. 1494; Conrad Russell, *LRB*, 6, 1984, 20–22; Genevieve Stattaford, *Publishers' Weekly*, 226, 1984, 134; Tom T. Tashiro, *LJ*, 109, 1984, 1849–50; Lorraine Charkabon, *UES*, 23, 1985, 44–45; Sidney Gottlieb, *MiltonQ*, 19, 1985, 113–14; John Morrill, *HT*, 35, 1985, 52–53; Byron Nelson, *SCN*,

43, 1985, 1–3; Theodore K. Rabb, *Book World*, 15, 1985, 4; David Underdown, *NYRB*, 32, 1985, pp. 41–44; Perez Zagorin, *JMH*, 58, 1986, 549–51; David Mulder, *SocSJ*, 24, 1987, 108–09.

174 Hill, Christopher. *Milton and the English Revolution.* London: Faber and Faber, 1977; New York: Viking, 1978; Harmondsworth: Penguin, 1979. xviii, 541pp.

"I believe that Milton's ideas were more directly influenced than is usually recognized by the events of the English Revolution in which he was an active participant: and that the influences brought to bear on him were much more radical than has been accepted." Reinterprets Milton the man and studies the political content of his poetry. Argues for the traditional date of *Samson Agonistes*. See Nos. 753, 841, and 1029. Reviews: David Daiches, *New Statesman*, 94, 1977, 477–78; John Kenyon, *Observer*, Oct. 2, 1977, p. 26; Austin Woolrych, *Listener*, 98, 1977, 451–52; Blair Worden, *TLS*, Dec. 2, 1977, pp. 1394–95; John B. Broadbent Jr., *English* (Oxford), 27, 1978, 38–44; Douglas Bush, *NR*, Jan. 7, 1978, pp. 30–31; Gerald Hammond, *CritQ*, 20, 1978, 83–85; G. K. Hunter, *SR*, 86, 1978, 414–21; Frank Kermode, *NYRB*, Mar. 5, 1978, pp. 10, 23, 26; William Lamont, *EHR*, 93, 1978, 621–26; Christopher Lehmann-Haupt, *IHT*, Mar. 14, 1978; *MiltonQ*, 12, 1978, 69–70; John Press, *ART*, 22, 1978, 34–38; Richard Schell, *SpenN*, 9, 1978, 5–6; Peggy Anne Streep, *Book World* (*Washington Post*), Feb. 26, 1978, p. 3; Michael Wilding, *Nation Review* (Melbourne), Nov. 10–16, 1978, p. 20; Perez Zagorin, *N&Q*, 25, 1978, 549–50; Naomi Bliven, *New Yorker*, Feb. 12, 1979, pp. 116–18; Julietta Harvey, *CQ*, 8, 1979, 265–73; Quentin Skinner, *NYRB*, Mar. 23, 1979, pp. 6–9; Raymond B. Waddington, *JMH*, 51, 1979, 108–12; Joseph Anthony Wittreich, Jr., *Rev*, 1, 1979, 123–64;

Michael Allen Mikolajczak, *SCN*, 38, 1980, 71–72; Frederick H. Shriver, *Historical Magazine of the Protestant Episcopal Church*, 49, 1980, 428–29; Roger Lejosne, *EA*, 34, 1981, 220–21; Jonathan Goldberg, *ELH*, 49, 1982, 514–42.

175 Hill, Elizabeth K. "Ring about Milton: A German Novelist's View." *MiltonQ*, 16, 1982, 97–98.

Comments on Max Ring's *John Milton und Seine Zeit* (1857; Stevens No. 2015), a blend of fact and fancy.

176 Hill, John Spencer. "Poet-Priest: Vocational Tension in Milton's Early Development." *MiltonS*, 8, 1975, 41–69.

"Milton's decision to become a poet, like that to become a minister, was taken early; and the vocational streams issuing from these twin and complementary resolves run parallel until at least 1637, when he composed *Lycidas*."

177 Hiwatashi, Masahiro. "John Hall and Milton: Towards an Understanding of Knowledge." *Studies in Milton* (Tokyo: Kinseido, 1974), pp. 154–74.

In Japanese. On the rigidity of learning effected under Cromwell, according to Thomas Sprat. Discusses Milton's influence on both men's pedagogical views.

178 Hobbs, Mary. *The Young Milton.* London: Macdonald; New York: Roy, 1968. 138pp.

A children's account of Milton's life through the publication of the long poems.

179 Hood, Edwin Paxton. *John Milton: The Patriot and Poet.* Folcroft, PA: Folcroft Library Editions, 1970, 1972.

Reprints of Stevens No. 1997, originally published in 1852.

180 Huckabay, Calvin. "John Milton: Poet as Politician." *Orev*, 5, 1976, 7–37.

Summarizes Milton's political activities to 1660, exploring why he served Cromwell and noting the irony that Milton's initial fame came from political pamphlets and his lasting fame from *Paradise Lost*.

181 Hughes, Merritt Y. "Milton as a Revolutionary." *Critical Essays on Milton from "ELH"* (Baltimore, MD, and London: Johns Hopkins Press, 1969), pp. 46–74.

Reprint of Huckabay No. 3221, originally published in 1943.

182 Hunter, Joseph. *Milton: A Sheaf of Gleanings.* Folcroft, PA: Folcroft Library Editions, 1976; Norwood, PA: Norwood Editions, 1977.

Reprints of Stevens No. 1677, originally published in 1850.

183 Hunter, William B., Jr. "Herbert and Milton." *SCRev*, 1, 1984, 22–37.

Notes that the literary careers of the Puritan Milton and the Anglican George Herbert were similar until the young, Anglican Milton was forced into the Puritan camp for "political and religious circumstances as he tried to deal with William Laud, the newly appointed primate of England."

184 Hunter, William B. "Milton and the Presbyterians." *The Descent of Urania: Studies in Milton, 1946–1988* (Lewisburg, PA: Bucknell Univ. Press; London and Toronto: Associated Univ. Presses, 1989), pp. 91–99.

Investigates the idea that Milton was a Presbyterian during his mid-thirties. Points out that he and the Presbyterians never disagreed about the issue of personal freedom. They were the "forcers of conscience" of his sonnet, but "it took him several years to recognize how completely at odds he was with them." Their position "had not yet hardened in 1644."

185 Hunter, William B., Jr. "Milton and the Waldensians." *SEL*, 11, 1971, 153–64. Reprinted in *The Descent of Urania: Studies in Milton, 1946–1988* (Lewisburg, PA: Bucknell Univ. Press; London and Toronto: Associated Univ. Presses, 1989), pp. 169–78.

Claims that Milton's doctrines reflect

his knowledge of and respect for the Waldensians.

186 Hutchinson, F. E. *Milton and the English Mind.* New York: Haskell House, 1974.

Reprint of Huckabay No. 3224, originally published in 1946.

187 Ivimey, Joseph. *John Milton: His Life and Times, Religious and Political Opinions with an Appendix Containing Animadversions upon Dr. Johnson's "Life of Milton."* Folcroft, PA: Folcroft Library Editions, 1970; Norwood, PA: Norwood Editions, 1974; Philadelphia, PA: R. West, 1977.

Reprints of Stevens No. 1666, originally published in 1833.

188 Jones, Esmor. "Milton." *Authors in Their Age Series* (Glasgow: Blackie and Son, 1977).

Relates the biographical and historical background to the development of Milton's syntax.

189 Keightley, Thomas. *An Account of the Life, Opinions, and Writings of John Milton with an Introduction to "Paradise Lost."* Ann Arbor, MI: Univ. Microfilms International, 1980 Books on Demand Reprints.

Reprint of Stevens No. 2007, originally published in 1855.

190 Kelley, Maurice. "Additions to: *Milton's Library.*" *MiltonQ,* 10, 1976, 93–94.

Offers constructive criticism to Jackson C. Boswell as he prepares a revised edition of *Milton's Library* (No. 9).

191 Kelley, Maurice. "Daniel Skinner and Milton's Trinity College Manuscript." *N&Q,* 24, 1977, 206–07.

Proposes Skinner, a friend of Pepys and Milton, as a possible donor of the Trinity Manuscript. Speculates about the date and circumstances of the donation.

192 Kelley, Maurice, and **Leo Miller.** "The Columbia Milton: Sixth Supplement." *N&Q,* 28, 1981, 43–44.

See No. 295. Comments on Miltonic

documents located through the courtesy of the Landesarchiv Schleswig-Holstein. Concerns Milton's work as Secretary for Foreign Tongues. Abs., *SCN,* 39, 1981, 100.

193 Kermode, Frank. "Milton and His Politics." *Daily Telegraph* (London), Nov. 9, 1974.

Surveys Milton's political career. Concludes that, judging from the number of people in his funeral procession, "Some Englishmen had already forgiven Milton for being great in the wrong way."

194 Kermode, Frank. "Milton in Old Age." *SoR,* 11, 1975, 513–29.

Concludes that "Milton's old age was a little too like the one Manoa planned for Samson—domestic comfort under the licence, dearly bought, of the Philistine lords." Abs., *MiltonQ,* 10, 1976, 27–28.

195 Kluncker, Karlhans. "Zu John Miltons *Epitaphium Damonis.*" *CPe,* 96, 1971, 57–89.

Traces Milton's youth, education, and friendship with Charles Diodati. Emphasizes his visit to Italy, where he learned of Diodati's death. When he returned to England, Milton was inspired to write *Epitaphium Damonis,* his last Latin poem, to honor his friend.

196 Komori, Teiji. "Milton's Victory over His Blindness." *MCJ News,* 4, 1980, 10–11.

Abstract of a paper presented at the Seventh Colloquium of MCJ in July, 1979. Concludes that "through his self-confidence and his faith in God, Milton could finally overcome his blindness and emerge victoriously."

197 Labriola, Albert C. "Milton's *Familiar Letters*: A Study in Intellectual Autobiography." *PLL,* 19, 1983, 239–48.

Traces Milton's changing perception of friendship as espoused in his *Familiar Letters* and as seen in his changing roles and vocations. Contends that "Milton's penchant for self-analysis" serves as a source for his poetic characters. Observes that "the *Familiar Letters*, as intellectual autobiography, may provide the link between Milton's prose and the major poetry." Abs., *SCN*, 36, 1978, 15.

198 Labriola, Albert C. "Portraits of an Artist: Milton's Changing Self-Image." *MiltonS*, 19, 1984, 179–94.
Examines Milton's literary transition from the pastoral to the epic genre as part of a changing self-image. Places *Epitaphium Damonis* at an important turning point in his life, including such events as Diodati's death and Milton's growing interest in Italian literature.

199 Lawson, McEwan. *Master John Milton of the Citie of London*. Folcroft, PA: Folcroft Library Editions, 1972; Norwood, PA: Norwood Editions, 1977.
Reprints of Stevens No. 2510, originally published in 1923.

200 Leach, A. F. "Milton as Schoolboy and Schoolmaster." *Essays on Milton* (Folcroft, PA: Folcroft Library Editions, 1970), pp. 295–318.
Reprint of Stevens No. 2305, originally published in 1907–08.

201 Macaulay, Rose. *Milton*. New York: Haskell House, 1974.
Reprint of Huckabay No. 3268, originally published in 1933.

202 Marsh, John Fitchett. *Papers Connected with Affairs of Milton and His Family*. Folcroft, PA: Folcroft Library Editions, 1974; Norwood, PA: Norwood Editions, 1977.
Reprints of Stevens No. 1679, originally published in 1851.

203 Martyn, W. Carlos. *Life and Times of John Milton*. Folcroft, PA: Folcroft Library Editions, 1970; Norwood, PA: Norwood Editions, 1977.
Reprints of Stevens No. 2048, originally published in 1866.

204 McClellan, Albert. "Was John Milton a Baptist?" *The Baptist Program* (Nashville, TN), April, 1977, p. 1.

Implies an affirmative answer.

205 McKenzie, D. F. "Milton's Printers: Matthew, Mary and Samuel Simmons." *MiltonQ*, 14, 1980, 87–91.
Offers evidence that Matthew, Mary, and Samuel Simmons were father, mother, and son.

206 Miller, Leo. "Before Milton was Famous: January 8, 1649/50." *MiltonQ*, 21, No. 1, 1987, 1–6.
Explores Milton's reaction to composing *Eikonoklastes* and the *First* and *Second Defence* at the request of the Commonwealth government. Identifies the men Milton believed were trying "to dissuade [him] from that task."

207 Miller, Leo. "The Date of Christoph Arnold's Letter." *N&Q*, 31, 1984, 323–24.
Contends that August 7 rather than October 7, 1651, is the correct date of Arnold's letter in Georg Richter's *Epistolae Selectiores*.

208 Miller, Leo. "Hermann Mylius' Baroque Letters to Milton and Weckherlin." *Acta Coventus Neo-Latini Guelpherbytani*. Ed. by Stella P. Revard and others (Binghamton, NY: Medieval and Renaissance Texts and Studies, 1988), pp. 233–40.
Studies the language and style of neo-Latin letters that Mylius sent to Milton and Weckherlin. One letter responds to Milton's request that Mylius voice his opinion on the antimonarchal pamphlets.

209 Miller, Leo. *John Milton among the Polygamophiles*. New York: Loewenthal Press, 1974. xii, 378pp.
Discusses Milton's personal reasons for believing in polygamy and outlines his argument for it in the *Christian Doctrine*. The body of this study traces the idea through western history and concludes with the case of King Charles II. Appendices: "Plural Marriage in Milton's *History of Britain*"; "Milton's Reputation as Polygamophile, 1644–1717"; "Discussion of Polygamy in England after Milton's Time: M.P.'s

and Methodists"; "Discussion of Polygamy in Germany after [Johan] Leyser: Thomasius, Willenberg"; and "Latter Day Polygamophiles."

210 Miller, Leo. *John Milton and the Oldenburg Safeguard: New Light on Milton and His Friends in the Commonwealth from the Diaries and Letters of Hermann Mylius, Agonist in the Early History of Modern Diplomacy.* New York: Loewenthal Press, 1985. xiv, 370pp.

Prints Mylius's writings from original manuscripts, with accompanying translations. Reviews: Christopher Hill, *Albion*, 18, 1986, 276–77; John T. Shawcross, *MiltonQ*, 20, 1986, 106–10; reply to Shawcross by Miller, *MiltonQ*, 21, No. 1, 1987, 31; rejoinder by Shawcross, pp. 31–32; Mara R. Wade, *German Quarterly*, 59, 1986, 674–76; Thomas N. Corns, *N&Q*, 34, 1987, 387–88; Robert Thomas Fallon, *RenQ*, 40, 1987, 377–80; Christopher Hill, *SCN*, 45, 1987, 53; Edward Le Comte, *JEGP*, 86, 1987, 251–54; John Morrill, *RES*, 38, 1987, 391–92; Gordon Campbell, *YES*, 18, 1988, 268–69; Amos C. Miller, *AHR*, 94, 1989, 437; Timothy C. Miller, *Expl*, 47, 1989, 10–12; J. Max Patrick, *SCN*, 47, 1989, 6.

211 Miller, Leo. "Milton and Lassenius." *MiltonQ*, 6, No. 4, 1972, 92–95.

On the relationship between Milton and Johan Lassenius, a Lutheran theologian and pastor of a German congregation in Copenhagen. Although Lassenius met Milton while in England and basked in reflected glory, he apparently was unsympathetic to Milton's ideas.

212 Miller, Leo. "Milton and the Mylius Papers." *Ringing the Bell Backward: The Proceedings of the First International Milton Symposium.* Ed. by Ronald G. Shafer. The IUP Imprint Series (Indiana: Indiana Univ. of Pennsylvania, 1982), pp. 37–42.

Offers preliminary information gleaned from the complete transcripts of Hermann Mylius's diary. Response by Calvin Huckabay, pp. 43–45.

213 Miller, Leo. "Milton and Vlacq." *PBSA*, 73, 1979, 145–207.

An account of the controversy and relationship between Adrian Vlacq and Milton and of Vlacq's career as a writer and printer. Corrections by Miller, *MiltonQ*, 15, 1981, 128. Abs., *MiltonQ*, 13, 1979, 160–61; *SCN*, 38, 1980, 20.

214 Miller, Leo. "Milton and Weckherlin." *MiltonQ*, 16, 1982, 1–3.

On Georg Rudolph Weckherlin's comments about Milton, who replaced him as Secretary for Foreign Tongues.

215 Miller, Leo. "Milton Dines at the Jesuit College: Reconstructing the Evening of October 30, 1638." *MiltonQ*, 13, 1979, 142–46.

Quotes the entry from the Pilgrim Book recording Milton's visit at the Jesuit hostelry, identifies other Englishmen present, and cites sentences from Milton's prose as answers to hypothetical taunts from his Jesuit hosts.

216 Miller, Leo. "Milton's Clash with Chappell: A Suggested Reconstruction." *MiltonQ*, 14, 1980, 77–87.

Proposes that Milton used several of his Latin compositions to satirize William Chappell and that Milton's learned wit led to their clash. Further suggests that *Elegy 7* and *Elegy 1* are records of Milton's stay in London during term time in 1627.

217 Miller, Leo. "Milton's *Personal Letters* and Daniel Skinner." *N&Q*, 30, 1983, 431–32.

Concludes that although Daniel Skinner prepared the manuscript of the *Personal Letters*, he did not supply the manuscript for the *Prolusions*.

218 Miller, Leo. *Milton's Portraits: An "Impartial" Inquiry into Their Authentication.* Athens, OH: Ohio Univ., 1976. 43pp.

Special issue of *MiltonQ*. Traces the three major Milton portraits, offering fact and conjecture about their origins, authenticity, and resemblance to the man himself. Corrects some details in J. M. French's (No. 160) and William Riley Parker's accounts (No. 230). Review: David Piper, *N&Q*, 26, 1979, 70–72.

219 Miller, Leo. "On the So-Called 'Portrait' of Sara Milton." *MiltonQ*, 15, 1981, 113–16.

Suggests that the painting does not portray the poet's mother; rather, it represents an unidentified woman painted by an unidentified artist.

220 Miller, Leo. "Portraits of Milton." *TLS*, Mar. 27, 1981, p. 351.

On the portraits' authenticity.

221 Miller, Leo. "Salmasius's *Responsio*: Addenda to the Milton *Life Records*." *N&Q*, 21, 1974, 95.

Adds two letters to those noted by J. M. French (No. 160) as indicating the posthumous appearance of Salmasius's work.

222 Miller, Leo. "Some Inferences from Milton's Hebrew." *MiltonQ*, 18, 1984, 41–46.

Describes and evaluates three cases that may clarify the "extent and quality of Milton's knowledge of the Hebrew language."

223 "Milton Wanted by the King, August, 1660." *JHS*, 1, 1968, 178–80.

Speculates about why Milton was not excepted from the king's pardon. Reproduces the proclamation of August 13, 1660, calling for the burning of the *First Defence* and *Eikonoklastes*.

224 Mohl, Ruth. *John Milton and His "Commonplace Book."* New York: Frederick Ungar, 1969. xi, 334pp.

"It is the purpose of this study . . . to examine as thoroughly as possible the relationship between Milton's reading and writing and to discover how valuable to him were the notes in this particular *Commonplace Book*." Reviews: *TLS*, July 10, 1969, p. 749; *MiltonN*, 3, 1969, 59–60; Robert W.

Ayers, *RenQ*, 23, 1970, 489–91; Virginia R. Mollenkott, *SCN*, 28, 1970, 26–27; D. D. C. Chambers, *RES*, 22, 1971, 208–10.

225 Morand, Paul Phelps. *The Effects of His Political Life upon John Milton.* Folcroft, PA: Folcroft Library Editions, 1969.

Reprint of Huckabay No. 3282, originally published in 1939.

226 Mortimer, Charles Edward. *An Historical Memoir of the Political Life of John Milton.* Ann Arbor, MI: Univ. Microfilms International, 1980 Books on Demand Reprints.

Reprint of Stevens No. 1838, originally published in 1805.

227 Mutschmann, Heinrich. *Milton's Eyesight and the Chronology of His Works.* Philadelphia, PA: R. West, 1977.

Reprint of Stevens No. 2540, originally published in 1924.

228 Mutschmann, Heinrich. *The Secret of John Milton.* Folcroft, PA: Folcroft Library Editions, 1969; Norwood, PA: Norwood Editions, 1975.

Reprints of Stevens No. 2560, originally published in 1925.

229 Paplova, Tatiana. *Winstanley.* Moscow: Young Guard, 1987. 302pp.

In Russian. On the life and works of Gerrard Winstanley. Milton mentioned throughout.

230 Parker, William Riley. *Milton: A Biography.* Oxford: Clarendon Press, 1968. 2 vols. xxi, 666pp.; pp. 667–1489.

See Huckabay No. 1644. See also Nos. 123, 207, 218, 231, 878, 1617, 1797, 4108, 4405, and 4456. Reviews: Douglas Bush, *VQR*, 43, 1968, 162–65; Michael Wilding, *New Statesman*, Aug. 23, 1968, pp. 222–23; *TLS*, Oct. 31, 1968, p. 1224; Albert W. Fields, *PBSA*, 63, 1969, 336–42; Andrew Breen Myers, *LJ*, 94, 1969, 185; J. Max Patrick, *SCN*, 27, 1969, 25; Kenneth Muir, *N&Q*, 16, 1969, 385–86; Isabel G. MacCaffrey, *RenQ*, 23, 1970, 203–06; Earl Miner, *ECS*, 3, 1970,

296–305; John N. Morris, *Nation*, 210, 1970, 23–24; Maurice Kelley, *SCN*, 28, 1970, 1; Barbara Kiefer Lewalski, *MP*, 68, 1970, 105–07; C. A. Patrides, *RES*, 21, 1970, 212–15; Nathaniel H. Henry, *SAB*, 36, 1971, 78–80; Merritt Y. Hughes, *MLR*, 66, 1971, xxi–xxxii; H. W. Donner, *ES*, 53, 1972, 162–66.

231 Parker, William Riley. "Problems in Milton Biography." *MiltonQ*, 5, 1971, 66–71.

Discusses the delays and uncertainties faced during almost thirty years of preparing *Milton: A Biography* (No. 230).

232 Pecheux, Sister M. Christopher. *Milton: A Topographical Guide.* Washington, DC: Univ. Press of America, 1981. viii, 139pp.

Gives information about the locations in England that are associated with Milton, including places where he lived and monuments to him. Reviews: Roy Flannagan, *MiltonQ*, 16, 1982, 20–21; Michael Allen Mikolajczak, *SCN*, 40, 1982, 42; Ted-Larry Pebworth, *C&L*, 32, 1983, 54–55.

233 Peck, Francis. *New Memoirs of the Life and Poetical Works of Mr. John Milton.* Ann Arbor, MI: Univ. Microfilms International, 1980 Books on Demand Reprints.

Originally published in 1740.

234 Petti, Anthony G. *English Literary Hands from Chaucer to Dryden.* London: Edward Arnold; Cambridge, MA: Harvard Univ. Press, 1977. ix, 133pp.

Gives notes on holographic material and characteristics of Milton's handwriting.

235 Piper, David. *Catalogue of Seventeenth-Century Portraits in the National Portrait Gallery, 1625–1714.* Cambridge: Cambridge Univ. Press, 1963. xxviii, 410pp.

Discusses Milton's portrait.

236 Pritchard, Allan. "Milton in Rome: According to Wood." *MiltonQ*, 14, 1980, 92–97.

Believes that Anthony Wood's account of Milton in Rome should be taken seriously because Wood was acquainted with English Roman Catholics who had been to Rome and his account parallels Milton's own narrative.

237 Racine, Louis. *Life of Milton: Together with Observations on "Paradise Lost."* Folcroft, PA: Folcroft Library Editions, 1973; Norwood, PA: Norwood Editions, 1976, 1977.

Reprints of Huckabay No. 3824, originally published in 1930.

238 Rama Sarma, M. V. "A Note on Milton's Blindness." *Triveni*, 36, 1967, 8–14.

Feels that Milton accepted his blindness as divine dispensation and continued to believe that he was one of the chosen few.

239 Rivers, Isabel. "The Making of a Seventeenth-Century Poet." *John Milton: Introductions.* Ed. by John Broadbent (Cambridge: Cambridge Univ. Press, 1973), pp. 75–107.

On Milton's education and development as a poet. Considerable background material on seventeenth-century poetry.

240 Rivers, Isabel. "Milton's Life and Times: Aids to Study." *John Milton: Introductions.* Ed. by John Broadbent (Cambridge: Cambridge Univ. Press, 1973), pp. 21–74.

Gives the chronology of Milton's life, lists his friends, discusses contemporary England, and examines his career as a public servant.

241 Rumrich, John Peter. "Mead and Milton." *MiltonQ*, 20, 1986, 136–39, 141.

Believes that Joseph Mead, a fellow at Christ's College, provided a personal example and an influence in biblical criticism for Milton.

242 Rusche, Harry. "A Reading of John Milton's Horoscope." *MiltonQ*, 13, 1979, 6–11.

From a chart preserved in the Bodleian Library and reproduced in the Columbia *Works* (No. 295).

243 Saillens, Émile. *John Milton: Man, Poet, Polemist.* Totowa, NJ: Rowman and Littlefield, 1971.

Reprint of Huckabay No. 3332, originally published in 1959.

244 Saino, Shiego. *The Life of Milton.* Tokyo: Kenkyusha, 1982. 195pp.

In Japanese.

245 Sánchez, Reuben Márquez, Jr. " 'Patria est, Ubicunque est Bene': The Milton-Heimbach Correspondence of 1666." *MiltonQ*, 22, 1988, 33–38.

Discusses Peter Heimbach's attempt to induce Milton to retire from public affairs and confine himself to literature. Concludes that while he is "Aware that his countrymen do not want him involved in public affairs and do not care about his well-being, Milton in his letter to Heimbach nevertheless asserts his confidence that God has not abandoned him. Like Samson, he too is ready to fulfill his public duty to God and country."

246 Schleiner, Louise. "Milton, G. B. Doni, and the Dating of Doni's Works." *MiltonQ*, 16, 1982, 36–42.

Finds no definite evidence of biographical connections between Milton and Giovanni Battista Doni but concludes that Milton was acquainted with his ideas about sung dramatic poetry.

247 Sekinaga, Mitsuhiko. "Milton at Chalfont St. Giles." *MCJ News*, 4, 1980, 6–7.

Abstract of paper presented. Discusses Milton's relationship with Thomas Ellwood and suggests that in his later years Milton was closer to Quakerism than to any other sect.

248 Senior, H. L. *John Milton, the Supreme Englishman.* Folcroft, PA: Folcroft Library Editions, 1969.

Reprint of Huckabay No. 3343, originally published in 1940.

249 Shawcross, John T. "Interferences of the Self: Mother Fixation and Milton's Life and Work." *SCN*, 44, 1986, 74–75.

Abstract of a paper presented at the Milton Seminar at Chicago's Newberry Library on May 17, 1986. "Milton's deliverance from the mother fixation which created repression and retentive anality did not occur until the late 1650s, when he was able to accept the death of his second wife and their child, the coming dissolution of the government he had put so much hope in, and the new future as creativity again took over, the ego still maintained."

250 Shawcross, John T. "Milton and Diodati: An Essay in Psychodynamic Meaning." *MiltonS*, 7, 1975, 127–63.

"A reading of *Epitaphium Damonis* implies a homoerotic relationship, with Diodati as the more dominantly 'masculine' and Milton as the more recessively 'feminine.' " Other evidence points to "Diodati's homosexual nature and Milton's latent homosexualism, which was repressed consciously and subconsciously from becoming overt, except perhaps with Diodati." Abs., *MiltonQ*, 9, 1975, 124–25.

251 Sherbo, Arthur. "More on Milton's Rustication." *MiltonQ*, 18, 1984, 22–24.

Considers the possibility that Milton was sent down from Cambridge. Quotes several letters from the *Gentleman's Magazine* stating that he was not.

252 Sirignano, Elizabeth Sewell. "To Be a True Poem." *John Milton: Introductions.* Ed. by John Broadbent (Cambridge: Cambridge Univ. Press, 1973), pp. 4–20.

Comments on Milton's attitude toward himself and his poetry. In spite of his rejection of traditional chivalry and heroism in his epic, Milton feels that "every free and gentle spirit . . . ought to be born a knight."

253 Sokolyansky, Mark. "Across the Mountains of Centuries." *Vsesvit*, Jan. 12, 1983, pp. 127–28.

In Ukrainian. Presents a biography of Milton and description of his literary work.

254 Sorsby, Arnold. "On the Nature of

Milton's Blindness." *Tenements of Clay: An Anthology of Medical Biographical Essays* (New York: Scribner's, 1974), pp. 97–114.

Reprint of Huckabay No. 3354, originally published in 1930. Brief notice *SCN*, 35, 1977, 36.

255 Spink, Ian. "Henry Lawes' 'Tunefull and Well Measur'd Song.'" *English Song: Dowland to Purcell* (London: B. T. Batsford; New York: Scribner's, 1974), pp. 75–100.

Discusses the relationship between Henry Lawes and Milton.

256 Sprunger, Keith L. *The Learned Doctor William Ames: Dutch Backgrounds of English and American Puritanism.* Urbana: Univ. of Illinois Press, 1972. xi, 289pp.

Provides information about Milton's educational background at Christ's College.

257 Stevens, David Harrison. *Milton Papers.* Folcroft, PA: Folcroft Library Editions, 1969; New York: AMS Press, 1975; Norwood, PA: Norwood Editions, 1977.

Reprints of Stevens No. 1813, originally published in 1927.

258 Swaim, Kathleen M. "A Fictional Gloss on the History of the 1640's." *MiltonQ*, 15, 1981, 97–98.

Mary Lee Settle's novel, *Prisons* (1973), which is set in revolutionary England.

259 Symmons, Charles. *The Life of John Milton.* New York: AMS Press, 1970.

Reprint of the third edition listed in Stevens No. 1650, originally published in 1822.

260 Takemura, Sanae. "Milton's Secretaryship and Cromwell." *MCJ News*, 5, 1981, 16–17.

Abstract of a paper presented at the Tenth Colloquium of MCJ in December, 1980. States that Cromwell and Milton admired each other.

261 Tanner, John S. "Making a Mormon of Milton." *BYUS*, 24, 1984, 191–206.

Cites parallels between Milton's theology and Mormonism, concluding that Milton was an "unbaptized Mormon."

262 Taylor, Don. "*Paradise Restored*: A Dramatization of the Life of John Milton." *Classic Theatre: The Humanities in Drama.* Introduction by Judith A. Kates. Ed. by Sylvan Barnet and others (Boston, MA: Educational Associates, Little, Brown and Co., 1975), pp. 190–222.

A play that first appeared on television in 1972 (see *MiltonQ*, 6, No. 1, 1972, 25) and that deals with Milton's life at Chalfont St. Giles. Contains flashbacks but focuses on the conflict between the poet and his daughter Mary. Review: *MiltonQ*, 9, 1975, 116–17.

263 Thorpe, James. *John Milton: The Inner Life.* [San Marino, CA]: Huntington Library, 1983. x, 191pp.

Discusses the workings of Milton's mind from youth to old age. In his poetry, "we can see, as in distant mirrors, reflections of Milton's governing ideas." Reviews: Roy Flannagan, *MiltonQ*, 18, 1984, 32–34; D. J. Enright, *TLS*, Nov. 25, 1983, p. 1306; Archie Burnett, *N&Q*, 32, 1985, 262–63; Calvin Huckabay, *C&L*, 34, 1985, 62–63; Thomas F. Healy, *YES*, 17, 1987, 280–82.

264 Todd, Henry John. *Some Account of the Life and Writings of John Milton.* Folcroft, PA: Folcroft Library Editions, 1970, 1977.

Reprints of Stevens No. 1663, originally published in 1826.

265 Toland, John. *The Life of John Milton.* Folcroft, PA: Folcroft Library Editions, 1969, 1972, 1976; Norwood, PA: Norwood Editions, 1977.

Reprints of the 1761 edition.

266 Trent, William P. *John Milton: A Short Story of His Life and Works.* Folcroft, PA: Folcroft Library Editions, 1970; New York: AMS Press, 1971.

Reprints of Stevens No. 2217, originally published in 1899.

267 Waddington, Raymond B. "Milton Turned Upside Down." *JMH*, 51, 1979, 108–12.

Review of Christopher Hill's *Milton and the English Revolution* (No. 174). Contends that Hill fails "to perceive that the profile of Milton the radical, the engaged political activist," has an immediate appeal to us. Thus, "an assessment of Milton's radicalism must resist the temptation to do the job the easy way, producing a study that . . . seems exactly right for the moment but will be quaint and dated tomorrow."

268 Wagenknecht, Edward C. *The Personality of Milton.* Norman: Univ. of Oklahoma Press, 1970. viii, 170pp.

"The man who was 'probably the most learned of all the very great poets' created by dramatizing his own personality. . . . He was not merely a great thinker or a man of immense learning or even a great poet, but a passionate and, if one understands him, lovable man." Reviews: Albert Johnston, *Publishers' Weekly*, 197, 1970, 57; *Booklist*, 67, 1971, 396; *TLS*, Apr. 23, 1971, p. 478; *MiltonQ*, 5, 1971, 23–24.

269 Warner, Rex. *John Milton.* Norwood, PA: Norwood Editions, 1978.

Reprint of Huckabay No. 1003, originally published in 1949.

270 Wedgwood, C. V. *Milton and His World.* London: Lutterworth Press; New York: Walck, 1969. 48pp.

An account of Milton's career. Review: *MiltonQ*, 6, No. 3, 1972, 14–15.

271 Willets, Pamela J., ed. *The Henry Lawes Manuscript.* London: Trustees of the British Museum, 1969. ix, 83pp.

Contains a reassessment of Lawes, a chronology of his life, an account of the manuscript's history, and a list of its contents. Abs., *MiltonQ*, 4, 1970, 12.

272 Williams, George G. *Guide to Literary London.* London: B. T. Batsford, 1973. 413pp.

Discusses twenty-one places associated with Milton.

273 Williamson, George C. *Milton.* Folcroft, PA: Folcroft Library Editions, 1969; Norwood, PA: Norwood Editions, 1975; Philadelphia, PA: R. West, 1978. Reprints of Stevens No. 2265, originally published in 1905.

274 Williamson, George C. *The Portraits, Prints and Writings of John Milton.* Exhibited at Christ's College, Cambridge, 1908, with an Appendix and Index by C. Sayle. New York: Burt Franklin Bibliography and Reference Series, 1967; Cambridge: Cambridge Univ. Press, 1968; Folcroft, PA: Folcroft Library Editions, 1969, 1973; Norwood, PA: Norwood Editions, 1976; Philadelphia, PA: R. West, 1978.

Reprints of Stevens No. 1774, originally published in 1908.

275 Wilson, A. N. *The Life of John Milton.* Oxford and New York: Oxford Univ. Press, 1983. i, 278pp.

Relates Milton's ideas to those of the twentieth century. Comments on his works, especially the long poems. Reviews: *BBN*, June, 1983, p. 385; *HT*, 33, 1983, 60; *Observer*, Jan. 23, 1983, p. 46; *Spectator*, 250, 1983, 22; *Publishers' Weekly*, 223, 1983, 75; D. J. Enright, *TLS*, Feb. 4, 1983, p. 100; Roy Flannagan, *MiltonQ*, 17, 1983, 49–51; Gerald Hammond, *CritQ*, 25, 1983, 81–84; Timothy Harris, *PN Review* (Manchester), 10, 1983, 63–64; Christopher Hill, *New Statesman*, 105, 1983, 22–23; Frank Kermode, *MGW*, Jan. 30, 1983, p. 22; Anthony Low, *C&L*, 34, 1983, 53–54; Colin MacCabe, *LitR*, 57, 1983, 5–6; John Mulryan, *Cithara*, 23, No. 1, 1983, 52–53; Rosamond Putzel, *LJ*, 108, 1983, 1364; Alan Watkins, *Listener*, 109, 1983, 21; Blair Worden, *LRB*, 5, 1983, 15–16; *Observer*, July 29, 1984, p. 21; *TLS*, Aug. 17, 1984, p. 927; *VQR*, 60, 1984, 12; David A. Loewenstein, *ELN*, 22, 1984, 70–72; John T. Shawcross, *RenQ*, 37, 1984,

148–52; Thomas Wheeler, *SR*, 92, 1984, 304–12; Michael Fixler, *RES*, 36, 1985, 269–70; Richard S. Ide, *Rev*, 7, 1985, 89–111; Thomas Healy, *MLR*, 82, 1987, 168–69.

276 Winston, Alexander. "John Milton: Poet as Politician." *History Today*, 22, 1972, 237–44.

Discusses Milton's early life, marriage, and political viewpoint as they are expressed in his writings. Concludes by discussing his political fall from grace and claims that he was "left to the design of poetry that he had sketched out in Cambridge days."

277 Wolfe, Don M. *Milton and His England*. Princeton, NJ: Princeton Univ. Press, 1971. xvi, 130pp.

Traces Milton's life in the context of public events and common scenes of his time. Reviews: *Booklist*, 68, 1972, 646; Henry G. Hahn, *LJ*, 97, 1972, 877; E. Keenelt, *SCN*, 30, 1972, 19–20; Michael Lieb, *Cithara*, 12, 1972, 85–106; *MiltonQ*, 6, No. 1, 1972, 17–18; *VQR*, 48, 1972, lxi; Roger Lejosne, *EA*, 26, 1973, 100; Lois Potter, *SCN*, 32, 1974, 4; Lois Potter, *ES*, 55, 1974, 477–79.

278 Woolrych, Austin. "Milton and Richard Heath." *PQ*, 53, 1974, 132–35. Offers evidence identifying the Richard Heath who served as vicar of St. Alkmund's, Shrewsbury, from 1650 to 1662 as the recipient of Milton's letter of December 13, 1652.

279 Yoshimura, Nobuo. "Milton and Marvell." *MCJ News*, 9, 1987, 16–17.

Abstract of paper presented. Studies the relationship between Milton and Andrew Marvell, suggesting that each man influenced the other—but not in literary matters. They were drawn together because they were "the last of the authentic Renaissance tribe."

280 Barker, Arthur E., ed. *"Samson Agonistes" and Shorter Poems*. Arlington Heights, IL: Harlan Davidson, 1975. xii, 115pp. Frequently reprinted.

New edition of Huckabay No. 196, originally published in 1950, with a revised introduction and bibliography.

281 Broadbent, John, gen. ed. The Cambridge Milton for Schools and Colleges. 10 vols. Cambridge: Cambridge Univ. Press, 1972–77.

This series is intended to supersede A. W. Verity's Pitt Press edition of Milton's poetry (Cambridge, 1891–96; Stevens No. 235) and contains the following volumes:

John Milton: Introductions. Ed. by Broadbent. 1973. xv, 344pp.

Contains a number of essays written by various authors. In this bibliography, each essay is listed according to author and classification. Reviews: *MiltonQ*, 8, 1974, 22–23; John Arthos, *RenQ*, 28, 1975, 288–91.

"Paradise Lost": Introduction. By Broadbent. 1972. x, 175pp.

Discusses various topics—such as themes, genre, structures, allusions, and style—and provides an extensive reading list. Reviews: R. E. C. Houghton, *RES*, 23, 1972, 497–99; *MiltonQ*, 6, No. 2, 1972, 40–41; Michael Lieb, *Cithara*, 12, 1972, 85–106; *SCN*, 30, 1972, 64–65; Joseph Anthony Wittreich, Jr., *RenQ*, 27, 1974, 258–61; Roger Lejosne, *EA*, 28, 1975, 347–48; Frank McCombie, *N&Q*, 22, 1975, 329–30.

"Paradise Lost": Books I–II. Ed. by Broadbent. 1972. x, 149pp.

Contains an extensive introduction and footnotes that frequently gloss Milton's vocabulary. Reviews: R. E. C. Houghton, *RES*, 23, 1972, 497–99; Michael Lieb, *Cithara*, 12, 1972, 85–106; *SCN*, 30, 1972, 65–66; Roger Lejosne, *EA*, 28, 1975, 347–48; Frank McCombie, *N&Q*, 22, 1975, 329–30.

"Paradise Lost": Books III–IV. Ed. by Lois Potter (Book 3) and Broadbent (Book 4). 1976. viii, 136pp.

Contains two appendices.

"Paradise Lost": Books V–VI. Ed. by Isabel G. MacCaffrey (Book V) and Robert Hodge (Book VI). 1975. viii, 159pp.

Includes an introduction by Broadbent. One appendix on each book. Review: C. Schaar, *ES*, 59, 1978, 218–24.

"Paradise Lost": Books VII–VIII. Ed. by David Aers (Book 7) and Mary Ann Radzinowicz (Book 8). 1974. viii, 146pp.

Includes an introduction by Broadbent and Jane Powell. Also contains an appendix to Book 7 and a list of resources for Book 8. Reviews: Michael J. O'Neal, *SCN*, 33, 1975, 58–59; Anthony Low, *MiltonQ*, 9, 1975, 20–27; C. Schaar, *ES*, 59, 1978, 218–24.

"Paradise Lost": Books IX–X. Ed. by J. Martin Evans. 1973. x, 189pp.

Extensive commentary precedes each book, followed by selected topics or issues. Review: *MiltonQ*, 8, 1974, 22.

"Paradise Lost": Books XI–XII. Ed. by Michael Hollington with Lawrence Wilkinson. 1976. vii, 115pp.

Extensive introduction by Hollington. Appendix: *A Fantasia upon Milton's Religious Doctrine*, by W. H. Auden.

Odes, Pastorals, Masques. Ed. by David

Aers, Winifred Maynard, Peter Mendes, Lorna Sage, and Broadbent. 1975. xii, 240pp.

Review: *MiltonQ*, 10, 1976, 91–93.

"Samson Agonistes," Sonnets, &c. Ed. by Broadbent and Robert Hodge, with translations of selected Latin and Italian poetry by Robert Hodge. 1977. xiv, 235pp.

Review: G. K. Hunter, *SR*, 86, 1978, 414–21.

282 Bush, Douglas, ed. *The Complete Poetical Works of John Milton.* London: Oxford Univ. Press, 1966. Frequently reprinted.

See Huckabay No. 128. Reviews: *TLS*, Sept. 1, 1966, p. 779; J. C. Maxwell, *N&Q*, 13, 1966, 397–99; Martin Mueller, *Archiv*, 204, 1968, 458–59; Irène Simon, *RLV*, 34, 1968, 540–41.

283 Bush, Douglas, ed. *The Essential Milton.* London: Chatto and Windus, 1969. 693pp.

A selection with some commentary.

284 Bush, Douglas, ed. *The Portable Milton.* New York: Viking Press, 1949. Frequently reprinted.

See Huckabay No. 85. Reprinted with an updated bibliography in 1968.

285 Campbell, Gordon, ed. *Complete English Poems, "Of Education," "Areopagitica."* Fourth edition. London: J. M. Dent and Sons, 1990. xxxvii, 620pp.

First published in c. 1909 (Stevens No. 254), revised by B. A. Wright in 1956 (Huckabay No. 113), and further revised by Campbell in 1980, with still further revisions in the present edition.

286 Carey, John, and **Alastair Fowler,** eds. *The Poems of John Milton.* Longmans Annotated English Poets. London and Harlow: Longmans, 1968; New York: W. W. Norton, 1972. xxii, 1181pp.

"We have modernized old spelling, but have reproduced old punctuation with diplomatic faithfulness." Contains extensive headnotes and footnotes and lengthy introductions, incorporating the achievements of recent scholarship. Second impression, with corrections, Longmans, 1980. See Nos. 300, 331, 1388, 1617, and 4109–10. Reviews: *TLS*, Apr. 17, 1969, p. 406; *MiltonN*, 3, 1969, 58–59; Emile Saillens, *EA*, 23, 1970, 444–46; Roberts W. French, *DR*, 50, 1970, 406–08; Maren–Sofie Røstvig, *SCN*, 28, 1970, 2–3; C. C. Barfoot, *DQR*, 1, 1971, 179–81; Merritt Y. Hughes, *MLR*, 66, 1971, xxi–xxxii. Review (of 1980 ed.): Roy C. Flannagan, *MiltonQ*, 15, 1981, 125–26.

287 Davies, Tony, ed. *Selected Shorter Poems and Prose Writings.* London: Routledge, 1988. viii, 265pp.

288 Eberhart, Richard, introd. *"Paradise Lost," "Paradise Regained," and "Samson Agonistes."* Garden City, NY: Doubleday, 1969.

Review: James A. McShane, *PrS*, 44, 1970, 368–69.

289 Frank, Joseph, ed. *Milton without Footnotes.* Harper Studies in Language and Literature. New York: Harper and Row, 1974. 48pp.

A collection of some of Milton's poetry and prose. Designed as an introduction for undergraduates. Review: Michael A. Mikolajczak, *SCN*, 33, 1975, 61–62.

290 Frye, Northrop, ed. *"Paradise Lost" and Selected Poetry and Prose.* New York: Holt, Rinehart, and Winston, 1973.

Reprint of Huckabay No. 88, originally published in 1951.

291 Hanford, James H., introd. *"Paradise Lost" and "Paradise Regained."* New York: Franklin Watts, 1971. xxviii, 443pp.

Hanford's critical profile is reprinted from the 1968 edition of the *Encyclopedia Americana*.

292 Le Comte, Edward, introd. *"Paradise Lost" and Other Poems.* New York: New American Library, 1981.

Reprint of Huckabay No. 118, originally published in 1961.

293 Lerner, L. D., ed. *Poems.* Harmondsworth: Penguin, 1985.

Reprint of Huckabay No. 110, originally published in 1953.

294 Patrides, C. A., gen. ed. The Macmillan Milton: The Poetry of John Milton. 5 vols. to date. London: Macmillan, 1972–74.

The following volumes have been published:

The Minor Poems in English. Ed. by John T. Shawcross. Introduction by A. D. Nuttall. Notes by Douglas Bush. London: Macmillan, 1972. 362pp.

Appendix: "On the Ode, The Masque, and The Pastoral Elegy," by Patrides.

"Paradise Lost" : Books I–II. Introduction by Philip Brockbank. Notes by Patrides. 1972. 230pp.

"Paradise Lost" : Book IV. Introduction and Notes by T. M. Gang. 1974. 136pp.

"Paradise Lost" : Book IX. Introduction and Notes by Rosemary Syfret. 1972. 168pp.

"Paradise Lost" : Book X. Introduction by E. A. J. Honigmann. Notes by Patrides. 1972. 150pp.

Review: R. E. C. Houghton, *RES*, 24, 1973, 488–90.

295 Patterson, Frank Allen, gen. ed. *The Works of John Milton*. New York: Columbia Univ. Press, 1931–38. 18 vols. in 21. Vols. 14 and 15 and two-volume index available on demand from Univ. Microfilms International.

See Huckabay No. 77. See Nos. 59, 192, 366 (Vol. 5), 3881, 3897, 3930, and 4140.

296 Sergeant, Howard, ed. *Pergamon Poets, 7: John Milton and William Wordsworth*. Pergamon English Library. Oxford: Pergamon, 1970. 107pp.

Milton selections, pp. 1–52. Contains seven of the shorter poems and selections from *Comus, Samson Agonistes, Paradise Lost*, and *Paradise Regained*.

297 Shawcross, John T., ed. *The Complete Poetry of John Milton*. Revised edition. New York: Doubleday Anchor Books, 1971.

Revised and enlarged version of Huckabay No. 122. Review: Michael Lieb, *Cithara*, 12, 1972, 85–106.

EDITIONS OF THE SHORTER POEMS

298 Burden, Dennis H., ed. *The Shorter Poems of John Milton.* New York: Barnes and Noble; London: Morrison and Gibb, 1970. x, 174pp.

Includes all the shorter English poems, except for some of Milton's Psalm translations. The text and order of the poems generally follow the 1673 edition. Review: N. W. Bawcutt, *N&Q*, 19, 1972, 198–200.

299 Butlin, Martin, ed. *"On the Morning of Christ's Nativity": Milton's Hymn with Illustrations by William Blake.* Andoversford: Whittington Press, Angscot Productions, 1981. xxii, 24pp.

A limited edition.

300 Carey, John, ed. *Complete Shorter Poems.* Longman Annotated English Poets Series. London: Longman, 1968, 1971. xx, 531pp.

Includes *Paradise Regained, Samson Agonistes,* and the shorter poems. Extensive introduction and notes. Modernized spelling but original punctuation. Reprints of the material in No. 286.

301 Crehan, T., ed. *The Minor Poems of John Milton.* Oxford and Elmsford, NY: Wheaton (Pergamon Press), 1976. 165pp. Review: David Russell, *SCN*, 35, 1977, 80.

302 Davies, Tony, ed. *Selected Shorter Poems and Prose Writings.* London and New York: Routledge, Chapman and Hall, 1988. viii, 265pp.

Contains an introduction, extensive critical commentary, notes, and bibliography.

303 Demaray, John G., afterword. *"Arcades": A Piece Taken from "Poems of Mr. John Milton, Both English and Latin, Composed at Several Times. Printed by His True Copies. London, 1645."* Lexington, KY: King Library Press, 1983. 23pp.

304 Enright, D. J., ed. *A Choice of Milton's Verse.* London: Faber and Faber, 1975. 128pp.

Selected passages from *L'Allegro, Il Penseroso, Comus, Lycidas, Paradise Lost, Paradise Regained,* and *Samson Agonistes.* Also includes the *Nativity Ode* and Sonnets 19, 22, and 23.

305 Etchells, Ruth, ed. *A Selection of Poems by John Milton, 1608–1674, Exploring His Pilgrimage of Faith.* Poets and Prophets Series. Sutherland, Australia: Tring Publishers, 1988. 48pp.

306 Keynes, Geoffrey, ed. *On the Morning of Christ's Nativity.* Folcroft, PA: Folcroft Library Editions, 1972.

Reprint of Stevens No. 395, originally published in 1923. Illustrations by William Blake.

307 Le Comte, Edward, ed. and trans. *"Justa Edovardo King": A Facsimile Edition of the Memorial Volume in which Milton's "Lycidas" First Appeared.* Norwood, PA: Norwood Editions, 1978; Folcroft, PA: Folcroft Library Editions, 1978. viii, 144pp.

Facsimile of the 1638 edition with a translation. See Nos. 1248, 1529–30, and 1573.

308 Milton, John. "The Bridgewater *Comus*: Text of *A Maske.*" *"A Maske at Ludlow": Essays on Milton's "Comus."* Ed. by John S. Diekhoff (Cleveland, OH: Press of Case Western Reserve Univ., 1968), pp. 207–40; reprinted Ann Arbor,

MI: Univ. Microfilms International, 1980 Books on Demand Reprints.

See Huckabay No. 2441. Harris Fletcher's transcription of the Bridgewater manuscript, reprinted from Huckabay No. 105.

309 Milton, John. *English Poems. "Comus" (1645).* Menston: Scolar Press, 1968. 120pp.

Facsimile of only the English poems in the 1645 volume.

310 Milton, John. *"Lycidas" : 1637–1645.* Students' Facsimiles. Menston: Scolar Press, 1970.

Contains the text from *Justa Edovardo King Naufrago* (1638); the text from the *Poems* (1645); the fragment of proof, corrected in Milton's hand, of the text of 1638; and the text from the Trinity Manuscript (1637). Review: John T. Shawcross, *SCN*, 28, 1970, 61–63.

311 Milton, John. *Milton's "L'Allegro" and "Il Penseroso."* London: Scolar Press, 1975.

Reprint of Stevens No. 505, originally published in 1860. Illustrated with etchings on steel by Birket Foster.

312 Milton, John. *"On the Morning of Christ's Nativity" and Other Poems.* London: Folio Press, 1987.

Engravings by B. Hanscomb.

313 Milton, John. *Poems.* Reproduced in Facsimile from the Manuscript in Trinity College, Cambridge. Menston: Scolar Press, 1970. N. pag.

Reprints the 1899 transcript of W. A. Wright (see Stevens No. 304). The introduction contains a brief history of the manuscript and a description of its present condition.

314 Milton, John. *"Poems" (1645); "Lycidas" (1638).* Menston and London: Scolar Press, 1970, 1973. [i], 233pp.

Facsimile. Includes the first edition of Milton's *Poems* and *Poemata*, along with the text of *Lycidas* from *Justa Edovardo King Naufrago.*

315 Milton, John, and **Henry Lawes.** "The Airs of the Songs by Henry Lawes with His Version of the Words." *"A Maske at Ludlow" : Essays on Milton's "Comus."* Ed. by John S. Diekhoff (Cleveland, OH: Press of Case Western Reserve Univ., 1968), pp. 241–50; reprinted Ann Arbor, MI: Univ. Microfilms International, 1980 Books on Demand Reprints.

See Huckabay No. 2441. "The text of the five songs from *Comus* is that prepared by Hubert J. Foss for *The Mask of Comus: The Poem, Originally Called 'A Mask Presented at Ludlow Castle, 1634, &c,' edited by E. H. Visiak. The Airs of the Five Songs Reprinted from the Composer's Autograph Manuscript, edited by Hubert J. Foss,* with a Foreword by the Earl of Ellesmere. Ornamented by M. R. H. Farrar. Bloomsbury: The Nonesuch Press, 1937."

316 Nellist, Brian, ed. *"Poems" of 1645 and "Comus."* Collins Annotated Student Texts. London, 1974. 272pp.

Review: Anthony Low, *MiltonQ*, 9, 1975, 20–27.

317 Nichols, Fred J., ed. and trans. *An Anthology of Neo-Latin Poetry.* New Haven, CT: Yale Univ. Press, 1979. xi, 734pp.

Ad Patrem and *Epitaphium Damonis* with Nichols's prose translations and critical summaries (pp. 632–51; notes, pp. 718–21).

318 Prince, F. T., ed. *"Comus" and Other Poems.* Oxford: Oxford Univ. Press, 1968. xvii, 197pp.

Reviews: *TLS*, Sept. 12, 1968, p. 1003; Francis E. Moran, *SCN*, 27, 1969, 26–27.

319 Skeat, W. W., trans. *Epitaphium Damonis.* Folcroft, PA: Folcroft Library Editions, 1969; Norwood, PA: Norwood Editions, 1977; Philadelphia, PA: R. West, 1977.

Reprints of Huckabay No. 226, originally published in 1933.

320 Skeat, Walter, trans. *"Lament for Damon" and Other Latin Poems.* Introduction by Edward Harold Visiak. Folcroft, PA: Folcroft Library, 1976; Norwood, PA: Norwood Editions, 1976, 1977; Philadelphia, PA: R. West, 1978; Ann Arbor, MI: Univ. Microfilms International, 1980 Books on Demand Reprints.

Reprints of Huckabay No. 232, originally published in 1935.

321 Sprott, S. E., ed. *John Milton: "A Maske," the Earlier Versions.* Toronto and Buffalo, NY: Univ. of Toronto Press, 1973. 230pp.

Provides parallel transcripts of the three earliest versions—the copy in the Trinity Manuscript, the Bridgewater Manuscript, and the 1637 printed text—and reconstructs a hypothetical manuscript that Milton probably wrote in 1634. Reviews: J. de Bruyn, *HAB*, 25, 1974, 350–52; Watson Kirkconnell, *DR*, 54, 1974, 570–72; *MiltonQ*, 8, 1974, 86–87; Anthony Low, *MiltonQ*, 9, 1975, 20–27; Winifred Maynard, *RES*, 26, 1975, 333–35; Michael Lieb, *Cithara*, 15, No. 2, 1976, 102–03; Lois Potter, *ES*, 57, 1975, 333–35.

322 Thomas, C. T., ed. *Lycidas.* London: Sangam Books, 1983. 51pp.

A student edition with extensive annotations and commentary.

323 Verity, Arthur Wilson, ed. *Comus.* Ann Arbor, MI: Univ. Microfilms International, 1980 Books on Demand Reprints.

Reprint of Stevens No. 453, originally published in 1921.

324 Verity, Arthur Wilson, ed. *Milton's "L'Allegro," "Il Penseroso," "Comus," "Lycidas."* Cambridge Series for Schools and Training Colleges. Ann Arbor, MI: Univ. Microfilms International, 1980 Books on Demand Reprints.

Reprint of Stevens No. 301, originally published in 1899.

325 Verity, Arthur Wilson, introd. *Milton's Sonnets.* Folcroft, PA: Folcroft Library Editions, 1973; Norwood, PA: Norwood Editions, 1978.

Reprints of Stevens No. 630 and Huckabay No. 227, originally published in 1895.

326 Asimov, Isaac, ed. *Asimov's Annotated "Paradise Lost."* Garden City, NY: Doubleday, 1974. 767pp.
Review: *MiltonQ*, 9, 1975, 27–28.

327 Bentley, Richard, ed. *Paradise Lost.* Nachdruck der Ausgabe London, 1732. Mit einer bibliographischen Notiz von Prof. Dr. M. Spevack, Münster. Leinen: Olms (Anglistica and Americana Series), 1972.
Reprint of the London edition, 1732. With a biographical note by Spevack.

328 Bentley, Richard, ed. *Paradise Lost.* New York: AMS Press, 1974.
Reprint of the 1732 edition.

329 Carey, James J., ed. *"Paradise Lost," Book I.* Dublin: Educational Co. of Ireland, 1969. 78pp.
Includes an essay that surveys modern Milton scholarship.

330 Elledge, Scott, ed. *Paradise Lost.* An Authoritative Text, Backgrounds and Sources, Criticism. A Norton Critical Edition. New York: W. W. Norton, 1975. xxix, 546pp.
A modernized, annotated text. Contents include selections from Milton's prose and the Bible, notes on important topics in the epic, and selections from modern and earlier Milton criticism. Review: *MiltonQ*, 10, 1976, 21–22.

331 Fowler, Alastair, ed. *Paradise Lost.* Longman Annotated English Poets. London: Longman, 1971, 1980. xx, 649pp.
Reprints, with some corrections, of the *Paradise Lost* section of No. 286.

332 Houghton, R. E. C., ed. *"Paradise Lost": Books IX–X.* London: Oxford Univ. Press, 1969. 244pp.

Uses Darbishire's text (see Huckabay No. 108), contains selected criticism, and provides appendices on the text, spelling, punctuation, and meter. Review: Anthony Low, *SCN*, 28, 1970, 45–46; reply to Low by Houghton and response to Houghton by Low, *SCN*, 29, 1971, 66–67.

333 Madsen, William G., ed. *Paradise Lost.* New York: The Modern Library College Edition by Random House, 1969. vii, 344pp.

334 Masson, David, introd. *"Paradise Lost," as Originally Published by John Milton.* Folcroft, PA: Folcroft Library Editions, 1972, 1976; Philadelphia, PA: R. West, 1978.
Reprints of Stevens No. 735, originally published in 1877. The ten-book first edition of *Paradise Lost.*

335 Milton, John. *Paradise Lost (1667).* Menston: Scolar Press, 1968, 1972, 1973. N. pag.
Facsimile of the epic in its ten-book first edition. See No. 4182. Review: *SCN*, 28, 1970, 12.

336 Milton, John. *Paradise Lost: A Poem in Twelve Books.* Ann Arbor, MI: Univ. Microfilms International, 1980 Books on Demand Reprints.
Reprint of the 1678 edition.

337 Prince, F. T., ed. *"Paradise Lost": Books I and II.* London: Oxford Univ. Press, 1969. 206pp.

338 Shepherd, Robert A., Jr. *"Paradise Lost": A Prose Rendition.* New York: Seabury Press, 1983. x, 166pp.
A prose paraphrase. Review: Philip J. Gallagher, *MiltonQ*, 18, 1984, 34–35.

339 Wesley, John, ed. *Milton for the Methodists*. Introduction by Frank Baker. London: Epworth Press, 1988. xvi, 90pp. First published in 1763. Edited and annotated extracts from *Paradise Lost*. In the introduction Baker discusses Milton's influence on Wesley and on his family.

EDITIONS OF *PARADISE REGAINED*

340 Dunster, Charles, ed. *Paradise Regained.* Norwood, PA: Norwood Editions, 1977.

Reprint of the 1795 edition, cited in Stevens No. 1102.

341 Milton, John. *"Paradise Regained"; "Samson Agonistes" (1671).* Menston: Scolar Press, 1968, 1973. [ii], 214pp. Facsimile.

342 Wittreich, Joseph Anthony, Jr., introd. *Milton's "Paradise Regained": Two Eighteenth-Century Critiques by Richard Meadowcourt and Charles Dunster.* 2 vols in 1. Gainesville, FL: Scholars' Facsimiles and Reprints, 1971. xv, 30; iv, 280pp. Facsimiles. Originally published in 1732 and 1795, respectively. Meadowcourt's work is a critique, with extensive quotations. Dunster's is an annotated edition. Wittreich's introduction relates these publications to the rise of Milton's reputation and to the history of Milton criticism.

343 Davis, Michael, ed. *Samson Agonistes.* Macmillan's English Classics. London: Macmillan; New York: St. Martin's Press, 1968. xliv, 163pp.

Modernized spelling and punctuation. Extensive notes facing each page of text.

344 Hunter, John, ed. *"Samson Agonistes" and "Lycidas."* Folcroft, PA: Folcroft Library Editions, 1977; Norwood, PA: Norwood Editions, 1978.

Reprints of Stevens No. 1134, published in the edition of 1870.

345 Medley, Robert, illustrator. *Samson Agonistes.* London: Bertram Rota and Basilisk Press, 1980.

Described by Roger Berthoud, *MiltonQ,* 15, 1981, 72, from the *Times,* Aug. 18, 1980.

346 Milton, John. *"Paradise Regained"; "Samson Agonistes" (1671).* Menston: Scolar Press, 1968, 1973. [ii], 214pp. Facsimile.

347 Milton, John. *Samson Agonistes.* London: Davis-Poynter, 1973. 52pp.

A playscript, "devised for practical use in the theatre, in schools, and by drama groups."

348 Phillips, Ann, ed. *Samson Agonistes.* London: Univ. Tutorial Press, 1974. 139pp.

Includes extensive introductory material and forty pages of notes.

349 Prince, F. T., ed. *Samson Agonistes.* London: Oxford Univ. Press, 1970.

Reprint of Huckabay No. 197, originally published in 1957.

350 Ainsworth, Oliver Morley, ed. *Milton on Education. The Tractate "Of Education" with Supplementary Extracts from Other Writings of Milton.* New York: AMS Press 1979.
Reprint of Stevens No. 1271, originally published in 1928.

351 Burton, Kathleen M., ed. *Prose Writings.* New York: E. P. Dutton, 1970, 1972.
Reprints of Huckabay No. 298, originally published in 1955.

352 Gabrieli, Vittorio, introd. *Selected Prose.* Biblioteca Italiana di Testi Inglesi. Bari: Adriatica Editrice, 1970. 381pp.
The general introduction, introduction to individual works, and notes are in Italian. Contents: *Private Letters, Commonplace Book, Of Reformation, Reason of Church-Government, Doctrine and Discipline of Divorce, Of Education, Areopagitica, Eikonoklastes, Second Defence, State Papers,* and *Readie and Easie Way.*

353 Jebb, Richard C., ed. *"Areopagitica," with a Commentary by Sir Richard C. Jebb, and with Supplementary Material.* Norwood, PA: Norwood Library Editions, 1977; New York: AMS Press, 1979.
Reprints of Stevens No. 1263, originally published in 1918.

354 Lea, K. M., ed. *"Areopagitica" and "Of Education."* Oxford: Clarendon Press, 1973. xxviii, 80pp.
Review: George Parfitt, *N&Q,* 23, 1976, 190–91.

355 Lockwood, Laura Emma, ed. *"Of Education," "Areopagitica," "The Commonwealth," with Early Biographies of Milton.* Ann Arbor, MI: Univ. Microfilms

International, 1980 Books on Demand Reprints.
Reprint of Stevens No. 1258, originally published in 1911.

356 Milton, John. *"Accedence" (1669).* Menston: Scolar Press, 1971. 65pp.
Facsimile of a copy of *Accedence Commenc't Grammar* in the Bodleian Library.

357 Milton, John. *A Complete Collection of the Historical, Political, and Miscellaneous Works of John Milton.* Ann Arbor, MI: Univ. Microfilms International, 1980 Books on Demand Reprints.
Reprint of the 1738 edition.

358 Mirsky, Prince D. S., ed. *A Brief History of Moscovia.* Folcroft, PA: Folcroft Library Editions, 1972.
Reprint of Huckabay No. 279, originally published in 1929.

359 Morley, Henry, ed. *English Prose Writings of John Milton.* Ann Arbor, MI: Univ. Microfilms International, 1980 Books on Demand Reprints.
Reprint of Stevens No. 1238, originally published in 1889.

360 Morris, Edward E., ed. *Tractate of Education.* Philadelphia, PA: R. West, 1978.
Reprint of Stevens No. 1241, originally published in 1895.

361 Patrides, C. A., ed. *John Milton: Selected Prose.* Harmondsworth: Penguin, 1974. 426pp. Revised edition. Columbia: Univ. of Missouri Press, 1985. 463pp.
Contains condensed versions, complete texts, and extracts of prose written between 1642 and 1660, and the early biographies by John Aubrey and Edward Phillips. Extensive bibliographies.

Reviews of 1974 ed.: *MiltonQ*, 8, 1974, 88–89; Anthony Low, *MiltonQ*, 9, 1975, 20–27. Reviews of 1985 ed.: Thomas N. Corns, *N&Q*, 34, 1987, 540–41; Elizabeth Skerpan, *SCN*, 46, 1988, 8–9.

362 Rivers, Isabel, ed. *Areopagitica. A Speech of Mr. John Milton for the Liberty of Unlicensed Printing to the Parliament of England.* Cambridge: Deighton, Bell and Co., 1973. xiv, 49pp.

A limited edition.

363 Sabine, George H., ed. *"Areopagitica" and "Of Education."* Arlington Heights, IL: Harlan Davidson, n.d.

Reprint of Huckabay No. 293, originally published in 1951.

364 Suffolk, J. C., ed. *Areopagitica.* London: Univ. Tutorial Press, 1968. vii, 147pp.

Extensive notes on pages facing the text.

365 Tillyard, Phyllis B., trans. *Milton: Private Correspondence and Academic Exercises.* Introduction by E. M. W. Tillyard. Folcroft, PA: Folcroft Library Editions, 1969; Ann Arbor, MI: Univ. Microfilms International, 1972; Norwood, PA: Norwood Library Editions, 1977; Philadelphia, PA: R. West, 1978.

Reprints of Huckabay No. 281, originally published in 1932.

366 Wolfe, Don M., gen. ed. *Complete Prose Works of John Milton.* 8 vols. in 10. New Haven, CT, and London: Yale Univ. Press, 1953–82.

Presents "annotated texts of Milton's prose in the ascertainable order of its composition, bringing to bear in notes, prefaces, and volume introductions the accumulated scholarship of the past century." This work appears in the following volumes:

Vol. 1, 1624–42: Introduction by Don M. Wolfe (volume editor). *Prolusions*: trans. by Phyllis B. Tillyard with notes and prefaces by Kathryn A. McEuen; Private Correspondence: trans., notes, and prefaces by W. Arthur Turner and Alberta T. Turner; *Commonplace Book*: trans., preface, and notes by Ruth Mohl; *Of*

Reformation: preface and notes by Wolfe and William Alfred; *Of Prelatical Episcopacy*: preface and notes by J. Max Patrick; *Animadversions*: preface by Rudolf Kirk with notes by Rudolf Kirk, assisted by William P. Baker; *Reason of Church-Government*: preface and notes by Ralph A. Haug; *An Apology against a Pamphlet*: preface and notes by Frederick L. Taft. Appendices: "Legal Index," trans. by Ruth Mohl with preface and notes by Maurice Kelley; "A Postscript," preface and notes by Wolfe; "The London Petition (December 11, 1640)"; "Constitutions and Canons Ecclesiastical (1640)"; "The Oath Ex-Officio," by Wolfe; "The Legion of Smec," by Frederick L. Taft and Ashur Baizer; "The Bishops," by Leo F. Solt, Ashur Baizer, Franklin R. Baruch, and J. Hillis Miller, Jr.; "Theme on Early Rising," trans., preface, and notes by Maurice Kelley and Donald Mackenzie; Textual Guide. 1953. xvi, 1073pp. See No. 3879.

Vol. 2, 1643–48: Introduction by Ernest Sirluck (volume editor). *Doctrine and Discipline of Divorce*: preface and notes by Lowell W. Coolidge; *Of Education*: preface and notes by Donald C. Dorian; *The Judgement of Martin Bucer*: preface and notes by Arnold Williams; *Areopagitica*: preface and notes by Sirluck; *Tetrachordon*: preface and notes by Arnold Williams; *Colasterion*: preface and notes by Lowell W. Coolidge; Private Correspondence: trans., notes, and prefaces by W. Arthur Turner and Alberta T. Turner; Textual Notes; *Doctrine and Discipline of Divorce*: Spelling and Punctuation Changes in 1644. Appendices: "The Star Chamber Decree of 1637," notes by Sirluck; "The Licensing Order of 1643," notes by Sirluck; "*Little Non-Such*: A Satire on Milton's Divorce Argument?" by Sirluck; "Milton as Translator: Notes on Milton's Method of Translation in *The Judgement of Martin Bucer*," by Arnold Williams. 1959. xii, 840pp. See Nos. 3841 and 3889.

Vol. 3, 1648–49: Introduction by Merritt

Y. Hughes (volume editor). *The Tenure of Kings and Magistrates*: preface and notes by Hughes; *Observations upon the Articles of Peace*: preface and notes by Hughes; *Eikonoklastes*: preface and notes by Hughes. Appendices: "Textual Notes on *The Tenure*"; "Textual Notes on *Eikonoklastes*." 1962. xii, 652pp.

Vol. 4, 1650–55: Introduction by Don M. Wolfe (volume editor). Part 1: *A Defence of the People of England*: preface and notes by William J. Grace, trans. by Donald Mackenzie; *A Second Defence of the English People*: preface and notes by Donald A. Roberts, trans. by Helen North. 1966. xvi, 686pp. Part 2: *Pro Se Defensio*: preface and notes by Kester Svendsen, trans. by Paul W. Blackford; Milton's Private Correspondence: trans., prefaces, and notes by W. Arthur Turner and Alberta T. Turner. Appendices: "The Phillips' *Response*," preface and notes by Robert W. Ayers, trans. by James I. Armstrong; "Salmasius: Opponent of Milton," by Kathryn A. McEuen; "Selections from *Defensio Regia* (May 11, 1649)," trans. by Kathryn A. McEuen; "Selections from Du Moulin, *Regii Sanguinis Clamor* (August, 1652)," preface and trans. by Paul W. Blackford; "Selections from More's *Fides Publica* (October, 1654) and *Supplementum* (April?, 1655)," preface and trans. by Paul W. Blackford; "Variants in London Editions of Milton's *Defensio*," by Robert W. Ayers; "Authorized Editions of Milton's *Defensio, Defensio Secunda*, and *Pro Se Defensio*," by Robert W. Ayers; "Corrections to the Columbia Text of Milton's *Pro Populo Anglicano Defensio*," by Robert W. Ayers. 1966. xivpp., Pp. 687–1166.

Vol. 5, 1648?–71: French Fogle (volume editor). Part 1: *History of Britain*: introduction and notes by Fogle; *The Digression*, preface and notes by Fogle; *Character of the Long Parliament*; *Digression*; Variants in Texts. 1971. lx, 467pp., plus unpaginated index. Part 2: *The Miltonic State Papers*: preface and

notes by J. Max Patrick, trans. by Paul W. Blackford. 1971. xivpp., Pp. 469–876, plus unpaginated index. See No. 4147.

Vol. 6, c. 1658–c. 1660: *Christian Doctrine*: prefaces by Maurice Kelley (volume editor) and John Carey; trans. by John Carey; introduction and notes by Kelley. Appendix: "Revisions in the Manuscript of Milton's *De Doctrina Christiana*," by Kelley. 1973. xxiv, 863pp. See Nos. 829, 1118, and 3796.

Vol. 7, 1659–60 (rev. ed.): Preface by Robert W. Ayers (volume editor) and Austin Woolrych. Historical Introduction by Austin Woolrych; *A Treatise of Civil Power*: preface and notes by William B. Hunter, Jr.; *Considerations Touching the Likeliest Means*: preface and notes by William B. Hunter, Jr.; *A Letter to a Friend*: preface and notes by Ayers; *Proposalls of Certaine Expedients*: preface and notes by Maurice Kelley; *The Readie & Easie Way* (first ed.): preface and notes by Ayers; *The Present Means and Brief Delineation of a Free Commonwealth*: preface and notes by Ayers; *The Readie and Easie Way* (second ed.): preface and notes by Ayers; *Brief Notes upon a Late Sermon*: preface and notes by Ayers; Private Correspondence: trans. and notes by W. Arthur Turner and Alberta T. Turner. Appendices: "Selections from *Aphorisms Political*, by James Harrington (1659)"; "Milton's Views on Church and State in 1659," by William J. Grace. 1974; rev. ed. 1980. xiii, 547pp. See Nos. 4146 and 4163.

Vol. 8, 1666–82: Preface by Maurice Kelley (volume editor). Private Correspondence: preface, trans., and notes by Robert W. Ayers; *Prose Accompanying "Paradise Lost"*: preface and notes by Robert J. Wickenheiser; *Accedence Commenc't Grammar*: introduction by David P. French; *Prose Preliminary to "Samson Agonistes"*: preface and notes by Robert J. Wickenheiser; *A Fuller Course in the Art of Logic*: ed. and trans. by Walter J. Ong, S. J., and Charles J. Ermatinger, introduction by Walter J. Ong, S. J.; *Of True Religion*: preface and notes by Keith W. F. Stavely; *A Declaration, or Letters Patents*: preface and notes by Kelley; *A Brief History of Moscovia*: preface and notes by George B. Parks. Appendices: "Milton's Outline for Tragedies (1639?–1642?)," preface and notes by John M. Steadman; "Notes on Milton's *Paradise Lost* and Other Biblical Scenarios," by James Holly Hanford, ed. by John M. Steadman; "*Diploma Electionis S. R. M. Poloniae*," preface by Kelley; "Russian-Language Criticism of Milton's *Moscovia*," by John B. Gleason. 1982. xv, 625pp. See No. 3988.

Reviews: Don Cameron Allen, *MLN*, 69, 1954, 116–20; *TLS*, July 30, 1954, p. 484; reply to Allen and *TLS* reviewer by Arthur Turner, *TLS*, Sept. 24, 1954, p. 609; Walter Taplin, *Spectator*, June 4, 1954, pp. 690–93; J. Max Patrick and others, *SCN*, 12, 1954, 1–4, 11–15; J. George, *AUR*, 36, 1955, 55–58; F. T. Prince, *RES*, 6, 1955, 316–18; Barbara Kiefer, *CH*, 25, 1956, 88–90; I. A. Shapiro, *MLR*, 51, 1956, 244–46; John B. Broadbent, Jr., *ES*, 38, 1957, 275–78; *SCN*, 17, 1959, 30; Arthur Axelrad, *SCN*, 17, 1959, 30–31; J. Max Patrick, *JMH*, 32, 1960, 279–80; G. B. Evans, *JEGP*, 59, 1960, 497–505; William Haller, *CH*, 29, 1960, 364–65; Ralph Laurence, *English* (Oxford), 13, 1960, 68–69; *QQ*, 67, 1960, 138; J. I. Cope, *RN*, 13, 1960, 250–52; *SCN*, 18, 1960, 7; *SCN*, 18, 1960, 13; *TLS*, Apr. 29, 1960, p. 274; Kenneth Muir, *MLR*, 56, 1961, 406–07; K. M. Lea, *RES*, 12, 1961, 204–07; *TLS*, Apr. 12, 1963, p. 250; William Haller, *ELN*, 1, 1963, 146–51; Joseph Frank, *SCN*, 21, 1963, 34-36; Samuel Mintz, *RN*, 16, 1963, 346–48; Walter J. Ong, S.J., *SEL*, 4, 1964, 178–79; Kenneth Muir, *MLR*, 59, 1964, 109; Alastair Fowler, *N&Q*, 11, 1964, 113–14; John M. Steadman, *JEGP*, 63, 1964, 516–21; K. M. Lea, *RES*, 15, 1964, 321–23; John R. Mulder, *SCN*, 24, 1966, 7–58; John M. Steadman, *RenQ*, 20, 1967, 395–400; C. V. Wedg-wood, *History*, 52, 1967, 86–87; John B. Broadbent, Jr., *ES*, 48, 1967, 243–46; Dennis H. Burden, *N&Q*, 15, 1968, 384–86; Barbara Kiefer Lewalski, *MP*, 65, 1968, 381–83; Edgar Mertner, *Anglia*, 86, 1968, 391–94; James H. Sims, *SHR*, 2, 1968, 385–87; William B. Hunter, Jr., *SCN*, 29, 1971, 61; George B. Parks, *SCN*, 29, 1971, 33–34; *MiltonQ*, 5, 1971, 57–59; Michael Lieb, *Cithara*, 12, 1972, 85–106; Leo Miller, *N&Q*, 19, 1972, 320, 474–78; Michael Fixler, *RES*, 24, 1973, 79–83; Roger Lejosne, *EA*, 26, 1973, 101–02; Valerie Pearl, *History*, 58, 1973, 448–49; Donald A. Roberts, *RenQ*, 26, 1973, 89–91; *MiltonQ*, 7, 1973, 50–52; Michael Fixler, *RES*, 25, 1974, 341–44; R. E. C. Houghton, *N&Q*, 21, 1974, 435–36; William B. Hunter, Jr., *SCN*, 32, 1974, 2–3; David R. Aers, *ES*, 56, 1975, 61–64; Joseph Anthony Wittreich, Jr., *MiltonQ*, 8, 1974, 15–21; Edwin B. Benjamin, *RenQ*, 28, 1975, 293–94; Roger Lejosne, *EA*, 28, 1975, 86–87; Barbara Kiefer Lewalski, *MP*, 72, 1975, 305–08; Michael Lieb, *Cithara*, 14, No. 2, 1975, 90–92; Anthony Low, *MiltonQ*, 9, 1975, 20–27; *MiltonQ*, 9, 1975, 52–53; Andrew M. McLean, *SHR*, 10, 1976, 362–69; J. S. Morrill, *EHR*, 91, 1976, 427; Sidney Warhaft, *Mosaic*, 9, 1976, 159–73; Roger Lejosne, *EA*, 30, 1977, 229–30; Mary Ann Radzinowicz, *SN*, 49, 1977, 158–58; C. Stuart Hunter, *RenQ*, 34, 1981, 627–29; Archie Burnett, *N&Q*, 29, 1982, 175–76; Robert Thomas Fallon, *SCN*, 40, 1982, 61–63; Blair Worden, *LRB*, 5, 1982, 15–16; Michael Fixler, *RES*, 34, 1983, 364–65; Michael Lieb, *Cithara*, 23, No. 2, 1983, 47–50; John T. Shawcross, *MiltonQ*, 18, 1984, 27–32; Gordon Campbell, *MLR*, 81, 1986, 444–45; Michael Fixler, *RES*, 36, 1985, 88–89.

TRANSLATIONS OF SELECTED POEMS

367 Albuquerque, Irene de, trans. *John Milton*. Lisboa: Verbo, n.d. 133pp.
In Portuguese.

368 Bolfan, Darko, and **Dusan Kosanovic,** trans. *Soneti*. Vranje: Nova Jugoslavija, 1986. 97pp.
Milton's sonnets in Serbo-Croatian.

369 Fuzier, Jean, trans. "Le *Lycidas* de Milton: Essai de Traduction en Vers." *CahiersE*, 2, 1972, 5–11.
A French translation of *Lycidas* along with an explanation of Fuzier's theory of translating English poetry.

370 Izzo, Carlo, trans. *Ode alla Natività. Ad un Concerto Sacro. Allegro, Penseroso. Arcadi. Como. Licida*. Firenze: G. C. Sansoni, 1974. xli, 272pp.
Italian translation of the *Nativity Ode*, "At a Solemn Music," *L'Allegro* and *In Penseroso, Arcades, Comus*, and *Lycidas*.

371 Izzo, Carlo, trans. *Sansone Agonista. Sonetti*. Firenze: G. C. Sansoni, 1974. xxxiv, 250pp.
Samson Agonistes and Milton's sonnets in Italian.

372 Janoshazy, Gyorgy, trans. *A Küzdö Sámson*. Bukarest: Kriterion, 1975, 1977. 95pp.
Samson Agonistes in Hungarian.

373 Janoshazy, Gyorgy, and others, trans. *Válogatott Költöi Müvei*. Budapest: Európa, 1978. 551pp.

374 Kisaichi, Motohiro, trans. *Milton no Comus*. Kyoto: Yamaguchi Shoten, 1980. 241pp.
Comus in Japanese.

375 Koizumi, Yoshio, trans. *Toshi-Samson*.

Tokyo: Yumi Shobo, 1980. 194pp.
Samson Agonistes in Japanese.

376 Kreipe, Christine, E., trans. *Samson Agonistes*. Introduction by Karl Denner. Folcroft, PA: Folcroft Library Editions, 1969; Norwood, PA: Norwood Editions, 1976.
Reprints of Huckabay No. 367, originally published in 1926 or 1949.

377 Laurens, Pierre, trans. and ed. *Mvsae Redvces: Anthologie de la Poésie Latine de l'Europe de la Renaissance*. 2 vols. Leiden: E. J. Brill, 1975. 444pp.; 536pp.
A French translation of *Mansus*, vol. 2, pp. 455–63.

378 Martinengo, G. S., trans. *Il Paradiso Riconquistato*. Introduction by S. Baldi. Studi di filol ingl., 3, Firenze, 1975.
Paradise Regained in Italian.

379 Onukiyama, Nobuo, trans. *Rakuen Kaifuku*. Urawa: Onukiyama Nobuo, 1980. 117pp.
Paradise Regained in Japanese. See the abstract of Onukiyama's paper, "On Translating *Paradise Regained*," in *MCJ News*, 5, 1981, 17–18.

380 Orest, Mikhail, trans. "Pro Shekspir." *Ukrainsk' a Shekspiriiana na Zakhodi*. Ed. by Yar Slavutych (Edmonton, Canada: Slavuta Publishers, 1987), p. 77.
Ukrainian translation of "On Shakespeare." Abs., *SCN*, 50, 1992, 31.

381 Parantaman, A. K., trans. *Kamakkalimakan Komas Allatu Karpin Verri*. Madras: Alli, 1975. 99pp.
Comus in Tamil.

382 Saillens, Émile, trans. *Lycidas. Sonnets*. Paris: Aubier, Montaigne, 1971. 212pp.

In French. Review: *MiltonQ*, 6, No. 3, 1972, 17–18.

383 Saravia Santander, A., trans. *Sonetos. Sansón Agonista.* Barcelona: Bosch, 1977. 325pp.

Milton's sonnets and *Samson Agonistes* in Spanish.

384 Shigeno, Tenrai, and **Yoichi Shigeno,** trans. *Rikisha Samson.* Tokyo: Kinseido, 1978. 249pp.

Comus and *Samson Agonistes* in Japanese.

385 Siddiqui, Zillur Rahman, trans. *Samson Agonistes.* Second edition. Dacca: Bangla Academy, 1985. 96pp.

In Bengali.

386 Sotillos, Eugenio, trans. *Miniclásicos.*

6 vols. Barcelona: Toray, 1978. In Spanish.

387 Sprusinski, Michal, trans. *Samson Walczacy.* Warsaw: Panstwowy Instytut Wydawniczy, 1977. 82pp.

Samson Agonistes in Polish.

388 Takeshi, Okazawa, trans. *Eibungaku no Sndai Aika.* Tokyo: Shinozaki Shorin, 1973. 337pp.

In Japanese. Contains Milton's *Lycidas,* Shelley's *Adonais,* and Tennyson's *In Memoriam.*

389 Toth, Arpad, trans. *Kisebb Költemények.* Budapest: Magvető, 1982. 30pp.

390 Yu, Yeong, trans. *Bogragweon.* Seoul: Eulunmunhwasa, 1975. 210pp.

Paradise Regained in Korean.

391 Arai, Akira, trans. *Rakuen no Soshitsu.* Tokyo: Taishukan Shoten, 1978. 403pp. In Japanese. Contains engravings by Denji Noma. Discusses the Miltonic universe and presents a chronology of Milton's life.

392 Avinoam, Reuven, trans. *Gan Ha-eden Ha-avud.* Givatayyim: Massadah, 1982. 253pp.
In Hebrew.

393 Celidze, Vahtang, trans. *Poterjannyj Raj. Vozvrascennyj Raj.* Tbilisi: Sabcota Sakartvelo, 1969. 446pp.
Paradise Lost and *Paradise Regained* in Georgian. Afterword, pp. 413–38, gives an account of Milton's life. Believes that the English revolution deeply influenced the composition of *Paradise Lost.* Sympathetic to Satan.

394 Changbae, I. *Sillakwon.* Seoul: Chungangmunhwasa, 1987. 546pp.
In Korean.

395 Conde Obregon, Ramon, trans. *El Paraíso Perdido.* Barcelona: Verón-Climent, 1975. 144pp. Frequently reprinted.
In Spanish.

396 Covaci, Aurel, trans. *Paradisul Pierdut.* Introduction by Petre Solomon. Bucuresti: Minerva, 1972. 456pp.
In Romanian.

397 Djilas, Milovan, trans. *Izgubljeni Raj.* New York: Harcourt, Brace and World, 1969. 402pp.
In Serbo-Croatian. Includes textual notes.

398 Espina, Antonio, trans. *El Paraíso Perdido.* Madrid: Mediterráneo, 1969. 145pp. Frequently reprinted.
In Spanish.

399 Fuster, Antonio, trans. *El Paraíso Perdido.* Barcelona: Iberia, 1968, 1985. x, 303pp.
In Spanish.

400 Hirai, Masao, trans. *Shitsurakuen.* Tokyo: Chikuma Shobo, 1979, 1981. 595pp.
In Japanese.

401 Janosy, Istvan, trans. *Elveszett Paradicson.* Budapest: Magyar Helikon, 1969. 419pp.
In Hungarian.

402 Janosy, Istvan, and **Gyorgy Janoshazy,** trans. *Elveszett Paradicson: A Kuezdo Samson.* Budapest: Europa, 1987. 471pp.
Paradise Lost and *Samson Agonistes* in Hungarian.

403 Jeong, Seong Gug, trans. *Sillagweon.* Seoul: Jemun, 1972. 360pp.
In Korean.

404 Mangion, F. X., trans. *Il-Genna Mitlufa: L-Ewwel erba' Kotba.* Malta: D. O. I., 1971. 108pp. Reprinted, Malta: Lux Press, 1973.
In Maltese.

405 Meier, Hans Heinreich, trans. *Das Verlorene Paradies.* Stuttgart: Reclam, 1969. 447pp. Frequently reprinted.
In German.

406 Messian, Pierre, trans. *Paradis Perdu: Quatrième Chant.* Paris: Les Bibliophiles de l'Automobile-club de France, 1974. lxxx, 15pp.
Book 4 in French.

407 Moritani, Mineo, trans. *Gokuraku Jodo Soshitsu.* Tokyo: Kazama Shobo, 1980. 250pp.
In Japanese.

408 Papi, Lazzaro, trans. *Il Paradiso*

Perduto. Milan: Bietti, 1972. 510pp. Reprinted, Ginevra: Ed. Ferni, 1976.
In Italian.

409 Paradiso Perduto. Milan: Mondadori, 1987. 318pp.
Books 7–12 in Italian.

410 El Paraíso Perdido. Barcelona: Verón, 1968. 143pp. Frequently reprinted.
In Spanish.

411 El Paraíso Perdido. Madrid: Alonso, 1969. 224pp.
In Spanish.

412 El Paraíso Perdido. Barcelona: Petronio, 1972. 400pp.
In Spanish.

413 El Paraíso Perdido. Barcelona: Ramón Sopena, 1975. 271pp.
In Spanish.

414 Poterjannyj Raj. Samson. Tbilisi: Sabcota Sakartvelo, 1978. 446pp.
Paradise Lost and *Samson Agonistes* in Georgian.

415 Pujals, Esteban, trans. *El Paraíso Perdido*. Madrid: Cátedra, 1986. 509pp.
In Spanish.

416 Ribera, J., trans. *El Paraíso Perdido*. Barcelona: Petronio, 1971. 384pp.
In Spanish.

417 Rosell, Cayetano, trans. *El Paraíso Perdido*. Second edition. Madrid: Ediciones y Reproducciones Internacionales, 1982. 128pp.
In Spanish.

418 Rosell, Cayetano, trans. *El Paraíso Perdido y Recobrado*. Barcelona: Editora de los Amigos del Círculo del Bibliófilo, 1980, 1982. 293pp.
Paradise Lost and *Paradise Regained* in Spanish.

419 Sanjuan, Dionisio, trans. *El Paraíso Perdido*. Madrid: Aguilar, 1969. 480pp. Frequently reprinted.
In Spanish.

420 Schumann, Bernhard, trans. *Das Ver-*
lorene Paradies. Berlin: Rütten and Loening, 1984. 421pp.
In Dutch.

421 Slomczynski, Maciej, trans. *Raj Utracony*. Warsaw: Panstwowy Instytut Wydawniczy, 1974, 1986. 414pp.
In Polish.

422 Sotto Maior, Conceição, G., trans. *O Paraiso Perdido*. Rio de Janeiro: Tecnoprint, 1982. 414pp.
In Portuguese.

423 Stejnberg, Arkadi, trans. *Poterjannyj Raj*. Moscow: Hudoz Lit., 1982. 414pp.
In Russian.

424 Stejnberg, Arkadi, and others, trans. *Poterjannyj Raj. Stihotvorenija. Samsonborec*. Moscow: Hudoz Lit., 1976. 573pp.
Paradise Lost, miscellaneous poems, and *Samson Agonistes* in Russian. Contains illustrations by Gustave Doré.

425 Surbanov, Aleksandar, trans. *Izgubenijat Raj*. Sofia: Narodna Kultura, 1981. 400pp.
In Bulgarian. The introduction discusses Milton's life and works in the context of the English revolution.

426 Thomas, Samuel Vedanayakam, trans. *Punkavanappiralayam*. Madras: CLS, 1978. xii, 122pp.
In Tamil.

427 Wasti, Shaukat, trans. *Firdaus-e-gum Gashtah*. Peshawar: Idarah-e-Ilm-o-Fun, 1979. 510pp.
In Urdu.

428 Wollschläger, Hans, trans. *Das Verlorene Paradies: Rappresentazione*. Mainz: Schott, 1978. 43pp.
Dutch translation of Krzysztof Penderecki's operatic adaptation; the libretto is by Christopher Fry (No. 2868).

429 Yüan, Shih Le, trans. *Ho Jui Hsiung*. Tainam: Kai San Book Store, 1968. 100pp.
In Chinese.

TRANSLATIONS OF THE PROSE WORKS

430 **Areopagitica: Discorso per la Libertà della Stampa.** Rome: Laterza, 1987. 129pp.

In Italian.

431 **Davidhazi, Péter,** and others, trans. *Milton, az Angol Forradalom Tükre. Válogatás Prózai Irásaibol.* Budapest: Gondolat, 1975. 210pp.

432 **Harada, Jun,** trans. *Igirisu Kakumei no Rinen.* Tokyo: Shogakukan, 1976. 451pp.

The volume includes the first Japanese translations of the *Doctrine and Discipline of Divorce, Tenure of Kings and Magistrates*, and *Readie and Easie Way*, along with new translations of *Areopagitica* and *Of Education*.

433 **Harada, Jun, Akira Arai,** and **Tanaka Hiroshi,** trans. *Ingurando Shukyo Kaikakuron.* Tokyo: Miraisha, 1976. 151pp.

Of Reformation in Japanese.

434 **John Milton und der Ursprung des Neuzeitlichen Liberalismus.** Hildesheim: Gerstenberg, 1980. 403pp.

435 **Kim, Deug Jung,** trans. *Ye-eoneui Haeseog.* Seoul: Concordia-sa, 1982. 203pp.

436 **Lee, Gun Ho,** trans. *Ha-na-nim-eui Chugbog-eui Eon-yagsuit-da.* Seoul: Concordia-sa, 1982. 286pp.

437 **Lutaud, Olivier,** ed. and trans. *For the Liberty of Unlicensed Printing: "Areopagitica." Pour la Liberté de la Presse sans Autorisation ni Censure: "Areopagitica."* Collection Bilingue des Classiques Etrangers. Paris: Aubier-Flammarion, 1969.

In French. Reprint of Huckabay No. 391, originally published in 1956.

438 **Rajandi, Henno.** *Areopagitica.* Tallin: Periodika, 1987. 56pp.

In Estonian.

439 **Siddiqui, Zillur Rahman,** trans. *Areopagitica.* Dacca: Central Board for Development of Bengali, 1971, 1981. 144pp.

In Bengali.

440 **Trattato dell'educazione.** Firenze: La Nuova Italia, 1975. xi, 295pp.

Of Education in Italian.

GENERAL CRITICISM AND MISCELLANEOUS ITEMS

441 Adams, Robert M. "One Man's Milton." *NYRB*, June 26, 1980, pp. 46–48.

Review essay on Louis L. Martz's *Poet of Exile* (No. 820).

442 Adamson, J. H. "The Creation." *Bright Essence: Studies in Milton's Theology.* By W. B. Hunter, C. A. Patrides, and Adamson (Salt Lake City: Univ. of Utah Press, 1971), pp. 81–102.

Reprint of Huckabay No. 398, originally published in 1962.

443 Adamson, J. H. "Milton's 'Arianism.'" *Bright Essence: Studies in Milton's Theology.* By W. B. Hunter, C. A. Patrides, and Adamson (Salt Lake City: Univ. of Utah Press, 1971), pp. 53–61.

Reprint of Huckabay No. 399, originally published in 1960.

444 Aers, David, and **Bob Hodge.** "'Rational Burning': Milton on Sex and Marriage." *MiltonS*, 13, 1979, 3–33. Reprinted in *Literature, Language and Society in England, 1580–1680*, ed. by Aers, Hodge, and Gunther Kress (Dublin: Gill and Macmillan; Totowa, NJ: Barnes and Noble, 1981), pp. 122–51.

Finds that an "underlying uncertainty is central to Milton's work and makes any final judgment on his 'position' deeply problematic."

445 Agari, Masahiko. "Miruton no Shi no Gengo ni okeru Rekishi Sei." *SELit*, 2, 1968, 1–12.

"Sources of Linguistic Expression in Milton's Poetry." In Japanese.

446 Aitken, David J. "Milton's Use of 'Stand' and the Doctrine of Perseverance." *ELN*, 19, 1982, 233–36.

Proposes that Milton's use of "stand" "carries with it the weight of New Testament teaching on Grace and . . . is central to the seventeenth-century debate on Perseverance." Abs., *MiltonQ*, 17, 1983, 99.

447 Akagawa, Yutaka. "Baroque and Milton." *Studies in Milton* (Tokyo: Kinseido, 1974), pp. 136–53.

In Japanese. Examines the baroque concept and mannerism as they pertain to Milton.

448 Allen, Don Cameron. *The Harmonious Vision: Studies in Milton's Poetry.* Enlarged edition. Baltimore, MD, and London: Johns Hopkins Press, 1970. xx, 146pp.

New edition of Huckabay No. 404, originally published in 1954, with one essay added, "The Descent to Light: Basic Metaphor in *Paradise Lost.*" This essay was first published in 1961 (see Huckabay No. 1082). Reviews: James R. McAdams, *SCN*, 29, 1971, 61–62; Mario A. Di Cesare, *RenQ*, 25, 1972, 512.

449 Allen, Don Cameron. *Mysteriously Meant: The Rediscovery of Pagan Symbolism and Allegorical Interpretation in the Renaissance.* Baltimore, MD, and London: Johns Hopkins Press, 1970. x, 354pp.

Briefly discusses Milton's attitude toward pagan myth in *Comus, Paradise Lost, Paradise Regained*, and the prose.

450 Alpers, Paul J. "The Milton Controversy." *Twentieth-Century Literature in Retrospect.* Ed. by Reuben A. Brower. Harvard English Studies, 2 (Cambridge, MA: Harvard Univ. Press, 1971), pp. 269–98.

An apologia for Milton's style. Believes that although F. R. Leavis is bitter over the Milton controversy (see Huckabay Nos. 695–96), he has honored the poet by initiating it. Regrets that the controversy has been a war, not a dialogue.

451 Ames, Kenneth J. "From Sowthistles and Brambles to a More Humanistic Response." *Teaching Milton to Undergraduates: Problems and Approaches.* Proceedings of the Special Session (537), Annual Meeting of the Modern Language Association, Dec. 28, 1976. Comp. by Paul L. Gaston ([Edwardsville: Southern Illinois Univ.], n.d.), pp. 17–20. Reprinted in *MiltonQ*, 12, 1978, 141–43.

Discusses problems of teaching Milton to contemporary students. "It is the vulnerability of man, the poignancy of man's predicament in a fallen world that Milton presents and that, I think, we should try to present to our students."

452 Ames, Percy, ed. *Milton Memorial Lectures.* New York: Haskell House, 1969.

Reprint of Stevens No. 2330 and Huckabay No. 746, originally published in 1909.

453 "Annual Convention, Northeast MLA, University of Vermont, April 8, 9, 10, 1976." *MiltonQ*, 10, 1976, 64.

Contains abstracts of papers on Milton and related topics read by Robert Crosman, Lawrence W. Hyman, William J. Kennedy, Sharon C. Seelig, and George William Smith, Jr.

454 Anonby, J. A. "Milton's Idea of a Christian Society." Doctoral diss., Univ. of Alberta, 1971.

455 Ansari, Asloob Ahmad, ed. *Essays on John Milton: A Tercentenary Tribute.* Aligarh: Aligarh Muslim Univ., 1976. vii, 170pp.

A collection of essays by Ansari, Ameen Ashraf, Amalendu Bose, A. G. George, P. K. Ghosh, Masoodul Hasan, M. H. Khan, Salamatullah Khan, M. K. Lodi, Harish Raizada, and

Zillur Rahman Siddiqui. In this bibliography, each essay is listed according to author and classification. Review: Archie Burnett, *N&Q*, 26, 1979, 72–73.

456 Arai, Akira. "Eliot no Futatsu no Milton-Ron: Dento-kan no Henyo." *Eliot to Dento.* Ed. by Shoichiro Yasuda (Tokyo: Kenkyusha, 1977), pp. 69–90.

"Eliot's Two Essays on Milton: Transfiguration of Sense of Tradition." In Japanese. Discusses T. S. Eliot's criticism of Milton (see Huckabay Nos. 530–31) and change of opinion during the 1930s and 1940s. Also, deals with Eliot's general effect on Milton criticism. Reprinted in No. 457.

457 Arai, Akira. *Miscellaneous Essays on Milton.* Tokyo: Chukyo Shuppan, 1979. 228pp.

In Japanese. A collection of twelve essays by Arai. In this bibliography, each essay is listed according to classification. The following come under general criticism:

"Eliot's Two Essays on Milton: A Departure from the Traditional View," pp. 127–52.

Reprint of No. 456.

"Hazlitt and Eliot—with Respect to Milton," pp. 118–26.

Believes that T. S. Eliot's Milton criticism (see Huckabay Nos. 530–31) reflects William Hazlitt's views.

"Milton and Nature," pp. 72–99.

Examines Milton's early and mature understanding of nature.

"Takeshi Fujii and Tenrai Han'ya," pp. 155–72.

Comments on the lives, criticism, and translations of two prominent Japanese Miltonists.

"Tenrai Han'ya and Milton," 186–213.

An appreciation of the life and writings of one of the first (1874–1933) and best Japanese Milton scholars and translators who was also a poet in his own right.

458 Arai, Akira. "Study of Milton: Present

State and Perspective." *EigoS*, 118, 1972, 410–12.

In Japanese. Deals with recent criticism on both sides of the Atlantic.

459 Archer, Stanley. "Review of *Milton Studies*, Vol. 7." *SCN*, 34, 1976, 1–2.

The volume, edited by Albert C. Labriola and Michael Lieb (No. 762), is a collection of eleven essays selected to illustrate the various current critical methodologies as applied to Milton's poetry. Archer tends to question the value of some of the methodologies.

460 Arnold, Marc Hadley. "The Logos Metaphor in Milton's Epics." Doctoral diss., Univ. of Wisconsin, 1973. 200pp. Abs., *DAI*, 34, 1973, 2546A.

Argues that the logos—or "speech and reasoning powers"—of Milton's epic characters unifies "the diverse parts" of *Paradise Lost* and *Paradise Regained*.

461 Arthos, John. *Dante, Michelangelo, and Milton.* Westport, CT: Greenwood Press, 1979.

Reprint of Huckabay No. 412, originally published in 1963.

462 Arthos, John. *Milton and the Italian Cities.* London: Bowes and Bowes, 1968. xiii, 224pp.

See Huckabay No. 2177. Reviews: *MiltonN*, 2, 1968, 30–31; *TLS*, July 25, 1968, p. 795; Hugh Maclean, *JEGP*, 68, 1969, 294–96; John M. Steadman, *IQ*, 13, 1969, 92–96; John Buxton, *RES*, 20, 1969, 344–45; Jackson I. Cope, *RenQ*, 22, 1969, 75–77; Michael Wilding, *MLR*, 65, 1970, 599–600.

463 Bailey, Margaret Lewis. *Milton and Jakob Boehme.* New York: Haskell House, 1969.

Reprint of Stevens No. 2410, originally published in 1914.

464 Balakrishnan, Purasu. "Blindness and the Great Task-Master's Eye: John Milton." *LHY*, 27, No. 2, 1986, 28–40.

Discusses Milton's references to his blindness in his poetry and in his prose. Insists that in spite of his affliction Milton became "a great man among little men."

465 Balota, Nicolae. "Miltoniana." *RoLit*, 5 (November 14), 1972, 49.

In Romanian. Discusses the poetry of Heliade Radulescu, who described Milton as a prophet and a fighter for human liberty. Also refers to *Paradise Lost* and contains general remarks about William Blake's attitude toward Milton.

466 Bargo, Martha Ellen Watson. "Milton's Biblical Concepts of Women." Doctoral diss., Georgia State Univ., 1984. 345pp. Abs., *DAI*, 46, 1985, 428A.

Examines the influence of biblical themes (such as "free will, freedom, and temptation") and types (including "the ideal, the fallen, and the restored ideal") on Milton's women characters.

467 Barker, Arthur E. "Calm Regained through Passion Spent: The Conclusions of the Miltonic Effort." *The Prison and the Pinnacle.* Ed. by Balachandra Rajan (Toronto and Buffalo, NY: Univ. of Toronto Press, 1973), pp. 3–48.

Asks about Milton's mood when he composed *Paradise Regained* and *Samson Agonistes* and whether they are companion poems or contrasting pieces. Surveys the movement of both poems. Feels that the brief epic leads into the Gospels, while the drama leads into the Epistles, especially Hebrews.

468 Barnes, C. L. *Parallels in Dante and Milton.* Folcroft, PA: Folcroft Library Editions, 1969, 1974; Norwood, PA: Norwood Editions, 1976; Philadelphia, PA: R. West, 1977; Darby, PA: Arden Library, 1979.

Reprints of the 1917 edition.

469 Barron, Porter Gable. "Milton as Prophet: His Concept of the Role and His View of History." Doctoral diss., Univ. of South Carolina, 1973. 290pp. Abs., *DAI*, 34, 1974, 5954A.

Asserts that Milton's prophetic interpretation of social, political, and historical events evolved from an insistence on broad social reform to "an effort to assure salvation to the worthy individual."

470 Barthel, Carol Ann. "Milton's Use of Spenser: The Early Poems and *Paradise Lost*." Doctoral diss., Yale Univ., 1974. 321pp. Abs., *DAI*, 36, 1975, 297A.

Analyzes Spenser's influence on Milton's adaptation of foreign literary forms, spiritual reinterpretation of traditional epic themes, discussion of moral virtues, use of allegory, and presentation of symbolic landscapes.

471 Bauman, Michael E. "Milton, Subordinationism, and the Two-Stage Logos." *WTJ*, 48, 1986, 173–82.

Insists that "the subordinationist/two-stage Logos movement within Milton criticism is based on a number of unfortunate theological misconceptions and, therefore, must be discarded." Argues that Milton is an Arian.

472 Bauman, Michael Edward. "Milton's Arianism: 'Following the Way which is Called Heresy.'" Doctoral diss., Fordham Univ., 1983. 235pp. Abs., *DAI*, 44, 1983, 1823A.

Consults patristic scholars, Milton critics, *Paradise Lost*, the *Christian Doctrine*, *Of True Religion*, and the *Art of Logic* to affirm Milton's Nicene Arianism.

473 Bauman, Michael. *Milton's Arianism.* Preface by John Peter Rumrich. Frankfurt am Main, Bern, and New York: Peter Lang, 1987. xvi, 378pp.

Surveys the history of the Arian controversy and the debate about Milton's alleged Arianism. Analyzes the *Christian Doctrine*, *Paradise Lost*, and *Of True Religion*. Believes that Milton was a Nicene Arian. Reviews: Roy Flannagan, *MiltonQ*, 21, No. 3, 1987, 113–17; Thomas N. Corns, *N&Q*, 36, 1989, 240–41.

474 Beck, Paula Gertzman. "Milton's Restorative Art: The Artist as Hero." Doctoral diss., St. John's Univ., 1974.

235pp. Abs., *DAI*, 35, 1975, 5337A.

Argues that the written, spoken, and sung art of Milton's heroes seeks to overcome temptation and restore humankind to "the 'unfallen' nature of pre-lapsarian Eden."

475 Becker, Robert Stephen. "Milton and Spenser: The Other Line of Wit." Doctoral diss., Univ. of California, Berkeley, 1973. 228pp. Abs., *DAI*, 35, 1974, 393A.

Investigates the ways in which the "narrative and syntactical organization" of the *Faerie Queene* and *Paradise Lost* involves and tries to improve on the reader's will.

476 Beers, Henry Augustin. *Milton's Tercentenary.* Folcroft, PA: Folcroft Library Editions, 1970; New York: AMS Press, 1973.

Originally published in 1910. An address delivered before the Modern Language Club of Yale University on the tercentenary of Milton's birth. Emphasizes Milton's Puritanism and the Puritan heritage of Yale University.

477 Behrendt, Stephen C. "The Polished Artifact: Some Observations on Imitative Criticism." *Genre*, 10, 1977, 47–62.

Proposes "a fresh consideration of the whole mode of imitative criticism" and points out the need for interdisciplinary criticism of works, such as *Comus*, which have both literary and theatrical aspects. Uses Blake's illustrations for *Comus* as a primary example of the need for good imitative criticism. Also mentions *Paradise Lost*, *L'Allegro*, and *Il Penseroso* in passing.

478 Belsey, Catherine. *John Milton: Language, Gender, Power.* Oxford and New York: Basil Blackwell, 1988. xi, 114pp.

Analyzes Milton's works by tying them to the birth of the modern epoch and examining the nature of meaning and its relation to power. Review: William Shullenberger, *MiltonQ*, 26, 1992, 86–89.

479 Bennett, Joan Pamela Secord.

"Milton's Prose Tracts as a Gloss on *Paradise Lost, Paradise Regained*, and *Samson Agonistes*." Doctoral diss., Stanford Univ., 1971. 330pp. Abs., *DAI*, 32, 1972, 4600A.

Relates civil, domestic, and ecclesiastical liberty, as discussed in Milton's prose tracts, to the interactions of Satan, humans, God, and the Son in the three long poems.

480 Bennett, Scott, and **Linda Hoffman,** eds. *Non Solus*. Urbana-Champaign: Univ. of Illinois Library Friends, 1980. 52pp.

A collection of tributes to Harris Francis Fletcher. Review: Michael A. Mikolajczak, *SCN*, 39, 1981, 85–86.

481 Benson, William. *Letters Concerning Poetical Translations (1739)*. Introduction by Timothy Webb. Menston: Scolar Press, 1973. [xiii], 83pp.

A facsimile of a copy in the Bodleian Library. Deals mainly with Virgil's and Milton's excellences.

482 Berkowitz, Morton Selig. "Not the Orphean Lyre: Milton's View of Himself as a Christian Poet." Doctoral diss., Univ. of Massachusetts, 1970. 256pp. Abs., *DAI*, 31, 1970, 2333A.

Contrasts the Renaissance reconciliation of Christian and pagan ideologies with Milton's attack on paganism, intended to "justify the ways of God to men."

483 Berry, Wendell. *Standing by Words*. San Francisco, CA: North Point Press, 1983. 213pp.

Several chapters make oblique references to Milton, placing him in relation to his time and place in European literature.

484 Blondel, Jacques. "Aspects de la Critique Miltonienne d'Aujourd'hui: *Paradise Lost*." *EA*, 27, 1974, 387–98.

Surveys recent criticism of Milton's works. "There has been an abundance of articles and books on Milton, especially *Paradise Lost*, and this criticism tries to be free of any preconceived religious or philosophical point of view

as well as from any effort to defend him."

485 Blondel, Jacques. "Milton et l'Actualité: Les *Milton Studies* (1981–1984)." *EA*, 39, 1986, 294–301.

Review of recent volumes of *Milton Studies*.

486 Blondel, Jacques. "Note de Lecture." *BSEAA*, 10, 1980, 127–31.

Review essay on Roger Lejosne's *La Raison dans l'Oeuvre de John Milton* (No. 780).

487 Bloom, Donald A. "The Idea of Despair in Four Protestant Authors: Spenser, Milton, Bunyan, and Richardson." *SPWVSRA*, 13, 1988, 66–72.

In *Samson Agonistes*, "there is a constant rising and falling of the character's awareness of his fall from grace, alternating with the patient endurance of his just punishment." Samson shows that despair is "a turning away from God even as it is *caused by* that turning away."

488 Bloom, Harold, ed. *John Milton*. Modern Critical Views. New York, New Haven, CT, and Philadelphia, PA: Chelsea House, 1986. x, 337pp.

"This volume offers a representative selection of the best literary criticism devoted to the work of John Milton over the last thirty years." William Flesch's essay is printed here for the first time and is listed under No. 2233. Reprinted authors include F. T. Prince, Isabel Gamble MacCaffrey, Sir William Empson, Thomas M. Greene, Northrop Frye, Geoffrey H. Hartman, Angus Fletcher, Stanley Eugene Fish, Leslie Brisman, Bloom, Mary Ann Radzinowicz, Louis L. Martz, John Hollander, William Wallace Kerrigan, Sanford Budick, and Peter M. Sacks.

489 Bloom, Harold. *A Map of Misreading*. New York: Oxford Univ. Press, 1975. [xi], 206pp. Reprinted, 1980. 224pp.

Contains two chapters relevant to Milton: "Milton and His Precursors," which uses *Paradise Lost* 1.283–313 to illustrate Milton's transcending his predecessors from Homer to Spenser, and deals with the poem's general allusiveness; and "In the Shadow of Milton," which interprets Wordsworth's *Ode on Intimations*, Shelley's *Ode to the West Wind*, Keats's *Ode to Psyche*, and Tennyson's *Ulysses* as poems that involve a "misprision or powerful misreading" of Milton. See No. 4557.

490 Blum, Abbe Marilyn. "Composing the Author: Milton's Writing in Its Social Contexts, 1643–1645." Doctoral diss., Yale Univ., 1987. 287pp. Abs., *DAI*, 48, 1988, 2632A–33A.

Describes Milton's presentation of an author image that responds to seventeenth-century "social opinion and legislation," including the development of print and debates on marital organization.

491 Bose, Amalendu. "Some Observations on Milton's Poetic Language." *Essays on John Milton: A Tercentenary Tribute.* Ed. by Asloob Ahmad Ansari (Aligarh: Aligarh Muslim Univ., 1976), pp. 16–34.

Discusses Milton's poetic language in the light of T. S. Eliot's criticism (see Huckabay Nos. 530–31). Concludes that Eliot's "disapproval of Milton's rhetorical style is thus invalid as a specific criticism of Milton's poetical language and is further invalid as a general theory of the language of poetry, and is, finally, denied by his own use of language."

492 Bouchard, Donald F. *Milton: A Structural Reading.* Montreal: McGill-Queen's Univ. Press; London: Edward Arnold, 1974. vii, 180pp.

A reading of selected shorter poems, *Paradise Lost*, *Paradise Regained*, and *Samson Agonistes*. Reviews: Jon S. Lawry, *QQ*, 82, 1975, 638–39; Anthony Low, *MiltonQ*, 9, 1975, 20–27; G. F. Waller, *DR*, 55, 1975, 369–71; D. D. C. Chambers, *RES*, 27, 1976, 72–74; Hannah Buchan, *MLR*, 71, 1976, 377–78; Hugh MacCallum,

ESC, 2, 1976, 471–74; Andrew M. McLean, *SHR*, 10, 1976, 362–69; Arnold Stein, *SR*, 84, 1976, 695–706; W. Reavley Gair, *Ren&R*, 12, 1976, 65–67; Hugh Maclean, *UTQ*, 46, 1977, 177–79; Claes Schaar, *ES*, 59, 1978, 218–24.

493 Brackney, Ross Clyde. "'By Fallacy Surpris'd': Logic and the Miltonic Hero." Doctoral diss., Stanford Univ., 1969. 233pp. Abs., *DAI*, 30, 1970, 5400A–01A.

Distinguishes Milton's heroes by their "accordance with Ramian logic" and with the poet's individualistic theology; concludes that Satan cannot be considered a hero.

494 Brennan, Thomas Augustus. "Idols and Idolatry in the Prose and Early Poetry of John Milton." Doctoral diss., Tulane Univ., 1970. 297pp. Abs., *DAI*, 31, 1970, 2868A.

Argues that Milton includes "demonic symbolism" in his prose and poetry to "confound good and evil," thereby forcing the Christian reader to restore God's truth "in the soul and in the world at large."

495 Briggs, Peter Miner. "The Children of Light: A Comparative Reading of Milton and Pope." Doctoral diss., Yale Univ., 1974. 309pp. Abs., *DAI*, 36, 1975, 267A.

Asserts that Milton and Pope dramatize "order in the world," explore spiritual heroism, affirm human dignity against "advocates of worldliness," typify human error through devils, and use themselves to validate their "moral outlook."

496 Brinkley, Robert A. "Romanticism and the Desire Called Milton." Doctoral diss., Univ. of Massachusetts, 1979. 426pp. Abs., *DAI*, 40, 1980, 4603A.

Locates "the dilemma of dialectic"—to mirror what one opposes—"in Wordsworth, charts its critique in Bloom, seeks its origin in Milton, and discovers its annihilation in Blake."

497 Brisman, Leslie. "Milton's Options." Doctoral diss., Cornell Univ., 1969. 374pp.

Abs., *DAI*, 30, 1970, 3936A.

Analyzes the relationship between choice and poetic structure, noting that the "fall of the measure, the carefully controlled suspensions and arrests, continually re-enact the Fall."

498 Broadbent, John, ed. *John Milton: Introductions.* Cambridge: Cambridge Univ. Press, 1973. xv, 344pp.

Contains essays on Milton's life, writing, and milieu by Broadbent, Roy Daniells, W. Reavley Gair, John Dixon Hunt, Winifred Maynard, Isabel Rivers, Lorna Sage, Elizabeth Sewell Sirignano, and J. B. Trapp. In this bibliography, each essay is listed according to author and classification. Reviews: R. E. C. Houghton, *RES*, 25, 1974, 344–45; John Arthos, *RenQ*, 28, 1975, 288–91.

499 Broadbent, John. "The Poets' Bible." *John Milton: Introductions.* Ed. by Broadbent (Cambridge: Cambridge Univ. Press, 1973), pp. 145–61.

Considers biblical texts, the Bible's language and the poetry, obscurities, and Milton and the Bible.

500 Broadbent, John B., Jr., and **Lorna Sage.** *Milton.* Sussex Tapes International Approach to Literary Criticism Series. New York: Holt Information Systems, 1973.

A recording of Broadbent and Sage's discussions about *Paradise Lost, Comus,* and *Samson Agonistes.* An accompanying booklet summarizes the discussions, and study notes by Peter Hollindale are provided. Review: *MiltonQ*, 7, 1973, 16–17.

501 Broadbent, John B., Jr., and **Lorna Sage.** "*Paradise Lost, Comus* and *Samson Agonistes.*" *English Poetry.* Ed. by Alan Sinfield (London: Sussex Publications, 1976), pp. 74–91.

Transcript of a discussion in which Broadbent questions Milton's attitudes and is troubled by the use of sheer force in *Paradise Lost,* the Lady's chastity in *Comus,* and Samson's sui-cide. Sage defends these, viewing Samson's death as a self-sacrifice.

502 Brodwin, Leonora Leet. "Milton and the Renaissance Circe." *MiltonS,* 6, 1974, 21–83.

"Milton's lifelong preoccupation with the Circe myth has not previously been given comprehensive analysis and, where noted, has been misjudged through exclusive reference to the allegorized Circe of Renaissance mythographers, an allegorical approach to brutishness Milton uniquely associates with political and psychological tyranny in his prose and continues to employ similarly in his last three major works."

503 Brooks, Cleanth. "Milton and the New Criticism." *A Shaping Joy: Studies in the Writer's Craft* (London: Methuen; New York: Harcourt Brace Jovanovich, 1971), pp. 330–48.

Reprint of Huckabay No. 453, originally published in 1951.

504 Brophy, James D. "Milton's 'Warble': The Trill as Metaphor of Concord." *MiltonQ,* 19, 1985, 105–09.

Asserts that "contexts of 'warble' throughout Milton's work confirm . . . that Milton, in employing the term, used and expected from his 'fit audience' a sophisticated musical knowledge of the trill, especially in its suggestion of harmony created from diversity and even discord."

505 Brückmann, Patricia, ed. *Familiar Colloquy: Essays Presented to Arthur Edward Barker.* Toronto: Oberon Press, 1978. 230pp.

Contains articles on Milton by Douglas Chambers, Hugh MacCallum, Diane McColley, and George Falle. In this bibliography, each article is listed according to author and classification. Also includes a selected list of Barker's publications and lectures compiled by Jane Couchman (see No. 5), with a list of theses and dissertations that he supervised.

506 Bryant, Joseph Allen, Jr. "The Evolution of Milton's Conception of History." Doctoral diss., Yale Univ., 1948. 421pp. Abs., *DAI*, 32, 1971, 1465A.

Explores Milton's attempt to unify "the Protestant interpretation of history as a gloss on scriptural prophecy" with a "cyclic interpretation of the world process."

507 Buck, Philo M., Jr. *Milton on Liberty.* Folcroft, PA: Folcroft Library Editions, 1960; Norwood, PA: Norwood Editions, 1978.

Reprints of Stevens No. 2548, originally published in 1925.

508 Budick, Sanford. *The Dividing Muse: Images of Sacred Disjunction in Milton's Poetry.* New Haven, CT, and London: Yale Univ. Press, 1985. ix, 213pp.

Argues that Milton's nonvisual imagery has a logical structure which is controlled by a dichotomizing dialectic. Interprets passages from the *Reason of Church-Government, Paradise Lost,* and *Paradise Regained* as displaying "sacred disjunction." Reviews: Georgia B. Christopher, *MLQ,* 46, 1985, 332–35; John Pitcher, *TLS,* Aug. 23, 1985, p. 932; Archie Burnett, *N&Q,* 33, 1986, 547–48; Mary Ann Radzinowicz, *JEGP,* 85, 1986, 267–69; Eugene R. Freed, *UES,* 24, 1986, 36–37; Thomas F. Healy, *MLR,* 82, 1987, 915–17; Albert C. Labriola, *RenQ,* 40, 1987, 828–29.

509 Budick, Sanford. "Milton and the Scene of Interpretation: From Typology toward Midrash." *Midrash and Literature.* Ed. by Geoffrey H. Hartman and Budick (New Haven, CT, and London: Yale Univ. Press, 1986), pp. 195–212.

States that Milton's poetry shows the "relationship between typology and other forms of exegesis." Points out that in the many interpretive modes found in such works, Milton "include[s] something that corresponds closely to one form of midrash." Concludes that "Milton revises and supplements conventional typology to reveal a hermeneutic reality of a different sort. Most particularly in *Paradise Lost,* he demonstrates that a Christian exegetical poetry can forcibly express interpretive necessities in which the fulfillment associated with one kind of typology is significantly deferred."

510 Budick, Sanford. "Milton's Epic Reclamations." *Poetry of Civilization: Mythopoeic Displacement in the Verse of Milton, Dryden, Pope, and Johnson* (New Haven, CT, and London: Yale Univ. Press, 1974), pp. 41–80.

Uses Sonnet 18 ("On the Late Massacre in Piemont"), *Samson Agonistes,* and *Paradise Lost* to show that Milton provided the Augustans with "a model for the supremacy of logos over mythos, of reason over Satanic idol-making." Review (of book): *MiltonQ,* 8, 1974, 61; Patricia Meyer Spacks, *JEGP,* 74, 1975, 126–28; Judy Tanis Parr, *CSR,* 5, 1976, 399–400; David Fairer, *N&Q,* 23, 1976, 527–28.

511 Buhagiar, A. "Tasso's *Discorsi del Poema Eroico* and Its Bearing on Milton's Epic Practice: A Translation and an Essay." M.A. thesis, Univ. of Wales, Swansea, 1971.

512 Burgess, Anthony. "The Milton Revolution." *Urgent Copy: Literary Studies* (London: Cape; New York: W. W. Norton, 1968), pp. 167–71.

Reprint of Huckabay No. 460, originally published in 1967.

513 Burns, Norman T. "The Major Spokesmen for Soul Sleeping: Overton, Milton, and Hobbes." *Christian Mortalism from Tyndale to Milton* (Cambridge, MA: Harvard Univ. Press, 1972), pp. 148–91.

Compares Overton's and Milton's ideas on the subject and speculates on their origins. Notes that Milton's thoughts about soul-sleeping are clearly stated only in the *Christian Doctrine.* Reviews (of book): *MiltonQ,* 7, 1973, 55; James R. McAdams, *SCN,* 32, 1974, 4–5; John F. Abbick, S. J., *CSR,* 4, 1974, 142–44.

514 Bush, Douglas. "Milton." *English Literature in the Earlier Seventeenth Century, 1600–1660.* Second edition (Oxford: Oxford Univ. Press, 1973), pp. 377–420.
Reprint of Huckabay No. 466, originally published in 1945.

515 Bush, Douglas. "Milton Three Hundred Years After." *The Undoing of Babel: Watson Kirkconnell, the Man and His Work.* Ed. by J. R. C. Perkin (Toronto: McClelland and Stewart, 1975), pp. 17–30.
"In the main, modern scholarship and criticism have brought a far richer understanding of Milton the man, the thinker, the crusader, and the poet than was ever formerly possible for anyone except a superhumanly ideal reader of the seventeenth century."

516 Buxton, Charles R. *Prophets of Heaven and Hell.* New York: Haskell House, 1970.
Reprint of Huckabay No. 476, originally published in 1945.

517 Cain, William E. "Reflections on the Milton Industry." *MLN,* 96, 1981, 1121–33.
Review essay. Believes that Milton criticism is in disrepair because writers are unaware of new critical theory and methodology and because most react to A. J. A. Waldock's *"Paradise Lost" and Its Critics* (Huckabay No. 1965) and Stanley Fish's *Surprised by Sin* (No. 2216). Comments on Robert Crosman, *Reading "Paradise Lost"* (No. 2091); James A. Freeman, *Milton and the Martial Muse* (No. 2248); Murray Roston, *Milton and the Baroque* (No. 2954); Roland Mushat Frye, *Milton's Imagery and the Visual Arts* (No. 620); Edward W. Tayler, *Milton's Poetry* (No. 1082); and G. K. Hunter, *Paradise Lost* (No. 2450).

518 Camé, J.-F. "Les Structures Fondamentales de l'Univers Imaginaire Miltonien." Doctoral Diss., Université of Nice, 1974. 594pp. Abs., *DAI,* 37, 1977, 3211C. Reproduced in typescript facsimile, Université of Lille, 1975. 2 vols. Paris: Didier, 1976. 594pp.
Psychological criticism that reveals Milton's obsessions by uncovering recurring themes, images, epithets, and descriptions in his works. Reviews: Jean Pironon, *CahiersE,* 10, 1976, 123–25; Michael Hollington, *DUJ,* 39, 1977, 110–11; Archie Burnett, *N&Q,* 25, 1978, 550–52; Raymond J. Cormier, *SCN,* 36, 1978, 10; Irène Simon, *RES,* 29, 1978, 209–14; Donald F. Bouchard, *YES,* 10, 1980, 272–73.

519 Campbell, Gordon. "Dinos Patrides: 1930–86." *MiltonQ,* 21, No. 1, 1987, 39–40.
In memoriam to C. A. Patrides.

520 Canavan, Francis. "John Milton and Freedom of Expression." *IJPP,* 7, No. 3, 1978, 50–65.
"To the extent, then, that Milton represents or, on a liberal interpretation of his thought, can be made to represent the intellectual tradition in favor of freedom of the press, the contemporary absolutist position on freedom of expression is not a development but a perversion of that tradition."

521 Candy, Hugh C. H. *Some Newly Discovered Stanzas Written by John Milton on Engraved Scenes Illustrating Ovid's "Metamorphoses."* Folcroft, PA: Folcroft Library Editions, 1972; Norwood, PA: Norwood Editions, 1975; Philadelphia, PA: R. West, 1977.
Reprints of Stevens No. 2673, originally published in 1924.

522 Carey, John. *Milton.* Literature in Perspective Series. London: Evans Brothers, 1969; New York: Arco, 1970. 154pp.
Includes a short account of Milton's life but focuses on his writing. Reviews: *TLS,* July 10, 1969, p. 749; Emile Saillens, *EA,* 23, 1970, 446–48.

523 Carver, Larry. "The Restoration Poets and Their Father King." *HLQ,* 40, 1977, 333–51.
Cites Milton as a critic of the idea that the king is the father of the nation. In

the *First Defence*, he attacks this analogy and in *Paradise Lost* continues the argument that "people choose their kings."

524 Cauthen, Irby B., Jr. "'A Complete and Generous Education': Milton and Jefferson." *VQR*, 55, 1979, 222–33.

Compares Milton's and Jefferson's ideas about what constituted "a complete and generous education." Both emphasized foreign languages as a tool and the orderly progression of subjects, and "both conceived of education as the basic foundation of the commonwealth, the essential and inescapable necessity for wise rule and citizenship."

525 Cawley, Robert Ralston. *Milton and the Literature of Travel.* Ann Arbor, MI: Univ. Microfilms International, 1980 Books on Demand Reprints.

Reprint of Huckabay No. 479, originally published in 1951.

526 Chambers, R. W. *Poets and Their Critics: Langland and Milton.* Norwood, PA: Norwood Library Editions, 1977.

Reprint of Huckabay No. 481, originally published in 1942.

527 Chatterjee, Visvanath. "Milton: After Three Hundred Years." *Bulletin of the Ramakrishna Mission Institute of Culture* (Calcutta), 58, 1977, 201–05.

In his writing, Milton sought truth and had a zeal for liberty; today, he is most significant because he can teach us "how to play the man" rather than the coward.

528 "Chicago, MLA and the Milton Society Dinner." *MiltonQ*, 12, 1978, 31–32.

Contains remarks on John Dixon Hunt's address, "Milton and the Making of the English Landscape Garden." Reported also in *SCN*, 36, 1978, 13.

529 Choi, Jung-Woon. "John Milton eui hugisi e natanan kidockgyojeok inbon sasang." *INH*, 16, 1988, 93–124.

"John Milton's Christian Humanism in His Later Poetry."

530 Christopher, Georgia B. *Milton and the Science of the Saints.* Princeton, NJ:

Princeton Univ. Press, 1982. xii, 264pp.

Uses Luther and Calvin as starting points for a study of Milton's poetry in view of his attitude toward sacred texts and his belief in their verbal sacrament. Reviews: Roy C. Flannagan, *MiltonQ*, 16, 1982, 98–99; Leland Ryken, *C&L*, 32, 1983, 47–49; Dayton William Haskin, *NDEJ*, 15, 1983, 105–08; Sarah Wintle, *TLS*, May 4, 1983, p. 211; Martin Evans, *RES*, 36, 1985, 270–72; Archie Burnett, *YES*, 16, 1986, 253–54.

531 Clark, Ira. "Milton and the Image of God." *JEGP*, 68, 1969, 422–31.

Traces Milton's use of the image of God in his prose and poetry. Concludes that it became the emblem he "learned to rely on in order to express his version of Christian history."

532 Clifford, Mallory Young. "The Storyteller's Apology: A Study of Truth and Storytelling in the *Odyssey*, Genesis, Spenser, Milton, and Blake." Doctoral diss., State Univ. of New York, Buffalo, 1979. 204pp. Abs., *DAI*, 40, 1980, 5041A.

Contends that the methods of storytelling in western literature—conspicuous authorship, transparent narrators, allegory, reference to Christian history, and praise of art—are designed to convey perceived truths.

533 Cogan, John James. "'For Contemplation Hee and Valor Form'd': The Dichotomy of the Active and the Contemplative Lives in John Milton's *Paradise Lost, Paradise Regained,* and *Samson Agonistes*." Doctoral diss., Marquette Univ., 1976. 355pp. Abs., *DAI*, 37, 1976, 2193A.

Discusses the interplay of the active epic, characterized by conquerors, and the contemplative pastoral, filled with rural figures, as it affects the reader in Milton's long poems.

534 Coleridge, S. T. *Seven Lectures on Shakespeare and Milton.* Introduction by J. Payne Collier. New York: Burt Franklin, 1968.

Reprint of Stevens No. 2008 and Huckabay No. 493, originally published in 1856.

535 Collett, Jonathan Howard. "Characteristic Uses of Classical Mythology by Marvell and Milton." Doctoral diss., Columbia Univ., 1967. 175pp. Abs., *DAI*, 31, 1970, 2871A.

Demonstrates how Marvell and Milton can denounce pagan mythology and yet use myths, "with all their qualifications intact, in often quite sophisticated ways that are central to the themes of their poems."

536 Collings, Michael Robert. "The Boundaries of Choice: Moral Freedom in Milton's Poetic Universe." Doctoral diss., Univ. of California, Riverside, 1977. 261pp. Abs., *DAI*, 38, 1977, 3513A.

Explores freedom of choice—limited only by the "Father's will and desires"—in humans and in God, the Son, and the angels.

537 "Commemorative Program." *MiltonQ*, 9, 1975, 65.

On a tercentenary tribute held at Southwestern University, Georgetown, Texas, on February 12–13, 1974.

538 Condee, Ralph Waterbury. *Structure in Milton's Poetry: From the Foundation to the Pinnacles.* University Park and London: Pennsylvania State Univ. Press, 1974. ix, 202pp.

Analyzes seventeen of Milton's poems, both early and late, to trace his developing ability to create "increasingly complex poetic structures." Reviews: Anthony Low, *MiltonQ*, 9, 1975, 20–27; Mary Ann Radzinowicz, *RenQ*, 28, 1975, 423–27; Hugh Maclean, *JEGP*, 75, 1976, 433–37; James H. Sims, *SCN*, 34, 1976, 92–93.

539 Conklin, George Newton. *Biblical Criticism and Heresy in Milton.* New York: Octagon Books, 1972.

Reprint of Huckabay No. 496, originally published in 1949.

540 Cooke, Michael G. *Acts of Inclusion: Studies Bearing on an Elementary Theory of Romanticism.* New Haven, CT, and London: Yale Univ. Press, 1979. xx, 289pp.

In "Elegy, Prophecy, and Satire in the Romantic Order," the author discusses *Lycidas* and compares it with Shelley's *Adonais*. In "Christ or Prometheus? The Norm of Consequences in English Romanticism," he discusses motives for Satan's fall in *Paradise Lost* and points out that Milton's Satan "occurs as a favorite in romantic thinking on consequences, and can serve as a model of the redefinition of consequences in the period."

541 Coombs, James H. "Wordsworth and Milton: Prophet-Poets." Doctoral diss., Brown Univ., 1985. 216pp. Abs., *DAI*, 46, 1986, 1946A–47A.

Argues that *Paradise Lost* and the *Prelude* each exhibit a structure that fulfills the author's prophetic goal—to lead readers "from carnal to spiritual vision and to induce faith and hope."

542 Cormican, L. A. "Milton's Religious Verse." *From Donne to Marvell.* Ed. by Boris Ford. The New Pelican Guide to English Literature, vol. 3. Revised edition (Harmondsworth: Penguin, 1982), pp. 219–38.

Cites three major reasons for critics' diverse opinions when dealing with Milton. He is often misread when a critic tries to make a distinction between the doctrinal content and the literary art of his work, his "greatness and the nature of his topics invite comparisons with Shakespeare and Dante," and "the very nature of his theme . . . separates him from the ordinary concerns and common experience of men." See Huckabay No. 499.

543 Courthope, W. J. "A Consideration of Macaulay's Comparison of Dante and Milton." *Essays on Milton* (Folcroft, PA: Folcroft Library Editions, 1970), pp. 259–74.

Reprint of Stevens No. 2300, originally published in 1907–08.

544 Courthope, W. J., and others. *Essays on Milton*. Folcroft, PA: Folcroft Library Editions, 1970.

Reprint of the *Proceedings of the British Academy*, 3, 1907–08. Contains essays by Courthope, R. C. Jebb, A. F. Leach, and by J. G. Robertson. In this bibliography, each item is listed according to author and classification.

545 Cox, Paul Hart. "The Rhetoric of Recovery: Moral Didacticism in Milton's Major Poetry." Doctoral diss., Univ. of Oklahoma, 1968. 223pp. Abs., *DA*, 29, 1969, 2669A–70A.

Claims that Milton's rhetorical techniques are designed to heighten the reader's moral awareness and create temptation scenes with even or uneven distribution of principles.

546 Craig, Terry Ann. "Witchcraft and Demonology in Renaissance English Literature: Selected Studies in Shakespeare, Donne, and Milton." Doctoral diss., Duquesne Univ., 1978. 216pp. Abs., *DAI*, 39, 1978, 1583A.

Explains the different purposes behind each writer's presentation of the occult arts—Shakespeare mocks fanatics, Donne emphasizes human sinfulness and the need for God, and Milton dramatizes the Fall.

547 Critical Essays on Milton from "ELH." Baltimore, MD, and London: Johns Hopkins Press, 1969. x, 290pp.

A selection of essays originally published in *ELH* between 1935 and 1968. Reprinted authors are Arnold Stein, Marjorie Nicolson, Merritt Y. Hughes, Kingsley Widmer, Richard Neuse, Gale H. Carrithers, Jr., Roger B. Wilkenfeld, Geoffrey Hartman, Arthur O. Lovejoy, Russell E. Smith, Jr., Mother Mary Christopher Pecheux, O. S. U., Albert R. Cirillo, Martin Mueller, Lee Sheridan Cox, and William O. Harris. In this bibliography, each reprinted essay is listed according to author and classification.

548 Crunelle, Anny. "Myth and Imagination in Milton's Images of Water." *CahiersE*, 15, 1979, 43–55.

Believes that Milton's whole work represents a variation of the themes of fall, separation, and return. Notes that his water images often suggest both violence and boundaries.

549 Cullen, Patrick. *Infernal Triad: The Flesh, the World, and the Devil in Spenser and Milton*. Princeton, NJ: Princeton Univ. Press, 1974. xxxvi, 267pp.

Explores the role of the medieval schema of the flesh, the world, and the devil in the *Faerie Queene* 1 and 2 and Milton's long poems. Three chapters on Milton: "*Paradise Lost*: The Infernal Triad in Hell and Eden"; "The Structure of *Paradise Regained*"; and "*Samson Agonistes*: Milton's Redefinition of Tragedy." Reviews: James S. Dean, *LJ*, 100, 1975, 584; *MiltonQ*, 9, 1975, 53–54; Sears Jayne, *JEGP*, 74, 1975, 576–79; K. Harper, *Ren&R*, 11, 1975, 136–37; A. Kent Hieatt, *SpenN*, 6, 1975, 1–3; John Mulryan, *Cithara*, 14, No. 2, 1975, 74–76; Howard C. Cole, *CSR*, 6, 1977, 358–59; Jean-François Camé, *EA*, 31, 1978, 384; P. G. Stanwood, *MP*, 76, 1978, 74–77; Dominic Baker-Smith, *SN*, 51, 1979, 151–53.

550 "Current Book Prices." *MiltonN*, 3, 1969, 22–23.

Surveys prices of a few items on the current market to help establish guidelines for acquiring Miltoniana.

551 "Current Book Prices." *MiltonQ*, 9, 1975, 66.

Quotes prices of first editions in a recent catalog from Bernard Quaritch of London.

552 Curry, Walter Clyde. *Milton's Ontology, Cosmogony, and Physics*. Lexington: Univ. of Kentucky Press, 1966.

Reprint of Huckabay No. 503, originally published in 1957.

553 Dahiyat, Eid. "Aspects of John Milton in Arabic." *MiltonQ*, 18, 1984, 5–13.

Considers works on Milton written in Arabic in countries of the Arab east. In four sections: Milton the Man and the Artist; Milton and Abū al-'Alá al-Ma'arrí (a tenth-century Arab poet); The Character of Satan; and Translations. Believes that Arabs have misunderstood Milton.

554 Dahiyat, Eid Abdallah. *John Milton and the Arab-Islamic Culture.* Amman: Shukayr and Akasheh, 1987. 138pp.

Concludes that Milton probably never studied Arabic but that he read translations of works by Arab and Muslim writers. Also mentions references to Arabia and Ottoman Turkey in Milton's works. Believes that the Romantic view of Satan has influenced Muslim critics.

555 Daiches, David. *A Critical History of English Literature.* 2 vols. London: Secker and Warburg, 1961, 1963, 1968, and 1969.

Reprints of Huckabay No. 505, originally published in 1960. Milton, vol. 1, pp. 390–457 and passim. Sees Milton as the "last English poet to take and use as his poetic heritage everything that Western civilization . . . had so far achieved."

556 Daniel, Clay Lee. "Some Aspects of Death in Milton's Poetry." Doctoral diss., Texas A&M Univ., 1988. 153pp. Abs., *DAI*, 49, 1989, 3367A.

Asserts that Milton's early poetry portrays death as "the providential consequence of God's good plan," or a divine punishment for lust.

557 Daniells, Roy. "Milton and Renaissance Art." *John Milton: Introductions.* Ed. by John Broadbent (Cambridge: Cambridge Univ. Press, 1973), pp. 186–207.

"In this chapter we shall be looking into the relation between Milton's poems and two comprehensive art forms known as Mannerism and Baroque." Feels that "Milton's Puritan temperament and sensibility make it inevitable" that he modify "certain dominant themes in continental art."

558 Danielson, Dennis R. "*Imago Dei*, 'Filial Freedom,' and Miltonic Theodicy." *ELH*, 47, 1980, 670–81.

Suggests that the traditional identification of human freedom with the divine image was important to Milton, examines his model of human freedom, and discusses the view of divine freedom implicit in his work. Proposes that in his theodicy "Milton did not quite tie together these three aspects of his thought."

559 Davidson, Clifford. "The Young Milton, Orpheus, and Poetry." *ES*, 59, 1978, 27–34.

Discusses the Orphic myth and relates various literary uses of it. Concludes that Milton's subject matter necessitated a level of Orphic height attained by a "sincere poet-priest."

560 Dawes, Winifred H. *Milton: Eagle-Sighted Prophet.* Bristol: Dawes, 1981. 21pp.

A brief survey of Milton's writing career. Sees Milton as the prophet of his age.

561 Denham, Robert D. *Northrop Frye and Critical Method.* University Park and London: Pennsylvania State Univ. Press, 1978. xii, 262pp.

Discusses Frye's *The Return of Eden* (No. 2262) and his essays on Milton, pp. 161–75. Suggests that in approaching Milton, Frye "specifically applies . . . principles set forth in *Anatomy of Criticism.*"

562 Devi, N. Parvathi. "Milton Criticism of Professor Rama Sarma." *The Laurel Bough: Essays Presented in Honour of Professor M. V. Rama Sarma.* Ed. by G. Nageswara Rao (Bombay: Blackie and Son, 1983), pp. 107–11.

An account of Rama Sarma's studies on Milton. Notes that many of Milton's ideas and epic characters parallel those in Hindu literature.

563 Dillon, Steven C. "Tragic Idyll: Studies in the Poetics of Virgil, Milton, and Tennyson." Doctoral diss., Yale Univ.,

1988. 287pp. Abs., *DAI*, 50, 1989, 1309A–10A.

Examines the tragic idyll as a recognizable epic characteristic, which is contrasted to a pastoral idyll by Virgil, set apart by Milton, and presented in succession by Tennyson.

564 Dobrée, Bonamy. "Milton and Dryden: A Comparison in Poetic Ideas and Poetic Method." *Milton to Ouida: A Collection of Essays* (London: Frank Cass; New York: Barnes and Noble, 1970), pp. 1–21.

Reprint of Huckabay No. 520, originally published in 1936.

565 Donnelly, Colleen Elaine. "The Semiotics of Romance." Doctoral diss., Univ. of Washington, 1986. 296pp. Abs., *DAI*, 47, 1987, 4381A–82A.

"The focus is on four great stylists, Chaucer, Milton, Hawthorne, and Faulkner, who worked within a tradition which develops a dialectic between societal-historical and individual visions."

566 Doolittle, Nancy Jean. "Landscape and Spatial Perspectives in Dante, Ariosto, and Milton." Doctoral diss., State Univ. of New York, Binghamton, 1983. 355pp. Abs., *DAI*, 43, 1983, 3901A.

Relates the landscape and setting of the *Divine Comedy*, *Orlando Furioso*, and *Paradise Lost* to each work's dominant motifs, treatment of humans and God, and characters' perceptions.

567 Dowd, John Andrew. "Simulacra Noctus for Voices and Instruments on a Latin Text by Milton." Doctoral diss., West Virginia Univ., 1973. 51pp. Abs., *DAI*, 34, 1974, 4310A.

Explains the composition of a "nontraditional work . . . suited to the possibilities of quadraphonic sound," based in part on Milton's "Naturam Non Pati Senium."

568 Dowling, John. "Two Views of Censorship: Saavedra Fajardo and Milton." *CH*, 1, 1979, 25–35.

Examines Fajardo's views in *República*

Literaria (1612) and Milton's in *Areopagitica* (1644). Contrasts the historically rigid Spanish censorship laws with the relaxed attitude of the Anglo-American world, especially since 1695.

569 Dowling, Paul M. "'The Scholastick Grosnesse of Barbarous Ages': The Question of the Humanism of Milton's Understanding of Virtue." *Milton and the Middle Ages.* Ed. by John Mulryan (Lewisburg, PA: Bucknell Univ. Press; London and Toronto: Associated Univ. Presses, 1982), pp. 59–72.

Milton's understanding of virtue in *Of Education* and *Areopagitica* indicates that he is closer to Thomas Aquinas than to Aristotle.

570 Duncan, Joseph E. "Creative Composition and Comparative Criticism in Teaching Milton." *Teaching Milton to Undergraduates: Problems and Approaches.* Proceedings of the Special Session (537), Annual Meeting of the Modern Language Association, Dec. 28, 1976. Comp. by Paul L. Gaston ([Edwardsville: Southern Illinois Univ.], n.d.), pp. 6–10.

On two kinds of writing assignments for students: creative modern versions of Milton's poems and comparisons between modern works and Milton's poems.

571 Duncan, Joseph E. "Paradise as the Whole Earth." *JHI*, 30, 1969, 171–86.

Examines the history of an idea which reached its fullest development in the sixteenth and seventeenth centuries, that "the biblical paradise was understood to be not a particular place, but the whole earth." Opponents regarded this interpretation as "dangerously unorthodox and absurd."

572 Eastland, Elizabeth Wilson. *Milton's Ethics.* Folcroft, PA: Folcroft Library Editions, 1969, 1971, 1976; Norwood, PA: Norwood Editions, 1977.

Reprints of Huckabay No. 526, originally published in 1942.

573 Edmundson, George. *Milton and*

Vondel: A Curiosity of Literature. Folcroft, PA: Folcroft Library Editions, 1969; Norwood, PA: Norwood Editions, 1974; Philadelphia, PA: R. West, 1975.

Reprints of Stevens No. 838, originally published in 1885.

574 Edmundson, Mark Wright. "Towards Reading Freud: Moments of Self-Representation in Milton, Wordsworth, Keats, Emerson, Whitman and Sigmund Freud." Doctoral diss., Yale Univ., 1985. 263pp. Abs., *DAI*, 46, 1986, 3357A.

Asserts that "Freud achieves his representations of self through strong revisions of the literary tradition," developing his "super-ego," for example, from the "anonymous voice" that manipulates Milton's Eve.

575 Egloff, Susan J. "'Our Darke Voyage': The Journey Motif in Milton's Poetry." Doctoral diss., Yale Univ., 1972. 298pp. Abs., *DAI*, 33, 1972, 2324A.

Argues that the various journeys in *Comus*, *Paradise Lost*, and *Paradise Regained* affirm the human ability to recognize evil and still prefer the righteous life of a "true wayfaring Christian."

576 Empson, William. "Milton and Bentley: The Pastoral of the Innocence of Man and Nature." *English Pastoral Poetry* (Freeport, NY: Books for Libraries Press, 1972), pp. 149–91.

Reprint of Huckabay No. 539, originally published in 1935.

577 Engle, Lars David. "Character in Poetic Narrative: Action and Individual in Chaucer and Milton." Doctoral diss., Yale Univ., 1983. 212pp. Abs., *DAI*, 45, 1984, 525A.

Explores the self-awareness—a character's ability to strain the boundaries of rhetoric or narrative through individual assertions—of Chaucer's Griselda and Theseus, and Milton's Satan, Adam, and Eve.

578 English Language Notes. *Milton Essays and Reviews*. Vol. 19, No. 3, Mar., 1982, 177–293.

A special issue on Milton edited by John M. Major and others. Contains essays by Edward Le Comte, C. A. Patrides, Mary D. Ravenhall, John Peter Rumrich, David J. Aitken, Charles A. Huttar, David S. Berkeley, and William Shullenberger, as well as reviews. In this bibliography, each essay is listed according to author and classification.

579 Entzminger, Robert L. *Divine Word: Milton and the Redemption of Language.* Pittsburgh, PA: Duquesne Univ. Press, 1985. x, 188pp.

Relates the distrust of eloquence in sixteenth-century England and examines Milton's idea that verbal and spiritual redemption was gained simultaneously. Studies Milton's attempt to harness the power of language to relate the Word of God. Reviews: Jacqueline T. Miller, *RenQ*, 39, 1986, 567–69; Boyd M. Berry, *JEGP*, 86, 1987, 113–15; Richard J. DuRocher, *SHR*, 21, 1987, 364–65; Anne Ferry, *MP*, 84, 1987, 322–23; Cheryl Fresch, *MiltonQ*, 21, No. 1, 1987, 24–25; Michael Murrin, *ELN*, 24, 1987, 81–82; G. R. Evans, *RES*, 38, 1987, 292.

580 Entzminger, Robert Lee. "Milton and Moral Aesthetics." Doctoral diss., Rice Univ., 1975. 189pp. Abs., *DAI*, 36, 1975, 2217A.

Outlines Milton's Protestant rebellion against Renaissance literary decorums though his "emphasis on grace and discipline," tightly controlled imagery, and "eschatological view of time."

581 Erlich, Victor. "Milton's Early Poetry: Its Christian Humanism." *AI*, 32, 1975, 77–112.

"Milton wrestles with both fantasy and theology. A dreamer, explainer and something more, he creates myths that sometimes embrace dogma and sometimes undermine it."

582 Études Anglaises. Vol. 27, no. 4, Oct.–Dec., 1974, 385–511.

A tercentenary issue containing a poem on Milton by Edwin Muir and essays by Jacques Blondel, Armand Himy, Roy Flannagan, Olivier Lutaud, Roger Lejosne, Kenneth Muir, Micheline Hugues, Lois Potter, Jean-François Camé, Barbara Kiefer Lewalski, and Louis Bonnerot. In this bibliography, each item is listed according to classification and author. Review: Anthony Low, *MiltonQ*, 9, 1975, 20–27.

583 Evans, G. Blakemore, ed. *Milton Studies in Honor of Harris Francis Fletcher.* Folcroft, PA: Folcroft Library Editions, 1974; Norwood, PA: Norwood Editions, 1975; Ann Arbor, MI: Univ. Microfilms International, 1980 Books on Demand Reprints.
Reprints of Huckabay No. 554, originally published in 1961.

584 Fallon, Robert Thomas. *Captain or Colonel: The Soldier in Milton's Life and Art.* Columbia: Univ. of Missouri Press, 1984. x, 272pp.
Examines parallels between Milton's experience of war and the martial figures in his works. Contains much background material and chapters on the War in Heaven, Satan, and the warriors in *Samson Agonistes*. Reviews: John Pitcher, *TLS*, Aug. 23, 1985, p. 932; Hugh M. Richmond, *JEGP*, 85, 1986, 565–67; Jackie DiSalvo, *AN&Q*, 24, 1986, 91–92; John Morrill, *RES*, 37, 1986, 258–60; Edward Jones, *MiltonQ*, 22, 1988, 28–29; James Egan, *SCN*, 48, 1990, 3–5.

585 Fallon, Robert T. "League with You I Seek: Milton's Epics and England's Relations with the Netherlands." *MiltonQ*, 9, 1975, 32.
Abstract of a paper presented at the University of Wisconsin, Milwaukee, Milton Tercentenary Conference, in November, 1974. Sees parallels between the First Dutch War (1652–54) and the Spanish War (1656–58) and Milton's definition of the cosmic struggle between good and evil.

586 Fallon, Robert Thomas. "Trials of the Interdisciplinary: A Review Article." *MiltonQ*, 16, 1982, 16–20.
On Andrew J. Milner's *John Milton and the English Revolution* (No. 841). Mostly animadversions on a sociologist who forces Milton into a preconceived mold.

587 Fallon, Stephen Michael. "'Degrees of Substance': Milton's Spirit World and Seventeenth-Century Philosophy." Doctoral diss., Univ. of Virginia, 1985. 328pp. Abs., *DAI*, 47, 1986, 535A.
Contrasts the monism of *Paradise Lost* to deterministic seventeenth-century thought, but admits that Milton's philosophy reflects the century's increasing materialism.

588 Fallon, Stephen M. "'To Act or Not': Milton's Conception of Divine Freedom." *JHI*, 49, 1988, 425–49.
"The immediate aim of this essay is to draw the boundary between the Cambridge Platonist and Arminian conception of divine freedom and Milton's own unusual view. The larger implicit aim is to begin the work of realigning Milton in the metaphysical and theological debates of his time. Associating Milton with the Cambridge Platonists might satisfy our rage for order, but it oversimplifies a complex web of intellectual relationships."

589 Fatch, Donald E. "Milton from John Locke's Library." *SCUL*, 1, 1969, 32–34.
Describes a copy of Milton's prose works once owned by Locke and now in the library of the University of California, Santa Barbara.

590 Feinstein, Blossom Grayer. "Creation and Theories of Creativity in English Poetry of the Renaissance." Doctoral diss., City Univ. of New York, 1967. 383pp. Abs., *DA*, 28, 1967, 1394A.
Associates Renaissance creation theories that incorporate Chaos and near-eastern philosophy with growing literary creativity, citing such authors as Spenser and Milton.

591 Fields, Albert W. "Author to Himself: Milton's Ethical Ideal." *SCB*, 35, 1975, 76.

Abstract of a paper presented at the 1975 MLA Convention. "Milton celebrated the spiritually elevating power of chosen good over the imbruting nature of chosen evil. The imbruting of both Adam and Samson was the consequence of their free choices of evil over good, while the spiritual elevation of Jesus proceeds from his choice of good over evil."

592 Findeisen, Helmut. "'Man Naturally Born Free': Zu Miltons Prosaschriften." *ZAA*, 23, 1975, 143–47.

Insists that the Miltonic and communist ideologies are not identical.

593 Fish, Stanley E. "Interpreting the *Variorum*." *CritI*, 2, 1976, 465–85. Reprinted in *Is There a Text in This Class? The Authority of Interpretive Communities* (Cambridge, MA, and London: Harvard Univ. Press, 1980), pp. 147–73.

On the first two volumes of the *Variorum Commentary* (Nos. 1236 and 1838), focusing on commentary on the sonnets. Opposes "the assumption that there *is* a sense, that it is embedded or encoded in the text, and that it can be taken in at a single glance." Replies by Douglas Bush (*CritI*, 3, 1976, 179–82) and Steven Mailloux (pp. 183–90). Rejoinder by Fish (pp. 191–96). See No. 773.

594 Fisher, Stephanie Ann. "Circean Fatal Women in Milton's Poetry: Milton's Concept of the Renaissance Woman." Doctoral diss., Univ. of Minnesota, 1971. 219pp. Abs., *DAI*, 32, 1971, 2639A.

Contends that the women of Milton's later poetry are fleshy femmes fatales, often depicted as sorceresses and constrained by domestic roles.

595 Fishman, Sylvia Barack. "The Watered Garden and the Bride of God: Patterns of Biblical Imagery in Poems of Spenser, Milton, and Blake." Doctoral diss., Washington Univ., 1980. 390pp.

Abs., *DAI*, 41, 1980, 1063A.

Discusses the effect of biblical allusion—especially to the Song of Solomon—on Spenser's presentation of sexuality, Milton's concept of history and contrast "between biblical and classical pastoral modes," and Blake's reinterpretation of biblical meanings.

596 Fix, Stephen. "The Contexts and Motives of Johnson's *Life of Milton*." *Domestick Privacies: Samuel Johnson and the Art of Biography.* Ed. by David Wheeler (Lexington: Univ. of Kentucky Press, 1987), pp. 107–32.

Discusses Johnson's contentiousness and prejudices against Milton's political and religious views. "But that contentiousness, I wish to argue, is largely connected with the project of rescuing Milton from the misplaced and misinformed enthusiasm of his admirers, and of articulating the standards upon which Milton's strongest case for fame as an artist may be built."

597 [Flannagan, Roy]. "International Milton Symposium: London, Chalfont St. Giles, July 7–9, 1981." *MiltonQ*, 15, 1981, 73–79.

A detailed account of the symposium, accompanied by photographs. Also reported in *SCN*, 39, 1981, 26.

598 Flannagan, Roy. "Look Homeward Angel: Milton Criticism in England and America." *Ringing the Bell Backward: The Proceedings of the First International Milton Symposium.* Ed. by Ronald G. Shafer. The IUP Imprint Series (Indiana: Indiana Univ. of Pennsylvania, 1982), pp. 63–68.

Discusses the traditional English ambivalence toward Milton, from Dryden to Carey and Fowler, and concludes that scholars on both sides of the Atlantic need each other deeply, to come together in balance.

599 Flannagan, Roy. "Milton Criticism, Present and Future." *EA*, 27, 1974, 399–403.

Argues that, even though Milton's

writings give critics infinite variety with which to work, there are no recent major adversaries, and criticism has become complacent. Looks for a time when exciting challenge may reenter Milton criticism.

600 Flannagan, Roy C. "Milwaukee Tercentenary Conference." *MiltonQ*, 8, 1974, 119–20.

Report on the conference.

601 Flannagan, Roy C. "MLA: Seminar Four, Milton Encyclopedia." *MiltonN*, 3, 1969, 8–9.

Fifteen members met to discuss the possibilities of a Milton encyclopedia.

602 Flannagan, Roy C. "Teaching Milton after the Revolution." *Teaching Milton to Undergraduates: Problems and Approaches.* Proceedings of the Special Session (537), Annual Meeting of the Modern Language Association, Dec. 28, 1976. Comp. by Paul L. Gaston ([Edwardsville: Southern Illinois Univ.], n.d.), pp. 3–5.

The American cultural revolution of the 1960s caused many teachers to try to make Milton appear relevant by misrepresenting his work. Since then, Miltonists have accommodated their teaching to undergraduates and their publishing to "the academic elite."

603 Flannagan, Roy. "Two on God, One on Satan." *MiltonQ*, 21, No. 3, 1987, 113–17.

Review essay of Hugh R. MacCallum, *Milton and the Sons of God* (No. 2637); Michael Bauman, *Milton's Arianism* (No. 473); and Neil Forsyth, *The Old Enemy* (No. 2241).

604 Fleming, James Francis. "Spenser's Influence on Milton's Changing Concept of the Active Life—1631–1644." Doctoral diss., Univ. of Illinois, Urbana, 1977. 167pp. Abs., *DAI*, 38, 1978, 6140A.

Follows Milton's poetic departure from "the superiority of contemplative detachment" in favor of "the active, wayfaring Christian who fully involves himself in the world."

605 Fletcher, Harris Francis. *Milton's Rabbinical Readings.* Folcroft, PA: Folcroft Library Editions, 1976; Norwood, PA: Norwood Editions, 1977; Philadelphia, PA: R. West 1978; Hamden, CT: Shoe String Press, 1979.

Reprints of Huckabay No. 557, originally published in 1930.

606 Fletcher, Harris Francis. *Milton's Semitic Studies and Some Manifestations of Them in His Poetry.* Folcroft, PA: Folcroft Library Editions, 1974; Norwood, PA: Norwood Editions, 1976; Philadelphia, PA: R. West, 1977.

Reprints of Stevens No. 2571 and Huckabay No. 558, originally published in 1926.

607 Fletcher, Ian. "Mimic Heavens: Milton's Century." *Encounter*, 55, 1980, 69–78.

Review essay that discusses the trends in Milton criticism and the difficulty in, for example, "diminishing . . . [the] disturbing substance [of *Paradise Lost*]: theme, pattern, structure, narrative."

608 Flinker, Norman. "Milton and Moses." Doctoral diss., New York Univ., 1973. 183pp. Abs., *DAI*, 34, 1974, 4198A.

Sees Moses as a demythologized human hero, "Christ-like yet also clearly fallen," recognized as the "author, editor and commentator on the Pentateuch," in Milton's prose and poetry.

609 Forster, Leonard. *The Poet's Tongues: Multilingualism in Literature.* Cambridge: Cambridge Univ. Press, in association with the Univ. of Otago Press, 1970. xii, 101pp.

Deals with Milton's multilingual abilities, in passing.

610 Fowler, Alastair. *A History of English Literature.* Cambridge, MA: Harvard Univ. Press, 1987, 1989, 1991. xiv, 409pp.

Discusses *Comus, L'Allegro* and *Il Penseroso, Paradise Lost*, and *Paradise Regained.* Calls *Paradise Lost* one of the most original poems ever written and offers fresh observations on the style of *Paradise Regained.*

Reviews: Thomas D'Evelyn, *Christian Science Monitor*, 80, 1988, 17; Martin Dodsworth, *TLS*, Apr. 8, 1988, p. 382; Donald Ray, *LJ*, 113, 1988, 61; *LRB*, 10, 1988, 8; *TES*, July 8, 1988, p. 25; Miranda Johnson Haddad, *SCN*, 47, 1989, 5–6.

611 Frank, Armin P. "Eliot on Milton: Tone as Criticism." *Miscellanea Anglo-Americana: Festschrift für Helmut Viebrock.* Ed. by Kuno Schuhmann, Wilhelm Hartmann, and Frank (München: Karl Pressler, 1974), pp. 184–201.

Surveys Eliot's comments on Milton. Argues that there is no substantial difference between the views expressed in Eliot's 1936 and 1947 essays (see Huckabay Nos. 530–31).

612 Frank, Joseph. "Exile and the Kingdom: The Incipient Absurdity of Milton and Shaw." *Mosaic*, 9, 1975, 111–21.

On *Samson Agonistes* and *Heartbreak House*. "Milton, despite his bleak metaphysics, manages to convey a message of Existential exhilaration; Shaw, despite his comic mask, conveys a message of Existential despair. In their differing responses to the absurdist dilemma each exiles himself from his own work."

613 Frank, Mortimer H. "Milton's Knowledge of Music: Some Speculations." *Milton and the Art of Sacred Song.* Ed. by J. Max Patrick and Roger Henry Sundell (Madison: Univ. of Wisconsin Press, 1979), pp. 83–98.

Believes that the music books Milton purchased in Italy point to his "interest in a wide range of composers, some of whom created the finest and most avant-garde music of the time." Hence some of his references to musical modes may have seventeenth-century implications and may not derive from classical sources.

614 Franson, John Karl, ed. *Milton Reconsidered: Essays in Honor of Arthur E. Barker.* Salzburg: Institut für Englische Sprache und Literatur, Universität Salzburg, 1976. v, 215pp.

Contains articles by Emory Elliott, Suzanne Blow, Karl Kiralis, John E. Grant, Ronald Primeau, Linda Draper Henson, William L. Kittle, Franson, and O. Glade Hunsaker. In this bibliography, each article is listed according to author and classification. Review: Virginia Ramey Mollenkott, *MiltonQ*, 12, 1978, 77–82.

615 Freedman, Morris. "Milton and Dryden on Tragedy." *English Writers of the Eighteenth Century.* Ed. by John H. Middendorf (New York and London: Columbia Univ. Press, 1971), pp. 158–71.

States that Milton was certain, traditional, unqualified, and brief, while Dryden was often tentative, prolific, exploratory, and sometimes apologetic. Deals briefly with the influence of *Samson Agonistes* on *All for Love.*

616 Freeman, James. "Milton's Roman Connection: Giovanni Salzilli." *MiltonQ*, 14, 1980, 71.

Abstract of a paper presented at the Binghamton Comparative Literature Conference in October, 1979. Notes Milton's high regard for the Italian academies and suggests that by "examining the poetry of Giovanni Salzilli, a member of Rome's *Fantastici*, we can see what influence academic ideas had upon Milton's practice."

617 French, Robert. "A Note from Milton's Cottage." *MiltonN*, 3, 1969, 17- 19.

Gives a brief history, describes the cottage and some of its contents, and notes that the Milton's Cottage Trust urgently needs funds for maintenance and improvements. Reply by Alyn C. Meiklejohn, wife of the curator (No. 830).

618 "The Friends of Milton's Cottage." *MiltonQ*, 10, 1976, 134.

Announces the formation of the organization and gives some details about the present condition of the cottage at Chalfont St. Giles. Also announced in *SCN*, 34, 1976, 94.

619 Frye, Roland Mushat. "In Memoriam: Constantine Apostolos Patrides, 1930–86." *MiltonQ*, 21, No. 1, 1987, 36–37.

Presented at the annual dinner of the Milton Society of America on December 29, 1986.

620 Frye, Roland Mushat. *Milton's Imagery and the Visual Arts: Iconographic Tradition in the Epic Poems.* Princeton, NJ: Princeton Univ. Press, 1978. xxv, 408pp.

"My purpose here is to study the ways in which artists represented the scenes, events, and characters that Milton treats poetically in his epic works." Extensive bibliography. Reviews: *MiltonQ*, 12, 1978, 107–08; John Mulryan, *Cithara*, 18, No. 1, 1978, 79–84; Joseph Anthony Wittreich, Jr., *Rev*, 1, 1979, 123–64; Barbara Kiefer Lewalski, *RenQ*, 32, 1979, 445–49; D. D. C. Chambers, *RES*, 30, 1979, 82–86; Hugh MacCallum, *UTQ*, 49, 1979–80, 176–80; Jacques Blondel, *EA*, 33, 1980, 211–12; Raymond B. Waddington, *MP*, 78, 1980, 84–87; William E. Cain, *MLN*, 96, 1981, 1121–33; Mario Praz, *ES*, 62, 1981, 566–69; J. B. Trapp, *MLR*, 77, 1982, 162–64. See also Nos. 2266 and 2688.

621 Frye, Roland Mushat. "Reason and Grace: Christian Epistemology in Dante, Langland, and Milton." *Action and Conviction in Early Modern Europe: Essays in Memory of E. H. Harbison.* Ed. by Theodore K. Rabb and Jerrold E. Seigel (Princeton, NJ: Princeton Univ. Press, 1969), pp. 404–22.

"Reason under grace, then, is a reason fulfilled and extended. It is what Milton and the Christian humanists called right reason."

622 Frye, Roland Mushat. "The Teachings of Classical Puritanism on Conjugal Love." *On Milton's Poetry: A Selection of Modern Studies.* Ed. by Arnold Stein (Greenwich, CT: Fawcett Publications, 1970), pp. 97–110.

Reprint of Huckabay No. 577, originally published in 1955.

623 Fujii, Haruhiko. "Milton's Walking Man—An Image of Christian Life." *Poetry and Faith in the English Renaissance.* Ed. by Peter Milward (Tokyo: Renaissance Institute, Sophia Univ., 1987), pp. 143–49.

Discusses various images of walking in Milton's poems and concludes that "in his sonnets and three major poems the figure of a walking man becomes one of the key images of Christian life on earth."

624 Gair, W. Reavley. "Milton and Science." *John Milton: Introductions.* Ed. by John Broadbent (Cambridge: Cambridge Univ. Press, 1973), pp. 120–44.

On Milton's interest in and attitudes toward scholasticism, empiricism, materialism, the humours, astronomy, and so forth.

625 Galdon, Joseph A., S. J. *Typology and Seventeenth-Century Literature.* De Proprietatibus Litterarum, Series Maior, 28. The Hague and Paris: Mouton, 1975. 164pp.

Discusses the typology in Milton's long poems, pp. 77–94, 98–99, and passim.

626 Gaston, Paul L., comp. *Teaching Milton to Undergraduates: Problems and Approaches.* Proceedings of the Special Session (537), Annual Meeting of the Modern Language Association, Dec. 28, 1976. [Edwardsville: Southern Illinois Univ.], n.d. 45pp.

Contains remarks by Roy C. Flannagan, Joseph E. Duncan, Susanne Woods, Kenneth J. Ames, Philip J. Gallagher, Bruce Henricksen, John Huntley, Marilyn R. Farwell, and Gary McCown. In this bibliography, each article is listed according to author and classification.

627 Geary, Robert F. "Milton, Pope, and Divine Harmony: Notes on the Secularization of Theodicy." *JMJ*, 35, 1977, 33–45.

Discusses the rational theodicy in Pope's *Essay on Man* as a departure from Milton's more traditional theodicy in *Paradise Lost* and believes that Pope's work is a step toward the secularization of western thought, as exemplified in Adam Smith's *Wealth of Nations.*

628 Geisst, Charles R. "Knowledge and Politics in the Thought of John Milton." Doctoral diss., London School of Economics and Political Science, 1972.

629 Geisst, Charles R. *The Political Thought of John Milton.* London and Basingstoke: Macmillan, 1984. vi, 127pp.
A general study organized around a topical outline. Devotes some attention to the evolution of Milton's political thought. Appendices: "The Problem of *Essence*"; "Hartlib and Comenius"; and "[Robert] Filmer's Critique of Milton [1652]." Review: Geoffrey M. Ridden, *MiltonQ*, 19, 1985, 23–24.

630 Gellinek, Christian. "Politik und Literatur bei Grotius, Opitz und Milton: Ein Vergleich Christlich Politischer Grundgedanken." *Daphnis*, 11, 1982, 637–68.
Discusses the relationships among the personalities and literary styles of Hugo Grotius, Milton, and Martin Opitz. Examines specific political and religious influences they shared, such as Calvinism, Catholicism, the Reformation, and issues concerning the rise of the middle class.

631 George, Diana Hume. "Is She Also the Divine Image? Values for the Feminine in Blake, Milton and Freud." Doctoral diss., State Univ. of New York, Buffalo, 1979. 491pp. Abs., *DAI*, 39, 1979, 7356A.
Evaluates Blake's concept of woman, preceded by Milton's unintentional feminine praise and followed by Freud's psychoanalysis, as a divine image victimized by the Fall.

632 Gérard, Albert. "Conformisme Ideologique et Révolte Individualiste dans le Classicisme Européen (Corneille, Milton, Vondel)." *PFSCL*, 11, 1979, 155–66.
During a period dominated by monarchies that tried to maintain absolute authority, Corneille, Milton, and Vondel found ways to question royal authority. One metaphor for this in Milton is the rebel angels' revolt against God.

633 Ghosh, P. K. "Milton's Idea of Freedom." *Essays on John Milton: A Tercentenary Tribute.* Ed. by Asloob Ahmad Ansari (Aligarh: Aligarh Muslim Univ., 1976), pp. 115–32.
States that because of Milton's inquiry into the whole range of nature and freedom, "he was able to hold out to the 'multitudes' a promise of liberation from the dark world of despondency resulting from a morbid preoccupation with the Original Sin in Pauline and Calvinistic doctrine."

634 Gilbert, A. J. "Milton and Pope." *Literary Language from Chaucer to Johnson* (London: Macmillan, 1979; Totowa, NJ: Barnes and Noble, 1980), pp. 111–31.
Examines the influence of Ramist logic in the two writers' poems, in terms of the plain, the middle, and the high styles.

635 Gnerro, Marco Lorenzo. "The Influence of Classical and *Cinquecento* Style Theory on British Invocatory Structure through Milton." Doctoral diss., The Catholic Univ. of America, 1971. 189pp. Abs., *DAI*, 32, 1971, 1471A.
Notes the impact of literary theory on the level of style, introductory pattern, narrator's attitude, and identity of the muse in Milton's invocations.

636 Goldberg, Jonathan. "Hesper-Vesper: Aspects of Venus in a Seventeenth-Century Trope." *SEL*, 15, 1975, 37–55.
Analyzes Milton's treatment of Venus in order to shed light on Donne's *Anniversaries.*

637 Goldberg, Jonathan. "Milton's Warning Voice: Considering Preventive Measures." *Voice Terminal Echo: Postmodernism and English Renaissance Texts* (New York and London: Methuen, 1986), pp. 124–58, 183–90.
Argues that, in his poetry, Milton is

obsessed with deferring beginnings and that he simultaneously appropriates and disappropriates Shakespeare and Spenser.

638 Goldberg, Jonathan. "The Politics of Renaissance Literature: A Review Essay." *ELH*, 49, 1982, 514–42.

Discusses some critics who espouse "the return to historical criticism," including Fredric Jameson, whose *Political Unconscious* (1981) is a "full scale attempt . . . to argue for a marxist theory of textual production." Disagrees with Jameson for having written the fall of feudalism into the text of *Paradise Lost*. Also examines Christopher Hill's *Milton and the English Revolution* (No. 174), which "confirms Jameson's predilection to read texts as one-for-one expressions of society."

639 Goldstein, Leonard. "The Good Old Cause and Milton's Blank Verse." *ZAA*, 23, 1975, 133–42.

Considers "whether John Milton's bourgeois revolutionary attitude also found expression in his prosody." Analyzes "Milton's rejection of rime for his larger works of his later years."

640 González Padilla, María Enriqueta, ed. *Ensayos sobre John Milton: Epopeya y Drama*. Facultad de Filosofía y Letras, Centro de Investigaciones de Letras Modernas y Arte Dramático (Mexico, D.F.: Universidad Nacional Autónoma de México, 1976). 79pp.

A collection of tercentenary essays by Magdalena García Amescua, González Padilla, Dianne Taylor William, Amelia G. Saravia de Farrés, and Encarnación Ventura y San Martín. In this bibliography, each essay is listed according to author and classification. Review: David Calderon, *Indice: Bibliográfico de la UNAM,* 16 (Oct. 1976), pp. 10–11.

641 Good, John Walter. *Studies in the Milton Tradition*. Univ. of Illinois Studies in Language and Literature, vol. 1, nos. 3–4. Ann Arbor, MI: Univ. Micro-

films International, 1980 Books on Demand Reprints.

Reprint of Stevens No. 2832, originally published in 1915.

642 Goslee, Nancy M. "'Promethean Art': Sculpture and Personification after Milton." *MiltonQ*, 17, 1983, 23–24.

Abstract of a paper presented at the 1982 MLA Convention. "Repeatedly associated with Milton's mythic figures and with his personifications, the analogue of sculpture for poetic creativity stimulates both the theory and practice of personification in the eighteenth century."

643 Grace, William J. *Ideas in Milton*. Notre Dame, IN, and London: Univ. of Notre Dame Press, 1968. viii, 205pp.

See Huckabay No. 592. Reviews: *MiltonN*, 2, 1968, 67–68; *TLS*, Dec. 26, 1968, p. 1457; James H. Sims, *SHR*, 3, 1969, 406–08; Anthony Low, *SCN* 27, 1969, 26; James Barcus, *Gordon Review*, 11, 1970, 300–01.

644 Greene, Edward Patrick. "The 'Benefit of Affliction': Verbal Continuity and Doctrinal Themes in Herbert and Milton." Doctoral diss., State Univ. of New York, Buffalo, 1976. 219pp. Abs., *DAI*, 37, 1977, 5141A–42A.

Explains the metaphoric significance of "affliction"—a painful need to revaluate one's relationship with God— in "Affliction," *Paradise Lost*, and *Samson Agonistes*.

645 Grierson, Herbert J. C. *Criticism and Creation: Essays and Addresses*. Folcroft, PA: Folcroft Library Editions, 1969, 1973; Norwood, PA: Norwood Editions, 1976; Philadelphia, PA: R. West, 1977.

Reprints of Huckabay No. 599, originally published in 1949.

646 Griffin, Dustin. "Milton and the Decline of Epic in the Eighteenth Century." *NLH*, 14, 1982, 143–54.

Questions the claim that Milton dried up or diverted the epic stream. Rather, "the progress of politeness and good sense made an essentially archaic form like the epic nearly impossible in an age of enlightenment, even in its Christianized forms."

647 Griffith, Philip Mahone. "A Short View of Joseph Warton's Criticism of Milton." *Papers on Milton.* Ed. by Griffith and Lester F. Zimmerman. Univ. of Tulsa Department of English Monograph Series, no. 8 (Tulsa, OK: Univ. of Tulsa, 1969), pp. 25–35.

Summarizes Warton's views on Milton, which were influenced by Longinus.

648 Griffith, Philip Mahone, and **Lester F. Zimmerman,** eds. *Papers on Milton.* Univ. of Tulsa Department of English Monograph Series, no. 8. Tulsa, OK: Univ. of Tulsa, 1969. 67pp.

Contains essays by David S. Berkeley, Ivy Dempsey, Griffith, James H. Sims, J. Patrick Tyson, and Zimmerman. In this bibliography, each essay is listed according to author and classification. See No. 1037. Review: Anthony Low, *SCN*, 28, 1974, 46.

649 Gros Louis, Kenneth R. R., and others, eds. *Literary Interpretations of Biblical Narratives.* Nashville, TN, and New York: Abingdon Press, 1974. 352pp.

A collection of essays by various hands. Designed as a textbook. Milton's handling of biblical narratives discussed, passim.

650 Grose, Christopher. *Milton and the Sense of Tradition.* New Haven, CT, and London: Yale Univ. Press, 1988. xiii, 240pp.

Believes that *Paradise Regained* and *Samson Agonistes* hark back to the Milton of the 1640s. Emphasizes the autobiographical importance of the *Apology.* Reviews: Robert L. Entzminger, *RenQ*, 42, 1989, 891–93; Neil Forsyth, *TLS*, Sept. 22–28, 1989, pp. 1036–37; Keith W. F. Stavely, *SCN*, 47, 1989, 36–37; M. J. Doherty, *MiltonQ*, 26, 1992, 46–52.

651 Guibbory, Achsah. "John Milton: Providential Progress or Cyclical Decay." *The Map of Time: Seventeenth-Century*

English Literature and Ideas of Pattern in History (Urbana and Chicago: Univ. of Illinois Press, 1986), pp. 169–211.

Views Milton's attitude toward time and change as the most radical of the century's major writers. Reviews (of book): Tom Hayes, *CLIO*, 17, 1988, 292–94; Edward W. Tayler, *RenQ*, 41, 1988, 360–62.

652 Guilfoyle, Cherrell. "'If Shape It Might be Call'd That Shape Had None': Aspects of Death in Milton." *MiltonS*, 13, 1979, 35–57.

Surveys references to death in Milton's poetry. Concludes that Milton was always concerned with aging and ultimate death but "in the end he mounted high like the young Lycidas, and [was] taken, like the aged Samson, home to his father's house."

653 Guillory, John David. "Poetry and Authority: Spenser, Milton, and Literary History." Doctoral diss., Yale Univ., 1979. 265pp. Abs., *DAI*, 40, 1980, 5874A.

Examines the conflict between sacred, inspired poetic creation, which Milton strongly advocates, and Renaissance faith in individual poetic authority.

654 Hagstrum, Jean H. "Milton and the Ideal of Heterosexual Friendship." *Sex and Sensibility: Ideal and Erotic Love from Milton to Mozart* (Chicago, IL, and London: Univ. of Chicago Press, 1980), pp. 24–49.

Sees Milton's idea of love and marriage as encompassing two extremes—the ideal of heterosexual friendship and the sin of narcissism. Reviews (of book): John A. Dussinger, *JEGP*, 80, 1981, 573–75; Patricia Brückmann, *UTQ*, 51, 1982, 298–303; Douglas Brooks-Davies, *MLR*, 77, 1982, 150–53.

655 Hale, John K. "Milton as a Translator of Poetry." *RenSt*, 1, 1987, 238–56.

Discusses Milton's purposes and methods of translation. Provides a checklist of the translations of poetry. Disagrees with recent criticism of Milton's ability to translate.

656 Hallam, A. D. "Milton's Knowledge and Use of Hebrew." *Milla wa-Milla* (Australia), 5, Dec., 1965, 18–22.

Feels that Milton had a basic knowledge of Hebrew, though he was not a Semitic scholar. Some of the Hebrew sources that he cited were not available in English translation.

657 Halley, Janet E. "Female Autonomy in Milton's Sexual Poetics." *Milton and the Idea of Woman.* Ed. by Julia M. Walker (Urbana and Chicago: Univ. of Illinois Press, 1988), pp. 230–53.

Surveys the feminist controversy surrounding Milton and examines the female figure in his early poems, the divorce tracts, and *Paradise Lost.* Insists that male intention is pervasive and that female autonomy comes only with male consent. Abs., *MiltonQ*, 24, 1990, 151.

658 Halley, Janet Elizabeth. "Voice and Sign in Seventeenth-Century Literature: Studies in Donne, Vaughan, Browne and Milton." Doctoral diss., Univ. of California, Los Angeles, 1980. 281pp. Abs., *DAI*, 41, 1980, 1609A–10A.

Explores the writers' efforts to unite language and imagery to their conception of God and the cosmos, noting that Milton transcends language and image in favor of "a direct sensuous participation in God."

659 Hamilton, Gary David. "Milton and Arminianism." Doctoral diss., Univ. of Wisconsin, 1968. 235pp. Abs., *DA*, 29, 1969, 4457A.

Argues that Milton, like Arminius, affirms human free will but stresses dependence on God's grace in the *Christian Doctrine* and *Paradise Lost.*

660 Hamilton, William Douglas, ed. *Original Papers Illustrative of the Life and Writings of John Milton.* New York: AMS Press, 1969.

Reprint of Stevens No. 1221A, originally published in 1859.

661 Hammil, Carrie Esther. "The Celestial Journey and the Harmony of the Spheres in English Literature, 1300–1700." Doctoral diss., Texas Christian Univ., 1972. 226pp. Abs., *DAI*, 33, 1972, 2326A.

Examines the celestial journey and harmony of the spheres, interrelated devices designed to harmonize the external universe with the internal soul, in the writings of Chaucer, Shakespeare, Milton, and Dryden.

662 Hanford, James Holly. *John Milton, Poet and Humanist: Essays by James Holly Hanford.* Foreword by John S. Diekhoff. Ann Arbor, MI: Univ. Microfilms International, 1980 Books on Demand Reprints.

Reprint of Huckabay No. 617, originally published in 1966.

663 Hanford, James Holly. "The Youth of Milton: An Interpretation of His Early Literary Development." *Studies in Shakespeare, Milton and Donne* (New York: Haskell House, 1972), pp. 89–163.

Reprint of Stevens No. 2556, originally published in 1925.

664 Hannay, Margaret Patterson. "Rehabilitations: C. S. Lewis' Contribution to the Understanding of Spenser and Milton." Doctoral diss., State Univ. of New York, Albany, 1976. 400pp. Abs., *DAI*, 37, 1976, 1564A.

Explains how Lewis defends the orthodoxy of Milton's creation theory, Christology, and presentation of Satan.

665 Harada, Jun. "Milton's View of the Antichristian Presbyterians." *MCJ News*, 7, 1984, 8–11.

Examines several of Milton's writings to reveal that "his final appraisal of the Presbyterians is that they are not essentially a principal Antichristian embodiment but a deserted apostate ally."

666 Harada, Jun. "Miruton no mohoron apurochi (1)." *Eigo Seinen*, 123, 1978, 517–19.

Milton follows Plato in believing that inspiration is the key to creativity. While Plato believes that imitation is one step removed from reality, Milton views divine inspiration as admirable. Milton sees himself as the correct interpreter of God's providence and his writing as the work of salvation in this world.

667 Harada, Jun. "Miruton no mohoron apurochi (2)." *Eigo Seinen*, 123, 1978, 582–84.

Renaissance humanist education taught Milton about classical ideas of imitation. By using imitation as a creative principle, Milton becomes one with his poetry.

668 Hardin, Richard F. "Ovid in Seventeenth-Century England." *CL*, 24, 1972, 44–62.

Briefly indicates that the story of *Comus* and the mention of pagan gods in *Paradise Lost* are related to Ovid's influence.

669 Harding, Davis Philoon. *Milton and the Renaissance Ovid*. Folcroft, PA: Folcroft Library Editions, 1968, 1976; Norwood, PA: Norwood Editions, 1977; Philadelphia, PA: R. West, 1978.

Reprints of Huckabay No. 628, originally published in 1946.

670 Hardison, O. B., Jr. "The Orator and the Poet: The Dilemma of Humanist Literature." *JMRS*, 1, 1971, 33–44.

"The case of John Milton, last and perhaps the greatest in the proud line of Christian humanists, illustrates both the ideal and the reason for its ultimate failure." Believes that *Areopagitica* and *Paradise Lost* 12 show Milton's rejection of humanism.

671 Hardison, O. B., Jr. *Toward Freedom and Dignity: The Humanities and the Idea of Humanity*. Baltimore, MD, and London: Johns Hopkins Press, 1972. xxvi, 166pp.

Considers Milton's ultimate rejection of humanism, pp. 72–79.

672 Harralson, David M. "Milton and Thomas Adams: A Study in Baroque Prose." *MiltonQ*, 9, 1975, 33.

Abstract of a paper presented at the University of Wisconsin, Milwaukee, Milton Tercentenary Conference, in November, 1974. Evidence points to common baroque stylistic elements.

673 Hartman, Geoffrey H. "False Themes and Gentle Minds." *PQ*, 47, 1968, 55–68. Reprinted in *Beyond Formalism: Literary Essays, 1958–1970* (New Haven, CT, and London: Yale Univ. Press, 1970), pp. 283–97; and in *On Milton's Poetry: A Selection of Modern Studies*. Ed. by Arnold Stein (Greenwich, CT: Fawcett Publications, 1970), pp. 53–59.

"It is clear that Milton is not the only master for the English mind. But he is among those who assured the survival of Romance by the very quality of his resistance to it."

674 Haskin, Dayton William. "The Light Within: Studies in Baxter, Bunyan, and Milton." Doctoral diss., Yale Univ., 1978. 290pp. Abs., *DAI*, 40, 1979, 270A.

Describes the conflict among the writers' kinds of faith in the authority of enlightened "personal insight," and seventeenth-century notions of the Bible as the exclusive source of "saving truth."

675 Haskin, Dayton. "Studies in the Poetry of Vision: Spenser, Milton, and Winstanley." *Thought*, 56, 1981, 226–39. Addendum, 56, 1981, 240.

Review essay. Applies Frank Kermode's *Genesis of Secrecy* and its thesis about intertextual reading and writing to several recent studies on Milton and others. Contains remarks on Virginia Mollenkott's essay in *Milton and the Art of Sacred Song* (No. 866); various essays from *Milton Studies*, vol. 12; Joan Malory Webber's *Milton and His Epic Tradition* (see No. 3210); Francis C. Blessington's *"Paradise Lost" and the Classical Epic* (No. 1955); and Joseph Anthony Wittreich, Jr.'s *Visionary Poetics* (No. 1152).

676 Hayes, Noreen Luceil. "Some Implications of Milton's Philosophy of History." Doctoral diss., Northwestern Univ., 1969. 237pp. Abs., *DAI*, 30, 1970, 4452A.

Notes the influence of Renaissance humanism and church history on Milton's application of scriptural analogy and "the deterioration of the universe" to history.

677 **Hayes, Thomas W.** "Natural Law and Milton's Attack on Corruption." *BuR*, 23, 1977, 13–32.

Argues that Milton's "attack on political corruption during the English Civil Wars and his concern over the origins and causes of mankind's moral corruption throughout his poetry have a common basis in the concept of natural law."

678 **Hayes, Thomas Wilson.** *Winstanley the Digger: A Literary Analysis of Radical Ideas in the English Revolution.* Cambridge, MA, and London: Harvard Univ. Press, 1979. xii, 258pp.

Contains scattered references to Milton's works. Compares the writers.

679 **Helgerson, Richard.** "Milton and the Sons of Orpheus." *Self-Crowned Laureates: Spenser, Jonson, Milton, and the Literary System* (Berkeley, Los Angeles and London: Univ. of California Press, 1983), pp. 185–282.

Examines Milton's relationship with his contemporaries and conception of his poetic mission. Reviews (of book): Annabel Patterson, *JDJ*, 2, 1983, 91–106; Richard S. Ide, *Rev*, 7, 1985, 89–111; Helen Cooper, *RES*, 37, 1986, 85.

680 **Hendrix, Howard Vincent.** "The Ecstasy of Catastrophe: A Study of Apocalyptic Narrative from Langland to Milton." Doctoral diss., Univ. of California, Riverside, 1987. 388pp. Abs., *DAI*, 48, 1988, 2635A.

Sees in apocalyptic literature a clash between "the ethical world that ought to be" and "the ontological world that is," noting Milton's "Apocalypse within" that can only become a "Paradise within" via a "Christ-like life."

681 **Heninger, S. K., Jr.** "Sidney and Milton: The Poet as Maker." *Milton and the Line of Vision.* Ed. by Joseph

Anthony Wittreich, Jr. (Madison and London: Univ. of Wisconsin Press, 1975), pp. 57–95.

"There is no direct evidence that Milton was familiar with, or even aware of, Sidney's *Defence of Poesy*. It might seem unwarranted, therefore, if not downright perverse, to suggest that this treatise underlies the poetic theory adopted by Milton in his best (and best-known) poetry."

682 **Henry, Nathaniel H.** *The True Wayfaring Christian: Studies in Milton's Puritanism.* American Univ. Studies, Series 4, Vol. 53. New York: Peter Lang, 1987. 178pp.

Examines the theological influences on Milton and maintains that his works express the Christian Renaissance and that he deserves the same respect given to such theologians as Luther, Aquinas, and Calvin.

683 **Herford, C. H.** *Dante and Milton.* Folcroft, PA: Folcroft Library Editions, 1971.

Reprint of Stevens No. 2533, originally published in 1924.

684 **Hibbard, G. R.** "Sequestration into Atlantick and Eutopian Polities: Milton on More." *Ren&R*, 4, 1980, 209–25.

Compares Milton and Henry More by portraying Milton as a realist who denied the possibility of Plato's best attainable state.

685 **Hieatt, A. Kent.** *Chaucer, Spenser, Milton: Mythopoeic Continuities and Transformations.* Montreal and London: McGill-Queen's Univ. Press, 1975. xvii, 292pp.

Traces the continuity from one poet to the other of certain myths "concerned with how we ought to behave towards those who are dear to us." Chapters on Milton: "*Faerie Queene* II, III and *Comus*"; "Milton's and Our *Faerie Queene* II"; "Spenser and *Paradise Lost*"; "Spenser and *Paradise Regained*"; "Symbolic Network and Rectilinear Narrative"; and "Afterthoughts

on Chaucer, Spenser, and Milton."
Reviews: Donald Cheney, *SpenN*, 7,
1976, 37–39; John Mulryan, *Cithara*,
16, No. 1, 1976, 75–76; Arnold Stein,
SR, 84, 1976, 695–706; *MiltonQ*, 11,
1977, 23–24; Elizabeth Dipple, *MLQ*,
38, 1977, 304–06; John Buxton, *RES*,
28, 1977, 345–46.

686 Hill, Christopher. "Covenant Theol-
ogy and the Concept of a Public Per-
son." *Powers, Possessions and Freedom:
Essays in Honour of C. B. MacPherson.*
Ed. by Alkis Kontos (Toronto: Univ. of
Toronto Press, 1979), pp. 3–22.

Considers "the theological concept . . .
of the representative person, or public
person, or common person." Includes
Milton, for "Adam and Eve were public persons in *Paradise Lost*; so was
the Son of God in *Paradise Regained*;
so was Samson."

687 Hill, Christopher. "George Wither and
John Milton." *English Renaissance Studies
Presented to Dame Helen Gardner in
Honour of Her Seventieth Birthday.* [Ed.
by John Carey] (Oxford: Clarendon Press,
1980), pp. 212–27. Reprinted in *The
Collected Essays of Christopher Hill*
(Amherst: Univ. of Massachusetts Press,
1985), vol. 1, pp. 133–56.

Draws attention "to the many points
of similarity between the political careers and the political and religious ideas
of the two poets." Believes that such
a comparison can help us to understand that Milton was no unique and
lonely genius.

688 Hill, Christopher. "Milton and Marvell." *Approaches to Marvell.* The York
Tercentenary Lectures. Ed. by C. A.
Patrides (London and Boston, MA:
Routledge and Kegan Paul, 1978), pp.
1–30. Reprinted in *The Collected Essays
of Christopher Hill* (Amherst: Univ. of
Massachusetts Press, 1985), vol. 1, pp.
157–87.

Finds many political parallels between
the men's attitudes from their first
cooperation in 1649 until Milton's death

in 1674. Both believed that the world
can be changed by human effort.

689 Hill, Christopher. "Milton the Radical." *TLS*, Nov. 29, 1974, pp. 1330–32.
Discusses Milton's radicalism and libertine beliefs. Claims that Milton was
secretly a theological liberal who denied the concept of Trinitarianism and
"no longer felt tuned in to God." See
also Paul Helm and James M. Lewis,
TLS, Dec. 13, 1974, p. 1416. Helm
asserts that Hill's proof of Milton's
radicalism is flawed and that Milton
"cannot be tarred with the same brush"
as his contemporaries. Lewis declares
that Hill weakens his case for Milton's
radicalism by comparing him with John
Reeve and Lodowick Muggleton.

690 Hill, Christopher. *The World Turned
Upside Down: Radical Ideas During the
English Revolution.* London: Temple
Smith; New York: Viking Press, 1972.
351 pp.

Milton mentioned extensively. Links
Milton's prose and poetry with the ideas
of the radicals. See also Appendix 2:
"Milton and Bunyan: Dialogue with
the Radicals." Reviews: *TLS*, Aug. 18,
1972, p. 969; David Caute, *New Statesman*, 83, 1972, 872; W. J. Fischman,
HT, 22, 1972, 748–49; Albert H.
Johnston, *Publishers' Weekly*, 202,
1972, 50; John Kenyon, *Spectator*, 229,
1972, 54–55; R. R. Rea, *LJ*, 97, 1972,
3586; *VQR*, 49, 1973, cxxiii; Charles
Bazerman, *Nation*, 216, 1973, 537;
Thomas Wilson Hayes, *SCN*, 31, 1973,
5–6; Richard Schlatter, *AHR*, 78, 1973,
1052–55; Claire Cross, *EHR*, 89, 1974,
183–84; *Observer* (London), Aug. 31,
1975, p. 18.

691 Hill, John Spencer. *John Milton: Poet,
Priest and Prophet: A Study of Divine
Vocation in Milton's Poetry and Prose.*
London and Basingstoke: Macmillan;
Totowa, NJ: Rowman and Littlefield,
1979. xiv, 233 pp.

Defines vocation as the act of God's
calling a person to a state of salvation

and to perform some special function. Discusses Milton's changing concept of his vocation from 1625 to 1660 (ministerial, poetic, and prophetic). Includes chapters on the three long poems. Reviews: J. Martin Evans, *RES*, 31, 1980, 354–56; Edward Jones, *MiltonQ*, 14, 1980, 24–25; Michael Lieb, *Cithara*, 21, 1981, 58–70.

692 Hill, John Spencer. "Servant of God: The Theme of Divine Vocation in Milton." Doctoral diss., Univ. of Toronto, 1972. Abs., *DAI*, 34, 1974, 5174A–75A.

Argues that Milton uses divine vocation to justify his poetic career, prophetic identity, and arguments about the limits of holy service.

693 Himy, Armand. "Milton et la Féminité." *BSEAA*, 20, 1985, 37–48.

Holds that while at first view, Milton's attitude toward women is negative, his work also offers a defense of women and an illustration of the new relationship with women which becomes evident in the eighteenth century. All negative attitudes toward women stem from a fear of them and a desire to protect man and preserve his freedom.

694 Hinman, Robert B. "'A Kind of a *Christmas* Ingine': Jonson, Milton, and the Sons of Ben in the Hard Season." *Classic and Cavalier: Essays on Jonson and the Sons of Ben.* Ed. by Claude J. Summers and Ted-Larry Pebworth (Pittsburgh, PA: Univ. of Pittsburgh Press, 1982), pp. 255–78.

Discusses the affinities between Milton and Jonson and his followers in dealing with life in a fallen world.

695 Hirai, Masao, ed. *Milton and His Age.* Tokyo: Kenkyusha, 1975. 430pp.

In Japanese. Reviews: Jun Harada, *EigoS*, 121, 1975, 75; Takero Oiji, *SELit*, 52, 1975, 194–98.

696 Hirakawa, Taiji. "Milton and the Sense of Hearing." *MCJ News*, 9, 1987, 9–12.

Examines Milton's references to music in such works as "At a Solemn Music" and *Paradise Lost.*

697 Hirakawa, Yasuji. *Spenser to Milton: Kanshoukara Jissene.* Kyoto: Apollon, 1988. 340pp.

Spenser and Milton: From Contemplation to Action.

698 Hollander, John. *The Figure of Echo: A Mode of Allusion in Milton and After.* Berkeley: Univ. of California Press, 1981. x, 155pp.

Shows how "poems seem to echo prior ones for the personal aural benefit of the poet, and of whichever poetic followers can overhear the reverberations." Surveys echoes in Milton's poetry, passim. Reviews: Roy C. Flannagan, *MiltonQ*, 16, 1982, 53; David Krause, *SCN*, 41, 1983, 1–3.

699 Honeygosky, Stephen Raymond. "Milton's House of God: Church, Scripture, Sacrament." Doctoral diss., Univ. of Wisconsin, Madison, 1988. 644pp. Abs., *DAI*, 49, 1989, 2667A.

Notes Milton's redefinition of ecclesiastical terms to express his theological faith in the individual's potential and dignity.

700 Honeygosky, Stephen Raymond. *Milton's House of God: The Invisible and Visible Church.* Columbia: Univ. of Missouri Press, 1993. xiv, 255pp.

701 Howard, Donald R. "Flying through Space: Chaucer and Milton." *Milton and the Line of Vision.* Ed. by Joseph Anthony Wittreich, Jr. (Madison and London: Univ. of Wisconsin Press, 1975), pp. 3–23.

"Chaucer's influence on Milton, compared with Dante's or Virgil's, seems *de minimis.* Milton did not feel Chaucer as a burden. Chaucer's influence did not cause him anxiety. Milton conceived of Chaucer as he wanted to—selectively, with the misunderstandings and projections of his time and his persuasion. It is no reason for us to condescend to Milton, for we read Chaucer in the same selective way."

702 Hudson, William Henry. *Milton and His Poetry.* Folcroft, PA: Folcroft Library

Editions, 1969; New York: AMS Press, 1971, 1972; Norwood, PA: Norwood Editions, 1977; Philadelphia, PA: R. West, 1978.

Reprints of Stevens No. 2342, originally published in 1919.

703 Hughes, Merritt Y. "The Miltonic Future." *MLR*, 66, 1971, xxi–xxxii.

Surveys recent Milton scholarship and remarks on work in progress. Criticizes numerologists and the use of statistical evidence to date the long poems. Mentions Carey and Fowler, eds., *The Poems of John Milton* (No. 286); William Riley Parker, *Milton: A Biography* (No. 230); Ronald David Emma, *Milton's Grammar* (Huckabay No. 1768); Mindele Treip, *Milton's Punctuation* (No. 3166); Gunnar Qvarnström, *The Enchanted Palace* (No. 2892); Isabel G. MacCaffrey, *"Paradise Lost" as "Myth"* (Huckabay No. 1535), and many other recent studies.

704 Hunsaker, Orvil Glade. "Calvinistic Election and Arminian Reparation: A Striking Contrast in the Works of Roger Williams and John Milton." Doctoral diss., Univ. of Illinois, Urbana-Champaign, 1970. 220pp. Abs., *DAI*, 31, 1971, 6553A.

Explains how Williams's faith in the salvation of the elect and Milton's belief in the reparation of the Fall affect their views on human goodness, the "Books of Nature and Scripture," separation of church and state, and the writer as God's mouthpiece.

705 Hunsaker, O. Glade. " 'Luxurious by Restraint': Is Milton Too Austere for Tomorrow's Readers?" *Milton Reconsidered: Essays in Honor of Arthur E. Barker.* Ed. by John Karl Franson (Salzburg: Institut für Englische Sprache und Literatur, Universität Salzburg, 1976), pp. 193–215.

Believes that future readers will appreciate Milton's emphasis on self-discipline and self-development in all areas of life. "The future of Milton's art seems very promising indeed."

706 Hunsaker, Orvil Glade. "Roger Williams and John Milton: The Calling of the Puritan Writer." *Puritan Influences in American Literature.* Ed. by Emory Elliott. Illinois Studies in Language and Literature, 65 (Urbana, Chicago, and London: Univ. of Illinois Press, 1979), pp. 3–22.

Contrasts Milton's and Williams's views of the writer's role in society. Observes that Milton's Arminianism and resistance to the doctrine of predestination provided a basis for his faith in the poet's corrective power while Williams's doctrinal views prevented his sharing this high regard for the writer's calling.

707 Hunter, G. K. "Milton in Our Time." *SR*, 86, 1978, 414–21.

Review essay. Conclusion: "I worry that the elaboration of the packaging may devalue the product." Discusses John M. Steadman, *Epic and Tragic Structure in "Paradise Lost"* (No. 3100); Arnold Stein, *The Art of Presence* (No. 3111); *Milton Studies*, vols. 9 and 10; Arnold Stein, *Answerable Style* (Huckabay No. 1878); Boyd M. Berry, *Process of Speech* (No. 1939); John Broadbent and Robert Hodge, eds., *"Samson Agonistes," Sonnets, &c.* (No. 281); Christopher Hill, *Milton and the English Revolution* (No. 174); Edward Le Comte, *Milton and Sex* (No. 774); and A. L. Rowse, *Milton the Puritan* (No. 984).

708 Hunter, William B., Jr. *The Descent of Urania: Studies in Milton, 1946–1988.* Lewisburg, PA: Bucknell Univ. Press; London and Toronto: Associated Univ. Presses, 1989. 285pp.

A collection of twenty-one of Hunter's previously published essays, with one new study (see No. 184). In this bibliography, each essay is listed according to its appropriate classification. Reviews: Joseph Anthony Wittreich, Jr., *SCRev*, 8, 1991, 76–78; Gordon Campbell, *MLR*, 87, 1992, 700–01; G. R. Evans, *RES*, 43, 1992, 139.

709 Hunter, William B., Jr. "Herbert and Milton." *SCRev*, 1, 1984, 22–37.

A comparison of the two poets, especially their sonnets. "Indeed, the careers of the two men offer greater likeness until political and religious circumstances forced Milton into the Puritan camp because he had to cope with Laud. Herbert did not, and that made the difference."

710 Hunter, William B., Jr. "John Milton: Autobiographer." *MiltonQ*, 8, 1974, 100–04. Reprinted in *The Descent of Urania: Studies in Milton, 1946–1988* (Lewisburg, PA: Bucknell Univ. Press; London and Toronto: Associated Univ. Presses, 1989), pp. 100–05.

Relates Milton's autobiographical utterances to the Arminian tradition, which ignores a central conversion experience, unlike the Calvinistic tradition, and which embraces prevenient grace.

711 Hunter, William B., Jr. *Milton on the Nature of Man: A Study in Late Renaissance Psychology.* Folcroft, PA: Folcroft Library Editions, 1969; Norwood, PA: Norwood Editions, 1977.

Reprints of Huckabay No. 662, originally published in 1946.

712 Hunter, William B., Jr. "Milton's Laundry Lists." *MiltonQ*, 18, 1984, 58–61.

Criticizes the lists of proper names in Milton's poetry. Believes that even with the help of annotations, the lists made the poetry burdensome in Milton's day and make it more burdensome today.

713 Hunter, W. B., C. A. Patrides, and **J. H. Adamson.** *Bright Essence: Studies in Milton's Theology.* Salt Lake City: Univ. of Utah Press, 1971. ix, 181pp.

A collection of essays by the three authors who in the mid-1950s "came independently to the conclusion that critics had misunderstood Milton's religious beliefs, that he was not an Arian." Each author feels that the Son is central in Milton's thought. All of the essays are reprints, some with revisions, of works listed according to classification in this bibliography, except Hunter's retitled study, "The War in Heaven: The Exaltation of the Son" (No. 2454). Reviews: Maurice Kelley, *SHR*, 6, 1972, 418–19; Michael Lieb, *Cithara*, 12, 1972, 85–106; Edward E. Ericson, Jr., *CSR*, 2, 1973, 352–54; Roland Mushat Frye, *RenQ*, 26, 1973, 242–44; R. E. C. Houghton, *N&Q*, 20, 1973, 191–93; D. T. Mace, *RES*, 24, 1973, 210–13; James R. McAdams, *SCN*, 31, 1973, 70–72; Stella P. Revard, *JEGP*, 72, 1973, 128–32; Philip Sheridan, *CarnM*, 12, 1973, 147–49; P. Ma-lekin, *SN*, 46, 1974, 270–75.

714 Huntington Library Quarterly. Vol. 33, No. 4, Aug., 1970, 315–400.

A special issue on Milton edited by John M. Steadman. Contains essays by Maurice Kelley, J. Max Patrick, John T. Shawcross, Sacvan Bercovitch, Charlotte Otten, Frank S. Kastor, and Lee A. Jacobus. In this bibliography, each essay is listed according to author and classification.

715 Hutchinson, Mary Anne. "The Devil's Gateway: The Evil Enchantress in Ariosto, Tasso, Spenser, and Milton." Doctoral diss., Syracuse Univ., 1975. 234pp. Abs., *DAI*, 36, 1976, 6656A.

Follows the evolution of women's allegorical significance from Ariosto's Satanic enchantress to Milton's Eve, an innocent figure who unconsciously represents "the nature of her evil."

716 Hyman, Lawrence W. *The Quarrel Within: Art and Morality in Milton's Poetry.* Port Washington, NY, and London: Kennikat Press, 1972. vii, 128pp.

Examines "the difference between the doctrines that went into the poems and the moral significance that comes out of the poems." Discusses the *Nativity Ode*, *Lycidas*, the three long poems, *Comus*, and the sonnets. Reviews: *MiltonQ*, 6, No. 4, 1972, 97–98; Douglas Bush, *MLQ*, 34, 1973, 78–84; Roger Henry Sundell, *SCN*, 32, 1974, 1–2.

717 Ichikawa, Shuji. "John Milton and the Metaphysicals." *Shiron*, 27, 1988, 39–53.

718 Ide, Richard S. "Five Versions of Milton at Horton." *Rev*, 7, 1985, 89–111.
Review essay of recent books, each of which presents a different picture of Milton's Horton years: A. N. Wilson, *The Life of John Milton* (No. 275); Maryann Cale McGuire, *Milton's Puritan Masque* (No. 1583); Richard Helgerson, *Self-Crowned Laureates* (see No. 679); John Guillory, *Poetic Authority* (No. 2358); and William Kerrigan, *The Sacred Complex* (No. 2519).

719 Ide, Richard S., and **Joseph Anthony Wittreich, Jr.,** eds. *Composite Orders: The Genres of Milton's Last Poems.* *MiltonS*, vol. 17. Pittsburgh, PA: Univ. of Pittsburgh Press, 1983. xiv, 318pp.
A special volume. Contains essays by Earl Miner, O. B. Hardison, Jr., Barbara K. Lewalski, Balachandra Rajan, Thomas Amorose, Stanley Fish, Annabel M. Patterson, Stuart Curran, John T. Shawcross, Mary Ann Radzinowicz, John C. Ulreich, Jr., Ide, and Wittreich. In this bibliography, each essay is listed according to author and classification. Reviews: Michael Fixler, *RES*, 37, 1986, 307; Thomas N. Corns, *MLR*, 83, 1988, 149–51.

720 Imai, Hiroshi. "On Milton's Partisanship." *MCJ News*, 3, 1979, 3–4.
Notes Milton's changing political and religious views from 1641 to 1660.

721 Imazeki, Tsuneo. "Church Discipline and Liberty of Conscience in Cromwell, Milton, and Baxter." *MCJ News*, 11, 1989, 7–10.
Argues that Milton, Cromwell, and Richard Baxter were at once "libertarians and disciplinarians who tried to solve their problem by finding such people as had an affinity for disciplined liberty." These are the people they believed should be the ruling class of a free commonwealth.

722 Inafuku, Hideo. "Milton's Idea of Divorce and Its Significance in the History of Legal Thought." *MCJ News*, 9, 1987, 1–4.
Contrasts the views of marriage and divorce of Hegel, Kant, and Milton. Examines modern ideas about divorce and traces their origins back to these men.

723 Jackson, Robert S. "Michelangelo's Ricetto of the Laurentian Library: A Phenomenology of the Alinari Photograph." *Art Journal* (New York), 28, 1968–69, 54–59.
Comments on views expressed by Roy Daniells in *Milton, Mannerism and Baroque* (Huckabay No. 509).

724 Jarvis, Robin. "Three Men in a Drunken Boat: Milton, Wordsworth, Bloom." *Diacritics*, 13, 1983, 44–56.
Considers texts of Milton, Wordsworth, and Bloom as having a "fundamental interplay between literal and figurative meanings."

725 Jenkins, R. B. *Milton and the Theme of Fame.* The Hague and Paris: Mouton, 1973. 71pp.
Traces Milton's references to fame in three periods of his life: 1608–39, 1640–60, and 1660–74. Shows that Milton began with classical concepts and ended his career desiring the approval of God alone. Reviews: J. Max Patrick, *SCN*, 33, 1975, 93; Anthony Low, *MiltonQ*, 9, 1975, 20–27; *MiltonQ*, 10, 1976, 60.

726 Johnson, James T. "The Covenant Idea and the Puritan View of Marriage." *JHI*, 32, 1971, 107–18.
Shows "how man-wife relations among Puritans are conceived on models drawn from covenantal theology." Contrasts Puritan marriage and high Anglican marriage doctrines.

727 Johnson, Lee M. "Milton's Blank Verse Sonnets." *MiltonS*, 5, 1973, 129–53.
"At critical points in their destinies, characters in Milton's last three poems often speak in blank verse sonnets to pledge their acceptance of one another,

of themselves, or of divine purposes. . . . Milton's blank verse sonnets appear throughout the major poems and always in the conclusions of narrative or dramatic actions, where they help him impart a final, Christian perspective and form to the larger forms and structural patterns he inherits from classical epic and dramatic traditions."

728 Johnston, James E. "Milton on the Doctrine of the Atonement." *Renascence*, 38, 1985, 40–53.

Endorses the view of such writers as Anselm and insists that Milton believed in the satisfaction theory of atonement, wherein Christ pays the penalty incurred by Adam's offense against God, thus restoring relations between God and humanity. Emphasizes Christ's voluntary obedience to pay for humanity's sins and this theme's centrality to Milton's conception of the atonement.

729 Jonas, Leah. "John Milton." *The Divine Science: The Aesthetic of Some Representative Seventeenth-Century English Poets* (New York: Octagon Books, 1972), pp. 166–200.

Reprint of Huckabay No. 670, originally published in 1940.

730 Jones, Kenneth B. "Unknown Artist." *Country Life* (London), Feb. 14, 1974, p. 314.

Sends a sketch of Milton's cottage at Chalfont St. Giles, "apparently executed in 1892," and asks for suggestions concerning the name of the artist, whose initials are "G. A. D."

731 Jones, R. I. Stephens. "Eighteenth-Century Criticism of the Miltonic Simile." *MiltonQ*, 10, 1976, 113–19.

Cites positive and negative eighteenth-century comments on the Miltonic simile. Critics were usually concerned with relevance, and less often with pagan imagery and disruption of syntax and action.

732 Jortin, John. *Remarks on Spenser's Poems.* New York: Garland Publishing, 1970.

A facsimile of a 1734 edition, which includes "Remarks on Milton," pp. 171–86.

733 Kang, Nae Heui. "The Renaissance Representation of the Other: Travel Literature, Spenser, Shakespeare, and Milton." Doctoral diss., Marquette Univ., 1986. 400pp. Abs., *DAI*, 47, 1987, 4396A–97A.

Discusses how "appropriation, allegorization, mimesis, and figurization" are employed to portray "the Other"—a figure outside the status quo who represents a larger group.

734 Kantra, Robert A. "Miltonic and Other Utopians." *All Things Vain: Religious Satirists and Their Art* (University Park and London: Pennsylvania State Univ. Press, 1984), pp. 75–92.

Believes that there is a general neglect of Milton today.

735 Kato, Kazutoshi. "Milton's 'Good Old Cause' and Future Visions of England." *MCJ News*, 11, 1989, 15–17.

Abstract of a paper presented at the Twenty-Fourth Colloquium of MCJ in July, 1988. Argues that Milton's appeal to the "Good Old Cause" promoted a "nostalgia for the regicide Parliament of love in the minds of the Left" and that he hoped England would adopt religious and civil liberties via the revolution to take a step toward the "beatific vision" to be regained in the kingdom of God.

736 Kaul, R. K. "Milton and Spinoza: Forerunners of the Enlightenment." *EnlE*, 2, 1971, 30–39.

Advances the idea that Milton and Spinoza anticipate the Enlightenment. Claims a Miltonic influence on Spinoza's writings. Concludes that the two "attempted to emancipate the human mind from superstition, dogma, and obscurantism . . . [and] they asserted the right of the individual to interpret God's word."

737 Keeble, N. H. *The Literary Culture of Nonconformity in Later Seventeenth-Century England.* Leicester: Leicester

Univ. Press; Athens: Univ. of Georgia Press, 1987. xi, 356pp.

Contains many scattered references to Milton on the subject of nonconformity.

738 Kelley, Maurice. "Milton and the Trinity." *HLQ*, 33, 1970, 315–20.

Asserts Milton's Arian views, which "constitute a classic example of Renaissance anti-Trinitarianism." Abs., *MiltonN*, 3, 1969, 14.

739 Kendrick, Christopher. "Milton: A Study in Ideology and Form." Doctoral diss., Yale Univ., 1981. 321pp.

See *DAI*, 43, 1983, 2354A.

740 Kendrick, Christopher. *Milton: A Study in Ideology and Form.* New York and London: Methuen, 1986. x, 240pp.

Studies *Areopagitica* and *Paradise Lost* "in relation to the collective agency of revolution and as determinate acts within that agency, as symbolic revolutionary acts themselves." Argues that Milton is an early proponent of the capitalist system. Reviews: Douglas Chambers, *RES*, 39, 1988, 108–09; Marshall Grossman, *RenQ*, 41, 1988, 175–77; Richard Helgerson, *JEGP*, 87, 1988, 582–83; David Norbrook, *LRB*, 10, 1988, 20–21; Gordon Campbell, *MLR*, 84, 1989, 127–28; P. J. Klemp, *MiltonQ*, 24, 1990, 71–76.

741 Kermode, Frank, with **Stephen Fender** and **Kenneth Palmer.** *English Renaissance Literature: Introductory Lectures.* London: Gray-Mills Publishing, 1974. 145pp.

Contains lectures on Milton's long poems by Kermode and by Palmer. In this bibliography, each lecture is listed by author under the appropriate classification.

742 Kerrigan, William. "An Encomium for Edward Le Comte." *MiltonQ*, 20, 1986, 64–66.

Remarks delivered to the Milton Society of America in Chicago, 1985.

743 Kerrigan, William. "The Heretical Milton: From Assumption to Mortalism." *ELR*, 5, 1975, 125–66.

Discusses the evolution of Milton's beliefs. His early poems suggest a temperamental discomfort with mortal severance. He often solicits a double consolation, implying that in a just world some rest for the body would be found comparable to the rest of the soul. His formulation of the mortalist heresy, by presenting death as the illusion of instantaneous translation, solved to some degree this conflict between wish and doctrine.

744 Kerrigan, William Wallace. "Milton and the Drama of Prophecy." Doctoral diss., Columbia Univ., 1971. 348pp. Abs., *DAI*, 34, 1974, 7193A–94A.

Examines the history of prophetic inspiration and discusses its effect on Milton's reaction to a secular England, creation of inspired narrators, and view of eternity.

745 Kerrigan, William. *The Prophetic Milton.* Charlottesville: Univ. Press of Virginia, 1974. xi, 285pp.

Considers various theories of the prophet's divine mission—ancient, medieval, and Renaissance—and focuses on Milton's belief in his own prophetic mission. Examines the long poems and several of the prose tracts in the context of prophetic inspiration. See No. 2358. Reviews: *MiltonQ*, 9, 1975, 28–30; Joan Malory Webber, *MLQ*, 36, 1975, 434–37; Robert H. West, *SCR*, 8, 1975, 70–72; Charles A. Huttar, *CSR*, 5, 1976, 284–87; Mary Ann Radzinowicz, *RenQ*, 29, 1976, 458–61; Arnold Stein, *SR*, 84, 1976, 695–706; Joseph H. Summers, *MP*, 74, 1977, 420–23; Roger H. Sundell, *SCN*, 38, 1980, 42.

746 Khan, M. H. "Milton Revalued: The Modernist Stance in Milton Criticism." *Essays on John Milton: A Tercentenary Tribute.* Ed. by Asloob Ahmad Ansari (Aligarh: Aligarh Muslim Univ., 1976), pp. 1–15.

Discusses the criticism of F. R. Leavis, T. S. Eliot, and others in relation to nineteenth-century criticism of Milton.

747 Kirkconnell, Watson. "Milton: A Tercentenary Stock-Taking." *DR*, 49, 1969–70, 549–56.

Discusses tercentenary volumes edited by Balachandra Rajan (No. 2899), Alan Rudrum (Huckabay No. 873), and C. A. Patrides (No. 2848).

748 Knapp, Steven Marshall. "Personification and Poetic Ambivalence from Milton to Keats." Doctoral diss., Cornell Univ., 1981. 210pp. Abs., *DAI*, 42, 1981, 1647A.

Examines attempts to reconcile the ambivalence between literal and metaphoric elements of allegorical personifications, starting with Milton's episode about Sin and Death.

749 Knight, G. Wilson. *Chariot of Wrath: The Message of John Milton to Democracy at War.* Folcroft, PA: Folcroft Library Editions, 1969; Norwood, PA: Norwood Editions, 1976; Philadelphia, PA: R. West, 1977.

Reprints of Huckabay No. 683, originally published in 1942.

750 Knight, George Wilson. *Poets of Action: Incorporating Essays from "The Burning Oracle."* London: Methuen; New York: Barnes and Noble, 1967; Lanham, MD: Univ. Press of America, 1982. xvi, 302pp.

Includes reprints of selected chapters from previously published works. See Huckabay Nos. 683–85.

751 Knott, John R., Jr. "Milton and the Spirit of Truth." *The Sword of the Spirit: Puritan Responses to the Bible* (Chicago, IL, and London: Univ. of Chicago Press, 1980), pp. 106–30.

Finds a relationship between Milton's attitude toward the authority of the Scriptures and his belief in the dynamic operation of the Holy Spirit. Believes that Milton modified his thinking but finds continuities ranging from ideas in *Of Reformation* to the final statement in *Paradise Regained*. Review (of book): Austin C. Dobbins, *ELN*, 19, 1982, 291–93.

752 Koehler, G. Stanley. "Milton's Use of Color and Light." *MiltonS*, 3, 1971, 55–81.

Deals with the influence of the emblematic tradition and of classical literatures. Review: Michael Lieb, *Cithara*, 12, 1972, 85–106.

753 Koizumi, Toru. "The Discovery of the 'Third Culture'—A Stream in the Historiography on the English Revolution." *MCJ News*, 7, 1984, 1–3.

Examines Christopher Hill's evolving attitude toward Milton and the Civil Wars in *Milton and the English Revolution* (No. 174).

754 Kolojeski, Paul Francis. "Milton and Mani: A Confrontation." Doctoral diss., Southern Illinois Univ., Carbondale, 1977. 241pp. Abs., *DAI*, 38, 1977, 2811A.

Uses *Paradise Lost* and the *Christian Doctrine* to study Milton's arguments against historical and contemporary notions of Manichean dualism.

755 Konecny, Lubomir. "Young Milton and the Telescope." *JWCI*, 37, 1974, 368–73.

Believes that the "long and dark Prospective glass" of *Prolusion 6* (1628) refers to the telescope and that Milton derived it from the emblem books. The image appears again in *At a Vacation Exercise*.

756 Kononenko-Moyle, Natalie. "Homer, Milton, and Asik Veysel: The Legend of the Blind Bard." *HUS*, 3–4, 1979–80, 520–29.

Contends that the legend of the blind bard "reflects the reality of being a minstrel," for minstrels have chosen this field not because of talent but out of need. Milton's blindness signifies greatness, since "blindness serves as a visible stigma which more clearly marks those selected by God."

757 Korshin, Paul J. *Typologies in England: 1650–1820.* Princeton, NJ: Princeton Univ. Press, 1982. xvii, 437pp.

Milton is mentioned extensively. "His

typological scope is wider, far wider, than that of almost any other English writer of his age, and the influence of his practice on eighteenth-century attitudes towards figuralism is enormous."

758 Koyama, Kaoru. "Milton's View of Virtue." *MCJ News*, 7, 1984, 17–18.
Abstract of a paper presented at the Sixteenth Colloquium of MCJ in December, 1983. Examines three ways in which Milton portrays virtue: as a beautiful goddess, as a "powerful and reliable existence which shows itself at its best under the trial of vice," and as an idea connected with freedom.

759 Kranidas, Thomas. "A View of Milton and the Traditional." *MiltonS*, 1, 1969, 15–29.
"I am not denying 'tradition' in reading Milton. I am only warning against an oversimplified view of Milton's allegiance to tradition."

760 Kudò, Hiromasa. "A View of [the] Cambridge Period of John Milton—A Process of His Mind for a Poet." *English Studies, Graduates of Ryukoku, the Association*, No. 5, Dec., 1976, pp. 34–50.

761 Labriola, Albert C. "Milton's Use of Neo-Latin Reference Books." *MiltonQ*, 13, 1979, 27–28.
Abstract of a paper presented at the 1978 MLA Convention. Notes that "The medieval and Renaissance encyclopedias, dictionaries, thesauri, and lexicons available to Milton . . . unify and harmonize numerous strands of thinking and interpretation." Although "This syncretistic tradition is the context in which to interpret Milton," "No one can say how, where, when, and through what sources Milton acquired his comprehensive and syncretistic vision."

762 Labriola, Albert C., and **Michael Lieb,** eds. *"Eyes Fast Fixt": Current Perspectives in Milton Methodology. MiltonS*, vol. 7. Pittsburgh, PA: Univ. of Pittsburgh Press, 1975. xii, 311pp.
A special volume. Contributors are A. B. Chambers, Stanley E. Fish, Chris-

topher Grose, Ernst Häublein, B. Rajan, Philip Rollinson, Jason P. Rosenblatt, John T. Shawcross, John M. Steadman, Labriola, and Lieb. In this bibliography, each essay is listed according to author and classification. Reviews: Stanley Archer, *SCN*, 34, 1976, 1–2; Arnold Stein, *SR*, 84, 1976, 695–706; D. D. C. Chambers, *RES*, 28, 1977, 218–21; Elizabeth MacKenzie, *MLR*, 74, 1979, 901–03.

763 Landy, Marcia. " 'A Free and Open Encounter': Milton and the Modern Reader." *MiltonS*, 9, 1976, 3–36.
"Literature embodies not universal or essential truths, but ideas and values which, like the reader's own, are conditioned and limited by history. Thus, Milton's views of authority relations, power, marriage, kinship relations, dominance and subordination, and his use of typification to define normative and deviant behavior, are subject to evaluation, rejection, or acceptance in the light of modern conceptions, drawn partly from anthropological and sociological research."

764 Langdon, Ida. *Milton's Theory of Poetry and Fine Art.* Ann Arbor, MI: Univ. Microfilms International, 1980 Books on Demand Reprints.
Reprint of Stevens No. 2536, originally published in 1924.

765 Langford, Beverly Young. " 'Some Great Change': Aspects of Ovidian Metamorphosis in the Poetry of Spenser and Milton." Doctoral diss., Georgia State Univ., 1981. 189pp. Abs., *DAI*, 42, 1982, 4833A.
Claims that, by asserting the functional value of metamorphosis poetry, "Spenser and Milton release Ovid's poem from the confines of two-dimensional allegorical interpretation."

766 Langton, Larry Bruce. "Milton, J. A. Comenius, and Hermetic Natural Philosophy." Doctoral diss., Univ. of Wisconsin, Madison, 1977. 219pp. Abs., *DAI*, 38, 1978, 6144A.

Relates Milton's and Comenius's educational theories to hermeticism, which emphasizes empirical knowledge as a path to spiritual transformation and truth.

767 Larson, Martin Alfred. *The Modernity of Milton: A Theological and Philosophical Interpretation.* Folcroft, PA: Folcroft Library Editions, 1969; Norwood, PA: Norwood Editions, 1977; Ann Arbor, MI: Univ. Microfilms International, 1980 Books on Demand Reprints.

Reprints of Stevens No. 2591, originally published in 1927.

768 Lawry, Jon S. *The Shadow of Heaven: Matter and Stance in Milton's Poetry.* Ithaca, NY: Cornell Univ. Press, 1968. xv, 416pp.

"In these discussions, I have followed Milton in calling his subjects 'matter.' The devices of participation within the subject by author and audience I call 'stance.'" Contains chapters on the early poetry but gives most attention to the three long poems. Reviews: Margaret Dalziel, *AUMLA*, 33, 1970, 119–21; Harry Rusche, *Criticism*, 12, 1970, 157–60; *TLS*, June 11, 1970, p. 641; F. T. Prince, *RES*, 22, 1971, 206–08.

769 Le Comte, Edward. "Ambiguous Milton." *Greyfriar*, 25, 1984, 25–36. Reprinted in *Milton Re-Viewed: Ten Essays* (New York and London: Garland Publishing, 1991), pp. 83–94.

Deals with obscure passages in Milton's poetry and prose. Appendix: "Something Old and Something New on That Two-Handed Engine."

770 Le Comte, Edward. "By Sex Obsessed." *MiltonQ*, 8, 1974, 55–56.

A rebuttal of John T. Shawcross (No. 3039), with a reply by Shawcross, pp. 56–57. Le Comte believes that Shawcross goes too far in finding sexual puns, and Shawcross is bothered most "that there are some people who simply can not accept even the possibility . . . that sexual matters can emerge consciously . . . from such moral authors as Milton."

771 Le Comte, Edward. *A Dictionary of Puns in Milton's English Poetry.* New York: Columbia Univ. Press; London: Macmillan, 1981. xxii, 238pp.

Finds seven classifications of puns in Milton's poetry and lists some 1,630 in alphabetical order. Contains an index of the poems' puns. Reviews: *BBN*, Aug., 1981, p. 500; Galbraith M. Crump, *SR*, 89, 1981, 628; Robert T. Logan, III, *HSL*, 13, 1981, 189–90; Robin Robbins, *TLS*, May 8, 1981, p. 522; *ARBA*, 13, 1982, 678; Archie Burnett, *MiltonQ*, 16, 1982, 12–16; reply by Le Comte, pp. 79–80.

772 Le Comte, Edward. "Douglas Bush Remembered." *The American Scholar*, 53, 1984, 390–95. Reprinted in *Milton Re-Viewed: Ten Essays* (New York and London: Garland Publishing, 1991), pp. 25–34.

An account of Bush's academic career, including his contributions to Milton studies.

773 Le Comte, Edward. "In Defence of *Variorum Commentary II.*" *MiltonQ*, 10, 1976, 122–24.

A response to criticisms of No. 1838, including Arthur Sherbo's remarks (No. 1027); the review of vol. 4 of the *Variorum Commentary* (No. 3386) in *MiltonQ*, 10, 1976, 58–59; and Stanley E. Fish's observations (No. 593).

774 Le Comte, Edward. *Milton and Sex.* New York: Columbia Univ. Press, 1978. x, 154pp.

Studies Milton's sexual orientation, views on marriage, and attitude toward women and sex. Reviews: *MiltonQ*, 12, 1978, 70; G. K. Hunter, *SR*, 86, 1978, 414–21; E. R. Gregory, *SCN*, 38, 1980, 42–43; Joseph Anthony Wittreich, Jr., *Rev*, 1, 1979, 123–64; John B. Broadbent, Jr., *TLS*, Mar. 17, 1978, p. 322; Fitzroy Pyle, *N&Q*, 26, 1979, 248–49; Mark Halliday, *EIC*, 29, 1979, 269–79; reply by Le Comte, *EIC*, 30, 1980, 189; Charles A. Huttar, *C&L*, 29, 1979, 62–64.

775 Le Comte, Edward. *Milton's Unchanging Mind: Three Essays.* Foreword by Douglas Bush. Port Washington, NY, and London: Kennikat Press, 1974. viii, 123pp.

Contains three essays: "Milton versus Time"; "*Areopagitica* as a Scenario for *Paradise Lost*"; and "The Satirist and Wit." The first essay is a psycho-biographical account of Milton's concept of time as it applied to his own career. The second provides details for the statement that *Areopagitica* looks back to the once planned Arthuriad and also contains hints of *Paradise Lost*. The third essay is a reprint of Huckabay No. 698, originally published in 1967. Reviews: *MiltonQ*, 8, 1974, 58–59; Pierre Legouis, *EA*, 28, 1975, 219–20; Anthony Low, *MiltonQ*, 9, 1975, 20–27; Andrew M. McLean, *SHR*, 10, 1976, 362–69; Edwin B. Benjamin, *RenQ*, 30, 1977, 125–27; Edgar F. Daniels, *SCN*, 35, 1977, 2.

776 Le Comte, Edward. "Remarks by Edward Le Comte as Honored Scholar at the Milton Society Dinner, Chicago, 12/28/85." *MiltonQ*, 20, 1986, 66–68.

Speaks mainly about his career as a Miltonist. Is appreciative of the work of other Milton scholars.

777 Le Comte, Edward. *Sly Milton: The Meaning Lurking in the Contexts of His Quotations.* East Meadow, NY: English Studies Collections, 1976. 15pp. Revised in *Greyfriar*, 19, 1978, 3–28. Reprinted in *Milton Re-Viewed: Ten Essays* (New York and London: Garland Publishing, 1991), pp. 51–81.

Uses quotations from *Elegy 3* through *Samson Agonistes* in light of their sources to show that "sly Milton" frequently makes sexual allusions in his poetry. Review: Edgar F. Daniels, *SCN*, 25, 1977, 1–2.

778 Le Comte, Edward. *Yet Once More: Verbal and Psychological Pattern in Milton.* New York: AMS Press, 1969.

Reprint of Huckabay No. 700, originally published in 1954. Review:

Gordon W. Huott, *SCN*, 28, 1970, 24–25.

779 Lejosne, Roger. "John Milton (1608–1674) et les Voies de Dieu." *Le Juste et L'injuste à la Renaissance et à l'Age Classique.* Institut d'Études de la Renaissance et de l'Age Classique (Publications de l'Université de Saint-Etienne, 1986), pp. 251–57.

Believes that human liberty and natural dignity are central to Milton's conception of human and divine justice.

780 Lejosne, Roger. *La Raison dans l'Oeuvre de John Milton.* Études Anglaises, 80. Paris: Didier-Erudition, 1981. 544pp.

Studies Milton's conception of reason and considers the contemporary relationship between human reason and divine revelation. Reviews: Jacques Blondel, *BSEAA*, 10, 1980, 127–31; Leo Miller, *MiltonQ*, 16, 1982, 78–79; Irène Simon, *EA*, 40, 1987, 209–11.

781 Lever, Katherine. "Classical Scholars and Anglo-Classic Poets." *CJ*, 64, 1969, 216–18.

Notes that both Milton and Chaucer concluded their poetic careers by testing the truth of the classics.

782 Levin, Harry. *The Myth of the Golden Age in the Renaissance.* Bloomington and London: Indiana Univ. Press, 1969; Oxford: Oxford Univ. Press, 1972. 231pp.

Discusses Milton, passim. Points out that "although Milton absorbed the whole of classical mythology in his world view, the golden age itself has a marginal place in that spacious prospect."

783 Lewalski, Barbara Kiefer. "Milton: Revaluation of Romance." *Four Essays on Romance.* Ed. by Herschel Baker (Cambridge, MA: Harvard Univ. Press, 1971), pp. 55–70.

Milton's poems frequently use romance elements—such as the perilous journey in *Comus* and the Garden of Eden in *Paradise Lost*—to revaluate the themes, motifs, and attitudes characteristic of this mode. Ultimately, however, Milton sees a heroic poem as one based on true events, not fables. Abs., *MiltonQ*, 4, 1970, 13. Review (of book): Joseph Anthony Wittreich, Jr., *Genre*, 5, 1972, 307–25.

784 Lewis, Linda Marlene. "Titanic Rebellion: The Promethean Iconography of Milton, Blake and Shelley." Doctoral diss., Univ. of Nebraska, Lincoln, 1987. 215pp. Abs., *DAI*, 48, 1988, 2067A.

Argues that Milton, Blake, and Shelley employ the Promethean myth "for their respective views on tyrant and rebel, power and impotence, revolution and the status quo."

785 Lieb, Michael. "Milton among the Monks." *Milton and the Middle Ages.* Ed. by John Mulryan (Lewisburg, PA: Bucknell Univ. Press; London and Toronto: Associated Univ. Presses, 1982), pp. 103–14.

Places Milton in the tradition of antimonastic satire and discusses his contempt for the monks, especially as expressed in the *History of Britain*.

786 Lieb, Michael. "Milton and the Kenotic Christology: Its Literary Bearing." *ELH*, 37, 1970, 342–60.

Claims that Milton has a kenotic interpretation, and that he reveals it in the *Christian Doctrine*. Disagrees with William B. Hunter, Jr. (Huckabay No. 661 and No. 2454) that Milton shuns this doctrine of Christ's "emptying himself of his Godhead." Points out kenotic references in *Paradise Lost* and other poems.

787 Lieb, Michael. "Milton and the Metaphysics of Form." *SP*, 71, 1974, 206–24.

Argues that Milton integrates "Platonic and Aristotelian conceptions of form."

788 Lieb, Michael. "Milton and the Organicist Polemic." *MiltonS*, 4, 1972, 79–99.

"The pervasive influence of organicism in the Renaissance is especially discernible in religious controversies that

distinguished between the visible and invisible church." Milton associates the body politic with outward concerns, the body ecclesiastical with inward ones. When the two bodies are unnaturally joined, a monster results. "Milton's organicist views, therefore, reflect not a desire to destroy, as might be charged, but a desire to make whole."

789 Lieb, Michael. "Recent Work on Milton: An Overview." *MiltonQ*, 11, 1977, 66–76.

Surveys more than thirty books published in 1975 and 1976, as well as a few that appeared in 1974. Discusses editions, Walter MacKellar's *Variorum Commentary*, vol. 4 (No. 3386), Jackson Campbell Boswell's *Milton's Library* (No. 9), collections of essays, and critical studies. Concludes that future scholarhip will be indebted to the achievements of the present works.

790 Lieb, Michael. "The Sinews of Ulysses: Exercise and Education in Milton." *JGE*, 36, 1985, 245–56.

Delineates Milton's positive regard for physical exercise as demonstrated in his writings.

791 Lieb, Michael. *The Sinews of Ulysses: Form and Convention in Milton's Works.* Pittsburgh, PA: Duquesne Univ. Press, 1989. 174pp.

Suggests different approaches to Milton's use of form and convention. Form and convention, conceived as pedagogical, metaphysical, polemical, theological, and generic categories, offer important evidence for understanding Milton's thought and practices as a writer. Reviews: John Mulryan, *Cithara*, 29, 1989, 74–75; James H. Sims, *SCN*, 49, 1991, 38–40; Alvin Snider, *PQ*, 70, 1991, 257–60; M. J. Doherty, *MiltonQ*, 26, 1992, 46–52; Stella P. Revard, *MP*, 89, 1992, 400–02; Nigel Smith, *RES*, 43, 1992, 110–14.

792 Lieb, Michael. "Some Recent Studies of Milton." *Cithara*, 21, 1981, 58–70.

Review essay that demonstrates how

"Milton scholarship continues to flourish in a number of forms." Discusses Raymond Anselment, *Betwixt Jest and Earnest* (see No. 3766); John Spencer Hill, *John Milton: Poet, Priest and Prophet* (No. 691); Clay Hunt, *"Lycidas" and the Italian Critics* (No. 1449); Thomas E. Maresca, *Three English Epics* (see No. 2653); Louis L. Martz, *Poet of Exile* (No. 820); Michael Murrin, *The Allegorical Epic* (see No. 2769); Mary Ann Radzinowicz, *Toward "Samson Agonistes"* (No. 3666); and Murray Roston, *Milton and the Baroque* (No. 2954).

793 Lieb, Michael. "A Survey of Recent Milton Scholarship: A Review Article." *Cithara*, 12, 1972, 85–106.

Examines books "that suggest consolidation [of information and of critical viewpoints] and those that suggest fresh lines of response" to the study of Milton: Douglas Bush, J. E. Shaw, A. Bartlett Giamatti, and A. S. P. Woodhouse, *Variorum Commentary*, vols. 1 and 2 (Nos. 1236 and 1838); *Milton Studies*, vol. 3; Joseph Anthony Wittreich, Jr., ed., *Calm of Mind* (No. 1142); W. B. Hunter, C. A. Patrides, and J. H. Adamson, *Bright Essence* (No. 713); John T. Shawcross, ed., *The Complete Poetry of John Milton* (No. 297); John Broadbent, *"Paradise Lost": Introduction* and an edition of Books 1 and 2 (No. 281); French Fogle and J. Max Patrick, eds., *Complete Prose Works of John Milton*, vol. 5 (No. 366); Don M. Wolfe, *Milton and His England* (No. 277); John R. Knott, Jr., *Milton's Pastoral Vision* (No. 2540); Harry Blamires, *Milton's Creation* (No. 1949); John E. Seaman, *The Moral Paradox of "Paradise Lost"* (No. 3020); Burton Jasper Weber, *The Construction of "Paradise Lost"* (No. 3212); and Angus Fletcher, *The Transcendental Masque* (No. 1358).

794 Lieb, Michael. "Three Monographs on Milton: An Assessment." *MP*, 74, 1976, 204–12.

Review essay of Burton Jasper Weber, *Wedges and Wings* (No. 3475); Keith W. Stavely, *The Politics of Milton's Prose Style* (No. 3986); and Hugh M. Richmond, *The Christian Revolutionary* (No. 971).

795 Liljegren, S. B. *Studies in Milton.* Folcroft, PA: Folcroft Library Editions, 1969.

Reprint of Stevens No. 2437, originally published in 1918.

796 "The Living Milton." *TLS*, Nov. 15, 1974, p. 1284.

Favorably reviews the Milton Exhibition held in the King's Library of the British Museum from 1973–75.

797 Lloyd, Markland Gale. "Milton and the Concept of Christian Liberty: A Study of the Influence of the Pauline Gospel on Milton's Major Poetry." Doctoral diss., Ohio Univ., 1975. 247pp. Abs., *DAI*, 36, 1976, 7439A.

Explores Milton's belief—influenced by Paul's letters—that Christian freedom is an internal surrender to God's grace, rather than an attempt to earn it, as expressed in his three long poems.

798 Loewenstein, David Andrew. "Milton and the Drama of History: From the Revolutionary Prose to the Major Poems." Doctoral diss., Univ. of Virginia, 1985. 353pp. Abs., *DAI*, 47, 1987, 3434A.

Explains Milton's view of history as "God's drama"—a dynamic process, full of conflicts both necessary and destructive.

799 Long, Anne B. "'She May Have More Shapes than One': Milton and the Modern Idea that Truth Changes." *MiltonS*, 6, 1974, 85–99.

"Controversies in science lead to new formulations of truth. When contradiction arises, individuals should wait patiently for the new paradigm. Milton similarly believes that God accommodates truth to man's abilities."

800 Lord, George de Forest. *Classical Presences in Seventeenth-Century English Poetry.* New Haven, CT, and London:

Yale Univ. Press, 1987. viii, 224pp.
A collection of previously published essays. Those dealing with Milton include the following: "Pretexts and Subtexts in Milton's Renaissance Homer"; "Milton's Translation of Epic Conventions"; and "Homeric Mockery in Milton and Pope." Reviews: David Hopkins, *N&Q*, 35, 1988, 530–31; John Steadman, *RenQ*, 41, 1988, 358–60; Raymond B. Waddington, *ELN*, 25, 1988, 94–96.

801 Low, Anthony. *Love's Architecture: Devotional Modes in Seventeenth-Century English Poetry.* New York: New York Univ. Press, 1978. xix, 307pp.
Mentions Milton often, sometimes in contrast with other poets.

802 Low, Anthony. "A Review of Milton Studies, 1974." *MiltonQ*, 9, 1975, 20–27; corrigendum, p. 126.
Concludes that 1974 was a good year for scholarship on Milton, even though the statistics on scholarly publishing are gloomy in general. Reviews several tercentenary volumes including David Shelley Berkeley, *Inwrought with Figures Dim* (No. 1200); Donald F. Bouchard, *Milton: A Structural Reading* (No. 492); Ralph Waterbury Condee, *Structure in Milton's Poetry* (No. 538); R. B. Jenkins, *Milton and the Theme of Fame* (No. 725); A. G. George, *Milton and the Nature of Man* (No. 2287); Edward Le Comte, *Milton's Unchanging Mind* (No. 775); Leo Miller, *John Milton among the Polygamophiles* (No. 838); Thomas Wheeler, *"Paradise Lost" and the Modern Reader* (No. 3229); *Milton Studies*, vol. 6; and a special issue of *Études Anglaises* (No. 582). Also reviews some editions: Samuel E. Sprott, ed., *"A Maske": The Earlier Versions* (No. 321); David Aers and Mary Ann Radzinowicz, eds., *"Paradise Lost," Books VII–VIII* (No. 281); C. A. Patrides, ed., *Selected Prose* (No. 361); and Robert W. Ayers, ed., *Complete*

Prose Works of John Milton, vol. 7 (No. 366).

803 Low, Sampson. *Giants of Literature: Milton.* Maidenhead: Sampson Low, 1977. 136pp.
First published in Italian (Milan: Arnoldo Mondadori Editore, 1968). Deals with Milton's life and times and gives background information. Contains extracts from *Paradise Lost* and comments on Milton's characters and changing reputation. Many illustrations from various artists, especially Blake.

804 Lowell, James Russell. *Essays on the English Poets.* Port Washington, NY: Kennikat Press, 1970.
Reprint of the 1888 edition. Includes an essay on Milton.

805 Lowery, William Raymond. "John Milton, Henry More, and Ralph Cudworth: A Study in Patterns of Thought." Doctoral diss., Northwestern Univ., 1970. 277pp. Abs., *DAI*, 31, 1971, 5413A.
Describes the differences among the writers' views of scriptural interpretation, the production and use of human knowledge, and religious toleration.

806 Lunger-Knoppers, Laura. "Happy Nuptial League: Milton's Covenantal Concept of Marriage." *CEA*, 48–49, 1986, 56–64.
Argues that the language of covenant and league is central to the long poems and that Milton first sets forth his theory of covenant in the divorce tracts.

807 Lutaud, Olivier, introd. *Prélude au Matin d'un Poète: Such Sights as Youthful Poets Dream: Traditions Humanistes chez le Jeune Milton.* Paris: Centre d'Histoire des Idées dans les Iles Britanniques, Université de Paris IV, Sorbonne, 1983. 77pp.
A collection of essays by Sarah Olivier, Angiola Maria Volpi, Jean Pironon, Marie-Madeleine Martinet, and Lutaud. In this bibliography, each essay is listed according to author and classification.

808 MacCabe, Colin. "'So Truth be in the Field': Milton's Use of Language." *Teaching the Text.* Ed. by Susanne Kappeler and Norman Bryson (London: Routledge and Kegan Paul, 1983), pp. 18–34.

Surveys twentieth-century commentary on Milton's use of poetic language. Defends Milton's works and discusses his language apart from its historical conditions.

809 MacCallum, Hugh. "Milton and Poetic Form." *UTQ,* 50, 1981, 314–23.

Review essay. Discusses Louis L. Martz, *Poet of Exile* (No. 820); Joseph Anthony Wittreich, Jr., *Visionary Poetics* (No. 1152); Edward W. Tayler, *Milton's Poetry* (No. 1082); Stella Purce Revard, *The War in Heaven* (No. 2926); and John G. Demaray, *Milton's Theatrical Epic* (No. 2128).

810 Mackail, J. W. *The Springs of Helicon: A Study in the Progress of English Poetry from Chaucer to Milton.* New York: Longmans, Green, and Co., 1976, 1984.

Reprints of Stevens No. 2345 and Huckabay No. 721, originally published in 1909.

811 Madsen, William G. *From Shadowy Types to Truth: Studies in Milton's Symbolism.* Ann Arbor, MI: Univ. Microfilms International, 1980 Books on Demand Reprints.

Reprint of Huckabay No. 727, originally published in 1968. Reviews: R. E. C. Houghton, *N&Q,* 213, 1968, 386–88; John R. Mulder, *SCN,* 27, 1969, 41; Karina Williamson, *SN,* 41, 1969, 432–34; J. M. Couper, *AUMLA,* 31, 1969, 97–99; Peter Malekin, *RES,* 20, 1969, 225–27; Ants Oras, *SR,* 77, 1969, 176–84; Earl Miner, *ECS,* 3, 1970, 296–305.

812 Magliocco, Maurine Marie Fisk. "The Function of Humor in the Works of John Milton." Doctoral diss., Univ. of Oklahoma, 1975. 307pp. Abs., *DAI,* 36, 1976, 6707A–08A.

Investigates Milton's use of humor "as an alternative vehicle for imparting serious meaning" or, less frequently, as an aesthetic device valuable in its own right.

813 Malekin, Peter. *Liberty and Love: English Literature and Society, 1640–88.* New York: St. Martin's Press, 1981. x, 219pp.

Contains scattered references to Milton and two chapters on him: "Milton: The Political Pamphlets and *Paradise Lost*" and "Milton: From Tracts on Divorce to *Paradise Lost.*" Believes that the publication of Milton's radical prose reflects a growing tolerance in England, that the substance of freedom is lacking in *Paradise Lost,* and that "Milton's insistence on the dignity of marriage and his advocacy of divorce for incompatibility . . . had a wider and beneficial influence."

814 Malpezzi, Frances M. "*Ministerium Verbi:* The Christian Aesthetics of the Renaissance and Seventeenth-Century Tuning Poets." Doctoral diss., Univ. of Nebraska, Lincoln, 1973. 203pp. Abs., *DAI,* 34, 1974, 7713A.

Asserts the tendency of Renaissance and seventeenth-century poets to act as guiding priests, often by creating a persona who has "undergone a tuning experience, i.e., the process of spiritual regeneration."

815 Manuel, M. *The Seventeenth Century Critics and Biographers of Milton.* Folcroft, PA: Folcroft Library Editions, 1977; Norwood, PA: Norwood Editions, 1978.

Reprints of Huckabay No. 729, originally published in 1962.

816 Marilla, Esmond Linworth. *Milton and Modern Man: Selected Essays.* Preface by Douglas Bush. Ann Arbor, MI: Univ. Microfilms International, 1980 Books on Demand Reprints.

Reprint of Huckabay No. 731, originally published in 1968. Review: Virginia R. Mollenkott, *SCN,* 27, 1969, 25–26.

817 Marshall, Margaret Willey. "Milton and Heresy: Guide Lines for a Sketch." *Critical Essays on English Literature.* Presented to Professor M. S. Duraiswami. Ed. by V. S. Seturaman (Madras: Orient Longmans, 1965), pp. 40–56.

Feels that the thrust of Milton's life and thought was dedicated to condemning the assumption that humans already know truth and need not seek further. To Milton, heresy is not knowing why one believes as one does.

818 Martindale, Charles. "Poetry in Eclipse." *TLS*, Feb. 5–11, 1988, p. 142.

Reviews recent studies of Milton. Believes that "Too often Miltonists seem to be talking mainly to each other" and that "it is a worrying thought that few ordinary educated persons interested in Milton would be likely to want to read any of these books." Discusses Joseph Wittreich, *Interpreting "Samson Agonistes"* (No. 3758); John M. Steadman, *Milton and the Paradoxes of Renaissance Heroism* (No. 1055); William Myers, *Milton and Free Will* (No. 882); Kathleen M. Swaim, *Before and After the Fall* (No. 3131); Hugh MacCallum, *Milton and the Sons of God* (No. 2637); and William B. Hunter, ed., *Milton's English Poetry: Being Entries from "A Milton Encyclopedia"* (No. 50).

819 Martyn, W. Carlos. *Life and Times of John Milton.* Philadelphia, PA: R. West, 1978.

Reprint of Stevens No. 2048, originally published in 1866.

820 Martz, Louis L. *Poet of Exile: A Study of Milton's Poetry.* New Haven, CT, and London: Yale Univ. Press, 1980. x, 356pp. Second edition (*Milton: Poet of Exile*), 1986.

Considers the body of Milton's poetic output and sees the 1645, 1667, and 1671 volumes as a triptych. The first is joyous; the second, somber; the third, austere. Contains two appendices: "*Paradise Regain'd* and the *Georgics*"

and "*Amor* and *Furor*: Anti-Heroic Themes and the Unity of Ovid's *Metamorphoses.*" Reviews: Roy Flannagan, *MiltonQ*, 14, 1980, 63–64; Robert M. Adams, *NYRB*, June 26, 1980, pp. 46–48; Michael Lieb, *Cithara*, 21, 1981, 58–70; Hugh MacCallum, *UTQ*, 50, 1981, 314–23; Don E. Ray, *Mosaic*, 12, 1981, 101–02; Edward W. Tayler, *RenQ*, 34, 1981, 292–94; Laurence Lerner, *CL*, 34, 1982, 76–78; Barbara Kiefer Lewalski, *JEGP*, 81, 1982, 262–64; Hugh M. Richmond, *CLIO*, 11, 1982, 302–04; Alan Rudrum, *ELN*, 19, 1982, 284–86; Joseph Anthony Wittreich, Jr., *MLQ*, 42, 1981, 184–91; William A. McQueen, *SHR*, 17, 1983, 77–79; David Loewenstein, *SCN*, 46, 1988, 7–8.

821 Masson, David. *The Three Devils: Luther's, Milton's, and Goethe's with Other Essays.* Norwood, PA: Norwood Editions, 1977.

Reprint of Stevens No. 2078, originally published in 1874.

822 Matar, N. I. "Milton and the Idea of the Restoration of the Jews." *SEL*, 27, 1987, 109–24.

Examines the inconsistencies between Milton's support in *Paradise Regained* of the restoration of the Jews and his lack of participation in a Cromwellian conference concerned with their admission into England in 1655. Concludes that this apparent irony was due to "Milton's limits of toleration which did not extend to Catholics or to unconverted Jews." Argues that Milton viewed Jews as "delayed Christians" and hoped that their restoration would lead to Christian conversion.

823 Mathew, Vempazatharayil John. "Milton's Conception of Heroism." Doctoral diss., St. Louis Univ., 1972. 257pp. Abs., *DAI*, 33, 1972, 1145A.

Clarifies "the relationship between Milton's conception of heroism and his idea of Christian magnanimity" in *Paradise Lost, Paradise Regained*, and *Samson Agonistes.*

824 Maynard, Winifred. "Milton and Music." *John Milton: Introductions.* Ed. by John Broadbent (Cambridge: Cambridge Univ. Press, 1973), pp. 226–57.

Discusses music in daily life and in education, especially Milton's; his interest in the music of the spheres; Milton and Henry Lawes. Lists some of Milton's works which have been set to music.

825 McCanles, Michael. "Milton and the Dialectic of Power." *MiltonQ*, 9, 1975, 34.

Abstract of a paper presented at the University of Wisconsin, Milwaukee, Milton Tercentenary Conference, in November, 1974. Discusses what *Paradise Lost*, *Paradise Regained*, and *Samson Agonistes* have in common regarding power.

826 McDill, Joseph Moody. *Milton and the Pattern of Calvinism.* Folcroft, PA: Folcroft Library Editions, 1969, 1974; Norwood, PA: Norwood Editions, 1975, 1976; Philadelphia, PA: R. West, 1977.

Reprints of Huckabay No. 739, originally published in 1942.

827 McKinney, Terri Rae. "Developing Theological Patterns in John Milton's Poetry." Doctoral diss., Louisiana State Univ., 1981. 177pp. Abs., *DAI*, 42, 1981, 1162A.

Discovers in Milton's poetry the beginnings of what would develop into an "unorthodox theological position: ex deo creation, mortalism, antitrinitarianism."

828 McLachlan, Herbert. *The Religious Opinions of Milton, Locke, and Newton.* Folcroft, PA: Folcroft Library Editions, 1970, 1974, 1975, 1976; Norwood, PA: Norwood Editions, 1976, 1977; Philadelphia, PA: R. West, 1977.

Reprints of Huckabay No. 740, originally published in 1941.

829 McLean, Andrew M. "Milton from Different Perspectives—A Review Essay." *SHR*, 10, 1976, 362–69.

Notes that "a sampling of some recent books and collections of essays on Milton appearing over the last six years indicates the variety and vitality of present Milton scholarship." Reviews *Milton Studies*, vols. 3–5; Michael Lieb and John T. Shawcross, eds., *Achievements of the Left Hand* (No. 3904); Edward Le Comte, *Milton's Unchanging Mind* (No. 775); Maurice Kelley, ed., *Complete Prose Works of John Milton*, vol. 6 (No. 366); Angus Fletcher, *The Transcendental Masque* (No. 1358); Joseph E. Duncan, *Milton's Earthly Paradise* (No. 2158); Anthony Low, *The Blaze of Noon* (No. 3615); Hugh M. Richmond, *The Christian Revolutionary* (No. 971); and Donald F. Bouchard, *Milton: A Structural Reading* (No. 492).

830 Meiklejohn, Mrs. Alyn C. "An Answer to A Note from Milton's Cottage." *MiltonN*, 3, 1969, 58.

The cottage curator's wife replies to Robert French (No. 617).

831 Meller, Horst. *Das Gedicht als Einübung: Zum Dichtungsverständnis William Empsons.* Heidelberg: Carl Winter—Universitätsverlag, 1974.

A 1968 dissertation for the University of Heidelberg. The entire work is a critical estimation of William Empson's ideas about poetry. In Part 3 ("Die Literarische Szene als Moralisches Tribunal: Zum Kontext von Milton's God," pp. 145–75), Meller writes four chapters evaluating Empson's approach to Milton. As an agnostic, Empson argues that much of the appeal of *Paradise Lost* lies in its subtle disparagement of the Christian concept of God.

832 Merrill, Harry G., III. "Climate of Opinion: Glanvill, Milton, Science in *Paradise Lost*." *TPB*, 19, 1982, 15–16.

Abstract of paper presented. "All existing statements by Milton show his thorough agreement with the Baconian objectives which moved the Royal Society."

833 Mikolajczak, Michael A., ed. "The Great Consult." *SCN*, 33, 1975, 53–58.

Abstracts of thirty-one papers delivered at the Milton tercentenary conferences of the University of Wisconsin, Milwaukee, Marquette University, and the University of Wisconsin, Parkside. Also includes commentary on the conferences.

834 Mikolajczak, Michael A. "The Second International Milton Symposium, August 8–12, 1983, Chalfont St. Giles and Christ's College, Cambridge. A Report with Abstracts of Papers." *SCN*, 42, 1984, 29–33.

835 Miller, David M. *John Milton: Poetry.* Twayne's English Authors Series. Boston, MA: Twayne Publishers; London: George Prior Publishers, 1978. 199pp.
A "spiritual" reading of several poems: the *Nativity Ode, L'Allegro* and *Il Penseroso, Comus, Lycidas, Paradise Lost, Paradise Regained,* and *Samson Agonistes.* Traces the emergence of Milton's central vision from the minor genres to the major ones. Reviews: Edward Jones, *MiltonQ,* 13, 1979, 22–23; Anna Karen Nardo, *SCN,* 37, 1979, 70–71; Lynn Veach Sadler, *C&L* 1980, 117–18.

836 Miller, George. "Teaching Milton to Undergraduates." *MiltonQ,* 12, 1978, 138–41.
Teaches Milton by using lectures and discussion periods, which are supplemented by tutorials.

837 Miller, Leo. "The Burning of Milton's Books in 1660: Two Mysteries." *ELR,* 18, 1988, 424–37.
In 1660, Charles II issued a royal proclamation to call in and burn certain books that defended the regicide sentence. But some books, including gift copies from Milton, were probably hidden in the Bodleian Library to avoid being burned; we cannot determine whether any books by Milton were at Cambridge University in 1660.

838 Miller, Leo. *John Milton among the*

Polygamophiles. New York: Loewenthal Press, 1974. xii, 378pp.
Discusses Milton's personal reasons for believing in polygamy and outlines his argument for it in the *Christian Doctrine.* The body of this study traces the idea through western history and concludes with the case of King Charles II. Appendices: "Plural Marriage in Milton's *History of Britain*"; "Milton's Reputation as Polygamophile, 1644–1717"; "Discussion of Polygamy in England after Milton's Time: M.P.'s and Methodists"; "Discussion of Polygamy in Germany after [Johan] Leyser: Thomasius, Willenberg"; and "Latter Day Polygamophiles." Reviews: *MiltonQ,* 8, 1974, 87–88; Anthony Low, *MiltonQ,* 9, 1975, 20–27; Christopher Hill, *N&Q,* 23, 1976, 27–28.

839 Miller, Leo. "The Tercentenary in Great Britain." *MiltonQ,* 8, 1974, 120–21.
Reports on miscellaneous events, including programs at Chalfont St. Giles, St. Giles Cripplegate, and Cambridge, and an exhibit at the British Museum.

840 Milner, Andrew J. "John Milton and the English Revolution: A Study in the Sociology of Literature." Doctoral diss., London School of Economics, 1977.

841 Milner, Andrew J. *John Milton and the English Revolution: A Study in the Sociology of Literature.* Totowa, NJ: Barnes and Noble; London: Macmillan, 1981. vii, 248pp.
Argues that the "'third circle' of Milton's views is homologous to the rationalist world vision of the revolutionary section of the English bourgeoisie" and discusses both the prose and the poetry from this point of view. Final chapter: "A Note on Christopher Hill's Milton" (see No. 174). Reviews: Archie Burnett, *N&Q,* 29, 1982, 441–42; Robert Thomas Fallon, *MiltonQ,* 16, 1982, 16–20; Robin Robbins, *TLS,* July 31, 1981, p. 888.

842 "Milton Center of Japan." *MiltonQ,* 9, 1975, 126.

On the inaugurating general assembly, held at Doshisha Women's College of Liberal Arts, Kyoto, on July 18, 1975. Also reported by J. Max Patrick, *SCN*, 25, 1977, 21–22.

843 "Milton Society Dinner." *MiltonQ*, 11, 1977, 21–22.

Reports on the 1976 meeting with a summary of J. Max Patrick's address, "Milton in Perspective." Also reported in *SCN*, 35, 1977, 14–15.

844 "Milton Society Dinner, 1974, and the M.L.A. Convention." *MiltonQ*, 9, 1975, 19–20.

Discusses the annual meeting and summarizes C. A. Patrides's talk, "Lude in Pace."

845 "Milton Society Meeting, San Francisco." *MiltonQ*, 10, 1976, 23–24.

Reports on the proceedings and contains an abstract of Joseph Wittreich's address, "From Pastoral to Prophecy: *Lycidas* in Context."

846 "Milton Society of America." *SCN*, 40, 1982, 9–10.

Report by Albert C. Labriola on the 1981 meeting, where John T. Shawcross was named honored scholar. See also *MiltonQ*, 16, 1982, 27–28.

847 "Milton Society of America. Report on Annual Meeting." *SCN*, 38, 1980, 14.

Report by Albert C. Labriola. James Thorpe was the principal speaker and Balachandra Rajan the honored scholar.

848 *Milton Tercentenary: Catalogue of an Exhibition Commemorative of the Tercentenary of the Birth of John Milton, 1608–1908, Including Original Editions of His Poetical and Prose Works, Together with Three Hundred and Twenty-Seven Engraved Portraits. Held at the Grolier Club . . . December 3, 1908 to January 9, 1909.* Folcroft, PA: Folcroft Library Editions, 1974; Norwood, PA: Norwood Editions, 1977; Philadelphia, PA: R. West, 1978.

Originally printed in 1908.

849 "Milton's Cottage." *PMLA*, 91, 1976, 300.

An appeal for assistance in preserving the cottage and its contents at Chalfont St. Giles. See also *MiltonQ*, 11, 1977, 122, and 14, 1980, 74.

850 Milward, Peter, S. J. "Milton." *The Continuity of English Poetry: Christian Tradition and Individual Poets* (Tokyo: Hokuseido Press, 1974), pp. 39–55.

A general discussion of Milton's prose and poetry. Feels that his poetry looks forward to the Romantic period.

851 Milward, Peter. "Milton's Idea of Woman." *English Literature and Language* (Tokyo), 19, 1983, 7–22.

Analyzes Milton's changing views on women. Believes that he never overcame his bitter experience with Mary Powell and that the Chorus in *Samson Agonistes* expresses his final unfavorable view.

852 Milward, Peter, S. J. "Puritan Endurance." *The Heart of England* (Tokyo: Hokuseido Press, 1976), pp. 38–48.

An appreciative account of Milton's poetry, focusing on the theme of Puritan endurance. "It is a pity there are so few students in Japan—even students of English Literature—who have read these poems."

853 Miner, Earl. "Milton and the Histories." *Politics of Discourse: The Literature and History of Seventeenth-Century England.* Ed. by Kevin Sharpe and Steven N. Zwicker (Berkeley: Univ. of California Press, 1987), pp. 181–203.

"In what follows I shall argue that Milton's sense of interpretation is 'literal' in the vexed Renaissance Protestant sense, and that although he assumed typology, analogy, and perhaps allegory, he essentially held to a single final sense that may be termed historical in a secular sense and a matter of faith inspired by the Holy Spirit in a religious sense."

854 Miner, Earl. "Plundering the Egyptians: or, What We Learn from Recent Books on Milton." *ECS*, 3, 1970, 296–305.

Review essay that welcomes the

apparent revival of historical scholarship and believes that it rests on sound critical assumptions. Discusses the following books: Anne Davidson Ferry, *Milton and the Miltonic Dryden* (No. 2201); Stanley Eugene Fish, *Surprised by Sin* (No. 2216); Barbara Kiefer Lewalski, *Milton's Brief Epic* (No. 3379); William G. Madsen, *From Shadowy Types to Truth* (No. 811); William Riley Parker, *Milton: A Biography* (No. 230); C. A. Patrides, *Milton and the Christian Tradition* (No. 933); and John M. Steadman, *Milton and the Renaissance Hero* (No. 1056).

855 **Miyagawa, Noboru.** "Genealogy of Similes—From Homer to Milton." *MCJ News*, 6, 1983, 10–11.
Abstract of paper presented. Milton's similes "are distinctly characteristic of him and not to be found in works by Homer, Virgil, or Dante."

856 **Mody, Jehangir R. P.** *Vondel and Milton.* Norwood, PA: Norwood Editions, 1977.
Originally published in 1942. Part 1 discusses the controversy about Vondel's alleged influence on Milton, and Part 2 provides a translation of Vondel's *Lucifer.*

857 **Mohanty, Christine.** "Death by Water in Milton." *MiltonQ*, 14, 1980, 122–26.
Surveys Milton's references to death by water but points out that the poet ultimately transcends his concern because of his belief in baptism by water.

858 **Mohanty, Christine Ann.** "Water Imagery in the Poetry of John Milton: Death and Regeneration." Doctoral diss., State Univ. of New York, Stony Brook, 1986. 320pp. Abs., *DAI*, 47, 1986, 1736A.
Identifies water as "a catalyst for transforming death into everlasting life" especially in *Lycidas*, but also in *Comus, Paradise Lost, Paradise Regained*, and *Samson Agonistes.*

859 **Mollenkott, Virginia Ramey.** "The Bible and Women Today." *TQ*, 16, 1973, 58–65.

Mentions Milton's concept of free will in the Fall. Concentrates on the idea of scriptural repression of women's liberation.

860 **Mollenkott, Virginia R.** "Milton and the Apocrypha." *MiltonQ*, 9, 1975, 34.
Abstract of a paper presented at the University of Wisconsin, Milwaukee, Milton Tercentenary Conference, in November, 1974. Shows that Milton reinforced "canonical support for various doctrines with references to the Apocrypha."

861 **Mollenkott, Virginia R.** "Milton and Women's Liberation: A Note on Teaching Method." *MiltonQ*, 7, 1973, 99–103.
Believes that Milton has been misread and that "clarification of Milton's position on issues as pressing as the equality of women must be made in the classroom by professors in full grasp both of contemporary problems and of Miltonic attitudes."

862 **Mollenkott, Virginia Ramey.** "Milton the Awakener." *Christianity Today*, 19, 1974, 120–27.
Believes that Milton can still "inspire us to climb toward the highest reaches of human nature" in a "technological world he could not possibly foresee."

863 **Mollenkott, Virginia Ramey.** "Milton's Mortalism: Treatise vs. Poetry." *SCN*, 26, 1968, 51–52.
"Milton's mortalist 'heresy' is confined to explicit statement in his theological treatise [the *Christian Doctrine*] and is not embodied in any of his poems."

864 **Mollenkott, Virginia R.** "Milton's Technique of Multiple Choice." *MiltonS*, 6, 1974, 101–11.
"Milton presented his readers with two or more possible interpretations of certain situations for the following purposes: to avoid committing himself on issues where he himself was doubtful; to recognize the mysteries of the universe; to make his plot more intriguing; to create a bridge between Hebraic mythological exclusiveness and

Hellenic richness; and to provide ironic commentary on the human condition."

865 Mollenkott, Virginia Ramey. "An Overview of Milton Studies, 1977." *MiltonQ*, 12, 1978, 77–82.

States that although there may be fewer publications on Milton, the quality remains high in 1977. Notes a trend to move away from viewing Milton in isolation and cites Paul Sherwin's *Precious Bane* (No. 4509) and *Milton Studies*, vol. 10 as attempts "to provide specific contexts for reading Milton." Also reviews John Karl Franson, ed., *Milton Reconsidered* (No. 614); Russell Fraser, *The Language of Adam* (No. 2244); S. Ramakrishnan, *The Epic Muse* (No. 2904); and Arnold Stein, *The Art of Presence* (No. 3111).

866 Mollenkott, Virginia Ramey. "The Pervasive Influence of the Apocrypha in Milton's Thought and Art." *Milton and the Art of Sacred Song*. Ed. by J. Max Patrick and Roger Henry Sundell (Madison: Univ. of Wisconsin Press, 1979), pp. 23–43.

Cites numerous examples of Milton's borrowings from the Apocrypha but concludes, "Both in his poetry and in his prose, Milton used the Apocrypha in a fashion which distinctively subordinated it to the Canon." See No. 675.

867 Moore, John Rees. "Milton and the Life to Come." *Shenandoah*, 31, 1980, 79–100.

Asserts that "the experience of freedom requires disobedience which requires death which requires sexual generation which requires guilt which requires . . . life as we know it. And only the miracle of Christ can lead to redemption."

868 Morahan, Richard Edward. "I. Samuel Johnson and William Lauder's Milton Forgeries. II. Poetry in Space: Disjunction in Language and Stage Action in Jonson's *Sejanus*. III. Jane Austen's Endings." Doctoral diss., Rutgers Univ., 1971. 123pp. Abs., *DAI*, 32, 1971, 3318A–19A.

Reinterprets Johnson's reaction to the claim of plagiarism brought against Milton as praise for the poet's "imitation of nature."

869 Morison, William. *Milton and Liberty.* Folcroft, PA: Folcroft Library Editions, 1970, 1972, 1976; Norwood, PA: Norwood Editions, 1977; Philadelphia, PA: R. West, 1978.

Reprints of Stevens No. 2346, originally published in 1909.

870 Morita, Katsumi. "The Operation of the Divine Spirit in Milton—From *Paradise Lost* to *Samson Agonistes*." *MCJ News*, 9, 1987, 22–23.

Abstract of a paper presented at the Nineteenth Colloquium of MCJ in July, 1985. Argues that in *Paradise Lost*, *Paradise Regained*, and *Samson Agonistes*, Milton uses the word "motion" to indicate the operation of divine grace on humans.

871 Morkan, Joel. "An Examination of Satiric Elements in the Early Works of John Milton." Doctoral diss., Northwestern Univ., 1969. 151pp. Abs., *DAI*, 30, 1970, 4418A.

Defines the satire in Milton's pre-revolutionary poetry and prose as "wrathful indignation" designed to purify the English church and society.

872 Morkan, Joel. "Wrath and Laughter: Milton's Ideas on Satire." *SP*, 69, 1972, 475–95.

Claims that Milton's defense of satire is within the Christian context and contends that Milton primarily discusses two areas of satire: its use and its nature. States that "satire is a shield" and ridicule a legitimate tool "in a war against the forces of evil, error, and superstition."

873 Morris, Joseph William. *John Milton: A Vindication, Specially from the Charge of Arianism.* Folcroft, PA: Folcroft Library Editions, 1977.

Reprint of Stevens No. 2039, originally published in 1862.

874 Moser, Willard Cummings. "The Meaning of 'Soul' and 'Spirit' in the Later Works of John Milton." Doctoral diss., Tulane Univ., 1968. 177pp. Abs., *DA*, 29, 1969, 3150A–51A.

Argues that Milton believes the soul to be immaterial but inseparable from the body—uniting, in fact, with the body as humans transform "from gross matter to pure spirit."

875 Muir, Kenneth. "Personal Involvement and Appropriate Form in Milton's Poetry." *EA*, 27, 1974, 425–35.

On Milton's private circumstances which colored his writings on marriage, politics, blindness, and human nature. Points out, however, that his own emotions were channeled for "precise purposes of art which Milton believed to be divinely inspired." He used memory for this purpose and sought the appropriate form, which he usually found.

876 Muldrow, George McMurry. *Milton and the Drama of the Soul: A Study of the Theme of the Restoration of Man in Milton's Later Poetry.* The Hague and Paris: Mouton, 1970. 270pp.

Studies the theme of human restoration in Milton's later poetry. Relies heavily on the *Christian Doctrine* as a gloss on the poems. Chapters on *Paradise Lost*, *Paradise Regained*, and *Samson Agonistes*. Appendix: "A Note on the Probable Date of *Samson Agonistes*." Accepts the traditional post-Restoration date. Reviews: *MiltonQ*, 5, 1971, 60–61; William B. Hunter, Jr., *RenQ*, 25, 1972, 373–74; Peter S. Macaulay, *EngS*, 54, 1973, 289–91.

877 Mulryan, John, ed. *Milton and the Middle Ages.* Lewisburg, PA: Bucknell Univ. Press; London and Toronto: Associated Univ. Presses, 1982. 189pp.

Contains essays by Paul Murphy Dowling, Ellen Goodman, Albert C. Labriola, Michael Lieb, William Melczer, Paul F. Reichardt, Jason P. Rosenblatt, Edward Sichi, Jr., and John C. Ulreich, Jr. In this bibliography, each essay is listed according to author and classification. Review: Roy C. Flannagan, *MiltonQ*, 17, 1983, 19–20.

878 Murray, Patrick. "Milton as Myth: A Reassessment." *Studies*, 63, 1974, 59–69.

Surveys the comments of Milton's detractors from Anthony Wood to T. S. Eliot. Concludes that Eliot's remarks amounted to propaganda and that apologetic criticism is no longer needed. Feels that William Riley Parker's *Milton: A Biography* (No. 230) has laid many myths to rest.

879 Mutschmann, Heinrich. *Milton's Eyesight and the Chronology of His Works.* Folcroft, PA: Folcroft Library Editions, 1969, 1971; New York: Haskell House, 1971; Norwood, PA: Norwood Editions, 1975; Philadelphia, PA: R. West, 1977.

Reprints of Stevens No. 2540, originally published in 1924.

880 Mutschmann, Heinrich. *Milton's Projected Epic on the Rise and Future Greatness of the Britannic Nation.* Folcroft, PA: Folcroft Library Editions, 1969; Norwood, PA: Norwood Editions, 1976.

Reprints of Huckabay No. 1618, originally published in 1936.

881 Mutsuura, Keison. "Milton and Science." *MCJ News*, 3, 1979, 29–30.

Abstract of a paper presented at the Fifth Colloquium of MCJ in July, 1978. Feels that science had moral connotations for Milton and that it opened new horizons to him.

882 Myers, William. *Milton and Free Will: An Essay in Criticism and Philosophy.* London, New York, and Sydney: Croom Helm, 1987. 258pp.

Argues against the deconstructors concerning free will and insists that Milton is its champion. Draws support from John Henry Newman, Henry James, Pope John Paul II, and "a cloud of other witnesses." Reviews: Stanley

Archer, *SCN*, 46, 1988, 8; Peter Barry, *English* (Oxford), 37, 1988, 74–81; Thomas N. Corns, *N&Q*, 35, 1988, 535–36; G. R. Evans, *RES*, 39, 1988, 604–05; Charles Martindale, *TLS*, Feb. 5–11, 1988, p. 142; Thomas F. Healy, *MLR*, 84, 1989, 717–18; P. J. Klemp, *MiltonQ*, 24, 1990, 71–76.

883 Myhr, Ivar Lou. *The Evolution and Practice of Milton's Epic Theory.* Folcroft, PA: Folcroft Library Editions, 1969, 1976; Norwood, PA: Norwood Editions, 1977; Philadelphia, PA: R. West, 1978.

Reprints of Huckabay No. 777, originally published in 1942.

884 Nagaoka, Kaoru. "Freedom and State in Milton's Thought." *MCJ News*, 1, 1976, 2–3.

Abstract of a paper presented at the First Annual Conference of MCJ in July, 1975. "It was the core of Milton's political philosophy . . . that a local society, a community, should be renovated into a free cooperative society, not into merely a reorganized one."

885 Nakano, Nancy Yoshiko. "The Authority of Narrative: Technique and Argument in Milton, Bunyan, Dryden, and John Reynolds." Doctoral diss., Univ. of California, Los Angeles, 1973. 203pp. Abs., *DAI*, 34, 1974, 7199A.

Explores the common purpose—"the manifestation of divine truth"—of seventeenth-century writers as expressed through various narrative techniques, such as the skewed plot of *Paradise Lost.*

886 Nakayama, Osamu. "The Development of Milton's Educational Thought from *Of Education* to *Paradise Lost.*" *SES*, 3, 1978, 1–15.

Analyzes *Of Education* and Milton's ideas about education in *Paradise Lost.* There are distinct differences, brought about mainly by the failure of the revolution.

887 Nelsen, Donald. "Laughter in Paradise: The Humor of John Milton." *ArtSci*, 66, 1966, 35–40.

Discusses humor in the poetry and the prose. Shows that Milton was a master of the satiric and ironic.

888 Nemoianu, Virgil. "Milton si Radicalii Sai." *SXX*, 20, 1972, 19–21.

Explores the radical ideas of Milton and other intellectual figures of seventeenth-century England. Focusing on Milton's pamphlets, compares his radicalism to Saint-Just's, and believes that Milton's ideas were those of a true revolutionary, rather than of a compromising reformer.

889 Neuse, Richard. "Milton and Spenser: The Virgilian Triad Revisited." *ELH*, 45, 1978, 606–39.

Points out similarities between the authors. Claims that Milton's roots are in Spenser, who drew from Virgil. Abs., *MiltonQ*, 11, 1977, 60.

890 Neve, Philip. *Cursory Remarks on Some of the Ancient English Poets, Particularly Milton.* Folcroft, PA: Folcroft Library Editions, 1969, 1978; Norwood, PA: Norwood Editions, 1980.

Reprints of the 1789 edition.

891 Newlyn, Lucy. "For the Fallen." *TLS*, Aug. 8, 1986, p. 871.

Review essay. Notes the influence of Harold Bloom and Stanley Fish on the books reviewed. Concludes that a modern Milton scholar must choose between Bloom's belief in a narrator who celebrates the Fall as a liberation from "Our Great Forbidder" or Fish's contention that "an omniscient narrator . . . betrays the reader into fallen assumptions as part of a humiliating programme of education and reform." Discusses Barbara Kiefer Lewalski, *"Paradise Lost" and the Rhetoric of Literary Forms* (No. 2592); Richard J. DuRocher, *Milton and Ovid* (No. 2161); Cedric C. Brown, *John Milton's Aristocratic Entertainments* (No. 1226); Richard Allen Shoaf, *Milton, Poet of Duality* (No. 1030); Paul Stevens, *Imagination and the Presence of Shakespeare* in *"Paradise Lost"* (No. 3116); and Dustin H. Griffin, *Regaining Paradise* (No. 4323).

892 Newman, John Kevin. "The English Tradition: Chaucer and Milton." *The Classical Epic Tradition* (Madison: Univ. of Wisconsin Press, 1986), pp. 339–98.

Exposes Milton's deep roots in and use of the classical tradition.

893 Nicolson, Marjorie Hope. *John Milton: A Reader's Guide to His Poetry.* London: Thames and Hudson, 1970; New York: Farrar, Straus and Giroux, 1973.

Reprints of Huckabay No. 786, originally published in 1963.

894 "Northeast MLA, April, 1976." *MiltonQ*, 10, 1976, 24.

Contains abstracts of papers by Lawrence W. Hyman, Robert Crosman, and Sharon C. Seelig.

895 Nordell, Roderick. "Words to the Wise, 1674–1974." *Christian Science Monitor*, Jan. 23, 1974, p. 1.

Offers several quotations from Milton's prose for the benefit of candidates during the 1974 American election campaign.

896 Norford, Don. "The Sacred Head: Milton's Solar Mysticism." *MiltonS*, 9, 1976, 37–75.

"Milton aspires to light, to free himself from the body. A celebrant of the solar Logos, he is preoccupied with the conflict between spirit and nature and the frightening possibility of the dissolution of consciousness. The central figures in Milton's poems are associated with the death and rebirth of the sun."

897 Norford, Don. "Some Versions of Milton." *MLQ*, 40, 1979, 292–306.

Reviews Mary Ann Radzinowicz, *Toward "Samson Agonistes"* (No. 3666); Joseph Anthony Wittreich, Jr., *Visionary Poetics* (No. 1152); and Joan Malory Webber, *Milton and His Epic Tradition* (see No. 3210).

898 Noro, Yuko. "Milton's Heroism—From a Single Great Leader to the 'Senate.'" *MCJ News*, 4, 1980, 12–13.

Abstract of a paper presented at the Eighth Colloquium of MCJ in December, 1979. Uses Sonnet 16 (to Cromwell) and Sonnet 17 (to Vane) to show that Milton "entertained two types of ideal hero, a single great leader in transition and a magistrate very similar to a member of 'the Senate,' which was later to become the core of his ideal state."

899 Nyquist, Mary Ellen, and **Margaret W. Ferguson,** eds. *Re-Membering Milton: Essays on the Texts and Traditions.* New York and London: Methuen, 1987. xviii, 362pp.

A collection of essays that "reconstruct" Milton's image as an author and cultural figure. Contributors include Abbe Marilyn Blum, Richard Bradford, Eleanor Cook, Terry Eagleton, Stanley Eugene Fish, Kenneth Gross, John Guillory, Richard Louis Halpern, Carolivia Herron, Robin Jarvis, Christopher Kendrick, Mary Loeffelholz, Herbert Marks, David Quint, David Riede, and Nyquist. In this bibliography, essays are listed according to author and classification. Reviews: *BBN*, Nov. 1987, p. 772; Thomas N. Corns, *N&Q*, 36, 1989, 394–95; Margarita Stocker, *TLS*, Jan. 27, 1989, p. 90; Rachel Trubowitz, *SCN*, 48, 1991, 55–56; Marilyn R. Farwell, *CL*, 44, 1992, 97–101.

900 O'Brien, Gordon W. "Milton, Hermes, and the Rhetoric of Mental Flight." *CaudaP*, 7, 1988, 1–8.

Discusses Milton's images of flight from the early poetry to *Paradise Lost*.

901 Ochi, Fumio. "The Aesthetics of Spiritual Exploration and Telescopic Vision in Milton's Poems." *AnRS*, 28, 1977, 38–67.

In Japanese. Discusses the images of flying in Milton's poetry, especially in *Paradise Lost*. Notes that the epic is structured around heaven, earth, and hell, which requires flying imagery. The many geographical references are a result of Milton's living in an age of discovery and exploration.

902 Ochi, Fumio. "A Note on the Recent Milton Revival, 1967–1971." *AnRS*, 23, 1972, 36–57.

In Japanese. Describes the rise of Milton studies in England, America, and Japan and discusses this revival in terms of the tercentenary of Milton's death.

903 Ochi, Fumio. "On the Occasion of the Establishment of 'The Milton Center of Japan.'" *MCJ News*, 1, 1976, 1–2.

On July 18, 1975, at Doshisha Women's College, Kyoto.

904 Ochi, Fumio. *Waga Milton tanbou: Kenkyu to Zuiso*. Tokyo: Sion-sha, 1986. vi, 236pp.

My Search for Milton: Studies and Essays.

905 Ogden, James. "Raleigh's Splendid Handbook on Milton." *Essays on Sir Walter Raleigh 1988*. Ed. by Asloob Ahmad Ansari (Aligarh: Aligarh Muslim Univ. Press, 1988), pp. 49–59.

An appreciative discussion of Raleigh's *Milton* (see Stevens No. 2226).

906 Ohkawa, Akira. "Milton and Tragedy." *CEMF*, 20, 1977, 13–21.

In Japanese. Discusses Milton's interest in drama and views on tragedy.

907 Ohkawa, Akira. "Milton's View of Shakespeare." *CEMF*, 19, 1975, 29–36. In Japanese.

908 Oiji, Takero. "Milton's Puritanism." *English Renaissance and Religion: From More to Milton*. Ed. by Shonosuke Ishii and Peter Milward (Tokyo: Aratake Press, 1975), pp. 159–201.

In Japanese. A brief history of Milton's reception in Japan since the Meiji period, mainly by Japanese Protestants, who introduced him primarily for his poetry's religious substance rather than its artistic value. Puritanism, which often blocks the acceptance of Milton, worked as a medium for his introduction in Japan.

909 O'Keeffe, Timothy J. *Milton and the Pauline Tradition: A Study of Theme and Symbolism*. Washington, DC: Univ. Press of America, 1982. xi, 343pp.

Discusses motifs in the Epistles "as symbolic strands providing a basis for interpreting the meaning of Christianity as Milton understood it." Focuses mainly on the prose and on *Paradise Lost*. Review: Philip J. Gallagher, *MiltonQ*, 16, 1982, 99–101.

910 O'Keeffe, Timothy J. "St. Paul, Milton, and the Reformation." *MiltonQ*, 9, 1975, 34–35.

Abstract of a paper presented at the University of Wisconsin, Milwaukee, Milton Tercentenary Conference, in November, 1974. Believes that the Pauline Epistles "generated a tradition of Commentaries, from St. John Chrysostom to John Calvin, which formed a basis for Milton's mature thought on the nature of man and evil."

911 Oleson, Clinton W. "Milton and the Concept of the Sovereignty of the State." Doctoral diss., Univ. of Chicago, 1968.

912 Olson, Mar Jean Lillian. "Emerson's Personal Search for a Hero: His Early Lectures on Shakespeare and Milton." Doctoral diss., Univ. of Florida, 1987. 280pp. Abs., *DAI*, 48, 1988, 2062A.

Describes Emerson's failure to locate a "perfect man"; Shakespeare is dismissed because of his "unsavory private life," and Milton because of his views on human depravity and necessary grace.

913 Ong, Walter J., S. J. "Logic and the Epic Muse: Reflections on Noetic Structures in Milton's Milieu." *Achievements of the Left Hand: Essays on the Prose of John Milton*. Ed. by Michael Lieb and John T. Shawcross (Amherst: Univ. of Massachusetts Press, 1974), pp. 239–68.

Discusses Ramist method and memory, Ramist logic and the epic as knowledge storage and retrieval, and logic and *Paradise Lost*.

914 Oram, William Allan. "The Disappearance of Pan: Some Uses of Myth in Three Seventeenth-Century Poets." Doctoral diss., Yale Univ., 1973. 324pp. Abs., *DAI*, 34, 1973, 3423A.

Analyzes Drayton's, Milton's, and Herrick's attempts to convey truth to a world that increasingly regarded mythology as "old-fashioned, false or simply meaningless."

915 Oram, William A. "Nature, Poetry, and Milton's Genii." *Milton and the Art of Sacred Song*. Ed. by J. Max Patrick and Roger H. Sundell (Madison: Univ. of Wisconsin Press, 1979), pp. 47–64.

Traces Milton's use of genii in the 1645 *Poems* and notices that "the model of Christ as the true poet-genius becomes increasingly explicit." In Milton's later poetry, the genius becomes the divine light, leaving the pagan world behind.

916 Oras, Ants. "Miltonic Themes." *SR*, 77, 1969, 176–84.

Believes that the five books under review have helped to balance two opposing views of Milton—as archrevolutionary and as man of the establishment: C. A. Patrides, *Milton and the Christian Tradition* (No. 933); William G. Madsen, *From Shadowy Types to Truth* (No. 811); Wayne Shumaker, *Unpremeditated Verse* (No. 3055); Dennis H. Burden, *The Logical Epic* (No. 2002); and Northrop Frye, *The Return of Eden* (No. 2262).

917 Oras, Ants. *Notes on Some Miltonic Usages: Their Background and Later Development.* Folcroft, PA: Folcroft Library Editions, 1969; Norwood, PA: Norwood Editions, 1974, 1976; Philadelphia, PA: R. West, 1977.

Reprints of Huckabay No. 802, originally published in 1938.

918 Orchard, Thomas Nathaniel. *Milton's Astronomy.* Folcroft, PA: Folcroft Library Editions, 1974; Norwood, PA: Norwood Editions, 1976; Philadelphia, PA: R. West, 1977.

Reprints of Stevens No. 939 and Huckabay No. 1638, first published in 1896.

919 Origo, Iris. "Additions to the Keats Collection." *TLS*, Apr. 23, 1970, pp. 457–58.

Discusses the most notable find as a "silver scallop-shell reliquary" containing two locks of hair: Milton's and Elizabeth Barrett Browning's.

920 Osgood, Charles Grosvenor. *The Classical Mythology of Milton's English Poems.* New York: Gordian Press, 1964; New York: Haskell House, 1969.

Reprints of Stevens No. 2225 and Huckabay No. 807, originally published in 1900.

921 Otten, Charlotte Fennema. "The Herbal Tradition in the Poetry of John Milton." Doctoral diss., Michigan State Univ., 1971. 185pp. Abs., *DAI*, 32, 1972, 6940A.

Explores the "medical, magic, ceremonial, horticultural, and aesthetic aspects" of the herbal tradition in *Paradise Lost, Comus,* and *Lycidas.*

922 Overton, Richard. *Mans Mortalitie.* Ed. by Harold Fisch. Liverpool: Liverpool Univ. Press, 1968. xxv, 102pp.

Argues "that Milton had seen Overton's tract when it first appeared in 1643/4 and that it helped to shape his views on the soul."

923 Padgett, Jeffrey Lynn. "The Monistic Continuity of the Miltonic Heresy." Doctoral diss., Ball State Univ., 1987. 440pp. Abs., *DAI*, 48, 1988, 2345A.

Contends that the heresies of the *Christian Doctrine*—monism, *ex deo* creation, anti-Trinitarianism, and mortalism—stem from Milton's "monistic conception of the cosmos."

924 Paramonova, T. I. "Dzhon Mil'ton v otsenke novoi kritiki." *VMU*, 4, 1972, 29–38.

"John Milton on the Appraisal of the New Criticism."

925 Parker, M. Pauline. "The Image of Direction in Dante, Spenser and Milton." *EM*, 19, 1968, 9–23.

Dante and Spenser deal with the "regeneration of a single human soul . . . from condemnation to sanctity," while Milton treats the reverse possibility by providing the alternative of irrevocable condemnation or redemption through repentance.

926 Partridge, A. C. *The Language of Renaissance Poetry: Spenser, Shakespeare, Donne, Milton.* London: Andre Deutsch, 1971. 348pp.

Contains two chapters on Milton's language: "Milton" and "*Paradise Lost* and *Samson Agonistes.*" The first consists mainly of an analysis of *Lycidas*, and the second contains an analysis of *Paradise Lost* 8.249–99 and *Samson Agonistes* 1721–58. "Milton's supreme accomplishment was the use he made of his ear for rhythm." Reviews: *TLS*, Feb. 11, 1972, p. 162; Masamichi Toyoda, *SELit*, 49, 1972, 111–15.

927 Paskus, John Martin. "Not Less but More Heroic: A Treatment of Myth and the Bible in the Poetry of John Milton." Doctoral diss., Univ. of Massachusetts, 1973. 465pp. Abs., *DAI*, 34, 1974, 6600A–01A.

Argues that Milton uses both biblical and mythological references to illustrate God's justice and emphasize the human need to "actively achieve salvation" through free choice.

928 Patrick, J. Max. "En Route." *SCN*, 31, 1973, 27–28.

Contains preliminary remarks on numerous recent publications on Milton and others.

929 Patrick, J. Max, and **Roger H. Sundell,** eds. *Milton and the Art of Sacred Song.* Madison: Univ. of Wisconsin Press, 1979. xiii, 154pp.

A collection of tercentenary essays. The authors are James H. Sims, Virginia R. Mollenkott, William A. Oram, Sundell, Mortimer H. Frank, Patrick, Stella P. Revard, and John T. Shawcross. In this bibliography, each essay is listed according to author and clas-

sification. Reviews: Joseph Anthony Wittreich, Jr., *SCN*, 38, 1980, 72–73; John L. Lievsay, *SAQ*, 79, 1980, 336–37; Thomas Werge, *C&L*, 31, 1980, 54–55.

930 Patrides, C. A. "Because We Freely Love: The Christian Idea of Love." *On Milton's Poetry: A Selection of Modern Studies.* Ed. by Arnold Stein (Greenwich, CT: Fawcett Publications, 1970), pp. 111–33.

Reprint of excerpts from *Milton and the Christian Tradition* (No. 933), originally published in 1966.

931 Patrides, C. A. *The Grand Design of God: The Literary Form of the Christian View of History.* London: Routledge and Kegan Paul, 1972. xviii, 157pp.

Discusses Milton's Christian view of history, pp. 84–90 and passim. Reviews: James H. Sims, *SCN*, 31, 1973, 74–75; William B. Hunter, Jr., *CSR*, 4, 1974, 141–42.

932 Patrides, C. A. "Milton and Arianism." *Bright Essence: Studies in Milton's Theology.* By W. B. Hunter, Patrides, and J. H. Adamson (Salt Lake City: Univ. of Utah Press, 1971), pp. 63–70.

Reprint of Huckabay No. 816, originally published in 1964.

933 Patrides, C. A. *Milton and the Christian Tradition.* Hamden, CT: Archon Books, Shoe String Press, 1979.

Reprint of Huckabay No. 818, originally published in 1966. Reviews: Douglas Bush, *JR*, 48, 1968, 109–10; Michael Fixler, *RES*, 19, 1968, 439–40; Mark Roberts, *N&Q*, 213, 1968, 389–94; Dieter Mehl, *Anglia*, 86, 1968, 229–32; Ants Oras, *SR*, 77, 1969, 176–84; John M. Steadman, *Archiv*, 205, 1969, 322–23; Edward E. Ericson, *Gordon Review*, 11, 1969, 231–34; Earl Miner, *ECS*, 3, 1970, 296–305.

934 Patrides, C. A. "Milton on the Trinity: The Use of Antecedents." *Bright Essence: Studies in Milton's Theology.* By W. B. Hunter, Patrides, and J. H.

Adamson (Salt Lake City: Univ. of Utah Press, 1971), pp. 3–13.

Reprint of part of *Milton and the Christian Tradition* (No. 933), originally published in 1966.

935 Patrides, C. A. *Premises and Motifs in Renaissance Thought and Literature.* Princeton, NJ: Princeton Univ. Press, 1982. xix, 236pp.

Makes several scattered references to Milton.

936 Patrides, C. A. "'Something like Prophetic Strain': Apocalyptic Configurations in Milton." *ELN*, 19, 1982, 193–207. Revised in *The Apocalypse in English Renaissance Thought and Literature* (Ithaca, NY: Cornell Univ. Press, 1984), pp. 207–37.

"The sum of Milton's poetry and, indeed, his prose: the Apocalypse ... attends the ambition after 'Something like Prophetick strain' that informs the *Nativity Ode* and *At a Solemn Musick*, *Comus* and *Lycidas*, the antiprelatical tracts of the early 1640s, *Areopagitica*, the sonnet on the Piedmontese massacre [Sonnet 18]—and ultimately both *Samson Agonistes* and, however odd its convolutions, *De Doctrina Christiana*. The impact of the Apocalypse can certainly be exaggerated, and it has been. But it is also possible to underestimate it much."

937 Patrides, C. A., and **Raymond B. Waddington,** eds. *The Age of Milton: Backgrounds to Seventeenth-Century Literature.* Manchester: Manchester Univ. Press; Totowa, NJ: Barnes and Noble, 1980. x, 438pp.

Intended to "provide varieties of contextualism for a fuller comprehension of the poetry and prose of Milton and his contemporaries." Contains the following chapters: G. E. Aylmer, "The Historical Background"; Austin Woolrych, "Political Theory and Political Practice"; Theodore K. Rabb, "Population, Economy and Society in Milton's England"; Kenneth Charlton, "The

Educational Background"; Samuel I. Mintz, "The Motion of Thought: Intellectual and Philosophical Backgrounds"; Patrides, "The Experience of Otherness: Theology as a Means of Life"; P. M. Rattansi, "The Scientific Background"; Peter le Huray, "The Fair Musick that All Creatures Made"; Philipp P. Fehl, "Poetry and the Entry of the Fine Arts into England: *Ut Pictura Poesis*"; Thomas O. Sloane, "Rhetoric, 'Logic' and Poetry: The Formal Cause"; and Waddington, "Milton among the Carolines." Also includes a chronological outline of seventeenth-century events in Europe, an introduction to the *Short-Title Catalogue*, and a bibliography of secondary sources. Reviews: James L. Balakier and Ann Stewart Balakier, *MiltonQ*, 15, 1981, 66, 68; Christopher Haigh, *EHR*, 97, 1982, 592–94; D. D. C. Chambers, *RES*, 34, 1983, 338–40.

938 Pecheux, Mother M. Christopher. "Milton and Eliot: Touched by a Common Genius." *Greyfriar*, 18, 1977, 29–44.

Surveys Eliot's scattered comments on Milton (see Huckabay Nos. 530–31) and compares the authors. "As an admirer of both writers, I can see so many resemblances between them and their work that I prefer to hyphenate their names not as opposites but as a familiar compound ghost." Abs., *MiltonQ*, 13, 1979, 62.

939 Pecheux, Mother M. Christopher. "Milton and *Kairos*." *MiltonS*, 12, 1978, 197–211.

Explains the Greek concept of kairos—the appointed time of opportunity—and discusses two lines found on the back of a letter Milton received from Henry Lawes. Concludes that Milton composed the lines in reference to a relief sculpture of the Greek god, Kairos, or as an image of opportunity inspired by an ode of Antonio Francini.

940 Pedley, Philip Edward. "Hierarchy in Milton: A Biography of an Idea."

Doctoral diss., Univ. of Pennsylvania, 1988. 422pp. Abs., *DAI*, 49, 1989, 2672A.

Examines Milton's tendency to attack social hierarchies by contrasting them to a more perfect, cosmic "homogeneous hierarchy."

941 Perez Gallego, Candido. "Prosa y Revolución en la Inglaterra del Siglo XVII." *CHA*, 351, 1979, 500–23.

Surveys the seventeenth-century English literary movement framed by contemporary historical events. Compares Hobbes's *Leviathan* with works by other British authors, including Milton.

942 Piehler, Paul. "Milton's Iconoclasm." *Evolution of Consciousness: Studies in Polarity in Honor of Owen Barfield.* Ed. by Shirley Sugerman (Middletown, CT: Wesleyan Univ. Press, 1976), pp. 121–35.

Deals mainly with *Comus* and *Paradise Lost.* Considers the epic to be "a major document in the history of consciousness, a prophetic book of iconoclasm, manifesting the destruction of the ancient participated cosmos."

943 Piltch, Charles Neil. "Inspiration and the Claim to Knowledge in Seventeenth-Century English Poetry." Doctoral diss., City Univ. of New York, 1968. 477pp. Abs., *DA*, 29, 1969, 2722A.

Traces the evolution of "exalted poetry," in which the author acquires supernatural knowledge via inspiration from a higher being, to its "culmination" in *Paradise Lost.*

944 Pironon, Jean. "La Critique de la Poésie Miltonienne: 1942–1978." Doctoral diss., Université Paul Valéry, Montpellier, 1979. 2 vols. 760pp.

Discusses the varied, complex, and interdependent factors which have determined the direction of Milton criticism and reviews the main critical controversies between 1942 and 1978.

945 Pitcher, John. "Towards the Universal Blank." *TLS*, Aug. 23, 1985, p. 932.

Review essay. Feels that the books discussed draw a universal blank: Sanford Budick, *The Dividing Muse*

(No. 508); John M. Steadman, *The Hill and the Labyrinth* (No. 1053) and *Milton's Biblical and Classical Imagery* (No. 1058); *Milton Studies*, vol. 20; James Sims and Leland Ryken, eds., *Milton and Scriptural Tradition* (No. 1038); and Robert Fallon, *Captain or Colonel* (No. 584).

946 Pointon, Marcia R. *Milton and English Art.* Manchester: Manchester Univ. Press; Toronto and Buffalo, NY: Univ. of Toronto Press, 1970, 1974. xliii, 276pp.

"This book comprises a historical survey of the illustrations to Milton's poetry executed in England between 1688 and 1860, including engraved designs incorporated in editions of Milton's poetry and exhibited works." Appendices: "Illustrations of Milton's Poetry from the 1870s to the Present Day"; "Sculpture on Miltonic Themes"; "Pictures of Milton's Life"; "J. H. Fuseli's Milton Gallery, 1799"; and "Blake's Illustrations to *Paradise Lost.*" Reviews: Johannes L. Dewton, *LJ*, 95, 1970, 42–46; Watson Kirkconnell, *DR*, 50, 1970, 413–14; *MiltonQ*, 4, 1970, 41–42; *TLS*, Dec. 25, 1970, p. 1515; John Holloway, *Spectator*, 224, 1970, 788–89; Lorna Sage, *New Statesman*, 80, 1970, 154–55; T. S. R. Boase, *MLR*, 66, 1971, 393–94; G. E. Bentley, Jr., *The Library*, 26, 1971, 356–59 (supplies addenda of illustrated British editions); Jacques Blondel, *EA*, 24, 1971, 530–31; J. R. Harvey, *DUJ*, 63, 1971, 244–46; *SCN*, 29, 1971, 62; Arthur Edward Barker, *AHR*, 77, 1972, 511–12; Roland Mushat Frye, *ELN*, 9, 1972, 205–06; Mario Praz, *ES*, 54, 1973, 73–74; *MiltonQ*, 7, 1973, 53–54.

947 Pollard, W. "Literature of Belief: A Comparative Study of Faith and Epistemology in Works of Milton, Bunyan and Dryden." M.Litt. thesis, Univ. of Cambridge, 1978.

948 Popham, Elizabeth Anne. "The

Concept of Arcadia in the English Literary Renaissance: Pastoral Societies in the Works of Sidney, Spenser, Shakespeare, and Milton." Doctoral diss., Queen's Univ., 1982. Abs., *DAI*, 43, 1983, 3326A. Asserts that the four writers reinterpret classical pastoral conventions to focus on an "anatomy of social and ethical behavior" in government and society.

949 Potter, Lois. *A Preface to Milton.* London: Longman; New York: Scribners, 1971. 180pp. Revised edition, 1986.

Contains sections on biography, the scientific background, the political and religious background, the literary background, and critical analyses. The revised edition presents an enlarged critical survey, proffering examples for study and discussion. Reviews: *MiltonQ*, 6, No. 3, 1972, 16; R. E. C. Houghton, *RES*, 23, 1972, 497–99.

950 Prince, F. T. "Milton's Blank Verse: The Diction." *On Milton's Poetry: A Selection of Modern Studies.* Ed. by Arnold Stein (Greenwich, CT: Fawcett Publications, 1970), pp. 151–66.

Reprint of a chapter from *The Italian Element in Milton's Verse* (Huckabay No. 834), originally published in 1954.

951 Proceedings of the American Philosophical Society. Symposium on John Milton. Vol. 120, No. 4, 1976, pp. 233–305.

A special issue. Contains papers presented in 1975 by Roland Mushat Frye, C. A. Patrides, John M. Steadman, and Walter J. Ong, S. J. In this bibliography, each paper is listed according to classification and author.

952 Quilligan, Maureen. *Milton's Spenser: The Politics of Reading.* Ithaca, NY, and London: Cornell Univ. Press, 1983. 249pp.

Studies Milton's incorporation of Spenser, especially in *Paradise Lost*. Relates the topic to politics and gender. Reviews: Anne Lake Prescott, *SpenN*, 15, 1984, 61–64; Joseph

Anthony Wittreich, Jr., *JEGP*, 84, 1985, 430–33.

953 Quinones, Ricardo J. "Milton." *The Renaissance Discovery of Time.* Harvard Studies in Comparative Literature, 31 (Cambridge, MA: Harvard Univ. Press, 1972), pp. 444–93.

Deals with Milton's conception of time (and fame) in the early works and the long poems. Milton usually associates time with mad forward movement, which contrasts strongly with God and Christ's patient virtues. Reviews (of book): G. F. Waller, *DR*, 52, 1972, 469–77; Robert E. Carter, *QQ*, 79, 1972, 560–61.

954 Radzinowicz, Mary Ann. " 'To Make the People Fittest To Chuse': How Milton Personified His Program for Poetry." *CEA*, 48–49, 1986, 3–23.

Discusses Milton's persona from the early poetry and prose to *Paradise Lost*. Concludes that "For four decades or so, Milton himself spoke to his nation in the figure of the recollective mediator and spoke to teach his people. If we learn anything to our own advantage now from Milton's poetry of the past, we learn how a poet put himself both in success and in failure at the service of a public program."

955 Rajan, Balachandra. "Browne and Milton: The Divided and the Distinguished." *Approaches to Sir Thomas Browne.* The Ann Arbor Tercentenary Lectures and Essays. Ed. by C. A. Patrides (Columbia: Univ. of Missouri Press, 1982), pp. 1–11.

Compares the authors' approaches to the Janus image.

956 Rajan, B. "The Cunning Resemblance." *MiltonS*, 7, 1975, 29–48.

"The continuing and prominent presence of parody in Milton's structures and the decisive part it plays in setting those structures in motion indicate that Milton's use of parody amounts to more than a poetic technique or literary strategy."

957 Rajan, Balachandra. *The Lofty Rhyme: A Study of Milton's Major Poetry.* Coral Gables, FL: Univ. of Miami Press; London: Routledge and Kegan Paul, 1970. viii, 190pp.

A collection of essays, most previously published, on the *Nativity Ode, Comus, Lycidas,* and the three long poems. See also No. 1155. Reviews: *MiltonQ,* 4, 1970, 27–28; *TLS,* June 11, 1970, p. 641; Larry S. Champion, *RenQ,* 24, 1971, 585–87; R. E. C. Houghton, *DUJ,* 63, 1971, 152–53; Irène Simon, *RBPH,* 50, 1972, 669–72; John Steadman, *YES,* 2, 1972, 268–69.

958 Rajan, Balachandra. "Milton, Humanism, and the Concept of Piety." *Poetic Traditions of the English Renaissance.* Ed. by Maynard Mack and George de Forest Lord (New Haven, CT, and London: Yale Univ. Press, 1982), pp. 251–69.

Believes that piety to Milton is a dedication to virtue and that he "follows an inward pull of piety nearly as far as he can without dissolving the entity that is Christian humanism."

959 Rajan, Balachandra. "Pinnacle of Peril." *CanL,* 61, 1974, 84–88.

Review of A. S. P. Woodhouse's *Heavenly Muse* (No. 1156). The book "is less than complete," but its "main strengths lay in knowledge of the background and the inheritance, a well-proportioned power of exposition and a firm grasp of main principles."

960 Rajan, Balachandra, ed. *The Prison and the Pinnacle.* Papers To Commemorate the Tercentenary of *Paradise Regained* and *Samson Agonistes* Read at The University of Western Ontario, March–April 1971. Toronto and Buffalo, NY: Univ. of Toronto Press, 1973. x, 163pp.

Essays by Arthur E. Barker, Barbara K. Lewalski, Rajan, Irene Samuel, and Northrop Frye. In this bibliography, each paper is listed according to author and classification. Reviews: Joseph Anthony Wittreich, Jr., *MiltonQ,*

8, 1974, 15–21; D. D. C. Chambers, *RES,* 26, 1975, 209–11; John Arthos, *RBPH,* 54, 1976, 206–08; Michael Lieb, *Cithara,* 16, No. 1, 1976, 89–90; Gerald J. Schiffhorst, *SHR,* 10, 1976, 181–82; R. E. C. Houghton, *N&Q,* 24, 1977, 88–89.

961 Rama Sarma, M. V. *The Heroic Argument: A Study of Milton's Heroic Poetry.* Madras and London: Macmillan, 1971. 171pp.

Studies *Comus, Paradise Lost, Paradise Regained,* and *Samson Agonistes.* Sees a distinct type of heroic conflict in each and feels that these poems comprise a tetralogy, "an organic, artistic unit upholding the great truth that virtue will be victorious against vice." The final chapter deals with Milton's use of eastern lore, particularly Indian. Reviews: *MiltonQ,* 5, 1971, 77–78; Irène Simon, *RES,* 23, 1972, 348–51; William B. Hunter, Jr., *SCN,* 30, 1972, 7.

962 Rama Sarma, M. V. *Things Unattempted: A Study of Milton.* New Delhi: Vikas Publishing House, 1982. x, 154pp.

States that Milton's poetry is "directed towards an exemplification of Miltonic doctrines, his concept of heroism, his knowledge of the East and India, and of the cross-cultural synthesis of the East and the West in his poetry." Also compares *Paradise Lost* and the *Mahabharata.* Reviews: William B. Hunter, Jr., *SCN,* 40, 1982, 42; Albert C. Labriola, *MiltonQ,* 16, 1982, 50–51.

963 Rapaport, Herman. *Milton and the Postmodern.* Lincoln: Univ. of Nebraska Press, 1983. xvi, 270pp.

Deals mainly with *Paradise Lost, Lycidas, Samson Agonistes,* and the prose works. Reviews: E. R. Gregory, *C&L,* 33, 1984, 63–65; Marshall Grossman, *MiltonQ,* 18, 1984, 99–102; Lachlan MacKinnon, *TLS,* Apr. 20, 1984, p. 60; Roger B. Rollin, *JEGP,* 84, 1985, 433–37; *SHR,* 19, 1985, 359; J. Martin Evans, *RES,* 37, 1986, 415–17; Thomas F. Healy, *YES,* 17, 1987, 280–82.

964 Rapaport, Herman. "The Uncouth Swain: A Post-Structuralist Reading of Milton." Doctoral diss., Univ. of California, Irvine, 1978. 261pp. Abs., *DAI*, 39, 1978, 1599A–1600A.

Contends that Eve, Christ, and even Milton are "'uncouth' (in the sense of humble, but also estranged, cut off) practicers of iconoclasm," which is self-destructive.

965 Readings, Bill. "On the New Forcers of Conscience: Milton's Critics." *OLR*, 7, 1985, 131–47.

Discusses some of the various ways of interpreting Milton that have developed since the 1960s.

966 Readings, W. J. "The Restoration and the Fall of Language: The Search for Meaning in the Poetry of Marvell and Milton." Doctoral diss., Oxford Univ., 1985. Abs., *IT*, 35, 1986, 45.

Examines the seventeenth-century theory of language use, focusing on Milton's attempt to achieve a "'natural language' which has the authority of Adamic naming."

967 Rees, Christine. "Some Seventeenth-Century Versions of the Judgment of Paris." *N&Q*, 24, 1977, 197–200.

Traces the line of continuity from sixteenth-century uses of the Judgment of Paris motif to its seventeenth-century variants in Milton (*Paradise Lost* 5) and others. Suggests that Milton's allusion to the motif in eulogizing Christina of Sweden in the *Second Defence* may have been prompted by Marvell's use of a variant on the motif to flatter her in "A Letter to Doctor Ingelo."

968 Reesing, John. *Milton's Poetic Art: "A Mask," "Lycidas," and "Paradise Lost."* Cambridge, MA: Harvard Univ. Press, 1968. x, 208pp.

See Huckabay No. 853. Reviews: *TLS*, Dec. 26, 1968, p. 1457; *MiltonN*, 3, 1969, 6–7; W. J. Barnes, *QQ*, 77, 1969, 726–29; Irène Simon, *RES*, 21, 1970, 209–11.

969 Rerecich, Marilyn Jean. "Milton on Marriage and Divorce." M.A. thesis, Adelphi Univ., 1975. Abs., *MA*, 13, 1975, 142.

970 Rhu, Lawrence Ford. "Literary Theory and the Practice of Narrative Poetry: Young Tasso's Heroic Project and the Epic Tradition from Homer to Milton." Doctoral diss., Harvard Univ., 1987. 273pp. Abs., *DAI*, 48, 1988, 2868A.

Examines elements of Tasso's epic theory—"the narrator's role, the imaginative uses of history and religion, unity of plot, allegory and mimesis, the tragic element in heroic poetry"—that were influenced by Homer and passed on to Spenser and Milton.

971 Richmond, Hugh M. *The Christian Revolutionary: John Milton.* Berkeley and London: Univ. of California Press, 1974. xi, 204pp.

Shows that "Milton's ultimate escape from idealism is a central factor in the triumphant art of his last three great poems, whose character specifically derives from his rejection of much of the pagan cult of the intellect. It is this final heroic escape that makes him truly exemplary for moderns." Reviews: *Christian Century*, 92, 1975, 316; *Literary Journal*, 100, 1975, 1131; *MiltonQ*, 9, 1975, 87–88; J. de Bruyn, *Ren&R*, 12, 1976, 133–35; Christopher Hill, *RenQ*, 29, 1976, 144–45; R. E. C. Houghton, *N&Q*, 23, 1976, 575–76; Charles A. Huttar, *CSR*, 5, 1976, 284–87; Babette M. Levy, *CH*, 45, 1976, 115; Michael Lieb, *MP*, 74, 1976, 204–12; Andrew McLean, *SHR*, 10, 1976, 362–69; Balachandra Rajan, *ELN*, 13, 1976, 302–04; William G. Riggs, *JEGP*, 75, 1976, 287–90; James H. Sims, *SCN*, 25, 1976, 1; Arnold Stein, *SR*, 84, 1976, 695–706.

972 Richmond, Hugh M. "Personal Identity and Literary Persona: A Study in Historical Psychology." *PMLA*, 90, 1975, 209–21.

Discusses several authors and pinpoints

Milton's "need parallel to [Pierre de] Ronsard's . . . systematic vindication of one's private identity."

973 Richmond, Hugh M. *Puritans and Libertines: Anglo-French Literary Relations in the Reformation.* Berkeley, Los Angeles, and London: Univ. of California Press, 1981. xii, 401pp.

Believes that French literature "evolved under the pressures of intense adversary relations generated by religious controversy" and that English literature profited from the distortions that resulted. Frequent references to the influence of French writers on Milton.

974 Ridden, Geoffrey M. *Studying Milton.* York Handbooks. Harlow: York Press, Longman Group, 1985. 182pp.

Intended as an introduction for the general reader and as a handbook for the student. Includes a chapter on the development of Milton criticism. Review: Archie Burnett, *YWES*, 66, 1985, 287.

975 Ring, Max. *John Milton and His Times: A Historical Novel in Three Parts.* Trans. by John Jefferson. Norwood, PA: Norwood Editions, 1977.

Reprint of Stevens No. 2161, originally published in 1889.

976 Rivers, Isabel. *Classical and Christian Ideas in English Renaissance Poetry: A Student's Guide.* London, Boston, MA, and Sydney: George Allen and Unwin, 1979. v, 231pp.

Discusses a wide range of subjects and uses several illustrative quotations from Milton's works. Reviews: Lawrence V. Ryan, *RenQ*, 33, 1980, 803–05; Caroline D. Eckhardt, *SCN*, 39, 1981, 16–17.

977 Rivers, Isabel. "John Milton: Reformation and Regeneration." *The Poetry of Conservatism, 1600–1745: A Study of Poets and Public Affairs from Jonson to Pope* (Cambridge: Rivers Press, 1973), pp. 74–100.

Discusses Milton's changing concept of the poet's role in public affairs.

Shows that although Milton began his career thinking that he could remake society, he moved far from that conservative belief after his recognition of political failure.

978 Roberts, Susan Ellen. "A Phenomenological Approach to Milton: From Typology to Existentialism." Doctoral diss., State Univ. of New York, Buffalo, 1970. 133pp. Abs., *DAI*, 31, 1971, 6566A–67A.

Uses existential phenomenology to identify Milton's major theme as anarchy or a "revolt against all systems that impinge upon the moral integrity of the individual."

979 Rosen, Alan David. "War and Peace in Milton's Prose and Poetry." Doctoral diss., Bryn Mawr College, 1972. 302pp. Abs., *DAI*, 33, 1973, 5195A.

Examines the effect of conflict (literal or figurative) and relative peace on political struggles, ecclesiastical clashes, civil liberty, and spiritual maturity in Milton's works.

980 Rosenberg, D. M. *Oaten Reeds and Trumpets: Pastoral and Epic in Virgil, Spenser, and Milton.* Lewisburg, PA: Bucknell Univ. Press; London and Toronto: Associated Univ. Presses, 1981. 287pp.

Chapters on Milton: "Milton's Pastoral Poetry"; "*Paradise Lost* (I)"; and "*Paradise Lost* (II)." Begins by discussing the early pastorals—the *Nativity Ode*, *L'Allegro* and *Il Penseroso*, *Arcades*, *Comus*, and *Lycidas*. Demonstrates that "the mutual inclusion of the genres reaches its culmination in Milton, in that he writes pastoral poems that are more heroic than those of his predecessors, and produces an epic in which the pastoral becomes the central setting, theme, and ideal." Deals with Milton's transformation of the pastoral. Reviews: P. J. Klemp, *SpenN*, 14, 1983, 9–11; Kitty Scoular Datta, *RenQ*, 35, 1982, 322–24; Harold E. Toliver, *CL*, 34, 1983, 278–79.

981 Ross, Aden Kathryn. *"Exeunt in Mysterium*: John Milton and the Trinitarian Controversy." Doctoral diss., Univ. of Utah, 1977. 349pp. Abs., *DAI*, 38, 1977, 2145A.

Analyzes the unorthodox Trinitarian views of the *Christian Doctrine*, in which the Holy Spirit is inferior and Christ is neither eternal nor a "primary, internally efficient cause of creation."

982 Ross, Malcolm MacKenzie. *Poetry and Dogma: The Transfiguration of Eucharistic Symbols in Seventeenth Century English Poetry.* New York: Octagon Books, 1969.

Reprint of Huckabay Nos. 870 and 1737, originally published in 1954.

983 Røstvig, Maren-Sofie. "Ars Aeterna: Renaissance Poetics and Theories of Divine Creation." *Mosaic*, 3, 1969–70, 40–61. Reprinted in *Chaos and Form.* Ed. by Kenneth McRobbie (Winnipeg: Univ. of Manitoba Press, 1972), pp. 101–19.

Shows "that the classical concept of harmony became an integral part of a theological tradition extending from the days of Augustine to those of John Milton, and that the nature of this tradition was such that it posited that all acts of creation, whether human or divine, consist in the application of a preconceived meaningful pattern."

984 Rowse, A. L. *Milton the Puritan: Portrait of a Mind.* London: Macmillan, 1977, 1985. 297pp.

An unsympathetic treatment. Feels that "Milton's unconscious was at war with his Puritan intellectual convictions." Reviews: *TES*, Oct. 28, 1977, p. 20; Alan Haynes, *HT*, 27, 1977, 824; R. C. Churchill, *Contemporary Review*, 232, 1978, 165; G. K. Hunter, *SR*, 86, 1978, 414–21; Roy Flannagan, *MiltonQ*, 14, 1980, 67–68; Leland Ryken, *C&L*, 28, 1979, 65–67.

985 Rudnytsky, Peter Lysiak. "Siege of Contraries: An Essay in Psychoanalytic Criticism." Doctoral diss., Yale Univ.,

1979. 391pp. Abs., *DAI*, 40, 1979, 3323A.

Psychoanalyzes "the relations between the myths of Oedipus and the Fall," comparing these myths to Milton's and Freud's "conception of themselves as heroes."

986 Rudrum, Alan. "On the Teaching of Poetry: Some Reflections and an Example." *Rendezvous*, 6, 1971, 45–50.

Contends that "the meaning and the esthetic effect of the poem" are primary concerns when teaching children poetry and uses *Paradise Lost* 1.1–26 for an example of how to teach poetry.

987 Rumrich, John Peter. "Milton and the Meaning of Glory." *MiltonS*, 20, 1984, 75–86.

Insists that the idea of glory pervades Milton's thought and that to him glory is a synthesis of the Hebrew word "kabod" and the Greek word "doxa." Glory ultimately reflects the relationship between God and human, or creator and creature.

988 Rumrich, John Peter. "Milton's Concept of Substance." *ELN*, 19, 1982, 218–33.

Argues that Milton perceives substance as a process rather than a "static condition of being." To him, substance is "the working out of God's will in the stuff of existence." Milton rejects the idea that evil is the result of "matter's reluctance to submit to God's will." Rather, the foundation of both good and evil is the acceptance or rejection of God once he has endowed matter with form.

989 Ruoff, James E. "John Milton." *Crowell's Handbook of Elizabethan and Stuart Literature* (New York: Thomas Y. Crowell Co., 1975), pp. 292–98.

Contains a concise biography and history of Milton criticism.

990 Rushdy, Ashraf H. A. "John M. Steadman: A Review of His Contribution to Milton Studies." *MiltonQ*, 21, No. 2, 1987, 71–74.

"Professor Steadman, it seems to me, has himself achieved the nice balance Dr. Johnson thought essential to the good critic: Learning borne up by the vigor of Wit, and Wit guided by the perspicacity of Learning."

991 Saez, Richard. *Theodicy in Baroque Literature.* New York: Garland Publishing, 1985. 190pp.

Examines the baroque treatment of pagan myths and the fortunate encounter with evil displayed in the works of Milton, Tasso, and Calderón.

992 Salvidio, Frank Anthony, Jr. "Dante, Milton and Kazantzakis: Poets of Salvation." Doctoral diss., Univ. of Connecticut, 1972. 188pp. Abs., *DAI*, 33, 1972, 2903A–04A.

Evaluates "the primordial myth of loss, search, and redemption" in the three poets' works, as characters journey toward truth by searching for order, imposing it, or both.

993 Sammons, Todd H. "A Note on the Milton Criticism of Ezra Pound and T. S. Eliot." *Paideuma*, 17, 1988, 87–97.

Pound influenced Eliot's conclusions about Milton (see Huckabay Nos. 530–31). Both modern writers dislike Milton as a person, believe that he had a bad influence on other authors, and fault his diction, syntax, and indefinite descriptions.

994 Sams, Horace, Jr. "Temptation in Imaginative Literature of Milton and Bunyan: Two Faces of the Puritan Persona." Doctoral diss., Univ. of South Florida, 1985. 259pp. Abs., *DAI*, 46, 1986, 3043A–44A.

Establishes the faith that both writers had in the ability of literature to help individuals overcome temptation, communicated equally by Milton's elevated and Bunyan's humble persona.

995 Samuel, Irene. *Dante and Milton: The "Commedia" and "Paradise Lost."* Ithaca, NY: Cornell Univ. Press, 1966. x, 299pp.

See Huckabay No. 1749. Concerned mainly with Milton's use of the *Commedia* in *Paradise Lost*, but the appendices list Milton's references to Dante before *Paradise Lost* and contain excerpts from studies on the relationship of the two poets. Reviews: William J. Grace, *MP*, 65, 1968, 379–81; James H. Sims, *BA*, 42, 1968, 129; A. C. Charity, *RES*, 20, 1969, 87–88; John M. Steadman, *JEGP*, 68, 1969, 515–17.

996 Samuel, Irene. "The Development of Milton's Poetics." *PMLA*, 92, 1977, 231–40.

Milton's views on poetics changed throughout his life, but unchanged were questions of the poet's inspiration, his relation to his audience, and his possible usefulness. The last poems suggest his final theory. Abs., *SCN*, 38, 1980, 21.

997 Samuel, Irene. "Milton and the Ancients on the Writing of History." *MiltonS*, 2, 1970, 131–48.

Observes Milton's scattered references to the writing of history, discusses the historians he had read, and shows how he came to differentiate rhetoric and oratory from history. Milton reversed his early opinions when he wrote the *History of Britain*. Traditional matter for historians, valorous deeds performed in battle, has no place in his history. Milton's point of view is echoed in *Paradise Lost* when Raphael declares that Satan's rebellious acts of war are "Cancell'd from Heaven and sacred memory."

998 Samuel, Irene. "Milton on Comedy and Satire." *HLQ*, 35, 1972, 107–30.

Discusses the influences of classical comic and satiric theory on Milton's development and the use of these styles throughout his earlier work. Suggests that greater attention be given to a comic vein in Milton's epics.

999 Samuel, Irene. "Milton on the Province of Rhetoric." *MiltonS*, 10, 1977, 177–93.

"My concern here is only to demonstrate his full respect for an art in which he himself was thoroughly grounded and which he expected his readers also to know. . . . Regarding the act of persuasion, he was both astute and informed: his constant invention for all the misleading speakers in his poems of the best possible arguments, not the most easily demolished, is so successful that they have often misled naive and careless readers, even when they are decisively answered by honest argument within the poems themselves."

1000 Samuel, Irene. "Milton on Style." *CLJ*, 9, 1969, 39–58.

Surveys Milton's scattered comments on style and his opponents' lack of style: "the true adequate style comes from a sinking of the mind in the matter . . . that allows the speaker to transcend himself, a concentration on what is to be said that finally sweeps away the concern with how it is to be said."

1001 Samuel, Irene. "Milton Speaks to Academe." *MiltonQ*, 4, 1970, 2–4.

Discusses Milton's views concerning educational reform in seventeenth-century England. Comments on his quarrel with the contemporary university system.

1002 Saunders, Frances Marie. "The Concept of Responsibility in Milton's Major Poetry." Doctoral diss., Univ. of Oklahoma, 1975. 184pp. Abs., *DAI*, 35, 1975, 6109A.

Examines humans' freedom and responsibility to choose the nature of their relationship with God, as presented in Milton's three long poems and influenced by Puritan thought.

1003 Saurat, Denis. *Gods of the People.* Folcroft, PA: Folcroft Library Editions, 1969, 1978; Norwood, PA: Norwood Editions, 1977.

Reprints of Huckabay No. 1762, originally published in 1947.

1004 Saurat, Denis. *Milton: Man and Thinker.* New York: Haskell House, 1970; New York: AMS Press, 1975.

Reprints of Stevens No. 2565, originally published in 1925.

1005 Schaar, C. "Milton on a Desert Island." *ES*, 59, 1978, 218–24.

Generally negative review essay of the editions of *Paradise Lost* 5–6 (by Robert Hodge and Isabel G. MacCaffrey) and 7–8 (by David Aers and Mary Ann Radzinowicz) in the Cambridge Milton for Schools and College series (No. 281); Donald F. Bouchard, *Milton: A Structural Reading* (No. 492); and Burton Jasper Weber, *The Construction of "Paradise Lost"* (No. 3212).

1006 Schindler, Walter Leo. "Voice and Crisis: The Pattern of Invocation in Milton's Poetry." Doctoral diss., Yale Univ., 1977. 174pp. Abs., *DAI*, 39, 1978, 1600A.

Asserts the pervasiveness, significance, and interpretive value of invocations in "the entire body of Milton's major poetry."

1007 Schindler, Walter Leo. *Voice and Crisis: Invocation in Milton's Poetry.* Hamden, CT: Archon Books, 1984. x, 130pp.

"This book aims to discover and interpret evidence of a fundamental unity in Milton's poetry: a pattern of invocation, of the poet's calling upon a source of inspiration." Explores Milton's long poems. Reviews: Thomas Kranidas, *RenQ*, 39, 1986, 148–49; James Egan, *SCN*, 44, 1986, 34–35; Thomas N. Corns, *MLR*, 83, 1988, 149–51.

1008 Schmidt, Michael. *A Reader's Guide to Fifty British Poets, 1300–1900.* London: Heinemann; Totowa, NJ: Barnes and Noble, 1980. 430pp.

Considers Milton, pp. 161–75.

1009 Schneider, Helen Margaret. "Three Views of Toleration: John Milton, Roger Williams, and Sir Henry Vane the Younger." Doctoral diss., State Univ. of

New York, Albany, 1977. 214pp. Abs., *DAI*, 38, 1978, 6750A.

Explores the effect of education and religious background on the three writers' independent theological ideas, especially those related to religious toleration.

1010 Sears, Donald, trans. "*La Tina*: The Country Sonnets of Antonio Malatesti as Dedicated to Mr. John Milton, English Gentleman." *MiltonS*, 13, 1979, 275–317.

A translation by Sears of fifty sonnets that Malatesti presented to Milton, probably before he left Florence in April, 1639. The sonnets are addressed to a rural mistress and contain imagery and words of double (usually sexual) meaning. The translator's preface includes background information.

1011 "The Second International Milton Symposium: Chalfont St. Giles and Cambridge, England, August 8–12, 1983." *MiltonQ*, 17, 1983, 101–08.

A detailed report and remarks on papers read.

1012 Seehase, Georg. "John Milton—der Dichter der englischen bürgerlichen Revolution." *ZAA*, 23, 1975, 93–107.

Surveys Milton's antifeudalist activities. Abs., *MiltonQ*, 10, 1976, 28–29.

1013 Segal, Charles. "The Magic of Orpheus and the Ambiguities of Language." *Ramus*, 7, 1978, 106–42.

Discusses Milton's use of the Orpheus myth.

1014 Sellin, Paul R. "The Last of the Renaissance Monsters: The *Poetical Institutions* of Gerardus Joannis Vossius, and Some Observations on English Criticism." *MiltonQ*, 11, 1977, 61.

Abstract of a paper presented at the William Andrews Clark Library Seminar on May 10, 1975. Believes that Milton's attitudes toward the arts resemble those of Vossius. Quotes several comments made by the Dutch critic in his 1647 work, comments that help us understand Milton's practices.

1015 Sellin, Paul R. "Le Pathétique

Retrouvé: Racine's Catharsis Reconsidered." *MP*, 70, 1973, 199–215.

Touches on the relationship between Daniel Heinsius and Milton in their respective approaches to tragedy.

1016 Sellin, Paul R. "Theories and Tragic Poets: Heinsius, Vondel, Milton and Racine." *MiltonQ*, 4, 1970, 13–14.

Abstract of a paper presented at the 1969 MLA Convention. Concerning Milton, Sellin says, "The power of tragedy is the ability to purge the mind of pity and fear; delight is concomitant; it stems from seeing those passions well imitated."

1017 Sen, R. K. "Invocation to the Muses as a Basis of Milton's Theory of Poetry." *Bulletin of the Department of English* (Calcutta Univ.), 10, No. 2, 1974–75, 1–12.

Argues that by the time Milton wrote *Paradise Lost*, he had accepted the doctrine of illumination rather than inspiration and that illumination became the basis of his aesthetics.

1018 [Shafer, Ronald G.] "International Milton Symposium, Day-by-Day Description." *The Newsletter of the Friends of Milton's Cottage*, 4, No. 2, 1981, 2–6.

Report on the symposium held on July 7–9, 1981 (see No. 1019). The issue also contains a list of participants and guests and reactions of participants.

1019 Shafer, Ronald G., ed. *Ringing the Bell Backward: The Proceedings of the First International Milton Symposium.* The IUP Imprint Series. Indiana: Indiana Univ. of Pennsylvania, 1982. iv, 150pp.

Lectures and responses presented at the symposium held on July 7–9, 1981. Introduction by Shafer, pp. 1–18. Includes papers by Dennis R. Danielson, Jackie DiSalvo, Roy Flannagan, Margaret P. Hannay, Leo Miller, Lois W. Parker, Estella Schoenberg, Edward Sichi, Jr., John Sears Tanner, and Austin Woolrych; and responses by Jon S. Lawry, Calvin Huckabay, Stella P. Revard, John T. Shawcross, Lynn

Veach Sadler, Charles A. Huttar, and Michael A. Mikolajczak. In this bibliography, each paper is listed according to author and classification. Reviews: Zenas J. Bicket, *C&L*, 34, 1983, 56–58; Edgar F. Daniels, *SCN*, 31, 1983, 42–43; Roger Lejosne, *YES*, 17, 1987, 277–79.

1020 Shafer, Ronald G. "In Search of Milton: A Visit to Chalfont St. Giles." *MiltonQ*, 11, 1977, 50–52.

Tells of a visit to Milton's cottage and of the efforts being made to restore and preserve its relics. Contrasts the place's modesty with the shrines of other English writers.

1021 Shaw, Robert Burns. "The Call of God: The Theme of Vocation in Donne, Herbert, and Milton." Doctoral diss., Yale Univ., 1974. 207pp. Abs., *DAI*, 36, 1975, 329A–30A.

Sees in the writings of Donne, Herbert, and Milton a progression from a Calvinistic vocational dependence on God to a more humanistic ideal that emphasizes works and free will.

1022 Shawcross, John T. "Milton and Covenant: The Christian View of Old Testament Theology." *Milton and Scriptural Tradition: The Bible into Poetry.* Ed. by James H. Sims and Leland Ryken (Columbia: Univ. of Missouri Press, 1984), pp. 160–91.

Reviews the scriptural foundation and historiography of covenant theology. Analyzes "Milton's attitudes toward the Old Covenant, that of the Old Testament as cited between God and Moses on Mount Sinai, and the New Covenant, that of the New Testament as exemplified through the Son."

1023 Shawcross, John T. "Pictorialism and the Poetry of John Milton." *HSL*, 13, 1981, 143–64.

Proposes that the pictorialism of Milton's poetry "involves linguistic and syntactic sounds as well as visualizations and thoughts. Its techniques are built on a scale of reality (not always vertical), on ambiguities (or dialectic) of vision, thought, and syntax, on tension because of the ambiguities, on a manipulation of time and space even when not 'baroque,' and on realistic illusion."

1024 Shawcross, John T. "*PL*: 'Erased.'" *MiltonQ*, 16, 1982, 80–81.

Notice of Ronald Johnson's rendition of a poem called *RADI OS* (Berkeley: Sand Dollar, 1977), which was composed by erasing words and lines from *Paradise Lost.*

1025 Shawcross, John T. "Some Literary Uses of Numerology." *HSL*, 1, 1969, 50–62.

In Renaissance and modern literature. Uses Dryden's *Ode on Mrs. Anne Killigrew* and *Lycidas* to demonstrate forms of numerological structure.

1026 Shawcross, John T. "Stasis, and John Milton and the Myths of Time." *Cithara*, 18, No. 1, 1978, 3–17.

Asserts that "Milton's perception of the myth of linear time . . . while always evidencing his belief and faith in the myth of God—suggests his agreement with the function of the social artist," for he shows "man what the world is like and how to change it."

1027 Sherbo, Arthur. "A Forgotten Miltonist." *MiltonQ*, 10, 1976, 31–39.

Thomas Holt White, a regular contributor to the *Gentleman's Magazine* starting in 1783, whose comments on Milton were used by Henry Todd and Thomas Warton. Feels that White deserves a place in the history of Milton studies. See also No. 773.

1028 Sherry, Beverley. "Approaches to Milton via the Visual Arts." *AUMLA*, 57, 1982, 31–39.

Discusses three approaches and suggests that the "Zeitgeist" approach is on the surest ground.

1029 Shibuya, Hiroshi. "Religio-Political Ideas of Puritanism—A Short Comment on C. Hill, *Milton and the English Revolution.*" *MCJ News*, 7, 1984, 3–6.

Rejects Christopher Hill's assertion (see No. 174) that there is "no common denominator" between Milton's "internalized religion" and the high Calvinism of his day.

1030 Shoaf, R. A. *Milton, Poet of Duality: A Study of Semiosis in the Poetry and the Prose.* New Haven, CT: Yale Univ. Press, 1985. xiv, 225pp.

Argues that "the dual and the duel (Satan versus Christ, for example) are powerful heuristic tools in the reading of Milton—this because he was a man and a poet deeply concerned with human and divine relationships, with the couples or pairs, man and woman, man (or woman) and God." Reviews: Lucy Newlyn, *TLS*, Aug. 8, 1986, p. 871; Lorraine Chaskalson, *UES*, 24, 1986, 34–35; Christopher Kendrick, *Criticism*, 28, 1986, 213–16; Irène Simon, *RES*, 37, 1986, 568–70; Archie Burnett, *N&Q*, 34, 1987, 86–87; Marshall Grossman, *JEGP*, 86, 1987, 418–21; Thomas F. Healy, *MLR*, 82, 1987, 917; William Kerrigan, *RenQ*, 40, 1987, 186–88; Roy C. Flannagan, *MiltonQ*, 24, 1990, 30–31.

1031 Shullenberger, William Arthur, II. "'The Omnific Word': Language in Milton." Doctoral diss., Univ. of Massachusetts, 1982. 407pp. Abs., *DAI*, 43, 1983, 2684A–85A.

Argues that Milton's theology, especially the "relationship of identity within difference between Father and Son," is reflected in the language and poetics of the *Christian Doctrine.*

1032 Siegmund-Schultze, Dorothea. "Milton und Toland." *ZAA*, 23, 1975, 148–53.

Points out that Toland links Milton to historical materialism and its relationship to the Enlightenment in England. Sees Milton as one of the best representatives of the middle-class Enlightenment.

1033 Simmonds, James D. "*Milton*

Studies: Tenth Anniversary Celebration." *MiltonQ*, 11, 1977, 122.

Mentions several celebration activities, including a reception hosted by *Milton Studies* and Don Parry Norford's lecture on "Milton's Eve and the Mythology of Women." See also *MiltonS*, 12, 1978, vii–xi.

1034 Simon, Roland Philip. "A Study of Dialectics in the Works of John Milton." Doctoral diss., Univ. of Southwestern Louisiana, 1980. 322pp. Abs., *DAI*, 42, 1981, 716A.

Examines Milton's dialectical ability to "argue both sides of a question" and traces the dialectics in his major works.

1035 Sims, James H. "Milton, Literature as a Bible, and the Bible as Literature." *Milton and the Art of Sacred Song.* Ed. by J. Max Patrick and Roger H. Sundell (Madison: Univ. of Wisconsin Press, 1979), pp. 3–21.

Submits that Milton would deny that the devotional and the literary approaches to the Bible are polar extremes and suggests that he read the Scriptures for delight as well as for instruction. Demonstrates also that Milton believed in the virtuous uses of nonbiblical writings. His long poems, then, "express from a single perspective more than sixteen centuries of concern with literature as a Bible and with the Bible as literature."

1036 Sims, James H. "The Miltonic Narrator and Scriptural Tradition: An Afterword." *Milton and Scriptural Tradition: The Bible into Poetry.* Ed. by Sims and Leland Ryken (Columbia: Univ. of Missouri Press, 1984), pp. 192–205.

Holds that Milton believed that "the individual Christian . . . must depend on the indwelling Spirit, the internal Scripture, to interpret the text, the external Scripture." This belief is reflected in the treatment of biblical episodes in his poetry.

1037 Sims, James H. "Symposium on Milton at the University of Tulsa." *SCN*, 27, 1969, 4–5.

Reports on papers read by Lester F. Zimmerman, Philip M. Griffith, John Patrick Tyson, David S. Berkeley, and Sims, and published in *Papers on Milton*, edited by Griffith and Zimmerman (No. 648). In this bibliography, each paper appears in its appropriate classification.

1038 Sims, James H., and **Leland Ryken,** eds. *Milton and Scriptural Tradition: The Bible into Poetry*. Columbia: Univ. of Missouri Press, 1984. xii, 212pp.

Contains essays by Harold Fisch, Michael Fixler, Michael Lieb, Sister M. Christopher Pecheux, Stella P. Revard, John T. Shawcross, Ryken, and Sims. In this bibliography, each essay is listed according to author and classification. Reviews: Roy C. Flannagan, *MiltonQ*, 19, 1985, 114–15; John Pitcher, *TLS*, Aug. 23, 1985, p. 932; John B. Gabel, *SAQ*, 85, 1986, 106–07; Archie Burnett, *N&Q*, 33, 1986, 416–17; Thomas N. Corns, *MLR*, 83, 1988, 149–51.

1039 Singh, Brijraj. *Milton: An Introduction*. Delhi, Bombay, Calcutta, and Madras: Macmillan Co. of India, 1977. xi, 87pp.

Discusses "various aspects" of many poems by Milton. Explores "the way in which the poet manipulates themes, techniques, character, language, verse or myth in order to express his belief in God's justice and providence." Chapters: "The Theme of Death in Milton's Early Poetry"; "Johnson on *Lycidas*: Some Notes"; "Balances in Milton's Sonnets"; "Eve in *Paradise Lost*"; "Milton's Style"; and "The Chorus in *Samson Agonistes*." Reviews: Virginia R. Mollenkott, *MiltonQ*, 12, 1978, 77–82; S. P. Appasamy, *LCrit*, 13, 1978, 72–75.

1040 Skerpan, Elizabeth Penley. "'The Living Labors of Public Men': Milton and the Political Writing of the English Revolution, 1642–1660." Doctoral diss., Univ. of Wisconsin, Madison, 1983. 553pp. Abs., *DAI*, 44, 1984, 2478A–79A.

Contends that Milton and other revolutionary pamphleteers use oratorical genres "determined by their intentions toward their audience, which in turn are governed by their ideology."

1041 Slights, Camille Wells. "Milton's Hero of Conscience." *The Casuistical Tradition in Shakespeare, Donne, Herbert, and Milton* (Princeton, NJ: Princeton Univ. Press, 1981), pp. 247–96.

Relates *Paradise Lost, Paradise Regained*, and *Samson Agonistes* to Renaissance Protestant casuistry but points out radical differences in conception and mode. Parts of this chapter appeared in No. 3712. Reviews (of book): Daniel Karlin, *TLS*, Nov. 20, 1981, pp. 1345–46; Diane Kelsey McColley, *C&L*, 31, 1982, 87–89; James Balakier, *MiltonQ*, 17, 1983, 53–54.

1042 Sloane, Thomas O. "Milton's Form." *Donne, Milton, and the End of Humanist Rhetoric* (Berkeley, Los Angeles, and London: Univ. of California Press, 1985), pp. 209–78.

Explores the disintegration of humanistic rhetoric and Milton's rhetoric. Concludes that once controversial thinking moved out of rhetoric and rhetoric became something added on to thinking done elsewhere, the nature of discourse changed radically. Sees Donne as more of a humanist than Milton because he was more of a rhetorician. Reviews (of book): Gerald Hammond, *THES*, Nov. 8, 1985, p. 18; Arthur F. Kinney, *JEGP*, 85, 1986, 450–54; Cedric C. Brown, *RES*, 38, 1987, 248–49; Brian Vickers, *RenQ*, 41, 1988, 525–28.

1043 Smith, A. J. "Humanity Vindicated: Milton's Pattern of Heroic Love." *The Metaphysics of Love: Studies in Renaissance Love Poetry from Dante to Milton* (Cambridge: Cambridge Univ. Press, 1985), pp. 323–27.

Argues that although Adam and Eve enter a fallen world of corrupt love in *Paradise Lost* 11–12, Michael teaches Adam that love will be necessary for humanity's well-being. Christ in *Paradise Regained* manifests his human love by being a man, suffering, and defeating temptation.

1044 Smith, George William, Jr. "Milton's 'Prompt Eloquence,' Debate and Rhetoric." Doctoral diss., Univ. of Virginia, 1975. 201pp. Abs., *DAI*, 36, 1975, 2225A.

Examines Milton's "rhetoric of error," use of symmetry to heighten the reader's involvement, presentation of speakers whose arguments transcend "narrative occasion," and "rhetoric of iteration."

1045 Smith, J. J. "A Comparison of the Imaginative Response of Donne and Milton to a Selection of Theological Doctrines." Doctoral diss., Oxford Univ., 1982. *IT*, 32, 1983, 197.

1046 Smith, Julia J. "Milton and Death." *DUJ*, 48, 1987, 15–22.

"What I propose to argue here is that the fear of mortality and its threat to himself had little power over Milton's imagination, and that this is entirely of a piece with his other emphases, doctrinal, emotional, and imaginative. Milton's picture of the world is characterized by self-confidence; an assurance of man's ability to control himself and to understand God; and a firm belief in the purpose and stability of his own existence, and the self-perpetuating power of nature."

1047 Smith, Logan Pearsall. *Milton and His Modern Critics.* Hamden, CT: Shoe String Press, 1967.

Reprint of Huckabay No. 917, originally published in 1940.

1048 Spaeth, Sigmund. *Milton's Knowledge of Music: Its Sources and Its Significance in His Works.* New York: Da Capo Press, 1973.

Reprint of Stevens No. 2407, originally published in 1913.

1049 Spellmeyer, Kurt Frederick. "Plo-

tinus and Seventeenth-Century Poetry: A Study of Donne, Milton and Traherne." Doctoral diss., Univ. of Washington, 1983. 347pp. Abs., *DAI*, 44, 1983, 1094A–95A.

Argues that the English writers' "aesthetic of self-creation" is affected by the Neoplatonic values of personal identity, self perception, and perfection through poetry.

1050 Spencer, Jeffry Burress. *Heroic Nature: Ideal Landscape in English Poetry from Marvell to Thomson.* Evanston, IL: Northwestern Univ. Press, 1973. xxx, 319pp.

Analyzes selected passages from *Paradise Lost* and *Paradise Regained*. Milton's landscapes "symbolically represent or objectify the poems' thematic content," and the epics themselves represented to Dryden "the harmonious mingling of fundamentally antithetical classes and baroque forms." Chapters on Milton: "Milton's Epic Landscapes: Responses to the Classical Baroque" and "Dryden and Milton." Reviews: Paul J. Korshin, *ELN*, 12, 1975, 203–06; James Sambrook, *JEGP*, 73, 1974, 246–47.

1051 Steadman, John M. "The Epic as Pseudomorph: Methodology in Milton Studies." *MiltonS*, 7, 1975, 3–27.

An introductory essay to a special issue of *Milton Studies*, which is devoted to current methodologies in Milton scholarship. Discusses the limitations as well as the potential of methodology in literary studies.

1052 Steadman, John M. "Heroes and Orators: Dialectical Process in Milton's Major Poetry." *Milton and the Paradoxes of Renaissance Heroism* (Baton Rouge and London: Louisiana State Univ. Press, 1987), pp. 173–93.

In the three long poems, Milton substitutes dialectical process for battlefields and right reason for martial valor. The role of orator-hero is filled by Satan, Christ, and Abdiel.

1053 Steadman, John M. *The Hill and the*

Labyrinth: Discourse and Certitude in Milton and His Near Contemporaries. Berkeley: Univ. of California Press, 1984. xiv, 185pp.

A reexamination of the relationship between style of discourse and epistemological method in seventeenth-century England. Brings into focus "certain late Renaissance and baroque tensions between conceptions of the role of language as a vehicle for traditional doctrines and accepted dogmas, as a weapon for attack or defense, and as an instrument of inquiry and discovery." Contains one chapter specifically on Milton, "The Dialectics of Temptation: Milton and the Idealistic View of Rhetoric." Reviews: John Pitcher, *TLS*, Aug. 23, 1985, p. 932; Heather Ross Asals, *RenQ*, 39, 1986, 356–58; Archie Burnett, *N&Q*, 33, 1986, 548–49; James Egan, *SCN*, 44, 1986, 6–7; Alvin Snider, *MP*, 84, 1986, 82–85; Frank Livingstone Huntley, *JEGP*, 85, 1986, 269–70; Charles A. Huttar, *C&L*, 36, 1987, 48–50; Thomas N. Corns, *YES*, 18, 1988, 269–70.

1054 Steadman, John M. *The Lamb and the Elephant: Ideal Imitation and the Context of Renaissance Allegory.* San Marino, CA: Huntington Library, 1974. xlvi, 254pp.

Milton discussed throughout, most extensively in the chapters on "Classical Tradition and Renaissance Epic" and "The Garment of Doctrine: Imitation and Allegory." Review: Anthony Low, *MiltonQ*, 9, 1975, 20–27.

1055 Steadman, John M. *Milton and the Paradoxes of Renaissance Heroism.* Baton Rouge and London: Louisiana State Univ. Press, 1987. viii, 264pp.

A collection of essays, many previously published, which deal mainly with the concept of heroism and spiritual combat in the three long poems. Reviews: David Loewenstein, *RenQ*, 41, 1988, 758–62; Thomas N. Corns, *N&Q*, 35, 1988, 535; Charles Martindale, *TLS*, Feb. 5–11, 1988, p. 142; Gordon Campbell, *MLR*, 85, 1990, 412–14; Nigel Smith, *RES*, 41, 1990, 123; *SHR*, 24, 1990, 79.

1056 Steadman, John M. *Milton and the Renaissance Hero.* Oxford: Clarendon Press, 1967. xiii, 209pp.

Considers Milton's "treatment of the heroic formulae commonly accepted as ethical and literary norms, his distinction between their valid and invalid modes, and his revaluation of the epic tradition in terms of this dichotomy." Discusses the critiques of fortitude, sapience, leadership, amor, and magnanimity. Reviews: *MiltonN*, 2, 1968, 8; *TLS*, Feb. 8, 1968, p. 134; L. R. N. Ashley, *BHR*, 30, 1968, 426–28; John Buxton, *RES*, 19, 1968, 319–20; D. J. Gordon, *RenQ*, 21, 1968, 491–93; Watson Kirkconnell, *DR*, 48, 1968, 260–61; Mark Roberts, *N&Q*, 213, 1968, 389–94; James H. Sims, *SCN*, 26, 1968, 2–3; James H. Sims, *SHR*, 2, 1968, 532–35; J. M. Couper, *AUMLA*, 31, 1969, 97–99; William G. Madsen, *CL*, 21, 1969, 89–90; Michael Wilding, *MLR*, 64, 1969, 142; Earl Miner, *ECS*, 3, 1970, 296–305; Ashraf H. A. Rushdy, *MiltonQ*, 21, No. 1, 1987, 71–74.

1057 Steadman, John M. "Milton and Renaissance Poetic Theory." *Medieval Epic to the Epic Theater of Brecht.* Ed. by Rosario P. Armato and John M. Spalek. Univ. of Southern California Studies in Comparative Literature, 1 (Los Angeles: Univ. of Southern California Press, 1968), pp. 109–24.

Believes that Milton turned to the Italians to help him understand how and what to imitate in classical poetry.

1058 Steadman, John M. *Milton's Biblical and Classical Imagery.* Duquesne Studies, Language and Literature Series, vol. 5. Pittsburgh, PA: Duquesne Univ. Press, 1984. 258pp.

Examines Milton's intertwining of biblical and classical imagery to take full advantage of both Greek and Hebrew etymologies. Most of the chapters are reprints of previously published articles. Reviews: John Pitcher, *TLS*, Aug. 23, 1985, p. 932; James H. Sims, *SCN*, 43, 1985, 1; G. R. Evans, *RES*, 37, 1986, 624; Charles A. Huttar, *C&L*, 36, 1987, 48–50; Thomas N. Corns, *MLR*, 83, 1988, 149–51.

1059 Steadman, John M. *Milton's Epic Characters: Image and Idol*. Chapel Hill: Univ. of North Carolina Press, 1968. xiii, 343pp.

"This volume explores the intellectual background of *Paradise Lost* and *Paradise Regained*, with particular emphasis on problems of characterization. Though its end is literary criticism, its method is primarily that of the history of ideas." Most of the chapters have been published previously but were revised for this study. Appendices: "Renaissance Definitions of the Hero"; "Heroes and Daemons"; and "Mazzoni on the Nature of the Hero." See No. 1060. Reviews: Hilda M. Hulme, *RenQ*, 22, 1969, 293–94; *MiltonN*, 3, 1969, 5–6; Michael Fixler, *RES*, 21, 1970, 358–61; Isabel Gamble MacCaffrey, *ELN*, 7, 1970, 219–22; James H. Sims, *SCN*, 28, 1970, 44–45; *TLS*, June 11, 1970, p. 641; Raymond B. Waddington, *MP*, 68, 1970, 201–04; Ashraf H. A. Rushdy, *MiltonQ*, 21, No. 1, 1987, 71–74.

1060 Steadman, John M. "The Suffering Servant." *Parnassus Revisited: Modern Critical Essays on the Epic Tradition*. Ed. by Anthony C. Low (Chicago, IL: American Library Assn., 1973), pp. 174–85.

Reprint of a chapter from No. 1059.

1061 Steadman, John M. *The Wall of Paradise: Essays on Milton's Poetics*. Baton Rouge and London: Louisiana State Univ. Press, 1985. 158pp.

Many chapters contain previously printed material and are noted elsewhere in this bibliography. Includes four new chapters: "Milton and the Art of Poetry: Rhetorical Contexts";

"Notes for an Ars Poetica: The Office of the Poet"; "Subject for Heroic Song: The Choice of an Epic Theme"; and "Argument More Heroic: Epic Theme as Didactic Exemplum." Reviews: Thomas N. Corns, *N&Q*, 34, 1987, 539–40; Galbraith M. Crump, *SR*, 95, 1987, 648–57; Balz Engler, *ES*, 68, 1987, 469–70; James Egan, *SCN*, 45, 1987, 6–7; Alastair Fowler, *TLS*, Jan. 30, 1987, p. 115; Ashraf H. A. Rushdy, *MiltonQ*, 21, No. 1, 1987, 71–74; David Loewenstein, *RenQ*, 41, 1988, 758–62.

1062 Stein, Arnold. "Justifying Milton's Ways." *SR*, 84, 1976, 695–706.

Review essay of the following recent studies: Donald F. Bouchard, *Milton: A Structural Reading* (No. 492); Galbraith Miller Crump, *The Mystical Design of "Paradise Lost"* (No. 2094); Austin C. Dobbins, *Milton and the Book of Revelation* (No. 2145); A. Kent Hieatt, *Chaucer, Spenser, Milton* (No. 685); William Kerrigan, *The Prophetic Milton* (No. 745); Anthony Low, *The Blaze of Noon* (No. 3615); Walter MacKellar, *Variorum Commentary*, vol. 4 (No. 3386); Hugh M. Richmond, *The Christian Revolutionary: John Milton* (No. 971); Thomas Wheeler, *"Paradise Lost" and the Modern Reader* (No. 3229); Joseph Anthony Wittreich, Jr., ed., *Milton and the Line of Vision* (No. 1146); *Milton Studies*, vols. 7 (No. 762) and 8.

1063 Stein, Arnold. "Milton and Metaphysical Art: An Exploration." *Critical Essays on Milton from "ELH"* (Baltimore, MD, and London: Johns Hopkins Press, 1969), pp. 1–14.

Reprint of Huckabay No. 933, originally published in 1949.

1064 Stein, Arnold, ed. *On Milton's Poetry: A Selection of Modern Studies*. Greenwich, CT: Fawcett Publications, 1970. xii, 273pp.

A selection of reprints of modern criticism by twenty authors. The introduction deals with the problems of Milton criticism from the seventeenth century to the present. In this bibliography, each selection is listed according to author and classification. Review: Mario A. Di Cesare, *RenQ*, 24, 1971, 587–90.

1065 Stephens, James. "Bacon and Milton." *MiltonQ*, 9, 1975, 36.

Abstract of a paper presented at the University of Wisconsin, Milwaukee, Milton Tercentenary Conference, in November, 1974. Believes that Bacon influenced Milton on matters of church reform, censorship, and education.

1066 Stevens, Paul. "Milton and the Icastic Imagination." *MiltonS*, 20, 1984, 43–73. Traces the continental background of the idea of the icastic imagination, which creates and reflects the good, and uses Adam's dreams in *Paradise Lost* as evidence of Milton's familiarity with it.

1067 Stock, A. G. "Classic Forms and Puritan Principles: A Note on Their Interaction in Milton's Poetry." *AJES*, 2, 1977, 1–10.

Believes that in Milton's mind there was always a struggle between the classical world and the Puritan Christian world. Shows that in his poetry Milton permits Christian values to distort classical forms.

1068 Stollman, Samuel S. "The Conceptualization and Role of Judaism and Pharisaism in Milton's 'Great Argument.'" *HUSL*, 8, 1980, 127–51.

Argues that Milton "distinguished between the Judaic and Hebraic factors of the Jewish heritage" and that the Pharisees taught erroneous doctrines and opposed Jesus and the Jews themselves.

1069 Stollman, Samuel S. "Milton's Dichotomy of 'Judaism' and 'Hebraism.'" *PMLA*, 89, 1974, 105–12.

Believes that Milton dichotomizes the Old Testament into Judaism and Hebraism and that "the undiscriminating use of 'Hebraic' or 'Judaic' as

interchangeable, all-inclusive designations for the contents of the Hebrew Bible has inadvertently contributed to the enigma of Milton's tolerationist psyche and the contradictions of Milton's 'judaistic motifs.'"

1070 Stollman, Samuel S. "Milton's Rabbinical Readings and Fletcher." *MiltonS*, 4, 1972, 195–215.

Questions Harris Fletcher's thesis (see Huckabay Nos. 557–58) that Milton used the Buxtorf rabbinical Bible and asserts that almost half of the rabbinical glosses cited by Fletcher have been mistranslated.

1071 Strasser, Gerhard Friedrich. "The Iconography of War in D'Aubigné, Gryphius, and Milton." Doctoral diss., Brown Univ., 1974. 287pp. Abs., *DAI*, 46, 1986, 2690A.

Correlates "visual representations of [Renaissance] warfare" in the three authors' works—including a sonnet by Milton and *Paradise Lost*—to the religious and political wars that affected them.

1072 Stroup, Thomas B. *Religious Rite and Ceremony in Milton's Poetry.* Ann Arbor, MI: Univ. Microfilms International, 1980 Books on Demand Reprints.

Reprint of Huckabay No. 943, originally published in 1968.

1073 Studies in Milton. Published by the Japan Society of Seventeenth-Century English Literature, Tohoku Gakuin Univ. Foreword by Eitaro Sayams. Ed. by Shonosuke Ishii and others. Tokyo: Kinseido, 1974. xxiv, 216pp.

A collection of essays by Naoyuki Yagyu, Akira Arai, Kazuaki Saito, Ishitaro Tamaki, Masahiko Agari, Takero Oiji, Haruhiko Fujii, Yutaka Akagawa, Mashahiro Hiwatashi, and Mitsuo Miyanishi. Also contains a selected Milton bibliography by Akira Arai. In this bibliography, each essay is listed according to author and classification.

1074 Summers, Claude J. "Remarks Occa-

sioned by the Death of C. A. Patrides."
MiltonQ, 21, No. 1, 1987, 37–39.

Delivered at the Seventh Biennial
Renaissance Conference at the University of Michigan, Dearborn, on
October 17, 1986.

1075 Summers, Joseph H. "The Crucifixion
in Milton's English Poems." *SCN*, 38,
1980, 46.

Abstract of a paper presented at the
1979 MLA Convention. "Within Milton's changing treatments of the crucifixion in his poems, it is possible to
glimpse something of the spiritual journey of a learned, confident, proud man
who came to accept the necessity—
and the possible triumphs—of suffering and death." Also abstracted in
MiltonQ, 14, 1980, 72.

1076 Summers, Joseph. "Milton and
Celebration." *MiltonQ*, 5, 1971, 1–7.

An address given at the annual Milton
Society of America dinner on December 29, 1970. "Milton's fascination with
the celebration of makings or events
or deeds . . . can be glimpsed continually in his prose as well as his poetry."

1077 Swan, Jim. "Difference and Silence:
John Milton and the Question of Gender." *The (M)other Tongue: Essays in
Feminist Psychoanalytic Interpretation.*
Ed. by Shirley Nelson Garner, Claire
Kahane, and Madelon Sprengnether
(Ithaca, NY, and London: Cornell Univ.
Press, 1985), pp. 142–68.

Discusses Milton's Renaissance view
of women, especially as it applies to
Samson and to Eve and Sin in *Paradise Lost*. Believes that the male fear
and rage are "not about woman at
all" but "about the double and divided subject, who suffers a fall into
language."

1078 Symes, M. W. R. "The Theme of
the Garden and Its Relation to Man in
the Poetry of Spenser, Milton, and Marvell, with Consideration of Some Other
Poetry of the Time." M.Phil. thesis, King's
College, London Univ., 1968.

1079 Takemura, Sanae. "Milton's View
of Ireland." *MCJ News*, 7, 1984, 12–13.

Abstract of paper presented. *Observations upon the Articles of Peace* and
the *History of Britain* show that Milton
viewed contemporary Irishmen as
"obdurate barbarians" while he maintained respect for the "cultured"
druids of seventh-century Ireland.

1080 Tanner, John Sears. "Milton among
the Mormons." *Ringing the Bell Backward: The Proceedings of the First
International Milton Symposium.* Ed.
by Ronald G. Shafer. The IUP Imprint
Series (Indiana: Indiana Univ. of Pennsylvania, 1982), pp. 123–32.

Notes several parallels between Miltonic and Mormon beliefs, such as the
War in Heaven and fortunate fall. In
the response, pp. 133–34, Michael A.
Mikolajczak suggests that the study
be expanded to include discussion of
what the parallels signify.

1081 Tate, Charles D., Jr. "The Christian
Humanism of John Milton." *"The Need
Beyond Reason" and Other Essays: College of Humanities Centennial Lectures,
1975–76* (Provo, UT: Brigham Young
Univ. Press, 1976), pp. 59–71.

Finds in all of Milton's works a
blending of the Christian and the
humanist. Sees no contradiction in the
two terms.

1082 Tayler, Edward W. *Milton's Poetry:
Its Development in Time.* Duquesne
Studies, Language and Literature Series,
vol. 2. Pittsburgh, PA: Duquesne Univ.
Press, 1979. x, 273pp.

Distinguishes between time as kairos
and time as chronos and is concerned
with the proleptic form of *Lycidas* and
the longer poems. Chapters: "Introduction"; "Occasional Experiments";
"*Lycidas* in Christian Time"; "*Paradise Lost*: From Shadows to Truth";
"*Samson Agonistes*: Found in the
Close"; "The Tempestivity of Time";
"*Paradise Regained*: Waiting to Stand";
and "Some Conclusions." Reviews:

P. J. Klemp, *MiltonQ*, 13, 1979, 153–55; Albert R. Cirillo, *RenQ*, 33, 1980, 486–88; William G. Madsen, *JEGP*, 79, 1980, 571–72; William E. Cain, *MLN*, 96, 1981, 1121–33; William Kerrigan, *MiltonQ*, 15, 1981, 71–72 (reply to Klemp); Edward Le Comte, *MiltonQ*, 15, 1981, 105 (contradicts Kerrigan); Hugh MacCallum, *UTQ*, 50, 1981, 314–23; J. Martin Evans, *RES*, 33, 1982, 318–23.

1083 Taylor, George. *Milton's Use of Du Bartas.* New York: Octagon Books, 1968. Reprint of Huckabay No. 955, originally published in 1934.

1084 "Tercentenary Conferences and Volumes." *MiltonN*, 2, 1968, 7.
Notice of the tercentenary celebrations at Goucher College, the College of Notre Dame of Maryland (Baltimore), and the University of York. Also announces recent publications, including the first volume of *Milton Studies*.

1085 "Tercentenary Conferences and Volumes." *MiltonN*, 2, 1968, 28–30.
On an exhibition at the John Rylands Library, a special issue of the *Huntington Library Quarterly* (see No. 714), and Shawcross and Emma's *Language and Style in Milton* (Huckabay No. 3429). Also includes Harry J. Mooney's report on papers read at the University of Pittsburgh.

1086 ["Tercentenary Festivals."] *MiltonQ*, 8, 1974, 95–97.
Reports on programs at Cambridge University, the University of Wisconsin, Milwaukee, Marquette University, the University of Wisconsin, Parkside, and Chalfont St. Giles.

1087 Teskey, Gordon. "From Allegory to Dialectic: Imagining Error in Spenser and Milton." *PMLA*, 101, 1986, 9–23.
Compares Milton to "his original" Spenser in his handling of "the gradations and subtleties that are called up as error, between [the two] extremes" when the poet acts as "interpreter of the best things" and hence also as "interpreter of the worst." Contrasts Spenser's representation of error and Milton's dialectical handling of error.

1088 Thickstun, Margaret Olofson. "Fictions of the Feminine: Puritan Doctrine and the Representation of Women." Doctoral diss., Cornell Univ., 1984. 181pp.

1089 Thompson, E. N. S. *Essays on Milton.* Folcroft, PA: Folcroft Library Editions, 1969.
Reprint of Stevens No. 2416, originally published in 1914.

1090 Thompson, E. P. "Milton the Radical." *TLS*, Mar. 7, 1975, p. 253.
"Hope[s] to throw new light on the possible relation between Milton's theology and Muggletonian doctrine."

1091 Thomson, John Morton, III. "'God Looking on th' Earth': Milton and the Reward of True Fame." Doctoral diss., Univ. of Iowa, 1983. 298pp. Abs., *DAI*, 44, 1984, 3699A–3700A.
Explores Milton's use of "self-consciousness" to handle the conflict between classical public heroism and true fame, claiming that Jesus's "self-identity as Son of God" is "a role at once personal and public."

1092 Tillyard, E. M. W. "John Milton." *British Writers.* Ed. by Ian Scott-Kilvert (New York: Charles Scribner's Sons, 1979), pp. 159–78.
Revision of Huckabay No. 973, originally published in 1952.

1093 Tippens, Darryl Lee. "John Milton and St. Paul: A Comparative Study." Doctoral diss., Louisiana State Univ., 1973. 270pp. Abs., *DAI*, 35, 1974, 1125A–26A.
Asserts Milton's agreement with the "Pauline context" when discussing *ex deo* creation, monism, subordination of women, anti-Trinitarianism, freedom from the law, and other "Miltonic problems."

1094 Titlestad, Peter James Hilary. "English Puritanism as a Literary Force from the Elizabethan Age to the Restoration." D.Litt. thesis, Univ. of Pretoria, 1976.

1095 Tobin, John Joseph Michael. "Milton's Concept of the Cardinal Virtue of Justice as Expressed in the Poetry." Doctoral diss., Univ. of Toronto, 1971. Abs., *DAI*, 32, 1972, 7013A.

Argues that context often defines justice in Milton's works, although "personal and retributive justice" consistently involves "private temperance and public retribution."

1096 Tomlinson, Mrs. M. R. "Milton Tercentenary." *MiltonQ*, 8, 1974, 68.

"I am writing . . . to tell you of the plans that are being made in Chalfont St. Giles to celebrate the tercentenary of the death of Milton in this year. . . ."

1097 Trapp, J. B. "Iconography." *John Milton: Introductions*. Ed. by John Broadbent (Cambridge: Cambridge Univ. Press, 1973), pp. 162–85.

Summarizes European iconography concerning biblical stories, from the creation to the Last Judgment. Contains sections on the iconography of Adam and Eve and Samson.

1098 Travers, Michael Ernest. "The Devotional Experience in Milton's Poetry." Doctoral diss., Michigan State Univ., 1985. 203pp. Abs., *DAI*, 46, 1986, 1954A.

Concludes that poetry was for Milton a devotional form of worship, communicated by his characters' search for God in the middle of earthy struggles.

1099 Travers, Michael Ernest. *The Devotional Experience in the Poetry of John Milton.* Lewiston, NY: Edwin Mellen Press, 1988. 163pp.

"I wish to examine . . . the experience of man's devotion to God . . . in Milton's poetic theories and his major poetry from 1629 to 1671. I wish to argue that Milton's own devotion to God is an active expression of his love for God and that he communicates this devotion in his view of poetry and in the experience of the speakers and characters in his poems." Reviews: George Musacchio, *C&L*, 38, 1989,

86–87; Rachel Trubowitz, *SCN*, 47, 1989, 7; John D. Morrison, *JETS*, 34, 1991, 403–04.

1100 Trevor-Roper, Hugh. "The Elitist Politics of Milton." *TLS*, June 1, 1973, pp. 601–03.

Believes that distinguishing between Milton as a poet and as a politician is a vain exercise, for his political ideas were an essential part of his personality, philosophy, and poetry.

1101 Trickett, Rachel. "Shakespeare and Milton." *E&S*, 31, 1978, 23–35.

Demonstrates that Milton echoes Shakespeare in *Lycidas, Comus,* and the long poems and suggests that these echoes "illustrate an aspect of the way in which the poetic imagination works."

1102 Turner, Amy Lee. "Milton and Millet." *SCB*, 30, 1970, 223–27.

Argues "that even though the artists were two centuries apart in time, lived in contrasting social backgrounds, yet still expressed the same subject matter, it is how each handles his media that determines the quality of his art."

1103 Turner, James Grantham. *The Politics of Landscape: Rural Scenery and Society in English Poetry, 1630–1660.* Cambridge, MA: Harvard Univ. Press, 1979. xiii, 237pp.

Studies "the literary depiction of rural places and the life they support." Discusses Milton's landscape, including references to *L'Allegro, Comus,* and *Paradise Lost.* Reviews: Kitty Scoular Datta, *RenQ*, 33, 1980, 482–84; J. S. Morrill, *RES*, 31, 1980, 466–67; Jeffry Burress Spencer, *JEGP*, 79, 1980, 121–24.

1104 Tuve, Rosemond. "Baroque and Mannerist Milton." *Essays by Rosemond Tuve: Spenser, Herbert, Milton.* Ed. by Thomas P. Roche, Jr. (Princeton, NJ: Princeton Univ. Press; London: Oxford Univ. Press, 1970), pp. 262–80.

Reprint of Huckabay No. 982, originally published in 1961.

1105 Tuve, Rosemond. "New Approaches to Milton." *Essays by Rosemond Tuve: Spenser, Herbert, Milton.* Ed. by Thomas P. Roche, Jr. (Princeton, NJ: Princeton Univ. Press; London: Oxford Univ. Press, 1970), pp. 255–61.

Reprint of Huckabay No. 3898, originally published in 1958.

1106 Ulreich, John C., Jr. "By Gradual Scale Sublimed: Ideas of Form in Milton's Poetry." Doctoral diss., Harvard Univ., 1969.

1107 Ulreich, John C., Jr. "Milton on the Eucharist: Some Second Thoughts about Sacramentalism." *Milton and the Middle Ages.* Ed. by John Mulryan (Lewisburg, PA: Bucknell Univ. Press; London and Toronto: Associated Univ. Presses, 1982), pp. 32–56.

An attempt "to reconcile the apparently anti-sacramental stance of Milton in most of his work, with those salient passages where Milton is decidedly in favor of the sacramental and even the Eucharistic tradition."

1108 Ulreich, John C. "Prophets, Priests, and Poets: Toward a Definition of Religious Fiction." *Cithara*, 22, No. 2, 1983, 3–31.

Discusses the two modes of religious poetry, as illustrated by Spenser, "the archetypal English maker of myth," and Milton, "almost certainly our greatest iconoclast."

1109 Utsunomiya, Hidekazu. "Milton's God." *MCJ News*, 8, 1985, 13–15.

Abstract of paper presented. Discusses Milton's comments about his blindness in Sonnet 19 ("When I consider") and *Paradise Lost*. Concludes that "Milton could overcome his physical blindness by believing in a biblical God who suffered with him (and us) in the person of Jesus of Nazareth, in history."

1110 Vicari, Patricia. "The Triumph of Art, the Triumph of Death: Orpheus in Spenser and Milton." *Orpheus: The Metamorphoses of a Myth.* Ed. by John Warden (Toronto, Buffalo, NY, and

London: Univ. of Toronto Press, 1982), pp. 207–30.

Believes that Orpheus has personal and emblematic significance for Milton. Traces his use of the Orpheus myth from the early poems to *Paradise Lost*.

1111 Visiak, Edward Harold. *The Animus against Milton.* Folcroft, PA: Folcroft Library Editions, 1970.

Reprint of Huckabay No. 992, originally published in 1945.

1112 Visiak, Edward Harold. *Milton Agonistes: A Metaphysical Criticism.* Folcroft, PA: Folcroft Library Editions, 1977; Norwood, PA: Norwood Editions, 1978.

Reprints of Stevens No. 2521, originally published in 1923.

1113 Visiak, Edward Harold. *The Portent of Milton: Some Aspects of His Genius.* Atlantic Highlands, NJ: Humanities Press, 1969.

Reprint of Huckabay No. 997, originally published in 1958.

1114 Vogler, Thomas A. "Romantic Form Consciousness: The Desire of Discourse and the Discourse of Desire." *English and German Romanticism: Cross-Currents and Controversies.* Ed. by James Pipkin (Heidelberg: Carl Winter Universitätsverlag, 1985), pp. 111–39.

Briefly mentions Milton in a study of cognitive structures which "can be read as self-descriptive in ways typical of a wide range of authors who shared the same form of pre-Romantic discourse."

1115 Voltaire, François. *Essay on Milton.* Ed. by Desmond Flower. Folcroft, PA: Folcroft Library Editions, 1970; Norwood, PA: Norwood Editions, 1977.

Reprints of Huckabay No. 1001, originally published in 1954.

1116 Wain, John. "Reflections on Johnson's *Life of Milton*." *William Empson: The Man and His Work.* Ed. by Roma Gill (London: Routledge and Kegan Paul, 1974), pp. 117–25.

Deals with the problem of liking a man's poetry but abhorring his political views. Feels that "Johnson approached the task of writing about Milton in very much the same way as I have, in recent years, approached the task of writing about [Ezra] Pound."

1117 Walker, Julia M., ed. *Milton and the Idea of Woman*. Urbana and Chicago: Univ. of Illinois Press, 1988. 262pp.

In "The Idea of Milton and the Idea of Woman," pp. 1–14, Walker introduces the volume, stating that "Poet, scholar, theologian, intellectual, man, John Milton was ill-equipped to come to terms with woman as an idea." Abs., *MiltonQ*, 24, 1990, 151. Includes essays by Richard Corum, Jackie DiSalvo, Lynn E. Enterline, Noam Flinker, Marshall Grossman, Janet Elizabeth Halley, Dayton William Haskin, S. J., Leah S. Marcus, Diane Kelsey McColley, John C. Ulreich, Jr., Walker, Kathleen Wall, and Susanne Woods. In this bibliography, each essay is listed by author and classification. Reviews: *ANQ*, 2, 1989, 110; Anne Ferry, *JEGP*, 88, 1989, 420–22; Raymond-Jean Frontain, *C&L*, 39, 1989, 96–98; Diane K. McColley, *ANQ*, 2, 1989, 110–20; Margaret Stocker, *TLS*, Jan. 27, 1989 90; Ann Baynes Coiro, *RenQ*, 43, 1990, 441–44; Marilyn R. Farwell, *CL*, 44, 1992, 97–101.

1118 Warhaft, Sidney. "'Thir Song was Partial': Some Recent Milton Publications." *Mosaic*, 9, 1976, 159–73.

Review essay that discusses the following: Michael Lieb and John T. Shawcross, eds., *Achievements of the Left Hand* (No. 3904); *Milton Studies*, vol. 5; Christopher Grose, *Milton's Epic Process* (No. 2345); and Maurice Kelley, ed., *Complete Prose Works of John Milton*, vol. 6 (No. 366). Concludes "that those critics serve Milton best who focus directly on his actual accomplishment without trying to make him over into their own image or somebody else's, and serve him least who come to him with inadequate scholarship or with inflexibile presuppositions

about the man, his times, and the genres he manipulated." Abs., *MiltonQ*, 12, 1978, 115–16.

1119 Warnke, Frank J. *Versions of Baroque: European Literature in the Seventeenth Century*. New Haven, CT, and London: Yale Univ. Press, 1972. xi, 229pp.

Uses the term "baroque" to describe a cluster of styles found in the period from 1580 to 1690. Contains many references to Milton's verse, including *L'Allegro* and *Il Penseroso*, *Lycidas*, and the three long poems. Reviews: Elias L. Rivers, *Diacritics*, 2, 1972, 22–24; Ronald M. Huebert, *SCN*, 31, 1973, 101–02.

1120 Waters, D. Douglas. "Milton's Use of the Sorcerer-Rhetorician." *MiltonQ*, 8, 1974, 113–16.

Shows that "Milton's complex connections between sorcery and false rhetoric may reveal something about his literary development in *Comus*, the anti-episcopal tracts, *Samson Agonistes*, *Paradise Regained*, and *Paradise Lost*."

1121 Watt, James Timothy. "The Prophecy of the Hero's Children in English Renaissance Epic: A Study of Heroic Futurity in Spenser, Milton, and Relevant Antecedents." Doctoral diss., Univ. of North Carolina, Chapel Hill, 1977. 426pp. Abs., *DAI*, 38, 1978, 7352A–53A.

Argues that both Spenser and Milton modify the classical prophecy concerning the nature of an epic hero's progeny, which will encompass all humanity, including the reader.

1122 Webber, Joan Malory. "Jumping the Gap: The Epic Poetry of Milton—and After." *MiltonQ*, 13, 1979, 107–11.

Points out the time lapse between previous epics and asserts that the epic genre is not dead. Claims that "We have not needed a new epic because Milton told us almost all we had to know about ourselves." Suggests that "Any epic poem today has to find its own philosophical or theological ground, and it probably has to come from outside the present western tradition of culture and power."

1123 Webber, Joan. "The Son of God and Power of Life in Three Poems by Milton." *ELH*, 37, 1970, 175–94.

Notices consistencies in Milton's treatment of the Christ character in the *Nativity Ode, Paradise Lost,* and *Paradise Regained.* Claims that throughout the forty-year period represented by these works, Milton portrays Christ as the giver of life, the shepherd of power, light, harmony, and peace.

1124 Webber, Joan. "Walking on Water: Milton, Stevens, and Contemporary American Poetry." *Milton and the Line of Vision.* Ed. by Joseph Anthony Wittreich, Jr. (Madison and London: Univ. of Wisconsin Press, 1975), pp. 231–68.

Uses Milton as an example for contemporary American poets, who should continue to speak out as prophets "even when they know they cannot succeed in changing the world." "Milton, crying out against the return of tyranny in 1660, when so many of his former allies were running for shelter, stood on the pinnacle of the temple. . . . Faith in creation, in life itself, enabled him to maintain his perilous balance. That kind of faith can sustain our poetry now."

1125 Wedgwood, C. V. "John Milton." *Seventeenth-Century English Literature.* Second edition (London: Oxford Univ. Press, 1970), pp. 84–93.

Revision of Huckabay No. 1010, originally published in 1950.

1126 Weiss, Brian. "Milton's Use of Ramist Method in His Scholarly Writings." Doctoral diss., City Univ. of New York, 1974. 264pp. Abs., *DAI*, 35, 1975, 4569A.

Considers Milton's deference to and departures from Ramist logic in the *Art of Logic, Accedence Commenc't Grammar,* and the *Christian Doctrine.*

1127 Whitehead, Oliver Henry. "Tele-

ology and the Function of Discourse in the Epics of Homer, Virgil, Dante and Milton." Doctoral diss., Univ. of Toronto, 1978. Abs., *DAI*, 39, 1979, 4229A.

Contends that all four writers present significant speeches that often express each poet's perception of his role and are increasingly influenced by the Christian Logos.

1128 Whiting, George W. *Milton and This Pendant World.* New York: Octagon Books, 1969.

Reprint of Huckabay No. 1017, originally published in 1958.

1129 Wight, Mary Elizabeth Merrill. "Milton's Conception of Regeneration." Doctoral diss., Univ. of Illinois, 1968. 515pp. Abs., *DA*, 29, 1969, 2689A.

Interprets the *Christian Doctrine* as "Milton's theological foundation" and *Paradise Lost* as the application of his religious ideas to life, especially the process of regeneration.

1130 Wilding, Michael. *Dragons Teeth: Literature in the English Revolution.* Oxford: Clarendon Press; New York: Oxford Univ. Press, 1987. 280pp.

Examines the major works of the English revolution in their contemporary historical and political context. The chapters on Milton are reprints, which are listed under their appropriate classification in this bibliography. Reviews: Thomas Healy, *English* (Oxford), 37, 1988, 155–64; Christopher Hill, *TLS*, Jan. 1, 1988, p. 17; David Norbrook, *LRB*, 10, 1988, 20–21.

1131 Wilkerson, James Carrell. "Milton's Ontology." Doctoral diss., Florida State Univ., 1973. 277pp. Abs., *DAI*, 34, 1973, 1875A.

Analyzes Milton's belief that God is the material center of the universe, he drew into himself to yield space to "individual beings," and all matter will return to an "immutable state."

1132 Williams, Kathleen. "Milton, Greatest Spenserian." *Milton and the Line of Vision.* Ed. by Joseph Anthony Wittreich,

Jr. (Madison and London: Univ. of Wisconsin Press, 1975), pp. 25–55.

"My intention here is merely to refer, in relation particularly to Milton and Spenser, to a poetic line, a community of poets extending through time and engaging, as often as not, in a kind of dialectic with the tradition of which they so strongly feel themselves a part."

1133 Williams, Meg Harris. *Inspiration in Milton and Keats.* London and Basingstoke: Macmillan, 1982. xi, 212pp.

Discusses the meaning of inspiration and considers Keats's and Milton's different attitudes toward it. Believes that Milton had a pervasive influence on Keats. Reviews: Anne Elliott, *RES*, 35, 1984, 541; John Barnard, *KSR*, 2, 1987, 145.

1134 Willis, Gladys J. *The Penalty of Eve: John Milton and Divorce.* New York and Berne: Peter Lang, 1984. 156pp.

"This book establishes the hypothesis that there are profound links between John Milton's 'rule of charity' as described in *The Doctrine and Discipline of Divorce* and St. Augustine's exegesis in *De Doctrina Christiana*—as it pertains to the Christian man and the primary factor that should determine his earthly actions."

1135 Willis, Gladys J. "The Rule of Charity in John Milton's Discussion of Marriage and Divorce: From the Divorce Tracts to *Paradise Lost* and *Samson Agonistes*." Doctoral diss., Princeton Univ., 1973. 181pp. Abs., *DAI*, 34, 1974, 5129A.

Uses Augustine's "rule of charity" to defend the orthodoxy of Milton's belief that divorce is justifiable when matrimony distracts from spiritual fulfillment.

1136 Willson, Robert F., Jr., ed. "Landmarks of Criticism: On Shakespeare and Milton—William Hazlitt." *ShN*, 24, 1974, 14.

From *Lecture 3*, in *Lectures on the English Poets* (1818).

1137 Wind, Barry. "On Aspects of Milton and Architecture." *SCN*, 34, 1976, 2–3.

Suggests that some of Milton's references to buildings may derive from books and some from stage architecture.

1138 Winegardner, Karl Lewis. "No Hasty Conclusions: Milton's Ante-Nicene Pneumatology." *MiltonQ*, 11, 1977, 102–07.

Reviews the ante-Nicene church fathers whom Milton read and examines their influence on his notion of the Holy Spirit. Observes that the "ambivalence which existed in the Fathers helped Milton formulate his own Trinitarian position which was heavily weighted toward the Father and progressively away from the Son and the Spirit."

1139 Winegardner, Karl Lewis. "To Sift and To Winnow: The Influence on Milton's Trinity of the Ante-Nicene Church Fathers." Doctoral diss., Bowling Green State Univ., 1974. 134pp. Abs., *DAI*, 35, 1975, 4465A.

Argues that Milton's beliefs in God's superiority, Christ's subordinate position as the "Second Adam," and the Holy Spirit's limited role are influenced by church fathers before Constantine.

1140 Wittreich, Joseph Anthony, Jr. "A. S. P. Woodhouse, *The Heavenly Muse: A Preface to Milton*." *SCN*, 32, 1974, 69–70.

Review essay. Feels that Woodhouse's study (No. 1156) is old fashioned in some respects, but "it opens vistas that we can now begin to explore."

1141 Wittreich, Joseph Anthony, Jr. "Beyond New Criticism: Literary History, Literary Criticism, and Milton Studies, 1973." *MiltonQ*, 8, 1974, 15–21.

Review essay. Notices that recent criticism has "developed new alliances, combining . . . the various 'criticisms' and yoking them irrevocably to sophisticated historical study." Discusses the following: Christopher Grose, *Milton's Epic Process* (No. 2345); Leslie Brisman, *Milton's Poetry of Choice* (No. 4232); Watson Kirkconnell, *Awake the Courteous Echo* (No. 3371); John

Collier, *Milton's "Paradise Lost":
Screen Play for Cinema of the Mind*
(No. 2068); Michael Lieb and John T.
Shawcross, eds., *Achievements of the
Left Hand* (No. 3904); Balachandra
Rajan, ed., *The Prison and the Pin-
nacle* (No. 960); Maurice Kelley, ed.,
Complete Prose Works of John Milton,
vol. 6 (No. 366); and *Milton Studies,*
vol. 5.

1142 Wittreich, Joseph Anthony, Jr.,
ed. *Calm of Mind: Tercentenary Essays
on "Paradise Regained" and "Samson
Agonistes" in Honor of John S. Diekhoff.*
Cleveland, OH, and London: Press of Case
Western Reserve Univ., 1971. xxiv, 342pp.
Reprinted Ann Arbor, MI: Univ. Microfilms International, 1980 Books on Demand Reprints.

Contains essays by J. B. Broadbent,
Albert R. Cirillo, Stuart Curran, Stanley
E. Fish, Merritt Y. Hughes, William
B. Hunter, Jr., William Riley Parker,
Mother Mary Christopher Pecheux,
O. S. U., Irene Samuel, John T. Shaw-
cross, John M. Steadman, Raymond
B. Waddington, and Wittreich. Appen-
dices (by Wittreich): "Illustrators of
Paradise Regained and Their Subjects
(1713–1816)" and "A Catalogue of
Blake's Illustrations to Milton." In
this bibliography, each essay is listed
according to author and classification.
Reviews: *MiltonQ*, 6, No. 1, 1972,
19–20; Michael Lieb, *Cithara*, 12,
1972, 85–106; D. T. Mace, *RES*, 24,
1973, 210–13; George F. Sensabaugh,
RenQ, 27, 1974, 376–81.

1143 Wittreich, Joseph. *Feminist Milton.*
Ithaca, NY, and London: Cornell Univ.
Press, 1987. xxiii, 173pp.

Studies women's observations on
Milton from about 1700 to 1830 and
contends that Milton was an early feminist. "This book reconstructs a female
perspective on and experience of *Paradise Lost* as a poem that was itself
engaged in the dethroning of authority
and in the formation of new gender
paradigms, as a poem inscribed with,

not by a received ideology concerning
the sexes which, instead of transmit-
ting, it would transform." Reviews:
Joseph Rosenblum, *LJ*, 112, 1987,
112–13; *NYRB*, 35, 1988, 45; Kim
Hamilton, *MiltonQ*, 22, 1988, 132–33;
Virginia R. Mollenkott, *C&L*, 38, 1988,
76–78; Diane K. McColley, *ANQ*, 2,
1989, 110–20; James Grantham Turner,
Criticism, 31, 1989, 193–200.

1144 Wittreich, Joseph. "In Happy
Consort, in Dubious Battle: The State
of Milton (and Renaissance) Criticism."
Rev, 5, 1983, 1–16.

Review essay that discusses the following studies: Stanley Fish, ed., *"ELH":
A Special Renaissance Issue in Honor
of Arnold Stein*, vol. 49, no. 2, 1982;
Michael Lieb, *Poetics of the Holy* (No.
2612); and John T. Shawcross, *With
Mortal Voice* (No. 3040).

1145 Wittreich, Joseph Anthony, Jr. "A
Little Onward . . . a Little Further On."
MLQ, 42, 1981, 184–91.

Review essay. Uses the following
studies to discuss the nature of modern Milton criticism: John Demaray,
Milton's Theatrical Epic (No. 2128)
and Louis L. Martz, *Poet of Exile*
(No. 820).

1146 Wittreich, Joseph Anthony, Jr., ed.
Milton and the Line of Vision. Madison
and London: Univ. of Wisconsin Press,
1975. xxi, 278pp.

Contains essays by Donald R. Howard,
Kathleen Williams, S. K. Heninger,
Jr., Wittreich, Jackie DiSalvo, James
Rieger, Stuart Curran, and Joan Webber.
In this bibliography, each essay is listed
according to author and classification.
Reviews: Arnold Stein, *SR*, 84, 1976,
695–706; Peter Malekin, *RES*, 28, 1977,
350–53; Luther Lee Scales, Jr., *KSJ*,
26, 1977, 150–52; A. M. Elliott, *N&Q*,
25, 1978, 77–79; Mary Ann Radzinowicz, *MLR*, 73, 1978, 404–05; Gary
A. Stringer, *SCN*, 36, 1978, 105–07.

1147 Wittreich, Joseph Anthony, Jr.

"Milton's Romantic Audience." *AN&Q*, 10, 1972, 147–50.

"Literary historians and critics have been extravagant, it seems, in their estimates of both the size and calibre of Milton's Romantic audience." For "both Milton and the Romantics... the ideal reader, the true critic... must bring a judgment 'equal or superior'— to that of the poet he professes to admire."

1148 Wittreich, Joseph Anthony, Jr. "Milton's 'Virtuoso' Forms: A Review Article." *Genre*, 5, 1972, 307–25.

The following recent studies "open the seals that have hidden its [Milton's art's] premises and its design from modern readers": Stanley Fish, "Discovery as Form in *Paradise Lost*" (No. 2215); Michael Fixler, "The Apocalypse within *Paradise Lost*" (No. 2222); Angus Fletcher, *The Transcendental Masque* (No. 1358); John R. Knott, Jr., *Milton's Pastoral Vision* (No. 2540); Barbara K. Lewalski, "Milton: Revaluation of Romance" (No. 783); and John T. Shawcross, "The Style and Genre of *Paradise Lost*" (No. 3038).

1149 Wittreich, Joseph. "The *New* Milton Criticism." *Rev*, 1, 1979, 123–64.

Review article. Believes that Milton criticism needs to return to its origins in the eighteenth century. Discusses Edward Le Comte, *Milton and Sex* (No. 774); Roland Mushat Frye, *Milton's Imagery and the Visual Arts* (No. 620); Christopher Hill, *Milton and the English Revolution* (No. 174); and Mary Ann Radzinowicz, *Toward "Samson Agonistes"* (No. 3666).

1150 Wittreich, Joseph Anthony, Jr. "'A Poet amongst Poets': Milton and the Tradition of Prophecy." *Milton and the Line of Vision*. Ed. by Wittreich (Madison and London: Univ. of Wisconsin Press, 1975), pp. 97–142.

"From the standpoint of literary history, prophecy is a link between... Milton's poetry and that of Chaucer, Langland, and Spenser.... From the perspective of literary history, Milton may thus be seen at the center of a poetic tradition that, extending from the Middle Ages into the modern world, also reaches beyond national boundaries to form cultural ones."

1151 Wittreich, Joseph Anthony, Jr. "The Poetry of the Rainbow: Milton and Newton among the Prophets." *Poetic Prophecy in Western Literature*. Ed. by Jan Wojcik and Raymond-Jean Frontain (Rutherford, NJ, Madison, WI, and Teaneck, NJ: Fairleigh Dickinson Univ. Press; London and Toronto: Associated Univ. Presses, 1984), pp. 94–105.

Despite their differences, Milton and Newton shared a concern for prophecy, particularly the Book of Revelation. The Romantics were interested in Newton, but Milton helped them "restore the poetry of the rainbow that Newton was accused of destroying."

1152 Wittreich, Joseph Anthony, Jr. *Visionary Poetics: Milton's Tradition and His Legacy*. San Marino, CA: Huntington Library, 1979. xxiv, 324pp.

Deals with the tradition of prophecy in Spenser and Milton, studies *Lycidas* as a prophetic work, and concludes by examining the prophetic elements in the three long poems. Gives special attention to the Miltonic legacy. Appendices: "Henry More's Explanation of His Own, and of Joseph Mede's, Table of Synchronisms" and "The English Poems from *Justa Edovardo King Naufrago*." Reviews: Charles A. Huttar, *C&L*, 29, 1979, 62–64; Don Parry Norford, *MLQ*, 40, 1979, 292–306; Foster Provost, *SpenN*, 10, 1979, 68–70; Archie Burnett, *N&Q*, 27, 1980, 368–69; Roy C. Flannagan, *MiltonQ*, 14, 1980, 23; Frank Livingstone Huntley, *RenQ*, 33, 1980, 490–92; Leonard Trawicks, *Blake*, 14, 1980, 100–02; J. Martin Evans, *RES*, 32, 1981, 329–31; Hugh R. MacCallum, *UTQ*, 50, 1981, 314–23; Gordon C. Campbell,

YES, 11, 1982, 255–56; Dayton William Haskin, S. J., *Thought*, 56, 1981, 226–39.

1153 Woo, Constance Ann. "Floralism in Milton's Poetry and Prose." Doctoral diss., Univ. of California, Los Angeles, 1979. 358pp. Abs., *DAI*, 40, 1979, 3327A.

Examines the use of floral imagery in Milton's canon, particularly "the bright consummate flow'r" of Raphael's speech in *Paradise Lost* 5.481.

1154 Wood, Louis Aubrey. *The Form and Origin of Milton's Antitrinitarian Conception.* Folcroft, PA: Folcroft Library Editions, 1971; Norwood, PA: Norwood Editions, 1975; Philadelphia, PA: R. West, 1978.

Reprints of Stevens No. 2382, originally published in 1911.

1155 Woodcock, George. "Balachandra Rajan: The Critic as Novelist." *WLWE*, 23, 1984, 442–51.

Deals with two of Rajan's novels— *The Dark Dancer* and *Too Long in the West*—and his study of Milton, *The Lofty Rhyme* (No. 957), which discusses the theme of the "wholeness" of a writer's work.

1156 Woodhouse, A. S. P. *The Heavenly Muse: A Preface to Milton.* Ed. by Hugh MacCallum. Toronto and Buffalo, NY: Univ. of Toronto Press, 1972. xii, 373pp.

Contains chapters on the study of Milton, Milton's early development, the short poems, Milton as reformer and theologian, and the three long poems. Reviews: Roy Daniells, *DR*, 53, 1973, 356–57; J. S. Lawry, *HAR*, 24, 1973, 329–31; Millar MacLure, *UTQ*, 43, 1973, 87–89; *MiltonQ*, 7, 1973, 85–86; Barbara Kiefer Lewalski, *RenQ*, 27, 1974, 261–64; Balachandra Rajan, *CanL*, 61, 1974, 84–88; Joseph Anthony Wittreich, Jr., *SCN*, 32, 1974, 69–70; Michael Fixler, *MP*, 72, 1975, 308–10; Dennis H. Burden, *RES*, 31, 1980, 211–12; Franklin Roy Baruch, *Ren&R*, 11, 1974, 61–63.

1157 Woodhouse, A. S. P. *Milton the Poet.*

Folcroft, PA: Folcroft Library Editions, 1969, 1973; Norwood, PA: Norwood Editions, 1977; Ann Arbor, MI: Univ. Microfilms International, 1980 Books on Demand Reprints.

Reprints of Huckabay No. 1056, originally published in 1955.

1158 Woods, Paula Mearia. "The Symbolic and Structural Significance of Music Imagery in the English Poetry of John Milton." Doctoral diss., North Texas State Univ., 1979. 253pp. Abs., *DAI*, 40, 1979, 1490A–91A.

Examines Milton's use of speculative, heard, and practical music—symbols of his theological beliefs—as well as his structural use of music imagery, designed to "frame" his poems.

1159 Woods, Susanne. "How Free are Milton's Women?" *Milton and the Idea of Woman*. Ed. by Julia M. Walker (Urbana and Chicago: Univ. of Illinois Press, 1988), pp. 15–31.

"To answer the question to this essay's title: Milton's women are not as free as his men, but they remain responsible for their actions. Milton comes to this position not out of misogyny but out of an original difference in matters of gender, informed and complicated by cultural and biblical attitudes toward men." Abs., *MiltonQ*, 24, 1990, 152.

1160 Woods, Susanne. "Teaching Milton to Sophomores: Some Suggestions." *Teaching Milton to Undergraduates: Problems and Approaches.* Proceedings of the Special Session (537), Annual Meeting of the Modern Language Association, Dec. 28, 1976. Comp. by Paul L. Gaston ([Edwardsville: Southern Illinois Univ.], n.d.), pp. 11–16.

Discusses ways to make Milton more accessible to students in poetry survey courses.

1161 Worden, Blair. "Milton among the Radicals." *TLS*, Dec. 2, 1977, pp. 1394–95.

Review article. Favors Christopher

Hill's *Milton and the English Revolution* (No. 174). "The novelty of Hill's thesis lies not in what he calls its 'historical approach,' but in his attempt to cut Milton off from his humanistic roots."

1162 Yaghjian, Lucretia Bailey. "The Poet and the Church: Visible Shapes and Invisible Images of *Ecclesia* in the Early Poetry and Prose of John Milton, 1634–1645." Doctoral diss., Univ. of Colorado, Boulder, 1976. 365pp. Abs.,

DAI, 37, 1977, 7770A–71A.

Reveals the influence of "a bipartite yet unified church, visible in particular congregations and invisible as the 'elect' of all ages," on *Comus*, *Lycidas*, and the antiprelatical tracts.

1163 Yeong, Yoo. "On the Structure of the Miltonic Idea of Liberty." *Yonsei Nonchong* (Seoul, Korea), 10, 1973, 57–74.

In Korean; abstract in English, p. 75. Discusses Milton's lifelong concern for liberty.

CRITICISM OF INDIVIDUAL WORKS: SHORTER POEMS

1164 Aasand, Hardin Levine. "Tiresias and the Stagekeeper: The Masque Visions of John Milton and Ben Jonson." Doctoral diss., Univ. of Toronto, 1986. Abs., *DAI*, 48, 1988, 2876A–77A.

Explores Milton's and Jonson's interpretations of the court masque, in which "royal and spiritual authority" are combined, and "the king's existence as a metaphorical creation of his nation's people places his absoluteness into the individual hands of the body politic."

1165 Ackert, Martha B. "The Biblical Last Judgment and Milton's Two-Handed Engine." *CCTEP*, 34, 1969, 11–18.

Traces Milton's precedent for the pastoral digression in which he vents his rage against the corrupt clergy and church while praising Lycidas for the good shepherd he would have been.

1166 Adams, Bernard S. "Miltonic Metaphor and Ramist 'Invention': The Imagery of the Nativity Ode." *MiltonS*, 18, 1983, 85–102.

Argues for the presence of a Ramist influence in Milton's works, especially in the early poetry. Finds Ramist metaphor and imagery in the *Nativity Ode*.

1167 Adams, J. E. "'Attend Me More Diligently': Guidance and Friendship in Milton's Sonnet 22." *MiltonQ*, 18, 1984, 13–17, 19.

Questions the lack of literary interest in Sonnet 22 ("Cyriack, this three years' day"). Believes the poem is transcendent in its assurance of finding guidance in God and friendship.

1168 Adams, Robert Martin. "Bounding *Lycidas*." *HudR*, 23, 1970, 293–304.

"The poem is unified, not as a structure of statements about the universe, or as a sequence of themes which fit naturally together, but as a momentary and fragile balance of centrifugal and centripetal focus within the reader's mind." See No. 1174.

1169 Adams, Robert M. "Reading *Comus*." *"A Maske at Ludlow": Essays on Milton's "Comus."* Ed. by John S. Diekhoff (Ann Arbor, MI: Univ. Microfilms International, 1980 Books on Demand Reprints), pp. 78–101.

Reprint of Huckabay No. 2335, originally published in 1953.

1170 Agari, Masahiko. "A Note on Milton's Trinity MS." *ELN*, 22, No. 2, 1984, 23–26.

Uses Milton's short-lived practice of writing the letter "a" with a distinctive downstroke to offer a partial solution to the dating of his early poems in the Trinity Manuscript.

1171 Allen, Don Cameron. "The Higher Compromise: *On the Morning of Christ's Nativity* and a Mask." *"A Maske at Ludlow": Essays on Milton's "Comus."* Ed. by John S. Diekhoff (Ann Arbor, MI: Univ. Microfilms International, 1980 Books on Demand Reprints), pp. 58–71.

Reprint of one chapter from Huckabay No. 2342, originally published in 1954.

1172 Allen, Don Cameron. "Milton as a Latin Poet." *Stuart and Georgian Moments.* Ed. by Earl Miner. Clark Library Seminar Papers on Seventeenth and Eighteenth Century English Literature (Berkeley, Los Angeles, and London: Univ. of California Press, 1972), pp. 23–45.

Reprint of Huckabay No. 2339, originally published in 1965.

1173 Alpers, Paul. "The Eclogue Tradition and the Nature of Pastoral." *CE*, 34, 1972, 352–71.

Suggests that the eclogue tradition concludes with *Lycidas*, in which Milton wants to find an appropriate form of commemoration, not to end with the vision of Lycidas in heaven. Abs., *MiltonQ*, 7, 1973, 20.

1174 Alpers, Paul. "*Lycidas* and Modern Criticism." *ELH*, 49, 1982, 468–96.

Considers recent criticism by Stanley Eugene Fish (No. 1343), Robert Martin Adams (No. 1168), and Donald M. Friedman (No. 1376) and presents a new reading. "The purpose of the poem, we more and more see, is not to 'pronounce lastly,' but to 'sing for Lycidas,' to recover human song."

1175 Anastaplo, George. "John Milton (1608–1674)." *The Artist as Thinker: From Shakespeare to Joyce* (Chicago, IL, Athens, OH, and London: Swallow Press, 1983), pp. 62–74.

Analyzes Sonnet 18 ("On the Late Massacre in Piemont") as perhaps one of the earliest international invocations of human rights.

1176 Arai, Akira. "The Epic Element in *Lycidas*." *EigoS*, 114, 1968, 312–13.

In Japanese. Studies Milton's purpose in writing *Lycidas*. Abs., *MiltonN*, 3, 1969, 32.

1177 Arai, Akira. "The Great Sword of *Lycidas*." *Miscellaneous Essays on Milton* (Tokyo: Chukyo Shuppan, 1979), pp. 23–30.

In Japanese. Agrees with those who maintain that the two-handed engine in *Lycidas* is a two-handed sword.

1178 Arai, Akira. "*Lycidas*: 'That Two-Handed Engine.'" *EigoS*, 117, 1971, 562–64.

In Japanese. Suggests that Milton's reference to the two-handed engine may have been influenced by Josua Sylvester's 1592 translation of Du Bartas's *La Sepmaine*, which refers to a "two-hand Sword" as crucial in the

destruction of Sennacherib. In *Paradise Lost* 6.250–53, Milton cites "the sword of Michael" brandished "with huge two-handed sway." Abs., *MiltonQ*, 6, No. 1, 1972, 21.

1179 Arai, Akira. "Milton's Heroism in His Sonnet XIX." *Research Bulletin, Department of General Education*, Nagoya Univ. (Japan), 12, 1968, 1–13.

Huckabay No. 2345. Abs., *MiltonN*, 2, 1968, 54.

1180 Archer, Stanley. "'Glutinous Heat': A Note on *Comus*, l. 917." *MiltonQ*, 7, 1973, 99.

Replies to James W. Flosdorf's query (No. 1359) about the meaning of "Smear'd with gums of glutinous heat." Suggests birdlime. See also Nos. 1243 and 3039.

1181 Asals, Heather. "Echo, Narcissus, and Ambiguity, in *Lycidas*." *SCN*, 38, 1980, 44; *MiltonQ*, 14, 1980, 31.

Abstract of a paper presented at the 1979 MLA Convention. Discusses the poem's frequent figures of repetition and grammatical reflexiveness as the "literary children of Echo and Narcissus" and examines their contributions to its ambiguity.

1182 Auffret, J. "Pagano-Christian Syncretism in *Lycidas*." *Anglia*, 87, 1969, 26–38.

Elaborates on the idea that *Lycidas* is Christian in spirit but pagan in form. Orpheus, Pan, and Apollo are Christ figures, and Apollo is a figure of the Holy Ghost.

1183 Baier, Lee. "Sin and Repentance in *Lycidas*." *PQ*, 67, 1988, 291–302.

Sees both the speaker and the poem evolving through a pattern of sin and repentance.

1184 Baker, Stewart A. "Eros and the Three Shepherds of *Comus*." *RUS*, 61, 1975, 13–26.

In *Comus*, Milton translates language into action as the songs are conjurations that actualize desire through language. This power is identified with the shepherd's role. Through the complex apposition of the three principal shepherds, Milton explores the role of the poet, poetry, and language.

1185 Baker, Stewart A. "Milton's Uncouth Swain." *MiltonS*, 3, 1971, 35–53.

"The swain's voice [in *Lycidas*] unifies the diverse modes of pastoral by translating the images of naturalistic and libertine pastoral into the symbols of Christian pastoral, and by employing a principle of inverse reduction, as defined by J. C. Scaliger."

1186 Bakopoulou-Halls, Alice. "Imagery in Milton's *Comus*." *Univ. of Thessaloniki School of Philosophy Yearbook*, 20, 1981, 11–25.

1187 Baldi, Sergio. "The Date of Composition of *Epitaphium Damonis*." *N&Q*, 25, 1978, 508–09.

Denies Shawcross's assumption (Huckabay No. 2712) that Milton wrote *Epitaphium Damonis* in October or November, 1639. Cites errors in harvest time calculations and asserts that autumn or winter of 1640 is more probable. Abs., *SCN*, 38, 1980, 18.

1188 Baldi, Sergio. *Studi Miltoniani*. Firenze: Università degli Studi di Firenze, Facoltà di Lettere e Filosofia, Istituto di Lingue e Letterature Germaniche, Slave e Ugrofinniche, [1985]. 173pp.

In Italian, including the translation of *Epitaphium Damonis*. Includes a discussion of Milton's Italian poetry. Review: Roy C. Flannagan, *MiltonQ*, 22, 1988, 26–27.

1189 Barber, C. L. "*A Mask Presented at Ludlow Castle*: The Masque as a Masque." *"A Maske at Ludlow" : Essays on Milton's "Comus."* Ed. by John S. Diekhoff (Ann Arbor, MI: Univ. Microfilms International, 1980 Books on Demand Reprints), pp. 188–206.

Reprint of Huckabay No. 2359, originally published in 1965.

1190 Baruch, Franklin R. "Milton's *Comus*: Skill, Virtue, and Henry Lawes." *MiltonS*, 5, 1973, 289–308.

"In *Comus*, Milton uses the great tradition of the *vir bonus dicendi peritus* ('a good man skilled in speaking') both to pay a masquing compliment to Henry Lawes and to provide central roles for all three Egerton children."

1191 Battersby, James L. *Rational Praise and Natural Lamentation: Johnson, "Lycidas," and Principles of Criticism.* Rutherford, NJ: Fairleigh Dickinson Univ. Press; London: Associated Univ. Presses, 1980. 282pp.

Discusses criticism as it applies to *Lycidas*, and then establishes the theoretical framework governing Samuel Johnson's criticism. Believes that, as a critic, Johnson has been misunderstood. Review: Howard D. Weinbrot, *ECS*, 15, 1982, 238–41.

1192 Baytop, Adrianne. "Milton's Sonnet Sequence: Strictest Measure." *LangQ*, 26, 1987, 20–22.

Examines excerpts from Milton's sonnets to find "the extent to which the interrelatedness between Pythagoras' stoic habits and his theory of the ordered control of the cosmos influenced the interplay·between Milton's life and art." Believes that a triadic form can be superimposed on the English sonnets.

1193 Beaumont, G. "*Lycidas*." *TLS*, July 16, 1970, p. 775.

Discusses the need to emend *Lycidas* 68–69: "To sport with *Amaryllis* in the shade, / Or with the tangles of *Neaera's* hair?" Believes it should read "Hid in" rather than "Or with." See also *TLS*, July 31, 1970, p. 855.

1194 Beckwith, Marc. "*Comus* and the *Zodiacus Vitae*." *MiltonQ*, 20, 1986, 145–47.

Asserts that Milton read Palingenius's *Zodiacus Vitae* and that it influenced the Attendant Spirit's opening and closing speeches in *Comus*.

1195 Bedford, R. D. "Right Spelling: Milton's *A Masque* and *Il Penseroso*." *ELH*, 52, 1985, 815–32.

On the meaning of "spell" in the two

works. Milton uses Welsh and other sources, which transcend Platonism and become allegorical, as the haemony of *Comus* shows.

1196 Bell, Arthur H. "Milton's *A Mask at Ludlow Castle*, 638." *Expl*, 28, 1970, Item 65.

Suggests that identification of the herb haemony with a variety of mustard offers new support for a theological reading of the masque.

1197 Bell, Barbara Currier. "*Lycidas* and the Stages of Grief." *L&P*, 25, 1975, 166–74.

Analyzes *Lycidas* in light of modern psychology to show that its structure parallels the four main stages of grief: denial, anger, depression, and resolution, with certain substages.

1198 Bennett, Joan S. "Virgin Nature in *Comus*." *MiltonS*, 23, 1987, 21–32.

Believes that Milton's doctrine of nature and chastity is in the humanistic tradition of Alain de Lille's *Complaint of Nature*.

1199 Bercovitch, Sacvan. "Milton's 'Haemony': Knowledge and Belief." *HLQ*, 33, 1970, 351–59.

Proposes "that one of the associations with haemony which Milton intended—homonymically, etymologically, and symbolically—pertains to the Hebrew word-root *aman*. Denoting in its various forms both 'knowledge' and 'belief,' it presents a striking parallel to *haimon* and as such . . . helps to clarify the herb's dramatic and allegorical function."

1200 Berkeley, David Shelley. *Inwrought with Figures Dim: A Reading of Milton's "Lycidas."* De Proprietatibus Litterarum, Series Didactica, vol. 2. The Hague and Paris: Mouton, 1974. 233pp.

Uses typology to relate major types—paradisal Cambridge, the sea, ship, eclipses, sea monsters, sun, and baptism—to their long traditions. Reviews: *MiltonQ*, 9, 1975, 85–86; Anthony Low, *MiltonQ*, 9, 1975, 20–27; Albert James

Smith, *RES*, 27, 1976, 350–52; Joseph Anthony Wittreich, Jr., *YES*, 6, 1976, 262–63.

1201 Berkeley, David S. " 'Light' in Milton's Sonnet XX." *PQ*, 61, 1982, 208–11.

When Milton specifies a "light" repast in Sonnet 20 (to Henry Lawrence), he deprecates foods that are "rich in *stercor*." He is "in effect inviting his young friend to an aristocratic dinner whose model . . ., if regularly consumed, would produce fine children, ward off insanity and the intellectual grossness of the peasantry, and prolong life."

1202 Berkowitz, M. S. "An Earl's Michaelmas in Wales: Some Thoughts on the Original Presentation of *Comus*." *MiltonQ*, 13, 1979, 122, 124–25.

Explores the use of Michaelmas festivities in *Comus* by pointing out such aspects of the early Michaelmas celebration as the "lawless hour" and a representation of the "Vegetation Spirit," which add even more importance to Milton's selection of time, place, and theme for his masque.

1203 Berkowitz, M. S. "Thomas Young's *Hopes Encouragement* and Milton's Sonnet XIX." *MiltonQ*, 16, 1982, 94–97.

Suggests that Young's sermon to Parliament on February 28, 1644, and Milton's Sonnet 19 ("When I consider") are similar in theme and that the sonnet was composed near Milton's thirty-fifth birthday.

1204 Blanchard, J. Marc. "The Tree and the Garden: Pastoral Poetics and Milton's Rhetoric of Desire." *MLN*, 91, 1976, 1540–68.

The danger to the Lady lies not in the overtness of Comus's appeal to sexual instincts but in his rhetoric, which robs the mystery from virginity's sacred and religious function. The Lady can find nothing wrong with his basic argument, but she builds her own rhetoric by avoiding the problem of "being strangl'd with her waste fertility" and emphasizing the protection of the individual through a system of temperance. Abs., *SCN*, 38, 1980, 18.

1205 Blanchard, Sheila. "Milton's Foothill: Pattern in the Piedmont Sonnet." *Genre*, 4, 1971, 39–44.

Examines the structure of Sonnet 18 ("On the Late Massacre in Piemont") and identifies biblical allusions. Concludes that justice will triumph, for the "blending of Biblical and classical allusion and the apparent destruction and recreation of the sonnet form . . . [provide] a typically Miltonic sense of energy and strength."

1206 Blondel, Jacques. "From *The Tempest* to *Comus*." *RLC*, 49, 1975, 204–16.

In many ways, the *Tempest* is a prelude to *Comus*, as both works extol restraint. Similarities in plot, structure, and mythical equipment move Milton's work away from court masque and closer to Shakespearean romance.

1207 Blondel, Jacques. "*Lycidas*: Panorama Critique et Interprétation." *EA*, 25, 1972, 104–15.

Points out that within the confines of the conventional elegiac form, Milton uses the rich mythology of *Lycidas* to present an ardent personal confession. The fiction opens the door to truth; the poet is also a prophet.

1208 Blondel, Jacques. "La Pastorale Anglaise: de Milton à Marvell. Le Thème de l'Eau." *Le Genre Pastoral en Europe du XVᵉ au XVIIᵉ Siècle*. Ed. by Claude Longeon (Sainte-Etienne: L'Université de Sainte-Etienne, 1980), pp. 169–75.

Notes that Milton integrates the classical with the Christian pastoral, without discord between the two worlds. For both Marvell and Milton (in *Comus* and *Lycidas*), water represents purity and purification; it is the source of life, death, and regeneration.

1209 Blow, Suzanne. "The Angel and the Sheep in *Lycidas*." *Milton Reconsidered: Essays in Honor of Arthur E. Barker*. Ed. by John Karl Franson (Salzburg: Institut für Englische Sprache und Literatur, Universität Salzburg, 1976), pp. 22–45.

Argues that the angel in *Lycidas* 163 is St. Michael, whom Milton invokes to look toward England and to protect the defenseless sheep from a corrupt clergy.

1210 Blythe, David-Everett. "Milton's 'Crisp.'" *Expl*, 41, 1982, 22–23.

"Milton's two uses of 'crisped' [in *Paradise Lost* 4.237 and *Comus* 984] each denote curledness, crimpedness, or unevenness (L. *crispus*)."

1211 Booth, Stephen, and **Jordan Flyer.** "Milton's 'How Soon Hath Time': A Colossus in a Cherrystone." *ELH*, 49, 1982, 449–67.

Emphasizes the last two lines of Sonnet 7, which is "a great poem—not only great in the metaphoric sense . . . but great in its literal sense: 'big.'"

1212 Bouchard, Gary Michael. "From Campus to 'Campus': The Relationship of the University World to the Literary Pastoral Worlds of Edmund Spenser, Phineas Fletcher, and John Milton." Doctoral diss., Loyola Univ. of Chicago, 1988. 262pp. Abs., *DAI*, 49, 1989, 1806A–07A.

Asserts that the three poets translate the "communal joys of youth, poverty, rivalry, and fellowship," experienced at Cambridge University, "into the pastoral joys of shepherds in the campus [field]."

1213 Bourdette, Robert E., Jr. "Mourning Lycidas: 'The Poem of the Mind in the Act of Finding What Will Suffice.'" *ELWIU*, 11, 1984, 11–20.

Contends that *Lycidas* traces the traditional psychological stages of grief. Concludes that "the stages of Milton's *Lycidas* show the searching mind acquiring and confirming for itself the enduring faith that triumphs over temporal death."

1214 Boyette, Purvis E. "Milton's Abstracted Sublimities: The Structure of

Meaning in *A Mask.*" *TSE*, 18, 1970, 35–58.

Examines how "Milton creates a basic figurative structure" in *Comus* and amplifies "the meaning of that figure in relation to the didactic intent of the masque as a whole." The settings and images metaphorically explain "the meaning of the essential action of the drama: the Lady's testing, bondage, and relief."

1215 Bradbrook, M. C. "Masque and Pastoral." *The Living Monument: Shakespeare and the Theatre of His Time* (Cambridge: Cambridge Univ. Press, 1976), pp. 245–57.

Connects *Comus* with Shakespeare and Jonson but concludes that it represents the rejection of the orthodox masque.

1216 Brand, Dana. "Self-Construction and Self-Dissolution in *L'Allegro* and *Il Penseroso.*" *MiltonQ*, 15, 1981, 116–19.

Perceives a dichotomy which determines the differences in the poems' structures. "*Il Penseroso* describes a process of development of a continuous self. *L'Allegro* describes what mental activity would be like without a continuous self."

1217 Breasted, Barbara. "Another Bewitching of Lady Alice Egerton, the Lady of *Comus.*" *N&Q*, 17, 1970, 411–12.

Suggests that a previously unpublished letter by Robert Napier (1632), which reveals Lady Bridgewater's fears that her daughter had been bewitched, is relevant to an understanding of the historical context of *Comus*.

1218 Breasted, Barbara. "*Comus* and the Castlehaven Scandal." *MiltonS*, 3, 1971, 201–24.

Argues that the Castlehaven scandal "provided a context for *Comus* that may have influenced the way the masque was written, the way it was cut for its first performance, and the way it was received by its first audience in 1634." See No. 1284. Review: Michael Lieb, *Cithara*, 12, 1972, 85–106.

1219 Breasted, Barbara. "I. *Comus* and the Castlehaven Scandal. II. Public Standards in Fiction: A Discussion of Three Nineteenth-Century Novels—George Eliot's *Middlemarch* and Jane Austen's *Pride and Prejudice* and *Emma*. III. *Antony and Cleopatra*: Theatrical Uses of the Self." Doctoral diss., Rutgers Univ. 1970. 194pp. Abs., *DAI*, 31, 1971, 4112A.

Describes the first private performance of *Comus* as an expression of sexual restraint, due to the Castlehaven scandal.

1220 Brisman, Leslie. "'All Before Them Where To Choose': *L'Allegro* and *Il Penseroso.*" *JEGP*, 71, 1972, 226–40.

Reads the poems as a "progress" in which the topic is "profoundly intertwined . . . with its process of creation. The poems are about choice, and make that choice as they go along. They create a unity of kind of experience and kind of poetry, building toward that identification, working in time to arrive at the definition of the subject matter culminated in their endings."

1221 Brock, Kathryn Gail. "Milton's Sonnet XVIII and the Language of Controversy." *MiltonQ*, 16, 1982, 3–6.

Sonnet 18 ("On the Late Massacre in Piemont") uses "language and imagery shared by Catholic and Protestant polemicists" and "shows that the Catholic attack on the Waldensians is one manifestation of the continual war of falsehood against true belief."

1222 Brockbank, Philip. "The Measure of *Comus.*" *E&S*, 21, 1968, 46–61.

Approaches the masque as a presentation and as a Neoplatonic allegory. Sees "three rival measures: the light fantastic of Comus, the chaste footing of the Lady, and . . . the Shropshire country dancers."

1223 Bromley, Laura Ann. "I. Continuity in Milton's Sonnets. II. Attitudes toward Love in *Venus and Adonis*. III. The Victorian 'Good Woman' and the Fiction of Charlotte Bronte." Doctoral diss.,

Rutgers Univ., 1973. 133pp. Abs., *DAI*, 34, 1973, 3336A.

Asserts the continuity but not the progression of Milton's sonnets through common themes, words, and images.

1224 Brooks-Davies, Douglas. "The Early Milton and the Hermetics of Revolution: *L'Allegro* and *Il Penseroso* and *Comus*." *The Mercurian Monarch: Magical Politics from Spenser to Pope* (Manchester: Manchester Univ. Press, 1983), pp. 124–49.

The three poems use a Hermetic theme to criticize a corrupt court and anticipate a golden age.

1225 Brown, Cedric C. "The Chirk Castle Entertainment of 1634." *MiltonQ*, 11, 1977, 76–86.

Describes a second masque, long unknown, believed to have been performed for the Earl of Bridgewater in 1634. Includes the text of the entertainment.

1226 Brown, Cedric C. *John Milton's Aristocratic Entertainments*. Cambridge: Cambridge Univ. Press, 1985. xii, 210pp.

Discusses *Arcades*, *Comus*, and *Lycidas*, focusing on the various stages of the texts and on the Egerton family. Reviews: William B. Hunter, *MiltonQ*, 20, 1986, 55–57; David A. Loewenstein, *SCN*, 44, 1986, 33–34; Lucy Newlyn, *TLS*, Aug. 8, 1986, p. 871; R. D. Bedford, *THES*, May 2, 1986, p. 20; John G. Demaray, *RenQ*, 40, 1987, 374–75; C. Schaar, *ES*, 68, 1987, 363; Martin Butler, *N&Q*, 34, 1987, 386–87; J. Martin Evans, *RES*, 38, 1987, 562–63; Gordon Campbell, *YES*, 18, 1988, 268–69.

1227 Brown, Cedric C. "The *Komos* in Milton." *JDJ*, 5, 1986, 235–66.

Discusses the literary and iconographic traditions of the word "komos" before Milton transliterated it into "Comus" for his masque.

1228 Brown, Cedric C. "Milton's *Arcades*: Context, Form, and Function." *RenD*, 8, 1977, 245–74.

Analyzes such aspects as literary devices, sources, motivation, and comic pretense.

1229 Brown, Cedric C. "Presidential Travels and Instructive Augury in Milton's Ludlow Masque." *MiltonQ*, 21, No. 4, 1987, 1–12.

Traces the Bridgewater family to Ludlow, where *Comus* was first performed. Discusses the Chirk Castle entertainment and offers ideas about the original performance. Includes letters written by the Earl of Bridgewater and Henry Lawes.

1230 Brown, Cedric C. "The Shepherd, the Musician, and the Word in Milton's *Masque*." *JEGP*, 78, 1979, 522–44.

"It is my contention that Haemony figures the word of God. In verbal allusion and metaphor Milton gave a whole host of clues that he intended the word to be ministered against the dangers of devilish deception and malign circumstance."

1231 Bryskett, Lodowick. *Literary Works*. Ed. by J. H. P. Pafford. Farnsburrough: Gregg International Publishers, 1972; Amersham: Demand Reprints, 1984. xxi, 332pp.

Includes a facsimile of the 1638 text of *Lycidas* because it contains echoes from Bryskett's poems.

1232 Burnett, Archie. *Milton's Style: The Shorter Poems, "Paradise Regained," and "Samson Agonistes."* London and New York: Longman, 1981. xiv, 187pp.

"This book has various aims: to give close readings of Milton's poems other than *Paradise Lost*; to take into account the criticism on these poems, focusing on major issues; and to investigate the variety and consistency of their style."

1233 Burnett, Archie. "Miltonic Parallels: (I) *L'Allegro* and *A Midsummer Night's Dream*; (II) *L'Allegro* and *Il Penseroso* and Theophrastan Character Literature." *N&Q*, 27, 1980, 332–34.

Discusses the contextual significance of a parallel between *L'Allegro* 127 and *A Midsummer Night's Dream* 1.1.19. Examines attempts to relate Milton's companion poems to early seventeenth-century Theophrastan character literature and offers additional parallels to support Milton's awareness of this mode of writing.

1234 Burnett, A. "Studies in the Language of Milton's English Poetry." Doctoral diss., Oxford Univ., 1976. Abs., *IT*, 27, 1979, 8.

1235 Burnett, Archie. "A Textual Crux in *L'Allegro*." *N&Q*, 29, 1982, 495–98. Concerning *L'Allegro* 103–04. Disagrees with John Creaser (No. 4111) and concludes that the 1673 version is superior to the 1645 text. See Creaser's response (No. 1286).

1236 Bush, Douglas, J. E. Shaw, and **A. Bartlett Giamatti.** *A Variorum Commentary on the Poems of John Milton.* Gen. ed. Merritt Y. Hughes. Vol. 1: The Latin and Greek Poems, by Bush; The Italian Poems, by Shaw and Giamatti. New York: Columbia Univ. Press, 1970. xi, 389pp.

In the Preface to Vol. 1, the General Editor Merritt Y. Hughes states: "Our object in this work is to furnish a body of variorum notes and discussions uniting all available scholarly illumination of the texts on all levels from the semantic and syntactical to those of deliberate or unconscious echoes of other works in all the languages known to Milton. In notes on the longer passages we have considered their inner rhetorical organization and involvements in the design of the poem as a whole, in the backgrounds of the literary traditions of which they themselves are outstanding developments, and in the many aspects of Milton's interests—theological, cosmological, hexameral, historical, psychological, and so on." See Nos. 1838 and 3386 for the other volumes of the *Variorum Commentary.* Reviews of Vol. 1: *MiltonQ*, 4, 1970, 66–67; *TLS*, Nov. 20, 1970, p. 1342; Mario

A. Di Cesare, *RenQ*, 24, 1971, 587–90; J. Max Patrick, *SCN*, 29, 1971, 1; John T. Shawcross, *SCN*, 29, 1971, 1–4; rejoinder to Patrick and Shawcross by Douglas Bush, *SCN*, 29, 1971, 4, 6 (see No. 1718); *TLS*, Aug. 6, 1971, p. 953; J. W. Binns, *MLR*, 67, 1972, 168–69; Michael Lieb, *Cithara*, 12, 1972, 85–106; Irene Samuel, *MLQ*, 33, 1972, 78–80; Roger Lejosne, *EA*, 26, 1973, 99–100; Stanley E. Fish, *CritI*, 2, 1976, 465–85 (see No. 593); replies by Douglas Bush, *CritI*, 3, 1976, 179–82, and Steven Mailloux, *CritI*, pp. 183–90; rejoinder by Fish, *CritI*, pp. 191–96.

1237 Butler, Martin. "A Provincial Masque of *Comus*, 1636." *RenD*, 17, 1986, 149–74. Examines the production of an "amateur masque" by studying records of the Clifford estate, whose entries include accounts of masque sponsorship. Parallels the Clifford masques to Milton's Ludlow masque in style and production.

1238 Byard, Margaret M. "Milton's 'On Time' and 'At a Solemn Musick.'" *Expl*, 41, No. 4, 1983, 13–14. Adopts Handel's approach to reading Milton's poetry with an awareness of rhythm and time values, as demonstrated in his musical adaptations of *L'Allegro* and *Il Penseroso*. Concludes that Milton created "an imitation in sound of the theme of both poems, the triumph of eternity over time itself."

1239 Byse, Fanny Lee. *Milton on the Continent: A Key to "L'Allegro" and "Il Penseroso."* Philadelphia, PA: R. West, 1977. Reprint of Stevens No. 545, originally published in 1903. Abs., *RenQ*, 32, 1979, 162.

1240 Cain, William E. "*Lycidas* and the Reader's Response." *DR*, 58, 1978, 272–84. States that "the reader's response to *Lycidas* continually develops and structures itself from line to line; and the history of the responses of different readers can be found in the critical work."

1241 Calhoun, Thomas O. "On John Milton's *A Mask at Ludlow*." *MiltonS*, 6, 1974, 165–79.

"Considered in the light of its occasion and performance, Milton's *A Mask at Ludlow* is a family drama about conflict among three age groups: children, adolescents, and adults. The adolescents—Lady Alice and 'the Spirit of Youth,' Comus—are distinguished from children and adults by their immediate concern with the problems of erotic love."

1242 Camé, Jean-François. "Les Éléments du Merveilleux dans *Comus* et *Paradise Lost*." *CahiersE*, 22, 1982, 41–49.

The world of *Comus* has its own laws, and Comus is the magician of the night who will fight the supernatural with his knowledge of the magic of plants.

1243 Camé, Jean-François. "More about Milton's Use of the Word 'Gums.'" *MiltonQ*, 9, 1975, 51–52.

Replies to James W. Flosdorf's query (No. 1359). Feels that Milton's attitude toward "gums" is contradictory. While he was sexually attracted by everything sticky, he "sensed the danger of this attraction" and preferred to describe smooth, morally safe substances. See also John T. Shawcross (No. 3039) and Stanley Archer (No. 1180).

1244 Camé, Jean-François. "Myth and Myths in Milton's *Comus*." *CahiersE*, 5, 1974, 3–24.

Shows that the masque's numerous mythological references are all connected with "a great mythical pattern, that of loss, search and rebirth."

1245 Campbell, Gordon. "Chequered Shades and Shadows in Shakespeare and Milton." *N&Q*, 28, 1981, 123.

"Chequer'd shade" of *L'Allegro* 95 and "chequer'd shadow" of Shakespeare's *Titus Andronicus* 2.3.15 probably derive from Virgil's *Eclogue* 7.46.

1246 Campbell, Gordon. "Imitation in *Epitaphium Damonis*." *MiltonS*, 19, 1984, 165–77.

Discusses Milton's borrowings from other poets. "In *Epitaphium Damonis* Milton has caught the flame of Theocritus and Virgil. In 1645 Milton placed *Epitaphium Damonis* at the end of his collection of poems. It is appropriate that his greatest Latin poem should have been accorded this important position, for it looks, Janus-like, back on Milton's achievement as a Latin poet and represents the culmination of his labors in that form, and looks forward to his achievement as the writer of the greatest English epic."

1247 Campbell, Gordon. "Milton and Aurora's Tears." *N&Q*, 26, 1979, 415.

Claims that Milton alludes to the work of Ovid. Asserts that incidents similar to Aurora's sprinkling of tears on the world may be found in *In Quintum Novembris* 133–36; "An Epitaph on the Marchioness of Winchester"; and *Paradise Lost* 5. Abs., *MiltonQ*, 14, 1980, 136.

1248 Campbell, Gordon. "'P. M. S.' and the Contributors to *Justa Edouardo King*." *MiltonQ*, 17, 1983, 58–59.

Challenges Edward Le Comte's identification of "P. M. S." (No. 1530). Also makes additional comments about the edition (see No. 307). See Le Comte's response (No. 1529) and No. 1573.

1249 Campbell, Gordon. "The Satire on Aristotelian Logic in Milton's *Vacation Exercise*." *ELN*, 15, 1977, 106–10.

Believes that this anti-Aristotelian work was the result of Milton's collegiate tradition and personal sentiment. Abs., *MiltonQ*, 12, 1978, 113.

1250 Campbell, Gordon. "A Sequence in Milton's 1645 *Poems*." *Káñina*, 5, 1981, 95–98.

Explains the connections among the "Passion," "On Time," and "Upon the Circumcision." Suggests that their sequence is intentional. Summary in Spanish.

1251 Candy, Hugh C. H. *Some Newly Discovered Stanzas Written by John Milton on Engraved Scenes Illustrating Ovid's "Metamorphoses."* Folcroft, PA: Folcroft Library Editions, 1972; Norwood, PA: Norwood Editions, 1975; Philadelphia, PA: R. West, 1977.

Reprints of Stevens No. 2673, originally published in 1924.

1252 Carpenter, Nan Cooke. "Milton and Music: Henry Lawes, Dante, and Casella." *ELR*, 2, 1972, 237–42.

Believes that Sonnet 13 (to Henry Lawes) closes with a reference to Dante and Casella because of a line from *Purgatorio* 2.106—"If a new law . . ."—which could be used as a bilingual pun on Lawes's name.

1253 Carrithers, Gale H., Jr. "Milton's Ludlow *Mask*: From Chaos to Community." *Critical Essays on Milton from "ELH"* (Baltimore, MD, and London: Johns Hopkins Press, 1969), pp. 103–22.

Reprint of Huckabay No. 2405, originally published in 1966.

1254 Carrithers, Gale H., Jr. "*Poems* (1645): On Growing Up." *MiltonS*, 15, 1981, 161–79.

Studies the English poems in the order of Milton's presentation, from the *Nativity Ode* to *Lycidas*. Believes that there is "a serious entertainment of movement from ahistoric, youthful incompleteness to realized, adult selfhood."

1255 Chambers, A. B. "Christmas: The Liturgy of the Church and English Verse of the Renaissance." *Literary Monographs, vol. 6: Medieval and Renaissance Literature.* Ed. by Eric Rothstein and Joseph Anthony Wittreich, Jr. (Madison and London: Univ. of Wisconsin Press, 1975), pp. 109–53, 179–82.

Discusses Milton's *Nativity Ode* in light of liturgical and poetic traditions.

1256 Chambers, A. B. "Milton's 'Upon the Circumcision': Backgrounds and Meanings." *TSLL*, 17, 1975, 687–97.

Compares the poem to other verses on the same subject by Crashaw, Herrick, Wither, Harvey, Beaumont, and Quarles, finding that Milton's work is more subtle and unusual than most readers have probably thought.

1257 Chatfield, Hale. "An Additional Look at the 'Meaning' of *Comus*." *MiltonQ*, 11, 1977, 86–89.

"This article will attempt to show that *Comus* is an artistic treatment of a relatively simple theme: a conflict between the idea that virtue is self-sufficient and the belief that it is not, the resolution of which conflict lies in an artistic statement that virtue, if it is not self-sufficient, is superior to its antithesis because it is favored by Heaven."

1258 Cheney, Patrick. "Alcestis and the 'Passion for Immortality': Milton's Sonnet XXIII and Plato's *Symposium*." *MiltonS*, 18, 1983, 63–76.

Sees Plato's *Symposium*, not Euripides's *Alcestis*, as the source for Milton's inspiration in Sonnet 23 ("Methought I saw").

1259 Christopher, G. B. "A Note on the 'Blind Mouths' of *Lycidas*." *N&Q*, 20, 1973, 379–80.

Interprets the phrase in *Lycidas* 119 in light of Calvin's teachings and suggests that it describes clergy who "preach without benefit of the Spirit."

1260 Christopher, Georgia B. "The Virginity of Faith: *Comus* as a Reformation Conceit." *ELH*, 43, 1976, 479–99.

Insists that the Reformation understanding of virginity and its opposites underlies the form of *Comus* and that Milton attempts to preserve the concept of faith against contamination of works. Abs., *MiltonQ*, 11, 1977, 92.

1261 Cipolla, E. M. C. "Pastoral Elements in Milton's Latin Poems." *UES*, 10, 1972, 1–16.

Discusses pastoral elements in *Elegy 5*, *Mansus*, and *Epitaphium Damonis*, which is the most successful.

1262 Cirtin, Diana Lee Mills. "Tipsy Dance

vs. Grand Dance: The Use of Dance in Milton's *Comus*." *BSUF*, 17, No. 2, 1976, 23–30.

States that "the use of dance in *Comus* [is] both literal and figurative." Proposes that dance "serves several purposes: it reinforces the belief that *Comus* is, indeed a masque; it emphasizes the theme of triumphant virtue, and it provides spectacular enjoyment for the audience." Abs., *MiltonQ*, 10, 1976, 96–97.

1263 Clanton, Jann Aldredge. "Love Descending: A Study of Spenser's *Fowre Hymnes* and Milton's *Nativity Ode*." Doctoral diss., Texas Christian Univ., 1978. 179pp. Abs., *DAI*, 39, 1978, 3593A.

Demonstrates an "affinity in lyric and philosophical traditions and in theme" between the *Fowre Hymnes* and the *Nativity Ode*.

1264 Clark, James Andrew. "Milton Naturans, Milton Naturatus: The Debate over Nature in *A Mask Presented at Ludlow*." *MiltonS*, 20, 1984, 3–27.

Analyzes the argument between the Lady and Comus, particularly its dramatic aspects. Believes that the appearance of Sabrina reconciles their conflicting attitudes.

1265 Clemen, Wolfgang. *Originalität und Tradition in der Englischen Dichtungsgeschichte*. München: Verlag der Bayerischen Akademie der Wissenschaften, 1978. 90pp.

Considers *Lycidas* the most prominent example of the interrelation between tradition and originality in seventeenth-century English poetry.

1266 Colaccio, John J. "'A Death Like Sleep': The Christology of Milton's Twenty-Third Sonnet." *MiltonS*, 6, 1974, 181–97.

In Sonnet 23 ("Methought I saw"), "Milton's 'late espoused Saint' appears at the center of two planes of spiritual movement, horizontal and vertical, each culminating in God and corresponding to the traditions of Christian typology and Christian Neoplatonism."

1267 Collette, Carolyn P. "Milton's Psalm Translations: Petition and Praise." *ELR*, 2, 1972, 243–59.

Claims that Milton's Psalm paraphrases, "in addition to being expressions of religious devotion and meditation," are "closely related to the themes of his major prose works and to events of the English Civil War and the Commonwealth period."

1268 Colvin, Daniel L. "Milton's *Comus* and the Pattern of Human Temptation." *C&L*, 27, 1978, 8–17.

Proposes that the question "Who am I?" is both "an individual psychological quest" and "an inclusive philosophical statement," an issue that Milton first addresses in *Comus*, where he "creates a dramatic picture of the nature of man and the possibility for significant action in a fallen world."

1269 "Comus at Oxford." *MiltonQ*, 7, 1973, 115.

Report on a production at Somerville Hall in 1972.

1270 "Comus on Stage." *SCN*, 41, 1983, 81.

Announces a celebration to mark the 350th anniversary of the masque, held at the State University College at Buffalo in 1984.

1271 Condee, R. W. "The Latin Poetry of John Milton." *The Latin Poetry of English Poets*. Ed. by J. W. Binns (London and Boston, MA: Routledge and Kegan Paul, 1974), pp. 58–92.

Traces the development of Milton's Latin poetry and analyzes each poem, especially *Epitaphium Damonis*, which marks both the high point and the end of his career as a Latin poet. Notes that Milton's pride in his Latin poems survived until his death.

1272 Condee, Ralph W. "Milton's Gawdy-Day with Lawrence." *Directions in Literary Criticism: Contemporary Approaches to Literature*. Ed. by Stanley Weintraub and Philip Young (University Park and London: Pennsylvania State

Univ. Press, 1973), pp. 86–92.

Believes that Sonnet 20 (to Henry Lawrence) "creates its unique character as a poem by means of an integration of its literary techniques with the non-literary situation which called it into being."

1273 Cornelius, David K., and **Kathryn Thompson.** "Milton's *Lycidas*, 119–27." *Expl*, 31, 1972, Item 25.

Concurs with Ruskin's interpretation of the corrupt clergy (the "blind mouths") as parasites rather than ministers. Adds that the symbolism may draw on "actual, rather than simply figurative, parasites," such as liver flukes—flesh-boring worms—which were the "scourge of sheep in the seventeenth century."

1274 Corns, Thomas N. "Ideology in the *Poemata* (1645)." *MiltonS*, 19, 1984, 195–203.

Believes that several of the Latin poems in the 1645 volume do not necessarily reflect Milton's current position about religion and politics. They reflect his concern with how others perceive him and his obsession with his developing genius.

1275 Corns, Thomas N. "*A Mask Presented at Ludlow Castle*, l. 231." *N&Q*, 29, 1982, 22–24.

Discusses the status of the apostrophe in "*Meander*'s margent green."

1276 Corse, Sandra. "Old Music and New in *L'Allegro* and *Il Penseroso*." *MiltonQ*, 14, 1980, 109–13.

Shows that in the companion poems, Milton contrasts two types of contemporary music, monodic and polyphonic.

1277 Council, Norman B. "*L'Allegro, Il Penseroso*, and 'The Cycle of Universal Knowledge.'" *MiltonS*, 9, 1976, 203–19.

"The subject of *L'Allegro* and *Il Penseroso* is the experience of education as Milton conceived it. All his statements on education assume the ideal expressed in the Seventh Prolusion: to aspire to a time 'when the

cycle of universal knowledge has been completed.'" Abs., *MiltonQ*, 11, 1977, 26–27.

1278 Cox, Gerard H. "Unbinding 'The Hidden Soul of Harmony': *L'Allegro, Il Penseroso*, and the Hermetic Tradition." *MiltonS*, 18, 1983, 45–62.

Suggests that "*L'Allegro* and *Il Penseroso* are complementary, that their reconciliation is a function of harmony, and that this conception of harmony derives from a sophisticated and self-conscious hermetic tradition."

1279 Cox, John D. "Poetry and History in Milton's Country Masque." *ELH*, 44, 1977, 622–40.

Claims that *Comus* refers to a sexual scandal in the Egerton family. Points out that Milton's major accomplishment is in the veracity of his historical references and concludes that the masque is "a model for vocation, a model for uniting history and poetry in the way that Milton later recommended to the aspiring poet."

1280 Cox, John D. "Renaissance Power and Stuart Dramaturgy: Shakespeare, Milton, and Dryden." *CompD*, 22, 1988, 323–58.

Sees *Comus* and *Samson Agonistes* as companion pieces and relates both to Milton's opposition to the Stuarts. Contrasts Milton's dramas with Shakespeare's and Dryden's.

1281 Crane, David. "Marvell and Milton on Cromwell." *N&Q*, 33, 1986, 464.

Asserts that in Sonnet 16 (to Cromwell), Milton "consciously reworks Marvell's equivocal image of Cromwell's lightning breaking out of the clouds in an energy as much hostile to friend as to foe."

1282 Creaser, John. "Dolphins in *Lycidas*." *RES*, 36, 1985, 235–43.

Refutes assertions that the dolphins in *Lycidas* allude to Arion, Melicertes, or Apollo. Rather, Milton draws on "a traditional and widespread stock of knowledge about the dolphin's response to man and known tendency to bring humans towards land."

1283 Creaser, John. "*Lycidas*: The Power of Art." *E&S*, 34, 1981, 123–47.

Concludes that at the end of the poem, "Milton and his solitary swain face the new experience that must be theirs resiliently and with faith restored, thanks to the power of art."

1284 Creaser, John. "Milton's *Comus*: The Irrelevance of the Castlehaven Scandal." *N&Q*, 31, 1984, 307–17. Revised in *MiltonQ*, 21, No. 4, 1987, 24–34.

Refutes the following hypotheses: "(i) that the [Castlehaven] scandal delayed Bridgewater's assumption of office; (ii) that it determined the theme of *Comus* and some of the treatment of that theme . . .; (iii) that its presence is suggested by the nature of the cuts in the performed text." See No. 1218.

1285 Creaser, John. "'The Present Aid of This Occasion': The Setting of *Comus*." *The Court Masque.* Ed. by David Lindley (Manchester and Dover, NH: Manchester Univ. Press, 1984), pp. 111–34.

Rejects the view that Comus was a children's entertainment staged "with borrowed costumes, limited or no spectacle, and amateurish performers." Claims that the masque was written for a major state event and performed with much splendor.

1286 Creaser, John. "A Textual Crux in *L'Allegro*: A Reply." *N&Q*, 31, 1984, 327–30.

Responds to Archie Burnett's reply (No. 1235) to Creaser's earlier article (No. 4111). Contends that Burnett's arguments for the 1673 edition of Milton's poems are "meticulous" but inevitably serve only to "reinforce [Creaser's] preference for *1645*."

1287 Crowley, Leslie-Anne. "The Unifying Function of Imagery in Milton's *Lycidas*: Theme, Polyvalence and Recall." *QLL*, 10, 1985, 5–27.

Concludes that "the artistic and emotive unity of the poem is achieved

largely by means of imagery: imagery which forms a series of continued figures or themes."

1288 Cullen, Patrick. "Imitation and Metamorphosis: The Golden-Age Eclogue in Spenser, Milton, and Marvell." *PMLA*, 84, 1969, 1559–70.

These poets imitate the golden-age or Messianic eclogue while transforming its conventional generic pattern. Milton's *Nativity Ode* uses the same formulas to praise the true Messiah, Christ, and to celebrate the new golden age, the new Eden, which his birth begins.

1289 Cumberland, Sharon, and **Lynn Veach Sadler.** "Phantasia: A Pattern in Milton's Early Poems." *MiltonQ*, 8, 1974, 50–55.

Defines "phantasia" in terms of high, low, and middle and applies these levels to the *Nativity Ode*, *Comus*, and other early poems.

1290 Cunnar, Eugene R. "Milton, *The Shepherd* of Hermas, and the Writing of a Puritan Masque." *MiltonS*, 23, 1987, 33–52.

Argues that in *Comus* Milton chose the masque form, which the Puritans traditionally opposed, to "express his commitment to reform those genres invested with ideologies and worldviews repugnant to his new calling of poet/prophet."

1291 Cunnar, Eugene R. "Milton's 'Two-Handed Engine': The Visionary Iconography of *Christus in Statera*." *MiltonQ*, 17, 1983, 29–38.

Surveys the topos of "Christus in statera" (Christ on the scales of the Cross). Demonstrates that, "given the Renaissance habit of reading moral meaning into works and of viewers completing the meaning of visual images in paintings, Milton's readers may well have apprehended the 'two-handed engine' as both the scales of St. Michael and as Christ on the scales of the Cross."

Abs., *SCN*, 38, 1980, 44; *MiltonQ*, 14, 1980, 31.

1292 Daiches, David. "Some Aspects of Milton's Pastoral Imagery." *More Literary Essays* (Edinburgh and London: Oliver and Boyd; Chicago, IL: Univ. of Chicago Press, 1968), pp. 96–114.
Reprint of Huckabay No. 2427, originally published in 1966.

1293 D'amico, Jack. *Petrarch in England: An Anthology of Parallel Texts from Wyatt to Milton.* Speculum Artium, no. 5. Ravenna: Longo Editore, 1979. 205pp.
Sees a Petrarchan influence in four of Milton's sonnets. Abs., *RenQ*, 32, 1979, 472.

1294 Daniel, Clay. "'The Blind *Fury*,' Providence, and the Consolations of *Lycidas*." *EIRC*, 13, 1987, 100–25.
Asserts that the poem's pagan and Christian elements are opposed, which ultimately shows the superiority of the latter, as in *Paradise Lost* and *Paradise Regained*.

1295 Daniels, Edgar F. "Milton's *Lycidas*." *Expl*, 39, No. 2, 1981, 18–19.
On Milton's use of ellipsis in the passage on fame. See No. 1834.

1296 Davies, H. Neville. "Laid Artfully Together: Stanzaic Design in Milton's *On the Morning of Christ's Nativity*." *Fair Forms: Essays in English Literature from Spenser to Jane Austen.* Ed. by Maren-Sofie Røstvig (Cambridge: D. S. Brewer; Totowa, NJ: Rowman and Littlefield, 1975), pp. 85–117, 213–19.
States that commentators are right "to split the poem into sections." Proposes that "the Ode is structured according to an exact and determinable plan, while an overall pattern of 'linked sweetness' unites the separate parts." Abs., *MiltonQ*, 13, 1979, 27.

1297 Davies, H. Neville. "*Lycidas*: Poem and Pattern." *CahiersE*, 14, 1978, 23–37.
Proposes a twofold structure in which "there is a simple contrast between Lycidas drowned and Lycidas wel-comed in heaven . . . and between versification disrupted by short lines and unrhymed lines and versification unbroken by such irregularities."

1298 Davies, H. Neville. "Milton's Nativity Ode and Drummond's *An Hymne of the Ascension*." *ScLJ*, 12, 1985, 5–23.
Compares the poems and decides that "Milton found the Ascension Hymn worthy of the most detailed scrutiny."

1299 Davis, Robert Leigh. "That Two-Handed Engine and the Consolation of *Lycidas*." *MiltonQ*, 20, 1986, 44–48.
Believes the two-handed engine in *Lycidas* holds an "unmistakable tone of judgment and [an] identification with the larger context of salvation."

1300 Dean-Smith, Margaret. "The Ominous Wood: An Investigation into Some Traditionary Sources of Milton's *Comus*." *The Witch Figure: Folklore Essays by a Group of Scholars in England Honouring the 75th Birthday of Katherine M. Briggs.* Ed. by Venetia Newall (London and Boston, MA: Routledge and Kegan Paul, 1973), pp. 42–71.
Deals with Robert Jamieson's and Joseph Jacobs's work, which provides "a series of those traditional tales or superstitions to which Warton believed Milton's genius to be sympathetic." The sources of *Comus* ultimately derive from primitive folklore, in which good and bad angels contend for the human soul.

1301 Demaray, John G. "*Arcades* as a Literary Entertainment." *PLL*, 8, No. 1, 1972, 15–26.
Imagines an actual production of the entertainment and reads it as "a work with a serious Christian meaning concealed beneath the allusions to pagan themes and figures."

1302 Demaray, John G. "Gunpowder and the Problem of Theatrical Heroic Form: *In Quintum Novembris*." *MiltonS*, 19, 1984, 3–19.
Shows that in the poem Milton synthesizes disparate theatrical, classical, and literary materials. Believes that this

youthful exercise points toward Satan's machinations in *Paradise Lost.*

1303 Demaray, John G. *Milton and the Masque Tradition: The Early Poems, "Arcades," and "Comus."* Cambridge, MA: Harvard Univ. Press, 1968. xii, 188pp. See Huckabay No. 2436. Reviews: *MiltonN*, 2, 1968, 8–9; John M. Wallace, *JEGP*, 68, 1969, 512–14; W. J. Barnes, *QQ*, 76, 1969, 726–29; Jonathan Price, *SCN*, 27, 1969, 65–66; Leonard Nathanson, *MP*, 67, 1970, 285–88.

1304 Demaray, John. "The Temple of the Mind: Cosmic Iconography in Milton's *A Mask.*" *MiltonQ*, 21, No. 4, 1987, 59–76. Discusses "the metaphor and the practice of cosmological dance in *A Mask.* Examining the masque tradition in France, Italy, and England, Demaray finds one of the great organizing principles of the masque in the very organization of the cosmos. In searching out that enormous metaphor, Demaray leads us into backwaters of cosmology, including hitherto unexamined adversary figures who sought to disrupt the order of things—necromancers, cheats, and jugglers—all like the character Comus" (from Roy Flannagan's Introduction, p. iv).

1305 Dempsey, Ivy. "To 'Attain to Something like Prophetic Strain.'" *Papers on Milton.* Ed. by Philip Mahone Griffith and Lester F. Zimmerman. Univ. of Tulsa Department of English Monograph Series, no. 8 (Tulsa, OK: Univ. of Tulsa, 1969), pp. 9–24. In *L'Allegro* and *Il Penseroso*, sees Mirth as thesis, Melancholy as antithesis, and their resolution as synthesis.

1306 Diehl, Huston. "Teaching Milton's Early Poetry." *CE*, 40, 1978, 46–54. Encourages the teaching of Milton's early poetry in light of both the seventeenth-century and modern contexts. The early poems help students understand the symbolism of *Paradise Lost.*

1307 Diekhoff, John S. "Appendix: The Text of *Comus*, 1634 to 1645." *"A Maske*

at Ludlow" : Essays on Milton's "Comus." Ed. by Diekhoff (Ann Arbor, MI: Univ. Microfilms International, 1980 Books on Demand Reprints), pp. 251–75. Reprint of Huckabay No. 2446, originally published in 1968.

1308 Diekhoff, John S., ed. *"A Maske at Ludlow" : Essays on Milton's "Comus."* Ann Arbor, MI: Univ. Microfilms International, 1980 Books on Demand Reprints. Reprint of Huckabay No. 2441, originally published in 1968. Review: John R. Mulder, *SCN*, 28, 1970, 3–4.

1309 Dillon, John B. "Renaissance Reference Books as Sources for Classical Myth and Geography: A Brief Survey, with an Illustration from Milton." *Acta Conventus Neo-Latini Bononiensis.* Ed. by R. J. Schoeck (Binghamton, NY: Medieval and Renaissance Texts and Studies, 1985), pp. 437–50. Believes that modern scholarship has erred by placing Aracynthus, from *In Quintum Novembris* 64–65, on the border between Boeotia and Attica.

1310 Dobin, Howard. "Milton's *Nativity Ode*: 'O What a Mask was There.'" *MiltonQ*, 17, 1983, 71–80. "The poem literally 'unmasks' the masque itself, stripping away the earthly level of metaphor designed to praise the glory of kings, and instead offering praise directly to the King of Glory."

1311 Dobler, Judith Margaret. "An Anatomy of Metaphor: A Method for Analyzing Figurative Language and Its Application to the Figures in *Lycidas, Adonais*, and *Thyrsis.*" Doctoral diss., Univ. of Iowa, 1983. 291pp. Abs., *DAI*, 44, 1984, 2137A. Locates fewer, simpler poetic figures, usually with rhetorical purposes, as poetic figurative language has changed between the Renaissance and the nineteenth century.

1312 Doke, Hiroichiro. "The Theme and Structure of *Lycidas.*" *MCJ News*, 2, 1978, 2–5.

Sees the figure of Lycidas as a poet, priest, and saint respectively in the past, present, and future, against the background of nature, society, and heaven. Abs., *MiltonQ*, 13, 1979, 159.

1313 Dorangeon, Simone. *L'Églogue Anglaise de Spenser à Milton.* Études Anglaises, 49. Paris: Didier, 1974. 594pp.

Studies the evolution of the English eclogue from 1579, the year Spenser was named the "New Poet," until 1637, when Milton chose the pastoral form on the death of a friend. In *Lycidas*, Milton adapts the Spenserian pastoral to suit the requirements of classical aesthetics.

1314 Doyle, Charles Clay. "Hobson's Oxford Fame: A 1651 Instance." *N&Q*, 16, 1969, 372–73.

Argues that the carrier Hobson of Milton's poems was probably known in Oxford circles of the mid-seventeenth century.

1315 Draper, R. P. *Lyric Tragedy.* London: Macmillan; New York: St. Martin's Press, 1985. vii, 231pp.

Discusses *Lycidas* and the traditional definition of lyrical tragedy. Believes that the elegy deals with the emotions of "grief, compassion, anxiety, resentment, indignation—and even, perhaps, a degree of self-pity" cathartically, as Milton uses a Christian standard that sees through anguish to divine order. Thus, "*Lycidas* is not lyric tragedy," though it exerts "a profound influence on the shape of lyric tragedy which comes after it."

1316 Driskill, Linda Lorane Phillips. "Cyclic Structure in Renaissance Pastoral Poetry." Doctoral diss., Rice Univ., 1970. 406pp. Abs., *DAI*, 31, 1970, 2872A–73A.

Analyzes and compares Spenser's *Shepheardes Calender*, Drayton's *Idea*, and Milton's *Lycidas* to understand the contributions of perspective, unity, and structure to cyclic pastoral poetry.

1317 Duckworth, George E. "Milton's Hexameter Patterns—Vergilian or Ovidian?" *American Journal of Philology*, 93, 1972, 52–60.

States that "Milton in his Latin poetry is both Vergilian and Ovidian." In his elegies, Milton "resembles Ovid more closely than do most Roman poets" and his hexameter poems follow Virgil's technique "to a degree."

1318 Du Rocher, Richard J. "The Wealth and Blood of Milton's Sonnet XI." *MiltonQ*, 17, 1983, 15–17.

Interprets Sonnet 11 ("A book was writ of late") as "Elizabethan verse satire" in which Milton alludes to his contemporaries as specific beasts. Believes that the phrase, "all this waste of wealth and loss of blood" refers to the English revolution, but it mainly insists "that natural, blood rights should be respected by law, and that valuable liberty may be achieved only with virtue and the discipline of truth."

1319 Dust, Philip. "Milton's *Epitaphium Damonis* and *Lycidas*." *HumLov*, 32, 1983, 342–46.

Questions the idea that Milton feels no great personal grief for Edward King and that he does for Charles Diodati. Finds many similarities between the two poems and argues that Milton borrowed from *Lycidas* to write the Latin elegy.

1320 Dust, Philip. "New Light on Milton's 'Two-Handed Engine': A Possible Neo-Latin Source." *HumLov*, 22, 1973, 320–24.

Suggests William Gager's poem on the gunpowder plot, *Pyramis*.

1321 Dye, E. H. "Milton's *Comus* and Boethius' *Consolation*." *MiltonQ*, 19, 1985, 1–7.

Asserts that *Comus* and the *Consolation of Philosophy* are complementary, for they share "the trials their protagonists suffer, the Circe myth, deprecation of the passions, a chaste ideal of temperance of Neoplatonic idealism, and the liberating intervention of divine grace that endows both heroine and hero with sufficient judgemental wisdom for them to achieve individual happiness."

1322 Dyson, A. E. "The Interpretation of *Comus*." *"A Maske at Ludlow": Essays on Milton's "Comus."* Ed. by John S. Diekhoff (Ann Arbor, MI: Univ. Microfilms International, 1980 Books on Demand Reprints), pp. 102–25.

Reprint of Huckabay No. 2458, originally published in 1955.

1323 Dyson, A. E. "Virtue Unwavering: Milton's *Comus*." *Between Two Worlds* (London: Macmillan, 1972), pp. 15–40. Reprinted in *Milton: "Comus" and "Samson Agonistes," a Casebook*. Ed. by Julian Lovelock (London and Basingstoke: Macmillan, 1975), pp. 106–33.

A revised version of Huckabay No. 2458, originally published in 1955.

1324 Easthope, Antony. "Towards the Autonomous Subject in Poetry: Milton 'On His Blindness.'" *1642: Literature and Power in the Seventeenth Century*. Ed. by Francis Barker and others (Colchester: Univ. of Essex, 1981), pp. 301–14. Reprinted in *Post-Structuralist Readings of English Poetry*. Ed. by Richard Machin and Christopher Norris (Cambridge: Cambridge Univ. Press, 1987), pp. 122–33.

Deals with the problems of "ordering" Milton's sonnets because they were written over a period of forty years. Sonnet 19 ("When I consider") "articulates both energetic rebellion against loss . . . and a controlled assertion that the loss be accepted. Progress across these two is enabled as the speaker's 'I' becomes the voice of the Father." The poem is theologically unorthodox because "there is still 'this deep strength of ego' deliberately asserting submission to superego."

1325 Edgerton, Larry. "Milton's 'On Time.'" *Expl*, 42, 1983, 14–16.

Demonstrates how "On Time" moves "from the mundane to the divine" and also employs rhythm and rhyme to show

that humanity can transcend time through the power of Christianity.

1326 El-Gabalawy, Saad. "Christian Communism in *Utopia*, *King Lear*, and *Comus*." *UTQ*, 47, 1978, 228–38.

Claims that "the sentiment of Christian communism reveals itself in the ideas that every man should have 'a moderate and beseeming share'; 'Nature's full blessings would be well dispens't / In unsuperfluous even proportion.'" Concludes that Milton implies that "equitable distribution is a sign of divine justice."

1327 Elliott, Emory. "Milton's Uncouth Swain: The Speaker in *Lycidas*." *Milton Reconsidered: Essays in Honor of Arthur E. Barker*. Ed. by John Karl Franson (Salzburg: Institut für Englische Sprache und Literatur, Universität Salzburg, 1976), pp. 1–21.

Believes that the last eight lines of *Lycidas* are unsettling and that Milton "raises the question of the continued vitality of the traditional poetic forms and the power of the Christian-humanist message."

1328 Ellrodt, Robert. "Milton's Unchanging Mind and the Early Poems." *MiltonQ*, 22, 1988, 59–62.

Asserts that Milton's poetry possesses "unbroken imaginative continuity" which can be recognized in the thematic and verbal similarities between his Cambridge poems and his later ones. Compares Milton and the metaphysical poets.

1329 Embry, Thomas Jerome. "The Ideal of Chastity in Milton's Early Poetry." Doctoral diss., Georgia State Univ., 1981. 283pp. Abs., *DAI*, 42, 1982, 3609A.

Relates Milton's emphasis on chastity to his youthful belief in inspiration and "marriage of the soul with Christ" before considering its impact on his entire poetic career.

1330 Embry, Thomas J. "Sensuality and Chastity in *L'Allegro* and *Il Penseroso*." *JEGP*, 77, 1978, 504–29.

Asserts that the symbolism of *Il Penseroso* applauds chastity, while in *L'Allegro* it opposes sensuality. Abs., *SCN*, 38, 1980, 19.

1331 Emerson, Cornelia Dozier. "Themes of Transformation in Spenser, Milton, and Shelley." Doctoral diss., Yale Univ., 1980. 225pp. Abs., *DAI*, 41, 1981, 4718A.

Demonstrates the persistence of transformation themes from the Renaissance to the nineteenth century and explores "changes in the relationship of man to nature in the selected poems" of Spenser, Shelley, and Milton.

1332 Emslie, Macdonald. "Milton on Lawes: The Trinity MS Revisions." *Music in English Renaissance Drama.* Ed. by John H. Long (Lexington: Univ. of Kentucky Press, 1968), pp. 96–102.

On the meaning of Milton's musical comments in Sonnet 13 (to Henry Lawes).

1333 Enterline, Lynn E. "'Myself/Before Me': Gender and Prohibition in Milton's Italian Sonnets." *Milton and the Idea of Woman.* Ed. by Julia M. Walker (Urbana and Chicago: Univ. of Illinois Press, 1988), pp. 32–51.

"By writing love sonnets and a *canzone* in Italian, Milton poses in his own way the problem of the poet's relation to language and gender, a problem that pervades Petrarch's *Canzoniere.* A psychoanalytic approach to these texts, in particular one that makes use of the writings of [Jacques] Lacan, offers a way of reading the issues of self, language, and gender in relation to one another." Abs., *MiltonQ*, 24, 1990, 150.

1334 Entzminger, Robert L. "The Epiphanies in Milton's *Nativity Ode.*" *RenP*, 1981, pp. 21–31.

Believes that the poem is more than a celebration of the birth itself, that it is an epiphany of God's making himself known to humanity.

1335 Evans, J. Martin. "Lycidas and the Dolphins." *N&Q*, 25, 1978, 15–17.

Claims that the dolphins allude to

Hesiod, one of Milton's favorite classical poets.

1336 Evans, J. Martin. "Lycidas, Daphnis, and Gallus." *English Renaissance Studies Presented to Dame Helen Gardner in Honour of Her Seventieth Birthday.* [Ed. by John Carey] (Oxford: Clarendon Press, 1980), pp. 228–44.

Questions the idea that Milton is merely imitating Theocritus's *Idyl* 1 and Virgil's *Eclogue* 10 in *Lycidas* 50–55. "Far from being just another pastoral hero who died young, Edward King emerges as the exact antithesis of Daphnis and Gallus, or, more precisely, of the Renaissance Daphnis and Gallus."

1337 Evans, J. Martin. *The Road from Horton: Looking Backwards in "Lycidas."* English Literary Studies Monograph Series, no. 28. [Victoria, BC]: English Studies, Univ. of Victoria, 1983. 90pp.

Argues that the poem is an "Age Thirty Transition" piece, that Milton's deepest anxieties lie beneath the surface of its lines, and that these anxieties would "eventually transform the retiring young virgin poet of Horton into the publicly outspoken, thrice married polemicist of Westminster." Review: Roy C. Flannagan, *MiltonQ*, 18, 1984, 133.

1338 Falle, George. "'A Solemne Measure . . . A Just Proportion.'" *Familiar Colloquy: Essays Presented to Arthur Edward Barker.* Ed. by Patricia Brückmann (Toronto: Oberon Press, 1978), pp. 209–26.

Compares the attitudes toward music in Milton's "At a Solemn Music" and Dryden's "Song for St. Cecilia's Day."

1339 Fallon, Robert Thomas. "Milton's 'Defenseless Doors': The Limits of Irony." *MiltonQ*, 13, 1979, 146–51.

Regards Sonnet 8 ("Captain or Colonel") as serious and its tone as one of quiet resolve. The poet will not be apart from the war and will play the traditional poet's role.

1340 Fawcett, Mary Laughlin. "'Such Noise as I Can Make': Chastity and

Speech in *Othello* and *Comus*." *RenD*, 16, 1985, 159–80.

Supports the idea that "speech peels away from the sexual state of chastity. Words cannot defend the chaste woman, and they may turn actively against her." Refutes the conception that the myth of Echo represents the ideal of the female chaste voice. Notes parallels between Desdemona of *Othello* and the Lady of *Comus*.

1341 Felsen, Karl E. "The 'Two-Handed Engine,' a Balanced View." *MiltonQ*, 9, 1975, 6–14.

With qualifications, supports Philip Rollinson's view (No. 1681) that the engine of *Lycidas* "is the balance or scales of judgment wielded by St. Michael at the Last Judgment." Rejoinder by Robert F. Fleissner (No. 1354) with a surrejoinder (No. 1342).

1342 Felsen, Karl. "That 'Two-Handed Engine' Once More." *MiltonQ*, 10, 1976, 124–26.

Answers Robert F. Fleissner's thesis (No. 1354) against Felsen's argument that the two-handed engine is the scale used at the Last Judgment (No. 1341).

1343 Fish, Stanley E. "*Lycidas*: A Poem Finally Anonymous." *Glyph*, 8, 1981, 1–18.

Contends "that the suppressing of the personal voice is the poem's achievement, and that the energy of the poem derives not from the presence of a controlling and self-contained individual, but from forces that undermine his individuality and challenge the fiction of his control." See No. 1174.

1344 Fish, Stanley E. "Problem Solving in *Comus*." *Illustrious Evidence: Approaches to English Literature of the Early Seventeenth Century*. Ed. by Earl Miner (Berkeley, Los Angeles, and London: Univ. of California Press, 1975), pp. 115–31.

Argues that "*Comus* is a device for the making true of its audience's ears, which are here tested, as they have been tested before, by their ability to

understand." Believes that the final "reward for reading *Comus* properly is not merely comprehension or even instruction, but conversion."

1345 Fish, Stanley. "The Temptation to Action in Milton's Poetry." *ELH*, 48, 1981, 516–31.

Discusses the view of action in "At a Solemn Music" and the *Nativity Ode*, showing that Milton regarded the impulse to ask for narrative action as "symptomatic of a desire to displace responsibility for moral decision from ourselves onto the world of circumstance."

1346 Fish, Stanley E. "What It's Like To Read *L'Allegro* and *Il Penseroso*." *MiltonS*, 7, 1975, 77–99. Reprinted in *Is There a Text in This Class? The Authority of Interpretive Communities* (Cambridge, MA, and London: Harvard Univ. Press, 1980), pp. 112–35.

"In the act of reading the poem [*L'Allegro*], we experience as a gift (from Milton) the care-less freedom which is its subject. In contrast, the activities required of us in reading *Il Penseroso* are consistently and self-consciously strenuous."

1347 Fiske, Dixon. "Milton in the Middle of Life: Sonnet XIX." *ELH*, 41, 1974, 37–49.

Concludes that in Sonnet 19 ("When I consider"), Milton writes "of his great trial" and "signals his critical and traditional confusion in the middle of life."

1348 Fiske, Dixon Davis. "Milton's Sonnets." Doctoral diss., Princeton Univ., 1969. 420pp. Abs., *DAI*, 31, 1970, 756A.

Addresses the problems of text, dating, and interpretation of Milton's sonnets.

1349 Fiske, Dixon. "The Theme of Purification in Milton's Sonnet XXIII." *MiltonS*, 8, 1975, 149–63.

"The controversy over the dating, subject, and meaning of Milton's Sonnet XXIII ['Methought I saw'] can be resolved in the context of Milton's ideas of purification [which is] . . . a major theme in the sonnet, and the key to Milton's use of it is to be found in the background of the sonnet's second simile. Milton's allusion there to the rites of purification under the old law is part of a thematic pattern in which the poet progressively refers to pagan, Jewish, and Christian images of purification."

1350 Fixler, Michael. "The Orphic Technique of *L'Allegro* and *Il Penseroso*." *ELR*, 1, 1971, 165–77.

Asserts that Milton used Orphic incantations and interwove them as a "technical secret . . . of creative imaginative force he was setting in action."

1351 Fixler, Michael. "'Unexpressive Song': Form and Enigma Variations in *Lycidas*, A New Reading." *MiltonS*, 15, 1981, 213–55.

"My object in what follows is specifically to identify two principal 'unheard' progressions in the formal and thematic movements of the poem, upon which the sounding harmonies largely depend." Identifies and discusses the poem's four movements, each of which ends in a rapture.

1352 Flannagan, Roy, ed. *"Comus": Contexts*. *MiltonQ*, 21, No. 4, 1987. iv, 76pp.

A special issue of *Milton Quarterly*. Contributors are Cedric C. Brown, John Creaser, John G. Demaray, David Lloyd, Leah Sinanoglou Marcus, and Michael Wilding. In this bibliography, each essay is listed according to author. Review: Stanley Archer, *SCN*, 47, 1989, 37–38.

1353 Fleissner, Robert F. "Milton's *Lycidas*, Lines 130–131." *Expl*, 41, No. 3, 1983, 23–25.

Argues that the two-handed engine in *Lycidas* is an apocalyptic allusion to the two keys that St. Peter wields. Further suggests that if the keys are envisaged as crossed, Milton may also have been hinting at a heraldic emblem, as in the papal coat of arms. This would associate the keys with both the door and the act of smiting.

1354 Fleissner, Robert F. "Scaling Down That 'Balanced' Engine." *MiltonQ*, 9, 1975, 82–83.

On the two-handed engine in *Lycidas*. Offers objections to Karl Felsen's views (No. 1341). Reply by Felsen (No. 1342).

1355 Fleissner, Robert F. "Some Gears for Milton's Two-Handed Engine: A Retrospect." *MiltonQ*, 16, 1982, 25.

Abstract of a paper presented at the 1981 Mid-Hudson MLA Conference. Surveys criticism about the two-handed engine and defends Kathleen Swaim's position (No. 1767).

1356 Fleissner, Robert F. "'The Two-Handed Engine': A Heraldic Emblem in *Lycidas*." *Anglia*, 91, 1973, 77–83.

Believes that St. Peter's keys should be "considered together as emblematically crossed, overlapping in the traditional heraldic manner."

1357 Fleming, Ray. "'Sublime and Pure Thoughts, without Transgression': The Dantean Influence in Milton's 'Donna leggiadra.'" *MiltonQ*, 20, 1986, 38–44.

Believes that Milton's Sonnet 2 ("Donna leggiadra") was influenced by Dante rather than Petrarch, specifically in its moral themes.

1358 Fletcher, Angus. *The Transcendental Masque: An Essay on Milton's "Comus."* Ithaca, NY, and London: Cornell Univ. Press, 1971. xvi, 261pp.

"This essay describes the mimetic character and magic symbolism of the masque, and . . . analyzes structural properties of *Comus* to show the transcendental form of that particular masque." Reviews: *MiltonQ*, 6, No. 3, 1972, 16–17; Robert M. Adams, *Diacritics*, 2, 1972, 2–5; Michael Lieb, *Cithara*, 12, 1972, 85–106; Shigeo Saino, *EigoS*, 118, 1972, 296; Claude J. Summers, *WHR*, 26, 1972, 284–85; Kathleen M. Swaim, *Mosaic*, 5, 1972, 191–95; Joseph Anthony Wittreich, Jr.,

Genre, 5, 1972, 307–25; J. H. Adamson, *SN*, 45, 1973, 452–53; Margaret M. Byard, *RenQ*, 26, 1973, 380–82; Ben Drake, *MLQ*, 34, 1973, 102–05; E. A. J. Honigmann, *RES*, 24, 1973, 75–76; A. H. Elliott, *N&Q*, 21, 1974, 439–40; Lois Potter, *ES*, 55, 1974, 477–79; Andrew M. McLean, *SHR*, 10, 1976, 362–69.

1359 Flosdorf, J. W. "'Gums of Glutinous Heat': A Query." *MiltonQ*, 7, 1973, 4–5.
Asks Miltonists to comment on the meaning of "gums of glutinous heat" in *Comus* 917. Suggests some possible interpretations. Replies by John Shawcross (No. 3039), Jean-François Camé (No. 1243), and Stanley Archer (No. 1180).

1360 Folsom, Lowell Edwin. "*L'Allegro* and *Il Penseroso*: The Poetics of Accelerando and Ritardando." *StHum*, 5, 1976, 39–41.
Suggests that each poem's title helps to create its mood and tempo, "one toward a happy brisk tempo—an allegro—and the other toward a solemn, meditative pace—a penseroso."

1361 Forker, Charles R. "Milton and Shakespeare: The First Sonnet on Blindness in Relation to a Speech from *Troilus and Cressida*." *ELN*, 11, 1974, 188–92.
Suggests that Milton "so feelingly absorbed the Shakespearean passage that both its vocabulary and its associations had become one with his own poetic impulses" in Sonnet 19 ("When I consider").

1362 Forrest, James F. "Milton and the Divine Art of Weaponry: 'That Two-Handed Engine' and Bunyan's 'Nameless Terrible Instrument' at Mouthgate." *MiltonS*, 16, 1982, 131–40.
Compares Bunyan's image in the *Holy War* with Milton's image in *Lycidas*. Believes that Milton's defies precise identification but relates it to the power of prayer.

1363 Forrest, James F. "The Significance of Milton's 'Mantle Blue.'" *MiltonQ*, 8, 1974, 41–48.
Suggests that the "'mantle blue' [*Lycidas* 192] ... may be associated with the symbolical garb traditionally worn by the Welsh bards."

1364 Forster, Harold. "Milton's *Lycidas*." *N&Q*, 25, 1978, 510.
Claims that Milton's intended spelling was "Lysidas." Abs., *SCN*, 38, 1980, 19.

1365 Fowler, Alastair. "'To Shepherd's Ear': The Form of Milton's *Lycidas*." *Silent Poetry: Essays in Numerological Analysis*. Ed. by Fowler (London: Routledge and Kegan Paul, 1970), pp. 170–84.
Concludes that "we have in *Lycidas* one of the best-built poems in our literature; though its architectural style is now an unfamiliar one." Feels that Milton intends "his poem's numbers to form in the reader the resolution its content describes."

1366 Franson, J. Karl. "An Anglo-Saxon Etymology for Milton's *Haemony*." *AN&Q*, 14, 1975, 18–19.
In *Comus*, "Haemony, with its own suggestion of opposites (dark unsightly root—bright golden flower; prickly leaves—medicinal powers) would thus draw together under a single emblem the whole dualism of human sexuality and the central concern of the mask."

1367 Franson, J. Karl. "Etymology of Edward King's Name." *MiltonQ*, 22, 1988, 127–28.
Asserts that Milton assigns the name of Edward King to the hero of *Lycidas* because it means "happy keeper" or "property guardian," and therefore King will protect ships from hidden rocks and reefs.

1368 Freeman, James A. "That Italianate Englishman, John Milton." *MiltonQ*, 16, 1982, 107.
Abstract of a paper given to the International Association for Neo-Latin Studies in St. Andrews, Scotland, in 1982. Shows that *Ad Salsillum* defines

Milton's view of himself and his poetry in relation to England and to Italy.

1369 Freeman, James A., and **Anthony Low,** eds. *Urbane Milton: The Latin Poetry. MiltonS*, vol. 19. Pittsburgh, PA: Univ. of Pittsburgh Press, 1984. xiii, 307pp.

A special volume. Contributors are Gordon Campbell, Christopher Collins, Thomas N. Corns, John G. Demaray, John B. Dillon, William J. Kennedy, Janet Leslie Knedlik, Albert C. Labriola, Diane Kelsey McColley, Stella P. Revard, William A. Sessions, Freeman, and Low. In this bibliography, each essay is listed according to author. Reviews: Thomas Healy, *Bulletin of the Society for Renaissance Studies*, 3, 1985, 82–83; Archie Burnett, *N&Q*, 33, 1986, 416.

1370 French, Roberts W. "A Note on Spenser and Milton." *N&Q*, 17, 1970, 412.

Suggests Spenser's *Epithalamion* 415–16 as the probable source of *L'Allegro* 121–22.

1371 French, Roberts W. "Reading a Poem: Two Sonnets by Milton." *CP*, 2, 1968, 11–16.

Shows how Milton reshapes the sonnet tradition in Sonnet 7 ("How soon hath Time") and Sonnet 19 ("When I consider").

1372 French, Roberts W. "Spenser and Sonnet XVIII." *MiltonQ*, 5, 1971, 51–52.

Suggests the influence of the *Faerie Queene* 1.8.36–37 on Milton's Sonnet 18 ("On the Late Massacre in Piemont").

1373 French, Roberts W. "Voice and Structure in *Lycidas*." *TSLL*, 12, 1970, 15–25.

Explains "the suddenness with which the poem turns from the despair of one section to the joy of the other." Feels that the "uncouth swain" speaks with two different voices.

1374 Friedman, Donald M. "*Comus* and the Truth of the Ear." *"The Muses Common-Weale": Poetry and Politics in the Seventeenth Century*. Ed. by Claude J. Summers and Ted-Larry Pebworth (Columbia: Univ. of Missouri Press, 1988), pp. 119–34.

Describes "Milton's use of neologisms to test those whose 'ears be true'" and shows that *Comus* points toward the young poet's mature vision of a reformed religion.

1375 Friedman, Donald. "Harmony and the Poet's Voice in Some of Milton's Early Poems." *MLQ*, 30, 1969, 523–34.

Believes that Milton's every act leads to the composition of *Paradise Lost* and that the early poems mark his attempts to master a persona.

1376 Friedman, Donald M. "*Lycidas*: The Swain's Paideia." *MiltonS*, 3, 1971, 3–34.

Focuses on the poem's consolation passage, in which "the poet speaks for the first time to a human audience, and takes on the double burden of knowledge and pastoral responsibility." The passage's language "leads directly to the new shepherd who prays for inspiration at the beginning of *Paradise Lost*." Review: Michael Lieb, *Cithara*, 12, 1972, 85–106. See No. 1174.

1377 Fruchter, Barry George. "Studies in the English Elegy." Doctoral diss., State Univ. of New York, Stony Brook, 1977. 134pp. Abs., *DAI*, 38, 1977, 1407A.

Sees in Donne's, Milton's, and Pope's and Gray's elegies the respective formation, maturation, and climax of a distinctively English elegy.

1378 Fry, Paul H. "Milton's Light-Harnessed Ode." *The Poet's Calling in the English Ode* (New Haven, CT, and London: Yale Univ. Press, 1980), pp. 37–48.

Believes that in the *Nativity Ode* Milton is concerned with his poetic vocation, as he is in *Lycidas*. Uses the Lucifer passage because it helps "to clarify Milton's subtly registered hesitancies as a hymnodist by tracing the influence of this passage elsewhere in the poem."

1379 Fujii, Haruhiko. "Iruka no yukue." *EigoS*, 117, 1971, 350–51.

On the location of the dolphins in *Lycidas* 164.

1380 Fujii, Haruhiko. "*Lycidas* and Spenser's Pastorals." *HSELL*, 19, 1972, 34–50.

In Japanese; English summary, pp. 51–52. On the affinities between Milton's poem and Spenser's November Eclogue and *Colin Clouts Come Home Again*.

1381 Fujii, Haruhiko. "Pastoral and the Sea: The Background of *Lycidas*, ll. 154–64." *Studies in Milton* (Tokyo: Kinseido, 1974), pp. 119–35.

In Japanese. Concludes that the passage presents the sea as a symbol of resurrection. The sea of *Lycidas* goes beyond those of pastoral tradition and is linked to the sea of Galilee, on which Jesus walked.

1382 Fujii, Haruhiko. "The Three Patterns of Movement in *Lycidas*." *MCJ News*, 2, 1978, 8–10.

"There are the scenes in which nothing moves, the scenes in which the movements are either unnatural or disordered, and the scenes in which everything moves rhythmically." Abs., *MiltonQ*, 13, 1979, 159.

1383 Fujii, Haruhiko. *Time, Landscape and the Ideal Life: Studies in the Pastoral Poetry of Spenser and Milton.* Doctoral diss., Osaka Univ. Kyoto: Apollon-sha, 1974. iv, 272pp.

Contains two chapters on *Lycidas*. "The Changing Landscape of *Lycidas*" shows that the landscape changes as the mourning shepherd's mood moves from sorrow to despair to hope. "Thomas Warton's Romantic Interpretation of *Lycidas*" points out that Warton's criticism illustrates how Spenser's and Milton's pastorals had lost their "fit audience" by the mid-eighteenth century.

1384 Gabler, Hans Walter. "Poetry in Numbers: A Development of Significa-

tive Form in Milton's Early Poetry." *Archiv*, 220, 1983, 54–61.

Explores Milton's use of numerical composition and symbolism to convey the governing ideas in such poems as "Song: On May Morning" and "At a Solemn Music."

1385 Gabler, Hans Walter. "The Synchrony and Diachrony of Texts: Practice and Theory of the Critical Edition of James Joyce's *Ulysses*." *TEXT*, 1, 1984, 305–26.

"The extant manuscript materials of works so diverse as John Milton's hymn 'At a Solemn Musick' and James Joyce's *Ulysses* . . . display alike in their revisions a progressive structuring of meaning by which the discrete textual states in each case are correlated."

1386 Gallagher, Philip J. "Milton's 'The Passion': Inspired Mediocrity." *MiltonQ*, 11, 1977, 44–50.

"The poet is concerned to depict not the Passion, but the psychological state of a speaker who is attempting—without success—to become inspired about that event."

1387 Gallo, Bruno. "La Struttura della *Nativity Ode* di J. Milton: Umanesimo, Redenzione e Storia." *QLL*, 3–4, 1978–79, 127–45.

Proposes an alternative structure for the *Nativity Ode*, based on Milton's knowledge of contemporary numerology. Believes that the poem has the same precision in its numerical scheme as *Paradise Lost*.

1388 Gaskell, Philip. "Milton, *A Maske (Comus)*, 1634." *From Writer to Reader: Studies in Editorial Method* (Oxford: Clarendon Press, 1978; Winchester: St. Paul's Bibliographies, 1984), pp. 29–61.

Discusses the problems of editing *Comus*. Gives some attention to the methods used by two recent editors of the poem, John T. Shawcross (No. 297) and John Carey (No. 286). See also No. 1710.

1389 Geckle, George L. "Miltonic Idealism: *L'Allegro* and *Il Penseroso*." *TSLL*, 9, 1968, 455–73.

Believes that a key to interpreting the poems lies in Milton's *Prolusions*, in which the writer speaks to two sides of a question. "The companion poems do not, however, express simple contrasts. They instead symbolize one principle, that of happiness, in two modes of existence and on two levels of perfection."

1390 Gibbs, A. M. " 'That Two-Handed Engine' and Some Renaissance Emblems." *RES*, 31, 1980, 178–83.

Suggests that Milton recalled the two-edged sword in Francis Quarles's *Emblemes* (1635) "when he wrote the splendidly resonant conclusion to St. Peter's speech in *Lycidas*." Abs., *SCN*, 39, 1981, 100.

1391 Gilbert, A. J. "Milton and Pope." *Literary Language from Chaucer to Johnson* (London: Macmillan; New York: Barnes and Noble, 1979), pp. 111–31.

Examines the influence of Ramist logic on *Lycidas* and Pope's *Elegy to the Memory of an Unfortunate Lady*. Suggests that Milton's poem synthesizes Ramist logic and traditional rhetorical decorum.

1392 Goekjian, Gregory F. "Deference and Silence: Milton's Nativity Ode." *MiltonS*, 21, 1985, 119–35.

Suggests that the poem's abrupt shifts reveal Milton's difficulty in dealing with poetic authority.

1393 Goldman, Jack. "Comparing Milton's Greek Rendition of Psalm 114 with that of the Septuagint." *ELN*, 21, No. 2, 1983, 13–23.

Compares Milton's Greek translation of Psalm 114 with that of the Septuagint "to determine its influence upon Milton, and to establish the degree to which Milton departs both from the original Hebrew text and from the Greek of the *LXX*, and composes his own, original version of the Psalm."

1394 Goldman, Jack. "Milton's Intrusion of Abraham and Isaac upon Psalm 114." *PQ*, 55, 1976, 117–26.

Uses the reference to Abraham as Terah's faithful son in Milton's 1624 English paraphrase of Psalm 114 and the introduction of Isaac into his 1634 Greek version of the same psalm to demonstrate his use and knowledge of both Christian and rabbinical sources.

1395 Goldman, Rabbi Jack. "Milton's Knowledge of Hebrew and His Renditions of the Psalms." Doctoral diss., Univ. of Detroit, 1973. 418pp. Abs., *DAI*, 35, 1974, 402A–03A.

Compares Milton's Psalm paraphrases to the Hebrew originals, concluding that "Milton is inexplicably inconsistent in his knowledge of Hebrew."

1396 Goldstein, Charles E. "The Hebrew Element in Milton's Sonnet XVIII." *MiltonQ*, 9, 1975, 111–14.

Shows how Sonnet 18 ("On the Late Massacre in Piemont") can be read as a kind of traditional Hebrew lament or call for revenge.

1397 Gorecki, John. "Milton's 'Fatal and Perfidious Bark' and the Argo." *MiltonQ*, 17, 1983, 89–91.

Compares Milton's use of the ship in *Lycidas* to classical uses of the ship. Though the *Argo* does not sink, it is "nevertheless like Milton's ship in bearing death to its passengers and to others."

1398 Gorecki, J. E. "Milton's Sonnet XXIII and Aeschylus' *Agamemnon*." *N&Q*, 25, 1978, 17.

Claims that the "frustrated feelings" expressed in Sonnet 23 ("Methought I saw") echo "Menalaos' dreams of clasping the abducted Helen once more in his arms."

1399 Gouws, John. "Milton's 'Three and Twentieth Year.' " *N&Q*, 31, 1984, 305–07.

Asserts that the number twenty-three signifies incompleteness in Sonnet 7 ("How soon hath Time") and "An Epitaph on the Marchioness of

Winchester." Reply by Jeremy Maule (No. 1572).

1400 Greenbaum, Sidney. "The Poem, the Poet, and the Reader: An Analysis of Milton's Sonnet 19." *Lang&S*, 11, 1978, 116–28.

Believes that Sonnet 19 ("When I consider") can best be analyzed "as consisting of two sentences . . . shared by three speakers": the poet-questioner, patience, and the poet-narrator.

1401 Greene, Thomas M. "The Meeting Soul in Milton's Companion Poems." *ELR*, 14, 1984, 159–74.

Compares *L'Allegro* and *Il Penseroso* in several literary and philosophical aspects.

1402 Gregory, E. R. "*L'Allegro* and *Il Penseroso*: The Eternal Generalities." *EANO Bulletin*, 8, 1970, 2–3.

Feels that if the companion poems have a special greatness, "It lies, I think, in their presenting to us eternal generalities."

1403 Gregory, E. R. "'Lift Not Thy Speare against the Muses Bowre': Essay in Historical Explication." *MiltonQ*, 11, 1977, 112–13.

Suggests that in Sonnet 8 ("Captain or Colonel"), line 9 may mean: "do not use violence against a place where arts and letters are taught."

1404 Gregory, E. R. "Milton and the Camenae." *EIRC*, 12, 1986, 1–18.

Shows that Milton's use of the Latin word "Camenae," a rough equivalent to the Greek for "muses," was especially appropriate in *Elegy 6*.

1405 Gregory, E. R. "The Road Not Taken: Milton's Literary Career and *L'Allegro-Il Penseroso*." *Discourse*, 12, 1969, 529–38.

Discusses the poetic options open to Milton when he wrote *L'Allegro* and *Il Penseroso*. Suggests that the two choices presented in the poems were honorable and that his mood is dispassionate.

1406 Griffin, Robert Westervelt. "The

Curious Knot: Three Pastoral Masques of the English Renaissance." Doctoral diss., Univ. of Virginia, 1979. 250pp. Abs., *DAI*, 40, 1979, 3315A.

Analyzes Jonson's *Pan's Anniversary* and Milton's *Arcades* and *Comus* to show how each work "combines pastoral and masque, as two distinct literary kinds, into a single complex whole."

1407 Griffith, Benjamin W. "Milton's Meditations and Sonnet XIX." *AN&Q*, 10, 1971, 7–8.

Suggests that Milton wrote Sonnet 19 ("When I consider") in June of 1655, rather than in April or May, because its wording resembles that found in the *Book of Common Prayer* for the Psalm "to be read on the Tuesday after the fourth Sunday after Trinity, which [is] in early June." Reply by William B. Hunter, Jr. (No. 1454).

1408 Grose, Christopher. "Lucky Words: Process of Speech in *Lycidas*." *JEGP*, 70, 1971, 383–403.

Discusses *Lycidas* 163 ("Look homeward Angel now, and melt with ruth") and the final narrative section to resolve problems of structural analysis.

1409 Grose, Christopher. "The Lydian Airs of *L'Allegro* and *Il Penseroso*." *JEGP*, 83, 1984, 183–99.

States that *L'Allegro* and *Il Penseroso* appear in Milton's pre-Puritan phase and show an important stage in his mental development. Examines their Lydian strains and traces the musical theme and the development of mythic allusion.

1410 Gros Louis, Kenneth R. R. "The Triumph and Death of Orpheus in the English Renaissance." *SEL*, 9, 1969, 63–80.

Notes that Milton refers to Orpheus in *L'Allegro, Il Penseroso, Elegy 6, Ad Patrem*, and *Prolusion 7*; recalls his death in *Lycidas*; and parallels his decline (and mythology) in *Paradise Lost*.

1411 Gross, Kenneth. "'Each Heav'nly

Close': Mythologies and Metrics in Spenser and the Early Poetry of Milton." *PMLA*, 98, 1983, 21–36.

Describes "certain revisionary relations between the two poets through an examination of Milton's use of a key metrical scheme [the hexameter] derived from the earlier poet." Abs., *MiltonQ*, 16, 1982, 107.

1412 Grossman, Allen. "Milton's Sonnet 'On the Late Massacre in Piedmont': A Note on the Vulnerability of Persons in a Revolutionary Situation." *TriQ*, 23–24, 1972, 283–301.

Explores the idea that "the effort to establish the new dispensation . . . entailed a corresponding devaluation of personal identity such as to suggest that the means of revolution and its ends are in conflict one with the other."

1413 Gu, Zhen. "Eliot's Criticism on Milton's Lyrical Poems: A Preliminary Analysis." *Waiguoyu*, 2, 1986, 12–14.

In Chinese.

1414 Guibbory, Achsah. "Natalis Comes and the Digression on Fame in Milton's *Lycidas*." *N&Q*, 18, 1971, 292.

Suggests parallels between Comes's Orpheus entry in *Mythologiae* and Milton's passages on fame and the corrupt clergy in *Lycidas*.

1415 Guillory, John. "'Some Superior Power': Spenser and Shakespeare in Milton's *Comus*." *Poetic Authority: Spenser, Milton, and Literary History* (New York: Columbia Univ. Press, 1983), pp. 68–93.

Asserts that the speakers of the dialogue in *Comus* "are not the children and friends of a noble family, but poets of the English Renaissance." Proposes that three ideas provide contexts for interpreting *Comus*: "the daemonic agents," "the relationship of desire to imagination," and "metamorphosis and transfiguration, or the effectuality of art."

1416 Haan, Estelle Anita. "John Milton's Latin Poetry: Some Neo-Latin and Vernacular Contexts." Doctoral diss., Queen's

Univ. of Belfast, 1987. 347pp. Abs., *DAI*, 49, 1988, 350C–51C.

Discusses "Ad Patrem" in the context of Renaissance theories of education, relates *In Quintum Novembris* to miniature Latin epics and other Latin poems, and connects such works as *Epitaphium Damonis*, *Elegy 5*, and "Naturam Non Pati Senium" to neo-Latin poetry. Finally, "offers a tentative study of the role of Latin and the vernacular in Milton's poetic career."

1417 Haas, Rudolf. "Anamnese und Interpretation: Möglichkeiten und Grenzen Biographisch Orientierter Erschliessung Literarischer Texte." *Theorie und Praxis der Interpretation: Modellanalysen Englischer und Amerikanischer Texte* (Berlin: Schmidt, 1977), pp. 118–44.

Argues that Sonnet 19 ("When I consider") lends itself to an anamnesic (recalling) approach since it contains biographical information about the poet himself.

1418 Hale, John K. "Milton's Greek Epigram." *MiltonQ*, 16, 1982, 8–9.

"Milton's solitary Greek epigram was composed so that William Marshall, having perpetrated the bad engraving of the poet for the title page of *Poems*, 1645, should engrave also a condemnation of his own workmanship, immediately underneath it."

1419 Hale, John. "Milton's Poems in Greek." *The Interpretative Power: Essays on Literature in Honour of Margaret Dalziel.* Ed. by C. A. Gibson ([Otago]: Dept. of English, Univ. of Otago, 1980), pp. 35–45.

Argues that Milton's "Philosophus ad Regem," though it has blemishes in "syntax and accidence, diction and scansion," is more controlled than critics generally concede. The Greek rendering of Psalm 114 has few technical problems and "more positive merit and indeed individuality," as Milton changes the Psalm's syntax and structure. While some satires have a greater or subtler sting, "In Effigiei Ejus Sculptorem" is a successful retaliation against the engraver William Marshall.

1420 Hale, John K. "Sion's Bacchanalia: An Inquiry into Milton's Latin in the *Epitaphium Damonis*." *MiltonS*, 16, 1982, 115–30.

Examines the diction and prosody and argues that "Latin is the living flesh of the poem, indispensable equally to its beauty and to its conviction."

1421 Halpern, Richard Louis. "The Divided God: Bacchic and Ascetic Strains in Milton's Early Poetry, 1629–1634." Doctoral diss., Yale Univ., 1983. 317pp. Abs., *DAI*, 44, 1984, 2771A–72A.

Correlates Milton's poetic fusion of Bacchic and ascetic themes to his "self-conscious training for epic verse."

1422 Halpern, Richard. "The Great Instauration: Imaginary Narratives in Milton's *Nativity Ode*." *Re-membering Milton: Essays on the Texts and Traditions*. Ed. by Mary Nyquist and Margaret W. Ferguson (New York and London: Methuen, 1987), pp. 3–24.

Uses Jacques Lacan's idea of the mirror stage to examine the *Nativity Ode*. Clarifies "certain structures in Milton's personal mythologies" and shows "how Milton anticipates Lacan's distaste for normalizing, pacifying, or reductive narratives of development."

1423 Halpern, Richard. "Puritanism and Maenadism in *A Mask*." *Rewriting the Renaissance: The Discourses of Sexual Difference in Early Modern Europe*. Ed. by Margaret W. Ferguson and others (Chicago, IL, and London: Univ. of Chicago Press, 1986), pp. 88–105.

"Milton's ideological project in *A Mask* . . . is to trace the line that leads from virginity to married chastity."

1424 Hammond, Gerald. "Milton's 'On Shakespeare.'" *SHR*, 20, 1986, 115–24.

Praises Milton for recognizing Shakespeare's brilliance at an early age. Discusses Milton's use of language in "On

Shakespeare" and compares the poem with Jonson's tribute to Shakespeare.

1425 Hannay, Margaret P. "'Psalms Done into Metre': The Common Measure Psalms of John Milton and of the Bay Colony." *Ringing the Bell Backward: The Proceedings of the First International Milton Symposium*. Ed. by Ronald G. Shafer. The IUP Imprint Series (Indiana: Indiana Univ. of Pennsylvania, 1982), pp. 91–104. Reprinted in *C&L*, 32, 1983, 19–29.

Examines Milton's use of the Bay Psalm Book when he translated the 1648 Psalms. Lynn Veach Sadler's response, pp. 105–08, suggests areas for further exploration.

1426 Harada, Jun. "A Monodic Approach to *Lycidas*." *MCJ News*, 2, 1978, 5–8.

The phrase "once more" in the opening line helps to shape the entire poem's texture and movement because "once more" becomes the repetitive "no more" at the end. The result is a creative synthesis in which the moment of recurrence and finality is realized. Abs., *MiltonQ*, 13, 1979, 159–60.

1427 Hardy, J. P. "*L'Allegro* and *Il Penseroso*." *Reinterpretations: Essays on Poems by Milton, Pope and Johnson* (London: Routledge and Kegan Paul, 1971), pp. 1–27.

States that *L'Allegro* and *Il Penseroso* should be read as a contrast between different kinds of poetic sensibility or different kinds of creative poetic potential, not as contrasting ways of life.

1428 Hardy, J. P. "*Lycidas*." *Reinterpretations: Essays on Poems by Milton, Pope and Johnson* (London: Routledge and Kegan Paul, 1971), pp. 28–49.

Discusses the appropriateness of placing *Lycidas* last in *Justa Edovardo King Naufrago*.

1429 Harned, Jon. "A Psycho-Biographical Reading of *Lycidas*." *CEA*, 48–49, 1986, 24–31.

Revives Tillyard's statement (Huckabay No. 972) that in *Lycidas* Milton is really writing about himself and that the poem is an attempt to forge an adult identity. Uses a letter to Charles Diodati to establish the elegy's biographical context.

1430 Hatlen, Burton Norval. "The Snake in the Garden: Milton's *Comus* as Pastoral." Doctoral diss., Univ. of California, Davis, 1971. 267pp. Abs., *DAI*, 32, 1972, 4001A–02A.

Follows Milton's initial separation and gradual reintegration of nature and spirit in *Comus* as they relate to the pastoral tradition.

1431 Heinzelman, Kurt. "'Cold Consolation': The Art of Milton's Last Sonnet." *MiltonS*, 10, 1977, 111–25.

In Sonnet 23 ("Methought I saw"), "Milton found his way by careful indirection, by not seeing what could not be seen, by seeing through Alcestis an analogue of Christian salvation. Through his singular use of similes, which by definition imply contrasts even as they name likenesses, Milton was able to manage the inferences behind his similes so that, in effect, he could imagine unspeakable heaven by explicitly not likening it too much." Abs., *MiltonQ*, 12, 1978, 155.

1432 Herz, Judith Scherer. "Epigrams and Sonnets: Milton in the Manner of Jonson." *MiltonS*, 20, 1984, 29–41.

Explores how the sonnets, "both individually and taken together, constitute Milton's most Jonsonian writing." Considers them to be Milton's response to Jonson's *Epigrammes*.

1433 Hester, M. Thomas. "Typology and Parody in 'Upon the Circumcision.'" *RenP*, 1985, pp. 61–71.

Does not believe that "Upon the Circumcision" is an inferior work. Studies its "liturgical and literary pre-texts . . . to suggest both its considerable achievement and its significance in Milton's unfolding conception of his poetic vocation."

1434 Hieatt, A. Kent. "Milton's Comus and Spenser's False Genius." *UTQ*, 38, 1969, 313–18.

Claims that these characters represent another parallel between Milton and Spenser, though the False Genius is a silent emblem, while Comus is outspoken in his temptations.

1435 Hill, Archibald A. "Imagery and Meaning: A Passage from Milton, and from Blake." *TSLL*, 11, 1969, 1093–1105.

On the "Blind mouths" metaphor in *Lycidas* 119 and the "Soldiers sigh" metaphor in Blake's *London*. Milton's metaphor illustrates the "ineffectiveness of negative imagery."

1436 Hill, Elizabeth K. "A Dream in the Long Valley: Some Psychological Aspects of Milton's Last Sonnet." *Greyfriar*, 26, 1985, 3–13.

Uses a psychoanalytical approach to dreams and concludes that the "late departed saint" in Sonnet 23 ("Methought I saw") is a composite of Milton's first two wives.

1437 Hill, Elizabeth K. "The Fierce Remedy: A Note on 'The Passion.'" *AN&Q*, 20, 1982, 134–35.

Contends that the word "fierce" in the "Passion" 24 is "a pun involving the Greek root," which is defined as "an antidote against a poisonous bite . . . especially against the bite of serpents." This usage appears again in *Paradise Lost*.

1438 Hill, John Spencer. "'Alcestis from the Grave': Image and Structure in Sonnet XXIII." *MiltonS*, 10, 1977, 127–39.

"Balancing loss against restoration, despair against triumph in delicate equilibrium, the poem ['Methought I saw'] traces an evolving definition of salvation ascending from flesh to spirit in three independent stages: pagan, Hebraic, and Christian." Abs., *MiltonQ*, 12, 1978, 155.

1439 Himy, Armand. "Bacchus et Comus." *EA*, 27, 1974, 436–49.

Believes that *Comus* treats Milton's main theme—that of a young virgin lost in a forest inhabited by the satyr—though in a more limited form.

1440 Hinnant, Charles H. "Freedom and Form in Milton's *Lycidas*." *PMASAL*, 53, 1968, 321–28.

Accounts for the "deliberate roughness" that Milton achieves by varying line lengths and stanzaic patterns: intense grief and the unlearned state of the persona, an actual shepherd.

1441 Hinz, Evelyn J. "New Light 'On His Blindness.'" *MSE*, 2, 1969, 1–10.

Substantiates Lysander Kemp's initial observation (Huckabay No. 2568) that Milton's Sonnet 19 ("When I consider") "owes its composition to a state of doubt and frustration . . . in relation to Milton's personal and political activities." Shows that "Milton's blindness is merely an *ex post facto* coincidence having no thematic relationship to the poem." Analyzes the sonnet as "one of Milton's many examinations of the Christian virtue of patience."

1442 Hirakawa, Taiji. "*Comus* and Spenser's Bower of Bliss." *MCJ News*, 2, 1978, 18–19.

Abstract of a paper presented at the Third Colloquium of MCJ in July, 1977. Suggests that although Milton borrows much from Spenser, they have different conceptions of temperance. While Spenser accepts the golden mean, Milton advocates an "idiosyncratically ethical" view. Abs., *MiltonQ*, 13, 1979, 160.

1443 Hiromoto, Katsuya. "A Comparison of the Chastity of *Comus* with the Free Love of Blake." *MCJ News*, 4, 1980, 5–6.

Abstract of paper presented. "One can conclude that *Comus* is a poem on sexual education and awareness in which Milton's white magic encompasses Blake and illuminates the falsity of Blake's treatise on free love [*Visions of the Daughters of Albion*]."

1444 Hiromoto, Katsuya. "*Comus* to *Visions of the Daughters of Albion*: seiai

ni kansuru nisakuhin." *SELit*, 57, 1980, 3–15.

"*Comus* and *Visions of the Daughters of Albion*: Two Works Concerning Sexual Love." In Japanese. Finds that Oathoon in *Visions* expresses ideas of sexual love quite similar to those of Comus. Suggests that Blake shared some of Milton's convictions expressed in the *Doctrine and Discipline of Divorce* and that Blake wrote *Visions* in order to correct the errors he perceived in *Comus*.

1445 Hofmann, Klaus. "Das Evangelium in der Idylle: Miltons *Lycidas*." *Anglia*, 88, 1970, 461–87.

Argues that Milton and his Protestant contemporaries require not aesthetic integrity in art, but rather historical integrity. The answers to the shepherd's questions are religious, not poetic, and *Lycidas* realizes the demand that poetry must escape its bonds and move from aesthetic appearance into historical reality.

1446 Hollander, John. "The Footing of His Feet: On a Line of Milton's." *On Poetry and Poetics*. Ed. by Richard Waswo (Zurich: Swiss Association of Univ. Teachers of English, 1985), pp. 11–30.

Uses *Il Penseroso* as a foundation for discussing Spenser's influence on Milton, which is often unconscious or unacknowledged.

1447 Holmer, Joan Ozark. "Milton's Hobson Poems: Rhetorical Manifestation of Wit." *MiltonQ*, 11, 1977, 16–21.

"Too long have Milton's Hobson poems been unappreciated as sophisticated examples of a particular kind of verse which the young poet was imitating very successfully"—metaphysical poetry.

1448 Humphreys-Edwards, Julia A. "Milton's *Il Penseroso*, 93–4." *N&Q*, 16, 1969, 93.

Notes "a close parallel between this couplet and several lists of daemons occurring in late Greek sources," one of which may have been known to Milton.

1449 Hunt, Clay. *"Lycidas" and the Italian Critics.* Preface by Irene Samuel. New Haven, CT, and London: Yale Univ. Press, 1979. x, 196pp.

Chapters: "The Poem and the Problem"; "Italian Criticism"; "The Pastoral"; "The Lyric"; and *"Lycidas."* Reviews: Jean-François Camé, *CahiersE*, 16, 1979, 124–25; Roy C. Flannagan, *MiltonQ*, 13, 1979, 54–55; Hugh Maclean, *JEGP*, 78, 1979, 411–14; Archie Burnett, *N&Q*, 27, 1980, 92–93; Richard H. Peake, *RenQ*, 33, 1980, 303–05; J. Martin Evans, *RES*, 32, 1981, 329–31; Michael Lieb, *Cithara*, 21, 1981, 58–70; Pauline Palmer, *MLR*, 77, 1982, 160–61.

1450 Hunter, William B., Jr. "The Date and Occasion of *Arcades.*" *ELN*, 11, 1973, 46–47.

Dates *Arcades* according to its scriptural content in conjunction with the *Book of Common Prayer.* Suggests the date was May 3, 1634, since the appropriate reading (1 Kings 10) fell on May 2, and the birthday of Alice, the Dowager Countess of Derby, fell on May 4, a Sunday.

1451 Hunter, William B., Jr. "The Date of Milton's Sonnet 7." *ELN*, 13, 1975, 10–14. Reprinted in *The Descent of Urania: Studies in Milton, 1946–1988* (Lewisburg, PA: Bucknell Univ. Press; London and Toronto: Associated Univ. Presses, 1989), pp. 179–83.

Suggests that "a date of December 1631 for the sonnet ['How soon hath Time'] is not inconsistent with all of the facts known about Milton's thinking at this time when he must have been deeply concerned about his ordination."

1452 Hunter, William B., Jr. "The Liturgical Context of *Comus.*" *ELN*, 10, 1972, 11–15.

Suggests that Milton was influenced by the *Book of Common Prayer* and "derived ideas for the masque from evening prayer on the 28th (I Cor. 13), morning prayer on the 29th (Psalms 139–41, Eccles. 39), and the communion service for St. Michael's day (the collect, Rev. 12.7ff., and Matt. 18.1ff.)."

1453 Hunter, William B., Jr. *Milton's "Comus": Family Piece.* Troy, NY: Whitston Publishing Co., 1983. xvi, 101pp.

Relates the composition of *Comus* to the Egerton family situation in 1634 and offers a text which recreates "what seem to have been Milton's original intentions that Lawes would carry out." Reviews: Roy C. Flannagan, *MiltonQ*, 19, 1985, 87–88; Philip B. Rollinson, *MR*, 2, 1985, 330–31; Paul Stevens, *Ren&R*, 9, 1985, 302–05.

1454 Hunter, Wm B., Jr. "Response to a Note on Milton and Common Prayer." *AN&Q*, 10, 1972, 117.

Suggests that Benjamin W. Griffith's article (No. 1407) makes the wrong assumption for the dating of Sonnet 19 ("When I consider"). Between 1643 and 1660, it was a crime to read the *Book of Common Prayer.* Thus, Milton did not still practice the liturgy and the date of the sonnet is not related to the church calendar.

1455 Huntley, John F. "The Poet-Critic and His Poem-Culture in *L'Allegro* and *Il Penseroso.*" *TSLL*, 13, 1972, 541–53.

Claims that the companion poems "stimulate an . . . insight into the . . . interaction of aesthetic criticism, worldly culture, and human destiny." Discusses the works as a release from the critical trap of cultural encapsulation.

1456 Hurley, Charles Harold. "The Alchemy of Genius: The Sources and Traditions of *L'Allegro* and *Il Penseroso.*" Doctoral diss., Univ. of Toledo, 1972. 185pp. Abs., *DAI*, 33, 1973, 5126A.

Reveals the indebtedness of Milton's two poems to general sources and relates them to the "melancholy, pastoral, and 'character' traditions."

1457 Hurley, C. Harold. "The Cheerful

Man's 'Sorrow': A Key to the Meaning of *L'Allegro*, 45–46." *ELN*, 11, 1974, 275–78.

Suggests that "the questions which lines 45–46 of *L'Allegro* seemingly pose cease to exist when we recognize that L'Allegro, whose disposition is naturally inclined toward sorrow and melancholy, comes to his window determined to combat his melancholy disorder by engaging in the pleasantries offered him each new day by 'heart-easing Mirth.'" Reply by John M. Major (No. 1558); rejoinder by Hurley, *ELN*, 12, 1975, 193–94.

1458 Hurley, C. Harold. "The Discovery of Beaumont and Fletcher's *Nice Valour* as a Source for Milton's *Il Penseroso*." *N&Q*, 20, 1973, 166–67.

Credits Thomas Seward, one of the coeditors of Beaumont's *Works* (1750), with the discovery.

1459 Hurley, C. Harold. "Thomas Warton and the Melancholy Sources of *L'Allegro* and *Il Penseroso*: Amendations of the *Variorum Commentary on the Poems of John Milton*." *MiltonQ*, 7, 1973, 46–47.

Offers the following corrections to the *Variorum Commentary* (No. 1838): Francis Peck, not Thomas Warton, first suggested Milton's debt to Robert Burton's "The Author's Abstract of Melancholy" in the companion poems, and Thomas Seward, not Warton, first pointed out similarities between John Fletcher's song on melancholy in *Nice Valour* and *Il Penseroso*.

1460 Hutchinson, Mary Anne. "*Comus* and Milton's Maturing Conception of Chastity." *Thoth*, 14, Nos. 2–3, 1974, 39–52.

Believes that in *Comus* Milton presents his early views on chastity and that in the divorce tracts and in *Paradise Lost* he sets forth a more complete view of married love.

1461 Hyman, Lawrence W. "Belief and Disbelief in *Lycidas*." *CE*, 33, 1972, 532–42.

Claims that "the distinctive nature of

the poem is not that it makes us *forget* what we believe and feel in real life, but that . . . the poetic experience can bring us to a level of conscience in which our beliefs do not matter."

1462 Hyman, Lawrence W. "Christ's Nativity and the Pagan Deities." *MiltonS*, 2, 1970, 103–12.

Feels that the disappearance of the pagan gods does not interfere with the unity of the *Nativity Ode*. Milton brings contradictory feelings into harmony.

1463 Hyman, Lawrence W. "*Comus* and the Limits of Interpretation." *Structuralist Review*, 2, 1981, 68–77.

In this investigation of interpretation and its limits in *Comus*, "the meaning that is not there is the allegorical meaning, the attempts to link the various actions and images into a coherent pattern. What is there are the discrepancies themselves, the gaps between the poem's ostensible theme . . . and the actions and images that contradict this message."

1464 Hyman, Lawrence W. "*Lycidas*—The 'False Surmise' and the 'True Revelation.'" *MiltonQ*, 17, 1983, 7–11.

Finds continuity "between the pastoral tradition that dominates the first two-thirds of the poem and the Christian revelation that follows. 'The false surmise' about the flowers, the painful truth about the drowned body of 'the hapless youth' *and* the youth who enters into 'the blest kingdoms meek of joy and love' are all related in a continuous web."

1465 Iinuma, Mariko. "Light, Darkness and Labyrinth—Milton's *Comus*." *Eigaku* (Heian Women's Junior College), 9, 1976, 1–14.

In Japanese. Emphasizes the contrast of light and darkness, and the vertical movement of spiritual beings going upward and downward in contrast to the humans' wandering in the perplexed paths of a labyrinth.

1466 Iinuma, Mariko. "On Milton's

Comus." *MCJ News*, 1, 1976, 5–6.

Abstract of a paper presented at the First Colloquium of MCJ in July, 1976. Focuses on the motif of light and darkness.

1467 Illo, John. "Miracle in Milton's Early Verse." *Costerus*, 1, 1972, 133–37.

"In his early verse, Milton's response to the miraculous progressed from a puerile interest in its phenomenal and external character to a mature conception of its religious and ethical meaning."

1468 Jacobs, Laurence H. " 'Unexpressive Notes': The Decorum of Milton's Nativity Ode." *ELWIU*, 1, 1974, 166–77.

Concludes that "the recurrent principle governing Milton's poetic choices, his special decorum in this poem, is to allow poetry its most eloquent statement of the significance of the Nativity of Christ only to discover that, in spite of its effectiveness, poetry cannot declare the full mystery."

1469 Jacobus, Lee A. "Milton Metaphrast: Logic and Rhetoric in Psalm I." *MiltonS*, 23, 1987, 119–32.

Studies the structure of Milton's translation of Psalm 1 to show his adherence to the "tradition of analysis represented by [William] Temple and [Richard] Bernard." Emphasizes Milton's use of the Psalm as strong Christian and political rhetoric.

1470 Jacobus, Lee A. "Milton's *Comus* as Children's Literature." *ChildL*, 2, 1973, 67–72.

Believes that the material in *Comus* "reminds us of so many children's stories that it becomes almost archetypal."

1471 Jayne, Sears. "The Subject of Milton's Ludlow *Mask*." *"A Maske at Ludlow": Essays on Milton's "Comus."* Ed. by John S. Diekhoff (Ann Arbor, MI: Univ. Microfilms International, 1980 Books on Demand Reprints), pp. 165–87.

Reprint of Huckabay No. 2559, originally published in 1959.

1472 Jenkins, R. B. "Invulnerable Virtue

in *Wieland* and *Comus*." *SAB*, 38, 1973, 72–75.

Discusses thematic parallels in the two works. States that Milton's virtue must be accompanied by divine grace and Charles Brockden Brown's by right reason.

1473 Johnson, Barbara A. "Fiction and Grief: The Pastoral Idiom of Milton's *Lycidas*." *MiltonQ*, 18, 1984, 69–76.

Asserts that the pastoral mode in *Lycidas* is successful despite its limitations.

1474 Jones, Edward John. "Milton's Sonnets: The Critical Comment, 1900–1985." Doctoral diss., Ohio Univ., 1985. 481pp. Abs., *DAI*, 47, 1986, 912A.

Uses descriptive essays and bibliographies to analyze the increasingly positive critical response to Milton's sonnets during the twentieth century.

1475 Jones, Nicholas R. "The Education of the Faithful in Milton's Piedmontese Sonnet." *MiltonS*, 10, 1977, 167–76.

"The process of the sonnet [Sonnet 18 ('On the Late Massacre in Piemont')]—education—becomes the subject of its concluding prayer. It is finally more than a personal outcry: it is a poem about the education of the faithful, a rhetorical demonstration of how the wisdom to recognize and conform to God's will can grow only in the presence of faith."

1476 Jordan, Richard D. "The Movement of the *Nativity Ode*." *SAB*, 38, 1973, 34–39.

Traces the poem's movements and stillnesses "to demonstrate that they have been arranged in a structure similar to that of the Pindaric ode." Concludes that "the everlasting movement [is] toward redemption."

1477 Judge, Philip G., S. J. "Hiding from the Sun: The Swain in Milton's *Lycidas*." *MiltonQ*, 21, No. 1, 1987, 6–11.

Believes that the speaker " 'uses' the body of the poem to find the 'word' of consolation for which he began his search." He finds this consolation in the concluding lines through "the rising of the sun each day" and the victory through Christ.

1478 Judkins, David Cummins. "Studies in Seventeenth Century Political Poetry of the English Civil War." Doctoral diss., Michigan State Univ., 1970. 202pp. Abs., *DAI*, 31, 1970, 2387A.

Places English poetry written between 1639 and 1653 in a political context, noting a strong royalist sentiment. Discusses Milton's sonnets.

1479 Jungman, Robert E. "Milton's *Lycidas*, Line 114." *Expl*, 41, No. 4, 1983, 11–13.

Explains the false shepherds who deceive their flocks "for their bellies' sake" by suggesting that the reference to "bellies" is from Philippians 3.18–19 and had been mentioned by many writers, including Jerome and Chaucer. Thus, the false shepherds are "the enemies of the cross of Christ: Whose end is destruction."

1480 Jungman, Robert E. "Milton's *Lycidas*, 128–29." *Expl*, 46, No. 2, 1988, 8–9.

Discusses the negative connotations of the word "privy" as applied to the Roman Catholic priests in *Lycidas* 128–29. In addition to "secrecy," "privy" can also suggest "theft," as well as the scatological references to a privy house.

1481 Jungman, Robert E. "Milton's Use of Catullus in *Lycidas*." *CF*, 32, 1978, 90–92.

Believes that Milton borrows from Catullus in *Lycidas* 165–73 but that he gives the image of the rising sun a particularly Christian meaning.

1482 Kandaswami, S. "An Echo of Chapman in Milton." *N&Q*, 29, 1982, 24.

The words "ruth" and "youth" in *Lycidas* recall Chapman's use of them in his elegy on the death of Prince Henry.

1483 Kastor, Frank S. "Miltonic Narra-

tion: *Christ's Nativity*." *Anglia*, 86, 1968, 339–52.

Believes that the narrative elements in Milton's *Nativity Ode* encompass the Christian view of history and serve as the poem's "framework and substance."

1484 Kell, Richard. "Thesis and Action in Milton's *Comus*." *EIC*, 24, 1974, 48–54.

Claims that Milton is preoccupied, not so much with chastity, but with "the psychology of resisting and lapsing." Concludes that there is a "discrepancy between thesis and action," possibly because he "gave as little thought to the mechanics of his drama as he did to the human realities underlying its theme."

1485 Kelly, L. G. "Contaminatio in *Lycidas*: An Example of Vergilian Poetics." *RUO*, 38, 1968, 588–98.

"Basically, then, *Lycidas* is a poem solidly based on Greek pastoral conventions, but to achieve this end Milton used Roman techniques as exemplified in Vergil." Likens Edward King to Gallus, Virgil's fellow student and the hero of *Eclogue* 10.

1486 Kelly, Stephen T. "Virgil and Milton: The Attempt at Natural Consolation." *CL*, 30, 1978, 193–208.

Concerned with the Virgilian pastoral tradition and Christian consolation in *Lycidas*. "What is remarkable . . . is the comparatively minor part Christian consolation actually plays in the poem."

1487 Kelly, V. V. "Milton's To the Lord General Cromwell." *Expl*, 41, 1983, 15–17.

Analyzes the genres, style, voice, tense, and rhyme scheme of Sonnet 16 (to Cromwell), suggesting that the two-fold military and political aspects of Cromwell's life allow him "to survive the transition from military to civic governor."

1488 Kendall, Lyle H., Jr. "Sonnet XIX and Wither's Emblem III. xlvii." *MiltonN*, 3, 1969, 57.

Suggests that Milton may have recalled a passage from George Wither's *Collection of Emblemes* in writing Sonnet 19 ("When I consider"). Notes verbal echoes and close correspondences in content.

1489 Kendrick, Christopher. "Milton and Sexuality: A Symptomatic Reading of *Comus.*" *Re-membering Milton: Essays on the Texts and Traditions.* Ed. by Mary Nyquist and Margaret W. Ferguson (New York and London: Methuen, 1987), pp. 43–73.

Studies the "chastity cult and generalized sexuality" in *Comus* from biographical, political-cultural, and socioeconomic perspectives.

1490 Kennedy, William J. "The Audiences of *Ad Patrem.*" *MiltonS*, 19, 1984, 73–86.

Examines "the poem's structure, tone, and comic resolution," focusing on Milton's diction and meter.

1491 Kent, Margo Anne. "Poetry as Liturgy: Poet as Priest in Some of Milton's Early Poetry." Doctoral diss., York Univ., Canada, 1981. Abs., *DAI*, 45, 1985, 2533A.

Defines Milton's poems from 1629 to 1637 as liturgies that parallel his initial "idiosyncratic brand of Puritan Anglicanism" that later evolved into a strong protest against the Church of England.

1492 Kessner, Carole Schwartz. "George Herbert and John Milton's Use of the Hebrew Psalms." Doctoral diss., State Univ. of New York, Stony Brook, 1975. 402pp. Abs., *DAI*, 36, 1976, 6705A.

Measures the impact of Psalm imagery, themes, and word connotations on some of Herbert's and Milton's works.

1493 Killeen, J. F. "A Homeric Usage in Milton's *L'Allegro*, 11–13." *N&Q*, 28, 1981, 42.

Notes that in the *Iliad*, Homer on four occasions uses different names from the language of gods and humans, as

Milton does in the passage about Euphrosyne-Mirth.

1494 Kingsley, Lawrence W. "Mythic Dialectic in the Nativity Ode." *MiltonS*, 4, 1972, 163–76.

"Milton works out a *discordia concors* in which Phaeton, Phoebus, Lucifer, Pan, and Hercules, together with the whole pantheon of dispossessed deities, collapse into the Christhead. This method of counterposing the pagan world, point for point, with spreading manifestations of Christ allows Milton to retain his predilection for classical heroes while still proclaiming their rejection."

1495 Kiralis, Karl. "Blake's Criticism of Milton's *L'Allegro* and *Il Penseroso* and of Its Author." *Milton Reconsidered: Essays in Honor of Arthur E. Barker.* Ed. by John Karl Franson (Salzburg: Institut für Englische Sprache und Literatur, Universität Salzburg, 1976), pp. 46–77.

Argues that Blake deliberately terminated the water-color designs and explains that "Blake thought Milton by no means ready for the role of poet-prophet on the strength of these companion poems."

1496 Kirkconnell, Watson. *Awake the Courteous Echo: The Themes and Prosody of "Comus," "Lycidas," and "Paradise Regained" in World Literature with Translations of the Major Analogues.* Toronto and Buffalo, NY: Univ. of Toronto Press, 1973. xxiv, 336pp.

Contains 39 analogues of *Comus* and 102 of *Lycidas*. Appendices: "On Metre"; "Biblical Epics"; and "Thomas Ellwood's Epic." Indices of persons and of analogues.

1497 Kisaichi, Motohiro. "Imagery of *Comus.*" *MCJ News*, 2, 1978, 16–18.

Abstract of a paper presented at the Second Colloquium of MCJ in December, 1976. Sees several levels of imagery, with the divine as "the highest element in the structural imagery of *Comus.*" This provides "the image of chastity as an indwelling virtue in humanity."

1498 Kisaichi, Motohiro. "An Introduction to Milton's *Comus*." *Studies in English Literature* (Konan Women's College), 12, 1976, 29–45.

1499 Klein, Joan Larsen. "The Demonic Bacchus in Spenser and Milton." *MiltonS*, 21, 1985, 93–118.

Argues that Milton created Comus in terms of the demonic tempters found in the *Faerie Queene* but that he moved away from the epic's later books as he resolved the conflict between the Lady and Comus.

1500 Knedlik, Janet Leslie. "High Pastoral Art in *Epitaphium Damonis*." *MiltonS*, 19, 1984, 149–63.

Compares the pastoral mode in *Lycidas* and in *Epitaphium Damonis*. Instead of renouncing the pastoral, the Latin poem transvalues it into a more Edenic pastoral mode.

1501 Knight, W. Nicholas. "Milton's Sonnet IX: The Lady in 'Lady That in the Prime.'" *PMPA*, 1, 1976, 14–23.

Discusses the lady's identity, the metrical and rhythmic patterns, biblical imagery, and such themes as the state of matrimony and the unity between spiritual preparedness and chastity.

1502 Knott, John R., Jr. "The Biblical Matrix of Milton's 'On the Late Massacre in Piemont.'" *PQ*, 62, 1983, 259–63.

Maintains that Sonnet 18's biblical context "includes the Old Testament as well as the New. The Waldensians appear . . . as descendants of the Israelites, who . . . [will be] brought together again by God."

1503 Kogan, Stephen. "John Milton and the Caroline Masque." *The Hieroglyphic King: Wisdom and Idolatry in the Seventeenth-Century Masque* (Rutherford, NJ: Fairleigh Dickinson Univ. Press; Cranbury, NJ: Associated Univ. Presses, 1986), pp. 229–65.

Argues that Milton thoroughly opposed the Caroline masque and that "the underlying basis of this quarrel is Milton's attitude toward idolatry and royal adoration." In *Comus*, he follows all of the genre's external requirements, but the opening speech "cuts through the rhetoric of royal love and divinity and both reasserts and intensifies the traditional contrast of heaven and earth."

1504 Koh, Myeong-Eun. "*Lycidas*: Its Allusiveness." *JELL*, 30, 1984, 265–84. In Korean; English summary, pp. 284–85. Discusses the poem from five angles of its allusiveness, leading up to its Christian statement at the end.

1505 Kohn, Terry Kidner. "Landscape in the Transcendent Masque." *MiltonS*, 6, 1974, 143–64.

"*Comus* transcends all other masques in its artistry and in the permanence of its moral fable. The treatment of landscape contributes both to Milton's artistic integration of traditional masque elements and to the philosophical content of *Comus*." In the masque, "Milton gives to landscape a degree of prominence and a richness of meaning surpassed only by the landscapes of *Paradise Lost*."

1506 Koizumi, Yoshio. "My View on Milton's *Lycidas*." *Bulletin of Aizu Junior College*, 34, 1977, 49–62.

In Japanese. Discusses flower and water imagery in the elegy and how Milton expresses his strong Christian thoughts through pagan pastoral images, forms, and conventions.

1507 Komori, Teiji. "Harmony and Discordant Sound in Milton's *Ode*." *MCJ News*, 10, 1988, 14–16.

Abstract of paper presented. Argues that in the *Nativity Ode* Milton uses examples of harmony and discordant sound to demonstrate the conflicts between Christianity and paganism.

1508 Komori, Teiji. "Milton's Recreation in Sonnets XX and XXI." *MCJ News*, 3, 1979, 6–7.

Abstract of paper presented. Suggests

that Sonnets 20 (to Henry Lawrence) and 21 ("Cyriack, whose Grandsire") show "that Milton had 'grown mellow, kindly, sweet-tempered, and lovable.'"

1509 Komori, Teiji. "Milton's Sonnets in Italian." *Journal of Obirin University and Junior College*, 16, 1976, 189–94.

Believes that Milton liked women of the "foreign type" and was in love with Emilia. Places him in the Petrarchan tradition.

1510 Komori, Teiji. "The Will of Heaven in Milton's Sonnet VII, 'How Soon Hath Time.'" *Journal of Obirin University and Junior College*, 17, 1977, 211–17.

Holds that Milton was in the process of abandoning any plans to enter the ministry when he wrote the sonnet.

1511 Kranidas, Thomas. "Milton's *Lycidas*." *Expl*, 38, 1979, 29–30.

Provides further evidence to substantiate Kathleen Swaim's interpretation (No. 1767) of the two-handed engine.

1512 Labriola, Albert C. "Self-Image and Self-Perception in Milton's *Epitaphium Damonis*." *SPWVSRA*, 10, 1985, 35–39.

Epitaphium Damonis, like *Lycidas*, is distinguished from Milton's other elegiac poems by an emphasis on "not only the death of a friend but also profound self-concern." Milton thus "transforms elegy into autobiography." Abs., *MiltonQ*, 15, 1981, 28.

1513 Lahiri, Krishna Chandra. "Woman in Four Sonnets of Milton." *Bulletin of the Department of English* (Calcutta Univ.), 10, 1974–75, 25–29.

Sonnets 9 ("Lady that in the prime"), 10 (to Margaret Ley), 14 (to Catharine Thomason), and 23 ("Methought I saw") "add to the sum total of the impression of women that the reader gathers from his writings." The sonnets are addressed to four beautiful types of womanhood: the virgin, the matron, the Christian woman, and the perfect wife.

1514 Lambert, Ellen Zetzel. "*Lycidas*:

Finding the Time and the Place." *Placing Sorrow: A Study of the Pastoral Elegy Convention from Theocritus to Milton*. Univ. of North Carolina Studies in Comparative Literature, no. 60 (Chapel Hill: Univ. of North Carolina Press, 1976), pp. 154–86.

Edward King is the sort of subject who would have been a candidate for the pastoral elegy form thirty years earlier—an academic, a poet, one who died before his prime. When Milton wrote *Lycidas*, however, this genre was decidedly out of fashion.

1515 Lambert, Ellen Zetzel. "The Pastoral Elegy from Theocritus to Milton: A Critical Study." Doctoral diss., Yale Univ., 1969. 331pp. Abs., *DAI*, 31, 1970, 1233A.

Describes *Lycidas* as informed by classical and Renaissance traditions, as well as Italian, French, and English elegies. Milton's poem is the climax and final transformation of the elegy genre.

1516 Landy, Marcia. "Language and Mourning in *Lycidas*." *AI*, 30, 1974, 294–312.

"By means of his poetic exploration of the experience of death and mourning with their disorganizing and organizing power, Milton was able not only to share with the reader his experience of objectifying his world through language, but also to re-create a universal structure—the poem—which is itself a form of objectification for the reader."

1517 Larson, Charles. "An Architectural Pun in Milton." *AN&Q*, 12, 1974, 101.

In Sonnet 22 ("Cyriack, this three years' day"), one meaning for "'orb' was an architectural term in use from the 14th through the 17th centuries. . . . It meant a *blind window*, a plain stone panel. The clever appropriateness tempers the pun's pathos."

1518 Latimer, Dan. *The Elegiac Mode in Milton and Rilke: Reflections on Death*. Berne: Herbert Lang; Frankfurt: Peter Lang, 1977. 56pp.

Studies Rainer Maria Rilke and the elegiac tradition and contrasts Milton and Rilke.

1519 Lautermilch, Steven J. "'That Fatal and Perfidious Bark': A Key to the Double Design and Unity of Milton's *Lycidas*." *RenQ*, 30, 1977, 201–16.

Claims that the duality of purpose in line 100 paves the way for further dual interpretations in the poem and reflects its theme: "the ultimate relationship between the Church and the state, the body and the soul." Points out that early church fathers used the ark to typify the church, and the ship image is reiterated in *Lycidas*.

1520 Lavoie, Thomas. "The Divine Vision of the Inward Eye: The Structural Hierarchy of the *L'Allegro-Il Penseroso* Sequence." *Thoth*, 16, No. 3, 1976, 3–17.

Interprets the poems as having one dominant theme, the apprehension and subsequent praise of God through artistic means.

1521 Lawry, Jon S. "'The Faithful Herdman's Art' in *Lycidas*." *SEL*, 13, 1973, 111–25.

Claims that the herdsman's art is fulfilled only when the speaker receives inspiration and resurrection from the three divine herdsmen—Apollo, Peter, and Michael. Suggests that the art of caring for the sheep parallels a priest's educating and uplifting the parish.

1522 Lawry, J. S. "Milton's Sonnet 18: 'A Holocaust.'" *MiltonQ*, 17, 1983, 11–14.

"As a holocaust in its own right, the sonnet ['On the Late Massacre in Piemont'], along with the Waldensians, establishes characteristic Miltonic stances: the justification of God to men, the glorification not so much of Passion as of nativity, or of achieved understanding, or of patient heroism within a fallen world, and an achieved confidence in the reality and the shadow of Heaven, rather than in the way of the world."

1523 Lawry, J. S. "Postscript and Prescript in Two Milton Sonnets." *MiltonS*, 18, 1983, 77–84.

Proposes a stylistic binary sequence of statement in many of Milton's works, focusing on Sonnets 7 ("How soon hath Time") and 19 ("When I consider"). Implies that this compositional form's continuity is universal in Milton's poetry.

1524 Le Comte, Edward. "Ambiguous Milton." *Greyfriar*, 25, 1984, 25–36. Reprinted in *Milton Re-Viewed: Ten Essays* (New York and London: Garland Publishing, 1991), pp. 83–94.

Deals with obscure passages in Milton's poetry and prose. Appendix: "Something Old and Something New on That Two-Handed Engine."

1525 Le Comte, Edward. "Did Milton Mistranslate Horace?" *MiltonQ*, 18, 1984, 128–29.

Questions whether Milton added the word "stern" to his translation of the last line in the "Fifth Ode of Horace." Pronounces Milton's translation correct.

1526 Le Comte, Edward. "A German Analogue to *Comus*." *MiltonQ*, 16, 1982, 72–73.

On similarities between Milton's poem and the diary that Christoph Haizmann kept after he made a pact with Satan in 1677.

1527 Le Comte, Edward. "The 'Haemony' Passage in *Comus*." *Poets' Riddles: Essays in Seventeenth-Century Explication* (Port Washington, NY, and London: Kennikat Press, 1975), pp. 67–99.

Reprint of Huckabay No. 2583, originally published in 1942.

1528 Le Comte, Edward. "Miltonic Echoes in *Elegia VII*." *ELR*, 14, 1984, 191–98. Reprinted in *Milton Re-Viewed: Ten Essays* (New York and London: Garland Publishing, 1991), pp. 119–27.

Determines that the themes of *Elegy 7* are about disobedience to divine law, punishment, repentance, and supplication. Discusses Milton's inspiration for writing the poem and concludes that it has a direct thematic link with *Paradise Lost*.

1529 Le Comte, Edward. "More on P. M. S." *MiltonQ*, 18, 1984, 135.

Objects to some of Gordon Campbell's supplement (No. 1248) to the notes in Le Comte's edition of *Justa Edovardo King* (No. 307). See further comments by Jeremy Maule (No. 1573). See also No. 1530.

1530 Le Comte, Edward. "'P. M. S.' in the Edward King Preface." *MiltonQ*, 16, 1982, 83.

Supplements his edition of *Justa Edovardo King* (No. 307) by suggesting that "P. M. S.," which appears at the head of the Latin prose panegyric following the title page, means "'Piis manibus sacrum' ('Consecrated to his pious shade')." See Gordon Campbell's response (No. 1248) and Nos. 1427 and 1573.

1531 Le Comte, Edward. "Shakespeare's Emilia and Milton's: The Parameters of Research." *MiltonQ*, 18, 1984, 81–84. Reprinted in *Milton Re-Viewed: Ten Essays* (New York and London: Garland Publishing, 1991), pp. 95–102.

Discusses the identity of Milton's poetic mistress with reference to Shakespeare's naming of his dark lady.

1532 Le Comte, Edward. "Something Old and Something New on That Two-Handed Engine." *Greyfriar*, 25, 1984, 34–36.

Offers evidence that the two-handed engine in *Lycidas* is a sword. Cites Sir Walter Scott's use of it in the *Talisman* (1825).

1533 Le Comte, Edward. "'That Two-Handed Engine' and Savonarola and the Blackfriars Fatal Vespers." *Poets' Riddles: Essays in Seventeenth-Century Explication* (Port Washington, NY, and London: Kennikat Press, 1975), pp. 100–28.

Reprint of Huckabay Nos. 2584–85, originally published in 1950 and 1952.

1534 Leishman, James B. *Milton's Minor Poems.* Ed. by Geoffrey Tillotson. London: Hutchinson, 1969; Pittsburgh, PA: Univ. of Pittsburgh Press, 1971. 360pp.

Contents: "The Young Milton"; "Some Remarks on Seventeenth-Century Poetry and Milton's Place in It"; "The Latin Poems"; "English Poems Written at Cambridge"; "Some Poems Written at Horton"; "*L'Allegro* and *Il Penseroso* in Their Relation to Seventeenth-Century Poetry"; "*Arcades*"; "*Comus*"; and "*Lycidas*." Appendix: "James Blair Leishman," by John Butt. Reviews: *TLS*, June 11, 1970, p. 641; R. E. C. Houghton, *N&Q*, 17, 1970, 429–30; *MiltonQ*, 5, 1971, 43–44; F. T. Prince, *RES*, 22, 1971, 206–08; Donald A. Roberts, *RenQ*, 26, 1973, 89–91; Claes Schaar, *ES*, 55, 1974, 80–82.

1535 Lerner, Laurence. "Farewell, Rewards and Fairies: An Essay on *Comus*." *JEGP*, 70, 1971, 617–31. Reprinted in *The Uses of Nostalgia: Studies in Pastoral Poetry* (London: Chatto and Windus; New York: Schocken Books, 1972), pp. 163–80.

Feels that Milton never resolved the conflict between the pagan and the Christian worlds, "until he extricated himself from it in *Paradise Regained*." This is especially apparent in *Comus*, where a pagan world reaches out to Christianity.

1536 Levitt, Annette S. "Comus, Cloud, and Thel's 'Unacted Desires.'" *CLQ*, 14, 1978, 72–83.

Studies the danger in comparing Blake's *Book of Thel* with *Comus*. Stresses the differences between the two works.

1537 Lieb, Michael. "Milton's 'Unexpressive Nuptial Song': A Reading of *Lycidas*." *RenP*, 1982, pp. 15–26.

Explores the poem's "ties with the amatory tradition of classical bucolic verse and the recasting of that tradition to accord with a Christian perspective" in both *Lycidas* and *Epitaphium Damonis*.

1538 Lieb, Michael. "Scriptural Formula and Prophetic Utterance in *Lycidas*." *Milton and Scriptural Tradition: The Bible into Poetry*. Ed. by James H. Sims and Leland Ryken (Columbia: Univ. of Missouri Press, 1984), pp. 31–42.

Asserts that Milton used the scriptural formulas of "once more" and "no more" "to bring into play an entire complex of nuances embodied in the formulaic language of Scripture and particularly in the language that characterizes the prophetical books."

1539 Lieb, Michael. "'Yet Once More': The Formulaic Opening of *Lycidas*." *MiltonQ*, 12, 1978, 23–28.

The poem's opening line is multifaceted: it invokes the entire pastoral elegiac tradition and alludes to Hebrews 12.26–29, which Milton associates "with the entire redemptive mission of Christ, culminating in the Last Judgment and the enjoyment of heavenly bliss by those who are saved."

1540 Lloyd, David. "Ludlow Castle." *MiltonQ*, 21, No. 4, 1987, 52–58.

Discusses Ludlow's history and the town as it is today.

1541 Lockerd, Ben. "'Sport That Wrinkled Care Unwrinkles'—A Pun in *L'Allegro*, line 31." *MiltonQ*, 17, 1983, 17–19.

Believes that in *Lycidas* 31, the English meaning of the word "derides" ("to mock") carries with it the French meaning ("to smooth").

1542 Lodi, M. K. "*Comus* as a Prelude to *Paradise Lost*." *Essays on John Milton: A Tercentenary Tribute*. Ed. by Asloob Ahmad Ansari (Aligarh: Aligarh Muslim Univ., 1976), pp. 35–47.

Discusses *Comus* as the "dawn or twilight" of *Paradise Lost*.

1543 Loeffelholz, Mary. "Two Masques of Ceres and Proserpine: *Comus* and *The Tempest*." *Re-membering Milton: Essays on the Texts and Traditions*. Ed. by Mary Nyquist and Margaret W. Ferguson (New York and London: Methuen, 1987), pp. 25–42.

"I propose to open a feminist inquiry into Shakespeare's presence in Milton's *Comus* by considering the relation of Prospero's interrupted betrothal masque of Ceres in *The Tempest* to Milton's masque."

1544 Loh, Bei-Yei. "A Note on Milton's 'On Shakespeare.'" *N&Q*, 30, 1983, 431.

Offers two motives for Milton's composition of "On Shakespeare": Milton knew Robert Allot, a bookseller who could have given him prior knowledge of a forthcoming second folio of Shakespeare's works; and evidence indicates that Milton's query, "What need'st thou such weak witness of thy name?" responds to "that wretched quatrain inscribed on Shakespeare's tombstone."

1545 Long, Anne B. "Coping with Milton's Power." *CEA*, 35, 1973, 33–35.

Explains a method of showing students the relevance and universal appeal of Milton through study of "On Time" coupled with Shakespeare's Sonnet 19 and a passage from Camus's *Plague*.

1546 Lovelock, Julian, ed. *Milton: "Comus" and "Samson Agonistes," a Casebook*. London and Basingstoke: Macmillan, 1975. 253pp.

Selected reprints of critical essays on both works, each divided into early criticism and twentieth-century criticism. Includes twentieth-century essays on *Comus* by C. L. Barber, John B. Broadbent, Jr., A. E. Dyson, Rosemond Tuve, and A. S. P. Woodhouse.

1547 Low, Anthony. "Amaryllis, Neaera, and Fame in Milton's *Lycidas*." *SCN*, 29, 1971, 34–35.

"Amaryllis and Neaera are not simply temptations to illicit love, but to all the affections that were classified as concupiscible; while Fame represents the temptation to indulge the irascible affections."

1548 Low, Anthony. "*Elegia Septima*: The Poet and the Poem." *MiltonS*, 19, 1984, 21–35.

Concludes that *Elegy 7* reveals "a more complicated young poet than most critics have admitted, and one far more in control of his art."

1549 Low, Anthony. *"Mansus*: In Its Context." *MiltonS*, 19, 1984, 105–26.

Examines *Mansus* with respect to the personal relationship between Manso and Milton and applies the classical allusions to Milton's intended glorification of his friend.

1550 Low, Anthony. "Milton's Last Sonnet." *MiltonQ*, 9, 1975, 80–82.

On the identity of the wife of Sonnet 23 ("Methought I saw"). "The evidence for Katherine is not conclusive; but for Mary Powell there is no evidence at all."

1551 Low, Anthony. "Some Notes on *Lycidas* and the *Aeneid*." *ELN*, 13, 1976, 175–77.

Notes that "the *Aeneid* is echoed in *Lycidas*: drowning in the midst of calm, being tossed about by the waves, washing up on the shore amid the surf, having no proper tomb, being cut off when young and full of promise, and concluding with the uselessness of mourning or flowers to reverse the fact of death."

1552 Low, Anthony. "The Unity of Milton's *Elegia Sexta*." *ELR*, 11, 1981, 213–23.

Suggests that the poem's final movement is integral, not digressive. Reads the poem as a Christmas elegy.

1553 Lutaud, Olivier. "'And Twitch't His Mantle Blue . . .': Thétis en *Lycidas*." *Prélude au Matin d'un Poète: "Such Sights as Youthful Poets Dream": Traditions Humanistes chez le Jeune Milton*. Introduction by Lutaud (Paris: Centre d'Histoire des Idées dans les Iles Britanniques, Université de Paris IV, Sorbonne, 1983), pp. 45–61.

Studies the biblical and classical influences in *Lycidas* and examines images, allusions, and events. Compares the poem with the works of William Browne.

1554 Lutaud, Olivier. *Arc de Guerre ou d'Alliance: L'Engin Énigmatique du Poème "Lycidas" de Milton*. Travaux du Centre d'Histoire des Idées dan les Iles Britanniques, no. 2. Paris: Université de Paris IV, Sorbonne, 1982. 42pp.

In *Lycidas* 130–31, the two-handed engine is the Anglicized form of the Latin "machina" and refers to the rainbow, which is the symbol of reconciliation between heaven and earth.

1555 Lyons, Bridget Gellert. "Epilogue: Milton's *Il Penseroso* and the Idea of Time." *Voices of Melancholy: Studies in Literary Treatments of Melancholy in Renaissance England* (London: Routledge and Kegan Paul; New York: Barnes and Noble, 1971), pp. 149–61.

Suggests that the speaker in *Il Penseroso* has a more "heightened awareness of time" than does the speaker in *L'Allegro*.

1556 MacCallum, Hugh. "The Narrator of Milton's *On the Morning of Christ's Nativity*." *Familiar Colloquy: Essays Presented to Arthur Edward Barker*. Ed. by Patricia Brückmann (Toronto: Oberon Press, 1978), pp. 179–95.

Examines the structure "with particular reference to the effect the poem creates of being sung or narrated by the poet."

1557 MacLaren, I. S. "Milton's Nativity Ode: The Function of Poetry and Structures of Response in 1629 (with a Bibliography of Twentieth-Century Criticism)." *MiltonS*, 15, 1981, 181–200.

Discusses Milton's conception of the poet's offices and holds that the poem's "embodiment of these functions of poetry and its integrity of form are . . . the features that distinguish *On the Morning of Christ's Nativity* from any of Milton's earlier poems."

1558 Major, John M. ["On L'Allegro."] *ELN*, 12, 1974, 124–25.

Replies to Charles Hurley (No. 1457). Contends that *L'Allegro* 45–46 refers to the lark. L'Allegro feels no sorrow, and the lark is singing in defiance of sorrow, on a cheerful note designed to awaken the young man to a day of carefree pleasures. Hurley replies (*ELN*, 12, 1975, 193–94) that Major has misread the poem, that his interpretation is a private one.

1559 Major, John M. "Ovid's *Amores* III.ix: A Source for *Lycidas*." *MiltonQ*, 6, No. 3, 1972, 1–3.

Suggests that the theme, tone, and form of *Lycidas* recall Ovid's lament for Tibullus.

1560 Mallette, Richard. *Spenser, Milton, and Renaissance Pastoral.* Lewisburg, PA: Bucknell Univ. Press; East Brunswick, NJ, London, and Toronto: Associated Univ. Presses, 1981. 224pp.

Examines "poems in which Spenser and Milton fashion and animate a shared proclivity toward pastoral" and accounts for "this peculiar form of literary artifice from the perspective the poets have in common." Chapters about Milton: "Spenser, Milton, and the Pastoral Tradition"; "Milton's Early Pastorals"; and "Spenser, Milton, and the Pastoral Elegy." Reviews: David A. Richardson, *SpenN*, 12, 1981, 57–59; Helen Cooper, *N&Q*, 29, 1982, 448–49; Anuradha Dingwaney Needham, *SCN*, 40, 1982, 65–66.

1561 Marcus, Leah. "The Earl of Bridgewater's Legal Life. Notes toward a Political Reading of *Comus*." *MiltonQ*, 21, No. 4, 1987, 13–23.

Claims that *Comus* "supports the Earl of Bridgewater against Laud by mirroring his analysis of the proper division of labor between the Council and the ecclesiastical courts. But simultaneously, the masque humbles the Council itself, implicitly measuring it against an ideal of judicial authority."

1562 Marcus, Leah Sinanoglou. "The Milieu of Milton's *Comus*: Judicial Reform at Ludlow and the Problem of Sexual Assault." *Criticism*, 25, 1983, 293–327. Revised in *Milton and the Idea of*

Woman. Ed. by Julia M. Walker (Urbana and Chicago: Univ. of Illinois Press, 1988), pp. 66–85.

Contends that Milton wrote *Comus* "as an analysis of the administration of justice—the difficulty of the task, its importance, and the stumbling blocks to be encountered in the course of carrying it out." Argues that the many parallels between the masque and the rape and robbery case of Margery Evans, for which the Earl of Bridgewater served as an investigator and judge, demonstrate Milton's familiarity with the case. Thus, the masque was meant to direct critical political allusions at the judges of the Council of Wales, who were present at the performance. Abs., *MiltonQ*, 24, 1990, 151.

1563 Marcus, Leah S. "Milton's Anti-Laudian Masque." *The Politics of Mirth: Jonson, Herrick, Milton, Marvell, and the Defense of Old Holiday Pastimes* (Chicago, IL, and London: Univ. of Chicago Press, 1986), pp. 169–212.

Argues that *Comus* "turns Anglican ritual against the Anglican establishment, symbolically freeing the church from the powerful influence of Laud." Provides information about the Egerton family. Reviews (of book): Richard Helgerson, *RenQ*, 40, 1987, 825–28; Robert C. Evans, *SCJ*, 19, 1988, 300–01; Jonathan Goldberg, *JEGP*, 87, 1988, 257–60; James E. Neufeld, *Ren&R*, 12, 1988, 234–37; David Norbrook, *LRB*, 10, 1988, 20–21; Lois Potter, *DUJ*, 80, 1988, 346; David Harris Sacks, *SQ*, 39, 1988, 477–79; Richard G. Barlow, *SCN*, 49, 1991, 45–46.

1564 Marjara, Harinder S. "Milton's 'Chromatick Jarres' and 'Tuscan Aire.'" *MiltonQ*, 19, 1985, 11–13.

Explains that Milton's sonnets show that he initially reacted negatively to the new Italian trend in music but later adopted a more positive attitude.

1565 Martin, Jeanne S. "Transformations

in Genre in Milton's *Comus*." *Genre*, 10, 1977, 195–213.

Points out that Milton departs from the masque's standard form and concludes that he denies the traditional "direct audience participation in an ideal world, and leaves them instead with a world which is . . . far from ideal." Abs., *MiltonQ*, 11, 1977, 93.

1566 Martin, Leonard Cyril. *Thomas Warton and the Early Poems of Milton.* Folcroft, PA: Folcroft Library Editions, 1977; Norwood, PA: Norwood Editions, 1978.

Reprints of Huckabay No. 2616, originally published in 1934.

1567 Martyn, J. R. C. "Milton's *Elegia Septima*." *Acta Conventus Neo-Latini Lovaniensis: Proceedings of the First International Congress of Neo-Latin Studies.* Ed. by Jozef Ijsewijn and Eckhard Kessler (München: Leuven Univ. Press, 1973), pp. 381–87.

Analyzes the poem's subtle tone, latent irony, and Ovidian wit.

1568 Martz, Louis L. "The Music of *Comus*." *Illustrious Evidence: Approaches to English Literature of the Early Seventeenth Century.* Ed. by Earl Miner (Berkeley, Los Angeles, and London: Univ. of California Press, 1975), pp. 93–113.

Believes that the masque draws from Shakespeare, Jonson, Theocritus, Euripides, and many others to exhibit poetry's music. "It is indeed a virtuoso display of poetical mastery, with the young Milton . . . showing himself now almost ready to embark upon the great work for which he has been so carefully preparing his powers."

1569 Martz, Louis L. "The Rising Poet, 1645." *On Milton's Poetry: A Selection of Modern Studies.* Ed. by Arnold Stein (Greenwich, CT: Fawcett Publications, 1970), pp. 37–52. Reprinted in *Literary Criticism: Idea and Act.* Ed. by W. K. Wimsatt (Berkeley, Los Angeles, and London: Univ. of California Press, 1974), pp. 402–22.

Reprint of Huckabay No. 2618, originally published in 1965.

1570 Martz, Louis L. "Who is Lycidas?" *YFS*, 47, 1972, 170–88.

Milton called his elegy *Lycidas* because the name is related to "the mature consciousness whose underlying presence in the poem has provided, from the opening line, the unrecognized or dimly apprehended signs of religious and poetical faith."

1571 Matsuda, Minori. "Ovidian and Spenserian Elements in *Comus*." *MCJ News*, 8, 1985, 2–4.

Studies echoes of Spenser's *Faerie Queene* and Ovid's *Metamorphoses* in *Comus*, with an emphasis on the Circe motif.

1572 Maule, Jeremy. "Milton's 'Three and Twentieth Year' Again." *N&Q*, 33, 1986, 32–33.

Disputes John Gouws's assertion (No. 1399) that the number twenty-three in Milton's "Epitaph on the Marchioness of Winchester" and Sonnet 7 represents incompleteness. Argues that it alludes to his nephew Edward Phillips's *Theatrum Poetarum*, which tells of the poet Arthur Johnston, who "was laureated at *Paris* before he had fully arriv'd to the 23d Year of his Age."

1573 Maule, Jeremy. "P. M. S. as Obituary Abbreviation." *MiltonQ*, 18, 1984, 135–36.

Believes that Gordon Campbell (No. 1248) is wrong to reject Edward Le Comte's emended reading of P. M. S. (see No. 1530) in his edition of *Justa Edovardo King Naufrago* (No. 307) because P. M. S. would not have been an obscure abbreviation to readers in 1637. See No. 1529.

1574 Maxwell, J. C. "*L'Allegro*, 25ff." *N&Q*, 17, 1970, 249.

Suggests that the passage echoes the topic and wording of one of Horace's *Odes*.

1575 Mazzaro, Jerome. "Gaining Authority: John Milton at Sonnets." *ELWIU*, 15, 1988, 3–12.

Discusses Milton's influence on the form of seventeenth-century sonnets. Analyzes the sources, imagery, religious implications, and syntax of several of his sonnets.

1576 McCarthy, B. Eugene. "*Comus* and Derrick's *A Poetical Dictionary.*" *MiltonN*, 3, 1969, 19–20.

Identifies additional passages in Samuel Derrick's work (see Huckabay No. 2507) which were falsely attributed to Milton but probably taken from John Dalton's 1738 *Comus*. Suggests that Derrick may have used Dalton's version for all quotations from the poem.

1577 McCarthy, William. "The Continuity of Milton's Sonnets." *PMLA*, 92, 1977, 96–109.

Traces the sequence of the sonnets as Milton rises from the role of Petrarchan apprentice to that of his community's conscience. Also examines his Christian career in a four-level structure of imagery: heaven, Eden, the fallen world, and the world of sin. Abs., *MiltonQ*, 11, 1977, 27–28.

1578 McCarthy, William Paul. "I. *The Lives of the Poets*: Johnson's Essay on Man. II. Stories from *The Secret Rose* by W. B. Yeats: A Critical Variorum Text. III. The Continuity of Milton's Sonnets." Doctoral diss., Rutgers Univ., 1974. 200pp. Abs., *DAI*, 35, 1974, 3692A.

Demonstrates a correlation between Milton's sonnet sequence and his "career both as poet and as Christian."

1579 McColley, Diane Kelsey. "Tongues of Men and Angels: *Ad Leonoram Romae Canentem.*" *MiltonS*, 19, 1984, 127–48.

Discusses seventeenth-century views of the angelic hierarchy and of angels and fallen humanity.

1580 McCord, Clare Finley. "'Various Style': Milton's Interpolated Sonnets and Their Tradition." Doctoral diss., Case

Western Reserve Univ., 1985. 171pp. Abs., *DAI*, 46, 1986, 3727A.

Reveals Milton's improvement of conventional and unconventional interpretations of the traditional sonnet, as well as his development of a blank-verse sonnet in *Comus*.

1581 McGuire, Mary Ann Cale. "Merriment Well Managed: A Study of Multiple Genres in Milton's *Comus.*" Doctoral diss., Brown Univ., 1975. 212pp. Abs., *DAI*, 37, 1976, 336A.

Examines Milton's defiance of masque tradition by including "elements from the romance, the entertainment, and the divine pastoral drama" in *Comus*.

1582 McGuire, Mary Ann. "Milton's *Arcades* and the Entertainment Tradition." *SP*, 74, 1978, 451–71.

Shows how Milton goes beyond the usual level of estate entertainment and presents in *Arcades* "a profound recognition of man's position and his responsibilities in a fallen world." Abs., *SCN*, 38, 1980, 20.

1583 McGuire, Maryann Cale. *Milton's Puritan Masque.* Athens: Univ. of Georgia Press, 1983. xi, 208pp.

Studies Milton's transformation of a royalist genre into a Puritan form. Suggests that *Comus* reveals his developing Puritan sympathies during the 1630s. Reviews: *TLS*, Apr. 20, 1984, p. 438; *VQR*, 60, 1984, 44; William P. Shaw, *MiltonQ*, 18, 1984, 95–97; *Ren&R*, 9, 1985, 302; Cedric C. Brown, *RenQ*, 38, 1985, 380; James L. Hedges, *C&L*, 34, 1985, 39–41; Richard S. Ide, *Rev*, 7, 1985, 93–97; Michael Fixler, *RES*, 37, 1986, 92–93.

1584 McQueen, William A. "Redeeming Time: Milton's *On the Morning of Christ's Nativity.*" *RenP*, 1975, pp. 53–61.

Argues that Milton's use of present and past tenses in the poem results in a subsuming of "any given moment in time, including . . . any future time" after the poem's composition in 1629.

1585 Meier, T. K. "Milton's *Nativity Ode*:

Sectarian Discord." *MLR*, 65, 1970, 7–10.

"The objective of this essay . . . is to demonstrate the victory of Puritan abstraction and harshness over the spirit of Anglican mildness in this early poem."

1586 Menascé, Esther. "Milton e i Valdesi." *Bollettino della Società di Studi Valdesi*, 121, July, 1967, 3–40.

Claims that Sonnet 18 ("On the Late Massacre in Piemont") "owes several ideas and turns of phrase to the diplomatic letters Milton was preparing as Cromwell's Latin secretary to various European rulers, and also to the account of the massacre officially published in 1655" (summary taken from *YWES*, 1968, p. 215).

1587 Mengert, James G. "The Resistance of Milton's Sonnets." *ELR*, 11, 1981, 81–95.

Discusses Milton's sonnets, especially in relation to their concluding lines. Shows that Milton's sonnet form "takes us up for a vision, a glimpse of the whole design, a glimpse made possible by a great effort of will to design; then it expels us into some form of that condition which occasions, even while it resists, such visions." Abs., *SCN*, 40, 1982, 81; *MiltonQ*, 16, 1982, 54.

1588 Mercer, LeMoyne Brooks. "Trinal Unity: The Sources, Traditions, and Craftsmanship of Milton's *On the Morning of Christ's Nativity*." Doctoral diss., Bowling Green State Univ., 1978. 102pp. Abs., *DAI*, 39, 1979, 4280A–81A.

Relates three themes in the *Nativity Ode*—"the universal peace, the music of the spheres, and the flight of the false gods"—to golden age tradition.

1589 Miles, Josephine. "Words as Themes in Milton's *Lycidas*." *Poetry and Change: Donne, Milton, Wordsworth, and the Equilibrium of the Present* (Berkeley, Los Angeles, and London: Univ. of California Press, 1974), pp. 84–90.

Reprint of Huckabay No. 2628, originally published in 1948. Reviews (of book): Denis Donoghue, *TLS*, Apr. 25, 1975, pp. 442–43; Hyatt H. Waggoner, *AL*, 47, 1975, 492–93; W. K. Wimsatt, *RenQ*, 28, 1975, 416–17.

1590 Miller, David M. "From Delusion to Illumination: A Larger Structure for *L'Allegro-Il Penseroso*." *PMLA*, 86, 1971, 32–39.

Discusses the poems' vertical structure, as they progress nearer to the contemplation of God. Parallel thematic units, the education of a superior mind, the subordination of flesh to mind and mind to spirit, and the progress of mind and soul through the complementary disorders of black melancholy and vain deluding joy culminate in the final section of *Il Penseroso*, which finally has no parallel in *L'Allegro*.

1591 Miller, Edmund. " 'The Late Massacre': Milton's Liturgical Sonnet." *CP*, 17, 1984, 43–50.

Discusses the possible sources and theological implications of Milton's seductive model prayer, Sonnet 18 ("On the Late Massacre in Piemont").

1592 Miller, George Eric. "A Video Tape Production of *Comus*." *MiltonQ*, 7, 1973, 107–09.

Produced by Miller's Milton class at the University of Delaware in 1973. See No. 1674.

1593 Miller, Leo. "Dating Milton's 1626 Obituaries." *N&Q*, 27, 1980, 323–24.

Deals with the poems written for Richard Ridding (*Elegy 2*), Lancelot Andrewes (*Elegy 3*), John Gostlin (*In Obitum Procancellarii*), and Nicholas Felton (*In Obitum Praesulis Eliensis*) and supplies new evidence about the date of Ridding's death. Conjectures that Milton began the poem for Gostlin at the age of sixteen and added material in 1626, after the death of Gostlin, to make it appropriate for a physician. Abs., *SCN*, 39, 1981, 100.

1594 Miller, Leo. "Milton's *Patriis Cicutis*." *N&Q*, 28, 1981, 41–42.

Argues that in line 89 of *Elegy 6*, Milton refers to his *Nativity Ode*, rather than to his Italian sonnets. Abs., *SCN*, 39, 1981, 100.

1595 Miller, William S. *The Mythology of Milton's "Comus."* Berkeley: Univ. of California Press, 1975. xii, 272pp. Reprinted, New York: Garland Publishing, 1988.

Argues that the importance of the mythologies and events in *Comus*, and their relevance to the poem's immediate surroundings, appears in its "aesthetic and social contexts."

1596 Morris, David B. "Drama and Stasis in Milton's *Ode on the Morning of Christ's Nativity*." *SP*, 68, 1971, 207–22.

Discusses the fusion of time with timelessness as it relates to the Incarnation in the *Nativity Ode*, based on Milton's interpretation of the Nativity as both an isolated, static event and "an essential episode in the comprehensive drama of history."

1597 Mortimer, Anthony. "*Comus* and Michaelmas." *ES*, 65, 1984, 111–19.

Believes that Michaelmas night gave Milton enough reason to write a masque about chastity and that *Comus* has no connection with the Castlehaven scandal.

1598 Mortimer, Anthony. "The Italian Influence on *Comus*." *MiltonQ*, 6, No. 1, 1972, 8–16.

On the sources of *Comus*. Argues that Milton did not know of Ottavio Tronsarelli's *La Catena d'Adone* and that, while Giambattista Marino's *Adone* may have directly influenced the plot, it is only one of a composite of influences. States that Tasso's *Aminta* was no model for Milton.

1599 Mueller, Janel M. "On Genesis in Genre: Milton's Politicizing of the Sonnet in 'Captain or Colonel.'" *Renaissance Genres: Essays on Theory, History, and Interpretation*. Ed. by Barbara Kiefer Lewalski (Cambridge, MA: Harvard Univ.

Press, 1986), pp. 213–40.

Discusses Milton's sonnets in relation to his life and prose. The political sonnets "provide an outlet for his constructive energies and vision during the period of his own political activity." This applies to Sonnet 8 ("Captain or Colonel").

1600 Mueller, Janel. "The Mastery of Decorum: Politics as Poetry in Milton's Sonnets." *CritI*, 13, 1987, 475–508.

Studies the political content of some of Milton's prose works and sonnets. Asserts that political poetry does not "falsify historical fact [and] may even help to shape it." As a form of philosophy, poetry has virtues such as "a saliency of image, a condensation of utterance, and a memorability induced by meter and other aspects of its verse design" that more traditional political media lack.

1601 Mulryan, John. "Aulus Gellius and Milton's *Il Penseroso*: 'Till Civil-Suited Morn Appear.'" *AN&Q*, supplementary vol. 1, 1978, 118–19.

Believes that Milton's use of the term "civil-suited" in *Il Penseroso* 122 is suggested by a passage in Gellius's *Attic Nights*. Abs., *SCN*, 38, 1980, 20.

1602 Mulryan, John. "The Iconography of Harmony and Chaos in Milton's 'Naturam Non Pati Senium.'" *MiltonQ*, 17, 1983, 25.

Abstract of a paper presented at the 1982 MLA Convention. The poem "treats the perennial problem of the artist—how to create something eternal and immutable in a world threatened by chaos and doomed to extinction."

1603 Mulryan, John. "Milton's *Lycidas* and the Italian Mythographers: Some Suggestive Parallels in Their Treatment of Mythological Subjects." *MiltonQ*, 15, 1981, 37–44.

"The purpose of this paper is simply to examine a number of images from Milton's *Lycidas*, and to point up passages of parallel interest in [Natalis] Conti's *Mythologiae* and [Vincenzo] Catari's *Imagini*." Abs., *MiltonQ*, 14, 1980, 32; *SCN*, 38, 1980, 46.

1604 Mundhenk, Rosemary Karmelich. "Dark Scandal and the Sun-Clad Power of Chastity: The Historical Milieu of Milton's *Comus*." *SEL*, 15, 1975, 141–52.

Asserts that "the particular occasion of *Comus* was a double one: the appointment of Bridgewater as Lord President and the deliverance of the entire family from the embarrassment of a recent scandal." Explains that references to chastity pertain to the sexual scandal recently weathered by the family. Abs., *MiltonQ*, 9, 1975, 62.

1605 Murley, Lyle Arthur. "Varieties of Manner in the English Lyrics of John Milton: A Critical Study." Doctoral diss., Northwestern Univ., 1969. 260pp. Abs., *DAI*, 30, 1970, 4418A–19A.

Contends that "the manner in which Milton presents his shorter English poems" affects variations in meaning, time, interpretation (of other works), and decorum.

1606 Naegele, Mary. "Milton and Other's Hobson Poems." *Expl*, 43, No. 3, 1985, 8–9.

Studies the use of puns involving the word "wain" in six poems commemorating Thomas Hobson's death, including one by Milton.

1607 Nardo, Anna Karen. "Milton's Sonnets and the Crisis of Community." Doctoral diss., Emory Univ., 1974. 311pp. Abs., *DAI*, 35, 1975, 4444A.

Analyzes Milton's use of the sonnet to describe an "ideal community" resembling a series of concentric circles centered on "man's isolated consciousness."

1608 Nardo, Anna K. *Milton's Sonnets and the Ideal Community*. Lincoln and London: Univ. of Nebraska Press, 1979. xii, 213pp.

Demonstrates that Milton's sonnets form a sequence and that they "present the larger communal ideal which Milton

envisioned for England." Offers background information about each sonnet and discusses Milton's use of the sonnet form. Reviews: Jean-François Camé, *CahiersE*, 19, 1981, 111–13; John L. Lievsay, *SAB*, 46, 1981, 124–27; Elizabeth McCutcheon, *RMR*, 35, 1981, 171–72; Mary Ann Radzinowicz, *RenQ*, 34, 1981, 463–66; Boyd M. Berry, *JEGP*, 81, 1982, 565–67; Archie Burnett, *N&Q*, 29, 1982, 79–80; Edward Jones, *MiltonQ*, 16, 1982, 21–22.

1609 Nardo, Anna K. "Renaissance Syncretism and Milton's Convivial Sonnets." *EIRC*, 4, 1978, 32–42.

Sonnets 20 (to Henry Lawrence) and Sonnet 21 ("Cyriack, whose Grandsire") "can provide us with vivid examples of how the syncretic spirit sought to harmonize humane, divine, and scientific wisdom, thereby fostering the Renaissance ideal of the magnanimous man."

1610 Nassar, Eugene P. "*Lycidas* as Pastiche." *The Rape of Cinderella: Essays in Literary Continuity* (Bloomington and London: Indiana Univ. Press, 1970), pp. 16–27.

"This is how I see the poem—patternless, save from the pattern of mindflow of an immensely well-read and sensitive man who has felt the patterns in works of the artists and thinkers of the past and manipulates these patterns at will."

1611 Negishi, Aiko. "John Milton *Comus*: Kyûtei Kamengeki no Saikôchiku." *Oberon*, 51, 1988, 103–12.

1612 Nelson, Byron C. "Milton's *Comus* as an Aristotelian Masque of Self-Restraint." *WVUPP*, 22, 1975, 10–20.

"For the philosophical substance and dramatic structure of the problem of adolescent sexuality, Milton turned to Aristotle and Spenser respectively.... Thus the Christian concept of Grace and the Aristotelian virtue of self-restraint would join to preserve the Lady from the temptations of sensual indulgence and by implication, together make virtue possible for the fallible but sincere Christian."

1613 Neuse, Richard. "Metamorphosis and Symbolic Action in *Comus*." *Critical Essays on Milton from "ELH"* (Baltimore, MD, and London: Johns Hopkins Press, 1969), pp. 87–102.

Reprint of Huckabay No. 2645, originally published in 1967.

1614 Nichols, Fred J. "*Lycidas, Epitaphium Damonis*, the Empty Dream, and the Failed Song." *Acta Conventus Neo-Latini Lovaniensis: Proceedings of the First International Congress of Neo-Latin Studies*. Ed. by Jozef Ijsewijn and Eckhard Kessler (München: Leuven Univ. Press, 1973), pp. 445–52.

Surveys the classical tradition underpinning Milton's elegies, especially *Epitaphium Damonis*, and concludes that he had to abandon the form and the language because the tradition had become distorted.

1615 Nitchie, George W. "Milton and His Muses." *ELH*, 44, 1977, 75–84.

Feels that in the *Nativity Ode* Milton offers "a prefiguring of *Paradise Regain'd*, with a divine hero and discomfited devils." He also presents a prefiguring of *L'Allegro* and *Il Penseroso*, and the tension found in them—"the apparent opposition that we do not so much choose between as assimilate, in an almost dialectical fashion."

1616 Norbrook, David. "The Politics of Milton's Early Poetry." *Poetry and Politics in the English Renaissance* (London and Boston, MA: Routledge and Kegan Paul, 1984), pp. 235–85, 327–35.

Deals mainly with the political content of the *Nativity Ode*, *Comus*, and *Lycidas*. Milton felt that his radicalism "was a logical extension of the insights of the greatest European and English poets." Reviews (of book): Robin Headlam Wells, *THES*, 23, 1984, 20; *BBN*, Mar. 1985, p. 179; Frank Ker-

mode, *TLS*, Jan. 18, 1985, pp. 65–66; Katharine Eisaman Maus, *WHR*, 39, 1985, 369–71; Blair Worden, *LRB*, 7, 1985, 13–14; *HT*, 36, 1986, 53; Christopher Hill, *N&Q*, 33, 1986, 226–27; John N. King, *HLQ*, 49, 1986, 277–80; *QQ*, 94, 1987, 133; Peter L. Rudnytsky, *RenQ*, 40, 1987, 153–55.

1617 Nuttall, A. D. "Milton's Arthurian Epic: *Mansus*, 80." *N&Q*, 35, 1988, 161.

Corrects a mistranslation of *Mansus* 80 in John Carey's edition (No. 286) and William Riley Parker's biography (No. 230).

1618 Oberhelman, Steven M., and **John Mulryan.** "Milton's Use of Classical Meters in the *Sylvarum Liber*." *MP*, 81, 1983, 131–45.

Demonstrates Milton's mastery of classical meters in his Latin poems. In such works, "meter is not merely an embellishment of theme and structure: it actually plays an active role in conveying the meaning of the poem."

1619 Obertino, James. "Milton's Use of Aquinas in *Comus*." *MiltonS*, 22, 1986, 21–43.

Argues that Milton's primary theological source is Thomas Aquinas, not Luther or Calvin. Discusses the continuity of nature and grace, with chastity an important virtue in its own right.

1620 Ogoshi, Kazuzo. "Milton Shoki no Jojoshi—Botsugo 300 Nen ni Chinande." *EigoS*, 120, 1974, 402–03.

"Milton's Early Lyrics: Specially Connected with the Tercentenary of Milton's Death." In Japanese.

1621 Ohkawa, Akira. "*Comus* and *Pleasure Reconciled to Virtue*." *CEMF*, 21, 1978, 41–50.

In Japanese. Compares Ben Jonson's masque and Milton's *Comus*. Points to Milton's emphasis on grace and believes that Jonson emphasizes dualism.

1622 Ohkawa, Akira. "On Reading *Comus* for Stage." *CEMF*, 31, 1988, 19–31.

On a theatrical production.

1623 O'Keeffe, Timothy J. "Line 181 of *Lycidas*." *MiltonQ*, 6, No. 1, 1972, 5–6.
Notes that a passage from Augustine's *City of God* "provides added enrichment" for the line.

1624 Olivier, Sarah. " 'Pretious Influence': The Native Tradition in Milton's *Nativity Ode*." *Prélude au Matin d'un Poète: "Such Sights as Youthful Poets Dream": Traditions Humanistes chez le Jeune Milton*. Introduction by Olivier Lutaud (Paris: Centre d'Histoire des Idées dans les Iles Britanniques, Université de Paris IV, Sorbonne, 1983), pp. 2–16.
Compares the native tradition with classical influence.

1625 Oram, William A. "The Invocation of Sabrina." *SEL*, 24, 1984, 121–39.
Studies sources of Sabrina in *Comus* as a figure who reconciles the work's opposites into a fruitful concord. Views her as an image of truth and as Milton's addition to the Circe myth.

1626 Ortego, Philip Darraugh. "*Comus*, Circe, and the Whole Bit." *UR*, 36, 1970, 287–91.
Emphasizes the masque's pastoral elements, which reinforce the allegory and the Puritan message.

1627 Oruch, Jack B. "Imitation and Invention in the Sabrina Myths of Drayton and Milton." *Anglia*, 90, 1972, 60–70.
"With Drayton's example in the *Poly-Olbion* (1612, 1622) to draw upon for plot outline, character traits, descriptive details, and phrasing, Milton must have felt he had adequate literary precedent for adapting the legend of Sabrina to suit his own purposes."

1628 Otten, Charlotte F. "Garlanding the Dead: The Epicedial Garland in *Lycidas*." *MiltonS*, 16, 1982, 141–51.
Insists that the poem's opening lines are funerary and that Milton selects three ancient plants whose berries are unripe in November.

1629 Otten, Charlotte F. "Milton's Daffadillies." *ELN*, 11, 1973, 48–49.

Denies that Milton's use of the word "daffadillies" in *Lycidas* 150 was simply colloquial and rustic. Asserts that in his day, "The three words—daffodil, daffadilly, and daffadowndilly ... are interchangeable."

1630 Otten, Charlotte. "Milton's Haemony." *ELR*, 5, 1975, 81–95.
"The criticism clustering around Milton's haemony [in *Comus*] has failed to take the botanico-medical tradition seriously. Haemony is andros-haemon(y), the ancient plant which Dioscorides called androsaemon and which contemporary botanists called hypericon, St. John's wart, fuga daemonum, perforata, and androsaemon. Botanically, this plant fits haemony down to the last detail." Abs., *MiltonQ*, 9, 1975, 122–23.

1631 Otten, Charlotte F. "Primrose and Pink in *Lycidas* (lines 142, 144)." *N&Q*, 31, 1984, 317–19.
Uses Louis D'Auxerre Liger's *Le Jardinier Fleuriste et Historiographe* to explain the mythological significance of the primrose and pink on Lycidas's hearse. Contends that Liger and Milton used the same unknown source for their information. The two accounts share such elements as a pastoral setting, "the God of the River," "the watry Urn," Fate cutting the thread of life, and even the name Lycidas.

1632 O'Valle, Violet. "Milton's *Comus* and Welsh Oral Tradition." *MiltonS*, 18, 1983, 25–44.
Proposes that significant elements in *Comus* are derived from Celtic (Welsh) oral tradition.

1633 Parfitt, George. "Funereal Verse for Private Figures: To Milton and Dryden." *English Poetry of the Seventeenth Century* (New York: Longman, 1985), pp. 100–11.
Examines other attempts to deal with issues similar to those found in *Lycidas* and then discusses how Milton handles them.

1634 Parks, Ward. "Metaphor in *Lycidas*: A Taxonomy." *Style*, 17, 1983, 1–15.

Subdivides the metaphors in *Lycidas* into three levels: ornamental, structural, and Lycidas/King. Discusses the cross references of facets of human/nonhuman and physical/abstract themes.

1635 Patrides, C. A., ed. *Milton's "Lycidas": The Tradition and the Poem*. Revised edition. Foreword by M. H. Abrams. Columbia: Univ. of Missouri Press, 1983. xviii, 370pp.

See Huckabay No. 2661. This new edition has extensively revised notes on *Lycidas*, a new bibliography, an appendix on the text of the poem, and newly included essays by Stanley E. Fish, Donald M. Friedman, Jon S. Lawry, Isabel G. MacCaffrey, Balachandra Rajan, and Edward W. Tayler. Some essays are deleted from the first edition. Review: Thomas F. Healy, *MLR*, 82, 1987, 915–16.

1636 Patterson, Annabel. "'Forc'd Fingers': Milton's Early Poems and Ideological Constraint." *"The Muses Common-Weale": Poetry and Politics in the Seventeenth Century*. Ed. by Claude J. Summers and Ted-Larry Pebworth (Columbia: Univ. of Missouri Press, 1988), pp. 9–22.

Believes that the early poems exhibit "signs of internal strain and disruption." Argues that Milton was "both a radical . . . and an elitist" throughout his life and that his poetry reflects these opposites.

1637 Patterson, Annabel. "*L'Allegro, Il Penseroso* and *Comus*: The Logic of Recombination." *MiltonQ*, 9, 1975, 75–79.

Considers the echoes of the companion poems in *Comus*. Feels that "in Milton's own mind the masque was intended to be the third in a sequence of three companion pastorals" and notes that "there is indeed an argumentative transfer of antitheses from the paired poems to the masque."

1638 Payne, Mildred Y. "Certain Folk Elements in Milton's *Comus*." *TFSB*, 34, 1968, 45–49.

Points out many similarities between Milton's poem and southern folklore, especially the tale of Tennessee's Bell Witch.

1639 Pecheux, Mother M. Christopher. "'At a Solemn Musick': Structure and Meaning." *SP*, 75, 1978, 331–46.

"An understanding of the significance of the octave both for the harmony of the solemn music and the progression of the theme not only illuminates the triumphant conclusion of the poem but shows as well how here, as in all great literature, structure and meaning become one." Abs., *MiltonQ*, 13, 1979, 62.

1640 Pecheux, Mother M. Christopher. "The Dread Voice in *Lycidas*." *MiltonS*, 9, 1976, 221–41.

"Why is the 'dread voice' which has just uttered the denunciation of the clergy said to shrink the streams? Examination of the biblical context of the lines indicates that the shrinking of the streams may be related to the drying up of the Red Sea at the Exodus. . . . Exegetical tradition, literary precedents, and Milton's other works support the theory that the figure [with the 'dread voice'] is a composite of Moses, Peter, and Christ." Abs., *MiltonQ*, 11, 1977, 28.

1641 Pecheux, Mother M. Christopher. "The Image of the Sun in Milton's *Nativity Ode*." *HLQ*, 38, 1975, 315–33.

Suggests that the sun is the controlling metaphor which organizes patterns of imagery and unites them with structure and theme. Abs., *MiltonQ*, 9, 1975, 91.

1642 Pecheux, Mother M. Christopher. "The Nativity Tradition in *Elegia Sexta*." *MiltonS*, 23, 1987, 3–19.

Examines the concluding lines of *Elegy 6* to determine whether the English poem to which Milton refers is his *Nativity Ode*. Determines that although the relationship between the two is close but not exact, "the former carries the concentrated weight of the same tradition that is diffused in the longer poem."

1643 Perri, Carmela Anne. "The Poetics of Dew: A Study of Milton's Sonnets." Doctoral diss., City Univ. of New York, 1977. 257pp. Abs., *DAI*, 38, 1978, 4184A–85A.

Explores "the kinds and degrees of poetic openness that Milton invents for the brief modern lyric in his sonnets."

1644 Petronella, Vincent F. "Milton's *L'Allegro* and *Il Penseroso*." *Expl*, 28, 1970, Item 40.

Suggests that Milton contrasts mirth and melancholy by using "light" in *L'Allegro* 33–34 and "even" in *Il Penseroso* 37–38 as "paralleled puns and submerged images pointing to the time of day associated with the two goddesses."

1645 Peutl, Ernst. "John Miltons Lateinische Gedichte und ihre Augusteischen Vorbilder." Doctoral diss., Wien, 1952. 102pp.

1646 Phelan, Herbert J. "What is the Persona Doing in *L'Allegro* and *Il Penseroso*?" *MiltonS*, 22, 1986, 3–20.

Relates the persona's whereabouts to cinematic technique. Contends that the poet lets the reader see the persona in some of the scenes but not in all of them.

1647 Pigman, George Wood, III. "Imitation and Pastoral Elegy." Doctoral diss., Yale Univ., 1977. 185pp. Abs., *DAI*, 39, 1978, 2239A–40A.

Uses allusion to examine Theocritus's *Idyll* 1, Virgil's *Eclogues* 5 and 10, and Milton's *Lycidas* as pastoral elegies designed to imitate and improve on previous models.

1648 Pigman, G. W., III. "Milton." *Grief and English Renaissance Elegy* (Cambridge: Cambridge Univ. Press, 1985), pp. 104–24.

Discusses grief in Milton's elegies, emphasizing *Lycidas* and noting its indebtedness to Virgil's lament for Gallus. Concludes that Milton's poem transcends the pastoral tradition.

1649 Pigman, G. W., III. "Versions of Imitation in the Renaissance." *RenQ*, 33, 1980, 1–32.

Uses Milton's *Lycidas* to illustrate the difference between imitation and emulation.

1650 Pironon, J. "'The Different Pace': Tradition et Innovation dans la Critique Récente du *Comus* de Milton." *Prélude au Matin d'un Poète: "Such Sights as Youthful Poets Dream": Traditions Humanistes chez le Jeune Milton*. Introduction by Olivier Lutaud (Paris: Centre d'Histoire des Idées dans les Iles Britanniques, Université de Paris IV, Sorbonne, 1983), pp. 33–44.

Reviews the interpretations (philosophical, historical, artistic, and social) which view *Comus* as an allegory as well as a moral debate and a courtly masque. Since the end of the 1950s, critics have seen it as a myth written to illustrate a moral principle: divine grace. The new criticism, however, has much in common with previous criticism.

1651 Pironon, J. "The Images of Woman in the Sonnets and Some Minor Poems of John Milton." *CahiersE*, 18, 1980, 43–52.

Suggests that the women of Milton's early poems prefigured the lifelong conflict in his mind.

1652 Poggioli, Renato. "Milton's *Lycidas*." *The Oaten Flute: Essays on Pastoral Poetry and the Pastoral Ideal* (Cambridge, MA: Harvard Univ. Press, 1975), pp. 83–104.

Discusses the poem's various sections in light of the pastoral tradition. Believes that the elegy is an artistic triumph which symbolically points to greener pastures and newer fields for Milton as poet.

1653 Pollock, John J. " 'On the University

Carrier': Comments on the Early Drafts." *AN&Q*, 13, 1974, 36–37.

Suggests that "the (apparent) revisions in the authorized texts . . . have the effect of intensifying both the negative view of death at the beginning of the poem and the positive view at the end and, consequently, the shift from the one to the other."

1654 Post, Jonathan F. S. "A Note on Milton's Wizards." *ELN*, 21, No. 1, 1983, 24–29.

Demonstrates the varied but predominantly negative connotations that the word "wizard" has in such works as the *Nativity Ode* and *Comus*.

1655 Radzinowicz, Mary Ann. "'To Play in the Socratic Manner': Oxymoron in Milton's *At a Vacation Exercise in the Colledge*." *HSL*, 17, No. 3, 1985, 1–11.

Explores Milton's extensive use of "oxymorons of genre, speaker, and action," giving examples of his wit through the paradoxical construction of events.

1656 Raizada, Harish. "Milton's 'Soul-Animating Strains': A Study of His Sonnets." *Essays on John Milton: A Tercentenary Tribute*. Ed. by Asloob Ahmad Ansari (Aligarh: Aligarh Muslim Univ., 1976), pp. 48–66.

Surveys the content of the sonnets and discusses their distinctive features.

1657 Raleigh, John Henry. "*Lycidas*: 'Yet Once More.'" *PrS*, 42, 1968, 303–18.

Proposes "to look at *Lycidas* from three points of view: first, as a personal document, that is, as an expression of Milton's character and circumstance; second, as a religious-historical document of English Renaissance Christianity; and third, as a timeless document, that is, what it means to any subsequent age, irrespective of its religious belief."

1658 Rama Sarma, M. V. "*Lycidas* and Milton's Mind." *Triveni*, 40, 1971, 65–72.

Deals mainly with Milton's feelings about death and his future. Offers several interpretations of the last line.

1659 Rapin, René. "Milton's Sonnet XIX." *N&Q*, 20, 1973, 380–81.

Quotes a passage from Goslicius to justify Milton's complaint that he had not reached "half [his] days."

1660 Rauber, D. F. "Milton's Sonnet XI—'I Did But Prompt. . . .'" *PQ*, 49, 1970, 561–64.

Suggests that in lines 8–9 Milton referred to the prefatory verses printed in many editions of the Geneva Bible and possibly intended an allusion to 2 Peter 2.

1661 Ray, Don E. "*Lycidas* and Milton's Epics." *MiltonQ*, 11, 1977, 28.

Abstract of a paper presented at the 1976 MLA Convention. "This paper argues that *Lycidas* and Milton's two epics *Paradise Lost* and *Paradise Regained* are reflections of one another not only in their Christian content but also in the 'parallel processes' by which the poems are developed and the reader led to understanding, catharsis, and reconciliation."

1662 Reader, Willie D. "Dramatic Structure and Prosodic Form in Milton's Sonnet 'On His Deceased Wife.'" *LangQ*, 11, Nos. 1 and 2, 1972, 21–25, 28.

Suggests that "the dramatic structure is reinforced by a carefully wrought prosodic pattern," for Sonnet 23 ("Methought I saw") "develops a strong sense of rising action in the first thirteen lines, then moves to an abrupt climax and falling action in the final line." Discusses the effect of the alliteration, rhyme pattern, and metrical inversions.

1663 Reilein, Dean A. "Milton's *Comus* and Sabrina's Compliment." *MiltonQ*, 5, 1971, 42–43.

Argues that the Earl of Bridgewater and his family "would have found the Sabrina episode to be the source of the chief compliment of the masque, a compliment showing that goodness, virtue, purity, charity, and the like can arise from a less than impeccable background."

1664 Relle, E. G. "Studies in the Presentation of Chastity, Chiefly in the Post-Reformation English Literature, with Particular Reference to Its Ecclesiastical and Political Connotations and to Milton's Treatment of the Theme in *Comus*." Doctoral diss., Cambridge Univ., 1970. *IT*, 20, 1973, 16.

1665 Revard, Stella P. "*Ad Joannem Rousium*: Elegiac Wit and Pindaric Mode." *MiltonS*, 19, 1984, 205–26.

"To trace how Milton progresses from the elegiac to the pindaric poet in this ode is to watch him bid farewell to one kind of poetry and to commit himself to another. At heart, then, *Ad Joannem Rousium* is a poem about John Milton and his role as a poet."

1666 Revard, Stella P. "*L'Allegro* and *Il Penseroso*: Classical Tradition and Renaissance Mythography." *PMLA*, 101, 1986, 338–50.

Considers the poems' classical form and the "mythic significance" of mirth and melancholy in antiquity and in the Renaissance. Believes that the poems are "serious devotions in which the poet explores his relationship to the patron deity of inspiration."

1667 Revard, Stella P. "The Seventeenth-Century Religious Ode and Its Classical Models." *"Bright Shootes of Everlastingness": The Seventeenth-Century Religious Lyric*. Ed. by Claude J. Summers and Ted-Larry Pebworth (Columbia: Univ. of Missouri Press, 1987), pp. 173–91.

Deals mainly with the odes of Milton, Crashaw, and Cowley in regard to their classical models. Points out that although the *Nativity Ode* is Christian in subject and concept, classical decorum guides Milton in structuring the poem.

1668 Richmond, H. M. "Milton." *Renaissance Landscapes: English Lyrics in a European Tradition* (The Hague and Paris: Mouton, 1973), pp. 89–108.

Focuses on the landscape and speaker in *L'Allegro* and *Il Penseroso*.

1669 Ricks, Christopher. "Milton: Part I. *Poems* (1645)." *English Poetry and Prose, 1540–1674*. Ed. by Ricks. Sphere History of Literature in the English Language, vol. 2 (London: Sphere Books, 1970), pp. 249–81. Revised edition, New York: Peter Bedrick Books, 1987.

Milton's *Poems* reveals a healthy tension between following literary convention and striving for originality or surprise. Review (of revised edition): Roy Flannagan, *MiltonQ*, 25, 1991, 108–09.

1670 Ridden, Geoffrey M. "Harmony and Harsh Horns: Music in *Lycidas* and *The Dippers Dipt*." *N&Q*, 31, 1984, 320–21.

Argues that Milton's publication of *Poems* (1645) "represents his effort to demonstrate his own command of the harmony of words after the slur on *Lycidas* in *The Dippers Dipt*, and to re-emphasize in the reprinting of *Lycidas* . . . that the original Puritan impetus for reform . . . had been associated with harmony and order."

1671 Ridden, Geoffrey M. "Henry Burton and a Possible Source for Milton's *Lycidas* and 'On the New Forcers of Conscience.'" *N&Q*, 31, 1984, 319–20.

Suggests Henry Burton's *For God, and the King* as a source for St. Peter's speech in *Lycidas*. Also argues that the theme of toleration present in "On the New Forcers of Conscience" makes Milton's supporter Burton a likely candidate for the allusion to Parliament's severing one's ears.

1672 Riggs, William G. "The Plant of Fame in *Lycidas*." *MiltonS*, 4, 1972, 151–61.

"Here, as elsewhere, Milton uses the metaphor of a plant which flowers 'aloft' to describe the workings of grace, and his use is grounded in the theological conception of being ingrafted in Christ."

1673 Riley, Joanne M. "Milton's Lycidas: New Light on the Title." *N&Q*, 24, 1977, 545.

Finds the title very significant in light of the name's Greek etymology, which means "deliverance from death," and of several examples of this usage in ancient Greek literature, including Homer's *Odyssey*.

1674 Roberts, Donald A. "A Note on a Campus Production of *Comus*." *MiltonQ*, 8, 1974, 58.

Doubts the validity of George Eric Miller's assertion (No. 1592) that productions of *Comus* have not been undertaken by college drama departments. Mentions a 1939 production at Vassar College.

1675 Roberts, Gareth. "Three Notes on Uses of Circe by Spenser, Marlowe and Milton." *N&Q*, 25, 1978, 433–35.

Speaks of Comus as the son of Bacchus and Circe, who surpasses his mother at her art. Abs., *SCN*, 38, 1980, 20–21.

1676 Roberts, Jeanne Addison. "Anxiety and Influence: Milton, Ovid, and Shakespeare." *SoAR*, 53, 1988, 59–75.

Claims that Milton's elegies demonstrate his use of Ovid's and Shakespeare's themes while "at the same time rejecting their implications and inverting their values." However, "As Milton's anxieties come to focus on the human perversions of the ideal and to reflect more fully his own experiences of doubt, disappointment, and defeat, the influence of both Ovid and Shakespeare recedes" in favor of conflicts generated by immediate experience.

1677 Robinson, David. "The Brothers' Debate in Milton's *Comus*." *SSCJ*, 41, 1975, 30–44.

Discusses Milton's use of the brothers' debate to increase audience interest. Claims that sympathy is initially with the Younger Brother's fear for the Lady's personal safety, but concludes that the Elder Brother's speech serves as a thematic statement. Believes that the Elder Brother points out the more important inner struggle.

1678 Rogal, Samuel J. "Emotion and Method in Milton's 'Death of a Fair Infant.'" *ILQ*, 33, No. 4, 1971, 42–51.

Considers "first these emotions and second the methods by which the seventeen-year-old Milton commemorated the death of Anne Phillips." Concludes that this poem "began a long series of Miltonic projects intended to 'assert Eternal Providence,/And justify the ways of God to man.'"

1679 Rollinson, Philip B. "The Central Debate in *Comus*." *PQ*, 49, 1970, 481–88.

Regards the exchange between the Lady and Comus in lines 666–799 as being of central importance. Argues for her effective use of logic in responding to his specious reasoning.

1680 Rollinson, Philip. "Milton's Nativity Poem and the Decorum of Genre." *MiltonS*, 7, 1975, 165–88.

"Although Milton's Nativity poem is usually considered to be an early example of the English ode, it is probably a literary hymn." Abs., *MiltonQ*, 9, 1975, 123.

1681 Rollinson, Philip. "The Traditional Contexts of Milton's 'Two-Handed Engine.'" *ELN*, 9, 1971, 28–35.

"I want to suggest that the two-handed engine which smites is a poetic conflation (employing the figure of metonymy) of two precise but closely related images associated with the Archangel Michael." See Nos. 1341–42 and Huckabay No. 3018.

1682 Romano, J. R. "Heaven's Youngest Teemed Star." *MiltonQ*, 15, 1981, 80–88.

Relates the "youngest teemed star" metaphor in the last stanza of the *Nativity Ode* to the homiletic tradition, "in which the Star of Bethlehem was for the edification of the faithful transformed into *nova*, sign, and servant."

1683 Rosen, Alan D. "Milton's 'War Sonnets': A Comparative Analysis of Theme and Form." *MCJ News*, 2, 1978, 14–15.

Abstract of paper presented. Attempts "to further our understanding of Milton's mind on the subject of war and peace." Abs., *MiltonQ*, 13, 1979, 161.

1684 Rosen, Alan D. "Milton's 'War Sonnets': A Comparative Analysis of Theme and Form." *SELit*, 59, 1978, 33–43.

Discusses Sonnets 15 (to Fairfax), 16 (to Cromwell), 17 (to Henry Vane), and 18 ("On the Late Massacre in Piemont"). Believes that they have a common thematic core which is fully articulated in the closing lines of the *Second Defence*, where Milton argues that the cessation of armed conflict is secondary to victories over spiritual enemies.

1685 Rosenberg, D. M. "Milton's Masque: A Social Occasion for Philosophic Laughter." *SP*, 67, 1970, 245–53.

Proposes to show that "comedy in *Comus* forms a significant part of the work as a whole." Claims that Milton closely follows the masque form's structure while presenting a story that resembles a Shakespearean comedy. Asserts that the concluding "ceremonial occasion brings . . . the masque [to] a definite, formal close."

1686 Rosenblatt, Jason P. "The Angel and the Shepherd in *Lycidas*." *PQ*, 62, 1983, 252–58.

Submits that the transition of the shepherd in *Lycidas* from depression to consolation is a function of "the swain's conception of the archangel Michael." Explores Milton's view of Moses's assumption and the application of the Mosaic ideal to Lycidas's character. Abs., *SCN*, 38, 1980, 46; *MiltonQ*, 14, 1980, 33.

1687 Røstvig, Maren-Sofie. "Elaborate Song: Conceptual Structure in Milton's *On the Morning of Christ's Nativity*." *Fair Forms: Essays in English Literature from Spenser to Jane Austen*. Ed. by Røstvig (Cambridge: D. S. Brewer; Totowa, NJ: Rowman and Littlefield, 1975), pp. 54–84.

Analyzes the concepts of "the circle, the centre, and the 'well-balanced world' hung on 'hinges.'" Argues that "these images have been worked into the structure of the poem to permit Milton's gift to the child to constitute an image of his acts as Creator and Redeemer." Abs., *MiltonQ*, 13, 1979, 28.

1688 Røstvig, Maren-Sofie. "Fra Bokstav til and. Litt om Allegorisk Fortolkning Sett i lys av Renessansens Synkretistiske Tenkning." *Edda*, 66, 1966, 101–16.

"From Letter to Spirit. A Note about Allegorical Interpretation in Light of Syncretistic Thinking during the Renaissance." In Norwegian. Uses the *Nativity Ode* as an example of Renaissance syncretism. Milton compares the baby Jesus with Hercules's slaying the snakes in the cradle. Viewed in a syncretistic light, it is natural for Milton to write allegorically of heathen myths, and the Hercules myth has just as much symbolic power as the story about Abraham and Isaac.

1689 Ruthven, K. K. "Serendipity and Scholarly Interpretations." *CritS*, 5, 1972, 292–98.

Proposes that Milton's Sonnet 9 ("Lady that in the prime") is about his own nickname and was written for an unknown lady during his Cambridge years.

1690 Ryan, Lawrence V. "Milton's *Epitaphium Damonis* and B. Zanchi's *Elegy on Baldassare Castiglione*." *HumLov*, 30, 1981, 108–23.

Believes that Basilio Zanchi's elegy formed part of the intricate background of Milton's lament for Charles Diodati. Abs., *SCN*, 40, 1982, 57.

1691 Sacks, Peter M. "Milton's *Lycidas*." *The English Elegy: Studies in the Genre from Spenser to Yeats* (Baltimore, MD, and London: Johns Hopkins Univ. Press, 1985), pp. 90–117.

Analyzes *Lycidas* in the context of the elegiac tradition that Milton modifies.

1692 Sadler, Lynn Veach. "Magic and the Temporal Scheme in *On the Morning of Christ's Nativity*." *BSUF*, 17, No. 2, 1976, 3–9.

Proposes that God's magic is the pure, white magic of the English fairy world, and as such is contrasted with its perversion, Satan's black magic. Suggests that "both are parodic, just as fallen nature, without grace, is a parody of prelapsarian nature or fallen man." Concludes that the "Great Magic of God" in the poem is "the Word made flesh and the subsequent redemption of time." Abs., *MiltonQ*, 10, 1976, 98.

1693 Safer, Elaine B., and **Thomas L. Erskine,** eds. *"L'Allegro" and "Il Penseroso."* Merrill Literature Casebook Series. Columbus, OH: Charles E. Merrill, 1970. vi, 146pp.

A collection of comments on the poems from Samuel Johnson to recent critics.

1694 Sage, Lorna. "The Coherence of *Comus*." *YES*, 1, 1971, 88–99.

Sees three levels in *Comus*—the worlds of the audience, the Attendant Spirit, and Comus—which Milton interweaves to produce a coherent work.

1695 Sage, Lorna. "Milton's Early Poems: A General Introduction." *John Milton: Introductions*. Ed. by John Broadbent (Cambridge: Cambridge Univ. Press, 1973), pp. 258–97.

Concludes that *Poems* (1645) looks complete and satisfying from one angle but "From another angle (as with everything of Milton's) the volume is a springboard into the future."

1696 Saillens, Emile. *Les Sonnets Anglais et Italiens de Milton.* Folcroft, PA: Folcroft Library Editions, 1974; Norwood, PA: Norwood Editions, 1976; Philadelphia, PA: R. West, 1977.

Reprints of Huckabay No. 354, originally published in 1930.

1697 Saito, Yasuyo. "John Milton and His

Psalm-paraphrases." *MCJ News*, 6, 1983, 26–27.

Abstract of a paper presented at the Twelfth Colloquium of MCJ in December, 1981. Discusses when and why Milton composed the Psalm paraphrases.

1698 Saito, Yasuyo. "On *Comus*: Its Form and Content." *MCJ News*, 8, 1985, 7–10.

Argues that Milton employed the masque form to demonstrate the Christian theme of humanity's spiritual development. States that his religious lesson is conveyed by allusion: "man lost and forlorn in the darkness regains his heavenly home by virtuous living and divine aid."

1699 Sampson, Alden. *Milton's Sonnets.* Folcroft, PA: Folcroft Library Editions, 1969, 1977; Norwood, PA: Norwood Editions, 1978; Philadelphia, PA: R. West, 1979.

Reprints of Stevens No. 629, originally published in 1886.

1700 Sarma, G. V. L. N. "Sublimity in Milton's Sonnets." *The Laurel Bough: Essays Presented in Honour of Professor M. V. Rama Sarma.* Ed. by G. Nageswara Rao (Bombay: Blackie and Son, 1983), pp. 99–105.

"Each sonnet sparkles like a gem and conveys an emotional experience that is unique."

1701 Sasek, Lawrence A. "'Ere Half My Days': A Note on Milton's Sonnet 19." *MiltonQ*, 15, 1981, 16–18.

In Sonnet 19 ("When I consider"), "Milton is saying literally not that less than half of his whole life is over but that he has more days of blindness ahead of him than behind him."

1702 Savage, J. B. "*Comus* and Its Traditions." *ELR*, 5, 1975, 58–80.

"Milton has created in *Comus* a self-consistent Platonic allegory of the soul, the principal concern of which is an ideal of the moral life and the point at which the moral life, fully achieved, transcends itself to be absorbed by the image of what it seeks." Abs., *MiltonQ*, 9, 1975, 124.

1703 Schenck, Celeste Marguerite. "'Unexpressive Nuptial Song': Milton's *Lycidas*." *Mourning and Panegyric: The Poetics of Pastoral Ceremony* (University Park and London: Pennsylvania State Univ. Press, 1988), pp. 91–106.

Focuses on the pastoral tradition, with some discussion of Spenser's influence. Believes that the Orphic myth is at the heart of *Lycidas* because Orpheus was the perfect courtier-bridegroom.

1704 Scher, Mark L. "Milton's 'Fallows Gray': *L'Allegro* 71." *ES*, 52, 1971, 518–20.

"Milton's gray is tinctured with a brownish, autumnal color" and is "suitable to the rest of the poem."

1705 Schoen, Raymond G. "The Hierarchy of the Senses in *A Mask*." *MiltonQ*, 7, 1973, 32–37.

Argues that Milton changed "heare" to "feele" in Comus's first speech to reflect a hierarchy of the senses in which vision dominates hearing and hearing prevails over touch. Concludes that Milton carefully develops references to this hierarchy "at every stage of his work on the mask."

1706 Schuyler, Sarah. "Their Ambivalent Adventures with a Mother: Freud, Milton, Sexton." *L&P*, 32, No. 4, 1986, 11–17.

Argues that Sonnet 23 ("Methought I saw") "invokes two women—a pure one and a tainted one—and they live in the same ghost, and their cohabitation is uneasy."

1707 Schweitzer, Edward C. "Milton's *Lycidas*, 164." *Expl*, 28, 1969, Item 18.

Replies to Thomas O. Mabbott (Huckabay No. 2604). Agrees that the line refers to the Palaemon myth but offers an additional version of it and suggests that this allusion's significance lies in its ambiguity.

1708 Scoufos, Alice-Lyle. "The Mysteries in Milton's *Masque*." *MiltonS*, 6, 1974, 113–42.

"In *Comus*, Milton appears to have used both stock characters and stock plot. Taking his cue from the liturgical text which the *Book of Common Prayer* listed for St. Michael's Day (Revelation xii: 7–13), he turned to the plot of the Woman Wandering in the Wilderness which had been the subject of the Advent plays of medieval drama." See No. 1758. Abs., *MiltonQ*, 9, 1975, 62–63.

1709 Seiters, John Douglas. "Milton's *Lycidas*: Background, Structure and Meaning." Doctoral diss., Florida State Univ., 1975. 214pp. Abs., *DAI*, 36, 1976, 8081A–82A.

Investigates the influence of the pastoral elegy tradition and Milton's intellectual development on the unified structure of *Lycidas*.

1710 Sekinaga, Mitsuhiko. "On the First Edition of *A Maske: Comus*, 1673 [sic]." *MCJ News*, 7, 1984, 13–15.

Abstract of paper presented. Believes that "any new edition of *A Maske* should be based on the 1637 edition supported by the Trinity Manuscript."

1711 Serpell, Michael. "Milton's Blind Mouths." *BC*, 35, 1986, 199–213.

Identifies the preacher Francis Rollenson as Milton's ultimate source of the "blind mouths" passage in *Lycidas*.

1712 Sessions, William A. "Milton and the Dance." *Milton's Legacy in the Arts*. Ed. by Albert C. Labriola and Edward Sichi, Jr. (University Park and London: Pennsylvania State Univ. Press, 1988), pp. 181–203.

Discusses the dance during Milton's time and his various references to it but focuses on productions of *Comus*, especially the 1942 ballet version, which starred Dame Margot Fonteyn.

1713 Sessions, William A. "Milton's 'Naturam.'" *MiltonS*, 19, 1984, 53–72.

Divides "Naturam Non Pati Senium" into four sections of proof. The poet concludes that "all of Nature, which cannot suffer decay and old age, must finally die in order to be transformed."

1714 Shapiro, S. C. "A Note on *L'Allegro* and *Il Penseroso*." *CEA*, 38, 1976, 18–19.

Believes that the relationship between the poems and seventeenth-century character writing merits further investigation.

1715 Shaw, Catherine M. "The Unity of *Comus*." *XUS*, 10, No. 1, 1971, 33–43.

Suggests that the drama's form further develops "the masque in which Milton has used the accepted masque structure but has elevated dramatic poetry to a dominant position in the performance and has reinforced the link between drama and masque.... The stage devices, the music, and the song, are made to serve the poetry and thus enhance the impact on the senses and the imagination."

1716 Shaw, William P. "*Lycidas* 130–131: Christ as Judge and Protector." *MLS*, 7, 1977, 39–42.

Explores the idea that the two-handed engine is Christ in his dual role as judge and protector.

1717 Shawcross, John T. "Form and Content in Milton's Latin Elegies." *HLQ*, 33, 1970, 331–50.

Examines the seven Latin elegies published in 1645. "In this paper I look at these elegies as literature and thus as precursors of the future greatness. For when examined past the customary nod, they herald the poetic themes, the ideological theses, and the mythic concepts of *Paradise Lost*."

1718 Shawcross, John T. "A Note of Correction." *SEL*, 14, 1974, 176.

Recognizes his errors in an earlier review of the *Variorum Commentary* (No. 1236) and identifies articles omitted from that book.

1719 Shawcross, John T. "A Note on the Piedmont Massacre." *MiltonQ*, 6, No. 2, 1972, 36.

Suggests the possible influence of a pamphlet entitled the *Barbarous and Inhumane Proceedings* on the writing of Milton's Sonnet 18 ("On the Late Massacre in Piemont").

1720 Shawcross, John T. "Two Comments." *MiltonQ*, 7, 1973, 97–98.

Replies to Hugh Maclean (No. 2644) by observing that *Paradise Lost* 5.661–62 and 664–65 "present 'the actual emergence of evil into the cosmos of' the poem better than line 666." Also replies to James W. Flosdorf's query (No. 1359) about the meaning of "gums of glutinous heat" in *Comus* 917. Offers a sexual interpretation. See also Edward Le Comte's reply (No. 770) and Shawcross's rejoinder, *MiltonQ*, 8, 1974, 56–57. See also Nos. 1180 and 1243.

1721 Sheidley, William E. "*Lycidas*: An Early Elizabethan Analogue by George Turbervile." *MP*, 69, 1972, 228–30.

Compares *Lycidas* and Turbervile's "Epitaph on the Death of Maister Arthur Brooke drowned in passing to New Hauen" (c. 1565).

1722 Sherry, Beverley. "Milton's 'Mystic Nativity.'" *MiltonQ*, 17, 1983, 108–16.

Believes that Milton's *Nativity Ode* and Sandro Botticelli's *Mystic Nativity* share a conceptual and prophetic quality. Furthermore, both works "conceive the Nativity as peace come down from heaven to earth at the First Coming and implied in this, despite suffering to come, the peace of the Second Coming." Both "'see' the Nativity existing mysteriously at a point in time and in all time and beyond," both claim "the defeat of Satan," and both carry "a sombre undertone."

1723 Shimizu, Hiroshi. "*Aminta* and *Comus*: A Comparative Study." *MCJ News*, 3, 1979, 32.

Abstract of a paper presented at the Sixth Colloquium of MCJ in December, 1978. Shows several parallels between Tasso's *Aminta* and Milton's *Comus*.

1724 Shinskey, Clare M. "*Lycidas*: Milton's Doric Song." *N&Q*, 28, 1981, 202–05.

On the "Doric lay" of *Lycidas* 189. Believes that Milton translates the pagan definition of the Dorian mode into Christian terms.

1725 Shullenberger, William. "Christ as Metaphor: Figural Instruction in Milton's Nativity Ode." *NDEJ*, 14, 1981, 41–58.

Examines the meaning of Incarnation and investigates its nature "as an idea about language, for Incarnation appears in the Nativity Ode to be a figure for the properly figurative power of language itself."

1726 Shullenberger, William A. "The Power of the Copula in Milton's Sonnet VII." *MiltonS*, 15, 1981, 201–12.

Notes that, to a biblically educated poet, Yahweh is associated with being and that "God's structuring presence is marked by the appearance and the varied reiteration of the copula which organizes the poem's [Sonnet 7's ('How soon hath Time')] sestet, its final and confirmatory utterance."

1727 Shumaker, Wayne. "W. K. Thomas on 'Mouths and Eyes in *Lycidas*.'" *MiltonQ*, 10, 1976, 6–7.

Questions W. K. Thomas's critical methods (No. 1775) for "going outside *Lycidas* to interpret a passage that is clear enough on its face."

1728 Simons, Louise. "'And Heaven Gates ore My Head': Death as Threshold in Milton's Masque." *MiltonS*, 23, 1987, 53–96.

Argues that in *Comus* the Lady's terrestrial journey to her father's residence foreshadows a celestial journey after death when she will be reunited with all her family. Thus death serves as a threshold or "release from terrestrial containment."

1729 Sims, James H. "Perdita's Flowers o' th' Spring and Vernal Flowers in *Lycidas*." *SQ*, 22, 1971, 87–90.

Discusses the flower passages as contrasting elements that emphasize the darker elements of Shakespeare's *Winter's Tale* and Milton's elegy. Rejoinder by Irene Dash, *SQ*, 23, 1972, 125; surrejoinder by Sims, p. 125.

1730 Skulsky, Harold. "Milton's Enrichment of Latin Love Elegy." *Acta Conventus Neo-Latini Lovaniensis: Proceedings of the First International Congress of Neo-Latin Studies.* Ed. by Jozef Ijsewijn and Eckhard Kessler (München: Leuven Univ. Press, 1973), pp. 603–11.

Discusses Milton's use of the pagan deities to act out the coming of spring in *Elegy 5*.

1731 Sledge, Linda Ching. *Shivering Babe, Victorious Lord: The Nativity in Poetry and Art.* Grand Rapids, MI: Wm. B. Eerdmans Publishing Co., 1981. x, 189pp.

Believes that the *Nativity Ode* reshaped the tradition of English Nativity poetry. Prints the poem, pp. 100–09.

1732 Sleeth, Charles R., and others. "Some Milton Questions." *TLS*, Oct. 2, 1970, p. 1137.

Contends that Neaera's hair in *Lycidas* 69 is pubic hair. Peyton Houston comments on the syntax in the elegy. J. Max Patrick discusses the use of the word "mewing" in *Areopagitica*.

1733 Smart, Alastair. "Milton's 'Talent.'" *TLS*, Jan. 25, 1974, p. 81; and Feb. 8, 1974, p. 134.

Refutes John Sparrow's thesis (No. 1739) that Milton's Sonnet 19 ("When I consider") has a sexual reference and connotation. See also David Knowles, Feb. 1, 1974, p. 108.

1734 Smith, Alan R. "Milton's 'Two-Handed Engine' and the Last Judgment." *AN&Q*, 20, 1981, 43–45.

Suggests that since Milton expected the Last Judgment to occur during his lifetime and since it "cannot be divorced from its place in God's divine plan," it "will end the reign of evil shepherds who supplanted Lycidas."

1735 Smith, Eric. "Milton—*Lycidas*." *By Mourning Tongues: Studies in English*

Elegy (Ipswich: Boydell Press; Totowa, NJ: Rowman and Littlefield, 1977), pp. 22–39.

"I think it must be felt that the poems after *Lycidas* draw on *Lycidas* and with it are part of an unbroken stream of poetry linking pastoral or 'nature' with elegy."

1736 Smith, George William, Jr. "Milton's Method of Mistakes in the Nativity Ode." *SEL*, 18, 1978, 107–23.

Argues that Milton uses the contrastive rhetoric of error as he celebrates "Christ's Nativity by describing a series of mistakes: mistaken attributions of Christ's role or his divinity to various propitious appearances and mistaken expectations of a more conspicuous alteration that has occurred." Abs., *MiltonQ*, 13, 1979, 63.

1737 Smith, George William, Jr. "Milton's Revisions and the Design of *Comus*." *ELH*, 46, 1979, 56–80.

Believes that Milton's major revisions give the debate more balance and that he deliberately leaves the issue unresolved. Abs., *SCN*, 38, 1980, 21.

1738 Snyder, Susan. "Nature, History, and the Waters of *Lycidas*." *HLQ*, 50, 1987, 323–35.

Discusses the aspects of *Lycidas* that make it a pastoral elegy, focusing on Lycidas's character.

1739 Sparrow, John. "Milton's 'Talent which is Death To Hide.'" *TLS*, Jan. 18, 1974, p. 54.

Claims that Sonnet 19 ("When I consider") refers to Milton's frustration over his sexual inadequacies. See Alastair Smart's response (No. 1733). See also Helen Gardner, Feb. 1, 1974, p. 108 and John Holloway, Mar. 1, 1974, p. 212.

1740 Spitzer, Leo. "On the Sonnet, 'Methought I Saw My Late Espoused Saint.'" *On Milton's Poetry: A Selection of Modern Studies*. Ed. by Arnold Stein (Greenwich, CT: Fawcett Publications, 1970), pp. 74–77.

Reprint of Huckabay No. 2740, originally published in 1951.

1741 Steadman, John M. "Iconography and Renaissance Drama: Ethical and Mythological Themes." *Research Opportunities in Renaissance Drama*, 13–14, 1970–71, 73–122. Revised in *Nature into Myth: Medieval and Renaissance Moral Symbols*. Duquesne Studies, Language and Literature Series, vol. 1 (Pittsburgh, PA: Duquesne Univ. Press, 1979), pp. 213–40.

Uses the mythographers and the lexicographers to trace the Comus tradition from Philostratus to the seventeenth century. Shows that "Milton's Comus betrays his Dionysian as well as his Circean ancestry" and that Milton undercuts the tradition.

1742 Stein, Arnold. *The House of Death: Messages from the English Renaissance*. Baltimore, MD: Johns Hopkins Univ. Press, 1986. xiii, 300pp.

Mentions Milton's treatment of death in *Lycidas*.

1743 Stevens, Paul. "Magic Structures: Comus and the Illusions of Fancy." *MiltonQ*, 17, 1983, 84–89.

Believes that Comus's language is the primary instrument of illusion. But Milton's language "imitates the operation of reason checking fancy by counterpoising Comus's appeal to visualization with a simultaneous appeal to analysis."

1744 Stevenson, Kay. "Inigo Jones' 'Glory' in Poems by Milton and Shirley." *MiltonQ*, 13, 1979, 46.

Suggests that Milton uses the word "glory," meaning "halo," in the 1673 version of the *Nativity Ode* because he was familiar with a stage design that Jones made for *Tempe Restored*.

1745 Stith, Joyce. "The Two-Handed Engine: A Personal Interpretation." *MiltonQ*, 18, 1984, 61–62.

Asserts that the two-handed engine in *Lycidas* refers to "Saint Peter, who, acting as God's agent, administers eternal reward or punishment."

Seventeenth-century definitions of "engine" show that the line would refer to a person rather than a mechanical object.

1746 Stollman, Samuel S. "Analogues and Sources for Milton's 'Great Task-Master.'" *MiltonQ*, 6, No. 2, 1972, 27–32.

Suggests the Hebrew tractate *Aboth* as a source for key material in Sonnet 7 ("How soon hath Time").

1747 Stone, C. F., III. "Milton's Self-Concerns and Manuscript Revisions in *Lycidas*." *MLN*, 83, 1968, 867–81.

Argues that *Lycidas* is a metaphor for "Milton's ability to shape and maintain a fiction in the presence of . . . problems." Focuses on the Orpheus passage and the flower passage.

1748 Stringer, Gary. "A Jot and Tittle More on Milton's 'How Soon Hath Time' and the *Letter to a Friend*." *SCN*, 36, 1978, 9–10.

Links the image of time as a thief to biblical origins in both Sonnet 7 and the *Letter to a Friend*. Abs., *MiltonQ*, 13, 1979, 63–64.

1749 Stringer, Gary A. "Milton's 'Thorn in the Flesh': Pauline Didacticism in Sonnet XIX." *MiltonS*, 10, 1977, 141–54.

Suggests that Sonnet 19 ("When I consider") is narrative, not lyric, and that Milton probably identified himself with Paul as a fellow sufferer. Abs., *MiltonQ*, 12, 1978, 156–57.

1750 Stringer, Gary. "The Unity of *L'Allegro* and *Il Penseroso*." *TSLL*, 12, 1970, 221–29.

"Specifically, I wish to show that *L'Allegro* portrays a young man who loves Mirth and that *Il Penseroso* concerns an older man who has come to prefer Melancholy." Sees mirth and melancholy as complementary, not contradictory.

1751 Stroup, Thomas B. "Dido, the Phoenix, and Milton's Sonnet XVIII." *MiltonQ*, 4, 1970, 57–60.

Suggests multiple associations and allusions in Sonnet 18 ("On the Late Massacre in Piemont"), including Dido's prayer and immolation in the *Aeneid* and Marlowe's Dido and Aeneas. Proposes that Milton fused these associations with the Cadmus myth, the phoenix myth, the parable of the sower, and one of Tertullian's aphorisms.

1752 Stroup, Thomas B. "'When I Consider': Milton's Sonnet XIX." *SP*, 69, 1972, 242–58.

Concludes that, in Sonnet 19 ("When I consider"), Milton "asserts Eternal Providence and justifies God's ways to men in so far as . . . infinite ways can be justified . . . to such finite beings."

1753 Stull, William Leonard. "The English Religious Sonnet from Wyatt to Milton." Doctoral diss., Univ. of California, Los Angeles, 1978. 417pp. Abs., *DAI*, 39, 1978, 2961A.

Explores the forms, rhetoric, and devotion themes used in religious sonnets between 1530 and 1660, including Milton's.

1754 Stull, William L. "Sacred Sonnets in Three Styles." *SP*, 79, 1982, 78–99.

Traces the English sonnet's development from Sir Thomas Wyatt to Ben Jonson, John Donne, and Milton. Shows that Milton models his heroic sonnets on those of Pietro Bembo, Torquato Tasso, and Giovanni della Casa. They are written in all three of the classical styles to great men and about significant contemporary events.

1755 Stull, William L. "'Why are Not *Sonnets* Made of Thee?': A New Context for the 'Holy Sonnets' of Donne, Herbert, and Milton." *MP*, 80, 1982, 129–35.

Presents "an alternative account of the background for the 'Holy Sonnets' of Donne, Herbert, and Milton, one that reveals the religious sonnet's steady development over the entire Renaissance period."

1756 Sullivan, Edward E., Jr. "Romans

16:18 and St. Peter's Speech in *Lycidas*." *N&Q*, 22, 1975, 542–43.

Points out "close correspondences in sense, phrasing and context" between the passages and suggests that Milton used the Bible as a source for St. Peter's speech. Abs., *MiltonQ*, 12, 1978, 114.

1757 Sullivan, Edward E., Jr. "'Sweet Societies That Sing': The Voice of the Saints in *Lycidas*." *ELWIU*, 3, 1976, 32–40.

Shows that in the framework of revelatory speeches "the climactic celebration of Lycidas' apotheosis is explicitly sung by the heavenly choir of angels and saints." Abs., *MiltonQ*, 10, 1976, 99.

1758 Suzuki, Shigeo. "A Three-Step Study of Milton's *Comus*." *SES*, 3, 1978, 99–112.

In Japanese. Surveys the transition in criticism about *Comus* from the 1940s to the 1970s. The three stages have to do with the masque's mysteries, as discussed by Alice-Lyle Scoufos (No. 1708), and with changes in the text caused by the Castlehaven scandal.

1759 Swaim, Kathleen M. "Allegorical Poetry in Milton's Ludlow Mask." *MiltonS*, 16, 1982, 167–99.

Considers the allegory and poetry in *Comus* to be matters of setting, character, structure, and theme and shows how Milton combines these elements to make a Christian statement.

1760 Swaim, Kathleen M. "Cycle and Circle: Time and Structure in *L'Allegro* and *Il Penseroso*." *TSLL*, 18, 1976, 422–32.

Explains that "diurnal imagery includes sunlight, moonlight, and starlight" and explores the poems' time categories. Reassesses the "structural design as essentially circular." Abs., *MiltonQ*, 12, 1978, 114–15.

1761 Swaim, Kathleen M. "'Heart-Easing Mirth': *L'Allegro*'s Inheritance of *Faerie Queene* II." *SP*, 82, 1985, 460–76.

Argues that Mirth in *L'Allegro* is a

"reshaping" of Phaedria in Spenser's *Faerie Queene* 2. Concludes that Milton is able "to ingest his predecessors while retaining or reinforcing his distinctness from them."

1762 Swaim, Kathleen M. "*Lycidas* and the Dolphins of Apollo." *JEGP*, 72, 1973, 340–49.

Examines the recurring motif of Apollo in *Lycidas* and analyzes the related image of the dolphins in line 164.

1763 Swaim, Kathleen M. "'Mighty Pan': Tradition and an Image in Milton's Nativity *Hymn*." *SP*, 68, 1971, 484–95.

Discusses the rationale behind Milton's use of Pan rather than other pagan deities. Concludes that Pan embodies "such aspects of deity as love, shepherding, and *all*-ness, and with the coming of . . . grace the traits Pan shares with Christ are redefined and Pan's nature transformed and newly perceived."

1764 Swaim, Kathleen M. "Milton and Transcendental Form." *Mosaic*, 5, 1972, 191–95.

Review essay that discusses Angus Fletcher's *The Transcendental Masque* (No. 1358) as "a remarkable and admirable production" that nevertheless has "problems with organization, proportions, and fully persuasive argument."

1765 Swaim, Kathleen M. "An Ovidian Analogue for *Comus*." *MiltonQ*, 9, 1975, 14–17.

Suggests several parallels between *Comus* and Ovid's version of the Picus-Canens-Circe tale.

1766 Swaim, Kathleen M. "'The Pilot of the Galilean Lake' in *Lycidas*." *MiltonQ*, 17, 1983, 42–45.

Asserts that the pilot is St. Peter. Believes further that a careful geographic study of the Sea of Galilee and the accompanying water imagery in the poem will provide a fuller understanding of *Lycidas*.

1767 Swaim, Kathleen M. "Retributive

Justice in *Lycidas*: The Two-Handed Engine." *MiltonS*, 2, 1970, 119–29.

"In brief, it is my contention that in the 'two-handed engine' Milton is conflating two images employed earlier in the poem—'th' abhorred shears' of Atropos and St. Peter's two keys." See Nos. 1355 and 1511.

1768 Swiss, Margo. "Crisis of Conscience: A Theological Context for Milton's 'How Soon Hath Time.'" *MiltonQ*, 20, 1986, 98–103.

Describes Sonnet 7 ("How soon hath Time") and the *Letter to a Friend* as Milton's attempts to justify his delay in vocational direction, a delay that he attributes to divine will.

1769 Taaffe, James G. "*Lycidas*—Line 192." *MiltonQ*, 6, No. 2, 1972, 36–38.

Suggests that the line—"At last he rose, and twitch't his Mantle blue"—alludes to 1 Kings 19.19–21 and 2 Kings 2.13–15, which describe the passing of Elijah's prophetic mantle to Elisha, his chosen successor.

1770 Taaffe, James G. "Michaelmas, the 'Lawless Hour,' and the Occasion of Milton's *Comus*." *ELN*, 6, 1969, 257–62.

Concludes that Milton "has taken three of the literal matters with which Michaelmas is concerned—its celebration of secular government, its remembrance of man's correspondent guardians in heaven, and its period of misrule and disorder—and he has shaped his materials by concentrating upon the symbolic significance of each." Abs., *MiltonN*, 3, 1969, 63–64.

1771 Takeda, Kiyoshi. "*Comus* in a Typological Perspective." *MCJ News*, 8, 1985, 4–7.

Interprets haemony as a symbol of the eucharist. Believes that the Epilogue's emblematic figures give full meaning to the earlier images, thus translating all that happens in the masque.

1772 Takeda, Kiyoshi. "Typological Progress of the Soul in *Comus*." *MCJ News*, 2, 1978, 13–14.

Abstract of paper presented. Sees Christian typology as the key to the spiritual movement of *Comus*. Abs., *MiltonQ*, 13, 1979, 161.

1773 Tamaki, Ishitaro. "Milton's Sonnet XX." *MCJ News*, 1, 1976, 4–5.

Abstract of a paper presented at the First Annual Conference of MCJ in July, 1975. On the meaning of "spare" in line 13 of Sonnet 20 (to Henry Lawrence).

1774 Tayler, Edward W. "*Lycidas* Yet Once More." *HLQ*, 41, 1978, 103–17. Reprinted in *Milton's Poetry: Its Development in Time*. Duquesne Studies, Language and Literature Series, vol. 2 (Pittsburgh, PA: Duquesne Univ. Press, 1979), pp. 45–59.

Argues for the suitability of the pastoral for *Lycidas*. "In using the pastoral as a standard from which to depart significantly, Milton reanimates the Christian commonplace that is the consolation for the loss of Lycidas." Abs., *MiltonQ*, 13, 1979, 62.

1775 Thomas, W. K. "Mouths and Eyes in *Lycidas*." *MiltonQ*, 9, 1975, 39–42.

In *Lycidas* 114–21 and 138–40, "Blind mouths" refers to rhetoricians who are spiritually blind, and the "sucking eyes" passage refers to flowers which draw moisture. Reply by Wayne Shumaker (No. 1727).

1776 Tillyard, E. M. W. "The Action of *Comus*." "*A Maske at Ludlow*": *Essays on Milton's "Comus.*" Ed. by John S. Diekhoff (Ann Arbor, MI: Univ. Microfilms International, 1980 Books on Demand Reprints), pp. 43–57.

Reprint of Huckabay No. 2773, originally published in 1942.

1777 Tillyard, E. M. W. *Milton's "L'Allegro" and "Il Penseroso.*" Folcroft, PA: Folcroft Library Editions, 1970.

Reprint of Huckabay No. 2774, originally published in 1932.

1778 Tobin, J. J. M. "*Metamorphoses* XI: An Influence on Milton's *Ad Patrem*." *N&Q*, 24, 1977, 206.

Asserts that Milton used Sandys's 1632 translation of Ovid's *Metamorphoses* and that *Ad Patrem* was composed in the middle of 1632. Abs., *MiltonQ*, 11, 1977, 121.

1779 Toliver, Harold E. "Milton: Platonic Levels and Christian Transformation." *Pastoral Forms and Attitudes* (Berkeley, Los Angeles, and London: Univ. of California Press, 1971), pp. 151–76.

Interprets *Comus* in Platonic terms. Although it "predicts the temptations and contests to which later Miltonic protagonists are subjected, it obviously does not have the same Christ-centered means of epiphany nor is its trial . . . as severe as Adam's exile from paradise." Sees *Lycidas* as a fusion of the Christian, heroic, and pastoral modes.

1780 Traister, Barbara Howard. "Heavenly Necromancy: The Figure of the Magician in Tudor and Stuart Drama." Doctoral diss., Yale Univ., 1973. 340pp. Abs., *DAI*, 34, 1973, 3438A.

Explains the magician figure's varied presentation as a nonhuman stereotype and a complex being torn between vaulting ambition and mortal limitations in Tudor plays and Stuart masques, including *Comus*.

1781 Treip, Mindele Anne. "*Comus* as 'Progress.'" *MiltonQ*, 20, 1986, 1–13.

Explores the play's "artistic structuring, its literary precedents, and the special circumstances at Ludlow, and also in the text itself, particulars of the masque's descriptions and language."

1782 Tromly, Frederic B. "Milton Responds to Donne: 'On Time' and 'Death be Not Proud.'" *MP*, 80, 1983, 390–93.

Argues that Milton's "On Time" was a response to Donne's "Death be Not Proud." Milton's persona resolves to face death "without fear or even regret," whereas Donne's persona "becomes progressively more uneasy and more vulnerable."

1783 Tromly, Frederic B. "Milton's 'Pre-

posterous Exaction': The Significance of 'The Passion.'" *ELH*, 47, 1980, 276–86.

Discusses the "Passion" as a failure resulting from Milton's immaturity and observes that he "tacitly diagnoses" this failure in *Of Education*, when he refers to the "preposterous exaction" of schoolmasters attempting to force immature minds to produce mature works. Analyzes *Lycidas* as a companion poem in which the more mature Milton "dramatizes the achievement of the understanding which eluded him in 'The Passion.'"

1784 Tsuji, Hiroko. "From *Prolusions* to *L'Allegro* and *Il Penseroso*." *Asphodel*, 18, 1984, 36–60.

Uses rhetorical elements and parallel imagery to demonstrate that the companion poems are in a line of development beginning with Milton's *Prolusions*.

1785 Tung, Mason. "Milton's Adaptation in *In Quintum Novembris* of Virgil's *Fama*." *MiltonQ*, 12, 1978, 90–95.

Shows that Milton's account of Rumor is Virgilian and discusses his skillful adaptation of passages from the *Aeneid*.

1786 Turlington, Bayly. "Milton's *Lycidas* and Horace's *Odes*, I.7." *TPB*, 6, No. 1, 1969, 2–12.

Shows that Horace's story of Teucer's banishment and travels influenced Milton's depiction of Edward King's death and heavenly bliss.

1787 Turner, Alberta T. "Milton and the Convention of the Academic Miscellanies." *YES*, 5, 1975, 86–93.

On Milton's contribution of *Lycidas* to *Justa Edovardo King Naufrago*. "The importance of the miscellany convention to Milton is that it formed part of the larger educational convention without which he would probably never have become a poet." Abs., *MiltonQ*, 12, 1978, 115.

1788 Turner, Alberta. "The Sound of Grief: A Reconsideration of the Nature and

Function of the Unrhymed Lines in *Lycidas.*" *MiltonQ*, 10, 1976, 67–73.

Concludes that *Lycidas* contains slant rhymes, but no truly unrhymed lines, and that these are a device to sustain the emotion of grief.

1789 Turner, W. Arthur. "The Quest of the Mysterious Engine." *MiltonQ*, 13, 1979, 17–20.

Reviews recent interpretations of the two-handed engine in *Lycidas*, admits that nobody has proved anything, and restates his earlier position (Huckabay No. 2779) that the engine is the lock on the door of heaven.

1790 Tuve, Rosemond. "Image, Form, and Theme in *A Mask.*" *"A Maske at Ludlow":* *Essays on Milton's "Comus."* Ed. by John S. Diekhoff (Ann Arbor, MI: Univ. Microfilms International, 1980 Books on Demand Reprints), pp. 126–64.

Reprint of one essay from Huckabay No. 2780, originally published in 1957.

1791 Tuve, Rosemond. "Theme, Pattern, and Imagery in *Lycidas.*" *On Milton's Poetry: A Selection of Modern Studies.* Ed. by Arnold Stein (Greenwich, CT: Fawcett Publications, 1970), pp. 60–73.

Reprint of part of one essay from Huckabay No. 2780, originally published in 1957.

1792 Ulreich, John C., Jr. "'And by Occasion Foretells': The Prophetic Voice in *Lycidas.*" *MiltonS*, 18, 1983, 3–23.

Emphasizes the poem's passage about St. Peter, particularly its prophetic strain.

1793 Ulreich, John C., Jr. "'A Bright Golden Flow'r': Haemony as a Symbol of Transformation." *SEL*, 17, 1977, 119–28.

States that haemony is an image of "spiritual growth." Asserts that the change in haemony is a symbolic transubstantiation present in human redemption (or "transplantation in Christ"). Haemony is "the symbol of a symbol, a *type* of atonement." Abs., *MiltonQ*, 12, 1978, 115.

1794 Ulreich, John C. "Typological Symbolism in Milton's Sonnet XXIII." *MiltonQ*, 8, 1974, 7–10.

Finds four typological levels and shows that lines 5–6 of Sonnet 23 ("Methought I saw") provide a valid starting point for a thorough explication.

1795 Vance, John A. "The Dating of Milton's Sonnet XV." *AN&Q*, 20, 1981, 45–46.

Milton wrote Sonnet 15 (to Fairfax) between June 14 and July 8, 1648, soon after hearing of Fairfax's stranglehold around Colchester.

1796 Vance, John A. "God's Advocate and His Pupils: Milton's Sonnets to Lawrence and Skinner." *SAB*, 42, No. 4, 1977, 31–40.

Holds that Sonnets 20 (to Henry Lawrence), 21 ("Cyriack, whose Grandsire"), and 22 ("Cyriack, this three years' day") comprise a trilogy whose concern is theological, as Milton gives spiritual advice to Lawrence and Skinner.

1797 Vance, John A. "The Sestet of Milton's Sonnet VIII." *MiltonQ*, 13, 1979, 48–49.

Disagrees with William Riley Parker (see No. 230) and others who find Sonnet 8 ("Captain or Colonel") humorous and ironic. Argues that the sestet shows Milton's serious concern for his own security and that of his property during the royalist uprising in 1642.

1798 Van den Berg, Sara. "Describing Sonnets by Milton and Keats: Roy Schafer's Action Language and the Interpretation of Texts." *Psychological Perspectives on Literature: Freudian Dissidents and Non-Freudians: A Casebook.* Ed. by Joseph Natoli (Hamden, CT: Shoe String Press, 1984), pp. 134–54.

Considers Milton's Sonnet 19 ("When I consider") and a sonnet by Keats ("When I have fears") in psychological terms. "Each poem is a process of revision: the poet redefines himself, changing his sense of what it means to 'stand' in his own time and place . . . to express his idea of his life."

1799 Van Sickle, Judy Lynn. "Song as Structure and Symbol in Four Poems of John Milton." Doctoral diss., Brown Univ., 1981. 296pp. Abs., *DAI*, 43, 1982, 456A–57A.

Argues that "John Milton makes use of song genres and musical structures in much more technically and formally precise ways that either Miltonists or music historians have hitherto appreciated."

1800 Varney, Andrew. "Milton's 'Uncouth Swain.'" *N&Q*, 29, 1982, 24–26.

Argues that "uncouth" in *Lycidas* 186 was intended to mean "lonely." Cites excerpts from Pepys's *Diary* (May 26, 1660) and Pope's *Rape of the Lock* to support this unusual usage.

1801 Via, John A. "Milton's 'The Passion': A Successful Failure." *MiltonQ*, 5, 1971, 35–38.

Argues that Milton included the "Passion" in the 1645 and 1673 editions of his shorter poems because it is "a successful failure that comments ironically on the experience of the regenerate man and the experience of the poet," two major thematic concerns of his verse and prose.

1802 Via, John A. "The Rhythm of Regenerate Experience: *L'Allegro* and *Il Penseroso*." *RenP*, 1969, pp. 47–55.

Holds that the poems "show the broad, rhythmic sweep of human experience, active and contemplative," in which the regenerate person can and should be involved.

1803 Viswanathan, S. "'In Sage and Solemn Tunes': Variants of Orphicism in Milton's Early Poetry." *NM*, 76, 1975, 457–72.

Outlines the evolution of Orphicism from the Greeks to the Renaissance and applies it to Milton's early poetry, especially *Il Penseroso*. Abs., *MiltonQ*, 13, 1979, 29–30.

1804 Viswanathan, S. "'That Two–Handed Engine,' Yet Once More." *Archiv*, 217, 1980, 108–11.

Believes that the Apocalypse influenced Milton, though he did not literally believe in its prophecies.

1805 Volpi, Angiola Maria. "*Pellegrina Bellezza*: Recherche du 'Peregrino' et Nostalgie Épique dans la Poésie Italienne du Jeune Milton." *Prélude au Matin d'un Poète: "Such Sights as Youthful Poets Dream": Traditions Humanistes chez le Jeune Milton*. Introduction by Olivier Lutaud (Paris: Centre d'Histoire des Idées dans les Iles Britanniques, Université de Paris IV, Sorbonne, 1983), pp. 17–32.

Examines the relationship between Milton's Italian poems and contemporary Italian poetry: sources, phrasing, irony, an interest in epic poetry, and the mysterious brown-haired lady.

1806 Wain, John. "Reflections on the First Night of *Comus*." *Encounter*, 48, 1977, 33–42.

Portrays "the first night of *Comus*, to see it as Yeats might have seen it, and as we see it now," as "a rich theme for meditation."

1807 Wall, Kathleen. "*A Mask Presented at Ludlow Castle*: The Armor of Logos." *Milton and the Idea of Woman*. Ed. by Julia M. Walker (Urbana and Chicago: Univ. of Illinois Press, 1988), pp. 52–65.

Believes that Milton derives both the plot and the concept of *Comus* from several mythological figures, such as Callisto, Zeus, Atalanta, and Cupid and Psyche. However, he transforms the Lady into "a receptacle of patriarchal virtues." Abs., *MiltonQ*, 24, 1990, 151–52.

1808 Weiland, Kurt F. "Michaelmas and Milton's Ludlow *Maske*: The Influence of the Christian Services." *MSE*, 10, 1986, 197–206.

Notes verbal and thematic echoes of the Michaelmas church service liturgy in *Comus*, a connection that places

Milton's masque in perspective as just one of the day's many events. Likewise, the sections of liturgy used by Milton indicate that *Comus* was presented before the evening service. The connection also demonstrates the young Milton's Christian faith.

1809 Weitzman, Arthur J. "The 'Babylonian Wo' of Milton's Piedmontese Sonnet." *MiltonN*, 3, 1969, 55–57.

Points out that Milton's reference in Sonnet 18 ("On the Late Massacre in Piemont") goes beyond the image of Babylon from the Bible and Puritan polemics. Suggests that Milton must have been aware of Babylon's symbolic importance within the Christian tradition, especially as Augustine developed it, and believes that the sonnet reflects this tradition.

1810 Welch, Dennis M. "Theme and Form in *Comus* and *Lycidas*." *Cithara*, 12, 1972, 74–84.

Describes Milton's "understanding of poetry as manifested in his masque and elegy."

1811 Wells, Claude Everett, Jr. "Sacramental Figuration and Milton's *Lycidas*." Doctoral diss., Purdue Univ., 1975. 193pp. Abs., *DAI*, 36, 1976, 6717A–18A.

Reveals Milton's use of sacramental figuration, in which poetic figures "convey the anagogical form that engenders and structures" a poem, as he creates "two narrational stances" in *Lycidas*.

1812 Wentersdorf, Karl P. "Allusion and Theme in the Third Movement of Milton's *Lycidas*." *MP*, 83, 1986, 275–79.

Studies the allusions "to the love of Alpheus for Arethusa, to the amorous element in the pastoral literary tradition believed to have been started by Theocritus, and to the amorous desires commonly attributed to and associated with dolphins [which] combine to reinforce the symbolic implications of the various flowers envisioned by Milton as being cast upon the imaginary hearse of the drowned young pastor."

1813 Wentersdorf, Karl P. "Images of 'Licence' in Milton's Sonnet XII." *MiltonQ*, 13, 1979, 36–42.

The "Owls and Cuckoos, Asses, Apes and Dogs" of Sonnet 12 ("I did but prompt") are Milton's detractors and images of moral turpitude. Milton uses the myth of Latona to point to their lack of wisdom in criticizing him for writing the divorce pamphlets.

1814 Wentersdorf, Karl P. "The 'Rout of Monsters' in *Comus*." *MiltonQ*, 12, 1978, 119–25.

In transforming the animals into images of sensuality, Milton was influenced by post-Homeric treatments of the Circe legend.

1815 Wentersdorf, Karl P. "The Thematic Significance of the Flower Catalogue in Milton's *Lycidas*." *ELH*, 47, 1980, 500–19.

Suggests that the flowers in the catalog are used primarily as symbols of romantic love or its potential and that the poem's third movement may, therefore, serve as a lament for Edward King's loss of "potential as a shepherd-lover."

1816 West, Michael. "*The Consolatio* in Milton's Funeral Elegies." *HLQ*, 34, 1971, 233–49.

Examines Milton's harmonizing of Christian and classical influences, particularly in his formal funeral elegies.

1817 White, Gail Lana. "Pastoral Plays and Masques of Shakespeare, Jonson, Milton." Doctoral diss., Univ. of California, Irvine, 1973. 353pp. Abs., *DAI*, 34, 1974, 7725A.

Analyzes the relationship of art and nature in Jonson's pastoral masques, Milton's *Comus*, and Shakespeare's *Winter's Tale* and *Tempest* as they combine the pastoral and masque genres.

1818 Whitehead, Louis Edward. "A Critical Study of Milton's Latin Elegies." Doctoral diss., Florida State Univ., 1976. 119pp. Abs., *DAI*, 37, 1977, 7769A–70A.

Sees in Milton's Latin elegies the poet's growing ability to relate form and content, use effective language, prepare to write later literary works, and infuse "life into a poem."

1819 Wilcher, Robert. "Milton's Masque: Occasion, Form and Meaning." *CritQ*, 20, No. 1, 1978, 3–20.

Finds that *Comus* is "an experiment, prompted by the unique opportunity offered by its occasion, in bringing together in a unified work of art the form of the aristocratic entertainment, the form of the academic disputation and a moral theme suited to both."

1820 Wilcox, Joel F. " 'Spending the Light': Milton and Homer's Light of Hope." *MiltonQ*, 18, 1984, 77–78.

Believes that Milton uses light in Sonnet 19 ("When I consider") in much the same way as Homer does in the *Iliad*, as "a 'gleam of hope' or a 'light of salvation.'" Milton thus becomes "a Christian Achilles whose inactivity is not tragic but is made to serve the purpose of a saving God."

1821 Wilding, Michael. "Milton's *A Masque Presented at Ludlow Castle, 1634*: Theatre and Politics on the Border." *Trivium*, 20, 1985, 147–79. Reprinted in *MiltonQ*, 21, No. 4, 1987, 35–51; revised in *Dragons Teeth: Literature in the English Revolution* (Oxford: Clarendon Press, 1987), pp. 28–88.

Discusses the political situation along the English-Welsh border at the time of the first production of *Comus*. Believes that Milton obliquely criticizes his noble patron, along with his aristocratic qualities.

1822 Wilkenfeld, Roger B. "The Seat at the Center: An Interpretation of *Comus*." *Critical Essays on Milton from "ELH"* (Baltimore, MD, and London: Johns Hopkins Press, 1969), pp. 123–50.

Reprint of Huckabay No. 2803, originally published in 1966.

1823 Williams, George Walton. "Milton's

L'Allegro, 135–36." *Expl*, 34, 1975, Item 15.

Suggests that the "*Lydian* Airs" were devised against "excessive cares and weariness of the spirit"; they refresh with relaxation and strengthen with delight.

1824 Williams, R. Darby. "Two Baroque Game Poems on Grace: Herbert's 'Paradise' and Milton's 'On Time.'" *Criticism*, 12, 1970, 180–94.

Proposes that the form of "On Time" succeeds because of the oblique reference to a clockwise motion that represents stages of grace.

1825 Williamson, Marilyn L. "The Myth of Orpheus in *L'Allegro* and *Il Penseroso*." *MLQ*, 32, 1971, 377–86.

Holds that the companion poems "represent complementary rather than competing values" and that Milton uses the Orpheus story as a point of transition between the poems.

1826 Williamson, Marilyn L. "A Reading of Milton's Twenty-Third Sonnet." *MiltonS*, 4, 1972, 141–49.

Sonnet 23 ("Methought I saw") is "structured on a progressive definition of salvation from death and of the human condition in this world. It contains a rising movement from physical salvation, according to the Alcestis legend, to ritualistic salvation, according to the Old Dispensation, to true Christian salvation, in which the saint is bride of the Lamb."

1827 Wilson, Gayle Edward. "Decorum and Milton's 'An Epitaph on the Marchioness of Winchester.'" *MiltonQ*, 8, 1974, 11–14.

Examines the poem in terms of genre, topoi, and style appropriate to the occasion. Shows how Milton makes the topos of descent the poem's unifying theme.

1828 Wilson, Gayle Edward. "Milton's Praise of 'A Fair Infant.'" *MiltonQ*, 22, 1988, 3–7.

Demonstrates how Milton follows the classical conventions of oration in "On the Death of a Fair Infant."

1829 Winter, June. "The Two-Handed Engine and the Fatal Bellman: *Lycidas* and *Macbeth*." *N&Q*, 26, 1979, 126–28.

Suggests that Milton's passage about the corrupt clergy in *Lycidas* 108–31 invokes Shakespeare's imagery of corruption and the Last Judgment in *Macbeth*. "Shakespeare's 'fatal bellman' became Milton's 'two-handed engine.'"

1830 Winter, Keith. "A Comprehensive Approach to *Lycidas*." *RS*, 36, 1968, 237–44.

Presents five approaches to *Lycidas* and shows how all have failed in important ways. Sees the poem as the consummation of a long tradition.

1831 Witte, Stephen Paul. "The Typological Tradition and *Beowulf*, the York Cycle, and Milton's Nativity Ode." Doctoral diss., Oklahoma State Univ., 1977. 270pp. Abs., *DAI*, 38, 1978, 5503A.

Weakens "the 'allegorical' approach to early Christian literature" by arguing that the church fathers believed biblical passages contained literal truth and "typological import," thereby influencing Christian writers.

1832 Wittreich, Joseph. "From Pastoral to Prophecy: The Genres of *Lycidas*." *MiltonS*, 13, 1979, 59–80.

Shows that *Lycidas* is a triumph of the imagination, involving the transcendence and transformation of the pastoral, the prophetic, and the epic forms.

1833 Wittreich, Joseph Anthony, Jr. "Milton's 'Destin'd Urn': The Art of *Lycidas*." *PMLA*, 84, 1969, 60–70.

Lycidas has "a formal, *circular* pattern carefully articulated by the poem's rhyme scheme . . . that, in its elusive regularity, supports the presiding themes of Milton's elegy." Through the rhyme scheme, Milton inscribes a series of circles, suggesting "the perfection and order of creation that is broken by King's death and . . .

restored with his resurrection." Reply by Anthony Low, *PMLA*, 86, 1971, 1032–33; rejoinder by Wittreich, pp. 1033–35.

1834 Wolfe, Ralph Haven. "Milton's *Lycidas*, Line 29." *Expl*, 41, No. 1, 1982, 23–24.

Supports Edgar F. Daniels's assertion (No. 1295) that in *Lycidas* 29, Milton's phrase "Batt'ning our flocks" refers to penning up the sheep rather than feeding them, as the *Variorum Commentary* claims (No. 1838). Cites the pastoral custom of driving flocks at the first appearance of the evening star, which Milton's shepherds would be violating had they been feeding their sheep rather than penning them.

1835 Wolpers, Theodor. "Miltons *L'Allegro* und *Il Penseroso*: Schatzhaus der Motive zwischen Renaissance, Barock, Klassizismus und Romantik." *Motive und Themen Romantischer Naturdichtung: Textanalysen und Traditionszusammenhänge im Bereich der Skandinavischen, Englischen, Deutschen, Nordamerikanischen und Russischen Literatur: Bericht über Kolloquien der Kommission für Literaturwissenschaftliche Motiv- und Themenforschung, 1981–1982*. Ed. by Wolpers (Göttingen: Vandenhoeck and Ruprecht, 1984), pp. 50–67.

Analyzes *L'Allegro* and *Il Penseroso*, focusing on recurring themes and motifs, which are aesthetic and spiritual elements designed to unite with the reader's mood.

1836 Woodhouse, A. S. P. "The Argument of Milton's *Comus*." *"A Maske at Ludlow": Essays on Milton's "Comus*." Ed. by John S. Diekhoff (Ann Arbor, MI: Univ. Microfilms International, 1980 Books on Demand Reprints), pp. 17–42.

Reprint of Huckabay No. 2810, originally published in 1941.

1837 Woodhouse, A. S. P. *"Comus Once More." "A Maske at Ludlow": Essays on Milton's "Comus*." Ed. by

John S. Diekhoff (Ann Arbor, MI: Univ. Microfilms International, 1980 Books on Demand Reprints), pp. 72–77.

Reprint of Huckabay No. 2811, originally published in 1950.

1838 Woodhouse, A. S. P., and **Douglas Bush.** *A Variorum Commentary on the Poems of John Milton.* Gen. ed. Merritt Y. Hughes. Vol. 2, Part 1: The Minor English Poems, by Woodhouse and Bush, 1972. xvii, 338pp.; Vol. 2, Part 2: The Minor English Poems, by Woodhouse and Bush, 1972. xi, pp. 339–734; Vol. 2, Part 3: The Minor English Poems, by Woodhouse and Bush, 1972. xi, pp. 735–1143.

In the Preface to Vol. 1, Hughes states, "Our object in this work is to furnish a body of variorum notes and discussions uniting all available scholarly illumination of the texts on all levels from the semantic and syntactical to those of deliberate or unconscious echoes of other works in all the languages known to Milton. In notes on the longer passages we have considered their inner rhetorical organization and involvements in the design of the poem as a whole, in the backgrounds of the literary traditions of which they themselves are outstanding developments, and in the many aspects of Milton's interests—theological, cosmological, hexameral, historical, psychological, and so on." Vol. 2, part 3 contains extensive information on *Comus*, some commentary on Psalms 1–8 and 80–88, an essay by Edward R. Weismiller ("Studies of Verse Form in the Minor English Poems"), and a bibliographical index. See Nos. 1236 and 3386 for the other volumes of the *Variorum Commentary.* See also No. 1459. Reviews of Vol. 2: *MiltonQ*, 6, No. 4, 1972, 95–96; *TLS*, Sept. 29, 1972, p. 1162; Michael Lieb, *Cithara*, 12, 1972, 85–106; William Blissett, *UTQ*, 43, 1973, 90–91; K. W. Gransden, *EIC*, 23, 1973, 302–10; Ralph Nash, *Criticism*, 15, 1973, 284–85; George F.

Sensabaugh, *RenQ*, 26, 1973, 92–95; William B. Hunter, Jr., *MP*, 71, 1974, 435–38; Timothy J. O'Keeffe, *SCN*, 32, 1974, 71–72; Roger Lejosne, *EA*, 28, 1975, 85–86; J. C. Maxwell, *N&Q*, 22, 1975, 572–74; Stanley E. Fish, *CritI*, 2, 1976, 465–85 (see No. 593); replies by Douglas Bush, *CritI*, 3, 1976, 179–82, and Steven Mailloux, pp. 183–90; rejoinder by Fish, pp. 191–96.

1839 Woodhouse, Christopher Reed. "'The Melting Voice': A Study of Milton's *L'Allegro* and *Il Penseroso* and Their Setting by Handel." Doctoral diss., Boston College, 1984. 205pp. Abs., *DAI*, 44, 1984, 3392A.

Uses a common theme of delight to unite Milton's imprecise, unconventional, and artificial *L'Allegro* and *Il Penseroso* with Handel's vivid, conventional, and passionate musical interpretation of the poems.

1840 Woods, Carrie Sue. "Style and Structure in *Comus*." Doctoral diss., Texas Christian Univ., 1971. 111pp. Abs., *DAI*, 32, 1971, 3337A.

Examines the union of idea and image as Milton uses verbal patterns, character movement, imagery, and drama to "reinforce on an intellectual level the allegorical meanings implicit in the visual spectacle" of *Comus*.

1841 Yagawa, Osamu. "Milton's *Comus*: An Escape from the Symbolic Features of the Masque." *Shiron*, 25, 1986, 23–43.

1842 Young, K. A. "*Lycidas* from the Manuscript in the Library of Trinity College Cambridge, Together with a Study of the Language of the Poem." M.Phil. thesis, Leeds Univ., 1975. *IT*, 25, 1977, 6.

1843 Younis, Raymond Aaron. "'And O Ye dolphins': Milton and Hesiod." *N&Q*, 35, 1988, 160.

Disputes comparisons of Lycidas to the mythological figures Arion and Palaemon-Melicertes and to Hesiod's account of dolphins.

1844 Zacharias, Greg W. "Young Milton's Equipment for Living: *L'Allegro* and *Il Penseroso*." *MiltonS*, 24, 1988, 3–15.

Believes that the poems form a circular movement and that they "can be read as Milton's attempt as he begins his poetic career to express symbolically his strategy to control the full range of experience."

1845 Adams, Robert Martin. "Contra Hartman: Possible and Impossible Structures of Miltonic Imagery." *Seventeenth-Century Imagery: Essays on Uses of Figurative Language from Donne to Farquhar.* Ed. by Earl Miner (Berkeley, Los Angeles, and London: Univ. of California Press, 1971), pp. 117–31.

Disagrees with Geoffrey Hartman's interpretation of *Paradise Lost* 8.253–56 (see No. 2399). Insists that Hartman has enriched the lines out of proportion.

1846 Adams, Robert M. "A Little Look into Chaos." *Illustrious Evidence: Approaches to English Literature of the Early Seventeenth Century.* Ed. by Earl Miner (Berkeley, Los Angeles, and London: Univ. of California Press, 1975), pp. 71–89.

Points out that Chaos intrudes again and again in *Paradise Lost.* "Its presence is felt in three contexts particularly: in the exterior structure of the world, in the history of man, and in his most inward workings, his psyche."

1847 Adamson, J. H. "The War in Heaven: The *Merkabah.*" *Bright Essence: Studies in Milton's Theology.* By W. B. Hunter, C. A. Patrides, and Adamson (Salt Lake City: Univ. of Utah Press, 1971), pp. 103–14.

Reprint of Huckabay No. 1076, originally published in 1958.

1848 Addison, Joseph. *Criticisms on "Paradise Lost."* Ed. by Albert S. Cook. Ann Arbor, MI: Univ. Microfilms International, 1980 Books on Demand Reprints.

Reprint of Stevens No. 860, originally published in 1892.

1849 Adelman, Janet. "Creation and the Place of the Poet in *Paradise Lost.*" *The Author in His Work: Essays on a Problem in Criticism.* Ed. by Louis L. Martz and Aubrey Williams (New Haven, CT, and London: Yale Univ. Press, 1978), pp. 51–69.

States that the epic shows a concern for the varieties of creation and for imitation and image-making, which reflect Milton's own anxiety about the process of poetic creation.

1850 Adkins, Camille. "In Adam's Room: Incarnation of the Divine Image in *Paradise Lost* and *Jerusalem.*" Doctoral diss., Texas Christian Univ., 1984. 127pp. Abs., *DAI*, 45, 1984, 1404A.

Compares Blake's and Milton's perceptions of the incarnation of God's image in humans and in the Son.

1851 Adkins, Joan F. "The Miltonic Style: Satan's Reincarnation as Serpent." *LCrit*, 10, 1973, 40–45.

Demonstrates that through poetic structure of sound and vision, Milton translates image into idea, shaping and dramatizing the aggressive and destructive nature of phallic symbolism.

1852 Adlard, John. "Milton's Harvest-Queen." *NM*, 71, 1970, 689–90.

Adds to Magoun's notes (No. 2646) by describing harvest queens in Cambridgeshire.

1853 Adler, Doris. "Imaginary Toads in Real Gardens." *ELR*, 11, 1981, 235–60.

On the toad of *Paradise Lost* 4.799–800. Asserts that the toad was a common symbol of cosmic jealousy in and before Milton's time.

1854 Agari, Masahiko. "Adam's Song of

Innocence." *USSE*, 13, 1985, 25–34.

1855 **Agari, Masahiko.** "Language as Epic Narrator: The Moral Aspect of Milton's Style." *Studies in English Language and Literature Presented to Professor Michio Masui*. Ed. by Hiroshige Yoshida (Tokyo: Kenkyusha, 1983), pp. 145–54.

Believes that the moral structure of *Paradise Lost* determines the form of its epic style. The mimetic nature of epic language works closely with the poet's intention.

1856 **Agari, Masahiko.** "Milton's Serious Rhetoric." *MCJ News*, 7, 1984, 16–17.

Abstract of a paper presented at the Fifteenth Colloquium of MCJ in July, 1983. Sees prelapsarian rhetoric as "belonging to both divine and human nature." This unity is broken when words and deeds no longer correspond. Postlapsarian humans can recover this "original, divine unity" through prevenient grace as they learn once more to unify word and deed.

1857 **Agari, Masahiko.** "Shitsurakuen no Gengo Hyogen ni Kansuru ichi Kosatsu." *Phoenix* (Hiroshima Univ.), 2, 1965, 1–8.

Studies linguistic expression in *Paradise Lost*.

1858 **Agari, Masahiko.** "Some Observations on the Language of *Paradise Lost*, with Special Reference to Its Formulaic Patterns." *HSELL*, 18, 1971, 12–28.

Points out some characteristics of the stylistic texture of *Paradise Lost* and places them in their historical context by citing other poets from Geoffrey Chaucer to Abraham Cowley.

1859 **Aitken, David J.** "Milton's Use of 'Stand' and the Doctrine of Perseverance." *ELN*, 19, 1982, 233–36.

Shows that Milton's use of the word "stand" in such works as *Paradise Lost* signifies that a character is in a state of perseverance while maintaining grace. "To 'stand' involved a conscious and continuous act of faith and obedience."

1860 **Akagawa, Yutaka.** "John Milton's Sense of Sight." *MCJ News*, 9, 1987, 8–9.

Argues that in *Paradise Lost* Milton demonstrates his reliance on an internal visual sense rather than the actual sense of sight. Even in the final scene, he refuses to fill "the gap between reality and appearance," for he forces Adam and Eve to "face reality, and spiritual truth coexistingly mingled" as they see the whole world.

1861 **Akagawa, Yutaka.** "The Structure of *Paradise Lost*." *SELit*, 48, 1971, 17–29.

In Japanese. Organizes *Paradise Lost* into four vertical blocks. The first deals with Satan's fall and man's revolt; the second, with the cosmic amplifier of Satan's position; the third, with God acting as a shock absorber; and the fourth, with humanity.

1862 **Alfonsi, Ferdinando.** "Satana in Milton e Dante." *CV*, 25, 1970, 587–92.

Presents physical and psychological differences in Satan as portrayed by Dante and Milton. Points out that Dante, conforming to medieval thought, presents Satan as the anti-God, while Milton, a Renaissance man, pictures him as the anti-Messiah.

1863 **Alkon, Paul K.** "Johnson's Conception of Admiration." *PQ*, 48, 1969, 59–81.

Considers "first Johnson's use of *admiration* as a critical term and then, in the light of that usage, the crux of his case against *Paradise Lost*: his assertion that it simultaneously evokes admiration and repels readers, forcing them to 'retire harassed and overburdened, and look elsewhere for recreation.'"

1864 **Allen, Don Cameron.** "Light and the Visual Image in *Paradise Lost*." *On Milton's Poetry: A Selection of Modern Studies*. Ed. by Arnold Stein (Greenwich, CT: Fawcett Publications, 1970), pp. 183–89.

Reprint of a chapter from No. 448 and

Huckabay No. 404, originally published in 1954.

1865 Altizer, Thomas J. J. "Milton and the English Revolution." *History as Apocalypse* (Albany: State Univ. of New York Press, 1985), pp. 137–73.

Discusses the *Christian Doctrine* and insists that *Paradise Lost* "is the grounding epic of the modern world."

1866 Alvarez De Toledo Morenés, M. "La Pregunta sobre el Mal en *Paradise Lost*, IV, 878–884." *RCEI*, 9, 1984, 87–93.

States that Milton treats the concept of evil with great seriousness in both moral and rational arguments. The conversation between Satan and Gabriel shows Milton's anguish over a mystical answer—evil exists because there is a will to do evil.

1867 Alvis, John. "Philosophy as Noblest Idolatry in *Paradise Lost*." *IJPP*, 16, 1988–89, 263–84.

Discusses the passage about "Vain wisdom . . . and false philosophy" in *Paradise Lost* 2.565. Believes that Adam and Eve's tendency for speculative philosophizing leads to the Fall.

1868 Amorose, Thomas Christopher. "The Glassy Sea: Action and Contemplation in *Paradise Lost*." Doctoral diss., Univ. of Washington, 1978. 289pp. Abs., *DAI*, 40, 1979, 841A.

Cites individual action and contemplation as the means of moving from a superficial existence to a liberating relationship with God, both in Milton's *L'Allegro* and *Il Penseroso* and in the works of his medieval predecessors.

1869 Amorose, Thomas. "Milton the Apocalyptic Historian: Competing Genres in *Paradise Lost*, Books XI–XII." *MiltonS*, 17, 1983, 141–62.

Examines the linear and cyclic views of history in Books 11–12 and shows that although Milton was familiar with ancient, medieval, and Renaissance perspectives, he developed one of his own. In the end, Adam learns that "God dwells with man and also works in the historical process." The competing genres are the historic, epic, and prophetic.

1870 Anand, Shahla. *Of Costliest Emblem: "Paradise Lost" and the Emblem Tradition.* Washington, DC: Univ. Press of America, 1978. xxi, 299pp.

Explores the images and ideologies in *Paradise Lost* in relation to the English emblem books by such authors as Geoffrey Whitney, Henry Peacham, Henry Hawkins, George Wither, Frances Quarles, and John Hall. Contains a chapter on the liturgical and dramatic icons in the epic, drawn mainly from Milton's unconscious use of the Anglican prayer book. Review: *MiltonQ*, 12, 1978, 108–10; reply by Mason Tung, *MiltonQ*, 13, 1979, 56–58; response by *MiltonQ* reviewer, p. 58.

1871 Anderson, Douglas. "Unfallen Marriage and the Fallen Imagination in *Paradise Lost*." *SEL*, 26, 1986, 125–44.

Contends that Milton's attempts to accommodate his divine subject to an earthly audience result in a nearly unbelievable portrayal of prelapsarian marriage in *Paradise Lost*.

1872 Anderson, Peter Slobin. "Obedient Ear: Hearing, Obedience, and the Narrative Structure of *Paradise Lost*." Doctoral diss., State Univ. of New York at Buffalo, 1978. 583pp. Abs., *DAI*, 39, 1979, 4925A–26A.

Explores various instances in *Paradise Lost* where hearing leads to obedience.

1873 Andersson, Theodore M. "Claudian, Tasso, and the Topography of Milton's Paradise." *MLN*, 91, 1976, 1569–71.

On *Paradise Lost* 4.131–45. Notes Milton's debt to Armida's mountain in Canto 15 of *Jerusalem Delivered* and observes that Tasso's principal model may be found in Claudian's *De Nuptiis Honorii et Mariae*. Suggests that Milton may have "used Claudian to supplement Tasso."

1874 Andrews, Michael. "A Note on the

Fall of Mulciber." *AN&Q*, 21, 1983, 69–70.

Argues that in additon to the *Iliad*, Milton draws on Thomas Heywood's *Brazen Age* for his account of Mulciber's fall in *Paradise Lost* 1.

1875 Angelo, Peter Gregory. *Fall to Glory: Theological Reflections on Milton's Epics.* New York: Peter Lang, 1987. xvi, 165pp.

Examines the idea of free will in *Paradise Lost*, specifically the seeming conflict between human free will and God's prescience, between the sinfulness of the fallen angels, who prefer their will to God's, and the deity of the Christ, who willfully accepts the burden of redemption.

1876 Angelo, Peter Gregory. "Free Will, Sin and Redemption in Milton's Epic Poetry." Doctoral diss., State Univ. of New York, Stony Brook, 1978. 171pp. Abs., *DAI*, 39, 1978, 890A.

Clarifies Milton's "understanding of the relationship between the free will of rational beings and the will of God" in *Paradise Lost* and *Paradise Regained.*

1877 Anikst, A. "Dzhon Mil'ton i ego poema Poteryannyi rai." *Nauka i religiya* (Moscow), 9, 1976, 54–57.

"John Milton and His Poem *Paradise Lost.*"

1878 Ansari, Asloob Ahmad. "Milton's Myth of the Garden of Eden in *Paradise Lost.*" *Essays on John Milton: A Tercentenary Tribute.* Ed. by Ansari (Aligarh: Aligarh Muslim Univ., 1976), pp. 80–95.

Analyzes the narrative that occurs in the garden, which becomes an impure archetype, while the paradise within represents the pure archetype.

1879 Anstice, Sir Robert H. *The Satan of Milton.* Folcroft, PA: Folcroft Library Editions, 1969; Norwood, PA: Norwood Editions, 1975; Philadelphia, PA: R. West, 1976.

Reprints of the 1910 edition.

1880 Arai, Akira. "Adam and the Redemp-

tive History." *The Bulletin of the Tokyo Univ. of Education, Literature Department*, 78, 1970, 1–23.

In Japanese; English summary, pp. 24–26. Defends *Paradise Lost* 11–12, pointing out that these books reveal a clear pattern of redemptive history that begins with Noah and ends with the Messiah.

1881 Arai, Akira. "*Paradise Lost* and Divorce Tracts: A Theory on the Escape from Paradise." *Studies in Milton* (Tokyo: Kinseido, 1974), pp. 19–30.

In Japanese. Milton's divorce tracts foreshadow the birth in *Paradise Lost* of a self-controlled being who stands in a kind of contractual relationship to God.

1882 Arai, Akira. "Toraji Tsukamoto's Colloquial Translation of the Bible and Milton's *Paradise Lost.*" *Miscellaneous Essays on Milton* (Tokyo: Chukyo Shuppan, 1979), pp. 217–24.

In Japanese. Tsukamoto's translation was the first into colloquial Japanese, giving the Japanese people easy access to the biblical story and hence to the background of *Paradise Lost.*

1883 Archer, Stanley. "*Paradise Lost*, XI–XII: The Vanity of Human Wishes." *SCB*, 35, 1975, 114–17.

The epic's final books deal with human vanity through the ages, and the only hope is to achieve the paradise within, through Christ.

1884 Archer, Stanley. "Satan and the Colures: *Paradise Lost* IX, 62–66." *ELN*, 10, 1972, 115–16.

Points out that, as described, Satan's dark journey from earth was "astronomically impossible." Suggests that Milton used the "Car of Night" as a poetic device to ensure darkness and associated Satan with the controversial colures in compliance with traditional demon lore.

1885 Armstrong, John. *The Paradise Myth.* London: Oxford Univ. Press, 1969. xi, 154pp.

Contains a chapter on *Paradise Lost.* Believes that Milton's "feeling for both the content of the Greek Hesperides myth and that of the parallel Sumerian myth of Inanna's Holy Garden broke the theoretical structure of his epic." Review: *MiltonQ*, 4, 1970, 44–45.

1886 Arnold, Marc H. "The Platan Tree in *Paradise Lost.*" *PLL*, 11, 1975, 411–14.
Discusses the meaning of the pun on Plato's name when Eve first sees Adam under a Platan tree in *Paradise Lost* 4.478, which may contain an allusion to Plato's *Phaedrus.* In the opening scene, Socrates tells Phaedrus about the difference between illusion and reality while the two sit under a plane tree. As Lysias will deceive Phaedrus with rhetoric, Satan will deceive Eve with lies and flattery. Abs., *MiltonQ*, 12, 1978, 113.

1887 Arnold, Marilyn. "Milton's Accessible God: The Role of the Son in *Paradise Lost.*" *MiltonQ*, 7, 1973, 65–72.
Holds that "whatever his personal beliefs on the matter might have been, Milton views the Son in *Paradise Lost* as the God of the earth, through whose person the God of heaven is made accessible to man."

1888 Arthos, John. "Milton, Andreini, and Galileo: Some Considerations on the Manner and Form of *Paradise Lost.*" *Approaches to "Paradise Lost."* The York Tercentenary Lectures. Ed. by C. A. Patrides (London: Edward Arnold; Toronto: Univ. of Toronto Press, 1968), pp. 163–79.
Contrasts the dramatic form of Giovanni Battista Andreini's *L'Adamo* and the epic form of *Paradise Lost* and discusses why the latter is necessarily epic. Notes differences between Milton's and Galileo's universes.

1889 Asahi, Satoru. "*Paradise Lost* Ko: Dai 2 kan to dai 11 kan no Taihi o Megutte." *Suga Yasuo, Ogoshi Kazugo: Ryokyoju Taikon Kinen Ronbunshu* (Kyoto: Apollonsha, 1980), pp. 238–50.
Compares Books 2 and 11.

1890 Ashraf, Ameen. "Milton and Iqbal." *Essays on John Milton: A Tercentenary Tribute.* Ed. by Asloob Ahmad Ansari (Aligarh: Aligarh Muslim Univ., 1976), pp. 148–69.
"Milton's Satan stands as an antithesis to God while Iblis in Iqbal is neither an adversary of God nor an enemy of Man."

1891 Ashworth, Ann. "Pandemonium and 'The Temple of Music.'" *MiltonQ*, 16, 1982, 10–11.
"It may be argued that Milton could and did associate architecture and music anyway, but the combination of bizarre architecture with music strongly suggests a Miltonic reminiscence of Fludd."

1892 Ashworth, Ann. "Psyche and Eve: Milton's Goddess without a Temple." *MiltonQ*, 18, 1984, 52–58.
Believes that Eve is similar to Psyche because she possesses the same beauty and pathos, lives in a paradise of ease and idyllic love, begins a creative process by breaking a taboo, is tempted by her curiosity and beauty, and desires death after the Fall.

1893 Ashworth, Ann. "Two Notes on Milton and Spenser." *N&Q*, 31, 1984, 324–25.
Argues that "Spenser's Titaness, who, like Satan, 'altered' the face of things and who was the enemy of constancy and of God," is the source of Milton's perception of mutability in *Paradise Lost.* Also cites the *Faerie Queene* as the source of the "two broad suns" described in *Paradise Lost* 6. In Spenser's work, only people whose "ethical judgement is unsound" see two suns, since one is merely an illusion.

1894 Astell, Ann W. "The Medieval *Consolatio* and the Conclusion of *Paradise Lost.*" *SP*, 82, 1985, 477–92.
Argues that Milton wrote *Paradise Lost* 11–12 in the form of a consolatio so readers could "experience [their] own redemption, the redemption of all mankind, through the psychological/

spiritual conversion of a single representative sinner and sufferer: Adam."

1895 Avery, Christine. *"Paradise Lost* and the Power of Language." *English* (Oxford), 19, 1970, 79–84.

Makes "a brief criticism of Milton's theological language and then . . . trace[s] one line emerging from it through the rest of his universe of discourse." Concludes that "the essential action in *Paradise Lost* has three aspects, semantic, poetic, and religious."

1896 Avigdor, Eva. "Une Traduction Française Inconnue du *Paradis Perdu* de Milton." *RLC*, 61, 1987, 69–79.

Studies the first French translation of the beginning of *Paradise Lost* 1, done by Jean Gaspar Scheuchzer between 1722 and 1729.

1897 Babb, Lawrence. *The Moral Cosmos of "Paradise Lost."* [East Lansing]: Michigan State Univ. Press, 1970. x, 166pp.

Examines the physical milieu of *Paradise Lost*. Chapters: "Preliminaries"; "Knowledge, Milton and Science"; "Earth, Men, and Angels"; "The Supralunar World"; "The New Astronomy"; "The Cosmos"; "Space, Matter, and Time"; and "Summary and Conclusion." Reviews: *MiltonQ*, 5, 1971, 23; *TLS*, Sept. 17, 1971, p. 1120; Frederick Lyons, *JEGP*, 71, 1972, 133–35; Edgar F. Daniels, *SCN*, 30, 1972, 6–7; D. D. C. Chambers, *RES*, 23, 1972, 207–09; Robert H. West, *MP*, 70, 1973, 360–64.

1898 Bacon, Alan. "Jane Eyre's Paintings and Milton's *Paradise Lost.*" *N&Q*, 31, 1984, 64–65.

Shows that Jane Eyre's paintings allude to scenes in *Paradise Lost*. The paintings of a cormorant, the evening star, and a huge head represent temptation, sin, and death.

1899 Baldi, Sergio. "Folte come le Foglie (e lo Scudo di Sàtana)." *Critical Dimensions: English, German and Comparative Literature Essays in Honour of Aurelio Zanco.* Ed. by Mario Curreli and Al-

berto Martino (Cuneo: SASTE, 1978), pp. 221–40.

Traces the history of the imagery concerning Satan's shield and the autumn leaves in *Paradise Lost* 1.

1900 Banfield, Ann M. "Stylistic Transformations: A Study Based on the Syntax of *Paradise Lost.*" Doctoral diss., Univ. of Wisconsin, Madison, 1973. 296pp. Abs., *DAI*, 34, 1973, 1265A–66A.

Examines "the relation of stylistic deviation to grammaticality" in *Paradise Lost*.

1901 Banschbach, John. "Allusions to the *Aeneid* in *Paradise Lost*, Books XI and XII." *TWA*, 74, 1986, 70–74.

Argues that the final books of *Paradise Lost* are constructed with care and that the many allusions to the *Aeneid* suggest "that Milton's own confidence in his artistic achievement had not diminished."

1902 Barbeau, Anne T. "Satan's Envy of the Son and the Third Day of the War." *PLL*, 13, 1977, 362–71.

Suggests that the episode of Christ's restoring nature in heaven shows that the "rebellious angels are, in the end, forced to oppose not only the Messiah's political authority but also his natural authority over the elements in Heaven, and over the celestial fabric that envelops and sustains them."

1903 Barfoot, C. C. "A Way with *Paradise Lost.*" *DQR*, 3, 1973, 111–22.

Argues that *Paradise Lost* should not be read historically and sets forth an idea of the relevance of certain passages to the modern reader. Sees Adam and Eve as allegorical figures within a symbolic psychological drama.

1904 Barker, Arthur E. *"Paradise Lost*: The Relevance of Regeneration." *"Paradise Lost": A Tercentenary Tribute.* Ed. by Balachandra Rajan ([Toronto]: Univ. of Toronto Press, 1969), pp. 48–78.

Feels that the final note in *Paradise Lost* reasserts "the dignity and the potentiality of not only redeemed but restored and regenerated human nature in its proper and destined human sphere." Sees this strand of hope, not despair, running throughout the poem.

1905 Barnish, Valerie L. *Notes on John Milton's "Paradise Lost."* Methuen Notes. London: Methuen, 1978. 116pp.

Contains background material and analyses of selected parts of the epic.

1906 Barolini, Helen. "Milton in Rome." *SAQ*, 74, 1975, 118–28.

Discusses Milton's trip to Rome around 1638–39 and its possible influence on *Paradise Lost.*

1907 Barr, Christopher Velten. " 'This Intellectual Being': Language and Being in *Paradise Lost.*" Doctoral diss., Purdue Univ., 1987. 252pp. Abs., *DAI*, 49, 1988, 1147A.

Argues that choice is the primary catalyst of human existence in *Paradise Lost*, affecting not only language but also revealing "the voice of Providence."

1908 Barthel, Carol. " 'Or of Reviv'd Adonis': Spenser and Milton's Images of Love." *MiltonQ*, 11, 1977, 26.

Abstract of a paper presented at the 1976 MLA Convention. In *Paradise Lost* Milton uses Spenserian motifs of love, "sometimes in a Spenserian, romantic manner and sometimes in a manner that criticizes romance and perhaps also Spenser."

1909 Baruch, Franklin R. "Milton's Blindness: The Conscious and Unconscious Patterns of Autobiography." *ELH*, 42, 1975, 26–37.

Claims that Milton attempts to subordinate the self to the demands of his epic. But elements concerning his blindness creep in because the poet sees a parallel between his condition and the spiritual state of humanity. Concludes that *Paradise Lost* blends personal and humanitarian considerations.

1910 Bauman, Michael. "Creation and the Son's Alleged Omnipresence." *MiltonQ*, 19, 1985, 110–12.

Rejects Gordon Campbell's assertion that Milton, in *Paradise Lost*, makes the Son omnipresent (No. 2019). Believes that Milton describes only the Father as omnipresent. See Campbell's response (No. 2020).

1911 Bauman, Michael. "Milton's Muse, Holy Light and the Son of God." *CP*, 17, 1984, 51–62.

Rejects W. B. Hunter's contention that the "holy Light" which Milton invokes in *Paradise Lost* 3 is the Son of God (Huckabay Nos. 1432 and 1434; see No. 2455). Contends that Milton should be taken literally—that he is indeed addressing "light" rather than the heavenly muse.

1912 Bauman, Michael. "Naming Satan's Heresies." *ELN*, 23, 1985, 31–35.

Argues that William B. Hunter's essay "The Heresies of Satan" is based on arguments that are fundamentally flawed (Huckabay No. 1430). Among the errors are the assertions that Satan repeatedly denies Christ's existence, that Milton's beliefs are the exact opposite of Satan's, that "*all* historians of early Christianity teach that dynamic monarchianism led in time to the Arianism that was condemned at Nicea," and that "dynamic monarchianism 'denies that the Son has any individual existence.' "

1913 Bauman, Michael. "A Reply to Professor Campbell." *MiltonQ*, 21, No. 3, 1987, 106–08.

Defends his view of the Father's exclusive omnipresence in *Paradise Lost* against Gordon Campbell's remarks (No. 2020; see also No. 2019).

1914 Baumgaertner, Jill. "*Felix Culpa* and Its Critics." *Cresset*, 42, No. 4, 1979, 23–24.

Defends Krzysztof Penderecki's operatic version of *Paradise Lost* (No. 2868). Contends that the critics do not understand "the whole nature of Christian tragedy."

1915 Baumgaertner, Jill. "Milton's Eve:

The Harlot and the Bride." *Cresset*, 40, No. 5, 1977, 8–11.

Believes that in *Paradise Lost* Milton uses the "defiled harlot [from the Book of Revelation] and the harlot restored in marriage [Israel] to point out essential similarities and significant differences between the characters of Eve and Sin. Although both become creatures of lust, Sin's description points toward the Whore of Babylon, whereas Eve's is ultimately connected with Israel, God's fallen line."

1916 Baumlin, James S. "Epic and Allegory in *Paradise Lost*, Book II." *CollL*, 14, 1987, 167–77.

Links moral choice to choice of genre; uses the Satanic council and the personifications of Sin and Death to show the bridge between genre (literary device with cultural reference) and morality (cultural ethics and standards).

1917 Bauso, Thomas Michael. "From Milton to Pope: Studies in Literary Displacement." Doctoral diss., Rutgers Univ., 1976. 271pp. Abs., *DAI*, 37, 1976, 293A.

Examines *Paradise Lost* "as the conduit for a variety of conventional images and motifs" for Augustan writers.

1918 Bayley, John. "The Epic Theme of Love." *Aspects of the Epic.* Ed. by Tom Winnifrith, Penelope Murray, and K. W. Gransden (London: Macmillan; New York: St. Martin's, 1983), pp. 64–79.

Deals with the theme of love in the epic tradition. Devotes several pages to unfallen and fallen sex in *Paradise Lost*. Review (of book): George de Forest Lord, *MLR*, 82, 1987, 156–57.

1919 Bedford, R. D. " 'The Ensanguind Field' of *Paradise Lost*." *ELN*, 21, 1984, 17–24.

Argues that Milton frequently uses the word "field" in *Paradise Lost* because it can connote either epic or pastoral values, or ambiguously refer to both.

1920 Bedford, R. D. "Milton's Logic." *EIC*, 27, 1977, 84–86.

A reply to K. W. Gransden (No. 2330).

Discusses Milton's view of predestination and foreknowledge and concludes that Gransden's consideration of logical determinism is in error.

1921 Bedford, R. D. "Similes of Unlikeness in *Paradise Lost*." *EIC*, 25, 1975, 179–96.

Discusses the epic similes in which people go about their everyday business. Milton sees them as subduers of the earth, "which involves subduing one's neighbour by force or guile."

1922 Bedford, R. D. "Time, Freedom, and Foreknowledge in *Paradise Lost*." *MiltonS*, 16, 1982, 61–76.

Argues that although Milton reveals a subtle sense of the philosophical and logical problems involved in discussing foreknowledge, fate, necessity, free will, and liberty, "his artistic and poetic solution to these problems depends largely on his resonantly ambiguous handling of the phenomenon of time in *Paradise Lost*."

1923 Beecham, R. G. "The Prometheus Myth as Tragic Metaphor in *Paradise Lost*." M.Litt. thesis, Oxford Univ., 1988. Abs., *IT*, 38, 1989, 527.

"Interprets the Prometheus myth . . . as a metaphor for tragic experience, and argues that the myth recurs as such in *Paradise Lost*."

1924 Bell, Robert H. " 'Blushing Like the Morn': Milton's Human Comedy." *MiltonQ*, 15, 1981, 47–55.

Develops Addison's suggestion that the colloquy between Adam and Raphael in *Paradise Lost* 8 is amusing to the imagination. Feels that it is a comic conversation and skillfully juxtaposed to the tragic action of Book 9.

1925 Benet, Diana. "Abdiel and the Son in the Separation Scene." *MiltonS*, 18, 1983, 129–43.

Discusses the separation scene in *Paradise Lost* 9. Suggests that Adam and Eve expect to emulate the Son and Abdiel, respectively, based on their understanding of Raphael's narration.

Contrasts Adam's and Eve's divergent concepts of trial and temptation.

1926 Benet, Diana. "Satan, God's Glory and the Fortunate Fall." *MiltonQ*, 19, 1985, 34–37.

Believes that through the Fall, Adam gains "a profound recognition of God's incomparable benevolence" and that God's glory is increased. Thus, Milton intended the Fall to be fortunate.

1927 Bennett, Joan S. " 'Go': Milton's Antinomianism and the Separation Scene in *Paradise Lost*, Book 9." *PMLA*, 98, 1983, 388–404.

Argues "that in Milton's view the first persons who had to deal with this dilemma of total spiritual liberty were unfallen man and woman, that the separation scene concerns not only relations between the sexes but the basic nature of human government, and that we will be rewarded by reading the quarrel between Adam and Eve in the light of Milton's answer to the epistemological question that faced ethical antinomianism."

1928 Bennett, Joan S. "God, Satan, and King Charles: Milton's Royal Portraits." *PMLA*, 92, 1977, 441–57.

Between the interpretation in Milton's prose works of Charles I's monarchy and the portrayal in *Paradise Lost* of Satan's tyranny, there exists an extensive and complex consistency based on the concept of the divine right of kings, a doctrine that informs the character and world view of Satan as well as King Charles. Replies by William Empson, *PMLA*, 93, 1978, 118, and Lawrence W. Hyman, 118–19. Further clarification by Bennett, pp. 119–20.

1929 Bensen, Robert Raymond. "Ecclesiastical History and Controversy in *Paradise Lost*." Doctoral diss., Univ. of Illinois, Urbana, 1974. 177pp. Abs., *DAI*, 35, 1975, 4500A.

Draws parallels between Milton's Satan and corruptions in and from the seventeenth-century Catholic church.

1930 Benskin, Michael, and **Brian Murdoch.** "The Literary Tradition of Genesis: Some Comments on J. Martin Evans' '*Paradise Lost' and the Genesis Tradition*." *NM*, 76, 1975, 389–403.

Reviews some of Evans's statements (No. 2182). "The present paper is a review in extenso of the pre-Miltonic sections of what is apparently the first attempt at a comprehensive and unified history of the literary tradition."

1931 Bentley, Richard. *Dr. Bentley's Emendations on the Twelve Books of Milton's "Paradise Lost."* Ann Arbor, MI: Univ. Microfilms International, 1980 Books on Demand Reprints.

Originally published in 1732.

1932 Berek, Peter. " 'Plain' and 'Ornate' Styles and the Structure of *Paradise Lost*." *PMLA*, 85, 1970, 237–46.

Milton contrasts plain and ornate speech to show the difference between perfection and imperfection, innocence and corruption in *Paradise Lost*. He makes the reader suspect the arts of language as devices for concealing or manipulating truth instead of stating or revealing it.

1933 Berger, Harry, Jr. "*Paradise Lost* Evolving: Books I–VI." *CentR*, 11, 1967, 483–531.

Concerned with the relationship between the speaker and the poem. Uses the axiom that cultural history is recapitulated in personal history and argues that "the dialectical pattern underlying both is enacted in the dynamic unfolding of *Paradise Lost*."

1934 Berkeley, David Shelley. "Michael's New Commandment 'With Promise': *Paradise Lost* 11.530–46." *PLL*, 24, 1988, 134–41.

Rebuts Michael's claim in *Paradise Lost* 11.530–46 that willful temperance in eating and drinking gives one hope for a long life and painless death. Concludes that "from the point of view of doctrine *Paradise Lost* is a

Christian-humanist epic rather than a strictly biblical poem."

1935 Berkeley, David Shelley. "The 'Mysterious' Marriage of Adam and Eve in *Paradise Lost.*" *PQ*, 66, 1987, 195–205.

Argues that Milton's use of the word "mysterious" to describe Adam and Eve's marriage in *Paradise Lost* is intended to allude to Christ's "marriage" to the church.

1936 Berkeley, David S. "Thematic Implications of Milton's Paradise of Fools." *Papers on Milton.* Ed. by Philip Mahone Griffith and Lester F. Zimmerman. Univ. of Tulsa Department of English Monograph Series, no. 8 (Tulsa, OK: Univ. of Tulsa, 1969), pp. 3–8.

The passage "supplies thematic contrast to the historically oriented catalogue in Books XI and XII of sinners endowed with some degree of right reason, some exercise of free will, and some acquaintance with divine truth or its authentic mouthpieces."

1937 Berkowitz, M. S. "'With Balanc't Air in Counterpoise': Milton and Robert Boyle." *MiltonQ*, 13, 1979, 15–17.

On *Paradise Lost* 4.996–1000 and the weighing of air. Argues that Milton was familiar with Robert Boyle's experiments.

1938 Berry, Boyd M. "Melodramatic Faking in the Narrator's Voice, *Paradise Lost.*" *MiltonQ*, 10, 1976, 1–5.

Cites a number of passages in which "the outcome of the event clashes directly with the expectations which the narrator's voice has aroused. In these cases, it is easy to judge that the melodrama evoked is misplaced and inappropriate to the event."

1939 Berry, Boyd M. *Process of Speech: Puritan Religious Writing and "Paradise Lost."* Baltimore, MD, and London: Johns Hopkins Univ. Press, 1976. xiii, 306pp.

Sets out to bridge the abyss between Puritan style and the style of *Paradise Lost.* Argues that Milton was perhaps the only genuine radical activist in English letters and that *Paradise Lost* is written in the style of Puritanism. Reviews: *MiltonQ*, 10, 1976, 89–90; James H. Sims, *SCN*, 35, 1977, 77–79; Anthony Raspa, *DR*, 57, 1977, 158–60; Calvin Huckabay, *CSR*, 7, 1978, 156–57; Everett H. Emerson, *ELN*, 15, 1978, 305–07; William E. Cain, *Criticism*, 19, 1978, 180–83; G. K. Hunter, *SR*, 86, 1978, 414–21; William G. Riggs, *RenQ*, 31, 1978, 117–20; Dominic Baker-Smith, *SN*, 51, 1979, 154–56; Dennis H. Burden, *RES*, 31, 1980, 214–16.

1940 Berry, Boyd M. "Puritan Soldiers in *Paradise Lost.*" *MLQ*, 35, 1974, 376–402.

"Just as military sermons provide a handy microcosm of the whole of Puritan divinity, so angelic warfare expresses the pattern of the whole poem."

1941 Berthold, Dennis. "The Concept of Merit in *Paradise Lost.*" *SEL*, 15, 1975, 153–67.

"The twenty-one references to 'merit' in *Paradise Lost* dramatically develop the concept of the Son's 'Merit' as a fusion of natural merit (justification by birthright) and earned merit (justification by works)." This is applied to Satan and to Adam and Eve.

1942 Black, James. "The Return to Pandemonium: Interlude and Antimasque in *Paradise Lost.*" *WascanaR*, 9, 1974, 139–98.

"As I see the return to Pandemonium in *Paradise Lost*, Milton has his masque after all, and his anti-masque, or a mystery play for good measure. The biblical plays were already very old in Milton's day, the anti-masque comparatively new. Both, however, were grist to the mill of one who agreed that the Book of Revelation could be regarded as a tragedy, and whose own poetic vision united both drama and epic in an 'adventrous' song."

1943 Blackburn, Thomas H. "Paradises Lost and Found: The Meaning and

Function of the 'Paradise Within' in *Paradise Lost*." *MiltonS*, 5, 1973, 191–211.

"The paradise promised Adam and his progeny in this world is that 'imperfect glorification' characterized in *Christian Doctrine*, Bk. II, ch. 25, as 'the state wherein . . . we are filled with a consciousness of present grace and excellency, as well as with an expectation of future glory, inasmuch that our blessedness is in a manner already begun.'"

1944 Blackburn, Thomas H. "'Uncloister'd Virtue': Adam and Eve in Milton's Paradise." *MiltonS*, 3, 1971, 119–37.

"Milton's conception of a knowledgeable, yet sinless, innocence not only is congruent with his analysis of virtue in *Areopagitica*, but also makes possible a narrative rendering of the Fall which is coherent, credible, and dramatic." Review: Michael Lieb, *Cithara*, 12, 1972, 85–106.

1945 Blake, Kathleen. "Toward a Utopian Psychology: The Quality of Life in Milton's Eden." *NDQ*, 46, No. 2, 1978, 29–37.

"I do wish to argue the power of Milton's evocation of the paradisaic state, a state different from the one we know, but still conceivably human and therefore of the utmost fascination because it gives a shape of human possibility both credible and astonishing."

1946 Blakemore, Steven. "Language and Logos in *Paradise Lost*." *SHR*, 20, 1986, 325–40.

Shows how Milton, believing names to be "a primary source of power and being" in *Paradise Lost*, reveals that the fallen angels have been stripped of their heavenly names. Likewise, "the Word's naming of the universe becomes the onomastic model for . . . all appropriate future naming."

1947 Blakemore, Steven. "Pandemonium and Babel: Architectural Hierarchy in *Paradise Lost*." *MiltonQ*, 20, 1986, 142–45.

"Thus the poem's 'architecture' suggests that all vain, human architecture can be traced back to Susa and Babel and, finally, to Pandemonium and Lucifer's palace."

1948 Blakemore, Steven. "'With No Middle Flight': Poetic Pride and Satanic Hubris in *Paradise Lost*." *KyR*, 5, 1985, 23–31.

Believes that the narrator's "attempt to soar and pursue 'things unattempted' is dangerously close to satanic ambition and pride." Nevertheless, he confronts and makes Christian the traditional epic boast.

1949 Blamires, Harry. *Milton's Creation: A Guide through "Paradise Lost."* London: Methuen; New York: Barnes and Noble, 1971. x, 308pp.

A book-by-book summary and analysis. "In escorting the reader through *Paradise Lost*, I have tried to answer the needs of the student who wants a bird's-eye view of the poem as a whole and also of the student who wants detailed help wherever the text is loaded or difficult." Reviews: *TLS*, Sept. 17, 1971, p. 1120; *DUJ*, 23, 1972, 165; *MiltonQ*, 6, No. 3, 1972, 16; Michael Lieb, *Cithara*, 12, 1972, 85–106; Roger Lejosne, *EA*, 26, 1973, 98; Samuel S. Stollman, *UWR*, 8, 1973, 113–15.

1950 Blau, Rivkah Teitz. "Various Praise: Psalms in *The Temple*, *Paradise Lost*, and *Samson Agonistes*." Doctoral diss., Columbia Univ., 1983. 268pp. Abs., *DAI*, 46, 1986, 2297A.

Illustrates the effect of Herbert's and Milton's inclusion, manipulation, and alteration of the Psalms in their poetry.

1951 Blessington, Francis C. "Abdiel and Epic Poetry." *MiltonQ*, 10, 1976, 108–13.

Believes that Abdiel belongs to the tradition of the epic malcontent, who opposes the hero and the assembly. But "Milton uses Abdiel more deliberately as a symbol of moral behavior. . . . Milton's malcontent is neither struck down nor ignored."

1952 Blessington, Francis C. "Autotheodicy: The Father as Orator in *Paradise Lost*." *Cithara*, 14, No. 2, 1975, 49–60.
Considers "the oratorical aids to . . . [the poem's] theological argument as they appear in the speeches of God the Father and Satan."

1953 Blessington, Francis C. "Maia's Son and Raphael Once More." *MiltonQ*, 8, 1974, 108–13.
Argues that Raphael's visit to Adam, while deriving from biblical sources, "echoes closely the descent of Mercury to Aeneas." Supplies many parallels that show "how Milton has consciously become the English Virgil."

1954 Blessington, Francis C. "Milton in the Shadow of Virgil." *English Review of Salem State College*, 3, 1975, 20–29.
Discusses Virgilian echoes in *Paradise Lost*. Believes that Virgil exerted more influence on this poem than anyone else.

1955 Blessington, Francis C. *"Paradise Lost" and the Classical Epic.* Boston, MA, London, and Henley: Routledge and Kegan Paul, 1979. xiii, 126pp.
Shows that "the relationship between *Paradise Lost* and the classical epic is more subtle and pervasive than has yet been recognized and that every aspect of the poem interacts with classical tradition." Reviews: Edward Jones, *MiltonQ*, 13, 1979, 156–57; David L. Russell, *SCN*, 38, 1980, 43–44; Earl Miner, *JEGP*, 79, 1980, 250–53; Isabel Rivers, *RenQ*, 33, 1980, 490; Mario A. Di Cesare, *ELN*, 17, 1980, 306–07; Stevie Davies, *CritQ*, 22, 1980, 86–87; Dayton Haskin, *Thought*, 56, 1981, 226–39; Archie Burnett, *MLR*, 77, 1982, 160; J. Martin Evans, *RES*, 33, 1982, 318–23; Philip J. Gallagher, *RMR*, 37, 1983, 217–34.

1956 Blessington, Francis Charles. *"Paradise Lost* and the Rhetoric of Justification." Doctoral diss., Brown Univ., 1972. 152pp. Abs., *DAI*, 33, 1973, 4332A–33A.
Analyzes the rhetoric—that is, "the persuasiveness of the argument of *Paradise Lost*"—used "to justify the ways of God to men."

1957 Blessington, Francis C. *"Paradise Lost"*: *Ideal and Tragic Epic.* Boston, MA: Twayne, 1988. xiv, 144pp.
Students' companion to the poem. Review: Michael Allen Mikolajczak, *SCN*, 47, 1989, 7–8.

1958 Blessington, Francis C. "'That Undisturbed Song of Pure Concent': *Paradise Lost* and the Epic-Hymn." *Renaissance Genres: Essays on Theory, History, and Interpretation.* Ed. by Barbara Kiefer Lewalski. Harvard English Studies, vol. 14 (Cambridge, MA, and London: Harvard Univ. Press, 1986), pp. 468–95.
Argues "that the dynamic opposition of epic and hymn constitutes a major generic paradigm for the theme of the poem and that Milton sums up and transcends the hymn of traditional epic poetry."

1959 Bligh, John. "Milton's *Paradise Lost*, VIII.654–56." *Expl*, 42, No. 2, 1984, 7.
On Adam's reference to Eve as being created "occasionally" in *Paradise Lost* 8.654–56. Argues that the word was taken from Thomas Aquinas's *Summa Theologica* in a quotation from Aristotle. The allusion shows that "God's primary and direct intention was to create Adam, and that the creation of Eve was occasioned by Adam's need of a helpmate in the work of procreating and rearing children."

1960 Blondel, Jacques. "Eve, Once More." *CahiersE*, 24, 1983, 61–72.
Examines Eve's actions and role in *Paradise Lost* to determine whether Milton was conveying a theme of misogyny based on biblical and patristic teachings. Concludes that these elements are present, but that Eve is nevertheless a vital part of the epic and a true mirror of human experience.

1961 Blondel, Jacques. "Des Limbes du *Paradis Perdu* à la Terre Gaste de *Childe*

Roland." *Repérages*, 8, 1986, 1–12.
Contrasts the use of quests and baroque art in the events in Milton's Paradise of Fools and the disturbing experience of Browning's Childe Rowland.

1962 Blondel, Jacques. *Milton, Poète de la Bible dans le "Paradis Perdu."* Folcroft, PA: Folcroft Library Editions, 1973; Norwood, PA: Norwood Editions, 1976.
Reprints of Huckabay No. 1127, originally published in 1959.

1963 Blondel, Jacques. "Le Paradis des Sots: *Paradise Lost*, III, 440–498." *Société d'Études Anglo-Américaines des XVIIe et XVIIIe Siècles* (Aix-en-Provence: Université de Provence, 1984), pp. 157–63.
The Paradise of Fools is not just an amusing digression but an integral part of the epic where fools and braggarts are now the sport of winds. None did evil to another, but all scorned humility and are reduced to the state of puppets.

1964 Bloom, Harold. "*Clinamen* or Poetic Misprision." *NLH*, 3, 1972, 373–91.
"Milton's Satan, archetype of the modern poet at his strongest, becomes weak when he reasons and compares, on Mount Niphates, and so commences that process of decline culminating in *Paradise Regained*, ending as the archetype of the modern critic at his weakest."

1965 Bloom, Lillian D. "Addison's Popular Aesthetic: The Rhetoric of the *Paradise Lost* Papers." *The Author in His Work: Essays on a Problem in Criticism.* Ed. by Louis L. Martz and Aubrey Williams (New Haven, CT, and London: Yale Univ. Press, 1978), pp. 263–81.
Relates Addison's criticism of *Paradise Lost* to his other works and shows that because Addison was familiar with his audience, he skirted intellectual rigor and elicited the delights of the imagination.

1966 Blythe, David-Everett. "Milton's Acanthus Ikon." *MiltonQ*, 16, 1982, 11–12.

On the implications of the acanthus plant's appearance in Adam's bower in *Paradise Lost* 4.695–96.

1967 Blythe, David-Everett. "Milton's 'Crisp.'" *Expl*, 41, 1982, 22–23.
"Milton's two uses of 'crisped' [in *Paradise Lost* 4.237 and *Comus* 984] each denote curledness, crimpedness, or unevenness (L. *crispus*)."

1968 Bøgholm, N. *Milton and "Paradise Lost."* New York: Haskell House, 1974.
Reprint of Huckabay No. 1133, originally published in 1932.

1969 Bolton, W. F. "A Further Echo of the Old English *Genesis* in Milton's *Paradise Lost*." *RES*, 25, 1974, 58–61.
Discusses the poem *Genesis* 413–17 and 1671–78 in relation to *Paradise Lost* 2.404–13 and 1.692–99. Concludes that Milton, within the framework of Renaissance translating, made use of the Old English poem.

1970 Bonham, Sister M. Hilda. "The Anthropomorphic God of *Paradise Lost*." *PMASAL*, 53, 1968, 329–35.
Demonstrates that Milton "could not have avoided humanizing God even if he had wanted to; that the poet of *Paradise Lost* so uses anthropomorphism that it serves both the structural unity and even perhaps the dramatic effectiveness of the poem."

1971 Boocker, Joseph David. "*Paradise Lost* as Reformation History." Doctoral diss., Univ. of Nebraska, Lincoln, 1988. 208pp. Abs., *DAI*, 50, 1989, 144A.
Examines "the extent of the effect of the millenarian movement on Milton and his art."

1972 Bourdette, Robert Edward, Jr. "'Advent'rous Song': A Study of the Theme of Inspiration, Action, and Fulfillment in the Invocations of Milton's *Paradise Lost*." Doctoral diss., Univ. of North Carolina, Chapel Hill, 1972. 305pp. Abs., *DAI*, 33, 1973, 4333A.
Shows how Milton's use of the invocation in *Paradise Lost* illustrates the transition from divine inspiration

to human action to regenerative fulfillment.

1973 Bourdette, Robert E., Jr. " 'To *Milton* Lending Sense': Richard Bentley and *Paradise Lost*." *MiltonQ*, 14, 1980, 37–49.

Examines Bentley's emendations and comments and concludes that they provide an insight into his own approach to the poem and "into the way Milton was being absorbed into the age of Newton." See No. 2365.

1974 Bowers, Fredson. "Adam, Eve, and the Fall in *Paradise Lost*." *PMLA*, 84, 1969, 264–73.

"The justification in *Paradise Lost* of the ways of God to men depends as much on Milton's dramatic and psychological motivation of the Fall as on its theological structure. In Milton's view Adam is the faultier of the two because of his conscious failure to assert the absolute authority of his reason over her misguided feelings."

1975 Boyd, William H. "The Secrets of Chaos." *MiltonQ*, 10, 1976, 83–87.

Discusses the concept of Chaos, its characteristics, Milton's use of it in the Christian cosmology in *Paradise Lost*, and its significance for an understanding of Milton's idea of creation.

1976 Boyette, Purvis E. "Milton and the Sacred Fire: Sex Symbolism in *Paradise Lost*." *Literary Monographs*, vol. 5. Ed. by Eric Rothstein (Madison and London: Univ. of Wisconsin Press, 1973), pp. 63–138, 196–207.

Argues that the male-female principle is a means "by which we conceptualize patterns and relationships that explain such diverse problems as Milton's cosmogony, the Christology of erotic love, the biological and ethical basis of human relationships, and the perversions of Satan." Reviews: *MiltonQ*, 7, 1973, 86; John B. Broadbent, Jr., *N&Q*, 22, 1975, 574.

1977 Boyette, Purvis E. "Sexual Metaphor in Milton's Cosmogony, Physics, and

Ontology." *RenP*, 1967, pp. 93–103.

"Christ, the sun, light, and Adam . . . are interchangeable ciphers in a divine equation that balances a feminine configuration made up of the earth, moon, and Eve, which two image clusters combine in turn to yield Milton's monistic God."

1978 Bradford, Richard. " 'Verse Only to the Eye'? Line Endings in *Paradise Lost*." *EIC*, 33, 1983, 187–204.

Supports the eighteenth-century critic Thomas Sheridan's view that the line endings in *Paradise Lost* are engineered very deliberately to create a "pause of suspension" at appropriate points.

1979 Brantlinger, Patrick. "To See New Worlds: Curiosity in *Paradise Lost*." *MLQ*, 33, 1972, 355–69.

Believes that the praise of God's worlds and the desire to see them are identical "so long as that desire is not tainted by pride." Satan's fate in the poem is a comment on the misuse of reason and curiosity.

1980 Brennan, William E. "Robert Fludd as a Possible Source for *Paradise Lost*, V.469–470." *MiltonQ*, 15, 1981, 95–97.

Suggests that the first two lines of Raphael's speech are Milton's recollection of a motto found on an engraving in Fludd's *Monochordum Mundi* (1622).

1981 Brennan, William Edward. "Standing on Earth: Self-Limitation in *Paradise Lost*." Doctoral diss., Princeton Univ., 1977. 268pp. Abs., *DAI*, 38, 1978, 4175A–76A.

Examines Milton's "attitude toward his material and toward the value of his enterprise," focusing on *Lycidas*, *Paradise Lost*, and other poems.

1982 Brian, Beverly. "Johnson's Criticism of *Paradise Lost* in the *Life of Milton*." *CCTEP*, 35, 1970, 22–26.

Details Johnson's criticism of *Paradise Lost* and compares it with other criticisms of the work, especially Addison's. "Johnson's admiration for

Milton's genius and his inability to enjoy his major work are not contradictory. . . . He finds the poem sublime, but not pleasurable."

1983 Bridges, Richard M. "Milton's Original Psalm." *MiltonQ*, 14, 1980, 12–16.
Uses *Paradise Lost* 7.602–32 to show that Milton, "like all who could read the Hebrew original, recognized the poetic properties of Hebrew parallelism and could even convey these qualities in English iambic pentameter, writing a Psalm."

1984 Brink, J. R. "*Paradise Lost* as Literary Myth." *Cithara*, 22, No. 1, 1982, 13–21.
Clarifies Milton's treatment of moral absolutes, demonstrates the central significance of grace over faith and works, and accounts for the epic's temporal disruption by underlining "the importance of vision to Milton's poetics."

1985 Brinkley, Robert A. "The Dilemma of *Paradise Lost*." *EIRC*, 7, 1981, 1–14.
"The dilemma of *Paradise Lost* is the sovereign expression of its voice, the kingly authority which its voice expresses. The dilemma of that authority is Milton's truth. God in Milton's poem imposes a choice on each of his subjects—to obey or to disobey his law—and *Paradise Lost* imposes the same choice on its readers, to oppose or to submit to its instruction."

1986 Brisman, Leslie. "Serpent Error: *Paradise Lost* X, 216–18." *MiltonS*, 2, 1970, 27–35.
The simile in these lines "carries the reader through a chain of associations at first sight uncomfortable but ultimately redemptive."

1987 Broadbent, John B. "Milton's 'Mortal Voice' and His 'Omnific Word.'" *Approaches to "Paradise Lost."* The York Tercentenary Lectures. Ed. by C. A. Patrides (London: Edward Arnold; Toronto: Univ. of Toronto Press, 1968), pp. 99–117.
On Milton's choice of language in *Paradise Lost*. "Mortal voice" refers to Milton's use of colloquial rhythms and diction and "omnific word" to his words that make "a concept out of nothing but syllables, and on the largest possible scale."

1988 Brockbank, Philip. "'Within the Visible Diurnal Spheare': The Moving World of *Paradise Lost*." *Approaches to "Paradise Lost."* The York Tercentenary Lectures. Ed. by C. A. Patrides (London: Edward Arnold; Toronto: Univ. of Toronto Press, 1968), pp. 199–221.
On the astronomy of *Paradise Lost*. Adam and Eve are encompassed by diurnal harmonies, but there are points of instability, aggravated by the Fall, which dislocate cosmic motions. In changed form, diurnal rhythm survives and life begins again under a new dispensation.

1989 Brodnax, Mary Margaret O'Bryan. "Medieval Analogues of *Paradise Lost*." Doctoral diss., Texas Christian Univ., 1968. 171pp. Abs., *DA*, 29, 1969, 2667A.
Demonstrates that, in composing *Paradise Lost*, Milton borrowed myths, paradoxes, and a "realistic and humorous spirit" from earlier English works, especially mystery plays.

1990 Brodwin, Leonora Leet. "The Dissolution of Satan in *Paradise Lost*: A Study of Milton's Heretical Eschatology." *MiltonS*, 8, 1975, 165–207.
"Though masked by a consistent strategy of ambiguity and omission, the apocalyptic passages in the epic suggest the heretical belief in the final dissolution of Satan, of the men and angels he perverted, and of hell itself, as contrasted with the exclusive resurrection of the just to eternal life."

1991 Broekhuysen, Maggie. "Difference between Man and Beast." *AN&Q*, 13, 1974, 2–3.
Discusses Milton's contrast between the human's upright stature and the beast's prone position.

1992 Brooks, Cleanth. "Eve's Awakening."

A Shaping Joy: Studies in the Writer's Craft (London: Methuen; New York: Harcourt Brace Jovanovich, 1971), pp. 349–66.

Reprint of Huckabay No. 1154, originally published in 1954.

1993 Brown, Barbara Hickingbottom. "Temporal Understanding and Narrative Technique in *Paradise Lost* and *Finnegans Wake*." Doctoral diss., Univ. of Illinois, Urbana, 1981. 283pp. Abs., *DAI*, 42, 1982, 4005A.

Examines Milton's and Joyce's "embodiment of temporal existence" as it relates to "ideas of time and history."

1994 Brown, J. N. "Golding and Milton's Versions of the Death of Orpheus." *N&Q*, 23, 1976, 232–33.

Claims that Milton leans more heavily on Arthur Golding's translation of Ovid's *Metamorphoses* than on the original.

1995 Brown, Mary Ruth. "*Paradise Lost* and John 15: Eve, the Branch and the Church." *MiltonQ*, 20, 1986, 127–31.

Believes that the branch imagery in *Paradise Lost* refers to John 15 and that Milton therefore implies that the Fall occurs because Adam and Eve no longer "remain unseparated and observe the proper hierarchy that God has ordained." Christ, on the other hand, is able to redeem because he "gives a directive to the Church to 'stay grafted to his side.'"

1996 Brown, Russell M. "Knowledge and the Fall of Man: Traherne's *Centuries* and Milton's *Paradise Lost*." *LURev*, 4, 1971, 41–49.

"Milton, a pragmatist and Puritan, feels man should learn only that which is directly useful for his future salvation or his present happiness. . . . Traherne, writing in the tradition of Christian mysticism, is not concerned with the usefulness of knowledge on any level other than that which heightens man's conception of God and his relationship to Him."

1997 Brown, Thomas Lewis. "Knowledgeable Virtue: An Analysis of the Fall in *Paradise Lost*." Doctoral diss., Univ. of South Florida, 1976. 101pp. Abs., *DAI*, 37, 1976, 2888A.

Explores the roles of sin and knowledge as they relate to the Fall in *Paradise Lost*.

1998 Browning, Judith Ellen. "Milton's Reformed Revision of the Medieval Circe in the Allegory of Sin and Death in *Paradise Lost*." Doctoral diss., Graduate Theological Union, 1987. 171pp. Abs., *DAI*, 48, 1987, 1207A.

Asserts that "Milton's allegory of Sin and Death provides a unique blend of ancient, medieval and Reformed traditions in seventeenth-century literature."

1999 Brückmann, Patricia. "Eve in the *Odyssey*." *AN&Q*, 22, 1984, 73.

Contends that the depiction of Calypso in Pope's translation of the *Odyssey* alludes to Milton's description of Eve in *Paradise Lost* 4.

2000 Buchwald, Emilie. "The Earthly Paradise and the Ideal Landscape: Studies in a Changing Tradition, through 1750." Doctoral diss., Univ. of Minnesota, 1971. 250pp. Abs., *DAI*, 32, 1971, 1465A–66A.

Studies "several manifestations of the idea of the earthly paradise as it has emerged in cartographic, literary, and aesthetic history from the fifth through the middle of the eighteenth century." Mentions Milton's *Comus*.

2001 Buckley, Elizabeth Wing. "The Double Helix: Contrariety as Structure in *Paradise Lost*." Doctoral diss., East Texas State Univ., 1984. 159pp. Abs., *DAI*, 45, 1985, 3643A.

Explains the contraries in *Paradise Lost* through a "double helix" model that "represents the duality of man and his universe and reflects the seventeenth century's confrontation between empiricism and rationalism, science and religion."

2002 Burden, Dennis H. *The Logical Epic: A Study of the Argument of "Paradise*

Lost." London: Routledge and Kegan Paul; Cambridge, MA: Harvard Univ. Press, 1967. ix, 206pp.

Identifies the epic's systematic and coherent structure by explaining that Milton's intention to assert God's providence is an exercise in clarification, finding order and rationality in what might appear random and inexplicable. Reviews: Stella P. Revard, *JEGP*, 67, 1968, 517–20; Rosalie L. Colie, *KR*, 122, 1968, 671–77; Mark Roberts, *N&Q*, 15, 1968, 389–94; Kenneth Connelly, *YR*, 57, 1968, 589–94; Michael Fixler, *RES*, 20, 1969, 227–29; Ants Oras, *SR*, 77, 1969, 176–84; Michael Wilding, *EC*, 11, 1969, 84–93.

2003 Burke, Kenneth. "Words Anent Logology: Perspectives in Literary Symbolism." *YCC*, 1, 1968, 72–82.

Disagrees with William Empson's views on Milton's God and the War in Heaven (see No. 2175).

2004 Burnet, R. A. L. "Some Echoes of the Genevan Bible in Shakespeare and Milton." *N&Q*, 27, 1980, 179–81.

Suggests that the Geneva Bible provides close parallels to *Paradise Lost* 1.392–96 (2 Kings 23.10) and 462–63 (1 Samuel 5.2 and 1 Chronicles 10.10) and to "On the New Forcers of Conscience" 5 (Leviticus 18.29).

2005 Bush, Douglas. "Milton." *On Milton's Poetry: A Selection of Modern Studies.* Ed. by Arnold Stein (Greewich, CT: Fawcett Publications, 1970), pp. 80–88.

Reprint of part of Huckabay No. 466, originally published in 1945.

2006 Bush, Douglas. "Three More Views of *Paradise Lost.*" *MLQ*, 34, 1973, 78–84.

Review essay on William G. Riggs, *The Christian Poet in "Paradise Lost"* (No. 2937); Lawrence W. Hyman, *The Quarrel Within* (No. 716); and Joseph E. Duncan, *Milton's Earthly Paradise* (No. 2158).

2007 Butler, Francelia. "The Holy Spirit and Odors in *Paradise Lost.*" *MiltonN*, 3, 1969, 65–69.

Suggests that fragrances are used to unify "the various identities of the Holy Spirit" and thus serve as "an ideal metaphor to explain the presence or absence of God."

2008 Byard, Margaret M. "Divine Wisdom-Urania." *MiltonQ*, 12, 1978, 134–37.

Speculates that in invoking Urania-Wisdom in *Paradise Lost*, Milton might have recalled seeing Andrea Sacchi's fresco on Divine Wisdom when visiting the Barberini Palace in Rome in 1639.

2009 Byard, Margaret Mather. "Note on the Illustration: St. Peter's and Pandaemonium?" *MiltonQ*, 9, 1975, 65–66.

The engraving on the cover of the May, 1975, issue of *MiltonQ* is of Giuseppe Tiburzio Vergelli's painting and "shows the interior of St. Peter's as Milton would have seen it in 1638 and 1639." The engraving suggests Milton's description in *Paradise Lost* 1.710–92.

2010 Byard, Margaret Mather. "Poetic Responses to the Copernican Revolution." *Scientific American*, 236, No. 6, 1977, 120–29.

Discusses Milton's view of the universe as Copernican versus Ptolemaic. Claims Milton's vision in *Paradise Lost* inspired others to write of world order. Asserts that "although Milton's message in *Paradise Lost* was theological and political, the awareness of space that was brought about by the revolutionary cosmology of Copernicus, Kepler and Galileo gave him a vast arena for his account of struggle between good and evil." Abs., *MiltonQ*, 12, 1978, 48.

2011 Camé, Jean-François. "Les Éléments du Merveilleux dans *Comus* et *Paradise Lost.*" *CahiersE*, 22, 1982, 41–49.

In *Paradise Lost*, Milton does not abandon the supernatural. The language suggestive of another world is lost when Adam and Eve fall from grace.

2012 Camé, Jean-François. "Spatial and

Temporal Variety in *Paradise Lost*." *CahiersE*, 8, 1975, 75.

Believes the juxtaposition of "grateful vicissitude" in *Paradise Lost* 6.8 and "sweet interchange" in 9.115 shows that "Milton enjoys as much the alternation of day and night and of seasons as he enjoys the mountains and plains, the valleys and hills."

2013 Camoin, François. "Milton's Satan." *MSE*, 1, 1967, 46–51.

Asserts that the character of Satan "belongs to a literary tradition that found its greatest expression some time before Milton, in the late works of Jacobean drama."

2014 Campbell, Gordon. "La Creación Según Ideas Theológicas y Literarias de Milton." *Káñina*, 2, 1978, 99–108. Translated as "Milton's Theological and Literary Treatments of the Creation." *JTS*, 30, 1979, 128–37.

Raphael's account of creation in *Paradise Lost* 7 is not intended to provide intellectual satisfaction, as is Milton's account in the *Christian Doctrine*. Rather, it "celebrates the wonder of creation so as to induce a worshipful attitude in Adam and in Milton's readers." Abs., *MiltonQ*, 14, 1980, 31.

2015 Campbell, Gordon C. "The Intellect and the Imagination: A Study of the Relationship between Milton's *De Doctrina Christiana* and *Paradise Lost*." Doctoral diss., Univ. of York, 1973. See *MiltonQ*, 7, 1973, 93.

2016 Campbell, Gordon. "Milton and Aurora's Tears." *N&Q*, 26, 1979, 415.

Claims that Milton alludes to the work of Ovid. Asserts that incidents similar to Aurora's sprinkling of tears on the world may be found in *In Quintum Novembris*, "An Epitaph on the Marchioness of Winchester," and *Paradise Lost* 5.

2017 Campbell, Gordon. "Milton's Catalogue of the Winds." *MiltonQ*, 18, 1984, 125–28.

Cites problems with Amy Lee Turner's assertion (No. 3173) that Milton used Jan Jansson's wind chart as a source for his catalog of the winds in *Paradise Lost* 10.695–707. Believes that Milton used Theophrastus's *De Ventis* and Aristotle's *Meteorologica* and *Problemata*.

2018 Campbell, Gordon C. "The Mortalist Heresy in *Paradise Lost*." *MiltonQ*, 13, 1979, 33–36.

In Book 3.245–49, Christ's statement points to the faultiness of Adam's statement in Book 10.789–92, which is not intended as a vehicle for Milton's mortalist sympathies.

2019 Campbell, Gordon. "The Son of God in *De Doctrina Christiana* and *Paradise Lost*." *MLR*, 75, 1980, 507–14.

Offers evidence that in the *Christian Doctrine*, "the philosophical arguments which Milton uses to deny these attributes [unity of essence, omnipresence, and eternity] to the Son were not formulated to shore up a specific theological point, but were drawn from his *Artis Logicae*, and that the degradation of the Son . . . is absent from *Paradise Lost* because in the poem the Son is not denied the attributes of God the Father." See Bauman's response (No. 1910). See also Nos. 1913 and 2020.

2020 Campbell, Gordon. "Son of Son of Lassie." *MiltonQ*, 21, No. 1, 1987, 104–05.

Defends his previous assertion of the Son's omnipresence in *Paradise Lost* (No. 2019), against Michael Bauman's arguments (No. 1910). See Bauman's response (No. 1913).

2021 Campbell, Gordon. "The Wealth of Ormus and of Ind." *MiltonQ*, 21, No. 1, 1987, 22–23.

Claims that Milton's reference to Ormus and Ind in *Paradise Lost* 2.2 indicates that "The wealth of Satan's throne is . . . associated with bloody conquest and bribery."

2022 Campbell, Gordon, and Roger Collins. "Milton's *Almansor*." *MiltonQ*, 17, 1983, 81–84.

Asserts that Milton refers to Almohad Emir Abū-Yusūf Ya'qūb al-Mansūr when he uses the title of Almansor in *Paradise Lost* 11.402–04. Also discusses the sources for Milton's political geography.

2023 Campbell, Gordon, and N. M. Davis. "*Paradise Lost* and the Norwich Grocers' Play." *MiltonQ*, 14, 1980, 113–16.

Notes that the 1565 play and *Paradise Lost* reflect Protestant views on conjugal feelings and that Milton's poem draws on popular Protestant traditions.

2024 Canfield, J. Douglas. "The Birthday of the Son in *Paradise Lost*." *ELN*, 13, 1975, 113–15.

Sees the lines "This day I have begot whom I declare / My only Son" (5.603–04) as referring to the Son's celestial birthday. Calls attention to the poem's grand, external chronology, measured by great years, until God shall be "All in All." The Messiah's birthday is the measurement not only of earthly time but heavenly time as well.

2025 Canfield, J. Douglas. "Blessed are the Merciful: The Understanding of the Promise in *Paradise Lost*." *MiltonQ*, 7, 1973, 43–46.

Concludes that the promise of the Redemption in *Paradise Lost* 10.171–81 "is judged 'best' to be given in 'mysterious terms' in order to provide Adam and Eve with the opportunity to do what Satan can never do: to be merciful to one another so that they can then comprehend God's mercy."

2026 Cann, Christian. *A Scriptural and Allegorical Glossary on Milton's "Paradise Lost."* Folcroft, PA: Folcroft Library Editions, 1972; Norwood, PA: Norwood Editions, 1976, 1977; Philadelphia, PA: R. West, 1977.

Reprints of Stevens No. 779, originally published in 1828.

2027 Cannon, Blanche. "The Haunted Stream: Rivers and Fountains in Milton's Poems." *RMR*, 23, 1969, 183–88.

Contends that in "the treatment of the river and fountain Christian and classical affinities are merged." Milton refers to rivers of the Old Testament to "place us geographically, and also to orient us spiritually in *Paradise Lost*. . . . With what sometimes appears to be greater poetic force, perhaps because of their association with 'the value of ideal–beauty,' he refers to the rivers of Greek mythology."

2028 Cappuzzo, Marcello. *Il "Paradise Lost" di John Milton.* Bari: Adriatica Editrice, 1972. 217pp.

Discusses Satan and God and includes chapters on Adam and Eve, the Fall and reconciliation, and concludes with a discussion of the paradise within.

2029 Cardell, Kerry. *On Reading "Paradise Lost": Myth in Literature and Society.* Victoria, BC: School of Humanities, Deakin Univ., 1980. 91pp.

"What follows here is not a study of the full myth . . . but a set of notes and exercises intended to facilitate your [the student's] initial reading of *Paradise Lost*." Discusses such topics as Genesis as the source, epic form, and style.

2030 Carlton, Susan R. "The Inward Image." *MiltonQ*, 15, 1981, 88–92.

Analyzes the use of the word "image" in *Paradise Lost* to show that an apprehension of God's image will enable Adam, Eve, and the reader to find the paradise within.

2031 Carnes, Valerie. "Time and Language in Milton's *Paradise Lost*." *ELH*, 37, 1970, 517–39.

Examines the use of language to suggest certain concepts of time in *Paradise Lost*. Claims that, through the use of language, "three distinct 'times' or epochs may be identified": time prior to the creation; time after the creation, but before the Fall; and time since the Fall. Shows the manipulation of sensory words such as "taste" and "light" to convey spiritual meanings.

2032 Carroll, Conard Paul. "Silence in *Paradise Lost*: A Study of the Divine, Human, and Demonic." Doctoral diss., State Univ. of New York, Buffalo, 1987. 273pp. Abs., *DAI*, 48, 1987, 1208A.

Explores the use of silence in *Paradise Lost* to explain why Eve engages the serpent in conversation.

2033 Carter, David. "'Frail is Our Happiness': Some Aspects of *Paradise Lost*." *CR*, 20, 1978, 3–14.

Discusses dramatic tension in *Paradise Lost* and the problem of obedience in the garden.

2034 Cauthen, Irby B., Jr. "Satan 'Squat Like a Toad.'" *MiltonQ*, 7, 1973, 95–97.

Examines the figure of Satan as toad in *Paradise Lost* 4.800 "in connection with the interpretation of traditional animal lore by Milton's near contemporaries."

2035 Cavanagh, Michael. "A Meeting of Epic and History: Books XI and XII of *Paradise Lost*." *ELH*, 38, 1971, 206–22.

Justifies the last two books, which are not "merely tacked on." "Since Adam lost Paradise . . . his task remaining is to acquire enough knowledge and experience to know why he lost it, to know what this loss bodes for the future, and to muster up enough courage to pronounce these consequences just." In his last speech, "Adam's final optimism would have been meaningless if it had been uttered in all ignorance of history."

2036 Chambers, A. B. "The Falls of Adam and Eve in *Paradise Lost*." *New Essays on "Paradise Lost."* Ed. by Thomas Kranidas (Berkeley, Los Angeles, and London: Univ. of California Press, 1969), pp. 118–30.

The "hierarchy of Paradise has been overturned. . . . This inversion of true order, with all that it implies, could not have taken its present form in

Paradise Lost were there not in the immediate background an analysis of sin, a psychology of temptation, as well as Augustine's understanding of St. Paul, all to insist that 'Adam was not deceived, but the woman being deceived was in the transgression.'" Abs., *MiltonQ*, 4, 1970, 34.

2037 Chambers, Douglas. "Darkness Visible." *Familiar Colloquy: Essays Presented to Arthur Edward Barker*. Ed. by Patricia Brückmann (Toronto: Oberon Press, 1978), pp. 163–78.

On Milton's treatment of light and dark imagery in relation to the Renaissance commentators and printers. Suggests that in *Paradise Lost* Milton is concerned "with a light that is moral, physical, spiritual, and dramatic" and that the light of Pandemonium is false, "the light of a confusion of tongues where speech is babel and rhetoric perverts truth."

2038 Chambers, Douglas. "'Discovering in Wide Lantskip': *Paradise Lost* and the Tradition of Landscape Description in the Seventeenth Century." *JGH*, 5, 1985, 15–31.

Observes that Milton's spelling of the word "lantskip" in Book 4.153 and 5.142 is indicative of art. In describing paradise, Milton remembers specific gardens and paintings in Italy and England.

2039 Chameev, A. A. *Dzhon Mil'ton i ego Poema Poteriânnyi rai*. Leningrad: Leningrad Univ. Press, 1987. 126pp.

John Milton and "Paradise Lost."

2040 Chameev, A. A. "Zhanrovo-kompozitsionnoe svoeobrazie poem Dzh: Miltona 'Poteriannyi rai.'" *Problemy Zhanra i Stilia Khudozhestvennogo Proizvedeniia*. Ed. by N. I. Velikaia (Dalnevost: Izdatel'stvo Dal'nevostochnogo Univ., 1988), pp. 212–20.

Discusses the cosmological and astronomical ideas in *Paradise Lost* and the various intellectual influences on Milton.

2041 Champagne, Claudia Maria. "Lacan's Mirror and Beyond: Dante, Spenser, and Milton." Doctoral diss., Tulane Univ., 1987. 473pp. Abs., *DAI*, 48, 1987, 778A.

Applies Jacques Lacan's theories concerning human psychic development to Satan, Adam, and Eve. Each presents a psychodrama which begins with what Lacan calls the "mirror stage."

2042 Chang, Y. Z. "Why Did Milton Err on Two Chinas?" *MLR*, 65, 1970, 493–98.

On *Paradise Lost* 11.376–96. "Milton did err on the subject of Cathay and China; he no doubt considered them as two countries. Obviously, his error was not the result of ignorance; it was the honest and excusable mistake of a sound and cautious scholar, unwilling to embrace a facile identification based on what he thought was flimsy and dubious evidence."

2043 Charlesworth, Arthur R. *Paradise Found.* New York: Philosophical Library, 1973. xxii, 273pp.

Believes that the *Christian Doctrine* should be read as a gloss on *Paradise Lost* and argues that Milton's epic is actually about paradise found. Review: *MiltonQ*, 9, 1975, 54.

2044 Cheung, King-Kok. "Beauty and the Beast: A Sinuous Reflection of Milton's Eve." *MiltonS*, 23, 1987, 197–214.

Argues that Eve's decision to eat the fruit must be viewed "as at least collusive, and not merely deceived." Contends that Milton likens Eve to the serpent by demonstrating that "external persuasion corresponds to personal desire."

2045 Cheung, King-Kok. "The Woe and Wonder of Despair: A Study of Doctor Faustus, Macbeth, and Satan." Doctoral diss., Univ. of California, Berkeley, 1984. 228pp. Abs., *DAI*, 46, 1985, 987A.

Recognizes that despair causes the potential for both good and evil in Doctor Faustus, Macbeth, and Milton's Satan.

2046 Choe, Ok Young. "A Study of Milton's Satan in *Paradise Lost*." *JELL*, 32, 1986, 219–33.

In Korean; English summary, pp. 234–35. Discusses the Satanist controversy in twentieth-century scholarship. Considers Satan to symbolize human depravity.

2047 Christopher, Georgia B. "The Improvement of God's 'Character' in *Paradise Lost*." *RenP*, 1982, pp. 1–8.

"More important than the deterioration of Satan as a character in *Paradise Lost* is the 'creation of the Deity,' as his face is carefully re-drawn during the course of Books I–VIII. The narrative structure of Milton's epic offers a *mimesis* of the perceptual drama that the Reformers ascribed to faith."

2048 Christopher, Georgia B. "Milton's Third Scripture." *SCN*, 38, 1980, 44.

Abstract of a paper presented at the 1979 MLA Convention. "The proximate models for Milton's assimilation of epic matter and manner to biblical story are Luther and Calvin."

2049 Christopher, Georgia B. "Satanic Aeneas and Virgilian Adam." *MiltonQ*, 14, 1980, 70.

Abstract of a paper presented at the 1979 MLA Convention. Sees "Satan as an ironically perfected Aeneas and Adam as the truly renovated Aeneas," who "shoulders an altogether new kind of destiny: he is to possess and establish a verbal kingdom."

2050 Christopher, Georgia B. "The Verbal Gate to Paradise: Adam's 'Literary Experience' in Book X of *Paradise Lost*." *PMLA*, 90, 1975, 69–77.

Shows that "Eve's loving gesture of reconciliation . . . has no direct bearing upon Adam's return to faith. At best, Eve serves as an unwitting but providential stimulus to memory." Reply by Jeanne C. Hunter (*PMLA*, 91, 1976, 115–16); rejoinder by Christopher, pp. 116–17.

2051 Church, Jo Hall. "Lucifer's Haven:

A Rhetorical Analysis of Book I, Lines 242–55 of *Paradise Lost.*" *CCTEP*, 48, 1983, 74–77.

Explains that Milton manipulates sound, word choice, and meter so that "the entire passage relies on Lucifer's sophistic reasoning conjoined with his rhetoric to persuade himself as well as his audience."

2052 Cinquemani, A. M. "Milton's *Paradise Lost*, IV, 460–473." *Expl*, 30, 1972, Item 56.

Suggests that Eve's discovery of her image in the water alludes to the murky image explained by Paul in 1 Corinthians 13.12 and to Narcissus.

2053 Cirillo, Albert R. " 'Hail Holy Light' and Divine Time in *Paradise Lost.*" *JEGP*, 68, 1969, 45–56.

Discusses the opening lines of Book 3 in order to explain the poem's twofold time scheme. "The address to light . . . represents a poetic conflation of the two realms of time and eternity under the single aspect of eternity."

2054 Cirillo, Albert R. "Noon-Midnight and the Temporal Structure of *Paradise Lost.*" *Critical Essays on Milton from "ELH"* (Baltimore, MD, and London: Johns Hopkins Press, 1969), pp. 210–33.

Reprint of Huckabay No. 1196, originally published in 1962.

2055 Cirillo, Albert R. "Tasso's *Il Mondo Creato*: Providence and the Created Universe." *MiltonS*, 3, 1971, 83–102.

Uses Tasso's poem as an aid to understanding the synthesis of earth and heaven, as explained by Raphael in *Paradise Lost* 7. Tasso also helps in explaining Raphael's description of the scale of nature in Book 5.

2056 Clark, David R. "Asmodeus and the Fishy Fume: *Paradise Lost*, IV, 153–171." *SEL*, 12, 1972, 121–28.

States that "the fishy fumes from which Asmodeus flees are thus made equivalent to Satan's flagrant and putrid sin, his dire attempt, which is its own punishment, and which will recoil on him

like that 'devilish Engine' in IV, 17, with a sulphurous smell, and 'with a vengeance' send him to where he will be 'fast bound.' "

2057 Clark, Mili N. "The Mechanics of Creation: Non-Contradiction and Natural Necessity in *Paradise Lost.*" *ELR*, 7, 1977, 207–42.

Sees "Sufficient to have stood, though free to fall" (*Paradise Lost* 3.99) as a contradiction but concludes: "It is the triumph of Christian logic, which is what Milton argues in the myth of *Paradise Lost*, that the contradiction in the Christian myth can be *overcome* by contradiction: that is, by those individuals rightfully exercising the power, theirs by virtue of natural necessity, to contradict themselves."

2058 Cockelreas, Joanne Lewis. "Much Deceiv'd, Much Failing, Hapless Eve: Iconography and Eve in Milton's *Paradise Lost.*" Doctoral diss., Univ. of New Mexico, 1973. 268pp. Abs., *DAI*, 34, 1974, 7184A–85A.

Compares "the portrayal of Eve in the visual arts with Milton's depiction of Eve in *Paradise Lost.*"

2059 Cohen, Kitty. "Milton's God in Council and War." *MiltonS*, 3, 1971, 159–84.

States that "Milton's presentation of God and Heaven not only embodies his seventeenth-century theology, but is also poetically convincing if various Hebraic elements, thematic and metaphorical, that are incorporated in Milton's descriptions of God in council and in war are closely examined."

2060 Cohen, Kitty. "A Note on Milton's Azazel." *PQ*, 49, 1970, 248–49.

On *Paradise Lost* 1.534. Suggests that "Milton was influenced by apocalyptic and late aggadic as well as cabbalistic literature, where Azazel is conceived of as a fallen angel and even as a prototype of Satan."

2061 Cohen, Kitty. "A Note on Milton's Semitic Studies." *MiltonQ*, 4, 1970, 7–10.

On *Paradise Lost* 1.19–22. Discusses

plausible sources from which Milton could have derived the meaning "brooding" for the Hebrew "merahephet" in Genesis 1.2.

2062 Cohen, Kitty O. "A Study of Selective Hebraic Elements in *Paradise Lost*." Doctoral diss., Yale Univ., 1968. 275pp. Abs., *DAI*, 30, 1969, 1556A.

Discusses the influence of Hebraic elements in the epic's different settings—hell, paradise, and heaven.

2063 Cohen, Kitty. *The Throne and the Chariot: Studies in Milton's Hebraism.* Studies in English Literature, vol. 97. The Hague and Paris: Mouton, 1975. xii, 194pp.

Studies Milton's use of the Hebrew Bible, which provides "an account of the relationship between Man, God and Nature in its permanent historical character." Deals with most of Milton's works, but especially with *Paradise Lost.* Appendix: "Milton's Editors from Hume to Hughes." Reviews: *MiltonQ*, 11, 1977, 57; Michael Lieb, *JEGP*, 76, 1977, 550–52; Michael Fixler, *RES*, 29, 1978, 214–15.

2064 Coiro, Ann Baynes. " 'To Repair the Ruins of Our First Parents': *Of Education* and Fallen Adam." *SEL*, 28, 1988, 133–47.

Compares the pedagogy in *Of Education* with that in *Paradise Lost* 11–12. Argues that Michael's instruction of Adam is a working model of Milton's educational approach revealed in *Of Education.* Also contends that education is both a central theme and a central action of *Paradise Lost.*

2065 Colaccio, John Jerry. "A Peculiar Dialectic: A Critical Study of Nature in Milton's Epic Paradise." Doctoral diss., New York Univ., 1975. 332pp. Abs., *DAI*, 36, 1975, 3725A–26A.

Explains nature in Milton's paradise as more than simple topography—it is instead "the psychic union of man, the visible creation, and God."

2066 Colie, Rosalie L. "*Paradise Lost* Re-

gained." *KR*, 30, No. 122, 1968, 671–77.

Review essay. Surveys the following studies: Dennis H. Burden, *The Logical Epic* (No. 2002); Ernest Sirluck, *"Paradise Lost": A Deliberate Epic* (No. 3076); Stanley E. Fish, *Surprised by Sin* (No. 2216); and Wayne Shumaker, *Unpremeditated Verse* (No. 3055).

2067 Collett, Jonathan H. "Milton's Use of Classical Mythology in *Paradise Lost*." *PMLA*, 85, 1970, 88–96.

Defines and discusses the three categories of myth in *Paradise Lost*: myths identifying the pagan gods with the fallen angels; myths used in comparisons with Eden, Adam, and Eve; and myths that are types of the Old and New Testament revelation that Adam will receive.

2068 Collier, John. *Milton's "Paradise Lost": Screenplay for Cinema of the Mind.* New York: Knopf, 1973. xiii, 144pp.

"A parade of scenes based on Milton's glorious and appalling images, peopled with hideous or radiant monsters, and with archetypes of human beings caught in the pregnant situations of the fable." Reviews: Timothy Foote, *Time*, June 25, 1973, pp. 90–91; Leo Braudy, *NYTB*, Aug. 5, 1973, pp. 6–7; Jay Martin, *NR*, 168, 1973, 28–29; Robert Evett, *Washington Star and Daily News*, May 20, 1973; reply to Evett by William W. Fee, *Washington Star and Daily News*, June 3, 1973 (reprinted in *MiltonQ*, 8, 1974, 67–68); Joseph Anthony Wittreich, Jr., *MiltonQ*, 8, 1974, 15–21.

2069 Collins, Anthony R. "*Paradise Lost* as a Baroque Poem." Doctoral diss., Michigan State Univ., 1969. 242pp. Abs., *DAI*, 30, 1970, 4940A.

Demonstrates that "*Paradise Lost* actually possesses most of the characteristics of the Seventeenth Century stylistic movement termed the Baroque."

2070 Collins, Christopher. "Milton's Early Cosmos and the Fall of Mulciber." *MiltonS*, 19, 1984, 37–52.

Suggests that Milton's cosmology changed as he matured and links *Elegy 7* with the fall of Mulciber, one of "those other men who had fallen victims to women."

2071 Collins, Dan S. "The Buoyant Mind in Milton's Eden." *MiltonS*, 5, 1973, 229–48.

"Although most critics interpret the prelapsarian action of the epic as a series of anticipations of the fall, Milton utilizes Eve's dream and Adam's comments on astronomy and the birth of his own consciousness, his search for a helpmeet, and his first experience of sexual attraction to demonstrate the mind's inherent buoyancy, in each episode rising further toward its angelic perfection by maintaining a willing dependence upon God's sustaining grace and exercising reason to discipline lesser faculties, particularly the imagination."

2072 Como, James. "C. S. Lewis in Milton Criticism." *CSLBull*, 3, No. 12, 1972, 5–6.

Believes that Lewis's greatest accomplishment in *A Preface to "Paradise Lost"* (see No. 2595) was to classify the poem as a secondary epic.

2073 Comstock, W. Richard. "Religion, Literature, and Religious Studies: A Sketch of Their Modal Connections." *NDEJ*, 14, 1981, 1–28.

Cites *Paradise Lost* as an example of the uniting of religion, literature, and scholarly study to form the whole. "Thus a solely religious reading of *Paradise Lost* may be overwhelmed by the weight of a seriousness that crushes it; while a strictly literary approach may cultivate a freedom that has lost touch with the deeper needs of the human spirit. . . . Each modality understood as an exclusive option seems incomplete."

2074 Condee, Ralph Waterbury. *Milton's Theories Concerning Epic Poetry: Their Sources and Their Influence on "Para-*

dise Lost." Ann Arbor, MI: Univ. Microfilms International, 1980 Books on Demand Reprints.

Reprint of Huckabay No. 1206, a doctoral dissertation from 1949.

2075 Condee, Ralph Waterbury. "No Local Wounds of Head or Heel: The Dynamic Structure of *Paradise Lost.*" *JGE*, 21, 1969, 91–106.

Maintains that Milton's handling of Greco-Roman literary tradition, as applied to Satan, Adam, and traditional heroism, "give[s] the poem its integrated forward thrust."

2076 Conley, James William. "Tasso and Milton: *I Discorsi, La Gerusalemme Liberata* and *Paradise Lost.*" Doctoral diss., Univ. of Wisconsin, Madison, 1974. 332pp. Abs., *DAI*, 36, 1975, 268A–69A.

Compares *Jerusalem Delivered* and *Paradise Lost* based on "the ideal subject, structure, and style of the heroic poem" as outlined in Tasso's *Discourses*.

2077 Connelly, Kenneth. "*Paradise Lost*: Explications." *YR*, 57, 1968, 589–94.

Review essay. Discusses Dennis H. Burden, *The Logical Epic* (No. 2002) and Wayne Shumaker, *Unpremeditated Verse* (No. 3055).

2078 Conner, William Fox. "Satan as Negative Consciousness in Milton, Blake and Shelley." Doctoral diss., Univ. of Missouri, Columbia, 1979. 226pp. Abs., *DAI*, 40, 1980, 4604A–05A.

Traces the evolution of Satan from a concrete figure to a vague "negative consciousness" as he is portrayed by Milton, Blake, and Shelley.

2079 Conners, John Reed. "The Crucifixion in *Paradise Lost, Paradise Regained* and *Samson Agonistes.*" Doctoral diss., Univ. of Rochester, 1982. 265pp. Abs., *DAI*, 44, 1983, 1460A.

Explores "the Son's nature, his place in the divine plan of salvation, and his example to be followed by all men and women" in Milton's three long poems.

2080 Cook, Eleanor. "Melos versus Logos, or Why Doesn't God Sing: Some Thoughts on Milton's Wisdom." *Re-membering Milton: Essays on the Texts and Traditions.* Ed. by Mary Nyquist and Margaret W. Ferguson (New York and London: Methuen, 1987), pp. 197–210.

Discusses melos (song) and logos (word), mainly in *Paradise Lost.* Logos is masculine, while melos is feminine. Expresses concern that Milton is not willing to give Eve a coequal relation with wisdom.

2081 Cope, Jackson I. *The Metaphoric Structure of "Paradise Lost."* Octagon Books. New York: Farrar, Straus and Giroux, 1979; Ann Arbor, MI: Univ. Microfilms International, 1980 Books on Demand Reprints.

Reprints of Huckabay No. 1209, originally published in 1962.

2082 Copeland, Thomas A. "Milton's Narrative Technique in the War in Heaven." *SPWVSRA,* 4, 1979, 16–20.

Believes that the War in Heaven trains the reader to perceive the structure of the poem as a whole because it marks an apex, with the other books ranged on either side in pairs. Contrasts the scenes in the war.

2083 Cormican, L. A. "Milton's Religious Verse." *From Donne to Marvell.* Ed. by Boris Ford. The New Pelican Guide to English Literature, vol. 3. Revised edition (Harmondsworth: Penguin, 1982), pp. 219–38.

Calls *Paradise Lost* the highest achievement of the Protestant mind. See Huckabay No. 499.

2084 Corum, Richard. "In White Ink: *Paradise Lost* and Milton's Ideas of Women." *Milton and the Idea of Woman.* Ed. by Julia M. Walker (Urbana and Chicago: Univ. of Illinois Press, 1988), pp. 120–47.

Concludes that "Milton's motive for poetry is that he *has* one parent but *had* two. What I have tried to do in this 'writing' of *Paradise Lost*'s white

ink is to suggest that the unsubmissive part of him would have us switch these verbs, and admit that monotheism, a narcissistic translation of parenting into a regressive, sadomasochistic dependency upon the 'kidnapped' son's endlessly grateful submission, tragically violates inalienable human rights— Eve's, Milton's, and our own." Abs., *MiltonQ,* 24, 1990, 150.

2085 Cox, Carrol B. "Citizen Angels: Civil Society and the Abstract Individual in *Paradise Lost.*" *MiltonS,* 23, 1987, 165–96.

Studies Milton's representation of angels in *Paradise Lost.* Argues that the cherub is the supreme example of Milton's art of presenting the "abstract-*isolated*-human individual." By isolating his characters from prior social relations, they are forced "by the choices they make . . . [to] create new social relations within which their action can take on meaning not inherent in the action itself."

2086 Cramer, Maurice Browning. "'A Woman's Last Word': *Paradise Lost* or Paradise Retained?" *BSNotes,* 6, No. 2, 1976, 3–17.

Discusses how to introduce Browning. Likens the situation in Browning's poems to Eve's having the last word as she leaves Adam to work alone in *Paradise Lost* 9.

2087 Crane, D. E. L. "Burton and Mulciber's 'Summer's Day.'" *N&Q,* 34, 1987, 324.

Cites Robert Burton's portrayal of Vulcan's fall from heaven in the *Anatomy of Melancholy* as the source for Milton's portrayal of Mulciber's fall.

2088 Craven, Robert R. "The Mists in *Paradise Lost.*" *ELN,* 18, 1980, 20–25.

Discusses Milton's poetic uses of the qualities attributed to rising and falling mists, especially as these qualities "ironically objectify Satan's travels in Eden."

2089 Crawford, John W. "Another Biblical

Allusion in *Paradise Lost.*" *Discourse: Essays on English and American Literature* (Amsterdam: Editions Rodopi N. V., 1978), pp. 62–64.

Reprint of Huckabay No. 1215, originally published in 1967.

2090 Crosman, Robert True. "Point of View in *Paradise Lost.*" Doctoral diss., Columbia Univ., 1971. 238pp. Abs., *DAI*, 34, 1974, 6634A.

Argues that Milton uses four points of view—"the satanic, the divine, the unfallen human and the fallen"—to present *Paradise Lost* as "a progressive revelation of truth."

2091 Crosman, Robert. *Reading "Paradise Lost.*" Bloomington and London: Indiana Univ. Press, 1980. xi, 262pp.

Views *Paradise Lost* not as an object but as an experience. Chapters: "Milton's Great Oxymoron (Books 1–2)"; "Light Invisible (Book 3)"; "Points of View in Paradise (Books 4–5)"; "Unfallen Narration (Books 5–6)"; "True Fiction (Books 7–8)"; "The Comedy of the Fall (Book 9)"; "The Curse (Book 10)"; and "Salvation through Reading (Books 11–12)." Reviews: Roy Flannagan, *MiltonQ*, 14, 1980, 131–32; William E. Cain, *MLN*, 96, 1981, 1121–33; Jean-François Camé, *CahiersE*, 19, 1981, 113–14; John B. Mason, *EIC*, 31, 1981, 362–68; Philip J. Gallagher, *RMR*, 37, 1983, 217–34.

2092 Crosman, Robert. "Some Doubts about 'The Reader of *Paradise Lost.*'" *CE*, 37, 1975, 372–82.

Critics often claim that *Paradise Lost* was written for the seventeenth-century reader or for an "ideal reader" encoded in the text. To understand the motive for such claims, we must see them in the context of the attack made on the intentional fallacy in the 1940s.

2093 Crump, Galbraith M., ed. *Approaches to Teaching Milton's "Paradise Lost.*" New York: Modern Language Association of America, 1986. x, 201pp.

Contents: Part 1: "Materials," by Crump; Part 2: "Approaches," containing essays on various approaches by Joseph E. Duncan, Sanford Golding, Robert W. Halli, Jr., Joan E. Hartman, Eugene D. Hill, George Klawitter, Michael M. Levy, Ellen S. Mankoff, Elizabeth McCutcheon, Leslie E. Moore, Anna K. Nardo, William Malin Porter, Anne Lake Prescott, Herman Rapaport, Hugh M. Richmond, Virginia Tufte, and John Wooten. Contains an extensive bibliography and a list of films and recordings. Review: Lois Potter, *MLR*, 84, 1989, 128.

2094 Crump, Galbraith Miller. *The Mystical Design of "Paradise Lost.*" Lewisburg, PA: Bucknell Univ. Press; London: Associated Univ. Presses, 1975. 194pp.

Demonstrates "the pervasiveness of a mystical, that is, anagogical level of meaning in *Paradise Lost*, embodied structurally and conceptually in the form of the circle, which represents both the cyclical rhythms of man's world and the eternal, immutable perfection of the Creator." Reviews: *MiltonQ*, 9, 1975, 54–56; Henry D. Janzen, *Ren&R*, 12, 1976, 136–37; Arnold Stein, *SR*, 84, 1976, 695–706; William B. Hunter, Jr., *SCN*, 35, 1977, 2–3.

2095 Crunelle, Anny. "La Dialectique du Dehors et du Dedans dans le *Paradis Perdu* de Milton." *BSEAA*, 16, 1983, 21–33.

In *Paradise Lost* Milton develops the image of enclosed space, usually a circular structure which protects the center and separates what is inside from what is outside: the Garden of Eden, the empyrean, and hell. The door always restricts those who enter and leave.

2096 Cunnar, Eugene R. "God's 'Golden Scales': Mercy and Justice in *Paradise Lost.*" *ELN*, 21, 1984, 13–21.

Promotes a theological and visual tradition of the scales as a symbol of both God's judgment and mercy. This interpretation anticipates Christ's embodiment of these two principles as he becomes judge and savior.

2097 Curran, Stuart. "The Siege of Hateful Contraries: Shelley, Mary Shelley, Byron, and *Paradise Lost.*" *Milton and the Line of Vision.* Ed. by Joseph Anthony Wittreich, Jr. (Madison and London: Univ. of Wisconsin Press, 1975), pp. 209–30.

Explores the younger Romantics' view, particularly Shelley's, of God and Satan in *Paradise Lost*. "What they also conceived was that God's revenge was equal in effect [to Satan's], as it was superior in design, and that the creation resulting from such antipathy must be reductive."

2098 Cyr, Marc D. "The Archangel Raphael: Narrative Authority in Milton's War in Heaven." *JNT*, 17, 1987, 309–16.

Explores the significance of Raphael's character as he narrates the War in Heaven to Adam. To establish authority and convey a scanty biblical account of the heavenly war, Milton makes Raphael a godlike and prestigious angel.

2099 Dabney, Dick. "Winter Light." *MiltonQ*, 14, 1980, 35. Reprinted from the *Washington Post*, December 18, 1979.

"For that old epic [Paradise Lost] is not 'irrelevant' to those who need some 'why' to go with the who, what, where and when."

2100 Dahiyat, Eid A. "The Separation Scene in John Milton's *Paradise Lost* Reconsidered." *Dirasat* (Univ. of Jordan), 12, 1985, 27–37.

Believes that "Milton gradually changes the characters of Adam and Eve from the prototypes of book 4 to ordinary frail man and woman by the end of book 8. . . . Had not Milton added the separation scene in which Adam and Eve reach a stage beneath their proper human level, the consequent temptation and fall would have struck the reader as an abrupt and sudden blow

rather than the steady gradual process Milton intended them to be."

2101 Daiches, David. "*Paradise Lost*: God Defended." *God and the Poets.* The Gifford Lectures, 1983 (Oxford: Clarendon Press, 1984), pp. 26–49.

Discusses how Milton's poem justifies God's ways. Review (of book): Martin Warner, *MLR*, 83, 1988, 127–28.

2102 Damrosch, Leopold, Jr. "Art and Truth in *Paradise Lost.*" *God's Plot and Man's Stories: Studies in the Fictional Imagination from Milton to Fielding* (Chicago, IL, and London: Univ. of Chicago Press, 1985), pp. 72–120.

Explains that, because doctrine requires imaginative recreation in the seventeenth century, Milton turns fiction into myth and myth into fiction. Reviews (of book): Paul Alkon, *JEGP*, 86, 1987, 421–23; Laurence Lerner, *CE*, 50, 1988, 575–76.

2103 Daniel, Clay. "Astraea, the Golden Scales, and the Scorpion: Milton's Heavenly Reflection of the Scene in Eden." *MiltonQ*, 20, 1986, 92–98.

Discusses astrology in *Paradise Lost*. Believes that Milton associates Eve with Virgo, and she is thus pure and just; he associates Gabriel with the golden scales and Libra, and he is powerful; finally, he associates Satan with the scorpion, or Scorpio, and he therefore appears in the context of corrupt sexuality.

2104 Daniel, Nathaniel Venable, Jr. "Biblical Proof Texts and Their Epic Contexts in *Paradise Lost.*" Doctoral diss., Univ. of Virginia, 1979. 163pp. Abs., *DAI*, 40, 1980, 4050A.

Defends the appropriateness of Milton's theology in *Paradise Lost* against claims that it is a weakness in an otherwise "great epic poem."

2105 Daniells, Roy. "A Happy Rural Seat of Various View." *"Paradise Lost": A Tercentenary Tribute.* Ed. by Balachandra Rajan ([Toronto]: Univ. of Toronto Press, 1969), pp. 3–17.

"My theme is the pleasure of living in the Garden of Eden, the skill with which Milton has managed its aspect and its prospect, the care with which he has provided everything Adam and Eve can require."

2106 Danielson, Dennis Richard. "Milton and the Problem of Evil: An Essay in Literary Theodicy." Doctoral diss., Stanford Univ., 1979. 318pp. Abs., *DAI*, 40, 1980, 4050A–51A.

Describes "Milton's theodicy—his justification of the ways of God—in conceptual, historical, and literary terms."

2107 Danielson, Dennis. "Milton's Arminianism and *Paradise Lost*." *MiltonS*, 12, 1978, 47–73.

Sees an affinity between Arminian theology and Milton's handling of human repentance, the intercession of Christ, and the grace of God at the end of Book 10 and the opening of Book 11. Discusses Milton's changing doctrinal views. Review: Dayton Haskin, *Thought*, 56, 1981, 226–39.

2108 Danielson, Dennis Richard. *Milton's Good God: A Study in Literary Theodicy.* Cambridge: Cambridge Univ. Press, 1982. xi, 292pp.

Argues that "Milton's theology informs and enhances his literary achievement, and that in fact his justification of God is all the more impressive for its being literary." Reviews: Gordon Campbell, *MiltonQ*, 16, 1982, 76, 78; E. Beatrice Batson, *C&L*, 34, 1983, 55–56; Joan S. Bennett, *JEGP*, 83, 1984, 120–22; Michael Fixler, *MP*, 82, 1985, 310–14; Roger Lejosne, *MLR*, 83, 1986, 717–18.

2109 Danielson, Dennis. "On Toads and the Justice of God." *MiltonQ*, 13, 1979, 12–14.

In associating Satan with the toad in *Paradise Lost* 4.800, Milton not only reflects contemporary belief, but also reinforces the poem's pervasive theme of the justice of divine judgment.

2110 Darbishire, Helen. *Milton's "Paradise Lost."* Folcroft, PA: Folcroft Library Editions, 1969; Oxford: Oxford Univ. Press, 1969; Norwood, PA: Norwood Editions, 1976; Philadelphia, PA: R. West, 1977.

Reprints of Huckabay No. 1234, originally published in 1951.

2111 Dasgupta, R. K. "Indian Response to *Paradise Lost*." *IndL*, 12, No. 1, 1969, 62–70.

Examines the critical response to *Paradise Lost* by Indian critics in the nineteenth and twentieth centuries and the epic's influence on certain Indian writers. Speculates about how early *Paradise Lost* might have been read and discussed in the Anglo-Indian community.

2112 Daub, Oscar C. "On the Ending of *Paradise Lost*." *RenP*, 1976, pp. 61–65.

Examines the poem's last five lines and the antithesis they posit. The narrator's manipulation leaves the reader feeling ambivalent but aware that God controls this world.

2113 Davidson, Clifford. "Sceptre and Keys as Visual Images in *Paradise Lost*." *DR*, 48, 1968–69, 539–49.

Repudiates T. S. Eliot's emphasis on Milton's blindness (see Huckabay No. 531), asserting instead the importance of Milton's imagery. Explicates the keys and scepter as symbols of divine authority in Scriptures, but also in classical myth and legend.

2114 Davies, James Mark Quentin. "Blake's Designs for *Paradise Lost*: A Critical Analysis." Doctoral diss., Univ. of Iowa, 1972. 410pp. Abs., *DAI*, 33, 1973, 6866A–67A.

Demonstrates that Blake's designs "are not literal illustrations but astute critical commentaries on the shortcomings of Milton's epic and the dualist, transcendental Christian world view it enshrines."

2115 Davies, Stevie. "An Analysis of Milton's *Paradise Lost*, Book One, Lines 589–669." *CritS*, 6, 1973, 21–25.

Argues for the significance of the themes of "the contending forces of light and darkness . . . [and] the conflict of revolutionary politics." The light here is "a moral and spiritual experience, and the politics take place on a cosmic scale."

2115A Davies, S. "Images of Kingship in John Milton's *Paradise Lost*." Doctoral diss., Manchester Univ., 1978. Abs., *IT*, 35, 1987, 543.

Explores Milton's attitude to kingship and its use in *Paradise Lost* in order to elucidate the apparent paradox of a royal God, a monarchal Satan, and a republican poet.

2116 Davies, Stevie. *Images of Kingship in "Paradise Lost" : Milton's Politics and Christian Liberty.* Columbia: Univ. of Missouri Press, 1983. vi, 248pp.

Distinguishes the kinds of kingship in the poem and reconciles them with the statements about monarchy in Milton's prose tracts. Reviews: James Egan, *SCN*, 42, 1984, 57; Jackie DiSalvo, *MiltonQ*, 18, 1984, 97–99; Georgia B. Christopher, *JEGP*, 84, 1985, 120–22; John Morrill, *RES*, 37, 1986, 258–60; Thomas F. Healy, *YES*, 17, 1987, 280–82; David Norbrook, *N&Q*, 34, 1987, 85–86.

2117 Davies, Stevie. "Milton." *The Idea of Woman in Renaissance Literature: The Feminine Reclaimed* (Brighton: Harvester, 1986), pp. 175–247. Reprinted as *The Feminine Reclaimed: The Idea of Woman in Spenser, Shakespeare and Milton.* Lexington: Univ. Press of Kentucky, 1986.

Argues that, in *Paradise Lost*, Milton explores his relationship with the feminine. Reviews (of book): S. J. Wiseman, *THES*, July 18, 1986, p. 17; Steven Mullaney, *RenQ*, 40, 1987, 573–78; Louise Simons, *MiltonQ*, 21, No. 2, 1987, 74–76; Jackie DiSalvo, *JEGP*, 87, 1988, 109–11; Jeanne Addison Roberts, *SQ*, 39, 1988, 370–71; Diane K. McColley, *ANQ*, 2, 1989, 110–20.

2118 Davies, Stevie. "The Quest for the One: Eve and Narcissus in *Paradise Lost*." *SMLit*, 3, 1983, 1–17.

Believes that Eve's account of admiring her reflection in the water is allegorical and stands for the human soul, as she becomes the central point in the creation of the universe.

2119 Davies, Stevie. "Triumph and Anti-Triumph: Milton's Satan and the Roman Emperors in *Paradise Lost*." *EA*, 34, 1981, 385–98.

"I suggest that the militaristic and pseudo-democratic climb of Satan to power within his own 'state' in Books I and II ingeniously parallels the Roman imperial model of gaining autocratic power, while the 'triumphal' re-entry into Hell after 'conquest' of the earth by Satan in Book X again alludes to elements of imperial ritual in Rome."

2120 Davies, Stevie, and William B. Hunter. "Milton's Urania: 'The Meaning, Not the Name I Call.'" *SEL*, 28, 1988, 95–111. Reprinted in *The Descent of Urania: Studies in Milton, 1946–1988* (Lewisburg, PA: Bucknell Univ. Press; London and Toronto: Associated Univ. Presses, 1989), pp. 31–45.

Argues that the muse Urania whom Milton invokes in *Paradise Lost* is actually the Christian Trinity. Focuses on the invocations in Books 1, 3, and 7, each of which "appeals to the whole threefold unity of God whilst the second and third each emphasize a different person of the Trinity."

2121 Davis, Donald M. "The Technique of Guilt by Association in *Paradise Lost*." *SAB*, 37, 1972, 29–34.

Displays evidence of Miltonic "guilt by association." Claims that the seventeenth-century reader's "feelings of horror" were aroused by insinuating that the actions of Adam and Eve were "modified repetitions of actions and attitudes of the very devils themselves."

2122 Davis, Patricia Elizabeth. "Covenant

and the 'Crowne of Life': A Figural Tapestry in *Paradise Lost*." *MiltonS*, 22, 1986, 141–50.

Discusses God's covenant with humanity, mainly in terms of the poem's flower imagery. The garland-crowns foreshadow humanity's redemption through Christ.

2123 Davis, Walter R. "The Languages of Accommodation and the Styles of *Paradise Lost*." *MiltonS*, 18, 1983, 103–27.

Characterizes the "styles or uses of language in *Paradise Lost* generally" and offers specific comments on all twelve books but deals mainly with the War in Heaven. Maintains that Milton shifts his use of language according to the narrative.

2124 Delasanta, Rodney. *The Epic Voice*. The Hague: Mouton, 1967. 140pp.

Paradise Lost discussed, pp. 82–109. Distinguishes Raphael's and Adam's restricted voices and the poet's omniscient voice. Finds a relationship between a writer's commitment to an "in medias res structure" and the ultimate use of restricted voice. Review: E. R. Gregory, *SCN*, 32, 1974, 50–51.

2125 Demaray, Hannah D. "The Literary Gardens of Andrew Marvell and John Milton." *Gardens and Culture: Eight Studies in History and Aesthetics*. Ed. by Demaray (Beirut: Eastern Press, 1969), pp. 115–42.

Argues that while Marvell mainly draws on contemporary gardening practices, Milton "depends more directly upon his vast knowledge of the Scripture, the classics, and his memory of the landscape and the art of Italy."

2126 Demaray, Hannah Disinger. "Milton's 'Perfect' Paradise and the Landscapes of Italy." *MiltonQ*, 8, 1974, 33–41.

Demonstrates that critical laboring over the supposed flaws of prelapsarian Eden "can be put to rest by recognizing that Milton, following traditional Italian painting and landscape conventions, placed controlled irregularities

and artificial elements into the Garden as a means of revealing its innate perfection."

2127 Demaray, John G. "Love's Epic Revel in *Paradise Lost*: A Theatrical Vision of Marriage." *MLQ*, 38, 1977, 3–20.

Suggests that in the opening episode in Eden (*Paradise Lost* 4.1–775), Milton transforms "a masque of Hymen" into epic mold, which forms a counterpart to the wanton revels indulged in by fallen humans. Abs., *MiltonQ*, 11, 1977, 92–93; *SCN*, 38, 1980, 19.

2128 Demaray, John G. *Milton's Theatrical Epic: The Invention and Design of "Paradise Lost."* Cambridge, MA, and London: Harvard Univ. Press, 1980. xix, 161pp.

Analyzes *Paradise Lost* against a backdrop of Renaissance pageants, baroque spectacles, masques, musical dramas, and continental heroic works and examines their influence on Milton. Reviews: Joseph Anthony Wittreich, Jr., *MLQ*, 42, 1981, 184–91; James L. Hedges, *C&L*, 30, 1981, 88–89; Anthony Low, *RenQ*, 34, 1981, 294–97; Linwood E. Orange, *SCN*, 39, 1981, 37; Eugene R. Cunnar, *ELN*, 19, 1982, 280–83; Gordon C. Campbell, *MLR*, 78, 1983, 679–80.

2129 Demetrakopoulos, S. A. "Eve as a Circean and Courtly Fatal Woman." *MiltonQ*, 9, 1975, 99–107.

Shows that "Milton's Eve is perhaps the earliest full embodiment in literature of what Mario Praz terms the 'Fatal Woman' in *The Romantic Agony*."

2130 De Palacio, Jean. "La Quête de l'Éden: Mary Wollstonecraft entre Milton et Rousseau." *RLC*, 49, 1975, 217–34.

Mary Wollstonecraft views Milton's and Jean-Jacques Rousseau's Edens as monumental errors. Milton's earthly paradise was based on the injustice of male domination and Rousseau's version in *Emile* was only a sham where sensual pleasure is present.

2131 Desai, Rupin W. "Adam's Fall as a Prefiguration of Christ's Sacrificing Himself for the Church." *MiltonQ*, 17, 1983, 121–25.

Interprets Adam's fall as a decision toward freedom and a loving self-sacrifice for Eve. Thus, his fall can prefigure Christ's Crucifixion.

2132 Devine, Paul Kevin. "Time Stands Fixt: The Theme of History in Milton's *Paradise Lost*." Doctoral diss., Vanderbilt Univ., 1982. 233pp. Abs., *DAI*, 43, 1982, 1150A.

Probes "the relationship between Milton's historical views and the historical thought of his age and shows how Milton uses his poetic skill to bring the reader of *Paradise Lost* to understand and embrace Milton's view of history."

2133 Di Benedetto, Vincent Paul. "Education, Poetic Restoration, and the Narrator of *Paradise Lost*." Doctoral diss., Univ. of Toronto, 1988. Abs., *DAI*, 49, 1989, 2666A.

Shows how education and poetry contribute to spiritual regeneration in *Paradise Lost*, especially for the narrator.

2134 Di Cesare, Mario. "The Dialectics of Allusion: *Paradise Lost* and Classical Epic." *SCN*, 38, 1980, 44–45.

Abstract of a paper presented at the 1979 MLA Convention. "Of the types of allusion, the evocative allusion—a demanding correspondence in language or detail which draws on the power and significance of the original—is the most challenging to the reader." Also abs., *MiltonQ*, 14, 1980, 70.

2135 Di Cesare, Mario A. "From Vergil to Vida to Milton." *Acta Conventus Neo-Latini Turonensis*. Series: De Pétrarque à Descartes, 38. Ed. by Jean-Claude Margolin (Paris: Vrin, 1980), pp. 153–61.

Argues that Vida's *Christiad* is a major link between the *Aeneid* and *Paradise Lost*.

2136 Di Cesare, M. A. "'Not Less but More Heroic': The Epic Task and the Renaissance Hero." *YES*, 12, 1982, 58–71.

Examines and defines the Renaissance epic, claiming that *Paradise Lost* was the last great epic. Describes the attributes that form epic heroes, including characters created by Homer, Virgil, Tasso, and Spenser.

2137 Di Cesare, Mario A. "*Paradise Lost* and Epic Tradition." *MiltonS*, 1, 1969, 31–50.

Analyzes "some of the ways in which Vergil and Milton modified the epic tradition." Sees *Paradise Lost* as a significant epic development beyond Virgil's writing.

2138 Diekhoff, John S. "Eve's Dream and the Paradox of Fallible Perfection." *MiltonQ*, 4, 1970, 5–7.

Surveys critical opinion about the paradox and responds in particular to Millicent Bell's arguments (Huckabay No. 1111) that Eve was created fallen and that her dream reveals her corrupt subconscious. Points out that the ability to disobey was a necessary part of perfection before the Fall and stresses that Satan's role in the dream cannot be overlooked. The dream springs from his consciousness, and Satan, not Eve, has fallen.

2139 Diekhoff, John S. "A Poem Doctrinal and Exemplary to the Dean." *MiltonQ*, 5, 1971, 71–73.

On the occasion of his retirement, Diekhoff draws tongue-in-cheek parallels between passages in *Paradise Lost* and the problems experienced by an academic dean.

2140 DiSalvo, Jacqueline. "Fear of Flying: Milton on the Boundaries between Witchcraft and Inspiration." *ELR*, 18, 1988, 114–37.

Discusses Milton's use of witch lore and nocturnal flights, especially in *Paradise Lost*. Believes that "we can identify a state of consciousness associated with women that Milton condemned and feared as a danger to his identity as a man and a poet." This fear "is paradoxically not just the enemy, but the source of his own poetic inspiration."

2141 DiSalvo, Jackie. "'In Narrow Circuit Strait'n'd by a Foe': Puritans and Indians in Milton's *Paradise Lost.*" *Ringing the Bell Backward: The Proceedings of the First International Milton Symposium.* Ed. by Ronald G. Shafer. The IUP Imprint Series (Indiana: Indiana Univ. of Pennsylvania, 1982), pp. 19–33.

Argues that Milton assimilated the experience of the new world "by envisioning it as a re-enactment of the original confrontation between God and Satan and the biblical encounter between the 'Chosen People' and the Canaanite pagans." Jon S. Lawry's response, pp. 34–36, offers several qualifications.

2142 DiSalvo, Jacqueline Anne. "War of Titans: Blake's Confrontation with Milton. *The Four Zoas* as Political Critique of *Paradise Lost* and the Genesis Tradition." Doctoral diss., Univ. of Wisconsin, Madison, 1977. 675pp. Abs., *DAI*, 38, 1977, 3456A–57A.

Explores Blake's belief that Milton's political contradictions and "the traditions he espoused" account for varying interpretations of the major themes of *Paradise Lost*—"love, reason, history, the conflict of God and Satan."

2143 DiSalvo, Jackie. *War of Titans: Blake's Critique of Milton and the Politics of Religion.* Pittsburgh, PA: Univ. of Pittsburgh Press; London: Feffer and Simons, 1983. xi, 391pp.

Studies Blake's interpretation of *Paradise Lost.* Sees the epic primarily as a political poem and deals with its apparent paradoxes. Reviews: Joseph Wittreich, *MiltonQ*, 18, 1984, 92–94; Andrew Lincoln, *RES*, 37, 1986, 105–07.

2144 Dixon, W. Macneile. *English Epic and Heroic Poetry.* New York: Haskell House, 1964.

Reprint of Stevens No. 2726, originally published in 1912.

2145 Dobbins, Austin C. *Milton and the Book of Revelation: The Heavenly Cycle.* Studies in the Humanities, no. 7, Literature. University: Univ. of Alabama Press, 1975. vi, 170pp.

Holds that the events of *Paradise Lost* 1–6 and 9 are more scriptural than epic. "The primary source of the heavenly cycle is the Bible, specifically the Book of Revelation. The incidents which have puzzled many readers . . . Milton based directly upon a well-known Renaissance interpretation of the Bible." Reviews: *MiltonQ*, 9, 1975, 86–87; Joseph Anthony Wittreich, Jr., *SCN*, 33, 1975, 92–93; Michael Lieb, *CSR*, 6, 1976, 225–26; Arnold Stein, *SR*, 84, 1976, 695–706; Christopher Hill, *English* (Oxford), 25, 1976, 38–42.

2146 Doke, Hiroichiro. "Celestial Light: The Irradiating Ideas of *Paradise Lost.*" *English Criticism in Japan: Essays by Younger Japanese Scholars on English and American Literature.* Ed. by Earl Miner (Tokyo: Tokyo Univ. Press, 1972), pp. 115–55.

Discusses the theology of *Paradise Lost* (including such issues as free will, God, the Fall, and redemption) and emphasizes Milton's Christian humanism.

2147 Donnelly, Colleen. "The Syntactic Counterplot of the Devils' Debates and God's Council." *Lang&S*, 19, 1986, 58–73.

Contrasts the language of the infernal debates with that of the heavenly council. Determines that God's and the Son's "forthright language" and use of the modals "will" and "shall" reflect their "certitude of omniscient sight; whereas the demons' use of many different modals coupled with their use of conditional clauses reveals their blindness."

2148 Donoghue, Denis. "God with Thunder." *TLS*, Nov. 3, 1972, pp. 1339–41.

Discusses T. S. Eliot's criticism of the Miltonic Eden (see Huckabay Nos.

530–31). Relates Milton's Christian epic to the pagan, mythological characters of Prometheus. Points out similarities in concepts of the creator, the flame of inspiration, the divine will, the cost of knowledge, the divine Logos, the transcription of the truth, the mind versus nature, and the imagination of the hero.

2149 Donoghue, Denis. "God with Thunder." *Thieves of Fire* (New York: Oxford Univ. Press, 1974), pp. 33–58.
Uses the Promethean myth to interpret *Paradise Lost*. Contrasts the Promethean motive with that of the Satanic, which subsides after the first two books.

2150 Douglas, John. *Milton No Plagiary; or, a Detection of the Forgeries Contained in Lauder's "Essay on the Imitation of the Moderns in 'Paradise Lost.'"* Folcroft, PA: Folcroft Library Editions, 1972; Norwood, PA: Norwood Editions, 1976; Philadelphia, PA: R. West, 1977.
Reprints of the 1756 edition.

2151 Dowie, William J. *"Paradise Lost*: A Hypothetical Fall." *Innisfree*, 4, 1977, 50–54.
Suggests that God "might have come off better" had Milton portrayed "an initial state of love between God and man" and that "the origin of the temptation lies within man rather than within God."

2152 Doyle, Charles Clay. "Nature's Fair Defect: Milton and William Cartwright on the Paradox of Woman." *ELN*, 11, 1973, 107–10.
Discusses the ambivalence of the seventeenth-century attitude toward women and states that Milton may have been influenced by William Cartwright's work.

2153 Drake, Gertrude C. "Satan's Councils in *The Christiad, Paradise Lost* and *Paradise Regained.*" *Acta Conventus Neo-Latini Turonensis*. Series: De Pétrarque à Descartes, 38. Ed. by Jean-Claude Margolin (Paris: Vrin, 1980), pp. 979–89.
Compares Milton's councils to Vida's.

Believes that Vida's *Christiad* provided material to help Milton dramatize the action in his poems.

2154 Dreher, Diane Elizabeth. "Diabolical Order in Hell: An Emblematic Inversion in *Paradise Lost.*" *SMy*, 8, 1985, 13–18.
Shows Milton's use of Hermetic lore and Neoplatonic emblems in a physical construct of his vision of heaven and hell, based on the Hermetic "trianguli" emblem.

2155 Dreher, Diane Elizabeth. "John Milton: The Four Estates in *Paradise Lost.*" *The Fourfold Pilgrimage: The Estates of Innocence, Misery, Grace, and Glory in Seventeenth-Century Literature* (Washington, DC: Univ. Press of America, 1982), pp. 99–155.
Examines Milton's use of the four estates and concludes that "Adam's lesson and ultimately the lesson of *Paradise Lost* is man's proper role in this world, as he sees his life within the pattern of the Four Estates. This awareness is the 'paradise within' with which Adam and Eve leave what had once been the State of Innocence and journey into our world of greater trials but also greater blessings." Reviews (of book): Robert Graalman, *SCN*, 31, 1983, 43–44; Dean Ebner, *C&L*, 32, 1983, 55–57.

2156 D'Souza, Peter Theodore. "The Sin of Adam in *Paradise Lost* Studied against the Background of Certain Doctrinal Traditions." Doctoral diss., Fordham Univ., 1971. 160pp. Abs., *DAI*, 32, 1971, 916A–17A.
Analyzes "Adam's sin in *Paradise Lost* in the light of Milton's own theology . . . for a better understanding of Milton's concept of the fall of man," and establishes "a thematic relationship between sin, fall, repentence and heroism."

2157 Duncan, Joseph E. "Archetypes in Milton's Earthly Paradise." *MiltonS*, 14, 1980, 25–58.
Uses anthropology, psychology, and

literary criticism to examine paradise and prelapsarian life in *Paradise Lost.* Concludes that Milton's paradise is "an intensive concentration of pattern central to the life of religion, the life of the psyche, and the life of the Western literary tradition."

2158 Duncan, Joseph E. *Milton's Earthly Paradise: A Historical Study of Eden.* Minnesota Monographs in the Humanities, vol. 5. Minneapolis: Univ. of Minnesota Press; London: Oxford Univ. Press, 1972. viii, 329pp.

"This work seeks to explain how Milton's conception of paradise is similar to or different from the conceptions of his predecessors, contemporaries, and successors . . . and how Milton's Paradise fits into the framework of Renaissance conceptions of paradise." Reviews: *MiltonQ,* 6, No. 3, 1972, 15–16; Lawrence Babb, *Criticism,* 5, 1973, 380–82; Michael Lieb, *Cithara,* 13, 1973, 112–17; Mary Ann Radzinowicz, *RenQ,* 26, 1973, 535–39; *TLS,* Feb. 16, 1973, p. 187; Douglas Bush, *MLQ,* 34, 1973, 78–84; Laurence H. Jacobs, *JEGP,* 72, 1973, 558–61; C. C. Barfoot, *DQR,* 4, 1974, 177–80; A. Bartlett Giamatti, *MP,* 71, 1974, 438–40; Isabel Gamble MacCaffrey, *ELN,* 12, 1974, 144–46; Gerald Stacy, *SCN,* 32, 1974, 2; Andrew M. McLean, *SHR,* 10, 1976, 362–69.

2159 Dunster, Charles. *Considerations on Milton's Early Reading and the Prima Stamina of His "Paradise Lost."* Ann Arbor, MI: Univ. Microfilms International, 1980 Books on Demand Reprints.

See Stevens No. 1817, originally published in 1800.

2160 Durkin, Sister Mary Brian. "Iterative Figures and Images in *Paradise Lost,* XI–XII." *MiltonS,* 3, 1971, 139–58.

The figures and images "merit praise and continued study, for the narrative, didactic, and rhetorical techniques in Books XI and XII are indisputable evidence of Milton's sustained power."

2161 DuRocher, Richard J. *Milton and Ovid.* Ithaca, NY, and London: Cornell Univ. Press, 1985. 241pp.

Compares *Paradise Lost* with the *Metamorphoses* to demonstrate the "effects of Ovidian allusions, analogues, and techniques on the style and significance of Milton's epic." Concludes that Milton's use of Ovid results in "a greater depth of characterization," "a broader range of expression," and "a wider scope of significance . . . than has yet been recognized." Reviews: Archie Burnett, *YWES,* 66, 1985, 291–92; Albert C. Labriola, *MiltonQ,* 20, 1986, 57–58; Lucy Newlyn, *TLS,* Aug. 8, 1986, p. 871; Margaret J. Arnold, *CML,* 7, 1987, 133–36; Daniel Javitch, *RenQ,* 40, 1987, 183–86; Charles Martindale, *CL,* 39, 1987, 181–83; William Porter, *CML,* 7, 1987, 136–39; Stella P. Revard, *ELN,* 24, 1987, 74–77; John M. Steadman, *JEGP,* 86, 1987, 249–51; Diane K. McColley, *ANQ,* 2, 1989, 110–20.

2162 Dyson, A. E., and Julian Lovelock. "Event Perverse: The Epic of Exile." *Milton: "Paradise Lost." A Casebook.* Ed. by Dyson and Lovelock (London: Macmillan, 1973), pp. 220–42; reprinted in *Masterful Images: English Poetry from Metaphysicals to Romantics* (London: Macmillan; New York: Barnes and Noble, 1976), pp. 47–70.

"While there can be no evading the ironies—so close to tragedy—in this material, there should be no overlooking the counterbalance of Christian Hope." *Paradise Lost* is, finally, a kind of divine comedy, as it moves from paradise to Fall to Incarnation to cross to empty tomb.

2163 Eagleton, Terry. "The God That Failed." *Re-membering Milton: Essays on the Texts and Traditions.* Ed. by Mary Nyquist and Margaret W. Ferguson (New York and London: Methuen, 1987), pp. 342–49.

"There are always those who, like the Koestlers and the Orwells, find it convenient and persuasive to blame the God that failed; but if we wanted a more accurate analogue of *Paradise Lost* in the twentieth century, we might do worse than take a look at Trotsky's *The Revolution Betrayed*."

2164 Earl, James W. "Eve's Narcissism." *MiltonQ*, 19, 1985, 13–16.

Discusses Eve's narcissism as a part of her psychological progression. Believes that all of the characters must find adequate images of themselves before they can proceed into maturity, but Eve is unable to do so until she has children.

2165 Easthope, Antony. "*Paradise Lost*: Ideology, Phantasy and Contradiction." *SoRA*, 20, 1987, 42–48.

Believes that the Fall in *Paradise Lost* is fortunate but much more so for Adam than for Eve, who becomes a slave to this archetypal man. Disagrees with Sandra Gilbert (No. 2293).

2166 Edgeworth, Robert J. "Milton's 'Darkness Visible' and *Aeneid 7*." *CJ*, 79, 1983–84, 97–99.

Believes that the "darkness visible" in *Paradise Lost* 1.63 actually refers to flames which give no light. Cites the *Aeneid* and the Zohar as possible sources for Milton's "radiant darkness."

2167 Edmundson, Mark. "Freudian Mythmaking: The Case of Narcissus." *KR*, 10, No. 2, 1988, 17–37. Reprinted in *Towards Reading Freud: Self-Creation in Milton, Wordsworth, Emerson, and Sigmund Freud* (Princeton, NJ: Princeton Univ. Press, 1990), pp. 55–86.

Notes Freud's love for *Paradise Lost* and uses Eve's infatuation with herself at the pool in Book 4 as a point of departure to discuss the development of Freud's theory of the human personality.

2168 Edwards, Karen L. "On Guile and Guyon in *Paradise Lost* and *The Faerie Queene*." *PQ*, 64, 1985, 83–97.

Contends that in *Paradise Lost*, guile can do no harm without its victim's consent. Contrasts this with Spenser's use of guile in the *Faerie Queene*.

2169 Edwards, Karen Leigh. "'Various Style': The Poetic Language of *Paradise Lost*." Doctoral diss., Yale Univ., 1979. 234pp. Abs., *DAI*, 40, 1979, 2692A–93A.

Demonstrates "that varieties of style in *Paradise Lost* stem from Milton's exploitation of two distinct traditions of elevated language"—ornateness and simplicity.

2170 Eller, Hans-Peter Michael. "'Light after Light Well Us'd': The Epic Conclusion of *Paradise Lost*." Doctoral diss., Univ. of New Mexico, 1972. 186pp. Abs., *DAI*, 33, 1973, 5674A–75A.

Defends the integration of Books 11 and 12 with the rest of *Paradise Lost*, asserting that they describe "an act of voluntary obedience, the overwhelming significance of which is that it shows the extent to which man is regenerated as he leaves Paradise to enter his troubled domain."

2171 Elliott, V. G. "The Neo-Classical Approach to *Paradise Lost*." B.Litt. thesis, Oxford Univ., 1970.

2172 Ellrodt, Robert. "Le Paradis Terrestre de Milton." *Annales: Faculté des Lettres et Sciences Humaines de Nice*, 3, 1968, 3–20. Revised as "Milton et la Vision Édénique." *Age d'or et Apocalypse*. Ed. by Ellrodt and Bernard Brugière (Paris: Publications de la Sorbonne, 1986), pp. 47–62.

Studies the terrestrial paradise of *Paradise Lost*, the attitudes of the middle ages and the Renaissance, geographic location, the landscape, and sacred aspects of the story of the Fall.

2173 Elyas, Adel Ata. "Two Ambitious Devils: Satan and Macbeth." *Journal of the College of Arts* (King Saud Univ.), 11, 1984, 71–81.

Compares Satan's ambition to that of Shakespeare's Macbeth.

2174 Emma, Ronald David. "The Exordium and *Paradise Lost*." *SAQ*, 71, 1972, 513–20.

On the diction, grammar, and prosody of the epic's first twenty-six lines, in which Milton weaves a texture that foreshadows the magnitude of the poem's verse.

2175 Empson, William. *Milton's God.* Cambridge: Cambridge Univ. Press, 1981. Reprint of Huckabay No. 1274 (with the addition of "Final Reflections," pp. 319–40), originally published in 1961 and revised in 1965.

2176 Engetsu, Katsuhiro. "Labor in *Paradise Lost*." *MCJ News*, 9, 1987, 24–25.
Abstract of a paper presented at the Twentieth Colloquium of MCJ in December, 1985. Studies the *Christian Doctrine* and *Paradise Lost* to gain insight into Milton's views on sabbatical labor. Contrasts the delight of prelapsarian labor with the mandatory nature of postlapsarian labor.

2177 Enozawa, Kazuyoshi. ["On the Importance of Adam."] *MCJ News*, 6, 1983, 14–15.
Abstract of a paper presented at the Eighth Annual Conference of MCJ in October, 1982. Believes that non-Christian readers should take a humanistic rather than a theological approach to *Paradise Lost*. Adam is the only character who exhibits humility and magnanimity. Milton might have identified with Adam "when he experienced an unhappy marriage with Mary Powell in 1642."

2178 Entzminger, Robert L. "Epistemology and the Tutelary Word in *Paradise Lost*." *MiltonS*, 10, 1977, 93–109.
Grace "subsequent to the Fall is first manifested in Adam as the restoration of memory, for he begins to overcome despair only when he remembers the prophecy in which the hope of mankind resides. But as Adam cannot forget his sin even when he is redeemed for it, neither are Milton's readers asked to recover paradise on the same terms our first parents held it."

2179 Entzminger, Robert L. "Michael's Options and Milton's Poetry: *Paradise Lost* XI and XII." *ELR*, 8, 1978, 197–211.
Discusses Michael's speeches in Books 11–12. "In Book XI, image has been subordinated to concept in response to the limitations of human epistemology. In Book XII, however, spectacle subsides altogether, to be replaced with narrative, while the thematic concern with the verbal medium becomes more explicit."

2180 Evans, Andy. "'By Some False Guile': The Temptation of Eve in *Paradise Lost*." *SPWVSRA*, 13, 1988, 79–82.
In the temptation scene, Satan's words come from a strong source—a beautiful beast—who is a friendly, dazzling flatterer. Satan twists appearances, truth, logic, and Eve's protest. His "effective presentation of himself and his arguments does not bring the end of man; it brings God's mercy."

2181 Evans, J. M. "Mortals' Chiefest Enemy." *MiltonS*, 20, 1984, 111–26.
Suggests that Adam and Eve's argument in *Paradise Lost* 9 revolves around a pun on the word "secure." Believes that Adam quibbles over its meaning before permitting Eve to depart.

2182 Evans, J. M. *"Paradise Lost" and the Genesis Tradition.* Oxford: Clarendon Press, 1968. xiv, 314pp.
Concerned "with the evolution of the Fall story . . . rather than with the precise connexions between the parallels themselves." Contents (abbreviated): "Introduction: The Study of a Tradition"; "The Exegetical Tradition"; "The Literary Tradition"; and "*Paradise Lost* and the Tradition." See also No. 1930. Reviews: *TLS*, Sept. 12, 1968, p. 1003; R. E. C. Houghton, *N&Q*, 15, 1968, 386–88; Watson Kirkconnell, *DR*, 48, 1968, 556–58; A. Fry, *Neophilologus*, 53, 1969, 234–35; James H. Sims, *SCN*, 27, 1969, 2–4; Michael Fixler, *RES*, 20, 1969, 499–501; J. M. Couper, *AUMLA*, 31, 1969, 97–99; W. J. Barnes, *QQ*, 76, 1969, 726–29.

2183 Evans, Robert C. "*Paradise Lost* and Renaissance Historiography." *POMPA*, 1984, pp. 69–87.

Discusses the Renaissance philosophy of history and shows that Milton's poem "shares with other histories of his age an explicitly educative purpose, an emphasis upon the exemplary nature of history, and a concomitant tendency to generalize from historical example."

2184 Everett, Barbara. "The End of the Big Names: Milton's Epic Catalogues." *English Renaissance Studies Presented to Dame Helen Gardner in Honour of Her Seventieth Birthday.* [Ed. by John Carey] (Oxford: Clarendon Press, 1980), pp. 254–70.

Concerned primarily with how Milton uses "big names" in Book 11's catalog, where they reveal the fallen world to Adam, and how they color the reader's developing reaction to *Paradise Lost*. Contradicts T. S. Eliot's belief (see Huckabay No. 531) that Milton uses them to show that he is a mouthpiece of philosophical and theological statement.

2185 Fallon, Robert Thomas. "Milton's Epics and the Spanish War: Toward a Poetics of Experience." *MiltonS*, 15, 1981, 3–28.

Begins with the premise that Milton's decade of government service affected his imagination. Proposes that during this decade, "England was involved in a war which in its broad design was quite similar to that which he describes in *Paradise Lost*, one which, moreover, contained incidents . . . which are suggestive of the actions of the angels."

2186 Fallon, Stephen M. "Milton's Sin and Death: The Ontology of Allegory in *Paradise Lost*." *ELR*, 17, 1987, 329–50.

Rejects the assertion by Samuel Johnson and others that the allegory of Sin and Death is out of place in *Paradise Lost*. Argues that "the nature of Sin and Death is consistent with Milton's Augustin-ian ontology of evil, and that Milton naturally turns to the 'lesser reality' of allegory to present characters who are the negation rather than the expression of substance."

2187 Fallon, Stephen M. "Satan's Return to Hell: Milton's Concealed Dialogue with Homer and Virgil." *MiltonQ*, 18, 1984, 78–81.

Cites examples from *Paradise Lost* which allude to the *Aeneid* and the *Odyssey*. "Milton's claim 'to soar/ Above th'Aonian Mount' must be evaluated not only in terms of Christian pride in the employment of a true myth, but also in terms of the genius with which he has woven Homer and Virgil into the texture of his poem and attempted to answer them there."

2188 Fallon, Stephen M. "'To Act or Not': Milton's Conception of Divine Freedom." *JHI*, 49, 1988, 425–49.

Examines the issue of divine freedom with respect to Milton's theology. Details how the perspectives of various thinkers—the Platonists, Thomas Hobbes, René Descartes, and Jacobus Arminius—affected the development and expression of Milton's depiction of divine will.

2189 Fallon, Stephen M. "The Uses of 'Seems' and the Spectre of Predestination." *MiltonQ*, 21, No. 3, 1987, 99–101.

Believes that Julia M. Walker "wrenches" Milton's use of "seems" in *Paradise Lost* (No. 3195) to arrive at a reading that suggests predestination rather than Milton's actual portrayal of free will. See Walker's response (No. 3196).

2190 Farmer, Alice Cruce. "John Milton: The Value of Mythic Parallels." Doctoral diss., Univ. of Southwestern Louisiana, 1976. 161pp. Abs., *DAI*, 37, 1977, 7761A.

Examines the archetypal images and myths behind the three worlds of *Paradise Lost*—heaven, paradise, and hell.

2191 Farwell, Marilyn. "Choosing by

Ambiguity: A Reconsideration of the Fall in *Paradise Lost*." *WascanaR*, 9, 1974, 213–20.

"If we are to see *Paradise Lost* as a unified work of art, we must provide an alternative answer at the Fall which will relate rather than separate the dramatic and theological elements. The argument to establish the inevitability of an alternative choice for Adam provides a means by which the dramatic and theological elements of the poem can be united."

2192 Farwell, Marilyn R. "Eve, the Separation Scene, and the Renaissance Idea of Androgyny." *MiltonS*, 16, 1982, 3–20.

Argues that "androgyny is inadequate and inaccurate as a description of the complex character of Eve and as a tool for the interpretation of the separation scene."

2193 Farwell, Marilyn R. "Puritanism and Zen: *Pradise Lost* and the Undergraduate." *Teaching Milton to Undergraduates: Problems and Approaches*. Proceedings of the Special Session (537), Annual Meeting of the Modern Language Association, Dec. 28, 1976. Comp. by Paul L. Gaston ([Edwardsville: Southern Illinois Univ.], n.d.), pp. 35–38.

Advocates approaching Milton by comparing his life to "the contemporary American experience of the last fifteen years."

2194 Faulds, Joseph Merkle. "The Son and Satan in *Paradise Lost*: An Inquiry into the Poetic Theodicy of John Milton in the Western Tradition." Doctoral diss., Univ. of Dallas, 1986. 233pp. Abs., *DAI*, 47, 1986, 909A.

Considers "the inter-relatedness of Milton's anti-Trinitarian christology and the problem of evil in *Paradise Lost* with comparative reference to four other works of the Western tradition: the *Aeneid*, Conrad's *Heart of Darkness*, the Resurrection narratives of the Lucan gospel, and Hemingway's *The Old Man and the Sea*."

2195 Featheringill, Ron Charles. "The Tension between Divine Will and Human Free Will in Milton and the Classical Epic Tradition." Doctoral diss., Univ. of California, Riverside, 1988. 317pp. Abs., *DAI*, 49, 1989, 1793A.

Focuses on epics from Virgil's *Aeneid* to *Paradise Lost* to investigate the strain created by human will's desire for independence confronting divine will's demand for submission.

2196 Featheringill, Ron Charles. *The Tension between Divine Will and Human Free Will in Milton and the Classical Epic Tradition.* New York and Frankfurt: Peter Lang, 1990. 339pp.

Traces the tension between divine will and human will in epic poetry, beginning with Hesiod and Homer and concluding with the Renaissance epics. Discusses Milton's concept of heroism and the epic tradition and the epic after Milton. Asserts that the epic is a "dead genre" today because in modern works the will of God is unknown and perhaps even nonexistent.

2197 Fee, William W. "A Letter about Milton." *Washington Star and Daily News*, June 3, 1973. Reprinted in *MiltonQ*, 8, 1974, 67–68.

A reply to Robert Evett's review in the *Star* (May 20, 1973) of John Collier's *Milton's "Paradise Lost": Screenplay for Cinema of the Mind* (No. 2068). Considers Milton extremely relevant to the modern mind.

2198 Feeney, D. C. "Epic Hero and Epic Fable." *CL*, 38, 1986, 137–58.

Argues that "there was available to Milton an idea of the form and nature of epic in which the figure of the 'generic hero' was not paramount." For Milton, "the question at the kernel of the genre was not the neoclassical 'What individual is the center of the poem?' but rather: 'What is the self-sufficient action which the poem represents?'" *Paradise Lost* has no single "great achiever."

2199 Fenderson, Lewis H. "The Onomato-Musical Element in *Paradise Lost*." *CLAJ*, 9, 1966, 255–64.

Examines the melodious quality of *Paradise Lost* by analyzing two of Milton's devices: his use of musical terms, references, and instruments as subject matter and his use of words that may or may not have musical meanings, but have connotations because of their euphonious or discordant nature or because the sequence of their syllables yields agreeable or disagreeable sounds.

2200 Ferguson, Faith A. "An Analysis and Reevaluation of the Themes of Deceit, Fate and Isolation in Milton's *Paradise Lost*." Doctoral diss., Indiana Univ. of Pennsylvania, 1988. 121pp. Abs., *DAI*, 49, 1988, 1149A.

Discusses the "unexplored ramifications" of "deceit, the nature of power and its exercise, the role of fate vs. Providence . . . and the consequences of isolation."

2201 Ferry, Anne Davidson. *Milton and the Miltonic Dryden.* Cambridge, MA: Harvard Univ. Press, 1968. 250pp.

Finds "an intricate pattern of connections" between *Paradise Lost* and *Absalom and Achitophel* and shows how Dryden "depicted human corruption by exploring the dangers of fallen language, in all its abuses and confusions." Reviews: *MiltonN*, 2, 1968, 64–65; Anthony Low, *SCN*, 26, 1968, 72–73; P. Joan Cosgrave, *JC*, 19, 1969, 172–73; Elizabeth MacKenzie, *RES*, 21, 1970, 82–84; Earl Miner, *ECS*, 3, 1970, 296–305.

2202 Ferry, Anne. "Milton's Creation of Eve." *SEL*, 28, 1988, 113–32.

A character study of Eve, including her relationship with Adam. Concludes that Milton was sympathetic to Eve because he endowed her with "those powers of the soul that belong especially to poetry."

2203 Ferry, Anne Davidson. *Milton's Epic Voice: The Narrator in "Paradise Lost."*

Chicago, IL: Univ. of Chicago Press, 1983; Ann Arbor, MI: Univ. Microfilm International, 1980 Books on Demand Reprints.

Reprints of Huckabay No. 1290 (with a new preface), originally published in 1963.

2204 Ferry, Anne D. "Point of View and Comment." *Parnassus Revisited: Modern Critical Essays on the Epic Tradition.* Ed. by Anthony C. Yu (Chicago, IL: American Library Association, 1973), pp. 132–38.

Reprint of a section from Ferry's *Milton's Epic Voice* (No. 2203).

2205 Fifer, Kenneth Paul. "The Heavenly Prospect in *Paradise Lost*." Doctoral diss., Univ. of Michigan, 1972. 160pp. Abs., *DAI*, 33, 1973, 6307A.

Describes Milton's use of viewpoint, epic form, and stylistic devices to bring the reader from a static, purely physical understanding of *Paradise Lost* to a "heavenly prospect"—"an eternal and simultaneous perception approaching God's own."

2206 Fink, Larry Earl. " 'By Temperance Taught': Food and Eating Imagery in the Bible and in Milton's *Paradise Lost*." Doctoral diss., Texas A&M Univ., 1987. 266pp. Abs., *DAI*, 49, 1988, 810A.

Analyzes "images which feature food and eating vehicles" in the Bible and in *Paradise Lost* to show how they express major themes and clarify "the relationship between the Bible's imagery and Milton's."

2207 Finnigan, David Francis. "Dark Designs: The Presentation of Evil in *Paradise Lost*." Doctoral diss., Univ. of Oregon, 1970. 247pp. Abs., *DAI*, 32, 1971, 387A.

Relates Milton's attractive portrayal of evil to his belief that it was "inextricably mixed with good and tended to imitate the good in order to corrupt it."

2208 Fiore, Peter A., O. F. M. " 'Account Mee Man': The Incarnation in *Paradise Lost*." *HLQ*, 39, 1975, 51–56.

Concludes that Milton's soteriological doctrine, with its central concern for fallen humanity, conforms to traditional Christian teaching about the Incarnation and redemption.

2209 Fiore, Peter Amadeus. "Freedom, Liability, and the State of Perfection in *Paradise Lost*." *MiltonQ*, 5, 1971, 47–51.

Investigates Eve's dream in light of the Augustinian tradition and comments on Adam's quest for knowledge and Eve's pool scene. Rejects the idea that the Fall occurs before Book 9.

2210 Fiore, Peter A. *Milton and Augustine: Patterns of Augustinian Thought in "Paradise Lost."* University Park and London: Pennsylvania State Univ. Press, 1981. ix, 118pp.

Study Augustine's influence on the three main doctrines inherent in the story of the Fall: paradise (preternatural world), which was lost (original sin), and finally recovered (redemption). Concludes that Milton draws widely from Augustine. Reviews: Roy Flannagan, *MiltonQ*, 15, 1981, 101–02; Michael A. Mikolajczak, *SCN*, 40, 1982, 63–64; Darryl Lee Tippens, *C&L*, 31, 1982, 91–94; J. Martin Evans, *RES*, 37, 1986, 260–62.

2211 Fiore, Peter A. "Milton and Kubrick: Eden's Apple or *A Clockwork Orange*." *CEA*, 35, 1973, 14–17.

Refutes the point of view of Stanley Kubrick's film *A Clockwork Orange*— humanity is basically evil—by citing Milton and Augustine, who believed that the Fall merely deprived humans of things that were additions. The basic goodness of humans was still intact, but they returned to their natural state.

2212 Fiore, Silvia Ruffo. "Patterns of Light and Morality in Dante and Milton: Illumination versus Justification." *NemlaIS*, 11–12, 1987–88, 5–13.

Suggests that "Dante's *Commedia* presents a definitive, clearcut portrayal of good and evil, with light and dark as corresponding symbolic alternatives."

On the other hand, Milton's symbolic use of light and dark to picture good and evil "does not consistently or comprehensively follow a clear vision or assertion." Milton's approach is oxymoronic, reflecting distortion, confusion, and uncertainty.

2213 Fisch, Harold. "Creation in Reverse: The Book of Job and *Paradise Lost*." *Milton and Scriptural Tradition: The Bible into Poetry.* Ed. by James H. Sims and Leland Ryken (Columbia: Univ. of Missouri Press, 1984), pp. 104–16.

Presents the Book of Job as a major influence on *Paradise Lost*. "In the obscure and strangely phantasmagoric world of Job, Milton found, if not a complete mythology, a striking pattern of images suggesting the direction for his imagination and conferring a biblical authority upon his invention."

2214 Fischer, Andreas. "Heinrich von Treitschke: *Milton*. Studien zum historischen Essay und zur historischen Porträtkunst an ausgewählten Beispielen." *Quellen und Forschungen zur Sprach- und Kulturgeschichte der Germanischen Völker*, N.F. no. 27 (Berlin: de Gruyter, 1968), pp. 63–78.

Part of a University of Hamburg dissertation completed in 1966. Treitschke's essay on Milton, written in 1860, illustrates a high regard for *Paradise Lost* and a desire to interpret it politically as a model for German rationalism.

2215 Fish, Stanley Eugene. "Discovery as Form in *Paradise Lost*." *New Essays on "Paradise Lost."* Ed. by Thomas Kranidas (Berkeley, Los Angeles, and London: Univ. of California Press, 1969), pp. 1–14.

"This description of *Paradise Lost*, as a poem concerned with the self-education of its readers, if it is accepted, throws a new light on some old questions. Specifically, it dictates a reorientation of the debate concerning the structure or form of the poem; for if the meaning of the poem is to be located in the reader's experience of it, the form of the poem is the form of that experience; and the outer or physical form, so obtrusive, and, in one sense, so undeniably there, is, in another sense, incidental and even irrelevant." Included in No. 2216. Abs., *MiltonQ*, 4, 1970, 33. Review: Joseph Anthony Wittreich, Jr., *Genre*, 5, 1972, 307–25.

2216 Fish, Stanley E. *Surprised by Sin: The Reader in "Paradise Lost."* Berkeley, Los Angeles, and London: Univ. of California Press, 1971.

Reprint of Huckabay No. 1301 (with an additional preface and appendix [a reprint of No. 2215]), originally published in 1967. Reviews: *TLS*, Aug. 17, 1967, p. 745; Rosalie L. Colie, *KR*, 122, 1968, 671–77; Alan Rudrum, *SoRA*, 3, 1968, 184–88; James H. Sims, *SHR*, 2, 1968, 532–35; Mark Roberts, *N&Q*, 15, 1968, 389–94; Barbara Kiefer Lewalski, *JEGP*, 68, 1969, 517–21; Gilbert Thomas, *English* (Oxford), 17, 1968, 58–59; John N. Morris, *SAQ*, 68, 1969, 134–37; Michael Fixler, *RES*, 20, 1969, 227–29; John R. Mulder, *SCN*, 27, 1969, 2; W. Arthur Turner, *RenQ*, 22, 1969, 420–22; Earl Miner, *ECS*, 3, 1970, 296–305; Patrick Grant, *Malahat Review*, 20, 1971, 129–30.

2217 Fish, Stanley. "Transmuting the Lump: *Paradise Lost*, 1942–1982." *Literature and History: Theoretical Problems and Russian Case Studies.* Ed. by Gary Saul Morson. Afterword by Richard Wortman (Stanford, CA: Stanford Univ. Press, 1986), pp. 33–56.

Traces the evolution of the critical response to Books 11–12 of *Paradise Lost* from rejection in 1942 to gradual acceptance by 1982. Disagrees with Raymond B. Waddington (No. 3193), who asserted that "the complexity of Books XI and XI was there all the while for those with eyes clear enough to see." Concludes that the complexity of those books which is "now as obvious and indisputable as Waddington says it is—came to be put there by

the labors of men and women like you and me."

2218 Fisher, S. A. "Milton's *Paradise Lost*." *Expl*, 33, 1974, Item 15.

Asserts that "Milton builds into Raphael's character a passionate sensuality that reinforces the erotic side of Adam and Eve's relationship," and that the angel flushes, not blushes, a passionate rosy hue. Suggests that "angelic body language adds another psychological motivation to the fall."

2219 Fitter, Christopher. "'Native Soil': The Rhetoric of Exile Lament and Exile Consolation in *Paradise Lost*." *MiltonS*, 20, 1984, 147–62.

Discusses the expulsion rhetoric in Book 11. Contends that Michael's statements "give greater comfort than might seem the case to us today." Finds exile consolation in Hellenistic rhetoric, Plutarch, Cicero, Seneca, and Renaissance literature, all of which Milton's contemporaries would have known.

2220 Fix, Stephen. "Johnson and the 'Duty' of Reading *Paradise Lost*." *ELH*, 52, 1985, 649–71.

On Johnson's statement that the reading of Milton's poem is a duty. Believes that Johnson really became "an intimidated reader, a reader forced by poetry to yield up so much control over his psychic and emotional experience, a reader who is mastered by another author."

2221 Fixler, Michael. "All-Interpreting Love: God's Name in Scripture and in *Paradise Lost*." *Milton and Scriptural Tradition: The Bible into Poetry.* Ed. by James H. Sims and Leland Ryken (Columbia: Univ. of Missouri Press, 1984), pp. 117–41.

Demonstrates that Milton's extensive use of the word "all" in *Paradise Lost* is both deliberate and significant. It represents "completeness" and, more importantly, stands for the name of God. By abandoning God's Old Testament names, such as Yahweh and Jehovah,

Milton reflects the sentiment of the New Testament where "the Father's name is known only through his Son." Thus, "the name of God is . . . the argument of Milton's poem."

2222 Fixler, Michael. "The Apocalypse within *Paradise Lost." New Essays on "Paradise Lost."* Ed. by Thomas Kranidas (Berkeley, Los Angeles, and London: Univ. of California Press, 1969), pp. 131–78.

Argues that Milton's poem itself is "an act of worship" and that in its structure it presents an elaborate systematic transformation of the Book of Revelation. "Beneath the epic vestments there is a sacramental postulant." Abs., *MiltonQ*, 4, 1970, 35. Review: Joseph Anthony Wittreich, Jr., *Genre*, 5, 1972, 307–25.

2223 Fixler, Michael. "Milton's Magnanimous Reader." *MP*, 82, 1985, 310–14.

Review essay. Discusses the following recent books: Dennis R. Danielson, *Milton's Good God* (No. 2108); Michael Lieb, *Poetics of the Holy* (No. 2612); and John T. Shawcross, *With Mortal Voice* (No. 3040).

2224 Fixler, Michael. "Milton's Passionate Epic." *MiltonS*, 1, 1969, 167–92.

Sees *Paradise Lost* as an act of worship intended to celebrate the mystery of God's providence. "The poem, in short, is indeed an argument, but no less a song of praise, a formal act of adoration celebrating the mystery of God's ways; and as such it is by the nature of its devotional energy more than an epic; it is a passionate epic."

2225 Fixler, Michael. "Plato's Four Furors and the Real Structure of *Paradise Lost." PMLA*, 92, 1977, 952–62.

Milton's invocations to the muse reveal the stages of a composing process that coordinates the levels of the poem's inspiration and overall design. This universal form both metaphysically and structurally underlies *Paradise Lost.*

2226 Flannagan, Roy. "Belial and 'Effeminate Slackness' in *Paradise Lost* and *Paradise Regained." MiltonQ*, 19, 1985, 9–11.

Compares the character of Belial (over-indulgent and over-sexed) to that of Jesus (strong and able to resist sexual temptation). Believes that "one reason Jesus is able to break the snares and spells of Satan is his success in resisting the sexual temptation that was the primary cause of Adam's fall: vehemence of love."

2227 Flannagan, Roy. "Eve's Choices in *Paradise Lost." MiltonQ*, 16, 1982, 106–07.

Abstract of a paper presented at the New York College English Association Meeting at Le Moyne College on October 8, 1982. Believes that Eve is completely responsible for her fall but "her earlier repentance carefully balances her precedence in sin."

2228 Flannagan, Roy C. *"Paradise Lost": Notes.* Lincoln, NB: Cliff Notes, 1970. Second edition, 1990. 83pp.

Contains summaries and commentaries.

2229 Flavin, Louise. "The Similar Dramatic Function of Prophetic Dreams: Eve's Dream Compared to Chauntecleer's." *MiltonQ*, 17, 1983, 132–38.

Believes that Eve's dream in *Paradise Lost* and Chauntecleer's dream in the *Nun's Priest's Tale* function in similar ways. Asserts that while "in neither case does the dream cause the character to fall, in each case the dream is instrumental in getting Eve and Chauntecleer in a position for the fall to take place."

2230 Fleissner, Robert F. "Milton and the Serpent." *AN&Q*, 9, 1971, 74.

Addresses the ambiguity of *Paradise Lost* 10.84: "Conviction to the Serpent none belongs." Believes that the "poor old snake is not to blame, that only the 'infernal' one is."

2231 Fleissner, R. F. "Milton and the Serpent Recoiled." *AN&Q*, 24, 1985, 8–9.

Argues that the word "conviction" alludes to castigation in the line "Conviction to the Serpent none belongs" (*Paradise Lost* 10.84). Cites Marlowe's *Doctor Faustus*, ideals of orthodox Judaism, and Freudian literary interpretation to support the claim that Milton granted the serpent a reprieve for its part in the Fall.

2232 Flesch, William Benjamin. "The Disconsolate: The Poetry of Irreparable Loss." Doctoral diss., Cornell Univ., 1986. 226pp. Abs., *DAI*, 47, 1986, 535A.

Examines "the type of affect elicited in and by literary response to loss that seems irreparable," citing Herbert's *Temple*, Milton's *Paradise Lost* and Percy Bysshe Shelley's "The Triumph of Life" as evidence.

2233 Flesch, William. "The Majesty of Darkness." *John Milton.* Modern Critical Views. Ed. by Harold Bloom (New York, New Haven, CT, and Philadelphia, PA: Chelsea House, 1986), pp. 293–311.

"On my reading, *Paradise Lost* dramatizes a series of more or less mistaken interpretations of God in order to claim a terrific prerogative for poetry as the only human endeavor pitched high enough to be adequate to the God the poem imagines."

2234 Flinker, Noam. "Cinyras, Myrrha, and Adonis: Father-Daughter Incest from Ovid to Milton." *MiltonS*, 14, 1980, 59–74.

Suggests that the parallels between Ovid's Myrrha and Sin in *Paradise Lost* represent "a mockery of the tradition which allegorized Ovid's heroine as the mother of Christ."

2235 Flinker, Noam. "Courting Urania: The Narrator of *Paradise Lost* Invokes His Muse." *Milton and the Idea of Woman.* Ed. by Julia M. Walker (Urbana and Chicago: Univ. of Illinois Press, 1988), pp. 86–99.

Asserts that "the narrator of *Paradise Lost* presents a statement about his attitude toward the Muse which includes a series of metaphors with striking psychosexual elements." However, the narrator avoids the behavior exhibited by Satan and Adam. Abs., *MiltonQ*, 24, 1990, 150.

2236 Flinker, Noam. "Father-Daughter Incest in *Paradise Lost*." *MiltonQ*, 14, 1980, 116–22.

Notes several examples of incest among the fallen angels mentioned in the catalog of Book 1 and points out that while fallen readers may initially find some of the angels attractive, our final attitude is one of repulsion.

2237 Foley, Jack. " 'Sin, Not Time': Satan's First Speech in *Paradise Lost*." *ELH*, 37, 1970, 37–56.

Analyzes *Paradise Lost* 1.84–124. Feels that Satan moves "further and further away from the horrible reality in front of him" and that the speech is a parody of Genesis 1.1–3 and John 1.1–5.

2238 Forrest, James F. "The Fathers on Milton's Evil Thought in Blameless Mind." *Canadian Journal of Theology*, 15, 1969, 247–67.

On the theological background of *Paradise Lost* 5.117–19, in which Adam explains Eve's dream.

2239 Forsyth, Neil Robert. " 'Full of Doubt I Stand': The Structure of *Paradise Lost*." *The Structure of Texts.* Ed. by Udo Fries (Tübingen: Narr, 1987), pp. 159–76.

Accounts for the changes between the first and second editions of *Paradise Lost*: "Ed. II [1674] makes clear what was only implicit in Ed. I [1667], that conversion, regeneration, the bringing of good from evil, are structural as well as doctrinal principles of *Paradise Lost*."

2240 Forsyth, Neil. "Homer in Milton: The Attendance Motif and the Graces." *CL*, 33, 1981, 137–55.

On the Graces that accompany Eve in *Paradise Lost*. Discusses Homer's use of the motif and shows how Milton enlarges, transforms, and finally denies it. Abs., *MiltonQ*, 14, 1980, 70; *SCN*, 38, 1980, 45.

2241 Forsyth, Neil Robert. *The Old Enemy: Satan and the Combat Myth.* Princeton, NJ: Princeton Univ. Press, 1987. xv, 506pp.

Traces the development of the Satan legend from its ancient beginning through its discussion by early Christian writers, including Paul, Origen, and Augustine. Points out that Milton accurately reflects "the essential ambivalence of the Judeo-Christian tradition when his narrator piles up the classical parallels and the folklore." Satan gradually emerged from a principle of evil to a narrative character. Review: Roy Flannagan, *MiltonQ*, 21, No. 3, 1987, 113–17.

2242 Forsyth, Neil Robert. "The Powers of Darkness Bound: The Rise to Power of Satan in Early Christian History and His Role in *Paradise Lost*." Doctoral diss., Univ. of California, Berkeley, 1976. 553pp. Abs., *DAI*, 38, 1977, 803A.

Traces Satan's rise and development in the early Christian church with his eventual portrayal in *Paradise Lost* as "the instrument of his own contradiction."

2243 Foster, Donald W. "Milton and the Universalists." *N&Q*, 27, 1980, 334.

Milton's "paraphrase in *Paradise Lost* of I Corinthians xv.22 and Romans v.15 represents a deliberate attempt to counter those who would use these biblical passages as universalist proof-texts."

2244 Fraser, Russell. *The Language of Adam: On the Limits and Systems of Discourse.* New York: Columbia Univ. Press, 1977. xiii, 288pp.

Reviews: *MiltonQ*, 12, 1978, 37; Virginia Ramey Mollenkott, *MiltonQ*, 12, 1978, 77–82.

2245 Freedman, Morris. "The 'Tagging' of *Paradise Lost*: Rhyme in Dryden's *The State of Innocence*." *MiltonQ*, 5, 1971, 18–22.

Compares passages in the two works in terms of Dryden's claims for rhyme.

Suggests that his dramatic adaptation of *Paradise Lost* "illustrates few of the advantages of rhyme he had argued for so vigorously" and that passages of merit result primarily from his talent as a dramatist and poet. Notes that Dryden eventually acknowledges the superiority of *Paradise Lost* and concludes that "His most serious critical failing . . . was not to recognize that the sheer massive scope of Milton's epic, its monumental vastness, was indispensable to its final and total greatness."

2246 Freeman, James Arthur. "Classic and Christian: Describing Deities in *Paradise Lost*." *MiltonQ*, 14, 1980, 71.

Abstract of a paper presented at the 1979 MLA Convention. "Milton carefully combines language from pagan epic and the Bible to describe supernatural beings in *Paradise Lost*. . . . He kidnaps the vigor associated with heathen works while he remains true to his religious convictions." Also abs., *SCN*, 38, 1980, 45.

2247 Freeman, James Arthur. "The Complexity of Satan in *Paradise Lost*." Doctoral diss., Univ. of Minnesota, 1968. 231pp. Abs., *DA*, 29, 1969, 2672A.

Asserts that Milton presents a multi-faceted and complex Satan to emphasize the common thread of malevolence that runs through his personality.

2248 Freeman, James A. *Milton and the Martial Muse: "Paradise Lost" and European Traditions of War.* Princeton, NJ: Princeton Univ. Press, 1980. xx, 253pp.

"Milton's dislike of war inspired a sustained, learned, and sophisticated poem to degrade systematic hostility." Chapters: "Public and Personal Responses to War"; "Satan's Soldiers"; "Satan the General"; and "War in Unexpected Places." Reviews: Jean Wilson, *TLS*, Apr. 10, 1981, p. 417; William E. Cain, *MLN*, 96, 1981, 1121–33; Philip J. Gallagher, *MiltonQ*, 15, 1981, 19–24; Archie Burnett, *N&Q*,

29, 1982, 441–42; Jean-François Camé, *CahiersE*, 20, 1981, 138–40; D. D. C. Chambers, *RES*, 34, 1983, 338–40; James H. Sims, *SCN*, 31, 1983, 33–34.

2249 Freeman, James. "Milton's Fable of the Bees: *Paradise Lost* I.768–776 in Its Renaissance Context." *MiltonQ*, 14, 1980, 71.

Abstract of a paper presented at the 1978 NEMLA Conference. Finds that instead of serving as a pastoral relief from the militarism of Satan and his army, the simile restates "the unpleasant facts we learn about fallen angels."

2250 Freeman, James A. "'The Roof was Fretted Gold.'" *CL*, 27, 1975, 254–66.

Milton molds his language to reflect both classical and Christian connotations, thus emphasizing the failure of Pandemonium by any standard. Not a gaudy but neutral detail, the golden fretwork on the ceiling is an index of Satan's reprehensible traits.

2251 Freeman, James A. "Satan, Bentley, and 'The Din of War.'" *MiltonQ*, 7, 1973, 1–4.

On *Paradise Lost* 1.663–69. Argues that Richard Bentley's note, in his 1732 edition of *Paradise Lost*, identifying Satan's fallen rebels with Roman soldiers clashing their arms is "not only historically inaccurate but also misleads us from the political and moral significance of martial approval."

2252 French, Roberts W. "Milton and Spenser." *N&Q*, 17, 1970, 249.

Notes that *Paradise Lost* 2.146–51, 911, and 914–16 and 10.476–77 echo the *Faerie Queene* 3.6.36.

2253 French, Roberts W. "*Paradise Lost* IV, 401–08: Lions and Tigers in Paradise." *MiltonQ*, 14, 1980, 21–22.

Disagrees with Robert Rex Meyers (No. 2721). Insists that the passage in question is not a poetic lapse. Reply by Meyers, p. 22.

2254 French, Roberts W. "Satan's Sonnet." *MiltonQ*, 11, 1977, 113–14.

Finds that Satan's call to reassemble the fallen angels in *Paradise Lost* 1.178–91 is a mock-sonnet. The sonnet form is incomplete, and "The suggested pattern only emphasizes Satan's inability to fulfill its promise."

2255 Fresch, Cheryl H. "'And Brought Her unto the Man': The Wedding in *Paradise Lost*." *MiltonS*, 16, 1982, 21–33.

Surveys various commentaries on the first wedding in light of Milton's account in Books 4 and 8. Observes that by permitting Eve to flee at first and then allowing Adam to woo her, Milton celebrates both human love and divine love as Adam and Eve come together in marriage.

2256 Fresch, Cheryl H. "'As the Rabbines Expound': Milton, Genesis, and the Rabbis." *MiltonS*, 15, 1981, 59–79.

Reexamines the controversy concerning the extent of Milton's rabbinical reading. Concludes that the source of the readings has yet to be identified (and may never be) but that the presence of a rabbinical influence in *Paradise Lost* is unmistakable.

2257 Fresch, Cheryl H. "The Hebraic Influence upon the Creation of Eve in *Paradise Lost*." *MiltonS*, 13, 1979, 181–99.

Examines three incidents—Adam's request for a mate, his sleep during the creation of Eve, and his first words at her presentation—to show that Milton was influenced by standard Hebrew interpretations, which demonstrated the kinship between ordinary humanity and the first two people in the garden.

2258 Fresch, Cheryl Hope. "Milton's Eve and the Problem of the Additions to the Command." *MiltonQ*, 12, 1978, 83–90.

Studies the theological responses to the discrepancy between Genesis 2.17 and 3.3 and Milton's concept of sin as the controlling factor in his solution to the problem in *Paradise Lost*. See also No. 2628.

2259 Fresch, Cheryl Hope. "Milton's Eve and the Theological Tradition." Doctoral diss., Cornell Univ., 1976. 179pp. Abs., *DAI*, 37, 1977, 5846A–47A.

Argues that Milton's perception of Eve in *Paradise Lost* is influenced by several theological traditions but is most closely aligned with the Hebraic "warm and human understanding of Eve."

2260 Froula, Christine. "When Eve Reads Milton: Undoing the Canonical Economy." *CritI*, 10, 1983, 321–47. Reprinted in *Canons*. Ed. by Robert von Hallberg (Chicago, IL, and London: Univ. of Chicago Press, 1984), pp. 149–75.

Believes that Eve becomes the "typical partriarchal woman" and that Adam desires to possess her. See rejoinder by Edward Pechter (No. 2864); and surrejoinder by Froula, *CritI*, 11, 1984, pp. 171–78.

2261 Frye, Northrop. "The Garden Within." *On Milton's Poetry: A Selection of Modern Studies*. Ed. by Arnold Stein (Greenwich, CT: Fawcett Publications, 1970), pp. 228–36.

Reprint of a chapter from Frye's *The Return of Eden* (No. 2262).

2262 Frye, Northrop. *The Return of Eden: Five Essays on Milton's Epics*. Toronto and Buffalo, NY: Univ. of Toronto Press, 1975.

Reprint of Huckabay No. 1322, originally published in 1965. See No. 561. Review: Ants Oras, *SR*, 77, 1969, 176–84.

2263 Frye, Northrop. "The Revelation to Eve." *"Paradise Lost": A Tercentenary Tribute*. Ed. by Balachandra Rajan ([Toronto]: Univ. of Toronto Press, 1969), pp. 18–47. Reprinted in *The Stubborn Structure: Essays on Criticism and Society* (Ithaca, NY: Cornell Univ. Press; London: Methuen, 1970; London: Univ. Paperbacks, 1974), pp. 135–59.

Uses the brief description of Eve's revelation in *Paradise Lost* 12.595–96 to relate "two great mythological structures" in literature—"one dominated by a male father-god" and the other by the mother-goddess.

2264 Frye, Northrop. "The Story of All Things." *On Milton's Poetry: A Selection of Modern Studies*. Ed. by Arnold Stein (Greenwich, CT: Fawcett Publications, 1970), pp. 89–96.

Reprint of a chapter from Frye's *The Return of Eden* (No. 2262).

2265 Frye, Northrop, and **Claude Mouchard,** trans. "Au Sujet de Milton." *Po&sie*, 46, 1988, 88–104.

2266 Frye, Roland Mushat. "Milton's *Paradise Lost* and the Visual Arts." *PAPS*, 120, 1976, 233–44. Reprinted in *Theology Today*, 34, 1977, 9–19.

Summarizes the findings to be presented in Frye's book (No. 620). "My thesis is that Milton's descriptions rely pervasively upon visual representations, and that his powers of description can neither be fully understood nor fully appreciated apart from the traditional iconography which he has transmuted into poetic forms."

2267 Fujii, Haruhiko. "Meanings of Space in *Paradise Lost*." *MCJ News*, 6, 1983, 11–12.

Abstract of paper presented. Examines some of the effects produced by Milton's description of space.

2268 Fujii, Haruhiko. "Yurameku Ensui-*Paradise Lost* to Mannerism teki Keitai." *EigoS*, 119, 1973, 458–59, 534–35.

Considers the mannerist elements in *Paradise Lost*.

2269 Fuller, Elizabeth Ely. "Flight toward Reality: A Kinesthetic Reading of Milton's *Paradise Lost*." Doctoral diss., City Univ. of New York, 1977. 506pp. Abs., *DAI*, 38, 1977, 1407A–08A.

Describes the joining of the epic's plot (the changing relationship "between modal reality and modal consciousness") to its "counterplot" (the reader's use of "aesthetic distancing" to comprehend a "kinesthetic and modal reality" within the poem).

2270 Fuller, Elizabeth Ely. *Milton's Kinesthetic Vision in "Paradise Lost."* Lewisburg, PA: Bucknell Univ. Press;

London and Toronto: Associated Univ. Presses, 1983. 321pp.

"Milton intends his poem to move the reader, not only in the emotional sense of that word but through all the faculties and capabilities of his/her being. The primary mode of both his vision and his poetry is kinesthetic." Part 1: "The Poetics of Milton's Counterplot"; Part 2: "Flight toward Reality: A Modal Reading of *Paradise Lost*"; Part 3: "Milton's Kinesthetic Vision: The Nature of the Universe." Contains an index of similes. Reviews: C. F. Main, *RenQ*, 37, 1984, 669–71; Georgia B. Christopher, *JEGP*, 84, 1985, 120–22; Paul Stevens, *UTQ*, 54, 1985, 285–88; John S. Tanner, *AN&Q*, 24, 1985, 61–63; Diana Benet, *MiltonQ*, 20, 1986, 110–11.

2271 Gagen, Jean. "Adam, the Serpent, and Satan: Recognition and Restoration." *MiltonQ*, 17, 1983, 116–21.

Explores Adam's ability to link the serpent with Satan. Believes that when Adam is finally able to make the connection, it marks the beginning of his "restoration to grace, with the reascendancy in him of right reason, and with his first inkling of God's plan to bring good out of Satanic evil."

2272 Gagen, Jean. "Anomalies in Eden: Adam and Eve in Dryden's *The State of Innocence*." *Milton's Legacy in the Arts*. Ed. by Albert C. Labriola and Edward Sichi, Jr. (University Park and London: Pennsylvania State Univ. Press, 1988), pp. 135–51.

Compares Milton's portrayal of Adam and Eve in *Paradise Lost* to that of Dryden in the *State of Innocence*. Emphasizes the more intellectual portrayal of Eve in Dryden's work.

2273 Gagen, Jean. "Did Milton Nod?" *MiltonQ*, 20, 1986, 17–22.

Discusses whether "Milton's failure to present a consistent explanation of the circumstances under which Eve was informed of Satan's malignant design"

was an intellectual conflict or simply an oversight. Reply by Edward Le Comte (No. 2578).

2274 Gair, Evelyn Mary Ann. "Milton's War in Heaven: A Study of the Commentators on the Revelation of St. John the Divine." Doctoral diss., Univ. of New Brunswick, 1974. Abs., *DAI*, 35, 1975, 7255A.

Insists that the Book of Revelation, "and seventeenth-century reactions to it, contribute directly to an understanding of some of the most difficult problems in *Paradise Lost*, especially to the War in Heaven in Books V and VI."

2275 Gallagher, Philip J. "Beyond the Oedipus Complex." *MiltonQ*, 18, 1984, 84–92.

Review essay. Believes that William Kerrigan's *The Sacred Complex* (No. 2519), which attempts to reinterpret Milton and his works in terms of neo-Freudian theory, is definitive despite instances of Kerrigan's subordinating Milton's world view to neo-Freudianism.

2276 Gallagher, Philip J. "Creation in Genesis and in *Paradise Lost*." *MiltonS*, 20, 1984, 163–204.

Analyzes Milton's reconciliation of apparent inconsistencies in the first three chapters of Genesis. Deals especially with the two accounts of creation and with Milton's handling of creation *ex deo*.

2277 Gallagher, Philip J. "Milton and Euhemerism: *Paradise Lost* X.578–84." *MiltonQ*, 12, 1978, 16–23.

Milton does not believe that the gods were deified heroes, and his use of the Ophion-Eurynome myth in the passage suggests that euhemerism has a Satanic origin.

2278 Gallagher, Philip J. "More Theirs by Being His: Teaching Milton to Undergraduates." *Teaching Milton to Undergraduates: Problems and Approaches.* Proceedings of the Special Session (537),

Annual Meeting of the Modern Language Association, Dec. 28, 1976. Comp. by Paul L. Gaston ([Edwardsville: Southern Illinois Univ.], n.d.), pp. 21–28. Reprinted in *MiltonQ*, 11, 1977, 4–9.

"I use an absolutely literalist and historicist method, one which disposes of the problem of contemporary relevance by ignoring it. . . . I insist that they [students] read *Paradise Lost* in its seventeenth-century context, that they examine the poem as a theodicy on *its* terms, not theirs."

2279 Gallagher, Philip J. "*Paradise Lost* and the Greek Theogony." *ELR*, 9, 1979, 121–48.

Argues that Milton is concerned with exposing as erroneous the Greek succession myth of Athena's birth as related by Hesiod. Also, Milton depicts the war among the Greek gods as "an internecine strife in which fallen angels fight among themselves to secure worship at various heathen shrines." The Titanomachia, then, is "a distortion of the War in Heaven."

2280 Gallagher, Philip Joseph. "*Paradise Lost* and the Promethean Tradition." Doctoral diss., Univ. of Massachusetts, 1972. 544pp. Abs., *DAI*, 33, 1973, 5122A.

Measures the impact of the Promethean myth on *Paradise Lost*, asserting that "Milton understands the entire ensemble of Promethean motifs . . . to be ill-remembered pagan redactions of the angelic War in Heaven and the fall of Adam and Eve in the Christian cosmos."

2281 Gallagher, Philip J. "*Paradise Lost* Text and Context: A Review Essay." *RMR*, 37, 1983, 217–36.

Review of Robert Crosman, *Reading "Paradise Lost"* (No. 2091); Stella P. Revard, *The War in Heaven* (No. 2926); and Francis C. Blessington, *"Paradise Lost" and the Classical Epic* (No. 1955).

2282 Gallagher, Philip J. " 'Real or Allegoric': The Ontology of Sin and Death

in *Paradise Lost*." *ELR*, 6, 1976, 317–35.

"The exegesis I propose not only insists in its theoretical underpinnings upon the absolute historicity of Sin and Death as creatures begotten by Satan; it also assumes that *Paradise Lost* offers its narrative of these personifications as the definitive account of their origin." Abs., *MiltonQ*, 10, 1976, 131.

2283 Gallagher, Philip J. "*Summa contra Pastorem et Lectorem.*" *MiltonQ*, 19, 1985, 53–60.

Asserts that the phrase "earth's hallow'd mould, / Of God inspir'd" in *Paradise Lost* 5.321–22 "is an epic epithet in the vocative case appositional to *Adam* and . . . that the phrase *small store* is the subject of the intransitive verb *will serve* (where *serve* means *suffice*)."

2284 Garber, Marjorie B. "Fallen Landscape: The Art of Milton and Poussin." *ELR*, 5, 1975, 96–124.

"Both artists were anthropocentric humanists who stress in their work a kind of 'fallen landscape,' a post-Arcadian or post-Edenic period in which man's mortal and finite state was celebrated as the necessary prelude to grace." Discusses Nicolas Poussin's painting and artistic theory. Abs., *MiltonQ*, 9, 1975, 120.

2285 Gardner, Helen. *A Reading of "Paradise Lost."* Oxford: Clarendon Press, 1965, 1967. xii, 131pp.

See Huckabay No. 1326. Reviews: Jacques Blondel, *EA*, 19, 1966, 449–50; Michael Wilding, *Southerly*, 26, 1966, 212–13; Basil Willey, *CritQ*, 8, 1966, 85–86; John B. Broadbent, Jr., *RES*, 18, 1967, 105–06; John M. Steadman, *Archiv*, 205, 1969, 403–05.

2286 Geisst, Charles R. "Milton and Ambrose on Evil." *N&Q*, 23, 1976, 233.

Finds that a passage in Ambrose's *De Paradiso* provides a "conceptual source" for *Paradise Lost* 5.117–19. Both Milton and Ambrose "held to the idea of moral good," as opposed to

Augustine's concept of ontological good, and "dealt with the topic when discussing Adam's prelapsarian state."

2287 George, A. G. *Milton and the Nature of Man: A Descriptive Study of "Paradise Lost" in Terms of the Concept of Man as the Image of God.* London: Asia Publishing House, 1974. xii, 168pp.

Argues that "we can only grasp Milton's concept of man in terms of the Biblical theocentric description of man as a being created in the image and likeness of God." Reviews: William B. Hunter, Jr., *SCN*, 32, 1974, 52; Anthony Low, *MiltonQ*, 9, 1975, 20–27; Mother Mary Christopher Pecheux, *CSR*, 6, 1976, 228–29.

2288 George, A. G. "Myth in *Paradise Lost*: A New Approach." *Essays on John Milton: A Tercentenary Tribute.* Ed. by Asloob Ahmad Ansari (Aligarh: Aligarh Muslim Univ., 1976), pp. 74–79.

"Indeed, Milton's special literary and mythic reconstruction of the story of Genesis lies in locating in time and history the biblical incidents mentioned in Genesis and incorporating the idea of mutability, thereby stressing the temporal and historical dimensions of experience."

2289 George, C. M. "The Wolf Image in Milton." *ES*, 52, 1971, 30–32.

On the political overtones of the wolf image in *Lycidas* and *Paradise Lost*. Feels that Milton refers mainly to the bishops.

2290 George, Diana Hume. "The Miltonic Ideal: A Paradigm for the Structure of Relations between Men and Women in Academia." *CE*, 40, 1979, 864–73.

Believes that women entering academia effect profound changes, which are "in some respects parallel to the changes wrought in Adam's life by Eve's creation in *Paradise Lost*." Includes a comment by Walter J. Ong, S. J.

2291 George, Rita Beatrice Lagacé. "Microcosmic Adam: Background Studies of a Renaissance Type." Doctoral diss., Univ.

of Minnesota, 1975. 298pp. Abs., *DAI*, 36, 1975, 2195A–96A.

Discusses the origin and impact of microcosmic theory—the individual human as "the little world" or "image of the cosmos"—on Christian culture and, more specifically, selected Renaissance writers.

2292 Gilbert, Allan H. *On the Composition of "Paradise Lost": A Study of the Ordering and Insertion of Material.* New York: Octagon Books, 1972.

Reprint of Huckabay No. 1336, originally published in 1947.

2293 Gilbert, Sandra M. "Patriarchal Poetry and Women Readers: Reflections on Milton's Bogey." *PMLA*, 93, 1978, 368–82. Printed in slightly revised form in *The Madwoman in the Attic: The Woman Writer and the Nineteenth-Century Literary Imagination.* By Gilbert and Susan Gubar (New Haven, CT, and London: Yale Univ. Press, 1979), pp. 187–212.

Believes that women from Wollstonecraft to Woolf have reread and misread *Paradise Lost* to allay anxieties aroused by Milton. See Nos. 2165 and 3211. Reply by Philip J. Gallagher, *PMLA*, 94, 1979, 319–21; rejoinder by Gilbert, pp. 321–22. Abs., *SCN*, 38, 1980, 19. Reviews (of book): Michele M. Leber, *LJ*, 104, 1979, 1698; Sara Plath, *Booklist*, 76, 1979, 590; Genevieve Stattaford, *Publishers' Weekly*, 216, 1979, 376; Frances Taliaferro, *Harper's Magazine*, 259, 1979, 78–79; Rosemary Ashton, *TLS*, Aug. 8, 1980, p. 901; Gillian Beer, *THES*, May 2, 1980, p. 15; Dean Flower, *HudR*, 33, 1980, 421–30; Shirley Foster, *Novel*, 14, 1980, 94–96; Suzanne Juhasz, *ELN*, 17, 1980, 308–10; Annette Kolodny, *AL*, 52, 1980, 128–32; Victoria S. Middleton, *Studies in the Novel*, 12, 1980, 383–85; Helen Moglen, *NCF*, 35, 1980, 225–29; Patricia Meyer Spacks, *YR*, 69, 1980, 266–70; Katherine Frank, *PQ*, 59, 1980, 381–83; Juliet Dusinberre, *N&Q*, 28, 1981, 351–52; Ingeborg Nordin Hennel, *Samlaren*,

102, 1981, 187–89; Mary Jacobus, *Signs*, 6, 1981, 517–23; Eva Simmons, *EIC*, 31, 1981, 252–58.

2294 Gilbertson, Carol. "'Many *Miltons* in This One Man': Marvell's Mower Poems and *Paradise Lost*." *MiltonS*, 22, 1986, 151–72.

Discusses the relationship between the mower poems and *Paradise Lost*. Feels that Marvell's poems reveal a problem of imitation, influence, and independence.

2295 Gilbertson, Carol Ann. "The Mower as a Type of Adam: Andrew Marvell's Mower Poems and *Paradise Lost*." Doctoral diss., Univ. of Minnesota, 1979. 614pp. Abs., *DAI*, 40, 1980, 5873A.

Examines the theme of self-destruction as it applies to Marvell's Mower and Milton's Adam.

2296 Gillham, D. G. "Milton's Gods." *The Sole Function: Essays, Poems, Reminiscences, and a Story Presented to Christina van Heyningen*. Ed. by J. A. Berthoud and C. O. Gardner (Pietermaritzburg: Univ. of Natal Press, 1969), pp. 57–65.

Contends that Milton "vacillates between an 'official' view of what is being described and a yielding at the critical moments, to the full imaginative promptings of his subject." Argues that "these alternatives . . . disclose a deeper purpose, a statement of the varying conditions of human belief and hence of the necessarily contradictory shape of human beliefs. The contradictions in *Paradise Lost* cannot be resolved metaphysically, but psychologically."

2297 Gilliland, C. Herbert, Jr. "Limitary Patterns in *Paradise Lost*." *SAB*, 43, 1978, 42–48.

Finds the polarity "between the creation and rupture of bounds." Stresses that "Milton does not employ a simple, passive contrast between circumscription on the one hand, and spaciousness on the other, but rather an active tension between the establishment of boundaries and their violation."

2298 Gilliland, Joan F. "'But Say I Could Repent': Satan's Decision." *BWVACET*, 5, 1979, 26–32.

Discusses the possibility of Satan's eventual repentance and salvation and concludes that "his inability to repent is not imposed from without but comes from 'The Hell within.'"

2299 Gilliland, Joan F. "*Paradise Lost* and the Youthful Reader." *CLAQ*, 10, 1985, 26–28.

An adaptation for children.

2300 Gilliland, Joan F. "Satan's Perverted Meditation." *SPWVSRA*, 5, 1980, 42–48.

Shows that Satan's first soliloquy in *Paradise Lost* 4 both follows and perverts the meditative pattern as outlined in Louis L. Martz's *The Poetry of Meditation* (Huckabay No. 2617).

2301 Gilliland, Joan F. "A Study of Despair in *Paradise Lost*." Doctoral diss., Vanderbilt Univ., 1977. 283pp. Abs., *DAI*, 38, 1977, 1408A.

Analyzes Satan's and Adam's despair in *Paradise Lost* "in light of theological and literary backgrounds and of psychoanalytic concepts."

2302 Gleason, Moriece. "What Surmounts the Reach of Human Sense." *Essays in Honor of Esmond Linworth Marilla*. Ed. by Thomas Austin Kirby and William John Olive. Louisiana State Univ. Studies, Humanities Series, no. 19 (Baton Rouge: Louisiana State Univ. Press, 1970), pp. 135–43.

On Milton's use of language "in his delineation of the spiritual by means of the corporeal" in *Paradise Lost*. The parallel council scenes in Books 2 and 3 illustrate the precise and lucid uses of language.

2303 Gnerro, Mark L. "Marian Typology and Milton's Heavenly Muse." *PPMRC*, 2, 1977, 39–48.

Holds the view that Milton invokes three muses in *Paradise Lost*: the Spirit (1.17–26), Holy Light (3.1–55), and Urania (1.1–16; 7.1–39; and 9.20–26 and 46–47). Proposes "to show that

Milton's familiarity with Marian typology rather than with Classical mythology was chiefly responsible for his invoking the beloved Urania in a tender and trusting manner, a tone markedly less formal than his addresses to the Spirit and to Holy Light."

2304 Godfrey, D. R. "The Ships in the Clouds and Milton's Flying Fiend." *HAB*, 22, 1971, 50–51.

Discusses the simile that compares Satan flying toward the gates of hell with a fleet of ships hanging in the clouds (*Paradise Lost* 2.636–43) and considers the possibility that these lines represent a mirage.

2305 Godshalk, William Leigh. "Marlowe, Milton, and the Apples of Hell." *MiltonQ*, 5, 1971, 34–35.

Suggests Marlowe's *Tamburlaine* as a possible source for Milton's infernal fruit tree in *Paradise Lost* 10. Notes Milton's probable familiarity with such a tree in the Moslem tradition stemming from the Koran, "The ultimate source of Marlowe's description." Marlowe's work thus gives a clue to Milton's source, if it is not the source itself.

2306 Gohain, H. "*Paradise Lost* and Aspects of the Seventeenth-Century Crisis." Doctoral diss., Cambridge Univ., 1969. *IT*, 19, 1971, 16.

2307 Goldberg, Jonathan. "*Virga Iesse*: Analogy, Typology, and Anagogy in a Miltonic Simile." *MiltonS*, 5, 1973, 177–90.

Raphael's analogy of a tree in *Paradise Lost* 5.469–502 should be viewed as "a spatial analogy for a temporal process." The tree thus acts "not only as an analogy but as a typological metaphor."

2308 Goldman, Jack. "Insight into Milton's Abdiel." *PQ*, 49, 1970, 249–54.

Discusses Abdiel's role as a "benign link between the fallen angels and the loyal, so to speak, untested, hosts of God." Regards Abdiel as a pivotal

figure in terms of "the religious and political backdrop of the age in which *Paradise Lost* was written." Suggests Noah, Phineas, and Elijah as possible models.

2309 Goldman, Jack. "Perspectives of Raphael's Meal in *Paradise Lost*, Book V." *MiltonQ*, 11, 1977, 31–37.

Argues that "the model for Milton's Feast with Raphael is the scene in Genesis 18, where Abraham feasts with the three angels."

2310 Goldwyn, Merrill H. "A Note on Milton's Borrowing from Marlowe's *Tamburlaine* in *Paradise Lost*." *ELN*, 22, No. 1, 1984, 22–23.

Reveals verbal echoes from the second part of Marlowe's *Tamburlaine* in Milton's poem.

2311 González Padilla, María Enriqueta. "La Epopeya del Libre Albedrío." *Ensayos sobre John Milton: Epopeya y Drama.* Ed. by González Padilla. Facultad de Filosofía y Letras, Centro de Investigaciones de Letras Modernas y Arte Dramático (Mexico, D.F.: Universidad Nacional Autónoma de México, 1976), pp. 13–38.

Shows that one reaches a state of harmony or an internal paradise only by the proper use of free will.

2312 González Padilla, María Enriqueta. "*El Paraíso Perdido* de John Milton." *Abside* (Mexico: S.N.), 38, 1974, 407–32.

Studies Satan in his revengeful opposition to God and examines the theme of Adam and Eve's life in paradise before the Fall. Describes Adam and Eve's fall from paradise, their disobedience to God's will, and the consequences.

2313 Goodfellow, William S. "Adam's Encounter with God in *Paradise Lost*." *MiltonQ*, 7, 1973, 103–07.

Believes that Milton is being deliberately vague about the identity of the divine personage in Book 8, as he is whenever this character appears to Adam. Holds that Adam has no need to know as long as he has learned what his visitor taught him.

2314 Goodman, Ellen. "The Design of Milton's World: Nature and the Fall in Christian Genesis Commentary and *Paradise Lost*." Doctoral diss., Brown Univ., 1976. 216pp. Abs., *DAI*, 38, 1977, 278A–79A.

Explores "the relationship between Milton's portrayal of nature and the subject of his epic, 'Man's First Disobedience,'" in light of commentary on Genesis.

2315 Goodman, Ellen. "Sway and Subjection: Natural Causation and the Portrayal of Paradise in the *Summa Theologica* and *Paradise Lost*." *Milton and the Middle Ages*. Ed. by John Mulryan (Lewisburg, PA: Bucknell Univ. Press; London and Toronto: Associated Univ. Presses, 1982), pp. 73–87.

In Milton's "vision of Eden . . . both the Thomistic and the Protestant elements are bent and blended to create an original, highly coherent treatment of relationships between superiors and subordinates in the hierarchy of causes."

2316 Gorecki, John E. "An Echo of *Julius Caesar* in *Paradise Lost*." *N&Q*, 33, 1986, 36.

Finds verbal echoes of the mob scene in Shakespeare's *Julius Caesar* in the first gathering of fallen angels in *Paradise Lost*. This analogy emphasizes the fickleness of both groups.

2317 Gorecki, John. "A Marlovian Precedent for Satan's Astronomical Journey in *Paradise Lost* IX.63–67." *MiltonQ*, 17, 1983, 45–47.

Argues that "Christopher Marlowe's *Doctor Faustus* contains a striking anticipation of Satan's journey in that a repeated orbiting of the earth is undertaken by two evil spirits."

2318 Gorecki, John Edward. "Milton's Similitudes for Satan and the Traditional Implications of Their Imagery." Doctoral diss., Univ. of South Carolina, 1974.

169pp. Abs., *DAI*, 35, 1975, 6665A–66A.

Argues by analogy that, if three metaphors in Milton's prose have traditional interpretations, the poet probably "intends traditional meanings to operate in the reader's response to the many epic similitudes for Satan for which prose analogues are lacking."

2319 Gorecki, John E. "A Note on *Paradise Lost* II.1011–16." *AN&Q*, 14, 1976, 129–30.

"The simile comparing Satan to a 'Pyramid of fire' . . . is quite probably based on a particular meteor known in Milton's time as the 'pyramidall burning pillar,'" or what we call a sun pillar or column of light caused by sunlight being reflected from ice particles. Milton probably intends the image to undercut Satan's boldness and grandeur by associating him with this image of transient brilliance.

2320 Gorecki, John E. "On a Misreading of the Word 'Balance' in *Paradise Lost* III.482." *AN&Q*, 15, 1977, 99–100.

The word "must refer to the condition or function of the crystalline sphere itself," not to the constellation Libra.

2321 Gorecki, J. E. "A Possible Platonic Echo in *Paradise Lost*, VI.99–102." *N&Q*, 26, 1979, 416–17.

Suggests that Milton's image of Satan in a chariot at the War in Heaven's outbreak alludes to Plato's image of the emerging tyrant in the *Republic* 8.

2322 Gorecki, John. "A Reply to Professor Lawrence W. Hyman's 'Satan and Historical Scholarship.'" *MiltonQ*, 12, 1978, 32–33.

Replies to Hyman's remarks (No. 2466). Feels that Satan must be judged on the basis of the object of his will. See No. 3849.

2323 Gorecki, John. "Satan among the Stars: *Paradise Lost* X.325–329." *ELN*, 15, 1978, 274–78.

Claims that Satan's purpose "among the stars" was not merely to hide from Uriel, but to align himself with the symbolic characteristics of the Centaur and Scorpion.

2324 Gossman, Ann. "Maia's Son: Milton and the Renaissance Virgil." *Studies in Medieval, Renaissance, American Literature: A Festschrift Honoring Troy C. Crenshaw, Lorraine Sherley, and Ruth Speer Angell.* Ed. by Betsy F. Colquitt (Ft. Worth: Texas Christian Univ. Press, 1971), pp. 109–19.

Believes that Milton's Raphael synthesizes Homer's Hermes, Virgil's Mercury (as the post-classical centuries had allegorized him), and the Neoplatonists' biblical angels.

2325 Gossman, Ann. "The Ring Pattern: Image, Structure, and Theme in *Paradise Lost*." *SP*, 68, 1971, 326–39.

Contends that the Christian-Platonic ring pattern is the poem's major image. The epic is "based on a series of good rings contrasted with circular mazes of error," a pattern that "not only governs images and determines structure, but explicates the main theme of *Paradise Lost*."

2326 Gossman, Ann. "Satan: From Toad to Atlas." *MiltonQ*, 10, 1976, 7–11.

"The apparent contradictions about Satan that run through the poem are resolved by Milton's brilliant synthesis of the classical view of evil with the medieval Christian one."

2327 Gottlieb, Sidney. "Milton's Land-Ships and John Wilkins." *MP*, 84, 1986, 60–62.

Suggests John Wilkins's *Mathematicall Magick* as a possible source of Milton's knowledge of the Chinese land-ship as presented in *Paradise Lost*.

2328 Grabes, Herbert. "Structure and Intention: Milton's *Paradise Lost* as a Theodicy." *Proceedings from the Second Nordic Conference for English Studies.* Ed. by Håkan Ringbom and Matti Rissanen (Åbo: Åbo Akademi, 1984), pp. 437–50.

Argues that Milton does justify the ways of God to man and that the sequence, selection, and intensity of the plot elements contribute to his initial intention of providing a theodicy.

2329 Graham, E. A. "Milton and Seventeenth Century Individualism: Language and Identity in *Paradise Lost, Paradise Regained* and *Samson Agonistes*." Doctoral diss., Manchester Univ., 1985. Abs., *IT*, 37, 1988, 439.

2330 Gransden, K. W. "Milton, Dryden, and the Comedy of the Fall." *EIC*, 26, 1976, 116–33.

Discusses the relation of *Paradise Lost* and Dryden's *State of Innocence* to the doctrine of the fortunate fall. States that "the sequence of events leading up to the Fall in *Paradise Lost* is closely followed by Dryden, who exposes the weaknesses and contradictions inherent in the story" and recognizes their "comic absurdity." Reply by R. D. Bedford (No. 1920).

2331 Gray, J. C. "Emptiness and Fulfillment as Structural Pattern in *Paradise Lost*." *DR*, 53, 1973, 78–91.

Discusses Milton's "frequent metaphorical conception of persons and places . . . as containers that are in the process of being filled and emptied." Points out that an expulsion begins and ends the epic. Concludes that "the poem moves from emptiness, to fulfillment, to a second emptiness, to the hope and vision and promise of a second fulfillment."

2332 Gray, J. C. "Paradox in *Paradise Lost*." *MiltonQ*, 7, 1973, 76–82.

Examines Milton's use of "a wide range of paradoxes to express demonic, divine, and human knowledge and modes of understanding" throughout *Paradise Lost*. Points out that unfallen Adam and Eve are too innocent to understand or use paradox and their ability to do so after the Fall reflects "their new knowledge and their new mode of understanding and expression." By the end of the poem, they have grasped the significance of "divinely revealed knowledge . . . expressed to them mysteriously in metaphors and paradox."

2333 Green, A. L. "Milton's Eve and Ovid's *Metamorphoses*." Doctoral diss., Univ. of Durham, 1985. Abs., *IT*, 35, 1987, 1084.

Argues that Milton presents Eve "obliquely, through the medium of a controlled and inspired evocation of figures from the *Metamorphoses*."

2334 Green, J. "A Kind of Another Species: Woman in Judeo-Christian Tradition from the Myth of the Fall to *Paradise Lost*." Doctoral diss., Univ. of Sussex, 1983.

2335 Greene, Thomas. "Milton." *The Descent from Heaven: A Study in Epic Continuity* (New Haven, CT, and London: Yale Univ. Press, 1970, 1975), pp. 363–418. Excerpts from this chapter reprinted in *On Milton's Poetry: A Selection of Modern Studies*. Ed. by Arnold Stein (Greenwich, CT: Fawcett Publications, 1970), pp. 200–14.

Reprint of Huckabay No. 1359, originally published in 1963. Review (of book): Donna G. Fricke, *SCN*, 31, 1973, 75–76.

2336 Greenfield, Concetta Carestia. "S. M. Eisenstein's *Alexander Nevsky* and John Milton's *Paradise Lost*: A Structural Comparison." *MiltonQ*, 9, 1975, 93–99.

Compares the film with *Paradise Lost*, especially Eisenstein's battle on the ice, which "faithfully repeats the structure of . . . Milton's Battle in Heaven."

2337 Gregerson, Linda. "The Limbs of Truth: Milton's Use of Simile in *Paradise Lost*." *MiltonS*, 14, 1980, 135–52.

Focuses primarily on the similes of Book 1, as they affect the reader's perception, and suggests five kinds of functions which they perform.

2338 Gregerson, Linda K. "Reforming Likeness: Idolatry and Interpretation in *The Faerie Queene* and *Paradise Lost*." Doctoral diss., Stanford Univ., 1987. 360pp. Abs., *DAI*, 47, 1987, 4396A.

Insists that Milton and Spenser use "mirror images" centered on the subject of erotic love to liven their rhetoric and protect against "arguments of Reformation iconoclasm."

2339 Gregory, E. R. "Three Muses and a Poet: A Perspective on Milton's Epic Thought." *MiltonS*, 10, 1977, 35–64.

Analyzes "the three interpretations that have been made of Milton's use of Clio: (a) as 'prime and general representative of poetry'; (b) as 'guardian of lustration'; and (c) as muse of history."

2340 Gribben, John L. "Steinbeck's *East of Eden* and Milton's *Paradise Lost*: A Discussion of *Timshel*." *Steinbeck Quarterly*, 5, 1972, 35–43.

Compares Milton's and John Steinbeck's views on freedom of choice.

2341 Griffin, Dustin H. "Milton's Evening." *MiltonS*, 6, 1974, 259–76.

"Not so much a precarious balance between day and night, evening is a moving moment, a 'grateful vicissitude,' just as Eden itself is marked not by physical and moral stasis, but by ceaseless change. After the Fall, as a measure of all that is lost, evenings become Virgilian—cold, damp, perilous."

2342 Griffin, Dustin. "Milton's Hell: Perspectives on the Fallen." *MiltonS*, 13, 1979, 237–54.

Focuses mainly on *Paradise Lost* 1 and 2. "For by pointing at them [the fallen angels] a judging finger and often *at the same time* drawing out our sympathy, Milton draws the reader in to see that the scene and the problem are ultimately his own."

2343 Griffin, Dustin. "Milton's Moon." *MiltonS*, 9, 1976, 151–67.

"The moonlit evening in Eden . . . is a supreme instance of that milder sublime and one of the great moments of the poem. At the climax of Milton's description of the arrival of evening, the moon 'unveil'd her peerless Light, / And o'er the dark her silver mantle threw.' This startling moment is an emblem of divine presence and protectiveness in unfallen Eden."

2344 Grimm, Clyde L., Jr. "Milton's *Paradise Lost*, II, 521–628." *Expl*, 31, 1972, Item 8.

Suggests that Satan's cohorts fall into six groups, which may correspond to six periods in the history of western civilization.

2345 Grose, Christopher. *Milton's Epic Process: "Paradise Lost" and Its Miltonic Background*. New Haven, CT, and London: Yale Univ. Press, 1973. xi, 268pp.

Studies the development of Milton's poetics and the relationship between image and discourse in *Paradise Lost*. The Miltonic background includes his prose and early poems, especially *Comus* and *Lycidas*. Reviews: *MiltonQ*, 7, 1973, 110–11; Richard J. Kelly, *LJ*, 98, 1973, 3003; Robert L. Pest, *SCN*, 32, 1974, 51–52; Joseph Anthony Wittreich, Jr., *MiltonQ*, 8, 1974, 15–21; John R. Knott, Jr., *JEGP*, 74, 1975, 447–49; Albert R. Cirillo, *RenQ*, 28, 1975, 427–29; R. E. C. Houghton, *N&Q*, 23, 1976, 191–92; Lois Potter, *ES*, 57, 1976, 173–75; Sidney Warhaft, *Mosaic*, 9, 1976, 159–73; Roger Lejosne, *EA*, 31, 1978, 384–85; Dennis H. Burden, *RES*, 31, 1980, 212–13.

2346 Gross, Kenneth. "'Pardon Me, Mighty Poet': Versions of the Bard in Marvell's 'On Mr. Milton's *Paradise Lost*.'" *MiltonS*, 16, 1982, 77–96.

Analyzes Andrew Marvell's dedicatory poem to the second edition of *Paradise Lost*. Believes that Marvell's lines "map out a truly inward critique of the epic and may introduce the reader of *Paradise Lost* to a subtler knowledge of its complexities than is evident on a first reading."

2347 Gross, Kenneth. "Satan and the Romantic Satan: A Notebook." *Re-membering Milton: Essays on the Texts and Traditions*. Ed. by Mary Nyquist and Margaret W. Ferguson (New York and London: Methuen, 1987), pp. 318–41.

Believes that the Romantic critics of Satan have wronged him, that he is the only character in *Paradise Lost* with a voice, attitude, and mind, even though he is in error.

2348 Gross, Nicolas P. "Zeus and Adam: Pagan Rhetoric in the Garden of Eden." *Classical Bulletin*, 52, 1975, 29–31.

Shows that Adam's seductive speech to Eve in *Paradise Lost* 9.1017–33 carefully manipulates Zeus's seductive speech to Hera in the *Iliad* 14.313–28.

2349 Grossman, Marshall. *"Authors to Themselves": Milton and the Revelation of History*. Cambridge and New York: Cambridge Univ. Press, 1987. xii, 243pp.

Studies "how the narrative form of *Paradise Lost* projects this new concept of the historical self through a dialectic that locates the narrated events at the intersection of prospective and retrospective points of view." Reviews: Thomas N. Corns, *N&Q*, 36, 1989, 395; David Loewenstein, *MiltonQ*, 24, 1990, 31–33; Keith W. F. Stavely, *SCN*, 49, 1991, 37–38.

2350 Grossman, Marshall. "Dramatic Structure and Emotive Pattern in the Fall: *Paradise Lost* IX." *MiltonS*, 13, 1979, 201–19.

Discusses the dramatic qualities of *Paradise Lost* 9. Shows that Milton follows the classical five-act tragic structure and encloses it in the atemporal Christian view of history.

2351 Grossman, Marshall. "Milton's Dialectical Visions." *MP*, 82, 1984, 23–39.

Argues that *Paradise Lost* presents an eschatology whose scope occurs on a dual level—humanity's corporeal world of imperfection and clouded understanding and God's world of perfection and enlightenment. Explains that the signifying act of Adam's eating of the apple forces these two worlds to unite and evolve toward the latter.

2352 Grossman, Marshall. "Milton's 'Transubstantiate': Interpreting the Sacrament in *Paradise Lost.*" *MiltonQ*, 16, 1982, 42–47.

In Milton's view, the ultimate miracle of transubstantiation is the transformation of experience into love and love into faith. The meal in the garden is thus a feast of words as well as fruits.

2353 Grossman, Marshall. "Servile/Sterile/Style: Milton and the Question of Woman." *Milton and the Idea of Woman.* Ed. by Julia M. Walker (Urbana and Chicago: Univ. of Illinois Press, 1988), pp. 148–68.

"*Paradise Lost*, by virtue of its exhaustive intention, discloses the suppressed and deferred authority of the Mother underlying the superimposition of subjectification and subjection in the Miltonic text." Abs., *MiltonQ*, 24, 1990, 150–51.

2354 Grossman, Marshall Scott. "Structure of the Poetic Affects in *Paradise Lost.*" Doctoral diss., New York Univ., 1977. 371pp. Abs., *DAI*, 38, 1978, 6142A.

Investigates the poetic effects of *Paradise Lost* as they "elucidate the poem's significant thematic concerns" and "stimulate reader-response."

2355 Grow, Gerald Owen. "*Paradise Lost* and the Renaissance Drama: Milton's Theme of Fall and Its Dramatic Counterpart in Marlowe, Shakespeare, Jonson, and Middleton." Doctoral diss., Yale Univ., 1968. 320pp. Abs., *DAI*, 30, 1969, 723A–24A.

Proposes "that *Paradise Lost* shows in open form some of the basic patterns which lie submerged beneath the 'realism' of the Renaissance drama," specifically the "pattern of Paradise, Fall, and Redemption."

2356 Grudzień, Anna. "Milton's God and *Paradise Lost.*" *ZRL*, 30, 1987, 63–81.

Discusses the poem's theology, drawing heavily on ideas expressed in the *Christian Doctrine*. Insists that form and doctrine cannot be separated.

2357 Guilfoyle, Cherrell. "Adamantine and Serpentine: Milton's Use of Two Con-

ventions of Satan in *Paradise Lost.*" *MiltonQ*, 13, 1979, 129–34.

Contends that in depicting Satan, Milton uses the mythological figure of the fallen god in *Paradise Lost* 1–6 and the figure of the deadly serpent or dragon of primitive fable in Books 7–12. Reply by Lawrence Hyman (No. 2465).

2358 Guillory, John. *Poetic Authority: Spenser, Milton, and Literary History.* New York: Columbia Univ. Press, 1983. xiii, 201pp.

Contains two chapters on *Paradise Lost*: "The Visible Saint: Miltonic Authority" and "Ithuriel's Spear: History and the Language of Accommodation." The first chapter discusses the relationship between power and authority in the epic, and the second studies Milton's methods of accommodation. Reviews: Anne Davidson Ferry, *RenQ*, 37, 1983, 133–35; Ronald Harvey, *MiltonQ*, 17, 1983, 138–41; Hugh Maclean, *SpenN*, 15, 1983, 31–34; Steven Mullaney, *Criticism*, 25, 1983, 383–93; David Krause, *SCN*, 42, 1984, 58–60; Gary Waller, *CLIO*, 14, 1984, 104–06; Richard S. Ide, *Rev*, 7, 1985, 89–111.

2359 Gurteen, S. Humphreys. *The Epic of the Fall of Man: A Comparative Study of Caedmon, Dante, and Milton.* New York: Haskell House, 1969; Ann Arbor, MI: Univ. Microfilms International, 1980 Books on Demand Reprints.

Reprints of Stevens No. 2718, originally published in 1896.

2360 Gutkin, Mildred. "Knowledge within Bounds: The Spatial Imagery in *Paradise Lost.*" *ESC*, 7, 1981, 282–95.

Interprets the epic as "a poem about space and infinity, conveying the human experience in terms of the one repeated metaphor of enclosures, of bounds, and of their violation."

2361 Gutkin, M. "'Sufficient To Have Stood': The Mimesis of Free Will in *Paradise Lost.*" *ESC*, 10, 1984, 11–21.

Examines the evolution of will in

Paradise Lost and studies the concept of free will in God's created world. States that "God's will functions as natural law" and that "power and freedom [of action] are in direct proportion to comprehension."

2362 Hagenbüchle, Roland. *Sündenfall und Wahlfreiheit in Miltons "Paradise Lost." Versuch einer Interpretation.* Bern: Francke Verlag, 1967. vii, 144pp.

See Huckabay No. 1369, a doctoral dissertation from 1964. Reviews: John M. Steadman, *Erasmus*, 21, 1969, 238–41; Joachim Stephan, *ZAA*, 19, 1971, 83–84.

2363 Hägin, Peter. *The Epic Hero and the Decline of Heroic Poetry: A Study of the Neoclassical English Epic with Special Reference to Milton's "Paradise Lost."* Folcroft, PA: Folcroft Library Editions, 1970; Norwood, PA: Norwood Editions, 1975; Philadelphia, PA: R. West, 1977.

Reprints of Huckabay No. 1370, originally published in 1964.

2364 Hainsworth, J. D. "Ups and Downs in *Paradise Lost.*" *EIC*, 33, 1983, 99–107.

Studies Milton's use of flight, dreams of flight, and height as a sign of achievement in *Paradise Lost.* Argues that an affinity for this symbolism comes from "Milton's association of the evils of his present situation with an experience of failure and frustration belonging to a much earlier period of his life"—namely, Milton's difficulty as a child learning to walk.

2365 Hale, John K. "More on Bentley's 'Milton.'" *MiltonQ*, 14, 1980, 131.

Response to No. 1973.

2366 Halewood, William H. *"Paradise Lost." The Poetry of Grace: Reformation Themes and Structures in English Seventeenth-Century Poetry* (New Haven, CT, and London: Yale Univ. Press, 1970), pp. 140–67.

Concerned with the structural use of the dualism between God and humanity and reconciliation by grace. Maintains that *Paradise Lost* has two

arguments and that their opposition constitutes one of the work's "planned *meanings.*" Appendix: "Milton's Arianism and Arminianism." Shows that the *Christian Doctrine* supports his reading of the poem and is completely a Reformation document. Reviews (of book): Virginia R. Mollenkott, *SCN*, 29, 1971, 40; Joseph H. Summers, *MLQ*, 33, 1972, 195–97; Joan Webber, *JEGP*, 71, 1972, 128–30; *MiltonQ*, 7, 1973, 54–55.

2367 Halkett, John. *Milton and the Idea of Matrimony: A Study of the Divorce Tracts and "Paradise Lost."* Yale Studies in English, 173. New Haven, CT, and London: Yale Univ. Press, 1970. ix, 162pp.

Studies Milton's comments on marriage in the divorce pamphlets and his presentation of marriage in *Paradise Lost.* Reviews: Virginia R. Mollenkott, *SCN*, 28, 1970, 63–64; Diane Kelsey McColley, *JEGP*, 70, 1971, 308–10; William Haller, *RenQ*, 25, 1972, 245–46; R. E. C. Houghton, *N&Q*, 19, 1972, 186–87; *MiltonQ*, 4, 1970, 28–29; Roger Lejosne, *EA*, 24, 1971, 331–32; *TLS*, Dec. 25, 1970, p. 1515.

2368 Hamilton, Gary D. "Milton's Defensive God: A Reappraisal." *SP*, 69, 1972, 87–100.

Discusses Milton's God as a spokesman for Arminianism. Believes that Milton saw God's speech in *Paradise Lost* 3 "as a most necessary part of his effort to produce a work which was 'doctrinal and exemplary to a nation.'" Concludes with a defense of God's voice as unanthropomorphic.

2369 Hamilton, G. Rostrevor. *Hero or Fool? A Study of Milton's Satan.* New York: Haskell House, 1969; Folcroft, PA: Folcroft Library Editions, 1969, 1971, 1974; Ann Arbor, MI: Univ. Microfilms International, 1980 Books on Demand Reprints.

Reprints of Huckabay No. 1735, originally published in 1944.

2370 Hamilton, K. G. *"Paradise Lost":
A Humanist Approach.* St. Lucia, London, and New York: Univ. of Queensland Press, 1981. xiii, 122pp.

Argues that humanity is the center of *Paradise Lost*. Also insists that *Paradise Regained* represents an ultimate failure to reconcile Christian and humanist values.

2371 Hamlet, Desmond McLawrence.
"Justice and Damnation in *Paradise Lost*." Doctoral diss., Univ. of Illinois, Urbana, 1973. 177pp. Abs., *DAI*, 34, 1974, 7705A.

Asserts that traditional concepts of the "Father's justice" and the "Son's mercy" describe qualities belonging "*both* to the Father and the Son" in *Paradise Lost*.

2372 Hamlet, Desmond M. *One Greater Man: Justice and Damnation in "Paradise Lost."* Lewisburg, PA: Bucknell Univ. Press; London: Associated Univ. Presses, 1976. 224pp.

Argues that in *Paradise Lost*, "God's justice is understood and portrayed by Milton more in terms of the essentially biblical concept of *righteousness* . . . with its significantly restorative and re-creative qualities, than in terms of the fundamentally Hellenistic sense of justice."

2373 Hamlet, Desmond M. "Recalcitrance, Damnation, and the Justice of God in *Paradise Lost*." *MiltonS*, 8, 1975, 267–91.

"The persistent notion of a dichotomy in *Paradise Lost* between the narrative idea and the affective dimension of the poetry—based on Milton's supposed subconscious repudiation of basic Christian doctrine—misrepresents both the poet's understanding of the nonsentimental character of the divine love and his complex portrayal of the essentially creative and restorative nature of divine justice."

2374 Hamlet, Desmond M. "Three Hundred Years Later: Heidegger, Milton and the Structure of *Paradise Lost*." *MiltonQ*, 9, 1975, 33.

Abstract of a paper presented at the University of Wisconsin, Milwaukee, Milton Tercentenary Conference, in November, 1974. Discusses the circular structure of *Paradise Lost* in light of Martin Heidegger's views on poetry.

2375 Hamm, Barbara E. "Adam and the Tragic Perspective in *Paradise Lost*." *Increase in Learning: Essays in Honor of James G. Van Buren.* Ed. by Robert J. Owens, Jr., and Hamm (Manhattan, KS: Manhattan Christian College, 1979), pp. 13–27.

Calls *Paradise Lost* a tragedy and examines the process by which Adam acquires a tragic perspective.

2376 Hamm, Barbara Elizabeth. "Multiple Perspectives in *Paradise Lost*: A Generic Approach." Doctoral diss., Kansas State Univ., 1979. 199pp. Abs., *DAI*, 40, 1980, 4606A.

Argues that Milton uses three perspectives in *Paradise Lost*—the demonic, divine, and human—and ties each to a generic tradition—"the heroic, the comic, and tragic," respectively.

2377 Han, Pierre. "Innocence and Natural Depravity in *Paradise Lost*, *Phèdre*, and *Billy Budd*." *RBPH*, 49, 1971, 856–61.

Explores the three works' shared theme of "the innocent person and his reaction—in the moment of greatest crisis—to the nature of evil."

2378 Hanley, Katherine, C. S. J. "Morning or Evening? The Conclusion of *Paradise Lost*." *EngR*, 22, 1971, 57–61.

In contrast with the rest of *Paradise Lost*, the conclusion does not contain a carefully defined time scheme. "Not only do we not know the hour of Adam's and Eve's dismissal, we cannot determine even whether it is morning or evening."

2379 Hanson, Larry Lee. "A Reconsideration of Books XI and XII of *Paradise Lost*." *EigoS*, 132, 1986, 324–27.

Argues that the books function as an integral part of the poem's complex structure. Also, defends their versification and rhetorical devices and notes differences in narrative technique between Book 11 and Book 12.

2380 Harada, Jun. "The Archetype and Ectypes of Belial in Milton's Epic Poems." *SELit*, 49, 1973, 171–83.

Sees Belial as a vice who "threatens even his master evil, Satan, to reduce his policy of war laid down before the council to a stand-still." Connects libertinism in Milton's prose with Belial, who tends to destroy any kind of discipline.

2381 Harada, Jun. "A Case Study of Milton's Busiris Simile." *SELit*, 50, 1974, 229–43.

Uses the simile in *Paradise Lost* 1.301–13 to show how Milton establishes a typological correspondence between the actual world and the visionary realm.

2382 Harada, Jun. "The Edenic Discipline of the Self as a Shadow." *SELit*, 52, 1976, 43–62.

Explains the process and significance of Milton's presentation of Eve's crisis when she sees her image in the water.

2383 Harada, Jun. "Jojishi ni okeru 'Michi' no Mochifu." *BG*, 47, 1979, 99–118.

"The Way Motif in Epics."

2384 Harada, Jun. "The Mechanism of Human Reconciliation in *Paradise Lost*." *PQ*, 50, 1971, 543–52.

On the reconciliation scene in Book 10. "Adam and Eve transcend self through the act of self-destruction (the Fall) and by the sacrifice of self (reconciliation), and thus . . . achieve the status of existence."

2385 Harada, Jun. "Mimesis to Metexis-Konnichi no Shitsurakuen Hihyo no Mondai." *EigoS*, 118, 1973, 584–85.

"Mimesis and Metexis in *Paradise Lost*."

2386 Harada, Jun. "On Marvell's 'On Mr. Milton's *Paradise Lost*.'" *MCJ News*, 9, 1987, 17–18.

Abstract of paper presented. Notes the "strangeness" of Marvell's approach to studying Milton in "On Mr. Milton's *Paradise Lost*." Specifies Marvell's initial "reserved recoil" that includes an insulting reference to Milton's blindness and also Marvell's reading the poem as if it were his first encounter with it.

2387 Harada, Jun. "Self and Language in the Fall." *MiltonS*, 5, 1973, 213–28.

"*Paradise Lost* provides for the reader a built-in reading device which, through saving him from a single uncritical reading of the epic, stimulates his self-knowledge as an ignorant sinner. This is fully observed in the function of the form of soliloquy uttered first by Eve and echoed by Adam at the Fall, the traditionally defined epic crisis in the poem."

2388 Harada, Jun. "Shitsurakuen ni okeru Dokusha no Kakawarikata." *EigoS*, 121, 1975, 116–17, 161–63.

"A Reader's Involvement in *Paradise Lost*."

2389 Harada, Jun. "Toward *Paradise Lost*: Temptation and Anti-Christ in the English Revolution." *MiltonS*, 22, 1986, 45–77.

Discusses Milton's political career, assuming that it is directly connected to *Paradise Lost*. Interprets the temptation scene and Satan in political terms.

2390 Harbinson, M. J. "'The Horrid Edge': Landsknecht Tactics and the Two-Handed Sword in Milton's War in Heaven." *N&Q*, 34, 1987, 325–27.

Compares Michael's actions during the War in Heaven in *Paradise Lost* to that of a Swiss "Landsknecht Doppelsöldner." Such a soldier was a model warrior and wielded a two-handed sword as does Michael. Further argues that Milton was influenced by Machiavelli and the *Arte della Guerra* for military details.

2391 Hardin, Richard F. "Milton's Nimrod." *MiltonQ*, 22, 1988, 38–44.

Explores the various interpretations of the myth of Nimrod, including Milton's in *Paradise Lost* 12. Believes that Milton views Nimrod as "yet another hunter of men who is self-tempted, self-depraved, and self-deceived."

2392 Harding, Davis P. *The Club of Hercules: Studies in the Classical Background of "Paradise Lost."* Illinois Studies in Language and Literature, vol. 50. Ann Arbor, MI: Univ. Microfilms International, 1980 Books on Demand Reprints.
Reprint of Huckabay No. 1382, originally published in 1962. Review: Maren-Sofie Røstvig, *ES*, 51, 1970, 258–61.

2393 Hardison, O. B., Jr. *"In Medias Res* in *Paradise Lost." MiltonS*, 17, 1983, 27–41.
Discusses Milton's options for beginning the narrative of *Paradise Lost*. Milton had read Horace and Aristotle, and he considered several beginning scenes. He finally decided to place Satan in hell in Books 1 and 2 to make him a credible example of evil.

2394 Hardison, O. B., Jr. "Written Records and Truths of Spirit in *Paradise Lost." MiltonS*, 1, 1969, 147–65.
On Milton's treatment of creation in Book 7. "There is a strong suggestion that creation is begun by a sexual impregnation of unformed matter, followed by an organic, almost evolutionary development of the physical world." Milton's view "illustrates the latitude of interpretation permitted those who read scripture in the light of the Spirit."

2395 Hardy, John. "'Distance and Distaste' in Milton's God's 'Ingrate.'" *N&Q*, 26, 1979, 422.
Suggests that God's reference to humanity as "ingrate" in *Paradise Lost* 3.97 has the latent meaning of "distasteful" and echoes the reference to "distance and distaste" in Book 9's opening lines. "The sensory connotations of 'ingrate' suggest just how

'distasteful' man will become to Milton's God."

2396 Harris, Neil. "Galileo as Symbol: The 'Tuscan Artist' in *Paradise Lost." Estratto da Annali dell' Istituto e Museo di Storia della Scienza di Firenze*, 10, 1985, 3–29.
Summarizes and discusses the controversy over Milton's visit to Galileo. Gives a detailed account of Galileo's imprisonment and believes that Milton did see Galileo. Argues that the Tuscan artist image in *Paradise Lost* 1 is a Satanic symbol "drawing on Florence's long history of schism and discord." Includes abstracts in English, Italian, German, and French.

2397 Harris, N. "Milton's 'Sataneid': The Poet and the Devil in *Paradise Lost*. A Study of Milton's Use in *Paradise Lost* of Dante's *Divina Commedia* and of Three Italian Renaissance Chivalric Epics." Doctoral diss., Univ. of Leicester, 1986. Abs., *IT*, 36, 1988, 911.
Studies the influence of the Italian chivalric epic on Milton's Satan and of Dante and Ariosto on the character of Milton's narrator.

2398 Harris, Victor. "The Iconography of *Paradise Lost." Brandeis Essays in Literature*. Ed. by John Hazel Smith (Waltham, MA: Department of English and American Literature, Brandeis Univ., 1983), pp. 37–49.
Surveys visual versions of scenes in Milton's poem. Deals especially with the Renaissance.

2399 Hartman, Geoffrey. "Adam on the Grass with Balsamum." *ELH*, 36, 1969, 168–92. Reprinted in *Beyond Formalism: Literary Essays, 1958–1970* (New Haven, CT, and London: Yale Univ. Press, 1970), pp. 124–50, and in *On Milton's Poetry: A Selection of Modern Studies*. Ed. by Arnold Stein (Greenwich, CT: Fawcett Publications, 1970), pp. 215–27.
On *Paradise Lost* 8.253–56. Claims that Adam's relationship with the sun is an archetype of blinded humanity's

relationship with the bright light of holiness. Explains that the poet uses the pagan phoenix as an image because it is associated with the sun. Finds various passages referring to "divine light," which Adam experiences both spiritually and physically. Reply by Robert M. Adams (No. 1845). Abs., *MiltonN*, 3, 1969, 80.

2400 Hartman, Geoffrey. "Milton's Counterplot." *Critical Essays on Milton from "ELH"* (Baltimore, MD, and London: Johns Hopkins Press, 1969), pp. 151–62. Reprinted in *Beyond Formalism: Literary Essays, 1958–1970* (New Haven, CT, and London: Yale Univ. Press, 1970), pp. 113–23.

Reprints of Huckabay No. 1391, originally published in 1958.

2401 Hartwell, Kathleen Ellen. *Lactantius and Milton.* New York: Haskell House, 1974; Folcroft, PA: Folcroft Library Editions, 1974.

Reprints of Huckabay No. 1392, originally published in 1929.

2402 Hasan, Masoodul. "The Ironic Mode in *Paradise Lost.*" *Essays on John Milton: A Tercentenary Tribute.* Ed. by Asloob Ahmad Ansari (Aligarh: Aligarh Muslim Univ., 1976), pp. 133–47.

Shows that, by using an ironic and contrastive structure in the epic, "Milton has built up moments of tension, heightened the poetic effect, and introduced some dramatic touches."

2403 Hasan, Nawal M. "Daughter of God and Man: A Re-Consideration of Milton's Eve in *Paradise Lost.*" *Al-Mustansiriya Literary Review* (Baghdad), 8, 1984, 123–44.

2404 Hatlen, Burton. "Milton, Mary Shelley, and Patriarchy." *BuR*, 28, 1983, 19–47.

Argues that *Paradise Lost* and Mary Shelley's *Frankenstein* have much in common, including a struggle between the mythos of patriarchy and the mythos of equality. Holds that "bourgeois literary criticism" has obscured the "revolutionary implications" of both works. Discusses Milton's God.

2405 Häublein, Ernst. "Milton's Paraphrase of Genesis: A Stylistic Reading of *Paradise Lost*, Book VII." *MiltonS*, 7, 1975, 101–25.

Evaluates Milton's "paraphrastic techniques in his adaptation of the biblical account of the Creation." Reassesses the structure of *Paradise Lost* 7.216–632 and Milton's way of distributing biblical quotations among "additions and amplifications."

2406 Hawkins, Deborah Blythe. "The Poetic Achievement of *Paradise Lost*, Books XI and XII." Doctoral diss., Yale Univ., 1978. 237pp. Abs., *DAI*, 40, 1979, 869A–70A.

Defends "the poetic richness and integrity" of *Paradise Lost* 11–12 against accusations of inferiority.

2407 Hawkins, Harriett. "'Of Their Vain Contest': Poetic and Critical Deadlocks in *Paradise Lost* and Spenser's Bower of Bliss." *Poetic Freedom and Poetic Truth: Chaucer, Shakespeare, Marlowe, Milton* (Oxford: Oxford Univ. Press, 1976), pp. 55–77.

During Adam and Eve's quarrel after the Fall, both have valid and invalid arguments. Milton feels that they are "guilty in dialectically opposite ways," but he "refuses to interfere with the freedom of his readers to reach their own conclusions about characters and situations in *Paradise Lost.*" Reviews (of book): *TLS*, Dec. 24, 1976, p. 1619; W. W. Robson, *RES*, 28, 1977, 342–44; M. C. Bradbrook, *MLR*, 74, 1979, 157–58.

2408 Heinsheimer, Hans. "*Paradise Regained.*" *Opera News* (New York), Nov., 1978, pp. 48, 50, 52, 55.

Announces the premiere of an opera based on *Paradise Lost*, at the Lyric Opera of Chicago, on November 29, 1978. Krzysztof Penderecki is the composer, and Christopher Fry wrote the libretto. See No. 2868.

2409 Heller, Ricki. "Opposites of Wife-hood: Eve and Dalila." *MiltonS*, 24, 1988, 187–202.

Relates Milton's discussion of marriage in the divorce tracts to the marriages of Adam and Eve and Samson and Dalila. "By depicting antithetical views of married life, *Paradise Lost* and *Samson Agonistes* serve to support Milton's conviction that marriage, if it is to benefit its partners, must create a spiritual unity that will naturally join them and urge them toward reconciliation even after a marital rupture."

2410 Helms, Randel. "'His Dearest Mediation': The Dialogue in Heaven in Book III of *Paradise Lost*." *MiltonQ*, 5, 1971, 52–57.

Examines the biblical models for the mediation scene and the assumptions about them in the biblical commentaries of Milton's day. Suggests that the dialogue in Book 3 follows the commonplace conception of foreordained mediation: "Milton too held the notion of God's pleasure in presenting a problem or asking a question to one of His creatures, the answer to which he already knows, simply for the sake of encouraging the one asked to demonstrate, by his answer, his intelligence or competence for some special role."

2411 Hemby, James Benjamin, Jr. "A Study of Irony in *Paradise Lost*." Doctoral diss., Texas Christian Univ., 1965. 226pp. Abs., *DAI*, 39, 1979, 5526A.

Demonstrates "how the various stylistic techniques of irony, as well as the broader ironies that involve the whole structure of the poem or the cosmic perspective of the poet, are related to one another in their service of the poet's vision of universal truth."

2412 Henry, Nathaniel H. "The Mystery of Milton's Muse." *RenP*, 1967, pp. 69–83.

Believes that "Milton's Muse is primarily a literary conceit" and that "divergent theologians may find in *Paradise Lost* confirmation of differing beliefs, that Trinitarian and anti-Trinitarian, Calvinist and Arminian may read *Paradise Lost* without offense or sense of contradiction."

2413 Henson, Linda Draper. "The Witch in Eve: Milton's Use of Witchcraft in *Paradise Lost*." *Milton Reconsidered: Essays in Honor of Arthur E. Barker.* Ed. by John Karl Franson (Salzburg: Institut für Englische Sprache und Literatur, Universität Salzburg, 1976), pp. 122–34.

"This paper proposes that Milton uses elements of witchcraft lore and Satanism in his portrayal of Eve, with her inordinate desire for a knowledge of good and evil, and in his dramatization of the initial corruption of man."

2414 Herron, Carol Olivia. "The Vacillating Epic: The Dialectic of Opposing World Views in the Expansion of the Epic Literary Genre." Doctoral diss., Univ. of Pennsylvania, 1985. 239pp. Abs., *DAI*, 46, 1985, 1271A–72A.

On Homer, Dante, and Milton. "Describes the manner in which the epic genre sustains its vitality through representing unanswerable metaphysical inquiries regarding world view."

2415 Herz, Judith Scherer. "*Paradise Lost* VIII: Adam, Hamlet, and the Anxiety of Narrative." *ESC*, 14, 1988, 259–69.

States that both *Hamlet* and *Paradise Lost* prolong the fatal action of plotting, heightening the readers' anxiety. Believes that "Adam both derives from and is Hamlet's original."

2416 Hieatt, A. Kent. "Eve as Reason in a Tradition of Allegorical Interpretation of the Fall." *JWCI*, 43, 1980, 221–26.

Surveys various allegorical interpretations of Adam and Eve, concluding that "Milton's imagination . . . seems more likely to have been the Augustinian than the Philonic one." Thus, "Eve signifies at one level the sciential part of the soul, open to sense-impressions, and Adam the knowledge of transcendent commands."

2417 Higgins, Dennis Vincent. "Intellect-Will in Poetry of the English Renaissance." Doctoral diss., Claremont Graduate School and Univ. Center, 1964. 180pp. Abs., *DA*, 28, 1968, 4130A–31A.

Follows the "medieval debate over the precedence of intellect or will as the supreme power in the scholastic schema of faculty psychology . . . in English renaissance poetry," ending with *Paradise Lost*.

2418 Higgs, Elton D. "The 'Thunder' of God in *Paradise Lost*." *MiltonQ*, 4, 1970, 24–27.

Asserts that "Milton uses the word [thunder] systematically to illuminate the psychology of the fallen Satan, to foreshadow the compounding of the devils' damnation, and to tie the fall of man poignantly (though not identically) to that of the rebellious angels. Through all three of these avenues, progressing to a climax in the third, Milton offers a commentary on the dominant theme of *Paradise Lost*, the justice of God."

2419 Himy, Armand. *John Milton: Pensée, Mythe et Structure dans le "Paradis Perdu."* Lille: Publications de l'Université de Lille 3, 1977. 526pp.

Uses a structuralist and archeological approach to study the apparent discordant elements within the larger structural framework of *Paradise Lost*. Reviews: G. Bullough, *EA*, 33, 1980, 74–77; Jean-François Camé, *CahiersE*, 16, 1987, 125–27.

2420 Himy, Armand. "Lire *Paradise Lost* Aujourd'hui." *BSEAA*, 13, 1981, 109–19.

Within the traditional subject matter in *Paradise Lost*, Milton gives a new and essentially literary interpretation to Christian antitheses and the biblical characters.

2421 Himy, Armand. "Milton et la Sortie de la Caverne." *Critique*, 26, 1970, 705–26.

Believes that the structure of *Paradise Lost* is based on the opposition of image

to simulacrum or counterfeit image, as suggested by Plato's shadows in the cave. Satan thus represents the counterfeit image. Notes that Milton's prose writings often treat this question of analogy.

2422 Hirai, Masao. "Invocation ni tsuite." *EigoS*, 119, 1974, 692–93.

"On Milton's Invocations." Divides *Paradise Lost* into four sections: hell, heaven, problems on earth, and the tragedy of Adam and Eve's loss of paradise.

2423 Hirai, Masao. "Shitsurakuen ni okeru Mokujiroku-teki Vision." *EigoS*, 134, 1988, 226–27, 289–91.

"The Apocalyptic Vision in *Paradise Lost*." Discusses the Apocalypse in *Paradise Lost* and the English revolution.

2424 Hirakawa, Taiji. *"Death* and Death—An Aspect of *Paradise Lost*." *MCJ News*, 4, 1980, 7–8.

Abstract of paper presented. Uses Spenser's Bower of Bliss to show that Death as a character cannot be distinguished from death as an abstract concept.

2425 Hodge, Bob. "Satan and the Revolution of the Saints." *L&H*, 7, 1978, 20–23. Reprinted in *Literature, Language and Society in England, 1580–1680.* Ed. by Hodge, David Aers, and Gunther Kress (Dublin: Gill and Macmillan; Totowa, NJ: Barnes and Noble, 1981), pp. 184–99.

Sees Satan as "the doomed champion of the old order, romanticised embodiment of what Milton felt was a richer civilisation than the bourgeoisie could show, with something of the heroism that the ordinary bourgeois so lamentably lacked."

2426 Hoffman, Nancy Y. "The Hard-Hearted Hell of Self-Delusion." *MiltonQ*, 7, 1973, 11–14.

Notices Satan's self-contradiction and self-delusion in *Paradise Lost* 1.242–55, which reflects his, and every individual's, ability to deceive himself in the face of evidence to the contrary, resulting in a hardening of the heart against the possibility of redemption.

2427 Hohne, Horst. "Peter Hacks' *Adam und Eva*, Milton und die Verarbeitung der Mythen." *ZAA*, 23, 1975, 154–59.

"Demonstrates how a recent comedy (1972) reduced the epic in order to make it palatable to Communists."

2428 Holahan, Michael. "Pastoral and History in *Don Quixote* and *PL*." *MiltonQ*, 4, 1970, 14.

Abstract of a paper presented at the 1969 MLA Convention. Sees a parallel in the works' final movements. In the end, Don Quixote faces reality, as Adam and the reader must do. *Paradise Lost* "thrusts us into a brazen world of history, and the very darkness of history is directly related to a sense of inward spiritual value expressed by the pastoral metaphor."

2429 Holland, Vivienne Kathleen. "*Paradise Lost* and Seventeenth-Century Pageantry." Doctoral diss., McMaster Univ., 1974. Abs., *DAI*, 35, 1975, 6716A.

Traces the influence of seventeenth-century court entertainment, especially its praising intentions, on *Paradise Lost*.

2430 Hollington, Michael. "Milton and the Baroque." *ES*, 60, 1979, 138–47.

Explores Milton's response to the baroque as it applies to the style and content of *Paradise Lost*. Believes that "Satan represents the baroque hero" in a negative way and cites baroque parallels.

2431 Holloway, Julia Bolton. "'Not *Babilon*, nor Great *Alcairo*.'" *MiltonQ*, 15, 1981, 92–94.

On the allusion to Babylon and Cairo in *Paradise Lost* 1.717–19. Milton's seventeenth-century readers "could see through the falsity of the poetic contrasting of Pandaemonium, Babylon, and Cairo, to a more truthful equation of them as a unity and trinity of infernality."

2432 Holoka, James P. "'Thick as Autum-

nal Leaves'—The Structure and Generic Potentials of an Epic Simile." *MiltonQ*, 10, 1976, 78–83.

Traces the epic simile in Homer and Virgil and notes Milton's poetic craftsmanship: "Far from being enfeebled beneath the weight of epic convention, *Paradise Lost* reanimated tradition, and nowhere more patently than in its similes."

2433 Holstun, James. "'Will You Rent Our Ancient Love Asunder'?: Lesbian Elegy in Donne, Marvell, and Milton." *ELH*, 54, 1987, 835–67.

Studies sapphic love in Donne's *Sappho to Philaenis*, Marvell's *Upon Appleton House*, and Eve's incident at the pool in *Paradise Lost* 4. Argues that Eve's account presents a scene of lesbian eroticism because she is "memorializing a lost sapphic moment."

2434 Hooker, Wallace Kurth. "Time, Process, and Moral Value in John Milton's *Paradise Lost*." Doctoral diss., Texas Christian Univ., 1966. 230pp. Abs., *DAI*, 39, 1979, 5526A–27A.

Investigates Milton's use of time in *Paradise Lost*, especially as it strengthens moral value and illuminates the process of salvation to humanity.

2435 Hopkins, David. "Milton's Sin and Shakespeare's *Richard III*." *N&Q*, 29, 1982, 502–03.

Notices similarities between Milton's portrayal of Sin in *Paradise Lost* 2 and "Queen Margaret's remarks to the Duchess of York in Act IV of Shakespeare's *Richard III*."

2436 Hornsby, S. G., Jr. "'Ambiguous Words': Debate in *Paradise Lost*." *MiltonQ*, 14, 1980, 60–62.

On the unfavorable connotation of the word "debate" in the New Testament. "But Milton seems to believe that as a tool in the hands of the repentant debate leads to truth; in the hands of the reprobate, it assists in the invention of evil."

2437 Hornsby, Samuel, Jr. "Penance Laden

with Fair Fruit: *PL*, X, 550." *MiltonQ*, 10, 1976, 119–22.

"That Milton knew the Protestant-Catholic dispute over the use of *penance* there is no doubt. That he deliberately wove the test passage of Matthew III:8 into the book of *Paradise Lost* where the nature of forgiveness, grace, and faith are central seems not unlikely."

2438 Howison, Patricia M. "Memory and Will: Selective Amnesia in *Paradise Lost*." *UTQ*, 56, 1987, 523–39.

Demonstrates that in *Paradise Lost*, "Milton illustrates how the proper co-operation of memory and will makes it possible to know and understand truths which cannot be apprehended merely through the evident facts."

2439 Hoy, James F. "A Meteorological Image in *Paradise Lost*." *MiltonQ*, 9, 1975, 17–18.

Believes that the meteorological imagery of *Paradise Lost* 1.594–98 portends foul weather and in essence captures Satan's role and character, while foreshadowing God's ultimate providence.

2440 Hoyle, James. "'If Sion Hill Delight Thee More': The Muse's Choice in *Paradise Lost*." *ELN*, 12, 1974, 20–26.

Explores the reasoning behind Milton's invoking the muse from two different locations in the poem's introductory lines. Concludes that Milton uses the two locations to epitomize stages of historical development, as he silently looks "forward through his own epic poem and the whole course of Christian history."

2441 Huckabay, Calvin. "The Beneficent God of *Paradise Lost*." *Essays in Honor of Esmond Linworth Marilla*. Ed. by Thomas Austin Kirby and William John Olive. Louisiana State Univ. Studies, Humanities Series, no. 19 (Baton Rouge: Louisiana State Univ. Press, 1970), pp. 144–57.

Shows how Milton uses contrasting scenes to portray God as a loving, constructive force in the universe and Satan as his opposite—hating and destructive.

2442 Hughes, Merritt Y. "Beyond Disobedience." *Approaches to "Paradise Lost."* The York Tercentenary Lectures. Ed. by C. A. Patrides (London: Edward Arnold; Toronto: Univ. of Toronto Press, 1968), pp. 181–98.

Discusses obedience and disobedience in *Paradise Lost*. "*Obedience* yields to *love* as the right word for what is meant. And the love may be either God's providential love for man or man's devoted but not blind love for God. Or both united."

2443 Hughes, Merritt Y. "Earth Felt the Wound." *ELH*, 36, 1969, 193–214.

On *Paradise Lost* 9.782–84 and 997–1004. Concerned with Milton's interpretation of the means by which humanity might "heal the wound inflicted on Nature by Adam's subjection of reason to the passions."

2444 Hughes, Merritt Y. "Milton's *Eikon Basilike*." *Calm of Mind: Tercentenary Essays on "Paradise Regained" and "Samson Agonistes" in Honor of John S. Diekhoff*. Ed. by Joseph Anthony Wittreich, Jr. (Cleveland, OH, and London: Press of Case Western Reserve Univ., 1971), pp. 1–24. Ann Arbor, MI: Univ. Microfilms International, 1980 Books on Demand Reprints.

Discusses Satan as a counterfeit *eikon basilike*, the Son as "a royal image reflected," and the Father as a divine royal image, with God "royal in the most refined sense of the doctrine that the king can do no wrong."

2445 Hugues, Micheline. "Le Mythe de Babel dans *Paradise Lost*." *EA*, 27, 1974, 450–60.

In Book 12, as in all the later books of *Paradise Lost*, the poet's imagination is replaced by liturgical verse as his role yields to that of the ardent Christian.

2446 Hugues, Micheline. "Le Sommeil

d'Adam et la Création d'Eve dans la Littérature Hexamérale des XVIᵉ et XVIIᵉ Siècles." *RLC*, 49, 1975, 179–203.

Traces the interpretations of Adam's sleep and Eve's creation in the works of sixteenth- and seventeenth-century poets and compares them to Milton's in *Paradise Lost*.

2447 Hulme, Hilda M. "Milton's Use of Colloquial Language in *Paradise Lost* (With a New Interpretation of 'Drugd as Oft' [X, 568])." *MLR*, 64, 1969, 491–99.

Discusses Milton's colloquial vocabulary and suggests that terms of physical description receive "new emphasis against the background of a more poetic language." Milton's past participle "drugd" means "having their mouths filled with dust" and may have been formed from the early seventeenth-century noun "drug," "with the sense, probably obsolescent, of 'dust, dirt.'"

2448 Hume, Patrick. *Annotations on Milton's "Paradise Lost."* Folcroft, PA: Folcroft Library Editions, 1971; Ann Arbor, MI: Univ. Microfilms International, 1980 Books on Demand Reprints.

A facsimile reproduction of the 1695 edition.

2449 Hunt, John Dixon. "Milton and the Making of the English Landscape Garden." *MiltonS*, 15, 1981, 81–105.

Discusses Milton's influence on the designs of English gardens from three aspects: the handling of water, the relationship of the garden to the surrounding countryside, and the manipulation of natural features inside the garden. Argues, however, that "Milton's description and use of the Garden of Eden in *Paradise Lost* was derived directly from Italian examples, as Addison wisely perceived."

2450 Hunter, G. K. *Paradise Lost.* The Unwin Critical Library. London, Boston, MA, and Sydney: Allen and Unwin, 1980. viii, 213pp.

Organized largely according to a diagram of descending and ascending

action. Chapters: "Introduction: The Manipulations of Genre"; "The Epic Mode"; "*Paradise Lost* as Drama"; "Style and Meaning"; "Subjective and Objective Vision, Book 6"; "A Tale of Two Falls, Books 2 and 10"; "Human History, Books 11 and 12"; "The Creation, Books 7 and 8"; "The Heart of the Poem (The Garden, Books 4 and 9 and Adam and Eve)"; and "Critical History, from Milton's Day to the Present." Reviews: William E. Cain, *MLN*, 96, 1981, 1121–33; Galbraith M. Crump, *SR*, 89, 1981, 62–78; Mary Ann Radzinowicz, *MLR*, 76, 1981, 930–32; *BBN*, Jan. 1981, p. 50; Archie Burnett, *N&Q*, 29, 1982, 79–80; D. D. C. Chambers, *RES*, 34, 1983, 338–40.

2451 Hunter, Jeanne Clayton. "Milton's *Paradise Lost*." *Expl*, 40, No. 4, 1982, 20–23.

Compares Satan and Christ and concludes, "by having Satan's language focus simultaneously on polarities . . ., Milton, yet once more, demands of the reader that a choice be made."

2452 Hunter, William B. "Belial's Presence in *Paradise Lost*." *MiltonQ*, 19, 1985, 7–9. Reprinted in *The Descent of Urania: Studies in Milton, 1946–1988* (Lewisburg, PA: Bucknell Univ. Press; London and Toronto: Associated Univ. Presses, 1989), pp. 243–45.

Believes that, after writing Book 1, Milton added Belial to the list of devils. States that Milton added Belial's speech urging "a more passive role in Hell . . . onto an otherwise continuous text" in Book 2.

2453 Hunter, William B., Jr. "The Center of *Paradise Lost*." *ELN*, 7, 1969, 32–34.

"Ascended," the first word of *Paradise Lost* 6.762, marks the poem's midpoint in the 1667 edition. "But Milton's additions in 1674 seem in part to reflect his express effort to correct the line numbering of 1667 so as to keep 'ascended' at the midpoint. He failed because the lineation of 1667 was wrong."

2454 Hunter, William B. "Milton on the Exaltation of the Son: The War in Heaven in *Paradise Lost*." *ELH*, 36, 1969, 215–31. Reprinted in *Bright Essence: Studies in Milton's Theology*. By Hunter, C. A. Patrides, and J. H. Adamson (Salt Lake City: Univ. of Utah Press, 1971), pp. 115–30.

On *Paradise Lost* 5.600–08. "I do not believe that Milton was an Arian. The purpose of the remainder of this paper is to explore what he meant by the begetting of the Son in *Paradise Lost* and to see how this meaning is basic to the War in Heaven." See No. 786.

2455 Hunter, W. B. "Milton's Muse." *Bright Essence: Studies in Milton's Theology*. By Hunter, C. A. Patrides, and J. H. Adamson (Salt Lake City: Univ. of Utah Press, 1971), pp. 149–56.

A partial reprint of Huckabay No. 1432, originally published in 1959. See No. 1911.

2456 Hunter, William B., Jr. "Some Reflections upon English Prosody and Especially *Paradise Lost*." *The Laurel Bough: Essays Presented in Honour of Professor M. V. Rama Sarma*. Ed. by G. Nageswara Rao (Bombay: Blackie and Son, 1983), pp. 15–24.

Discusses the principles of English prosody in general and applies them to Milton's poem with an emphasis on stress.

2457 Huntley, Frank L. "Before and After the Fall: Some Miltonic Patterns of Systasis." *Approaches to "Paradise Lost."* The York Tercentenary Lectures. Ed. by C. A. Patrides (London: Edward Arnold; Toronto: Univ. of Toronto Press, 1968), pp. 1–14.

Compares Adam and Eve's pre- and postlapsarian states to show that the pattern of systasis or the union of two complementary objects functions centrally in *Paradise Lost*. Milton weaves four modes of systasis: "(1) the mar-

riage between *male* and *female*; (2) the conflict and reconciliation in plot of the *union-with* and *separation-from* good; (3) the terms *good* and *evil* within the propositions of his 'great argument'; and (4) the relationship between *Creator* and *creature* in theology." Abs., *MiltonN*, 3, 1969, 77.

2458 Huntley, Frank Livingstone. "Vultures, Chinese Land-Ships, and Milton's 'Paradise of Fools.'" *Essays in Persuasion: On Seventeenth-Century English Literature* (Chicago, IL, and London: Univ. of Chicago Press, 1981), pp. 133–41.

Defends Milton's inclusion of the Paradise of Fools passage in *Paradise Lost* 3. Relates it to the rest of the poem and finds that it "is not a gratuitous blemish in an otherwise well-constructed whole. Milton justifies its inclusion and position not only by the simile of the vulture landing in China, but also by his whole plot, his cosmic setting, and his moral intention. Its anti-Catholicism, there by history, ceases to be topical as it is raised by Milton's artistry to become a symbol of pride." Combines two earlier articles (Huckabay Nos. 1438–39).

2459 Huntley, John F. "Body Sickness and Social Sickness in Milton's Figure of Satan." *L&P*, 18, 1968, 101–08.

"Clearly Satan and Adam (during the time of his Satanic inspiration) are not sick in any natural or clinical sense of the word. . . . Both are 'healthy' in body and mind though dedicated to evil, pain-producing goals."

2460 Huntley, John F. "Gourmet Cooking and the Vision of Paradise in *Paradise Lost*, 5, 321–49." *XUS*, 8, 1969, 44–54.

"Adam and Eve feed themselves in a highly civilized and sophisticated manner in Paradise. This part of Milton's vision is emphasized in a very particular way. Milton describes their pleasure in language which echoes, while it reverses, some traditional satiric jabs against the glutton and his works. How Milton does this, and how much gourmandizing can simultaneously reflect the purity of innocent people in an innocent world and the impulse of those who would destroy them are the questions pursued in this essay."

2461 Huntley, John. "Mapping Milton." *Teaching Milton to Undergraduates: Problems and Approaches.* Proceedings of the Special Session (537), Annual Meeting of the Modern Language Association, Dec. 28, 1976. Comp. by Paul L. Gaston ([Edwardsville: Southern Illinois Univ.], n.d.), pp. 32–34. Reprinted as "Teaching Milton: Some Thoughts on Manipulation and Mapping." *MiltonQ*, 12, 1978, 144–45.

To prepare for an in-depth discussion of *Paradise Lost*, students draw "diagrammatic maps" to clarify the geography and present Milton's "convoluted chronology . . . in linear sequence."

2462 Hyman, Lawrence W. "Against Reconstructing *Paradise Lost.*" *Greyfriar*, 28, 1987, 18–27.

Suggests that the "discontinuities and paradoxes in *Paradise Lost*" should remain as part of the imaginative experience.

2463 Hyman, Lawrence W. "The Ambiguity of *Paradise Lost* and Contemporary Critical Theory." *MiltonQ*, 13, 1979, 1–6.

Declares that critics who have made Satan into a monster have failed because of the poem's deep ambiguity. Insists that contradictions in *Paradise Lost* are not problems to be solved but deliberate intensifications of the poetic experience.

2464 Hyman, Lawrence W. "Must We Pin Milton's Shoulders to the Mat?" *MiltonQ*, 21, No. 3, 1987, 122–23.

Disagrees with William Shullenberger's article (No. 3054), which he terms a literary and political battle against the feminist critics.

2465 Hyman, Lawrence W. "A Note on Satan as Serpent." *MiltonQ*, 14, 1980, 62.

Disagrees with Cherrell Guilfoyle (No. 2357), who links the Promethean Satan with heroic action and the serpentine Satan with ignoble action.

2466 Hyman, Lawrence W. "Satan and Historical Scholarship: A Letter from Lawrence W. Hyman." *MiltonQ*, 11, 1977, 94–95.

Responds to No. 3849. Holds that Satan cannot be reduced to a figure of scorn and impotence. Reply by John Gorecki (No. 2322).

2467 Ide, Richard S. "Adam's Hyacinthine Locks." *MiltonQ*, 19, 1985, 80–82.

Believes the reference to Adam's "hyacinthine locks" in *Paradise Lost* 4.301 alludes to a passage in Book 23 of the *Odyssey* "likening Odysseus to a god." Therefore, Milton's Adam "is 'Godlike' in a 'more Heroic' sense."

2468 Ide, Richard S. "On the Begetting of the Son in *Paradise Lost.*" *SEL*, 24, 1984, 141–55.

Questions the view that God's announcement of the Son's begetting in *Paradise Lost* 5.600–06 refers metaphorically to the Resurrection and ascension to the right hand of the Father. Instead, "the moment heralds a new epoch in angelic history, the beginning of a Christian dispensation. . . . But the advent of the Son as anointed king separates that past era from this new era."

2469 Ide, Richard S. "On the Uses of Elizabethan Drama: The Revaluation of Epic in *Paradise Lost.*" *MiltonS*, 17, 1983, 121–40.

Points to the Elizabethan influence on Milton's Satan and the "tragedy of damnation," which is contrasted to the comedy of forgiveness. Relates the influence of these opposing genres to Milton's theology.

2470 Iinuma, Mariko. "Milton and Taste." *MCJ News*, 9, 1987, 12–16.

Finds two significant roles that the sense of taste plays in *Paradise Lost*. Argues that since it is considered the basest of the five senses, taste as related to the eating of the forbidden fruit is connected with the Fall. Conversely, this sense "is blessed when it is used to express the just enjoyment of what God gives bounteously for man to enjoy, and shows the essence of true blessedness."

2471 Iinuma, Mariko. "Milton no Rakuen: Neo-Platonism-teki Ichimen o Otte." *Suga Yasuo, Ogoshi Kazugo: Ryokyoju Taikan Kinen Ronbunshu* (Kyoto: Apollonsha, 1980), pp. 251–63.

Deals with Platonism in *Paradise Lost*.

2472 Iinuma, Mariko. ["On Neoplatonic Love in *Paradise Lost*."] *MCJ News*, 6, 1983, 15–18.

Discusses "the nature of the love enjoyed by Adam and Eve in their prelapsarian condition of perfect happiness" in Books 4, 5, and 8.

2473 Inamochi, Shigeo. "Milton's Inner Paradise." *SES*, 1, 1976, 25–36.

"The inner paradise of innocence and the external paradise fuse to form a complex symbol of a certain spiritual state, while the inner life of Satan and devils fuses with the external feature of Hell to form a symbol of just the opposite significance."

2474 Inoue, Misako. "William Empson on Milton's God." *MCJ News*, 6, 1983, 24–25.

Abstract of paper presented. Summarizes Empson's ideas about this character in *Paradise Lost* (see No. 2175).

2475 Itzoe, Linda V. "Adam's Speech before and after His Fall: A Comparison." *CP*, 13, 1980, 33–39.

Contrasts the language and rhetoric of *Paradise Lost* 9.343–58 and 1136–86. "In the earlier speech Adam demonstrates his ability to see God and creation clearly." In the second speech, Adam lacks clear perspective; his words and ideas exhibit confusion.

2476 Jackson, Holly. "Ovid's *Metamorphoses* and Milton's *Paradise Lost*: The Pattern of Allusions." Doctoral diss., Stanford Univ., 1975. 271pp. Abs., *DAI*, 36, 1975, 3653A.

Argues that, instead of taking isolated events from Ovid's *Metamorphoses* to make a moral point, Milton employs subtle variations of entire themes, moods, and criticisms from Ovid's work in creating *Paradise Lost*.

2477 Jackson, James L. "The Angel Michael's 'Huge Two-Handed Sway.'" *Expl*, 35, No. 1, 1976, 16–17.

Recalls that "Milton prided himself on his . . . knowledge of fencing." Gives a physical, historical, and martial description of the sword.

2478 Jacobs, Glenda. "John Milton: Division in Authority in *Paradise Lost*." *ESA*, 27, 1984, 93–105.

Examines the division of authoritative voice and action between Milton and Satan and this division's impact on the thematic and literal action. The epic's style and structure indicate that Milton cannot be aligned exclusively with God or with the human couple without destroying the message of *Paradise Lost*.

2479 Jacobsen, Eric. "'Stationing' in *Paradise Lost* and *The Scarlet Letter*." *Americana-Norvegica Dedicated to Sigmund Skard*. Ed. by Brita Seyersted. Norwegian Contributions to American Studies, vol. 4 (Oslo: Universitets Forlaget, 1973), pp. 107–22.

Believes that Milton serves his doctrinal purposes by placing characters in relation to spatial objects. Compares Milton's and Hawthorne's techniques.

2480 Jacobson, Howard. "A Rabbinic Argument in Milton's *Paradise Lost*." *ES*, 52, 1971, 423–24.

Milton employs a rabbinical argument in *Paradise Lost* 10.143.

2481 Jacobus, Lee Andree. "The Problem of Knowledge in *Paradise Lost*." Doctoral diss., Claremont Graduate School and Univ. Center, 1968. 383pp. Abs., *DA*, 29, 1969, 2676A.

Relates Milton's discussion of self-knowledge, sensory perception, logic, and knowledge of God to philosophies of the seventeenth century and earlier.

2482 Jacobus, Lee A. "Self-Knowledge in *Paradise Lost*: Conscience and Contemplation." *MiltonS*, 3, 1971, 103–18.

In Satan and in Adam and Eve. "Milton supports Calvin by treating the two forms of knowledge [self-knowledge and knowledge of God] as wholly reliant on one another and as being forms of conscience and contemplation."

2483 Jacobus, Lee A. *Sudden Apprehension: Aspects of Knowledge in "Paradise Lost."* Studies in English Literature, vol. 94. The Hague and Paris: Mouton, 1976. 225pp.

Studies the history of epistemological philosophies before Milton's age and examines "the uses of knowledge, from the knowledge of self to the knowledge of God, in *Paradise Lost*." Reviews: *MiltonQ*, 10, 1976, 90–91; Tim D. P. Lally, *SCN*, 35, 1977, 79–80; Anthony Low, *RenQ*, 31, 1978, 121–23.

2484 Jacobus, Lee A. " 'Thaumaturgike' in *Paradise Lost*." *HLQ*, 33, 1970, 387–93.

Feels that Milton probably knew John Dee's discussion of "Thaumaturgike" in his preface to Billingsley's translation of Euclid's *Elements* (1570). Suggests that Milton's use of thaumaturgy, or wonder-working, helps to explain the use of natural sciences in *Paradise Lost*.

2485 Jameson, Fredric. "Religion and Ideology." *1642: Literature and Power in the Seventeenth Century*. Ed. by Francis Barker and others (Colchester: Univ. of Essex, 1981), pp. 315–36. Reprinted, London and New York: Methuen, 1986, pp. 35–56.

Explores the political content of *Paradise Lost* and reads the poem in terms of class struggle.

2486 Janzen, Henry D. "Milton's *Paradise Lost*, IV.156–65." *Expl*, 45, No. 2, 1987, 13–15.

Explains the lines' nautical significance, proposing the Gulf of Aden or the Red Sea as the ship's probable destination rather than India, as one might suppose.

2487 Javanaud, R. "Faith and Reason: Some Aspects of Milton's Theology." M.Phil. thesis, Univ. of Liverpool, 1983. Abs., *IT*, 35, 1986, 45.

On *Christian Doctrine* and *Paradise Lost*.

2488 Jefferson, D. W. "Milton's Austerity and Moral Disdain." *The Morality of Art: Essays Presented to G. Wilson Knight by His Colleagues and Friends*. Ed. by Jefferson (London: Routledge and Kegan Paul, 1969), pp. 156–64.

On Milton's role as poet in *Paradise Lost* and other poems. His verse achieves magnificent severity, but not austerity.

2489 Jennings, Margaret. "Typological Dialectic in Milton's Major Poems." *BSUF*, 17, No. 2, 1976, 16–22.

Points out the use of the Adamic type of Christ in *Paradise Lost* and *Samson Agonistes*. States that "the Adamic typology enunciated by Saint Paul and poetically described by Milton is the grand analogue of the Christian life." Concludes that "With the coming of Christ, temporal/physical sequences are abrogated and Eden, the Promised Land, and the kingdom of heaven become, in Milton's typological dialectic, the same place."

2490 Jobe, Don. "Milton's *Paradise Lost*, I.242–245." *Expl*, 42, 1983, 16–17.

Points out that when Satan says, "Is this the Region, this the Soil, the Clime," as he sees hell for the first time in *Paradise Lost* 1.242, Milton metrically represents his fall from heaven. In that line, a word is subtracted in each successive utterance, thus diminishing from four words in the first question to only two in the last. This lyrically represents Satan's tumble from "completeness."

2491 Johnson, Hershel C. "The Problem of Abdiel's 'Contradiction' of the Father, *Paradise Lost*, Book V, Lines 822–823." *Studies in English Language and Literature* (Seinan Gakuin Univ.), 25, 1984, 1–14.

Discusses Abdiel's speech in *Paradise Lost* 5.822–31 concerning the Son's origin and role in the creation of the angels. Believes that in *Paradise Lost* 5.600–15, God uses the word "begot" in the sense of announcing the Son's existence and enthroning him.

2492 Johnson, Lee M. "Milton's Mathematical Symbol of Theodicy." *Computers and Math with Applications*, 12B, 1986, 617–27. Reprinted in *Symmetry: Unifying Human Understanding*. Ed. by Istvan Hargittai (Oxford: Pergamon, 1986), pp. 617–27.

"Symmetry in literature usually calls attention to thematic relationships, and at times even has a distinctly mathematic character. . . . Milton uses the Fibonacci series to construct golden sections in the epic *Paradise Lost* and in the pastoral elegy *Lycidas*." Believes that the golden sections in these works symbolize the poet's theodicy or divine imperatives in relationship to the possibilities of human destiny.

2493 Johnstone, Robert Beede. "The Language of Satan." Doctoral diss., Univ. of Washington, 1970. 185pp. Abs., *DAI*, 31, 1971, 3506A.

Examines Satan's corrupt and abused language as it attempts to warp God's words and allow the devil to "exist absolved from guilt, obligation, loyalty—answerable only to the demands of self."

2494 Jones, Myrl Guy. "Word-Repetition as a Technique Emphasizing Characterization and Theme in *Paradise Lost*." Doctoral diss., Univ. of Houston, 1973. 150pp. Abs., *DAI*, 34, 1973, 1860A.

Correlates patterns of word repetition as they appear "by book and character" in *Paradise Lost*.

2495 Jones, Nicholas R. "'Stand' and 'Fall' as Images of Posture in *Paradise Lost*." *MiltonS*, 8, 1975, 221–46.

"A major example of the unique conjunction of physical and metaphysical action which characterizes *Paradise Lost* is the multiple use of the verbs 'stand' and 'fall.' These words signify not only the moral aspect of the epic—obedience and disobedience—but also, simultaneously, its physical adjuncts—posture and position within the cosmos."

2496 Jones, Roger Ioan Stephens. "The Epic Simile in *Paradise Lost*." B.Litt. thesis, Oxford Univ., 1968.

2497 Jordan, Richard D. "John Abbot's 1647 *Paradise Lost*." *MiltonQ*, 20, 1986, 48–51.

Discusses the biography of John Abbot and his epic, *Devout Rhapsodies*, which explores some of the same theological matters, political issues, and biblical events that appear in *Paradise Lost*.

2498 Juhnke, Anna K. "Remnants of Misogyny in *Paradise Lost*." *MiltonQ*, 22, 1988, 50–58.

Claims that Milton portrays the misogynist tradition in *Paradise Lost*. While clearing Eve of the weight of the blame for the Fall, he draws out her similarities to Sin and Cain's corrupted daughters and, therefore, carries out the tradition of women as the temptresses of mankind.

2499 Julian, Jane. "A Medieval Interpretation of Milton's Garden of Eden." *KyR*, 2, 1968, 41–50.

Analyzes Milton's paradise from a medieval perspective. Suggests that the garden's structure and imagery resemble those of Geoffrey Chaucer's and Guillaume de Lorris's gardens.

2500 Kastor, Frank S. "By Force or Guile Eternal War: *Paradise Lost*, IV, 776–1015." *JEGP*, 70, 1971, 269–78.

Asserts that the encounter of Satan and the angelic guard "brings the opposing forces into direct confrontation, furthers the action, and projects it to its inevitable climax."

2501 Kastor, Frank S. *Milton and the Literary Satan.* Amsterdam: Editions Rodopi N. V., 1974. 119pp.

"A study of the character of Satan in this literary tradition, through a large number of literary versions of the story, reveals a very definite pattern of Satanic characterization. This pattern, I believe, explains the controlling and artistic principles of Milton's Satan." Review: *MiltonQ*, 9, 1975, 30.

2502 Kastor, Frank S. "Milton's Tempter: A Genesis of a Subportrait in *Paradise Lost.*" *HLQ*, 33, 1970, 373–85.

"The role of the Tempter and its characterization, which appear only in Books IV and IX, amount to a subportrait: an almost separable part of the satanic portrait and one which differs markedly from the rest, yet is absolutely self-consistent. My purpose is simply to present a genesis and explanation of that subportrait." Discusses Milton's analogues.

2503 Kates, Judith A. "The Revaluation of the Classical Heroic in Tasso and Milton." *CL*, 26, 1974, 299–317.

Reaffirms *Paradise Lost* as a Christian epic. Outlines the intent of Tasso's *Jerusalem Delivered*, in which "the classical idea of the heroic life is not only defeated but morally rejected as admirable but insufficient." Claims that Milton's use of the heroic epic has the same intent as he relates Satan's proud exploits.

2504 Kates, Judith A. *Tasso and Milton: The Problem of Christian Epic.* Lewisburg, PA: Bucknell Univ. Press; London and Toronto: Associated Univ. Presses, 1983. 181pp.

Proposes "to make sense of Tasso's continuing presence for Milton" when he wrote *Paradise Lost.* Suggests analogies between *Jerusalem Delivered* and *Paradise Lost.*

2505 Kato, Kazutoshi. "Satan and the Idea of Free Competition—A Historical Approach to Milton's *Paradise Lost.*" *MCJ News*, 7, 1984, 6–8.

Contends that rather than being a "revolutionary fighting against the absolute monarch," Satan represents "a pseudo-revolutionary or an anti-revolutionary" who "not only impeded the revolutionary progress 'to establish a free commonwealth' but brought about the counter-revolution in England."

2506 Katsurayama, Kohji. "The Poet in the Poem—Antithetical Structures in the Invocations of *Paradise Lost.*" *MCJ News*, 9, 1987, 31–32.

Abstract of a paper presented at the Twenty-Second Colloquium of MCJ in December, 1986. Studies "rise and fall" and "light and dark" imagery in *Paradise Lost.* Argues that these antithetical images parallel "the contention that the basic conflict of the poem lies especially between God and Adam, and Adam and Eve."

2507 Kauffman, Corinne E. "Adam in Paradox." *ArlQ*, 1, 1968, 111–17.

Considers various aspects of Adam's paradoxical position in *Paradise Lost.* Feels that in losing paradise, Adam "gained the mysterious wound, the misery and grandeur of man."

2508 Kaufmann, U. Milo. *Paradise in the Age of Milton.* Victoria, BC: Univ. of Victoria, 1978. 84pp.

Notes that Milton refuses to specify any particular place as a home for Adam and Eve but points out that home means transcendence, not merely human inwardness. Eden's garden involves two modes of transcendence—the heavenly and the abyssal. Review: James H. Sims, *C&L*, 30, 1980, 116–17.

2509 Keating, Elizabeth F. "El Diablo en Calderon de la Barca y John Milton." *CHA*, 333, 1978, 417–34.

Compares Calderón's treatment of Satan to Milton's treatment of the devil in *Paradise Lost*, *Paradise Regained*, and *Comus*. Concludes that "Calderón managed to avoid the dangers into which Milton fell. They both make Satan the main character of the work. Calderón's description of Satan comes closer to the truth than Milton's description because he followed closely the teachings of Saint Thomas. Milton's system of values differs from the ones that a sincere orthodox Christian, Catholic, or Evangelic, would have."

2510 Keener, Frederick M. "Parallelism and the Poets' Secret: Eighteenth-Century Commentary on *Paradise Lost*." *EIC*, 37, 1987, 281–302.

Examines the commentaries of Patrick Hume, Richard Bentley, Zachary Pearce, the Jonathan Richardsons, Thomas Newton, and Henry John Todd. Finds it curious that "They and their contemporaries only infrequently give evidence of noticing internal parallels, and, when pursuing the ramifications of such parallels do so only very modestly, if at all." Remarks on the absence of commentary about Satan, Sin, and Death.

2511 Keet, James Calvin. "The Plateaus of Correspondence: A Critical Interpretation of the Epic Similes of *Paradise Lost*." Doctoral diss., Northwestern Univ., 1969. 243pp. Abs., *DAI*, 30, 1970, 2971A.

Explores the effect of the epic similes' integration on "the total imagery and structure" of *Paradise Lost* and on "the reader's response to action and character."

2512 Keller, Eve. "Tetragrammic Numbers: Gematria and the Line Total of the 1674 *Paradise Lost*." *MiltonQ*, 20, 1986, 23–25.

Believes that by "juxtaposing the Hebrew letters which correspond to each number" in the line total of *Paradise Lost*, Milton creates "the Hebrew Tetragrammaton, the most holy Name of

God." Asserts that this explains his addition of fifteen lines to the poem's 1674 edition.

2513 Kelley, Maurice. "*Paradise Lost* and the Christian Theory of History." *SAB*, 37, 1972, 3–11.

States the theory theologically as "a fall, a redemption, and a perfect glorification for the righteous." Asserts that a great need exists in modern education that can be filled only by the Christian theory of history.

2514 Kellogg, Robert. "The Harmony of Time in *Paradise Lost*." *OT*, 2, 1987, 260–72.

Argues that a harmony of time exists in *Paradise Lost*, in which "historical, legendary, mythological figures [are] organized and understood in one grand intellectual and poetic scheme." By "experiencing simultaneously both historical time and a divine spirit in which all times are one," the poet is able both to "lift us up to Heaven" and "bring Heaven down to earth."

2515 Kendrick, Christopher. *Milton: A Study in Ideology and Form.* New York and London: Methuen, 1986. x, 240pp.

Studies *Areopagitica* and *Paradise Lost* "in relation to the collective agency of revolution and as determinate acts within that agency, as symbolic revolutionary acts themselves." Argues that Milton is an early proponent of the capitalist system. Reviews: Douglas Chambers, *RES*, 39, 1988, 108–09; Marshall Grossman, *RenQ*, 41, 1988, 175–77; Richard Helgerson, *JEGP*, 87, 1988, 582–83; David Norbrook, *LRB*, 10, 1988, 20–21; Gordon Campbell, *MLR*, 84, 1989, 127–28; P. J. Klemp, *MiltonQ*, 24, 1990, 71–76.

2516 Kennedy, William J. "The Epic Genre and Varieties of Form." *Rhetorical Norms in Renaissance Literature* (New Haven, CT, and London: Yale Univ. Press, 1978), pp. 128–88.

Discusses Ariosto, D'Aubigné, and *Paradise Lost*. "It remained for Milton . . . to find for his own audience the historical and mythic equivalent of Virgil's subject and through the rhetorical strategies . . . [to] exploit their potentials to the full."

2517 Keogh, J. G. "Milton's *Paradise Lost*, II, 552." *Expl*, 31, 1973, Item 61.

Responds to Gerald Stacy's note (No. 3095) on Milton's use of "partial" in *Paradise Lost*. Offers a musical interpretation of the lines in question. Cites musical metaphors such as "partes," "harmony," and "suspension." Proposes that a blending of the interpretations might be more correct.

2518 Kermode, Frank. "Adam Unparadised." *On Milton's Poetry: A Selection of Modern Studies*. Ed. by Arnold Stein (Greenwich, CT: Fawcett Publications, 1970), pp. 134–50. Reprinted in *Shakespeare, Spenser, Donne: Renaissance Essays* (London: Routledge and Kegan Paul; New York: Viking Press, 1971), pp. 260–97.

Reprint of Huckabay No. 1478, originally published in 1960.

2519 Kerrigan, William. *The Sacred Complex: On the Psychogenesis of "Paradise Lost."* Cambridge, MA, and London: Harvard Univ. Press, 1983. x, 348pp.

Uses the theories of Paul Ricoeur, Freud, and others to relate Milton's works, beginning with *Comus*, to his psychological development. Discusses the religious symbolism of *Paradise Lost*. Reviews: Philip J. Gallagher, *MiltonQ*, 18, 1984, 84–92; Herman Rapaport, *Philosophy and Literature*, 8, 1984, 307–08; Christopher Grose, *HSL*, 15–16, 1985, 129–35; Richard S. Ide, *Rev*, 7, 1985, 89–111; Michael Lieb, *RenQ*, 38, 1985, 183–85; George Parfitt, *TLS*, Jan. 18, 1985, p. 66; William G. Riggs, *Criticism*, 27, 1985, 409–13; J. Martin Evans, *RES*, 37, 1986, 415–17; Richard C. Frushell, *Review of Metaphysics*, 39, 1986, 568–71; Edward Le Comte, *Thought*, 61, 1986, 176–79.

2520 Kerrigan, William, and **Gordon Braden.** "Milton's Coy Eve: *Paradise Lost* and Renaissance Love Poetry." *ELH*, 53, 1986, 27–51.

Surveys the Ovidian and the Petrarchan traditions of love poetry and discusses Milton's depiction of Adam and Eve's sexual relationship before and after the Fall.

2521 Kessner, Carole S. "Psalm 92 and Milton's Sabbath Hymn." *MiltonQ*, 10, 1976, 75–77.

Details the similarities and differences between Psalm 92 and the angels' sabbath hymn in *Paradise Lost* 7.594–632, concluding that the latter is "profoundly indebted" to the former.

2522 Khan, Salamatullah. "The Doctrine of Love and Mercy in the Last Three Books of *Paradise Lost*." *Essays on John Milton: A Tercentenary Tribute*. Ed. by Asloob Ahmad Ansari (Aligarh: Aligarh Muslim Univ., 1976), pp. 96–114.

Shows that the divine promise of love and mercy in *Paradise Lost* 3.173–82 is fulfilled by the "exposition of Man's restoration in the last three books."

2523 Kiehl, James M. "Observations on Richard Upton's *Credo*: A Sketch from John Milton's *Paradise Lost*." *Salmagundi*, 15, 1971, 65–77.

Believes that Milton, "by ordering *Paradise Lost* on the Lucifer-Adam-Abdiel-Christ-God axis," conclusively established the concept of making an ordinary plebeian man the hero. Also, like the successive episodes in *Paradise Lost*, the sequence of lithographs in Upton's *Credo* "coincides with all states of being."

2524 Kiernan, V. J. "Milton in Heaven." *Reviving the English Revolution: Reflections and Elaborations on the Work of Christopher Hill*. Ed. by Geoff Eley and William Hunt (London: Verso, 1988), pp. 161–80.

Discusses *Paradise Lost*, mainly in political terms. Relates the War in Heaven to the English revolution, concluding that Milton completed his poem at the end of one era and the beginning of another.

2525 Kilborn, Judith Margaret. "Presence and Absence: Goodness and Evil in *Paradise Lost*." Doctoral diss., Purdue Univ., 1985. 242pp. Abs., *DAI*, 46, 1986, 3360A.
Investigates the creation, behavior, interaction, and theological background of good and evil as they appear in *Paradise Lost*.

2526 King, Dixie Lee. "Marriage and Sexuality in *Paradise Lost*: Milton and the Puritans." Doctoral diss., Univ. of California, Davis, 1988. 326pp. Abs., *DAI*, 49, 1988, 1463A.
Asserts "that a complete understanding of married life in Milton's Eden can only come from an equally good understanding of what marriage and sexuality meant to Milton's Puritan peers and to Milton as a Puritan."

2527 King, John N. "Milton's Bower of Bliss: A Rewriting of Spenser's Art of Married Love." *Ren&R*, 10, 1986, 289–99.
Argues that Spenser's Bower of Bliss in the *Faerie Queene* parodies medieval and Renaissance traditions. Shows how Spenser's Protestant doctrine of chaste love influenced Milton, especially in the blissful bower where Adam and Eve experienced prelapsarian love.

2528 Kivette, Ruth. "My Will is Fate." *MiltonQ*, 16, 1982, 107.
Abstract of a paper presented at the New York College English Association Meeting at Le Moyne College on October 8, 1982. Believes that narrative problems in *Paradise Lost* "are caused by God's 'permissive will' and His unleashing of Satan from Hell to ensure the ruin of Adam and Eve."

2529 Klein, Jürgen. "John Milton." *Astronomie und Anthropozentrik Die Copernicanische Wende bei John Donne, John Milton und den Cambridge Platonists* (Frankfurt am Main, Berne, and New York: Peter Lang, 1986), pp. 217–78.
Discusses the seventeenth-century view of the cosmos, paying special attention to Milton's description of the six-day creation. Believes that Raphael and Adam's conversation in *Paradise Lost* 8 reflects the contemporary astronomical controversy.

2530 Klemp, Paul Jerald. "'The Garden of God': A Study of the Green World in *The Faerie Queene* and *Paradise Lost*." Doctoral diss., Univ. of Toronto, 1979. Abs., *DAI*, 40, 1980, 6271A–72A.
Contrasts Spenser's faith in elaborate allegory with Milton's straightforward "Adamic tongue" as their different styles affect the presentation of their poems' pastoral settings.

2531 Klemp, P. J. "'Now Hid, Now Seen': An Acrostic in *Paradise Lost*." *MiltonQ*, 11, 1977, 91–92.
"It can hardly be coincidental that the name 'S-A-T-A-N' accompanies the description of the serpent in the acrostic formed by lines 510–514 [of Book 9]. . . . The acrostic appears at a very dramatic moment in the narrative and is perfectly suited to its context."

2532 Klemp, P. J. "Take Five: A Review-Essay." *MiltonQ*, 24, 1990, 71–76.
Discusses the following books: Christopher Kendrick, *Milton: A Study in Ideology and Form* (No. 740); Thomas Merrill, *Epic God-Talk* (No. 2716); Leonard Mustazza, *Such Prompt Eloquence* (No. 2775); William Myers, *Milton and Free Will* (No. 882); and Kathleen M. Swaim, *Before and After the Fall* (No. 3131). Believes that these five books give a fair representation of the shape of Milton scholarship in the past decade. Wishes, however, "that critics with similar interests would listen to each other, allowing potentially fruitful dialogue to replace soliloquy."

2533 Klotz, Günther. "Biblische Figuration und Irdische Notwendigkeit: Zu Miltons *Paradise Lost*." *ZAA*, 23, 1975, 123–32.

Examines Milton's strict Calvinistic treatment of Adam and Eve, which is also laced with a hint of humanism that strays from orthodox Puritan values. Furthermore, one of Milton's purposes was to combine medieval heroism, Christian beliefs, feudalistic elements, and a strong biblical influence to make a sociopolitical statement concerning the English people's motivation.

2534 Klotz, Günther. "Shakespeare und Milton in dem Geschichtlichen Pro-zess von der Reformation zur Revolution." *Jahrbuch der deutschen Shakespeare-Gesellschaft Ost. Weimar*, 120, 1984, 77–84.

Notes similarities between Adam and Eve in *Paradise Lost* and Ferdinand and Miranda in the *Tempest*, as well as between Milton's garden of Eden and the garden scene in *Richard II*.

2535 Knedlik, Janet Leslie. "Fancy, Faith, and Generative Mimesis in *Paradise Lost*." *MLQ*, 47, 1986, 19–47.

Discusses the Renaissance perception of fancy, faith, and mimesis and offers evidence of the presence of a "generative mimesis" in *Paradise Lost*.

2536 Knoespel, Kenneth J. "The Limits of Allegory: Textual Expansion of Narcissus in *Paradise Lost*." *MiltonS*, 22, 1986, 79–99.

Extends Milton's use of Ovid's story beyond Eve to Satan and Adam. "In the broadest sense, Milton transforms the fable from a narrative about love to a narrative about understanding."

2537 Knopp, Bradley A. "'Whence Comest Thou?': Milton's Satan and the Peripatetic Genesis of Evil." *CCTEP*, 52, 1987, 36–41.

"Consequently, when one asks of Milton's Satan, 'Whence comest thou?', one discovers from *Paradise Lost* and *Paradise Regained* that the Fiend's 'wand'rings' originate in his rebellion against the Author of all movement and that his rejection of Divine Order condemns him to everlasting digres-

sion. In this respect, his journeys are ceaseless affirmations of God's justice."

2538 Knoppers, Laura Lunger. "'League with You I Seek': Milton's Concept of Covenant." Doctoral diss., Harvard Univ., 1986. 315pp. Abs., *DAI*, 47, 1987, 4089A.

Believes that understanding three covenants—"spiritual, marital, and political"—in terms of Puritan thought "provides an interpretive key to the relationships between God and man, husband and wife, and ruler and subject in *Paradise Lost*, *Paradise Regained*, and *Samson Agonistes*."

2539 Knott, John R., Jr. "Milton's Heaven." *PMLA*, 85, 1970, 487–95.

Milton's heavenly paradise offers the consolation of a bliss which resembles Eden and also a higher festive joy. It resembles the biblical New Jerusalem in God's regality and power and synthesizes a resemblance to Eden and the omnipotence in the victory of Christ in the Revelation.

2540 Knott, John R., Jr. *Milton's Pastoral Vision: An Approach to "Paradise Lost."* Chicago, IL, and London: Univ. of Chicago Press, 1971. xv, 180pp.

"When Milton made the earthly paradise rather than the battlefield the main stage for the action of his epic, he replaced heroic values with others that can be characterized as pastoral. I am not suggesting that Milton returned in spirit or in style to the pastoral exercises of his early career or that he is guilty of a confusion of genres. . . . But the very habit of thinking in terms of genres with fixed conventions may blind one to the fact that *Paradise Lost* is an epic with a pastoral center." Reviews: *MiltonQ*, 5, 1971, 59–60; John C. Ulreich, Jr., *ArQ*, 27, 1971, 370–79; John G. Demaray, *ELN*, 10, 1972, 50–52; Haruhiko Fujii, *EigoS*, 117, 1972, 107–12; Michael Lieb, *Cithara*, 12, 85–106; James G. Taaffe, *JEGP*, 71, 1972, 130–33; Joseph Anthony Wittreich, Jr., *Genre*, 5, 1972, 307–25;

TLS, Feb. 18, 1972, p. 184; Joseph Frank, *MP*, 71, 1973, 87–89; Warner Rice, *MQR*, 12, 1973, 202–04; Albert James Smith, *RES*, 24, 1973, 76–79.

2541 Knott, John R., Jr. *"Paradise Lost and the Fit Reader."* *MLQ*, 45, 1984, 123–43.

Claims that the "fit reader" of *Paradise Lost* must have a capacity for awe, empathy, and self-correction.

2542 Knott, John R., Jr. "Symbolic Landscape in *Paradise Lost."* *MiltonS*, 2, 1970, 37–58.

Milton's Eden resembles a "Christianized Arcadia" and reflects the perfection of heaven, while hell parodies this perfection. When Adam leaves the garden, "he must replace the *otium* of his life in Eden with an inner peace, self-attained and independent of the external world."

2543 Knott, John R., Jr. "The Visit of Raphael: *Paradise Lost*, Book V." *PQ*, 47, 1968, 36–42.

Suggests that Milton uses the meal in Book 5 as a means of enhancing Adam and Eve's dignity and majesty.

2544 Knowles, Julie Nall. *"The Course of Time*: A Calvinistic *Paradise Lost."* *MiltonS*, 18, 1983, 173–93.

Compares Robert Pollok's *Course of Time* (1827) and *Paradise Lost*. Believes that Pollok's poem provides "an insight into the problems that Milton faced in rejecting Calvinism—and a much better realization of the greatness of *Paradise Lost."*

2545 Ko, Myoung-Eun. "Milton's Understanding of Human Freedom and the Polarized Symmetries of *Paradise Lost."* Doctoral diss., Sogang Univ., Seoul, 1988.

2546 Koehler, G. Stanley. "Milton and the Art of Landscape." *MiltonS*, 8, 1975, 3–40.

"Milton's description of Eden, which is on one level the English countryside, on another the ideal place of legend, is on still a third level an elaborately developed landscape in the

informal style of the seventeenth century, including effects which the eighteenth century would label 'picturesque.'"

2547 Koehler, G. Stanley. "Milton's Milky Stream." *JAF*, 82, 1969, 155–66.

Suggests that the "milky stream" in *Paradise Lost* 5.303–07 relates to other creation-paradise myths in which fertility, birth, and nourishment are important and that Milton's "nutrient stream" stands in the tradition of "marvelously fortified rivers, symbolic of abundance" as well as fertility. Characterizes Eve in the earth-mother pattern.

2548 Koehler, G. Stanley. "Satan's Journey in *Paradise Lost."* *Fabula*, 10, 1969, 100–06.

On Satan's journey in search of paradise. "But Eden becomes even more the longed-for place, the target for aspiration as well as envy, if we can look on Satan not merely as an instrument of evil, but as a pilgrim to an archetypal garden."

2549 Kogan, P. "The Political Theme of Milton's *Paradise Lost."* *L&I*, 4, 1969, 21–40.

Sees *Paradise Lost* as Milton's effort to champion the rights of the bourgeoisie and destroy the remnants of feudal culture, which Satan represents.

2550 Kohn, Terry Ann Kidner. "The Treatment of Landscape in Four Early Poems of Milton and in *Paradise Lost."* Doctoral diss., Bryn Mawr College, 1971. 295pp. Abs., *DAI*, 32, 1972, 5742A.

Asserts that, in Milton's poetry, "Man, or any animate creature, reveals his relationship to the landscape, and in so doing reveals himself."

2551 Kolin, Philip C. "Milton's Use of Clouds for Satanic Parody in *Paradise Lost."* *ELWIU*, 5, 1978, 153–62.

Discusses God's clouds and Satan's distortion of them. Believes that clouds "promise hope and assure defeat; they are instruments of punishment as well as objects of parody." Abs., *MiltonQ*, 13, 1979, 61.

2552 Koltai, Tamás. *"Paradise Lost*: On the Stage." *Hungarian Review*, 10, 1970, 22.

In Hungarian. Report on a production staged in Budapest during the summer of 1970. God is presented as a high-ranking official from the city. Satan and the fallen angels are hippies. The forbidden fruit is a drug. See also No. 3188.

2553 Komori, Teiji. ["On Love in *Paradise Lost*."] *MCJ News*, 6, 1983, 18–22.

Abstract of a paper presented at the Eighth Annual Conference of MCJ in October, 1982. Examines Milton's concept of an ideal marriage in *Paradise Lost*.

2554 König, Edgar. "Die Tropen Metonymie, Synekdoche und Antonomasie in Miltons *Paradise Lost*." Doctoral diss., Wien, 1951. 81pp.

2555 Koyama, Kaoru. "'Lowliness Majestic'—The Meaning of 'Humility' in *Paradise Lost*." *MCJ News*, 8, 1985, 11–12.

Abstract of paper presented. Contrasts the sincere humility and dignity of prelapsarian Adam and Eve with the pride of Satan and his followers.

2556 Kraker, John Joseph. "Milton, *Paradise Lost*, and the Human Condition." Doctoral diss., Case Western Reserve Univ., 1973. 159pp. Abs., *DAI*, 34, 1974, 5107A.

Relates Homer's ideas on the human condition to Milton and *Paradise Lost*. Also points out similarities between Milton's work and Gabriel Marcel's concepts of incarnation, communion, and transcendence.

2557 Kramer, Melinda G. "Taking the Solitary Way through Eden: An Allegorical Reading of *Paradise Lost*." *GyS*, 1, 1974, 40–51.

"Milton skillfully subordinates all else to where the real drama lies—in how well Adam and Eve understand the definition of their relationship. Man cannot live alone; learning what this means is the story of *Paradise Lost*."

2558 Kranidas, Thomas. "Decorum in the Verse." *On Milton's Poetry: A Selection of Modern Studies*. Ed. by Arnold Stein (Greenwich, CT: Fawcett Publications, 1970), pp. 190–99.

Reprint of Huckabay No. 1491, originally published in 1965.

2559 Kranidas, Thomas, ed. *New Essays on "Paradise Lost."* Foreword by Arnold Stein. Berkeley, Los Angeles, and London: Univ. of California Press, 1969. xv, 180pp.

Contains essays by Stanley Eugene Fish, John T. Shawcross, Harold E. Toliver, Isabel G. MacCaffrey, Barbara Kiefer Lewalski, A. B. Chambers, and Michael Fixler. In this bibliography, each essay is listed according to author. Reviews: *TLS*, Dec. 25, 1970, p. 1515; Micheline Hugues, *RLC*, 45, 1971, 267–69; Roger Lejosne, *EA*, 24, 1971, 332–34; Maren-Sofie Røstvig, *ES*, 52, 1971, 457–59; Joseph Anthony Wittreich, Jr., *Genre*, 5, 1972, 307–25.

2560 Kröner, Jörg. "A Genre Interpretation and Pedagogical Consequences of Milton's *Paradise Lost*." Doctoral diss., East Texas State Univ., 1973. 207pp. Abs., *DAI*, 34, 1973, 2566A–67A.

Investigates *Paradise Lost* based on the approaches of C. S. Lewis, Northrop Frye, and Emil Staiger to suggest new methods of teaching Milton's epic in the classroom.

2561 Kuby, Lolette. "The World is Half the Devil's: Cold-Warmth Imagery in *Paradise Lost*." *ELH*, 41, 1974, 182–91.

Describes dualistic imagery in *Paradise Lost*, relating the deadly cold of Chaos with Satan and warmth with the Son. Reaffirms Milton's monism.

2562 Kyle, Linda Davis. "Milton's Eden: Cyclical Amplification of Spenser's Gardens." *SELit*, 55, 1978, 1–14.

"I would like to emphasize this cyclical amplification of Milton's Garden of Eden as landscape before and after the fall with Spenser's Garden of Prosperpina and Garden of Adonis and to compare the relationships of Spenser's characters to his moralized landscapes with those of Milton's characters to his more natural landscape."

2563 Labriola, Albert C. "The Aesthetics of Self-Diminution: Christian Iconography and *Paradise Lost*." *MiltonS*, 7, 1975, 267–311.

"As these same events of the Old Testament are depicted in the iconography of the Middle Ages and the Renaissance, a similar visual context is used. Most importantly, these iconographic depictions tend to interrelate persons and events of the Old Testament with counterparts from the New Testament. . . . To a very great extent iconographic conceptualization is reflected in the development of character and action in *Paradise Lost*, in the elaboration of central themes, and in the selection of imagery."

2564 Labriola, Albert C. "*Christus Patiens*: The Virtue Patience and *Paradise Lost*, I–II." *The Triumph of Patience: Medieval and Renaissance Studies.* Ed. by Gerald J. Schiffhorst (Orlando: Univ. Presses of Florida, 1978), pp. 138–46. Expanded version published as "The Medieval View of Christian History in *Paradise Lost*." *Milton and the Middle Ages.* Ed. by John Mulryan (Lewisburg, PA: Bucknell Univ. Press; London and Toronto: Associated Univ. Presses, 1982), pp. 115–32.

Believes that Milton uses icons from the medieval tradition to discuss sacred history. Focuses on the story of Noah and shows that "Satan throughout *Paradise Lost* is characterized as the demonic counterpart of Noah and of the suffering and triumphant Christ."

2565 Labriola, Albert C. "'God Speaks': Milton's Dialogue in Heaven and the Tradition of Divine Deliberation." *Cithara*, 25, No. 2, 1986, 5–30.

Uses the tradition of deliberation (discourse among members of the Trinity) on fallen humanity as a context with which to interpret the dialogue in heaven in *Paradise Lost* 3. Sees Milton's deliberation scene as a religious drama whose themes are drawn from the transfiguration.

2566 Labriola, Albert C. "'Thy Humiliation Shall Exalt': The Christology of *Paradise Lost*." *MiltonS*, 15, 1981, 29–42.

Shows that the Son's humiliation and exaltation and Satan's parodic enactments of them are balanced throughout the epic and concludes that the poem's Christology reflects Milton's theology of humiliation. Abs., *SCN*, 38, 1980, 45.

2567 Labriola, Albert C. "The Titans and the Giants: *Paradise Lost* and the Tradition of the Renaissance Ovid." *MiltonQ*, 12, 1978, 9–16.

"The present study will consider how the Typhon myth is recounted in Ovid, interpreted by Sandys [in his 1632 translation of the *Metamorphoses*], and adapted by Milton." Emphasizes George Sandys's allegorized commentary on Ovidian myth.

2568 Landy, Marcia. "'Bounds Prescrib'd': Milton's Satan and the Politics of Deviance." *MiltonS*, 14, 1980, 117–34.

"The power and originality of Milton's portrait of Satan lies in its power to capture and capitalize on the terror of deviant reality: ridicule, ostracism, and death."

2569 Landy, Marcia. "Kinship and the Role of Women in *Paradise Lost*." *MiltonS*, 4, 1972, 3–18.

"In *Paradise Lost*, Milton places marriage at the center of social institutions. It is from the point of view of marriage that all social roles and attitudes are defined and judged valuable or destructive. . . . In general, worldly activity belongs to the man: he is artist, ruler, intellect. The woman's role is to be procreative, skilled in domesticity, and obedient to her husband, upon whom she depends for education and guidance."

2570 Largent, Regina M. "A Multilevel Celebration: Milton's Morning Hymn." *MiltonQ*, 22, 1988, 63–66.

Believes that Milton, in the morning hymn in *Paradise Lost* 5, "not only signifies the fall of Satan, but also portends the creation story of Book 7." Thus, "Adam and Eve intuitively possess a knowledge of creation which they are not formally taught until Book[s] 6 and 7."

2571 Latimer, Dan. "Sex in *Paradise Lost*: Neurosis in the Blissful Bower." *L&P*, 30, No. 1, 1980, 18–25.

Asserts that "Milton was unwise to portray sex in Eden because it is difficult, if not impossible, to imagine sexual excitement as uncolored by neurosis." Insists that Milton was guilty of "self-deception and the confounding of what he knew sex to be with what he and the Reformation divines tried in theory to force it to be."

2572 Latt, David J. "Praising Virtuous Ladies: The Literary Image and Historical Reality of Women in Seventeenth-Century England." *What Manner of Woman: Essays on English and American Life and Literature*. Ed. by Marlene Springer (New York: New York Univ. Press, 1977), pp. 39–64.

Notes that Milton gives prominence to women's fortitude, piety, and procreative ability, not to their sexuality and companionship in marriage.

2573 Lauck, John H., II. "*Paradise Lost* IX.1084–90 and Luke 23:28–30." *AN&Q*, 21, 1983, 132–33.

Argues that the lines allude to both Luke and Revelation, unify the poem, and place Adam's preceding speech of despair in context with the idea of judgment.

2574 Law, Jules David. "Eruption and Containment: The Satanic Predicament in *Paradise Lost*." *MiltonS*, 16, 1982, 35–60.

"Satan's predicament is defined . . . by his very inability to fill up the enormous physical and rhetorical space given to him."

2575 Lawry, Jon S. "Travelers in Pandemonium." *BSUF*, 11, 1970, 72–80.

Relates Milton's account of linguistic falls in *Paradise Lost* to the confusion concerning the Greek languages learned in Greece today—classical, modern standard, and vulgar. Alludes indirectly to the influence of classical Greece on Milton.

2576 Lawson, Anita. "'The Golden Sun in Splendor Likest Heaven': Johannes Kepler's *Epitome* and *Paradise Lost*, Book 3." *MiltonQ*, 21, No. 2, 1987, 46–51.

Believes that Milton uses Kepler's *Epitome of Copernican Astronomy* (1618–21) as a source of inspiration for the astronomical imagery in *Paradise Lost* and for his religious convictions as revealed through the cosmos.

2577 Le Comte, Edward. "Dubious Battle: Saving the Appearances." *ELN*, 19, 1982, 177–93. Reprinted in *Milton Re-Viewed: Ten Essays* (New York and London: Garland Publishing, 1991), pp. 3–23.

Surveys several critical views of *Paradise Lost* 6. Concludes that as a materialist, Milton graphically depicts the War in Heaven to achieve solidity on the heavenly battlefield. Milton's distaste for symbolism further forced him to portray this event realistically.

2578 Le Comte, Edward. "Milton Did *Not* Nod: A Response to Jean Gagen." *MiltonQ*, 21, No. 1, 1987, 30.

A reply to No. 2273. Argues that readers have not noticed alleged contradictions in Adam and Eve's conversation in *Paradise Lost* 9 because they do not exist.

2579 Lee, Chang-Kuk. "Miltonic Humor: The Comic Vision in *Paradise Lost*." Doctoral diss., Sogang Univ., Seoul, 1988.

2580 Legouis, Pierre. "Dryden plus Miltonien que Milton?" *Aspects du XVII*

Siècle (Paris: Didier, 1973), pp. 159–67. Reprint of Huckabay No. 1506, originally published in 1967.

2581 Leitch, V. B. "The Landscape of Hell in *Paradise Lost*, Book I." *XUS*, 9, 1970, 26–30.

The "clusters of concrete images" that Milton uses to portray hell may have "an underlying proleptic structure," but they function primarily "on a descriptive level, creating without question the unique and memorable concrete landscape in *Paradise Lost*, Book I."

2582 Leonard, J. K. "Names and Naming in *Paradise Lost*." Doctoral diss., Cambridge Univ., 1985. Abs., *IT*, 35, 1987, 543–44.

Studies *Paradise Lost* in the context of seventeenth-century theories about the origin of language.

2583 Leonard, John. *Naming in Paradise: Milton and the Language of Adam and Eve.* Oxford: Clarendon Press, 1990. x, 304pp.

Discusses "Milton's distinction between prelapsarian and postlapsarian language, particularly as this is reflected in his employment of names." Examines Adam's naming of Eve and the animals and argues that Satan's followers are quite nameless throughout *Paradise Lost*. Analyzes the naming of Satan and explores his corruption of language in seducing the angels and deceiving Eve. Finally, considers Milton's role as narrator and his various attempts to recover a prelapsarian state of language. Reviews: Cedric C. Brown, *N&Q*, 38, 1991, 541–42; Dennis H. Burden, *EIC*, 41, 1991, 331–39; Diana Treviño Benet, *MiltonQ*, 26, 1992, 131–32; Nigel Smith, *RES*, 43, 1992, 110–14.

2584 Leonard, John. "'Once Fawn'd and Cring'd': A Song and Dance about Satan's Servility." *MiltonQ*, 19, 1985, 101–05.

Discusses how "Satan's participation for one full Heavenly day in 'song and dance' which, for him, display only seeming pleasure, amounts to fawning, cringing and servile adoration," rather than the genuine service he once carried out. This change causes Satan to move "from eternity to time; from a world of song to a World where all consciousness is a dead weight."

2585 Leonard, John. "'Though of Thir Names': The Devils in *Paradise Lost*." *MiltonS*, 21, 1985, 157–78.

Argues "that Satan's followers (but not Satan himself) are without names throughout the action of *Paradise Lost*." They address each other by grand titles and later get new names.

2586 Lerner, Laurence. "The Loss of Paradise." *The Uses of Nostalgia: Studies in Pastoral Poetry* (London: Chatto and Windus; New York: Schocken Books, 1972), pp. 197–212.

Milton's garden is nature itself, bursting with abundance and fertility, and it is closely linked to the pastoral tradition because Eden is doomed. Feels that nostalgia is the basic emotion of pastoral.

2587 Levenback, Karen. "The Elements in *Paradise Lost*." *MiltonQ*, 10, 1976, 11–14.

"It is man now corrupted who corrupts the elements; air, earth, fire, and water will always be pure in essence. The original loss of Love separates man from the elements and makes them adversaries: man no longer rules the elements but struggles against them."

2588 Lewalski, Barbara K. "The Genres of *Paradise Lost*: Literary Genre as a Means of Accommodation." *MiltonS*, 17, 1983, 75–103.

Explores the use of multiple genres in *Paradise Lost*, stating that Milton models his writings after the form that best suits his need for a vehicle in which to convey meaning to the audience. Focuses on Raphael and Michael (the epic's "subordinate narrators") as examples of Milton's use of literary accommodation. Abs., *MiltonQ*, 14, 1980, 71–72; *SCN*, 38, 1980, 45–46.

2589 Lewalski, Barbara Kiefer. "Innocence and Experience in Milton's Eden." *New Essays on "Paradise Lost."* Ed. by Thomas Kranidas (Berkeley, Los Angeles, and London: Univ. of California Press, 1969), pp. 86–117.

"This imagination of the Life in Innocence is emphatically antiromantic, anti-Arcadian, anti-escapist, anti-individualistic: it is an exaltation of humanism, maturity, civilization in happiest conjunction with vitality, change, growth. Such an imagination of the State of Innocence sets the Fall in the proper tragic perspective in the poem, as the event which blasted man's opportunity to develop—without suffering, violence, despair and death, though not in the least without tension and trial—the rich resources and large potentialities of the human spirit." Abs., *MiltonQ*, 4, 1970, 34. Review: Joseph Anthony Wittreich, Jr., *Genre*, 5, 1972, 307–25.

2590 Lewalski, Barbara K. "Literary Forms for Wholeness: Mixed Modes and the *Vita Beata* of Milton's Angels." *MiltonQ*, 17, 1983, 24.

Abstract of a paper presented at the 1982 MLA Convention. "Angelic society in *Paradise Lost* is portrayed through a mix of literary modes, displaying the angels' ready and continuous access to the entire spectrum of feelings and values the several literary modes embody, presenting thereby an ideal of integrity and wholeness."

2591 Lewalski, Barbara K. "Milton on Women—Yet Once More." *MiltonS*, 6, 1974, 3–20.

"Responding to a feminist study of *Paradise Lost* in terms of sociological role definitions, this article asserts the limitations of such analyses in assessing the true complexity of Milton's literary treatment of women, and the universality of the poem's concerns."

2592 Lewalski, Barbara Kiefer. *"Paradise Lost" and the Rhetoric of Literary Forms.* Princeton, NJ: Princeton Univ. Press, 1985. xi, 378pp.

Proposes that "Milton makes constant, complex, and highly conscious use of the Renaissance genre system, and the cultural significances and moral values associated with the several kinds, as a means of imagining his unimaginable subject, and as a rhetorical strategy to educate his readers and to guide their responses." Reviews: Roy C. Flannagan, *MiltonQ*, 19, 1985, 113; Lucy Newlyn, *TLS*, Aug. 8, 1986, p. 871; Michael Lieb, *MP*, 84, 1986, 225–28; Joseph Anthony Wittreich, Jr., *RenQ*, 39, 1986, 567–72; Christopher Kendrick, *Criticism*, 28, 1986, 213–16; Boyd M. Berry, *JEGP*, 86, 1987, 247–49; Thomas F. Healy, *MLR*, 82, 1987, 917; C. Schaar, *ES*, 68, 1987, 362–63; John M. Steadman, *CL*, 40, 1988, 181–82.

2593 Lewalski, Barbara Kiefer. *Protestant Poetics and the Seventeenth-Century Religious Lyric.* Princeton, NJ: Princeton Univ. Press, 1979. xiv, 536pp.

Proposes that "the major seventeenth-century religious lyricists owe more to contemporary, English, and Protestant influences than to Counter Reformation, continental, and medieval Catholic resources." Points out that the most fruitful study of Milton in these terms would focus on the lyrical passages of *Paradise Lost*. Reviews: Alison Heinemann, *LJ*, 104, 1979, 1258; Ilona Bell, *MLQ*, 41, 1980, 93–96; Georgia B. Christopher, *JEGP*, 79, 1980, 248–50; Earl Miner, *C&L*, 29, 1980, 75–79; W. Brown Patterson, *SR*, 88, 1980, 651–54; Carl J. Rasmussen, *SCJ*, 11, 1980, 99–102; Hugh M. Richmond, *RenQ*, 33, 1980, 289–99; Mary Ellen Rickey, *GHJ*, 3, 1980, 82–89; John Stachniewski, *TLS*, Mar. 7, 1980, p. 272; Bettie Ann Doebler, *RMR*, 35, 1981, 314–15; William H. Halewood, *SCN*, 39, 1981, 86–87; Janel M. Mueller, *JR*, 61, 1981, 81–87; Steven N. Zwicker, *MQR*, 20, 1981, 473–76; John N. King,

RES, 33, 1982, 81–83; Louis L. Martz, *MP*, 80, 1982, 168; Elizabeth Mac-Kenzie, *N&Q*, 29, 1982, 438–40; Anthony Raspa, *Ren&R*, 6, 1982, 71–73; William Halewood, *SCN*, 41, 1983, 68–69; Kim Hamilton, *MiltonQ*, 19, 1985, 88–89.

2594 Lewalski, Barbara Kiefer. "Typological Symbolism and the 'Progress of the Soul' in Seventeenth-Century Literature." *Literary Uses of Typology from the Late Middle Ages to the Present.* Ed. by Earl Miner (Princeton, NJ: Princeton Univ. Press, 1977), pp. 79–114.

Gives some attention to the typology in *Paradise Lost* and *Paradise Regained.*

2595 Lewis, C. S. *A Preface to "Paradise Lost."* London: Oxford Univ. Press, 1960, 1963, 1965, 1967, 1971, 1975, 1979.

Reprints of Huckabay No. 1513, originally published in 1942. See Nos. 2939 and 4327.

2596 Lewis, C. S. "Primary Epic: Technique and Subject." *Parnassus Revisited: Modern Critical Essays on the Epic Tradition.* Ed. by Anthony C. Yu (Chicago, IL: American Library Association, 1973), pp. 29–41.

Reprint of a chapter from No. 2595, originally published in 1942.

2597 Lewis, Linda Marlene. "Titanic Rebellion: The Promethean Iconography of Milton, Blake and Shelley." Doctoral diss., Univ. of Nebraska, Lincoln, 1987. 215pp. Abs., *DAI*, 48, 1988, 2067A.

Asserts that in *Paradise Lost*, the *Four Zoas*, and *Prometheus Unbound*, the authors exploit the Promethean myth "for their respective views on tyrant and rebel, power and impotence, revolution and the status quo."

2598 Liang, Yisan. "A Tentative Comment on the Nature and the Theme of *Paradise Lost*: Also Illustrating the Ideological Tendency of the Poet." *FLS*, 26, 1984, 27–37.

2599 Lieb, Michael. "'The Chariot of Paternal Deitie': Some Visual Render-

ings." *Milton's Legacy in the Arts.* Ed. by Albert C. Labriola and Edward Sichi, Jr. (University Park and London: Pennsylvania State Univ. Press, 1988), pp. 21–58.

Studies the various ways in which Milton's chariot of paternal deity has been visually depicted. Concludes that twentieth-century world warfare endowed Carlotta Petrina with the necessary experience to illustrate this vehicle more powerfully.

2600 Lieb, Michael. "'Cupid's Funeral Pile': Milton's Projected Drama on the Theme of Lust." *RenP*, 1977, pp. 29–41.

Discusses Milton's plans for a drama on lust, as outlined in the Trinity Manuscript, concluding that the Cupid material, associated with the Sodomites, becomes the pageantry of the fallen angels in *Paradise Lost.*

2601 Lieb, Michael. *The Dialectics of Creation: Patterns of Birth and Regeneration in "Paradise Lost."* [Amherst]: Univ. of Massachusetts Press, 1970. 262pp.

Finds that the poem's common referent deals with creation or birth in all its aspects. Suggests that "Milton as a poet speaks in a language of birth in order to dramatize such events as the warring of good and evil, the fall of angels and men, the redemption of man through grace, God's creation of the universe, and the poet's creation of the poem." Reviews: *TLS*, Dec. 25, 1970, p. 1515; *MiltonQ*, 4, 1970, 29–30; Robert H. West, *MP*, 70, 1973, 360–64; Virginia R. Mollenkott, *SCN*, 29, 1971, 33–34.

2602 Lieb, Michael. "Further Thoughts on Satan's Journey through Chaos." *MiltonQ*, 12, 1978, 126–33.

Believes that the anality of hell causes Satan's journey "to take on distinctly unsavory overtones." Discusses the voyage in scatological terms and relates it to ancient and contemporary thought. Abs., *MiltonQ*, 11, 1977, 94.

2603 Lieb, Michael. "'Hate in Heav'n':

Milton and the *Odium Dei*." *ELH*, 53, 1986, 519–39.

Discusses divine hate and divine love from the perspectives of the Bible and Reformation commentators. In *Paradise Lost* the Son exhibits "odium Dei" when he mounts the chariot of paternal deity and drives the rebel angels out of heaven. "The chariot performs a twofold function: that of destruction and that of reclamation."

2604 Lieb, Michael. "'Holy Name': A Reading of *Paradise Lost*." *HTR*, 67, 1974, 321–39.

Examines "the fundamental attitude toward Holy Name expressed in *Paradise Lost* . . . [which] draws upon the full potentialities of Holy Name implicit in the traditions that shape religious thought."

2605 Lieb, Michael. "'Holy Place': A Reading of *Paradise Lost*." *SEL*, 17, 1977, 129–47.

In *Paradise Lost*, Milton considers the idea of entering a divine enclosure from a number of different perspectives. Concludes that he "successfully accommodates Old and New Testament renderings of holy place to the Christian vision that permeates his epic."

2606 Lieb, Michael. "'Holy Rest': A Reading of *Paradise Lost*." *ELH*, 39, 1972, 238–53.

Explains "holy rest" as an innate factor in the unfallen human state, a necessary backdrop for the works of good against evil, and a proper reward for seeking God. Believes that it is "intimately associated with the pattern of return" and "the achievement of eternal rest after the fall."

2607 Lieb, Michael. "Milton's 'Chariot of Paternal Deitie' as a Reformation Conceit." *JR*, 65, 1985, 359–77.

Investigates the Reformation underpinnings of the chariot of paternal deity in *Paradise Lost* 6. Identifies Ezekiel's chariot as the most immediate antecedent to Milton's; according to John

Calvin's *Commentaries on . . . Ezekiel*, this correlation designates the chariot as "a divine instrument for reforming what is corrupt and as a weapon against all who would oppose the workings of God."

2608 Lieb, Michael. "Milton's 'Dramatick Constitution': The Celestial Dialogue in *Paradise Lost*, Book III." *MiltonS*, 23, 1987, 215–40.

Examines the dialogue in heaven in *Paradise Lost* 3 to demonstrate Milton's endorsement of "a reading of Scripture consistent with the practice of conceiving the biblical text as the highest form of drama, one comparable even to the 'Dramatick constitutions' of Sophocles and Euripides."

2609 Lieb, Michael. "*Paradise Lost* and the Myth of Prohibition." *MiltonS*, 7, 1975, 233–65.

"In accord with the J text of Genesis, Milton incorporates into *Paradise Lost* the mythic and nonrational elements implicit in the prohibition against eating the fruit. In so doing, he formulates a view of the prohibition that at once dismisses the prevailing rationalist interpretation based upon a covenant theology and embraces a nonrationalist outlook that has ties with something associated with a covenant theology."

2610 Lieb, Michael. "*Paradise Lost* and the Twentieth Century Reader." *Cithara*, 9, No. 1, 1969, 27–42.

Contends that *Paradise Lost* is applicable today, for it "provides a way of reconciling the human dilemma both with respect to man's present circumstances and with respect to man's ultimate future."

2611 Lieb, Michael. "*Paradise Lost*, Book III: The Dialogue in Heaven Reconsidered." *RenP*, 1974, pp. 39–50.

Relates Abraham's and Moses's dialogues with God and their relationship to the dialogue between the Father and the Son in *Paradise Lost*. Feels that Milton's handling of this material moves the epic "beyond tragedy" and causes it "to provide an education in the meaning of grace."

2612 Lieb, Michael. *Poetics of the Holy: A Reading of "Paradise Lost."* Chapel Hill: Univ. of North Carolina Press, 1981. xxi, 442pp.

Focuses on *Paradise Lost* "as a sacral document, one that gives rise to a hierophantic outlook that complements and reinforces the vatic point of view." Discusses the basic contexts by which the holy may be understood, the aesthetic dimensions of the concept, and the fundamental aspects of sacral phenomena in *Paradise Lost*. Reviews: Roy C. Flannagan, *MiltonQ*, 16, 1982, 47–49; James H. Sims, *SCN*, 31, 1983, 33–34; Paul J. Klemp, *C&L*, 32, 1982, 63–65; Raymond B. Waddington, *RenQ*, 36, 1983, 485–89; Joseph Anthony Wittreich, Jr., *Rev*, 5, 1983, 1–16; Barbara K. Lewalski, *JEGP*, 82, 1983, 560–62; Martin Evans, *RES*, 35, 1984, 538–39; Gordon C. Campbell, *MLR*, 80, 1985, 905–06; Michael Fixler, *MP*, 82, 1985, 310–14.

2613 Lieb, Michael. "S. B.'s '*In Paradisum Amissam*': Sublime Commentary." *MiltonQ*, 19, 1985, 71–73, 75–78.

Believes that Samuel Barrow's "In Paradisum Amissam," as the earliest commentary on *Paradise Lost*, is as important as and comparable to Marvell's "On *Paradise Lost*." Reproduces the Latin poem and supplies an English translation. Notes that Barrow's poem "merits close and detailed scrutiny both for its critical insights and for its eloquence of expression."

2614 Lifson, Martha R. "Creation and the Self in *Paradise Lost* and the *Confessions*." *CentR*, 19, 1975, 187–97.

Sees similarities between Augustine's and Milton's doctrines, but notes that Milton is telling a story. Describes the use of imagery in both works and discusses parallel themes.

2615 Lifson, Martha. "The Mediating Muse

of *Paradise Lost*: Guide to Spiritual Transformation." *NDEJ*, 13, 1981, 45–60.

Focuses on "the prologues as the specific locus for spiritual transformation in the poem, on the imagery used, and . . . on the muse as the necessary agent for such change."

2616 Lifson, Martha Ronk. "The Theme of Creation in *Paradise Lost*." Doctoral diss., Yale Univ., 1968. 265pp. Abs., *DA*, 29, 1969, 3976A.

Examines the creation in *Paradise Lost* 7 of a "physically concrete, unfallen golden world" that is characterized by unity and analogous to other works of creation in Milton's epic.

2617 Lim, Walter Swee Huat. "Biblical Analogy and the Heroic Paradigm in *Paradise Lost* and *Paradise Regained*." Doctoral diss., Univ. of Toronto, 1988. Abs., *DAI*, 49, 1988, 811A.

Believes that Milton partly modeled his epic heroes (the preexistent Son, Adam, Eve, the incarnate Son) mainly on Old Testament figures to infuse "the actions of his protagonists with greater dramatic and theological significance" and to clarify the poet's own "role as prophet to the English New Jerusalem."

2618 Lindenbaum, Peter. "Lovemaking in Milton's Paradise." *MiltonS*, 6, 1974, 277–306. Revised in *Changing Landscapes: Anti-Pastoral Sentiment in the English Renaissance* (Athens and London: Univ. of Georgia Press, 1986), pp. 136–79.

Discusses various aspects of prelapsarian life in paradise, including lovemaking and work. Concludes that Milton is actually making a statement about the human condition and that his epic can continue to speak forcefully to the modern reader. Reviews (of book): Alastair Fowler, *THES*, Aug. 7, 1987, p. 19; Alvin Kernan, *YR*, 77, 1987, 86–102; Michael G. Brennan, *RES*, 39, 1988, 541–42; Sukanta Chaudhuri, *N&Q*, 35, 1988, 526; Terry Comito, *RenQ*, 41, 1988, 349–52; Matthew

N. Proser, *SCN*, 46, 1988, 1–3; J. C. A. Rathmell, *TLS*, Jan. 22, 1988, p. 91; Charles L. Squier, *JRMMRA*, 9, 1988, 179–80; Michael L. Hall, *SR*, 97, 1989, 456–62; Theodore B. Leinwand, *MR*, 4, 1989, 273–75.

2619 Lippincott, Henry F., Jr. "Marvell's 'On *Paradise Lost*.'" *ELN*, 9, 1972, 265–72.

Suggests that Marvell's work is not just an attack on Dryden, but the product of a dispute with Samuel Parker on the value of Milton's occasional use of internal rhyme. "In context, there is a contrast between Milton (the true poet) of his 'own sense secure' . . . and the 'Town-Bayes' (the false poets) who spend their time hunting the rhyme to 'set off' their matter."

2620 Lisbeth, Terrence L. "Major Latinisms in the Miltonic Theme of the Fall." *CF*, 26, 1972, 83–93.

Analyzes "the meanings and contexts of some of the major Latinisms in *Paradise Lost*, that is, the Latinisms that contribute their several associative meanings to the Fall of Satan and Adam."

2621 Lockwood, Deborah H. "Observing Decorum in *Paradise Lost*, Books XI and XII." *ELWIU*, 11, 1984, 21–33.

Examines the elements of prophecy in Michael's visions and narrative.

2622 Lord, George de Forest. *Heroic Mockery: Variations on Epic Themes from Homer to Joyce*. Newark: Univ. of Delaware Press; London: Associated Univ. Presses, 1977. 162pp.

Discusses Milton's War in Heaven, pp. 67–77. Believes that Milton borrows from Homer in letting gods fight against gods and that the war "purges this epic at its very center from the traditional epic fallacy of force."

2623 Lord, George de F. "Milton's Dialogue with Omniscience in *Paradise Lost*." *The Author in His Work: Essays on a Problem in Criticism*. Ed. by Louis L. Martz and Aubrey Williams (New Ha-

ven, CT, and London: Yale Univ. Press, 1978), pp. 31–50.

Deals with Milton's preoccupation with himself and with the process of poetic creation and examines the ways in which the poet qualifies as hero.

2624 Lord, George de Forest. "Pretexts and Subtexts in 'that Fair Field of Enna.'" *MiltonS*, 20, 1984, 127–46.

On *Paradise Lost* 4.268–87. Notes that in this comparison of the garden to pagan paradises, Milton goes far beyond Ovid and suggests that he knew the Homeric *Hymn to Demeter*.

2625 Lovejoy, Arthur O. "Milton and the Paradox of the Fortunate Fall." *Critical Essays on Milton from "ELH"* (Baltimore, MD, and London: Johns Hopkins Press, 1969), pp. 163–81.

Reprint of Huckabay No. 1526, originally published in 1937.

2626 Low, Anthony. "Angels and Food in *Paradise Lost*." *MiltonS*, 1, 1969, 135–45.

"The meal in the Garden . . . is a symbol of hospitality, of an ideal relationship between man and angel. Its abundance reveals God's goodness, while its simplicity underlines man's innocence."

2627 Low, Anthony. "The Astronomy of *Paradise Lost*." *ELN*, 8, 1971, 263–67.

Claims that "Milton's universe in *Paradise Lost* is Ptolemaic."

2628 Low, Anthony. "Eve's Additions to the Command: Milton and Donne." *MiltonQ*, 13, 1979, 20.

In *Paradise Lost* 9, Eve's words in her rationalization that she would not die are similar to those in a sermon by John Donne. By choosing to view Eve's modification of God's command, Milton makes her represent all of us. See also No. 2258.

2629 Low, Anthony. "The Image of the Tower in *Paradise Lost*." *SEL*, 10, 1970, 171–81.

Suggests that Nimrod's tower symbolizes rebellion against God and the prideful attempts of Satan (and later humanity) to parody and make themselves God's equal. Concludes that "the ambivalence of the Tower, with its splendor, glory, and pride balanced against impiety, foolishness, and vanity, its heavenly meaning countered by worldly corruption, makes it especially effective as a central image in *Paradise Lost*."

2630 Low, Anthony. "Milton and the Georgic Ideal: *Paradise Lost*." *The Georgic Revolution* (Princeton, NJ: Princeton Univ. Press, 1985), pp. 310–22.

Argues that the poem moves from pastoral to georgic.

2631 Low, Anthony. "Milton's God: Authority in *Paradise Lost*." *MiltonS*, 4, 1972, 19–38.

"*Paradise Lost* presents . . . a vision of God's ideal justice, corresponding to the vision of bliss in Eden."

2632 Low, Anthony. "'No Middle Flight': *Paradise Lost*, I.14." *MiltonN*, 3, 1969, 1–4.

Explains that Milton divided the atmosphere into three layers and placed the pagan gods and fallen angels in the middle air. Concludes that *Paradise Lost*, through reliance on the muse, would not enter the realm of the classical and pagan gods, but would rise above to the realm of divinity.

2633 Low, Anthony. "Siloa's Brook: *Paradise Lost*, I.11." *MiltonQ*, 6, No. 3, 1972, 3–5.

Holds that Siloa's brook in *Paradise Lost* 1.11–12 "becomes in its context a Christian Aganippe" and that Milton alludes to both Isaiah 8 and John 9. Comments on "the metaphorical connection Milton makes between these passages" and discusses their thematic appropriateness to *Paradise Lost*, especially to Book 3.21–32. See No. 2730.

2634 Luxton, Andrea Thomasing Joy. "Milton's Hermeneutics: An Intertextual Study of the Epistle to the Hebrews and *Paradise Lost*." Doctoral diss., The Catholic Univ. of America, 1986. 387pp. Abs., *DAI*, 47, 1986, 1334A.

Notes Milton's "imaginative reinterpretation" of the Epistle to the Hebrews in discussing the Father and Son's interaction, "images of Mount Sion and Mount Sinai," and other theological concepts in *Paradise Lost*.

2635 MacCaffrey, Isabel G. "The Theme of *Paradise Lost*, Book III." *New Essays on "Paradise Lost."* Ed. by Thomas Kranidas (Berkeley, Los Angeles, and London: Univ. of California Press, 1969), pp. 58–85.

"In the overall structure, the third book marks a major narrative transition. Within the cosmography of *Paradise Lost*, it is also a transition from one area to another since, through Book VI, narrative structure and spatial plan are virtually identified. This shift in perspective coincides with a concentration of thematic focus upon a particular aspect of Milton's enormous subject. The poem treats the ways of God to men; Book III deals specifically with divine epistemology, the ways whereby men can know, or come to know, God." Abs., *MiltonQ*, 4, 1970, 34.

2636 MacCallum, Hugh. "Memory and the Recovery of Man in *Paradise Lost*." *SCN*, 38, 1980, 46.

Abstract of a paper presented at the 1979 MLA Convention. Observes that Milton's treatment of Adam and Eve in *Paradise Lost* "provides his most extended and dramatic commentary on the role of memory. There are three crucial moments in which memory contributes to Adam's progress through repentance to restoration: his responses to the judgment of the Son, to the news of his banishment, and to the lessons of history." Also abs., *MiltonQ*, 14, 1980, 72.

2637 MacCallum, Hugh. *Milton and the Sons of God: The Divine Image in Milton's*

Epic Poetry. Toronto, Buffalo, NY, and London: Univ. of Toronto Press, 1986. x, 325pp.

Examines Milton's perception and uses of sonship, which is the key for him in understanding the relationship between God and man. Reviews: Roy Flannagan, *MiltonQ*, 21, No. 3, 1987, 113–17; Albert C. Labriola, *RenQ*, 40, 1987, 376–77; Ira Clark, *C&L*, 37, 1988, 53–54; G. R. Evans, *RES*, 39, 1988, 294–95; Charles Martindale, *TLS*, Feb. 5–11, 1988, p. 142; Stella P. Revard, *RSR*, 14, 1988, 149; Julia J. Smith, *N&Q*, 35, 1988, 91–92; Richard J. DuRocher, *JEGP*, 88, 1989, 237–40.

2638 MacCallum, Hugh. "'Most Perfect Hero': The Role of the Son in Milton's Theodicy." *"Paradise Lost": A Tercentenary Tribute*. Ed. by Balachandra Rajan ([Toronto]: Univ. of Toronto Press, 1969), pp. 79–105.

Places Milton in the Socinian tradition, which puts primary emphasis on human values, but notes several departures in his thinking.

2639 MacDonald, Ronald Russell. "The Burial-Places of Memory: Epic Underworlds in Vergil, Dante, and Milton." Doctoral diss., Yale Univ., 1983. 219pp. Abs., *DAI*, 44, 1984, 2755A.

Investigates the three epic poets' use of the underworld to link themselves and their characters to the past.

2640 MacDonald, Ronald R. "Milton: Traditions and the Individual Talent." *The Burial-Places of Memory: Epic Underworlds in Vergil, Dante, and Milton* (Amherst: Univ. of Massachusetts Press, 1987), pp. 118–82.

Suggests that "Milton found his primary defense against the past in the trope of metalepsis and that *Paradise Lost* is in a special sense a meditation on priority.... Milton manages to convey something like the impression that previous epics were really trying to tell the story of *Paradise Lost* with

very partial success. It is only apparently a paradox that in choosing the story furthest back in the past, the story of origins, Milton claims the future and achieves a conspectus of all history from Creation to Last Judgment." Reviews (of book): *VQR*, 64, 1988, 7; Sara Mandell, *Classical Bulletin*, 64, 1988, 99–100; James V. Mirollo, *RenQ*, 41, 1988, 512–14; John Moore, *SCN*, 46, 1988, 71–72; D. M. Rosenberg, *CentR*, 32, 1988, 217–18; R. J. Schork, *RSR*, 14, 1988, 366; K. W. Gransden, *MLR*, 85, 1990, 131–32.

2641 MacKellar, Walter. "On Two English Metamorphoses." *Poetry and Poetics from Ancient Greece to the Renaissance: Studies in Honor of James Hutton*. Cornell Studies in Classical Philology, 38. Ed. by G. M. Kirkwood (Ithaca, NY, and London: Cornell Univ. Press, 1975), pp. 207–17.

On the metamorphoses in Pope's *Windsor Forest* and Milton's *Paradise Lost*. Notes that Satan's metamorphosis into a serpent in Book 10 is based in part on Ovid, though Milton gives the scene a symbolic and moral meaning.

2642 MacKenzie, Elizabeth. "The Growth of Plants: A Seventeenth-Century Metaphor." *English Renaissance Studies Presented to Dame Helen Gardner in Honour of Her Seventieth Birthday*. [Ed. by John Carey] (Oxford: Clarendon Press, 1980), pp. 194–211.

On the Christian tradition of comparing human life with the life of a tree or a plant. Discusses Raphael's conversation with Adam in *Paradise Lost* 5.308–505 and Raphael's answer concerning angelic digestion, the chain of being, and Adam's place in it.

2643 MacLaren, I. S. "Arctic Exploration and Milton's 'Frozen Continent.'" *N&Q*, 31, 1984, 325–26.

Cites journals of Arctic explorers such as Richard Hakluyt's *Divers Voyages* and Thomas James's *Strange and*

Dangerous Voyage as sources of Milton's "frozen Continent" in hell found in *Paradise Lost* 2.

2644 Maclean, Hugh. *"Paradise Lost* (1674) V.636–40, and 666." *MiltonQ*, 7, 1973, 8–11.

The lines that Milton added to the 1674 edition help to maintain numerical balance and also "enable readers to estimate the significance of Satan's revolt more fully and more precisely than the edition of 1667 will allow." Reply by John T. Shawcross (No. 3039).

2645 Madathiparampil, George J. "Epics of India and *Paradise Lost*: Convergence of Visions." *SLRev*, 5, 1988, 43–55.

Shows that the *Ramayana*, the *Mahabharata*, and *Paradise Lost* share the theme that "the ultimate victory in the affairs of mankind belongs to the forces of good."

2646 Magoun, F. P., Jr. "Two Notes on *Paradise Lost*." *NM*, 70, 1969, 723–24.

In *Paradise Lost* 1, Tammuz's blood flows purple during the spring, not summer, when the red earth is washed down from the mountains. In *Paradise Lost* 9, perhaps Milton had seen harvest queens in rural England, and this accounts for the garland which Adam weaves for Eve. Supplemented by No. 1852.

2647 Mahood, Molly M. *Poetry and Humanism.* New York: W. W. Norton, 1970.

Reprint of Huckabay No. 1545, originally published in 1950.

2648 Maier, Harald. "Kontrast und Parallele als strukturbildende Elemente in Vergils *Aeneis* und Miltons *Paradise Lost*." Doctoral diss., Tübingen, 1974.

"Contrast and Parallel as Structural Constitutive Elements in Virgil's *Aeneid* and Milton's *Paradise Lost*."

2649 Major, John M. "Eve's 'Experience.'" *MiltonQ*, 4, 1970, 39–40.

In *Paradise Lost* 9.807–10 and 988–89, Eve's tributes to her experience in eating the forbidden fruit "serve to make more complex the circumstance of her Fall" and provide an ironic commentary on the Renaissance educational doctrine that learning should be ratified by experience. In these passages and in *Paradise Regained* 3.232–43, "The Milton of the last years, for whom the active life had turned sour, is . . . placing experience in a bad light, as schooling of the Devil."

2650 Maltz, Harold P. "Lucifer's Fall: Freewill and the Aetiology of Evil in *Paradise Lost*." *Theoria*, 72, 1988, 63–73.

Argues that the Fall is insufficient to explain the origin of evil and that Milton had to turn to an earlier fall, that of Lucifer-Satan from heaven. Emphasizes the angels' free will.

2651 Maltz, Harold P. *"Paradise Lost*, Genesis and Job: A Reconstruction of Authorial Choices." *Theoria*, 71, 1988, 23–34.

Suggests that Milton could have based his theodicy on the book of Job, rather than Genesis 1–3. Concludes that Job was not adaptable and in many ways contradicted the moral principles displayed in *Paradise Lost*.

2652 Manion, Frederick P. *"Paradise Lost* IX, 445–466 and *L'Allegro*, ll. 37–80." *MiltonQ*, 14, 1980, 130.

Contrasts the cheerful man's walk in *L'Allegro* and Satan's reaction to the sight of Eve alone in *Paradise Lost* 9. "The contrast points the truth that fallen man can enjoy the beauties of the world without guilt; but an evil motive, a perverse intention, destroys the goodness of Paradise itself."

2653 Maresca, Thomas E. "Milton: *Paradise Lost*." *Three English Epics: Studies of "Troilus and Criseyde," "The Faerie Queene," and "Paradise Lost"* (Lincoln and London: Univ. of Nebraska Press, 1979), pp. 75–142.

Argues that "the motif of the descent to Hell forms the spine of English epic tradition." Interprets Milton's epic in terms of structure, of several ascents and descents, including the poet's own requests for the descent of divine inspiration. Reviews (of book): Albert C. Labriola, *SpenN*, 11, 1980, 4–7; Michael Lieb, *Cithara*, 21, 1981, 58–70; John M. Steadman, *JEGP*, 80, 1981, 234–37; John J. O'Connor, *RenQ*, 34, 1981, 149–51; Christina von Nolcken, *RES*, 33, 1982, 196–97.

2654 Marilla, Esmond Linworth. *The Central Problem of "Paradise Lost": The Fall of Man.* Folcroft, PA: Folcroft Library Editions, 1971, 1977; Norwood, PA: Norwood Editions, 1978.

Reprints of Huckabay No. 1552, originally published in 1953.

2655 Marjara, Harinder S. "Angelic Motion and Moloch's False Rhetoric." *MiltonQ*, 19, 1985, 82–87.

Asserts that Moloch's speech about the angels' capability of ascending to heaven is false rhetoric because they are physically heavy and predetermined to fall through Chaos eternally.

2656 Marjara, Harinder. "'Beauty' and 'Grace' in *Paradise Lost*." *MiltonQ*, 18, 1984, 50–52.

Discusses Milton's definition of the words "beauty" and "grace" and the origin of his understanding in Renaissance art theory. Views the words as logical contraries, grace being the superior quality.

2657 Marks, Herbert. "The Blotted Book." *Re-membering Milton: Essays on the Texts and Traditions.* Ed. by Mary Nyquist and Margaret W. Ferguson (New York and London: Methuen, 1987), pp. 211–33.

Uses the fallen angels' names in *Paradise Lost* 1 to illustrate Milton's exploitation of etymology.

2658 Marks, Herbert John. "The Language of Adam: Biblical Naming and Poetic Etymology." Doctoral diss., Yale Univ., 1985. 194pp. Abs., *DAI*, 47, 1986, 1311A.

Studies the use of etymology as it clarifies "the essential identity of the thing or being named" and illuminates the literal meaning of the Bible, the *Divine Comedy*, and *Paradise Lost*.

2659 Markus, Helmut. "Die Funktion der Parenthese in Miltons *Paradise Lost*." Doctoral diss., Freiburg, 1965. 289pp. "On the Function of Parenthesis in Milton's *Paradise Lost*."

2660 Marotta, Richard Joseph. "Milton and the Art of the Catalogue." Doctoral diss., City Univ. of New York, 1977. 256pp. Abs., *DAI*, 38, 1977, 2142A.

Discusses the Homeric and Virgilian origins of five types of catalogs in Milton's poetry—triumphal, epic, temptation, thaumaturgic, and prophetic.

2661 Martindale, Charles. "The Epic of Ideas: Lucan's *De Bello Civili* and *Paradise Lost*." *CCrit*, 3, 1981, 133–56.

Examines Milton's allusions to *De Bello Civili* "and account[s] for certain broad similarities of poetic strategy in *Paradise Lost* and *De bello civili* that arguably arise essentially from similarities of purpose, and which thus might have existed even if Milton had not read a word of Lucan's epic."

2662 Martindale, C. A. "A Homeric Formula in Milton." *N&Q*, 24, 1977, 545–47.

Finds that the passages describing the going forth of Adam (*Paradise Lost* 5.350–57) and Eve (8.59–63) are complementary and that they represent adaptations of a common Homeric formula in which a character's status is reflected by attendants. Since Adam is unaccompanied yet loses no status, Milton advances the view that "there is no connection between virtue and the external trappings of rank."

2663 Martindale, Charles A. *John Milton and the Transformation of Ancient Epic.* London and Sydney: Croom Helm, 1986. 239pp.

Discusses Milton's attitude toward the classics and explores the influence of Homer, Virgil, Ovid, and Lucan. Emphasizes the importance of biblical influence. Reviews: Francis C.

Blessington, *MiltonQ*, 21, No. 1, 1987, 25–26; Paul Hammond, *THES*, Sept. 19, 1986, p. 20; Balz Engler, *ES*, 68, 1987, 468–69, Alastair Fowler, *TLS*, Jan. 30, 1987, p. 115; J. Martin Evans, *RES*, 39, 1988, 552–53; Claes Schaar, *SN*, 60, 1988, 268–70; Julia J. Smith, *N&Q*, 35, 1988, 91–92; George de Forest Lord, *MLR*, 84, 1989, 927–28.

2664 Martindale, Charles. "Paradise Metamorphosed: Ovid in Milton." *CL*, 37, 1985, 301–33.
Examines "some of the reasons that may have drawn Milton to Ovid" and describes "the nature of the Ovidian presence in *Paradise Lost*."

2665 Martz, Louis L. "*Paradise Lost*: The Power of Choice." *Ventures*, 10, 1970, 37–41.
Adam and Eve's conversation at the beginning of Book 9 demonstrates that "nothing stands alone, but everything lives best in the linked universe of love, with respect for those above and care for those below."

2666 Martz, Louis L. "*Paradise Lost*: Princes of Exile." *ELH*, 36, 1969, 232–49.
Sees a parallel between Satan's exile and Milton's Restoration exile. "Without ignoring ancient analogies, I would like to explore the poem's reliance on the individual consciousness, by comparing it briefly with a modern analogy, the poetry of the greatest of living French poets, St. John Perse."

2667 Martz, Louis L. "*Paradise Lost*: The Realms of Light." *ELR*, 1, 1971, 71–88.
Claims that Books 1 and 2 emphasize darkness, yet their real appeal is in "the fact that they deal with the . . . effort of the fallen . . . to retain consciousness and hope to struggle toward the light."

2668 Martz, Louis L. "*Paradise Lost*: The Solitary Way." *The Author in His Work: Essays on a Problem in Criticism*. Ed. by Martz and Aubrey Williams (New Haven, CT, and London: Yale Univ. Press, 1978), pp. 71–84.

Discusses "solitary" as it applies to Adam and Eve, Satan, and the poet. Believes that the ending of Milton's poem is ambiguous and paradoxical.

2669 Mason, H. A. "The Sum of Things." *N&Q*, 22, 1975, 309–10.
On *Paradise Lost* 6.667–74. Suggests Virgil's *Aeneid* as a likely source for Milton's use of the phrase "Consulting on the sum of things." Reply by H. J. Real (No. 2907).

2670 Massey, William. *Remarks upon Milton's "Paradise Lost": Historical, Geographical, Philological, Critical and Explanatory*. Folcroft, PA: Folcroft Library Editions, 1970, 1977; Norwood, PA: Norwood Editions, 1978.
Reprints of the 1761 edition.

2671 Masson, David. *The Three Devils: Luther's, Milton's, and Goethe's*. Folcroft, PA: Folcroft Library Editions, 1969; New York: AMS Press, 1970; Norwood, PA: Norwood Editions, 1977; Philadelphia, PA: R. West, 1978.
Reprints of the 1874 edition and of Stevens No. 2078.

2672 Mathews, Alice M. "Eve's Sense of Separateness: The Path to the Fall in *Paradise Lost*." *CCTEP*, 53, 1988, 22–28.
Argues that Eve's fall is a result of cumulative experience, beginning with her first, when she sees and admires her reflection in the pool. Emphasizes the significance of her dream.

2673 Mathews, Alice M. "Milton's *Paradise Lost*, XI.126–29." *Expl*, 40, 1982, 20.
Says that "the reference to the 'double *Janus*' may be explained by considering the thematic implications," which Milton associates "with God's indictment of sinners."

2674 Mathews, Alice McWhirter. "The Path to Paradox: The Effects of the Falls in Milton's *Paradise Lost* and Conrad's *Lord Jim*." Doctoral diss., North Texas State Univ., 1987. 302pp. Abs., *DAI*, 48, 1987, 655A.
Argues that both *Paradise Lost* and

Lord Jim contain a fall or separation, the fragmenting effects of which are ultimately overcome by paradox—"the joining of polarities to form one truth."

2675 Mathis, Gilles. *Analyse Stylistique du "Paradis Perdu" de John Milton: L'Univers Poétique, Echoes et Correspondances.* Thèse de Doctorat d'Etat Présentée devant l'Université d'Aix Marseille, 1979. 3 vols. Marseille: Université de Provence Service des Publications, 1987. 1490pp.

A stylistic analysis that considers the manner and means of expression in *Paradise Lost.* Compares Milton's epic with the Bible and the epics of Homer, Virgil, Dante, Du Bartas, and Spenser. Reviews: Thomas F. Healy, *MLR*, 84, 1989, 717–18; Leo Miller, *MiltonQ*, 23, 1989, 83–84; Mary Ann Radzinowicz, *RenQ*, 42, 1989, 146–49.

2676 Mathis, Gilles. "Mémoire et Création dans *Le Paradis Perdu.*" *Mémoire et Création dans le Monde Anglo-Américain aux XVIIᵉ et XVIIIᵉ Siècles.* Société d'Études Anglo-Américaines des XVIIᵉ et XVIIIᵉ Siècles (Strasbourg: Université de Strasbourg II, 1984), pp. 147–67.

Stresses the importance of both the author's and the reader's memory in creating the world of *Paradise Lost.*

2677 Matsuda, Minori. "A. J. A. Waldock and G. A. Wilkes on *Paradise Lost.*" *MCJ News*, 4, 1980, 9–10.

Abstract of a paper presented at the Seventh Colloquium of MCJ in July, 1979. Summarizes Waldock's position (Huckabay No. 1965) and argues that Wilkes (Huckabay No. 2007) successfully refutes it without resorting to historical criticism.

2678 Matsuda, Minori. "Virgil and Milton, The *Aeneid* and *Paradise Lost.*" *MCJ News*, 6, 1983, 28–31.

Abstract of a paper presented at the Thirteenth Colloquium of MCJ in July, 1982. Points to Milton's echoes of Virgil's words and plot.

2679 Matsunami, Ayako. "The Meta-physics of Love in *Paradise Lost.*" *MCJ News*, 7, 1984, 15–16.

Abstract of paper presented. Argues that in Milton's epic, the love of God is merely the negation of love and hatred, while Satan "first gave rise to love and hatred."

2680 Maurer, Iris Sue. "Allusions to the Epistle to the Romans in *Paradise Lost*: A Comparison of Their Contexts in the Light of Reformation Theology." Doctoral diss., Catholic Univ. of America, 1981. 311pp. Abs., *DAI*, 42, 1981, 713A–14A.

Uses the epic's allusions to the Epistle to the Romans to describe Milton's ideas about God, sin, and salvation.

2681 McAdams, James Roberts. "Milton's Epic Synthesis: A Study of the Association of *Paradise Lost* and *Paradise Regained.*" Doctoral diss., New York Univ., 1966. 260pp. Abs., *DAI*, 30, 1970, 4458A–59A.

Examines the thematic relationship between *Paradise Lost* and *Paradise Regained*, revealing a common organizational pattern—internally parallel events, temptation, and resolution.

2682 McCanles, Michael. "*Paradise Lost* and the Dialectic of Providence." *Dialectical Criticism and Renaissance Literature* (Berkeley, Los Angeles, and London: Univ. of California Press, 1975), pp. 120–55.

Suggests that "Milton, in explaining the original causes of division and fragmentation in the created world, provides us with the ultimate mythic account of why dialectic comes to straiten men in their fallen state." Review (of book): Dennis B. Quinn, *JEGP*, 76, 1977, 131–34.

2683 McCanles, Michael. "Signs of Power and the Power of Signs in Milton's Last Poems." *SHR*, 17, 1983, 327–38.

Examines *Paradise Lost*, *Paradise Regained*, and *Samson Agonistes* to show that "Milton envisions physical power as possessing the potentiality both for parodying and perverting spiritual, divine power; and becoming its outward sign and manifestation. . . . The dialectic between these two potentialities parallels . . . another dialectic, that between invisible spiritual reality and outward, physical symbol of that reality."

2684 McCarthy, B. Eugene. "Defoe, Milton, and Heresy." *MiltonN*, 3, 1969, 71–73.

"Defoe's accusations against the theology of *Paradise Lost* are, thus, notable mainly because he was the first to label the epic unequivocally heretical, but also because his critical remarks on Milton's poetry have been so long ignored that a new look at some of his esoteric works casts light upon his own attitude of insistence upon scripturally founded orthodoxy and upon the attitude of his time toward Milton's epic."

2685 McCarty, Willard. "The Catabatic Structure of Satan's Quest." *UTQ*, 56, 1986–1987, 283–307.

Perceives Satan's fall into hell as Milton's attempt to parody the catabasis of the classical hero who "descends into death . . . but who bursts forth in glorious and revolutionary triumph."

2686 McChrystal, Deirdre. "Responses to 'Wrestling with the Angel.'" *MiltonQ*, 21, No. 3, 1987, 121–22.

A response to William Shullenberger (No. 3054). Emphasizes Eve's grace.

2687 McClung, William Alexander. "The Architectonics of *Paradise Lost*." *VIA 8*, 1986, 32–39.

Discusses the architecture of Pandemonium, *Paradise Lost*, and heaven. Believes that "Milton creates a physical universe of Art coequal and in harmonious tension with Nature."

2688 McClung, William A. "The Architecture of Pandaemonium." *MiltonQ*, 15, 1981, 109–12.

Suggests that the case against St. Peter's in Rome, as argued by Amy Lee Turner

(No. 49; *A Milton Encyclopedia* 1: 90–102) and Roland Mushat Frye (No. 620), will not stand up to close examination.

2689 McColley, Diane Kelsey. "'Daughter of God and Man': The Callings of Eve in *Paradise Lost*." Doctoral diss., Univ. of Illinois, Urbana, 1974. Abs., *DAI*, 35, 1975, 4438A–39A.

Challenges portrayals of Eve as weak and corruptible with Milton's presentation of her as "truly free and sufficient."

2690 McColley, Diane. "'Daughter of God and Man': The Subordination of Milton's Eve." *Familiar Colloquy: Essays Presented to Arthur Edward Barker*. Ed. by Patricia Brückmann (Toronto: Oberon Press, 1978), pp. 196–208.

Discusses Eve's subordination to Adam in *Paradise Lost* as a positive role resembling the subordination of the Son to the Father and of humanity to the Son. Suggests that "Eve's calling as Adam's meet help embodies a principle enacted throughout the poem: obedience to God and to those He calls to leadership gives each individual the largest possible scope for the development of his or her distinctive character and talents: this is the service which is perfect freedom."

2691 McColley, Diane. "Eve and the Arts of Eden." *Milton and the Idea of Woman*. Ed. by Julia M. Walker (Urbana and Chicago: Univ. of Illinois Press, 1988), pp. 100–19.

"I should like therefore to consider Eve's part in the arts of Eden, beginning with what I perceive as her role as the embodiment of Milton's defense—and, at her fall, his critique—of poesy." Abs., *MiltonQ*, 24, 1990, 151.

2692 McColley, Diane. "Eve's Dream." *MiltonS*, 12, 1978, 25–45.

Rejects the idea that Milton believed in a fortunate fall and that Eve's dream is a step toward the Fall. Rather, the dream "allows a growth in moral understanding and the proper use of fancy that might have proceeded in innocence; and their [Adam and Eve's] response to it prepares for the first steps in their regeneration." Review: Dayton Haskin, *Thought*, 56, 1981, 226–39.

2693 McColley, Diane Kelsey. "Free Will and Obedience in the Separation Scene of *Paradise Lost*." *SEL*, 12, 1972, 103–20.
Analyzes Milton's doctrine of free will, stating that Adam and Eve fell by choice, not by a tragic flaw. Further indicates that free will was merely the vehicle, not the cause, of their fall.

2694 McColley, Diane K. "The Iconography of Eden." *MiltonS*, 24, 1988, 107–21.
Discusses various illustrations of Genesis 3, particularly those from the seventeenth century.

2695 McColley, Diane Kelsey. *Milton's Eve*. Urbana: Univ. of Illinois Press, 1983. ix, 233pp.
"This study is an effort to extricate Eve from a reductive critical tradition, as Milton sought to extricate her from a reductive literary and iconographic tradition, and to establish a regenerative reading of her role: that is, to show that Milton has fashioned an Eve who . . . is a pattern and composition of active goodness and a speaking picture of the recreative power of poetry itself." Reviews: Rosamond Putzel, *LJ*, 108, 1983, 1364; Thelma Scott Kiser, *Sunday Independent* (Ashland, KY), Sept. 4, 1983, p. 43; Roy Flannagan, *MiltonQ*, 18, 1984, 32–34; Lachlan MacKinnon, *TLS*, Apr. 20, 1984, p. 438; *VQR*, 60, 1984, 7; Raymond B. Waddington, *RenQ*, 37, 1984, 672–74; Frederick J. Crosson, *Key Reporter*, Spring, 1985, p. 5; C. Duncan, *CLAJ*, 28, 1985, 357–60; G. R. Evans, *RES*, 36, 1985, 623; Carolyn Heilbrun, *JEGP*, 84, 1985, 110–13; Patrick G. Hogan, Jr., *SCJ*, 16, 1985, 383–84; Richard DuRocher, *SHR*, 19, 1985, 267.

2696 McColley, Diane Kelsey. "Shapes of Things Divine: Eve and Myth in *Paradise Lost*." *SCJ*, 9, 1978, 47–55.
Examines "Milton's habit of comparing Eve, even before the Fall, to such archetypal temptresses as Circe, Pandora and Venus or Ida . . . for their regenerative connotations."

2697 McColley, Diane. "Subsequent or Precedent? Eve as Milton's Defense of Poesie." *MiltonQ*, 20, 1986, 132–36.
Asserts that "Eve personifies poesy in her work, in the imagery associated with her, and in the method of her vocation." The Fall "represents the abuse of [this] poesy."

2698 McColley, Diane. "The Voice of the Destroyer in Adam's Diatribes." *MP*, 75, 1977, 18–28.
"Far from being Milton's 'own voice,' Adam's diatribes give tongue to the voice of 'our Destroyer' (4.749). They epitomize stale antifeminine commonplaces still lingering in Milton's lifetime, they are based on a dualistic *contemptus mundi* which Milton thought blasphemous, and they contradict his firm belief that true obedience requires freedom." Milton refutes these diatribes "both in the reasoning voice of his prose and in his representation of original and regenerate righteousness in *Paradise Lost*."

2699 McCown, Gary M. "Milton and the Epic Epithalamium." *MiltonS*, 5, 1973, 39–66.
"In *Paradise Lost* Milton alludes to conventions of the classical epithalamium both to praise the wedding of Adam and Eve and, ironically, to adumbrate its desecration." He develops traditions of the epic epithalamium to "elevate proper marital virtues." "Milton's version follows Christian humanists' qualifications of certain topics found in secular epithalamia."

2700 McCown, Gary. "Milton Recycled." *Teaching Milton to Undergraduates: Problems and Approaches*. Proceedings of the

Special Session (537), Annual Meeting of the Modern Language Association, Dec. 28, 1976. Comp. by Paul L. Gaston ([Edwardsville: Southern Illinois Univ.], n.d.), pp. 39–45.

Proposes teaching *Paradise Lost* early in a course and then returning to specific passages when studying different works for the remainder of the semester.

2701 McKee, John B. "Milton's *Paradise Lost*, IX, 952–959." *Expl*, 33, 1975, Item 48.

Asserts that Milton "feels that submerging the self too readily in another can be as harmful as selfish love."

2702 McLaren, John. "John Milton: The Poet as God." *CR*, 15, 1972, 23–28.

Asserts that Milton fails to achieve his purpose because he dramatizes God within his argument.

2703 McLaughlin, Agnes Veronica. "Time Symbols in *Paradise Lost* Reflecting Satan at Midnight and the Noon-Day Devil." *Horizontes*, 33–34, 1973–74, 127–39.

Focuses on those symbols that relate to "Satan at Midnight and the Noon-Day Devil which are central themes molding the epic into a temporal-eternal framework." Demonstrates that *Paradise Lost* "expresses an organic unity through John Milton's significant use of time symbols to beat out the cyclical rhythms of rise and fall throughout the epic."

2704 McLoone, George Hughes. "Contemplative Symbols in *Paradise Lost* and *Paradise Regained*." Doctoral diss., George Washington Univ., 1982. 339pp. Abs., *DAI*, 43, 1982, 810A–11A.

Discusses God's use of contemplative symbols—visual images such as the cosmos, the earth, and the human body—to help humans intuitively understand what is right, thereby forcing them to choose between obedience and rebellion.

2705 McManus, Hugh F. "The Pre-

existent Humanity of Christ in *Paradise Lost*." *SP*, 77, 1980, 271–82.

Suggests that in Book 5.603–15, "Milton has depicted the begetting of the human nature of Christ" and feels that this hypothesis may solve problems in interpreting the Messiah's offer to be mediator in Book 3.236–56, the presence of the Son at the creation of the angels, and the motives for Satan's rebellion.

2706 McMaster, Belle Miller. "'Accomplisht Eve': The Interrelation of Character, Tradition, and Structure in Milton's *Paradise Lost*." Doctoral diss., Univ. of Louisville, 1974. 283pp. Abs., *DAI*, 35, 1975, 7261A–62A.

Explains Milton's efforts to portray Eve as a balanced figure, free to make the right choice but responsible for making the wrong one.

2707 McQueen, William A. "'The Hateful Siege of Contraries': Satan's Interior Monologues in *Paradise Lost*." *MiltonQ*, 4, 1970, 60–65.

Examines the pattern and functions of Satan's interior monologues in Book 4, before the first view of paradise, and in Book 9, before the temptation. Suggests that they reveal a "hateful siege of contraries" operating on several levels: between Satan and the setting, between the juxtaposed characters of Satan and Adam and Eve, and within Satan himself. Concludes that the monologues dramatically represent the psychology of Satan's fall and foreshadow Adam and Eve's moral choice.

2708 McQueen, William. "*Paradise Lost* V, VI: The War in Heaven." *SP*, 71, 1974, 89–104.

Claims that the battle "is an enactment on a colossal scale of the analogous battle which Adam must fight against Satan ... within his own soul." Asserts that the war contrasts God's creative power with his destructive power.

2709 McQueen, William A. "Point of View

in *Paradise Lost*: Books I–IV." *RenP*, 1967, pp. 85–92.

Shows how Milton manipulates the point of view from hell to heaven to earth in order to "establish Satan as a serious adversary and at the same time assert God's omnipotence."

2710 McShane, James Arthur. "The Discerning Vision of *Paradise Lost*." Doctoral diss., Emory Univ., 1968. 504pp. Abs., *DA*, 29, 1968, 1515A–16A.

Defends *Paradise Lost*'s coherence, intelligence, and, especially, use of metaphor.

2711 Meadows, A. J. *The High Firmament: A Survey of Astronomy in English Literature*. Leicester: Leicester Univ. Press; New York: Humanities Press, 1969. xiii, 207pp.

Begins with the medieval universe and continues through the Victorian reaction. Contains many scattered references to Milton's universe in *Paradise Lost*.

2712 Melchior, Bonnie. "Teaching *Paradise Lost*: The Unfortunate Fall." *CollL*, 14, 1987, 76–84.

Sees most students as literary taxonomists instead of literate readers and suggests some strategies for dealing with them.

2713 Mengert, James Grant. "Modulation of Style in *Paradise Lost*." Doctoral diss., Yale Univ., 1972. 223pp. Abs., *DAI*, 33, 1972, 760A.

Investigates how Milton's modulations of style affect the ability of his words to sustain multiple meanings.

2714 Mengert, James G. "Styling the Strife of Glory: The War in Heaven." *MiltonS*, 14, 1980, 95–115.

Notes parallels between the War in Heaven and the wars of history and epic tradition but insists that the "strife of glory" phrase is Satan's, not the poet's, and that Milton ultimately exposes and refuses to endorse Satan's ambitions in Book 6.

2715 Merchant, Paul. *The Epic*. London: Methuen, 1971. viii, 103pp.

Examines the development of the epic

form. Believes that *Paradise Lost* is still read because of Milton's exact awareness of psychology and capacity for visual description.

2716 Merrill, Thomas. *Epic God-Talk: "Paradise Lost" and the Grammar of Religious Language*. Jefferson, NC, and London: McFarland and Co., 1986. 132pp.

Proposes that recent techniques of analyzing religious language can help revive the unspoken connections underlying *Paradise Lost* and deflate the secular aloofness which obscures the work that Milton wrote as a religious document. Review: P. J. Klemp, *MiltonQ*, 24, 1990, 71–76.

2717 Merrill, Thomas F. "Miltonic God-Talk: The Creation in *Paradise Lost*." *Lang&S*, 16, 1983, 296–312.

Explains how the semantic behavior of language is dictated by a commitment to a logical premise, especially the relationship between grammar and logic. Analyzes Raphael's account of the creation in *Paradise Lost* as a representative example of the religious dynamics of language, especially as a parallel to the language in Genesis.

2718 Merrill, Thomas F. "Milton's Satanic Parable." *ELH*, 50, 1983, 279–95.

"Satan, then, functions as an instrument of divine insight by providing Christian readers with a parabolic awareness of God's presence. Until book IX he is the only character with this capability."

2719 Merrill, Thomas F. "*Paradise Lost* and the Hazards of Semantic Idolatry." *NM*, 77, 1976, 387–410.

Advocates "a *religious* reading of *Paradise Lost*, one which recognizes that religious and literary claims are not always compatible," and shows that "many crucial *narrative* difficulties in the epic make compelling *religious* sense."

2720 Merton, Thomas. "Can We Survive Nihilism?" *SatR*, 50, April 15, 1967, pp. 16–19.

On the ultimate self-destructive tendencies of Milton's Satan. "Camus has shown in his study of revolt [*Myth of Sisyphus*] how this kind of nihilism has in fact entered into the very essence of all the modern power structures that now are in conflict."

2721 Meyers, Robert Rex. "Milton's *Paradise Lost*, IV, 401–08: Fierce Lions and Tigers in Paradise?" *MiltonQ*, 13, 1979, 126.

Finds that Satan's assuming the disguise of a postlapsarian lion and tiger is one of Milton's more interesting lapses "occasioned by a conflict between consistent theology and the need for realism in the narrative." Milton forgets "that he has told us moments before how utterly harmless these creatures were in Paradise." Rejoinder by Roberts W. French (No. 2253).

2722 Meyers, Robert R. "Was There a Toad in the Bower?" *MLQ*, 33, 1972, 37–43.

Argues that Milton did not put Satan into the shape of a toad in *Paradise Lost* 4.

2723 Miller, George. "Archetype and History: Narrative Technique in *Paradise Lost*, Books XI and XII." *MLS*, 10, 1980, 12–21.

Not only are "the dialectical exchange between Michael and Adam in Book XI and the summary paraphrase of biblical history in Book XII . . . discursive in form rather than dramatic," but they also embody a "general movement from the material to the spiritual, from the historical to the metaphoric, that forms the structure of Michael's prophecy."

2724 Miller, George Eric. "Didactic Form and Function in *Paradise Lost*." Doctoral diss., Univ. of Connecticut, 1970. 207pp. Abs., *DAI*, 31, 1970, 1283A.

Analyzes the process of moral instruction "as it is carried on in Raphael's narration of the War in Heaven in Book VI and in Michael's prophecy in Books XI–XII."

2725 Miller, George Eric. "Dismissive Comparisons as a Descriptive Technique in *Paradise Lost*." *NM*, 78, 1977, 57–61.

"Dismissive comparisons serve to remind the reader that normal descriptive techniques are not adequate in the pre-fall world for everything there is diverse from and greater than the experiential world."

2726 Miller, George E. "'Images of Matter': Narrative Manipulation in Book VI of *Paradise Lost*." *ArielE*, 11, 1980, 5–13.

Argues that "once Raphael's narration of the War begins in Book VI, it becomes increasingly difficult for the reader to respond to the War as being in any sense metaphoric or symbolic. The vehicle (epic warfare) serves to condition and confine our response. Everything in Raphael's narration of the War is confined within material 'limits.' The effect is intentional and not simply the result of the choice of the vehicle."

2727 Miller, George. "Milton's *Topothesias*: Some Rhetorical Aspects of Description in *Paradise Lost*." *CahiersE*, 16, 1979, 45–58.

Discusses Milton's rhetorical description of places in *Paradise Lost*—hell, Chaos, and paradise.

2728 Miller, George Eric. "Stylistic Rhetoric and the Language of God in *Paradise Lost*, Book III." *Lang&S*, 8, 1975, 111–26.

Analyzes God's speeches in Book 3 to show how Milton uses rhetorical figures to create a distinctly poetic style for his God, "a style which helps to foster the illusion of authority." Abs., *MiltonQ*, 12, 1978, 114.

2729 Miller, Leo. "On the Author, 12." *Expl*, 29, 1971, Item 52.

Shows that Milton's answer to Dryden that he might "tagge his verses" was not an original metaphor. The phrase had been used in a 1656 edition of Osborne's *Advice to a Son*.

2730 Miller, Leo. "'Siloa's Brook' in *Paradise Lost*: Another View." *MiltonQ*, 6, No. 3, 1972, 5–7.

Notes that Milton would not have found the form "Siloa" (*Paradise Lost* 1.11) in the versions of the Bible available to him and suggests Josephus as a likely source. Contends that a reference to the "Siloam pool" of John 9 is plausible but open to question. See No. 2633.

2731 Miller, Mark Crispin. "Beelzebub and Adam and 'The Worst that Can Be.'" *MiltonS*, 10, 1977, 65–76.

"Despite Hell's grand atmosphere and Milton's bold images of half-glorious, unspeakable menace in Books I and II of *Paradise Lost*, Satan's underlings seem too quickly mollified by his high words. . . . Satan is the poem's one truly terrifying figure, the only inmate who has a mind to match hell's 'floods and whirlwinds of tempestuous fire.'"

2732 Miller, Ronald Fiek. "Before the Fall: Five Judgments of *Paradise Lost*." Doctoral diss., Univ. of Connecticut, 1969. 231pp. Abs., *DAI*, 30, 1969, 730A.

Traces the reception of Milton's epic by using the criticism of Joseph Addison, Samuel Johnson, Samuel Taylor Coleridge, Walter Savage Landor, and Walter Raleigh.

2733 Mills, Jerry Leath. "Satan as Cormorant, *Paradise Lost*, IV, 196." *N&Q*, 17, 1970, 414–15.

Considers the cormorant simile as an ironic allusion to the outcome of Satan's mission in the fortunate fall.

2734 Milowicki, Edward, and **Rawdon Wilson.** "'Character' in *Paradise Lost*: Milton's Literary Formalism." *MiltonS*, 14, 1980, 75–94.

Discusses the interplay of character development in the epic. Demonstrates Milton's "remarkably original" characterization and pays special attention to Ovid's influence.

2735 Milward, Peter. "Milton's *Paradise Lost*." *The Meaning of English Master-* *pieces*. Ed. by Hideo Okamoto and Takao Suzuki (Tokyo: Kaibunsha, 1974), pp. 42–51.

Reviews Milton's career and concludes that in spite of his Puritanism, his sympathies ultimately are with Satan.

2736 Miner, Earl. "*Felix Culpa* in the Redemptive Order of *Paradise Lost*." *PQ*, 47, 1968, 43–54.

Believes "that there is a carefully calculated redemptive order in *Paradise Lost* inclusive of all God's angelic and human creatures."

2737 Miner, Earl. "Milton's Laws Divine and Human." *The Restoration Mode from Milton to Dryden* (Princeton, NJ: Princeton Univ. Press, 1974), pp. 198–268.

Focuses on *Paradise Lost* and *Paradise Regained*. Considers the dominant character of our experience as we read the poems and their relation to Milton's life and times. See also No. 3400. Reviews (of book): *MiltonQ*, 8, 1974, 116–17; Gerard Reedy, *Thought*, 50, 1975, 318–19; Robert Ellrodt, *EA*, 29, 1976, 219–21; William Myers, *RES*, 27, 1976, 75–77; Gary Stringer, *SHR*, 11, 1977, 311; Masa'aki Imanishi, *EigoS*, 120, 1975, 495–96.

2738 Miner, Earl. "The Reign of Narrative in *Paradise Lost*." *MiltonS*, 17, 1983, 3–25.

Explains why narrative rules over dramatic and lyric elements in *Paradise Lost*.

2739 Misek, Linda Douglas. "Computing a Context: Style, Structure, and the Self–Image of Satan in *Paradise Lost* (Volumes I and II)." Doctoral diss., Case Western Reserve Univ., 1972. 1180pp. Abs., *DAI*, 33, 1972, 281A–82A.

Explains Satan's ability to involve the reader in *Paradise Lost* and join disparate elements of the epic. Clarifies the effect of his goal—to exist independent of God—on his identity.

2740 Misek, Linda Douglas. *Context Concordance to John Milton's "Paradise Lost."* Cleveland, OH: Andrew R. Jennings

Computing Center, Press of Case Western Reserve Univ., 1971. 661pp.

"This Interactive Context Concordance presents not only the full text (no words omitted) of *Paradise Lost* with Key-Word-In-Context including upper/lower case and full punctuation, but also the communication situation relative to every usage: actual names and cycles for settings, speakers, and addresses. Linguistic data accompanies all entries in place, and separate Rank/Frequency and Synoptic Dictionaries conclude the volume." Reviews: Jason P. Rosenblatt, *CHum*, 7, 1973, 421–24; Edward R. Weismiller, *RenQ*, 27, 1974, 255–57.

2741 Miyanishi, Mitsuo. "On Milton's 'Paradise.'" *MCJ News*, 1, 1976, 7–8.

Argues that Milton believed paradise really existed in Eden, that it was not merely an Arcadian dreamland.

2742 "MLA Conference on Milton." *MiltonN*, 2, 1968, 5–6.

Reports on three tercentenary papers on *Paradise Lost* presented at the 1967 MLA Convention: Louis Martz, "'A Poem Written in Ten'" (see No. 820); Stanley Fish, "Discovery as Form in *Paradise Lost*" (see No. 2215); and B. Rajan, "The Providence of Style" (see No. 2901).

2743 Mollenkott, Virginia R. "Milton's Rejection of the Fortunate Fall." *MiltonQ*, 6, No. 1, 1972, 1–5.

"While he clearly demonstrates that a gracious God brings good out of evil by providing redemption, Milton suggests through Raphael that the alternative might have been even *more* glorious."

2744 Mollenkott, Virginia R. "Some Implications of Milton's Androgynous Muse." *BuR*, 24, No. 1, 1978, 27–36.

The heavenly muse of *Paradise Lost* 1 appears to be patriarchal, but its androgyny becomes evident in Book 7 when it is identified with the female figure of Urania.

2745 Mollenkott, Virginia R. "The Wheat, the Chaff, and the Aborted Duel." *CP*, 6, 1973, 38–43.

States that the functions of the aborted duel in *Paradise Lost* 4 are to foreshadow Satan's defeat; to stress God's omnipotence; and to symbolize the restraint the "warfaring Christian must practice as long as he is living in this world."

2746 Moore, Frank Harper. "Astraea, the Scorpion, and the Heavenly Scales." *ELH*, 38, 1971, 350–57.

Explains the symbolism of the three constellations mentioned in *Paradise Lost*: Astraea (Virgo) is used as a symbol for justice; the Scorpion (Scorpio) is a type of Satan and his serpentine sting; and the Scales (Libra) imply the weighing of consequences of the two courses of action open to Satan, and the weighing of Satan himself.

2747 Moore, Leslie Ellen. "Milton's Poetics of Redemption: Incarnation and Simile in *Paradise Lost* and *Paradise Regained*." Doctoral diss., Yale Univ., 1981. 257pp. Abs., *DAI*, 42, 1981, 2144A.

Argues that "a particular theological issue, the conflict between Incarnational redemption and sacrificial atonement, is connected to Milton's use of simile within the larger narrative of *Paradise Lost* and *Paradise Regained*."

2748 Morita, Katsumi. "Milton and the Perseverance of the Saints." *MCJ News*, 3, 1979, 8–9.

Abstract of paper presented. Uses Michael's speech in *Paradise Lost* 12.575–605 to show Milton's conditional definition of the perseverance of the saints.

2749 Morita, Katsumi. ["On Love in *Paradise Lost*."] *MCJ News*, 6, 1983, 22–24.

Believes that Adam fell because of his passion for Eve and that he is regenerated through a process of true love. Eve's line, "Forsake me not thus, Adam" (10.914), is the turning point in *Paradise Lost*. True love comes after Michael's instruction in the poem

(12.581–85): "This is godly love which is not dominated by passion."

2750 Morita, Katsumi. "The Role of the Son in *Paradise Lost*." *MCJ News*, 11, 1989, 17–18.

Abstract of a paper presented at the Twenty-Fourth Colloquium of MCJ in July, 1988. Contends that the Son plays a dual role in *Paradise Lost*: "the generation of the Son takes place in time as an execution of the Father's decree"; "the Son receives the divine attributes from the Father as gifts 'in accordance with the Father's decree and will.'"

2751 Morita, Katsumi. "The Theme of Hope in *Paradise Lost*." *MCJ News*, 1, 1976, 6–7.

Abstract of a paper presented at the First Colloquium of MCJ in July, 1976. Adam achieves hope in the epic's closing lines.

2752 Moritz-Siebeck, Berta. *Untersuchungen zu Miltons "Paradise Lost": Interpretation der beiden Schlüssbucher.* QFSK, 12. Berlin: Walter de Gruyter, 1963. vii, 275pp.

See Huckabay No. 1601. Reviews: Rainer Lengeler, *GGA*, 219, 1967, 242–54; J. P. Willems, *RLV*, 35, 1969, 102–04.

2753 Morris, Robert James. "An Enriching of Art: *Paradise Lost* and the Genre Question." Doctoral diss., Michigan State Univ., 1971. 223pp. Abs., *DAI*, 32, 1972, 5192A–93A.

Challenges the notion that *Paradise Lost* is an epic, exploring it as a "long narrative poem containing discrete epic and tragic-dramatic plots, each with an appropriate set of conventional attributes and each with its own hero."

2754 Morrison, Nan D. "The Third Council in *Paradise Lost*." *RenP*, 1976, pp. 51–59.

Regards the council between Adam and Eve in Book 10 as a parallel scene to the councils in Books 2 and 3 and as crucial to the epic's structure and theme of regeneration.

2755 Morsberger, Katharine M. "Darkness Visible: Imagination and Evil in *Paradise Lost*." *Odyssey*, 3, 1978, 3–12.

Studies the importance of the imaginative process in human redemption. "Since salvation is in the realm of the spirit, it is especially important for man to recognize the complexity of the imaginative process.... Imagination ranges from 'the devil's grand lurking place' to a pure vision of the Holy Spirit."

2756 Moseley, C. W. R. D. "A Note on Possible Acrostics in *Paradise Lost*." *N&Q*, 35, 1988, 162–63.

Suggests that Milton used acrostics in *Paradise Lost*. See Edward Jones, *N&Q*, 37, 1990, 288.

2757 Moyles, R. G. "Orthography and the Text of *Paradise Lost*: A Final, Final Word." *ESC*, 6, 1980, 1–12.

Shows "that [David] Masson was indeed correct when he suggested that the so-called emphatic spellings should be relegated to that list of spellings which need not be preserved."

2758 Moyles, R. G. *The Text of "Paradise Lost": A Study in Editorial Procedure.* Toronto, Buffalo, NY, and London: Univ. of Toronto Press, 1985. x, 188pp.

Examines "the textual and bibliographical state of *Paradise Lost*," including "a thorough description of the transmission of the text and its treatment at the hands" of various prominent editors during the past three centuries. Reviews: Roy Flannagan, *MiltonQ*, 19, 1985, 22–23; Claud A. Thompson, *ESC*, 12, 1986, 346–50.

2759 Mueller, Martin. "*Paradise Lost* and the *Iliad*." *CLS*, 6, 1969, 292–316.

Asserts that *Paradise Lost* fuses epic and tragic conventions and is structurally patterned after the *Iliad*. States that Milton created a Christian epic which revaluated classical heroic ideals.

2760 Mueller, Martin. "The Tragic Epic: *Paradise Lost* and the *Iliad*." *Children* *of Oedipus and Other Essays on the Imitation of Greek Tragedy, 1550–1800* (Toronto, Buffalo, NY, and London: Univ. of Toronto Press, 1980), pp. 213–30.

Discusses thematic "affinities which not only illuminate the principles of organization of *Paradise Lost* but also invite us to reconsider the nature of Milton's attitude towards the epic tradition."

2761 Mulder, John R. "'Ambiguous Words and Jealousies': A Secular Reading of *Paradise Lost.*" *MiltonS*, 13, 1979, 145–79.

Regards *Paradise Lost* as only incidentally a theological poem. Hypothesizes that the narrator's voice "is not identical with Milton but is rather the voice of a persona who illustrates the loss of paradise in his inspirations, his motives, his reasoning, and his counsel."

2762 Mulder, John R. "The Lyric Dimension of *Paradise Lost.*" *MiltonS*, 23, 1987, 145–63.

Suggests that *Paradise Lost* be read from the perspective of modern liberal theology. Argues that the alleged contradictions that the Romantics discovered in the epic are the result of Milton's understanding "the deconstructive possibilities of the arguments in his poem and [using] apparent contradictions for a purpose."

2763 Mulder, John R. *The Temple of the Mind: Education and Literary Taste in Seventeenth-Century England.* Pegasus Backgrounds in Literature. New York: Pegasus, 1969. x, 165pp.

Studies significant aspects of seventeenth-century education and includes Milton mainly in connection with *Paradise Lost.*

2764 Muldrow, George M. "Satan's Last Words: 'Full Bliss.'" *MiltonQ*, 14, 1980, 98–100.

Notes the irony of Satan's last two words in *Paradise Lost* 10.502–03. His bliss "is an insatiable energy which

ultimately finds no satisfaction and is self-defeating."

2765 Murakami, Shin. "A Study of Milton's Language in *Paradise Lost.*" *English Research Association of Hiroshima,* 5, 1967, 31–32.

In Japanese. Discusses the poem's repetitive language and recurrent structure.

2766 Murota, Goro. "On the Death in *Paradise Lost.*" *MCJ News,* 5, 1981, 13–14.

Abstract of a paper presented at the Ninth Colloquium of MCJ in July, 1980. On Adam and Eve's gradual realization that death will not be an instant experience for them after the Fall.

2767 Murray, Patrick. *Milton: The Modern Phase. A Study of Twentieth-Century Criticism.* London: Longmans; New York: Barnes and Noble, 1967. ix, 163pp.

See Huckabay No. 1614. Reviews: Gilbert Thomas, *English* (Oxford), 17, 1968, 58–59; Jonathan Price, *SCN*, 27, 1969, 27.

2768 Murray, Patrick. "Milton's Theology: A New Perspective." *Irish Ecclesiastical Record,* 3, 1968, 372–80.

Suggests that the heresies of the *Christian Doctrine* are obscured in *Paradise Lost* by the poem's artistry. The reader is thus free to choose the most amenable interpretation.

2769 Murrin, Michael. "The Language of Milton's Heaven." *MP*, 74, 1977, 350–65. Revised in *The Allegorical Epic: Essays in Its Rise and Decline* (Chicago, IL, and London: Univ. of Chicago Press, 1980), pp. 153–71.

Holds that because Milton was a literalist in his interpretation of Scripture, he did not allegorize the war of the angels in *Paradise Lost.* This choice signals the end of a tradition that began with attempts to allegorize the fighting of Homer's gods. Reviews (of book): Michael Lieb, *Cithara*, 21, 1981, 58–70; Foster Provost, *SpenN*, 12, 1981, 3–14.

2770 Murti, K. V. S. "Milton's Poetry: A

Symbol of Trinity (A Note with Special Reference to Book IX of *Paradise Lost*)." *BP*, 21, 1976, 41–56.

Argues that Milton's "three major works spring out of the self-same matrix, the poet's generative experience which is a symbol of Trinity."

2771 Musacchio, George Louis. "Fallible Perfection: The Motivation of the Fall in Reformation Theology and *Paradise Lost*." Doctoral diss., Univ. of California, Riverside, 1971. 239pp. Abs., *DAI*, 32, 1971, 2649A–50A.

Asserts the plausibility of the Fall by combining Adam and Eve's original righteousness with four kinds of innate fallibility: "(1) physical; (2) mental; (3) individual incompleteness; (4) the need to maintain temperance."

2772 Musacchio, George. *Milton's Adam and Eve: Fallible Perfection.* New York: Peter Lang, 1991. xii, 214pp.

Surveys the issue of the original righteousness in human nature, as discussed by the Reformers and by recent critics, and focuses on four episodes which foreshadow the act of sin. Concludes that Adam and Eve are not morally flawed by their creator. Review: Faye Pauli Whitaker, *C&L*, 41, 1992, 353–55.

2773 Mustazza, Leonard. "Meaning in an Interposed Scene: *Paradise Lost* 5.711–42." *MiltonQ*, 21, No. 1, 1987, 11–14.

Asserts that Milton promotes "his theodicean intent" by interposing the scene of the Father and Son's brief exchange within Raphael's account of the War in Heaven.

2774 Mustazza, Leonard. "'Such Prompt Eloquence': Language as Agency and Character in Milton's Epics." Doctoral diss., State Univ. of New York, Stony Brook, 1983. 246pp. Abs., *DAI*, 44, 1983, 1802A.

Argues that the language of Satan, Adam and Eve, God, and the Son reflects each character's internal developments and conflicts.

2775 Mustazza, Leonard. *"Such Prompt Eloquence": Language as Agency and Character in Milton's Epics.* Lewisburg, PA: Bucknell Univ. Press; London and Toronto: Associated Univ. Presses, 1988. 173pp.

Studies Satanic language, human language, and divine language in *Paradise Lost* and *Paradise Regained.* Shows that "the two epics are really of a piece, the later poem merely amplifying the larger contest between good and evil words that is evident in the larger epic." Reviews: Rachel Trubowitz, *SCN*, 47, 1989, 35–36; P. J. Klemp, *MiltonQ*, 24, 1990, 71–76; Thomas H. Blackburn, *RES*, 42, 1991, 113–14.

2776 Mustazza, Leonard. "'To Hear New Utterance Flow': Language before the Fall in *Paradise Lost*." *CLAJ*, 30, 1986, 184–209.

Examines Edenic language, both verbal and nonverbal, in *Paradise Lost*, especially the language/mode of communication of Adam and Eve, Raphael, and Satan. Discusses how Milton uses language to establish a sense of knowledge, innocence, and authority. Claims that language after the Fall must become increasingly necessary because God and the angels have grown silent.

2777 Muto, Susan Annette. "The Symbolism of Evil: A Hermeneutic Approach to Milton's *Paradise Lost*." Doctoral diss., Univ. of Pittsburgh, 1970. 221pp. Abs., *DAI*, 31, 1971, 6561A–62A.

Asserts that Milton centers "his hermeneutics of evil within the Adamic myth," as it is defined in Paul Ricoeur's *Symbolism of Evil.*

2778 Mutschmann, Heinrich. *Further Studies Concerning the Origin of "Paradise Lost".* Folcroft, PA: Folcroft Library Editions, 1977; Norwood, PA: Norwood Editions, 1979.

Reprints of Huckabay No. 1617, originally published in 1934.

2779 Mutschmann, Heinrich. *Studies*

Concerning the Origin of "Paradise Lost."
New York: Haskell House, 1971.
> Reprint of Stevens No. 987, originally published in 1924.

2780 Nagel, Alan Frederick. "An Approach to the Narrator of *Paradise Lost.*" Doctoral diss., Cornell Univ., 1969. 185pp. Abs., *DAI*, 30, 1970, 3951A.
> Uses analogies between the narrator's language and that of major characters to explore Milton's idea of a right relationship with God.

2781 Nakayama, Osamu. "The Ceres Simile—Milton's Disjunctive Simile." *MCJ News*, 8, 1985, 12–13.
> Abstract of paper presented. Argues that *Paradise Lost* 4.268–72 includes an ancient iconographic motif, the rape of Proserpina. In this typological pattern, Ceres is associated with Christ and Proserpina with humanity.

2782 Nakayama, Osamu. "'Fairest Fruit and Humid Bow': Milton's Epic Simile and Conception of Time in *Paradise Lost.*" *Poetry and Faith in the English Renaissance.* Ed. by Peter Milward and others (Tokyo: Renaissance Institute, Sophia Univ., 1987), pp. 151–59.
> Uses *Paradise Lost* 4.146–52 to show that Milton's similes reveal "significant moments . . . when God's eternal providence is present even in our postlapsarian world." Focuses on the words "fruit" and "rainbow."

2783 Nakayama, Osamu. "Time in Eden." *MCJ News*, 9, 1987, 20–21.
> Abstract of a paper presented at the Nineteenth Colloquium of MCJ in July, 1985. Delineates Milton's treatment of time and time imagery in *Paradise Lost.* Views the Fall as the destroyer of cyclical time.

2784 Nardo, A. K. "The Submerged Sonnet as Lyric Moment in Miltonic Epic." *Genre*, 9, 1976, 21–35.
> Claims that Milton used many sonnet-like lyrics in *Paradise Lost*, some of which are reminiscent of his sonnets.

2785 Nash, Victor Thomas. "The Other Satan: A Study of the Watcher Devil in Patristics, Folklore, and English Literature." Doctoral diss., Univ. of Oregon, 1977. 217pp. Abs., *DAI*, 38, 1977, 3459A.
> Traces the "folkloristic and pseudigraphical" origins of the watcher devil to his appearance in "three works of English literature: the Caedmonian *Genesis B*, Milton's *Paradise Lost*, and Byron's *Heaven and Earth.*"

2786 Nelson, Alfred L., and **Robert Brainard Pearsall.** "Milton Invents a Matron." *AN&Q*, 11, 1972, 20–22.
> Writing of Belial's sons, Milton uses "exposed a Matron" in *Paradise Lost* 1.505 to express dramatic intensity. The use of the word "matron" creates shock and dismay, as the word "concubine" would not have because concubines had a lower status than matrons in Genesis and in Judges, the sources of Milton's passage.

2787 Nelson, Byron. "Milton's Son of God and the Aristotelian Ideal of Magnanimity." *BWVACET*, 1, 1974, 22–39.
> Uses Aristotle's definition of magnanimity, as modified by the Catholic, Protestant, and Neoplatonist traditions, to conclude that "the career of the Son of God is the story of martial prowess, in which the Son of God far outstrips his epic competitors by his bravery and strength; . . . the whole of the story is marked by a fortitude and compassion . . . unmatched elsewhere in epic literature."

2788 Neves da Silva, Rosa Maria. "Adam and Eve: Actors?" *EAA*, 3–4, 1979–80, 31–43.
> Sees Adam and Eve as actors whom Milton manipulates in order to perform the roles he wanted to have in life.

2789 Newman, Robert D. "Entanglement in Paradise: Eve's Hair and the Reader's Anxiety in *Paradise Lost.*" *IJIAC*, 16, 1985, 112–15.
> Cites instances of Milton's use of the word "hair" in the poem, especially as they apply to Eve. "While evoking a

remarkably appealing sense of sensuality and femininity through his depiction of Eve's hair, Milton manages to load his description with terms that, taken independently, elicit a response that is certainly disconcerting."

2790 Newmeyer, Edna. "The Language of a 'Butchers Stall': Wordsworth on Milton's Description of Abel's Sacrifice." *MiltonQ*, 8, 1974, 69–72.

On Wordsworth's criticism of the language of *Paradise Lost* 11.429–43. Shows that the Bible contains the details of Abel's sacrifice and that "Milton accommodated Biblical language to contemporary taste and sensibility."

2791 Newton, J. M. "A Speculation about Landscape." *CQ*, 4, 1969, 273–82.

On Milton's use of images of height and erectness in his descriptions of paradise.

2792 Nicolson, Marjorie. "Milton and the Telescope." *Critical Essays on Milton from "ELH"* (Baltimore, MD, and London: Johns Hopkins Press, 1969), pp. 15–45.

Reprint of Huckabay No. 1626, originally published in 1935.

2793 Nieman, Lawrence J. "The Justness of Milton's Heaven." *LHR*, 10, 1968, 7–16.

Books 3–5 of *Paradise Lost* address the "*central* question of the justness of the universe—telescoped into the justness of Heaven." Concludes that "if one would refrain from interpreting the action solely from Satan's point of view, the legitimacy of God's just rule over the angels and man could be accepted unconditionally."

2794 Nimis, Stephen Albert. "The Epic Simile from Homer to Milton." Doctoral diss., Univ. of Minnesota, 1981. 269pp. Abs., *DAI*, 42, 1982, 4442A–43A.

Examines the epic simile as it affects "the modes of text production" in Homer, Virgil, Dante, and Milton.

2795 Nobumori, Hiromitsu. "Ariosto's Influence on Milton." *MCJ News*, 3, 1979, 24–26.

Abstract of paper presented. Discusses Milton's fondness for Ariosto and suggests that he might have been influenced by the epic structure of the *Orlando Furioso*.

2796 Noda, Motoko. "*Paradise Lost* as a Christian Apologetic—Centering around Restorative Motif—The Son as Pantokrator." *MCJ News*, 5, 1981, 10–12.

Abstract of paper presented. Argues that Milton describes the Son as a divine Christ in heaven, not with the bloody image of him on the cross, and that this is consistent with Protestantism and Puritanism.

2797 Nohrnberg, James. "Comparative Epic and Epic Comparison in *Paradise Lost*." *MiltonQ*, 14, 1980, 72.

Abstract of a paper presented at the 1979 MLA Convention. Relates the various kinds of epics to *Paradise Lost*.

2798 Norford, Don Parry. "The Devouring Father in *Paradise Lost*." *HUSL*, 8, 1980, 98–126.

Argues that Satan's rebellion is analogous to the father-son relationships among Uranus, Cronus, and Zeus.

2799 Norford, Don Parry. "'My Other Half': The Coincidence of Opposites in *Paradise Lost*." *MLQ*, 36, 1975, 21–53.

Believes that the relationship between several pairs of opposites—male and female, spirit and matter, good and evil—parallels the Platonic notion that the shadows were as necessary to the sun of the intellectual heavens as the sun to the shadows. Abs., *SCN*, 38, 1980, 20.

2800 Norford, Don Parry. "The Separation of the World Parents in *Paradise Lost*." *MiltonS*, 12, 1978, 3–24.

Deals with the universal myth of the separation of the world parents and maintains that Eve is a creative principle in *Paradise Lost* because "her act generates time and the evolution of consciousness through the movement of history." Believes that "For Milton, woman was and ever remained a snare and delusion." Abs., *MiltonQ*, 12, 1978, 47–48.

2801 North, Michael. "Expressing the Spirit: The Significance of Certain Repetitions in *Paradise Lost*." *ELWIU*, 7, 1980, 167–78.

Shows that the repetition of words by Adam and Raphael and then Adam and Michael refines Adam's understanding and furthers his education. Language and action come together when Adam and Eve repent.

2802 Northrop, Douglas A. "The Double Structure of *Paradise Lost*." *MiltonS*, 12, 1979, 75–90.

Combines sequential and geometric analyses by considering the double perspectives of time and eternity. Insists that the two views always interact, clarifying and enriching each other.

2803 Northrup, Mark D. "Milton's Hesiodic Cosmology." *CL*, 33, 1981, 305–20.

Believes that Milton's source of the "nethermost . . . Realm" in *Paradise Lost* 2.968–72 is Hesiod's *Theogony* instead of Plato and the Neoplatonists.

2804 Norton-Smith, John. "Virgil's Influence on Milton's Similes." *Virgil in a Cultural Tradition: Essays To Celebrate the Bimillenium*. Ed. by Richard A. Cardwell and Janet Hamilton (Nottingham: Univ. of Nottingham, 1986), pp. 106–14.

Discusses the function of the similes in the *Aeneid* and argues that "All of Milton's similes may be analysed in accordance with the principles of Virgilian poetic invention, and all will yield the same exactitude of symbolic expressiveness."

2805 Nuttall, A. D. *"Paradise Lost."* Over-heard by God: Fiction and Prayer in Herbert, Milton, Dante and St. John (London and New York: Methuen, 1980), pp. 83–111.

Argues that Milton chooses a story that espouses Satan's cause, and the God of *Paradise Lost* ends up being inde-

fensible. Reviews (of book): Sidney Gottlieb, *MiltonQ*, 15, 1981, 103–05; C. H. Cissen, *TLS*, Apr. 24, 1981, p. 458; Virginia R. Mollenkott, *JEGP*, 81, 1982, 418–21; Helen Wilcox, *N&Q*, 29, 1982, 169–71; Rebecca S. Beal, *C&L*, 31, 1982, 67–70.

2806 Nye, Peter. "On *Paradise Lost*." *Spectrum* (Univ. of California, Santa Barbara), 21, 1979, 101–12.

Points out many instances of the poet's commentary as the poem progresses: "Milton is constantly stepping back from the events he's relating to praise or celebrate, lament or blame—to point out larger significances and make you aware of moral points."

2807 Nyquist, Mary. "Fallen Differences, Phallogocentric Discourses: Losing *Paradise Lost* to History." *Post-Structuralism and the Question of History*. Ed. by Derek Attridge and others (Cambridge: Cambridge Univ. Press, 1987), pp. 212–43.

Deals with the misinterpretations of *Paradise Lost* 9.1059–63, when Adam and Eve awake after their first fallen lovemaking. Argues that Milton's relations with his wives is present in his works and that he was a misogynist.

2808 Nyquist, Mary. "The Father's Word/ Satan's Wrath." *PMLA*, 100, 1985, 187–202.

In both *Paradise Lost* and *Paradise Regained*, the Father's revelation of his Son (his Word) "initiates a new order and in both has the immediate effect of inciting Satan, another Son, to rebellion."

2809 Nyquist, Mary. "The Genesis of Gendered Subjectivity in the Divorce Tracts and in *Paradise Lost*." *Re-membering Milton: Essays on the Texts and Traditions*. Ed. by Nyquist and Margaret W. Ferguson (New York and London: Methuen, 1987), pp. 99–127.

Discusses Milton's combining the two accounts of creation in Genesis 1 and 2. Sees his view of marriage as masculine and radically bourgeois.

2810 Nyquist, Mary. "Gynesis, Genesis, Exegesis, and the Formation of Milton's Eve." *Cannibals, Witches, and Divorce: Estranging the Renaissance*. Selected Papers from the English Institute, 1985. Ed. by Marjorie Garber (Baltimore, MD, and London: Johns Hopkins Univ. Press, 1987), pp. 147–208.

Argues that Milton gives the J text in Genesis priority over the P text. In *Paradise Lost*, he develops a patriarchal bourgeois society. Adam articulates the doctrine of marriage in his soliloquy in Book 8, but in Book 4 Eve's speech about her first experiences acts out its discipline.

2811 Nyquist, Mary. "Reading the Fall: Discourse in Drama in *Paradise Lost*." *ELR*, 14, 1984, 199–229.

Analyzes the theological, social, and psychological implications of the Fall in *Paradise Lost*. Focuses on Adam and Eve's prelapsarian psychosocial development.

2812 Nyquist, Mary Ellen. "The Temptation against the Word in Reformation Theology and in Milton's *Paradise Lost* and *Paradise Regained*." Doctoral diss., Univ. of Toronto, 1978. Abs., *DAI*, 40, 1979, 274A.

Contrasts the Reformation view that the Fall involves "dualism of faith and unbelief in the Word" with Augustinian thought, especially as it affects *Paradise Lost* and *Paradise Regained*.

2813 Nyquist, Mary. "Textual Overlapping and Dalilah's Harlot-Lap." *Literary Theory/Renaissance Texts*. Ed. by Patricia Parker and David Quint (Baltimore, MD, and London: Johns Hopkins Univ. Press, 1986), pp. 341–72.

Believes that modern patriarchal critics have misread the Samson simile in *Paradise Lost* 9.1059–62.

2814 Obertino, James Russell, Jr. "The Political Vision of *Paradise Lost*: Milton's Use of the Two Cities." Doctoral diss., Univ. of Illinois, Urbana, 1975. 163pp. Abs., *DAI*, 36, 1975, 2852A.

Relates "Milton's use of the Augustinian model of the two cities" to "the conflict between heaven and hell in *Paradise Lost*."

2815 O'Brien, Robert J. "Name Calling and the Dissolution of the Marriage of Adam and Eve." *BWVACET*, 2, 1975, 32–44.

Examines the pre- and postlapsarian epithets of address and suggests that their absence after the Fall stands as a clear signal "of the divinely ordained personal relationship collapsing as a result of rebellion against God."

2816 Ochi, Fumio. "Gleanings from Milton." *MCJ News*, 9, 1987, 32–33.

Abstract of a paper presented at the Twenty-Second Colloquium of MCJ in December, 1986. Argues that in *Paradise Lost* 4.758–59, Milton's technique of changing plural personal pronouns into singular ones parallels "a delicate shift of impersonal restraint toward personal liberation of emotion in the poet's mind." In *Comus* 375–80, Wisdom's "birdshape" alludes to Pallas Athene's owl.

2817 Ogden, James. "Milton's Ideal of Innocence." *CritQ*, 24, 1982, 17–23.

Compares Dryden's and Milton's concepts of innocence. To grasp Milton's theology of innocence, readers should consider *Paradise Lost* not as historical but as idyllic.

2818 Ogilvy, James Angus. "Visions of God: Accommodation and the Reader in the Epics of Homer, Virgil, Vida and Milton." Doctoral diss., Univ. of Toronto, 1978. Abs., *DAI*, 40, 1979, 239A.

Asserts that each of the four poets "shows the gods to be ineffable, yet attempts so to manipulate the language of his poem as to carry the reader beyond the literal meaning to a vision greater than can be given by direct statement."

2819 Ogoshi, Kazuso. *Kami takuma tono Aida de*. Kyoto: Aporonsha, 1971. 289pp.

Analyzes *Paradise Lost*.

2820 Ohinata, Gen. "Book X of *Paradise Lost*." *MCJ News*, 6, 1983, 27–28.

Abstract of a paper presented at the Thirteenth Colloquium of MCJ in July, 1982. Points out that almost all of the poem's characters make appearances in this book, which also contains a diversity of settings.

2821 Ohinata, Gen. "Hesitation and Retrogression in *Paradise Lost*." *Kwansei Gakuin University Annual Studies*, 30, 1981, 49–55.

"In *Paradise Lost* Milton tries to delay the progression toward the Fall through motifs and images of hesitation and retrogression."

2822 Ohinata, Gen. "The New Heaven and New Earth." *MCJ News*, 10, 1988, 4–6.

Studies Milton's references to the new heaven and new earth in *Paradise Lost*, focusing on the revelation of this future event to Adam and the poet's longing for the end of time.

2823 Ohinata, Gen. *Shiturakuen No Sekai*. Tokyo: Sougen, 1987. 340pp.

The World of "Paradise Lost."

2824 O'Keeffe, Timothy J. "An Analogue to Milton's 'Sin' and More on the Tradition." *MiltonQ*, 5, 1971, 74–77.

Points out an analogue to Milton's Sin in the portrayal of Lechery in the *Famous and Renowned History of Morindos a King of Spain*, an anonymous piece of seventeenth-century short fiction. Comments on Milton's theological intentions and on the "long and richly developed tradition" to which both allegories belong.

2825 Ong, Walter J., Jr. "Milton's Logic and the Evolution of Epic Consciousness." *MiltonQ*, 8, 1974, 26.

Abstract of a paper presented at the 1973 MLA Convention. "In *Paradise Lost* the knowledge storage and retrieval traditions of the old oral epic and of Ramist logical 'method' meet."

2826 Ong, Walter J., S. J. "Milton's Logical Epic and Evolving Consciousness." *PAPS*, 120, 1976, 295–305. Reprinted in *Interfaces of the Word: Studies in the Evolution of Consciousness and Culture* (Ithaca, NY: Cornell Univ. Press, 1977), pp. 189–212.

"*Paradise Lost* is no longer strongly formulaic in the old conventional way, it is controlled by the noetic economy of the old-style epic hardly at all and its structure is shaped not by communal forces but by a logic which its author has reflectively appropriated and interiorized."

2827 Onishi, Naoki. "Paradise Within in *Paradise Lost*." *MCJ News*, 3, 1979, 22–24.

Abstract of paper presented. Adam and Eve's belief in the promise of the second Adam, "together with the happy memories of the prelapsarian life, constitute the new 'paradise within.'"

2828 Orchard, Thomas N. *The Astronomy of Milton's "Paradise Lost."* New York: Haskell House, 1969.

Reprint of Stevens No. 939, originally published in 1896.

2829 Osler, Alan. "John Marchant's Lectures on *Paradise Lost*." *MiltonQ*, 20, 1986, 52–53.

Discusses an announcement of a public lecture on *Paradise Lost* in 1758, the identity of the lecturer, and the nature of public lectures in the historical context.

2830 Otten, Charlotte. "Homer's Moly and Milton's Rue." *HLQ*, 33, 1970, 361–72.

Examines the rue, euphrasie, and water of *Paradise Lost* 11.411–22. Connects rue with the Homeric tradition and surveys its treatment in Renaissance herbals.

2831 Otten, C. F. "Milton's Myrtles." *EIC*, 24, 1974, 105.

Points out that Milton refers to the small dark tree five times in *Paradise Lost* and that botanic information is more valid than poetic precedent in this instance.

2832 Otten, Charlotte F. "'My Native Element': Milton's Paradise and English

Gardens." *MiltonS*, 5, 1973, 249–67.

"It is Milton's willingness to incorporate in his 'delicious Paradise' some of the features of the actual garden of his day and the practices of contemporary gardeners that makes him able to bridge the gap between the mythical and the real, between Art and Nature."

2833 Palmer, Kenneth. *English Renaissance Literature: Introductory Lectures.* By Frank Kermode, Stephen Fender, and Palmer. London: Gray-Mills Publishing, 1974. 151pp.

Contains the following essays by Palmer on *Paradise Lost*:

"A Few General Notes on the Heroic Poem," pp. 113–17.

Traces the development of a national language and heroic poetry. Discusses the universality of *Paradise Lost* and Milton's choice of sacred history for his epic.

"Milton: *Paradise Lost* I," pp. 96–100.

Discusses Milton the man, his background, beliefs, and attitudes, showing him to be the "traditional, elevated, Orphic poet."

"Milton: *Paradise Lost* II," pp. 101–07.

Examines the garden's change after the Fall. Adam and Eve experience a similar change and move from the first week of the creation down to the seventeenth century in a few seconds.

"Milton: *Paradise Lost* III," pp. 108–12.

Analyzes the function of myth in creating the image of the unfallen paradise for postlapsarian readers and the function and flow of space and time— all places and times seen at once—in the structure of *Paradise Lost*.

2834 "Paradise Lost Dramatization." *MiltonQ*, 8, 1974, 121.

Report on a reading of *Paradise Lost* on November 17, 1974, at the Theatre Royal in York, England. Sir John Gielgud appeared as Milton.

2835 Parfitt, George. "Milton and Epic." *English Poetry of the Seventeenth Century* (New York: Longman, 1985), pp. 183–98.

Believes that *Paradise Lost* presents issues "which bear powerfully on the seventeenth century," including chances missed, the pathos of failure, the heroism of resistance, the dignity of choice, and the wonder of experience. Notes that Milton's work "provides the last truly important achievement in epic of the seventeenth century." Review (of book): Achsah Guibbory, *MLR*, 83, 1988, 671–72.

2836 Parish, John E. "Milton and the Well-Fed Angel." *EM*, 18, 1967, 87–109.

"In examining the episode of Raphael's visit with Adam and Eve, I shall show how much of its charm derives from subtle allusions to the familiar stories, biblical and classical, of heavenly visitors on earth, stories which all stress the exemplary hospitality of the mortals honored by such celestial guests."

2837 Parker, David. "The Love Poems of *Paradise Lost* and the Petrarchan Tradition." *ArielE*, 3, 1972, 34–43.

Cites *Paradise Lost* 4.641–56 and 8.546–59 as passages that may be read as independent love poems. Contends that "the love poems of *Paradise Lost* contain certain tensions, betray certain inclinations, that tend to subvert orthodox Petrarchan attitudes. These are best seen when we compare the passages from *Paradise Lost* with Elizabethan poems on similar themes."

2838 Parker, Gillian. "Aspects of the Millenarian Tradition in England—A Preface to *Paradise Lost*." *MiltonQ*, 11, 1977, 60.

Abstract of a paper presented at the 1976 MLA Convention. In *Paradise Lost*, the "English Revolution was a re-enactment of the Civil War in Heaven, itself a prefiguring of the Apocalypse. After Christ's victory, the earthly kingdom, the millenium, would be established."

2839 Parker, Gillian Edith. "I. The Loss of the Millennium: *Paradise Lost* and the English Revolution. II. Patterns of Duality in Defoe's Narratives: *Robinson Crusoe* and *A Journal of the Plague Year.* III. Lineage and History in *Tess of the D'Urbervilles.*" Doctoral diss., Rutgers Univ., 1977. 302pp.
See *DAI*, 38, 1978, 6747A.

2840 Parker, Lois Wilson. "The Muse of *Paradise Lost*: The Holy Spirit." Doctoral diss., Southern Illinois Univ., 1970. 173pp. Abs., *DAI*, 31, 1971, 5371A.
Argues that the muse of *Paradise Lost* is the Holy Spirit, that "only this muse informs the entire poem, and that she does so by her capacities for illumination, edification, and harmony."

2841 Parker, Lois Wilson. *Not Too Easy Won: Milton's Muse.* East Meadow, NY: English Studies Collections, 1977. 49pp.
Identifies the muse as the Holy Spirit.

2842 Parker, Patricia. "Eve, Evening, and the Labor of Reading in *Paradise Lost.*" *ELR*, 9, 1979, 319–42.
Discusses the various evenings in *Paradise Lost.* "Dwelling on the twilight space of creation or created figure is clearly in Milton part of the lesson of patience, of submission to the discipline of time or temperance, in contrast to the apocalyptic impulse in its Satanic form." Abs., *MiltonQ*, 17, 1983, 55.

2843 Parker, Patricia A. "Milton." *Inescapable Romance: Studies in the Poetics of a Mode* (Princeton, NJ: Princeton Univ. Press, 1979), pp. 114–58.
Believes that Milton rejects the romance genre. Discusses "the interval in which Eve reflects upon her own image in the pool, and the extension of the implications of that interval to Book IV's temporal image of suspension, the realm of evening or twilight, poised between the Either-Or of darkness and light."

2844 Paterson, James. *A Complete Commentary with Etymological, Explanatory, Critical and Classical Notes on Milton's*

Paradise Lost." Ann Arbor, MI: Univ. Microfilms International, 1980 Books on Demand Reprints.
Originally published in 1744.

2845 Paterson, L. "Satan and Lucifer: A Comparison of Their Metamorphoses from Angel to Devil in Milton's *Paradise Lost* and Vondel's *Lucifer* and *Adam in Ballingschap.*" M.A. Thesis, Rhodes Univ., 1979.

2846 Patrick, J. Max. "A Reconsideration of the Fall of Eve." *EA*, 28, 1975, 15–21.
"In short, Eve was not obliged to fall by her nature or by any inferiority or by preconditioning. Milton invented and arranged her story to demonstrate that she had sufficient warning and understanding, knowledge and experience, sophistication and reasoning power to have stood against the temptation." Abs., *MiltonQ*, 12, 1978, 114.

2847 Patrick, John M. *Milton's Conception of Sin as Developed in "Paradise Lost."* Philadelphia, PA: R. West, 1978.
Reprint of Huckabay No. 1651, originally published in 1960.

2848 Patrides, C. A., ed. *Approaches to "Paradise Lost."* The York Tercentenary Lectures. London: Edward Arnold; Toronto: Univ. of Toronto Press, 1968. xii, 265pp.
Includes essays by John Arthos, J. B. Broadbent, Philip Brockbank, Bernard Harris, Merritt Y. Hughes, Frank L. Huntley, Brian Morris, F. T. Prince, Mary Ann Radzinowicz, Irene Samuel, T. J. B. Spencer, Joseph H. Summers, and J. B. Trapp. This bibliography lists each essay according to author. Reviews: Watson Kirkconnell, *DR*, 49, 1969, 549–56; James H. Sims, *SCN*, 27, 1969, 66; *TLS*, Apr. 17, 1969, p. 406, Margaret Dalziel, *AUMLA*, 33, 1970, 119–21; Robert W. Ayers, *RenQ*, 23, 1970, 339–42; Rosalie L. Colie, *CanL*, 52, 1972, 99–102; Michael Fixler, *RES*, 21, 1970, 358–61.

2849 Patrides, C. A. "The Godhead in

Paradise Lost: Dogma or Drama?" *Bright Essence: Studies in Milton's Theology.* By W. B. Hunter, Patrides, and J. H. Adamson (Salt Lake City: Univ. of Utah Press, 1971), pp. 71–77.

Reprint of Huckabay No. 1655, originally published in 1965.

2850 Patrides, C. A. "Milton and the Arian Controversy; or, Some Reflexions on Contextual Settings and the Experience of Deuteroscopy." *PAPS*, 120, 1976, 245–52.

Rather than being an Arian document, "*Paradise Lost* resists our efforts to regard the limited literal dimension, and constantly invites us to behold the entire design." To equate the ideas of the *Christian Doctrine* with those of *Paradise Lost* "would be to endorse the dangerous premise that 'grammatical similarity means logical kinship.'"

2851 Patrides, C. A., ed. *Milton's Epic Poetry: Essays on "Paradise Lost" and "Paradise Regained."* Harmondsworth: Penguin, 1967. 428pp.

See Huckabay No. 1660. Reviews: *MiltonN*, 2, 1968, 9–10; John R. Mulder, *SCN*, 28, 1970, 3.

2852 Patrides, C. A. "*Paradise Lost* and the Language of Theology." *Bright Essence: Studies in Milton's Theology.* By W. B. Hunter, Patrides, and J. H. Adamson (Salt Lake City: Univ. of Utah Press, 1971), pp. 165–78.

Reprint of Huckabay Nos. 819 and 1661, originally published in 1967.

2853 Patrides, C. A. "*Paradise Lost* and the Theory of Accommodation." *Bright Essence: Studies in Milton's Theology.* By W. B. Hunter, Patrides, and J. H. Adamson (Salt Lake City: Univ. of Utah Press, 1971), pp. 159–63.

Reprint of Huckabay No. 1663, originally published in 1963.

2854 Patrides, C. A. "'Something Like Prophetic Strain': Apocalyptic Configurations in Milton." *ELN*, 19, 1982, 193–207. Reprinted in *The Apocalypse in English Renaissance Thought and Litera-*

ture. Ed. by Patrides and Joseph Wittreich (Ithaca, NY: Cornell Univ. Press, 1984), pp. 207–37.

Contends that, while we can exaggerate the impact of the Apocalypse on *Paradise Lost*, "it is also possible to underestimate it much."

2855 Patterson, Lee W. "'Rapt With Pleasaunce': Vision and Narration in the Epic." *ELH*, 48, 1981, 455–75.

Examines several instances of the entranced gaze on a significant image in medieval and Renaissance literature, including Satan's contemplation of Eve in *Paradise Lost*.

2856 Pavlock, Barbara Rose. "Epic and Romance: *Genera Mixta* in Vergil, Ovid, Ariosto, and Milton." Doctoral diss., Cornell Univ., 1977. 168pp. Abs., *DAI*, 38, 1978, 4148A.

Links the *Aeneid*, *Heroides*, *Orlando Furioso*, and *Paradise Lost* through the use of antiromantic irony, themes of madness, literary imitation, and relationships between the author and his characters.

2857 Pearce, Zachary. *A Review of the Text of "Paradise Lost."* Ann Arbor, MI: Univ. Microfilms International, 1980 Books on Demand Reprints.

Originally published in 1732–33.

2858 Pebworth, Ted-Larry. "*Paradise Lost* and Freshman Composition." *CEA Forum*, 19, 1989, 10–12.

Recounts the decision to change his freshman composition text from an essay anthology to an edition of Milton's poems. Asserts that the focus on the text and the use of literature improved the course's structure and increased the students' enthusiasm.

2859 Pecheux, Sister M. Christopher. "The Council Scenes in *Paradise Lost*." *Milton and Scriptural Tradition: The Bible into Poetry.* Ed. by James H. Sims and Leland Ryken (Columbia: Univ. of Missouri Press, 1984), pp. 82–103.

Asserts that Milton's divine and demonic council scenes are influenced by both classical references and Scripture. Abs., *MiltonQ*, 15, 1981, 28–29.

2860 Pecheux, Mother M. Christopher, O. S. U. "Milton's *Paradise Lost*." *Expl*, 32, 1973, Item 28.

Comments on Charles L. Regan's note (No. 2910) concerning Eve's origin. Draws attention to the "similarities between the birth of Eve from Adam and that of Sin from Satan." Notes Milton's choice of the left side for extraction of man's rib because it is nearer to the heart and suggests that consideration of the Latin word for "left," sinister, with its English derivative, is significant.

2861 Pecheux, Mother Mary Christopher, O. S. U. "The Second Adam and the Church in *Paradise Lost*." *Critical Essays on Milton from "ELH"* (Baltimore, MD, and London: Johns Hopkins Press, 1969), pp. 195–209.

Reprint of Huckabay No. 1678, originally published in 1967.

2862 Pecheux, Mother M. Christopher, O. S. U. "Spenser's Red Cross and Milton's Adam." *ELN*, 6, 1969, 246–51.

States that "St. George is . . . a representative of mankind surveying mankind's path through life, just as Adam, also the man of earth, looks across the vistas of time on the history of his descendants." Suggests that the vision of Milton's Adam reflects a vision given to Spenser's Red Cross Knight.

2863 Pecheux, Mother M. Christopher. "'Their Place of Rest': *Paradise Lost* XII.647." *MiltonQ*, 6, No. 4, 1972, 73–75.

"It seems, then, in the light of the biblical background and of the careful preparation in the poem itself, that we should read line 647 of Book XII with full awareness of the eschatological overtones of the 'place of rest.'"

2864 Pechter, Edward. "When Pechter Reads Froula Pretending She's Eve Reading Milton; or, New Feminist is but Old Priest Writ Large." *CritI*, 11, 1984, 163–70.

Disagrees with Christine Froula (No. 2260), who disputes the claim that *Paradise Lost* is "an attempt to affirm orthodox authority by mystifying it." Froula's surrejoinder, pp. 171–78.

2865 Pecorino, Jessica Prinz. "Eve Unparadised: Milton's Expulsion and Iconographic Tradition." *MiltonQ*, 15, 1981, 1–10.

Shows how "Milton's departure from pictorial conventions establishes not only a different kind of God, but a different Eve as well." Whereas the iconographic tradition suggests Eve's greater culpability, Milton's Eve leaves paradise as Adam's moral equal.

2866 Peczenik, Fannie. "Adam's Other Self: A Reading of Milton's Eve." Doctoral diss., City Univ. of New York, 1981. 332pp. Abs., *DAI*, 41, 1981, 5110A.

Proposes that Milton, contrary to seventeenth-century prejudices, created "an Eve who sums up all that is female without summing up all that is inferior and secondary."

2867 Peczenik, F. "Fit Help: The Egalitarian Marriage in *Paradise Lost*." *Mosaic*, 17, 1984, 29–48.

Argues that "in Eden Adam and Eve are equals and that the perception of a hierarchy between them is a misreading caused by ascribing fallen values and prejudices to their innocent state." The Fall, however, "perverts the human marriage from God's intent, and the restored relation between man and woman is alloyed by their demonic misreading of Eve's status and their acceptance of the devil's misogyny."

2868 Penderecki, Krzysztof. *Paradise Lost.* Libretto by Christopher Fry.

An opera whose premier production was at the Lyric Opera in Chicago on Nov. 29, 1978. Reviews: Manuela Hoelterhoff, *Wall Street Journal*, Dec. 14, 1978, p. 18; Michael Lieb, *MiltonQ*, 12, 1978, 151–52; Stella Revard, *MiltonQ*, 13, 1979, 23–25; Roy Flannagan, *MiltonQ*, 13, 1979, 25–26; Harold C.

Schonberg, *New York Times*, Dec. 10, 1978, p. 21D; Robert Jacobson, *Opera News*, 43, 1979, 32.

2869 Peniche Vallado, Leopoldo. "John Milton, el Homero Inglés: Caracter Polémico de *El Paráiso Perdido*." *CA*, 156, 1968, 174–87.

Discusses the polemical aspects of *Paradise Lost*.

2870 Perkins, Anne Peper. "Divine Epiphany in Epic: Supernatural Episodes in the *Iliad*, the *Odyssey*, the *Aeneid*, and *Paradise Lost*." Doctoral diss., Washington Univ., 1986. 331pp. Abs., *DAI*, 47, 1987, 3028A–29A.

Classifies supernatural encounters in the four poems as epiphanies, non-epiphanies, ghost encounters, episodes with infernal spirits, and episodes with other subordinate spirits, examining the origins of each and their ability to bind the poems together.

2871 Perlmutter, Eila Siren. "Milton's Three Degrees of Grace: A Study of Predestination in *Paradise Lost* and the *De Doctrina Christiana*." Doctoral diss., State Univ. of New York, Albany, 1971. 202pp. Abs., *DAI*, 33, 1972, 2901A–02A.

Believes Milton challenges Augustinian-Calvinist views on predestination by subjecting humanity to three degrees of grace, determined by one's choice to instruct, obey, or rebel.

2872 Peter, Brother Baldwin, F. S. C. "Milton's Hell Hounds and the Children of God." *MiltonQ*, 8, 1974, 1–3.

In *Paradise Lost* "the Cerberean dogs are a distortion of the Christian concept of the sons of God and thus complete the trinitarian parody."

2873 Petty, Jane M. "The Voice at Eve's Ear in *Paradise Lost*." *MiltonQ*, 19, 1985, 42–47.

Believes that while Eve thinks she dreams, she actually subconsciously listens to Adam and Michael and finds knowledge to confront the real world after she leaves Eden. Reply by Edward Le Comte (No. 4139).

2874 Pickering, Frederick P. *Augustinus oder Boethius? Geschichtsschreibung und Epische Dichtung im Mittelalter und in der Neuzeit, II: Darstellender Teil.* Philologische Studien und Quellen, no. 80. Berlin: Erich Schmidt Verlag, 1976. 243pp.

Discusses *Paradise Lost* in Chapter 6, "Aus dem Nachreformatorischen Zeitalter: Die Elisabethaner, der Deutsche Barock, Milton." Examines the tendency to follow an Augustinian or a Boethian model in explicitly Christian historical works or in literature. Finds that Milton follows a Boethian model in *Paradise Lost*.

2875 Pironon, Jean. *Le Temps Figé et L'Inexprimable Distance: Les Images de la Fixité et du Mouvement dans le "Paradis Perdu" de John Milton.* Adosa: Université de Clermont, 1984. 96pp.

Analyzes images of fixity and movement in *Paradise Lost* and reviews the sources for the images of time and space. Applies the principles of the four-dimensional universe to the poem.

2876 Plotkin, Frederick. "Milton's Hell and the Typology of Anonymity." *Greyfriar*, 11, 1970, 21–30.

Discusses types and their place in *Paradise Lost*. Believes that as they become more ideal, they also become more anonymous, as Milton's Satan and hell reveal.

2877 Plotkin, Frederick. *Milton's Inward Jerusalem: "Paradise Lost" and the Ways of Knowing.* The Hague and Paris: Mouton, 1971. 155pp.

Discusses the ontological ideas concerning reality and existence in *Paradise Lost*, focusing on problems related to thought, knowledge, time, and perception.

2878 Porter, William Malin. "Milton and Horace: The Post-Bellum Muse." *CL*, 35, 1983, 351–61.

Asserts that Milton makes political statements in *Paradise Lost* by alluding to Horace's "Descende caelo."

2879 Porter, William Malin. "*Paradise*

Lost's Allusive Interpretation of the *Aeneid*." Doctoral diss., Boston Univ. Graduate School, 1980. 205pp. Abs., *DAI*, 40, 1980, 6264A.

Asserts that Milton's allusions to the *Aeneid* explode, invert, and evaluate Virgil's epic.

2880 Porter, William Malin. "A View from 'Th'Aonian Mount': Hesiod and Milton's Critique of the Classics." *CML*, 3, 1982, 5–23.

Suggests "that in *Paradise Lost*, Milton brazenly contradicts Hesiod's text, but this is neither a conclusive victory, rendering the pagan poems obsolete, nor a 'misprision' . . . due to Milton's or the seventeenth century's inability to perceive and accept Hesiod's meaning in its own terms."

2881 Potter, Lois. "Paradise and Utopia: Human Interest in *Paradise Lost*." *EA*, 27, 1974, 461–70.

2882 Poulsen, Søren Refskou. "Milton's Stil i *Paradise Lost*: Et Litteraturkritisk Problem. En Redegørelse og Diskussion med Saerligt Henblik på T. S. Eliot og F. R. Leavis' Milton-kritik." *Extracta*, 4, 1972, 177–79.

2883 Powell, Don Lance. "Ear, Eye, and Redemption in Milton's *Paradise Lost*." Doctoral diss., Univ. of Illinois, Urbana, 1975. 225pp. Abs., *DAI*, 36, 1976, 6118A–19A.

Contrasts Milton's faith in the "distinctly oral character of Biblical revelation" with his relegation of "the eye to a decidedly inferior role in the acquisition of spiritual knowledge."

2884 Priest, Dale G. "Toward a Poetry of Accommodation: The Invocation to Book III of *Paradise Lost*." *SCB*, 41, 1981, 112–14.

Believes that in Book 3, Milton "establishes the paradox of 'vision-in-blindness' that furnishes an immediate paradigm for the poetic process of accommodation."

2885 Primeau, Ronald. "Regeneration and

Motorcycle Maintenance in *Paradise Lost*." *Milton Reconsidered: Essays in Honor of Arthur E. Barker*. Ed. by John Karl Franson (Salzburg: Institut für Englische Sprache und Literatur, Universität Salzburg, 1976), pp. 103–21.

Believes that Milton's "wholistic view of regeneration [is an] ongoing response to experience" and shows that the "educative process of repairing the ruins is the subject of the entire poem."

2886 Prince, F. T. "Milton and the Theatrical Sublime." *Approaches to "Paradise Lost."* The York Tercentenary Lectures. Ed. by C. A. Patrides (London: Edward Arnold; Toronto: Univ. of Toronto Press, 1968), pp. 53–63.

Examines the use of organized and enacted spectacle in *Paradise Lost*. Concludes that Milton abandoned the dramatic form because he realized that his subject could be treated more dramatically in the epic form.

2887 Pujals, Esteban. "Estructura, Contenidos y Significado de el *Paraíso Perdido* de Milton." *Historia y Estructura de la Obra Literaria* (Madrid: Consejo Superior de Investigaciones Científicas, 1971), pp. 123–33.

Points out that the poem's structure is necessitated by the unity of the theological theme and the demands of settings, which include the traditions and the scientific knowledge of the time.

2888 Pujals, Esteban. "*El Paráiso Perdido*, de Milton, en su Tercer Centenario." *CHA*, 216, 1967, 481–506.

Studies the origins, structure, and significance of *Paradise Lost*. "The internal structure is focused on broadening the Biblical story about the fall of mankind, from the rebellion and fall into Hell of the heavenly angels, to Satan's flight to Earth to conquer Paradise, and, finally, to the temptation and punishment of the first couple and the promise of Revelation."

2889 Qui, Shaolong. "Wai kuo wen Hsüeh

yen Chiu." *FLS*, 23, 1984, 25–31.
On *Paradise Lost* and the images of Satan.

2890 Quilligan, Maureen. "Milton's Spenser: The Inheritance of Ineffability." *Ineffability: Naming the Unnamable from Dante to Beckett.* Ed. by Peter S. Hawkins and Anne Howland Schotter (New York: AMS, 1984), pp. 65–79.

Compares Spenser's and Milton's visions. Spenser's *Faerie Queene* enabled Milton to make the giant leap across the ineffable. By changing the genre from drama to epic when writing *Paradise Lost*, he was able to present Adam and Eve as prelapsarian characters.

2891 Quint, David. "The Boat of Romance and Renaissance Epic." *Romance: Generic Transformation from Chrétien de Troyes to Cervantes.* Ed. by Kevin Brownlee and Marina Scordilis Brownlee (Hanover, NH, and London: Published for Dartmouth College by Univ. Press of New England, 1985), pp. 178–202. Trans. as "La Barca dell'Avventura nell'Epica Rinascimentale." *Intersezioni*, 5, 1985, 467–88. Revised in *Epic and Empire: Politics and Generic Form from Virgil to Milton* (Princeton, NJ: Princeton Univ. Press, 1993), pp. 248–67.

Argues that, while Tasso incorporates romance into his epic's "plot of conquest and manifest political destiny," Milton in *Paradise Lost* "satirically collapses such epic plots into the bad romance of Satan, while . . . the story of Adam and Eve . . . reclaims and revalorizes the open-endedness and contingency of romance." If Camoëns celebrates the exploits of discovery in the *Lusíads*, Milton demotes them from the rank of epic and turns them into "the pattern of adventure."

2892 Qvarnström, Gunnar. *The Enchanted Palace: Some Structural Aspects of "Paradise Lost."* Stockholm: Almqvist and Wiksell, 1967.

See Huckabay No. 1702. Reviews:

James H. Sims, *SCN*, 26, 1968, 69–70; John B. Broadbent, Jr., *N&Q*, 16, 1969, 117–18; Olav Lansund, *Edda*, 69, 1969, 130–33; Peter Malekin, *RES*, 20, 1969, 225–27; George F. Sensabaugh, *RenQ*, 22, 1969, 71–74; E. N. Tigerstedt, *SN*, 41, 1969, 186–90; Michael Wilding, *MLR*, 64, 1969, 644–46; Merritt Y. Hughes, *MLR*, 66, 1971, xxi–xxxii; Russell A. Peck, *ES*, 52, 1971, 550–53.

2893 Raber, Joseph, and **David V. Lieberman.** "Text Comparison: Principles and a Program." *The Computer in Literary and Linguistic Studies.* Proceedings of the Third International Symposium. Ed. by R. F. Churchhouse and Alan Jones (Cardiff: Univ. of Wales Press, 1976), pp. 297–308.

Describes a computer program used to demonstrate the influence of *Paradise Lost* on Shelley's *Prometheus Unbound*.

2894 Radzinowicz, Mary Ann. "'Man as a Probationer of Immortality': *Paradise Lost* XI–XII." *Approaches to "Paradise Lost."* The York Tercentenary Lectures. Ed. by C. A. Patrides (London: Edward Arnold; Toronto: Univ. of Toronto Press, 1968), pp. 31–51.

"Milton has shaped the last two books to show Adam that patience and heroic martyrdom are more than an inner condition; they are a species of ethical behaviour. The action proposed to Adam is an inner and a public struggle between good and evil."

2895 Radzinowicz, Mary Ann. "The Politics of *Paradise Lost*." *Politics of Discourse: The Literature and History of Seventeenth-Century England.* Ed. by Kevin Sharpe and Steven N. Zwicker (Berkeley: Univ. of California Press, 1987), pp. 204–29.

Shows that *Paradise Lost* is neither a poem of political disengagement nor of political encryption. "I will argue that in line with Milton's humanistic understanding of the nature and function of heroic poetry, *Paradise Lost* has a public role to play in the poet's own day. Milton responds to the expectation of a 'fit audience' for epic poetry that it will 'imbreed and cherish in a great people the seeds of vertu, and publick civility.'"

2896 Radzinowicz, Mary Ann. "Psalms and the Representation of Death in *Paradise Lost*." *MiltonS*, 23, 1987, 133–44.

Contends that "the personification allegories of the birth of Sin and Death and of their bridge to earth draw on Psalms xlix and lxxxix; the Father's version of their arrival on earth then displaces those personification allegories by a typology of death through Psalm xxii."

2897 Raizis, Marios Byron. "The Case of Milton's Satan." *From Caucasus to Pittsburgh: The Prometheus Theme in British and American Poetry* (Athens, 1983), pp. 53–61.

Argues that R. J. Zwi Werblowsky (see Huckabay No. 1982) "does not succeed in convincing any informed reader that Milton's epic is a multiple failure and that Prometheus is one of the archetypes of the devil."

2898 Rajan, B. "Osiris and Urania." *MiltonS*, 13, 1979, 221–35.

On the ambiguity of Raphael's "lik'ning spiritual to corporal forms" in *Paradise Lost* 5.563–76. Suggests that "Raphael's statement is poised between two views of the structure of reality and that these views can be related to and perhaps originate in two views of the nature of language and the possibility of poetry." Milton's muse is Urania, but his poem is dedicated to Osiris in that the poet is attempting to bring together the "torn body of truth."

2899 Rajan, Balachandra, ed. *"Paradise Lost": A Tercentenary Tribute.* [Toronto]: Univ. of Toronto Press, 1969. xi, 140pp.

Includes contributions by Roy Daniells, Northrop Frye, Arthur E. Barker, Hugh MacCallum, and Rajan. In this bibliography, each essay is listed according to author. Reviews: Watson Kirkconnell, *DR*, 49, 1969, 549–56; *TLS*, June 11, 1970, p. 641; C. A. Patrides, *YES*, 1, 1971, 254–55; Rosalie L. Colie, *CanL*, 52, 1972, 99–102.

2900 Rajan, Balachandra. "*Paradise Lost* and the Balance of Structures." *UTQ*, 41, 1972, 219–26.

Claims that the universe in *Paradise Lost* is structured homocentrically. Points out the use of numerology and Milton's abandonment of the midpoint. Asserts that the poem has not one structure, but several.

2901 Rajan, B. "*Paradise Lost*: The Providence of Style." *MiltonS*, 1, 1969, 1–14.

Holds that *Paradise Lost* has more than one style, that Milton's tactic with language "springs out of the basic needs of the poem."

2902 Rajan, Balachandra. "*Paradise Lost*: The Uncertain Epic." *MiltonS*, 17, 1983, 105–19. Revised in *The Form of the Unfinished: English Poetics from Spenser to Pound* (Princeton, NJ: Princeton Univ. Press, 1985), pp. 104–27.

Recognizes that Milton's epic has many genres whose major strains run to tragedy and epic. States that *Paradise Lost* forms its literary structure, esoteric meaning, and spiritual identity from the contest between the two forms. Further argues that the poem's structural uncertainty magnifies its final impact on the audience.

2903 Rajan, Balachandra. "*Paradise Lost*: The Web of Responsibility." *"Paradise Lost": A Tercentenary Tribute.* Ed. by Rajan ([Toronto]: Univ. of Toronto Press, 1969), pp. 106–40.

Argues that free will and humanity's responsibility for its own destiny stand at the center of *Paradise Lost*.

2904 Ramakrishnan, S. *The Epic Muse: The "Ramayana" and "Paradise Lost."* Foreword by T. P. Meenakshisundaran.

New Delhi: People's Publishing House, 1977. xix, 215pp.

Discusses the two poets as they work within their cultures and epic traditions. Believes that while *Paradise Lost* ends tragically, the Tamil epic "almost exonerates and even praises Kaikeyi by depicting her fall entirely out of character." Reviews: *MiltonQ*, 12, 1978, 36; Virginia Ramey Mollenkott, *MiltonQ*, 12, 1978, 77–82.

2905 Rauber, D. F. "The Metamorphoses of Eve." *LHR*, 12, 1971, 54, 59–70.

Contends that Eve "is almost buried under a riotous mass of classical allusions, parallels, and identifications." Argues that "there is no better example in the entire poem of the wideness of Milton's views or of the depth to which he pursues his lonely investigation of the universe at large and its microcosm, the human psyche."

2906 Ravenhall, Mary D. "Sources and Meaning in Dr. Aldrich's 1688 Illustrations of *Paradise Lost*." *ELN*, 19, 1982, 208–18.

Cites a number of sources.

2907 Real, H. J. "The Sum of Things Once More." *N&Q*, 24, 1977, 547.

Believes that H. A. Mason (No. 2669) is "wrong in dismissing Virgil as a possible source for Milton's 'Consulting on the sum of things' (*Paradise Lost*, VI, 673)."

2908 Reamer, Owen J. "The Human Drama of *PL*." *MiltonQ*, 4, 1970, 50.

Abstract of a paper presented at the 1970 South-Central Renaissance Conference held at Centenary College. Argues that "Milton persuades us to accept truths of the Christian Gospel by dramatizing them." Notes that "Adam and Eve in their perfection are not at all colorless as often charged; afterward their gamut of common behavior is overwhelming evidence of their humanity."

2909 Rebhorn, Wayne A. "The Humanist Tradition and Milton's Satan: The Conservative as Revolutionary." *SEL*, 13, 1973, 81–93.

Sees Satan's soliloquy in the opening of Book 4 as a study of the fallen mentality. Satan adopts a pseudo-conservative stance and ignores a basic tenet of Christian humanism—merit. His use of political terms suggests a perverse misunderstanding of God and his ways.

2910 Regan, Charles L. "Milton's *Paradise Lost*." *Expl*, 30, 1972, Item 49.

Suggests that through the "recurrence of the theme of the physical origin of their union, Milton dramatizes the tensions of the relationship of Adam and Eve." Adam's uxoriousness is increased, and Eve's wifely rebellion is born by their preoccupation with the creation of Eve from Adam's rib. Reply by Mother M. Christopher Pecheux, O. S. U (No. 2860).

2911 Reichert, John. "'Against His Better Knowledge': A Case for Adam." *ELH*, 48, 1981, 83–109.

Examines Milton's handling of Adam's paradoxical knowledge of "the chief good" and rejection of it in *Paradise Lost* 9. Reviews the state of Adam's unfallen knowledge and analyzes the separation scene and Adam's response to Eve's offer. Concludes that "Milton shared Augustine's view of Adam's fall, and his desire to follow scripture in seeing him as undeceived."

2912 Reid, David Stuart. "The Humanism of *Paradise Lost*." Doctoral diss., Univ. of British Columbia, 1976. Abs., *DAI*, 38, 1977, 287A–88A.

Uses the *Lusíads*, *Jerusalem Delivered*, *Paradise Lost*, and *Absalom and Achitophel* to "examine how neoclassical humanism developed as a study of man and how it accommodated the Christian study of the will" in Milton's epic.

2913 Reid, David. "Ovid's Golden Age in Drummond and Milton." *N&Q*, 34, 1987, 307–08.

Contends that Milton's description of

the brooks that "ran nectar" in *Paradise Lost* 4.236–46 was either directly influenced by Ovid's *Metamorphoses* or indirectly influenced by Ovid via Drummond of Hawthornden.

2914 Reist, John S., Jr. "Reason as a Theological-Apologetic Motif in Milton's *Paradise Lost*." *Canadian Journal of Theology*, 16, 1970, 232–49.

Analyzes reason's role "to show that Milton is perhaps one of the greatest of the early cultural theologians of the modern era, and that in his *Paradise Lost* one can find one of the first grand Protestant attempts at constructive theology."

2915 Reiter, Robert E. "Milton's *Paradise Lost*, XII, 648." *Expl*, 28, 1969, Item 2.

Suggests that, at key points in the epic, Milton uses Adam's and Eve's hands "as a kind of symbol for their relationship to God." Observes that "When their hands are separated, disobedience follows; when they are 'hand in hand,' they are properly obedient to God."

2916 Revard, Carter, and **Stella Revard.** "Milton's *Amerc't*: The Lost Greek Connection." *MiltonQ*, 12, 1978, 105–06.

On the meaning and derivation of the word "amerc't" in *Paradise Lost* 1.609–10. Concludes that Milton introduced the word directly from the Greek. Corrections of Greek spellings, p. 159.

2917 Revard, Stella P. "Eve and the Doctrine of Responsibility in *Paradise Lost*." *PMLA*, 88, 1973, 69–78.

Notes that Eve's temptation is analogous to Abdiel's. Although Adam's consenting to her departure might be a tactical error, Eve is ultimately responsible. If her failure is to have any meaning, "we must grant with our whole hearts that she possessed the capacity for success."

2918 Revard, Stella P. "The Heroic Context of Book IX of *Paradise Lost*." *JEGP*, 87, 1988, 329–41.

Believes that while Milton claimed to leave "the better fortitude / Of Patience and Heroic Martyrdom / Unsung" (*Paradise Lost* 9.31–33), he ultimately reached "the heroic achievements of the Classic and Christian standard." He did this, not through Adam or Satan, but through the Son, "who both endures the trials of patience and heroic martyrdom and triumphs over his foe in single contest."

2919 Revard, Stella P. "Milton's Gunpowder Poems and Satan's Conspiracy." *MiltonS*, 4, 1972, 63–77.

"The influence of the gunpowder sermons [preached annually to celebrate the discovery of Guy Fawkes's plot in 1605], is apparent in the many striking resemblances between them and Milton's work, early and late." They "bring into sharp relief some political contours of *Paradise Lost*."

2920 Revard, Stella P. "Milton's Muse and the Daughters of Memory." *ELR*, 9, 1979, 432–41.

Discusses similarities between Milton's muse and those of Homer, Hesiod, and Pindar and shows how Milton skillfully combines the classical Greek and the Hebraic experiences. Abs., *MiltonQ*, 17, 1983, 55.

2921 Revard, Stella P. "Neo-Latin Sources for Milton's War in Heaven: *Paradise Lost* and Renaissance Heroics." *Acta Conventus Neo-Latini Turonensis*. Series: De Pétrarque à Descartes, 38. Ed. by Jean-Claude Margolin (Paris: Vrin, 1980), pp. 1047–55.

Concentrates on five neo-Latin poems to show that Milton had ample precedent for staging the War in Heaven. But he criticizes rather than glorifies the battle.

2922 Revard, Stella P. "The Renaissance Michael and the Son of God." *Milton and the Art of Sacred Song*. Ed. by J. Max Patrick and Roger H. Sundell (Madison: Univ. of Wisconsin Press, 1979), pp. 121–35.

Notes that Milton is the only Renaissance poet who arms the Son of God, not Michael, and uses him as the agent to drive Satan out of heaven. By restricting Michael's role in the War in Heaven, Milton emphasizes the Son's transcendence. Abs., *MiltonQ*, 9, 1975, 35.

2923 Revard, Stella P. "Satan's Envy of the Kingship of the Son of God: A Reconsideration of *Paradise Lost*, Book 5, and Its Theological Background." *MP*, 70, 1973, 190–98.

Points out that Milton first mentions envy, not pride, as the cause of Satan's revolt in *Paradise Lost*, examines Protestant theological opinion on the cause, and shows how envy results in Satan's desire to duplicate the thing envied (kingship), with an inevitable, catastrophic distortion.

2924 Revard, Stella P. "Vergil's *Georgics* and *Paradise Lost*: Nature and Human Nature in a Landscape." *Vergil at 2000: Commemorative Essays on the Poet and His Influence.* Ed. by John D. Bernard (New York: AMS Press, 1986), pp. 259–80.

Demonstrates that Virgil's *Georgics* influences *Paradise Lost* in two ways: "it presents man in an idealized relationship to nature and the gods of nature" and "it shows how man has 'fallen' from that ideal state and must struggle with himself and nature in a hostile world."

2925 Revard, Stella P. "Vision and Revision: A Study of *Paradise Lost* 11 and *Paradise Regained*." *PLL*, 10, 1974, 353–62.

Demonstrates that the full significance of the recovery of the Edenic vision in *Paradise Regained* "cannot be understood unless we realize that in some ways Milton has begun in book 11 [of *Paradise Lost*] to prepare us for that recovery."

2926 Revard, Stella Purce. *The War in Heaven: "Paradise Lost" and the Tradition of Satan's Rebellion.* Ithaca, NY, and London: Cornell Univ. Press, 1980. 315pp.

Approaches the War in Heaven "knowing and responding to the political, religious, and poetical traditions Milton was aware of." Interprets the war as a central episode which reflects those traditions and "lends manifold meaning to the whole of *Paradise Lost*." Reviews: Roy C. Flannagan, *MiltonQ*, 14, 1980, 102–03; Miriam K. Starkman, *RenQ*, 34, 1981, 290–92; Hugh MacCallum, *UTQ*, 50, 1981, 314–23; D. J. Enright, *TLS*, June 25, 1982, p. 699; Anthony Low, *C&L*, 31, 1982, 76–77; Gordon Campbell, *MLR*, 78, 1983, 140–41; D. D. C. Chambers, *RES*, 34, 1983, 338–40; Philip J. Gallagher, *RMR*, 37, 1983, 217–34.

2927 Revard, Stella P. "The Warring Saints and the Dragon: A Commentary upon Revelation 12:7–9 and Milton's War in Heaven." *PQ*, 53, 1974, 181–94.

Argues that the passage in Revelation is important to Book 6 and to *Paradise Lost* in general. The coming of the Son in Book 6 is "not just a flashback but a prophetic vision, balancing structurally as well as thematically that final vision of Michael in Book XII."

2928 Rewak, William J., S. J. "Book III of *Paradise Lost*: Milton's Satisfaction Theory of the Redemption." *MiltonQ*, 11, 1977, 97–102.

Discusses two theological positions concerning Christ's satisfaction for Adam's original sin and the sins of humanity: the older view of the church fathers, as represented by Aquinas, and the Reformation theory of Luther and Calvin. Examines Milton's sources and finds that *Paradise Lost* 3 recalls the Calvinistic doctrine "that Christ had to experience the full punishment of eternal death."

2929 Reynolds, Rickey J. "Milton's Adam and the Angels: A Dialogue between Classicism and Christianity in *Paradise*

Lost." Doctoral diss., Univ. of Dallas, 1980. 218pp. Abs., *DAI*, 42, 1981, 2145A–46A.

Considers "the interplay of Hellenistic and Judeo-Christian ideas on the hierarchy of being and their bearing upon the drama of Adam's fall."

2930 Rice, Robert Van Volson, Jr. "Heaven of Heavens Presumed: A Study of Milton's Use of Accommodation in *Paradise Lost.*" Doctoral diss., Univ. of Michigan, 1969. 276pp. Abs., *DAI*, 31, 1970, 734A–35A.

Examines Milton's agreement with and rare departures from the theory of biblical accommodation that asks Bible investigators to "conceive of an invisible, immaterial God in human terms."

2931 Richard, Jeremy. "Latin Narrative Syntax in Virgil and Milton." *JNT*, 14, 1984, 193–200.

Shows that the complex and unique language of *Paradise Lost* has its roots in Latin literary epic style. Compares the syntax and language of *Paradise Lost* and the *Aeneid*.

2932 Richmond, Hugh M. "*Paradise Lost*: Performance as Criticism." *MiltonQ*, 22, 1988, 17–20.

Outlines the video performance of *Paradise Lost* at the University of California, Berkeley. Concludes that performance intensifies "the dramatic verse and conviction of individual speeches . . . [and] provides critical insight into the power of Milton's poetry."

2933 Ricks, Christopher. "Sound and Sense in *Paradise Lost.*" *EDH*, 39, 1977, 92–111. Reprinted in *The Force of Poetry* (Oxford: Clarendon Press, 1984), pp. 60–79.

States that the use of sound, especially rhyme, aids in the interpretation of *Paradise Lost.* Concludes that "it is the relationship of sound to sense which most enables a poet's words to be at once fully an experience and fully an understanding."

2934 Ridden, Geoffrey. "*Paradise Lost*,

IX.119–22." *MiltonQ*, 7, 1973, 109–10.

Suggests that "torment" is used in the passage as a contrast to "pleasures" and also "because of its connotative connection with 'siege' in this strictly etymological sense."

2935 Rieger, James. "Wordsworth Unalarm'd." *Milton and the Line of Vision.* Ed. by Joseph Anthony Wittreich, Jr. (Madison and London: Univ. of Wisconsin Press, 1975), pp. 185–208.

Argues that Wordsworth and his contemporaries were free from the anxiety of influence: "there simply was no 'Milton problem.' Like Johnson, Mary Shelley, Dickens, and many others, Wordsworth saw that the Christian scheme of Creation → Fall → Redemption conforms to the structure of secular experience. Because Milton's poem definitively expresses that pattern, allusion to it in Milton's own words reminds the reader that any significant human life resonates in myth."

2936 Riggs, William George. "'Advent'rous Song': The Christian Poet in *Paradise Lost.*" Doctoral diss., Univ. of California, Berkeley, 1968. 219pp. Abs., *DAI*, 30, 1969, 1148A.

Compares the ambitions, struggles, and innovations of Milton's narrator to those of the epic's main characters.

2937 Riggs, William G. *The Christian Poet in "Paradise Lost."* Berkeley, Los Angeles, and London: Univ. of California Press, 1972. x, 194pp.

"My approach to Milton's poem seeks to locate the poet's vantage point, and I find, in pursuing the Christian poet in *Paradise Lost*, that Milton has presented himself to his reader as the prime example of the relevance of his biblical epic to fallen men." Discusses the poet's relationship to Satan, paradise, the angelic narrators (Raphael and Michael), and the Son. The Afterword discusses "*Paradise Regained* and the Miltonic Hero" (see No. 3434). Reviews: Stanley Eugene Fish, *MP*, 70,

1972, 194–97; Frank Livingstone Huntley, *RenQ*, 27, 1974, 267–68; Roger Lejosne, *EA*, 28, 1975, 84–85; Joan Malory Webber, *JEGP*, 73, 1974, 124–25; *MiltonQ*, 6, No. 4, 1972, 98–99; C. H. Sundall, *SCN*, 31, 1973, 689; C. A. Patrides, *CSR*, 3, 1973, 202–03; Lawrence Babb, *Criticism*, 15, 1973, 380–82; Michael Lieb, *Cithara*, 13, 1973, 112–17; R. E. C. Houghton, *N&Q*, 21, 1974, 116–17; Douglas Bush, *MLQ*, 34, 1973, 78–84; *TLS*, June 15, 1973, p. 697.

2938 Riggs, William G. "The Poet and Satan in *Paradise Lost*." *MiltonS*, 2, 1970, 59–82.

In *Paradise Lost*, Milton "anticipates the Satanist response by repeatedly asking us to compare his portrait of the poet with his portrait of Satan."

2939 Roberts, Donald A. "A Preface to *Paradise Lost*." *CSLBull*, 3, 1972, 2–5.

Calls C. S. Lewis's *Preface to "Paradise Lost"* (see No. 2595) a sensitive and perceptive study.

2940 Robson, W. W. "*Paradise Lost*: Changing Interpretations and Controversy." *From Donne to Marvell*. Ed. by Boris Ford. The New Pelican Guide to English Literature, vol. 3. Revised edition (Harmondsworth: Penguin, 1982), pp. 239–59.

Surveys commentary about *Paradise Lost* written during the past three centuries.

2941 Rognoni, Francesco. "A Death like Sleep. Significato e Stile dell'Educazione Umana alla Morte nel *Paradise Lost*." *LeS*, 23, 1988, 403–26.

Contrasts the allegorical image of Death in the poem with Adam and Eve's constantly redefined understanding of death.

2942 Rollin, Roger B. "Milton's 'I's': The Narrator and the Reader in *Paradise Lost*." *Renaissance and Modern Essays in Honor of Edwin M. Moseley*. Ed. by Murray J. Levith (Saratoga Springs, NY: Skidmore College, 1976), pp. 33–55.

Discusses the identity of the hero and the function of the narrator in *Paradise Lost*. Argues that Milton's narrator is only one of several hero-figures.

2943 Rollin, Roger B. "*Paradise Lost*: 'Tragical-Comical-Historical-Pastoral.'" *MiltonS*, 5, 1973, 3–37.

"*Paradise Lost* is more than a highly dramatic poem: it is 'an epic built of dramas,' an encyclopedic work composed of three distinct yet interlocking plots, each of which approximates the theoretic form of a different genre of Renaissance drama."

2944 Rosenberg, Fredrica Lehrman. "Milton's Satan: A Study in Monarchy." Doctoral diss., Univ. of Virginia, 1969. 165pp. Abs., *DAI*, 31, 1970, 1240A.

Asserts that Milton's Satan is a tyrannical royalist monarch designed to express contempt for "Stuart doctrines of sovereignty."

2945 Rosenblatt, Jason P. "Adam's Pisgah Vision: *Paradise Lost*, Books XI and XII." *ELH*, 39, 1972, 66–86.

Uses the last books of the Pentateuch as the context for Michael's statement to Adam (*Paradise Lost* 12.307–14) concerning Moses, who was deprived from entering Canaan. Like Moses, Adam will have only a foretaste of the Promised Land. Closure comes after Adam realizes that he can attain eternal life by faith in God through Christ.

2946 Rosenblatt, Jason Philip. "Angelic Tact: Raphael on Creation." *Milton and the Middle Ages*. Ed. by John Mulryan (Lewisburg, PA: Bucknell Univ. Press; London and Toronto: Associated Univ. Presses, 1982), pp. 21–31.

Examines Raphael's account of "the angelic hymns celebrating the creation of the *Ur-Licht* on the first day [of creation] and the Sabbath on the seventh, and the creation of the sun on the fourth day." Suggests a strong medieval rabbinical influence.

2947 Rosenblatt, Jason P. "'Audacious

Neighborhood': Idolatry in *Paradise Lost*, Book I." *PQ*, 54, 1975, 553–68.

Paul's insistence on separation from idols in 2 Corinthians 6.14–17 is relevant to three events in *Paradise Lost*: Satan's confinement in hell, the catalog of the fallen angels, and the fall of Adam.

2948 Rosenblatt, Jason P. "Celestial Entertainment in Eden: Book V of *Paradise Lost*." *HTR*, 62, 1969, 411–27.

Explores the parallel between Abraham and Adam in Book 5, particularly the resemblances between the angels' visit to Abraham at Mamre and Raphael's descent to Eden. Milton's language indicates that he was familiar with the original Hebrew texts of Genesis.

2949 Rosenblatt, Jason Philip. "Milton's Bee-lines." *TSLL*, 18, 1977, 609–23.

Describes the bee simile in *Paradise Lost* 1.768–75 as "pivotal, proleptic, and ironic." Asserts that the bees appear in this context because the demons will exercise their transformational powers to assume such a shape.

2950 Rosenblatt, Jason P. "The Mosaic Voice in *Paradise Lost*." *MiltonS*, 7, 1975, 207–32.

"A limited perception of Moses' relation to the epic narrator in *Paradise Lost* derives from the tendency to regard his brief role as hierophant in an early draft of a tragedy as a paradigm of his role in the great epic. . . . Though lines ought not be drawn too sharply, it is generally true that the epic voice depends on the neo-Platonic tradition of Moses as a poet-illuminator in passages that describe a prelapsarian world."

2951 Rosenblatt, Jason Philip. "A Revaluation of Milton's Indebtedness to Hebraica in *Paradise Lost*." Doctoral diss., Brown Univ., 1969. 233pp. Abs., *DAI*, 31, 1970, 368A.

Notes the profound effect of Rashi's *Commentary* on the Hebraic elements of *Paradise Lost*.

2952 Rosenblatt, Jason P. "Structural Unity and Temporal Concordance: The War in Heaven in *Paradise Lost*." *PMLA*, 87, 1972, 31–41.

Explains how "the war in heaven, appearing at the exact center of the poem and overlaid with elements of the Exodus account," contributes to our "apprehension of the poem as a wholly unified structure." However, Milton maintains the Old Testament conception of the Exodus and takes pains to preserve its literal meaning.

2953 Ross, Charles Stanley. "Raphael's Animals." *MiltonQ*, 15, 1981, 120–22.

In *Paradise Lost* 7, Raphael's description involves historical accommodation and artistic patterning, but no mode of analysis can account for the complete list.

2954 Roston, Murray. *Milton and the Baroque*. London: Macmillan; Pittsburgh, PA: Univ. of Pittsburgh Press, 1980. ix, 192pp.

Discusses the baroque style in *Paradise Lost* and the relationships between literature and the baroque visual arts. Emphasizes the change in the baroque vision of the universe from finite to infinite. Reviews: Roy C. Flannagan, *MiltonQ*, 15, 1981, 24–25; Joan Pamela Secord Bennett, *RenQ*, 34, 1981, 466–68; William E. Cain, *MLN*, 96, 1981, 1121–33; Michael Lieb, *Cithara*, 21, 1981, 58–70; Robin Robbins, *TLS*, Oct. 24, 1980, p. 1196; Barbara Kiefer Lewalski, *JEGP*, 81, 1982, 260–62; Roland Mushat Frye, *MLR*, 77, 1982, 410–12; Michael Lieb, *Cithara*, 21, 1981, 58–70; John Joseph Michael Tobin, *ELN*, 34, 1981, 466–68.

2955 Røstvig, Maren-Sofie. "Fra Bokstav til and. Litt om Allegorisk Fortolkning Sett i lys av Renessansens Synkretistiske Tenkning." *Edda*, 66, 1966, 101–16.

"From Letter to Spirit. A Note about Allegorical Interpretation in Light of Syncretistic Thinking during the Renaissance." In Norwegian. Claims that the syncretistic tradition, a Hermetic-cabbalistic form of Neoplatonism, is neglected as the main influence on the allegorical tendencies in Renaissance prose and poetry. This tradition inspired many of the subtle symbolic and allegorical effects in *Paradise Lost*, which has an inner meaning that a modern reader unfamiliar with the syncretistic tradition will not notice.

2956 Rudat, Wolfgang E. H. "Adam's and Eve's Oneness: *Paradise Lost* and Virgilian Allusion." *MiltonQ*, 22, 1988, 120–26.

Believes that Milton in *Paradise Lost* 9 (specifically in the sections that describe the earth's reactions to Adam and Eve's separate falls) alludes to Virgil's *Aeneid*.

2957 Rudat, Wolfgang E. H. "Augustinian Theology and Milton's 'Manhood' in *Paradise Lost*." *JEP*, 6, 1985, 12–15.

Argues that in using the words "subjection" and "sway" in *Paradise Lost* 4.307–11, Milton implies that, "in terms of their sexual relationship, Adam expresses his government over Eve through his own body movements—while she lies perfectly still underneath. For this is exactly how in *The City of God* St. Augustine had presented the role of the woman during the prelapsarian sex act."

2958 Rudat, Wolfgang E. H. "'Back to the Thicket Slunk': Another Look at Milton's Serpent." *AN&Q*, 22, 1983, 7–9.

On *Paradise Lost* 9.780–87. "Slinking 'Back to the Thicket' the Serpent symbolizes the postlapsarian phallus—i.e., the sexual problems and inadequacies which were inflicted on man as a punishment for having disobeyed God."

2959 Rudat, Wolfgang E. H. "Godhead and Milton's Satan: Classical Myth and Augustinian Theology in *Paradise Lost*." *MiltonQ*, 14, 1980, 17–21.

Believes that the serpent's movements in *Paradise Lost* 9.494–528 reflect Milton's reading of Augustine's de-scription of the prelapsarian phallus and that Satan avenges himself on God by emulating the godhead of Jupiter and Juno as they are described in 4.497–504. Discusses the sexual images and themes in *Paradise Lost* before and after the Fall.

2960 Rudat, Wolfgang E. H. "Milton and the *Miller's Tale*: Chaucerian Allusions in *Paradise Lost*." *Euphorion*, 80, 1986, 417–26.

Uses Augustine's discussion of human sexuality as a context and sees a relationship between the John-Alison-Nicholas-Absolom quadrangle and Adam and Eve's Fall.

2961 Rudat, Wolfgang E. H. "Milton, Freud, St. Augustine: *Paradise Lost* and the History of Human Sexuality." *Mosaic*, 15, 1982, 109–21.

Believes that Augustine's and Freud's theories are complementary. Milton argues that "the male became subject to impotency when . . . he relinquished his manhood and allowed woman to usurp his sexual adamness."

2962 Rudat, Wolfgang E. H. "Milton's Dido and Aeneas: The Fall in *Paradise Lost* and the Vergilian Tradition." *CML*, 2, 1981, 33–46.

Believes that Adam's remark, "certain to go," in *Paradise Lost* 9.952–53 alludes to Aeneas's phrase, "certuo eundi," and that Milton brings the classical and Christian traditions to bear on each other.

2963 Rudat, Wolfgang E. H. "Milton's *Paradise Lost*: Augustinian Theology and Fantasy." *AI*, 42, 1985, 297–313.

Analyzes Augustine's theory of original sin in Freudian terms: "the phallic demonstration which inspires Eve with awe is a transformation of Milton's homoerotic childhood fantasies and/or adolescent fantasies."

2964 Rudat, Wolfgang E. H. "Milton's Satan and Virgil's Juno: The 'Perverseness' of Disobedience in *Paradise Lost*." *Ren&R*, 3, 1979, 77–82.

Discusses Milton's use of Virgil's epic questions in the *Aeneid*. There is an allusive connection in the contrast between Juno and Satan.

2965 Rudat, Wolfgang E. H. "Milton's Treatment of Sexuality in *Paradise Lost*: New Light from Augustine and Chaucer." *MiltonQ*, 9, 1975, 35.

Abstract of a paper presented at the University of Wisconsin, Milwaukee, Milton Tercentenary Conference, in November, 1974. Argues that Adam and Eve do not have sexual relations before the Fall.

2966 Rudat, Wolfgang E. H. *The Mutual Commerce: Masters of Classical Allusion in English and American Literature.* Heidelberg: Carl Winter Universitäts-verlag, 1985. 144pp.

Compares Aeneas and Dido's relationship with Adam and Eve's. Believes that "Milton identifies with a Satan who is rebelling against the 'universal Dame.'" Insists that Milton derives his ideas on human sexuality from Augustine.

2967 Rudat, Wolfgang E. H. "Ovid's *Art of Love* and Augustinian Theology in *Paradise Lost*." *MiltonQ*, 21, No. 2, 1987, 62–65.

Asserts that in *Paradise Lost*, Milton uses Augustine "to parody Ovid by poetically ruining what the poet of *The Art of Love* had described as ideal sex."

2968 Rudat, Wolfgang E. H. " 'Thy Beauty's Heav'nly Ray': Milton's Satan and the Circean Eve." *MiltonQ*, 19, 1985, 17–19.

Believes that in comparing Eve to Circe, Milton establishes Eve as a femme fatale who unwittingly charms Satan with her sexual beauty and thus causes the Fall.

2969 Ruddick, William. *"Paradise Lost" I and II.* Notes on English Literature Series. Oxford: Basil Blackwell, 1969. iv, 91pp. Reprinted, 1973, 1982.

An introduction designed primarily for the university student.

2970 Rudrum, Alan. "Polygamy in *Paradise Lost*." *EIC*, 20, 1970, 18–23.

Claims that Milton argues, "not merely for the innocence of sexual relations within marriage, but for their innocence within polygamous marriages." Concludes that *Paradise Lost* 4.761–62 refers to "Milton's belief that it was the tyrant Custom, operating through the laws of the land, and not anything essential to Christianity, which prevented men of his own time from contracting polygamous marriages."

2971 Rumrich, John Peter. *Matter of Glory: A New Preface to "Paradise Lost."* Pittsburgh, PA: Univ. of Pittsburgh Press, 1987. xii, 208pp.

Investigates the Hebrew and Greek roots of the word "glory" and discusses "the remarkable civil and religious synthesis of these disparate traditions, particularly as it appears in Renaissance literature and in the life and works of John Milton." Reviews: Joseph Rosenblum, *LJ*, 112, 1987, 112–13; *VQR*, 64, 1988, 54; Carey C. Newman, *MiltonQ*, 23, 1989, 34–37; Paul Stevens, *JEGP*, 88, 1989, 417–20; Michael Bauman, *MiltonQ*, 24, 1990, 114–15; Gordon Campbell, *MLR*, 85, 1990, 412–14; J. Martin Evans, *RES*, 41, 1990, 564; James Reidy, *SCN*, 49, 1991, 41; John K. Hale, *MiltonQ*, 26, 1992, 89–90.

2972 Rumrich, John Peter. "Matter of Glory: Motivation in *Paradise Lost*." Doctoral diss., Univ. of Virginia, 1981. 211pp. Abs., *DAI*, 42, 1982, 3168A.

Locates "the principle of identity in *Paradise Lost* in Milton's concept of glory: the final cause of creation, the destination of the blessed, the unrealized goal of the damned, and the substance of the relationship between creature and creator."

2973 Rumrich, John Peter. "Metamorphosis in *Paradise Lost*." *MCJ News*, 10, 1988, 17–18.

Abstract of a paper presented at the Twenty-Third Colloquium of MCJ in

July, 1987. Proposes alchemy, the Bible, and Ovid as sources of Milton's conception of metamorphosis. Studies examples of metamorphosis in *Paradise Lost* and argues that Milton's intent is "to convey the nature of both fallen and unfallen worlds as well as the relations between them."

2974 Rumrich, John Peter. "Milton, Duns Scotus, and the Fall of Satan." *JHI*, 46, 1985, 33–49.

Contends that the premises for Satan's rebellion in *Paradise Lost* 5.577–907 "resemble principles of Duns Scotus regarding the play between the will of God and that of His creatures."

2975 Rumrich, John Peter. "Milton's Concept of Substance." *ELN*, 19, 1982, 218–33.

Finds "a crucial Miltonic deviation from Aristotle's concept of substance" in *Paradise Lost*. Abs., *MiltonQ*, 17, 1983, 100.

2976 Ryken, Leland. *The Apocalyptic Vision in "Paradise Lost."* Ithaca, NY, and London: Cornell Univ. Press, 1970. vii, 239pp.

Uses the word "apocalyptic" to "designate a transcendental state that is not located in history and the order of nature but that is placed either above or prior to ordinary time." In *Paradise Lost*, this realm "includes Heaven and the prelapsarian Garden of Eden, and the agents which move within these areas (God, the angels, and Adam and Eve)." Reviews: Anthony Low, *SCN*, 28, 1970, 62–63; Dean Ebner, *CSR*, 1, 1970, 51–54; *MiltonQ*, 4, 1970, 43–44; Calvin Huckabay, *GaR*, 25, 1971, 378–80; Anne Davidson Ferry, *JEGP*, 70, 1971, 306–08; Michael Fixler, *MP*, 69, 1971, 163–65; Merritt Y. Hughes, *MLR*, 66, 1971, xxi–xxxii; Micheline Hugues, *RLC*, 45, 1971, 270–72; Maren-Sofie Røstvig, *ES*, 53, 1972, 463–64; J. R. Scrutchins, *SHR*, 6, 1972, 95–97.

2977 Ryken, Leland. "Milton and the Apocalyptic." *HLQ*, 31, 1968, 223–38.

Identifies and illustrates the poetic theories and philosophical outlook with which Milton approached the problem of portraying the "apocalyptic in humanly comprehensible terms." Feels that he was strongly influenced by the medieval and Renaissance theory of accommodation and even by Platonism.

2978 Ryken, Leland. "Milton's Apocalyptic Vision." Doctoral diss., Univ. of Oregon, 1968. 341pp. Abs., *DA*, 29, 1969, 2227A.

Argues that the "techniques of contrast, negation, analogy, distance, and apocalyptic imagery combine to form the unified apocalyptic vision of *Paradise Lost*."

2979 Ryken, Leland. "Milton's Dramatization of the Godhead in *Paradise Lost*." *MiltonQ*, 9, 1975, 1–6.

Discusses the ambiguity of the Godhead, especially in Books 7, 8, and 10, noting "that the most decisive reason underlying Milton's ambiguous portrayal of the deity was his adherence to his biblical model."

2980 Ryken, Leland. "*Paradise Lost* and Its Biblical Epic Models." *Milton and Scriptural Tradition: The Bible into Poetry*. Ed. by James H. Sims and Ryken (Columbia: Univ. of Missouri Press, 1984), pp. 43–81.

Unifies the ideas that Milton employed Genesis, Exodus, and Revelation as "biblical epic models" and that *Paradise Lost* is demonstrably an anti-epic. Points to the poem's emphasis on "domestic values . . . [and] divine greatness and human smallness . . . and spiritualized epic motifs."

2981 Safer, Elaine B. "'Sufficient To Have Stood': Eve's Responsibility in Book IX." *MiltonQ*, 6, No. 3, 1972, 10–14.

Responds to critical arguments supporting Adam's accountability for Eve's fall. Contends that though Eve is subordinate to Adam's authority, she is independently responsible for her own transgression.

2982 Safer, Elaine B. "The Use of Contraries: Milton's Adaptation of Dialectic in *Paradise Lost.*" *ArielE*, 12, No. 2, 1981, 55–69.

"I wish to suggest that in the 'diffuse' epic *Paradise Lost* there are a variety of dialectical exchanges. This complex process enables the silent participant— the reader—to refine his vision so that he gradually can distinguish truth from falsehood, good from evil."

2983 Saito, Kazuaki. "Humor in *Paradise Lost.*" *Studies in Milton* (Tokyo: Kinseido, 1974), pp. 31–53.

In Japanese. Although Milton is not usually seen as a purveyor of humor, the modern reader can apprehend a genuinely humorous sensitivity in his writings, particularly in situations where one's expectations, based on foreshadowing, are betrayed.

2984 Saito, Kazuaki. "Rakuen no Jigoku: Shitsurakuen Dai q Kan ni tsuite." *Kirisutokyo to Bungaku* (Dai 3 Shu). Ed. by Tomoichi Sasabuchi (Tokyo: Kasama Shoin, 1975), pp. 28–47.

"Hell in Paradise: Book 9 of *Paradise Lost.*" Deals with the discordant element between Adam and Eve at the beginning of *Paradise Lost* 9 and their relationship after the Fall. Their long quarrel at the end of the book indicates that hell is already in paradise.

2985 Salewic, Mary Margaret. "Reciprocity in Milton's *Paradise Lost:* A Structural Analysis." Doctoral diss., Univ. of Pittsburgh, 1976. 137pp. Abs., *DAI*, 37, 1976, 2901A.

Illustrates the power of reciprocity— "the oppositions of giving and receiving"—to protect against excessive knowledge, disruption between heaven and earth, marital strife, and Satan's irrationality.

2986 Sammons, Todd H. "'As the Vine Curls Her Tendrils': Marriage Topos and Erotic Countertopos in *Paradise Lost.*" *MiltonQ*, 20, 1986, 117–27.

Believes that Milton uses the classical images of the vine curling around the elm to symbolize prelapsarian marital union and of the ivy clinging to the tree to symbolize postlapsarian eroticism. He again uses the elm and the vine to reestablish "conjugal harmony between Adam and Eve at the end of Book 10."

2987 Sammons, Todd Hunter. "Stylistic Variation in Milton's *Paradise Lost.*" Doctoral diss., Stanford Univ., 1980. 382pp. Abs., *DAI*, 40, 1980, 5879A.

Asserts that Milton pairs different rhetorical styles with different speakers, but uses recognizable figures of speech within a given style to distinguish it from other styles.

2988 Samuel, Irene. "*Paradise Lost.*" *Critical Approaches to Six Major English Works: "Beowulf" through "Paradise Lost."* Ed. by R. M. Lumiansky and Herschel Baker (Philadelphia: Univ. of Pennsylvania Press, 1968; London: Oxford Univ. Press, 1969), pp. 209–53.

Surveys many of the critical approaches that took place between the 1940s and the late 1960s. Sees C. S. Lewis's *A Preface to "Paradise Lost"* (No. 2595) as a starting point. Discusses subsequent major critical works, including studies of style, patterns of structural development, tragedy or comedy, theodicy or *paideia*, and the epic tradition. "My own assumption is that the work is an epic poem in tragic vein about the losing of Paradise, designed as a *paideia.*"

2989 Samuel, Irene. "*Paradise Lost* as Mimesis." *Approaches to "Paradise Lost."* The York Tercentenary Lectures. Ed. by C. A. Patrides (London: Edward Arnold; Toronto: Univ. of Toronto Press, 1968), pp. 15–29.

Sees *Paradise Lost* primarily as a poem representing human action and implying a complex of desirables and undesirables. Feels that Milton understands a wide range of human experiences and that when Adam and Eve leave the garden, they "have cut themselves down to our stature, have cut *us* down to our stature."

2990 Samuels, Peggy. "Milton's Use of Sonnet Form in *Paradise Lost.*" *MiltonS*, 24, 1988, 141–54.

Shows that the embedded sonnets help to control prolixity of discourse and increase the feeling that there can be no resting at false solutions.

2991 Sano, Hiroko. "Milton and the Tradition of Love Poetry." *MCJ News*, 7, 1984, 11–12.

Abstract of paper presented. Reconsiders Milton's view of women in *Paradise Lost* with respect to his involvement in English love poetry. Rejects the idea that Milton was a misogynist.

2992 Sano, Hiroko. "Milton's Idea of Matrimony in *Paradise Lost* and the Divorce Pamphlets." *SES*, 1, 1976, 5–24.

2993 Saravia de Farrés, Amelia G. "Coherencia y Optimismo en el Desenlace de *El Paraíso Perdido.*" *Ensayos sobre John Milton: Epopeya y Drama.* Ed. by María Enriqueta González Padilla. Facultad de Filosofía y Letras, Centro de Investigaciones de Letras Modernas y Arte Dramático (Mexico, D.F.: Universidad Nacional Autónoma de México, 1976), pp. 55–65.

Discusses the structure of the last three books of *Paradise Lost*. Shows that Books 11–12 were not an unnecessary addition; they complement the poem's formal structure and underline the unity of Milton's thought.

2994 Sarkar, Malabika. "Satan's Astronomical Journey, *Paradise Lost*, IX.63–66." *N&Q*, 26, 1979, 417–22.

Analyzes the structure of the universe in *Paradise Lost* and traces Satan's seven-day orbit in space between the first and second temptations of Eve. Feels that this journey "reveals Satan's increasing assurance and power."

2995 Sarkar, Malabika. " 'The Visible Diurnal Sphere': Astronomical Images of Space and Time in *Paradise Lost.*" *MiltonQ*, 18, 1984, 1–5.

Discusses time and space in terms of the Copernican revolution's effect on seventeenth-century poetry, particularly *Paradise Lost*; of Milton's progression into an expanding universe; and of Satan's movement within a framework of sequential time as opposed to Adam and Eve's sense of timelessness.

2996 Savage, J. B. "Freedom and Necessity in *Paradise Lost.*" *ELH*, 44, 1977, 286–311.

Claims that Milton's humanism is of such a "moral dimension and derived so closely from a view of the proper values of human nature" that it must include innate freedom. Points out that all areas of his work relate to the idea of freedom. Concludes that divine liberty gave humanity free will, which provides for both the Fall and regeneration.

2997 Sawai, Katsuko. "Redemption of Adam and Eve." *MCJ News*, 3, 1979, 31–32.

Abstract of a paper presented at the Sixth Colloquium of MCJ in December, 1978. Raphael's account of redemption undergirds the peace that Adam and Eve feel as they leave paradise.

2998 Schaar, C. " 'The Blasted Starrs Lookd Wan.' " *ES*, 60, 1979, 261–66.

Cites several examples of the "blasted stars" motif, including *Paradise Lost* 10.406–10, and suggests that to seventeenth-century readers it would have had "a huge cluster of meanings and connotations, by resemblance or by contrast."

2999 Schaar, C. " 'Each Stair Mysteriously was Meant.' " *ES*, 58, 1977, 408–10.

Discusses the various meanings of the line in the title (*Paradise Lost* 3.516). Claims that Milton's stairs are similar in meaning to the symbol of Jacob's ladder seen in Dante's *Paradiso*.

3000 Schaar, Claes. *The Full Voic'd Quire*

Below": Vertical Context Systems in "Paradise Lost." Lund Studies in English, No. 60. Lund: C. W. K. Gleerup, 1982. 354pp.

Analyzes various examples of vertical context systems in Paradise Lost, organizing the material in "a series of increasing semantic complexity." Abs., MiltonQ, 17, 1983, 56. Reviews: Beverley Sherry, AUMLA, 60, 1983, 311–13 (reprinted in MiltonQ, 17, 1983, 95–96); Archie Burnett, N&Q, 31, 1984, 122–23; John M. Steadman, YES, 16, 1986, 254–55.

3001 Schaar, Claes. "Linear Sequence, Spatial Structure, Complex Sign, and Vertical Context System." Poetics, 7, 1978, 377–88.

Mentions the linear sequence and spatial structure in Paradise Lost, especially as they apply to Satan and Raphael.

3002 Schaar, C. "A Note on Paradise Lost VIII.42–47." ES, 68, 1987, 313–15.

Traces precursors of Milton's depiction of flowers blooming in the presence of Eve. Shows that allusions to earlier writers cast Eve in both a negative and positive light.

3003 Schaar, C. "Paradise Lost IV.977–85 and V.706–10." ES, 56, 1975, 215–16.

Refutes the interpretation of "threshing" as final judgment. Suggests that Milton wishes to express God's concern as overseer of the battleground or angelic "threshing floore."

3004 Schaar, Claes. "The Sospetto d'Herode and Paradise Lost." ES, 50, 1969, 511–16.

Assesses the extent of Giambattista Marino's and Richard Crashaw's influence on Milton. Proposes a "vertical reading" of Paradise Lost to appreciate the extent to which Milton drew on literature of the past.

3005 Schiffhorst, Gerald J. "Patience and the Education of Adam in Paradise Lost." SoAR, 49, 1984, 55–63.

Holds that Milton views patience as "a key to other major virtues." Thus, in Paradise Lost, an understanding of patience helps "Adam and the reader learn about the ideal of Christian heroism."

3006 Schiffhorst, Gerald J. "Patience and the Humbly Exalted Heroism of Milton's Messiah: Typological and Iconographic Background." MiltonS, 16, 1982, 97–113.

Examines the background of Milton's portrayal of the Messiah in Paradise Lost 6. Concludes that he "is the timeless, majestic soldier and the triumphant future Judge of Revelation . . . whose past humiliation and exaltation make him the perfect, eternally present pattern of heroic Christian patience."

3007 Schiffhorst, Gerald J. "Satan's False Heroism in Paradise Lost as a Perversion of Patience." C&L, 33, 1984, 13–20.

Believes that Milton views patience as a key "to the other major virtues." Argues that he uses its opposite in Paradise Lost to teach this lesson by endowing the antihero, Satan, with a penchant for impatience and conversely having Adam be taught the virtue of patience.

3008 Schlösser, Anselm. "Paradise Lost als Erbeproblem." ZAA, 23, 1975, 108–22.

Examines Milton's humanism, political beliefs, and religious philosophy with special emphasis on Paradise Lost. The reader can easily see Milton's propensity for blindly accepting certain religious teachings as truthful. However, his desire to obtain more philosophical knowledge is also apparent. He was a revolutionary thinker who was ahead of his time.

3009 Schoen, Raymond George. "Cosmology, Angelic Eating, and Free Will in Paradise Lost: A Study in Milton's Poetic Technique." Doctoral diss., Univ. of Wisconsin, 1971. 229pp. Abs., DAI, 32, 1971, 931A.

Insists that Milton describes angels eating earthly food to emphasize the union of spirituality and materialism in a Platonic universe where humans have the free will to sin, and thus deserve their punishment.

3010 Schork, R. J. "Hordes, Hounds, and a Comma: Milton's Negative Similes." *MiltonQ*, 21, No. 2, 1987, 51–62.

"In this study I review the characteristics of that figure [the negative simile] and offer analyses of three examples from *Paradise Lost*. My discussion of the negative comparison at 1.351–55 (the '*Hordes*') is composed of juxtaposed positive and negative elements, a rhetorical technique which highlights the subtle contrasts in a seemingly conventional series of mythological allusions. Finally, I suggest the elimination or repositioning of a minor, but exceedingly obtrusive, point in 1.574 (a '*Comma*')."

3011 Schrey, Helmut. *Das Verlorene Paradies: Auf dem Wege zu Miltons "Fit Audience though Few": Untersuchungen zur Rezeptionsgeschichte und Rezeptionsgegenwart von "Paradise Lost" unter Literaturdidaktischem Aspekt.* St. Augustin: Richarz, 1980. 311pp.

Investigates the literary-didactic qualities of *Paradise Lost* in relation to its historical reception. Focuses on the ways *Paradise Lost* was taught and understood. In European schools and universities, teaching Milton became a means of didactic manipulation of literary materials. Examines the poem's reception in England, on the continent, and particularly in Germany.

3012 Schricker, Gale C. "Epic Innovator: Milton's Persona in *Paradise Lost*." *CEA*, 46, 1984, 38–47.

Points out that "Milton is the first English poet not only to introduce extended personal meditations into the impersonal epic genre but also purposefully to forge a structural poetic persona from the empirical details of his own life."

3013 Schücking, Levin L. "Milton's Conception of Marriage." *The Puritan Fam-*

ily: A Social Study from Literary Sources. Trans. by Brian Battershaw (London: Routledge and Kegan Paul, 1969), pp. 103–14.

Translation of Huckabay No. 1770. Draws material mainly from *Paradise Lost*. Sees a contradiction between Milton as a man of the Renaissance and as a Puritan.

3014 Schwartz, Harriet Berg. "Minerva's Tower: Right Reason in *Paradise Lost* and the Fourth Voyage of *Gulliver's Travels*." Doctoral diss., Columbia Univ., 1972. 234pp. Abs., *DAI*, 35, 1975, 6733A.

Contrasts Milton's faith in the possibility of gaining right reason—a reliance on faith even when it contradicts reason—with Swift's view of it as an "impossible ideal."

3015 Schwartz, Regina. "From Shadowy Types to Shadowy Types: The Unendings of *Paradise Lost*." *MiltonS*, 24, 1988, 123–39.

Describes Michael's final narration to Adam in *Paradise Lost* as replete with conclusions that will not finish, moments of revelation that are incomplete, and flashes of insight that turn out to be apprehensions.

3016 Schwartz, Regina. "Milton's Hostile Chaos: '. . . And the Sea was No More.'" *ELH*, 52, 1985, 337–74.

Emphasizes the creative process of *Paradise Lost* and points out that Raphael's account of creation is the poem's centerpiece. Milton describes a good Chaos because it is vital to the success of his theodicy.

3017 Schwartz, Regina M. *Remembering and Repeating: Biblical Creation in "Paradise Lost."* Cambridge: Cambridge Univ. Press, 1988. ix, 144pp. Reprinted with a new preface as *Remembering and Repeating: On Milton's Theology and Poetics*. Chicago, IL: Univ. of Chicago Press, 1993. xiv, 144pp.

Studies the poem's use of beginnings, repetition, and struggle between chaos and creation. Focuses on Milton's use of the Bible. Reviews: Neil Forsyth, *TLS*, Sept. 22, 1989, p. 1036; *VQR*, 66, 1990, 86; Wendy Furman, *RSR*, 16, 1990, 338; David Patterson, *MiltonQ*, 24, 1990, 33–35; Thomas H. Blackburn, *RES*, 42, 1991, 113–14; Richard DuRocher, *SHR*, 25, 1991, 176–79; J. Martin Evans, *MP*, 89, 1991, 117–19; Dayton Haskin, *JEGP*, 90, 1991, 128–30; Jason P. Rosenblatt, *RenQ*, 44, 1991, 175–79.

3018 Schwartz, Regina Mara. "The Return of the Beginning: The Repetition of the Creation Motif in *Paradise Lost* and the Bible." Doctoral diss., Univ. of Virginia, 1985. 219pp. Abs., *DAI*, 48, 1987, 400A–01A.

Associates God's creation of earth with his ability to organize good out of chaotic evil, making it worthy of remembrance and repetition.

3019 Scott, F. S. "Some Observations on the Syntax of *Paradise Lost*." *Australasian University Language and Literature Association*. Proceedings and Papers of the 12th Congress Held at the Univ. of Western Australia, 5–11 February 1969. Ed. by A. P. Treweek (Sydney: AULLA, 1970), pp. 211–23.

Explains why poetic syntax departs from normal English word order and applies the conclusions to *Paradise Lost*. Feels that Milton's manipulation of syntax displays experienced professional control.

3020 Seaman, John E. *The Moral Paradox of "Paradise Lost."* The Hague and Paris: Mouton, 1971. 135pp.

"I believe that Milton's heroic standard is more Homeric than current interpretation allows." Chapters: "Milton's Epic Hero"; "Satan the Anti-Hero"; and "The Epic Roles of Adam and Eve." Reviews: *MiltonQ*, 6, No. 1, 1972, 18–19; *TLS*, Feb. 18, 1972, p. 184; Michael Lieb, *Cithara*, 12, 1972, 85–106; Gary Stringer, *SCN*, 31, 1973, 69–70; Irène Simon, *RES*, 23, 1972, 348–51.

3021 Seigel, Catharine F. "The Reconciliation in Book X of *Paradise Lost*." *MLR*, 68, 1973, 260–63.

Believes that Eve is "not the changed woman" eulogized by various critics and observes that her two speeches of reconciliation contain "repugnant reminders of the wilful, egocentric, self-indulgent, light-minded Eve of Book IX." Finds that Adam "takes the initial step—the positive action—in their real reconciliation, that is, in their reunion with God, and the dramatic act which leads ultimately to the redemption of man."

3022 Sestito, Marisa. *L'Illusione Perduta: Saggio su John Milton.* Rome: Bulzoni, 1987. 198pp.

Contrasts Adam's and Eve's roles in *Paradise Lost*. Adam's passion for Eve leads him to eat the forbidden fruit only for fear of losing her. Eve pursues a continuous quest for self-realization—the subconscious tendency to be away from Adam, to be alone, and finally, knowingly to eat the fruit.

3023 Sethna, K. D. "The Inspiration of *Paradise Lost*." *Sri Aurobindo Circle* (Bombay), 24, 1968, 83–102.

Discusses the invocations as a part of the lyric element in *Paradise Lost* and traces the development of Milton's belief in inspiration.

3024 Shaheen, Naseeb. "Milton's Muse and the *De Doctrina*." *MiltonQ*, 8, 1974, 72–76.

Believes that all five invocations in *Paradise Lost* and *Paradise Regained* are to the Holy Spirit and that "a reading of the *De Doctrina* in its proper context will reveal that the way some have interpreted Milton's discussion of the Holy Spirit and applied it to the epic is open to serious question."

3025 Shaheen, Naseeb. "Of *Oreb*, or of *Sinai*." *ELN*, 9, 1971, 25–28.

Suggests that in the opening lines of *Paradise Lost*, the confusion over the scene of Moses's inspiration "lies in the fact that the Pentateuch is itself a compilation of earlier documents." Milton avoids the problem by mentioning both names.

3026 Shaklee, Margaret E. "Grammatical Agency and the Argument for Responsibility in *Paradise Lost.*" *ELH*, 42, 1975, 518–30.

Analyzes Satan's shunning of responsibility by the use of rhetoric and explains the abstract nature of God's speeches in *Paradise Lost.*

3027 Sharpless, F. Parvin. *The Myth of the Fall: Literature of Innocence and Experience.* Rochelle Park, NJ: Hayden Book Co., 1974. 242pp.

Includes excerpts from *Paradise Lost,* with discussion questions.

3028 Shaw, William Peter. "Book IX of *Paradise Lost*: The 'Tragedy' of Adam." Doctoral diss., Ohio Univ., 1971. 170pp. Abs., *DAI*, 32, 1971, 2653A.

Believes Milton uses the Greek model of tragedy to compose Book 9 by uniting action, time, and place; including a tragic hero; and exploring "somber themes."

3029 Shaw, William P. "The Euripidean Influence on Milton's 'Tragedy of Adam.'" *MiltonQ*, 19, 1985, 29–34.

Asserts that Euripides's influence on Milton is apparent in the philosophical principles of liberty and reason and the rhetorical devices of *Paradise Lost* 9.

3030 Shaw, William P. "Milton's Choice of the Epic for *Paradise Lost.*" *ELN*, 12, 1974, 15–20.

Discusses aspects of epic and tragedy as alternative styles for *Paradise Lost.* Claims that aspects of all genres appear in the epic form. Asserts that Milton chose the epic genre "on the basis of this theory of inclusiveness."

3031 Shawcross, John T. "The Bee-Simile Once More." *MiltonQ*, 15, 1981, 44–47.

Suggests similarities between the bee simile in *Paradise Lost* 1.759–76 and passages in Richard Hakluyt's *Principall Navigations* and Samuel Purchas's *Hakluytus Posthumus* and *Theatre of Politicall Flying-Insects.*

3032 Shawcross, John T. "The Hero of *Paradise Lost* One More Time." *Milton and the Art of Sacred Song.* Ed. by J. Max Patrick and Roger H. Sundell (Madison: Univ. of Wisconsin Press, 1979), pp. 137–47.

Notes Milton's rejection of traditional heroism in the proem to Book 9 and concludes that "The hero of *Paradise Lost* is thus not just an ordinary hero of literature, not a specific personage within the work, but rather every man who follows the path, who learns like Adam the sum of wisdom. . . . The hero of *Paradise Lost* is the fit audience; the hero may be you." Abs., *MiltonQ*, 9, 1975, 36.

3033 Shawcross, John T. "*Paradise Lost* and 'Novelistic' Technique." *JNT*, 5, 1975, 1–15.

Argues that Milton in *Paradise Lost* is "still so frighteningly present and futural! His concern in the epic has certainly encompassed the concerns of the novelists of our time."

3034 Shawcross, John T. "*Paradise Lost* and the Theme of Exodus." *MiltonS*, 2, 1970, 3–26.

Sees the Exodus myth as "moving linearly through time, rather than by cyclic recurrence." Feels that it is interwoven into the fabric of *Paradise Lost,* especially in Books 11 and 12. "The aim of successive exoduses is to transform the hardened heart into 'th'upright heart and pure,' to achieve the Paradise within."

3035 Shawcross, John T. "The Poet in the Poem: John Milton's Presence in *Paradise Lost.*" *CEA*, 48–49, 1986, 32–55.

"This amazing poem keeps offering instance after instance of its author's craft, and thus his presence, leading us with amazement to weigh the philosophic issues it encompasses, the psychological beings we are or may be, and above all the craft which is open to all readers, ideal or not. But Milton's presence is also a living presence for later writers."

3036 Shawcross, John T. "The Rhetor as Creator in *Paradise Lost*." *MiltonS*, 8, 1975, 209–19.

"In *Paradise Lost* Milton simulates the role of creator by certain rhetorical aims and techniques: Milton's creation is to aid the replenishment of heaven with true, faithful, and loving spirits by asserting God's great love seen in his eternal providence and by countering the antiheroic element that sees God as unjust and tyrannic."

3037 Shawcross, John T. "The Simile of Satan as a Comet, *PL* II, 706–11." *MiltonQ*, 6, No. 1, 1972, 5.

In this passage, "Milton has not made an astronomical error," as some readers have claimed. Discusses the simile's significance.

3038 Shawcross, John T. "The Style and Genre of *Paradise Lost*." *New Essays on "Paradise Lost."* Ed. by Thomas Kranidas (Berkeley, Los Angeles, and London: Univ. of California Press, 1969), pp. 15–33.

"It is my hope to show that the poem's genre, though epic, is a modification of tradition not previously noted, while abiding by the 'rules'; to illustrate that its generic classification depends upon point of view; to establish the style as complex in range; and to argue that the style is calculated to drive home Milton's 'message.'" Abs., *MiltonQ*, 4, 1970, 33. Review: Joseph Anthony Wittreich, Jr., *Genre*, 5, 1972, 307–25.

3039 Shawcross, John T. "Two Comments." *MiltonQ*, 7, 1973, 97–98.

Replies to Hugh Maclean (No. 2644) by observing that *Paradise Lost* 5.661–62 and 664–65 "present 'the actual emergence of evil into the cosmos of'

the poem better than line 666." Also replies to James W. Flosdorf's query (No. 1359) about the meaning of "gums of glutinous heat" in *Comus* 917. Offers a sexual interpretation. See also Edward Le Comte's reply (No. 770) and Shawcross's rejoinder, *MiltonQ*, 8, 1974, 56–57. See also Nos. 1180 and 1243.

3040 Shawcross, John T. *With Mortal Voice: The Creation of "Paradise Lost."* Lexington: Univ. Press of Kentucky, 1982. x, 198pp.

This book's "subject is Milton's achievement in *Paradise Lost* as a creative artist, and its thesis is that the evaluation of the epic as one of the truly great masterpieces of artistic creation should depend upon the viability of its literary approaches." Chapters: "The Rhetor as Creator"; "Inspiration and Meaning"; "The Thesis and the Theme"; "The Hero"; "Structural Patterns"; "Numerological Relationships"; "Sources as Meaning and Structure"; "The Genre"; "The Style"; "The Myth of Return"; "The Myth of Exodus"; "The Poem as Novelistic Technique"; and "The Poem as Entity." Appendix: "The Dates of Composition." Reviews: Lachlan MacKinnon, *TLS*, Dec. 3, 1982, p. 1332; Roy C. Flannagan, *MiltonQ*, 16, 1982, 49–50; Michael Lieb, *C&L*, 32, 1983, 49–50; Joseph Anthony Wittreich, Jr., *Rev*, 5, 1983, 1–16; Albert C. Labriola, *Cithara*, 23, No. 1, 1983, 50–52; Anne Davidson Ferry, *RenQ*, 36, 1983, 313–14; David L. Russell, *SCN*, 42, 1984, 6; Michael Fixler, *MP*, 82, 1985, 310–14; Martin Evans, *RES*, 36, 1985, 270–72.

3041 Shea, Michael Timothy. "I. The 'Uncreating Word': The Poetical Identities of William Cowper. II. Milton: The 'Sociable Angel' of *Paradise Lost*. III. Browning and Tennyson and the Uses of the Past." Doctoral diss., Rutgers Univ., 1973. 143pp. Abs., *DAI*, 34, 1973, 2578A–79A.

Examines Milton's emphasis on redemption through his poetic treatment of the Fall.

3042 Sheldon, Leslie E. "'That Anaconda of an Old Man' and Milton's Satan." *Extracts*, 26, 1976, 11.

3043 Sherbo, Arthur. "'Mazie Error': *Paradise Lost* IV.239." *MLR*, 67, 1972, 745–51.

Uses Milton's "mazie error" as a point of departure to question some critics' conclusions about the presence of Latin words in *Paradise Lost*.

3044 Sherry, Beverley. "Milton's Raphael and the Legend of Tobias." *JEGP*, 78, 1979, 227–41.

"The presence of the Tobias story at once highlights the opposition of Raphael and Satan and betrays its imbalance: in the crucial action of *Paradise Lost* the Adversary will outweigh the Friend; Raphael is not strong enough to crush the Serpent's head."

3045 Sherry, Beverley. "Not by Bread Alone: The Communication of Adam and Raphael." *MiltonQ*, 13, 1979, 111–14.

Claims that the meal in *Paradise Lost* 5 is secondary to Raphael and Adam's conversation. Asserts that emphasis on the Apocryphal story of Tobias gives a better perspective to the angelic conversation than the scene of Abraham's angelic visitation would have done.

3046 Sherry, Beverley. "Speech in *Paradise Lost*." *MiltonS*, 8, 1975, 247–66.

"In the sixteenth and seventeenth centuries several treatises (religious, philosophical, and rhetorical) discussed the Fall of Man as involving a corruption of mankind's speech. In *Paradise Lost* we witness a dramatization of that corruption."

3047 Shiratori, Masataka. "On the Judgement after the Fall in *Paradise Lost* Book X." *MCJ News*, 3, 1979, 26–27.

Abstract of a paper presented at the Fourth Colloquium of MCJ in December, 1977. Expresses concern about whether the Judge is the Father or the Son.

3048 Shiratori, Masataka. "The Vision of God—On the Beatific Vision of *Paradise Lost*." *MCJ News*, 11, 1989, 14–15.

Abstract of paper presented. Discusses God's many dimensions in the poem— as God himself, as God in the Son, and as God in man.

3049 Shirley, Charles G., Jr. "The Four Phases of the Creation: Milton's Use of Accommodation in *Paradise Lost* VII." *SAB*, 45, 1980, 51–61.

In Book 7, the creation is divided into four phases of action, each on a different level of accommodation: action in heaven, action in Chaos, action in forming and filling the earth, and action in the Son's return to the Father.

3050 Shitaka, Hideyuki. "How Does Milton 'Justify the Ways of God' in *Paradise Lost*, Book 6?" *Memoirs of the Faculty of Education of Fukui University*, Series 1, No. 31, Jan. 30, 1982, pp. 1–16.

Analyzes the rhetorical devices that Raphael uses to narrate the War in Heaven. Feels that Milton sufficiently prepares Adam and Eve to withstand the temptation if they will "Remember, and fear to transgress."

3051 Shitaka, Hideyuki. "Man's Mutuality, Love, and Language in *Paradise Lost*." *HSELL*, 30, 1985, 25–35.

Studies Adam and Eve's mutual love before and after the Fall. Believes that Milton's seemingly simple verbal patterns syntactically stress their relationship to each other and reflect the divine relationship or its infernal counterpart.

3052 Shitaka, Hideyuki. "Regeneration of Adam's Language." *MCJ News*, 7, 1984, 18–20.

Abstract of a paper presented at the Sixteenth Colloquium of MCJ in December, 1983. Claims that, after the Fall, Adam and Eve's language degenerates to resemble Satan's. Examines how "their language, corrupted by Satan, gradually regenerates in Books

10, 11, and 12, under the influence of 'Prevenient Grace' (11.3) from God, the teachings of Michael, and the 'gentle Dreams' (12.595) sent to Eve."

3053 Shitaka, Hideyuki. "Worship of God and Idolatry in *Paradise Lost.*" *MCJ News*, 10, 1988, 1–3.

Studies Milton's views on the worship of God as stated in the *Christian Doctrine* and as exemplified in *Paradise Lost.* Claims that Milton views the Son's worship of the Father as ideal. Also studies the various idols that humans and Satan worship instead of God.

3054 Shullenberger, William. "Wrestling with the Angel: *Paradise Lost* and Feminist Criticism." *MiltonQ*, 20, 1986, 69–85.

Believes that although *Paradise Lost* portrays a patriarchal paradigm, it also portrays one in which the sexes complement each other and in which Milton "continually tests and complicates an apparent ideology of male superiority." Responses by Deirdre McChrystal (No. 2686) and Lawrence Hyman (No. 2464).

3055 Shumaker, Wayne. *Unpremeditated Verse: Feeling and Perception in "Paradise Lost."* Princeton, NJ: Princeton Univ. Press, 1967. x, 230pp.

See Huckabay No. 1799. Reviews: *TLS*, Dec. 26, 1968, p. 1457; Rosalie L. Colie, *KR*, 122, 1968, 671–77; Kenneth Connelly, *YR*, 57, 1968, 589–94; Patrick Crutwell, *HudR*, 21, 1968, 197–207; James R. McAdams, *SCN*, 26, 1968, 49–50; Alan Rudrum, *SoRA*, 3, 1968, 184–88; Robert B. Hinman, *JA*, 28, 1969, 255–56; Ants Oras, *SR*, 77, 1969, 176–84; F. T. Prince, *RES*, 20, 1969, 501–03.

3056 Sichi, Edward, Jr. "Milton and the *Roman de la Rose*: Adam and Eve at the Fountain of Narcissus." *Milton and the Middle Ages.* Ed. by John Mulryan (Lewisburg, PA: Bucknell Univ. Press; London and Toronto: Associated Univ. Presses, 1982), pp. 153–82.

Analyzes the poems' narcissistic epi-

sodes and suggests that "*Paradise Lost* is an interpretation of love . . . incorporating much of the setting, imagery, allegory, and philosophy utilized four centuries earlier by Guillaume de Lorris and Jean de Meun."

3057 Sichi, Edward, Jr. "The Serpent with Carbuncle Eyes: Milton's Use of 'Carbuncle' in *Paradise Lost.*" *MiltonQ*, 14, 1980, 126–30.

Discusses the metaphoric meaning of carbuncle in terms of its association with water, fire, and sex and suggests that the serpent's eyes assist in the seduction of Eve.

3058 Sichi, Edward, Jr. "'These Two Imparadis't': A Comparative Study of the Gardens in *Paradise Lost* and the *Roman de la Rose.*" Doctoral diss., Duquesne Univ., 1977. 228pp. Abs., *DAI*, 38, 1977, 1369A.

Asserts that the two works use images of an enclosed garden to emphasize the difference between earthly and divine love.

3059 Sigmon, Dennis H. "The Negatives of *Paradise Lost*: An Introduction." *SP*, 73, 1976, 320–41.

Analyzes the negative constructions, which appear constantly because the epic's subject is God, "who must be defined by what he is *not.*"

3060 Silk, Edmund T. "Claudian's *In Rufinum* and the Congress of Fallen Angels in *Paradise Lost.*" *MiltonQ*, 11, 1977, 37–38.

"For the resemblance between Claudian's council of underworld spirits in the *In Rufinum* and the congress of fallen angels in *Paradise Lost* is so close that I believe one provided the model for the other."

3061 Simons, John. "All about Eve: Woman in *Paradise Lost.*" *Jacobean Poetry and Prose: Rhetoric, Representation, and the Popular Imagination.* Ed. by Clive Bloom (London: Macmillan; New York: St. Martin's Press, 1988), pp. 213–25.

Uses the context of Jacques Lacan's rereading of Freud to examine Eve's arrival in the poem and Milton's treatment of her. Believes that she is a threat to *Paradise Lost* and "the dark presence which disturbs the master signifier of the phallocentric discourse."

3062 Simons, John. "Bees and Fallen Angels: A Note on *Paradise Lost*." *MiltonQ*, 21, No. 1, 1987, 21–22.

Believes that Milton uses the simile of the bees in *Paradise Lost* 1.768–75 as a "savage warning" about the institution of monarchy and to provide "an ironic glance at Satan's regime."

3063 Simons, John. "A Possible Reference to *Timon of Athens* in *Paradise Lost*." *N&Q*, 31, 1984, 326–27.

Cites Shakespeare's *Timon of Athens* as the source of *Paradise Lost* 5.396. Such an allusion extends Milton's condemnation of "the tedious pomp" of "social jockeying" begun in line 354.

3064 Simons, Louise. "Death's Household, Death's Threshold: Representations of Death in Shakespeare and Milton." Doctoral diss., Univ. of Maryland, College Park, 1987. 295pp. Abs., *DAI*, 48, 1988, 2070A.

Contrasts Shakespeare's presentation of death as "a box that closes on the poet" with Milton's "prophecy that opens on the future."

3065 Simons, Louise. "A Summer Institute for College Professors on *Paradise Lost*." *MiltonQ*, 19, 1985, 89–91.

Report on a six-week course at Arizona State University, led by John T. Shawcross.

3066 Sims, James H. "Camoëns, Milton, and Myth in the Christian Epic." *RenP*, 1971, pp. 79–87.

Shows that the poets added to and extended the myths and "put both old and new myths in the service of a Christian truth that partakes of but transcends mythological and historical truth." Lists studies of Camoëns's possible influence on Milton.

3067 Sims, James H. "Camoëns' *Lusíads* and Milton's *Paradise Lost*: Satan's Voyage to Eden." *Papers on Milton*. Ed. by Philip Mahone Griffith and Lester F. Zimmerman. Univ. of Tulsa Department of English Monograph Series, no. 8 (Tulsa, OK: Univ. of Tulsa, 1969), pp. 39–46.

Suggests that Satan's voyage to Eden echoes passages from Camoëns's epic of Vasco da Gama's pioneer voyage to the east.

3068 Sims, James H. "Christened Classicism in *Paradise Lost* and *The Lusíads*." *CL*, 24, 1972, 338–56.

Discounts barriers to Milton's knowledge of Camoëns's Portugese epic and draws attention to similarities in the handling of pagan themes in a Christian context.

3069 Sims, James H. "'Delicious Paradise' in *Os Lusíadas* and in *Paradise Lost*." *Ocidente*, número especial, Nov., 1972, pp. 163–72.

Shows how Camoëns's and Milton's descriptions of paradise conform to and depart from tradition. Milton's paradise "is clearly used symbolically to represent the bliss of communion with God that man has lost and may, through Christ, regain." Abs. in Portuguese, p. 172.

3070 Sims, James H. "Echoes of Camoëns' *Lusíads* in Milton's *Paradise Lost* (I–IV)." *RCam*, 3, 1971, 135–44.

Shows "how Milton's allusions to Camoëns' epic of Vasco da Gama's pioneer voyage to the East intensify the reader's fascination with and understanding of Satan's voyage from Pandemonium to Hellgate and through Chaos to this World and Eden."

3071 Sims, James H. "Enter Satan as Esau, Alone; Exit Satan as Belshazzar: *Paradise Lost*, Book (IV)." *Costerus*, 7, 1973, 183–91.

Shows that the opening and closing scenes of Book 4 demonstrate Milton's use of biblical allusion in the style of Marlowe and Shakespeare.

3072 Sims, James H. "The Epic Narrator's Mortal Voice in Camoës and Milton." *RLC*, 51, 1977, 374–84.

Notes parallels in the narrators' self-characterization in the *Lusíads* and *Paradise Lost*.

3073 Sims, James. "Further Thoughts on Milton's 'Pattern of a Christian Hero.'" *MiltonQ*, 13, 1979, 151.

Questions the accuracy of several of Robert J. Wickenheiser's quotations and statements (No. 3231). Reply by Wickenheiser, p. 152, insists on the validity of his original interpretation of the Christian hero.

3074 Sims, James H. "A Greater than Rome: The Inversion of a Virgilian Symbol from Camoës to Milton." *Rome in the Renaissance: The City and the Myth*. Ed. by P. A. Ramsey. Medieval and Renaissance Texts and Studies, vol. 18 (Binghamton, NY: Medieval and Renaissance Texts and Studies, 1982), pp. 333–44.

"Milton turns the ideal inward, rejecting outer pomp and power as ultimately insignificant and focusing, instead, on the human heart, indwelt by God's grace and Spirit, as the source of true greatness." Abs., *MiltonQ*, 14, 1980, 72.

3075 Sims, James H. "*Os Lusíadas*: A Structural Prototype of *Paradise Lost*?" *EIRC*, 4, 1978, 70–75.

Favors the idea that Milton knew and was influenced by the Portuguese epic. Sees parallels between the poems' narrators and structural divisions.

3076 Sirluck, Ernest. *"Paradise Lost": A Deliberate Epic*. Churchill College, Cambridge, Overseas Fellowship Lecture No. 1. Cambridge: W. Heffer and Sons, 1967. 30pp.

See Huckabay No. 1805. Reviews: Rosalie L. Colie, *KR*, 122, 1968, 671–77; *TLS*, Feb. 8, 1968, p. 1134; Michael Wilding, *YES*, 1, 1971, 152–53.

3077 Slogsnat, Helmut. *Das Dramatische Epos: Studien zu Miltons "Paradise Lost."* Doctoral dissertation, Univ. of Heidelberg. Frankfurt: Haag and Herchen, 1978. 465pp.

Analyzes the originality of *Paradise Lost* against the background of sixteenth-century theories of poetry, five dramas that also deal with the Fall, and movements in the history of ideas during the English revolution.

3078 Smith, A. James. "The Bond of Kind: *Paradise Lost*." *The Metaphysics of Love: Studies in Renaissance Love Poetry from Dante to Milton* (Cambridge: Cambridge Univ. Press, 1985), pp. 114–40.

Examines Adam and Eve's relationship. Reviews (of book): Alastair Fowler, *TLS*, Nov. 8, 1985, p. 1260; Warren Chernaik, *THES*, Mar. 29, 1985, p. 23; Michael G. Brennan, *N&Q*, 33, 1986, 537; Jonathan F. S. Post, *RenQ*, 39, 1986, 539–41; Ilona Bell, *JEGP*, 86, 1987, 413–15; Cedric C. Brown, *RES*, 38, 1987, 65–66; Anne Ferry, *CL*, 39, 1987, 277–78; Raymond B. Waddington, *SCJ*, 18, 1987, 133–34.

3079 Smith, A. James. "From Dante to Milton." *The Metaphysics of Love: Studies in Renaissance Love Poetry from Dante to Milton* (Cambridge: Cambridge Univ. Press, 1985), pp. 140–45.

"*Paradise Lost* persuades us that we have our right state when we fulfil our own nature, in the body and in our fit place in the created order. We would recover the Fall not by rising above human kind, or denying some part of our nature, but by regaining our full humanity." If Milton's conception of love "commits him to a universe of dynamic activity," "Dante always looks to the still centre."

3080 Smith, A. James. "Sense and Innocence: Two Love Episodes in Dante and Milton." *An English Miscellany Presented to W. S. Mackie*. Ed. by Brian S. Lee (Capetown, London, and New York: Oxford Univ. Press, 1977), pp. 119–30. Reprinted in *The Metaphysics of Love:*

Studies in Renaissance Love Poetry from Dante to Milton (Cambridge: Cambridge Univ. Press, 1985), pp. 14–28.

Studies the changing European attitudes toward sexual and spiritual love. Contrasts Dante's handling of the story of Paolo and Francesca in the *Divine Comedy* and Milton's treatment of unfallen sexuality in *Paradise Lost*.

3081 Smith, Eric. *"Paradise Lost." Some Versions of the Fall: The Myth of the Fall of Man in English Literature.* Foreword by J. I. M. Stewart (Pittsburgh, PA: Univ. of Pittsburgh Press, 1973), pp. 21–66.

Examines various works containing the theme of the Fall. Identifies three strands running through *Paradise Lost*: the bare biblical story, the Miltonic associations of divine and human obedience, and the living relationship of Adam and Eve. The Fall is seen as an ordinary act from which humanity will recover through understanding of both good and evil. Reviews (of book): Martin Lebowitz, *YR*, 63, 1973, 311–12; John R. Marvin, *LJ*, 98, 1973, 3004; Harold H. Watts, *MFS*, 19, 1973, 664–67; *MiltonQ*, 8, 1974, 59–60; *VQR*, 50, 1974, xx; C. C. Barfoot, *DQR*, 4, 1974, 177–80; J. Martin Evans, *N&Q*, 21, 1974, 114–16; Stephen Medcalf, *RES*, 25, 1974, 365–66; Robert H. West, *GaR*, 28, 1974, 374–75; William C. James, *JR*, 55, 1975, 485–86; Charles E. Lloyd, *SR*, 83, 1975, xxii; Charlotte F. Otten, *CSR*, 5, 1976, 398–99.

3082 Smith, George William, Jr. "Iterative Rhetoric in *Paradise Lost*." *MP*, 74, 1976, 1–19.

Studies the frequency of iterative schemes in fifty-seven speeches in *Paradise Lost*. Concludes that "with the partial exception of ploce and polyptoton, . . . the schemes of iteration accomplish specific grammatical and rhetorical purposes and set forth logical and other recurring relationships. They are individually functional in Milton's verse, rather than superficially decorative."

3083 Smith, Russell E., Jr. "Adam's Fall." *ELH*, 35, 1968, 527–39. Reprinted in *Critical Essays on Milton from "ELH"* (Baltimore, MD, and London: Johns Hopkins Univ. Press, 1969), pp. 182–94.

"Milton deviates from the traditional explanations of Adam's fall in that his Adam falls for the same reason as does his Eve." Feels that Adam, like Eve, aspires and is ambitious.

3084 Snare, Gerald. "Milton's 'Siloa's Brook' Again." *MiltonQ*, 4, 1970, 55–57.

Disagrees with George Whiting and Ann Gossman (Huckabay No. 2003), who accept the reading of "Siloa's Brook" in *Paradise Lost* 1.11 as mainly a scriptural analogy to the muses' "dark-coloured spring." Argues that Milton's biblical allusion primarily refers to John 9.

3085 Snider, Alvin. "The Self-Mirroring Mind in Milton and Traherne." *UTQ*, 55, 1986, 313–27.

Uses Jacques Lacan's theory of a mirror stage of childhood development to compare Thomas Traherne's mirror imagery in "Shadows in the Water" to Milton's use of this motif in *Paradise Lost* 4. Concludes that both authors' "mirrors function as symbols of the tangled relation between original and replica, object and symbol, the world and the self."

3086 Song, Hong-Han. "Milton's Prophetic View of History in *Paradise Lost*." *Pegasus* (Soungjeon Univ., Korea), 8, 1985, 34–52.

3087 Southall, Raymond. *"Paradise Lost and the Puritan Debacle." Literature and the Rise of Capitalism: Critical Essays Mainly on the Sixteenth and Seventeenth Centuries* (London: Lawrence and Wishart; New York: Beekman, 1973), pp. 113–33.

Sees a conflict in *Paradise Lost* between two views of human nature—one heroic and the other sinful. The English revolution's failure has its roots in the growth of the latter view.

3088 Speck, Paul Surgi. "Clouds, Rain, Rivers, Serpents, and Birth: The Imagistic Structure of *Paradise Lost*, Books VI and VII." *Innisfree*, 2, 1975, 22–31.

Suggests the extent to which Milton's images have been purposefully blended. "The storm . . . produces rain. The rain is itself a water of purgation . . . and as such becomes the source of worldly evil. . . . But the actual image of watery purgation is delayed until the third day of Creation where—pictured not only as an image of justice and potential destruction, but also as an image of love, birth and regeneration—it must be considered not as an isolated act of God's wrath but as a justifiable part of God's merciful Providence."

3089 Spencer, Jeffry Burress. "Five Poetic Landscapes, 1650–1750: Heroic and Ideal Landscape in English Poetry from Marvell to Thomson." Doctoral diss., Northwestern Univ., 1971. 473pp. Abs., *DAI*, 32, 1971, 3271A.

Examines the impact of traditional visual styles on theme in descriptions of landscape by Marvell, Milton, Dryden, Pope, and Thomson.

3090 Spencer, T. J. B. "*Paradise Lost*: The Anti-Epic." *Approaches to "Paradise Lost."* The York Tercentenary Lectures. Ed. by C. A. Patrides (London: Edward Arnold; Toronto: Univ. of Toronto Press, 1968), pp. 81–98.

"It is now at last obvious what *Paradise Lost* is. It is the anti-epic. Wherever we turn we find the traditional epic values inverted. It closed the history of this poetic genre in England. . . . It closed the history of the epic."

3091 Sproxton, Judith. "D'Aubigné, Milton and the Scourge of Sin." *JES*, 11, 1981, 262–78.

Uses Agrippa d'Aubigné's *Les Tra-*

giques and Milton's *Paradise Lost* to show that the two writers understood sin in a similar way.

3092 Stacy, Gerald. "Books XI and XII of *Paradise Lost*." *MiltonQ*, 11, 1977, 94.

Abstract of a paper presented at the 1977 NEMLA Convention. "In Books XI and XII of *Paradise Lost*, Milton enlarges the scope of the poem so that the repentant but sinful Adam becomes the symbol of fallen man being prepared by God for redemption."

3093 Stacy, G. J. "Christ and the Repentance of Adam: Book X, *Paradise Lost*." *MiltonQ*, 9, 1975, 36–37.

Abstract of a paper presented at the University of Wisconsin, Milwaukee, Milton Tercentenary Conference, in November, 1974. Argues that Christ, through his judgment, "begins the redemptive process by becoming the example which spurs Adam to true repentance."

3094 Stacy, Gerald Joseph. "The Influence of Senecan Stoicism on Milton's *Paradise Lost*." Doctoral diss., Bowling Green State Univ., 1972. 167pp. Abs., *DAI*, 33, 1973, 6326A–27A.

Follows "the interplay between Augustinian and Stoic ethics" through "Adam and Eve's prelapsarian perfection, their mortal sin, and their repentance from sin."

3095 Stacy, Gerald. "Milton's *Paradise Lost*, II, 552." *Expl*, 30, 1971, Item 30.

Contends that the correct interpretation of "partial" is "imperfect," but not "biased," as has previously been suggested. Reply by J. G. Keogh (No. 2517).

3096 Startzman, L. Eugene. "Wisdom and Beauty: Two Principles in *Paradise Lost*." *C&L*, 36, 1987, 26–39.

Concludes that "Mortal Beauty . . . reflects Mortal Truth; action and love complement and complete knowledge." This point is demonstrated by Satan, in whom beauty and wisdom are eternally separated. Milton thus shows

"That possibility exists, but such need not be the fate of mankind."

3097 Stavely, Keith W. F. "*PL* and Christian Politics." *MiltonQ*, 10, 1976, 29.

Abstract of a paper presented at the 1975 MLA Convention. In *Paradise Lost* "we do see the collective historical experience of mankind under the rule of Satan; and the poem is written from the perspective that the present moment of history is one acute crisis."

3098 Stavely, Keith W. F. *Puritan Legacies: "Paradise Lost" and the New England Tradition, 1630–1890.* Ithaca, NY, and London: Cornell Univ. Press, 1987. xiv, 294pp.

Analyzes the development of Puritan culture in New England and relates the Fall of Adam and Eve to comparable stories of representative New Englanders and other Americans. Reviews: Susan A. Stussy, *LJ*, 112, 1987, 183; *VQR*, 64, 1988, 81; Theodore Dwight Bozeman, *EAL*, 23, 1988, 345–48; Christopher Hill, *NYRB*, 35, 1988, pp. 45–48; Deborah L. Jones, *JAS*, 22, 1988, 495–96; Laura L. Knoppers, *SCN*, 46, 1988, 73–74; James Holstun, *William and Mary Quarterly*, 45, 1988, 791–93; K. P. Van Anglen, *AL*, 60, 1988, 660–61; Mason I. Lowance, Jr., *AHR*, 94, 1989, 840–41; Dustin Griffin, *Criticism*, 31, 1989, 103–07; Robert I. Headley, *MiltonQ*, 23, 1989, 81–83; Margarita Stocker, *TLS*, Jan. 27, 1989, p. 90; James G. Turner, *RenQ*, 42, 1989, 593–97; Stephen M. Fallon, *JEGP*, 89, 1990, 144–47; Gordon Campbell, *MLR*, 85, 1990, 412–14; Joseph Conforti, *RSR*, 16, 1990, 172; Robin Grey, *MP*, 88, 1990, 198–201.

3099 Steadman, John M. "Allegory and Verisimilitude: The 'Impossible Credible.'" *The Wall of Paradise: Essays on Milton's Poetics* (Baton Rouge and London: Louisiana State Univ. Press, 1985), pp. 143–50.

Reprint of Huckabay No. 1822, originally published in 1963.

3100 Steadman, John M. *Epic and Tragic Structure in "Paradise Lost."* Chicago, IL, and London: Univ. of Chicago Press, 1976. xi, 189pp.

"I shall be concerned primarily with the plot as 'idea' or formal cause of the epic poem, examining the three principal parts of the epic or tragic fable—reversal, recognition, and 'scene of suffering'—against the background of Renaissance critical theory." Reviews: *MiltonQ*, 11, 1977, 22–23; Ralph W. Condee, *JEGP*, 76, 1977, 455–58; C. A. Patrides, *TLS*, July 8, 1977, p. 838; Douglas Bush, *RenQ*, 31, 1978, 120–21; Stella P. Revard, *MP*, 77, 1979, 89–92; Earl Miner, *CL*, 31, 1979, 92–93; Ashraf H. A. Rushdy, *MiltonQ*, 21, 1987, 71–74.

3101 Steadman, John M. "The Idea of Satan as the Hero of *Paradise Lost.*" *PAPS*, 120, 1976, 253–94.

Analyzes the Satanist controversy from Dryden to the present. Sees Satan as a false hero with classical and Machiavellian features, but feels that the parodic relationship between Satan's role and that of the Father and Son is more significant than his literary origins. In *Paradise Lost*, Satan presents an example of "spiritual *decreation.*"

3102 Steadman, John M. "'Memphian Chivalry': Milton's Busiris, Etymology and Chronography." *UR*, 37, 1971, 215–31. Revised in *Nature into Myth: Medieval and Renaissance Moral Symbols.* Duquesne Studies in Language and Literature, vol. 1 (Pittsburgh, PA: Duquesne Univ. Press, 1979), pp. 185–212.

This chapter also includes a revised version of Huckabay No. 1826, originally published in 1961, and Huckabay No. 1830, originally published in 1960. Examines *Paradise Lost* 1.306–11 and its background. Discusses the implications of the Busiris and Leviathan allusions in the light of Renaissance etymological techniques, Milton's identification of Pharaoh against the background of Christian historiography, and the relationship between Busiris and Memphis in the passage. The Appendix contains theories about the name of the Pharaoh during the Exodus.

3103 Steadman, John M. *Milton and the Renaissance Hero.* Oxford: Clarendon Press, 1967. xx, 210pp.

See Huckabay No. 932. Reviews: *MiltonN*, 2, 1968, 8; *TLS*, Feb. 8, 1968, p. 134; John Buxton, *RES*, 19, 1968, 319–20; D. J. Gordon, *RenQ*, 22, 1968, 491–93; Watson Kirkconnell, *DR*, 48, 1968, 260–01; Mark Roberts, *N&Q*, 15, 1968, 389–94; James H. Sims, *SHR*, 2, 1968, 532–35; J. M. Couper, *AUMLA*, 31, 1969, 97–99; William G. Madsen, *CL*, 31, 1969, 89–90; Michael Wilding, *MLR*, 64, 1969, 142; Ashraf H. A. Rushdy, *MiltonQ*, 21, 1987, 71–74.

3104 Steadman, John M. "Milton: Part II. *Paradise Lost.*" *English Poetry and Prose, 1540–1674.* Ed. by Christopher Ricks. Sphere History of Literature in the English Language, vol. 2 (London: Sphere Books, 1970), pp. 281–98. Revised edition, New York: Peter Bedrick Books, 1987.

Explains that *Paradise Lost* is "a literary victory won out of personal and political defeats, private and public humiliations. But it is also the reflection of a moral triumph, the outcome of his [Milton's] hard-fought struggle with himself."

3105 Steadman, John M. "Milton's *Paradise Lost* and the Apotheosis Tradition." *Antike und Abendland: Beiträge zum Vertändnis der Griechen und Römer und ihres Nachlebens*, 20, no. 2 (Berlin and New York: Walter de Gruyter and Co., 1974), pp. 110–34. Reprinted in *Milton's Biblical and Classical Imagery* (Pittsburgh, PA: Duquesne Univ. Press, 1984), pp. 167–89.

Focuses on Milton's deviation from the tradition. "Instead of apotheosizing human virtue, it [*Paradise Lost*] ex-poses the vanity of human merits. Instead of eulogizing the capacities of human reason, it emphasizes the limitations of man's intellect."

3106 Steadman, John M. "Milton's Rhetoric: Satan and the 'Unjust Discourse.'" *MiltonS*, 1, 1969, 67–92. Reprinted in *Milton and the Paradoxes of Renaissance Heroism* (Baton Rouge and London: Louisiana State Univ. Press, 1987), pp. 111–35.

"Satan's role in *Paradise Lost* reflects the Socratic-Aristophanic contrast between Just and Unjust Discourse, or true and false eloquence. Through such devices as verbal echoes, explicit rebuttal, and inherent contradictions, Milton portrays in Satan the character of the arch-sophist."

3107 Steadman, John M. "*Paradise Lost* and the Misery of the Human Condition." *Archiv*, 209, 1972, 283–309.

Emphasizes Milton's conception of the regenerate: "All mankind is involved in Adam's fall, but only a fraction of his posterity will share his repentance and act of faith." Concludes that *Paradise Lost* tends to deflate, rather than exalt, its epic hero.

3108 Steadman, John M. "*Paradise Lost*: Milton's 'Sin.' The Problem of Literary Indebtedness." *Nature into Myth: Medieval and Renaissance Moral Symbols.* Duquesne Studies in Language and Literature, vol. 1. (Pittsburgh, PA: Duquesne Univ. Press, 1979), pp. 174–84.

Revised versions of Huckabay Nos. 1870–71 and 1875, originally published in 1961, 1956, and 1960, respectively.

3109 Steadman, John M. "Rhetoric and Character in *Paradise Lost.*" *Milton and the Paradoxes of Renaissance Heroism* (Baton Rouge and London: Louisiana State Univ. Press, 1987), pp. 136–70.

Reprint of Huckabay No. 1831, originally published in 1967.

3110 Steadman, John M. "Satan in Orbit and Medieval Demonology (*Paradise*

Lost, IX, 64–66)." *ELN*, 12, 1975, 161–63.
Considers Milton's depiction of Satan's flight astronomically correct and in accord with the medieval demonology linking demons and the colures.

3111 Stein, Arnold. *The Art of Presence: The Poet and "Paradise Lost."* Berkeley, Los Angeles, and London: Univ. of California Press, 1977. ix, 190pp.
Focuses on the poet's hand as he arranges and shapes episodes for his poem. Argues that Milton the poet-prophet, not Milton the man, has a direct presence in *Paradise Lost*. The reader examines the artistic choices that define the poem. Reviews: *MiltonQ*, 11, 1977, 55–57; Joan Malory Webber, *MLQ*, 38, 1977, 398–401; Dan Stead Collins, *RenQ*, 31, 1978, 261–62; G. K. Hunter, *SR*, 86, 1978, 414–21; Virginia Ramey Mollenkott, *MiltonQ*, 12, 1978, 77–82; William George Riggs, *JEGP*, 77, 1978, 438–41; Stella P. Revard, *MP*, 77, 1979, 89–92; Roger Henry Sundell, *SCN*, 29, 1981, 3–4.

3112 Stein, Arnold. "On Milton's Unfortunate Lovers." *MiltonQ*, 7, 1973, 59.
Abstract of a paper presented to the Milton Society of America on December 27, 1972. Deals with the problem of both horizontal and vertical love in *Paradise Lost*, especially as it affects Adam and Eve's relationship.

3113 Stein, Arnold. "Satan's Metamorphoses: The Internal Speech." *MiltonS*, 1, 1969, 93–113.
"The internal speech demonstrates how he [Satan] maneuvers himself freely expressing the passions, motives, and selective awareness by which he moves, but which govern him—so that he is at once 'voluntary' agent and victim."

3114 Steinke, Arthur Russell. "When It Comes: The Sense of Time in *Paradise Lost*." Doctoral diss., State Univ. of New York, Stony Brook, 1977. 249pp. Abs., *DAI*, 38, 1977, 3523A–24A.
Explores Milton's use of "perspectives,

of close-ups and fade-outs," in creating "authentic temporal contexts for the mystery of supernatural and unfallen modes of experience."

3115 Stevens, Paul. "The Evidence of Things Not Seen: Faith and Imagination in *Paradise Lost*." Doctoral diss., Univ. of Toronto, 1983. Abs., *DAI*, 44, 1983, 762A.
Analyzes the extremes of imagination's potential—a path to seduction when separated from reason, but a gate to truth when educated—in *Paradise Lost*.

3116 Stevens, Paul. *Imagination and the Presence of Shakespeare in "Paradise Lost."* Madison: Univ. of Wisconsin Press, 1985. ix, 270pp.
Discusses Shakespeare's presence in *Comus* but especially in *Paradise Lost*. Explicates "some of the more extensive patterns of Shakespearean echo and allusion . . . in conjunction with similar patterns from other influences, especially Milton's 'original,' Spenser." Reviews: Georgia Christopher, *SQ*, 38, 1987, 392–94; Paul Yuckman, *MiltonQ*, 21, No. 3, 1987, 119–20; Nigel Smith, *RES*, 38, 1987, 249–50; Gordon Campbell, *MLR*, 83, 1988, 677.

3117 Stevenson, Kay Gilliland. "Eve's Place in *Paradise Lost*." *MiltonQ*, 22, 1988, 126–27.
Believes that Milton gives Eve dignity and complicates her placement in the earthly and heavenly hierarchies because of her "special place in Paradise," the "inversion of male-female stereotypes" in Book 9, and "the order of the final speeches in Book 12."

3118 Stevenson, Kay Gilliland. "'No More . . . No End': *Paradise Lost* IX." *RenP*, 1983, pp. 103–09.
Believes that the words "No more" at the beginning and "no end" at the end of Book 9 frame a five-act tragedy which preserves the unities of time, place, and action. "The recurrent motif of the tragedy is separation, physical or psychological."

3119 Stocker, Margarita. "God in Theory: Milton, Literature and Theodicy." *L&T*, 1, 1987, 70–88.

Relates D. J. Enright's *Love Almighty and Ills Unlimited* (1966) and *Paradise Illustrated* (1978) to the theodicy of *Paradise Lost*. Believes that Milton avoids clear-cut answers to theological questions and discusses multiple meanings.

3120 Stocker, Margarita. *"Paradise Lost": An Introduction to the Variety of Criticism.* London: Macmillan; Atlantic Highlands, NJ: Humanities Press International, 1988. 95pp.

Examines approaches to the poem through its theme, form and genre, historical context, psychology and myth, and reader and text.

3121 Stoenescu, Stefan. "Milton: *Paradisul Pierdut.* La Tricentenarul unei Opere Fundamentale." *SXX*, 20, No. 7, 1974, 52–58.

"Milton: *Paradise Lost.* On the Tercentenary of a Basic Work." In Romanian. Focuses on Milton's use of language in the poem, especially the lexico-grammatical and syntactic effects. Mentions the effects created by broken verse and the Homeric influence on Milton's work.

3122 Stollman, Samuel S. "Satan, Sin, and Death: A Mosaic Trio in *Paradise Lost.*" *MiltonS*, 22, 1986, 101–20.

Believes that "the personifications of Sin and Death and their encounters with Satan act out one of Milton's major doctrines, namely his . . . antinomian view of the Mosaic Law and of the Law's impediment to the attainment of Christian liberty."

3123 Stroup, Thomas B. *"Paradise Lost." Religious Rite and Ceremony in Milton's Poetry* (Lexington: Univ. of Kentucky Press, 1968), pp. 15–47.

See Huckabay No. 1893. Reviews (of book): *MiltonN*, 2, 1968, 10; Robert M. Davis, *SHR*, 3, 1969, 204–06; Davis P. Harding, *RenQ*, 23, 1970,

206–07; Michael Wilding, *YES*, 1, 1971, 152–53.

3124 Sullivan, Ernest W. "The Bible and Satanic Deceit: *Paradise Lost* X, 460–572." *ES*, 61, 1980, 127–29.

Discusses Proverbs 20.17 and Romans 3.13–19 as probable sources for many details in the episode when Satan announces the deception of Adam and Eve to his followers. Points out that the transformation of food in the mouth and the loss of speech experienced by Satan and his followers represent the punishments for deceivers illustrated in these biblical passages.

3125 Summers, Joseph H. "The Embarrassments of *Paradise Lost.*" *Approaches to "Paradise Lost."* The York Tercentenary Lectures. Ed. by C. A. Patrides (London: Edward Arnold; Toronto: Univ. of Toronto Press, 1968), pp. 65–79.

Notes that *Paradise Lost* provides some embarrassments and cannot be used as propoganda either by representatives of the status quo or its opponents. Concludes that it is a remarkably modern poem which stands as the center of the English literary tradition.

3126 Summers, Joseph H. *The Muse's Method: An Introduction to "Paradise Lost."* Binghamton, NY: Medieval and Renaissance Texts and Studies, 1981.

Reprint of Huckabay No. 1896, originally published in 1962.

3127 Sundell, Roger H. "The Singer and His Song in the Prologues of *Paradise Lost." Milton and the Art of Sacred Song.* Ed. by J. Max Patrick and Sundell (Madison: Univ. of Wisconsin Press, 1979), pp. 65–80.

Analyzes the functions of the four prologues, which, when taken together, comprise a poem about making a sacred poem. Suggests a tonal progression from confidence to something like presumption, to apprehension, and finally to regained confidence.

3128 Suzuki, Shigeo. "Anti-Feminism in

Paradise Lost." *MCJ News*, 10, 1988, 16–17.

Abstract of a paper presented at the Twenty-Third Colloquium of MCJ in July, 1987. Claims that in its portrayal of women, *Paradise Lost* is simultaneously antifeminist and not misogynistic. Attributes this apparent contradiction to the Puritan view of women who "though making a success of founding a new tradition of treating men and women on an equal basis, subconsciously took a negative attitude toward incorporating within their organization the feminine principles and femininity."

3129 Suzuki, Shigeo. "Shitsurakuen no Ansoku." *EigoS*, 131, 1986, 607–08.

Comments on the sin of sloth in *Paradise Lost*.

3130 Swaim, Kathleen M. "The Art of the Maze in Book IX of *Paradise Lost.*" *SEL*, 12, 1972, 129–40.

"Maze is a very skillfully manipulated physical, spatial, verbal, intellectual, and spiritual pattern in which Milton richly embodies the internal and external action of the Fall and an extended . . . commentary on the import of that action."

3131 Swaim, Kathleen M. *Before and After the Fall: Contrasting Modes in "Paradise Lost."* Amherst: Univ. of Massachusetts Press, 1986. xiv, 291pp.

Compares Raphael's prelapsarian instruction to Adam in Books 5–8 of *Paradise Lost* with Michael's post-lapsarian lessons in Books 11–12. Studies "the radically different principles and epistemologies that govern the unfallen and fallen universes and the alterations in the conduct of human life and relationship to deity." Reviews: Charles Martindale, *TLS*, Feb. 5–11, 1988, p. 142; Irène Simon, *RES*, 39, 1988, 295–97; Frederick M. Keener, *YES*, 19, 1989, 321–22; Jacqueline T. Miller, *RenQ*, 42, 1989, 365–67; P. J. Klemp, *MiltonQ*, 24, 1990, 71–76.

3132 Swaim, Kathleen M. "Flower, Fruit, and Seed: A Reading of *Paradise Lost.*" *MiltonS*, 5, 1973, 155–76.

"Milton's predominantly floral prelapsarian cosmos employs imagery relating flowers to character, place, and theme. . . . Milton's poetry like his fiction shifts from floral to fruitful, from paradise without to paradise within, from innocence to experience, from praise to prayer, from discursive to intuitive apprehension."

3133 Swaim, Kathleen M. " 'Hee for God Only, Shee for God in Him': Structural Parallelism in *Paradise Lost.*" *MiltonS*, 9, 1976, 121–49.

"Three sections of *Paradise Lost*—Eve's love song and astronomical query in Book IV and Adam's parallel dealings with Raphael in Book VIII, Adam and Eve's fateful parting and their fallen evaluations of it in Book IX, and the reconciliation and reunion through prayer in Book X—illuminate the thematic relationship of the epistemologies of experience and faith in the poem. Eve's relationship with Adam parallels Adam's with divine agency."

3134 Swaim, Kathleen M. "The Mimesis of Accommodation in Book 3 of *Paradise Lost.*" *PQ*, 63, 1984, 461–75.

Believes that in *Paradise Lost* 3, Milton uses light to provide "a mimesis of accommodation, a sort of 'metaphoric structure' for mediating between divine mysteries and human limitations as well as capacities."

3135 Swaim, Kathleen M. "The Morning Hymn of Praise in Book 5 of *Paradise Lost.*" *MiltonQ*, 22, 1988, 7–16.

Explores the material Milton draws on and alludes to in Adam and Eve's prelapsarian morning hymn of praise in *Paradise Lost* 5.153–208: the Apocrypha and such books as Psalms, Daniel, and Genesis.

3136 Swaim, Kathleen M. "Some Dante and Milton Analogues." *Renascence*, 37, 1984, 43–51.

Demonstrates Milton's indebtedness to Dante by finding verbal echoes of his work in *Paradise Lost*. Shows how Milton "reorient[s] this inherited literary material in his own Protestant directions."

3137 Swift, John N. "Similes of Disguise and the Reader of *Paradise Lost*." *SAQ*, 79, 1980, 425–35.

Examines similes of disguise and shows that, in God's eyes, they are all transparent. Because "the truest purpose of any simile is itself to be a likeness," then "The reader who understands this purpose, who discards the Satanic sense of simile as equality and accepts its typological nature, finds himself drawn unerringly toward God."

3138 Symes, M. W. R. "A Paradise within Thee?: The Relationship between the Garden and Man in *Paradise Lost*." *YES*, 3, 1973, 94–107.

Sees the garden as a counterpart to Adam because it reflects his general state of being—perfection. Ultimately, the garden becomes internal or "the Eden within man. . . . The poem is about man and not about a garden."

3139 Szenczi, M. J. "Milton's Dialectic in *Paradise Lost*: Some Patterns of Interpretation." *Angol Bes Amerikai Filolbogiai Tanulmbanyok*, 1, 1971, 58–92.

Argues that *Paradise Lost* has "a permanent appeal independent of the time and place of its origin," in spite of its apparent contradictions and foundation in primeval myths.

3140 Szigeti, Jeno. "Milton Elveszett Paradicsom-a Magyarországon." *IK*, 74, 1970, 205–13.

Discusses *Paradise Lost* in Hungary.

3141 Szittya, Brenda Bethel. "'If Art Could Tell': Negative Theology in *Paradise Lost*." Doctoral diss., Univ. of Virginia, 1972. 153pp. Abs., *DAI*, 33, 1972, 1697A.

Draws parallels between the God of *Paradise Lost* and the incomprehensible Old Testament God examined in negative theology.

3142 Takaku, Shin-Ichi. "Some Dubious Angels in Heaven." *Lang&C*, 4, 1983, 1–17.

In Japanese; English summary, pp. 18–19. Argues that some of the angels were secretly corrupted, even before they openly rebelled against God.

3143 Takizawa, Masahiko. "'Tears, Such as Angels Weep' (*Paradise Lost* I, 619–20) and *Genesis B*." *MCJ News*, 8, 1985, 15–16.

Abstract of a paper presented at the Seventeenth Colloquium of MCJ in July, 1984. Insists that *Paradise Lost* was influenced by the Old English poem *Genesis B*. Argues that the Christian notion of pride as a sin crushes the Germanic sense of pride as "one of the worthiest virtues" and leads Satan to shed "Tears, such as Angels weep."

3144 Tamaki, Ishitaro. "The Fortunate Fall in *Paradise Lost*." *MCJ News*, 9, 1987, 18–20.

Abstract of paper presented. Studies the structural implications of the paradox of the fortunate fall in *Paradise Lost* 12.473–78. Views the work as a five-act play in which the paradox is "the culmination around which the theme of the whole poem is organized."

3145 Tamaki, Ishitaro. "Milton's Punctuation in *Paradise Lost*." *MCJ News*, 9, 1987, 26–27.

Abstract of a paper presented at the Twentieth Colloquium of MCJ in December, 1985. Collates the punctuation of the second edition of *Paradise Lost* (1674) with that of Masson's edition (1874; see Huckabay No. 3273). Concludes that "Milton's punctuation in *PL* originated from the metrics of his own abounding in enjambement and caesura or diaeresis, carrying the sense over from one line to the next."

3146 Tamaki, Ishitaro. "The Text of *Paradise Lost*." *Studies in Milton* (Tokyo: Kinseido, 1974), pp. 54–73.

In Japanese. Surveys the various texts,

paying special attention to spelling and punctuation.

3147 Tanner, John S. "Anxiety in Eden: Eve and the Psychology of Sin in *Paradise Lost* and *The Concept of Anxiety*." *L&B*, 7, 1987, 41–48.

Milton "imagines paradise as a state of bliss qualified by anxiety, especially for Eve. His conception of Eve's dreamfall and actual fall is remarkably compatible with the prelapsarian Eden Kierkegaard describes in *The Concept of Anxiety*."

3148 Tanner, John Sears. "The Dreadful Garden: *Paradise Lost* and *The Concept of Dread*." Doctoral diss., Univ. of California, Berkeley, 1980. 242pp. Abs., *DAI*, 42, 1981, 232A.

Uses Kierkegaard's ideas on the nature of the Fall, the origin of sin, and the path to salvation to illuminate *Paradise Lost*.

3149 Tanner, John S. "'Say First What Cause': Ricoeur and the Etiology of Evil in *Paradise Lost*." *PMLA*, 103, 1988, 45–56.

Employs Paul Ricoeur's theories of the Adamic myth and original sin to study the etiology and symbolism of evil in *Paradise Lost*. Divides sin into three categories: Satanic evil, which "occurs in heaven among Satan and his followers"; Adamic evil, which "transpires in Eden and involves Adam and Eve"; and historical evil, which is "foreseen among the descendants of Adam and Eve."

3150 Tayler, Edward W. "Milton's Grim Laughter and Second Choices." *Poetry and Epistemology: Turning Points in the History of Poetic Knowledge*. Ed. by Roland Hagenbüchle and Laura Skandera (Regensburg: Pustet, 1986), pp. 72–93.

The rational reader might agree with some of Satan's statements, but Milton as narrator encourages a second choice. God's laughter occurs several times in *Paradise Lost*, sometimes grim and sometimes playful.

3151 Teague, Anthony G. "The Fall of Satan and the Harrowing of Hell: Literary Preludes to Milton." *JELL*, 32, 1986, 407–30.

Discusses the tradition of the harrowing of hell and believes that the theme of hope at the end of *Paradise Lost* preserves its essential meaning. Studies the development of the story of the War in Heaven.

3152 Teague, Frances. "Milton and the Pygmies." *MiltonQ*, 20, 1986, 31–32.

Believes that the pygmy warriors in *Paradise Lost* 1.573–76 are drawn from Ovid's story of Anarche and Minerva in the *Metamorphoses*. Milton thus associates the battles of the pygmies and the cranes with overweening pride punished by divine wrath.

3153 Teskey, Gordon. "Milton and Modernity." *Diacritics*, 18, 1988, 42–53.

Asserts that it is foolish to constantly attempt new meanings of *Paradise Lost*. Instead, the reader must both appreciate Milton's epic for the time in which it was written and extract meaning from it in relation to the world we inhabit now.

3154 Teskey, Gordon. "Milton's Choice of Subject in the Context of Renaissance Critical Theory." *ELH*, 53, 1986, 53–72.

Discusses various Renaissance opinions concerning proper subjects for an epic, including Milton's. Believes that Milton finally chose his subject when he decided that the Fall was proper for epic as well as for drama.

3155 Thickstun, Margaret Olofson. "Effeminate Slackness Substantially Expressed: Woman as Scapegoat in *Paradise Lost*." *Fictions of the Feminine: Puritan Doctrine and the Representation of Women* (Ithaca, NY, and London: Cornell Univ. Press, 1988), pp. 60–86.

A reading of *Paradise Lost* by "a scholar and a feminist, from within and without, to try to reconcile the attention to religious and historical context . . . with sensitivity to the inconsistency in

Milton's message concerning women's moral sufficiency that feminist readings recognize." Explores the influence of Puritan theology and domestic theory on the representation of women in English narrative. Believes that in treating the relationship between man and woman, Milton follows the Pauline tradition, but both Adam and Eve sin because they put their personal needs above God. Review (of book): Diane K. McColley, *ANQ*, 2, 1989, 110–20.

3156 Thomas, Raymond Lawrence. "Neo-Classical, Romantic, and Twentieth-Century Interpretations of Milton's Satan, 1695–1967." Doctoral diss., Pennsylvania State Univ., 1968. 113pp. Abs., *DAI*, 30, 1969, 1185A–86A.

Examines the critical response to Milton's Satan, asserting that religious prejudices and passing ideologies have long prevented an objective, contextual view of him.

3157 Thorne-Thomsen, Sara. "'Hail Wedded Love': Milton's Lyric Epithalamium." *MiltonS*, 24, 1988, 155–85.

Relates the hymn in *Paradise Lost* 4.750–73 to the tradition of the marriage hymn from classical literature to Spenser.

3158 Thorne-Thomsen, Sara. "Milton's 'Advent'rous Song': Lyric Genres in *Paradise Lost*." Doctoral diss., Brown Univ., 1985. 260pp. Abs., *DAI*, 46, 1986, 1953A–54A.

Argues that Milton uses various lyric genres—such as the epithalamium, the sonnet, the aubade, the serenade, the lament, and the hymn—to validate "a definition of love that substantiates his justification of God's ways."

3159 Threadgold, Terry. "What Did Milton Say Belial Said and Why Don't the Critics Believe Him?" *Linguistics in a Systemic Perspective.* Ed. by James D. Benson and others (Amsterdam: Benjamins, 1988), pp. 331–92.

"It will be my argument that the consistent semantic patternings and

lexico-grammatical structures that are accessible to analysis in the Milton text *are* generically predictable; that this is a text which is constrained by not one but many intertextual generic systems, and that this is the source of much of the text's polysemy and ambiguity."

3160 Tobin, J. J. M. "A Note on Luther, Arius and *PL*, X, 504ff." *MiltonQ*, 11, 1977, 38–43.

Advances the idea that Milton was not a supporter of Arius, that he knew of a source for the image of Arius as a serpent, and that he recognized the many similarities between Arius's and Satan's careers and fused them.

3161 Toliver, Harold E. "Milton's Household Epic." *MiltonS*, 9, 1976, 105–20.

"Formal epic is both consummated and altered by Milton in *Paradise Lost* and *Paradise Regained*, which absorb much of the tradition but recast it. The focus in *Paradise Lost* on Adam and Eve is part of Milton's conscious resistance to chivalric epic on behalf of Puritan and domestic values."

3162 Toliver, Harold E. "The Splinter Coalition." *New Essays on "Paradise Lost."* Ed. by Thomas Kranidas (Berkeley, Los Angeles, and London: Univ. of California Press, 1969), pp. 34–57.

Discusses the hollow machinations of Satan and his allies. Sees him, finally, as a diplomat who has been completely undermined. Abs., *MiltonQ*, 4, 1970, 33–34.

3163 Toliver, Harold. "Symbol-Making and the Labors of Milton's Eden." *TSLL*, 18, 1976, 433–50.

Claims that poetic language is natural to Adam and Eve and that the same naturalness of purpose inspires the use of symbols in Eden. Abs., *MiltonQ*, 12, 1978, 115.

3164 Toole, William B. "'The Attractions of the Journey': A Comment on the Structure of *Paradise Lost*." *ArlQ*, 1, 1968, 18–37.

Sees *Paradise Lost* as a series of

complex and specific correspondences, such as those between Satan and Christ, Satan and Eve, and Satan and Adam. Milton constructs various scenes to show parallelism with contrast.

3165 Treip, Mindele Anne. *"Descend from Heav'n Urania": Milton's "Paradise Lost" and Raphael's Cycle in the "Stanza della Segnatura."* Victoria, BC: Univ. of Victoria, 1985. 84pp.

Compares one room of Raphael's ceiling frescoes in the Vatican and Milton's poetry. Reviews: Roy Flannagan, *MiltonQ*, 20, 1986, 55; Gordon Campbell, *MLR*, 83, 1988, 677.

3166 Treip, Mindele. *Milton's Punctuation and Changing English Usage, 1582–1676.* London: Methuen; New York: Barnes and Noble, 1970. xiv, 189pp.

Focuses on the punctuation of the manuscript of *Paradise Lost* 1. Considers variants in the 1667 edition. Shows the interdependence between Milton's punctuation and rhythm and meaning. Recognizes affinities between Milton's punctuation and that of the Elizabethans. Reviews: *SELit*, 48, 1971, 132–35; John S. Diekhoff, *JEGP*, 70, 1971, 553–55; Merritt Y. Hughes, *MLR*, 66, 1971, xxi–xxxii; Michael Lieb, *SCN*, 29, 1971, 35; *MiltonQ*, 5, 1971, 78–79; John T. Shawcross, *ELN*, 8, 1971, 326–31; Alan Ward, *RES*, 23, 1972, 78–80; Roger Lejosne, *EA*, 26, 1973, 101.

3167 Tsuji, Hiroko. "Oratory at Pandacmonium with a Focus on Belial's Speech." *MCJ News*, 2, 1978, 11–12.

Abstract of paper presented. There is a distinct difference between appearance and reality in Belial's speech in *Paradise Lost* 2, resulting in a kind of sophistry which Milton would condemn, as would Plato and Cicero. Abs., *MiltonQ*, 13, 1979, 161.

3168 Tsuji, Hiroko. "Paradise and Language." *MCJ News*, 10, 1988, 6–11.

Argues that since biblical stories "were real to Milton," he "seems to restore the value of the literal meanings of the language as well as the metaphorical implications" when he "transfigures a biblical myth directly into his epic."

3169 Tsuji, Hiroko. "The 'Tragic Notes' and the Language of *Paradise Lost*, Book IX." *MCJ News*, 8, 1985, 16–17.

Abstract of a paper presented at the Eighteenth Colloquium of MCJ in December, 1984. Identifies tragic elements in Book 9.

3170 Tsuji, Hiroko. "The 'Tragic Notes' and the Language of *Paradise Lost*, Book IX." *SELit*, 63, 1986, 41–59.

Analyzes the tragic structure of Book 9, using an Aristotelian context. Divides the book into five parts, with the last episode serving as a denouement and Book 10 as its continuation. Follows other critics in noticing the close relationship between epic and tragedy.

3171 Tucker, Herbert F., Jr. "Gravity and Milton's Moral Physics." *MiltonQ*, 12, 1978, 96–100.

"Proceeding from God the grantor of Milton's cosmos and of every force that sustains it, the principle of gravity expresses and illuminates fundamental principles sustaining Milton's poem [*Paradise Lost*] as well. Milton's exploitation of a moral physics, and particularly of certain paradoxes inherent in the laws governing falling bodies, makes possible some of his most distinctive poetic effects."

3172 Tucker, John Arthur. *"Paradise Lost* and the Masque." *ESC*, 5, 1979, 140–53.

Discusses the masque form's influence on *Paradise Lost* in such aspects as visual effects and symbolic reference. Compares various masques with Milton's epic.

3173 Turner, Amy Lee. "Milton and Jansson's Sea Atlas." *MiltonQ*, 4, 1970, 36–39.

Does not believe that Milton's blindness would have prevented his using Jan Jansson's international wind chart for the image of the original winds in

Paradise Lost 10.695–707. Notes that the chart first appeared in Jansson's *Atlas Maritimus* (1650), before Milton's blindness, and that Milton probably had access to a copy. Reply by Gordon Campbell (No. 2017).

3174 Turner, Amy Lee. "Milton and Jodocus Hondius the Elder." *MiltonN*, 3, 1969, 26–30.

Suggests that the allegory of Sin, Death, and Satan as depicted by Hondius on his "Christian Knight Map of the World" influenced Milton's dramatic groupings of the infernal triad in *Paradise Lost* 2.648–889 and 10.229–409.

3175 Turner, Amy Lee. "Milton and the Moon." *ForumH*, 4, 1965, 32–36.

Although Milton's cosmology essentially follows that of the Aristotelian-Ptolemaic system, his moon is mostly Galilean. Milton admired Galileo, and the revelations of the telescope had a profound effect on his work.

3176 Turner, James Grantham. "Love Made in the First Age: Edenic Sexuality in *Paradise Lost* and Its Analogues." *One Flesh: Paradisal Marriage and Sexual Relations in the Age of Milton* (Oxford: Clarendon Press, 1987), pp. 230–309.

Holds that *Paradise Lost* "represents the climax of Milton's lifelong struggle to create a vision of Eros based on his reading of Genesis." His reconstruction of Adam and Eve's love is an imaginary reversal of the incompatibility of his early prose. Notes that Satan's most intense outbursts come when he observes Eve's sexuality because he is an erotic fallen angel. Reviews (of book): C. H. Sisson, *TLS*, Dec. 4, 1987, p. 1357; Roy C. Flannagan, *MiltonQ*, 22, 1988, 129–32; Thomas Healy, *English* (Oxford), 37, 1988, 155–64; James Holstun, *SCN*, 46, 1988, 72; Diane K. McColley, *ANQ*, 2, 1989, 110–20; Marilyn L. Williamson, *Criticism*, 31, 1989, 480; Christopher Hill, *EHR*, 105, 1990, 735–36; Nigel Smith,

RES, 41, 1990, 123; Susan Staves, *MP*, 88, 1990, 193–98.

3177 Turner, J. G. "Milton's Hollow Cube." *N&Q*, 25, 1978, 17–18.

Claims that Milton derived Satan's strategy of the hollow cube from contemporary military handbooks.

3178 Turner, Richard. "The Interpretation of Dreams and Audience Response in *Paradise Lost* and *Paradise Regained*." *PLL*, 19, 1983, 361–74.

Believes that the knowledge of dream lore that Milton's readers possessed allowed them to interpret both the cause and the significance of dreams in *Paradise Lost* and *Paradise Regained*. Contends that "the dreams instruct the readers and prepare them for confrontations with Satan both in the narrative structure of the poems and in their everyday lives." Also argues that Milton's presentation of dreams requires a reader-response approach and a literary history approach to interpret it.

3179 Tyson, J. Patrick. "The Satan Tragedy in *Paradise Lost*." *Papers on Milton*. Ed. by Philip Mahone Griffith and Lester F. Zimmerman. Univ. of Tulsa Department of English Monograph Series, no. 8 (Tulsa, OK: Univ. of Tulsa, 1969), pp. 47–56.

"All of the elements of the Greek tragic structure are . . . evident in the portions of *Paradise Lost* which deal with Satan. His actions form a unified plot with a beginning, middle, and end."

3180 Ulreich, John C., Jr. "A Paradise Within: The Fortunate Fall in *Paradise Lost*." *JHI*, 32, 1971, 351–66.

Argues that regeneration begins from the outside, but is consummated within, supernaturally. Milton wants to demonstrate God's justice and not to prove the Fall necessary for humanity's ultimate glory and salvation.

3181 Ulreich, John C. "'Sufficient To Have Stood': Adam's Responsibility in Book IX." *MiltonQ*, 5, 1971, 38–42.

Holds that after Eve's fall, Adam has

the responsibility to trust God and realize his own capacity for love. Suggests that Adam, like Christ, could have chosen to offer himself as a redeemer, dying *"for* Eve rather than *with* her. . . . The real issue of the Fall is not the justice or apparent awfulness of the punishment but the responsibility and integrity of the creature; self-sacrifice is the response of genuine love. Adam, of course, does not have the benefit of Christ's example, but he does have, until he loses it, his love for Eve and God. And there is no reason to suppose that his sacrifice would have been any less acceptable than Christ's."

3182 Valtz Mannucci, Loretta. *Ideali e Classi nella Poesia di Milton: La Nàscita dell'Eròe Borghese Puritano in "Paradise Lost" e "Paradise Regained."* Saggi di Cultura Contemporanea, 116. Milano: Edizioni di Comunità, 1976. 284pp.
Deals mainly with Adam's education.

3183 van den Berg, Sara. "Eve, Sin, and Witchcraft in *Paradise Lost.*" *MLQ*, 47, 1986, 347–65.
Concludes that, when Milton portrayed Eve and Sin in *Paradise Lost*, seventeenth-century debates about witchcraft gave him "languages with which to sort out ideas about gender relations and about matters common to men and women: imagination, desire, and identity."

3184 van den Berg, Sara. " 'Return Me to My Native Element': A Reading of *PL* (Bks. VII–VIII)." *MiltonQ*, 10, 1976, 26.
Abstract of a paper presented at the 1975 MLA Convention. *Paradise Lost* turns inward in Books 7 and 8 and the native element becomes the self and Adam's other self becomes Eve.

3185 Van Sickle, Judy Lynn. "Song as Structure and Symbol in Four Poems of John Milton." Doctoral diss., Brown Univ., 1981. 296pp. Abs., *DAI*, 43, 1982, 456A–57A.
Argues that "John Milton makes use

of song genres and musical structures in much more technically and formally precise ways that either Miltonists or music historians have hitherto appreciated."

3186 Vaughn, Mark. "More than Meets the Eye: Milton's Acrostics in *Paradise Lost.*" *MiltonQ*, 16, 1982, 6–8.
Discusses several acrostics that appear in the epic, some of which have a relation to the text. Notes that "SATAN" and "WOE" are the most pertinent.

3187 Vent, Maryanne. "The Fall of Man and the Poetry of Love in *Paradise Lost.*" *MiltonQ*, 17, 1983, 26.
Abstract of a paper presented at the 1982 MLA Convention. While *Paradise Lost* 4 develops love based on the Old Testament view, Books 8–9 develop love based on an "antithetical philosophy of love . . . from the poetry of the troubadours and their successors in Italy."

3188 Vesenyi, Paul. "Milton on Stage behind the Iron Curtain." *MiltonQ*, 5, 1971, 16–17.
Review of Karoly Kazimir's 1970 adaptation of *Paradise Lost* for the Thalia Theater of Budapest, Hungary. Notes shortcomings but concludes that "in this bold interpretation of *Paradise Lost*, Milton did not get lost." See also No. 2552.

3189 Vessels, Elizabeth Jane. "A Mythic Light on Eve: The Function of Mythological Allusion in Defining Her Character and Role in the Epic Action of *Paradise Lost.*" Doctoral diss., Fordham Univ., 1972. 56pp. Abs., *DAI*, 33, 1973, 3605A.
Considers the impact of Christian mythology on Milton's Eve "because of the special link existing between her, the focal point of devilish deceit in *Paradise Lost*, and pagan mythology, the product of devilish 'falsities and lies.' "

3190 Vetö, Miklos. "Des Livides Flammes à l'Endurcissement: La Doctrine du Mal dans *Paradis Perdu.*" *RMM*, 84, 1979, 446–66.

Shows that *Paradise Lost* develops classical ideas about the origin and manifestation of evil by integrating Protestant theology and classical humanism expressed in a metaphysical doctrine. Rejects Calvinistic predestination and looks instead to frailties in human nature to explain why some refuse salvation.

3191 Viswanathan, S. "Milton and the 'Seasons' Difference.'" *SEL*, 13, 1973, 127–33.

Discusses references to the seasons in *Paradise Lost*, concluding that Milton felt the climate had an influence on poetic faculties and believed Eden had an eternal spring. But he also asserts that the seasons were implemented as further punishment for human sin.

3192 Viswanathan, S. "The Sun and the Creation of Adam: *Paradise Lost*, VIII. 253–55." *MiltonQ*, 8, 1974, 80–82.

On Renaissance ideas concerning the sun's role in the process of creation. Milton's passage is in line with the thinking of Marsilio Ficino and others.

3193 Waddington, Raymond B. "The Death of Adam: Vision and Voice in Books XI and XII of *Paradise Lost*." *MP*, 70, 1972, 9–21.

Argues that Milton shifts from vision in Book 11 to narration in Book 12 to show that Adam's life must end during the first age (before the flood). See No. 2217.

3194 Waddington, Raymond B. "Here Comes the Son: Providential Theme and Symbolic Pattern in *Paradise Lost*, Book 3." *MP*, 79, 1982, 256–66.

Shows that Milton uses light and sight imagery to depict the Fall, the prediction of it, and its consequences. Maintains that, in *Paradise Lost* 3.56–59, the eye of God "directly evokes the Old Testament descriptions of 'th'Almighty Father,' but simultaneously suggests the *oculus mundi*, the sun of the physical world, a symbolic sun which potentially figures both the Holy Trinity and the Son of God." Abs., *MiltonQ*, 14, 1980, 33; *SCN*, 38, 1980, 46.

3195 Walker, Julia M. "'For Each Seem'd Either': Free Will and Predestination in *Paradise Lost*." *MiltonQ*, 20, 1986, 13–16.

Asserts that "although the reader finds Free Will clearly defined in an unambiguous passage, the rival reality of Predestination is more subtly presented throughout the length of the poem, presented through the shifting uses of the verb 'seems.'" See Stephen M. Fallon's response (No. 2189) and Walker's surrejoinder (No. 3196).

3196 Walker, Julia M. "Free Will, Predestination, and Ghost-Busting." *MiltonQ*, 21, No. 3, 1987, 101–02.

Disagrees with Stephen M. Fallon's assertion (No. 2189) that she "assumes 'that the only alternatives [in *Paradise Lost*] are a necessitated will or an irrational random will.'" Also claims that Fallon has a "'flawed reading of Milton's use of the verb "seems."'"

3197 Wallace, Laurie Ann. "The Renaissance Transformation of Eve." Doctoral diss., Texas Christian Univ., 1985. 118pp. Abs., *DAI*, 46, 1986, 3364A.

Demonstrates how Milton and Spenser affirm the Renaissance "woman in her role as wife while establishing the integrity of her full humanity within the universal hierarchy."

3198 Walsh, Marcus. "Literary Annotation and Biblical Commentary: The Case of Patrick Hume's *Annotations* on *Paradise Lost*." *MiltonQ*, 22, 1988, 109–14.

Discusses Patrick Hume's 1695 *Annotations* for *Paradise Lost*. Contends that "The purpose of Hume's paraphrase is not to offer, in substitution for Milton's meaning, . . . a sense of his own, but to explicate, to unfold to his reader, Milton's meaning itself." Hume fulfills this purpose through biblical commentary.

3199 Wanamaker, Melissa C. *Discordia Concors: The Wit of Metaphysical Poetry.* Port Washington, NY: Kennikat Press, 1975. 166pp.

Examines *Paradise Lost* through the context of discordia concors, focusing on the similes.

3200 Wang, Xiao-Gin. "A Tentative Analysis of the Guiding Idea in the Creation of *Paradise Lost.*" *FLS*, 20, 1983, 78–85. In Chinese.

3201 Warhaft, Sidney. "The Assertion of Providence after the Fall in *Paradise Lost.*" *ESC*, 2, 1976, 262–79.

Discusses postlapsarian providence's obligations—including punishment, preservation, and restoration—and the conflict between such obligations. Milton resolves it "by asserting eternal providence, by showing that providence achieves its ends indirectly, through adaptation and accommodation, when it cannot do so directly (that is, through miracles); and by so asserting he affects fundamentally the structure and style of the last books of his poem."

3202 Warren, William Fairfield. *The Universe as Pictured in Milton's "Paradise Lost."* Folcroft, PA: Folcroft Library Editions, 1969, 1973.

Reprints of Stevens No. 946, originally published in 1915.

3203 Watson, Thomas Ramey. "Milton's Pyramids." *AN&Q*, 24, 1986, 132–34.

Argues that in *Paradise Lost*, Milton incorporates a pyramidal motif in the construction of the universe. Points out that Satan imitates this motif, which symbolizes perfection.

3204 Watson, Thomas Ramey. "Milton's Use of Bees in *Paradise Lost.*" *AN&Q*, 24, 1985, 38–39.

Notices the difference between the bees' prelapsarian and postlapsarian behavior. In hell they are perversions that hiss and swarm, while in paradise they are productive members of their community.

3205 Watson, Thomas Ramey. "Perversions, Originals, and Redemptions: Typological Patterns Underlining Theme in *Paradise Lost* Based upon Augustine's *De Civitate Dei.*" Doctoral diss., Univ. of Louisville, 1981. 157pp. Abs., *DAI*, 42, 1982, 3170A.

Compares historical themes in *Paradise Lost* and the *City of God*, especially Satan's continuous perversion of divine perfection, which is opposed by God's evolving plan of redemption for humanity.

3206 Watson, Thomas Ramey. "The Typological Pattern of Noonday in Milton's *Paradise Lost.*" *MiltonQ*, 21, No. 1, 1987, 14–20.

Argues that Milton uses the noonday motif in *Paradise Lost* to portray the dichotomy of spiritual light and darkness, the time of temptation, and the light to come: Jesus Christ.

3207 Weathers, Winston. "*Paradise Lost* as Archetypal Myth." *The Archetype and the Psyche: Essays in World Literature* (Univ. of Tulsa Department of English Monograph Series, No. 4, 1968), pp. 46–52.

Reprint of Huckabay No. 1972, originally published in 1952–53.

3208 Webber, Joan. "Milton and the Politics of Epic." *MiltonQ*, 10, 1976, 30.

Abstract of a paper presented at the 1975 MLA Convention. Believes that the design of *Paradise Lost* "is intended to initiate the release of the central forces of destruction and creation outward into their material realization of history as described at the beginning (in the catalog of devils) and at the end."

3209 Webber, Joan. "Milton's God." *ELH*, 40, 1973, 514–31.

States that "the traditional Christian God is at once celebrated and subverted, as Milton thus both accepts the paradoxical epic tradition and tries to find the source and reason for its paradoxes."

3210 Webber, Joan Malory. "*Paradise*

Lost." *Milton and His Epic Tradition* (Seattle and London: Univ. of Washington Press, 1979), pp. 101–63.

Shows how Milton transforms the epic tradition to suit his own purposes. Interprets epics as essentially subversive and as representing turning points in human consciousness. Reviews (of book): Roy C. Flannagan, *MiltonQ*, 13, 1979, 155–56; David Norbrook, *TLS*, Nov. 30, 1979, p. 74; Don Parry Norford, *MLQ*, 40, 1979, 292–306; Stevie Davies, *CritQ*, 22, 1980, 86–87; Mario A. Di Cesare, *ELN*, 17, 1980, 303–06; William B. Hunter, Jr., *C&L*, 29, 1980, 79–80; Earl Miner, *JEGP*, 79, 1980, 250–53; Isabel Rivers, *RenQ*, 33, 1980, 488–90; James H. Sims, *SCN*, 38, 1980, 69–71; John C. Ulreich, Jr., *Cithara*, 20, No. 1, 1980, 57–60; C. A. Patrides, *CLIO*, 10, 1981, 101–02; Archie Burnett, *MLR*, 77, 1982, 160–61; J. Martin Evans, *RES*, 33, 1982, 318–23.

3211 Webber, Joan Malory. "The Politics of Poetry: Feminism and *Paradise Lost.*" *MiltonS*, 14, 1980, 3–24.

Demonstrates that although Milton accepted male dominance, he himself "searched beyond it as much as anyone in his age," and points out that ultimately the Christ of *Paradise Regained* rejects "all of the so-called masculine values." Does not believe that Milton is "misogynistic and patriarchal." See No. 2293.

3212 Weber, Burton J. *The Construction of "Paradise Lost."* Foreword by John Gardner. Carbondale and Edwardsville: Southern Illinois Univ. Press; London and Amsterdam: Feffer and Simons, 1971. xxxi, 248pp.

Argues that *Paradise Lost* is a unified defense of God made through a moral analysis of his creatures. Discusses the secondary plot, the main plot, the major and minor characters, and concludes by demonstrating "the structural and thematic connections between the separate elements." Reviews: *MiltonQ*, 5, 1971, 79; *TLS*, Mar. 3, 1972,

p. 252; Michael Lieb, *Cithara*, 12, 1972, 85–106; Irène Simon, *RES*, 23, 1972, 348–51; Claes Schaar, *ES*, 59, 1978, 218–24.

3213 Weber, Burton J. "The Non-Narrative Approaches to *Paradise Lost*: A Gentle Remonstrance." *MiltonS*, 9, 1976, 77–103.

"The non-narrative critics offer structural and thematic objections to the narrative view; but Milton's handling of his materials accords with Aristotelian principles, and Milton *can* achieve his stated didactic ends by narrative means." Abs., *MiltonQ*, 11, 1977, 29.

3214 Webster, Margaret Wilmot Simpson. " 'The Soul of All the Rest': Choice as Love in *Paradise Lost.*" Doctoral diss., Univ. of Toronto, 1975. Abs., *DAI*, 37, 1977, 6519A–20A.

Contends that free will in *Paradise Lost* is "grounded in love and rewarded by joy."

3215 Weidhorn, Manfred. "The Literary Debate on the Dream Problem." *MiltonQ*, 5, 1971, 27–34.

Identifies four basic philosophical approaches to the problem of dreams and surveys key examples of dream debates in western literature. Suggests that Eve's dream in *Paradise Lost* is shaped by this tradition and notes especially the similarities between Chaucer's *Nun's Priest's Tale* and Milton's account. Milton added to the tradition by being explicit about the source and nature of Eve's dream.

3216 Weidhorn, Manfred. "Milton." *Dreams in Seventeenth-Century English Literature.* Studies in English Literature, vol. 57 (The Hague and Paris: Mouton, 1970), pp. 130–55.

Discusses dreams in Milton's works but deals mainly with *Paradise Lost.* Sees Eve's dream as wish-fulfillment.

3217 Weinbrot, Howard D. "John Clarke's *Essay on Study* and Samuel Johnson on *Paradise Lost.*" *MP*, 72, 1975, 404–07.

Claims that Johnson's discussion of

Paradise Lost owes a great deal to Clarke. Concludes that the *Essay on Study* suggested "both the examination of Satan's blasphemy and the inconsistent materiality of angels, each of which Johnson then improved in his own way."

3218 Weinhouse, Linda. "The Urim and Thummim in *Paradise Lost*." *MiltonQ*, 11, 1977, 9–12.

Milton evokes the image of the Old Testament priests by using the image of their Urim and Thummim in describing the chariot of paternal deity in *Paradise Lost* 6.750–62. In the epic, he assumes that the priesthood served as a type of Christ, who subsumed all former types of himself.

3219 Weinkauf, Mary S. "The Escape from the Garden." *TQ*, 16, No. 3, 1973, 66–72.

Claims that "One of the chief motivations for leaving utopia, in fact one of the most clearly stated reasons for Eve's fall in *Paradise Lost*, is a search for something even better than Eden."

3220 Weinkauf, Mary S. "Eve and the Sense of Beauty." *TSL*, 14, 1969, 103–10.

Suggests that "what critics have called vanity is a manifestation of an innocent love for beauty of the sensuous world." Claims that Satan perverted Eve's sense of beauty into vanity and desire for sensual pleasure. Concludes that after her repentance, vanity is no longer her controlling passion.

3221 Weiss, Dolores. "Milton's Poetics of the Sacred: The Limits of the Poet in *Paradise Lost* and *Paradise Regained*." Doctoral diss., Indiana Univ., 1986. 325pp. Abs., *DAI*, 47, 1987, 3438A–39A.

Examines the poet's struggle to translate unaltered divine truth into epic form, an action that is continually frustrated by the inadequacy of epic language.

3222 Wells, Claude E. "Milton's 'Vulgar Readers' and 'The Verse.'" *MiltonQ*, 9, 1975, 67–70.

On Milton's explanation of why *Para-dise Lost* "Rimes not." "His attack was not directed at rhyme *per se*, but at the readers who were so bound to jingling rhyme that they were deaf to gentle phonetic harmonies."

3223 Wentersdorf, Karl P. "*Paradise Lost* IX: The Garden and the Flowered Couch." *MiltonQ*, 13, 1979, 134–41.

Discusses the tree and flower symbolism, especially that of *Paradise Lost* 9.1034–45, which describes Adam and Eve's postlapsarian couch. The flowers in this passage are associated with eros, beauty, death, lust, and the loss of physical and spiritual immortality.

3224 Werblowsky, R. J. Zwi. *Lucifer and Prometheus: A Study of Milton's Satan.* Introduction by C. G. Jung. Norwood, PA: Norwood Editions, 1978.

Reprint of Huckabay No. 1982, originally published in 1952.

3225 Werman, Golda Spiera. "Midrash in *Paradise Lost*: *Capitula Rabbi Eliezer*." *MiltonS*, 18, 1983, 145–71.

"I propose that Milton got the bulk of his Jewish learning, except for the Bible and possibly the Targum, from translations into languages he knew well. Furthermore, I propose a specific translation of a Jewish midrashic work as a possible source used in *Paradise Lost*, Vorstius' Latin translation of *Pirkei* (chapters) *de-Rabbi Eliezer* of 1644."

3226 Werman, Golda Spiera. "*Paradise Lost* and Midrash." Doctoral diss., Indiana Univ., 1982. 527pp. Abs., *DAI*, 43, 1983, 2686A.

Notes the influence of *Pirkei de-Rabbi Eliezer*—a Latin translation of much of the rabbinical midrash—on Milton's theological interpretations of biblical texts.

3227 Werman, Golda. "Repentance in *Paradise Lost*." *MiltonS*, 22, 1986, 121–39.

Discusses Milton's belief in free will and repentance. Believes that Milton used midrashic commentary in constructing the repentance scene in Book 10.

3228 Weston, Peter. *"Paradise Lost": A Critical Study*. New York: Viking Penguin, 1987. 163pp.

Study companion that examines the epic in a day-by-day manner, referring to relevant criticism and ideas.

3229 Wheeler, Thomas. *"Paradise Lost" and the Modern Reader*. Athens: Univ. of Georgia Press, 1974. xi, 132pp.

"Because the modern reader does not accord any peculiar authority to the biblical material on which *Paradise Lost* is based, he will demand that the poem establish its own authority." Chapters: "Milton's Epic"; "The Voices"; "Formulas"; "Freedom"; "Adam and Eve"; "Satan"; "John Milton"; and "Our Epic." Reviews: Andrew M. McLean, *SCN*, 32, 1974, 71; *MiltonQ*, 8, 1974, 89–90; Anthony Low, *MiltonQ*, 9, 1975, 20–27; Leland Ryken, *CSR*, 5, 1975, 209–11; Gerald J. Schiffhorst, *SHR*, 10, 1976, 181–82; Arnold Stein, *SR*, 84, 1976, 695–706.

3230 White, Robert B., Jr. "Milton's Allegory of Sin and Death: A Comment on Backgrounds." *MP*, 70, 1973, 337–41.

Asserts that Milton inverted Augustine's doctrine of the Holy Trinity in creating Satan, Sin, and Death, who represent a parody of the Father, Son, and Holy Spirit. Examines Milton's infernal triad within the context of this orthodox doctrine and concludes that "the allegory of Sin and Death is integrated into the doctrinal structure of *Paradise Lost* as well as into the narrative structure."

3231 Wickenheiser, Robert J. "Milton's 'Pattern of a Christian Hero': The Son in *Paradise Lost*." *MiltonQ*, 12, 1978, 1–9.

Interprets the Son's actions as exemplary of Milton's pattern of true Christian heroism. Before leaving the garden, Adam relates this pattern in his speech in *Paradise Lost* 12.557–73. See James H. Sims's response (No. 3073).

3232 Widmer, Kingsley. "The Iconography of Renunciation: The Miltonic Simile." *Critical Essays on Milton from "ELH"* (Baltimore, MD, and London: Johns Hopkins Press, 1969), pp. 75–86.

Reprint of Huckabay No. 2005, originally published in 1958.

3233 Wigler, Stephen. "Outrageous Noise and the Sovereign Voice: Satan, Sin, and Syntax in Sonnet XIX and Book VI of *Paradise Lost*." *MiltonS*, 10, 1977, 155–65.

"Milton's affecting little poem on his blindness and his extravagantly written epic battle illuminate each other. The protagonist of the one and the antagonist of the other suggest that confusion of the individual voice or word with God's sovereign voice or Word is an important aspect of the satanic personality."

3234 Wigler, Stephen. "The Poet and Satan before the Light: A Suggestion about Book III and the Opening of Book IV of *Paradise Lost*." *MiltonQ*, 12, 1978, 59–64.

Book 3 and the opening of Book 4 "imaginatively recreate and celebrate" the Son's decision to wreak vengeance on his enemies but to give pity to humans. "The security and self-assurance of Milton's introduction, and the anxiety and self-loathing of Satan's contrasted coda, are a carefully structured expression of the consequence of that decision."

3235 Wilding, Michael. "Jonson, Sin and Milton." *N&Q*, 17, 1970, 415.

Asserts that Milton's description of Sin in *Paradise Lost* 2.650–57 echoes a passage in Ben Jonson's "The Poet to the Painter."

3236 Wilding, Michael. "The Last of the Epics: The Rejection of the Heroic in *Paradise Lost* and *Hudibras*." *Restoration Literature: Critical Approaches*. Ed. by Harold Love (London: Methuen, 1972), pp. 91–120.

Notes that both Milton and Samuel

Butler question the traditional epic's basic values and suggests that this revaluation stems from the tragic experience of civil war. Focuses on Milton's Satan.

3237 Wilding, Michael. *Milton's "Paradise Lost."* Sydney Studies in Literature. Sydney: Sydney Univ. Press; London: International Book Services, 1969. 128pp.

Chapters: "An Approach to the Poem"; "Satan and Hell, Heaven, Earth"; and "The Critics." Reviews: John Colmer, *Australian Book Review*, July, 1969, 186; *MiltonN*, 3, 1969, 73; W. M. Beckett, *ESA*, 13, 1970, 419–21; Margaret M. Byard, *RenQ*, 23, 1970, 487–89; Pierre Legouis, *EA*, 24, 1971, 532–33; R. E. C. Houghton, *N&Q*, 19, 1972, 400; Richard Douglas Jordan, *SCN*, 30, 1972, 66; *TLS*, Mar. 3, 1972, p. 252; Albert James Smith, *RES*, 24, 1973, 76–79.

3238 Wilding, M. *"Paradise Lost*: The Parliament of Hell." *Teaching of English* (English Teachers Association of New South Wales, 1970), pp. 14–27.

On the political aspects of Book 2 and of the epic in general. Argues that Milton is not sympathetic to Satan. Analyzes the demonic council to show that Milton has much to communicate to us today about war, militarism, political manipulation, and tyranny.

3239 Wilding, Michael. "Regaining the Radical Milton." *The Radical Reader*. Ed. by Stephen Knight and Wilding (Sydney: Wild and Woolley, 1977), pp. 119–43.

Demonstrates that Milton draws attention to his previous religious and political opinions and associations throughout *Paradise Lost*. Believes that with *Paradise Regained* and *Samson Agonistes*, "Milton established a pointed contrast between the old heroic ambition of military glory . . . and the new values [such as pacifism] that the Messiah actually brought."

3240 Wilkes, G. A. "'Full of Doubt I Stand': The Final Implications of *Paradise Lost*." *English Renaissance Studies Presented to Dame Helen Gardner in Honour of Her Seventieth Birthday*. [Ed. by John Carey] (Oxford: Clarendon Press, 1980), pp. 271–78.

Holds that the poem's last two books demonstrate that the Fall is irreversible and that the second Eden is remote, in spite of Adam's "O goodness infinite" speech in *Paradise Lost* 12.469–78.

3241 Wilkes, G. A. *The Thesis of "Paradise Lost."* Norwood, PA: Norwood Editions, 1977.

Reprint of Huckabay No. 2007, originally published in 1961. Review: *RenQ*, 32, 1979, 169.

3242 Willan, William Robert. "Milton and 'Sensible Things': Instruction in *Paradise Lost*." Doctoral diss., Purdue Univ., 1987. 243pp. Abs., *DAI*, 48, 1988, 2639A.

Describes Milton's use of the senses and physical experience to teach his readers about spiritual "intellective abstractions."

3243 William, Dianne Taylor. "Satán, ¿héroe de *El Paraíso Perdido?*" *Ensayos sobre John Milton: Epopeya y Drama*. Ed. by María Enriqueta González Padilla. Facultad de Filosofía y Letras, Centro de Investigaciones de Letras Modernas y Arte Dramático (Mexico, D.F.: Universidad Nacional Autónoma de México, 1976), pp. 39–53.

Explains why Satan is not the hero of *Paradise Lost*.

3244 Willson, Robert F., Jr. "*Paradise Lost* II.310–416: Beelzebub's Satanic Solution." *CEA*, 37, 1975, 12–15.

"In setting the stage for Satan's heroic scouting expedition, Beelzebub manages to satisfy the apparent factions represented by each of the main speakers and, in doing so, molds his audience into fanatical followers of the supreme 'sacrificer.'"

3245 Wilson, Gayle Edward. "'His Eyes He Op'n'd': The Abel-Cain Vision, *Paradise Lost*, XI.427–448." *MiltonQ*, 14, 1980, 6–12.

Analyzes Milton's technique in transforming the Genesis account of the murder into a paradigm that is intended to deter not only Adam but everyone from such sins.

3246 Wilson, Sister Jeremy, S. S. M. "Milton's Use of the Image Relationship in *Paradise Lost*." *Discourse*, 15, 1968, 199–204.

Examines Milton's Platonic heritage and "the complex series of relationships he constructs in *Paradise Lost* by the use of the 'image-archetype' relation."

3247 Wilson, Talbot. "The Narrator of *Paradise Lost*: Divine Inspiration and Human Knowledge." *SR*, 79, 1971, 349–59.

Explains that the narrator asks for two things: "divine inspiration, insight into the nature of Creation and God's purposes," and "the ability to become a poet-guide, to compose a poem which will direct men toward an understanding of Creation and of God."

3248 Winn, James A. "Milton on Heroic Warfare." *YR*, 66, 1976, 70–86.

Discusses Milton's attitude toward the arms in *Paradise Lost*, which are mostly references to the arms of the rebel angels. Cites examples of "arma" (arms) and "brachia" (fleshly arms) being used as puns; notes many references to arms and war in Milton's other works. Concludes that "an important part of the message of the War in Heaven is that the *logos* is more powerful than heroic arms." Abs., *MiltonQ*, 10, 1976, 133.

3249 Wittreich, Joseph. "'All Angelic Natures Joined in One': Epic Convention and Prophetic Interiority in the Council Scenes of *Paradise Lost*." *MiltonS*, 17, 1983, 43–74.

States that the council scenes in *Paradise Lost* 2 and 3 confer prophetic character and create a parallel genre to the work's epic qualities, reinforcing the epic tradition and interiorizing and

psychologizing the poem to support the proposed prophetic voice.

3250 Wittreich, Joseph Anthony, Jr. "Perplexing the Explanation: Marvell's 'On Mr. Milton's *Paradise Lost*.'" *Approaches to Marvell*. The York Tercentenary Lectures. Ed. by C. A. Patrides (London and Boston, MA: Routledge and Kegan Paul, 1978), pp. 280–305.

Examines the circumstances surrounding the composition of Marvell's *Rehearsal Transpros'd* and his complimentary poem on *Paradise Lost*. Suggests that they reflect Milton's writings and reveal Marvell's own mind and art.

3251 Woelfel, Harry Walter, III. "*Paradise Lost* and the Four Degrees of Death." Doctoral diss., Auburn Univ., 1980. 195pp. Abs., *DAI*, 41, 1980, 2623A.

Relates the four degrees of death in the *Christian Doctrine*—"the punishments which are preludes to death, spiritual death, temporal death, and eternal death"—to obedience and disobedience in *Paradise Lost*.

3252 Wollaeger, Mark A. "Apocryphal Narration: Milton, Raphael, and the Book of Tobit." *MiltonS*, 21, 1985, 137–56.

Sees the Apocryphal Book of Tobit as a sort of counternarrative, which enters *Paradise Lost* "as a human voice that is firm in its proclamation of salvation."

3253 Wood, Elizabeth Jane. "'Improv'd by Tract of Time': Metaphysics and Measurement in *Paradise Lost*." *MiltonS*, 15, 1981, 43–58.

Discusses several metaphors of time and measurement and of motion and space in *Paradise Lost* and shows that they demonstrate Milton's concern for the philosophic-scientific revolution of the sixteenth and seventeenth centuries.

3254 Wood, John Michael. "A Nation Delivered from Satan: The Homiletic Structure of Deliverance in *The Faerie Queene* and *Paradise Lost*." Doctoral diss.,

Univ. of Maryland, 1977. 233pp. Abs., *DAI*, 38, 1978, 4189A.

Demonstrates a correspondence between deliverance sermons celebrating England's divine protection from the evils of Catholicism and the paths to salvation in the *Faerie Queene* and *Paradise Lost*.

3255 Wood, Nancy Hagglund. "Satan as Orator: A Rhetorical Analysis of the Persuasion of Eve in *Paradise Lost*." Doctoral diss., Rutgers Univ., 1972. 238pp. Abs., *DAI*, 33, 1972, 1701A.

Asserts that Satan's use and modification of classical modes of persuasion— ethos, pathos, and logos—give his words special weight when presented to Milton's contemporaries.

3256 Woodhull, Marianna. *The Epic of "Paradise Lost" : Twelve Essays*. Folcroft, PA: Folcroft Library Editions, 1969; Norwood, PA: Norwood Editions, 1976; Philadelphia, PA: R. West, 1977.

Reprints of Stevens No. 908, originally published in 1907.

3257 Woodman, Ross G. "Milton's Urania and Her Romantic Descendants." *UTQ*, 48, 1979, 189–208.

Contends that Milton's "invocation to the Muse celebrates the Christian liberty that confers prophethood upon the Lord's people. The inspired company of Christian poet and chosen readers is Milton's challenging answer to the Restoration."

3258 Woods, Marjorie Curry. "Milton's Interruption of Genesis: A Note on the Structure of Books VII and VIII of *Paradise Lost*." *N&Q*, 28, 1981, 205–07.

Argues that Milton's use of Genesis and Hugo Grotius's *Adamus Exul* shows that Adam's questions in Book 8 interrupt and divert the biblical narrative and are inappropriate.

3259 Wooten, John. "The Comic Milton and Italian Burlesque Poets." *Cithara*, 22, 1982, 3–12.

"The ridicule, satiric jest, and burlesque debunking in *Paradise Lost*" reflect the influence of Italian writers such as Pulci and Folengo.

3260 Wooten, John. "From Purgatory to the Paradise of Fools: Dante, Ariosto, and Milton." *ELH*, 49, 1982, 741–50.

Believes that Milton transcends both Dante and Ariosto in *Paradise Lost* 3. "What we have in Milton's Paradise of Fools is a very sophisticated and highly allusive piece of literary and theological criticism."

3261 Wooten, John Calvin. "Hero and Harlequin: Burlesque Comedy in *Paradise Lost*." Doctoral diss., Vanderbilt Univ., 1976. 185pp. Abs., *DAI*, 37, 1976, 3657A–58A.

Argues that burlesque comedy influences Milton's juxtaposition of high and low, use of the grotesque to provoke laughter, and mixture of comedy with satire.

3262 Wooten, John. "The Metaphysics of Milton's Epic Burlesque Humor." *MiltonS*, 13, 1979, 255–73.

Focuses on the Paradise of Fools passage in Book 3 to define burlesque and finds affinities between Milton's use of the absurd and modern black humor.

3263 Wooten, John. "Satan, Satire, and Burlesque Fables in *Paradise Lost*." *MiltonQ*, 12, 1978, 51–58.

"The satire of *Paradise Lost*, then, is part of the burlesque manner which functions organically in the epic world of the poem. The satire is part of a burlesque because Milton creates elaborate fables which depend on comic distortion and incongruity of an openly mimetic nature to achieve the satiric purpose."

3264 Wren, Robert Allen. "The Scheme of the Battle: The War in Heaven and Graeco-Roman Military Tradition." Doctoral diss., Univ. of Texas, Austin, 1987. 184pp. Abs., *DAI*, 48, 1987, 1213A.

Uses classical historians and histories to interpret confrontations that "illustrate Milton's use of Greek and Roman military practice and ethics to inform and imagine the Empyreal combatants."

3265 Wright, B. A. "A Milton Crux." *N&Q*, 15, 1968, 377.

Suggests that in *Paradise Lost* 5.412, "concoct" means "digest, assimilate," not just "digest."

3266 Wurtele, Douglas. "Milton, Satan, and the Sophists." *Ren&R*, 3, 1979, 189–200.

"One way of understanding Milton's complex treatment of Satan, indeed, is to regard the Prince of Darkness as an evilly inclined orator skilled in sophistic rhetoric and logic, a kind of demonic prototype for the deceptive sophists of Milton's own day."

3267 Wurtele, Douglas. "'Persuasive Rhetoric': The Techniques of Milton's Archetypal Sophist." *ESC*, 3, 1977, 18–33.

Examines Milton's attitude toward sophists and false rhetoricians and analyzes the sophistic rhetoric and logic exhibited in Satan's public utterances.

3268 Yaghjian, Lucretia B. "Between the Alpha and the Omega: A Study of History, Prophecy, and Apocalypse in *Paradise Lost*, Book XII." *CSR*, 6, 1976, 180–95.

Argues that in *Paradise Lost* 12 Milton presents a strategic simultaneity of history and prophecy, which creates both a sense of an ending and a scenario of beginnings. Abs., *MiltonQ*, 12, 1978, 116.

3269 Yagyu, Naoyuki. "*Paradise Lost* and the Modern Reader." *Studies in Milton* (Tokyo: Kinseido, 1974), pp. 3–18.

In Japanese. Feels that the temptation motif is the principal concern of Milton's major works.

3270 Yang, Zhouhan. "Milton's 'Canie Waggon Light': A Note on Cross-Cultural Impact." *Cowrie*, 1, 1986, 29–45.

Believes that the image of the Chinese sailing wagons in *Paradise Lost* 3.437–39 shows Milton's vast knowledge of geography.

3271 Yeong, Yoo. "The Literary Study of the Subjectivistic Idea in Milton's Epic." *Inmun Kwahak* (Yonsei Univ., Seoul), 31, 1974, 47–74.

In Korean; English summary, pp. 317–18.

3272 Yeong, Yoo. *Paradise Lost.* Seoul: Yonsei Univ. Press, 1981. xvii, 455pp.

Includes previously published essays.

3273 Yeong, Yoo. "A Study of Milton's Satan: The Formation and Characteristics." *Dongguk Review* (Dongguk Univ., Seoul), 5–6, 1974, 53–74.

In Korean.

3274 Yoon, Kee-Ho. "Satan eui myosa e natanan Milton eui hyeonsilgwan." *RRCNU*, 32, 1986, 69–80.

"Milton's View of Reality in *Paradise Lost*."

3275 Yost, George. "Milton's Sin and Her Pelican Daughters." *RenP*, 1972, pp. 37–42.

Relates the religious allegory of the pelican, which is devoured by its own offspring, to the allegory of Sin, the counterpart of Christ, and her children.

3276 Yost, George. "A New Look at Milton's Paradise." *MiltonS*, 10, 1977, 77–91.

"This article will be confined to the background in ancient historical records of the geographical and topographical description that Milton chose for his Paradise." Abs., *MiltonQ*, 12, 1978, 157.

3277 Yu, Anthony C. "Life in the Garden: Freedom and the Image of God in *Paradise Lost*." *JR*, 60, 1980, 247–71.

Points out that in presenting Adam and Eve, Milton uses "the scriptural declaration that man was made in the image of God." The poet also explicates a complex of ideas, echoes various motifs, and follows Reformation theology in depicting Adam and Eve's growing sense of selfhood. In stressing human intellectual prowess, Milton anticipates modern Protestant thought.

CRITICISM: PARADISE LOST 355

Abs., *MiltonQ*, 14, 1980, 33; *SCN*, 38, 1980, 46.

3278 Zacharasiewicz, Waldemar. *Die "Cosmic Voyage" und die "Excursion" in der Englischen Dichtung des 17. und 18. Jahrhunderts.* Doctoral diss., Univ. of Graz. Vienna: Verlag Notring, 1969. viii, 204pp.

Contains some discussion of Milton.

3279 Zarov, Herbert. "Milton and the Rhetoric of Rebellion." *MiltonQ*, 7, 1973, 47–50.

Responds to Satanist arguments linking Milton's rebellion against Charles I with Satan's revolt against God in *Paradise Lost*. Compares Milton's political pamphlets with his epic to show "that the imagery and language which Milton associated with Charles in order to illuminate that tyrant's psychology parallel remarkably those he later associated with Satan in *Paradise Lost* for the same purpose." Concludes "that the arguments of the 'political Satanists' are fallacious and that Milton's sympathy, unconscious or otherwise, was not with his Satan."

3280 Zeong, Yun-Shig. "Shakespeare and Milton: A Poetic Approach through Aristotle's *Poetics* and Longinus' *The Sublime*: *Macbeth* and *Paradise Lost*." Doctoral diss., Univ. of Arkansas, 1984. 218pp. Abs., *DAI*, 46, 1986, 3729A.

Examines the definition, causes, devices, effects, and purpose of tragedy—criteria established by Aristotle and Longinus—in *Macbeth* and *Paradise Lost*.

3281 Zeong, Yun-Shig. "Sihak mit Shinhakjeok Cheukmyeon esuh gochalhan Bigeukjeok yoin gwa geu hyogwa: Milton eui *Paradise Lost* reul jungsim euro." *JELL*, 32, 1986, 3–20.

"An Approach to the Tragic Causes and Effects: Milton's *Paradise Lost* and Aristotle's *Poetics*." In Korean; English summary, pp. 20–21. Believes that in Aristotelian terms, both Satan and Adam are tragic heroes. Classi-

fies *Paradise Lost* as an epic tragedy.

3282 Zieky, Michael Jan. "An Automated Aid to the Study of Literature: The Application of Content Analytic and Statistical Techniques to *Paradise Lost*." Doctoral diss., Univ. of Connecticut, 1969. 149pp. Abs., *DAI*, 30, 1969, 700A.

Groups the words written about every character in *Paradise Lost* under nine different attribute categories in an attempt to match similar characters before and after the Fall.

3283 Zimmerman, Lester F. "'And Justify the Ways . . .'—A Suggested Context." *Papers on Milton.* Ed. by Philip Mahone Griffith and Zimmerman. Univ. of Tulsa Department of English Monograph Series, no. 8 (Tulsa, OK: Univ. of Tulsa, 1969), pp. 57–66.

"It is my purpose to examine the justice motif in *Paradise Lost* and then to relate it to the context of a central Protestant concern of the British Seventeenth Century."

3284 Zimmerman, Shari Ann. "'In Unity Defective': Transformations of Identity in *Paradise Lost*." Doctoral diss., State Univ. of New York, Buffalo, 1984. 204pp. Abs., *DAI*, 45, 1985, 2864A.

Investigates the influence of fear and desire on Adam's, Eve's, and Satan's awakening—realization of self.

3285 Zimmerman, Shari A. "Milton's *Paradise Lost*: Eve's Struggle for Identity." *AI*, 38, 1981, 247–67.

Studies Eve's desire for selfhood. "Hidden amid the poem's many mis-readings of her character, Eve's actions and language recreate and illuminate the universal desire for identity."

3286 Zimmermann, Edward J. "'Light out of Darkness': A Study of the Growth and Structure of Evil in Milton's *Paradise Lost*." Doctoral diss., State Univ. of New York, Buffalo, 1970. 220pp. Abs., *DAI*, 31, 1971, 4741A–42A.

Examines Milton's "ideas of the necessity of evil, the mode of its proliferation, and its essential function as a vehicle for good in God's plan."

3287 Zitelli, Joanne Janet. "Poetry Unparadised: *Paradise Lost* and Rimbaud's Prose Poetry." Doctoral diss., Univ. of California, Irvine, 1981. 220pp. Abs., *DAI*, 42, 1981, 1139A–40A.

Compares the poets' presentations of hell, analyses of social institutions, poetic structures, and allusions to other works.

3288 Ades, John I. "*Paradise Regained*: The Gospel According to John Milton." *CEA*, 51, 1988, 74–87.

Argues that Milton makes Luke's Jesus as human as possible and that "the final Temptation of the Tower shows to Satan, to Jesus, and to the reader, the divine figure, the Son of God declared in the Baptism."

3289 Agari, Masahiko. "The Language of Canaan Restored." *MCJ News*, 5, 1981, 6–7.

Believes that in *Paradise Regained* Milton presents a double structure—the reader's imitation of Jesus as exemplar and the preparation of Jesus for saving humanity.

3290 Agari, Masahiko. "The Style of *Paradise Regained*: Its Anxiety and Silence." *Studies in Milton* (Tokyo: Kinseido, 1974), pp. 74–100.

In Japanese. Believes that it is unfair to compare *Paradise Regained* with the dazzling linguistic architectonics of *Paradise Lost*. Examines the brief epic's language and those elements (such as silence) which transform it externally.

3291 Agari, Masahiko. "The Word and Language of Canaan: The Double Structure of *Paradise Regained*." *USSE*, 16, 1988, 45–68.

3292 Anderson, Wayne C. "Is *Paradise Regained* Really Cold?" *C&L*, 32, 1983, 15–23.

Argues that "from Milton's own perspective, piety, patience, fortitude and magnanimity are not cold at all." Rather, they are heroic.

3293 Angelo, Peter Gregory. "Free Will, Sin and Redemption in Milton's Epic Poetry." Doctoral diss., State Univ. of New York, Stony Brook, 1978. 171pp. Abs., *DAI*, 39, 1978, 890A.

Clarifies Milton's "understanding of the relationship between the free will of rational beings and the will of God" in *Paradise Lost* and *Paradise Regained*.

3294 Arai, Akira. "The Trial of Christ in *Paradise Regained*." *Otsuka Review* (Tokyo Univ. of Education), 8, 1971, 1–16.

Says that the temptations are real, there is room for vulnerability, and to some degree they are related to temptations in Milton's own life. Abs., *MiltonQ*, 6, No. 2, 1972, 44.

3295 Asahi, Satoru. "The Symmetrical Design of *Paradise Regained*." *MCJ News*, 5, 1981, 7–9.

Believes that the temptations are arranged symmetrically from the crudest (food) to the subtlest (divinity).

3296 Asals, Heather. "Milton's *Paradise Regained*, IV.514–521." *Expl*, 40, 1981, 19–20.

Explicates "the logical proof provided by Satan . . . that he, too, is a son of God."

3297 Aycock, Roy E. "Illusion in *Paradise Regained*." *CLAJ*, 24, 1980, 194–202.

"There necessarily must be the illusion that Satan's temptations of Christ are not absolutely futile. Otherwise there is no dramatic conflict between Satan and Christ because Satan's temptations would not be temptations at all."

3298 Baker, Stewart Addison. "The Brief Epic: Studies in the Style and Structure of the Genre of *Paradise Regained.*" Doctoral diss., Yale Univ., 1964. 334pp. Abs., *DAI*, 32, 1971, 1464A.

Defines the brief epic (exemplified by *Paradise Regained*) as a reconciliation between classical heroism and New Testament morality, often centered on "one brief significant episode," and characterized by a "middle style."

3299 Banschbach, John. "The Names of Jesus in *Paradise Regained.*" *MiltonQ*, 21, No. 3, 1987, 96–98.

Emphasizes the integration of Christ's roles of Son of God, Savior, Messiah, and Jesus.

3300 Blythe, David-Everett. "On Low's Georgic References." *MiltonQ*, 18, 1984, 136.

Responds to No. 3384 by providing new material and clarifying other information.

3301 Blythe, Joan Heiges. "The Cloistered Virtue: Rhetorical Posture in *Paradise Regained.*" *NM*, 89, 1988, 324–32.

Examines Jesus's character in *Paradise Regained* and draws a parallel between this work and Albertano da Brescia's *Del Arte Loquendi et Tacendi*.

3302 Broadbent, J. B. "The Private Mythology of *Paradise Regained.*" *Calm of Mind: Tercentenary Essays on "Paradise Regained" and "Samson Agonistes" in Honor of John S. Diekhoff.* Ed. by Joseph Anthony Wittreich, Jr. (Cleveland, OH, and London: Press of Case Western Reserve Univ., 1971), pp. 77–92. Ann Arbor, MI: Univ. Microfilms International, 1980 Books on Demand Reprints.

Believes that in *Paradise Regained* Milton expresses his anxieties concerning parents, wives, and sexual frustrations. Review: Michael Lieb, *Cithara*, 12, 1972, 85–106.

3303 Burnett, Archie. "Milton's *Paradise Regained*, I.314–19." *N&Q*, 25, 1978, 509–10.

Asserts that the old shepherd gathering sticks to make a fire "presents a test of the Son's critical ability and

Biblical knowledge." Claims that this pitiful creature is mentioned in reference to Old Testament accounts.

3304 Burnett, Archie. *Milton's Style: The Shorter Poems, "Paradise Regained," and "Samson Agonistes."* London and New York: Longman, 1981. xiv, 187pp.

"This book has various aims: to give close readings of Milton's poems other than *Paradise Lost*; to take into account the criticism on these poems, focusing on major issues; and to investigate the variety and consistency of their style." Reviews: Dustin H. Griffin, *RenQ*, 36, 1983, 482–85; C.A. Patrides, *YWES*, 62, 1981, 234–35; Roger Henry Sundell, *SCN*, 41, 1983, 34–36; Mary Ann Radzinowicz, *MLR*, 81, 1986, 171–72.

3305 Bush, Douglas. "Milton." *On Milton's Poetry: A Selection of Modern Studies.* Ed. by Arnold Stein (Greenwich, CT: Fawcett Publications, 1970), pp. 238–46.

Reprint of the sections on *Paradise Regained* and *Samson Agonistes* in Huckabay No. 466, originally published in 1945.

3306 Cain, William E. "Learning How To Read: A Note on *Paradise Regained*, IV.321–30." *MiltonQ*, 13, 1979, 120–21.

Reopens the controversy sparked by the Son's rejection of learning in *Paradise Regained*. Asserts that Milton's Jesus felt reading was worthwhile only if the reader had special moral insight. But if a reader possessed such an informed moral vision, there would be no need to read.

3307 Camé, Jean-François. "La Structure Mythique de *Paradise Regained.*" *EA*, 27, 1974, 471–80.

3308 Campbell, Gordon. "Milton's *Paradise Regained*, IV, 244–245." *Expl*, 41, 1982, 23.

Argues that "Academe" refers to Academus, "the mythical hero after whom the area was thought to be named."

3309 Carpenter, Mary Wilson. "Milton's Secret Garden: Structural Correspondences between Michael's Prophecy and *Paradise Regained.*" *MiltonS*, 14, 1980, 153–82.

Accepts Richard Douglas Jordan's thesis (No. 3365) that the brief epic contains ten temptations and demonstrates that there is "a carefully ordered and elaborately symmetrical series of thematic correspondences between the ten temptations in *Paradise Regained* and ten sections of Michael's prophecy in Books XI and XII of *Paradise Lost.*"

3310 Carson, Michael Joseph. "The Moral Use of Rhetoric in *Paradise Regained.*" Doctoral diss., Ohio State Univ. in cooperation with Miami Univ. (Ohio), 1976. 279pp. Abs., *DAI*, 37, 1976, 982A.

Argues that Milton communicates regenerative truth in *Paradise Regained* through Jesus's "plain, logically based rhetoric," which is opposed to Satan's elaborate but self-condemning speech.

3311 Chambers, A. B. "The Double Time Scheme in *Paradise Regained.*" *MiltonS*, 7, 1975, 189–205.

Discusses the two different concepts of time—linear and cyclic—and the resulting interreactions of alternate chronologies for divine and human history.

3312 Choi, Jung-Woon. "Milton eui gang-yeolhan seosasi e natanan Satan gwa Jesus eui image." *INH*, 14, 1987, 197–220. "The Images of Satan and Jesus in Milton's Brief Epic."

3313 Christopher, Georgia B. "The Secret Agent in *Paradise Regained.*" *MLQ*, 41, 1980, 131–50.

The secret agent is God's Word, which Jesus understands because, unlike Satan, he is under the influence of the Holy Spirit.

3314 Clark, Ira. "Christ on the Tower in *Paradise Regained.*" *MiltonQ*, 8, 1974, 104–07.

Argues that the central emblem of *Paradise Regained* is the Son's stand during Satan's fall, for there Christ

"supplants Satan" and "visually prophesies himself to be the new king of the middle air," as he regains the kingdom that Satan usurped.

3315 Clark, Ira. "*Paradise Regained* and the Gospel According to John." *MP*, 71, 1973, 1–15.

Proposes "the Gospel according to John as the primary inspiration for *Paradise Regained.*"

3316 Condee, Ralph Waterbury. "Milton's Dialogue with the Epic: *Paradise Regained* and the Tradition." *YR*, 59, 1970, 357–75.

Believes that as Milton's theories of epic poetry developed from his youth to the end of his life, they were more consonant with *Paradise Regained* than with *Paradise Lost. Paradise Lost* represents a transitional stage.

3317 Conners, John Reed. "The Crucifixion in *Paradise Lost, Paradise Regained* and *Samson Agonistes.*" Doctoral diss., Univ. of Rochester, 1982. 265pp. Abs., *DAI*, 44, 1983, 1460A.

Explores "the Son's nature, his place in the divine plan of salvation, and his example to be followed by all men and women" in Milton's three long poems.

3318 Cook, Albert. "Imaging in *Paradise Regained.*" *MiltonS*, 21, 1985, 215–27.

Asserts that in *Paradise Regained*, the invocation's brevity indicates a different focus and register from those of *Paradise Lost*. The difference rests primarily in the imaging that each performs.

3319 Cope, Jackson I. "*Paradise Regained*: Inner Ritual." *MiltonS*, 1, 1969, 51–65.

Sees *Paradise Regained* as the culmination of an interwoven series of literary events, "where the pattern which Dryden presented dramatically [in *Almanzor*] is re-enacted in a ritualistic context appropriate to the divine, suprahistorical point of view which Milton evokes in a number of ways."

3320 Cunningham, Merrilee Allison. "Narrative Strategies in John Milton's *Paradise Regained*." Doctoral diss., Vanderbilt Univ., 1978. 247pp. Abs., *DAI*, 39, 1978, 2286A.

Discusses the function and context of the brief epic's narrative techniques— orations, meditations, angelic choruses, and narrator's entrances.

3321 Curran, Stuart. "*Paradise Regained*: Implications of Epic." *MiltonS*, 17, 1983, 209–24.

Examines the epic character of *Paradise Regained*, pointing to the *Aeneid* as Milton's primary source for epic parallels; discusses the modifications Milton makes to the epic structure, as he revitalizes epic patterns to further the transcendental and psychological aspects of Jesus's temptations.

3322 Das Gupta, Amlan. "The Debate on Learning in *Paradise Regained*." *JDECU*, 21, 1986–87, 86–107.

Views Christ's rejection of learning as "relative rather than absolute, a rejection ultimately of the terms that Satan offers," and points out parallels in Augustine.

3323 Dillon, John B. "'Peeling Thir Provinces': A Tiberian Allusion in *Paradise Regained*." *MiltonQ*, 11, 1977, 109–11.

Explores the significance of a possible allusion to Tiberius in *Paradise Regained* 4.135–37.

3324 Doherty, Mary Jane Margaret. "The Mistress-Knowledge: Literary Architectonics in the English Renaissance." Doctoral diss., Univ. of Wisconsin, Madison, 1977. Abs., *DAI*, 38, 1978, 4840A.

Concludes with a chapter on the "portrayal of the practice of self-knowledge in the archetypal Poet and Prophet of *Paradise Regained*."

3325 Drake, Gertrude C. "Satan's Councils in *The Christiad, Paradise Lost* and *Paradise Regained*." *Acta Conventus Neo-Latini Turonensis*. Series: De Pétrarque à Descartes, 38. Ed. by Jean-Claude Margolin (Paris: Vrin, 1980), pp. 979–89.

Compares Milton's council to Vida's. Believes that Vida's *Christiad* provided material for Milton.

3326 Dwight, Sheila Dana. "Satan's Motivations: A Reinterpretation of Milton's *Paradise Regained*." Doctoral diss., Univ. of California, Riverside, 1975. 204pp. See *DAI*, 38, 1977, 276A.

3327 Elliott, Emory. "Milton's Biblical Style in *Paradise Regained*." *MiltonS*, 6, 1974, 227–41.

"Through the very words and phrases of Scripture, he [Milton] draws into the poem essential details of the encircling framework of Christ's total career and teaching, and he thereby puts the particular episode of the temptations into a biblical perspective."

3328 Engel, Wilson F., III. "Christ in the Winepress: Backgrounds of a Sacred Image." *GHJ*, 3, 1979–80, 45–63.

Discusses Milton's portrayal of Christ in *Paradise Regained* as one who is "self-assured and righteous," while George Herbert emphasizes Christ's sufferings. Abs., *SCN*, 38, 1980, 16.

3329 Ettin, Andrew V. "Milton, T. S. Eliot, and the Virgilian Vision: Some Versions of Georgic." *Genre*, 10, 1977, 233–58.

Studies "some important ways in which *Paradise Regained* and the *Four Quartets* can be related to Virgil's *Georgics*." Shows how each work is tempered by the author's experience and emphasizes the stylistic traits of Milton's epic.

3330 Fish, Stanley E. "Inaction and Silence: The Reader in *Paradise Regained*." *Calm of Mind: Tercentenary Essays on "Paradise Regained" and "Samson Agonistes" in Honor of John S. Diekhoff.* Ed. by Joseph Anthony Wittreich, Jr. (Cleveland, OH, and London: Press of Case Western Reserve Univ., 1971), pp. 25–47. Ann Arbor, MI: Univ. Microfilms International, 1980 Books on Demand Reprints.

"The main plot works itself out in terms of the Son's response to Satan, the reader's plot in terms of his response to the Son's response to Satan." As readers go through the poem, they gradually discard values in which the dignity of the self adheres and substitute for them the all-inclusive value of obedience to God.

3331 Fish, Stanley. "Things and Actions Indifferent: The Temptation of Plot in *Paradise Regained*." *MiltonS*, 17, 1983, 163–85.

Paradise Regained reveals humanity's physical versus spiritual orientation. Satan shows both temptation as a pathway by which the metaphysical (obedience to the law of God) is transmuted to the plot of a physical existence and the supremacy of Christ's resistance against devaluing the spiritual fortress of obedience. See No. 3343.

3332 Fisher, Alan. "Why is *Paradise Regained* So Cold?" *MiltonS*, 14, 1980, 195–217.

"Milton, radical though he was, came finally to think that excitement and faith were vastly different experiences." Thus, *Paradise Regained* is a cold poem "because Milton chose to exchange intimacy for responsibility, the power to act for the power to endure."

3333 Flannagan, Roy. "Belial and 'Effeminate Slackness' in *Paradise Lost* and *Paradise Regained*." *MiltonQ*, 19, 1985, 9–11.

Compares the character of Belial (over-indulgent and over-sexed) to the character of Jesus (strong and able to resist sexual temptation). Believes that "one reason Jesus is able to break the snares and spells of Satan is his success in resisting the sexual temptation that was the primary cause of Adam's fall."

3334 Forsyth, Neil. "Having Done All To Stand: Biblical and Classical Allusion in *Paradise Regained*." *MiltonS*, 21, 1985, 199–214.

Shows that Milton prepares the reader for the final confrontation on the pinnacle with a series of parallel images and allusions. Biblical allusions are adapted to classical form—"distant or muted for Christ, emphatic and explicit for Satan."

3335 Fortin, René E. "The Climactic Similes of *Paradise Regained*: 'True Wisdom' or 'False Resemblance'?" *MiltonQ*, 7, 1973, 39–43.

In *Paradise Regained* 4.560–76, the similes comparing Christ to Hercules and Oedipus "serve a dual and paradoxical function: while they initially enlarge the meaning of Christ's victory by offering very rich analogies drawn from the classical world, they also . . . underscore the crucial differences between the pagan and Christian worlds" and thus reflect Milton's ambivalence toward classical culture.

3336 Fowler, Alastair. "*Paradise Regained*: Some Problems of Style." *Medieval and Pseudo-Medieval Literature*. The J. A. W. Bennett Lectures, Perugia, 1982–1983. Ed. by Piero Boitani and Anna Torti (Tübingen: Gunter Narr; Cambridge: D. S. Brewer, 1984), pp. 181–89.

Believes that the style of *Paradise Regained* is innovative. It resembles the style of Virgil's *Georgics* and anticipates that of Augustan poetry.

3337 Franson, John Karl. "Bread and Banquet as Food for Thought: Experiential Learning in *Paradise Regained*." *Milton Reconsidered: Essays in Honor of Arthur E. Barker*. Ed. by Franson (Salzburg: Institut für Englische Sprache und Literatur, Universität Salzburg, 1976), pp. 154–92.

Believes that a close reading of the poem reveals a focus on Christ's divine nature and that the bread and banquet temptations constitute a progressive learning experience for Christ and Satan.

3338 Franson, J. Karl. "'By His Own Independent Power': Christ on the Pinnacle in *Paradise Regained*." *MiltonQ*, 14, 1980, 55–60.

Sees the final temptation as "a subtle ploy by Satan, not to discover Christ's identity, but to discover the degree of Christ's divinity, Christ's perception of that divinity, and the degree to which Christ can exercise it." Supplemented by Jack W. Herring (No. 3355).

3339 Franson, John Karl. "Knowledge of Christ's Nature and Mission as Central Motif of Milton's *Paradise Regain'd.*" Doctoral diss., Univ. of Illinois, Urbana, 1972. 160pp. Abs., *DAI*, 33, 1973, 5677A.
Argues that both Satan's brief successes and ultimate failure are caused by his temptations of Christ, which are actually veiled attempts to gain divine knowledge.

3340 Fujimaki, Noriko. "Why is *Paradise Regained* So Cold?" *Poetry and Drama in the Age of Shakespeare: Essays in Honour of Professor Shonosuke Ishii's Seventieth Birthday.* Ed. by Peter Milward and Tetsuo Anzai (Tokyo: Renaissance Institute, Sophia Univ., 1982), pp. 199–217.
Believes that Jesus's alleged coldness in *Paradise Regained* is a result of Milton's not being able to create a worthy antagonist for Satan.

3341 Fulton, Pauline Robinson. "Milton's Use of the Book of Job in *Paradise Regained* and *Samson Agonistes.*" Doctoral diss., Univ. of North Carolina, Chapel Hill, 1983. 210pp. Abs., *DAI*, 44, 1983, 1092A.
Analyzes Milton's use of dialogue and the suffering hero of faith from the Book of Job in *Paradise Regained* and *Samson Agonistes.*

3342 Gearreald, Karen L. "Milton's Majestic Style: Studies in the Diction and Syntax of *Paradise Regained.*" Doctoral diss., Harvard Univ., 1969.

3343 Goldsmith, Steven. "The Muting of Satan: Language Redemption in *Paradise Regained.*" *SEL*, 27, 1987, 125–40.
Rejects Stanley Fish's assertion (No. 3331) that in *Paradise Regained*, Jesus must "eradicate speech on his way toward a perfect passivity and obedience embodied in silence." Rather, "the

Son steadily speaks at greater length and in the process of debate consistently renders Satan mute until the adversary's final silence is the emblem of nonexistence, spiritual substance-lessness."

3344 González Padilla, María Enriqueta. "La Epopeya del Libre Albedrío." *Ensayos sobre John Milton: Epopeya y Drama.* Ed. by González Padilla. Facultad de Filosofía y Letras, Centro de Investigaciones de Letras Modernas y Arte Dramático (Mexico, D.F.: Universidad Nacional Autónoma de México, 1976), pp. 13–38.
Shows that one reaches a state of harmony or an internal paradise only by the proper use of free will.

3345 Graham, E. A. "Milton and Seventeenth-Century Individualism: Language and Identity in *Paradise Lost, Paradise Regained* and *Samson Agonistes.*" Doctoral diss., Manchester Univ., 1985. Abs., *IT*, 37, 1988, 439.

3346 Grant, Patrick. "Time and Temptation in *Paradise Regained.*" *UTQ*, 43, 1973, 32–47. Reprinted in *Images and Ideas in Literature of the English Renaissance.* Ed. by Grant (Amherst: Univ. of Massachusetts Press; London: Macmillan, 1979), pp. 129–53.
Explicates the iconography of time in *Paradise Regained* and shows that Milton embraces modern perspectives on time, material nature, and faith. Believes that he rejects Neoplatonic and emblematic imagery and that the poem's single image is the Son.

3347 Graves, Allan Rolf. "Puritan Empiricism in *Paradise Regained* and *Samson Agonistes.*" Doctoral diss., Univ. of Wisconsin, 1973. 279pp. Abs., *DAI*, 34, 1973, 2561A.
Contends that Puritan empiricism, which emphasizes learning by doing, affects Jesus's education in *Paradise Regained* and the "alchemical symbolism" of *Samson Agonistes.*

3348 Guss, Donald L. "A Brief Epic: *Para-*

dise Regained." *SP*, 68, 1971, 223–43.

Agrees that *Paradise Regained* is a moral romance in the tradition of Spenser and Tasso but argues that Milton's subject is epic. Refutes the notion that *Paradise Regained* is "not nearly so fine a poem as *Paradise Lost.*"

3349 Hamilton, Gary D. "Creating the Garden Anew: The Dynamics of *Paradise Regained.*" *PQ*, 50, 1971, 567–81.

On the theme and structure of *Paradise Regained* and its relationship to *Paradise Lost.* Argues that Michael's advice to Adam regarding the "paradise within" in *Paradise Lost* 12.575–87 "can be of considerable help in explaining the dynamics of *Paradise Regained*, and that the development of Christ in the course of the poem can be seen as a movement toward achieving that state of inner Paradise about which Michael speaks."

3350 Harada, Jun. "Epic Doctrinal and Exemplary: An Introduction to *Paradise Regained.*" *SELit*, 1978, 45–63.

Discusses *Paradise Regained* from the reader's point of view: "He is brought into self-examination and enlightenment at every turn of Christ's refutation of Satan."

3351 Hardwick, Lillian Beth. "Identification and Adaptation in Satan's Rhetoric in *Paradise Regained.*" Doctoral diss., Univ. of Texas, Austin, 1978. 297pp. Abs., *DAI*, 39, 1978, 2290A.

Examines "the persona, context, message, style, and audience within each speech situation" to explain why Satan's orations persuade his followers but not Christ.

3352 Haskin, Dayton. "Matthew, Mary, Luke and John: The Mother of the Work [sic] in Milton's Poetry." *PPMRC*, 10, 1987, 75–86.

Believes that "In view of the widely circulating belief in our time that Milton stands prominently in the first rank among antifeminist writers, it is important to begin taking into account . . .

his distinctive portrait of Mary in *Paradise Regained.*"

3353 Haskin, Dayton. "Milton's Portrait of Mary as a Bearer of the Word." *Milton and the Idea of Woman.* Ed. by Julia M. Walker (Urbana and Chicago: Univ. of Illinois Press, 1988), pp. 169–84.

Surveys Reformation views of Mary and notes that Milton gives her considerable attention in *Paradise Regained* by presenting her as someone "who mediates the Word—first to Jesus himself, then to the New Testament writers, and ultimately to Christians in any age." Abs., *MiltonQ*, 24, 1990, 151.

3354 Haskin, Mary Anne, and **Dayton Haskin, S. J.** "*Paradise Regained* Adapted for the Stage." *MiltonQ*, 13, 1979, 30–32.

Review of a stage version produced in New York City in August, 1978, at the Performing Garage by a company called the Victory Theatre. Charles Frederick prepared the script, and Matthew Causey served as director.

3355 Herring, Jack W. "Christ on the Pinnacle in *Paradise Regained.*" *MiltonQ*, 15, 1981, 98.

Supplements J. Karl Franson's article (No. 3338). Christ defeats Satan by using only human powers and demonstrates that human redemption is viable.

3356 Hunter, William B., Jr. "The Double Set of Temptations in *Paradise Regained.*" *MiltonS*, 14, 1980, 183–93. Reprinted in *The Descent of Urania: Studies in Milton, 1946–1988* (Lewisburg, PA: Bucknell Univ. Press; London and Toronto: Associated Univ. Presses, 1989), pp. 261–70.

Believes that the narrative flaws and repetitions of lines in the poem are the result of two different versions of the same event, "written perhaps at different times." One version derives from Luke and the other from the baptismal service in the prayer book.

3357 Hunter, William B., Jr. "The Obedience of Christ in *Paradise Regained.*" *Calm of Mind: Tercentenary Essays on "Paradise Regained" and "Samson Ago-*

nistes" in Honor of John S. Diekhoff. Ed. by Joseph Anthony Wittreich, Jr. (Cleveland, OH, and London: Press of Case Western Reserve Univ., 1971), pp. 67–75. Ann Arbor, MI: Univ. Microfilms International, 1980 Books on Demand Reprints. Reprinted in *The Descent of Urania: Studies in Milton, 1946–1988* (Lewisburg, PA: Bucknell Univ. Press; London and Toronto: Associated Univ. Presses, 1989), pp. 106–13.

In his brief epic, Milton presents the concept of active obedience as found in the Old Testament and ultimately combines it with passive obedience.

3358 Huttar, Charles A. *"Paradise Regained,* the Hermeneutical Circle, and Christian Anticipations of Post-Modern Theory." *R&L,* 19, 1987, 15–26.

Focuses on the hermeneutics of Milton's ultimate meaning as interpreted according to the perceptions of the individual reader or audience. Relates this meaning to Milton's portrayal of Christ and his actions based on the understanding of the said meaning.

3359 Huttar, Charles A. "The Passion of Christ in *Paradise Regained." ELN,* 19, 1982, 236–60.

States that while the Passion is not explicit in *Paradise Regained,* "redemption by the Cross . . . is nevertheless an essential part of the poem." Points out several allusions to the Atonement.

3360 Hyman, Lawrence W. "Christ on the Pinnacle: A New Reading of the Conclusion to *Paradise Regained." MiltonQ,* 18, 1984, 19–22.

Believes that the Son frustrates the reader's expectations of a savior and his victory. However, "the contradictory qualities of a Christ who both can and cannot be '*our* Saviour' . . . are intertwined." One quality cannot exist without its negation.

3361 Hyman, Lawrence W. "The Reader's Attitude in *Paradise Regained." PMLA,* 85, 1970, 496–503.

The poem's emotional center is provided for the reader in the tension created as the Son moves from the human to the divine, renouncing hope of redeeming the world in human or secular terms. The reader's inability to identify with the Son is, therefore, essential to the poem's success.

3362 Ide, Richard S. "Satan and the Mask of Apollo in *Paradise Regained." MiltonQ,* 9, 1975, 33–34.

Abstract of a paper presented at the University of Wisconsin, Milwaukee, Milton Tercentenary Conference, in November, 1974. Deals with two topics: "the self-destructive nature of evil and the function of typology in *Paradise Regained."*

3363 Jenkins, R. B. "Revelation in *Paradise Regained." JEP,* 6, 1985, 269–83.

Emphasizes the role of divine revelation in illuminating Jesus regarding his earthly mission and its absence in the mind of Satan, who remains ignorant of his great adversary.

3364 Jordan, Richard Douglas. *"Paradise Regained:* A Dramatic Analogue." *MiltonQ,* 12, 1978, 65–68.

Cites the medieval mystery plays and especially Jean Michel's *Le Mystère de la Passion,* which was printed many times during the late fifteenth and early sixteenth centuries.

3365 Jordan, Richard Douglas. *"Paradise Regained* and the Second Adam." *MiltonS,* 9, 1976, 261–75.

"While some modern critics have tried to read *Paradise Regained* as a psychologically realistic dramatic presentation, the text itself does not support such a reading. The poem is rather an exploration of Christ's role as the second Adam, and it is meant to be read as a sequel to *Paradise Lost* offering certain typological contrasts between Adam and Christ." See No. 3309.

3366 Kato, Kazutoshi. "Satan's Temptation of 'the Kingdoms of the World': Meanings of His Stratagems in Offering the

Kingdoms." *JCSS*, 11, 1976, 73–97.

In Japanese; English summary. Believes that Satan's stratagems reflect some important questions at issue in the English revolution.

3367 Kelsall, Malcolm. "The Historicity of *Paradise Regained.*" *MiltonS*, 12, 1978, 235–51.

Proposes that Milton's Christ reflects the philosophy, politics, and history of the Roman empire as he discusses godly virtues and personal heroism.

3368 Kermode, Frank. "Interpretive Continuities and the New Testament." *RAR*, 1, 1982, 33–49.

Cites Milton as an example of one who reinterprets the narrative of Christ's temptation. "So Milton uses a good measure of interpretive freedom, but still he preserves, in this new discourse [*Paradise Regained*], such elements of the tradition as satisfied him."

3369 Kermode, Frank. "Milton: *Paradise Regained.*" *English Renaissance Literature: Introductory Lectures.* By Kermode, Stephen Fender, and Kenneth Palmer (London: Gray-Mills Publishing, 1974), pp. 118–31.

Discusses the difficulties in presenting Jesus as a traditional epic hero, while retaining the poem's quiet mood and portraying him as man and God resisting all temptations.

3370 Kerrigan, William. "The Riddle of *Paradise Regained.*" *Poetic Prophecy in Western Literature.* Ed. by Jan Wojcik and Raymond-Jean Frontain (Rutherford, NJ, Madison, WI, and Teaneck, NJ: Fairleigh Dickinson Univ. Press; London and Toronto: Associated Univ. Presses, 1984), pp. 64–80.

Analyzes the similes in *Paradise Regained* 4.549–87, especially the one concerning Oedipus. "Suffering the punishment of Oedipus, blind Milton revealed in his latent tribute at the climax of *Paradise Regained* the fate out of which was born the prophetic power within himself and his myth."

3371 Kirkconnell, Watson. *Awake the Courteous Echo: The Themes and Prosody of "Comus," "Lycidas," and "Paradise Regained" in World Literature with Translations of the Major Analogues.* Toronto and Buffalo, NY: Univ. of Toronto Press, 1973. xxiv, 336pp.

Contains 25 analogues of *Paradise Regained.* Appendices: "On Metre"; "Biblical Epics"; and "Thomas Ellwood's Epic." Indices of persons and of analogues. See No. 3402. Reviews: *MiltonQ*, 7, 1973, 111–12; Claes Schaar, *RenQ*, 27, 1974, 601–02; Martin Mueller, *CRCL*, 2, 1974, 188–89; Joseph Anthony Wittreich, *MiltonQ*, 8, 1974, 15–21; Michael Lieb, *Cithara*, 15, 1975, 118–19; A. H. Elliott, *N&Q*, 23, 1976, 28–29.

3372 Kittle, William L. "The Temptation to *Acedia* in *Paradise Regained.*" *Milton Reconsidered: Essays in Honor of Arthur E. Barker.* Ed. by John Karl Franson (Salzburg: Institut für Englische Sprache und Literatur, Universität Salzburg, 1976), pp. 135–53.

Suggests that "an analysis of the Satanic temptations to acedia (spiritual apathy) will increase our awareness of the richness of *Paradise Regained*, both in terms of the Christian tradition . . . and of the homiletic function of poetry."

3373 Knight, W. N. " 'To Enter Lists with God': Transformation of Spenserian Chivalric Tradition in *Paradise Regained.*" *Costerus*, 2, 1972, 83–108.

Suggests "that in setting, language, and action *Paradise Regained* owes more to the chivalric tradition than to any other save its Biblical sources."

3374 Knopp, Bradley A. "Whence Comest Thou?: Milton's Satan and the Peripatetic Genesis of Evil." *CCTEP*, 52, 1987, 36–41.

"Consequently, when one asks of Milton's Satan, 'Whence comest thou?', one discovers from *Paradise Lost* and *Paradise Regained* that the Fiend's 'wand'rings' originate in his rebellion against the Author of all movement and that his rejection of Divine Order condemns him to everlasting digression."

3375 Kuratsune, Sumiko. "Christ's Suffering of Humble Death—A Reading of *Paradise Regain'd.*" *MCJ News*, 11, 1989, 13–14.

Abstract of paper presented. Argues that only by suffering a humble death can Jesus break the "trap of egoistic faith, into which not only Satan but Adam, Eve and Samson in *Samson Agonistes* were once caught."

3376 Langford, Thomas. "The Nature of the Christ of *Paradise Regained.*" *MiltonQ*, 16, 1982, 63–67.

Argues that while "Milton's Christ is divine in some sense, it is as a man that he faces Satan in *Paradise Regained.*" Notes parallels and contrasts between Christ and Adam.

3377 Laskowsky, Henry J. "A Pinnacle of the Sublime: Christ's Victory of Style in *Paradise Regained.*" *MiltonQ*, 15, 1981, 10–13.

Contrasts Christ's increasingly terse, didactic style with Satan's growing verbosity. Finds that Christ's last ten words and the narrator's following four words in the final temptation scene in *Paradise Regained* 4.540–61 "represent not simply a final repudiation of Satan's style, but also, and more significantly, the apotheosis of the didactic style of Christ." Discusses line 561 as the substantive sublime's "stylistic triumph" and notes a parallel with the style of *Paradise Lost* 9.781, where Eve eats the fruit.

3378 Le Comte, Edward. "Satan's Heresies in *Paradise Regained.*" *MiltonS*, 12, 1978, 253–66. Reprinted in *Milton Reviewed: Ten Essays* (New York and London: Garland Publishing, 1991), pp. 35–49.

Explicates Christ's temptations and relates Satan's offers and inquiries to moral errors and heresies common in

the first century, such as gnosticism and the Pharisaic heresy.

3379 Lewalski, Barbara Kiefer. *Milton's Brief Epic: The Genre, Meaning, and Art of "Paradise Regained."* Providence, RI: Brown Univ. Press; London: Methuen, 1966. ix, 436pp.

See Huckabay No. 2094. Reviews: Christopher Ricks, *NYRB*, June 9, 1966, pp. 27–28; Kenneth Muir, *CritQ*, 8, 1966, 282–83; William G. Madsen, *MP*, 65, 1968, 251–53; Samuel I. Mintz, *RenQ*, 21, 1968, 367–69; Alan Rudrum, *SoRA*, 3, 1968, 184–88; Dieter Mehl, *Anglia*, 87, 1969, 261–65; Earl Miner, *ECS*, 3, 1970, 296–305; Michael Wilding, *MLR*, 65, 1970, 599–600.

3380 Lewalski, Barbara. "Time and History in *Paradise Regained.*" *The Prison and the Pinnacle.* Ed. by Balachandra Rajan (Toronto and Buffalo, NY: Univ. of Toronto Press, 1973), pp. 49–81.

Shows how conceptions of time and history contribute to the poem's thematic subtleties, advance its dramatic action, and assist in characterizing its principal personages. Considers the Roman conception of fortune and fate and the Machiavellian conception of the ruler.

3381 Lewalski, Barbara Kiefer. "Typological Symbolism and the Progress of the Soul in Seventeenth-Century Literature." *Literary Uses of Typology from the Late Middle Ages to the Present.* Ed. by Earl Miner (Princeton, NJ: Princeton Univ. Press, 1977), pp. 79–114.

Gives some attention to the typology in *Paradise Lost* and *Paradise Regained.*

3382 Lim, Walter Swee Huat. "Biblical Analogy and the Heroic Paradigm in *Paradise Lost* and *Paradise Regained.*" Doctoral diss., Univ. of Toronto, 1988. Abs., *DAI*, 49, 1988, 811A.

Believes that Milton partly modeled his epic heroes (the preexistent Son, Adam, Eve, the incarnate Son) mainly on Old Testament figures to infuse "the actions of his protagonists with greater dramatic and theological significance" and to clarify the poet's own "role as prophet to the English New Jerusalem."

3383 Lord, George de Forest. "Folklore and Myth in *Paradise Regain'd.*" *Poetic Traditions of the English Renaissance.* Ed. by Maynard Mack and Lord (New Haven, CT, and London: Yale Univ. Press, 1982), pp. 229–49. Reprinted in *Trials of the Self: Heroic Ordeals in the Epic Tradition* (Hamden, CT: Archon Books, 1983), pp. 93–109.

"In his unannounced departure from home . . . and in going back to his mother in the end . . . Jesus is tracing the monomyth in the essentially private and domestic mode of the fairy tale."

3384 Low, Anthony. "Milton, *Paradise Regained*, and Georgic." *PMLA*, 98, 1983, 152–69.

"*Paradise Regained* contains neither swords nor pruning hooks, but its structure, style, and spirit, as well as much of its imagery, are georgic." See David-Everett Blythe's response (No. 3300).

3385 MacCallum, Hugh. "Jesus as Teacher in *Paradise Regained.*" *ESC*, 14, 1988, 135–51.

States that Milton's view of Jesus in *Paradise Regained* moves away from his earlier vision of Christ as mediator and redeemer. Examines Christ's use of literary and dialectical techniques to defeat Satan.

3386 MacKellar, Walter. *A Variorum Commentary on the Poems of John Milton.* Gen. ed. Merritt Y. Hughes. Vol. 4: *Paradise Regained.* New York: Columbia Univ. Press, 1975. xxiv, 379pp.

In the Preface to Vol. 1, the General Editor Merritt Y. Hughes states: "Our object in this work is to furnish a body of variorum notes and discussions uniting all available scholarly illumination of the texts on all levels from the semantic and syntactical to those of deliberate or unconscious echoes of other works in all the languages known to Milton. In notes on the longer passages we have considered their inner rhetorical organization and involvements in the design of the poem as a whole, in the backgrounds of the literary traditions of which they themselves are outstanding developments, and in the many aspects of Milton's interests— theological, cosmological, hexameral, historical, psychological, and so on." Contains a documented introduction, meticulous commentary, and an essay by Edward R. Weismiller, "Studies of Style and Verse Form in *Paradise Regained.*" See Nos. 1236 and 1838 for the other volumes of the *Variorum Commentary.* See also Nos. 773 and 789. Reviews: *MiltonQ*, 10, 1976, 58–60; reply by Edward Le Comte, pp. 122–24; Arnold Stein, *SR*, 84, 1976, 695–706; Alastair Fowler, *MLR*, 72, 1977, 657–59; Michael Lieb, *Cithara*, 16, No. 2, 1977, 140–42; George F. Sensabaugh, *RenQ*, 30, 1977, 127–31; Irène Simon, *RES*, 28, 1977, 347–48.

3387 Marilla, E. L. "Milton on the Crucifixion." *EA*, 22, 1969, 7–10.

Cites several passages from Milton's works to show that he regarded "the Crucifixion as essential to salvation." It does not appear in *Paradise Regained* "for the simple reason that the context provides no place for it."

3388 Marsh, Dwight Chaney. "'Above Heroic': A Theological Explication of *Paradise Regained* as Anti-Epic." Doctoral diss., Univ. of Nebraska, Lincoln, 1968. 133pp. Abs., *DA*, 29, 1969, 2219A.

Argues that *Paradise Regained* cannot be judged by the same standards as *Paradise Lost* because it often abandons "pagan epic forms" when they are "incompatible with Christian doctrines."

3389 McAdams, James Roberts. "Milton's Epic Synthesis: A Study of the Association of *Paradise Lost* and *Paradise*

Regained." Doctoral diss., New York Univ., 1966. 260pp. Abs., *DAI*, 30, 1970, 4458A–59A.

Examines the thematic relationship between *Paradise Lost* and *Paradise Regained*, revealing a common organizational pattern—internally parallel events, temptation, and resolution.

3390 McAdams, James R. "The Pattern of Temptation in *Paradise Regained.*" *MiltonS*, 4, 1972, 177–93.

"The debate of Christ and Satan concerning 'zeal and duty' to Israel is the most significant temptation in *Paradise Regained*. In it, Milton sums up the main themes, reveals the antagonists definitively, and foreshadows the remaining action and resolution."

3391 McCaffrey, Phillip. "*Paradise Regained*: The Style of Satan's Athens." *MiltonQ*, 5, 1971, 7–14.

Analyzes Satan's depiction of Athens in *Paradise Regained* 4.212–84. Argues that the reader "errs in attributing any detachable, objective validity to the devil's presentation of Greek culture." Holds that the passage contains both undeniable poetic beauties and "a pervasive, damning commentary of symbolism, allusion, and irony," which discredits Satan's proposal.

3392 McCanles, Michael. "Signs of Power and the Power of Signs in Milton's Last Poems." *SHR*, 17, 1983, 327–38.

Examines *Paradise Lost*, *Paradise Regained*, and *Samson Agonistes* to show that "Milton envisions physical power as possessing the potentiality both for parodying and perverting spiritual, divine power; and becoming its outward sign and manifestation. . . . The dialectic between these two potentialities parallels . . . another dialectic, that between invisible spiritual reality and outward, physical symbol of that reality."

3393 McCarron, William E. "The 'Persuasive Rhetoric' of *Paradise Regained.*" *MiltonQ*, 10, 1976, 15–21.

Examines Satan's speech in *Paradise Regained* 3.204–22, which contains the essential reason for his temptation of the Son. States that the swarm of flies simile in 4.15–20 is both a metaphor for the Son's present treatment at Satan's hands and also proleptic of his redemptive mission.

3394 McClung, W. A. "The Pinnacle of the Temple." *MiltonQ*, 15, 1981, 13–16.

Discusses the complex and ambiguous history of and the various explanations for the pinnacle of the temple in *Paradise Regained* 4.549–50. Suggests that Milton intended a model "roughly on the lines of King's College Chapel."

3395 McLoone, George Hughes. "Contemplative Symbols in *Paradise Lost* and *Paradise Regained.*" Doctoral diss., George Washington Univ., 1982. 339pp. Abs., *DAI*, 43, 1982, 810A–11A.

Discusses God's use of contemplative symbols—visual images such as the cosmos, earth, and body—to help humans intuitively understand what is right, thereby forcing them to choose between obedience and rebellion.

3396 Mikolajczak, Michael Allen. "Opposite Kindred: Comparisons and Contrasts of *Paradise Regained* and *Samson Agonistes.*" Doctoral diss., Univ. of Wisconsin, Milwaukee, 1982. 241pp. Abs., *DAI*, 44, 1983, 176A–77A.

Argues that the stylistic similarities between *Paradise Regained* and *Samson Agonistes* form "a vision of true heroism" involving "surrender to divine will."

3397 Miller, Edmund. "The Godhead of the Son in *Paradise Regained.*" *MHLS*, 5, 1982, 39–52.

Addresses the extent to which the poem expounds an orthodox Trinitarian view of Christ, "the extent to which the Son of God as a character in the poem seems to know His true nature, . . . [and] the extent to which the nature of the Son of God . . . is known to Satan."

3398 Miller, Timothy Charles. "Milton's *Paradise Regained.*" *Expl*, 47, 1988, 10.

Claims that in *Paradise Regained* Satan knows that God has proclaimed Jesus the Son of God. But Satan incorrectly attributes this pronouncement to John the Baptist, hoping to make Jesus attempt to prove that he is the divine Son and thus show distrust in God's pronouncement.

3399 Miller, Timothy Charles. "A Study of *Paradise Regained* in the Context of Milton's Religion of the Spirit." Doctoral diss., State Univ. of New York, Binghamton, 1982. 136pp. Abs., *DAI*, 43, 1983, 1555A–56A.

Explains how Milton's faith in the Holy Spirit's supreme authority influences the portrayal of Jesus in *Paradise Regained*.

3400 Miner, Earl. "Recovered Paradise." *The Restoration Mode from Milton to Dryden* (Princeton, NJ: Princeton Univ. Press, 1974), pp. 268–87.

Discusses *Paradise Regained* as a poem of related perspectives—Satan's, the Son's, the narrator's, and the reader's.

3401 Moore, Leslie Ellen. "Milton's Poetics of Redemption: Incarnation and Simile in *Paradise Lost* and *Paradise Regained.*" Doctoral diss., Yale Univ., 1981. 257pp. Abs., *DAI*, 42, 1981, 2144A.

Argues that "a particular theological issue, the conflict between Incarnational redemption and sacrificial atonement, is connected to Milton's use of simile within the larger narrative of *Paradise Lost* and *Paradise Regained.*"

3402 Murdoch, Brian O. "Thematic Analogues of *Paradise Regained*: Some Notes on a Recent Milton Handbook." *EA*, 31, 1978, 203–07.

Adds to and emends Watson Kirkconnell's collection of analogues of *Paradise Regained* in No. 3371.

3403 Mustazza, Leonard. "Language as Weapon in Milton's *Paradise Regained.*" *MiltonS*, 18, 1983, 195–216.

Examines Milton's use of language and linguistic patterns in the interplay between Christ and Satan. Suggests that *Paradise Regained* moves from verbosity to silence—Satan's silence in defeat and Christ's silence of victory.

3404 Mustazza, Leonard. "'Such Prompt Eloquence': Language as Agency and Character in Milton's Epics." Doctoral diss., State Univ. of New York, Stony Brook, 1983. 246pp. Abs., *DAI*, 44, 1983, 1802A.

Argues that the language of Satan, Adam and Eve, God, and the Son reflects each character's internal developments and conflicts.

3405 Mustazza, Leonard. *"Such Prompt Eloquence": Language as Agency and Character in Milton's Epics.* Lewisburg, PA: Bucknell Univ. Press; London and Toronto: Associated Univ. Presses, 1988. 173pp.

Studies Satanic language, human language, and divine language in *Paradise Lost* and *Paradise Regained*. Shows that "the two epics are really of a piece, the later poem merely amplifying the larger contest between good and evil words that is evident in the larger epic."

3406 Nakayama, Osamu. "Christology and John Milton—From the Viewpoint of Kenosis." *MCJ News*, 5, 1981, 9–10.

Abstract of paper presented. Argues that Milton considers Christ the anthropos in *Paradise Regained* and that kenosis is not the basis for the poem's dramatic tension.

3407 Nelson, Byron. "Milton's Son of God and the Aristotelian Ideal of Magnanimity." *BWVACET*, 1, 1974, 22–39.

Uses Aristotle's definition of magnanimity, as modified by the Catholic, Protestant, and Neoplatonist traditions, to conclude that "the career of the Son of God is the story of martial prowess, in which the Son of God far outstrips his epic competitors by his bravery and strength; . . . the whole of the story is marked by a fortitude and compassion . . . unmatched elsewhere in epic literature."

3408 Nelson, Cary Robert. "Christ's Body and Satan's Head: Incarnate Space in *Paradise Regained*." *The Incarnate Word: Literature as Verbal Space* (Urbana and London: Univ. of Illinois Press, 1973), pp. 80–100.

"Neither Christ nor Satan ever really sees space in the other's terms, though the same spaces lie before them both. There is no real conflict, because their alternative visions of incarnate space . . . are mutually exclusive."

3409 Nohrnberg, James. "*Paradise Regained* by One Greater Man: Milton's Wisdom Epic as a 'Fable of Identity.'" *Centre and Labyrinth: Essays in Honour of Northrop Frye.* Ed. by Eleanor Cook and others (Toronto, Buffalo, NY, and London: Univ. of Toronto Press, 1983), pp. 83–114.

Argues that "the poem takes a deeply retrospective view of Milton's own vocational history." Believes that in *Paradise Regained* the epic poet reaffirms the wisdom of his choice of vocation and subject.

3410 North, Michael. "Language and the Struggle of Identity in *Paradise Regained*." *Ren&R*, 6, 1982, 273–83.

"All of Satan's temptations can be seen as temptations to accept a definition of language as a provisional thing, and all of his attacks on Christ strike at language first, as a way of destroying the messenger by distorting his message."

3411 Nyquist, Mary. "The Father's Word/ Satan's Wrath." *PMLA*, 100, 1985, 187–202.

In both *Paradise Lost* and *Paradise Regained*, the Father's revelation of his Son (his Word) "initiates a new order and in both has the immediate effect of inciting Satan, another Son, to rebellion."

3412 Nyquist, Mary Ellen. "The Tempta-

tion against the Word in Reformation Theology and in Milton's *Paradise Lost* and *Paradise Regained*." Doctoral diss., Univ. of Toronto, 1978. Abs., *DAI*, 40, 1979, 274A.

Contrasts the Reformation view that the Fall involves "dualism of faith and unbelief in the Word" with Augustinian thought, especially as it affects *Paradise Lost* and *Paradise Regained*.

3413 Ohinata, Gen. "Ambiguity in *Paradise Regain'd*." *MCJ News*, 9, 1987, 28–29.

Abstract of a paper presented at the Twenty-First Colloquium of MCJ in July, 1986. Reviews various instances of ambiguity.

3414 Ohki, Hideo. "From William Ames (1576–1633) towards Milton Concerning the Development of the Puritan Covenant Theology." *MCJ News*, 3, 1979, 2–3.

Suggests that Milton, rather than Ames, contributed to the downfall of "corpus Christianorum."

3415 Oleyar, Rita Balkey. "The Biblical Wilderness in Vaughan, Herbert, and Milton." Doctoral diss., Univ. of California, Irvine, 1968. 166pp. Abs., *DAI*, 30, 1969, 287A–88A.

Contends that "the Israelite trek through the desert of Sinai" serves as a metaphor for a Christian's life journey toward God in the three writers' works.

3416 Ono, Kosei. "*Paradise Regained* and Exodus." *MCJ News*, 10, 1988, 12–14.

Abstract of paper presented. Describes allusions to the Book of Exodus in *Paradise Regained*. Emphasizes the religious significance of Milton's use of the words "stand" and "fall" and their relation to the Exodus.

3417 Patrides, C. A., ed. *Milton's Epic Poetry: Essays on "Paradise Lost" and "Paradise Regained."* Harmondsworth: Penguin, 1967. 428pp.

See Huckabay No. 2119.

3418 Patterson, Annabel M. "*Paradise Regained*: A Last Chance at True Ro-

mance." *MiltonS*, 17, 1983, 187–208.
Delineates background sources and currents in the romantic tradition from which Milton could have received his views. Traces the development of his chivalric and romantic themes from *Il Penseroso* through *Paradise Regained* and discusses the antiromantic attitude expressed in the latter.

3419 Pearce, James Morris, Jr. *"Paradise Regained*: The Human and the Divine." Doctoral diss., Stanford Univ., 1979. 199pp. Abs., *DAI*, 40, 1979, 873A–74A.
Counters modern criticism by arguing that "Christ and Satan are both aware of Christ's identity."

3420 Pearce, James M. "The Theology of Representation: The Meta-Argument of *Paradise Regained*." *MiltonS*, 24, 1988, 277–96.
Argues that "the humanist rhetorical tradition furnished Milton with the set of assumptions which . . . governed the way in which he depicted Christ." He uses Cicero's concept of "controversia," which provides the meta-argument and is the vehicle through which Christ's nature is realized.

3421 Pecheux, Mother Mary Christopher, O. S. U. "Sin in *Paradise Regained*: The Biblical Background." *Calm of Mind: Tercentenary Essays on "Paradise Regained" and "Samson Agonistes" in Honor of John S. Diekhoff.* Ed. by Joseph Anthony Wittreich, Jr. (Cleveland, OH, and London: Press of Case Western Reserve Univ., 1971), pp. 49–65. Ann Arbor, MI: Univ. Microfilms International, 1980 Books on Demand Reprints.
Proposes "to examine the principal biblical themes of sin as they relate to the action of *Paradise Regained*." Sins of error appear in the poem's first two books and those of rebellion in the last two. The theme of humanity's slavery to sin and the Son's victory over it forms the poem's conclusion.

3422 Quint, David. "David's Census: Milton's Politics and *Paradise Regained*."

Re-membering Milton: Essays on the Texts and Traditions. Ed. by Mary Nyquist and Margaret W. Ferguson (New York and London: Methuen, 1987), pp. 128–47. Reprinted in *Epic and Empire: Politics and Generic Form from Virgil to Milton* (Princeton, NJ: Princeton Univ. Press, 1993), pp. 325–40.
Studies the anti-Restoration political undercurrents in *Paradise Regained*. Specifically deals with the contradiction of Milton, a staunch anti-royalist, arguing for extreme individualism.

3423 Radzinowicz, Mary Ann. "*Paradise Regained* as Hermeneutic Combat." *HSL*, 15–16, 1983–84, 99–107.
Demonstrates that the poem's theology is indebted to Luke, Hebrews, and the Psalms.

3424 Rajan, Balachandra. "'To Which is Added *Samson Agonistes*—.'" *The Prison and the Pinnacle*. Ed. by Rajan (Toronto and Buffalo, NY: Univ. of Toronto Press, 1973), pp. 82–110.
Discusses the methodical use of hills and plains in *Paradise Lost* and finds an extension of it in *Paradise Regained* and *Samson Agonistes*. *Paradise Regained* is a poem of the hill and *Samson Agonistes* is a drama of the plain to which fallen Adam must descend. Christ standing on the pinnacle and Samson tearing down the temple of Dagon are complementary climaxes. "'To which is added Samson Agonistes' must be taken as indicating that the end is both what it should be and what it was felt to be from the beginning."

3425 Reedy, Gerard, S. J. "Noumenal and Phenomenal Evidence in England, 1662–1682." *EnlE*, 2, 1971, 137–48.
Briefly examines *Paradise Regained* "as a sample of Restoration biblical hermeneutic in practical subservience to the arts." Discusses Milton's reliance on typology and his use of Scripture as a base, but not the complete source, to prove the Son's humanity. Claims that Milton's theology allows

him to succumb to dramatic expediency to make his epic feasible.

3426 Renaker, David. "The Horoscope of Christ." *MiltonS*, 12, 1978, 213–33.
Claims that Satan's horoscope of Christ in *Paradise Regained* 4.382–93 is a rational effort to determine the course of future events. It is in this form, and incomplete, because Satan had access to the entire Greco-Roman civilization, but was unaided by a belief in the Old Testament prophets.

3427 Revard, Stella P. "The Gospel of John and *Paradise Regained*: Jesus as 'True Light.'" *Milton and Scriptural Tradition: The Bible into Poetry*. Ed. by James H. Sims and Leland Ryken (Columbia: Univ. of Missouri Press, 1984), pp. 142–59.
Asserts that *Paradise Regained* relies on the Gospel of John for its characterization of Jesus, its enhancement of scenes taken from other sources, its treatment of Christ's realization of his role as the Son of God, and its portrayal of Satan's temptation of Christ. *Paradise Regained* thus reflects the idea of Christ's role as "true Light," which is central to the Gospel of John. Abs., *MiltonQ*, 15, 1981, 29.

3428 Revard, Stella P. "Milton and Classical Rome: The Political Context of *Paradise Regained*." *Rome in the Renaissance: The City and the Myth*. Ed. by P. A. Ramsey. Medieval and Renaissance Texts and Studies, vol. 18 (Binghamton, NY: Medieval and Renaissance Texts and Studies, 1982), pp. 409–19.
Believes that Milton's portrait of Rome reflects his continual insistence on applying the lessons of history. "On the one hand was the luxurious court of Rome ruled by Tiberius, with no son for an heir, and on the other was Whitehall and the luxuries of Charles, also heirless."

3429 Revard, Stella P. "Vision and Revision: A Study of *Paradise Lost* 11 and *Paradise Regained*." *PLL*, 10, 1974, 353–62.

Demonstrates that the full significance of the recovery of the Edenic vision in *Paradise Regained* "cannot be understood unless we realize that in some ways Milton has begun in Book 11 [of *Paradise Lost*] to prepare us for that recovery."

3430 Revere, Linda Sanders. "Deconstructing Satan: The Hermeneutics of Milton's *Paradise Regained*." Doctoral diss., Rice Univ., 1982. 235pp. Abs., *DAI*, 43, 1982, 812A–13A.
Defines *Paradise Regained* as "a decentered text, a poem that questions itself as other than a supplement to the Biblical Word."

3431 Rhodes, Byne. "Milton's Banquet in the Wilderness." *AN&Q*, 15, 1976, 20–23.
Milton adds the banquet scene to provide a focal point for understanding Christ's role in the poem "as a protagonist rather than a theological abstraction."

3432 Ricks, Christopher. "Milton: Part III. *Paradise Regained* and *Samson Agonistes*." *English Poetry and Prose, 1540–1674*. Ed. by Ricks. Sphere History of Literature in the English Language, vol. 2 (London: Sphere Books, 1970), pp. 299–316. Revised edition, New York: Peter Bedrick Books, 1987.
Argues that the style of *Paradise Regained* is inferior to that of *Paradise Lost*. Because the temptations are easy to refuse, the conflict between Christ and Satan lacks drama.

3433 Ridden, Geoffrey M. "*Paradise Regained* and *Eikon Basilike*." *MiltonQ*, 17, 1983, 26–27.
Claims that in *Paradise Regained* 2.457–65, Milton's attack on the divine right theory is specifically aimed at Charles I and *Eikon Basilike*. Notes that Milton's lines provide an antithetical response to the fourteen-line verse in the frontispiece of *Eikon Basilike*.

3434 Riggs, William G. "Afterword: *Paradise Regained* and the Miltonic

Hero." *The Christian Poet in "Paradise Lost"* (Berkeley, Los Angeles, and London: Univ. of California Press, 1972), pp. 183–90.

Deals with Milton's choosing the subject of the temptation rather than the Passion. Christ's temptations "represent the *process* of recovery, the recovery of a paradise within."

3435 Roskoski, Stanley John. "No New Device: Milton's *Paradise Regained* in the Light of His *De Doctrina Christiana*." Doctoral diss., Indiana Univ., 1971. 235pp. Abs., *DAI*, 32, 1972, 4632A.

Contends that *Paradise Regained* agrees with the *Christian Doctrine* on ideas considered orthodox by Protestant standards, but downplays or ignores unorthodox views.

3436 Rushdy, Ashraf H. A. "Of *Paradise Regained*: The Interpretation of Career." *MiltonS*, 24, 1988, 253–75.

Develops the idea that "the interpretation of one's career—in both the sense of 'vocation' and 'motion' toward or away from God—is the basic temptation in the poem." Satan can interpret the Son's career only to a degree.

3437 Sabir, S. I. "Milton's One Greater Man and the Form of *Paradise Regained*: A Study of the Coinage in the Context of the Poem's Controversial Form." M.Litt. thesis, Univ. of Strathclyde, 1976.

3438 Safer, Elaine B. "The Socratic Dialogue and 'Knowledge in the Making' in *Paradise Regained*." *MiltonS*, 6, 1974, 215–26.

"An examination of the dialogue form in *Paradise Regained* illuminates Milton's method of educating the reader by involving him as an indirect participant in a Platonic-Socratic dialectic between Christ and Satan. . . . Involvement in the dialectic process helps us to separate falsity from truth in order to reach the ultimate joy of the good life: a glimpse of paradise regained for mankind."

3439 Samaha, Edward E., Jr. "Light and

Dark in the Setting of *Paradise Regained*." *ELN*, 7, 1969, 98–105.

Shows that in his brief epic Milton continues to experiment "with degrees of light and shades of darkness to indicate the presence of temptation and the conflict between good and evil." The poet draws from Neoplatonic and Hermetic traditions and his own treatment of light and dark to weave "a tapestry of subtle shades and a final glorious outburst [shaped according to] the opposing forces of good and evil."

3440 Samuel, Irene. "The Regaining of Paradise." *The Prison and the Pinnacle.* Ed. by Balachandra Rajan (Toronto and Buffalo, NY: Univ. of Toronto Press, 1973), pp. 111–34.

Disagrees with the commonly held view that *Paradise Regained* is centrally concerned with establishing the identity of its hero. "What Milton chiefly does is elaborate the temptations into arguments and the rejections into counter-arguments, so that every man may see in the exemplary answers a complete program for regaining Eden."

3441 Sasek, Lawrence A. "Milton's Criticism of Greek Literature in *Paradise Regained*." *Essays in Honor of Esmond Linworth Marilla.* Ed. by Thomas Austin Kirby and William John Olive. Louisiana State Univ. Studies, Humanities Series, no. 19 (Baton Rouge: Louisiana State Univ. Press, 1970), pp. 158–65.

Suggests that Christ's rejection of classical literature in *Paradise Regained* 4.331–52 is not the rejection of Milton the poet but of Christ as a dramatic figure who must believe that Hebrew poetry is far superior to Greek imitations.

3442 Schoen, Raymond G. "Milton's Similes and the Idea of Temporal Flow." *MiltonQ*, 9, 1975, 35–36.

Abstract of a paper presented at the University of Wisconsin, Milwaukee, Milton Tercentenary Conference, in November, 1974. Demonstrates that the Antaeus simile in *Paradise Regained* 4.563 accepts classical values.

3443 Shawcross, John T. "The Etymological Significance of Biblical Names in *Paradise Regain'd*." *LOS*, 2, 1975, 34–57.

Concludes that "examining biblical names in *Paradise Regain'd* has direct significance for a recognition of Milton's citation of their meanings, for an understanding of ironies and deeper texture, for a mythic context, sometimes arising from the Bible, and for a realization that, explicitly and implicitly, Milton enhanced his message and art by word-play on names."

3444 Shawcross, John T. "The Genres of *Paradise Regain'd* and *Samson Agonistes*: The Wisdom of Their Joint Publication." *MiltonS*, 17, 1983, 225–48.

Builds a definition of brief epic and places *Paradise Regained* in that genre; states that the "genre of *Samson Agonistes* . . . is drama by form and characteristics, but poem by execution and structure." Assigns a comic mode to *Paradise Regained* and a tragic mode to *Samson Agonistes*. Asserts that *Paradise Regained* and *Samson Agonistes* are companion works literally (in publication), structurally (by contrast of style), metaphysically (in the comparison and contrast of the Son and Samson), and theologically (in that Milton's overall doctrine of religious interiority is fully set forth only by comprehending the poems' heroes as companion spirits).

3445 Shawcross, John T. *"Paradise Regain'd": Worthy T'Have Not Remain'd So Long Unsung*. Pittsburgh, PA: Duquesne Univ. Press, 1988. 150pp.

Examines the themes of self-knowledge, life as a battlefield, and the patient hero in *Paradise Regained*. Argues that Milton asks us not to imitate the Son's heroism, but to internalize it. Reviews: Michael Allen Mikolajczak, *SCN*, 47, 1989, 34–35; Roy Flannagan, *MiltonQ*, 26, 1992, 25–27.

3446 Shawcross, John T. "The Structure and Myth of *Paradise Regained*." *The Laurel Bough: Essays Presented in Honour of Professor M. V. Rama Sarma*. Ed. by G. Nageswara Rao (Bombay: Blackie and Son, 1983), pp. 1–14.

"In this paper I shall explore these implications: the structure that delineates the battlefield, the achievement of self-knowledge, and the power or energy to be victorious on the battlefield, and the mythic concept of the patient hero wherewith the crown of life may be attained."

3447 Shawcross, John. "The Structure of *Paradise Regain'd* as Meaning." *MiltonQ*, 7, 1973, 91.

Abstract of a paper presented at the 1973 North Central Conference of the Renaissance Society of America. The poem's 1:3 structure "indicates the primacy of the first book," and *Paradise Regained* "presents the transcendence of the man Jesus into the man-God Jesus."

3448 Shiratori, Masataka. "On the Satan of *Paradise Regained*—A Reconsideration." *MCJ News*, 5, 1981, 2–6.

Examines the historical Satan and the ironies in Milton's presentation of him.

3449 Sims, James H. "A Greater than Rome: The Inversion of a Virgilian Symbol from Camoëns to Milton." *Rome in the Renaissance: The City and the Myth*. Ed. by P. A. Ramsey. Medieval and Renaissance Texts and Studies, vol. 18 (Binghamton, NY: Medieval and Renaissance Texts and Studies, 1982), pp. 333–44.

"Milton turns the ideal inward, rejecting outer pomp and power as ultimately insignificant and focusing, instead, on the human heart, indwelt by God's grace and Spirit, as the source of true greatness." Abs., *MiltonQ*, 14, 1980, 72.

3450 Sims, James H. "Psalm 90 and the Pattern of Temptation in *A Dialogue of Comfort* and *Paradise Regained*: From 'Solicitations' to 'Furiose Force.'" *Moreana*, 19, 1982, 27–37.

Argues that Milton explicitly uses Psalm 90's pattern of temptation "in Satan's temptation on the pinnacle of the Temple and implicitly in his contrast of the nature of the final temptation with that of those which build towards it. . . . [The] force/fraud dichotomy in temptation . . . takes on special significance in the dramatic development of [Thomas] More's and Milton's narratives."

3451 Smith, Carolyn H. "The Virgin Mary in *Paradise Regain'd*." *SAQ*, 71, 1972, 557–64.

On the poem's characterization of Mary, whom Milton sees as "perceptive, frank with Jesus about his divine birth, and capable of having and controlling such emotions as impatience and anxiety."

3452 Smith, Grant William. "Religious Language in *Paradise Regained*." Doctoral diss., Univ. of Delaware, 1975. 249pp. Abs., *DAI*, 37, 1976, 2902A–03A.

Examines Milton's tendency to qualify religious models in *Paradise Regained*.

3453 Steadman, John M. "*Paradise Regained*: The Crossroads Motif and the Ordeal of Initial Choice." *Milton and the Paradoxes of Renaissance Heroism* (Baton Rouge and London: Louisiana State Univ. Press, 1987), pp. 194–212.

In *Paradise Regained*, Jesus uses the rejection motif to establish his knowledge, holiness, and "filial freedom." The poem represents "the process of man's gradual renewal in knowledge after the image of the Creator"—a "paradigm of regeneration."

3454 Steadman, John M. "Satanic *Paideia*: The Devil as Humanist." *Milton and the Paradoxes of Renaissance Heroism* (Baton Rouge and London: Louisiana State Univ. Press, 1987), pp. 213–23.

Satan offers Jesus readings in Hellenic literature and philosophy, "the same kind of training that Horace had recommended for the poet and that Quintilian and Cicero had proposed for the orator." When Milton describes the temptation of Athens in *Para-

dise Regained*, he "surely had the humanist educational program partly in mind."

3455 Stein, Arnold. *Heroic Knowledge: An Interpretation of "Paradise Regained" and "Samson Agonistes."* Hamden, CT: Shoe String Press, 1968.

Reprint of Huckabay No. 2149, originally published in 1957.

3456 Stein, Robert A. "Eloquence as Power: Another Dimension of the Hercules Simile, *Paradise Regained*, IV, 562–8." *MiltonQ*, 4, 1970, 22–24.

States that "the simile reminds us of Jesus' physical and spiritual power" and indirectly recalls his "decision to employ eloquence in his battle for men's souls."

3457 Stein, Robert A. "*Paradise Regained* in the Light of Classical and Christian Traditions of Criticism and Rhetoric." Doctoral diss., Brandeis Univ., 1968. 151pp. Abs., *DA*, 29, 1969, 2685A–86A.

Describes the traditions that influenced Milton's combination of Christian themes with pagan forms in *Paradise Regained*.

3458 Stein, Robert A. "The Sources and Implications of the Jobean Analogies in *Paradise Regained*." *Anglia*, 88, 1970, 323–33.

"The Jobean analogies in *Paradise Regained* owe more to the allusive habits of Renaissance writers than to The Book of Job itself. They stem from widely shared conventions. . . . They do not imply the poem's model (if, indeed, there is one)."

3459 Sumers-Ingraham, Alinda. "John Milton's *Paradise Regained* and the Genre of the Puritan Spiritual Biography." Doctoral diss., George Washington Univ., 1984. 425pp. Abs., *DAI*, 45, 1984, 193A.

Argues that "Puritan hagiology influences the heroism of the Son, the psychology of Satan's assault, the structure and order of temptation, and the severity of tone in *Paradise Regained*."

3460 Sundell, Roger H. "The Narrator

as Interpreter in *Paradise Regained.*" *MiltonS*, 2, 1970, 83–101.

"In the temptation episodes . . . the narrator shares with the hero the role of interpreter."

3461 Swaim, Kathleen M. "Hercules, Antaeus, and Prometheus: A Study of the Climactic Epic Similes in *Paradise Regained.*" *SEL*, 18, 1978, 137–53.

Explores the epic similes in *Paradise Regained* 4.562–81, which compare Satan and Christ with Antaeus and Hercules and with Sphinx and Oedipus. The two similes require readers "to search, interpret, and apply classical mythology to the thematic purposes of the brief epic."

3462 Swanson, Donald. "Milton's Scholarly Jesus in *Paradise Regained.*" *Cithara*, 27, No. 2, 1988, 3–10.

Addresses the magnitude of Christ's omniscience and suggests that his education was in the Greco-Roman tradition.

3463 Szenher, Phillip John. " 'Poetry, Both in Divine and Human Things': A Rhetorical Reading of *Paradise Regained.*" Doctoral diss., Univ. of Connecticut, 1975. 269pp. Abs., *DAI*, 36, 1975, 1539A–40A.

Describes the rhetoric and logic of *Paradise Regained* as a confirmation of its purpose—"Recover'd Paradise to all mankind."

3464 Tashjian, Carol M. "Studies in Renaissance Rhetoric and Literature." Doctoral diss., Brandeis Univ. 1974. 281pp. Abs., *DAI*, 35, 1974, 1063A–64A.

Examines the influence of rhetorical training on mimesis, praise, deliberation, debate, and rational inquiry in Renaissance works, including *Paradise Regained.*

3465 Tatum, James. "Apollonius of Rhodes and the Resourceless Hero of *Paradise Regained.*" *MiltonS*, 22, 1986, 255–70.

Examines *Paradise Regained* and the *Argonautica* to establish a new type

of heroic character who is incapable of true heroic action.

3466 Teskey, Gordon. "Balanced in Time: *Paradise Regained* and the Centre of the Miltonic Vision." *UTQ*, 50, 1981, 269–83.

Paradise Regained should be appreciated not only for its theme, the return of one man representing humanity, but also for Milton's larger, inexhaustible vision.

3467 Teunissen, John James. "Of Patience and Heroic Martyrdom: The Book of Job and Milton's Conception of Patient Suffering in *Paradise Regained* and *Samson Agonistes.*" Doctoral diss., Univ. of Rochester, 1967. 406pp. Abs., *DA*, 28, 1967, 1797A.

Argues that Christ's perfect and Samson's imperfect suffering is marked by a heroic patience modeled after the Book of Job.

3468 Tsuji, Hiroko. "Rhetoric and Truth in Milton's *Paradise Regained.*" *AnRS*, 20, 1969, 348–69.

Asserts that Milton's education at St. Paul's taught him to distinguish between true and false rhetoric and that the true rhetoric of *Paradise Regained* ultimately comes from the Bible.

3469 Turner, Richard. "The Interpretation of Dreams and Audience Response in *Paradise Lost* and *Paradise Regained.*" *PLL*, 19, 1983, 361–74.

Believes that the knowledge of dream lore that Milton's readers possessed allowed them to interpret both the cause and the significance of dreams in *Paradise Lost* and *Paradise Regained.* Contends that "the dreams instruct the readers and prepare them for confrontations with Satan both in the narrative structures of the poems and in their everyday lives." Also argues that Milton's presentation of dreams requires a reader-response approach and a literary history approach to interpret it.

3470 Valtz Mannucci, Loretta. *Ideali e Classi nella Poesia di Milton: La Nàscita* *dell'Eròe Borghese Puritano in "Paradise Lost" e "Paradise Regained."* Saggi di Cultura Contemporanea, 116. Milano: Edizioni di Comunità, 1976. 284pp.

Deals mainly with the conflict between Jesus and Satan. Both are sons of God, but they are distinguished by grace.

3471 Valtz Mannucci, Loretta. "Milton e la Trasfigurazione Poetica del Borghese." *Comunità*, 39, 1975, 305–89.

Contrasts Jesus's and Satan's roles in terms of psychology. Jesus's victory shows that salvation occurs through the human context, which is directed toward a future founded on human effort.

3472 Wallace, Meta Sehon. "The Christian Pattern of Temptation, Trial, and Grace in Four Renaissance Works: *Paradise Regained, Samson Agonistes, The Faerie Queene*, Book One, and *Macbeth*." Doctoral diss., Univ. of Arkansas, 1978. 176pp. Abs., *DAI*, 39, 1978, 3607A–08A.

Describes a four-part pattern—the annunciation of a mission, temptation based on "the Flesh, the World, and the Devil," the need to accept grace, and the resolution of the mission—in all four works.

3473 Webber, Joan Malory. *"Paradise Regained." Milton and His Epic Tradition* (Seattle and London: Univ. of Washington Press, 1979), pp. 165–209.

"Jesus and Satan illustrate the opposite uses that modern man might make, or has made, of the modern world."

3474 Weber, Burton Jasper. "The Schematic Structure of *Paradise Regained*: A Hypothesis." *PQ*, 50, 1971, 553–66.

Suggests structural units for the poem, especially as they apply to the second day's temptations. Feels that each temptation contains a multiplicity of elements.

3475 Weber, Burton Jasper. *Wedges and Wings: The Patterning of "Paradise Regained."* Carbondale and Edwardsville: Southern Illinois Univ. Press; London and Amsterdam: Feffer and Simons, 1975. xiv, 130pp.

Analyzes the poem's structure. Sets *Paradise Regained* against the epic genre's history. Reviews: *MiltonQ*, 9, 1975, 56–57; Michael Lieb, *MP*, 74, 1976, 204–07; Hugh Maclean, *JEGP*, 75, 1976, 433–37.

3476 Weiss, Dolores. "Milton's Poetics of the Sacred: The Limits of the Poet in *Paradise Lost* and *Paradise Regained*." Doctoral diss., Indiana Univ., 1986. 325pp. Abs., *DAI*, 47, 1987, 3438A–39A.

Examines the poet's struggle to translate unaltered divine truth into epic form, an action that is continually frustrated by the inadequacy of epic language.

3477 Wilson, Gayle Edward. "Emblems in *Paradise Regained*." *MiltonQ*, 6, No. 4, 1972, 77–81.

Discusses various emblems that Milton used in *Paradise Regained* to develop characters and heighten themes.

3478 Wittreich, Joseph Anthony, Jr., ed. *Milton's "Paradise Regained": Two Eighteenth-Century Critiques, by Richard Meadowcourt and Charles Dunster.* Gainesville, FL: Scholar's Facsimiles and Reprints, 1971. xv, 310pp.

Contains facsimile reprints of Meadowcourt's discussion (1732) and Dunster's edition (1795), which includes extensive notes from various authors. Argues that "Meadowcourt precipitated a revaluation of the brief epic," while "Dunster effected a new understanding of the poem, based upon a comprehension of the genre to which *Paradise Regained* belongs and a perception not only of the poem's integrity but also of its mythic dimensions."

3479 Wittreich, Joseph Anthony, Jr. "Strange Text! '*Paradise Regain'd* . . . To Which is Added '*Samson Agonistes*.'" *Poems in Their Place: The Intertextuality and Order of Poetic Collections.* Ed. by Neil Fraistat (Chapel Hill and London: Univ. of North Carolina Press, 1986), pp. 164–94.

On the intertextual connection between the two poems: "typological patterning, generic organization, self-quotation and echo, imagistic and thematic repetition, a common subtext, all of which are conspicuously evident in Milton's 1671 volume. *Paradise Regained* and *Samson Agonistes* have not a separate but shared syntax; these poems together form a totality, with the individual poems themselves becoming like fragments."

3480 Allen, Don Cameron. "Despair and *Samson Agonistes.*" *On Milton's Poetry: A Selection of Modern Studies.* Ed. by Arnold Stein (Greenwich, CT: Fawcett Publications, 1970), pp. 257–73.

Reprint of excerpts from a chapter in Huckabay No. 404, originally published in 1954.

3481 Andrews, John F. "'Dearly Bought Revenge': *Samson Agonistes, Hamlet,* and Elizabethan Revenge Tragedy." *MiltonS,* 13, 1979, 81–107.

Compares *Samson Agonistes, Hamlet,* and other revenge tragedies, based on the assumption that Milton's drama is a revenge tragedy.

3482 Arai, Akira. "On the Writing of Tenrai Han'ya's Milton's *Samson Agonistes.*" *Miscellaneous Essays on Milton* (Tokyo: Chukyo Shuppan, 1979), pp. 173–85.

In Japanese. Comments on Tenrai Shigeno's pioneering translation and analysis of *Samson Agonistes.*

3483 Arai, Akira. "Samson's 'Death So Noble.'" *SELit,* 53, 1972, 43–59.

Deemphasizes the Greek element in *Samson Agonistes.* Sees it rather as a Puritan Christian drama which relates a threefold pilgrimage: despair, hope, and glorification.

3484 Arnold, Margaret J. "*Graeci Christiani*: Milton's Samson and the Renaissance Editors of Greek Tragedy." *MiltonS,* 18, 1983, 235–54.

Compares Milton's Samson with Renaissance Christian readings of Sophocles's *Ajax,* Euripides's *Heracles,* and Aeschylus's *Prometheus Bound.* Shows how Milton's blend of classical and Christian heroism develops Samson to heroic proportions.

3485 Arthos, John. "Milton and Monteverdi: A Consideration of Music and Drama in Italy in Relationship to *Samson Agonistes.*" *Milton and the Italian Cities* (London: Bowes and Bowes, 1968), pp. 129–205.

See Huckabay No. 2177.

3486 Arthos, John. "Milton and the Passions: A Study of *Samson Agonistes.*" *MP,* 69, 1972, 209–21.

Samson Agonistes shows "Milton's idea of the part the passions play in the nature of men, his idea of how they interact with thought and fancy, how they ally themselves with virtue as well as vice, and how they prepare the way for action, all in accord with a divine scheme." Abs., *MiltonQ,* 6, No. 2, 1972, 44.

3487 Asals, Heather. "In Defense of Dalila: *Samson Agonistes* and the Reformation Theology of the Word." *JEGP,* 74, 1975, 183–94.

"Although Milton's Dalila once caused Samson's fall through her ability with words, she makes possible his regeneration by acting as an effective agent of God's word when she comes to him in the poem."

3488 Asals, Heather. "Rhetoric Agonistic in *Samson Agonistes.*" *MiltonQ,* 11, 1977, 1–4.

"My purpose here is to examine the three tempters [Manoa, Dalila, and Harapha] in the framework of the three divisions of debate rhetoric: deliberative, forensic, and epideictic."

3489 Atkinson, Michael. "The Structure

of the Temptations in Milton's *Samson Agonistes.*" *MP*, 69, 1972, 285–91.

Focuses on the nature and structure of Samson's three temptations, which negatively define the end of his spiritual progress—wholeness in his relationship to God. Finds that "each of the three temptations itself contains three temptations, and each has the same basic structure."

3490 Baruch, Franklin R. "Time, Body, and Spirit at the Close of *Samson Agonistes.*" *ELH*, 36, 1969, 319–39.

"Manoa and the Chorus . . . share a final and vital place in the poet's fusion of intellectual, dramatic, and aesthetic forces to reveal distorted perception and values." Does not believe that the Chorus at the end becomes the poet's mouthpiece.

3491 Bennett, Joan S. "Liberty under the Law: The Chorus and the Meaning of *Samson Agonistes.*" *MiltonS*, 12, 1978, 141–63.

Explains that Samson's faith and victory are based on a rational, not ritual, interpretation of Old Testament law. Even God does not contradict his law, but Samson's penitent and sacrificial actions fulfill its intent. Concludes that the Chorus errs in opposing these truths. Review: Dayton Haskin, *Thought*, 56, 1981, 226–39.

3492 Bennett, Joan S. "'A Person Rais'd': Public and Private Cause in *Samson Agonistes.*" *SEL*, 18, 1978, 155–68.

Considers Milton's prose works as a gloss on the issue of revolution in the play. Reveals "the political positions assumed by Dalila and Harapha to be parodic versions of Samson's genuine commitment to the public good."

3493 Berkeley, David S. "Dalila as Amphisbaena." *PLL*, 19, 1983, 87–92.

Sees Dalila in *Samson Agonistes* 997–98 as an amphisbaena, a serpent with a head on each end. Disputes the notion that she is portrayed as a scorpion.

3494 Berkeley, David S. "On a Common

Error Respecting Samson's Size and Musculature." *ELN*, 19, 1982, 260–62.

Although Milton refers to "Herculean Samson" in *Paradise Lost* 9.1060 and in the drama invites readers to think of Samson as a Herculean figure in *Samson Agonistes* 149–50, "his analogy does not and cannot extend to size or body development." Such an "attribution of gigantic size or extraordinary physical development" would make "Samson's deeds . . . his own, not God's."

3495 Berkeley, David S., and **Salwa Khoddam.** "Samson the Base versus Harapha the Gentle." *MiltonQ*, 17, 1983, 1–7.

Claims that Milton challenges the Renaissance belief in the gentry's superiority by portraying Samson as baseborn, "made more rank by wretched conditions." Reply by Leo Miller (No. 3634). Rejoinder to Miller by Berkeley and Khoddam, *MiltonQ*, 18, 1984, 129–31, with a surrejoinder by Miller, p. 131; Noam Flinker extends Miller's disagreement with them in *MiltonQ*, 19, 1985, 19–20; Berkeley and Khoddam further defend their article, p. 34.

3496 Blakemore, Steven. "Milton's *Samson Agonistes*, Lines 80–82." *Expl*, 42, 1984, 17–18.

Proposes Deuteronomy 28.29 as the source of *Samson Agonistes* 80–82. Argues that "the allusion establishes a causal connection between Samson's disobedience and his blindness, and it highlights the moral metaphor of darkness 'amid the blaze of noon.'"

3497 Blau, Rivkah Teitz. "Various Praise: Psalms in *The Temple, Paradise Lost*, and *Samson Agonistes.*" Doctoral diss., Columbia Univ., 1983. 268pp. Abs., *DAI*, 46, 1986, 2297A.

Illustrates the effect of Herbert's and Milton's inclusion, manipulation, and alteration of the Psalms in their poetry.

3498 Blondel, Jacques. "La Tentation dans *Samson Agonistes.*" *EA*, 30, 1977, 158–68.

Argues that Manoa, Dalila, and Harapha unsuccessfully tempt Samson to abandon his faith and become an atheist.

3499 Bonneau, Danielle. "Art et Artifice dans *Samson Agonistes*; ou, Milton contre Dalila." *Aspects du Theatre Anglais (1594–1730)*. Ed. by Nadia Rigaud (Aix-en-Provence: Université de Provence, 1987), pp. 39–58.

Studies the poetic devices Milton uses to develop Dalila as a reflection of Eve and Satan, woman and snake. Samson succumbs, like Adam, knowing the consequences.

3500 Boswell, Jackson Campbell. "Samson's Bosom Snake." *MiltonQ*, 8, 1974, 77–80.

On the image in *Samson Agonistes* 763. Cites other references to embosomed serpents. See No. 3607.

3501 Bouchard, D. F. "Samson as Medicine Man: Ritual Function and Symbolic Structure in *Samson Agonistes*." *Genre*, 5, 1972, 257–70.

Proposes that *Samson Agonistes* is "good medicine" because it gives critics food for thought. Presents a consensus of criticism on major points about the work, such as themes of regeneration, imagery, characters, and the war of opposites.

3502 Bowers, Fredson. "*Samson Agonistes*: Justice and Reconciliation." *The Dress of Words: Essays on Restoration and Eighteenth Century Literature in Honor of Richmond P. Bond*. Ed. by Robert B. White, Jr. Univ. of Kansas Publications, Library Series, 42 (Lawrence: Univ. of Kansas Libraries, 1978), pp. 1–23.

Interprets *Samson Agonistes* as a redemptive tragedy, traces the redemptive process that occurs, and argues that in pulling down the temple, Samson once more becomes God's champion and wins a victory analogous to the fortunate fall in *Paradise Lost*.

3503 Buchanan, Edith. "Milton's True Knight." *SAQ*, 71, 1972, 480–87.

Deals with "the references in *Samson Agonistes* to arms, knightly combat, trophies, and the nature of the chivalric hero common to romance," concluding that Milton makes Samson "reminiscent of a medieval knight."

3504 Burnet, R. A. L. "Two Further Echoes of the Genevan Margin in Shakespeare and Milton." *N&Q*, 28, 1981, 129.

The marginal note to Isaiah 47.2 may have influenced Milton when he wrote the "Eyeless in Gaza" passage in *Samson Agonistes* 40–42.

3505 Burnett, Archie. *Milton's Style: The Shorter Poems, "Paradise Regained," and "Samson Agonistes."* London and New York: Longman, 1981. xiv, 187pp.

"This book has various aims: to give close readings of Milton's poems other than *Paradise Lost*; to take into account the criticism on these poems, focusing on major issues; and to investigate the variety and consistency of their style."

3506 Bush, Douglas. "Milton." *On Milton's Poetry: A Selection of Modern Studies*. Ed. by Arnold Stein (Greenwich, CT: Fawcett Publications, 1970), pp. 238–46.

Reprint of the sections on *Paradise Regained* and *Samson Agonistes* in Huckabay No. 466, originally published in 1945.

3507 Camé, J.-F. "A Note on Shakespeare's Cleopatra and Milton's Dalila." *CahiersE*, 12, 1977, 69–70.

Concludes that "Dalila is a degraded Cleopatra, still able to seduce, but obviously unable to love."

3508 Camé, J.-F. "*Samson Agonistes* (68–109): A Summary of Essential Elements in Milton's Imaginary Universe." *CahiersE*, 11, 1977, 63–71.

Considers the opposition between "death and its associations . . . and life and its associations" and the facility of these images, for "it is easy to cross the borderline from life to death, through sin, as is the case with Adam, or through despair, . . . as is the case with Samson."

3509 Camé, Jean-François. "The World

Picture in Milton's *Samson Agonistes*." *CahiersE*, 14, 1978, 39–48.

Believes that Milton's drama reflects the Elizabethan world picture. Discusses the disruption and reestablishment of the play's world order.

3510 Canale, Ann. "Paradigms and Reflections: A Discussion of the *Oresteia* and of *Samson Agonistes*." Doctoral diss., Univ. of Massachusetts, 1981. 278pp. Abs., *DAI*, 42, 1981, 1135A.

Argues that interpretation is guided by the similarities between the works' action and characters and their various models.

3511 Christopher, Georgia B. "Homeopathic Physic and Natural Renovation in *Samson Agonistes*." *ELH*, 37, 1970, 361–73.

Believes that the curing steps in Samson's regeneration echo his steps to spiritual darkness. Explains the "homeopathic cure" as a process of purging.

3512 Cirillo, Albert R. "Time, Light, and the Phoenix: The Design of *Samson Agonistes*." *Calm of Mind: Tercentenary Essays on "Paradise Regained" and "Samson Agonistes" in Honor of John S. Diekhoff*. Ed. by Joseph Anthony Wittreich, Jr. (Cleveland, OH, and London: Press of Case Western Reserve Univ., 1971), pp. 209–33. Ann Arbor, MI: Univ. Microfilms International, 1980 Books on Demand Reprints.

"In its meaning and in its affective relation to its audience, the story of Samson's death is the story of a death that is a life, a triumph for the reader *now*. In this sense, it is timeless and eternal, for it asserts that man's spirit does rise, like the Phoenix, out of the darkness . . . into the noon-light of eternal life."

3513 Clayton, Thomas. "Catharsis in Aristotle, the Renaissance, and Elsewhere." *JRMMRA*, 2, 1981, 87–95.

Discusses various interpretations of catharsis and argues that the most

defensible one appears in Milton's Preface to *Samson Agonistes*.

3514 Cohen, Michael. "Rhyme in *Samson Agonistes*." *MiltonQ*, 8, 1974, 4–6.

Believes that the functions of rhyme in *Samson Agonistes* are manifold and that "Regardless of the disclaimer in the Preface to *Paradise Lost*, Milton was sensitive to the possibilities of rhyme configuration for metrical, rhetorical, and semantic effects."

3515 Collins, Douglas P. "Ronsard and a Simile in *Samson Agonistes*." *N&Q*, 21, 1974, 95–96.

Suggests that Pierre de Ronsard's elegy to Mary Stuart influenced *Samson Agonistes* 710–18.

3516 Colony, Joyce. "An Argument for Milton's Dalila." *YR*, 66, 1977, 562–75.

Dalila is the catalyst for Samson's conscious reawakening as he experiences a revelation of his renewed potential as God's champion. The decisive action is Dalila's reaching for Samson's hand by which she, having destroyed his will, acts unconsciously to restore it.

3517 Conners, John Reed. "The Crucifixion in *Paradise Lost, Paradise Regained* and *Samson Agonistes*." Doctoral diss., Univ. of Rochester, 1982. 265pp. Abs., *DAI*, 44, 1983, 1460A.

Explores "the Son's nature, his place in the divine plan of salvation, and his example to be followed by all men and women" in Milton's three long poems.

3518 Coppola, Antonella Piazza. "Critical Interpretation and Textual Analysis of *Samson Agonistes*." *Studi di Letteratura e di Linguistica*. Quaderno 3, by various authors. Pubblicazioni dell'Università degli Studi de Salerno, Sezione di Studi Filologici, Letterari, e Artistici, 7 (Naples: Edizioni Scretifiche Italiane, 1984), pp. 29–50.

Emphasizes the importance of the Dalila scene but does not believe that the work is a tragedy.

3519 Cox, John D. "Renaissance Power and Stuart Dramaturgy: Shakespeare, Milton, and Dryden." *CompD*, 22, 1988, 323–58.

Sees *Comus* and *Samson Agonistes* as companion pieces and relates both to Milton's opposition to the Stuarts. Contrasts Milton's dramas with Shakespeare's and Dryden's.

3520 Cox, Lee Sheridan. "Natural Science and Figurative Design in *Samson Agonistes*." *Critical Essays on Milton from "ELH"* (Baltimore, MD, and London: Johns Hopkins Press, 1969), pp. 253–76. Reprint of Huckabay No. 2190, originally published in 1968.

3521 Crenshaw, James L. *Samson: A Secret Betrayed, A Vow Ignored*. Atlanta, GA: John Knox Press, 1978. 173pp.

"In Milton's hands he [Samson] comes alive as an intensely suffering human being, struggling with God, struggling with himself—much more like Job than the legendary giant of Judges."

3522 Dahiyat, Eid A. "Harapha and Baalzebub/Ashtaroth in Milton's *Samson Agonistes*." *MiltonQ*, 16, 1982, 60–62.

"My purpose in this paper is to show that Harapha, the giant of Gath and the champion of Dagon and Philistia, is properly shown as invoking Baalzebub and Ashtaroth."

3523 Dahiyat, Eid. "The Philistine Deity *Dagon*: The Semitic Origin and Two Possible Derivations." *SAP*, 20, 1987, 213–16.

The name of the Philistine deity Dagon, who appears in *Samson Agonistes*, may be derived from the Hebrew word "dag," meaning fish; his name was associated with the Semitic noun "dagan," meaning corn (he was thus also an agricultural deity). Echoing the Semitic words, the Arabic "tajin" refers to a cooking pot and, in the Arabic dialect spoken in southern Jordan, "tajun" means "a big eater or a glutton."

3524 Dahiyat, Eid A. "The Portrait of the Philistines in John Milton's *Samson Agonistes*." *SAP*, 14, 1982, 293–303.

Contends that the "portrait of the Philistines in *Samson Agonistes* is framed by the Hebraic spirit of the Old Testament and rabbinical writings," from which Milton occasionally deviates "to give a bright picture of the Philistines or simply to present a different point of view."

3525 Dale, James. "*Samson Agonistes* as Pre-Christian Tragedy." *HAB*, 27, 1976, 377–88.

Relates aspects of the drama to their Old Testament context to emphasize the play's tragic quality.

3526 Damico, Helen. "Duality in Dramatic Vision: A Structural Analysis of *Samson Agonistes*." *MiltonS*, 12, 1978, 91–116.

Discusses the scene involving Dalila and Samson as the center of *Samson Agonistes* and as "the keystone of the work's bipartite framework and its fusion of comic and tragic forms." States that the scene may be comprehended on two levels: in the human sense, as a clash between Samson and Dalila—his other self; and in the divine sense, as a conflict between Samson and God.

3527 Dickey, Harold A. "*Samson Agonistes*: Exposition, Dialogue, Imagery." *Aegis*, 2, 1973, 29–38.

Focuses on the scenes involving Dalila and Harapha in terms of holocaust imagery. Sees the play as Samson's attempt to escape the Mosaic idea of self-destruction.

3528 Dickey, Harold Alexander. "*Samson Agonistes*: The Dramatic Role of Ratiocination." Doctoral diss., Univ. of Nebraska, Lincoln, 1968. 189pp. Abs., *DA*, 29, 1969, 2208A–09A.

Analyzes the discovery of "one's own sin" in *Samson Agonistes*, as Samson realizes that the reasoning displayed by Dalila and Harapha is the same kind that led to his fall.

3529 DiSalvo, Jackie. "Intestine Thorn: Samson's Struggle with the Woman

Within." *Milton and the Idea of Woman.* Ed. by Julia M. Walker (Urbana and Chicago: Univ. of Illinois Press, 1988), pp. 211–29.

"In *Samson Agonistes*, I propose, while endorsing the goals of male psychogenesis, Milton also presents its agonizing contradictions and terrible costs, both to the male Samson, who overcomes mutilation and inward festering only to be outwardly destroyed, and the female Dalila, who must be viciously denigrated in the process." This describes "the interpersonal and intrapsychic web of our gender dynamics." Abs., *MiltonQ*, 24, 1990, 150.

3530 DiSalvo, Jackie. "'The Lord's Battells': *Samson Agonistes* and the Puritan Revolution." *MiltonS*, 4, 1972, 39–62.

"Samson was a culture hero for the Puritan revolution, held up as a spiritual model by the preachers. *Samson Agonistes* expresses the central values of that revolution. Samson is an active hero with a divine vocation who eschews the idle life represented by Dalila, just as the Puritan middle class rejected the leisure values of the aristocracy."

3531 DiSalvo, Jacqueline. "Make War Not Love: On *Samson Agonistes* and *The Caucasian Chalk Circle*." *MiltonS*, 24, 1988, 203–31.

Compares Milton's and Bertolt Brecht's treatments of gender and war. "As a feminist Miltonist, I may often criticize him, as here for the ways he exalts warriors to denigrate women, but I do so with some humility, realizing that the effort to resolve such contradictions will require his virtues of courage and fortitude, or what one might call a valiant Miltonic feminism."

3532 Duerling, Nancy Suman. "*Samson Agonistes* and *Oedipus Tyrannus* as Affirmations of the Truth of Prophecy." Doctoral diss., American Univ., 1981. 28pp. Abs., *DAI*, 42, 1981, 1158A.

Contends that prophecy, whether pagan or Christian, "motivates the actions of Samson and Oedipus and, consequently, structures the plots."

3533 "An 18th-Century Non-Performance of Samson Agonistes." *SCN*, 27, 1969, 66–67.

Discusses a playbill that outlines a performance of *Samson Agonistes* which never took place.

3534 Entzminger, Robert L. "*Samson Agonistes* and the Recovery of Metaphor." *SEL*, 22, 1982, 137–56.

After his blinding, Samson distrusts the polysemous quality of words, but he gradually recovers by conversing with the Chorus and the other characters.

3535 Fallon, Robert T. "Samson and the Inner Life." *MiltonQ*, 16, 1982, 25.

Abstract of a paper presented at the 1981 MLA Convention. Feels that "Samson is the thwarted soldier of God who longs to act, and finally does so in obedience to the word of God."

3536 Fish, Stanley. "Question and Answer in *Samson Agonistes*." *CritQ*, 11, 1969, 237–64. Reprinted in *Milton: "Comus" and "Samson Agonistes," a Casebook.* Ed. by Julian Lovelock (London and Basingstoke: Macmillan, 1975), pp. 209–45.

Deals with such issues as the cause of Samson's betrayal of himself to Dalila and her motivation. Feels that the lines of cause and effect are deliberately blurred. See No. 3649.

3537 Flower, Annette C. "The Critical Context of the Preface to *Samson Agonistes*." *SEL*, 10, 1970, 409–23.

States that the Preface falls into two sections: the justification of tragedy and the introduction to *Samson Agonistes*. Concludes that the Preface exhibits the highly compressed treatment of complex critical problems, such as the unities, catharsis, structure, and use of the Chorus.

3538 Freedman, Morris. "The Date of *Samson Agonistes*—Still?" *MiltonQ*, 14, 1980, 62.

Notes that Ernest Sirluck's discussion of the date does not appear in the table of contents of that issue of *JEGP* because it forms an appendix to his main essay (Huckabay No. 2735). See reply by Edward Le Comte (No. 3606).

3539 Freedman, Morris. "Waiting for Samson: The Modernity of *Samson Agonistes*." *MiltonQ*, 13, 1979, 42–45.

Believes that Samson looks forward to modern drama because his transformation to a man of dignity prepares us for the reaffirmation of human dignity implicit in such plays as *Death of a Salesman* and *Long Day's Journey into Night*.

3540 French, Roberts W. "Rhyme and the Chorus of *Samson Agonistes*." *LauR*, 10, 1970, 60–67.

Demonstrates that "rhyme has the effect of ironic qualification in that it tends to undercut certain of the Chorus' speeches in ways of which the speakers are not at all aware."

3541 Frye, Northrop. "Agon and Logos: Revolution and Revelation." *The Prison and the Pinnacle*. Ed. by Balachandra Rajan (Toronto and Buffalo, NY: Univ. of Toronto Press, 1973), pp. 135–63. Reprinted in *Spiritus Mundi: Essays on Literature, Myth, and Society* (Bloomington and London: Indiana Univ. Press, 1976), pp. 201–27.

Points out that *Samson Agonistes* exhibits a parallel conflict between the Word of God within Samson and the temptations, which consist of a sequence of dialogues. Deals with Milton's transformations of classical tragedy into Christian drama and of the barbaric Samson of Judges into a Miltonic hero.

3542 Frye, Roland Mushat. "Theological and Non-Theological Structures in Tragedy." *ShakS*, 4, 1969, 132–48.

"As a literary work *Samson Agonistes* operates on a tightly wrought plot line, in which dramatic action is so integrally related to theological doctrine that the tragedy itself cannot be fully understood and appreciated apart from its inherent theological structure."

3543 Fulton, Pauline Robinson. "Milton's Use of the Book of Job in *Paradise Regained* and *Samson Agonistes*." Doctoral diss., Univ. of North Carolina, Chapel Hill, 1983. 210pp. Abs., *DAI*, 44, 1983, 1092A.

Analyzes Milton's use of dialogue and the suffering hero of faith from the Book of Job in *Paradise Regained* and *Samson Agonistes*.

3544 Furman, Wendy. "*Samson Agonistes* as Christian Tragedy: A Corrective View." *PQ*, 60, 1981, 169–81.

In contrast with Irene Samuel's contention (No. 3694) that it is an Aeschylean tragedy because of "the hero's final exercise of his unrectified flaw," sees *Samson Agonistes* as a Christian tragedy because it is "a terrible but necessary 'episode in the divine comedy.'"

3545 Gallagher, Philip J. "On Reading Joseph Wittreich: A Review Essay." *MiltonQ*, 21, No. 3, 1987, 108–13.

Questions the evidence and conclusions presented in No. 3758. Refutes Wittreich's claim that Milton's Samson is unregenerate.

3546 Gallagher, Philip J. "The Role of Raphael in *Samson Agonistes*." *MiltonS*, 18, 1983, 255–94.

"To be specific, I will argue that excepting differences necessitated by the formal demands of genre, the descent of Raphael in *Paradise Lost* is precisely analogous to the marriage of Samson to the Woman of Timna in *Samson Agonistes*. Both angel and woman are embodiments of prevenient grace sent by the deity to initiate the regeneration of fallen man before he has fallen." Abs., *MiltonQ*, 16, 1982, 25.

3547 Gilman, Ernest B. "Milton's Contest 'Twixt God and Dagon.'" *Iconoclasm and Poetry in the English Reformation: Down Went Dagon* (Chicago, IL, and London: Univ. of Chicago Press, 1986), pp. 149–77.

Discusses Milton's iconoclasm from *Comus* to *Samson Agonistes*, mainly with respect to genre. Stresses the effect that Milton's blindness had on his drama's structure. "With Milton the iconoclastic impulse of the Reformation is amplified and transmuted into a revolutionary aesthetic that replaces the filial piety of imitatio with the sharper antagonism of a trial of strength." Reviews (of book): Maurice Charney, *SCN*, 45, 1987, 33; Ira Clark, *C&L*, 36, 1987, 42–44.

3548 Goldman, Jack. "Milton's Samson and the Halacha." *MiltonQ*, 9, 1975, 90. Abstract of a paper presented at the University of Wisconsin, Milwaukee, Milton Tercentenary Conference, in November, 1974. Internal evidence reveals Milton's knowledge and use of the Halacha, the body of Jewish law.

3549 Goldman, Jack. "The Name and Function of Harapha in Milton's *Samson Agonistes*." *ELN*, 12, 1974, 84–91. Claims that "the encounter between Samson and Harapha more closely resembles Elijah's on Mount Carmel with the 850 priests of the Baalim and the Ashtaroth." Further suggests that "the function of the Philistine giant in the poem is to epitomize Samson's struggle as the great, and perhaps eternal psychomachia."

3550 Goldsmith, Robert H. "Triumph and Tragedy in *Samson Agonistes*." *RenP*, 1968, pp. 77–84. Concludes that it is irrelevant whether *Samson Agonistes* is a tragedy or Christian drama. Samson's "death is his triumph, as his will finally becomes merged with the divine will."

3551 Graham, E. A. "Milton and Seventeenth-Century Individualism: Language and Identity in *Paradise Lost*, *Paradise Regained*, and *Samson Agonistes*." Doctoral diss., Manchester Univ., 1985. Abs., *IT*, 37, 1988, 439.

3552 Graves, Allan Rolf. "Puritan Empiricism in *Paradise Regained* and *Samson*

Agonistes." Doctoral diss., Univ. of Wisconsin, 1973. 279pp. Abs., *DAI*, 34, 1973, 2561A. Contends that Puritan empiricism, which emphasizes learning by doing, affects Jesus's education in *Paradise Regained* and the "alchemical symbolism" of *Samson Agonistes*.

3553 Green, Paul D. "Milton's *Samson* and *The Faerie Queene*." *SPWVSRA*, 7, 1982, 14–21. Cites numerous parallels between *Samson Agonistes* and the *Faerie Queene* 1, concluding that Milton absorbed much of the structure of the Red Cross Knight's quest and reshaped it for his own purposes.

3554 Grose, Christopher. "'His Uncontrollable Intent': Discovery as Action in *Samson Agonistes*." *MiltonS*, 7, 1975, 49–76. "As suggested in *An Apology* and *Paradise Lost*, the conception of a 'virtuous wisdom' uniting word with 'event' provides the model for a Miltonic action that rejoins the two plots of *Samson Agonistes*."

3555 Guillory, John. "Dalila's House: *Samson Agonistes* and the Sexual Division of Labor." *Rewriting the Renaissance: The Discourses of Sexual Difference in Early Modern Europe*. Ed. by Margaret W. Ferguson and others (Chicago, IL, and London: Univ. of Chicago Press, 1986), pp. 106–22. Believes that Milton superimposes his own ideas about sexuality and marriage into the biblical story and that conflict arises because of the sexual division of labor. Labor belongs to the male, and sexuality to the female. At the center of the story is Samson's refusal of Dalila's offer to take him to her house rather than to his father's house.

3556 Guillory, John David. "The Father's House: *Samson Agonistes* in Its Historical Moment." *Re-membering Milton: Essays on the Texts and Traditions*. Ed.

by Mary Nyquist and Margaret W. Ferguson (New York and London: Methuen, 1987), pp. 148–76.

"Lodged between the narratives of saint and artist, the narrative of Samson's life records for Milton the transformation of the father's talents, the money-lender's material capital . . . into 'talent,' symbolic capital."

3557 Guillory, John David. "The Strength of Usurpation." *Poetic Authority: Spenser, Milton, and Literary History* (New York: Columbia Univ. Press, 1983), pp. 172–78.

Notes that Milton alters his source (Judges 16.28) in the description of Samson's positioning between the pillars (*Samson Agonistes* 1629–39). In letting Samson pray for revenge because of his loss of sight, Judges is crudely barbaric. But Milton reverts to the phoenix myth and the idea of "self-begetting." The loss of vision "throws the poet back upon an inner resource: Samson's 'inward eyes.'" Readers have difficulty with the ending of *Samson Agonistes* because they do not want to recognize merely human authority.

3558 Gunn, K. "The Infusion of Doubt in *Samson Agonistes*." M.Phil. thesis, Oxford Univ., 1985. *IT*, 35, 1986, 45.

3559 Hagedann, Wolfgang. "Die Verschmelzung Klassisch-Heidnischer und Alttestament-Lich-Christlicher Gehalte in Miltons *Samson Agonistes*." Doctoral diss., Frankfurt, 1967. 188pp.

3560 Han, Pierre. "Baroque Foreground and Background in *Samson Agonistes*." *RBPH*, 50, 1972, 807–13.

Considers "the later Milton as participating in the larger cultural movement of the seventeenth century: what is designated by literary critics and historians as the Baroque." Observes that "the architectonic perfection of its [the play's] construction . . . epitomizes the Baroque triumph."

3561 Han, Pierre. "Vraisemblance and Decorum: A Note on the Baroque in *Samson Agonistes* and *Bérénice*." *SCN*, 29, 1971, 67–68.

To Milton and Louis Racine the terms are "a sign not of order, but of harmony of discordant elements held together by artistic creativity."

3562 Hanford, James Holly. "*Samson Agonistes* and Milton in Old Age." *Studies in Shakespeare, Milton and Donne.* By Members of English Department of the Univ. of Michigan (New York: Haskell House, 1972), pp. 167–89.

Reprint of Stevens No. 1182, originally published in 1925.

3563 Hardin, Richard F. "Milton's Radical 'Admirer' Edward Sexby, with a Note on Samson's Revenge." *MiltonQ*, 15, 1981, 59–61.

On the allusion to Milton in *Killing No Murder* (1657). Suggests that the poet's reply comes in *Samson Agonistes* 1211–14, when Samson distinguishes between private revenge and divine vengeance.

3564 Harris, William O. "Despair and 'Patience as the Truest Fortitude' in *Samson Agonistes*." *Critical Essays on Milton from "ELH"* (Baltimore, MD, and London: Johns Hopkins Press, 1969), pp. 277–90.

Reprint of Huckabay No. 2228, originally published in 1963.

3565 Haskin, Dayton, S. J. "Divorce as a Path to Union with God in *Samson Agonistes*." *ELH*, 38, 1971, 358–76.

Feels that Dalila proves an unfit wife by not providing genuine spiritual conversation. Thus, Samson's spiritual regeneration involves an individual restoration of order brought about only by divorce from her.

3566 Haskin, Dayton. "*Samson Agonistes* on the Stage at Yale." *MiltonQ*, 19, 1985, 48–53.

Follows the production of *Samson Agonistes* at Yale Univ. from the decision to perform it through the performance. Believes that the team made unusual changes in Milton's drama, and although they had some difficulty, "The show was acted valiantly by a cast whose varied talents went some distance" toward realizing the playwright's ambitious hopes.

3567 Hawkins, Sherman H. "Samson's Catharsis." *MiltonS*, 2, 1970, 211–30.

Sees a relationship between Adam's catharsis in *Paradise Lost* 11–12 and that of Samson. "Samson's fall thus conforms him to the image of the first Adam; his sacrificial self-offering renews him in the image of the second, completing the pattern of human history and of Milton's three great poems."

3568 Heller, Ricki. "Opposites of Wifehood: Eve and Dalila." *MiltonS*, 24, 1988, 187–202.

Relates Milton's discussion of marriage in the divorce tracts to the marriages of Adam and Eve and Samson and Dalila. "By depicting antithetical views of married life, *Paradise Lost* and *Samson Agonistes* serve to support Milton's conviction that marriage, if it is to benefit its partners, must create a spiritual unity that will naturally join them and urge them toward reconciliation even after a marital rupture."

3569 Henricksen, Bruce. "Samson and the Drama of Decision." *Teaching Milton to Undergraduates: Problems and Approaches*. Proceedings of the Special Session (537), Annual Meeting of the Modern Language Association, Dec. 28, 1976. Comp. by Paul L. Gaston ([Edwardsville: Southern Illinois Univ.], n.d.), pp. 29–31.

Explores how Samson's actions show "a vicious and dangerous ethic" from the student's twentieth-century perspective. But from Milton's perspective, Samson played a role in the "divinely prompted punishment of God's enemies."

3570 Hill, John Spencer. "Milton's Agonistes: The Date of *Samson Agonistes*." *John Milton: Poet, Priest and Prophet:*

A Study of Divine Vocation in Milton's Poetry and Prose (London and Basingstoke: Macmillan; Totowa, NJ: Rowman and Littlefield, 1979), pp. 195–203.

Argues for a 1660–61 date by using biographical evidence.

3571 Hill, John S. "Vocation and Spiritual Renovation in *Samson Agonistes*." *MiltonS*, 2, 1970, 149–74.

"It is in the resolution of the tension between prophecy and fact, between Samson's promised vocation as God's champion and Israel's deliverer and his actual position as a Philistian bondslave, that the true meaning of Samson's inward and spiritual growth, his regeneration, must ultimately be seen."

3572 Hilty, Deborah Pacini. "*Samson Agonistes*: Poem, Tradition and Genre." Doctoral diss., Case Western Reserve Univ., 1969. 268pp. Abs., *DAI*, 31, 1970, 2881A.

Agrees with Johnson's claim that *Samson Agonistes* has no middle, but attributes this to a circular—as opposed to a linear—form.

3573 Hoffman, Nancy Y. "Samson's Other Father: The Character of Manoa in *Samson Agonistes*." *MiltonS*, 2, 1970, 195–210.

"Manoa is the too-human father, trapped by the limitations of his own vision and by his relationship to his son. The ambiguity of the drama... perhaps derives from the polarities of father and son."

3574 Hornsby, Samuel. "Penance of the Hyaena in *Samson Agonistes*." *PQ*, 57, 1978, 353–58.

Believes that Milton consciously distinguishes between penance and repentance in the Dalila episode. Her show of penance is self-indulgent, idolatrous, and, to Milton, Catholic.

3575 Howard, J. E. "Studies in the Language and Style of Milton's *Samson Agonistes*." M.Phil. thesis, Univ. College, London Univ., 1972.

3576 Hunter, William B., Jr. "New Evidence for Dating Milton's *Samson*

Agonistes." *SCN*, 37, 1979, 9–10. Reprinted in *The Descent of Urania: Studies in Milton, 1946–1988* (Lewisburg, PA: Bucknell Univ. Press; London and Toronto: Associated Univ. Presses, 1989), pp. 219–23.

Presents statistical evidence dealing with Milton's changing preference for my/thy over mine/thine before vowels and suggests that this "strongly indicates that *Samson* postdates all of Milton's other poetry."

3577 Huttar, Charles A. "Samson's Identity Crisis and Milton's." *Imagination and the Spirit: Essays in Literature and the Christian Faith Presented to Clyde S. Kilby.* Ed. by Huttar (Grand Rapids, MI: Wm. B. Eerdmans Publishing Co., 1971), pp. 101–57.

Traces Samson's search for his identity (self-knowledge) and insists that Milton's quest follows a similar pattern.

3578 Hyman, Lawrence W. "The 'True Experience' of *Samson Agonistes.*" *MiltonQ*, 13, 1979, 90–95.

Asserts that Milton does not strive to reveal hidden religious or philosophical truths to justify God's ways. Explains that Samson's great event is fitting vengeance, yet it does not answer the question of God's justice. Believes that we must read the poem as an imaginative document to receive the experience that Milton intended.

3579 Hyman, Lawrence W. "The Unwilling Martyrdom in *Samson Agonistes.*" *TSL*, 13, 1968, 91–98.

Argues that Samson's "final action represents his own ineradicable desire to act like a military hero" and that he is never reconciled to God's ways.

3580 Inamochi, Shigeo. "Manoa, Dalila and Harapha in *Samson Agonistes.*" *MCJ News*, 2, 1978, 10–11.

Abstract of paper presented. Regards Manoa, Dalila, and Harapha as temptation figures and the drama itself as perhaps Milton's most convincing presentation of the theme of temptation.

3581 Srinivasa Iyengar, K. R. "*Samson Agonistes.*" *The Laurel Bough: Essays Presented in Honour of Professor M. V. Rama Sarma.* Ed. by G. Nageswara Rao (Bombay: Blackie and Son, 1983), pp. 65–73.

Compares the structure of *Samson Agonistes* with that of Greek drama and offers an autobiographical interpretation.

3582 Jacobson, Howard. "Milton's Harapha." *AN&Q*, 24, 1986, 70–71.

Contends that rather than simply meaning "the giant," Milton's invented word "haraphah" in *Samson Agonistes* 1068 is actually a proper noun.

3583 Jacobson, Howard. "Some Unnoticed Echoes and Allusions in Milton's *Samson Agonistes.*" *N&Q*, 29, 1982, 501–02.

Compares passages in Milton's drama with those in the Bible, Virgil, and other writers and concludes that the profundity of Milton's knowledge makes it impossible to determine whether his echoes are deliberate or unconscious.

3584 Jebb, R. C. "*Samson Agonistes* and the Hellenic Drama." *Essays on Milton* (Folcroft, PA: Folcroft Library Editions, 1970), pp. 341–48. Reprinted in *Milton: "Comus" and "Samson Agonistes," a Casebook.* Ed. by Julian Lovelock (London and Basingstoke: Macmillan, 1975), pp. 175–84.

Reprints of Stevens No. 1172, originally published in 1907–08.

3585 Jose, Nicholas. "*Samson Agonistes*: The Play Turned Upside Down." *EIC*, 30, 1980, 124–50. Reprinted in *Ideas of the Restoration in English Literature, 1660–71* (Cambridge, MA: Harvard Univ. Press, 1984), pp. 142–63.

Accepts a late date of composition and interprets the drama politically. "In *Samson Agonistes* a two-fold restoration is achieved through a two-fold destruction." The drama becomes, then, Milton's spiritual answer to the political Restoration.

3586 Kato, Kazutoshi. "Milton's Plot Design in *Samson Agonistes*: A First Step toward the Interpretation of the Tragedy." *MCJ News*, 3, 1979, 20–21.

Abstract of paper presented. Argues that the Manoa, Dalila, and Harapha episodes constitute the middle of the drama.

3587 Kaufmann, R. J. "Bruising the Serpent: Milton as a Tragic Poet." *CentR*, 11, 1967, 371–86.

Discusses *Samson Agonistes* as an example of the violence and voice of Milton's tragedy.

3588 Kawaguchi, Makiko. "From Death to Death: Concerning Sin and Salvation in *Samson Agonistes*." *Annual Reports of English and American Literature* (Osaka Shoin Women's College), 13, 1976, 25–39.

In Japanese. The poem is about the process of Samson's suffering, from his confrontation with death as a result of sin to his vision of a death which achieves God's will and leads to salvation. In this process, change occurs in the middle section. *Samson Agonistes* successfully unifies the Hebraic and Hellenic worlds.

3589 Kawasoko, Shogo. "*Samson Agonistes* and Greek Tragedy: On Prophecy and Frustration." *MCJ News*, 2, 1978, 15–16.

Abstract of paper presented. Suggests that Samson has a double frustration—his enemies and his own death—and that this leads to a fulfillment of God's prophecy. Compares Samson's situation with that in *Oedipus* and *Prometheus Unbound*.

3590 Kerman, Sandra. "George Buchanan and the Genre of *Samson Agonistes*." *Lang&S*, 19, 1986, 21–25.

Asserts that George Buchanan's two Christian tragedies—*Jephthes, sive Votum* and *Baptistes sive Calumnia*—may have influenced *Samson Agonistes*. Suggests that Milton may have translated the latter into English.

3591 Kermode, Frank. "Milton: *Samson Agonistes*." *English Renaissance Litera-ture: Introductory Lectures.* By Kermode, Stephen Fender, and Kenneth Palmer (London: Gray-Mills Publishing, 1974), pp. 132–45.

Argues that *Samson Agonistes* is a late work. Compares it to Sophocles's plays, disproves the theory that nothing happens in the work, and shows that it reflects the tension between notions of providence and the experience of suffering.

3592 Kerrigan, William. "The Irrational Coherence of *Samson Agonistes*." *MiltonS*, 22, 1986, 217–32.

Examines Milton's view of religious heroism and the necessity of making the wrong choice for the right choice to be possible. Analyzes Samson and the regeneration of his heroic quality through his moral and spiritual fall and reclamation.

3593 Kessner, Carole S. "Milton's Hebraic Herculean Hero." *MiltonS*, 6, 1974, 243–58.

"Unlike other Renaissance dramatists, whose conception of the Herculean hero derived from traditional versions . . . and who portrayed Hercules in all his *areté*, Milton's conception rested on the much more humanized hero of Euripides' *Heracles*. Comparison of *Heracles* with *Samson Agonistes* reveals many similarities in theme, structure, and character."

3594 Khan, Salamatullah. "The Thematic Structure of *Samson Agonistes*." *AJES*, 1, 1976, 244–59.

Studies the drama's "thematic structure" and traces the pattern of Samson's regeneration.

3595 Kim, Hwaja. "The Self and the Anti-self in *Samson Agonistes* and *The Death of Cuchulain*." Doctoral diss., Univ. of Iowa, 1976. 125pp. Abs., *DAI*, 37, 1976, 2896A.

Contends that, although Milton's and Yeats's visions of self-completeness differ, the writers share the goal of "trying to show life steadily with a meaning."

3596 Kimbrough, Ray Alan. "'Passions Well Imitated': *Samson Agonistes* and the Reader." Doctoral diss., Brown Univ., 1974. 496pp. Abs., *DAI*, 35, 1975, 7258A–59A.

Measures the effectiveness of Milton's tragedy: its agreement with classical models, its power to elicit an aesthetic response, and its ability to educate the reader.

3597 Kirkconnell, Watson. *That Invincible Samson: The Theme of "Samson Agonistes" in World Literature with Translations of the Major Analogues.* Toronto: Univ. of Toronto Press, 1964, 1968. viii, 218pp.

See Huckabay No. 2235.

3598 Kolin, Philip C. "Milton's *Samson Agonistes*, 393–412." *Expl*, 30, 1972, Item 43.

Analyzes Milton's use of puns in *Samson Agonistes* and claims that "unlock'd," "shook," and "capital secret" all refer to Samson's hair.

3599 Korach, Alice Florence. "The Dialectic Structure of English Renaissance Literature." Doctoral diss., Univ. of Texas, Austin, 1980. 197pp. Abs., *DAI*, 41, 1980, 1612A; *SCN*, 39, 1981, 100.

Argues that Renaissance authors, including Milton in *Samson Agonistes*, often ask their readers to accept both sides of conflicting "thematic or epistemological orientations."

3600 Kranidas, Thomas. "Manoa's Role in *Samson Agonistes*." *SEL*, 13, 1973, 95–109.

Claims that the character of Manoa reminds Samson of his follies and achievements, thus stimulating his conscience to repentance. Discusses various stage interpretations possible for the character of Manoa.

3601 Kuykendall, Radford B. "Milton's Neglected Drama." *SSCJ*, 37, 1971, 186–94.

Examines the relevance of Milton's writing today. Suggests that *Samson Agonistes*, though not written to be performed, has an appeal for contemporary interpreters and audiences.

3602 Labriola, Albert C. "Divine Urgency as a Motive for Conduct in *Samson Agonistes*." *PQ*, 50, 1971, 99–107.

Argues that Samson's "'rousing motions' betoken an exercise of free will to do good, whereas Samson's Philistine marriages, which were sinful deeds prompted by evil temptation, revealed his former state of spiritual death and his forfeiture of free will to do good because of subjection to sin."

3603 Landy, Marcia. "Language and the Seal of Silence in *Samson Agonistes*." *MiltonS*, 2, 1970, 175–94.

Sees Milton's preoccupation with the nature of language in *Samson Agonistes* as a significant vehicle for describing psychic processes. Emphasizes the metaphor of hearing, for when Samson "finally listens with his inner ear, there is no more language, but there is illumination."

3604 Le Comte, Edward. "The Date of *Samson Agonistes*." *MiltonQ*, 13, 1979, 153.

Notes that his own and other recent arguments against the idea that *Samson Agonistes* is not Milton's last poem should discourage any inclination to state that one dating is as good as another, since none can be proved. See Nos. 3538 and 3606.

3605 Le Comte, Edward. "New Objections to a Pre-Restoration Date for *Samson Agonistes*." *Poets' Riddles: Essays in Seventeenth-Century Explication* (Port Washington, NY, and London: Kennikat Press, 1975), pp. 129–60.

Replies to William Riley Parker (Huckabay Nos. 2272–73) and others. "A pre-Restoration conjecture is gratuitous and against the grain and a futile exercise in skepticism for skepticism's sake that rapidly turns into a new faith, the more stubbornly clung to the more it is assailed."

3606 Le Comte, Edward. "On the Dangers

of Complaining without Reading: A Reply to Morris Freedman." *MiltonQ*, 14, 1980, 101.

Points out that Freedman (No. 3538) did not pay sufficient attention to Le Comte's comments on the date of *Samson Agonistes* (No. 3604).

3607 Le Comte, Edward. "Samson's Bosom Snake Again." *MiltonQ*, 9, 1975, 114–15.

Adds to Jackson Campbell Boswell's analogues (No. 3500) to *Samson Agonistes* 763–65. In Aeschylus's *Choephori*, Orestes is the serpent in Clytemnestra's dream.

3608 Lewalski, Barbara Kiefer. "Milton's *Samson* and the 'New Acquist of True [Political] Experience.'" *MiltonS*, 24, 1988, 233–51.

Lists four kinds of experience as suggested in Milton's tracts and poetry and applies them to *Samson Agonistes*. Concludes that the drama contains no definitive answers.

3609 Lewalski, Barbara K. "*Samson Agonistes* and the 'Tragedy' of the Apocalypse." *PMLA*, 85, 1970, 1050–62.

Links *Samson Agonistes* with the Book of Revelation, identified by Pareus as a tragedy on the basis of form and subject. The spiritual combat between the elect and the Antichrist presents Samson as the suffering elect and assists in the interpretation of his judgeship (or his role as deliverer of God's people and executor of his wrath).

3610 Libby, Nancy D. "Milton's Harapha." *SAQ*, 71, 1972, 521–29.

Sees Harapha as a "comic figure of the braggart soldier" who awakens in Samson a recognition of his earlier personal pride.

3611 Lieske, Stephan. "Zur Geschlechterpolitik in John Miltons *Simson der Kämpfer*." *Literarische Diskurse und Historischer Prozess: Beiträge zur Englischen und Amerikanischen Literatur und Geschichte.* Ed. by Brunhild de la Motte (Potsdam: Pädagogische Hochschule

Karl Liebnecht, 1988), pp. 48–56.

Interprets *Samson Agonistes* in terms of politics and social structure.

3612 Lochman, Daniel T. "'If There be Aught of Presage': Milton's Samson as Riddler and Prophet." *MiltonS*, 22, 1986, 195–216.

"This study will trace Samson's spiraling progress from a destructive obsession with past promise and present suffering to a unity of present action and providence."

3613 Lovelock, Julian, ed. *Milton: "Comus" and "Samson Agonistes," a Casebook.* London and Basingstoke: Macmillan, 1975. 253pp.

Selected reprints of critical essays on both works, each divided into early criticism and twentieth-century criticism. Includes twentieth-century essays on *Samson Agonistes* by Don Cameron Allen, Stanley Eugene Fish, Sir Richard C. Jebb, and Mary Ann Radzinowicz. Reviews: Elizabeth MacKenzie, *MLR*, 71, 1976, 630–32; Frank McCombie, *N&Q*, 24, 1977, 89.

3614 Low, Anthony. "Action and Suffering: *Samson Agonistes* and the Irony of Alternatives." *PMLA*, 84, 1969, 514–19.

Suggests that the irony of alternatives is based on a proposition with alternatives posited by one character; both choices eventuate, although they appear to be mutually exclusive. All are ironically resolved in the catastrophe, which combines alternatives and reveals the simplifying power of providence.

3615 Low, Anthony. *The Blaze of Noon: A Reading of "Samson Agonistes."* New York and London: Columbia Univ. Press, 1974. ix, 236pp.

"The more one looks at various aspects of *Samson Agonistes*, the more clearly it appears how well Milton has succeeded in writing a play that is both a tragedy and a story of religious regeneration and triumph." Reviews: *MiltonQ*, 8, 1974, 85–86; Peter Verney,

DR, 54, 1974, 775–77; Boyd M. Berry, *MLQ*, 36, 1975, 84–86; Michael Lieb, *WHR*, 29, 1975, 192–94; Laurence Michel, *JEGP*, 74, 1975, 449–52; Michael Allen Mikolajczak, *SCN*, 33, 1975, 89–90; A. B. Chambers, *RenQ*, 29, 1976, 303–06; R. E. C. Houghton, *N&Q*, 23, 1976, 274–75; Andrew M. McLean, *SHR*, 10, 1976, 362–69; Geoffrey M. Ridden, *TLS*, Mar. 26, 1976, p. 352; Arnold Stein, *SR*, 84, 1976, 695–706.

3616 Low, Anthony. "Milton's Samson and the Stage, with Implications for Dating the Play." *HLQ*, 40, 1977, 313–24.

Considers the probability that *Samson Agonistes* was the kind of play Milton wanted the authorities to produce in public theaters during the 1640s. The five-act structure is used, although act and scene divisions are not marked.

3617 Low, Anthony. "No Power but of God: Vengeance and Justice in *Samson Agonistes*." *HLQ*, 34, 1971, 219–32.

Analyzes the theme of vengeance, which shows Samson's actions to be based not on personal vengeance, but on his role as God's deputy, "a revenger to execute wrath upon him that doeth evil." Seventeenth-century ideas of justice validate Samson's acts.

3618 Low, Anthony. "The Phoenix and the Sun in *Samson Agonistes*." *MiltonS*, 14, 1980, 219–31.

Discusses the second semichorus (*Samson Agonistes* 1687–1707) and the implications of the phoenix image, including its ancient and contemporary connotations and specific applications to Samson. "Like the phoenix, he has died and been reborn, and has risen into the heavens to join the noonday sun."

3619 Low, Anthony. "*Samson Agonistes*: Theology, Poetry, Truth." *MiltonQ*, 13, 1979, 96–102.

Asserts that Milton's poem is not to be considered a theological treatise, and that it is, for various reasons, some-times reticent. Concludes that Milton is not content to create "imaginary poetic worlds," but prefers "to imitate, interpret, and give new form to God's own truth." Responses by Joseph H. Summers, pp. 102–06, and Roy C. Flannagan, p. 106.

3620 Low, Anthony. "Tragic Pattern in *Samson Agonistes*." *TSLL*, 11, 1969, 915–30.

Discusses Samson as a monster and a scapegoat, concluding that he has not only human weaknesses, but human strengths, much like Job, Oedipus, and Lear.

3621 MacCallum, Hugh. "*Samson Agonistes*: The Deliverer as Judge." *MiltonS*, 23, 1987, 259–90.

Argues that *Samson Agonistes* "is deeply concerned throughout with the contrast between Mosaic law as external prescription and the inner, rational freedom best fulfilled in the gospel." Further contends that this contradiction "receives only a partial resolution and that the process of discovery thus remains tragically imperfect."

3622 Mackin, Cooper R. "Strength and Silence in *Samson Agonistes*." *Odyssey*, 5, 1982, 3–10.

Focuses on the Dalila episode, which gives Samson an opportunity to restore his power of reason and speech and to right the moral order. Abs., *MiltonQ*, 17, 1983, 24–25.

3623 Mankin, Philip H. "*Samson Agonistes*." *TLS*, Aug. 28, 1969, p. 955.

Points out a misprint in *Samson Agonistes* 144. Asserts that "fell" should be "felld (or felled)" to parallel the preterite "pulld" in line 146.

3624 Martz, Louis L. "Chorus and Character in *Samson Agonistes*." *MiltonS*, 1, 1969, 115–34.

Sees a contrast between Samson and the Chorus, which stresses Samson's grandeur, Manoa's weakness and ordinariness, Dalila's complexity, and Harapha's boastfulness.

3625 Mason, John B. "Multiple Perspectives in *Samson Agonistes*: Critical Attitudes toward Dalila." *MiltonS*, 10, 1977, 23–33.

"Dalila is not the hero of *Samson Agonistes*, but she is more than just Samson's means of rejecting lust, effeminacy, and ease." From Samson's perspective, "she is a confusion, something alien to him and to the mental struggle which has engaged him"; from the Chorus's exaggerated perspective, "she is impressive but also evil"; from her own perspective, "she is forgiving, loyal, and sensible."

3626 Mathewson, Mary Elizabeth. "Irony, Image, and Idea in *Samson Agonistes*." Doctoral diss., Univ. of Iowa, 1971. 233pp. Abs., *DAI*, 32, 1971, 1480A–81A.

Relates the evolving imagery of *Samson Agonistes* to Milton's attempt to justify God's ways and analyzes the irony behind ambivalent images.

3627 Mathis, Gilles. "Rhétorique(s) et Stylistique(s)." *Actes du Congrès de Poitiers.* Ed. by Société des Anglicistes de l'Enseignement Supérieur (Paris: Didier Erudition, 1984), pp. 505–30.

Studies the stylistic and rhetorical devices that Milton uses to develop Dalila's character.

3628 Matsuda, Minori. "On the Spirit of *Samson Agonistes*: With Special Emphasis on Its Hellenic, Hebraic and Christian Elements." *MCJ News*, 3, 1979, 7–8.

Abstract of paper presented. Argues that all three elements are present, but concludes that "*Samson Agonistes* is a Christian enlightenment under Greek and Hebraic veils."

3629 Maurin, Jill. "A Stylistic Approach to *Samson Agonistes*: Poem or Play?" *Démarches Linguistiques et Poétiques.* Travaux 19 (Saint-Étienne: Centre Interdisciplinaire d'Étude et de Recherche sur l'Expression Contemporaine, 1977), pp. 235–52.

Analyzes the work's poetic qualities—such as structure, rhythm, language,

style, and theme—and concludes that it is more poetic than dramatic because it lacks external causality and Samson's mental changes "are not a dramatic or rather theatrical possibility."

3630 Mayer, Joseph Gerson. "Heroic Magnitude of Mind: A Re-interpretation of *Samson Agonistes*." Doctoral diss., Boston Univ., 1975. 189pp. Abs., *DAI*, 35, 1975, 7873A.

Argues that Samson is a regenerate saint from the beginning of *Samson Agonistes* and that his perceived "sinful pride" is actually "heroic magnitude of mind."

3631 McCanles, Michael. "Signs of Power and the Power of Signs in Milton's Last Poems." *SHR*, 17, 1983, 327–38.

Examines *Paradise Lost*, *Paradise Regained*, and *Samson Agonistes* to show that "Milton envisions physical power as possessing the potentiality both for parodying and perverting spiritual, divine power; and becoming its outward sign and manifestation. . . . The dialectic between these two potentialities parallels . . . another dialectic, that between invisible spiritual reality and outward, physical symbol of that reality."

3632 McCarthy, B. Eugene. "Metaphor and Plot in *Samson Agonistes*." *MiltonQ*, 6, No. 4, 1972, 86–92.

Responds to Christopher Ricks's objection (Huckabay No. 3478) to mixed metaphors in *Samson Agonistes*. Suggests that they "function dramatically to reflect the mind of the speaker, structurally to provide links and preparations for coming events, and thus give important thematic clues."

3633 Mikolajczak, Michael Allen. "Opposite Kindred: Comparisons and Contrasts of *Paradise Regained* and *Samson Agonistes*." Doctoral diss., Univ. of Wisconsin, Milwaukee, 1982. 241pp. Abs., *DAI*, 44, 1983, 176A–77A.

Argues that the stylistic similarities between *Paradise Regained* and *Samson*

Agonistes form "a vision of true heroism" involving "surrender to divine will."

3634 Miller, Leo. "Milton's Heroic Samson: In Response to Berkeley and Khoddam." *MiltonQ*, 18, 1984, 25–27.

Responds to No. 3495 by stating that Samson's tribe of Dan was not of illegitimate birth, Harapha was not gentle-born, and the tribe of Dan and Manoa is not "despicable."

3635 Miller, Milton. "A Contrary Blast: Milton's Dalila." *Drama, Sex and Politics.* Ed. by James Redmond (Cambridge: Cambridge Univ. Press, 1985), pp. 93–108.

"Milton in his characterization of Dalila touches on the Renaissance figure of the temptress and the tradition behind it in ways reminiscent of Shakespeare's treatment of Cleopatra, but he also incorporates another dimension altogether, that of the seventeenth-century woman who has newly perceived possibilities of an independent moral status."

3636 Milo, Malka. "*Samson Agonistes* et les Commentaires Bibliques." *RLC*, 49, 1975, 260–70.

In *Samson Agonistes*, Milton does not radically change the Old Testament narrative, but he chooses those elements that suit his point of view. Samson represents Milton himself and, by extension, the English people, who in betraying their trust, have fallen from grace. The requirements of Greek tragedy shape the work's structure. Points out similarities between sixteenth- and seventeenth-century biblical commentaries and Milton's interpretation.

3637 Miyazaki, Junko. "Milton's Idea of Patience through an Analysis of *Samson Agonistes*." *MCJ News*, 10, 1988, 11–12.

Abstract of paper presented. Studies Milton's use of the word "serve" in *Samson Agonistes* to demonstrate his perception of patience as an active rather than a passive process.

3638 Mollenkott, Virginia R. "Relativism in *Samson Agonistes*." *SP*, 67, 1970, 89–102.

Asserts that Milton's "absolute" point of view in *Paradise Lost* is not to be read into *Samson Agonistes*. Because the drama deals with a human rather than an ultimate struggle, it requires a relative outlook. Concludes, however, that the reader must be aware of two levels of conflict (God versus Dagon and Samson versus self).

3639 Mori, Michiko. "On *Samson Agonistes* and *Antigone*." *MCJ News*, 3, 1979, 30–31.

Abstract of a paper presented at the Fifth Colloquium of MCJ in July, 1978. Notes that the two works have a common theme—an individual's struggle against tyranny.

3640 Moriyasu, Aya. "Samson and the Chorus." *MCJ News*, 5, 1981, 18–20.

Abstract of a paper presented at the Eleventh Colloquium of MCJ in July, 1981. "I think the Christian spirit is represented by Samson, the Hebrew spirit by Manoa and the Greek spirit by the chorus."

3641 Morrow, Laurie P. "The 'Meet and Happy Conversation': Dalila's Role in *Samson Agonistes*." *MiltonQ*, 17, 1983, 38–42.

Suggests that Dalila "plays a significant role in Samson's development and in the revelation of his character and thus contributes substantially to our understanding of the tragedy as a whole." Analyzes the tone and purpose of her speeches, their effect on Samson, and "the larger function this encounter [between Samson and Dalila] serves relative to the poem as a whole."

3642 Moses, Judith A. "*Samson Agonistes*: Love, Authority, and Guilt." *AI*, 44, 1987, 331–45.

Examines "how the poem connects Samson's problems with love, authority, and guilt in ways that suggest this connection's crucial role in the development of the self."

3643 Mueller, Martin. "*Pathos* and *Katharsis* in *Samson Agonistes*." *Critical Essays on Milton from "ELH"* (Baltimore, MD, and London: Johns Hopkins Press, 1969), pp. 234–52.

Reprint of Huckabay No. 2264, originally published in 1964.

3644 Mueller, Martin. "Time and Redemption in *Samson Agonistes* and *Iphigenie auf Tauris*." *UTQ*, 41, 1972, 227–45.

Discusses Milton's and Goethe's works in terms of shared Greek sources. Central to both is the interdependence of time and redemption (or the Greek word kairos).

3645 Mueller, Martin. "The Tragedy of Deliverance: *Samson Agonistes*." *Children of Oedipus and Other Essays on the Imitation of Greek Tragedy* (Toronto, Buffalo, NY, and London: Univ. of Toronto Press, 1980), pp. 193–212.

Believes that Milton uses many plot elements from *Oedipus at Colonus* and *Prometheus Bound*.

3646 Mulryan, John. "The Heroic Tradition of Milton's *Samson Agonistes*." *MiltonS*, 18, 1983, 217–34.

Clarifies the play's Greek and Hebrew elements. Demonstrates that Milton's choice of traditional elements was deftly employed and suggests that the models for his Samson were the biblical Samson and the Greek Heracles. The legends of Oedipus and Sisyphus were secondary sources.

3647 Muskin, Miriam. "Milton's Understanding of Hebraism and *Samson Agonistes*." Doctoral diss., Case Western Reserve Univ., 1977. 298pp. Abs., *DAI*, 38, 1977, 1414A.

Analyzes Hebraic elements in *Samson Agonistes* "to help decipher puzzles concerning characterization, prosodic and linguistic features, and the direction of the drama."

3648 Muskin, Miriam. "'Wisdom by Adversity': Davidic Traits in Milton's Samson." *MiltonS*, 14, 1980, 233–55.

Believes that Milton sees parallels between the biblical accounts of Samson and David and combines them in his dramatic portrayal of Samson. Each character sins but becomes a suppliant seeking God's mercy.

3649 Mustazza, Leonard. "The Verbal Plot of *Samson Agonistes*." *MiltonS*, 23, 1987, 241–58.

Applies Stanley Fish's idea (No. 3536) of a verbal plot where speech diminishes in complexity and volubility to a point of silence. Sees this progression as tripartite, consisting of Samson's verbal exchanges with domestic figures, with Dalila and Harapha, and finally with the Philistines.

3650 Neifosh, Eileen B. "Spiritual Humanism in John Milton's Drama, *Samson Agonistes*." M.A. thesis, Adelphi Univ., 1974. 428pp. Abs., *MA*, 12, 1974, 428.

3651 Nestrick, William V. "*Samson Agonistes* and Trial by Combat." *SN*, 63, 1971, 246–51.

Samson's challenge to Harapha "serves as a false image of the trial of fortitude that must be rejected before the truly heroic exercise of patience can begin."

3652 Obourn, Theodore Douglas. "The Rhetoric of Milton's *Samson Agonistes* in the Context of English Literature from Spenser to Bunyan." Doctoral diss., Univ. of Rochester, 1982. 221pp. Abs., *DAI*, 43, 1982, 1981A.

Explains how the rhetoric of *Samson Agonistes* reinforces the various stages of Samson's spiritual journey and gives deeper meaning to the dialogue.

3653 Oiji, Takero. "The Hero of *Samson Agonistes*." *Studies in Milton* (Tokyo: Kinseido, 1974), pp. 101–18.

In Japanese. Examines the political themes of *Samson Agonistes*, in which Milton issues a political literary challenge to the imperial Restoration and a prophecy of its defeat.

3654 Onuska, John T., Jr. "The Equation of Action and Passion in *Samson Agonistes.*" *PQ*, 52, 1973, 69–84.

Discusses the critical debate about the principles of action versus passion in *Samson Agonistes* and examines their role in the play's thematic conflict. When Samson resigns himself to God's will, both he and the Chorus learn that in God's eyes the two principles are identical. "In His work, action equals passion."

3655 Parker, William Riley. "The Date of *Samson Agonistes* Again." *Calm of Mind: Tercentenary Essays on "Paradise Regained" and "Samson Agonistes" in Honor of John S. Diekhoff.* Ed. by Joseph Anthony Wittreich, Jr. (Cleveland, OH, and London: Press of Case Western Reserve Univ., 1971), pp. 163–74. Ann Arbor, MI: Univ. Microfilms International, 1980 Books on Demand Reprints.

Still favors an early date. Seeks "to explain the problem, and then to put into my reader's possession all the relevant bits of evidence as I now see them." See No. 3657.

3656 Parker, William Riley. *Milton's Debt to Greek Tragedy in "Samson Agonistes."* New York: Barnes and Noble, 1970.

Reprint of Huckabay No. 2276, originally published in 1937.

3657 Patrick, J. Max. "Milton's Revolution against Rime, and Some of Its Implications." *Milton and the Art of Sacred Song.* Ed. by Patrick and Roger H. Sundell (Madison: Univ. of Wisconsin Press, 1979), pp. 99–117.

Argues against William Riley Parker's early dating of *Samson Agonistes* (Huckabay Nos. 2272–73) and offers evidence that Milton dictated it in 1665–67 and had not yet begun to dictate *Paradise Regained.* His revolution against rhyming "was probably precipitated by his composing its [the play's] intricate rimed passages." Appendix: "A Caveat against Parker" offers further comment against the case for an early date (No. 3655).

3658 Patrides, C. A. "The Comic Dimension in Greek Tragedy and *Samson Agonistes.*" *MiltonS*, 10, 1977, 3–21.

"*Samson Agonistes* reflects explicitly through its Chorus what is implicit in its protagonist: a gradual transition from risible vulgarities to the noble conception of a mysterious universe under the control of 'th'unsearchable dispose of Highest Wisdom.'"

3659 Peck, James William. "Variation in Milton's *Samson Agonistes*: A Study of Its Occurrence in Syntax, in Diction, in Phonology, and in Metrics." Doctoral diss., Univ. of Alabama, 1970. 210pp. Abs., *DAI*, 31, 1971, 3517A.

Uses statistics to analyze stylistic and other variations in *Samson Agonistes*, noting that they occur more frequently in climactic passages.

3660 Peek, George S. "*Samson Agonistes* and the Masque Tradition." *Cithara*, 15, 1975, 37–44.

Suggests that one way to reduce the "flaws or inconsistencies in Milton's use of Greek tragedy in *Samson Agonistes*" is to recognize that he draws on the masque tradition.

3661 Price, Reynolds. "Poem Doctrinal and Exemplary to a Nation: A Reading of *Samson Agonistes.*" *Shenandoah*, 23, 1971, 3–36. Reprinted in *Things Themselves: Essays and Scenes* (New York: Atheneum, 1972), pp. 214–59.

A scene-by-scene analysis, with critical comment.

3662 Primeau, Ronald. "Samson and Manoa: Rescue or Regeneration?" *BSUF*, 17, 1976, 10–15.

States that "Manoa's repeated attempts at rescue are a reminder to Samson that the regenerate state is an ongoing process rather than an accomplished fact." Argues that the rescue offered by Manoa is a temptation which opposes the true regenerative process.

3663 Quay, James Donald. "'Expose Thyself To Feel What Wretches Feel': *Doctor Faustus* and *Samson Agonistes* as Tragedies of Despair." Doctoral diss., Univ. of California, Berkeley, 1981. 232pp. Abs., *DAI*, 42, 1982, 3167A.

Contends that despair in both tragedies veils a destructive hope—Faustus's hope for eternal life and Samson's hope to be "the deliverer of his people."

3664 Radzinowicz, Mary Ann. "The Distinctive Tragedy of *Samson Agonistes.*" *MiltonS*, 17, 1983, 249–80.

Sees Samson's life as "the story of a failed man who, after reassessing his nature, deeds, and failure becomes a good man, the passion faced in the encounters with other characters brought to a harmony under reason."

3665 Radzinowicz, Mary Ann. "Medicinable Tragedy: The Structure of *Samson Agonistes* and Seventeenth-Century Psychopathology." *English Drama: Forms and Development: Essays in Honour of Muriel Clara Bradbrook.* Ed. by Marie Axton and Raymond Williams (Cambridge: Cambridge Univ. Press, 1977), pp. 94–122.

Shows that Samson "is depicted in the light of seventeenth-century melancholy." The work's "structure imitates the cure of a disturbed mind through the recognition and reintegration of its conflicting passions." The play's "theme is the difficult, tragic but life-affirming possibility of human change" and "its tragic effect is the alteration of the sensibility of the audience."

3666 Radzinowicz, Mary Ann. *Toward "Samson Agonistes": The Growth of Milton's Mind.* Princeton, NJ: Princeton Univ. Press, 1978. xxiii, 436pp.

Studies *Samson Agonistes* in relation to Milton's other works to show how he arrives at ideas brought together in the play and what light it throws on its predecessors. Organizes the chapters around six contexts: Milton's dialectic, conception of history, politics, ethics, theology, and poetics. Contains an appendix on the date of *Samson Agonistes.* Reviews: Roy C. Flannagan,

MiltonQ, 13, 1979, 21–22; Don Parry Norford, *MLQ*, 40, 1979, 292–306; Balachandra Rajan, *JEGP*, 78, 1979, 552–54; John M. Steadman, *RenQ*, 32, 1979, 449–52; Joseph Anthony Wittreich, Jr., *Rev*, 1, 1979, 123–64; J. Martin Evans, *RES*, 31, 1980, 353–54; Michael Lieb, *Cithara*, 21, 1981, 58–70; Mary Christopher Pecheux, *ELN*, 17, 1980, 145–47; Charles D. Murphy, *ModA*, 25, 1981, 104–06; James H. Sims, *SCN*, 39, 1981, 81–83; Gordon C. Campbell, *YES*, 11, 1982, 256–57.

3667 Rajan, Balachandra. "'To Which is Added *Samson Agonistes*——.'" *The Prison and the Pinnacle.* Ed. by Rajan (Toronto and Buffalo, NY: Univ. of Toronto Press, 1973), pp. 82–110.

Discusses the methodical use of hills and plains in *Paradise Lost* and finds an extension of it in *Paradise Regained* and *Samson Agonistes. Paradise Regained* is a poem of the hill and *Samson Agonistes* is a drama of the plain to which fallen Adam must descend. Christ standing on the pinnacle and Samson tearing down the temple of Dagon are complementary climaxes. "'To which is added Samson Agonistes' must be taken as indicating that the end is both what it should be and what it was felt to be from the beginning."

3668 Rama Sarma, M. V. *The Eagle and the Phoenix (A Study of "Samson Agonistes").* Madras: Macmillan, 1976. vi, 102pp.

Considers such topics as the date of composition, the autobiographical fallacy, and Samson's regeneration. Also discusses the theme of martyrdom in *Samson Agonistes, Saint Joan,* and *Murder in the Cathedral.* Review: Syed Amanuddin, *JIWE*, 7, 1979, 70–72.

3669 Rama Sarma, M. V. "'The Unsearchable Dispose of Highest Wisdom': *Samson Agonistes.*" *MiltonQ*, 13, 1979, 85–89.

Explores the parallels between *Samson Agonistes* and Greek tragedy. Relates

Samson's triumphant destruction to Hebraic, Hellenic, and Christian forms of tragedy, which Milton fuses.

3670 Reaske, Christopher R. "Milton's Dramatic Poem: A Study of Thought, Tension, Drama, and Catharsis in *Samson Agonistes.*" Doctoral diss., Harvard Univ., 1965.

3671 Rees, B. R. *Aristotle's Theory and Milton's Practice: "Samson Agonistes."* Birmingham: Univ. of Birmingham, 1972. 25pp.

Concludes that Aristotle's theory in the *Poetics* and Milton's practice converged, creating *Samson Agonistes.*

3672 Reichardt, Paul F. "Milton's Samson and the Iconography of Worldly Vice." *SIcon*, 5, 1979, 135–45. Reprinted in *Milton and the Middle Ages.* Ed. by John Mulryan (Lewisburg, PA: Bucknell Univ. Press; London and Toronto: Associated Univ. Presses, 1982), pp. 135–49.

Shows that the connections between the three worldly vices of 1 John 2.16 and the characters in *Samson Agonistes* are established through Christian iconography.

3673 Revard, Stella P. "Dalila as Euripidean Heroine." *PLL*, 23, 1987, 291–302.

Argues that Dalila in *Samson Agonistes* is a complex Euripidean heroine. Contends that in her final speech, she succeeds in "attaining her full potential as an antagonist of Samson and proving herself the only character in the play who has been a match for him." By thus "testing his powers," Dalila becomes the vehicle by which Samson attains rehabilitation. Milton generally "used his female characters to challenge the assumptions of a male-dominated society."

3674 Ricks, Christopher. "Milton: Part III. *Paradise Regained* and *Samson Agonistes.*" *English Poetry and Prose, 1540–1674.* Ed. by Ricks. Sphere History of Literature in the English Language, vol. 2 (London: Sphere Books, 1970), pp. 299–316. Revised edition, New York:

Peter Bedrick Books, 1987.

States that the style of *Samson Agonistes* lacks "delicacy, spontaneity or suppleness." Many of Samuel Johnson's criticisms about the play are valid.

3675 Ridden, Geoffrey M. "*Samson Agonistes* in Edinburgh." *MiltonQ*, 17, 1983, 96–97.

On a performance at the Edinburgh Festival Fringe in 1983, with all of the roles played by a single actor.

3676 Ridden, Geoffrey M. "A Stylistic Investigation of John Milton's *Samson Agonistes,* with a View to Determining the Date of Composition." M.Phil. thesis, Univ. of Leeds, 1971.

3677 Robertson, Duncan. "Metaphor in *Samson Agonistes.*" *UTQ*, 38, 1969, 319–38.

Analyzes such issues as strength and weakness, freedom and slavery, nature and sex, Samson as Adam and Christ, and the fortunate fall.

3678 Rosenberg, D. M. "Milton, Dryden, and the Ideology of Genre." *CompD*, 21, 1987, 1–18.

Argues that *Samson Agonistes* was written as an antidote to Dryden's heroic plays and that Milton had no respect for the Restoration theater and society.

3679 Rosenberg, Donald Maurice. "*Samson Agonistes*: Proverb'd for a Fool." *CentR*, 32, 1988, 65–78.

Studies "the conflict between folly and wisdom in *Samson Agonistes* and show[s] how Samson's foolishness ultimately pulls down the fleshly wisdom of the world."

3680 Roston, Murray. *Biblical Drama in England: From the Middle Ages to the Present Day.* Evanston, IL: Northwestern Univ. Press, 1968. 335pp.

Considers Milton's scattered references to the stage and analyzes *Samson Agonistes* as "the finest flowering of the Protestant biblical drama." Contains three sections on Milton: "Milton and the Stage"; "*Samson Agonistes*";

and "Samson and Job." Review: *MiltonN*, 3, 1969, 20–21.

3681 Roston, Murray. "Milton's Herculean Samson." *MiltonQ*, 16, 1982, 85–93.

Interprets Samson as a baroque hero. Sees the play as a drama of anguish like Job's within Samson's muscular body and of a Herculean struggle with the self, culminating in the work's final movement.

3682 Rudrum, Alan. *A Critical Commentary on Milton's "Samson Agonistes."* Macmillan Critical Commentaries. London: Macmillan; New York: St. Martin's Press, 1969. 70pp.

Contains a scene-by-scene analysis.

3683 Rusbar, Alice M. "Heroic Martyrdom in Milton's *Samson Agonistes*." Doctoral diss., Tulane Univ., 1982. 192pp. Abs., *DAI*, 43, 1982, 1982A.

Compares Samson to the traditional Christian martyr, asserting that "disgrace, torture, imprisonment, and death" lead him to "a faith based on suffering, regeneration, and intellectual acceptance."

3684 Russo, John P. "'Diffus'd Spirits': Scientific Metaphor in *Samson Agonistes*." *PLL*, 7, 1971, 85–90.

On Milton's three uses of the word "diffus'd" in *Samson Agonistes* 96, 118, and 1141 and the scientific status it had acquired by 1671. For Milton, the word had both poetic and theological significance.

3685 Sadler, Lynn Veach. *Consolation in "Samson Agonistes": Regeneration and Typology.* Elizabethan and Renaissance Studies, 82. Salzburg: Universität Salzburg, Institut für Anglistik und Amerikanistik, 1979. vi, 332pp.

Discusses current criticism of *Samson Agonistes* and offers a regenerative and typological reading.

3686 Sadler, Lynn Veach. "Coping with Hebraic Legalism: The Chorus in *Samson Agonistes*." *HTR*, 66, 1973, 353–68.

Demonstrates how the Chorus experiences change through Samson's action, which purges them from their dependence on Old Testament wisdom and legalism. Although the Chorus cannot grasp "the full Christian implications of Samson's experience, . . . it is expected to amend its legalistic interpretation through a prophetic reading of experience."

3687 Sadler, Lynn Veach. "The Problem of the Ending of *Samson Agonistes*: Aristotle Plus Reorientation." *NM*, 76, 1975, 642–50.

"The audience, including Manoa and the Chorus, should learn the process of regeneration from him [Samson], for it is in the Miltonic basic scheme: every individual must become regenerated or remain damned in the Fall." Abs., *MiltonQ*, 13, 1979, 28–29.

3688 Sadler, Lynn Veach. "Regeneration and Typology: *Samson Agonistes* and Its Relation to *De Doctrina Christiana*, *Paradise Lost*, and *Paradise Regained*." *SEL*, 12, 1972, 141–56.

Suggests that other works by Milton describe Samson as a type, not only of Christ, but of the regenerative power of faith in God.

3689 Sadler, Lynn Veach. "Relations between Alchemy and Poetics in the Renaissance and Seventeenth Century, with Special Glances at Donne and Milton." *Ambix*, 24, 1977, 69–76.

Discusses "the use of alchemical analogies and doctrine in treatises on poetry" and surveys "alchemical techniques in Donne's 'The Triple Foole' and Milton's *Samson Agonistes*."

3690 Sadler, Lynn Veach. "The Samson Figure in Milton's *Samson Agonistes* and Stowe's *Dred*." *NEQ*, 56, 1983, 440–48.

Notes many similarities between *Samson Agonistes* and Harriet Beecher Stowe's *Dred: A Tale of the Great Dismal Swamp*, both of which draw on the biblical story of Samson. Concludes that both authors move "toward that great biblical rhythm of oppression and recall that speaks to all dispensations."

3691 Sadler, Lynn Veach. "Typological Imagery in *Samson Agonistes*: Noon and the Dragon." *ELH*, 37, 1970, 195–210.

Asserts that noon is an image of the Gospel, and Revelation is the midnight of the dispensatory process. States that these images of light and darkness are equated with the noon despair of Christ's Crucifixion and the midnight of judgment. The dragon is associated with heraldic animals, as well as scenes of judgment and havoc. Concludes that Samson's triumph is in his rechanneling of the powers symbolized by noon and the dragon.

3692 Saito, Kazuaki. "The Theme of *Samson Agonistes*." *MCJ News*, 3, 1979, 13–16.

Uses the drama's nautical imagery to show that Samson's "interior vision" is "so clear that his will becomes one with God's will, and his wind becomes God's Tempest to destroy the Temple of Dagon."

3693 "Samson on Stage." *MiltonQ*, 12, 1978, 75.

Report on a production in Ann Arbor in 1978. The St. Andrew's Players performed a modern adaptation of *Samson Agonistes* by Frank L. Huntley of the University of Michigan. Thomas Strode composed music especially for the production.

3694 Samuel, Irene. "*Samson Agonistes* as Tragedy." *Calm of Mind: Tercentenary Essays on "Paradise Regained" and "Samson Agonistes" in Honor of John S. Diekhoff*. Ed. by Joseph Anthony Wittreich, Jr. (Cleveland, OH, and London: Press of Case Western Reserve Univ., 1971), pp. 235–57. Ann Arbor, MI: Univ. Microfilms International, 1980 Books on Demand Reprints.

Insists that there is no support for the idea that Samson dies regenerate. "Milton called *Samson Agonistes* a tragedy, not a martyr play; its subject cannot be Samson restored to divine favor." See No. 3544. Review: Michael Lieb, *Cithara*, 12, 1972, 85–106.

3695 San Juan, Epifami, Jr. "On the Motif of Incongruence in *Samson Agonistes*." *OL*, 23, 1968, 221–24.

Examines the discord between the characters' external gestures and internal motivation.

3696 Sano, Hiroko. "Milton's Dalila." *SES*, 3, 1978, 16–29.

Holds that Dalila should be viewed through seventeenth-century eyes and that Milton attempted to place her in the tradition of married love established by Spenser.

3697 Sellin, Paul R. "Milton and Heinsius: Theoretical Homogeneity." *Medieval Epic to the Epic Theater of Brecht*. Ed. by Rosario P. Armato and John M. Spalek. Univ. of Southern California Studies in Comparative Literature, 1 (Los Angeles: Univ. of Southern California Press, 1968), pp. 125–34.

Believes that Milton "appropriated the core ideas of his view of tragedy" from Heinsius's interpretation of Aristotle.

3698 Sellin, Paul R. "Milton on Tragedy." *Daniel Heinsius and Stuart England* (Leiden: Leiden Univ. Press; London: Oxford Univ. Press for the Sir Thomas Browne Institute, 1968), pp. 164–77.

Proposes that Milton "borrowed his theory [of tragedy] from Heinsius' commentary, a congenial interpretation of the *Poetics* that was both famous and readily accessible."

3699 Shapiro, Marta Berl. "*Samson Agonistes* and the Hebraic Tradition." Doctoral diss., St. John's Univ., 1974. 350pp. Abs., *DAI*, 36, 1976, 5328A.

Explains Milton's inclusion of Hebraic motifs in *Samson Agonistes* in terms of his identification with Samson, faithfulness to decorum, and changing theological views.

3700 Shaw, William P. "Producing *Samson Agonistes*." *MiltonQ*, 13, 1979, 69–79.

Describes a readers' theater performance of *Samson Agonistes* at the second annual Le Moyne Forum on
Religion and Literature. Believes that
a production gives rewards and insights
beyond private reading and offers suggestions for subsequent productions.

3701 Shawcross, John T. "The Genres of
Paradise Regain'd and *Samson Agonistes*:
The Wisdom of Their Joint Publication."
MiltonS, 17, 1983, 225–48.

Builds a definition of brief epic and
places *Paradise Regained* in that genre;
states that the "genre of *Samson
Agonistes* . . . is drama by form and
characteristics, but poem by execution
and structure." Assigns a comic mode
to *Paradise Regained* and a tragic mode
to *Samson Agonistes*. Asserts that
Paradise Regained and *Samson Agonistes* are companion works literally
(in publication), structurally (by contrast of style), metaphysically (in the
comparison and contrast of the Son
and Samson), and theologically (in that
Milton's overall doctrine of religious
interiority is fully set forth only by
comprehending the poems' heroes as
companion spirits).

3702 Shawcross, John T. "Irony as Tragic
Effect: *Samson Agonistes* and the Tragedy of Hope." *Calm of Mind: Tercentenary Essays on "Paradise Regained"
and "Samson Agonistes" in Honor of John
S. Diekhoff*. Ed. by Joseph Anthony Wittreich, Jr. (Cleveland, OH, and London:
Press of Case Western Reserve Univ.,
1971), pp. 289–306. Ann Arbor, MI: Univ.
Microfilms International, 1980 Books on
Demand Reprints.

Argues that there are two versions of
tragedy in *Samson Agonistes*: "the tragedy of the self, the individual man
subject to temptation, to waste, and to
blindness in his lack of understanding
of self and life" and "the tragedy of
hope which repeatedly dogs man, blinding him to realities, to full recognition
of self, and to lasting achievement."

Review: Michael Lieb, *Cithara*, 12,
1972, 85–106.

3703 Shimizu, Hiroshi. "Samson and Providence—Rhetorical Features in Their
Relation." *MCJ News*, 1, 1976, 3–4.

Abstract of a paper presented at the
First Annual Conference of MCJ in
July, 1975. Three rhetorical features
develop thematic arguments about
Samson and providence: development
from the Preface through the main
argument, antithetical argument and
inference, and rhetorical figures characteristic of emotional appeals and
exhortation.

3704 Shitaka, Hideyuki. "The Language
of *Samson Agonistes*—Some Devices for
Emotional Expression." *MCJ News*, 3,
1979, 21–22.

Abstract of paper presented. Points out
that Milton uses various linguistic
devices, such as repetition, antithesis,
variation, and manipulation of syntax,
to reveal each speaker's mental state.

3705 Siddiqui, Zillur Rahman. "On Rereading *Samson Agonistes*." *Essays on
John Milton: A Tercentenary Tribute*. Ed.
by Asloob Ahmad Ansari (Aligarh: Aligarh Muslim Univ., 1976), pp. 67–73.

Emphasizes Samson's heroic qualities
and feels that his death bridges the gap
between his country and him.

3706 Simon, Ulrich. "Samson and the
Heroic." *Ways of Reading the Bible*. Ed.
by Michael P. Wadsworth (Brighton:
Harvester; Totowa, NJ: Barnes and Noble,
1981), pp. 154–67.

The Samson story's abiding theme "is
the propriety of violence and the ultimate justification of self-sacrifice. . . .
Without that godly brand of heroism
[of the English fighter pilots] the race
is doomed."

3707 Simons, June Haig. "Recognition and
Reversal in *Samson Agonistes*." Doctoral
diss., Univ. of New Mexico, 1972. 156pp.
Abs., *DAI*, 34, 1973, 339A.

Argues that *Samson Agonistes* grows
out of the divine drama tradition. Uses

recognition and reversal to chart Samson's inner growth and explain his actions.

3708 Sims, James H. "Milton Society of America. Report of Annual Dinner and Meeting." *SCN*, 27, 1969, 5.

Describes the meeting and includes an abstract of "Catharsis in *Samson Agonistes*," a paper read by Sherman Hawkins (see No. 3567).

3709 Sircar, Prabirkumar. *Milton's Samson: Studies in Character and Construction.* Kalyani, West Bengal: Univ. of Kalyani, 1977. xi, 83pp.

Studies character and structure in the drama. Chapters: "Disintegration in *Samson Agonistes*: A Study in Character and Construction"; "Peripeteia and Anagnorisis in *Samson Agonistes*"; "Milton's Treatment of Samson's Moral Failure"; and "The Last Picture of Samson: A Significant Deviation from the Bible." Review: Archie Burnett, *N&Q*, 26, 1979, 72.

3710 Slaymaker, William Earl. "A Comparison of the Concepts of Freedom in Aeschylus' *Oresteia*, Milton's *Samson Agonistes*, and Sartre's *Les Mouches*." Doctoral diss., Indiana Univ., 1975. 277pp. Abs., *DAI*, 36, 1976, 7400A–01A.

Examines the effect of divine or supernatural will, individual disposition, traditional portrayals of women, and political conflicts on each author's concept of liberty.

3711 Slaymaker, William Earl. "Tragic Freedom: Milton's Samson and Sartre's Orestes." *StHum*, 6, 1978, 36–43.

Maintains that Milton's and Sartre's heroes, as paradigms of faith, share the struggle for personal freedom, even though Sartre's foundations for freedom are antireligious.

3712 Slights, Camille W. "A Hero of Conscience: *Samson Agonistes* and Casuistry." *PMLA*, 90, 1975, 395–413. Revised in *The Casuistical Tradition in Shakespeare, Donne, Herbert, and Milton*

(Princeton, NJ: Princeton Univ. Press, 1981), pp. 247–96.

"Such casuistical concepts as the supremacy of the individual conscience, the relevance of circumstances to moral law, and the role of reason in resolving doubt illuminate the conflicting moral judgments that form the dramatic texture of *Samson Agonistes*."

3713 Smith, Albert James. "No Failing Hero: A Reassessment of *Samson Agonistes*." *CIFM*, 1974, pp. 176–92.

"For all its austerity of effect *Samson Agonistes* is in many ways a consummation of Milton's artistic career."

3714 Stacy, Gerald. "The Senecan Messenger in *Samson Agonistes*." *BSUF*, 14, 1973, 32–34.

Contends that Milton modeled his messenger after the one in Seneca's *Trojan Women*. Points out similarities in tone, place, person, event, and pattern but notes that Milton offers "a striking commentary on the weakness of the classical Stoic ideal in contrast to the power of Hebraic Christianity."

3715 Steadman, John M. "Milton's Summa Epitasis: The End of the Middle of *Samson Agonistes*." *MLR*, 69, 1974, 730–44.

Locates the point of highest tension or "summa epitasis" in the scene with the Philistine officer. Studies Milton's use of the term "epitasis" in his dramatic sketches and his critical terminology in the Preface to *Samson Agonistes*. Analyzes the play's structure, surveying critical opinion and examining Milton's techniques in relation to various contemporary schemes of dramatic analysis.

3716 Steadman, John M. "Paradoxes of Magnanimity: Heroic Action and Inaction in *Samson Agonistes*." *Milton and the Paradoxes of Renaissance Heroism* (Baton Rouge and London: Louisiana State Univ. Press, 1987), pp. 224–59.

Examines the problem of heroic model,

the question of decorum in character and literary genre, and the interrelationship between character and action. A central problem in the drama is the paradox of the enslaved deliverer. As a heroic image, Samson meets two of the demands of Renaissance critics, but he combines a variety of heroic norms. *Samson Agonistes* is ultimately a political drama that embodies the failure of the Good Old Cause. We may not know when Milton wrote his drama, but we do know when he published it (1671).

3717 Steadman, John M. "'Passions Well Imitated': Rhetoric and Poetics in the Preface to *Samson Agonistes*." *Calm of Mind: Tercentenary Essays on "Paradise Regained" and "Samson Agonistes" in Honor of John S. Diekhoff.* Ed. by Joseph Anthony Wittreich, Jr. (Cleveland, OH, and London: Press of Case Western Reserve Univ., 1971), pp. 175–207. Ann Arbor, MI: Univ. Microfilms International, 1980 Books on Demand Reprints.

Concludes that the principal source of Milton's Preface is Aristotle, as seen through Renaissance eyes, and that most of its main ideas were conventional in contemporary criticism.

3718 Stein, Arnold. "Dalila." *On Milton's Poetry: A Selection of Modern Studies.* Ed. by Stein (Greenwich, CT: Fawcett Publications, 1970), pp. 247–56.

Reprint of a chapter from No. 3719, originally published in 1957.

3719 Stein, Arnold. *Heroic Knowledge: An Interpretation of "Paradise Regained" and "Samson Agonistes."* Hamden, CT: Shoe String Press, 1968.

Reprint of Huckabay No. 2149, originally published in 1957.

3720 Stollman, Samuel S. "Milton's Samson and the Jewish Tradition." *MiltonS*, 3, 1971, 185–200.

Feels that Milton's Samson is "significantly different from the Samson of Jewish tradition," for this character acts "as the Old Testament precursor of Christian liberty."

3721 Stollman, Samuel S. "Milton's Understanding of the 'Hebraic' in *Samson Agonistes*." *SP*, 69, 1972, 334–47.

Discusses Milton's choice of a Hebraic hero to typify Christian principles. Claims that Milton dichotomizes Judaic and Hebraic concepts and religious values. Contends that Hebraic doctrine complements Christian doctrines of love and mercy, while Judaic laws confuse and stifle spiritual freedom and growth.

3722 Stollman, Samuel S. "Samson as Dragon and a Scriptural Tradition." *ELN*, 7, 1970, 186–89.

Uses Genesis 49.16–18 to show that the dragon image in *Samson Agonistes* 1692–93 is not pejorative. Rather, it connotes a spiritual dimension and is appropriate to the prophecy concerning Samson.

3723 Stroup, Thomas B. "'All Comes Clear at Last,' but 'The Readiness is All.'" *CompD*, 10, 1976, 61–75.

Discusses right reason as seen from several viewpoints. Concludes that *Samson Agonistes* is the "finest illustration" of Milton's argument, as Samson reacts to the inner voice of right reason. Abs., *MiltonQ*, 12, 1978, 114.

3724 Swaim, Kathleen M. "The Doubling of the Chorus in *Samson Agonistes*." *MiltonS*, 20, 1984, 225–45.

Discusses the drama's various kinds of structural and thematic doubleness. Focuses on the second semichorus's imagery in *Samson Agonistes* 1687–1707.

3725 Takizawa, Masahiko. "Worldly Logic of Samson." *MCJ News*, 3, 1979, 11–13.

Believes that under "the seemingly simple structure of *Samson Agonistes* is hidden the complicated intellectual development of human enlightenment in the seventeenth century." Samson has to learn that wisdom, not strength, is his solution. However, his final act should be regarded as open terrorism.

3726 Tamaki, Ishitaro. "Literary Origins of the Chorus in *Samson Agonistes*." *MCJ News*, 5, 1981, 14–15.

Abstract of a paper presented at the Ninth Colloquium of MCJ in July, 1980. Concludes that Milton owes as much to the " 'Grecians' of Italy in the *cinquecento*" as he does to the ancients.

3727 Tamaki, Ishitaro. "Milton's Concept of *Katharsis*." *MCJ News*, 3, 1979, 16–20.

Concludes that in *Samson Agonistes*, Milton's concept of the term is a synthesis; he had read several definitions and formulated a theory of his own.

3728 Tayler, Edward W. "Milton's Firedrake." *MiltonQ*, 6, No. 3, 1972, 7–10.

Contends that the "ev'ning Dragon" in *Samson Agonistes* 1692 refers to the meteorological phenomenon known in the Renaissance as the firedrake or fire dragon.

3729 Tayler, Edward W. "Milton's Samson: The Form of Christian Tragedy." *ELR*, 3, 1973, 306–21. Reprinted in *Milton's Poetry: Its Development in Time*. Duquesne Studies, Language and Literature Series, vol. 2 (Pittsburgh, PA: Duquesne Univ. Press, 1979), pp. 105–22.

Argues that the reader must "in effect attend to two lines of development— the movements of the plot and the progressive revelation of form." Discounts those who attempt to divide *Samson Agonistes* into acts and proposes that patient reading allows a culmination of a regenerative theme.

3730 Teunissen, John James. "Of Patience and Heroic Martyrdom: The Book of Job and Milton's Conception of Patient Suffering in *Paradise Regained* and *Samson Agonistes*." Doctoral diss., Univ. of Rochester, 1967. 406pp. Abs., *DA*, 28, 1967, 1797A.

Argues that Christ's perfect and Samson's imperfect suffering is marked by a heroic patience modeled on the Book of Job.

3731 Thornton, Peter John. "*Samson Agonistes* and the Search for Christian Trag-edy." Doctoral diss., Stanford Univ., 1974. 257pp. Abs., *DAI*, 35, 1975, 6112A–13A.

Contends that a "Christian humanistic perspective" explains the small action of *Samson Agonistes* and answers "whether it can be considered a tragedy."

3732 Tippens, Darryl. "The Kenotic Experience of *Samson Agonistes*." *MiltonS*, 22, 1986, 173–94.

Discusses the kenotic tradition which Milton inherited. Believes that kenosis is the unifying pattern that links his last great poems.

3733 Tippens, Darryl. " 'Race of Glory, Race of Shame': Kenotic Thought in *Samson Agonistes*." *MiltonQ*, 19, 1985, 96–100.

Explains that *Samson Agonistes* is primarily Christian in thought because of its kenotic paradigm, or its theme of glory through humiliation.

3734 Tisch, J. H. *"Samson Agonistes" and Milton's Ideas of Worldly and Religious Immortality*. Hobart: Univ. of Tasmania, 1984. 4pp.

In German. Discusses Samson's relationship with God, focusing on the concept of glory.

3735 Tobin, John Joseph Michael. "A Macaronic Pun in *Samson Agonistes*." *AN&Q*, 14, 1975, 37–38.

" 'Aerie flight' [see *Samson Agonistes* 971–74] is not only evocative of loftiness, but metonymically descriptive of Fame's vehicle of propaganda." The expression "aerie flight" is "simultaneously a precise filial evocation of his [Milton's] Classical predecessors and a macaronic pun which links Fame's flight with its instrument."

3736 Tobin, John Joseph Michael. "Milton's *Samson Agonistes*, 19–20." *Expl*, 32, 1974, Item 77.

Suggests that Milton's use of the word "hornet" has three purposes: its obvious meaning as stinging agents of conscience, its reference to cuckoldry, and its conscious and subconscious play on whore-nets.

3737 Tobin, J. J. M. "A Note on Dalila as 'Hyaena.'" *MiltonQ*, 11, 1977, 89–91.

"The imperative, 'Out, out hyaena' is a manifestation of Samson's growing awareness that 'All wickedness is weakness'" and that "Dalila is in some basic sense the embodiment of his own spiritual uncleanness." The hyena is also connected with Ovid's *Metamorphoses*.

3738 Tobin, John Joseph Michael. "Samson and Sea-Imagery Again." *ELN*, 15, 1977, 23–27.

Suggests that Milton's nautical coloring in *Samson Agonistes* is derived from Virgil's *Aeneid*. Claims that Virgil's use of the Persian word "gaza" (later the name of the pertinent city) remained in Milton's mind and inspired his imagery.

3739 Tobin, John Joseph Michael. "The Trojan Harapha." *ELN*, 12, 1975, 273–79.

Investigates the source of Harapha. Concludes that Harapha and Samson's conflict parallels the one between Dares and Entellus in Virgil's *Aeneid* and that Milton fuses elements from Scripture and the classics.

3740 Ulreich, John C., Jr. "'Beyond the Fifth Act': *Samson Agonistes* as Prophecy." *MiltonS*, 17, 1983, 281–318.

Considers the play "essentially parabolic: like Samson's riddle in the Book of Judges, the story of Samson (as Milton tells it) is a parable of deliverance."

3741 Ulreich, John C., Jr. "Incident to All Our Sex: The Tragedy of Dalila." *Milton and the Idea of Woman*. Ed. by Julia M. Walker (Urbana and Chicago: Univ. of Illinois Press, 1988), pp. 185–210.

Defends Dalila in "an attempt to rescue her from a hostile critical tradition." Sees her ultimately as a tragic figure "fatally flawed rather than radically corrupt." Abs., *MiltonQ*, 24, 1990, 151.

3742 Ulreich, John C., Jr. "Samson's Riddle: Judges 13–16 as Parable." *Cithara*, 18, No. 2, 1979, 3–28.

Explains the drama's paradoxes. Sees *Samson Agonistes* as a parable of deliverance in which Samson is a figure of judgment and a type of Israel itself. He recapitulates that nation's pragmatic historical cycle.

3743 Ulreich, John C., Jr. "'This Great Deliverer': *Samson Agonistes* as Parable." *MiltonQ*, 13, 1979, 79–84.

Asserts that Samson's life is not merely a type of Christ's, but a figurative tale of individual and national redemption. States that "Milton transforms the history of Samson into a parable of man's eternal deliverance from spiritual oppression."

3744 Van Devender, George William. "The Prosody of Milton's *Samson Agonistes*." Doctoral diss., Univ. of Mississippi, 1973. 323pp. Abs., *DAI*, 34, 1974, 5209A.

Treats English and Greek rhythms, differentiating between lyric and stichic meters.

3745 Ventura y San Martin, Encarnación. "Apuntes para la Lectura de *Sansón Agonista*." *Ensayos sobre John Milton: Epopeya y Drama*. Ed. by María Enriqueta González Padilla. Facultad de Filosofía y Letras, Centro de Investigaciones de Letras Modernas y Arte Dramático (Mexico, D.F.: Universidad Nacional Autónoma de México, 1976), pp. 67–79.

Explains that the poem is the culmination of Milton's attempt to justify God's ways to humans.

3746 Waddington, Raymond B. "Melancholy against Melancholy: *Samson Agonistes* as Renaissance Tragedy." *Calm of Mind: Tercentenary Essays on "Paradise Regained" and "Samson Agonistes" in Honor of John S. Diekhoff*. Ed. by Joseph Anthony Wittreich, Jr. (Cleveland, OH, and London: Press of Case Western Reserve Univ., 1971), pp. 259–87. Ann Arbor, MI: Univ. Microfilms

International, 1980 Books on Demand Reprints.

Considers the drama in relation to the melancholy tradition and the literature of despair.

3747 Waddington, Raymond B. "The Politics of Metaphor in *SA*." *MiltonQ*, 10, 1976, 29–30.

Abstract of a paper presented at the 1975 MLA Convention. "The understanding of the particulars in *SA* lead[s] us to the conclusion that these particularities reflect the crises of religious and political authority in Milton's time."

3748 Wall, John N., Jr. "The Contrarious Hand of God: *Samson Agonistes* and the Biblical Lament." *MiltonS*, 12, 1978, 117–39.

Claims that *Samson Agonistes* parallels the biblical story of Job. Suggests that Samson's faithfulness to his lament brings about his restoration to God's will. Review: Dayton Haskin, *Thought*, 56, 1981, 226–39.

3749 Wallace, Meta Sehon. "The Christian Pattern of Temptation, Trial, and Grace in Four Renaissance Works: *Paradise Regained*, *Samson Agonistes*, *The Faerie Queene*, Book One, and *Macbeth*." Doctoral diss., Univ. of Arkansas, 1978. 176pp. Abs., *DAI*, 39, 1978, 3607A–08A.

Describes a four-part pattern—the annunciation of a mission, temptation based on "the Flesh, the World, and the Devil," the need to accept grace, and the resolution of the mission—in all four works.

3750 Weber, Burton J. "The Schematic Design of the *Samson* Middle." *MiltonS*, 22, 1986, 233–54.

Systematically refutes the typological three-section design of the play's center portion. Analyzes plot, character construction and motivation, and structural logistics. States that the play's schematic design reveals the workings of a supernatural presence whose plan is to "establish the meaning and the terms of Samson's change."

3751 Weinkauf, Mary S. "Dalila: The Worst of All Possible Wives." *SEL*, 13, 1973, 135–47.

Argues that Dalila is "a tempting seductress who violates all the Renaissance rules for wifehood and commits what amounts to marital treason." Her "motives are not love, affection, altruism, regret, helpfulness, generosity, or any such pleasantness, but sheer pride."

3752 Welcher, Jeanne K. "The Meaning of Manoa." *MiltonQ*, 8, 1974, 48–50.

Manoa's name in Hebrew means "resting place" and indicates the alternative against which Samson must struggle. His final resting place is death and burial in his father's tomb, not rest in his father's home.

3753 West, Robert H. "Samson's God: 'Beastly Hebraism' and 'Asinine Bigotry.'" *MiltonS*, 13, 1979, 109–28.

Contends that Samson's own testimony about his God can impress us favorably and contains no persisting doubt about God's goodness. Samson accepts the divine mystery.

3754 Wilcher, Robert. "*Samson Agonistes* and the Problem of History." *RMS*, 26, 1982, 108–33.

Argues that Milton's drama "was calculated to engage with a number of the problematic issues which the failure of the English Revolution had made unavoidable for those of his contemporaries who saw history as 'God manifesting himself' and who had once shared a vision of the imminent establishment of Christ's Kingdom by the specially appointed Saints of God."

3755 Williams, Mima. "Milton's Biblical Adaptations for *Samson Agonistes*." *CCTEP*, 40, 1975, 58–64.

Milton changes the biblical story by developing the main characters, changing their actions, and adding characters. "Milton converts the inner strivings of Samson into a progressive psychological change; none of this is suggested in Judges, but rather in Job."

3756 Wimsatt, James I. *"Samson Agonistes* and the Tradition of Boethius." *RenP,* 1972, pp. 1–10.

Points out aspects of the drama which look back to Boethius's *Consolation of Philosophy* and shows that Samson's conclusion differs radically from that found in the medieval treatise.

3757 Witte, Stephen Paul. "Milton's *Samson Agonistes." Expl,* 36, 1977, 26–27.

Shows that in the poetic form of the Chorus's last speech, elements converge from the Italian and the English sonnet forms.

3758 Wittreich, Joseph. *Interpreting "Samson Agonistes."* Princeton, NJ: Princeton Univ. Press, 1986. xxxii, 394pp.

Discusses the present state of criticism about *Samson Agonistes* and the various versions of the Samson story. Finds Samson an unregenerate character. See No. 3545. Reviews: Anthony Low, *JEGP,* 86, 1987, 415–18; Roger Rollin, *SCR,* 19, 1987, 59–60; James Thorpe, *CLIO,* 16, 1987, 282–84; Gordon Campbell, *N&Q,* 35, 1988, 537; J. Martin Evans, *RES,* 39, 1988, 109–11; Wendy Furman, *PQ,* 67, 1988, 389–93; Charles Martindale, *TLS,* Feb. 5–11, 1988, p. 142; Thomas F. Healy, *MLR,* 84, 1989, 128–29; Janel Mueller, *MP,* 86, 1989, 300–04; James H. Sims, *SCN,* 49, 1991, 38–40.

3759 Wittreich, Joseph Anthony, Jr. "Strange Text! *'Paradise Regain'd' ... To Which is Added 'Samson Agonistes.'" Poems in Their Place: The Intertextuality and Order of Poetic Collections.* Ed. by Neil Fraistat (Chapel Hill and London: Univ. of North Carolina Press, 1986), pp. 164–94.

On the intertextual connection between the two poems: "typological patterning, generic organization, self-quotation and echo, imagistic and thematic repetition, a common subtext, all of which are conspicuously evident in Milton's 1671 volume. *Paradise Regained* and *Samson Agonistes* have not a separate but shared syntax; these poems together form a totality, with the individual poems themselves becoming like fragments."

3760 Wolf, Melvin H. "The Unity of *Samson Agonistes." EngR,* 17, 1967, 32–36.

"The current journey follows the 'structural unity' approach—one which invites repeated passage; its vehicle is an analysis of the work's component parts and their interrelationships; its itinerary includes considerations of PLOT, THEME, and CHARACTERIZATION; its destination is the recognition of *Samson Agonistes* as an artistically unified literary work of art."

3761 Wood, Derek N. C. "Exil'd from Light: The Darkened Moral Consciousness of Milton's Hero of Faith." *UTQ,* 58, 1988–89, 244–62.

Perceives Samson as a hero of faith who is neither saintly nor Satanic. Argues that "the play dramatizes a fictional Old Testament consciousness in all its personages. . . . Samson's ethic and consciousness contrast with Christ's. In this negative way, *Samson Agonistes* points . . . to the centrality of Christ in Milton's thought."

3762 Zeong, Yun-Shig. "A Poetic Paradigm: The 'Middle' of *Samson Agonistes." JELL,* 33, 1987, 3–15.

Believes that *Samson Agonistes* has a middle that involves the Chorus, Manoa, Dalila, and Harapha. The play's structure agrees with the poetic system outlined by Aristotle and Longinus.

CRITICISM: PROSE WORKS

3763 Aers, David, and **Gunther Kress.** "Historical Process, Individuals and Communities in Milton's *Areopagitica*." *Literature, Language and Society in England, 1580–1680.* Ed. by Aers, Kress, and Bob Hodge (Dublin: Gill and Macmillan; Totowa, NJ: Barnes and Noble, 1981), pp. 152–83.

"Milton's freedom from ever having *had* to work as a hired labourer . . ., his freedom from the labour market, his freedom from . . . the commercial sector of society or the landed gentry, this social and economic freedom is a shaping factor . . . in his whole experience" and resulted in "imaginative failure and intellectual closure."

3764 Aers, David, and **Gunther Kress.** "Historical Process, Individuals and Communities in Milton's Early Prose." *1642: Literature and Power in the Seventeenth Century.* Ed. by Francis Barker and others (Colchester: Univ. of Essex, 1981), pp. 283–300.

"In this paper we concentrate on Milton's version of historical process and communities in *Areopagitica*, hoping to shed light on Milton's worldview and to sketch a form of inquiry which could be extended fruitfully to his other writings and those of his contemporaries, both the more radical and the conservative ones." Abs., *MiltonQ*, 15, 1981, 27–28.

3765 Anjum, A. R. *Milton's Philosophy of Education.* Lahore: Polymer, 1985. 128pp.

3766 Anselment, Raymond A. "John Milton *contra* Hall." *"Betwixt Jest and Earnest": Marprelate, Milton, Marvell,* *Swift and the Decorum of Religious Ridicule* (Toronto, Buffalo, NY, and London: Univ. of Toronto Press, 1979), pp. 61–93.

Deals mainly with *Animadversions* and the *Apology*. "In teaching through exposure by zealous laughter, the satires are themselves a lesson in decorum." Reviews (of book): Annabel M. Patterson, *RenQ*, 33, 1980, 816–18; James Egan, *SCN*, 39, 1981, 12–14; Michael Lieb, *Cithara*, 21, 1981, 58–70; H. A. Marshall, *N&Q*, 28, 1981, 192; P. G. Stanwood, *JEGP*, 80, 1981, 253–55; Edmund Miller, *C&L*, 31, 1982, 75–76; Leo Miller, *MiltonQ*, 15, 1981, 64–66; reply to Leo Miller by Edward Le Comte, p. 105.

3767 Arai, Akira. "Milton and 1644." *Miscellaneous Essays on Milton* (Tokyo: Chukyo Shuppan, 1979), pp. 31–44.

In Japanese. Discusses the reasons for Milton's sudden change from pro- to anti-Presbyterian with the publication of *Areopagitica* in 1644.

3768 Arai, Akira. "Milton's *Defensio Secunda*." *Otsuka Review,* 5, 1968, 3–9.

In Japanese. In the praise of Cromwell and others, including Milton himself, Milton states that true heroism resides in right principles and in the right behavior of an individual who lives with self-restraint, led by right reason. Abs., *MiltonN*, 3, 1969, 32.

3769 Arai, Akira. "Milton's Divorce Tracts: The Exodus from Paradise." *The Bulletin of the Tokyo Univ. of Education, Literature Department,* 93, 1973, 23–34.

In Japanese; English summary, pp. 35–36. Believes that when Milton writes the divorce tracts, he anticipates some of the ideas in *Paradise Lost*, such as the view that Adam's exodus from paradise is heroic, not tragic. Abs., *MiltonQ*, 17, 1973, 89.

3770 Arai, Akira. "Milton's Heroism in His Tractate *Of Education*." *The Bulletin of the Tokyo Univ. of Education, Literature Department*, 73, 1969, 1–11.

In Japanese; English summary, pp. 12–13. Believes that in *Of Education*, Milton equates magnanimity and godliness, which in turn produces true heroism.

3771 Auksi, Peter. "Milton's 'Sanctifi'd Bitternesse': Polemical Technique in the Early Prose." *TSLL*, 19, 1977, 363–81.

Concludes that in the antiprelatical tracts, Milton rises above "his own sanctified bitterness and the stridency of his literary fruit."

3772 Austin, M. A. "*Areopagitica*: Milton's Optimism and the Mode of Its Expression." *Opus* (Univ. of Rhodesia), second series, 1, 1977, 8–11.

Emphasizes Milton's idealism, inability to grasp reality, and view of England's future grandeur, as expressed in his prose.

3773 Ayers, Robert W. "The Editions of Milton's *Readie and Easie Way To Establish a Free Commonwealth*." *RES*, 25, 1974, 280–91.

Modifies and corrects prior assumptions concerning the period of composition and asserts that internal evidence strengthens the case for publication in February, 1660. Recalls the crucial political events of the months and days preceding February 22 of that year.

3774 "B. B. C. Milton Broadcast." *MiltonQ*, 5, 1971, 46.

Reports on a B. B. C. taped broadcast called *Milton's Left Hand*, by Austin Woolrych, which "deals with Milton's turn to prose (1649–1654) despite his hopes for success in poetry."

3775 Banschbach, John. "Ethical Style in Milton's *The Readie and Easie Way*." *Lang&S*, 17, 1984, 79–91.

Discusses how Milton's style suits his arguments in the tract.

3776 Banschbach, John Michael. "The Prose Styles of John Milton's *The Readie and Easie Way*." Doctoral diss., Indiana Univ., 1979. 165pp. Abs., *DAI*, 40, 1980, 5448A.

Claims that Milton's disordered style and suspended sentences are caused by his "hatred of monarchy" and "awareness of the desperateness of his cause."

3777 Barker, Arthur E. *Milton and the Puritan Dilemma, 1641–1660*. Toronto: Univ. of Toronto Press, 1976. Frequently reprinted.

Reprint of Huckabay No. 2824, originally published in 1942.

3778 Barker, Francis. "In the Wars of Truth." *SoRA*, 20, 1987, 111–25.

Combines "some description, in Milton [*Areopagitica*] and Hobbes [*Leviathan*], of the tropes of true discourse or Truth and the warlike violence with which they are associated, with some reflection on the theory of discourse today."

3779 Bauman, Michael E. "Heresy in Paradise and the Ghosts of Readers Past." *CLAJ*, 30, 1986, 59–68.

Contends that Milton espoused heretical Arian views in the *Christian Doctrine* and that they are evident in *Paradise Lost*.

3780 Bauman, Michael E. "Milton's Theological Vocabulary and the Nicene Anathemas." *MiltonS*, 21, 1985, 71–92.

Examines certain key words in Milton's vocabulary to conclude that "By any honest reckoning, Milton is an Arian."

3781 Benjamin, Edwin B. "Milton and Tacitus." *MiltonS*, 4, 1972, 117–40.

Milton drew frequently from Tacitus's work, using parallels with the process by which Roman liberty was extinguished under the empire. "His adaptations of passages from Tacitus in the *History [of Britain]* seem at times to imitate directly the wit and concision of the Latin, and it is likely that some of these features are carried over into the style of the epics."

3782 Berghaus, Günter. "A Case of Censorship of Milton in Germany: On an Unknown Edition of the *Pro Populo Anglicano Defensio.*" *MiltonQ*, 17, 1983, 61–70.

Discusses the European reaction to the English revolution, citing attempts to publish and repress translations of *First Defence* in Germany.

3783 Blum, Abbe. "The Author's Authority: *Areopagitica* and the Labour of Licensing." *Re-membering Milton: Essays on the Texts and Traditions.* Ed. by Mary Nyquist and Margaret W. Ferguson (New York and London: Methuen, 1987), pp. 74–96.

Examines the contradictions between Milton's message in *Areopagitica* and his later activities as a Commonwealth licenser. Argues that such inconsistencies demonstrate that Milton wished "to repudiate and to embrace a discourse of power associated with a principle of authorial autonomy."

3784 Boehrer, Bruce. "Elementary Structures of Kingship: Milton, Regicide, and the Family." *MiltonS*, 23, 1987, 97–117.

Contends that Milton's arguments in *Eikonoklastes* and *First* and *Second Defence* do not justify regicide or "refute a concept of kingship that manifested itself, on the personal level, in the figurations of family order." Notes the "royalist triumph of the father-king over Milton's rhetoric."

3785 Boehrer, Bruce Thomas. "Monarchy and Incest in Renaissance England: Literature from Henry VIII to Charles I." Doctoral diss., Univ. of Pennsylvania, 1986. 317pp. Abs., *DAI*, 47, 1987, 2591A.

Follows the degeneration of the Renaissance family, influenced by political developments, using Milton's *Eikonoklastes* and other works as evidence.

3786 Bowers, Anthony Robin. "John Milton as Controversialist: Rhetorical Influences on the Structure of the Three *Defences.*" Doctoral diss., Princeton Univ., 1968. 230pp. Abs., *DA*, 29, 1969, 2667A.

Analyzes the effect of the Milton-Salmasius controversy on the mature rhetoric of Milton's three *Defences.*

3787 Bowers, A. Robin. "Milton and Salmasius: The Rhetorical Imperatives." *PQ*, 52, 1973, 55–68.

Compares the structure and rhetorical strategies of Salmasius's *Defensio Regia* and Milton's rebuttal in the *First Defence.* Evaluates the effectiveness of Milton's work and concludes that "its immediate rhetorical success proved that its author was indeed found 'nowise wanting' to his cause."

3788 Boyette, Purvis E. "Milton's Divorce Tracts and the Law of Marriage." *TSE*, 17, 1969, 73–92.

On Milton's idealistic conception of marriage. Argues that "the polemical bias of the divorce pamphlets requires us to separate the content of the tracts from their form."

3789 Bradley, S. A. J. "Ambiorix Ariovistus, Detractor of Milton's *Defensio*, Identified." *MP*, 73, 1976, 382–88.

Identifies Henrik Ernst (1603–65), professor of jurisprudence in Denmark, as the author of the *Anonymous Answer* to Milton's *First Defence.*

3790 Brennan, William. "Milton's *Of Education* and the *Translatio Studii.*" *MiltonQ*, 15, 1981, 55–59.

On Milton's views of the transmission of learning from east to west, as reflected in *Of Education.* Believes that Milton yearned for an enlightenment of his countrymen so they would no longer go to Italy to become educated but instead "foreigners would flock to England as the newly restored fount of wisdom."

3791 Burroughs, Franklin G., Jr. "Milton's Historical Thought: The Backgrounds of the *History of Britain* and Its Place in His Intellectual Development." Doctoral diss., Harvard Univ., 1970.

3792 Cable, Lana F. "Carnal Rhetoric: Image and Truth in Milton's Polemics." Doctoral diss., Johns Hopkins Univ., 1986. 258pp. Abs., *DAI*, 47, 1987, 4394A.

Outlines Milton's changing views of truth and imagery—originally incompatible, gradually codependent, and finally fulfilled by human action—in his polemical prose.

3793 Cable, Lana. "Coupling Logic and Milton's Doctrine of Divorce." *MiltonS*, 15, 1981, 143–59.

Shows that, in the divorce tracts, Milton "constructs his argument upon the framework of a distinctive pattern of logic which, on examination, proves consistent, rational and even elegantly appropriate."

3794 Cable, Lana. "Shuffling up Such a God: The Rhetorical Agon of Milton's Antiprelatical Tracts." *MiltonS*, 21, 1985, 3–33.

Studies the conflict between the "startling images" in Milton's prose tracts and the historical and rational level of argument.

3795 Camé, J.-F. "Images in Milton's *Areopagitica*." *CahiersE*, 6, 1974, 23–37.

Discusses the many images drawn from various fields of daily life.

3796 Campbell, Gordon. "Alleged Imperfections in Milton's *De Doctrina Christiana*." *MiltonQ*, 12, 1978, 64–65.

Questions some of the imperfections listed by Maurice Kelley in his introduction to the *Christian Doctrine* in the Yale *Complete Prose Works* (No. 366).

3797 Campbell, Gordon. "*Bara, Ktizein, and Creare* Again." *N&Q*, 28, 1981, 42–43.

Replies to Bill Coggin (No. 3804), offering evidence that Milton had ample support in denying that the Hebrew, Greek, and Latin words "to create" mean "to create something out of nothing."

3798 Campbell, Gordon. "*De Doctrina Christiana*: Its Structural Principles and Its Unfinished State." *MiltonS*, 9, 1976, 243–60.

"A series of deleted notes in the manuscript [of the *Christian Doctrine*] shows that the treatise once stood in ten parts. Milton had apparently completed the reorganization of everything except the sixth part. *De Doctrina Christiana* must accordingly be seen as unfinished." Abs., *MiltonQ*, 11, 1977, 26.

3799 Campbell, Gordon C. "The Intellect and the Imagination: A Study of the Relationship between Milton's *De Doctrina Christiana* and *Paradise Lost*." Doctoral diss., Univ. of York, 1973. See *MiltonQ*, 7, 1973, 93.

3800 Campbell, Gordon. "Milton's *Accedence Commenc't Grammar*." *MiltonQ*, 10, 1976, 39–48.

Discusses Milton's qualified endorsement of the Ramist method in grammar "in the context of the inroads Ramism had already made into the teaching of grammar in England."

3801 Campbell, Gordon. "Milton's *Index Theologicus* and Bellarmine's *Disputationes De Controversiis Christianae Fidei Adversus Huius Temporis Haereticos*." *MiltonQ*, 11, 1977, 12–16.

Proposes "that Milton's index [the lost *Index Theologicus*] was compiled in preparation for a polemical treatise directed against Bellarmine's *Disputationes*."

3802 Carter, Ronnie D. "Syntax and Style in Milton's English Prose." Doctoral diss., Univ. of Wisconsin, 1972. 150pp. Abs., *DAI*, 33, 1973, 6343A–44A.

Uses statistics to analyze the static, evolving, and genre-controlled elements of syntax and style in six of Milton's prose works.

3803 Cavanaugh, Sister Mary Hortense, S. S. J. "John Milton's *Prolusions* Considered in the Light of His Rhetorical and Dialectical Education at St. Paul's Grammar School and Cambridge University." Doctoral diss., Fordham Univ., 1968. 352pp. Abs., *DA*, 29, 1969, 2668A–69A.

Measures the impact of Milton's schooling—a system formed by classical, medieval, and Renaissance influences that stressed grammar, rhetoric, and logic—on his *Prolusions*.

3804 Coggin, Bill. "A Semantic Problem in John Milton's *Christian Doctrine*." *N&Q*, 26, 1979, 422–24.

Finds that Milton's position in the *Christian Doctrine* that the world was created out of preexisting matter is contradicted by contemporary Hebrew, Latin, and Greek lexicons, which indicate that verbs meaning "to create" "would be used to signify to create out of nothing." Reply by Gordon Campbell (No. 3797).

3805 Corns, Thomas N. *The Development of Milton's Prose Style*. Oxford: Clarendon Press; New York: Oxford Univ. Press, 1982. xiv, 118pp.

A computer-aided study in historical linguistics, which compares each group of Milton's tracts with pamphlets by other writers who dealt with the same controversies. "I have attempted to reconstruct the genre expectations of Milton's first readers, so that . . . we may rediscover some of the genuine freshness and innovation which his original audience would have appreciated." Examines lexical features (such as word frequencies), syntactic features, sentence structure, and imagery. Reviews: Edmund Miller, *C&L*, 32, 1982, 50–52; Roy C. Flannagan, *MiltonQ*, 16, 1982, 75–76; Archie Burnett, *N&Q*, 30, 1983, 470–71; William George Riggs, *RenQ*, 36, 1983, 479–82; Georgia B. Christopher, *JEGP*, 83, 1984, 118–20; Alan Ward, *RES*, 35, 1984, 539–40; Brian Vickers, *MLR*, 83, 1988, 673–77.

3806 Corns, Thomas N. "Imagery in Civil War Polemic: Milton, Overton and the *Eikon Basilike*." *MiltonQ*, 14, 1980, 1–6.

Investigates patterns of reiterated imagery in Milton's vernacular political tracts and compares his practice with that of contemporary writers who use the same genre.

3807 Corns, Thomas N. "Obscenity, Slang and Indecorum in Milton's English Prose." *PSt*, 3, No. 1, 1980, 5–14.

Argues that Milton offers a new decorum of abuse, in terms of both polemical strategy and range of reference. Deals mainly with the antiprelatical tracts. Abs., *MiltonQ*, 14, 1980, 136.

3808 Corns, Thomas N. "Punctuation in Milton's Vernacular Prose." *N&Q*, 25, 1978, 18–19.

"Milton's contemporaries, whether quoting his prose or setting it up in type, favoured alterations which bring the punctuation in line with modern, syntactical criteria. This certainly suggests that Miltonic punctuation, in prose as well as in his poetry, contained elements which seemed aberrant by mid-century standards and which his original readers neither appreciated nor respected."

3809 Corns, T. N. "Studies in the Development of Milton's Prose Style." Doctoral diss., Oxford Univ., 1976. *IT*, 27, 1979, 8.

3810 Corns, T. N., W. A. Speck, and **J. A. Downie.** "Archetypal Mystification: Polemic and Reality in English Political Literature, 1640–1750." *ECLife*, 7, No. 3, 1982, 1–27.

Discusses Milton's representation of royalists in the *Readie and Easie Way*.

3811 Crawford, John W. "Early Proponents of Modern Educational Theory." *Journal of Adventist Education*, Feb.-Mar., 1969, pp. 10–12.

"This article compares Milton's thoughts on education with those of John Comenius" (summary from *MiltonQ*, 4, 1970, 17).

3812 Cupps, William Donald. "The Ethical Milieu of John Milton's *De Doctrina Christiana*." Doctoral diss., Univ. of Illinois, Urbana, 1973. 349pp. Abs., *DAI*, 34, 1974, 5905A.

Follows Milton's defense of Aristotelian principles against seventeenth-century Christian ethics, as shown in the *Christian Doctrine*.

3813 Curet, Peggy Joann. "The Rhetoric of Humor in Milton's *Areopagitica*." Doctoral diss., Univ. of Southwestern Louisiana, 1976. 159pp. Abs., *DAI*, 38, 1977, 801A–02A.

Explores Milton's use of ostensible humor directed at "papist practices" to hide an attack on "the Long Parliament which used the licensing order of 1643."

3814 Dahlø, Rolf. "The Date of Milton's *Artis Logicae* and the Development of the Idea of Definition in Milton's Works." *HLQ*, 43, 1979, 25–36.

Considers possible dates for the *Art of Logic* and concludes "that the passage on definition in the *Tetrachordon* should be seen not as a logical digression of peripheral interest, but as a fundamental element in Milton's mode of thought."

3815 Davies, David, and Paul Dowling. "'Shrewd Books, with Dangerous Frontispices': *Areopagitica*'s Motto." *MiltonQ*, 20, 1986, 33–37.

Believes that "Milton has playfully mistranslated Euripides in order to establish a kind of Greek/English dialectic which previews important arguments of the *Areopagitica*."

3816 Davies, Tony. "Milton's Blind Fury." *MiltonQ*, 15, 1981, 28.

Abstract of a paper presented at the 1980 Essex Sociology of Literature Conference. Focusing on *Of Education*, discusses "the historical transformations of public and private life, the secularization of social power, and the representation in the 1640's of emergent (bourgeois) conceptions of civil and domestic subjectivity."

3817 Davis, Norman. "'God and Good Men.'" *N&Q*, 15, 1968, 376.

Points out that Milton uses the phrase "God and good men" in *Areopagitica*.

Discusses reference by C. T. Onions in *TLS*, Aug. 13, 1931.

3818 Dillon, John B. "*Surdeo*, Saumaise, and the Lexica: An Aspect of Milton's Latin Diction." *HumLov*, 27, 1978, 238–52.

Concludes that Milton's use of the Latin word "surdeat" was correct, despite Salmasius's objections.

3819 Dowling, Paul M. "*Areopagitica* and *Areopagiticus*: The Significance of Isocratic Precedent." *MiltonS*, 21, 1985, 49–69.

Believes that Milton uses Isocrates's work as his model but uses Plato's *Republic* and *Laws* for content in an ironic fashion. Insists that *Areopagitica* is concerned with the art of legislating morality.

3820 Dowling, Paul Murphy. "Milton's Prose Style: Argument and Style in Four Classical Republican Pamphlets." Doctoral diss., Indiana Univ., 1973. 189pp. Abs., *DAI*, 34, 1973, 1902A–03A.

Asserts that the styles of *Of Education*, *Areopagitica*, the *Tenure of Kings and Magistrates*, and the *Readie and Easie Way* reflect their respective arguments—graduated, balanced education; the constant exercise of reason; reasonable tyrannicide; and an English commonwealth.

3821 Dowling, Paul Murphy. "Milton's Use (or Abuse) of History in *Areopagitica*." *Cithara*, 23, No. 1, 1983, 28–37.

Compares the modern definition of history to the classical vision of "historia." Shows that the historical errors in *Areopagitica* found by modern critics disappear if viewed from the classical standpoint. Also addresses Milton's "highly prejudiced history" and his adaptations of content to serve his needs.

3822 Dowling, Paul M. "'The Scholastick Grosnesse of Barbarous Ages': The Question of the Humanism of Milton's Understanding of Virtue." *Milton and the Middle Ages*. Ed. by John Mulryan

(Lewisburg, PA: Bucknell Univ. Press; London and Toronto: Associated Univ. Presses, 1982), pp. 59–72.

Milton's understanding of virtue in *Of Education* and *Areopagitica* indicates that he is closer to Thomas Aquinas than to Aristotle.

3823 Dust, Philip. "Another Copy of Milton's *Pro Populo Anglicano Defensio.*" *Library*, 3, 1981, 143–44.

Traces the text of his own 1652 copy.

3824 Dzelzainis, M. M. "The Ideological Context of John Milton's *History of Britain.*" Doctoral diss., Cambridge Univ., 1984.

3825 Egan, James. *The Inward Teacher: Milton's Rhetoric of Christian Liberty.* SCN Editions and Studies, vol. 2. University Park: Pennsylvania State Univ., 1980. iv, 99pp.

Reviews rhetorical conventions of Renaissance prose genres, demonstrates that Milton selected his genres according to the intended audience, points out a transformation to a simple style during his prose period, and concludes that Milton gradually realized the difficulties of reforming an intractable nation. Reviews: Joseph Allen Bryant, Jr., *C&L*, 31, 1982, 89–91; James Stephens, *SCN*, 40, 1982, 9.

3826 Egan, James. "Milton and the Conventions of Prose Controversy: A Generic Analysis." *MiltonQ*, 10, 1976, 130–31.

Abstract of a paper presented at the University of Michigan, Dearborn, in 1976. "Unlike those of the typical pamphleteer, Milton's works generally transcend purely personal abuse and reach important and enduring levels of meaning."

3827 Egan, James. "Milton and the Marprelate Tradition." *MiltonS*, 8, 1975, 103–21.

"The decorum of seventeenth-century controversy demanded that Milton reply in kind to opponents who had ridiculed the positions he championed in his prose tracts. In the Marprelate tra-

dition he found the appropriate weapon. Milton's *Animadversions* (1641) and *Colasterion* (1645) display not only a variety of characteristics identified with the Marprelate genre, but also several Miltonic innovations in that genre."

3828 Egan, James. "Public Truth and Personal Witness in Milton's Last Tracts." *ELH*, 40, 1973, 231–48.

Explains Milton's methods of doctrinal clarification through abbreviation of "lengthy explication" and "verbal ambiguity." Contrasts his diction, which ranges from "highly personal" in the *Apology* to "devoid of suggestive force" in *Of Civil Power*. Discusses the use of the "regenerate voice."

3829 Egan, James. "The Satiric Wit of Milton's Prose Controversies." *SLitI*, 10, No. 2, 1977, 97–104.

Discusses "how Milton's witty allusions, innuendo[e]s and lampooning in works such as *Animadversions* (1641), *Colasterion* (1645), and *Eikonoklastes* (1649) create satire by enlarging upon the normal 'dialectic[al] process of statement, proof, and refutation' that characterizes controversial prose in the seventeenth century." Abs., *MiltonQ*, 13, 1979, 27; *SCN*, 38, 1980, 19.

3830 Egan, James J., Jr. "The 'Shattr'd Idoll': Milton's *Eikonoklastes* and Renaissance Satiric Theory." *SCN*, 38, 1980, 14–15.

Abstract of a paper read at Villanova University in 1978. "The satire of *Eikonoklastes*, then, tells us a good deal about Milton's tactics as a prose satirist, anticipates some of his strategies of denigration in *Paradise Lost*, and suggests an indebtedness in virtually all of his works to Renaissance satiric theory."

3831 Egan, James Joseph, Jr. "The Varieties of Style in Milton's Prose." Doctoral diss., Univ. of Notre Dame, 1971. 241pp. Abs., *DAI*, 32, 1972, 3948A.

Examines the interdependence of style and content, as well as a "movement from public to personal," in Milton's four prose styles—oratorical, pamphlet, disputative, and plain.

3832 Fallon, Robert Thomas. "Milton in the Anarchy, 1659–1660: A Question of Consistency." *SEL*, 21, 1981, 123–46.

Argues that in his prose written in 1659–60, Milton "was consistent throughout in his support of the English Army and in his conviction that only an English legislative body, be it a perpetual senate or a readmitted Rump, could legitimize disestablishment of the Church." Abs., *SCN*, 39, 1981, 99–100.

3833 Firth, Charles Harding. *Milton as an Historian.* Folcroft, PA: Folcroft Library Editions, 1969, 1974; Norwood, PA: Norwood Editions, 1976; Philadelphia, PA: R. West, 1977.

Reprints of Stevens No. 1311, originally published in 1908.

3834 Fish, Stanley. "Critical Legal Studies: Unger and Milton." *RAR*, 7, No. 2, 1987, 1–20.

Uses Milton's works, mainly *Areopagitica*, to illustrate the ideas presented in Roberto Unger's works. "Unger poses a politics that is the direct descendant of Milton's, a politics of perpetual distrust and perpetual progression."

3835 Fish, Stanley. "Driving from the Letter: Truth and Indeterminacy in Milton's *Areopagitica*." *Re-membering Milton: Essays on the Texts and Traditions.* Ed. by Mary Nyquist and Margaret W. Ferguson (New York and London: Methuen, 1987), pp. 234–54.

"Specifically, I will argue that Milton is finally, and in a profound way, not against licensing, and that he has almost no interest at all in the 'freedom of the press' as an abstract or absolute good (and, indeed, does not unambiguously value freedom at all)."

3836 Fish, Stanley E. "Reasons That Imply Themselves: Imagery, Argument, and the Reader in Milton's *Reason of Church Government*." *Seventeenth-Century Imagery: Essays on Uses of Figurative Lan-* *guage from Donne to Farquhar.* Ed. by Earl Miner (Berkeley, Los Angeles, and London: Univ. of California Press, 1971), pp. 83–102. Revised in *Self-Consuming Artifacts: The Experience of Seventeenth-Century Literature* (Berkeley, Los Angeles, and London: Univ. of California Press, 1972), pp. 265–302.

In the *Reason of Church-Government*, "the focus of meaning is not the printed page . . . but the mind of the reader, where everything is happening."

3837 Fish, Stanley E., ed. *Seventeenth-Century Prose: Modern Essays in Criticism.* New York: Oxford Univ. Press, 1971. xi, 572pp.

Essays on Milton are by Kester Svendsen (Huckabay No. 3732A) and Thomas Kranidas (No. 3891). Reviews: F. Costa, *EA*, 26, 1973, 478; Jørn Carlsen, *RLV*, 40, 1974, 576–79.

3838 Fletcher, Harris Francis. *The Use of the Bible in Milton's Prose.* Folcroft, PA: Folcroft Library Editions, 1969; New York: Haskell House, 1970; Ann Arbor, MI: Univ. Microfilms International, 1980 Books on Demand Reprints.

Reprints of Huckabay No. 2875, originally published in 1929.

3839 French, Roberts W. "Milton's *Areopagitica*." *The Humanist*, 28, No. 2, 1968, 15.

In Milton's work, "the humanist ideals of intellectual freedom, of dependence upon reason, and of faith in man find enduring expression."

3840 Friedman, Lester David. "Bold Inquirers: A Study of the Political Prose of Milton and Shelley." Doctoral diss., Syracuse Univ., 1975. 319pp. Abs., *DAI*, 36, 1976, 6701A.

Analyzes Milton's influence on Shelley's work and both writers' responses to "basic questions about the role of the imaginative artist and his work within a framework of political ideas."

3841 Gatti, Hilary. "Some Amendments to E. Sirluck's Textual Notes on *Areopagitica*." *N&Q*, 29, 1982, 499–500.

"Sirluck's textual notes [see No. 366] . . . suggest that his 'A' text is in fact less reliable than the other texts examined; for in five cases he finds printing errors in the Thomason copy which he reports as corrected in all or most of the other copies he collates with."

3842 Gatti, Hilary. "The 'Twenty Ingrossers' of Milton's *Areopagitica*." *N&Q*, 29, 1982, 498–99.

Clarifies Milton's "apparent mistake" in *Areopagitica*, when he lists only twenty censors by counting the "individual appointments," rather than "the appropriate professional groups."

3843 Geisst, Charles R. "Milton and Brutus: Born To Command." *N&Q*, 21, 1974, 412–13.

Notes parallel phrasing in Milton's *Tenure of Kings and Magistrates* and a late sixteenth-century regicide tract by the pseudonymous Stephen Junius Brutus.

3844 Geisst, Charles R. "Milton's 'Laborious Ascent.'" *N&Q*, 21, 1974, 94–95.

Finds Plato's *Laws* a possible source for Milton's use of the phrase early in *Of Education*.

3845 George, C. M., Rev. "The 'Learned English Writer' in *Of Reformation*." *MiltonN*, 3, 1969, 54–55.

Agrees that Milton refers to Francis Bacon.

3846 Gershgoren, Sid Carl. "Millennarian and Apocalyptic Literature from Thomas Burnet to William Blake." Doctoral diss., Univ. of California, Davis, 1969. 316pp. Abs., *DAI*, 31, 1970, 2385A.

Traces the movement of apocalyptic literature in the seventeenth and eighteenth centuries from conservative summaries of doctrine to radical apocalyptic recreations (*Areopagitica*), and then to scientific approaches, and finally to a conflict between the narrator and the cosmos.

3847 Gilman, Wilbur Elwyn. *Milton's Rhetoric: Studies in His Defense of Lib-*erty. Folcroft, PA: Folcroft Library Editions, 1969; Norwood, PA: Norwood Editions, 1977.

Reprints of Huckabay No. 2892, originally published in 1939.

3848 Gilmartin, Kevin. "History and Reform in Milton's *Readie and Easie Way*." *MiltonS*, 24, 1988, 17–41.

Relates the tract to Milton's earlier, more optimistic prose works and insists that "the final disintegration of the parliamentary cause has brought about a sobering recognition that the course of human history is uncertain, and has forced Milton to abandon his confident 'apocalyptic progressivism.'"

3849 Gorecki, John. "Milton's Similitudes for Satan and the Traditional Implications of Their Imagery." *MiltonQ*, 10, 1976, 101–08.

Shows "the correspondence between Milton's stated meanings for some images in his prose [such as locusts, cones, pyramids, triangles, and the darkened sun] and the traditional implications of those images." Reply by Lawrence W. Hyman (No. 2466); surrejoinder by Gorecki (No. 2322).

3850 Greene, Donald. "Milton Questions." *TLS*, Aug. 14, 1970, p. 903.

Insists that "mewing" is unacceptable, and "renewing" should be substituted in *Areopagitica*. See also *TLS*, Aug. 21, p. 928; Sept. 4, p. 975; Oct. 2, p. 1137.

3851 Greene, Douglas G. "A Note on *Eikon Basilike*." *N&Q*, 19, 1972, 176.

Offers evidence to support the accuracy of the memorandum by Arthur Annesley, Earl of Anglesey, naming Bishop John Gauden as author.

3852 Gregory, E. R. "Milton's Use of *Musae Mansuetiores* in His First Prolusion." *MiltonQ*, 22, 1988, 66–68.

Examines "an early instance of . . . [Milton's] use of the Ciceronian phrase, *musae mansuetiores*, in his first Prolusion."

3853 Grose, Christopher. "Milton on

Ramist Similitude." *Seventeenth-Century Imagery: Essays on Uses of Figurative Language from Donne to Farquhar.* Ed. by Earl Miner (Berkeley, Los Angeles, and London: Univ. of California Press, 1971), pp. 103–16.

Concerned with the degree of Ramist influence on Milton and his departure from it in the *Art of Logic.*

3854 Grose, Christopher. "'Unweapon'd Creature in the Word': A Revision in Milton's *Letter to a Friend.*" *ELN,* 21, No. 1, 1983, 29–34.

Behind both versions of the letter lies the notion of a special calling that indicates Milton's concern about his mission in life. Feels that there are reasons for retaining the phrase "unweapon'd creature in the word," which pertains to the young poet's hopes and fears in his long preparation for pastoral work.

3855 Hale, David G. "Intestine Sedition: The Fable of the Belly." *CLS,* 5, 1968, 377–88.

Sees the fable in *Of Reformation* as "an example of the traditional correspondence between man the microcosm and the body politic."

3856 Halkett, John. *Milton and the Idea of Matrimony: A Study of the Divorce Tracts and "Paradise Lost."* Yale Studies in English, 173. New Haven, CT, and London: Yale Univ. Press, 1970. ix, 162pp.

Studies Milton's comments on marriage in the divorce pamphlets and his presentation of marriage in *Paradise Lost.*

3857 Haller, William. "Church-Outed by the Prelates." *On Milton's Poetry: A Selection of Modern Studies.* Ed. by Arnold Stein (Greenwich, CT: Fawcett Publications, 1970), pp. 26–36.

Reprint of a section of Huckabay No. 2901, originally published in 1938.

3858 Hamabayashi, Masao. "Milton in the History of English Educational Thought." *MCJ News,* 6, 1983, 5–7.

Discusses *Of Education* in reference to seventeenth-century educational thought.

3859 Hannay, Margaret. "Milton's Doctrine of the Holy Scriptures." *CSR,* 5, 1976, 339–49.

Finds that in the *Christian Doctrine,* Milton declares that the Bible must be available to all, every Christian has the obligation diligently to study the Scriptures, the uneducated can comprehend all that is necessary to salvation, and the scholar must pursue biblical truth with every exegetical tool available. Probably the most vital implication of Milton's biblical doctrine appears in his reiterated pleas for tolerance. Abs., *MiltonQ,* 12, 1978, 113.

3860 Harnack, Harvey Andrew. "The Typological Divine: A Study in the Figural Expression of Renaissance Kingship." Doctoral diss., Oklahoma State Univ., 1976. 223pp. Abs., *DAI,* 37, 1977, 5851A.

Follows the expansion and subsequent criticism of typology about the monarch in Spenser's poetry, Shakespeare's *Cymbeline,* and Milton's prose.

3861 Haskin, Dayton, S. J. "Milton's Strange Pantheon: The Apparent Tritheism of the *De Doctrina Christiana.*" *Heythrop Journal,* 16, 1975, 129–48.

Explores "Milton's views on the Father, Son, and Spirit in the light of certain assumptions about revelation and doctrine which he relies on and aims to sort out the quarrel over Milton's alleged 'Arianism.'" Abs., *MiltonQ,* 9, 1975, 90.

3862 Helgerson, Richard. "Milton Reads the King's Book: Print, Performance, and the Making of a Bourgeois Idol." *Criticism,* 29, 1987, 1–25.

Studies class-coding in Renaissance culture and the stigma against a gentleman's publishing. Applies these to the works of King James and to Milton's attack on King Charles in *Eikonoklastes.*

3863 Himy, Armand. "La *Logique* de

Milton." *Revue Philosophique*, 98, 1973, 155–70.

Ramus influenced Milton's A*rt of Logic* in two ways: concepts of logic which provide a foundation for his philosophical and theological speculations and a method in which dichotomy is fundamental.

3864 Hiroichiro, Doke. "Milton and Mortalism." *MCJ News*, 9, 1987, 29–30.

Abstract of a paper presented at the Twenty-First Colloquium of MCJ in July, 1986. Studies the *Christian Doctrine* to demonstrate Milton's belief in mortalism. Milton's view is consistent with early Christian views, as opposed to the Greeks' belief in the immortality of the soul.

3865 Hoffman, Richard L. "The Rhetorical Structure of Milton's *Second Defence of the People of England*." *SN*, 43, 1971, 227–45.

Analyzes the *Second Defence* in terms of "the classical oration, as identified by Quintilian and illustrated by Cicero."

3866 Hughes, Merritt Y. "Milton's Treatment of Reformation History in *The Tenure of Kings and Magistrates*." *The Seventeenth Century: Studies in the History of English Thought and Literature from Bacon to Pope*. Ed. by Richard Foster Jones and others (Stanford, CA: Stanford Univ. Press; London: Oxford Univ. Press, 1969), pp. 247–63.

Reprint of Huckabay No. 2918, originally published in 1951.

3867 Huguelet, Theodore L. "The Rule of Charity in Milton's Divorce Tracts." *MiltonS*, 6, 1974, 199–214.

Milton "observed that doctrinal charity becomes the 'supreme axiom' in the *method* of Scripture, or the art of divinity. Hence, by the axiom of charity, a literal, merciless interpretation of Christ's words on divorce would invert the Law and the Gospel and violate the divine dialectics of Scripture. Milton's confidence in his divorce argument was bolstered by his perception of divine method behind 'the all-interpreting voice of Charity.'"

3868 Hunter, W. B. "Further Definitions: Milton's Theological Vocabulary." *Bright Essence: Studies in Milton's Theology*. By Hunter, C. A. Patrides, and J. H. Adamson (Salt Lake City: Univ. of Utah Press, 1971), pp. 15–25.

Reprint of Huckabay No. 2926, originally published in 1964.

3869 Hunter, W. B. "Milton on the Incarnation." *Bright Essence: Studies in Milton's Theology*. By Hunter, C. A. Patrides, and J. H. Adamson (Salt Lake City: Univ. of Utah Press, 1971), pp. 131–48.

Reprint of Huckabay Nos. 661 and 2923, originally published in 1960.

3870 Hunter, W. B. "Milton's Arianism Reconsidered." *Bright Essence: Studies in Milton's Theology*. By Hunter, C. A. Patrides, and J. H. Adamson (Salt Lake City: Univ. of Utah Press, 1971), pp. 29–51.

Reprint of Huckabay No. 2924, originally published in 1959.

3871 Hunter, William B., Jr. "The Theological Context of Milton's *Christian Doctrine*." *Achievements of the Left Hand: Essays on the Prose of John Milton*. Ed. by Michael Lieb and John T. Shawcross (Amherst: Univ. of Massachusetts Press, 1974), pp. 269–87. Reprinted in *The Descent of Urania: Studies in Milton, 1946–1988* (Lewisburg, PA: Bucknell Univ. Press; London and Toronto: Associated Univ. Presses, 1989), pp. 73–90.

Accepts a 1655–60 date of composition and identifies the readers for whom Milton composed the treatise: the traditional Calvinists, the moderates, and the radicals. He hoped "to bring together these separate sects on a common Christian ground."

3872 Huntley, Frank Livingstone. "Who 'Confuted' John Milton in 1642?" *Essays in Persuasion: On Seventeenth-Century English Literature* (Chicago, IL, and London: Univ. of Chicago Press, 1981), pp. 77–85.

Supports the view that the "Confuter" provoking Milton's *Apology* was "not Bishop Hall but the Reverend Robert Dunkin, a loyal and little known vicar in Hall's own diocese."

3873 Huntley, John F. "The Images of Poet and Poetry in Milton's *The Reason of Church-Government*." *Achievements of the Left Hand: Essays on the Prose of John Milton.* Ed. by Michael Lieb and John T. Shawcross (Amherst: Univ. of Massachusetts Press, 1974), pp. 83–120.

Argues that "the organization of Milton's pamphlet was acutely and subtly conceived, and that its 'digression' served as keystone in Milton's rhetorical and argumentative strategy."

3874 Illo, John. "*Areopagitica*s Mythic and Real." *PSt*, 11, 1988, 3–23.

Examines Milton's political and religious viewpoint and ascribes popular misreadings of *Areopagitica* to reactionary movements of Milton's critics away from the enlightened viewpoint from which he wrote.

3875 Illo, John. "The Misreading of Milton." *Radical Perspectives in the Arts.* Ed. by Lee Baxandall (Harmondsworth and Baltimore, MD: Penguin, 1972), pp. 178–92.

Reprint of Huckabay No. 2928, originally published in 1965. Abs., *MiltonQ*, 7, 1973, 57; corrected on p. 94.

3876 Jacobson, Howard. "Milton's *Second Defence* and Sallust." *N&Q*, 31, 1984, 327.

Asserts that Milton based the Preface of the *Second Defence* on that of Sallust's *Catilinae Coniuratio*.

3877 Javanaud, R. "Faith and Reason: Some Aspects of Milton's Theology." M.Phil. thesis, Univ. of Liverpool, 1983. Abs., *IT*, 35, 1986, 45.

On *Christian Doctrine* and *Paradise Lost.*

3878 Jebb, Richard Claverhouse. *Milton's "Areopagitica."* Folcroft, PA: Folcroft Library Editions, 1969, 1974; Norwood, PA: Norwood Editions, 1977; Philadelphia, PA: R. West, 1978.

Reprints of Stevens No. 1263, originally published in 1918.

3879 Jochums, Milford C. "Yale Prose Milton—A Correction." *N&Q*, 28, 1981, 205.

Offers evidence that in *Of Reformation*, Milton's reference to the Paphnutius story derives from Socrates's *Scholasticus*. See No. 366.

3880 Johnson, Clarence O. "A Note on Milton's Use of *Gamut* in *Areopagitica*." *ELN*, 14, 1977, 187–89.

"The suggestion that the censors even bother with such a mutant is a decidedly sharp Miltonic barb. If we consider *gamut* as it was originally used, i.e., *gam ut* (*ut* being the lowest note in the scale *gamma*), the implication is that the censors would sink to their lowest endeavor in licensing this music."

3881 Kelley, Maurice. "Considerations Touching the Right Editing of John Milton's *De Doctrina Christiana*." *Editing Seventeenth Century Prose.* Ed. by D. I. B. Smith (Toronto: Hakkert for the Committee of the Conference on Editorial Problems, 1972), pp. 31–50.

Demonstrates that both Charles Sumner and the editors of the Columbia Edition of the *Works* (see No. 295) take too much liberty with the text and suggests that any future editor follow the style and format of Milton's amanuensis, Jeremie Picard. Concludes, however, that it is impossible to reconstruct the manuscript as Milton left it in 1674 because of the changes made by another amanuensis, Daniel Skinner.

3882 Kelliher, W. Hilton. "Erasmus' *Adagia* and Milton's *Mane Citus Lectum Fuge*." *MiltonQ*, 5, 1971, 73–74.

Suggests that Milton's quotation from Homer in his school theme on early rising was taken at second hand from Erasmus's *Adagia.*

3883 Kendrick, Christopher. "Ethics and the Orator in *Areopagitica*." *ELH*, 50, 1983, 655–91.

Argues that Milton is a monist and that he invokes natural law rather than divine law because of the controversy over toleration.

3884 Kendrick, Christopher. *Milton: A Study in Ideology and Form.* New York and London: Methuen, 1986. x, 240pp.

Studies *Areopagitica* and *Paradise Lost* "in relation to the collective agency of revolution and as determinate acts within that agency, as symbolic revolutionary acts themselves." Argues that Milton is an early proponent of the capitalist system.

3885 Keplinger, Ann. "Milton: Polemics, Epic, and the Woman Problem, Again." *Cithara*, 10, No. 2, 1971, 40–52.

Considers Milton's motive for entering the divorce controversy, his polemical techniques, and his arguments.

3886 Keplinger, Ann. "Milton's *An Apology for Smectymnuus.*" *Expl*, 30, 1972, Item 66.

Asserts that in the *Apology* the reference to man as "a true poem" is directly related to the use of the Greek word "poieo" in Ephesians 2.10, which describes man as a "product" of God. Suggests that Milton's early works are based as solidly on theological doctrine as his later ones.

3887 King, James Roy. "Psyche's Tasks— Milton's Sense of Self." *Studies in Six Seventeenth Century Writers* (Athens: Ohio Univ. Press, 1966), pp. 193–218.

Uses Milton's allusion to the Amor and Psyche myth in *Areopagitica* to explain some of the important motifs in his poetry.

3888 Kirby, R. Kenneth. "Milton's Biblical Hermeneutics in *The Doctrine and Discipline of Divorce.*" *MiltonQ*, 18, 1984, 116–25.

Believes that Milton demonstrates the "Protestant Scholastic" priority of reason over faith by departing from a literal interpretation of Christ's teachings on divorce.

3889 Kivette, Ruth M. "The Ways and Wars of Truth." *MiltonQ*, 6, No. 4, 1972, 81–86.

Discusses the origin and appropriateness of the textual change from "wayfaring Christian" to "warfaring Christian" in the edition of *Areopagitica* in the Yale *Complete Prose Works* (No. 366). Argues that Milton intended "wayfaring."

3890 Kouchi, Saburo. "Modernity of *Areopagitica.*" *MCJ News*, 4, 1980, 4–5.

Believes that pamphlets such as Milton's had little or no influence over policy decisions.

3891 Kranidas, Thomas. "'Decorum' and the Style of Milton's Antiprelatical Tracts." *Seventeenth-Century Prose: Modern Essays in Criticism.* Ed. by Stanley E. Fish (New York: Oxford Univ. Press, 1971), pp. 475–88.

Reprint of Huckabay No. 2956, originally published in 1965.

3892 Kranidas, Thomas. "Milton on Teachers and Teaching." *MiltonQ*, 20, 1986, 26–29.

Discusses Milton's views on the office of teacher. Believes that Milton is harsh toward formal education because he holds that the teacher's role is sacred: "the teacher is included with the poet and preacher in the vocation of Evangelist—speakers of the Word unmediated."

3893 Kranidas, Thomas. "Milton's *Of Reformation*: The Politics of Vision." *ELH*, 49, 1982, 497–513.

Throughout *Of Reformation*, "the rational mind has sought to establish praise and blame, to urge the reader on to judgment in the final great vision of a judging and merciful God revealed at the last day as rational beyond our comprehension."

3894 Kranidas, Thomas. "Milton's Trinculo." *N&Q*, 26, 1979, 416.

Suggests that Milton's Trinculo in the *Apology* is a fusion of the Trinculo figures in Thomas Tomkys's *Albumazar* and Shakespeare's the *Tempest*. Discusses the anonymous *Plot Discovered and Counterplotted* as another possible source.

3895 Kranidas, Thomas. "Polarity and Structure in Milton's *Areopagitica*." *ELR*, 14, 1984, 175–90.

Argues that *Areopagitica* has both an oratorical structure and a structure based on polarization.

3896 Kranidas, Thomas. "Style and Rectitude in Seventeenth-Century Prose: Hall, Smectymnuus, and Milton." *HLQ*, 46, 1983, 237–69.

Views Milton's prose tracts within their contemporary context and defends his language, especially that found in *Animadversions*.

3897 Kranidas, Thomas. "Two Notes on Milton's *An Apology*." *MiltonQ*, 17, 1983, 47–48.

Argues that in the *Apology*, Milton intends the word "chafe" to stand and disagrees with the editors of the Columbia Edition of the *Works* (see No. 295) that it should be emended to "chase." Also believes that Milton's attack on academic drama in the work responds to Archbishop Laud, "who had prosecuted William Prynne for the *Histriomastix* (1633) and who was known to favor masques and stageplays."

3898 Kranidas, Thomas. "Words, Words, Words, and the Word: Milton's *Of Prelatical Episcopacy*." *MiltonS*, 16, 1982, 153–66.

States that the work's argument demonstrates "rigorous rational humanity" in its emphasis on the study of the Scriptures.

3899 Labriola, Albert C. "Milton's *Familiar Letters*: A Study in Intellectual Autobiography." *MiltonQ*, 12, 1978, 43–44.

Abstract of a paper presented at the 1977 MLA Convention. Focuses on the idea of friendship to suggest "how the *Familiar Letters* provide many insights into a psychobiographical

portrait of a man who was as versatile as he was erudite."

3900 Larson, Charles. "Milton and 'N. T.': An Analogue to *The Tenure of Kings and Magistrates*." *MiltonQ*, 9, 1975, 107–10.

Notes similarities between N. T.'s *The Resolver; or, A Short Word to the Large Question of the Times* (1649) and Milton's work.

3901 Le Comte, Edward. "*Areopagitica* as a Scenario for *Paradise Lost*." *Milton's Unchanging Mind* (Port Washington, NY, and London: Kennikat Press, 1973), pp. 69–98. Reprinted in *Achievements of the Left Hand: Essays on the Prose of John Milton*. Ed. by Michael Lieb and John T. Shawcross (Amherst: Univ. of Massachusetts Press, 1974), pp. 121–41.

Explains how *Areopagitica* looks back to the planned Arthuriad and also contains hints of *Paradise Lost*.

3902 Lejosne, Roger. "Nature Humaine et Loi Divine dans le *Tetrachordon*." *EA*, 27, 1974, 415–24.

Analyzes the places in *Tetrachordon* where Milton comments on the four principal biblical texts about marriage—Genesis, Deuteronomy, Matthew, and 1 Corinthians. Shows that the institution of marriage includes the possibility of divorce.

3903 Lieb, Michael. "Milton's *Of Reformation* and the Dynamics of Controversy." *Achievements of the Left Hand: Essays on the Prose of John Milton*. Ed. by Lieb and John T. Shawcross (Amherst: Univ. of Massachusetts Press, 1974), pp. 55–82.

Considers "Milton's tract thematically and structurally as a way of determining the fundamental issues underlying polemical discourse." Contends that Milton "drew upon prevailing modes of discourse in order to transcend them."

3904 Lieb, Michael, and **John T. Shawcross,** eds. *Achievements of the Left Hand: Essays on the Prose of John Milton*. Amherst: Univ. of Massachusetts Press, 1974. viii, 396pp.

A collection of essays by William B. Hunter, Jr., John F. Huntley, Edward S. Le Comte, Walter J. Ong, S. J., Florence Sandler, Harry Smallenburg, Joseph Anthony Wittreich, Jr., Austin Woolrych, Lieb, and Shawcross. In this bibliography, each essay is listed according to classification and author. Reviews: Joseph Anthony Wittreich, Jr., *MiltonQ*, 8, 1974, 15–21; Marcia Landy, *SCN*, 33, 1975, 59–61; Andrew M. McLean, *SHR*, 10, 1976, 362–69; Donald A. Roberts, *RenQ*, 29, 1976, 141–43; Sidney Warhaft, *Mosaic*, 9, 1976, 159–73.

3905 Limouze, Henry Sanford. "The Context and Method of Milton's Early English Prose." Doctoral diss., Johns Hopkins Univ., 1977. 260pp. Abs., *DAI*, 41, 1980, 669A.

Explains common themes of individuality, choice, and virtue, along with Milton's repeated use of dichotomization (often through imagery) in his early prose.

3906 Limouze, Henry S. "'The Surest Suppressing': Writer and Censor in Milton's *Areopagitica*." *CentR*, 24, 1980, 103–17.

Argues that "Milton's tract spoke to its readers, and speaks to them still, as reasonable moral beings, and that his subject throughout is the free choice of the individual." Abs., *MiltonQ*, 10, 1976, 132.

3907 Loewenstein, David A. "*Areopagitica* and the Dynamics of History." *SEL*, 28, 1988, 77–93.

Contends that "*Areopagitica* concerns the interconnection between renovation and revolution in history" by arguing that "historical renewal occurs as a consequence of continual friction between opposing forces and ideologies . . . which paradoxically contribute to '*the unity of Spirit*' . . . in church and state alike."

3908 Low, Anthony. "Milton's Eagle and Pindar's *Olympia II*." *ELN*, 18, 1981, 179–80.

Suggests the image of the eagle and the crows in Pindar's ode as a possible source for Milton's image comparing the English nation to a mighty eagle surrounded by "a gabbling flock of birds" in *Areopagitica*.

3909 Low, Anthony. "'Plato, and His Equall Xenophon': A Note on Milton's *Apology for Smectymnuus*." *MiltonQ*, 4, 1970, 20–22.

Interprets Milton's use of the term "equall" and suggests that "the *Cyropaedia* may have been in Milton's mind when he coupled Xenophon with Plato as a philosopher in the *Apology*."

3910 Lusignam, Francine. "L'*Artis Logicae Plenior Institutio* de John Milton: État de la Question et Position." Doctoral diss., Université of Montreal, 1974.

3911 Lutaud, Olivier. "Le 'Savant Instituteur' et les 'Labour'd Studies of the French' (*Of Education* en Français et en France)." *EA*, 27, 1974, 404–14.

Traces and documents the incomplete knowledge of the tract in France and asserts the need for a definitive French translation of it.

3912 Manuszak, David. "Milton's *Apology against a Pamphlet* and the Communion Liturgy." *ELN*, 22, No. 3, 1985, 39–41.

Examines Milton's criticism of church liturgy, especially its use in communion, in the *Apology*. Shows how Milton at one point parodies a section of the prayer book.

3913 Martinet, Marie-Madeleine. "'British Troy': Milton entre l'Éternel Retour des Origines Antiques et la Liberté Anglaise Toujours Recommencée: de l'Histoire Mythique à l'Histoire Critique." *Prélude au Matin d'un Poète: "Such Sights as Youthful Poets Dream": Traditions Humanistes chez le Jeune Milton*. Introduction by Olivier Lutaud (Paris: Centre d'Histoire des Idées dans les Iles Britanniques,

Université de Paris IV, Sorbonne, 1983), pp. 62–76.

In the *History of Britain*, mythological allusions are integrated into Milton's historiography as he studies the revolution of time and examines the succession of empires.

3914 Mason, Julian. "Milton Modifies a Metaphor: 'Veritas Filia Temporis.'" *MiltonQ*, 12, 1978, 101–04.

Examines the allusion, in the *Doctrine and Discipline of Divorce*, to an allegorical tradition that truth is the child of time, which is part of a larger allegorical tradition that attributes a cause and effect relationship to truth and time.

3915 McCabe, Richard. "The Form and Methods of Milton's *Animadversions upon the Remonstrant's Defence against Smectymnuus.*" *ELN*, 18, 1981, 266–72.

Suggests that Milton used the form and methods of his adversary Bishop Joseph Hall. "The devastating style and methods of the *Animadversions*, suggested ironically by the techniques of Hall's well-known *Apologie* of 1610, were designed to counteract the effect of the bishop's powerful rhetoric on the episcopal debate by treating him as disrespectfully as he had treated his opponents."

3916 McGuire, Mary Ann. "'A Most Just Vituperation': Milton's Christian Orator in *Pro Se Defensio.*" *SLitI*, 10, No. 2, 1977, 105–14.

Rejects the argument that the abusive rhetoric in the *First Defence* is simply "a lapse in taste." Rather, contends that Milton followed the example of other Puritan writers who "frequently used abusive language to castigate opponents." Concludes that he "defends vituperation as a necessary tool of the wayfaring, warfaring Christian," justifying invective as both an end and a means to attain it.

3917 Melczer, William. "Looking Back without Anger: Milton's *Of Education.*"

Milton and the Middle Ages. Ed. by John Mulryan (Lewisburg, PA: Bucknell Univ. Press; London and Toronto: Associated Univ. Presses, 1982), pp. 91–102.

Denies that the pamphlet is a humanistic document; insists instead that it reflects a return to Aristotelianism on several levels.

3918 Mendelsohn, Leonard R. "Milton and the Rabbis: A Later Inquiry." *SEL*, 18, 1978, 125–35.

"But by examining Milton's prose works from a perspective centered in a knowledge of rabbinic writings, it is possible to demonstrate that, although some of his material was ultimately from rabbinic sources, Milton did not, and in all likelihood could not, read the rabbinic commentators." Abs., *MiltonQ*, 13, 1979, 61–62.

3919 Miller, Anthony. "'Scotus or Aquinas'—and Horace." *MiltonQ*, 22, 1988, 1–3.

Claims that in *Areopagitica*, Milton "follow[s] Horace in elevating the poet as ethical teacher by dismissing two of the poet's rivals with such conspicuous and magisterial off-handedness."

3920 Miller, Leo. "Another Milton State Paper Recovered and a Mystery Demystified." *ELN*, 25, No. 1, 1987, 21–33.

Clarifies the dating of a letter from the Council of State to the Duke of Tuscany and furnishes details about the protocol involved in the composition of the letters of state.

3921 Miller, Leo. "The Burning of Milton's Books in 1660: Two Mysteries." *ELR*, 18, 1988, 424–37.

Discusses the burning of certain books by Milton, such as *Eikonoklastes* and the *First Defence*. Relates these burnings to the return of Charles II when he condemned people and books that had a bearing on his father's death.

3922 Miller, Leo. "Establishing the Text of Milton's State Papers." *TEXT*, 2, 1985, 181–86.

Emphasizes the importance of the State

Papers, discusses the history of their publication, and concludes that a definitive text is needed.

3923 Miller, Leo. "The Italian Imprimaturs in Milton's *Areopagitica.*" *PBSA*, 65, 1971, 345–55.

Tentatively concludes that the imprimatur "in Galileo's *Dialogo* is unique and supplied the third example" in Milton's *Areopagitica* of "books published in Italy whose imprimaturs testified that they had been 'approv'd and licenc't under the hands of 2 or 3 glutton Friers.'"

3924 Miller, Leo. "Milton Edits Freigius' *Life of Ramus.*" *Ren&R*, 8, 1972, 112–14.

Describes how Milton edited and cut Freigius's *Life of Peter Ramus* for inclusion in the 1672 publication of the *Art of Logic.*

3925 Miller, Leo. "Milton, Salmasius and Hammond: The History of an Insult." *Ren&R*, 9, 1973, 108–15.

Describes Milton's teasing of "Salmasius for sensitivity to the epithet *Grammaticus,*" which the Reverend Henry Hammond bestowed on him, with the result that Salmasius called Hammond a "nebulo" (knave). In effect, Milton set two Stuart defenders into needling each other.

3926 Miller, Leo. "Milton, Salmasius and 'Vapulandum': Who Should be Flogged?" *MiltonQ*, 9, 1975, 70–75.

On Milton's criticizing Salmasius's use of "persona" meaning "person," in the *First Defence*, while at the same time using an apparently incorrect Latin form, "vapulandum." Justifies Milton's use of the form.

3927 Miller, Leo. "Milton's *Apology.*" *Expl*, 44, No. 2, 1986, 20–21.

Discusses Milton's use of the word "humm'd" in his condemnation of Oxford and Cambridge sermons in the *Apology.* Explains that humming was a contemporary form of applause.

3928 Miller, Leo. "Milton's Conversations with Schlezer and His Letters to

Brandenburg." *N&Q*, 34, 1987, 321–24.

Discusses Milton's letters to Friedrich Wilhelm, Elector of Brandenburg, and his relationship with Johann Friedrich Schlezer. Prints a newly discovered letter. See No. 3933.

3929 Miller, Leo. "Milton's *Eikon Alethine* Located." *MiltonQ*, 9, 1975, 64.

Found in the New York Public Library.

3930 Miller, Leo. "Milton's State Letters: The Lünig Version." *N&Q*, 17, 1970, 412–14.

Describes a previously unnoticed text printed in Leipzig in 1712 and notes differences between it and the 1676, 1690, and Columbia editions (see No. 295).

3931 Miller, Leo. "Milton's State Papers: 'Spirensis Camera,' 'Ann of Foy,' and Other Obscurities." *N&Q*, 16, 1969, 95–96.

Identifies various geographical references in the letters of state and notes some inaccurate translations in Edward Phillips's English version of 1694.

3932 Miller, Leo. "Some Inferences from Milton's Hebrew." *MiltonQ*, 18, 1984, 41–46.

On Milton's knowledge of the Hebrew Scriptures. Claims that three questionable spellings "*must be ascribed to errors in printing Milton's psalm paraphrases in 1673 with inadequate proof reading.*" Milton's rebuttal of Salmasius's *Defensio Regia* shows his "*grasp of the subtleties to be found in the language of the Hebrew Scriptures.*" Finally, the miswritten Hebrew words in the *Christian Doctrine* suggest that the Skinner transcript "*was not begun until the very last days of Milton's life; or even more likely, it was not begun until after Milton was dead.*"

3933 Miller, Leo. "Two Milton *State Letters*: New Dates and New Insights." *N&Q*, 33, 1986, 461–64.

Uses evidence such as revisions in Milton's Latin versions of letters of state to ascertain dates. Concludes that other State Papers translated by Milton may be discovered in the future. Corrects the spelling of "vester" to "vestro" in No. 3928.

3934 Morkan, Joel. "Milton's *Areopagitica*: A Reason for the Title." *N&Q*, 20, 1973, 167–68.
Suggests that Milton wanted to evoke the earlier Anglican-Puritan (Hall-Smectymnuus) debates on church government.

3935 Nagaoka, Kaoru. "The Basic Ideas To Maintain Milton's Political Theories." *MCJ News*, 3, 1979, 4–5.
"It is essential to remember that politics for Milton was deeply rooted in the soil of religion; for him, politics was not influenced solely by economic factors."

3936 Nordell, Roderick. "Words to the Wise, 1674–1974." *Christian Science Monitor*, Jan. 23, 1974, p. 1.
Offers several quotations from Milton's prose for the benefit of candidates during the 1974 American election campaign.

3937 Noro, Yuko. "Liberty and Slavery in *Pro Populo Anglicano Defensio*." *MCJ News*, 11, 1989, 3–7.
Abstract of a paper presented at the Fourteenth Annual Conference of MCJ in October, 1988. States that in the *First Defence*, Milton answers critics of the Commonwealth by comparing them to slaves who would rather blindly follow a tyrant than depose him. Conversely, "liberty" is present only when "the public body, grounded upon right reason," chooses a king who can be deposed if he becomes a tyrant.

3938 Nyquist, Mary. "The Genesis of Gendered Subjectivity in the Divorce Tracts and in *Paradise Lost*." *Re-membering Milton: Essays on the Texts and Traditions*. Ed. by Nyquist and Margaret W. Ferguson (New York and London: Methuen, 1987), pp. 99–127.
Argues that the divorce tracts contain "deeply masculinist assumptions . . . in Milton's articulation of a radically bourgeois view of marriage." Milton gives Adam priority in the divorce tracts, not because of the order of his creation, but because of the divine words instituting marriage in Genesis 2.18.

3939 Nyquist, Mary. "Gynesis, Genesis, Exegesis, and the Formation of Milton's Eve." *Cannibals, Witches, and Divorce: Estranging the Renaissance*. Selected Papers from the English Institute, 1985. Ed. by Marjorie Garber (Baltimore, MD, and London: Johns Hopkins Univ. Press, 1987), pp. 147–208.
Surveys studies of the J and P texts of Genesis. Observes that J's creation story has been used through the centuries to oppress women. Questions the assumption that the J account should receive the precedence that Milton gives it. In the divorce tracts, he sometimes uses plural pronouns to refer to the married couple, but often his argument comes to rest with the nongenerically masculine "he." Milton ultimately promotes the patriarchal system.

3940 Ohkawa, Akira. "On Milton's *Of Education*." *CEMF*, 24, 1981, 11–18.
In Japanese. Surveys the background of Milton's tract and discusses his conception of the goals of education.

3941 O'Keeffe, Timothy J. "The Imaginal Strategy of John Milton's *Eikonoklastes*." *BSUF*, 11, No. 4, 1970, 33–45.
Points out some of the many clusters of images aimed against Charles I and gives examples of imagery concerning him (as a slave and oriental tyrant) and the church (the sword of judgment). Concludes that Milton uses an imaginal strategy to appeal "to logic, emotion, and even prejudice."

3942 Olsen, V. Norskov. *The New Testament Logia on Divorce: A Study of Their Interpretation from Erasmus to Milton*. Tübingen: J. C. B. Mohr (Paul Siebeck), 1971. vi, 161pp.

Examines Reformation interpretations, including Milton's, of the New Testament divorce texts.

3943 Ong, Walter J. "Printer's Legerdemain in Milton's *Artis Logicae Plenior Institutio.*" *TCBS*, 6, 1974, 167–74.

Studies the collation of the first edition of the *Art of Logic* and explains the printer's cutting out of leaves and substituting others with faked signatures.

3944 Paramonova, T. I. "Antiepikkopal'nye traktaty Dzhona Mil'tona." *Uchenye Zapiski Turkmenskogo Universiteta* (Ashkhabad), 63, 1971, 107–26.

"John Milton's Anticlerical Tracts."

3945 Patrick, J. Max. "Significant Aspects of the Miltonic State Papers." *HLQ*, 33, 1970, 321–30.

Explores the importance of the State Papers and how their rhetoric and style, their characterizations and ideas illuminate Milton's other works.

3946 Patterson, Annabel. "The Civic Hero in Milton's Prose." *MiltonS*, 8, 1975, 71–101.

"In wrestling with the problematical role of the intellectual in times of crisis, and in trying to define that role as heroic, Milton created a linguistic and metaphoric synthesis of action and contemplation which differs from the passive fortitude of the great poems." Abs., *MiltonQ*, 9, 1975, 123.

3947 Perlette, John M. "Anthony Ascham's 'Of Marriage.'" *ELR*, 3, 1973, 284–305.

Believes that "if the treatise is in fact a reply to Milton, it is the only genuinely rational and reasonable one which we know of." Compares Milton's and Ascham's views on marriage and divorce. Abs., *MiltonQ*, 7, 1973, 91.

3948 Perlette, John M. "Milton, Ascham, and the Rhetoric of the Divorce Controversy." *MiltonS*, 10, 1977, 195–215.

Believes that Anthony Ascham's brief essay, "Of Marriage" (1647–48), constitutes a refutation of Milton's thesis on divorce. Abs., *MiltonQ*, 12, 1978, 156.

3949 Perlmutter, Eila Siren. "Milton's Three Degrees of Grace: A Study of Predestination in *Paradise Lost* and the *De Doctrina Christiana.*" Doctoral diss., State Univ. of New York, Albany, 1971. 202pp. Abs., *DAI*, 33, 1972, 2901A–02A.

Believes Milton challenges Augustinian-Calvinist views on predestination by subjecting humanity to three degrees of grace, determined by one's choice to instruct, obey, or rebel.

3950 Pittion, J.-P. "Milton, La Place, and Socinianism." *RES*, 23, 1972, 138–46.

Identifies a source that Milton discusses in the *Christian Doctrine*, Josué de La Place's *Disputationes*, and assesses its significance in "the context of seventeenth-century theological controversies on Socinianism." Shows "how this source can help to date chapter five of the first book of Milton's treatise."

3951 Potts, James Basil, Jr. "Milton's Deviations from Standard Biblical Interpretation in the Discussion of Divorce." Doctoral diss., Univ. of Mississippi, 1968. 276pp. Abs., *DA*, 29, 1968, 1213A.

Analyzes Milton's unorthodox arguments—used only when discussing divorce—that the Holy Spirit can lead an "individual to disobey the written word" and that biblical charity refers to temporal good.

3952 Proudfoot, D. S., and D. Deslandres. "Samuel Purchas and the Date of Milton's *Moscovia.*" *PQ*, 64, 1985, 260–65.

Uses Samuel Purchas's *Hakluytus Posthumus* to argue that Milton wrote the *Brief History of Moscovia* in 1626 while attending Cambridge.

3953 Rajan, Balachandra. "*Areopagitica* and the Images of Truth." *The Form of the Unfinished: English Poetics from Spenser to Pound* (Princeton, NJ: Princeton Univ. Press, 1985), pp. 85–103.

Points out that "human effort can only approximate . . . the truth, and a final act of integration remains reserved for a force of coherence beyond time." Just as Isis never found all the pieces of Osiris's body, so *Areopagitica* is another example of the unfinished.

3954 Ramage, Sarah Thorpe. "Milton's Nationalism as Exemplified in His Early Prose." Doctoral diss., Yale Univ., 1942. 279pp. Abs., *DAI*, 43, 1983, 3605A.

Examines the three components of Milton's nationalism—a call to improve the church and state, use of the native English language, and reference to earlier English writers—in his eleven reform pamphlets.

3955 Richek, Roslyn. "Thomas Randolph's *Salting* (1627), Its Text, and John Milton's Sixth Prolusion as Another Salting." *ELR*, 12, 1982, 103–31.

Focuses on Randolph's "salting" and the tradition of salting or initiation of freshmen by seniors into the various colleges at Cambridge. Contends that Milton's *Prolusion 6* is an account of a salting in the tradition of Randolph.

3956 Ridden, Geoffrey M. "Winstanley's Allusion to Milton." *N&Q*, 31, 1984, 321–23.

States that Milton's contemporary Gerrard Winstanley alluded to *Eikonoklastes* in the *Law of Freedom in a Platform*.

3957 Rosenberg, D. M. "Parody of Style in Milton's Polemics." *MiltonS*, 2, 1970, 113–18.

Shows how in *Animadversions* and the *Apology*, Milton exposes his adversaries' styles by impersonating them.

3958 Rosenberg, D. M. "Satirical Techniques in Milton's Polemical Prose." *SNL*, 8, 1971, 91–97.

Believes that the techniques of satire dominate Milton's persuasive rhetoric.

3959 Rosenberg, D. M. "Style and Meaning in Milton's Anti-Episcopal Tracts." *Criticism*, 15, 1973, 43–57.

Asserts that Milton's tracts are prayers attempting to clarify his idea of religious freedom. Claims that Milton "deliberately strove for the prophetic

style which transcends the sacramentalism . . . and . . . the formalities of pulpit preaching, pamphleteering, and conventional prayer."

3960 Rosenberg, D. M. "Theme and Structure in Milton's Autobiographies." *Genre*, 2, 1969, 314–25.

"Careful study of the autobiographies [the *Reason of Church-Government*, the *Apology*, and the *Second Defence*] will reveal Milton's gradual shift of emphasis from inward, emergent structures which reflect doubt and divisive uncertainty, to more stable and integrated structures which are built formally from without."

3961 Rosenberg, Martin E. "Truth and Power in *Areopagitica*: De Man's 'The Rhetoric of Blindness' and Milton's Epic Insight." *RaJAH*, 1988, pp. 59–86.

Deals mainly with the contradictions in *Areopagitica* and various critics' responses to them. Regards the work as a dilemma which produces an unresolvable tension.

3962 Rosenblatt, Jason P. "Milton's Chief Rabbi." *MiltonS*, 24, 1988, 43–71.

Acknowledges Milton's limited knowledge of Hebrew but argues that John Selden, his most learned contemporary in England and "the author of a half dozen immense rabbinical works, is the principal source of Milton's Jewish learning."

3963 Rosenblatt, Jason P. "*The Plot Discovered and Counterplotted.*" *ELR*, 15, 1985, 318–52.

Examines a copy of the *Plot Discovered* owned by Sir Edward Dering, who attributed the authorship to Milton. Offers no conclusive evidence that Milton wrote the tract.

3964 Rosenblatt, Jason P. "Sir Edward Dering's Milton." *MP*, 79, 1982, 376–85.

Offers evidence that Milton wrote the *Plot Discovered*, an anonymous antiprelatical pamphlet, but questions the attribution.

3965 Rusk, Robert R. "Milton." *The*

Doctrines of the Great Educators (London: Macmillan; New York: St. Martin's Press, 1969), pp. 112–26.

Discusses *Of Education.*

3966 Sadler, Lynn Veach. "Regeneration and Typology: *Samson Agonistes* and Its Relation to *De Doctrina Christiana*, *Paradise Lost*, and *Paradise Regained*." *SEL*, 12, 1972, 141–56.

Suggests that other works by Milton describe Samson as a type, not only of Christ, but of the regenerative power of faith in God.

3967 Sánchez, Reuben Márquez, Jr. "Persona and Decorum in Milton's Prose." Doctoral diss., Cornell Univ., 1986. 214pp. Abs., *DAI*, 47, 1987, 3051A.

Accounts for variations in persona by noting Milton's observance of decorum in different prose tracts, but asserts that "the persona is always a [principled] teacher."

3968 Sánchez, Reuben Márquez, Jr. "'The Worst of Superstitions': Milton's *Of True Religion* and the Issue of Religious Tolerance." *PSt*, 9, No. 3, 1986, 21–38.

Examines Milton's anticatholicism, puritanical outlook, and toleration toward all Protestant sects. States that each Miltonic tract has a distinct persona. In *Of True Religion*, that persona's manner of teaching ensnares the interpretive process of a sometimes unwilling audience.

3969 Sandler, Florence. "Icon and Iconoclast." *Achievements of the Left Hand: Essays on the Prose of John Milton.* Ed. by Michael Lieb and John T. Shawcross (Amherst: Univ. of Massachusetts Press, 1974), pp. 160–84.

Discusses King Charles's attitude toward himself and toward monarchy, the religious and political background of his trial and execution, and the aftermath. Suggests that Milton avoids crucifixion scenes in his poetry because Charles had equated his martyrdom with Christ's.

3970 Sasek, Lawrence A. "'*Plato*, and

His Equall *Xenophon*.'" *ELN*, 7, 1970, 260–62.

Believes that Milton's line in the *Apology* refers to Xenophon's equality "as teacher, not as literary craftsman or philosopher."

3971 Schoen, Raymond G. "Milton and Spenser's Cave of Mammon Episode." *PQ*, 54, 1975, 684–89.

Finds that in *Areopagitica*, "Milton revises Spenser not because of their differing ethical persuasions, but because Milton is thinking in terms of poetic rather than philosophic traditions." Abs., *MiltonQ*, 10, 1976, 133; *SpenN*, 7, 1976, 27.

3972 Sewell, Arthur. *A Study in Milton's "Christian Doctrine."* Oxford: Oxford Univ. Press, 1966, 1967; Hamden, CT: Archon Books, 1967; Folcroft, PA: Folcroft Library Editions, 1969; Norwood, PA: Norwood Editions, 1975; Philadelphia, PA: R. West, 1977.

Reprints of Huckabay No. 3036, originally published in 1939.

3973 Sharma, Vinod C. "Johnson's Criticism of Milton's Scheme of Education." *Univ. of Rajasthan Studies in English*, 4, 1969, 32–43.

Concludes that Samuel Johnson's criticism of Milton's theories of education is justified, "that nobody can learn all these subjects in a limited period of nine years as Milton intended."

3974 Shawcross, John T. "A Contemporary Letter Concerning Milton's State Papers." *MiltonQ*, 15, 1981, 119–20.

Presents a transcript of a letter dated November 6, 1676, from Sir Leoline Jenkins to Sir Joseph Williamson, which disparages Milton because of his position with the Interregnum government.

3975 Shawcross, John T. "The Higher Wisdom of *The Tenure of Kings and Magistrates*." *Achievements of the Left Hand: Essays on the Prose of John Milton.* Ed. by Michael Lieb and Shawcross (Amherst: Univ. of Massachusetts Press, 1974), pp. 142–59.

Argues that Milton's *Tenure* is modern in its radical views; yet it is a failure because Milton did not achieve his goals. Like idealists of our own time, Milton pays insufficient attention to his audience and is wrong in assuming that people will listen to right reason.

3976 Shawcross, John T. "A Survey of Milton's Prose Works." *Achievements of the Left Hand: Essays on the Prose of John Milton.* Ed. by Michael Lieb and Shawcross (Amherst: Univ. of Massachusetts Press, 1974), pp. 291–391.

"This survey of Milton's prose attempts to pull together all known information about editions, dates of composition, public reaction to and knowledge of the works, and general scholarly discussions of them."

3977 Shullenberger, William. "Linguistic and Poetic Theory in Milton's *De Doctrina Christiana*." *ELN*, 19, 1982, 262–78.

Examines "the structural principles of language and metaphor implicit in *De Doctrina Christiana*, and . . . suggest[s] their importance in Milton's high estimation of his treatise." Abs., *MiltonQ*, 17, 1983, 100.

3978 Smallenburg, Harry R. "Contiguities and Moving Limbs: Style as Argument in *Areopagitica*." *MiltonS*, 9, 1976, 169–84.

The tract's "intuitive, imaginative" and "logical, discursive" argumentative modes are integrated and "suggest that truth, which has a divine life of its own, must be allowed to appear freely, unconstrained by the necessarily limited forms and perceptions of human beings."

3979 Smallenburg, Harry. "Government of the Spirit: Style, Structure and Theme in *Treatise of Civil Power*." *Achievements of the Left Hand: Essays on the Prose of John Milton.* Ed. by Michael Lieb and John T. Shawcross (Amherst: Univ. of Massachusetts Press, 1974), pp. 219–38.

"The mood of the *Treatise* is unity and harmony, easy conjunction of elements

that have been in conflict. The style of the tract answers to the decorum of the entities represented; they in turn have been created in response to a need in the polity."

3980 Smallenburg, Harry Russell. "Structures of Truth: Milton's Affective Polemic." Doctoral diss., Univ. of California, Berkeley, 1970. 230pp. Abs., *DAI*, 32, 1971, 985A.

Demonstrates that "Milton's prose style is intentional and functional"; every tract is "a vital and active representation and enactment of the truth for which it argues."

3981 Smith, James Robert. "A Linguistic Description of Milton's Prose Style." Doctoral diss., Univ. of Alabama, 1972. 192pp. Abs., *DAI*, 33, 1972, 2954A.

Analyzes the grammar and syntax of a sample of Milton's prose to describe his style in "objective, quantitative terms."

3982 Spear, Gary Neil. "Milton and the Political Text." Doctoral diss., Stanford Univ., 1987. 238pp. Abs., *DAI*, 48, 1988, 2882A.

Maps "a strategy for reading Milton's political works as works which both mediate and reproduce the historical, social, and economic struggles of the English Revolution."

3983 Speer, Diane Parkin. "Freedom of Speech: Milton's View of Polemic and His Polemical Works." Doctoral diss., Univ. of Iowa, 1970. 221pp. Abs., *DAI*, 31, 1970, 1241A–42A.

Examines the rhetorical ideas governing Milton's "polemical approach and the influences of opposing works" on the tactics of his answers.

3984 Speer, Diane Parkin. "Milton's *Defensio Prima*: Ethos and Vituperation in a Polemic Engagement." *QJS*, 56, 1970, 277–83.

Analyzes Milton's "response within a rhetorical situation" to show "his mastery of persuasive technique and refutation, most notably in countering the *ethos* of his opponent and constructing his own *ethos* to reinforce the arguments against the monarchy."

3985 Stavely, Keith Williams. "The Evolution of Milton's Prose Rhetoric." Doctoral diss., Yale Univ., 1969. 260pp. Abs., *DAI*, 31, 1970, 1296A.

Argues that modifications of "imagination, reason, and emotion" in Milton's prose are responses to "private enthusiasms" and later to "the changing public patterns of the Puritan Revolution."

3986 Stavely, Keith W. *The Politics of Milton's Prose Style.* Yale Studies in English, 185. New Haven, CT, and London: Yale Univ. Press, 1975. ix, 136pp.

Deals with the style of Milton's political tracts from *Of Reformation* to the *Readie and Easie Way*. Sees his prose as "a medium of imaginative expression" that is worthy of the literary critic's scrutiny. Ironically, the "'poetic' texture limits the political effectiveness of Milton's prose instead of extending and enriching it." Reviews: James Egan, *SCN*, 33, 1975, 90–92; *VQR*, 51, 1975, 154; Gerald L. Evans, *LJ*, 100, 1975, 856; *MiltonQ*, 10, 1976, 126–28; Christopher Grose, *JEGP*, 75, 1976, 430–33; Michael Lieb, *MP*, 74, 1976, 204–12; Geoffrey Ridden, *TLS*, Mar. 26, 1976, p. 352.

3987 Stavely, Keith W. "The Style and Structure of Milton's *Readie and Easie Way*." *MiltonS*, 5, 1973, 269–87.

"When Milton contemplates the forces leading England to the Restoration, his coordinate, linear style implies that the situation is beyond rational control. When he proposes his ready and easy way, his more structured style generates an image of the politics of pure reason. These two styles alternate throughout the tract and create a pattern of futile but heroic political struggle."

3988 Sterne, Laurence, and **Harold H. Kollmeier,** gen. eds. *A Concordance to the English Prose of John Milton.* Medi-

eval and Renaissance Texts and Studies, vol. 35. Binghamton, NY: Medieval and Renaissance Texts and Studies, 1985. xxii, 1491pp.

Takes the place of an index originally planned for the Yale *Complete Prose Works* (No. 366), the text on which it is based. Reviews: Roy Flannagan, *MiltonQ*, 20, 1986, 103–05; Michael Fixler, *RES*, 38, 1987, 594.

3989 Stevens, Paul. "Discontinuities in Milton's Early Public Self-Representation." *HLQ*, 51, 1988, 261–80.

Portrays Milton's stand against the bishops' tyranny in 1641–42 as heroic and romantic. Shows how his political philosophy manifested itself in his writings, especially the pamphlets.

3990 Stewart, Stanley. "Milton Revises *The Readie and Easie Way*." *MiltonS*, 20, 1984, 205–24.

Analyzes the prose tract's two versions to show that Milton did more than develop arguments advanced in the first edition. "He also enriched the tract by reinterpreting the political situation in biblical terms. And he amplified his own voice by inviting associations of it with prophetic models."

3991 Stollman, Samuel S. "Samson's 'Sunny Locks the Laws': An Hebraic Metaphor." *SCN*, 26, 1968, 71–72.

Explains that the Samson-sun-law imagery in the *Reason of Church-Government* derives from Milton's knowledge of Hebrew and perhaps from his awareness of the rabbinical tradition.

3992 Stollman, Samuel S. "'To Grind in the Mill . . .': Milton's Etymology, Exegesis and Euphemism." *SCN*, 29, 1971, 68–69.

Believes that in the *Doctrine and Discipline of Divorce*, "to grind in the mill" has a sexual connotation.

3993 Sugimoto, Makoto. "Milton's Freedom of Speech, Thought." *MCJ News*, 4, 1980, 1–2.

Analyzes the argument of *Areopagitica*.

3994 Suzuki, Masayuki. "Milton in the Western History of Education." *MCJ News*, 6, 1983, 8–10.

Compares "Milton's thoughts on education as found in *Of Education* and those revealed in his other works."

3995 Svendsen, Kester. "Science and Structure in Milton's *Doctrine of Divorce*." *Seventeenth-Century Prose: Modern Essays in Criticism*. Ed. by Stanley E. Fish (New York: Oxford Univ. Press, 1971), pp. 462–74.

Reprint of Huckabay No. 3064, originally published in 1952.

3996 Swaim, Kathleen M. "Milton in 1825." *MiltonQ*, 22, 1988, 44–50.

Studies two essays published on the *Christian Doctrine* in 1825. The first, written by Thomas Babington Macaulay, "develops an expansive contrast between Milton and Greek tragedians and Milton and Dante, and applauds the special affective qualities of Milton's poetry." The second, by Henry Hart Milman, "elaborates the concerns of a thoughtful, conservative, religiously oriented Englishman of the early nineteenth century . . . about Milton's unorthodoxy and . . . conscientious pursuit of the implications of his own argument."

3997 Takemura, Sanae. "Milton and before the Restoration." *MCJ News*, 11, 1989, 10–13.

Abstract of a paper presented at the Fourteenth Annual Conference of MCJ in October, 1988. Gives a brief history of Milton's pre-Restoration pamphlets that continued to defend the Commonwealth.

3998 Tanner, John S. "Milton and the Early Mormon Defense of Polygamy." *MiltonQ*, 21, No. 2, 1987, 41–46.

Discusses the printing in 1854 of excerpts about polygamy from Milton's *Christian Doctrine* in the *Latter-day Saints' Millennial Star*, a Mormon weekly. "Beset by salacious innuendo and moral outrage from every side,

Mormon Elders enlisted support . . . by calling upon the revered name of John Milton. . . . Theirs has been a forgotten response to the *Christian Doctrine*."

3999 Teunissen, John J. "The Book of Job and Stuart Politics." *UTQ*, 43, 1973, 16–31.

Discusses *Eikonoklastes* as a response to *Eikon Basilike* and uses Milton's negative reaction to Charles I's statement of Job-like suffering to outline the reaction of contemporary Puritans.

4000 Thompson, Claud Adelbert. "Milton's *The Doctrine and Discipline of Divorce*: A Bibliographical Study." Doctoral diss., Univ. of Wisconsin, 1971. 146pp. Abs., *DAI*, 32, 1971, 1487A.

Studies four early editions of Milton's pamphlet to affirm "William Riley Parker's general conclusions" concerning its publication and to "identify the corrected states of . . . variant sheets" in the second edition.

4001 Tsuji, Hiroko. "From Quintilian to Milton's *Of Education*." *AnRS*, 27, 1976, 1–20.

Draws parallels between Quintilian's *Institutio Oratoria* and Milton's *Of Education*. Concludes that "Milton's theory of education aims at educating the whole man based on the classical view and the Christian view of man, in the perspective of rhetoric."

4002 Tsuji, Hiroko. "From Quintilian to Milton's *Of Education*." *MCJ News*, 6, 1983, 2–5.

Abstract of a paper presented at the Seventh Annual Conference of MCJ in October, 1981. "Milton was a sound adherent of the humanistic tradition" in education and "not a pioneer of modern education."

4003 Turner, James Grantham. "The Intelligible Flame: Paradisal Eros and Old Testament Divorce in Milton's Prose." *One Flesh: Paradisal Marriage and Sexual Relations in the Age of Milton* (Oxford: Clarendon Press, 1987), pp. 188–229.

Analyzes Milton's views of marriage

in the divorce tracts: marriage must retain its prelapsarian bliss and must not be grounded in procreation but in "a mutual fitness to the final causes of wedlock, help and society." Without this "cheerful society of wedlock," the individual is incomplete, and the solution is divorce. Feels that the overwhelming impression of the divorce tracts is one of violence. The tensions exhibited in the tracts propel Milton toward *Paradise Lost*.

4004 Van Anglen, Kevin P. "'That Sainted Spirit'—William Ellery Channing and the Unitarian Milton." *Studies in the American Renaissance*. Ed. by Joel Myerson (Charlottesville: Univ. Press of Virginia, 1983), pp. 101–27.

Feels that Channing, in his review of the *Christian Doctrine*, "reaches for a new and broader understanding of Milton than the Whig tradition could provide" and "sums up the past and points towards the future, and the Milton of Emerson and Thoreau."

4005 Via, John A. "Milton's Antiprelatical Tracts: The Poet Speaks in Prose." *MiltonS*, 5, 1973, 87–127.

Milton's tracts of 1641–42 present harsh attacks on the English church's corruption, while developing "the major themes and principal imagistic patterns of his academic exercises and early poetry."

4006 Via, John A. "Theme and Image in Milton's *Prolusions* 6 and 7." *MiltonQ*, 9, 1975, 37.

Abstract of a paper presented at the University of Wisconsin, Milwaukee, Milton Tercentenary Conference, in November, 1974. "Both exercises reveal Milton's early attitude toward the person and function of the poet—an idea persistently present in his later works."

4007 Von Maltzahn, N. "Milton's *History of Britain* in Its Historical Context." Doctoral diss., Oxford Univ., 1985. Abs., *IT*, 38, 1989, 528.

Surveys Milton's response to a demand for a national history and shows that his reappraisal of the national myth in the *History of Britain* "indicates his disillusionment with his original historical project and reflects his changing opinion of the national character."

4008 Watanabe, Noboru. "The Doctrine and the Conception of *Areopagitica*." *MCJ News*, 4, 1980, 2–4.

Abstract of a paper presented at the Fifth Annual Conference of MCJ in October, 1979. Believes that the religious basis of Milton's argument leads to contradictions and limitations. Abs., *MiltonQ*, 16, 1982, 55.

4009 Watanabe, Noboru. "Milton's Divorce Pamphlets and the Bible." *MCJ News*, 9, 1987, 4–5.

Abstract of a paper presented at the Eleventh Annual Conference of MCJ in October, 1985. Argues that in the divorce pamphlets, Milton values the spiritual aspect above the physical one in matrimony. Claims that his goal is "to explain that the Biblical teachings on divorce are not mutually contradictory, even though they may seem so superficially."

4010 Waters, D. Douglas. "Milton and the 'Mistress-Missa' Tradition." *MiltonQ*, 6, No. 1, 1972, 6–8.

Discusses Milton's use of the tradition in the antiprelatical tracts as "central to an understanding of his argument against the English liturgy."

4011 Webber, Joan. "John Milton: The Prose Style of God's English Poet." *The Eloquent "I": Style and Self in Seventeenth-Century Prose* (Madison, Milwaukee, and London: Univ. of Wisconsin Press, 1968), pp. 184–218.

See Huckabay No. 3073. Reviews (of book): Robert Adolph, *Style*, 3, 1969, 202–03; L. A. Beaurline, *GaR*, 23, 1969, 103–05; Jonathan Goldberg, *RenQ*, 22, 1969, 204–06; Judith Levinson, *SAQ*, 68, 1969, 271; Leonard Nathanson, *Criticism*, 11, 1969, 209–11; *TLS*, May

15, 1969, p. 537; Janel M. Mueller, *MP*, 68, 1970, 109–10.

4012 Weitzel, Roy Lee. "Eloquence and Truth in Milton's Prose." Doctoral diss., Washington Univ., 1973. 250pp. Abs., *DAI*, 34, 1974, 7724A–25A.

Analyzes Milton's assertion of truth over rhetoric in *Of Reformation*, the *Treatise of Civil Power*, and the *Likeliest Means To Remove Hirelings*.

4013 Werman, Golda. "Milton's Use of Rabbinic Material." *MiltonS*, 21, 1985, 35–47.

Does not believe that Milton was an accomplished Semitic scholar. Demonstrates instead that he, along with many contemporary Protestants, used English and Latin translations.

4014 West, Michael. "'Not without Dust and Heat': A Ciceronianism in Milton's *Areopagitica*." *RES*, 29, 1978, 181–85.

Claims that *Areopagitica* has "no scriptural parallel worth remarking, but suggest[s] an echo of Cicero's *De Oratore*." Abs., *SCN*, 38, 1980, 21.

4015 Whitaker, Juanita. "'The Wars of Truth': Wisdom and Strength in *Areopagitica*." *MiltonS*, 9, 1976, 185–201.

"For Milton, complete wisdom and strength is man's dedicated struggle to know God's truth, and the occasion of the treatise clearly manifests the *topos*: Books (wisdom) are fighting (strength) to exist in England. The book metaphor admits the full epistemological scope of a free press: Society has all options for positive or perverted wisdom and strength."

4016 Wilding, Michael. "Milton's *Areopagitica*: Liberty for the Sects." *PSt*, 9, 1986, 7–38. Reprinted in *The Literature of Controversy: Polemical Strategy from Milton to Junius*. Ed. by Thomas N. Corns (London: Frank Cass, 1987), pp. 7–38.

Believes that Milton goes beyond the subject of publication of books and argues for the freedom of the sects and common people.

4017 Williams, Philip. "John Milton, Historian." *ESELL*, 53–54, 1968, 1–14.

The *History of Britain* shows Milton's "concern with the interpretation of God's providential hand in world history, bringing good out of evil."

4018 Wittreich, Joseph Anthony, Jr. "Another 'Jest' in Milton's 'Sportive Exercises.'" *MiltonQ*, 7, 1973, 5–8.

Discusses Milton's use of irony in the oratorical section of *Prolusion 6*. Observes that "The 'jest'—the irony—lies in the fact that Milton, assuming the posture of 'idiocy,' imposes a literal interpretation on a received allegory and then invites his audience of 'learned men' to accept it."

4019 Wittreich, Joseph Anthony, Jr. "'The Crown of Eloquence': The Figure of the Orator in Milton's Prose Works." *Achievements of the Left Hand: Essays on the Prose of John Milton*. Ed. by Michael Lieb and John T. Shawcross (Amherst: Univ. of Massachusetts Press, 1974), pp. 3–54.

Explains that, to Milton, the oratorical tradition rested with Cicero and Quintilian, and he applied it to his prose works, including the antiprelatical tracts and *Areopagitica*, and finally to his epics. "Milton not only draws his moral character from the orator; he derives from him his epic stance as well."

4020 Wittreich, Joseph Anthony, Jr. "Milton's *Areopagitica*: Its Isocratic and Ironic Contexts." *MiltonS*, 4, 1972, 101–15.

"Through his title, Milton means to establish a set of correspondences between himself and Isocrates, between Parliament and the General Assembly." He exploits "the initial equation just long enough to elicit the good will of his audience (that is, to fulfill the rhetorical demands of his exordium); then he allows the Pauline allusion to emerge and ironic inconsistencies to tumble forth."

4021 Wittreich, Joseph Anthony, Jr.

"Milton's Idea of the Orator." *MiltonQ*, 6, No. 2, 1972, 38–40.

Shows that in the prose works, Milton identifies "his orator with the poet-prophet-priest," thus bringing together "the secular and the religious in a higher conjunction than that suggested by classical or Renaissance theorists."

4022 Wittreich, Joseph Anthony, Jr. "Pico and Milton: A Gloss on *Areopagitica*." *ELN*, 9, 1971, 108–10.

Points out Milton's recollection of Pico in *Areopagitica* and parallels their works. Adds that "for both, man's freedom to choose and, choosing, to determine his destiny is what distinguishes him from other forms of created life."

4023 Woolrych, Austin. "The Date of the Digression in Milton's *History of Britain*." *For Veronica Wedgewood These: Studies in Seventeenth-Century History*. Ed. by Richard Ollard and Pamela Tudor-Craig (London: Collins, 1986), pp. 217–46.

Asserts that the widely accepted date of 1648 is problematical: in the digression, Milton has negative attitudes toward Britain's future, but his other writings from that year reveal a positive attitude. Proposes 1660 as the probable year of the digression's composition.

4024 Woolrych, Austin. "Milton and Cromwell: 'A Short but Scandalous Night of Interruption'?" *Achievements of the Left Hand: Essays on the Prose of John Milton*. Ed. by Michael Lieb and John T. Shawcross (Amherst: Univ. of Massachusetts Press, 1974), pp. 185–218.

The prose of 1659–60 shows that Milton became disillusioned with Cromwell and "identified himself completely with the Protector's republican enemies."

4025 Woolrych, Austin. "Milton and the Good Old Cause." *Ringing the Bell Backward: The Proceedings of the First International Milton Symposium*. Ed. by Ronald G. Shafer. The IUP Imprint Series (Indiana: Indiana Univ. of Pennsylvania, 1982), pp. 135–50.

Surveys what the cause meant to Milton in 1640 and in 1660.

4026 Woolrych, Austin. "Milton's Political Commitment: The Interplay of Puritan and Classical Ideals." *WascanaR*, 9, 1974, 166–88.

Milton "drew mainly on his arsenal of classical learning when he wrote in Latin against Salmasius and du Moulin, for he was defending the regicide state before a European audience which would share few of the presuppositions of the English parliamentarians. Equally naturally, he drew more largely on the Scriptures and on Christian writers when he addressed his fellow countrymen in their own language."

STYLE AND VERSIFICATION

4027 Bose, Amalendu. "Some Observations on Milton's Poetic Language." *Bulletin of the Department of English* (Calcutta Univ.), 10, 1974–75, 48–62.

Replies to T. S. Eliot's charges (see Huckabay No. 531) against Milton's poetic language.

4028 Bradford, Richard. "Milton's Graphic Poetics." *Re-membering Milton: Essays on the Texts and Traditions.* Ed. by Mary Nyquist and Margaret W. Ferguson (New York and London: Methuen, 1987), pp. 179–96.

Concludes that "if there is to be a serious reassessment of the relationship between author, text and reader in *Paradise Lost*, then it must be acknowledged that the stylistic features of the poem represent a fundamental challenge to the assumptions of critical practice, from . . . the new metrists to the sensitive close readings."

4029 Bridges, Robert. *Milton's Prosody.* Folcroft, PA: Folcroft Library Editions, 1970, 1972.

Reprints of Stevens No. 2767, originally published in 1921.

4030 Brisman, Leslie. "'More Glorious To Return': Miltonic Repetition." *YES*, 1, 1971, 78–87.

On the effects of repetition in Milton's poetry.

4031 Brogan, T. V. F. *English Versification, 1570–1980: A Reference Guide with a Global Appendix.* Baltimore, MD: Johns Hopkins Univ. Press, 1981. xxix, 794pp.

Contains an annotated list of books and articles on Milton's style and versification under several classifications, such as rhythm, meter, syntax and grammar.

4032 Burnett, Archie. "Compound Words in Milton's English Poetry." *MLR*, 75, 1980, 492–506.

Demonstrates that Milton's use of compound words "identifies him with early apologists for English, reveals many 'sources' in other authors and his adaptation of them to his own literary ends, locates him firmly between the Elizabethans and the Augustans, and illuminates his stylistic development."

4033 Burnett, Archie. "*A Dictionary of Puns in Milton's English Poetry.*" *MiltonQ*, 16, 1982, 12–16.

Review essay of Le Comte's *Dictionary* (No. 771). Concludes that "even with its considerable shortcomings, it stands as an indictment of those who have denied the qualities of flexibility and ambivalence to Milton's style." Reply by Le Comte, pp. 79–80.

4034 Burnett, Archie. "'The Fifth Ode of Horace, Lib. I,' and Milton's Style." *MiltonQ*, 16, 1982, 68–72.

Believes that Milton's translation of Horace's ode is not characteristic of his own poetry. It is actually a metaphrase, not a translation.

4035 Burnett, Archie. *Milton's Style: The Shorter Poems, "Paradise Regained," and "Samson Agonistes."* London and New York: Longman, 1981. xiv, 187pp.

"This book has various aims: to give close readings of Milton's poems other than *Paradise Lost*; to take into account the criticism on these poems, focusing on major issues; and to investigate the variety and consistency of their style."

4036 Burnett, A. "Studies in the Language of Milton's English Poetry." Doctoral diss., Oxford Univ., 1976. *IT*, 27, 1979, 8.

4037 Burnett, Archie. " 'Wandering Steps and Slow' and 'Vast Profundity Obscure': Two Miltonic Adjective Formations." *ELN*, 21, No. 3, 1984, 25–38.

Studies adjective-noun-adjective phrases in Milton's poetry—such as "forc'd fingers rude" in *Lycidas* and "sad task and hard" in *Paradise Lost*—and shows that other poets used them, though Milton did so more often and more distinctively. "The statistical frequency reflects an awareness, which no other poet matches, of their full dramatic, mimetic, and evocative potential. For this reason they are rightly to be called Miltonic."

4038 Buss, Karen Orton Hodges. "Stress Placement in Milton's Verse: Implications for the Halle-Keyser Theory of English Iambic Pentameter." Doctoral diss., Brandeis Univ., 1974. 297pp. Abs., *DAI*, 35, 1974, 3727A–28A.

Examines Milton's placement of nontraditional stresses, concluding that his patterns agree with Halle-Keyser's general assertions, but sometimes contradict specific points.

4039 Camé, Jean-François. "Modulations Poétiques Miltoniennes." *Linguistique, Civilisation, Littérature*. Ed. by André Bordeaux (Paris: Didier, 1980), pp. 218–29.

Studies the poetic modulations of intentional repetition in Milton's works: plural/singular; tense changes; the comparative; inversion; compression; substitution; and opposition.

4040 Candy, Hugh C. H. *Milton: The Individualist in Metre*. Folcroft, PA: Folcroft Library Editions, 1969; Norwood, PA: Norwood Editions, 1976; Philadelphia, PA: R. West, 1977.

Reprints of the expanded version of Huckabay No. 3412, originally published in 1934.

4041 Carter, Ronnie D. "Syntax and Style in Milton's English Prose." Doctoral diss., Univ. of Wisconsin, 1972. 150pp. Abs., *DAI*, 33, 1973, 6343A–44A.

Uses statistics to analyze the static, evolving, and genre-controlled elements of syntax and style in six of Milton's prose works.

4042 Copeland, Thomas Arthur. "A Theory of Metrical Structure with Special Emphasis on Milton's Epic Blank Verse." Doctoral diss., Northwestern Univ., 1971. 335pp. Abs., *DAI*, 32, 1971, 3244A–45A.

Examines "prevalent theories of meter, particularly the debate over metrical 'imposition' or distortion," using the meter of Milton's two epics to describe verse structure.

4043 Corns, Thomas N. *The Development of Milton's Prose Style*. Oxford: Clarendon Press; New York: Oxford Univ. Press, 1982. xiv, 118pp.

A computer-aided study in historical linguistics, which compares each group of Milton's tracts with pamphlets by other writers who dealt with the same controversies. "I have attempted to reconstruct the genre expectations of Milton's first readers, so that . . . we may rediscover some of the genuine freshness and innovation which his original audience would have appreciated." Examines lexical features (such as word frequencies), syntactic features, sentence structure, and imagery.

4044 Corns, Thomas N. "New Light on the Left Hand: Contemporary Views of Milton's Prose Style." *DUJ*, 72, 1980, 177–81.

Explains "how highly Milton and his contemporaries regarded his prose style" and "how remarkable it seemed to them."

4045 Corns, T. N. "Studies in the Development of Milton's Prose Style." Doctoral diss., Oxford Univ., 1976. Abs., *IT*, 27, 1979, 8.

4046 Cox, R. G. "Milton: Humanist and Puritan." *From Donne to Marvell.* Ed. by Boris Ford. The New Pelican Guide to English Literature, vol. 3. Revised edition (Harmondsworth: Penguin, 1982), pp. 74–78.

General remarks on the development of Milton's style.

4047 Davies, Hugh Sykes. "Milton and the Vocabulary of Verse and Prose." *Literary English since Shakespeare.* Ed. by George Watson (London: Oxford Univ. Press, 1970), pp. 175–93.

Believes that Milton's prose vocabulary, unlike his poetic vocabulary, favors words from the Latin and Romance languages over Anglo-Saxon words.

4048 Dillon, George L. "Clause, Pause, and Punctuation in Poetry." *Linguistics,* 169, 1976, 5–20.

Reports experiments which "attempt to shed light on the pausing strategies used by readers in reading passages of iambic pentameter, primarily Miltonic blank verse. The chief passage is *Paradise Lost* II.604–28."

4049 Emma, Ronald David, and **John T. Shawcross,** eds. *Language and Style in Milton: A Symposium in Honor of the Tercentenary of "Paradise Lost."* New York: Frederick Ungar, 1967. xii, 371pp.

See Huckabay No. 3429. Review: H. W. Donner, *ES,* 52, 1971, 173–74.

4050 Goekjian, Gregory F. "The Function and Effect of Rhyme." Doctoral diss., Univ. of Pittsburgh, 1970. 189pp. Abs., *DAI,* 31, 1971, 4714A.

Argues that rhyme, by coupling significant words, manipulates audience expectation to reveal unique poetic meanings in the works of Milton, Pope, and Pound.

4051 Hunter, William B., Jr. "Some Reflections upon English Prosody and Especially *Paradise Lost.*" *The Laurel Bough: Essays Presented in Honour of Professor M. V. Rama Sarma.* Ed. by G. Nageswara Rao (Bombay: Blackie and Son, 1983), pp. 15–24.

Sets forth several linguistic and prosodic principles that apply to our reading of poetry and observes "how Milton employed these principles in the development of his distinctive prosody."

4052 Keener, Frederick M. "Parallelism and the Poets' Secret: Eighteenth-Century Commentary on *Paradise Lost.*" *EIC,* 37, 1987, 281–302.

Demonstrates that Miltonic parallelism—the poets' secret—remained elusive to eighteenth-century critics. Rejects the modern view that eighteenth-century critics were aware of parallelism.

4053 Knights, L. C. "Hooker and Milton: A Contrast of Styles." *Public Voices: Literature and Politics with Special Reference to the Seventeenth Century.* The Clark Lectures for 1970–71 (London: Chatto and Windus, 1971), pp. 52–70.

Sees "reasonableness and courtesy" in Richard Hooker's prose but finds "a strain in Milton's political writing that makes against the humanistic virtues that he wished to promote."

4054 Le Comte, Edward. "In Imitation of Milton, Judges xi." *MiltonQ,* 11, 1977, 64–65.

Asks students to identify the traits of Milton's style in Le Comte's own poetic version of the passage from Judges.

4055 Limouze, Henry S. "Joseph Hall and the Prose Style of John Milton." *MiltonS,* 15, 1981, 121–41.

Questions the view that the Ciceronian Milton takes on the Senecan Hall and examines their styles "to show that a case can be made for their interaction which helps explain some of the difficult features of Milton's early prose style."

4056 Marshall, Donald Glenn. "The Development of Blank-Verse Poetry from Milton to Wordsworth." Doctoral diss., Yale Univ., 1971. 405pp. Abs., *DAI,* 32, 1971, 1480A.

Follows the development of metonymic language, characterized by "repetition at various intervals, by succession, and by continuity," in poetry from *Paradise Lost* to the *Prelude*.

4057 Martindale, C. A. "Milton and the Homeric Simile." *CL*, 33, 1981, 224–38.

Studies the relationship between Milton's similes and Homer's and Virgil's. Believes that Milton's have a greater degree of homologation between simile and narrative.

4058 McDavid, Raven I., Jr. "Sandhi-Alternation of Attributive Genitives in Milton's Works." *SAQ*, 71, 1972, 530–33.

Examines Milton's use of my/mine and thy/thine.

4059 Miyagawa, Noboru. "Genealogy of Similes—From Homer to Milton." *MCJ News*, 6, 1983, 10–11.

Abstract of paper presented. Milton's similes "are distinctly characteristic of him and not to be found in works by Homer, Virgil, or Dante."

4060 Musacchio, George L. "Milton's Feminine Pronouns with Neuter Antecedents." *JEngL*, 2, 1968, 23–28.

"Milton's usage of a possessive feminine pronoun with a neuter antecedent . . . seems to have various causes rather than a single one."

4061 Olsen, Leslie Ann. "A Description of the Blank Verse Prosodies of John Milton, James Thomson, Edward Young, William Cowper, and William Wordsworth." Doctoral diss., Univ. of Southern California, 1974. 703pp. Abs., *DAI*, 35, 1974, 3002A.

Uses computer programs based on the Halle-Keyser theory of prosody to analyze the poets' verse, noting that "Wordsworth and Milton share more prosodic characteristics with each other than with the three eighteenth-century poets."

4062 Park, B. A. "Milton and Classical Meters." *MiltonQ*, 6, No. 4, 1972, 75–77.

Explains how Milton's translation of the "Fifth Ode of Horace" imitates the original's verse form, allowing for the different structures of Latin and English.

4063 Piper, William Bowman. "The Invulnerability of Poetic Experience." *SCRev*, 4, 1987, 11–23.

Discusses Milton's and Pope's poetry, focusing on passages from *Lycidas* and the *Essay on Man*. Also examines Dryden's poetry and notes variations in these three writers' poetic styles.

4064 Ricks, Christopher. *Milton's Grand Style*. London: Oxford Univ. Press, 1965, 1967, 1968, 1978, 1979, and 1983.

Reprints of Huckabay No. 3478, originally published in 1963.

4065 Ricks, Christopher. "Tincture or Reflection." *On Milton's Poetry: A Selection of Modern Studies*. Ed. by Arnold Stein (Greenwich, CT: Fawcett Publications, 1970), pp. 167–82.

Reprint of a chapter from No. 4064.

4066 Sadler, Lynn Veach. "Relations between Alchemy and Poetics in the Renaissance and Seventeenth Century, with Special Glances at Donne and Milton." *Ambix*, 24, 1977, 69–76.

Discusses "the use of alchemical analogies and doctrine in treatises on poetry" and surveys "alchemical techniques in Donne's 'The Triple Foole' and Milton's *Samson Agonistes*."

4067 Schaar, Claes. *"The Full Voic'd Quire Below": Vertical Context Systems in "Paradise Lost."* Lund Studies in English, no. 60. Lund: C. W. K. Gleerup, 1982. 354pp.

Analyzes various examples of vertical context systems in *Paradise Lost*, organizing the material in "a series of increasing semantic complexity." Abs., *MiltonQ*, 17, 1983, 56.

4068 Schaar, Claes. "Vertical Context Systems." *Style and Text: Studies Presented to Nils Erik Enkvist*. Ed. by Håkan Ringbom and others (Stockholm: Språkförlaget Skriptor, 1975), pp. 146–57.

Discusses the vertical context and methods of allusion in *Paradise Lost*.

4069 Shawcross, John T. "The Prosody of Milton's Translation of Horace's Fifth Ode." *TSL*, 13, 1968, 81–89.

Suggests that Milton used quantitative rules for English words. Sees a relationship between the prosody of this translation (1646–48) and that of *Samson Agonistes.*

4070 Sloane, Thomas O. "Reading Milton Rhetorically." *Renaissance Eloquence: Studies in the Theory and Practice of Renaissance Rhetoric.* Ed. by James J. Murphy (Berkeley, Los Angeles, and London: Univ. of California Press, 1983), pp. 394–410.

Proposes a rhetorical reading of Milton's poetry because that approach "presupposes a certain attitude toward language: language reflects a speaker's designs as he confronts an audience, who he assumes are not possessed of *tabulae rasae* but of minds filled with associations, conventions, expectations, which he must direct, control, or take advantage of."

4071 Smallenburg, Harry. "Milton's Cosmic Sentences." *Lang&S*, 5, 1972, 108–14.

Uses examples from the *Tenure of Kings and Magistrates* to show that Milton's sentences "are 'cosmic' in this sense: the reader must be continually aware, as he moves from word to word, clause to clause, paragraph to paragraph . . . that he is constantly being engaged in a progressive and ongoing activity—what Milton in *Areopagitica* calls 'closing up truth to truth as we find it.'"

4072 Smallenburg, Harry Russell. "Structures of Truth: Milton's Affective Polemic." Doctoral diss., Univ. of California, Berkeley, 1970. 230pp. Abs., *DAI*, 32, 1971, 985A.

Demonstrates that "Milton's prose style is intentional and functional"; every tract is "a vital and active representation and enactment of the truth for which it argues."

4073 Sprott, S. Ernest. *Milton's Art of Prosody.* Folcroft, PA: Folcroft Library Editions, 1969, 1970, 1977; Norwood, PA: Norwood Editions, 1978.

Reprints of Huckabay No. 3492, originally published in 1953.

4074 Stavely, Keith Williams. "The Evolution of Milton's Prose Rhetoric." Doctoral diss., Yale Univ., 1969. 260pp. Abs., *DAI*, 31, 1970, 1296A.

Argues that modifications of "imagination, reason, and emotion" in Milton's prose are responses to "private enthusiasms" and later to "the changing public patterns of the Puritan Revolution."

4075 Stavely, Keith W. *The Politics of Milton's Prose Style.* Yale Studies in English, 185. New Haven, CT, and London: Yale Univ. Press, 1975. ix, 136pp.

Deals with the style of Milton's political tracts from *Of Reformation* to the *Readie and Easie Way.* Sees his prose as a medium of imaginative expression that is worthy of the literary critic's scrutiny. Ironically, the poetic texture "limits the political effectiveness of Milton's prose instead of extending and enriching it."

4076 Steadman, John M. "'Verse without Rime': Milton's Debt to Italian Defenses of Blank Verse." *The Wall of Paradise: Essays on Milton's Poetics* (Baton Rouge and London: Louisiana State Univ. Press, 1985), pp. 131–42.

Slightly revised version of Huckabay No. 3494, originally published in 1964.

4077 Toliver, Harold. *Transported Styles in Shakespeare and Milton.* University Park: Pennsylvania State Univ. Press, 1989. 283pp.

Argues that for Shakespeare and Milton, the more sublimely poetic the language the more it is at odds with a conservative reinstatement of social order. Review: Alexander Leggatt, *SQ*, 41, 1990, 535–37.

4078 Tricomi, A. H. "Milton and the Jonsonian Plain Style." *MiltonS*, 13, 1979, 129–44.

Believes that between 1630 and 1632, Milton began to assimilate into his poetry characteristics that are common in Ben Jonson's—lucidity, simplicity, understatement, unity of tone, and clarity of emotional response.

4079 Ulreich, John C., Jr. "The Typological Structure of Milton's Imagery." *MiltonS*, 5, 1973, 67–85.

"The seeming abstractness of Milton's imagery results from its intellectual structure, particularly from the way metaphors are recreated through typological fulfillment. . . . Milton's imagery is not sacramental; neither is it simply abstract, for Milton re-creates his own incarnational symbolism by a process of analysis, purification, and reembodiment."

4080 Vallely, M. "Milton and Metaphor." M.Litt. thesis, Glasgow Univ., 1971.

4081 Van Devender, George William. "The Prosody of Milton's *Samson Agonistes*." Doctoral diss., Univ. of Mississippi, 1973. 323pp. Abs., *DAI*, 34, 1974, 5209A.

Treats English and Greek rhythms, differentiating between lyric and stichic meters.

4082 Ward, Alan. "Milton's Spellings Again." *Five Hundred Years of Words and Sounds: A Festschrift for Eric Dobson*. Ed. by Douglas Gray and E. G. Stanley (Cambridge: Brewer, 1983), pp. 157–64.

Examines Milton's use of "-'n" and "-en" in his poetry, focusing mainly on *Paradise Lost*. Proposes that Milton used "-'n" to indicate syllabic "n" in all cases, whether or not it was in fact metrically syllabic, leaving "-en" to indicate /ən/ or /in/.

4083 Waters, Lindsay. "Milton, Tasso, and the Renaissance Grand Style: Syntax and Its Effect on the Reader." *StIR*, 2, 1981, 81–92.

Contends that Milton's grand style demonstrates "the virtues of syntactic confusion and the resulting obscurity." Many readers consider his ambiguous syntax as a defect, but the virtue of this defect is that although "It retards the reader's movement through the poem, . . . it draws him soul and body into the poem."

4084 Whaler, James. *Counterpoint and Symbol: An Inquiry into the Rhythm of Milton's Epic Style*. New York: Haskell House, 1970.

Reprint of Huckabay No. 3509, originally published in 1956.

4085 Winnifrith, T. "Milton's Similes." *KM 80: A Birthday Album for Kenneth Muir, Tuesday, 5 May, 1987* (Liverpool: Liverpool Univ. Press, 1987), p. 146.

Deals with the contrastive elements in the similes of *Paradise Lost*.

4086 Allentuck, Marcia. "Henry Fuseli on Engravings of His Milton Paintings: An Unpublished Letter." *Burlington Magazine*, 116, 1974, 214.

Comments on "an unpublished letter [of September 27, 1802] from Fuseli to the publisher Du Roveray, demonstrating Fuseli's concern about William Bromley's engravings of his work in the 1802 edition of *Paradise Lost*, which sheds further light upon Fuseli's long devotion, as a 'poetical painter,' to the spirit and letter of Milton's text."

4087 Amory, Hugh. "Things Unattempted Yet: A Bibliography of the First Edition of *Paradise Lost*." *BC*, 32, 1983, 41–66.

Analyzes the order of printing of the first six issues of the first edition of *Paradise Lost*, examining their structural differences, title pages, and binding orders and creating a timeframe for printings and revisions.

4088 Arai, Akira. "On the Writing of Tenrai Han'ya's Milton's *Samson Agonistes*." *Miscellaneous Essays on Milton* (Tokyo: Chukyo Shuppan, 1979), pp. 173–85.

In Japanese. Comments on Tenrai Shigeno's pioneering translation and analysis of *Samson Agonistes*.

4089 "Arthur Annesley's Copy of the Areopagitica." *MiltonQ*, 9, 1975, 128.

Describes a copy of the first edition that once belonged to "A. A.," identified in Bernard Quaritch's catalog as Annesley, "who was later the close friend of Milton and certainly responsible in part for Milton's survival after the Restoration."

4090 Assmann, Aleida. "Vom Verlustigten Paradeiss zum *Verlorenen Paradies*." *Archiv*, 211, 1974, 309–19.

Surveys approaches to the translation of *Paradise Lost* from the seventeenth to the twentieth century, including translations by Theodor Haak, Johann Jacob Bodmer, Johann Gottsched, and Friedrich Wilhelm Zachariä. Finally, examines Adolf Böttger's translation of 1869 and J. Meier's of 1969.

4091 Avigdor, Eva. "Une Traduction Française Inconnue du *Paradis Perdu* de Milton." *RLC*, 61, 1987, 69–79.

Studies the first French translation of the beginning of *Paradise Lost* 1, done by Jean Gaspar Scheuchzer between 1722 and 1729.

4092 Balakier, James J. "Annotations to *Paradise Lost*." *MiltonQ*, 22, 1988, 128–29.

Discusses the annotations that Francis Atterbury, Bishop of Rochester and Dean of Westminster (1662–1732), made for *Paradise Lost*.

4093 Behrendt, Stephen C. "Blake's Illustrations to Milton's *Nativity Ode*." *PQ*, 55, 1976, 65–95.

Feels that Blake's two sets of designs for the poem show his belief that "the *Ode* is as much about the apocalyptic conclusion as it is about the glorious beginning of the Christian era."

4094 Behrendt, Stephen C. "Bright Pilgrimage: William Blake's Designs for *L'Allegro* and *Il Penseroso*." *MiltonS*, 8, 1975, 123–47.

"Blake visually associates the poet of *L'Allegro* with the material, physical world of experience and with the inferior, conventionalized poetry of the merely average versifier. He associates the poet of *Il Penseroso* with the imaginatively superior world of higher innocence and directly with the poetic genius of Milton."

4095 Behrendt, Stephen C. "*Comus* and *Paradise Regained*: Blake's View of Trial in the Wilderness." *M&R*, 3, 1977, 8–13.
Compares Blake's designs for these two poems. Blake ultimately sees the Lady as a failure, Christ a success. Abs., *MiltonQ*, 13, 1979, 60.

4096 Behrendt, Stephen C. "Liberating the Awakener: William Blake's Illustrations to John Milton's Poetry." Doctoral diss., Univ. of Wisconsin, 1974. 308pp. Abs., *DAI*, 35, 1975, 4415A.
Argues that Blake's illustrations of Milton's major works remove obscuring "narrative and doctrinal detail" and infuse the "traditional iconography with new meanings."

4097 Behrendt, Stephen C. "The Mental Contest: Blake's *Comus* Designs." *BlakeS*, 8, 1978, 65–88.
Regards the designs as "the fullest and most sensitive" ever done, for they "attempt both to refocus and to correct the tradition of *Comus* illustration." Notes that Blake disagrees with Milton's views on chastity.

4098 Behrendt, Stephen C. *The Moment of Explosion: Blake and the Illustration of Milton.* Lincoln and London: Univ. of Nebraska Press, 1983. xvi, 211pp.
"This study considers Blake's Milton illustrations from several perspectives: in light of Blake's direct comments on Milton as man and thinker, in light of his vision and revision of Milton's ideas and works, and in light of the rich tradition of Milton illustration with which Blake, as a commercial artist, was particularly conversant and upon whose iconography he drew significantly." Reviews: Karl Kroeber, *Blake*, 19, 1984, 75; Joseph Wittreich, *MiltonQ*, 18, 1984, 92–94; Dennis M. Welch, *PQ*, 64, 1985, 424–26; David

W. Lindsay, *YES*, 17, 1987, 304–05.

4099 Bender, Wolfgang. "Johann Jacob Bodmer und Johann Miltons *Verlohrnes Paradies*." *JDSG*, 11, 1967, 225–67.
Relates the process that Bodmer used to improve his German translation of *Paradise Lost*, focusing on differences in language and syntax. Concludes that a German translation will necessarily be longer than the English original, and its length will be influenced by the time period in which it is written.

4100 Bennett, Stuart. "Jacob Tonson: An Early Editor of *Paradise Lost*?" *Library*, 10, 1988, 247–52.
Deals mainly with Tonson's early work on Milton's text and his criticism of Richard Bentley's edition. Believes that Tonson anticipates modern textual principles.

4101 Berthoud, Roger. "Searching for the Image of Milton." *MiltonQ*, 15, 1981, 72.
Reprinted from the *London Times*, August 18, 1980. Describes Robert Medley's illustrations for an edition of *Samson Agonistes*.

4102 Bindman, David. "Hogarth's *Satan, Sin and Death* and Its Influence." *Burlington Magazine*, 112, 1970, 153–58.
Discusses an illustration of Milton's Satan, Sin, and Death in *Paradise Lost*.

4103 Bond, W. H. "Thomas Hollis and Baron's Milton: A Strange Device." *BC*, 35, 1986, 381.
A query concerning Richard Baron's 1756 edition of *Eikonoklastes*.

4104 Bonnerot, Louis. "Chateaubriand Traducteur de Milton." *EA*, 27, 1974, 501–11.
Suggests the need for more study of Chateaubriand's unique translation of *Paradise Lost* and shows that Chateaubriand was a methodical student and erudite critic of Milton.

4105 Boorsch, Suzanne. "The 1688 *Paradise Lost* and Dr. Aldrich." *Metropolitan Museum Journal*, 6, 1972, 133–50.
Discusses the designer of the unsigned

illustrations in the fourth edition of *Paradise Lost* (1688). Suggests that Medina did not design them. Shows how Dr. Henry Aldrich was associated with these three illustrations. See also Nos. 4169 and 4174.

4106 Bourdette, Robert E., Jr. "A Sense of the Sacred: Richard Bentley's Reading of *Paradise Lost* as 'Divine Narrative.'" *MiltonS*, 24, 1988, 73–106.

Argues that Bentley's emendation of "secret" to "sacred" in the opening lines of *Paradise Lost* provides a thesis for many of his subsequent emendations and that he imposed his will on the text. But Bentley "was a far more astute reader of the poem than has been acknowledged."

4107 Cable, Carole. "The Doves Press Edition of *Paradise Lost*." *LCUT*, 1974, pp. 30–35.

Describes the physical characteristics of this edition and reports on the decisions made to produce it.

4108 Coleridge, K. A. "Some Amendments to W. R. Parker's Census of Seventeenth-Century Editions of Milton." *N&Q*, 19, 1972, 175–76.

Lists additional copies found and more precisely identifies some copies already recorded by Parker (see No. 230).

4109 Creaser, John. "Editorial Problems in Milton: Part I." *RES*, 34, 1983, 279–303.

Studies the variations in typography and spelling in the range of Milton's works. Points out his preferred idiosyncratic spellings and how editors have influenced the final printed versions of his prose. Examines the use of capitalization in the printed text of *Paradise Lost* and in the Trinity Manuscript.

4110 Creaser, John. "Editorial Problems in Milton (Concluded)." *RES*, 35, 1984, 45–60.

Focuses on editorial dilemmas caused by punctuation in Milton's works. Offers several solutions, such as adding accent marks to identify inflections, but proposes an eclectic approach. Reviews some recent editors' practices.

4111 Creaser, John. "Textual Cruces in Milton's Shorter Poems." *N&Q*, 29, 1982, 26–28.

"Four discrepancies between the texts of the two contemporary editions of Milton's shorter poems are especially important, and any editor's view of the relative merits of these two editions—*1645* and *1673*—is bound to be strongly influenced by his assessment of them." See Archie Burnett's response (No. 1235) and Creaser's surrejoinder (No. 1286).

4112 Davies, James Mark Quentin. "Blake's Designs for *Paradise Lost*: A Critical Analysis." Doctoral diss., Univ. of Iowa, 1972. Abs., *DAI*, 33, 1973, 6866A–67A.

Demonstrates that Blake's designs "are not literal illustrations but astute critical commentaries on the shortcomings of Milton's epic and the dualist, transcendental Christian world view it enshrines."

4113 Dunbar, P. M. "A Study of Blake's Illustrations to the Poetry of Milton." Doctoral diss., Cambridge Univ., 1973. *IT*, 23, 1975, 7.

4114 Dunbar, Pamela M. *William Blake's Illustrations to the Poetry of Milton.* New York: Oxford Univ. Press; Oxford: Clarendon Press, 1980. xvi, 207pp.

Studies Blake's illustrations for *Paradise Lost, Paradise Regained, Comus,* the *Nativity Ode,* and *Il Penseroso.* Examines their relationship with the texts and with Blake's own poetry. Reviews: J. Karl Franson, *MiltonQ*, 15, 1981, 99–101; Marcia R. Pointon, *Burlington Magazine,* 123, 1981, 313–14; Désirée Hirst, *RES*, 34, 1983, 222–24.

4115 Duncan, Ivar L. "John Wesley Edits *Paradise Lost.*" *Essays in Memory of Christine Burleson in Language and Literature by Former Colleagues and Students.* Ed. by Thomas G. Burton (Johnson

City: East Tennessee State Univ. Press, 1969), pp. 73–85.

Discusses Wesley's 1763 abridged edition of Milton's epic and his inclusion of poems by Milton, his favorite poet, in the 1744 anthology of English poetry.

4116 England, Martha Winburn. "John Milton and the Performing Arts." *BNYPL*, 80, 1976, 19–70.

Deals mainly with musical versions of *Comus*, *Paradise Lost*, and *Samson Agonistes*, but also discusses the development of English music after the Restoration.

4117 Feaver, William. *The Art of John Martin.* Oxford: Clarendon Press, 1975. xv, 256pp.

Refers to Milton throughout and places Martin's illustrations of *Paradise Lost* in their context.

4118 [Flannagan, Roy C.] "Editor's Note." *MiltonN*, 2, 1968, 58.

Calls attention to the reproductions of paintings and mosaics included in this issue.

4119 Franson, J. Karl. "Christ on the Pinnacle: Interpretive Illustrations of the Crisis in *Paradise Regained*." *MiltonQ*, 10, 1976, 48–53.

Discusses several illustrative interpretations of *Paradise Regained* 4.560–62. Concludes that Blake's view is "consistent with the whole text of *Paradise Regained* and also with the Christology of Milton's *The Christian Doctrine*."

4120 Geduld, Harry M. "Tonson and *Paradise Lost*." *Prince of Publishers: A Study of the Work and Career of Jacob Tonson* (Bloomington: Indiana Univ. Press, 1969), pp. 111–32.

Discusses editions of *Paradise Lost* by Tonson and by his heirs.

4121 Gilbert, Allan H. "Bentley Redivivus: Some Emendations in *Paradise Lost*." *RenP*, 1975, pp. 43–51.

Offers several emendations but cautions against Richard Bentley's excesses.

4122 Gleckner, Robert F. "Blake's Illustration of the Third Temptation in *Paradise Regained*." *Blake*, 11, 1977, 126–27.

Observes that Blake "via the positional dynamics and spatial movement of his entire illustration, enacts the several complexities and implicit contrasts in Milton's poem."

4123 Grant, John E. "Blake's Designs for *L'Allegro* and *Il Penseroso*, with Special Attention to *L'Allegro*; 1, 'Mirth and Her Companions': Some Remarks Made and Designs Discussed at MLA Seminar 12: 'Illuminated Books by William Blake,' 29 December 1970." *BlakeN*, 4, 1971, 117–34.

Includes reproductions of Blake's watercolors.

4124 Grant, John E. "The Meaning of Mirth and Her Companions in Blake's Designs for *L'Allegro* and *Il Penseroso*. Part II: Of Some Remarks Made and Designs Discussed at the MLA Seminar 12: 'Illuminated Books by William Blake,' 29 December 1970." *BlakeN*, 5, 1972, 190–202.

"The evidence indicates that despite their prepossessing characteristics Mirth and her Companions are all in jeopardy, though some more clearly than others."

4125 "Grolier Club Exhibition." *MiltonQ*, 8, 1974, 30.

Describes the Milton exhibition called *The Poet Illustrated* (December 19, 1973–February 14, 1974) and calls attention to a smaller exhibition at the Morgan Library, New York.

4126 Hale, John K. "More on Bentley's 'Milton.'" *MiltonQ*, 14, 1980, 131.

Sheds some light on Thomas Bentley's letter to Zachary Pearce (April 20, 1731), mainly concerning the emendation of *Paradise Lost* 4.250 and the attitude of Bentley's nephew toward his uncle. See Nos. 1973, 4127, and 4130.

4127 Hale, John K. "Notes on Richard Bentley's Edition of *Paradise Lost* (1732)." *MiltonQ*, 18, 1984, 46–50.

Believes that Bentley's corrections of *Paradise Lost* are not "typical of Augustan recreations," but rather were meant to provoke his contemporaries. See Nos. 1973 and 4126.

4128 Hale, John K. "The Personal Element in Some Renderings of Milton's *Paradise Lost*." *Literature in Translation: From Cultural Transference to Metonymic Displacement*. Ed. by Pramod Talgeri and S. B. Verma (Bombay: Popular Prakashan, 1988), pp. 92–102.

Argues that while all renderings of Milton's epic—including editions (such as Bentley's), adaptations (Dryden's), and translations (by Trapp, Haak, Chateaubriand, Paolo Rolli, and Voltaire)— "are sure of being ridiculous somewhere," they also reveal the sublime or "the interaction of poem and version."

4129 Hale, John K. "The Significance of the Early Translations of *Paradise Lost*." *PQ*, 63, 1984, 31–53.

Examines Latin, German, Dutch, French, and Italian translations of *Paradise Lost* for approximately one hundred years after it was written. Contends that the careful reading required for translation may yield new information about a work.

4130 Hale, J. K. "Thomas Bentley to Dr. Pearce: New Light on Richard Bentley's Edition of *Paradise Lost*." *Turnbull Library Record* (Wellington, New Zealand), 14, 1981, 23–34.

With a bibliographical note by Kathleen Coleridge. The letter is to Dr. Zachary Pearce, who had reviewed Bentley's edition. Thomas Bentley, the editor's nephew, had tried to dissuade his uncle from making some of the emendations. See No. 4126.

4131 Hammelmann, Hanns. *Book Illustrators in Eighteenth-Century England*. New Haven, CT, and London: Yale Univ. Press, 1975. xiv, 120pp.

Lists the principal works relevant to Milton's poetry.

4132 Hodgson, Judith Feyertag. "Human Beauty in Eighteenth-Century Aesthetics." Doctoral diss., Univ. of Pennsylvania, 1973. 331pp. Abs., *DAI*, 34, 1974, 5175A.

Uses the changing illustrations of *Paradise Lost* to show "the disappearance of the possibility for masculine beauty and feminine sublimity" in the eighteenth century.

4133 Hodgson, Judith F. "Satan Humanized: Eighteenth-Century Illustrations of *Paradise Lost*." *ECLife*, 1, 1974, 41–44.

Claims that "the overwhelmingly visual effects of *Paradise Lost* on its eighteenth-century readers transformed their ideas of human beauty and sublimity." Points out that Satan, the poem's most visible character, is its hero.

4134 Hunt, John Dixon. "Milton's Illustrators." *John Milton: Introductions*. Ed. by John Broadbent (Cambridge: Cambridge Univ. Press, 1973), pp. 208–25.

Discusses illustrators from John Baptist de Medina to Gustave Doré. Sees an illustration as an example of a critical experience and as a definition of an artist's and age's attitudes.

4135 "Invest in John Milton: Some Current Book Prices." *MiltonQ*, 10, 1976, 65.

On the high prices of early editions of Milton.

4136 Irwin, Helen. "Samuel Palmer, Poet of Light and Shade: His Last Years at Reigate, Surrey." *Apollo*, 114, 1981, 109–13.

Studies Palmer's etchings and paintings of scenes from Milton's works, particularly *L'Allegro* and *Il Penseroso*.

4137 Jagosova, Anezka. "Milton's *Samson Agonistes*." *Acta Universitatis Caroliniae: Philologica*, 18, 1984, 97–104.

4138 Kreuder, Hans-Dieter. "Noch Einmal Frühe Deutsche Milton-Übersetzungen." *Archiv*, 214, 1977, 80–82.

Discusses early German translations of Milton.

4139 Le Comte, Edward. "Comments on Waddington and Petty." *MiltonQ*, 20, 1986, 53.

Finds fault with Raymond B. Waddington's article (No. 4193), stating that "in Cheron Sin is not blind but blindfolded." Also disputes Jane M. Petty's assertion (No. 2873) that Adam's voice sets off Eve's dream. Believes that Satan is responsible.

4140 Le Comte, Edward. "The Index to the Columbia Milton: Its Virtues and Defects." *Greyfriar*, 28, 1987, 3–17. Reprinted in *Milton Re-Viewed: Ten Essays* (New York and London: Garland Publishing, 1991), pp. 103–18.

Compares Patterson and Fogle's index (see No. 295) with its rivals and concludes that it has no substitute.

4141 Lieb, Michael. "'The Chariot of Paternal Deitie': Visual Renderings." *MiltonQ*, 17, 1983, 24.

Abstract of a paper presented at the 1982 MLA Convention. Explores "some of the most representative illustrations of 'the Chariot of Paternal Deitie' in *Paradise Lost*."

4142 Lincoln, Eleanor Terry. "Jean Dassier's Milton Medal: A Further Note." *PULC*, 37, 1975, 24–28.

Suggests that the reverse side of the medal by John Dassier illustrates the opening lines of *Paradise Lost*. See No. 4143.

4143 Lincoln, Eleanor T. "Jean Dassier's Milton Medal: An Oversight." *MiltonQ*, 10, 1976, 73–75.

Relates the medal's history and points out that "Dassier's tribute deserves on its merits to be recognized and enjoyed among the 'portraits, books, and other objects which have interest by their relation to Milton' and are a measure of his fame." See No. 4142.

4144 Miller, Leo. "Milton and Rupert Brooke." *MiltonQ*, 15, 1981, 134.

On the sale of Brooke's copy of Milton's *Poetical Works* (1896). De-scribes Brooke's comments and marks in the edition.

4145 Miller, Leo. "Milton's *Areopagitica*: Price 4d." *N&Q*, 22, 1975, 309.

Gives the original sale price of a previously unrecorded first edition.

4146 Miller, Leo. "A Note on the Revised Yale *Prose Works*, Volume VII." *MiltonQ*, 15, 1981, 25–26.

Compares the two versions of the volume (see No. 366) and suggests that errors in the preceding volumes be noted in the final one.

4147 Miller, Leo. "[Review Article on the *Complete Prose Works of John Milton*, Volume V, Part II]." *N&Q*, 19, 1972, 474–78.

States that this edition (see No. 366) is not definitive.

4148 "Milton Going Up." *MiltonQ*, 10, 1976, 135.

Announces a first edition of *Paradise Lost* for sale.

4149 "Milton Going Up." *MiltonQ*, 13, 1979, 11.

Reproduces a sale notice for a first edition of *Paradise Lost*.

4150 Milton Illustrated: Visions of Paradise. An Exhibition in the Reference Library, Language and Literature Department. Birmingham Public Libraries, 1978. Introduction by Phillip N. Allen. [Birmingham: Birmingham Public Libraries, 1978.] 31pp.

Lists fifty-eight editions and illustrators who range from John Baptist de Medina to Blair Hughes-Stanton.

4151 Molnár, Judit, and **István Pálffy.** "The Intellectual Contacts of Debrecen, the 'Capital' of Eastern Hungary with England in the 17th and 18th Centuries." *HSE*, 18, 1985, 23–33.

Discusses the development of Hungarian interest in English letters. Milton became a favorite, and there were several attempts to translate *Paradise Lost* into Hungarian.

4152 Morris, Edward. "John Gibson's Satan." *JWCI*, 34, 1971, 397–99.

Gibson's drawing, *Fall of the Rebel Angels* (1808–11), is based on Michelangelo's *Last Judgment* in the Sistine Chapel, but Michelangelo's figure of Christ as judge becomes Gibson's Satan.

4153 Moyles, R. G. "Edward Capell (1713–1781) as Editor of *Paradise Lost*." *TCBS*, 6, 1975, 252–61.

Studies Capell's 1759 unpublished edition. Capell was, "in terms of his treatment of the substantive text, his awareness of the authoritative editions, and his inclusion of a textual apparatus, more than a hundred years ahead of his time."

4154 Moyles, R. G. "On Editing *Paradise Lost*: A Study of the Textual Problems, with Special Reference to Edward Capell's Unpublished Edition of the Poem Preserved at Trinity College Library, Cambridge." Doctoral diss., Birkbeck College, London, 1969. *IT*, 19, 1971, 16.

4155 Moyles, R. G. "The Text of *Paradise Lost*: A Stemma for the Early Editions." *SB*, 33, 1980, 168–82.

"One important area . . . [of study] has been entirely neglected: the treatment of the text itself. When did editors of *Paradise Lost* begin to seek a definitive text? When did they become aware of the state of the original editions—of the variants between them? When did they begin to use what W. W. Greg calls 'reasoned editorial judgment'? This paper represents an attempt to remedy that neglect and to answer those questions by examining two aspects of the text: editorial treatment of the Quarto and Octavo variants; and the perpetuation of progressive error."

4156 Moyles, R. G. *The Text of "Paradise Lost": A Study in Editorial Procedure.* Toronto, Buffalo, NY, and London: Univ. of Toronto Press, 1985. x, 188pp.

Examines "the textual and bibliographical state of *Paradise Lost*," including

"a thorough description of the transmission of the text and its treatment at the hands" of various prominent editors during the past three centuries.

4157 Mulhallen, Karen. "William Blake's Milton Portraiture and Eighteenth Century Milton Iconography." *CLQ*, 14, 1978, 7–21.

"This paper will examine the Milton iconographic tradition as it is reflected in three portraits by William Blake." Compares Blake and other artists who portrayed Milton.

4158 Noble, Margaret Mary. "Twentieth-Century Illustrations of John Milton's *Paradise Lost*." Doctoral diss., Univ. of Toledo, 1977. 133pp. Abs., *DAI*, 38, 1978, 6697A.

Notes varying degrees of accuracy among five modern illustrators of *Paradise Lost*, as well as a heightened focus on the "human relationship of Adam and Eve."

4159 "A Note on Our Cover." *MiltonQ*, 8, 1974, 31.

On two of William Hogarth's illustrations of *Paradise Lost*, possibly intended for Jacob Tonson's edition (1725).

4160 Onukiyama, Nobuo. "On Translating *Paradise Regained*." *MCJ News*, 5, 1981, 17–18.

Abstract of a paper presented at the Eleventh Colloquium of MCJ in July, 1981. Discusses problems the author encountered when translating *Paradise Regained* into Japanese.

4161 Oras, Ants. *Milton's Editors and Commentators from Patrick Hume to Henry John Todd (1695–1801): A Study in Critical Views and Methods.* London: Oxford Univ. Press, 1969.

Reprint of Huckabay No. 3588, originally published in 1931.

4162 Paley, Morton D. "'To Realize after a Sort the Imagery of Milton': Samuel Palmer's Designs for *L'Allegro* and *Il Penseroso*." *HLQ*, 46, 1983, 48–71.

Uses the correspondence between Leonard Rowe Valpy and Palmer as a means of discussing the latter's interest in Milton's poetry.

4163 Patrick, J. Max. "Why was a Revised Volume VII of the Yale Milton Issued?" *SCN*, 40, 1982, 63.

Gives several reasons for the numerous errors in the first version of the volume (No. 366).

4164 Paulson, Ronald. "The Miltonic Scripture." *Book and Painting: Shakespeare, Milton and the Bible. Literary Texts and the Emergence of English Painting* (Knoxville: Univ. of Tennessee Press, 1982), pp. 99–151.

Studies verbal structures that "impressed themselves on English painting," focusing on the illustrators of Satan, Sin, and Death. Reviews (of book): Estella Schoenberg, *MiltonQ*, 17, 1983, 51–52; Kenneth Garlick, *RES*, 36, 1985, 424–26.

4165 Pointon, Marcia R. *Milton and English Art.* Manchester: Manchester Univ. Press; Toronto and Buffalo, NY: Univ. of Toronto Press, 1970. xliii, 276pp.

"This book comprises a historical survey of the illustrations to Milton's poetry executed in England between 1688 and 1860, including engraved designs incorporated in editions of Milton's poetry and exhibited works."

4166 Ravenhall, Mary D. "Francis Atterbury and the First Illustrated Edition of *Paradise Lost.*" *MiltonQ*, 16, 1982, 29–36.

Argues that "A fresh examination of eighteenth[-] and nineteenth-century biographical sources pertaining to Atterbury indicates that he, not [John] Somers, is the person most likely to have served as advisor to [John Baptist de] Medina and Bernard Lens, the designer of a single plate for Book IV."

4167 Ravenhall, Mary D. "Francis Hayman and the Dramatic Interpretation of *Paradise Lost.*" *MiltonS*, 20, 1984, 87–109.

Shows that Hayman, in his illustrations for the 1749 edition, depicts the poem as a series of dramatic actions and bases his work on mid-eighteenth-century critical opinion.

4168 Ravenhall, Mary Dennis. "Illustrations of *Paradise Lost* in England, 1688–1802." Doctoral diss., Univ. of Illinois, Urbana, 1980. 966pp. Abs., *DAI*, 41, 1980, 442A.

Argues that eighteenth-century illustrations of *Paradise Lost* show "a shift in emphasis from moral and theological meaning to dramatic action," often centered on Satan, Adam, or Eve.

4169 Ravenhall, Mary D. "Sources and Meaning in Dr. Aldrich's 1688 Illustrations of *Paradise Lost.*" *ELN*, 19, 1982, 208–18.

Continues the work in No. 4105. Attributes three plates to Dr. Henry Aldrich and studies his sources "as visual keys to the seventeenth-century reader's interpretation of Milton's poem."

4170 Rose, Edward J. "Blake's Illustrations for *Paradise Lost, L'Allegro,* and *Il Penseroso*: A Thematic Reading." *HSL*, 2, 1970, 40–67.

Shows that Blake's illustrations for *Paradise Lost* and the companion poems, like his poem *Milton*, are a commentary on Milton. Milton himself is the chief figure in the designs for *L'Allegro* and *Il Penseroso*, appearing as the "piper of innocence, the bard of experience; the image of the reptilizing rebel dominates the designs for *Paradise Lost.*"

4171 Schoenberg, Estella. "The Face of Satan, 1688." *Ringing the Bell Backward: The Proceedings of the First International Milton Symposium.* Ed. by Ronald G. Shafer. The IUP Imprint Series (Indiana: Indiana Univ. of Pennsylvania, 1982), pp. 47–59.

Suggests that Satan's depiction in Plates 1 and 2 of Jacob Tonson's edition of *Paradise Lost* (1688) resembles contemporary statues of Charles II and James II. Response by Stella P. Revard, pp. 60–61.

4172 Schoenberg, Estella. "Picturing Satan for the 1688 *Paradise Lost.*" *Milton's Legacy in the Arts.* Ed. by Albert C. Labriola and Edward Sichi, Jr. (University Park and London: Pennsylvania State Univ. Press, 1988), pp. 1–20.

Believes that in their 1688 edition, Jacob Tonson knew of the epic's political content and John Baptist de Medina reflected a bias toward the Stuarts in his illustrations.

4173 Sellin, Paul R. "Lieuwe van Aitzema and the Dutch Translation of Milton on Divorce." *Papers from the Second Interdisciplinary Conference on Netherlandic Studies Held at Georgetown University 7–9 June 1984.* Ed. by William H. Fletcher (Washington, DC: Univ. Press of America, 1985), pp. 105–11.

Discusses van Aitzema's letter of January 29, 1655, informing Milton that he had commissioned a Dutch translation of Milton's "Tractlet" on divorce. The translation has never been found, but there were important domestic and political reasons for commissioning it.

4174 Shawcross, John T. "The First Illustrations for *Paradise Lost.*" *MiltonQ,* 9, 1975, 43–46.

Replies to No. 4105. On the 1688 edition. See No. 4178.

4175 Shawcross, John T. "A Note on Milton's Latin Translator, M. B." *MiltonQ,* 21, No. 2, 1987, 65–66.

Argues that Michael Bold wrote the Latin translation of *Paradise Lost* 1 (1702). Discusses his biography and other works.

4176 Shawcross, John T. "A Note on T. P.'s Latin Translation of *Paradise Lost.*" *MiltonQ,* 21, No. 2, 1987, 66–68.

Discusses Thomas Power's Latin translation of *Paradise Lost* (1691), his methods of translation, and his various manuscripts.

4177 Shawcross, John T. "Scholarly Editions: Composite Editorial Principles of Single Copy-Texts, Multiple Copy-Texts, Edited Copy-Texts." *TEXT,* 4, 1988, 297–317.

Discusses some of an editor's problems, particularly when several textual variations exist, as in the case of Milton's poems, especially the shorter ones.

4178 Sims, James H. "Corrections Concerning 'The First Illustrations for *Paradise Lost.*'" *MiltonQ,* 9, 1975, 126–27.

Replies to John Shawcross's article (No. 4174) by stating that John Baptist de Medina accurately reflects the content of *Paradise Lost* 3.64–69 and 11.185–90.

4179 Stanley, E. G. "Richard Bentley's Use of *Persona,* 1732." *N&Q,* 30, 1983, 442.

Believes that Bentley invented a "supposed 'editor'" of *Paradise Lost* in order to justify his "corrections."

4180 Sullivan, Ernest W., II. "Illustration as Interpretation: *Paradise Lost* from 1688 to 1807." *Milton's Legacy in the Arts.* Ed. by Albert C. Labriola and Edward Sichi, Jr. (University Park and London: Pennsylvania State Univ. Press, 1988), pp. 59–92.

Traces the pictorial representations of Satan, Sin, and the Fall to show that illustrations of *Paradise Lost* reveal changing interpretations of the poem.

4181 Tayler, Irene. "Blake's *Comus* Designs." *BlakeS,* 4, 1972, 45–80. Reprinted in *Blake's Sublime Allegory: Essays on the "Four Zoas," "Milton," and "Jerusalem."* Ed. by Stuart Curran and Joseph Anthony Wittreich, Jr. (Madison: Univ. of Wisconsin Press, 1973), pp. 233–58.

"What I am suggesting, in brief, is that Blake saw the lady's encounter with Comus as the product of that frightened girl's fantasy: her bondage, the bondage of sexual fears; her release, the release from them."

4182 "Tercentenary Conferences and Volumes." *MiltonN,* 2, 1968, 46–47.

On the facsimile edition of *Paradise Lost* (1667; see No. 335) published by the Scolar Press and a special issue of the *Huntington Library Quarterly* (see No. 714), which contains illustrations from the Huntington Art Gallery collection.

4183 Tisch, J. H. "Between Translation and Adaptation: *Paradise Lost* in German 1682–1760." *Expression, Communication and Experience in Literature and Language*. Proceedings of the XIIth Congress of the International Federation for Modern Languages and Literatures Held at Cambridge University, 20 to 26 August, 1972. Ed. by Ronald G. Popperwell and others (London: Modern Humanities Research Association, 1973), pp. 282–85.

Compares Simon Grynäus's version and F. W. Zachariä's versions, with comments on Bodmer's influence.

4184 Tisch, J. H. "Between Translation and Adaptation: The 'Poetic Theology' (Bodmer) of *Paradise Lost* in German 1682–1793." *Abstracts of Papers, AULLA 26th Congress* (Univ. of Western Australia and Murdoch Univ.), 1991, pp. 37–38.

Simon Grynäus's verse translation (1758) is "literary" and Friedrich Wilhelm Zachariä's (1760) is "religious," though both reflect the influence of Bodmer's prose translation.

4185 Tisch, J. H. *A Critical Assessment of the German Translation of "Paradise Lost." Book 1 by Simon Grynäus*. Hobart: Univ. of Tasmania, 1980. 13pp.

In German. Portrays Bodmer as the forerunner of German translations with his version of *Paradise Lost* (1732) and his powerful influence on others, such as Friedrich Wilhelm Zachariä and especially Simon Grynäus.

4186 Tisch, J. Hermann. "*Paradise Lost* 'in der Vollen Pracht des Deutschen Hexameters': Eine Kritische Würdigung der Milton-Übersetzung von Simon Grynäus." *Akten des VI. Internationalen Germanisten-Kongresses, Basel, 1980, III*. Ed. by Heinz Rupp and Hans-Gert Roloff (Berne: Peter Lang, 1980), pp. 46–52.

Compares the poetic language of *Paradise Lost* when translated into German and examines changes in meter and diction in Simon Grynäus's translation (1758).

4187 Tisch, J. H. "*Paradise Lost* 'in der Vollen Pracht des Deutschen Hexame-

ters': Observations on the Milton Translations by F. W. Zachariä and Simon Grynäus." *Seminar*, 9, 1973, 187–201.

On eighteenth-century German verse translations of *Paradise Lost* which rely heavily on Bodmer's prose translation. Abs., *SCN*, 34, 1976, 21.

4188 Trapp, J. B. "The Iconography of the Fall of Man." *Approaches to "Paradise Lost."* The York Tercentenary Lectures. Ed. by C. A. Patrides (London: Edward Arnold; Toronto: Univ. of Toronto Press, 1968), pp. 223–65.

Surveys illustrations of the Fall from early Christian times to the seventeenth century.

4189 Tufte, Virginia. "Evil as Parody in the Paradise That was Lost: Three Illustrators Interpret Milton's Book 4." *Mosaic*, 21, Nos. 2–3, 1988, 37–58.

Focuses on various illustrators of Book 4—Bernard Lens (1688), William Blake (1807–08), and Mary Groom (1937)—who "draw on traditional iconography as they interpret facets of the epic, in particular the nature of Eden and of evil as parody of good."

4190 Tufte, Virginia. "Protection and Peril: Bernard Lens's View of Milton's Eden." *MiltonQ*, 21, No. 3, 1987, 90–96.

Claims that Lens's 1688 illustration for *Paradise Lost* 4 emphasizes the garden's "protective features and at the same time the evil that lurks there," particularly through animal symbolism.

4191 Turman, Kathryn Lee Green. "The Illumination of the Paradise Within: An Iconological Analysis of *Milton, a Poem in 2 Books*." Doctoral diss., Univ. of Texas, Austin, 1987. 554pp. Abs., *DAI*, 48, 1987, 1213A.

Inspects the iconography of *Paradise Lost* and Blake's work, testing "the utility of a critical method based on C. G. Jung's theory of archetypal analysis and Owen Barfield's theory of idolatry."

4192 Waddington, Raymond B. "The Iconography of Jean Dassier's Milton Medal." *MiltonQ*, 19, 1985, 93–96.

Analyzes Dassier's medal (1730), "focusing upon the iconography of both the Milton portrait and the *Paradise Lost* scene of the reverse."

4193 Waddington, Raymond B. "Louis Cheron's Illustration of Milton's 'Sin.'" *MiltonQ*, 19, 1985, 78–80.

Argues that in Tonson's edition of Milton's *Works* (1720), Cheron's illustration of Sin deviated "from the considerably more complicated anatomy described by Milton" and looked instead to Cesare Ripa's *Iconologia* "for an established visual formula." Reply by Edward Le Comte (No. 4139).

4194 Welch, Dennis M. "Blake's Critique of Election: *Milton* and the *Comus* Illustrations." *PQ*, 64, 1985, 509–31.

Studies Blake's illustrations of *Comus*. Argues that *Milton* shows that Blake saw the conflicts in *Comus* as Milton's internal struggle "between his enthusiasm for religion, reason, and restraint and his impulse toward nature, feeling, and experience."

4195 Werner, Bette Charlene. *Blake's Vision of the Poetry of Milton: Illustrations to Six Poems.* Lewisburg, PA: Bucknell Univ. Press; London: Associated Univ. Presses, 1986. 319pp.

Examines what Blake's illustrations reveal about his perception of Milton's work. Reviews: J. M. Q. Davies, *PQ*, 68, 1989, 280–82; Mary Lynn Johnson, *JEGP*, 88, 1989, 429–34.

4196 Werner, Bette Charlene. "Milton's Sixfold Emanation Redeemed in the Designs of Blake: William Blake's Illustrations to Six Poems by John Milton." Doctoral diss., Univ. of Toledo, 1981. 442pp. Abs., *DAI*, 42, 1981, 2693A.

Contends that, in illustrating Milton's major works, "Blake casts off what he perceives as error in order to highlight areas of eternal verity."

4197 Wills, James T. " 'For I Discern Thee Other then Thou Seem'st': An Extra Illustration for Blake's *Paradise Regained* Series." *BlakeS*, 8, 1979, 109–19.

Believes that a drawing in the Frick Collection "should now be seen as a legitimate extra illustration for the Milton text."

4198 Wittreich, Joseph Anthony, Jr. "Appendix A: Illustrators of *Paradise Regained* and Their Subjects (1713–1816)." *Calm of Mind: Tercentenary Essays on "Paradise Regained" and "Samson Agonistes" in Honor of John S. Diekhoff.* Ed. by Wittreich (Cleveland, OH, and London: Press of Case Western Reserve Univ., 1971), pp. 309–29. Ann Arbor, MI: Univ. Microfilms International, 1980 Books on Demand Reprints.

A catalog prepared after examining the editions of *Paradise Regained* in a number of American libraries.

4199 Wittreich, Joseph Anthony, Jr. "Appendix B: A Catalogue of Blake's Illustrations to Milton." *Calm of Mind: Tercentenary Essays on "Paradise Regained" and "Samson Agonistes" in Honor of John S. Diekhoff.* Ed. by Wittreich (Cleveland, OH, and London: Press of Case Western Reserve Univ., 1971), pp. 331–42. Ann Arbor, MI: Univ. Microfilms International, 1980 Books on Demand Reprints.

Organizes the illustrations in three groupings: Engravings after Others' Designs, Separate Designs, and Sets of Designs.

4200 Wittreich, Joseph Anthony, Jr. "Milton's 'First' Illustrator." *SCN*, 32, 1974, 70–71.

Henry Aldrich, not John Baptist de Medina. Believes that the Satanist controversy began with these two illustrators, with Aldrich "remaining faithful in spirit if not always in details to *Paradise Lost*, Medina choosing instead to bring Milton's revolutionary conception of Satan into line with orthodoxy."

4201 Wittreich, Joseph Anthony, Jr. "William Blake: Illustrator-Interpreter of *Paradise Regained*." *Calm of Mind: Tercentenary Essays on "Paradise Re-*

gained" and "Samson Agonistes" in Honor of John S. Diekhoff. Ed. by Wittreich (Cleveland, OH, and London: Press of Case Western Reserve Univ., 1971), pp. 93–132. Ann Arbor, MI: Univ. Microfilms International, 1980 Books on Demand Reprints.

"In a series of twelve designs, Blake has presented with magnificent clarity the grand lines of the myth that informs Milton's poem [*Paradise Regained*] and has explored, then defined, Milton's relation to both theological and poetical traditions."

4202 Wolvekamp-Baxter, B. M. "*Het Paradijs Verloren*: Alex Gutteling's Translation of Milton's *Paradise Lost*, Books I–VI.*" European Context: Studies in the History and Literature of the Netherlands Presented to Theodoor Weevers.* Ed. by P. K. King and P. F. Vincent. Publications of the Modern Humanities Research Association, 4 (Cambridge: Modern Humanities Research Association, 1971), pp. 268–301.

Analyzes Gutteling's methodology as he translated *Paradise Lost* into Dutch (1910–12).

4203 Adler, Joshua. "A Further Note on Tennyson's 'Subtle Beast.'" *N&Q*, 22, 1975, 437–39.

Reinforces the thesis that Tennyson's use of the phrase "Subtle Beast" in *Guinevere* was influenced by Milton's references to Satan in *Paradise Lost*.

4204 Adler, Thomas P. "The Uses of Knowledge in Tennyson's *Merlin and Vivien*." *TSLL*, 11, 1970, 1397–1403.

Proposes "to use Book 9 of *Paradise Lost*, which exhibits some striking similarities to *Merlin and Vivien*, as a way of approaching Tennyson's poem and opening it up to a more substantive understanding."

4205 Alvis, John. "The Miltonic Argument in Caroline Gordon's *The Glory of Hera*." *SoR*, 16, 1980, 560–73.

Sees Hercules's career ending in "a comic denouement for which we are prepared by the novel's Miltonic transvaluation of classical material." Contends that "Gordon's Zeus prefigures Milton's 'bright effluence of bright essence increate,'" notes the similarity between Gordon's Ophion and Milton's Satan, and associates Hercules with Milton's Samson.

4206 Anand, Shahla. "Isa Charan Sada: A Twentieth-Century Urdu Poet: 1870–1957." *MiltonQ*, 12, 1978, 74.

Abstract of a paper presented at the 1977 MLA Convention. Mentions Sada's translations of Milton's major works into Urdu poetry.

4207 Anand, Shahla. *Magnificent Quest. Isa Charan Sada: Urdu Poet and Milton Scholar.* Foreword by John T. Shawcross. Delhi: I. S. P. C. K., 1986. xx, 509pp.

Discusses Milton's influence and Sada's translations of his work into Urdu poetry.

4208 Anderson, David R. "Milton's Influence on Thomson: The Uses of Landscape." *MiltonS*, 15, 1981, 107–20.

"Milton taught [James] Thomson to associate walking through nature with meditation upon it and led him from that meditation to praise of nature's God." Emphasizes the verbal parallels between *Il Penseroso* and the *Seasons*. Also suggests that *Spectator* 425 is a mixture of Miltonic and Thomsonian materials.

4209 Andreach, Robert J. "*Paradise Lost* and the Christian Configuration of *The Waste Land*." *PLL*, 5, 1969, 296–309.

Argues that "in the two pivotal scenes of *The Waste Land* it is Milton as well as Dante who asserts his immortality most vigorously." Suggests that Eliot's pronouncements on Milton have thrown critics off guard—that Milton was a positive influence in the *Waste Land*.

4210 Anozie, Sunday O. "Soyinka and the *Jihad* of the Pen; or, Style as Intertextuality." *Matatu*, 1, 1987, 73–83.

The resemblance between Milton and the Nigerian author Wole Soyinka "is lodged in both the structure and the intensity of allusiveness of their poetic language."

4211 Arai, Akira. "Milton and Modern Poetry." *Miscellaneous Essays on Milton* (Tokyo: Chukyo Shuppan, 1979), pp. 103–17.

In Japanese. Discusses Milton's impact on certain modern poets, including Arnold, Bridges, Eliot, Hopkins, and Pound.

4212 Arner, Robert D. "Nehemiah Walter: Milton's Earliest American Disciple?" *EAL*, 8, 1973, 62–65.

Denies earlier assertions that Cotton Mather was "the first American to leave a clear record of Milton's impress" and claims that title for Increase Mather's son-in-law, Nehemiah Walter. Places the earliest date of Milton's influence in America at 1687.

4213 Avrakhova, Liudmyla. "Dolia Odnoho Zadumu." *Vsesvit*, 1, 1987, 170–71. "Destiny of One Idea." In Ukrainian. Discusses the Ukrainian poet Lesya and her interest in Milton's literary works.

4214 Bagchi, P. "A Note on Wordsworth's 'Artegal and Eliduré.'" *N&Q*, 18, 1971, 377–78.

On Wordsworth's misreading of a passage in Milton's *History of Britain.*

4215 Baker, Christopher P. "Milton's Nativity Ode and *In Memoriam CVI.*" *VP*, 18, 1980, 202–03.

Suggests that Tennyson's "known appreciation of Milton, the repetition of the phase 'Ring out,' and the thematic parallel of the death of an old order and the inception of a new, specifically Christian, hope in both poems, all suggest that Milton's ode may have aided Tennyson's conception of his own poem of religious faith."

4216 Beer, Gillian. "Richardson, Milton, and the Status of Evil." *RES*, 19, 1968, 261–70.

Samuel Richardson imitates Milton's technique for portraying evil, for Milton at first presents Satan attractively. Then the reader's disillusionment with his character "make[s] evil recognizable."

4217 Berryman, John. "Wash Far Away." *American Review*, 22, 1975, 1–26.

A short story that deals with a professor who is moved and shaken by the experience of teaching Milton's *Lycidas.* See No. 4288.

4218 Beyette, Kent. "Milton and Pope's *The Rape of the Lock.*" *SEL*, 16, 1976, 421–36.

Suggests that elements of Pope's *Rape of the Lock* are directly related to the works of Milton, particularly *Comus* and *Paradise Lost.* Claims that "for comic purposes he [Pope] employs Milton's idea that the fate of mankind depends on the resolution of a lovers' quarrel."

4219 Bidney, Martin. "*Christabel* as Dark Double of *Comus.*" *SP*, 83, 1986, 182–200. Argues that "*Christabel* reads in large part like a darkly ironic re-evaluation of the moral world-view conveyed in *Comus.*"

4220 Bidney, Martin. "Of the Devil's Party: Undetected Words of Milton's Satan in Arnold's *Dover Beach.*" *VP*, 20, 1982, 85–89.

Examines "verbal and imaginal echoes and parallels" of Milton's *Paradise Lost* in Arnold's *Dover Beach.* Finds most significant Arnold's use of Milton's Satanic dialogue which draws a parallel between hell and earth.

4221 Bieman, Elizabeth. "Devils' Yule and Mountain-Birth: Miltonic Echoes in Coleridge's *Dejection Ode.*" *M&R*, 2, 1976, 16–22.

"The effects to be noted in the final stanzas of *Dejection* are achieved through images and verbal echoes that point, via certain passages in Milton's *Ode on the Morning of Christ's Nativity* and in *Paradise Regained*, to the triumphant coming of love to the world."

4222 Blessington, Francis C. "The Portrait in the Spoon: George Eliot's Casaubon and John Milton." *MiltonQ*, 20, 1986, 29–31.

Asserts that George Eliot's Casaubon in *Middlemarch* is a parody of Milton. He "resembles Milton in social status, education, intellectual interests, domestic life, and temperament," but he also has "pompous epistolary and conversational styles," a "condescending and pretentious manner," and an "inherent weakness of character." Reply by Sister Bridget Marie Engelmeyer (No. 4273).

4223 Blondel, Jacques. "Du Périple des Sots à la Quete de *Childe Roland*." *Le Voyage Romantique et ses Réécritures.* Ed. by Christian La Cassagnère. Faculté des Lettres et Sciences Humaines de l'Université de Clermont-Ferrand II, vol. 26 (Clermont-Ferrand: Faculté des Lettres et Sciences Humaines de Clermont-Ferrand, Centre du Romantisme Anglais, 1987), pp. 119–28.

Contrasts the use of quests and baroque art in the events in Milton's Paradise of Fools and the disturbing experience of Browning's Childe Roland.

4224 Bloom, Harold. *The Anxiety of Influence: A Theory of Poetry.* New York: Oxford Univ. Press, 1973; Oxford: Oxford Univ. Press, 1975. 157pp.

Considers Milton to be "the central problem in any theory and history of poetic influence in English." He is "the great Inhibitor, the Sphinx who strangles even strong imaginations in their cradles." See No. 4557.

4225 Blumenthal, Friedrich. *Lord Byron's Mystery "Cain" and Its Relation to Milton's "Paradise Lost" and Gessner's "Death of Abel."* Philadelphia, PA: R. West, 1976; Folcroft, PA: Folcroft Library Editions, 1977.

Reprints of Stevens No. 863, originally published in 1892.

4226 Bostich, June. "Miltonic Influence in *The Rape of the Lock*." *EnlE*, 4, No. 1, 1973, 65–72.

Claims that the machinery of the sylphs was derived from Milton's treatment of the angels in *Paradise Lost*. Also points out similarities between Eve and Belinda and finds echoes of Satan in the lover's retaliation. Concludes that Pope's imitation is not "slavish" but an integral part, an echo of and allusion to Milton's "moral context."

4227 Brand, Dana. "Milton's Presence in Wordsworth's London: A Discussion of the Structure of Book VII of the *Pre-*

lude." *CEA*, 48–49, 1986, 70–75.

Shows how *Paradise Lost* 7 provides a structural framework for the *Prelude* 7. Believes that Milton played an important role in Wordsworth's effort to define his creative identity.

4228 Briggs, Peter M. "The Jonathan Richardsons as Milton Critics." *SECC*, 9, 1979, 115–30.

Examines the Richardsons' celebration and defense of Milton, especially against Richard Bentley's "notorious 'corrected' edition of *Paradise Lost*."

4229 Brink, J. R. "Johnson and Milton." *SEL*, 20, 1980, 493–503.

Shows that Johnson admires Milton more than is commonly thought and that in his *Life* "Johnson's view of the literary biographer as a guardian of public taste and morals helps to explain his critical stance toward Milton."

4230 Brinkley, Robert A. "Vagrant and Hermit: Milton and the Politics of 'Tintern Abbey.'" *WC*, 16, 1985, 126–33.

"The cherished spot that Wordsworth revisits in 'Tintern Abbey' is transformed from an elegiac scene into the kind of internalized landscape, the 'paradise within' which Milton associated with prophetic obligation. . . . As such, the topographical elegy gains a particular political significance."

4231 Brisman, Leslie. "Keats, Milton, and What One May 'Very Naturally Suppose.'" *M&R*, 1, No. 1, 1975, 4–7.

To Keats, Milton originated the awareness of the difference between natural and intellectual succession. Feels that Keats identified Milton with Apollonius, the "sage of cold philosophy" in *Lamia*.

4232 Brisman, Leslie. *Milton's Poetry of Choice and Its Romantic Heirs.* Ithaca, NY, and London: Cornell Univ. Press, 1973. xv, 335pp.

Choice refers to subtleties of language, method, and style, and of meanings that are beyond the words. The Romantic heirs include Keats, Shelley, Blake, and Wordsworth. Reviews:

MiltonQ, 7, 1973, 86–87; Leslie Tannenbaum, *BlakeS*, 6, 1973, 55–68; Roberts W. French, *SCN*, 32, 1974, 52; Joseph Anthony Wittreich, Jr., *JEGP*, 73, 1974, 435–39, and *MiltonQ*, 8, 1974, 15–21; Florence Sandler, *BlakeN*, 8, 1975, 127–28; Dennis H. Burden, *RES*, 31, 1980, 213–14.

4233 Brodwin, Leonora Leet. "Miltonic Allusion in *Absalom and Achitophel*: Its Function in the Political Satire." *JEGP*, 68, 1969, 24–44.

Demonstrates Milton's influence on Dryden, mainly from *Paradise Lost* but also from *Samson Agonistes* and *Comus*.

4234 Bromberg, Pamela Starr. "Blake and the Spectre of Milton." Doctoral diss., Yale Univ., 1973. 323pp. Abs., *DAI*, 34, 1973, 2548A–49A.

Examines Blake's poetic relationship with Milton, who is recognized in the *Marriage of Heaven and Hell*, parodied in *Europe*, challenged in the *Four Zoas*, and confronted in *Milton*.

4235 Brunel, Pierre. "Claudel Lecteur et Juge de Milton." *RLC*, 49, 1975, 249–59.

"Claudel senses the heresy in Milton (materialism, arianism, gnosticism, defense of polygamy) and makes of *Paradise Lost* the mirror of schismatic England. Milton became, for Claudel, the poet of Satan and thus superior to Dante. This judgement is possible only by reduction."

4236 Buchan, Hannah. "*Absalom and Achitophel*: A Patron's Name or a Patriot's?" *YES*, 7, 1977, 86–90.

Considers the echoes of Milton in Dryden, especially in the words "patron" and "patriot."

4237 Burch, Beth. "A Miltonic Echo in Faulkner's *The Hamlet*." *NConL*, 8, No. 4, 1978, 3–4.

Believes that "the Ike Snopes-Houston's cow scene from *The Hamlet* . . . is analogous to Milton's pastoral *Elegia Quinta*."

4238 Burnett, Archie. "Echoes and Parallels in Tennyson's Poetry." *N&Q*, 34, 1987, 40–41.

Includes addenda to echoes and parallels of Milton noted in Christopher Ricks's edition of the *Poems of Tennyson* (1969).

4239 Burnett, Archie. "Miltonic Echoes and Parallels in Matthew Arnold's Poetry." *N&Q*, 34, 1987, 493–94.

Addenda to the parallels and echoes of Milton noted in the second edition of Miriam Allott's text of the *Poems of Matthew Arnold* (1979).

4240 Burnett, Archie. "Tennyson's 'Mariana': Two Parallels." *N&Q*, 27, 1980, 207–08.

Suggests that "Mariana" 78 echoes *Il Penseroso* 7–8.

4241 Bush, Douglas. "The Milton of Keats and Arnold." *MiltonS*, 11, 1978, 99–114.

Keats's "notes on *Paradise Lost*, however brief, give us insight into both Milton and himself. Arnold's much fuller comments on Milton and the epic in particular remain classic formulations of general attitudes and ideas which existed before him and which he did much to establish as orthodoxy."

4242 Camé, Jean-François. "Milton and Marvell." *CahiersE*, 15, 1979, 73–74.

Believes that Marvell's poetry reflects Milton's "diffuse influence."

4243 Campbell, Gordon. "Francini's *Permesso*." *MiltonQ*, 15, 1981, 122–23.

On Antonio Francini's tribute to Milton included in the *Poems* (1645). The allusion to the stream of Permessus "acknowledges Milton's accomplishment as an elegiac poet, but also gracefully anticipates his destiny as an epic poet."

4244 Chatterjee, Visvanath. "Milton's Significance for Us." *Bulletin of the Department of English* (Calcutta Univ.), 10, 1974–75, 13–24.

Says that Milton teaches us how to "play the man" and discusses his influence on Indian writers.

4245 Chavy, Paul. "Baroque Miltonien et

Paysages de Chateaubriand." *CAIEF*, 29, 1977, 65–79.

Chateaubriand was fascinated by *Paradise Lost* and Milton. He found many parallels between their personal lives and literary interests. Traces Milton's influence on Chateaubriand's works.

4246 Clifford, James L. "Johnson and Lauder." *PQ*, 54, 1975, 342–56.

Discusses Johnson's initial trust in William Lauder's accusation that Milton plagiarized "largely unknown" modern writers in *Paradise Lost*.

4247 Cole, Phyllis. "The Purity of Puritanism: Transcendentalist Readings of Milton." *SIR*, 17, 1978, 129–48.

Claims that earlier transcendentalists, such as Channing and Emerson, "read Milton's work as an expression of his progress toward redemption and as a means toward their own redemption." Concludes that Lowell spoke for the later transcendentalists when he gave "limited praise" to Milton and more lavish praise to Dante, "who embodied the full power of visual imagination in complete removal from complicating issues of Puritan egotism."

4248 Collins, Douglas P. "Milton et 'Le Beau Navire.'" *BBaud*, 9, No. 1, 1973, 3–5.

The Chorus's description of Dalila coming "like a stately Ship" is a possible source for the image of the ship in Pierre Charles Baudelaire's "Le Beau Navire."

4249 Connors, S. G. "Living within the Light of High Endeavours: Wordsworth's Poetry of 1800–1805 and the Influence of John Milton." Doctoral diss., Univ. of Wales, 1986. Abs., *IT*, 39, 1990, 32.

4250 Cook, Albert. "Blake's *Milton*." *Costerus*, 6, 1972, 27–33.

The "very high-handedness with which he [Blake] treated Milton only marks the assuredness with which he was able . . . to adapt Milton for his own poetic purposes."

4251 Cook, Eleanor. "Birds in Paradise:

Uses of Allusion in Milton, Keats, Whitman, Stevens and Ammons." *SIR*, 26, 1987, 421–43.

Milton's nightingale in *Paradise Lost* is "the true paradisal bird, whether in Eden or as image for his poetic voice in the invocation to Light." Keats, Whitman, Stevens, and A. R. Ammons all echo Milton's bird image and deal with the issue of mimic fancy.

4252 Cox, Lee Sheridan. "In Praise of a Master Magician." *MiltonQ*, 14, 1980, 97.

An appreciative poem.

4253 Crawford, John W. "*Absalom and Achitophel* and Milton's *Paradise Lost*." *UDR*, 7, No. 2, 1971, 29–37. Reprinted in *Discourse: Essays on English and American Literature* (Amsterdam: Editions Rodopi N. V., 1978), pp. 65–76.

Suggests that Dryden exhibits considerable indebtedness to Milton.

4254 Curran, Stuart. "The Mental Pinnacle: *Paradise Regained* and the Romantic Four-Book Epic." *Calm of Mind: Tercentenary Essays on "Paradise Regained" and "Samson Agonistes" in Honor of John S. Diekhoff.* Ed. by Joseph Anthony Wittreich, Jr. (Cleveland, OH, and London: Press of Case Western Reserve Univ., 1971), pp. 133–62. Ann Arbor, MI: Univ. Microfilms International, 1980 Books on Demand Reprints.

"The brief epic, as defined by *Paradise Regained*, is clearly the prototype for the four-book epics of the Romantic period: Keats' *Endymion*, Blake's *Jerusalem*, and Shelley's *Prometheus Unbound*."

4255 Cutts, John P. "Garrick's Use of Milton in His Versions of *A Midsummer Night's Dream*." *NM*, 80, 1979, 78–80.

Quotes several passages adapted from *Arcades* and *L'Allegro* in Garrick's 1755 production.

4256 Dahiyat, Eid A. "Milton and Franklin." *EAL*, 21, 1986, 44–48.

Demonstrates that Benjamin Franklin was a great admirer of Milton and that their thinking had much in common.

4257 Danielson, Dennis R. "Milton and Early America: 'Evangelical Strains.'" *Ringing the Bell Backward: The Proceedings of the First International Milton Symposium.* Ed. by Ronald G. Shafer. The IUP Imprint Series (Indiana: Indiana Univ. of Pennsylvania, 1982), pp. 75–84.

Shows that some early American authors, such as Joseph Bellamy, echo Milton's language, while Horace Bushnell and others echo Milton but present a non-Miltonic theodicy. Response by John T. Shawcross, pp. 85–90.

4258 Dargan, Tom. "Blake and Hayley in Wittreich's *Angel of Apocalypse.*" *BlakeN*, 10, 1977, 130–35.

Disagrees with Joseph Anthony Wittreich, Jr. (No. 4555), who holds that William Hayley shaped Blake's conception of Milton.

4259 D'Avanzo, Mario L. "The Literary Sources of *My Kinsman, Major Molineux*: Shakespeare, Coleridge, Milton." *SSF*, 10, 1973, 121–36.

Discusses Milton's hell and Pandemonium as probable sources for elements in Hawthorne's *My Kinsman*.

4260 Davies, Stevie. *Emily Brontë.* London: Harvester-Wheatsheaf; Bloomington: Indiana Univ. Press, 1988, xii, 180pp.

Points out that Brontë was influenced by Milton, especially *Paradise Lost*.

4261 Desser, David. "*Blade Runner*: Science Fiction and Transcendence." *LFQ*, 13, No. 3, 1985, 172–79.

Shows that biblical allusions and borrowings from *Paradise Lost* contribute to Scott Ridley's mythic structure and reveal his "redemptive, transcendental vision." The film's citiscape is compared to Milton's hell, and various characters in *Blade Runner* parallel Milton's characters.

4262 Dillon, Steven C. "Milton and Tennyson's 'Guinevere.'" *ELH*, 54, 1987, 129–55.

Detects Milton's presence throughout Tennyson's poem. Believes that Tennyson draws especially from *Paradise Lost*

4, but points out that the fall of Camelot is more gradual than the Fall in Milton's poem.

4263 DiSalvo, Jackie. "Blake Encountering Milton: Politics and the Family in *Paradise Lost* and *The Four Zoas.*" *Milton and the Line of Vision.* Ed. by Joseph Anthony Wittreich, Jr. (Madison and London: Univ. of Wisconsin Press, 1975), pp. 143–84.

"Blake's encounter with Milton is . . . always historically self-conscious. The very goal of Blake's epics is a revelation of the historical and political basis of cultural symbols and cultural influence."

4264 DiSalvo, Jacqueline. "The Intertextuality of Doris Lessing's *The Good Terrorist* and Milton's *Samson Agonistes.*" *DLN*, 12, 1988, 3–4.

Explains that Miltonic elements are clearly present in Lessing's *Canopus in Argos* series. Lessing, Dorothy Mellings in the *Good Terrorist*, and Milton "merge as former revolutionaries in retreat, reading Samson as an image of futility in their 'brave' and disillusioned epiphany of political defeatism."

4265 DiSalvo, Jacqueline. "Milton and Shaw Once More: *Samson Agonistes* and *St. Joan.*" *MiltonQ*, 22, 1988, 115–20.

Believes that the feminism in *St. Joan* differs from Milton's, but that Shaw still builds on "that Puritan affirmation of personal and historical self-determination most uncompromisingly articulated by Milton not only in *Samson Agonistes* but throughout his works."

4266 DiSalvo, Jacqueline Anne. "War of Titans: Blake's Confrontation with Milton. *The Four Zoas* as Political Critique of *Paradise Lost* and the Genesis Tradition." Doctoral diss., Univ. of Wisconsin, Madison, 1977. 675pp. Abs., *DAI*, 38, 1977, 3456A–57A.

Explores Blake's belief that Milton's political contradictions and "the traditions he espoused" account for varying interpretations of the major themes of *Paradise Lost*—"love, reason, history, the conflict of God and Satan."

4267 DiSalvo, Jackie. *War of Titans: Blake's Critique of Milton and the Politics of Religion.* Pittsburgh, PA: Univ. of Pittsburgh Press; London: Feffer and Simons, 1983. xi, 391pp.

Studies Blake's interpretation of *Paradise Lost*. Sees the epic primarily as a political poem and deals with its apparent paradoxes. Reviews: Joseph Wittreich, *MiltonQ*, 18, 1984, 92–94; Andrew Lincoln, *RES*, 37, 1986, 105–07.

4268 Dollarhide, Louis E. "The Paradox of Ruskin's Admiration of Renaissance English Writers." *UMSE*, 8, 1967, 7–12.

"There is no evidence that [John] Ruskin knew Milton very well, but there is evidence that he had little sympathy for what he did know."

4269 Doudna, Martin K. "Echoes of Milton, Donne, and Carlyle in *Civil Disobedience*." *TJQ*, 12, No. 3, 1980, 5–7.

Cites a passage from *Areopagitica* which influenced Thoreau's *Of Civil Disobedience*.

4270 Dowden, Edward. *Milton in the Eighteenth Century (1701–1750).* Folcroft, PA: Folcroft Library Editions, 1969.

Reprint of Stevens No. 2819, originally published in 1907–08.

4271 Ende, Stuart A. "Keats's Music of Truth." *ELH*, 40, 1973, 90–104.

Comments on Keats's powerful emotional response to Milton, as shown in his notes on *Paradise Lost*.

4272 Ende, Stuart A. "Milton and the Subjective Drama of the Eighteenth-Century Sublime Poem." *Keats and the Sublime* (New Haven, CT: Yale Univ. Press, 1976), pp. 1–31.

On the Miltonic legacy and the consequences of choosing Milton as a poetic model.

4273 Engelmeyer, Sister Bridget Marie. "In Defense of Milton, Aspersed." *MiltonQ*, 21, No. 3, 1987, 103–04.

Replies to Francis C. Blessington (No. 4222). States that he has a weak basis for comparing Eliot's Casaubon and Milton. Rather, Milton was a "presence in the mind of George Eliot, a presence not uncommon in the minds of nineteenth-century novelists."

4274 Engelmeyer, Sister Bridget Marie. "Graves' Milton Redivivus: Another View." *MiltonQ*, 14, 1980, 101.

Criticizes the republication of Robert Graves's *Wife to Mr. Milton* (No. 4317).

4275 England, Martha Winburn. "John Milton and the Performing Arts." *BNYPL*, 80, 1976, 19–70.

Examines the eighteenth-century attitude toward Milton, which caused his works to be discussed, read out loud, and performed. Discusses musical performances of *Comus*, *Samson Agonistes*, *L'Allegro*, and *Il Penseroso*. Notes performances of ballets, puppet shows, and oratorios of Milton.

4276 Erdman, David V. "Milton! Thou Shouldst be Living." *WC*, 19, 1988, 2–8.

Notes that Wordsworth hoped his fourteen "Sonnets dedicated to Liberty" "would be trumpet-calls to wake England from lethargy and ledger-worship at a time when *English freedom* and the freedom of all nations . . . was being weighed in the balance." The sonnet had been a trumpet for Milton, and Wordsworth "wanted to put it to immediate use" for his country and the world.

4277 Evans, D. R., and **J. P. Hardy.** "Dylan Thomas." *TLS*, June 23, 1972, p. 719.

Discusses a source in Milton for Thomas's fourth religious sonnet, "What is the metre of this dictionary?"

4278 Falzarano, James V. "Adam in Houyhnhnmland: The Presence of *Paradise Lost*." *MiltonS*, 21, 1985, 179–97.

Studies the complex presence of *Paradise Lost* in *Gulliver's Travels*. Asserts that Swift joins Gulliver with Satan and contrasts him with Adam.

4279 Falzarano, James Vincent. *"Paradise Lost* and *The Prelude*: Toward a More Comprehensive Model of Poetic Influence." Doctoral diss., Brown Univ., 1982. 304pp. Abs., *DAI*, 43, 1983, 3602A.

Argues that Wordsworth's allusions to *Paradise Lost* in the *Prelude* illustrate the poets' differing conceptions of the sublime, poetic creation, poetic vision, and symbolism.

4280 Fee, William W. "Of Reformation in England—and America." *MiltonQ*, 8, 1974, 82–85.

On the relevance of Milton's words to contemporary American society. Finds in his life an "inspiring example" and "believes that scholars and teachers have a special responsibility to emulate Milton in contributing to the reformation of their country."

4281 Fisch, Harold. "Blake's Miltonic Moment." *William Blake: Essays for S. Foster Damon*. Ed. by Alvin H. Rosenfeld (Providence, RI: Brown Univ. Press, 1969), pp. 36–56.

Argues that "in spite of the depth and force" of their affinity, "Blake's poetry belongs in the last analysis to a tradition essentially different from Milton's."

4282 Fisher, Sidney. "A Miltonic Parallel in Coleridge." *N&Q*, 29, 1982, 204.

Believes that Samuel Coleridge drew from *Samson Agonistes* 710ff. in Part 3, stanzas 7, 10, and 11 of the *Rime of the Ancient Mariner*.

4283 Flannagan, Roy. "Handel's *L'Allegro, il Penseroso ed il Moderato* in a New Recording." *MiltonQ*, 17, 1983, 92–95.

Believes that Handel's composition of *L'Allegro* and *Il Penseroso* is faithful to Milton's themes, just as John Eliot Gardiner and the English Monteverdi Choir are faithful to Handel in the work's new recording.

4284 Fleissner, Robert F. "The Rape of Milton's Locks." *MiltonQ*, 9, 1975, 32.

Abstract of a paper presented at the University of Wisconsin, Milwaukee, Milton Tercentenary Conference, in November, 1974. On Pope's use of *Lycidas* in the *Rape of the Lock*.

4285 Folkenflik, Robert. "Pope's Timon: A Possible Allusion to His Literary Identity." *EA*, 28, 1975, 72–74.

Believes that Pope's Timon echoes Milton's treatment of Mulciber in *Paradise Lost*.

4286 Fox, Susan. *Poetic Form in Blake's "Milton."* Princeton, NJ: Princeton Univ. Press, 1976. xvi, 242pp.

Discusses Blake's argument with Milton by focusing "on those passages in which it is instrumental in the poem's structure." Review: Mary Lynn Johnson, *M&R*, 2, 1976, 1–10.

4287 Freedman, William. "The Garden of Eden in *The Rape of the Lock*." *Renascence*, 34, 1981, 34–40.

Shows how "Pope works pointed variations of Satan's temptation of Eve, the principal effect of which is . . . to admonish with a realistic sense of where we have come from and to what we have arrived."

4288 French, Roberts W. "'Wash Far Away': A Reading of *Lycidas*." *MiltonQ*, 10, 1976, 133–34.

Reports on John Berryman's short story "Wash Far Away," from his recently published collection, *The Freedom of the Poet* (1976; see No. 4217).

4289 French, Roberts W. "Wordsworth's *Paradise Lost*: A Note on 'Nutting.'" *StHum*, 5, No. 1, 1976, 42–45.

Asserts that "Nutting" is an account of the Fall, which illustrates the inevitable gulf between humans and nature in the pattern and language of *Paradise Lost*.

4290 Friedenreich, Kenneth. "Loutherbourg's *Eidophusikon* and Two Scenes from *Paradise Lost*." *BNYPL*, 80, 1976, 71–83.

Argues that Loutherbourg produced two scenes from *Paradise Lost* 1 because they complement the *Eidophusikon* and have dramatic phrasing.

4291 Frost, William. "*Aureng-Zebe* in Context: Dryden, Shakespeare, Milton, and Racine." *JEGP*, 74, 1975, 26–49.

Points out parallels between *Samson Agonistes* and Dryden's play, especially in the "delineation of sexual and marital dilemmas."

4292 Frye, Roland Mushat. "The Dissidence of Dissent and the Origins of Religious Freedom in America: John Milton and the Puritans." *PAPS*, 133, 1989, 475–88.

Traces the gradual development of the idea of dissent in England and America and notes that men such as John Adams and Thomas Jefferson often quoted Milton.

4293 Furia, Philip. "Nuances of a Theme by Milton: Wallace Stevens's 'Sunday Morning.'" *AL*, 46, 1974, 83–87.

Believes that Stevens alludes "to Milton only to present a diametrically opposed vision."

4294 Gast, Marlene. "Wordsworth and Milton: Varieties of Connection." Doctoral diss., Boston College, 1985. 198pp. Abs., *DAI*, 46, 1986, 2299A.

Examines the verbal connections to Milton in Wordsworth's sonnets, arguing that they embody the latter writer's "poetic empowerment" and "visionary authority."

4295 Gavriliu, Eugenia. "A Contribution to Establishing the Earliest Romanian Contacts with Milton's Work: Milton in the First Romanian Periodicals." *Limba si Literatura*, 3, 1980, 7–14.

In Romanian.

4296 Gerber, Gerald E. "Milton and Poe's 'Modern Woman.'" *PN*, 3, 1970, 25–26.

Compares Milton's Eve with Edgar Allan Poe's Signora Psyche Zenobia: both "are motivated in similar ways," pursue "new experiences," and manifest outwardly "the condition of the soul."

4297 Gibson, William A. "Literary Influences on Robert Morris's First Excursion in Architectural Theory." *Rendezvous*, 6, No. 2, 1971, 1–14.

Cites Milton as a literary influence on Robert Morris, who quotes *Paradise Lost* 1.714–16 and 738–39, passages that "identify the style of Pandemonium with that of Greek architecture."

4298 Gilbert, Sandra M. "Patriarchal Poetry and Women Readers: Reflections on Milton's Bogey." *PMLA*, 93, 1978, 368–82. Reprinted in *The Madwoman in the Attic: The Woman Writer and the Nineteenth-Century Literary Imagination*. By Susan Gubar and Gilbert (New Haven, CT, and London: Yale Univ. Press, 1979), pp. 187–212.

Discusses "Milton's bogey," as Virginia Woolf terms it, and how women writers have reacted to Milton's alleged misogyny. Relates Mary Shelley's *Frankenstein* and Emily Brontë's *Wuthering Heights* to Milton.

4299 Gillet, Jean. "Milton dans *Cromwell*." *Victor Hugo et la Grande-Bretagne*. Actes du Deuxieme Colloque Vinaver, Manchester, 1985. Vinaver Studies in French, 3. Ed. by A. R. W. James (Liverpool: Francis Cairns, 1986), pp. 39–47.

Discusses Milton's influence on Hugo's *Odes* and appearance as a character in his play *Cromwell*. Focuses on Milton's republicanism and Oliver Cromwell's Satanic, Promethean ambition.

4300 Gillet, Jean. "Milton et le Mot de la Fin dans *Cinq-Mars*." *RLC*, 49, 1975, 235–48.

"In letting Milton—an ambiguous figure in the eyes of the royalist romantics—have the last word in his novel, Alfred de Vigny already has a feeling about what direction his own revolt will take."

4301 Gillet, Jean. *Le "Paradis Perdu" dans la Littérature Française de Voltaire à Chateaubriand*. Paris: Librairie Klincksieck, 1975. 668pp.

Studies the reception, interpretation, and translation of *Paradise Lost* in French literature. Voltaire became interested in it during his stay in England and was the most important French critic of Milton during this period. Concludes by discussing Milton's influence on Chateaubriand and his translation of *Paradise Lost*. Review: Jean-François Camé, *CahiersE*, 10, 1976, 125–28.

4302 Gillham, D. G. "Blake's Debt to Milton." *UCTSE*, 5, 1974, 34–48.

"Blake's thought was profoundly influenced by his reading of Milton's prose and poetry, and this may be shown by taking the theme of the Fall, particularly as it is dealt with in *Paradise Lost* and *The Songs of Innocence and Experience*."

4303 Gilmore, Michael T. "Calvinism and Gothicism: The Example of Brown's *Wieland*." *Studies in the Novel*, 9, 1977, 107–18.

Concludes that "it is fitting that *Wieland* is built on the fable of *Paradise Lost*." By turning back to Milton, Charles Brockden Brown also addresses "the promise of America, . . . the 'paradise lost' in *Wieland*."

4304 Glavin, John J. "'The Exercise of Saints': Hopkins, Milton, and Patience." *TSLL*, 20, 1978, 139–52.

Claims that Gerard Manley Hopkins's "Patience" does not echo the optimism of Milton's Sonnet 19 ("When I consider").

4305 Glavin, John J. "*The Wreck of the Deutschland* and *Lycidas*: Ubique Naufragium Est." *TSLL*, 22, 1980, 522–46.

Cites parallels between the *Wreck* and *Lycidas* which "seem to point beyond their own individual and local significance to an overall pattern of much more profound connection."

4306 Gleckner, Robert F. "Blake and the Four Daughters of God." *ELN*, 15, 1977, 110–15.

Cites *Paradise Lost* 3.403–11 and 12.547–51 as sources of Blake's Mercy and Peace.

4307 Gleckner, Robert F. "Blake's Miltonizing of Chatterton." *Blake*, 11, 1977, 27–29.

Milton's lines, not Thomas Chatterton, are most often Blake's ultimate source.

4308 Gleckner, Robert F. "Keats's 'How Many Bards' and Poetic Tradition." *KSJ*, 27, 1978, 14–22.

Deals with Milton's influence, especially on Keats's early poetry, including "How Many Bards." Notes that it is difficult to distinguish between Milton's direct influence and his eighteenth-century imitators' indirect influence.

4309 Golden, Morris. "A Decade's Bent: Names in the *Monthly Review* and the *Critical Review*, 1760–1769." *BNYPL*, 79, 1976, 336–61.

Makes brief references to Milton and claims that his works were used for common literary allusions during this period. Reply by Kathleen Swaim (No. 4519).

4310 Gorecki, J. "Graham Greene's 'The Destructors' and *Paradise Lost*." *PLL*, 21, 1985, 336–40.

Finds echoes of Milton's account of the War in Heaven in Graham Greene's short story.

4311 Goslee, Nancy M. "From Marble to Living Form: Sculpture as Art and Analogue from the Renaissance to Blake." *JEGP*, 77, 1978, 188–211.

Concludes that Blake's use of sculpture in *Milton* reshapes the "historical character both of *Milton* and of sculpture itself."

4312 Goslee, Nancy Moore. "Mutual Amity: *Paradise Lost* and the Romantic Epic." Doctoral diss., Yale Univ., 1968. 524pp. Abs., *DAI*, 30, 1969, 723A.

Shows how the Romantic poets' long works are affected by Milton's understanding of Satan's role, focus on the individual, and tendency to place a "figure within a closely-observed part of the natural setting."

4313 Goslee, Nancy Moore. "'Promethean Art': Personification and Sculptural Imagery after Milton." *Milton's Legacy in the Arts*. Ed. by Albert C. Labriola and

Edward Sichi, Jr. (University Park and London: Pennsylvania State Univ. Press, 1988), pp. 219–36.

Discusses Milton's use of allegorical personifications of abstract concepts and sculptural molding in *Paradise Lost*, beginning with his description of Death. Feels that his influence is apparent in mid-eighteenth-century English odes.

4314 Goslee, Nancy M. "'Under a Cloud in Prospect': Keats, Milton, and Stationing." *PQ*, 53, 1974, 205–19.

Notes that Milton places his objects to point out the universe's hierarchical and horizontal nature, but Keats redefines stationing. The Titans in the *Fall of Hyperion* are no longer stationed in a landscape but rather stand as "memorials to the efficacy of the imagination."

4315 Gottlieb, Sidney. "Milton's 'On the Late Massacre in Piemont' and Eisenstein's *Potemkin*." *MiltonQ*, 19, 1985, 38–42.

Believes Sergei M. Eisenstein's Odessa Steps sequence in *Potemkin* parallels Milton's scene in Sonnet 18 ("On the Late Massacre in Piemont").

4316 Grant, John E. "The Female Awakening at the End of Blake's *Milton*: A Picture Story, with Questions." *Milton Reconsidered: Essays in Honor of Arthur E. Barker*. Ed. by John Karl Franson (Salzburg: Institut für Englische Sprache und Literatur, Universität Salzburg, 1976), pp. 78–99.

Discusses some of the plates in *Milton* and concludes that with the last one, Blake shows that "the leadership of a woman is necessary to the fulfillment of time."

4317 Graves, Robert. *Wife to Mr. Milton: The Story of Marie Powell.* Chicago, IL: Academy Chicago, 1979.

Reprint of Huckabay No. 3194, originally published in 1943. See No. 4274. Reviews: Roy Flannagan, *MiltonQ*, 14, 1980, 27–29; James Egan, *SCN*, 40, 1982, 44.

4318 Gray, J. M. "An Allusion to *Paradise Regained* in *Merlin and Vivien*." *TRB*, 1971, p. 150.

Believes that when Tennyson's Merlin tempts Vivien, he echoes Belial's suggestion in *Paradise Regained* 2.165–71 that Jesus be tempted by woman.

4319 Gray, James. "'Postscript to the *Odyssey*': Pope's Reluctant Debt to Milton." *MiltonQ*, 18, 1984, 105–16.

Asserts that Pope's statement about his translation of the *Odyssey*—"Some use has been made . . . of the style of Milton"—is an understatement. Believes that "Pope was influenced by Milton, not only in his poetic vision, but also in his poetic style."

4320 Gregory, John Michael. "Milton's Use of Myth in *Paradise Lost* and Its Bearing on Keats's Use of Myth in *Hyperion*." Doctoral diss., Texas Christian Univ., 1978. 178pp. Abs., *DAI*, 39, 1979, 4948A.

Argues that Keats's "pagan account of . . . the fall of the Saturnian or Golden Age innocence" borrows from Milton's Christian description of the Fall.

4321 Griffin, Dustin. "The Bard of Cyder-Land: John Philips and Miltonic Imitation." *SEL*, 24, 1984, 441–60.

Contends that Philips, the "first poet in English to imitate Milton and to see the parodic possibilities of Miltonic blank verse," was the literary pioneer who influenced Pope, Thomson, Cowper, and others to make creative use of Milton's works.

4322 Griffin, Dustin. "Cowper, Milton, and the Recovery of Paradise." *EIC*, 31, 1981, 15–26.

Discusses Milton's influence on Cowper.

4323 Griffin, Dustin. *Regaining Paradise: Milton and the Eighteenth Century.* Cambridge and New York: Cambridge Univ. Press, 1986. ix, 299pp.

Refutes the suggestion that eighteenth-century literature suffered from Milton's influence. Argues that poor writers sought to emulate superficial aspects of his work and great writers gained inspiration and direction from its themes and framework. Reviews: Lucy Newlyn, *TLS*, Aug. 8, 1986, p. 871; James Sambrook, *THES*, Aug. 1, 1986, p. 17; Balz Engler, *ES*, 68, 1987, 470–71; David Hopkins, *N&Q*, 34, 1987, 388–89; Ashraf H. A. Rushdy, *EIC*, 37, 1987, 67–71; Frederick M. Keener, *YES*, 18, 1988, 285–86.

4324 Grundy, Joan. "Hardy and Milton." *THA*, 3, 1985, 3–14.

Believes that Hardy was influenced by Milton's divorce pamphlets and sees his extensive influence in *Tess of the d'Urbervilles* and *Jude the Obscure.*

4325 Grundy, Joan. "*Samson Agonistes* and *The Prelude.*" *KM 80: A Birthday Album for Kenneth Muir: Tuesday, 5 May, 1987* (Liverpool: Liverpool Univ. Press, 1987), pp. 60–61.

Notices similarities between the two works' opening lines. By associating himself with Samson, Wordsworth indicates that he is to be the hero, the central figure of his poem.

4326 Gunny, Ahmad. "Milton, Alexandre Tanevot and the Fall of Man." *Neohelicon*, 7, No. 1, 1979, 241–51.

Discusses Tanevot's *Adam et Eve; ou, la Chute de l'Homme* (1742), which is based on *Paradise Lost.*

4327 Hannay, Margaret P. "A Preface to *Perelandra.*" *The Longing for a Form: Essays on the Fiction of C. S. Lewis.* Ed. by Peter J. Schakel (Kent, OH: Kent State Univ. Press, 1977), pp. 73–90.

Approaches Lewis's Edenic myth through his criticism of Milton, especially his *Preface to "Paradise Lost"* (No. 2595).

4328 Hansen, Marlene R. "*Rasselas*, Milton, and Humanism." *ES*, 60, 1979, 14–22.

Believes that *Paradise Lost* 4 influenced Johnson when he created the Happy Valley in *Rasselas* and regards Milton's poem as a minor source.

4329 Harris, Bernard. "'That Soft Seducer, Love': Dryden's *The State of Innocence and Fall of Man.*" *Approaches to "Paradise Lost."* The York Tercentenary Lectures. Ed. by C. A. Patrides (London: Edward Arnold; Toronto: Univ. of Toronto Press, 1968), pp. 119–36.

Concerned with Dryden's appreciation of *Paradise Lost* and his intention in the *State of Innocence.*

4330 Hatlen, Burton. "Milton, Mary Shelley, and Patriarchy." *BuR*, 28, No. 2, 1983, 19–47.

Argues that *Paradise Lost* and Mary Shelley's *Frankenstein* have much in common, such as a struggle between the mythos of patriarchy and the mythos of equality.

4331 Haven, Richard. "Coleridge on Milton: A Lost Lecture." *WC*, 3, 1972, 21–24.

Cites the *Rifleman*, 4 (January 26, 1812), p. 30, which contains "a moderately detailed account by 'T. T.' (possibly Thomas Talfourd) of a lecture on Milton." This report is apparently "the only extant account of the lecture."

4332 Haworth, Helen E. "The Titans, Apollo, and the Fortunate Fall in Keats's Poetry." *SEL*, 10, 1970, 637–49.

Compares the ideology and characters in Keats's *Hyperion* and *Fall of Hyperion* with those in *Paradise Lost.*

4333 Hazen, James. "Blake's Tyger and Milton's Beasts." *BlakeS*, 3, 1971, 163–70.

Suggests that "the animal imagery of *Paradise Lost* is an important source of Blake's poem and an important clue to its meaning."

4334 Helgerson, Richard. "Milton and the Sons of Orpheus." *Self-Crowned Laureates: Spenser, Jonson, Milton, and the Literary System* (Berkeley, Los Angeles, and London: Univ. of California Press, 1983), pp. 185–282.

Notes the general neglect of the early seventeenth-century minor poets and the gradual emergence of Milton, who is never grouped with them and who in 1667 became the true laureate.

4335 Herron, Carolivia. "Milton and

Afro-American Literature." *Re-membering Milton: Essays on the Texts and Traditions.* Ed. by Mary Nyquist and Margaret W. Ferguson (New York and London: Methuen, 1987), pp. 278–300.

Analyzes the acceptance or rejection of Milton's works by African-American writers from different periods in American history—Phillis Wheatley, John Boyd, Charles W. Chesnutt, and Ishmael Reed. Concludes that their progressively negative view of Milton demonstrates "the historical development of an Afro-American tradition of epic literature."

4336 Herz, Judith Scherer. "Milton and Marvell: The Poet as Fit Reader." *MLQ*, 39, 1978, 239–63.

Speculates that the two poets influenced each other, especially during the early 1650s.

4337 Hinz, E. J., and J. J. Teunissen. "Milton, Whitman, Wolfe and Laurence: *The Stone Angel* as Elegy." *DR*, 65, 1985–86, 474–91.

Uses *Lycidas* to begin discussing the elegiac tradition, to which Margaret Laurence's novel belongs.

4338 Hoagwood, Terence Allan. "Shelley, Milton, and the Poetics of Ideological Transformation: *Paradise Lost* and the Prologue to Hellas." *RPP*, 10, No. 2, 1986, 25–48.

Notes the complexity of Shelley's relationship to Milton but insists on his centrality (especially through *Paradise Lost*) "to virtually every major work of Shelley's maturity."

4339 Hogan, Patrick Colm. "Lapsarian Odysseus: Joyce, Milton, and the Structure of *Ulysses*." *JJQ*, 24, 1986, 55–72.

Examines the parallels between James Joyce's *Ulysses* and *Paradise Lost*.

4340 Hopkins, David. "Dryden's *Baucis and Philemon* and *Paradise Lost*." *N&Q*, 29, 1982, 503–04.

In *Baucis and Philemon*, "the words 'savoury' and 'appetite' occur twice in close conjunction in Milton's de-

scriptions of Adam and Eve's divinely-favored meals."

4341 Horváth, Károly. "Ádám Alakjának Világirodalmi Elõzményeihez." *IK*, 88, 1984, 52–57, 128–30.

Discusses Milton's influence on Imre Madách (1823–64), whose drama *Az Ember Tragédiája* (*The Fall of Man*) contains a reenactment of the Fall.

4342 Howard, John. *Blake's "Milton": A Study in the Selfhood.* Cranbury, NJ: Fairleigh Dickinson Univ. Press; London: Associated Univ. Presses, 1976. 300pp.

Discusses Blake's opinion of Milton the man.

4343 Hubert, Thomas. "Simms's Use of Milton and Wordsworth in *The Yemassee*: An Aspect of Symbolism in the Novel." *SCR*, 6, No. 1, 1973, 58–65.

Shows that Milton contributed to the symbolism that conveys one of the novel's major themes.

4344 Hunt, Bishop C., Jr. "Wordsworth's Marginalia on *Paradise Lost*." *BNYPL*, 73, 1969, 167–83.

Discusses Wordsworth's life and attitudes as reflected in his notations in a 1674 edition of *Paradise Lost*.

4345 Jackson, Robert L. "Miltonic Imagery and Design in Puskin's *Mozart and Salieri*: The Russian Satan." *American Contributions to the Seventh International Congress of Slavists, Warsaw, August 21–27, 1973.* Vol. 2, Literature and Folklore. Ed. by Victor Terras (The Hague: Mouton, 1973), pp. 261–70.

Contends that Aleksandr Sergeevich Pushkin's Salieri belongs among the significant Romantic metamorphoses of Satan but believes that Pushkin's response is not typically Romantic.

4346 Jacobus, Lee A. "*Lycidas* in the 'Nestor' Episode." *JJQ*, 19, 1982, 189–94.

Argues that for Stephen in James Joyce's *Ulysses*, *Lycidas* signals "the anxiety of early death, failure of achievement, separation, loss, and that other anxiety of influence: the ghost of Milton as a father of poets, for whom

Stephen, as poet, is himself among the dearest pledges."

4347 Jain, Nalini. "Echoes of Milton in Johnson's *Irene*." *AN&Q*, 24, 1986, 134–36.

Cites several echoes from *Paradise Lost* and *Comus* in Samuel Johnson's blank-verse drama.

4348 Jarvis, Robin. "Love between Milton and Wordsworth." *Re-membering Milton: Essays on the Texts and Traditions*. Ed. by Mary Nyquist and Margaret W. Ferguson (New York and London: Methuen, 1987), pp. 301–17.

Examines whether Wordsworth had a loving remembrance of Milton and contrasts the two different meanings of love in *Paradise Lost* and the *Prelude*.

4349 Jarvis, Robin. "Shades of Milton: Wordsworth at Vallombrosa." *SIR*, 25, 1986, 483–504.

Wordsworth uses *Paradise Lost* 1.302–04 to preface his poem, "At Vallombrosa." Examines the father-son rivalry to see whether Wordsworth could "still be rehearsing that primal scene of the 'trespass of teaching,' in which new poets struggle against the 'forms and presence of a precursor,' and 'wrestle with the internalized violence' which that struggle involves them in." Wordsworth's deferred visit to Vallombrosa "effects metonymically a postponed encounter with Milton."

4350 Jeffrey, Lloyd N. "Shelley's 'Plumèd Insects Swift and Free.'" *KSJ*, 25, 1976, 103–21.

Points to Milton's influence on Shelley's note on the sick worm.

4351 Jin, Sunju. "Joyce wa Milton: Disobedience Theme eui Jungsim Euro." *JELLC*, 28, 1986, 185–211.

"Joyce and Milton: On the Theme of Disobedience."

4352 Johnson, Lee Milford. "Wordsworth and the Sonnet." Doctoral diss., Princeton Univ., 1970. 280pp. Abs., *DAI*, 31, 1971, 4167A.

Notes the Miltonic sonnet's contribu-

tions to the internal unity, sequential integration, three-part structure, and rhetorical development of Wordsworth's sonnets.

4353 Johnson, Mary Lynn. "Recent Reconstruction of Blake's Milton and *Milton: A Poem*." *M&R*, 2, 1976, 1–10.

Review essay that focuses on Joseph Anthony Wittreich, Jr.'s *Angel of Apocalypse* (No. 4555), and Susan Fox's *Poetic Form in Blake's "Milton"* (No. 4286).

4354 Jump, John D. "Literary Echoes in Byron's *Don Juan*." *N&Q*, 14, 1967, 302.

Mentions Byron's allusion to *Lycidas* 68: "To sport with *Amaryllis* in the shade."

4355 Ka, Eimei. "The Influence of *Paradise Lost* on Poe's *Al Aaraaf*." *MCJ News*, 3, 1979, 5–6.

Abstract of paper presented. Regards Poe's poem as a lyrical version of *Paradise Lost*.

4356 Kang, Sun-Koo. "William Blake eui Milton." *JELLC*, 29, 1987, 5–31.

On William Blake's understanding of Milton.

4357 Kesterson, David B. "Milton's Satan and Cooper's Demonic Chieftains." *SCB*, 29, 1969, 138–42.

"When Magua and Mahtoree are compared with Satan, when their actions and relationships to their followers and enemies are examined, it is obvious that Cooper must have had Milton's 'Prince of Darkness' in mind."

4358 King, James. "Cowper, Hayley, and Samuel Johnson's 'Republican' Milton." *SECC*, 17, 1987, 229–38.

Argues that Cowper's reaction to two of Milton's biographers, William Hayley and Samuel Johnson, reveals the influence of Milton's republican ideas.

4359 Kneale, Douglas. "Milton, Wordsworth, and the 'Joint Labourers' of *The Prelude*." *ESC*, 12, No. 1, 1986, 37–54.

Discusses the structural and verbal echoes of Milton in the *Prelude*.

4360 Knuth, Deborah J. "Blackmore, Milton, and *Peri Bathous*." *AN&Q*, 18, 1980, 108–10.

Cites Milton's Satan as a source for Richard Blackmore's *Prince Arthur*.

4361 Kramer, Jerome A. "'Virtue, Religion, and Patriotism': Some Biographies of Milton in the Romantic Era." *M&R*, 3, 1977, 1–7.

Studies biographies of Milton between 1796 and 1836 by Sir Egerton Brydges, William Carpenter, William Hayley, Joseph Ivimey, John Mitford, Charles Edward Mortimer, Charles Symmons, and Henry John Todd. They present Milton as a patriot, prophet, nonconformist rebel and hero, sublime poet, and great thinker. Abs., *MiltonQ*, 13, 1979, 61.

4362 Kreuder, Hans-Dieter. *Milton in Deutschland: Seine Rezeption im Latein- und Deutschsprachigen Schrifttum Zwischen 1651 und 1732*. Quellen und Forschungen zur Sprach- und Kulturgeschichte der Germanischen Völker, no. 43. Doctoral diss. Berlin: Walter de Gruyter, 1971. xvi, 257pp.

Examines the earliest period of Milton's influence in Germany until Bodmer's translation of *Paradise Lost* (1732).

4363 Kreuder, Hans-Dieter. "Noch Einmal frühe Deutsche Milton-Übersetzungen." *Archiv*, 214, 1977, 80–82.

Discusses how Milton's writings, especially *Paradise Lost*, became famous in Germany and the German intellectuals who studied Milton.

4364 Kropf, C. R. "Miscreation: Another Miltonic Allusion in *The Dunciad*." *PLL*, 10, 1974, 425–27.

Pope's *Dunciad* 1.54–78 alludes to Milton's account of the third day of creation in *Paradise Lost*. Abs., *MiltonQ*, 12, 1978, 113.

4365 Kuroda, Kenjiro. "Some Aspects of Milton's Reception in Japan (1887–1945)." *MCJ News*, 8, 1985, 17–19.

Abstract of a paper presented at the Eighteenth Colloquium of MCJ in December, 1984. Studies the influence of Milton on the works of Sohoh Tokutomi, Tenrai Shigeno, Takeshi Fujii, and Tadao Yanaihara.

4366 La Borsiere, C. R. "Wordsworth's 'Go Back to Antique Ages, if Thine Eyes,' and *Paradise Lost*, XII, 23–47." *N&Q*, 22, 1975, 63.

Feels that "Milton's account of the beginnings of future political dissension" in *Paradise Lost* 12 is a "likely source" for Wordsworth's reference to the hunting of men, not beasts, in his sonnet.

4367 Labriola, Albert C. "'Insuperable Highth of Loftiest Shade': Milton and Samuel Beckett." *Milton's Legacy in the Arts*. Ed. by Labriola and Edward Sichi, Jr. (University Park and London: Pennsylvania State Univ. Press, 1988), pp. 205–17.

Compares *Paradise Lost* and Beckett's *Waiting for Godot* to show that Beckett may be intentionally "participating in a dialectical encounter with Milton." Abs., *MiltonQ*, 16, 1982, 26; *SCN*, 40, 1982, 10.

4368 Labriola, Albert C., and Edward Sichi, Jr., eds. *Milton's Legacy in the Arts*. University Park and London: Pennsylvania State Univ. Press, 1988. xii, 239pp.

A collection of essays about Milton's influence on the arts other than poetry. Contributors are Jean Gagen, Nancy Moore Goslee, Michael Lieb, Leo Miller, Stella P. Revard, Estella Schoenberg, William A. Sessions, Ernest W. Sullivan, II, and Labriola. In this bibliography, each essay is listed according to author and classification. Reviews: Steven C. Dillon, *Choice*, 26, 1989, 928; Douglas Chambers, *RES*, 42, 1991, 603–05; Roy Flannagan, *MiltonQ*, 26, 1992, 133–34.

4369 Lacey, William R. "An Eighteenth-Century Adaptation of Milton." *CCTEP*, 37, 1972, 29–33.

Joseph Addison intermittently admired *Paradise Lost* and the Roman stoic

Cato. In *Cato*, "Addison combined both interests." Compares the two works.

4370 Lacy, Lloyd B. "Samuel Johnson and William Lauder: Malevolence in the Criticism of Milton." *NRam*, C7, 1969, pp. 38–44.

Feels that Johnson entered into the Lauder accusations with ill will toward Milton.

4371 Lammers, John Hunter. "*Caliban upon Setebos*: Browning's Divine Comedy." *SBrown*, 12, 1984, 94–119.

Studies religious influences on *Caliban upon Setebos*, particularly Genesis and *Paradise Lost*. Caliban and Setebos resemble Milton's Satan and the fallen angels.

4372 Lams, Victor J., Jr. "Ruth, Milton, and Keats's *Ode to a Nightingale*." *MLQ*, 34, 1973, 417–35.

Argues that key echoes of Milton in the *Ode* and "Keats's handling of the Ruth figure in stanza 7 . . . clarify the religious aspects of the intense personal struggle of understanding and choice that the *Ode* memorializes."

4373 Leggett, B. J. "The Miltonic Allusions in Housman's 'Terence, This is Stupid Stuff.'" *ELN*, 5, 1968, 202–07.

Suggests that A. E. Housman's allusions to *Paradise Lost* show that "both works spring from an attempt to deal with man's loss of innocence and his recognition of the human condition as characterized by mutability and death."

4374 Lewalski, Barbara Kiefer. "On Looking into Pope's Milton." *EA*, 27, 1974, 481–500. Reprinted in *MiltonS*, 11, 1978, 29–50.

"Pope's characteristic stance toward Milton is one of judicious admiration and evaluation. . . . It will be evident that Pope's extensive, intelligent, and creative use of Milton is a tribute of the highest order."

4375 Lewis, Hanna B. "Hofmannsthal and Milton." *MLN*, 87, 1972, 732–41.

Discusses the influence of *Comus*, *L'Allegro*, and *Il Penseroso* on Hugo von Hofmannsthal's *Ariadne auf Naxos*.

4376 Liebman, Sheldon W. "Hawthorne and Milton: The Second Fall in *Rappaccini's Daughter*." *NEQ*, 41, 1968, 521–35.

Claims that Hawthorne mirrors the Fall and the warfare between good and evil in *Paradise Lost*.

4377 Liebman, Sheldon W. "Hawthorne's *Comus*: A Miltonic Source for 'The Maypole of Merry Mount.'" *NCF*, 27, 1972, 345–51.

Shows that Hawthorne's "Maypole" owes a great debt to *Comus* in terms of message, symbols, and setting.

4378 Liu, Yulin. "Style as Deviation from the Norm, I and II." *Waiguoyu*, 3, No. 25, 1983, 6–12 and 4, No. 26, 1984, 18–23.

In Chinese. Compares Milton's style with that of James Joyce's *Ulysses*.

4379 Lockwood, Deborah H. "The Eighteenth-Century Response to *Paradise Lost*'s Last Two Books." *ELN*, 21, No. 4, 1984, 22–32.

Examines eighteenth-century readers' "subdued and sometimes even negative response" to Milton's account of fallen history in *Paradise Lost* 11–12. Attributes that response to the contemporary definition of "sublimity" in literature, to which the final two books of *Paradise Lost* do not adhere.

4380 Loomis, Jeffrey B. "Miltonic Patterns in Flannery O'Connor's *A Good Man is Hard To Find*." *Cithara*, 24, No. 1, 1984, 41–58.

Argues that O'Connor's collection of short stories, *A Good Man is Hard To Find*, "imitates the chronological order of events in *Paradise Lost*" and emphasizes Milton's theme of "the importance to human relations of Christlike charity."

4381 "Lord Byron Agonistes." *MiltonQ*, 10, 1976, 99.

Points out that in a review of Byron's letters and journals in *TLS*, July 30, 1976, p. 962, Jerome J. McGann discusses Byron's identification with Milton.

4382 Lord, George de Forest. "Homeric Mockery in Milton and Pope." *Classical Presences in Seventeenth-Century English Poetry* (New Haven, CT, and London: Yale Univ. Press, 1987), pp. 173–91.

Believes that there is a "brilliant assimilation" of Homer and Milton in the *Rape of the Lock* and the *Dunciad*, especially in scenes of mocking, such as battles.

4383 Low, Lisa Elaine. "Ending in Eden: Mind and Nature in Milton, Marvell, Wordsworth, and Wallace Stevens." Doctoral diss., Univ. of Massachusetts, 1986. 202pp. Abs., *DAI*, 47, 1987, 3435A.

Contends that Milton, like the later poets, believes that one must first define an internal existence—an "inner paradise"—before confronting the outer, "morally neutral world."

4384 Lutaud, Olivier. "Des Révolutions d'Angleterre à la Révolution Française: L'Exemple de la Liberté de Presse ou Comment Milton 'Ouvrit' les Etats Généraux." *La Légende de la Révolution.* Ed. by Christian Croisille and others (Clermont-Ferrand: Université Blaise-Pascal, 1988), pp. 115–25.

Traces how Comte de Mirabeau encountered Milton's works and published an adaptation of *Areopagitica* called *Sur la Liberté de la Presse* (1788).

4385 Mahanti, J. C. "States of Mind and Feeling: T. S. Eliot on Seventeenth Century Verse." Doctoral diss., Univ. of New Brunswick, 1978. Abs., *DAI*, 39, 1978, 1553A.

Examines Eliot's criticism of seventeenth-century poetry, focusing on his belief "that with Milton and Dryden imagination split into magniloquence and levity."

4386 "The Man Who Fell to Earth and Paradise Lost." *MiltonQ*, 10, 1976, 100.

Points out that the movie is a modern version of the Adam and Eve story, based on a book by Walter Tevis, "who once held most of *PL* in his mind."

4387 Marcuse, Michael J. "The *Gentle-*

man's Magazine and the Lauder/Milton Controversy." *BRH*, 81, 1978, 179–209.

"Combines a systematic survey . . . of all items related to the controversy which appeared in the *GM* (1746–50) with a discussion of aspects of the relation between the controversy and the *GM* intended to bring problem areas into relief for further attention."

4388 Marcuse, Michael J. "The Lauder Controversy and the Jacobite Cause." *Studies in Burke and His Time*, 18, 1977, 27–47.

Analyzes William Lauder's political activities, including his motives for attacking Milton.

4389 Marcuse, Michael J. "Miltonoklastes: The Lauder Affair Reconsidered." *ECLife*, 4, 1977, 86–91.

Discusses Lauder's falsified evidence which alleged that Milton was a forger and plagiarist. Explains John Douglas's exposure of the falsification and details his political and social rationale. Points out that Lauder had the support of Johnson, who forced him to renounce all claims when the falsification of Milton's works was discovered.

4390 Marcuse, Michael J. "The Pre-Publication History of William Lauder's *Essay on Milton's Use and Imitation of the Moderns in His 'Paradise Lost.'*" *PBSA*, 72, 1978, 37–57.

Refutes Sir John Hawkins's recollection of the prepublication history, which involved Samuel Johnson. Argues that Johnson was not the author of the preface and postscript, as Hawkins, and later James Boswell, alleged.

4391 Marcuse, Michael J. "'The Scourge of Imposters, the Terror of Quacks': John Douglas and the Exposé of William Lauder." *HLQ*, 42, 1979, 231–61.

Examines Douglas's exposé of Lauder, who sought "to serve the Jacobite cause by accusing Milton, apologist for regicide, of having plagiarized *Paradise Lost* from a variety of neo-Latin poems."

4392 Martin, Peter Edward. "Pope and the Garden: A Background, Biographical, and Critical Study." Doctoral diss., Syracuse Univ., 1967. 244pp. Abs., *DAI*, 28, 1968, 4604A–05A.

Examines the influence of the "wild, visual pattern" of Milton's earthly paradise on Pope's "symbolic use of the Garden of Eden."

4393 Mason, J. R. "To Milton through Dryden and Pope: or, God, Man and Nature: *Paradise Lost* Regained?" Doctoral diss., Cambridge Univ., 1987. Abs., *IT*, 37, 1988, 439.

Argues that based on Dryden's and Pope's uses of Milton's epic in producing their own verse, these two later poets recognize "the permanent worth" of *Paradise Lost*, a verdict radically unlike any view expressed from Wordsworth's death to the present.

4394 McCarthy, B. Eugene. "More Imitations of Milton before 1750." *N&Q*, 16, 1969, 182–83.

Notes previously unrecorded imitations from the late seventeenth and eighteenth centuries.

4395 McGann, Jerome J. "Milton and Byron." *KSMB*, 25, 1974, 9–25.

Discusses Milton's twofold influence on Byron's works: the first "has to do with Byron's Satanism and the poetic tradition of the criminal hero"; the second "involves Byron's interpretation and imaginative use of Milton's life."

4396 McGregor, Rob Roy. "Camus' Absurd Man: A Metamorphosis of Milton's Satan." *Francofonia*, 4, 1983, 45–54.

Describes the parallels between Camus's Absurd Man and Milton's Satan, defining their viewpoints, actions, and methods of "revolt."

4397 McHaney, Thomas L. "*The Confidence-Man* and Satan's Disguises in *Paradise Lost*." *NCF*, 30, 1975, 200–06.

Connects Herman Melville's use of disguise in the *Confidence-Man* and the biblical rationale for Milton's choices of Satanic disguise in *Paradise Lost*.

4398 McInerney, Peter. "Satanic Conceits in *Frankenstein* and *Wuthering Heights*." *M&R*, 4, 1980, 1–15.

Discusses the resemblances among Milton's Satan, Mary Shelley's Victor, and Emily Brontë's Heathcliff. Feels that many Romantics have misinterpreted all three—each author disapproves of the character's actions.

4399 McNally, Paul. "Milton and the *Immortality Ode*." *WC*, 11, 1980, 28–33.

Regards Milton's invocation to light in *Paradise Lost* 3 as an important presence in Wordsworth's *Ode*. "Generally, both are about lost powers of outward sight and renewed powers of insight."

4400 Middleman, Louis I. "Borges, Milton, and the Game of the Name." *MLN*, 87, 1972, 967–71.

In "Death and the Compass," Jorge Luis Borges "has dreamed up, in very short compass indeed, a heterodox version of *Paradise Lost* in which Satan emerges victorious."

4401 Miller, Leo. "Anne Manning's *The Masque at Ludlow*." *MiltonQ*, 11, 1977, 107–09.

Describes an idyllic Victorian novelette on the composing of *Comus* and its performance at the Michaelmas gala in 1634. The story consists of twenty-five imaginary letters dated June 30 to September 30, 1634.

4402 Miller, Leo. "Melville *Milton* Marginalia Discovered." *MiltonQ*, 18, 1984, 67.

Describes marginalia in an edition of Milton's *Poetical Works* owned by Herman Melville.

4403 Miller, Leo. "Milton Cited in Germany, 1652: A Further Note." *MiltonQ*, 12, 1978, 28–31.

Finds a citation in Wilhelmus a Kospoth's *Oratio de Quaestione Bisgemina*. Kospoth shows that he has read Milton's *First Defence*.

4404 Miller, Leo. "Milton, Fichlau, Bensen and Conring: Addenda to the *Life Records of John Milton*." *PBSA*, 68, 1974, 107–18.

Provides addenda to No. 160 to explain Milton's leap to celebrity status after the publication of the *First Defence*. Abs., *MiltonQ*, 8, 1974, 94.

4405 Miller, Leo. "Milton's Contemporary Reputation: A Footnote to Parker and French." *MiltonQ*, 17, 1983, 56–57.

Discusses an English translation of a 1659 *Defensio* by French writer Jean Nicholas de Parival that initially appears to express "something favorable in writing about Milton's defense of the sovereignty of the people." However, the "English translator obviously 'edited' the text to suit the Commonwealth market." See Nos. 3808 and 230.

4406 Miller, Leo. "Milton's *Defensio* Ordered Wholesale for the States of Holland." *N&Q*, 33, 1986, 33.

Cites an order placed by the Dutch envoy for twenty-five copies of the *First Defence* to be sent to officials in Holland. Contends that this order shows "the sudden transition of John Milton from insular obscurity . . . to widespread fame among circles of the learned in western Europe following the publication of his *Pro Populo Anglicano Defensio*."

4407 Miller, Leo. "'Why was Spontini's Opera *Milton* Sponsored by Empress Josephine?'" *Milton's Legacy in the Arts*. Ed. by Albert C. Labriola and Edward Sichi, Jr. (University Park and London: Pennsylvania State Univ. Press, 1988), pp. 151–79.

Examines the events leading to the production of the one-act opera *Milton*, as well as the supportive role of the Empress Josephine, to whom it was dedicated. Abs., *MiltonQ*, 17, 1983, 25.

4408 Miner, Earl. "Dryden's Admired Acquaintance, Mr. Milton." *MiltonS*, 11, 1978, 3–27.

Discusses Milton's influence on Dryden as a classic and a contemporary. Concludes that "Dryden spent about thirty years being original—and indebted to Milton as well as to other writers. Only

after that long sonhood did he become completely his own man in the generous epic of his *Fables Ancient and Modern*."

4409 Minnick, Thomas Ludwig. "On Blake and Milton: An Essay in Literary Relationship." Doctoral diss., Ohio State Univ., 1973. 237pp. Abs., *DAI*, 34, 1973, 2641A.

Traces Milton's influence on Blake's developing mythology, from the latter's disagreement about the "capacity of man" to his subsequent view of Milton as "the archetypal poet-prophet."

4410 Miyanishi, Mitsuo. "Milton and Japan." *Studies in Milton* (Tokyo: Kinseido, 1974), pp. 175–203.

In Japanese. Discusses Milton's reception in Japan, beginning in 1841. Notes that in 1954 Japanese scholars of English and American literature placed *Paradise Lost* at the top of a "Best Twelve Books" list, above the *Canterbury Tales* and *Hamlet*.

4411 Mori, Michiko. "Christ's Temptation in the Wilderness—Milton and Dostoevsky." *MCJ News*, 9, 1987, 5–6.

Abstract of paper presented. Compares Milton's treatment of the Son's temptation in the wilderness in *Paradise Regained* with that of Ivan and Alyosha in the *Brothers Karamazov*.

4412 Morkan, Joel. "Milton's *Eikonoklastes* and Blake's Mythic Geography: A Parallel." *BlakeN*, 7, 1974, 87, 89.

Notes that the "fusion of English and biblical geography" in *Eikonoklastes* has parallels in Blake's works.

4413 Morris, Brian. "'Not without Song': Milton and the Composers." *Approaches to "Paradise Lost."* The York Tercentenary Lectures. Ed. by C. A. Patrides (London: Edward Arnold; Toronto: Univ. of Toronto Press, 1968), pp. 137–61.

"Augustan society, to come to terms with Milton's epic, found it necessary to humanise it, to reduce the proportions of its cosmic vision, to domesticate it."

4414 Morton, Bruce. "Browning and Milton: The Bridgewater Book in *Mr.*

Sludge, the Medium." *N&Q*, 24, 1977, 407. Suggests that the reference to the "Bridgewater Book" in Robert Browning's poem alludes to *Comus*. The poet may have intended "a foil, in the form of absolutes," to the "convincing, albeit convoluted, rationale" of Sludge's monologue on morality.

4415 Mounts, Charles Eugene. "Hawthorne's Echoes of Spenser and Milton." *NHJ*, 1973, 162–71.

"From Milton he [Hawthorne] appears to derive much less than can be precisely pin-pointed, but what he does derive, as in 'Young Goodman Brown' and *The Marble Faun*, is both better assimilated and directed into channels of speculation more distinctly his own."

4416 Mustazza, Leonard. "Vonnegut's Tralfamadore and Milton's Eden." *ELWIU*, 13, 1986, 299–312.

Shows that Kurt Vonnegut's *Slaughterhouse-Five* parallels Milton's Eden in several ways. Both authors believe "a paradise can be attained within each individual."

4417 Myers, Robert Manson. *Handel, Dryden, and Milton.* Folcroft, PA: Folcroft Library Editions, 1970; Norwood, PA: Norwood Editions, 1977.

Reprints of Huckabay No. 3793, originally published in 1956.

4418 Nath, Prem. "Johnson Agonistes and Milton's *Samson*." *AN&Q*, 20, 1982, 69–71.

Explores echoes of *Samson Agonistes* in Samuel Johnson's *Vanity of Human Wishes*.

4419 Nelson, Byron. "John Milton as a Character in Howard Barker's *Victory*." *MiltonQ*, 17, 1983, 52–53.

Animadversions on the portrayal of Milton in this play and on the play itself, which premiered in London on March 23, 1983.

4420 Nelson, Carl. "The Ironic Allusive Texture of *Lord Jim*: Coleridge, Crane, Milton, and Melville." *Conradiana*, 4, No. 2, 1972, 47–59.

Claims similarities in certain aspects of *Lord Jim* and *Paradise Lost*. Concludes that Conrad used allusions to Milton in a negative sense to denote a "nominally religious context."

4421 Newey, Vincent. "Keats, Cowper, and Adam's Dream." *KM 80: A Birthday Album for Kenneth Muir: Tuesday, 5 May, 1987* (Liverpool: Liverpool Univ. Press, 1987), pp. 106–07.

Discusses Keats's and Cowper's use of Adam's account of his dream in *Paradise Lost* 8.

4422 Newmeyer, Edna. "Paradise Preserved or *Paradise Regained*: Milton and Wordsworth on the Scale of Love." *M&R*, 2, 1976, 11–15.

Relates Wordsworth's ideas on intellectual love to *Paradise Lost* 5 and 8.

4423 Newmeyer, Edna. "Wordsworth on Milton and the Devil's Party." *MiltonS*, 11, 1978, 83–98.

Wordsworth and Coleridge "were unique among their contemporaries in recognizing Milton's Satan as the arch-enemy of human freedom and well-being, not their champion: the prototype of all that is evil, tyrannical, and murderous."

4424 Nicholls, Graham. "Two Notes on Pope's *Epistle to Bathurst*." *N&Q*, 21, 1974, 251–52.

Suggests a parallel between lines in the *Epistle* and "Milton's description of Mammon's influence on mankind" in *Paradise Lost* 1.

4425 Nijland-Verwey, Mea. "Wat heeft Albert Verwey aan John Milton te Danken?" *European Context: Studies in the History and Literature of the Netherlands Presented to Theodoor Weevers.* Ed. by P. K. King and P. F. Vincent. Publications of the Modern Humanities Research Association, 4 (Cambridge: Modern Humanities Research Association, 1971), pp. 248–67.

In Dutch. Shows how the Dutch scholar admired Milton and his works.

4426 O'Connell, Michael, and John Powell. "Music and Sense in Handel's Setting of Milton's *L'Allegro* and *Il Penseroso*." *ECS*, 12, 1978, 16–46.

Praises Handel's use of word painting to achieve a synthesis of music and poetry in *L'Allegro* and *Il Penseroso*. Points out that composers held music capable of portraying particular emotions and states of mind.

4427 Ogawa, Shizue. "Milton's Influence on John Keats." *MCJ News*, 11, 1989, 18–19.

Abstract of a paper presented at the Twenty-Fifth Colloquium of MCJ in December, 1988. Argues that Keats was influenced by Milton to a greater degree than by Spenser, Shakespeare, or Dante. Suggests that Keats's rhetorical technique in *Hyperion* echoes *Paradise Lost*.

4428 Oiji, Takero. "Milton and Mukyôkai." *RenB*, 2, 1975, 8–12.

Discusses the achievements of the Mukyôkai (nonchurch) people in introducing Milton to Japan.

4429 O'Neal, Michael J. "Miltonic Allusions in *Bishop Blougram's Apology*." *VP*, 15, 1977, 177–82.

Believes that Robert Browning uses allusions from *Lycidas* and *Paradise Regained* to undermine Bishop Blougram's rhetoric.

4430 O'Sullivan, Maurice J., Jr. "Matthew Arnold: Un Milton Jeune et Voyageant." *MiltonQ*, 7, 1973, 82–84.

Discusses Milton's influence on Arnold and explores Arnold's views of Milton. Points out that a passage near the end of *Dover Beach* echoes the conclusion of *Paradise Lost*, offering "both an agnostic critique of Milton's version of Christian optimism and an undespairing, if somber, substitute for it."

4431 Parker, Lois W. "The Milton Window." *Ringing the Bell Backward: The Proceedings of the First International Mil-*

ton Symposium. Ed. by Ronald G. Shafer. The IUP Imprint Series (Indiana: Indiana Univ. of Pennsylvania, 1982), pp. 69–73.

Describes the panels in the window in St. Margaret's Church, London. See No. 4432.

4432 Parker, Lois W. "The Milton Window, the Americans, and Matthew Arnold." *MiltonQ*, 13, 1979, 50–53.

On the window (No. 4431) given by an American journalist, George William Childs, in 1888. Reprints Matthew Arnold's address on the occasion, which emphasizes Milton's poetic excellence, not his libertarianism.

4433 Parker, Patricia. "The Progress of Phaedria's Bower: Spenser to Coleridge." *ELH*, 40, 1973, 372–97.

Discusses some of Milton's poems— such as *Paradise Lost*, *L'Allegro*, and *Lycidas*—as intermediate steps in the journey from Spenser to Coleridge.

4434 Parker, William Riley. *Milton's Contemporary Reputation: An Essay, Together with a Tentative List of Printed Allusions to Milton, 1641–1674, and Facsimile Reproductions of Five Contemporary Pamphlets Written in Answer to Milton*. New York: Haskell House, 1971; Norwood, PA: Norwood Editions, 1977.

Reprints of Huckabay No. 3804, originally published in 1940.

4435 Paulson, Kristoffer F. "Rochester and Milton: The Sound, Sense, and Sources of Pope's Portraits of Bufo, Atticus, and Sporus in *An Epistle to Dr. Arbuthnot*." *PLL*, 12, 1976, 299–310.

Shows that Milton's influence is most evident when Pope uses Belial as his model for Atticus.

4436 Pearce, Donald. "Thoughts on the Autumn Ode of Keats." *ArielE*, 6, No. 3, 1975, 3–19.

Contends that "the diction and syntax of 'To Autumn' constituted a deliberate literary experiment," for Keats sought "to compose in a diction from which all trace of Milton had been excluded."

4437 Pease, Donald. "Blake, Crane, Whitman, and Modernism: A Poetics of Pure Possibility." *PMLA*, 96, 1981, 64–85.

Discusses Milton's influence on Blake.

4438 Perry, Robert L. "*Billy Budd*: Melville's *Paradise Lost*." *Midwest Quarterly*, 10, 1969, 173–85.

Explores the similarities between Satan and Claggart, compares Billy to Adam and Eve, and concludes with "some reflections about the meaning of the phrase 'knowledge of good and evil.'"

4439 Persoon, James L. "Hardy's Pocket Milton: An Early Unpublished Poem." *ELN*, 25, No. 3, 1988, 49–52.

Examines Thomas Hardy's pocket-sized volume of Milton's poetry. Studies both Hardy's markings in the book and an early unpublished poem also contained in the volume to show Milton's influence on the young Hardy's style.

4440 Persoon, James L. "'Once More to the Darkling Thrush': Hardy's Reversals of Milton." *CEA*, 48–49, 1986, 76–86.

Links the word "darkling" in the title of Thomas Hardy's poem to Milton's use of it in the invocation to *Paradise Lost* 3, but points out that Hardy has a different view of nature.

4441 Peterfreund, Stuart. "'In Free Homage and Generous Subjection': Miltonic Influence on *The Excursion*." *WC*, 9, 1978, 173–77.

Suggests that the "many allusions to and quotations of Milton throughout *The Excursion* indicates that Wordsworth seized upon the consolations held out by Milton's vision to restructure his own increasingly Christian vision, however revisionary it might have been."

4442 Peterfreund, Stuart. "Wordsworth, Milton, and the End of Adam's Dream." *M&R*, 3, 1977, 14–21.

On the young Wordsworth's personal problems, inability to complete the *Recluse*, and realization that he could not surpass Milton. Abs., *MiltonQ*, 13, 1979, 62–63.

4443 Petry, Alice Hall. "Longfellow's *The Cross of Snow* and Milton." *ELWIU*, 11, 1984, 299–304.

Argues that Milton's Sonnet 23 ("Methought I saw") is as likely to be a source for the *Cross of Snow* as is Dante.

4444 Piper, H. W. "The Two Paradises in *Kubla Khan*." *RES*, 27, 1976, 148–58.

Proposes Milton as one of three sources for the first paradise in *Kubla Khan*.

4445 Ponsford, Michael. "Milton and Traherne: A Shared Pun on 'Guilt.'" *ELN*, 25, No. 2, 1987, 37–40.

Suggests that Thomas Traherne's pun on guilt/gilt in the *City* was borrowed from Milton's use of it in the "Passion."

4446 Pritchard, R. E. "Milton's Satan and Empson's Old Lady." *N&Q*, 34, 1987, 59–60.

Cites several Miltonic echoes in William Empson's poetry and believes that between 1928 and 1930, Empson was "obsessed" with Milton.

4447 Proffitt, Edward. "Samson and the Intimations Ode: Further Evidence of Milton's Influence." *WC*, 11, 1980, 197.

Discusses the similarities between Milton's description of Samson and Wordsworth's description of the boy in his ode.

4448 Proudfit, Charles L. "Landor on Milton: The Commentators' Commentator." *WC*, 7, 1976, 3–12.

Believes that "Landor's criticism of Milton is at once both derivative and original, both closely linked with the critical methods of late seventeenth- and eighteenth-century commentators on Milton and with the enthusiasm of the early nineteenth-century readers of Milton."

4449 Rajan, Balachandra. "Milton and Eliot: A Twentieth-Century Acknowledgement." *MiltonS*, 11, 1978, 115–29.

Shows that despite T. S. Eliot's position on Milton's influence, his works constitute a tribute to Milton, especially in "East Coker" and "Little Gidding."

4450 Rajan, B., ed. *The Presence of Milton.* *MiltonS*, vol. 11. Pittsburgh, PA: Univ. of Pittsburgh Press, 1978. xiv, 129pp.

A special volume. Essays by Douglas Bush, Barbara K. Lewalski, Earl Miner, Edna Newmeyer, Joseph Anthony Wittreich, Jr., and Rajan. In this bibliography, each essay is listed according to author. The term presence, rather than influence, is used because it is "ample enough to accommodate the many forms of relationship that arise from and declare the Miltonic continuity." These essays examine the varieties of Miltonic presence in Arnold, Blake, Dryden, Eliot, Keats, Pope, and Wordsworth. Reviews: Stanley Archer, *SCN*, 37, 1979, 69–70; John Carey, *RES*, 32, 1981, 79–80.

4451 Regan, John V. "Orpheus and the *Dunciad*'s Narrator." *ECS*, 9, 1975, 87–101.

Believes that the Orpheus myth in Pope's *Dunciad* derives from Milton's use of it in *Lycidas* and *Paradise Lost*.

4452 Reinhart, Charles William. "The Universal Brotherhood: Blake, Milton, and the Reader in Blake's *Milton*." Doctoral diss., Indiana Univ., 1978. 315pp. Abs., *DAI*, 39, 1979, 4283A.

Explores Blake's attempt to involve the reader in Milton's prophetic vision—one which, in Blake's view, "yet needed to be corrected and expanded."

4453 Revard, Stella P. "From the State of Innocence to the Fall of Man: The Fortunes of *Paradise Lost* as Opera and Oratorio." *Milton's Legacy in the Arts.* Ed. by Albert C. Labriola and Edward Sichi, Jr. (University Park and London: Pennsylvania State Univ. Press, 1988), pp. 93–134.

Studies representative songs, choral pieces, oratorios, and operas inspired by *Paradise Lost* during the eighteenth, nineteenth, and twentieth centuries "to convey something of the musical character of each age as well as its attitude toward Milton and his epic."

4454 Revard, Stella P. "Handel's *Samson*: London, 1985." *MiltonQ*, 21, No. 1, 1987, 28–30.

Review of the Royal Opera's production of the oratorio *Samson*, adapted from Milton's drama.

4455 Ricks, Christopher. "Allusion: The Poet as Heir." *Studies in the Eighteenth Century III: Papers Presented at the Third David Nichol Smith Memorial Seminar, Canberra, 1973.* Ed. by R. F. Brissenden and J. C. Eade (Canberra: Australian National Univ. Press; Toronto and Buffalo, NY: Univ. of Toronto Press, 1976), pp. 209–40.

Mentions Milton's influence. Does not believe that Milton inhibited Dryden or Pope.

4456 Ridden, Geoffrey M. "Milton and Phillip's [sic] *New World of Words*." *MiltonQ*, 7, 1973, 29–32.

Does not believe that *Samson Agonistes* influenced the revisions and additions in any edition of Edward Phillips's *New World of Words* (1671).

4457 Riffe, Nancy Lee. "A Study of Milton's Eighteenth Century Reputation in British Periodicals, 1711–1778." Doctoral diss., Univ. of Kentucky, 1963. 347pp. Abs., *DAI*, 30, 1969, 2497A.

Suggests that most eighteenth-century readers praised *Paradise Lost*, ignored Milton's politics and religion, and criticized his use of English, archaisms, foreign words, puns, and blank verse.

4458 Robertson, J. G. "Milton's Fame on the Continent." *Essays on Milton* (Folcroft, PA: Folcroft Library Editions, 1970), pp. 319–40.

Reprint of Stevens No. 2313, originally published in 1907–08.

4459 Robinson, Charles E. *Shelley and Byron: The Snake and Eagle Wreathed in Fight.* Baltimore, MD, and London: Johns Hopkins Univ. Press, 1976. xi, 292pp.

Concerned throughout with Milton's influence.

4460 Rogal, Samuel J. "The Role of *Paradise Lost* in Works by John and Charles Wesley." *MiltonQ*, 13, 1979, 114–19.

Claims that certain hymns and various works by the Wesleys (notably John) reflect the doctrine and phrasing of *Paradise Lost*.

4461 Rogal, Samuel J. "Some Versions of Milton's Psalm Paraphrases." *MiltonQ*, 10, 1976, 53–58.

Discusses various cento (patchwork) versions of five of Milton's paraphrases, which "were essentially efforts to transform these paraphrases into practical hymns for congregational worship."

4462 Rose, Marilyn Gaddis. "Milton, Chateaubriand, and Villiers de L'Isle-Adam: *Paradise Lost* and *Axël*." *SIR*, 9, 1970, 37–43.

Suggests that George Villiers was influenced by Chateaubriand's reading of *Paradise Lost*.

4463 Rosenblum, Joseph. *"The Pickwick Papers* and *Paradise Lost."* *DQu*, 3, 1986, 47–54.

Argues that Dickens "was consciously echoing an epic concerned with the Edenic." He invokes *Paradise Lost* to heighten the novel's "comedic elements" and deepen its moral vision.

4464 Rosenheim, James M. "An Early Appreciation of *Paradise Lost*." *MP*, 75, 1978, 280–82.

Examines initial reactions to the publication of *Paradise Lost* contained in two letters by Sir John Hobart, which refer to the work's fine quality. Abs., *MiltonQ*, 13, 1979, 28.

4465 Rudat, Wolfgang E. H. "Dickinson and Immortality: Virgilian and Miltonic Allusions in 'Of Death I Try To Think Like This.'" *AN&Q*, 16, 1978, 85–87.

Contends that Emily Dickinson alludes to *Paradise Lost* 9.977–85 by "making the 'Flower Hesperian' something analogous to the Forbidden Fruit, and she would be extending this analogy to the 'Purple Flower.'"

4466 Rudat, Wolfgang E. H. "The Sev'nfold Fence: Pope's Belinda and Milton's Eve." *CEA*, 48–49, 1986, 65–69.

Discusses Milton's use of the word "fenc't" in *Paradise Lost* 9.1119–21 and Pope's use of "fence" in the *Rape of the Lock* 2.117–19. Believes that Belinda, like Eve, suffers from post-coital depression and that Pope was "keenly aware" of Milton's borrowing the idea of "Post coitum omnia animalia tristia sunt" from Augustine.

4467 Rudat, Wolfgang E. H. "Sex-Role Reversal and Miltonic Theology in Pope's *Rape of the Lock*." *JEP*, 8, 1987, 48–61.

Believes that "Pope makes Milton's treatment of sexuality in *Paradise Lost* allusively operative in his mock-epic about the battle of the sexes in order to point to the sinfulness of Belinda playing *ombre/man/adam*, and in order to express that sinfulness in sexual terms."

4468 Ruoff, A. Lavonne. "Landor's Conception of the Great Leader." *WC*, 7, 1976, 38–50.

Asserts that "Milton represented for [Walter Savage] Landor the Ciceronian ideal of the man of great intellectual power who devoted himself to the welfare of his country without concern for personal gain and who achieved both high position and respect through merit rather than through inheritance."

4469 Sage, Lorna. "Milton in Literary History." *John Milton: Introductions*. Ed. by John Broadbent (Cambridge: Cambridge Univ. Press, 1973), pp. 298–341.

Summarizes Milton's reputation and influence from the seventeenth century to the present. "His work provides a point of reference writers cannot afford to dispense with."

4470 Salle, J. C. "'Forlorn' in Milton and Keats." *N&Q*, 19, 1972, 293.

Suggests *Paradise Lost* 9.908–10 as a possible source for Keats's use of "forlorn" in his *Ode to a Nightingale*.

4471 Samuel, Irene. "The Legacy of Milton's Poetics." *MiltonQ*, 16, 1982, 54.

Abstract of a paper presented at the 1981 MLA Convention. Believes that Milton is better understood when placed alongside his predecessors and successors.

4472 Sandler, Florence. "The Iconoclastic Enterprise: Blake's Critique of 'Milton's Religion.'" *BlakeS*, 5, 1972, 13–57.

Studies Blake's *Milton* and his reaction to Milton's religion and life. Regards Blake's critique as "a prophecy for the Age."

4473 Sarkar, Malabika. "The Quest for Paradise: Milton and the Romantics." *The Romantic Tradition*. Ed. by Visvanath Chatterjee (Calcutta: Jadavpur Univ., 1984), pp. 53–63.

Discusses Milton's influence on Byron, Coleridge, Keats, Shelley, and Wordsworth, especially as it pertains to the description of the landscape in *Paradise Lost* 4.

4474 Saunders, Hermine Peregoy. "Samson Hath Quit Himself Like Samson: A Study of the Treatment Accorded *Samson Agonistes* in the Restoration and Eighteenth Century Reflecting Aesthetic Theory and Practice." Doctoral diss., Univ. of Maryland, 1971. 403pp. Abs., *DAI*, 32, 1971, 3329A.

Follows the reception of *Samson Agonistes*: first rejected because it lacked external action, later accepted as a closet drama, and finally given public expression in Handel's oratorio.

4475 Scales, Luther Lee, Jr. "Miltonic Elements and the Humanization of Power in Shelley's Poetry, Culminating in *Demogorgon's Song*." Doctoral diss., Drew Univ., 1969. 395pp. Abs., *DAI*, 30, 1969, 2043A.

Argues that the song "epitomizes aspects of Milton's verse which Shelley most frequently echoes and transforms: elements having to do with the attainment of visionary power and elements

suggestive of Eden and the inner Paradise."

4476 Scales, Luther L., Jr. "The Poet as Miltonic Adam in *Alastor*." *KSJ*, 21–22, 1972–73, 126–44.

Claims that Shelley's *Alastor* reflects the poet's desire to seek out and reinhabit the elements of paradise known by Milton's Adam in the Garden of Eden.

4477 Scanland, Sylvia Iris Bellamy. "The Place of Addison in Neo-Classical Criticism of Milton's *Paradise Lost*." Doctoral diss., Univ. of Utah, 1970. 238pp. Abs., *DAI*, 31, 1971, 4135A.

As a critic, Addison gave clear and enthusiastic accounts of each book of *Paradise Lost* and treated the poem in such a way that he became "one of the first Romantic critics of Milton."

4478 Scharnhorst, Gary. "Paradise Revisited: Twain's 'The Man That Corrupted Hadleyburg.'" *SSF*, 18, 1981, 59–64.

Reconciles "Twain's moralism and determinism" by recognizing "that in this story Twain recast major sections of *Paradise Lost* . . . to fashion a modern, though no less paradoxical, parable of the Fortunate Fall."

4479 Scherer, Barrymore Laurence. "Chainèd Heroics." *Opera News*, 50, Mar. 1, 1986, pp. 10–13.

Proposes *Samson Agonistes* as Handel's inspiration for his *Samson*; examines librettist Newburgh Hamilton's work in reassigning several Miltonic sources into the final *Samson*. Shows how this view of Samson differs from Milton's view in *Samson Agonistes*.

4480 Scherpbier, Herman. *Milton in Holland*. Folcroft, PA: Folcroft Library Editions, 1969, 1976.

Reprints of Huckabay No. 3847, originally published in 1933.

4481 Schmitt-Von Mühlenfels, Franz. "Die Rettung Miltons durch Davenant: Eine Anekdote als Opernstoff Spontinis." *Archiv*, 211, 1974, 382–91.

Discusses the political relationship between William Davenant and Milton. Focuses on an opera (based on a poem by Chateaubriand), in which Milton dictates *Paradise Lost* to Davenant's son, who is in love with Milton's daughter.

4482 Schroeder, Natalie. "Echoes of *Paradise Lost* in *The Mystery of Edwin Drood*." *DSN*, 13, 1982, 42–47.

Points out verbal echoes of *Paradise Lost* in Charles Dickens's *Mystery of Edwin Drood* and likens Dickens's characterization of Edwin, Rosa, and John Jasper to Milton's Adam, Eve, and Satan, respectively.

4483 [Sears, Donald A.] "Milton! Thou Should'st be Living at This Hour." *CEA Forum*, 7, 1977, 8–9.

Reports on undergraduate responses to an optional question on a recent final examination: "What in Milton seems to you most vital and valuable to a 20th century reader?" Their answers praised "Milton's intellect, his social conscience, his vitality of religion, his humanism including the inspiration provided by his own life, and his achievements in style." Responses in *MiltonQ*, 11, 1977, 64.

4484 Seely, Clinton B. "Homeric Similes, Occidental and Oriental: Tasso, Milton, and Bengal's Michael Madhusudan Dutt." *CLS*, 25, 1988, 35–56.

Believes that Michael Madhusudan Dutt was impressed by the similes in *Paradise Lost* and used them in the *Slaying of Meghanada* to make his villain attractive.

4485 Sen, Sunil Kanti. "Changing Images of Milton." *Bulletin of the Department of English* (Calcutta Univ.), 10, No. 2, 1974–75, 30–47.

Comments on Milton's reputation from the eighteenth century to the present.

4486 Sena, John F. "A Miltonic Echo in *The Enthusiast*." *RS*, 46, 1978, 202–03.

Sees a parallel between the style of Thomas Warton's comparison of Addison and Shakespeare and the style of "Milton's praise of Shakespeare in *L'Allegro*."

4487 Sensabaugh, George F. "Milton and the Attempted Whig Revolution." *The Seventeenth Century: Studies in the History of English Thought and Literature from Bacon to Pope*. Ed. by Richard Foster Jones and others (Palo Alto, CA: Stanford Univ. Press; London: Oxford Univ. Press, 1969), pp. 291–305.

Reprint of Huckabay No. 3855, originally published in 1951.

4488 Sensabaugh, George F. "That Vile Mercenary, Milton." *PCP*, 3, 1968, 5–15.

Traces the legend from 1649 to the present that Milton was a vile mercenary as Secretary for Foreign Tongues.

4489 Severino, Alexandrino Eusébio. "A Presença de Milton Numa Ode de Álvaro de Campos." *Colóquio*, 58, 1970, 57–60.

Shows that two Portuguese authors, Alvaro de Campos and Fernando de Pessoa, wrote poems in imitation of *L'Allegro* and *Il Penseroso*.

4490 Sharma, K. L. *Milton Criticism in the Twentieth Century.* New Delhi: S. Chand; Mystic, CT: Verry, 1971. xii, 191pp.

Surveys Milton's reputation among the Victorians and deals specifically with his "dislodgement," which was followed "by his enthronement on a higher pedestal."

4491 Sharoni, Edna G. "'Peace' and 'Unbar the Door': T. S. Eliot's *Murder in the Cathedral* and Some Stoic Forbears." *CompD*, 6, 1972, 135–53.

Points out parallels between Eliot's play and *Samson Agonistes*.

4492 Sharratt, Bernard. "The Appropriation of Milton." *E&S*, 35, 1982, 30–44.

Discusses "the influence of Milton upon later readers, his own conception of 'the poet' and the role of Milton's work in the development of that deeply ideological practice we now call 'literary criticism.'" Concludes that Milton's work can still be easily appropriated by those against whom he fought.

4493 Shawcross, John T. "An Early Echo of Milton's *Comus*." *MiltonQ*, 4, 1970, 19–20.

Notes a manuscript commonplace book that contains "Ld. Lucas his Ghost," a poem that echoes the Attendant Spirit's speeches. Dated from about 1686–87, the manuscript is one of the earliest allusions to Milton's masque.

4494 Shawcross, John T. "An Eighteenth-Century Epigram on Milton." *ANQ*, 1, 1988, 130–32.

"The thrust of the epigram is decidedly to put down 'slashing' Bentley, who postulated a redactor between the blind Milton and his text."

4495 Shawcross, John T. "Further Remarks on Milton's Influence: Shelley and Shaw." *MiltonQ*, 20, 1986, 85–92.

Believes that Shelley admired and imitated Milton, while Shaw rebelled against Milton in his writing.

4496 Shawcross, John. "Influence for the Worse? Bernard Shaw and Hart Crane Rethink Milton." *MiltonQ*, 16, 1982, 54–55.

Abstract of a paper presented at the 1981 MLA Convention. Although negative in their attitude toward Milton, "both poets rethink Milton's craft and ideas and are influenced in a positive way."

4497 Shawcross, John T. "Influence for the Worst? Hart Crane Rethinks Milton." *The Visionary Company*, 1–2, 1982, 71–89.

4498 Shawcross, John T., ed. *Milton: The Critical Heritage*. London: Routledge and Kegan Paul; New York: Barnes and Noble, 1970. xi, 276pp.

Uses comments by Milton and others to survey his reputation from 1628–1731. Contains three appendices: "Publication of the Works"; "Selected Secondary References and Collections Similar to the Present Volume"; and "Noteworthy Criticism Omitted in This Selection." Continued in No. 4499. Reviews: *TLS*, June 11, 1970, p. 641;

Lorna Sage, *New Statesman*, 80, 1970, 154; *Booklist*, 67, 1971, 396.

4499 Shawcross, John T., ed. *Milton, 1732–1801: The Critical Heritage*. London and Boston, MA: Routledge and Kegan Paul, 1972. xi, 439pp.

Continuation of No. 4498. Contains three appendices: "Selected Secondary References"; "Additional Significant Criticism Omitted in This Selection"; and "Important Editions, 1732–1801." Reviews: *Economist*, Dec. 9, 1972, p. 64; *MiltonQ*, 6, No. 4, 1972, 96–97; *TLS*, June 15, 1973, p. 697.

4500 Shawcross, John T. "A Note on *Grogam*: Light after Light." *Factotum*, No. 4, 1978, 6.

Points out several Miltonic echoes in the *Vision of Grogam*. Addenda to D. A. Warren in *Factotum*, No. 3.

4501 Shawcross, John T. "'They That Dwell under His Shadow Shall Return': Joyce's *Chamber Music* and Milton." *New Alliances in Joyce Studies: "When It's Aped To Foul a Delfian."* Ed. by Bonnie Kime Scott (Newark: Univ. of Delaware Press; London and Toronto: Associated Univ. Presses, 1988), pp. 200–09.

Sees Milton's presence in James Joyce's *Chamber Music*.

4502 Sheldon, Leslie E. "Another Layer of Miltonic Allusion in *Moby-Dick*." *MSEx*, 35, 1978, 15–16.

Suggests that Melville "used images from Book I of *Paradise Lost* to create particular effects in this frenetic scene in which Ahab delivers his God-defying challenge to the 'clear spirit of clear fire.' The allusion is most evident just before and just after Ahab's diatribe against Divinity."

4503 Sheldon, Leslie Elmer. "The Illimitable Ocean: Herman Melville's Artistic Response to *Paradise Lost* in *Moby-Dick*, *Typee*, and *Billy Budd*." Doctoral diss., Univ. of Toronto, 1980. Abs., *DAI*, 41, 1980, 2608A.

Contends that Melville's understanding of *Paradise Lost* is deeper than has been recognized and that his allusions are individualized, complex, and frequently ambivalent.

4504 Sherwin, Paul Stuart. "Collins and the Miltonic Legacy: A Study in Poetic Influence." Doctoral diss., Yale Univ., 1974. 342pp. Abs., *DAI*, 36, 1975, 330A.

Suggests that, while Collins fails to capture Milton's "unselfconscious freedom" or "sublime visionary experience," he successfully "accommodates himself to the poetry of Milton's 'evening ear.'"

4505 Sherwin, Paul. "Dying into Life: Keats's Struggle with Milton in *Hyperion*." *PMLA*, 93, 1978, 383–95.

"Entering the threatening ancestral space of Miltonic epic and sublime fable, Keats endeavors to occupy and master it, making it his own by subduing the phantom he raises." But Milton will not maintain his place in the past; he "returns 'uncannily' to bewilder Keats's sense of time and self, subverting Keats as powerfully as Keats subverts him."

4506 Sherwin, Paul S. *Precious Bane: Collins and the Miltonic Legacy*. Austin and London: Univ. of Texas Press, 1977. ix, 137pp.

Believes that the Miltonic legacy both liberated and constrained the Romantics and interprets William Collins's poetry in that context. "What remains to be seen is how Collins malforms and individuates himself in relation to the 'precious bane' of the Miltonic legacy." Reviews: *MiltonQ*, 11, 1977, 114–15; Pat Rogers, *TLS*, Feb. 3, 1978, p. 111; Oliver F. Sigworth, *JEGP*, 77, 1978, 441–43; John Dawson Carl Buck, *SCN*, 36, 1978, 10–11; Virginia Ramey Mollenkott, *MiltonQ*, 12, 1978, 77–82; Patrick G. Hogan, Jr., *Texas Books in Review*, 3, 1979, 6; Merle Brown, *SIR*, 18, 1979, 311–16; Richard Wendorf, *MP*, 77, 1980, 440–44.

4507 Sichi, Edward, Jr. "Milton, Mayhew and Thoreau: In Search of a Heritage; or, The Choice and Master Spirits of Any Age." *Ringing the Bell Backward: The Proceedings of the First International Milton Symposium*. Ed. by Ronald G. Shafer. The IUP Imprint Series (Indiana: Indiana Univ. of Pennsylvania, 1982), pp. 109–17.

Believes that Milton's *First Defence* influenced Jonathan Mayhew's *Concerning the Unlimited Submission to the Higher Powers* and Henry David Thoreau's *Of Civil Disobedience*. Response by Charles A. Huttar, pp. 118–21.

4508 Siegmund-Schultze, Dorothea. "Milton und Toland." *ZAA*, 23, 1975, 148–53.

Discusses John Toland's affinity for and use of Milton to support his Enlightenment ideas. Believes that Toland's materialism and belief in reason's power are firmly rooted in Milton's writings. Stresses the republican ideas that Toland admired in Milton's works.

4509 Stackhouse, Janifer Gerl. "Early Critical Response to Milton in Germany: The *Dialogi* of Martin Zeiller." *JEGP*, 73, 1974, 487–96.

Points out that "recognition of Zeiller's *Dialogi* as the first known commentary in German on Milton's *Defensio* changes previous estimates of the early critical response to Milton in Germany."

4510 Stanculescu, Liana. "The Continuity of the Poetic Image and Milton's Contribution to the Language of the Poets." *AnUBLG*, 20, 1971, 101–14.

Shows how Milton's images reappear in the writing of Pope and the Romantic poets.

4511 Stanculescu, Liana. "The Miltonic Vision in Thomas Hardy's *Tess of the d'Urbervilles*." *AnUBLG*, 19, 1970, 163–73.

Demonstrates that Hardy's novel "is a modern social visualization of the Miltonic Adam and Eve myth as Milton's *Paradise Lost* had been a visualization of the Book of Genesis."

Interprets Tess's story as a study of the Fall and its consequences.

4512 Standley, Fred L. "An Echo of Milton in *The Crucible*." *N&Q*, 15, 1968, 303.

Feels that a passage in Arthur Miller's play parallels one in Milton's Hobson poems. Reply by Oliver H. P. Ferris, *N&Q*, 16, 1969, 268.

4513 Stavely, Keith W. F. *Puritan Legacies: "Paradise Lost" and the New England Tradition, 1630–1890.* Ithaca, NY, and London: Cornell Univ. Press, 1987. xiv, 294pp.

Analyzes the relationship between Milton's English Puritanism and the Puritanism of colonial New England.

4514 Stevenson, Warren. *Divine Analogy: A Study of the Creation Motif in Blake and Coleridge.* Salzburg Studies in English Literature. Salzburg: Institut für Englische Sprache und Literatur, Universität Salzburg, 1972. x, 403pp.

Compares Milton's and Blake's treatments of creation and discusses Blake's *Milton* and *Jerusalem*.

4515 Stock, Reed Clark. "Milton in Musical and Theatrical Adaptation." Doctoral diss., Rutgers Univ., 1968. 153pp. Abs., *DAI*, 29, 1969, 3985A.

Examines approximately 150 musical and theatrical adaptations of Milton from 1677 to the present, noting interpretive shifts and giving special attention to Dryden and Handel.

4516 Surbanov, Aleksandar. "Pronikvaneto na Miltan v Balgaria 1864–1944." *Literaturna Misal* (Sofia), 30, 1986, 66–87.

"Milton's Influence in Bulgaria, 1864–1944." Points out that Milton's fame reached Bulgaria in the middle of the nineteenth century, when he was mentioned along with Shakespeare as the greatest English poet. Also deals with various attempts to translate *Paradise Lost*.

4517 Sutton, William A. "In Memory of Milton." *CEA Forum*, 6, No. 2, 1975, 11.

On the inability of many college students to identify Milton.

4518 Swaim, Donna Elliott. "Milton's Immediate Influence on Dryden." Doctoral diss., Univ. of Arizona, 1978. 137pp. Abs., *DAI*, 39, 1978, 904A.

Asserts that after reading *Paradise Lost* in the winter of 1668–69, Dryden reexamined "moral instruction in drama," the "patient martyrdom" of heroes, and the "heroic play."

4519 Swaim, Kathleen. "Milton: Not a Major Reference?" *MiltonQ*, 10, 1976, 99.

Replies to Morris Golden (No. 4309) by listing references to Milton and others in the *Monthly Review* and *Critical Review* from 1760 to 1769.

4520 Swaim, Kathleen M., with **Margaret Culley.** "Anne Manning on John Milton." *MiltonQ*, 10, 1976, 88–89.

Discusses two of Manning's works: the *Maiden and Married Life of Mary Powell, Afterwards Mistress Milton* (1849) and *Deborah's Diary: A Fragment* (1858).

4521 Tannenbaum, Leslie. "From Filthy Type to Truth: Miltonic Myth in *Frankenstein*." *KSJ*, 26, 1977, 101–13.

Claims that "in *Frankenstein* Mary Shelley is engaged in a continual dialogue with Milton, expressed by direct and oblique allusions to *Paradise Lost*." Proposes the young Dr. Frankenstein as a Satanic figure in rebellion against God's creative powers.

4522 Tarr, Rodger L. "'The Eagle' versus 'the Mole': The Wisdom of Virginity in *Comus* and *The Book of Thel*." *BlakeS*, 3, 1971, 187–94.

"The fundamental difference, then, between the philosophies advanced in *Comus* and *The Book of Thel* regarding virginity is still another register of the basic conflict in ideas between Milton and Blake, especially in their formative years."

4523 Tate, J. O. "Flannery O'Connor's Counterplot." *SoR*, 16, 1980, 869–78.

"Milton's *distancing*, his spatial interventions and foreshortenings, and most of all his celebration of the great theme of Creation, of the blessings of Providence, find echoes . . . throughout O'Connor's work."

4524 Telleen, John Martin. *Milton dans la Littérature Française.* New York: Burt Franklin, 1972.

Reprint of Stevens No. 2813, originally published in 1904.

4525 Tintner, Adeline R. "The Countess and Scholastica: Henry James's *L'Allegro* and *Il Penseroso.*" *SSF*, 11, 1974, 267–76.

Believes that "James's invocation of Milton is implicit in the theme of *Benvolio*: the necessary and refreshing contrast between the life of social activity and the life of scholarly seclusion."

4526 Tintner, Adeline R. "*Paradise Lost* and *Paradise Regained* in James's *The Wings of the Dove* and *The Golden Bowl.*" *MiltonQ*, 17, 1983, 125–31.

Claims that throughout his life, Henry James admired and imitated Milton. Believes that the *Wings of the Dove* alludes to *Paradise Lost* and the *Golden Bowl* alludes to *Paradise Regained* rather than the Bible. However, "James modifies the Miltonic argument by insisting that the fruit of the tree of knowledge *must* be eaten, since consciousness and awareness are necessary for a real paradise."

4527 Tisch, J. H. "Between the Idyllic and the Sublime—Some Aspects of the Reception of Milton in Switzerland." *Affinities: Essays in German and English Literature. Dedicated to the Memory of Oswald Wolff (1897–1968).* Ed. by R. W. Last (London: Oswald Wolff, 1971), pp. 3–18.

Shows that "theological and pietistic circles were prominently involved in the reception of the 'Christian Homer' in Germany and Switzerland." Deals especially with Milton's influence on Johannn Jacob Bodmer and Simon Grynäus.

4528 Tisch, J. H. "Irregular Genius: Some Aspects of Milton and Shakespeare on the Continent at the End of the Eighteenth Century." *Studies in Eighteenth-Century Literature.* Ed. by Miklos J. Szenczi and others (Budapest: Akademiai Kiado, 1974), pp. 301–23.

4529 Tisch, J. H. "Milton and the German Mind in the Eighteenth Century." *Studies in the Eighteenth Century: Papers Presented at the David Nichol Smith Memorial Seminar, Canberra, 1966.* Ed. by R. F. Brissenden (Canberra: Australian National Univ. Press and Oxford Univ. Press; Toronto: Univ. of Toronto Press, 1968), pp. 205–29.

Surveys Milton's reception and influence, focusing on Bodmer, Klopstock, Goethe, and Schiller. "Milton, for many, became just as overwhelming, exalting, and transforming an experience as the Shakespeare of the great tragedies."

4530 Tisch, J. H. "Milton's *Paradise Lost* and the German Enlightenment Critics." *Proceedings and Papers of the Fourteenth Congress of the Australasian Univ. Language and Literature Association* (Dunedin: AAULA, 1972), pp. 155–56.

An abstract. "The paper traces . . . the main stages in the reception of *Paradise Lost* by German Enlightenment critics as a significant part of the 'English revolution of German letters.'"

4531 Tisch, J. H. "'Poetic Theology': *Paradise Lost* between Aesthetics and Religion in Eighteenth-Century Switzerland." *RLC*, 49, 1975, 270–83.

Demonstrates that *Paradise Lost* "dealt with higher Christian truths" and that it was "rooted in religious as well as in aesthetic foundations, in a predilection for Milton's 'poetic theology' and for epic literature that exemplifies and inculcates Christian beliefs." Characterizes "the style of argumentation adopted by Milton's most vocal and effective Enlightenment apologist," Johann Jacob Bodmer.

4532 Tisch, J. H. "Von Satan bis Mephistopheles: Milton und die Deutsche Klassik." *Proceedings of the Australian Goethe Society*, 1969, 90–118.

4533 Ulreich, John C. "Prophets, Priests, and Poets: Toward a Definition of Religious Fiction." *Cithara*, 22, No. 2, 1983, 3–31.

Deals with Spenser's and Milton's influence on C. S. Lewis.

4534 Ursache, Magda. "Panait Cerna. Simbolica Relevanta." *ALIL*, 29, 1983–84, 171–79.

In Romanian; French abstract, pp. 179–80. Shows how Cerna was influenced by *Paradise Lost* and how he used Adam as his model.

4535 Van Anglen, Kevin Patrick. "*That Sainted Spirit*: Milton and the American Renaissance." Doctoral diss., Harvard Univ., 1983. 298pp. Abs., *DAI*, 44, 1983, 1794A–95A.

Argues that Milton's exploration of the imagination, support of religious freedom, and Puritan background encouraged American writers from Macaulay to Channing to Emerson.

4536 Vanderbeets, Richard. "Milton in Early America: The Example of Benjamin Franklin." *MiltonQ*, 6, No. 2, 1972, 33–36.

Discusses Milton's influence on Franklin's ideas about religion, politics, and education.

4537 Vieth, David M. "Pope, Belinda, and Milton: Another Allusion." *N&Q*, 24, 1977, 231–32.

Suggests an allusion to *Paradise Lost* 2.477 in the *Rape of the Lock* 1.128. Compares Satan's "sacred rites of Pride" with those of Belinda's toilet.

4538 Vogler, Thomas A. *Preludes to Vision: The Epic Venture in Blake, Wordsworth, Keats, and Hart Crane.* Berkeley, Los Angeles, and London: Univ. of California Press, 1971. 231pp.

Frequently discusses Milton's influence.

4539 Wade, Philip. "Shelley and the Miltonic Element in Mary Shelley's *Frankenstein.*" *M&R*, 2, 1976, 23–35.

Holds that Percy Shelley is the source of the Miltonic elements in *Frankenstein*.

4540 Wagner, John Carl. "The Making of an Authority: Evolving Attitudes among Milton's Eighteenth-Century Commentators toward Addison's Essays on *Paradise Lost*." Doctoral diss., Case Western Reserve Univ., 1972. 166pp. Abs., *DAI*, 33, 1972, 1746A–47A.

Contends that "Milton's eighteenth-century commentators were responsible for both preserving and refining Addison's remarks and for establishing him as the period's outstanding critical authority" on *Paradise Lost*.

4541 Walzer, Arthur E. "An Allusion to *Paradise Lost* in Eliot's 'Gerontion.'" *NMAL*, 2, 1977, Item 6.

Eliot's use of "squat" borrowed the feelings Milton gave it when "In *Paradise Lost* [4.800] Satan's metamorphosis from a rebel boldly defying God to a toad furtively seducing Eve is epitomized in Satan's position squat at the sleeping Eve's ear."

4542 Ware, Thomas C. "A Miltonic Allusion in Joyce's 'The Dead.'" *JJQ*, 6, 1969, 273–74.

In the final story of James Joyce's *Dubliners*, Gabriel Conroy quotes from the *Reason of Church-Government*.

4543 Ware, Tracy. "A New Miltonic Echo in Shelley's *Defence*." *ELN*, 19, 1981, 120–22.

Argues that the ambivalent view of Milton as "the Romantic starting point and the Romantic adversary . . . is observable in *A Defence of Poetry*, in that Shelley regards Milton as a great exemplar of inspiration, but he dislikes his predecessor's account of poetic composition."

4544 Wasser, Henry. "John Quincy Adams on the Opening Lines of Milton's *Paradise Lost*." *AL*, 42, 1970, 373–75.

Shows that Adams, in his criticism of *Paradise Lost*, reveals both a rich mind and unjust comments.

4545 Weissman, Judith. "A Note on the Pleasant Bank by Moonlight in *The Marriage of Heaven and Hell*." *N&Q*, 24, 1977, 321–22.

Discusses Blake's work as "a poetic commentary on *Paradise Lost*." Whereas Milton's moonlit scene at the end of Book 1 suggests "the danger of imagination," an "ally of desire against reason," Blake's scene reverses Milton's judgment and presents the poetic imagination as the divine element of human nature.

4546 Wellens, Oskar. "A Coleridgean Borrowing from the *Critical Review*?" *N&Q*, 28, 1981, 308–09.

A quotation in Samuel Taylor Coleridge's notebook may have originated from a misquotation of *Paradise Lost* 3.380–81 in the *Critical Review*.

4547 Whang, Ho-Soon. "Survey over the Milton Controversy." *JELL*, 30, 1984, 287–308.

In Korean; English abstract, pp. 308–09. Believes that the attacks on Milton by Ezra Pound (Huckabay No. 828), T. S. Eliot (Huckabay No. 531), and others reveal deep prejudices against Milton himself, as well as against his ideas. Also discusses the replies of his defenders.

4548 White, Gail. "Milton's Eve." *MiltonQ*, 9, 1975, 37.

A lyric poem about Milton's three wives.

4549 Wilding, Michael. "Allusion and Innuendo in *MacFlecknoe*." *EIC*, 19, 1969, 355–70.

Believes that in *MacFlecknoe*, John Dryden's references to the Bible and *Paradise Lost* "fill out the meaning, from innuendo to the vulgar and scatological."

4550 Wilding, Michael. "*Paradise Lost* and *Fanny Hill*." *MiltonQ*, 5, 1971, 14–15.

Suggests that the scene of Fanny's sexual initiation in John Cleland's *Fanny Hill* alludes to the first act of postlapsarian intercourse in *Paradise Lost*.

4551 Wilkie, Brian. "Epic Irony in *Milton*." *Blake's Visionary Forms Dramatic*. Ed. by David V. Erdman and John E. Grant (Princeton, NJ: Princeton Univ. Press, 1970), pp. 359–72.

Deals with Blake's understanding of the epic tradition and tangentially with Milton's influence.

4552 Williams, Anne. "*The Intimations Ode*: Wordsworth's Fortunate Fall." *RPP*, 5, 1981, 1–13.

Claims that the divergent strains in Wordsworth's *Intimations Ode* are subservient to "the myth of the fortunate fall, as told by Milton." Believes that various allusions to *Paradise Lost* show "a consistent analogy of situation and a consistent pattern of psychological response."

4553 Williams, M. C. "The Concept of Inspiration as Discovered in the Early Poetry of Milton and in the Poetry of Keats." M.Litt. thesis, Oxford Univ., 1979. Abs., *IT*, 29, 1982, 188.

4554 Wilson, James D. "Hank Morgan, Philip Traum and Milton's Satan." *MTJ*, 16, 1973, 20–21.

Sees "a significant relationship" among Mark Twain's Hank Morgan in *Connecticut Yankee*, Philip Traum in the *Mysterious Stranger*, and Milton's Satan, who invents the devilish engines during the War in Heaven.

4555 Wittreich, Joseph Anthony, Jr. *Angel of Apocalypse: Blake's Idea of Milton*. Madison: Univ. of Wisconsin Press, 1975. xxiii, 332pp.

Discusses Blake's idea of Milton as revealed in his portrayals of Milton, illustrations for Milton's poetry, critique of the poet in the *Marriage of Heaven and Hell*, and celebration of him in *Milton*. Reviews: Purvis E. Boyette, *Blake*, 10, 1976–77, 88–89; Tom Dargan, *BlakeN*, 10, 1977, 130–35; Christopher Hill, *N&Q*, 23, 1976, 461–62; Mary Lynn Johnson, *M&R*,

2, 1976, 1–10; William F. Halloran, *SCN*, 35, 1977, 101–04; Peter Malekin, *RES*, 28, 1977, 350–53; *MiltonQ*, 11, 1977, 54–55; J. M. Q. Davies, *MLR*, 73, 1978, 886–87; H. B. DeGroot, *ES*, 60, 1979, 670–72; Florence Sandler, *MP*, 77, 1979, 228–34.

4556 Wittreich, Joseph Anthony, Jr. "Blake's Milton: 'To Immortals, . . . a Mighty Angel.'" *MiltonS*, 11, 1978, 51–82.

On the Miltonic tradition as Blake interpreted it and the poetics of influence, which he delivered to future artists through his poem *Milton*.

4557 Wittreich, Joseph Anthony, Jr. "Cartographies: Reading and Misreading Milton and the Romantics." *M&R*, 1, No. 1, 1975, 1–3.

Discusses Harold Bloom's *A Map of Misreading* (No. 489) and *Anxiety of Influence* (No. 4224) in relation to Spenser and Milton and the Romantics. Feels that "Milton is the 'starting point' for the English Romantic poets and now is becoming a focal point for assessing their poems, as well as the cultural moment that produced them."

4558 Wittreich, Joseph Anthony, Jr. "'Divine Countenance': Blake's Portrait and Portrayals of Milton." *HLQ*, 38, 1975, 125–60.

Blake portrays Milton and illustrates his work based on the understanding of him as a poet who "spent an entire career breaking loose from convention, undermining orthodoxy, and revolutionizing forms to encompass his radically new vision."

4559 Wittreich, Joseph. "'The Illustrious Dead': Milton's Legacy and Romantic Prophecy." *M&R*, 4, 1980, 17–32.

For all the Romantics, particularly Blake, Wordsworth, and Shelley, Milton was "the founder of a city of art that these poets would make endure through the centuries."

4560 Wittreich, Joseph Anthony, Jr. "In

Copious Legend, or Sweet Lyric Song: Typology and the Perils of the Religious Lyric." *Bright Shootes of Everlastingnesse.* Ed. by Claude J. Summers and Ted-Larry Pebworth (Columbia: Univ. of Missouri Press, 1987), pp. 192–215.

Explores how the various views of Samson affected the "sweet lyric song" of the seventeenth century. Believes that the notion of Samson as God's great heroic servant remains untested.

4561 Wittreich, Joseph Anthony, Jr. "Opening the Seals: Blake's Epics and the Milton Tradition." *Blake's Sublime Allegory: Essays on "The Four Zoas," "Milton," "Jerusalem."* Ed. by Stuart Curran and Wittreich (Madison: Univ. of Wisconsin Press, 1973), pp. 23–58.

"For Blake, the Milton tradition was comparable to the classical epic tradition; it was created by Milton with the hope that his successors would use it in the same way that he used the poems of Homer, Virgil, and Ovid— imaginatively, not imitatively. . . . The Milton tradition, for Blake, was characterized not by its bonds with the past but by its freedom from them—not by its compliance with precedents but by its disregard of them."

4562 Wittreich, Joseph Anthony, Jr., ed. *The Romantics on Milton: Formal Essays and Critical Asides.* Cleveland, OH, and London: Press of Case Western Reserve Univ., 1970. xxiii, 594pp.

"A studied look at the commentaries and critical asides of the Romantic poets and critics . . . reveals that they knew their Milton well, that they raised the issues and grappled with the questions that modern criticism is trying so desperately to resolve. These critics . . . are the shapers of 'modern attitudes' toward Milton; they are the unacknowledged architects of Milton criticism as we know it today." Reviews: *MiltonQ*, 4, 1970, 65–66; *TLS*, Aug. 6, 1971, p. 953; Kenneth Muir, *N&Q*, 20, 1973, 77–78; Andy P. Antippas, *BlakeN*, 6,

1973, 55; John R. Mulder, *SCN*, 32, 1974, 4.

4563 Wittreich, Joseph Anthony, Jr. "'Sublime Allegory': Blake's Epic Manifesto and the Milton Tradition." *BlakeS*, 4, No. 2, 1972, 15–44.

"Out of centuries of experimentation, Milton forged a tradition that was regarded by Blake, and should be recognized by us, as the Milton tradition. Blake was the first poet to ensconce himself within this tradition; and by doing so he created a poetry of contexts with Milton's poems serving as a backdrop for his own."

4564 Woodhouse, Christopher Reed. "'The Melting Voice': A Study of Milton's *L'Allegro* and *Il Penseroso* and Their Setting by Handel." Doctoral diss., Boston College, 1984. 205pp. Abs., *DAI*, 44, 1984, 3392A.

Uses a common theme of delight to unite Milton's imprecise, unconventional, and artificial *L'Allegro* and *Il Penseroso* with Handel's vivid, conventional, and passionate musical interpretation of the poems.

4565 Woodman, Ross. "The Death and Resurrection of Milton According to the Gospel of Blake." *ESC*, 3, 1977, 416–32.

"What, in the fiction he was devising, Blake offered the Milton who was a part of it, was a hero whose sole task was to enact the process of creation according to the dictates of desire within a radically new kind of epic whose process was its form. Blake's fictional Milton accepts the offer partly because Blake's vision of the Last Judgement in the earlier prophetic works had persuaded him it was at hand, partly too because he himself in *Paradise Lost* had failed to bring it off."

4566 Woodman, Ross. "Milton's Satan in

Wordsworth's 'Vale of Soul-making.'" *SIR*, 23, 1984, 3–30.

Notes that in Wordsworth's poetry, the narrator—in each case, an adult observing children—resembles "Milton's Satan confronting the still innocent Eve." Wordsworth's narrators, however, have no evil intent, but they often have to check their feelings of grief, of "tragic enmeshment in the world."

4567 Woolford, John. "Wordsworth Agonistes." *EIC*, 31, 1981, 27–40.

Discusses the Miltonic elements in the 1805 version of the *Prelude*.

4568 Wooten-Hawkins, Anna. *Satan Speaks of Eve in Seven Voices, after the Fall.* Raleigh, NC: Joseph C. Woodard Printing Co., 1986. N. pag.

A collection of poems dealing mainly with Satan's reaction from Eve's Fall to the expulsion scene. Contains brief quotations from *Paradise Lost.*

4569 Yokozawa, Shiro. "The Adamic Fall in Nathaniel Hawthorne's Literary Works." *MCJ News*, 9, 1987, 6–7.

Abstract of paper presented. Traces the influence of the fortunate fall in *Paradise Lost* on Hawthorne's works, especially the *Marble Faun.*

4570 Youngblood, Ed. "To Milton by Motorcycle: An Unlikely Progress." *MiltonQ*, 11, 1977, 52–54.

An account of a trip by motorcycle, including a visit to Milton's cottage at Chalfont St. Giles. Qualifies some of his remarks, p. 95.

4571 Zitelli, Joanne Janet. "Poetry Unparadised: *Paradise Lost* and Rimbaud's Prose Poetry." Doctoral diss., Univ. of California, Irvine, 1981. 220pp. Abs., *DAI*, 42, 1981, 1139A–40A.

Compares the poets' presentations of hell, analyses of social institutions, poetic structures, and allusions to other works.

INDEX

References are to item numbers

Petrina, Carlotta, 2599
Petronella, Vincent F., 1644
Petry, Alice Hall, 4443
Petti, Anthony G., 234
Petty, Jane M., 2873, 4139
Peutl, Ernest, 1645
Phelan, Herbert J., 1646
Philipps, Jenkin Thomas, 72
Philips, John, 4321
Phillips, Ann, 348
Phillips, Anne, 1678
Phillips, Edward, 361, 1572, 3931, 4456
Picard, Jeremie, 3881
Pickering, Frederick P., 2874
Pico della Mirandola, Giovanni, 4022
Piehler, Paul, 942
Pigman, George Wood, III, 1647–49
Piltch, Charles Neil, 943
Pindar, 2920, 3908
Pinto, V. de Sola, 90
Piper, David, 218, 235
Piper, H. W., 4444
Piper, William Bowman, 4063
Pipkin, James, 1114
Pironon, Jean, 91, 518, 807, 944,
    1650–51, 2875
Pitcher, John, 508, 584, 945, 1038,
    1053, 1058
Pittion, J.-P., 3950
Plath, Sara, 2293
Plato, 588, 666, 684, 787, 1195, 1258,
    1702, 1779, 1886, 2225, 2321, 2421,
    2471, 2799, 2803, 2977, 3009, 3167,
    3246, 3438, 3819, 3844, 3909
Plotinus, 1049
Plotkin, Frederick, 2876–77
Plutarch, 2219
Pocock, J. G. A., 173
Poe, Edgar Allan, 4296, 4355
Poggioli, Renato, 1652
Pointon, Marcia R., 946, 4114, 4165
Pollard, W., 947
Pollock, John J., 1653
Pollok, Robert, 2544
Ponsford, Michael, 4445
Pope, Alexander, 495, 510, 627, 634,
    800, 1377, 1391, 1427–28, 1800,
    1917, 1999, 2641, 3089, 4050, 4063,
    4218, 4226, 4284–85, 4287, 4319,
    4321, 4364, 4374, 4382, 4392–93,

4424, 4435, 4450–51, 4455, 4466–67,
    4487, 4510, 4537
Popham, Elizabeth Anne, 948
Popperwell, Ronald G., 4183
Porter, William Malin, 2093, 2161,
    2878–80
Post, Jonathan F. S., 1654, 3078
Potter, Lois, 277, 281, 321, 582, 949,
    1358, 1563, 2093, 2345, 2880
Potts, James Basil, Jr., 3951
Poulsen, Søren Refskou, 2882
Pound, Ezra, 993, 1116, 3953, 4050,
    4211, 4547
Poussin, Nicolas, 2284
Powell, Don Lance, 2883
Powell, Jane, 281
Powell, John, 4426
Power, Thomas, 4176
Praz, Mario, 620, 946, 2129
Prescott, Anne Lake, 952, 2093
Press, John, 174
Price, Jonathan, 1303, 2767
Price, Reynolds, 3661
Priest, Dale G., 2884
Primeau, Ronald, 614, 2885, 3662
Prince, F. T., 318, 337, 349, 366, 488,
    768, 950, 1534, 2848, 2886, 3055
Pritchard, Allan, 236
Pritchard, R. E., 4446
Proffitt, Edward, 4447
Proser, Matthew N., 2618
Proudfit, Charles L., 4448
Proudfoot, D. S., 3952
Provost, Foster, 1152, 2769
Prynne, William, 3897
Pujals, Esteban, 415, 2887–88
Pulci, Luigi, 3259
Purcell, Henry, 255
Purchas, Samuel, 3031, 3952
Pushkin, Aleksandr Sergeevich, 4345
Putzel, Rosamond, 275, 2695
Pyle, Fitzroy, 774

Quarles, Francis, 1256, 1390, 1870
Quay, James Donald, 3663
Qui, Shaolong, 2889
Quilligan, Maureen, 952, 2890
Quinn, Dennis B., 2682